Fodor's 9
Worldwide Cruises and Ports of Call

"When it comes to information on regional history, what to see and do, and shopping, these guides are exhaustive."

—*USAir Magazine*

"Usable, sophisticated restaurant coverage, with an emphasis on good value."

—Andy Birsh, *Gourmet Magazine* columnist

"Valuable because of their comprehensiveness."

—*Minneapolis Star-Tribune*

"Fodor's always delivers high quality...thoughtfully presented...thorough."

—*Houston Post*

"An excellent choice for those who want everything under one cover."

—*Washington Post*

Fodor's Travel Publications, Inc.
New York • Toronto • London • Sydney • Auckland
http://www.fodors.com/

ISBN 0-679-03198-7

Fodor's Worldwide Cruises and Ports of Call

Editor: M. T. Schwartzman
Contributors: Robert Blake, Shannon Craig, Janet Foley, Amy Fried, Mary Ann Hemphill, Herb Hiller, Lori Lincoln, Dina Long, Rebecca Miller, Kate Pennebaker, Melissa Rivers, Heidi Sarna, Mary Ellen Schultz, Theodore W. Scull, Jordon Simon, Jonathan Siskin, Dinah A. Spritzer, Heidi Waldrop Bay, Simon Worrall, Jane E. Zarem
Creative Director: Fabrizio La Rocca
Cartographer: David Lindroth
Technical Illustration: Christopher A. Wilson
Illustrator: Karl Tanner
Cover Photograph: Harvey Lloyd/The Stock Market
Cover Design: John Olenyik
Design: Vignelli Associates

Special Sales

Fodor's Travel Publications are available at special discounts for bulk purchases for sales promotions or premiums. Special editions, including personalized covers, excerpts of existing guides, and corporate imprints, can be created in large quantities for special needs. For more information, contact your local bookseller or write to Special Markets, Fodor's Travel Publications, 201 East 50th Street, New York, NY 10022. Inquiries from Canada should be directed to your local Canadian bookseller or sent to Random House of Canada, Ltd., Marketing Department, 1265 Aerowood Drive, Mississauga, Ontario L4W 1B9. Inquiries from the United Kingdom should be sent to Fodor's Travel Publications, 20 Vauxhall Bridge Road, London SW1V 2SA, England.

PRINTED IN THE UNITED STATES OF AMERICA
10 9 8 7 6 5 4 3 2 1

Contents

At Sea with Fodor's

A good cruise guide is like a trusted adviser. It's a place you can turn to for honest reviews of more than 125 ships. It tells you how to find a knowledgeable travel agent, recommends the best shore excursions, and gives you inside tips for enjoying your time in port. In the creation of *Worldwide Cruises and Ports of Call 1997,* we at Fodor's have gone to great lengths to provide you with the very best of all possible cruise companions, and, by extension, to make your cruise the best of all possible vacations.

About Our Writers

The information on these pages is courtesy of a roster of extraordinary writers.

Veteran travel-industry reporter **Dinah Spritzer** can help you answer the two questions most commonly asked about cruising: "How do I get a good deal?" and "How do I find a good travel agent?" Dinah's insightful tips and strategies can be found in our Cruise Primer.

One of the newest hot spots in cruising is Asia, and this year, we asked **Lori Lincoln** to compile a new ports-of-call section for this emerging cruise destination. Lori was especially well qualified for this assignment. As the cruise editor of *Travel Weekly,* she sailed aboard more than 20 ships. Before covering cruising, she wrote about Asia and the Pacific from a land point of view. Lori also contributed our new ports section on Europe and the Mediterranean.

Helping Lori to get all the latest information on Asia was **Heidi Waldrop Bay,** who sailed from Singapore to Hong Kong aboard the *Island Princess.* Since 1991, Heidi has been a major contributor to this book, and this year was no exception as Heidi reviewed numerous cruise lines.

Cruising is more than oceangoing liners, and this year, we asked well-known cruise expert **Ted Scull** to expand our section on special-interest cruises. These wide-ranging cruise options are now featured in a brand-new chapter. Ted also wrote reviews of Orient Lines, Royal Olympic Cruises, and Cunard Line's *Vistafjord.*

Competition among cruise lines is heating up in the dining rooms. Several lines have announced programs to upgrade their menus by joining forces with famous chefs and academies (*see* What's New, *below*). Among the first of these was Windstar Cruises, reviewed this year by cruise writer **Jon Siskin.** Jon also sailed aboard Seawind Cruise Line's *Seawind Crown* and Commodore Cruise Line's *Enchanted Isle* in preparation of this edition.

Meanwhile, back in New York, editor **M. T. Schwartzman** boarded Holland America's *Westerdam* to sample that line's new "Signature" cuisine. Schwartzman also went aboard the *Century* to taste the new desserts and dishes that Michel Roux has created for Celebrity. Not to be outdone, Silversea trumpeted its new partnership with Le Cordon Bleu at a New York luncheon aboard the *Silver Wind*. Our editor reports that the cuisine was most satisfactory.

What's New

One cruise-line executive recently asked us if reviewing new ships had become harder. After all, she said, today's megaships are so similar. But as with so many things, the difference lies in the details, which is one of the emerging stories in cruising. From the outside, many megaships have a cookie-cutter look. But inside, a design war is being waged as cruise lines play a game of "top this."

These design wars are being waged in the spas, the dining rooms, and the showrooms. Greco-Roman imagery, double-decker designs, and 10,000-square-foot spas vie for attention. Private verandas, once reserved for only the best cabins, are increasingly common in standard accommodations. Princess Cruises is the leader in private verandas. Fleetwide the line has nearly 1,000 cabins with balconies in a variety of price categories. On its newest ship, the *Sun Princess*, 38% of the cabins have private verandas. On Royal Caribbean's new *Legend of the Seas* and *Splendour of the Seas*, 25% of the cabins have balconies. Holland America's *Statendam* series of ships have verandas in 23% of their cabins. Meanwhile, a technology revolution is under way, with interactive video systems and computer learning centers taking their place on the cruise ships of the Information Age.

Who's In, Who's Out

First Royal Viking Line, now Royal Cruise Line—Kloster Cruise Ltd.'s stable of cruise lines continues to shrink. In May of 1996, the cruise world bid good-bye to an old friend, RCL. The line's ships were distributed to new owners: the *Crown Odyssey* was transferred to Royal's sister line, Norwegian Cruise Line, the last of Kloster's operating cruise entities. The ship is now known as the *Norwegian Crown*. Others went to Seabourn and Europe's Fred Olsen Lines.

Regency Cruises is also history. The line shut down suddenly in late 1995. At press time, the disposition of its ships remained unresolved.

A sad farewell is being said to the 38-year-old *Rotterdam*. Holland America announced that it will retire the ship in September 1997, so this may be your last chance to sail aboard one of the last of the classic liners that is still in its original condition. But while the ship will soon sail into the sunset, the name will live on: Holland America has said that its next vessel, a 62,000-ton ship currently under construction, will be christened the SS *Rotterdam VI*.

The choppy waters of cruising haven't discouraged new entrants. Cape Canaveral Cruise Line (800/910–7447), a fledgling line out of Florida's Port Canaveral, has begun operating two-day cruises to the Bahamas aboard the *Dolphin IV*, formerly of Dolphin Cruise Line. Another new name is Royal Seas Cruise Line, which was launched in March of 1996 by OdessAmerica Cruise Company (800/221–3254). The line's namesake ship, the *Royal Seas*, was built in 1976 as the *Ukraina* and carries a

Ukranian crew. Two-night cruises to nowhere and five-night cruises to Merida and Cancún leave from Tampa.

Record-Breaking Boats The major cruise lines continue to expand as well. Among the many new ships now being built are cruising's first 100,000-tonners. The first, Carnival Cruise Lines' 101,000-ton *Destiny*, was scheduled to debut in November of 1996. And come early 1998, Princess Cruises' *Grand Princess* will claim the title of world's biggest cruise ship at 105,000 tons.

Finally, we look ahead to next year, when Disney Cruise Line (tel. 407/939–3500) launches its first ship, the 85,000-ton *Disney Magic*. The vessel won't sail its inaugural cruise until February 1998, but Disney is already taking bookings for what is sure to be one of the most anticipated events in cruising.

How to Use This Book

Organization For many first-time cruisers (and some experienced passengers as well) choosing a ship is a mind-boggling proposition. To help lay the groundwork for your choice, we begin this book with a Cruise Primer. Within its pages you'll find definitions of all the different types of ships you're likely to encounter, a discussion of the cruise experiences you'll have aboard, advice on where to find the best deals—and how to choose a travel agent. You'll find out about the choices you have for dining and the cuisine and special diets available aboard most ships. And you'll learn everything you need to know for a satisfying and safe cruise vacation.

Cruise Ships and Lines Chapter 1 is the heart of this book. The discussion of each cruise line begins with the Fleet, which summarizes the vessels—are they big ships or small ships, new ships or old ships? Following the Fleet is the Cruise Experience, a detailed account of the onboard lifestyle each line cultivates. This section includes information on activities, dining, entertainment, service, and tipping. Finally, each ship has its own review, the Ship's Log, which describes the highlights of each vessel.

Special-Interest Cruises Cruising means different things to different people. To most, a cruise is a seagoing affair aboard a floating resort. But to many others, a cruise is an educational experience, an adventure ashore, or a chance to travel in the company of an international complement of people. For these readers, we have Chapter 2, Special-Interest Cruises.

Ports of Call In Chapter 3, you'll find our choices for the best ashore in every major port of call around the globe. We'll tell you how and where you'll come ashore and how to get around, where the best museums are, and how to arrange for your favorite activities. All the most popular destinations are covered, whether you're heading for Antarctica, Alaska, the Bahamas, Bermuda, the Caribbean, Europe and the Mediterranean, New England and Canada, the Panama Canal Zone, South America, or Southeast Asia.

For each port, we've chosen the shore excursions that we think you'll like best. We've also highlighted the most interesting attractions, keeping in mind the time limitations facing passengers ashore just for a short port call. Many cruise passengers like to play tennis or golf while in port, so we've identified those courts, and courses that welcome cruise passengers. We've selected the best restaurants ashore as well.

The following credit-card abbreviations are used: **AE,** American Express; **D,** Discover; **DC,** Diners Club; **MC,** MasterCard; and **V,** Visa. Discover is not accepted outside the United States.

Itineraries After you've read about the ships and armchair-traveled to their different ports of call, you'll surely want to know which ships go where. So in Chapter 4, we've listed all the latest cruise itineraries for the late-1996 to mid-1997 cruise season.

Please Write to Us

Everyone who has worked on *Worldwide Cruises and Ports of Call 1997* has taken enormous care to ensure the accuracy of the text. All prices and opening times we quote are based on information supplied to us at press time. However, the passage of time will always bring changes, so it's always a good idea to call ahead to confirm information in this guide when it matters—particularly if you have to travel far from your ship. Fodor's cannot accept responsibility for any errors that may have occurred.

Was your ship as we described it? Was the food better? The service worse? The cabins smaller? Did our restaurant picks exceed your expectations? Did you find a museum we recommended a waste of time? Positive and negative, we love your feedback. So please send us a letter or postcard (we're at 201 East 50th Street, New York, NY 10022). If you have complaints, we'll look into them and revise our entries when the facts warrant it. We'll look forward to hearing from you. And in the meantime, have a wonderful cruise!

Cruise Primer

Choosing Your Cruise

The right ship is one that makes you comfortable. Every ship has its own personality, depending upon its size, when it was built, and its purpose. Big ships are more stable and offer a huge variety of activities and facilities. Smaller ships feel intimate, like private clubs. Each type of ship satisfies a certain type of passenger, and for every big-ship fan there is somebody who would never set foot aboard one of these "floating resorts."

Comparing Ships

In order to compare cruise ships, you need to speak "ship talk." Vessels are generally described according to their passenger capacity, gross registered tonnage, passenger-to-crew ratio, and space ratio. A ship's passenger capacity is usually based on double occupancy, meaning the normal cruise complement of the vessel with two passengers in each cabin. This does not include third or fourth passengers in a cabin, which on some ships can greatly increase the total passenger count. Gross registered tonnage is commonly used to measure a vessel's size. Technically, it is a measurement of the ship's volume, with one cubic foot equal to one gross registered ton. Passenger-to-crew ratio indicates the number of passengers served by each crew member—the lower the ratio, the better the level of service. Space ratio, the ship's tonnage divided by its passenger capacity, allows you to compare a ship's roominess. The higher the ratio, the more spacious a vessel will feel. The roomiest ships have ratios of 40:1 or better; ships with ratios of less than 28:1 may feel cramped.

But when choosing your cruise, the size of the ship isn't the only factor to consider. You also need to find out about the nature of the experience you will have—the lifestyle and activities available by day and after dark, the mealtime hours and dining-room dress codes, how roomy the ship is, and how good the service is apt to be. Equally important are your itinerary, the accommodations, and the cost of the cruise.

Types of Ships

Although all ocean liners are equipped with swimming pools, spas, nightclubs, theaters, and casinos, there are three distinct types: classic liners, cruise liners, and megaships. Many **classic liners,** ships constructed between 1950 and 1969 for transatlantic or other ocean crossings, are still sailing in the fleets of many cruise lines. Beginning in the 1960s, ship lines began to create vessels specifically for cruising. Some of these **cruise liners** were brand new; others were converted ferries or freighters. Vessels known as **megaships,** the biggest cruise ships ever built, first appeared in the late 1980s and, with their immense proportions and passenger capacities, immediately established a new standard of cruise-ship design.

Cruises are also available aboard a number of specialty ships: cruise yachts, expedition ships, motor-sailing ships, riverboats, and coastal cruisers.

Classic Liners With their long, sweeping hulls and stepped-back passenger decks, these vessels defined passenger-ship design for decades. Now serving cruise duty, they were originally configured to keep passengers happy during long ocean crossings. Typically, their cabins and closets are larger than those on vessels built for cruising. Deck space is sheltered, with fully or partially enclosed promenades that allow you to relax on deck even during foul weather. A few are still steam powered, without the vibrations sometimes associated with diesel power. Rich wood panels the walls, and fixtures may be the original brass. Smaller ships may feel cramped because of low ceilings in the lobby and corridors. But on the most opulent vessels, public spaces designed to inspire still do. There are balconies above the dining room, where musicians can serenade diners; stained glass graces the cinemas and other public spaces; and grand staircases lead from one deck to another. Such traditional features have proved so enduring they have been incorporated in the plans for some of today's newest vessels.

Although classic ships typically carry between 600 and 1,000 passengers and register between 20,000 and 30,000 tons, a couple of them are among the largest passenger ships afloat.

Cruise Liners When shipbuilders stopped constructing vessels for transportation and started designing them for vacationing, the cruise liner entered the scene. On these ships, outdoor deck space is plentiful; stateroom space is not. Many have a wraparound outdoor promenade deck that allows you to stroll or jog the perimeter of the ship. Older cruise liners resemble the transatlantic ships from which they are descended: Decks are stacked one atop the other in steps, and the hull amidships may appear to droop, so the bow and stern seem to curve upward. In the newest cruise liners, traditional meets trendy. You find atrium lobbies and expansive sun and sports decks, picture windows instead of portholes, and cabins that open onto private verandas. The smallest cruise liners carry 500 passengers and are no bigger than 10,000 tons, while the largest accommodate 1,500 passengers, exceed 50,000 tons, and are stuffed with diversions—almost like megaships.

Megaships The centerpiece of most megaships is a three-, five-, or seven-story central atrium. However, these giant vessels are most easily recognized by their boxy profile: The hull and superstructure rise straight out of the water, as many as 14 stories tall, topped out by a huge sun or sports deck with a jogging track and swimming pool, which may be Olympic size. Some megaships, but not all, also have a wraparound promenade deck. Like the latest cruise liners, picture windows are standard equipment, and cabins in the top categories have private verandas. From their casinos and discos to their fitness centers, everything is proportionally bigger and more extravagant than on other ships. Between 1,500 and 2,500 passengers can be accommodated, and tonnage ranges from 60,000 to 70,000 or more.

Cruise Yachts At the opposite end of the spectrum from the megaship is the tiny cruise yacht. These intimate vessels carry from 100 to 300 passengers, register between 4,000 and 15,000 tons, and are like miniature ocean liners, with big-ship amenities such as fitness centers, casinos, lounges, and swimming pools. What sets these yachts apart from typical ocean liners is that passengers are treated like royalty. Cabins are all outside suites equipped with every creature comfort on the high seas—from VCRs and stocked minibars to marble baths. Built into the stern of some of these vessels are retractable platforms, which are lowered for water sports when the ship is at anchor in calm waters.

Expedition Ships Vessels of this type are designed to reach into the most remote corners of the world. Shallow drafts allow them to navigate up rivers, close to coastlines, and into shallow coves. Hulls may be hardened for sailing in Antarctic ice. Motorized rubber landing craft known as Zodiacs, kept on board, make it possible for passengers to put ashore almost anywhere. However, because the emphasis during cruises aboard expedition ships tends to be on learning and exploring, the ships don't have casinos, showrooms, multiple bars and lounges, and other typical ocean-liner diversions. Instead, they have theaters for lectures, well-stocked libraries, and enrichment programs, led by experts, as entertainment. The smallest expedition ships carry fewer than 100 passengers and register just over 2,000 tons. The largest carries nearly 200 people and registers 9,000 tons.

Motor-Sail Vessels A number of cruise vessels were designed as sailing ships. With their sails unfurled, they are an impressive sight. But since they must keep to a schedule, they cannot rely solely on wind power. So all are equipped with engines as well. Usually they employ both means of propulsion, a technique known as motor sailing, to put on a good show and make the next port on time. These vessels range from small windjammers carrying a handful of passengers to rather large clipper-style ships that approach the size of a small ocean liner and accommodate almost 400 passengers.

Riverboats Most riverboats sailing in today's cruise fleet are replicas of those that sailed the nation's rivers in the 19th century. The feeling is definitely Victorian: Parlors are furnished with Tiffany lamps and leather wing chairs, and rocking chairs line the outer decks. Smaller riverboats offer just a lounge or two and a dining room. Bigger ones may add a small health club, theater, and a few other amenities, while still retaining their traditional character. But even the largest riverboat, which carries more than 400 passengers, registers only 3,000 tons.

Coastal Cruisers Closely related to the riverboat is its modern-day equivalent, the coastal cruiser. Designed more for exploring than entertaining, these yachtlike ships are able to sail to remote waterways and ports. Some have forward gangways for bow landings or carry a fleet of Zodiac landing craft. Unlike larger expedition ships, they do not have ice-hardened hulls. Registering no more than 100 tons and carrying only about 100 passengers, coastal cruisers offer few onboard facilities and public spaces—perhaps just a dining room and a multipurpose lounge.

The Cruise Experience

Your cruise experience will be shaped by several factors, and to determine whether a particular ship's style will suit you, you need to do a bit of research. Is a full program of organized activities scheduled by day? What happens in the evening? Are there one or two seatings in the dining room? If there is more than one, you will not be allowed to arrive and exit as the spirit moves you but instead must show up promptly when service begins—and clear out within a specified time. What kind of entertainment is offered after dark? And how often do passengers dress up for dinner? Some cruises are fancier than others.

Although no two cruises are quite the same, even aboard the same ship, the cruise experience tends to fall into three categories.

Formal Formal cruises embody the ceremony of cruising. Generally available on ocean liners and cruise yachts sailing for seven days or longer, formal cruises recall the days when traveling by ship was an event in itself. By day, shipboard lifestyle is generally unstructured, with few organized activities. Tea and bouillon may be served to the accompaniment of music from a classical trio in the afternoon. Ashore, passengers may be treated to a champagne beach party. Meals in the dining room are served in a single seating, and passengers are treated to the finest cuisine afloat. Jackets and ties for men are the rule for dinner, tuxedos are not uncommon, and the dress code is observed faithfully throughout the evening. Pianists, cabaret acts, and local entertainers provide nighttime diversion. Service is extremely attentive and personalized. Passenger-to-crew and space ratios are best. Because these cruises tend to attract destination-oriented passengers, shore excursions—such as private museum tours—sometimes are included in the fare, as are pre- or post-cruise land packages and sometimes even tips.

Semiformal Semiformal cruises are a bit more relaxed than their formal counterparts. Meals are served in two seatings on ocean liners or one seating on specialty ships, menu choices are plentiful, and the cuisine is on a par with that available in better restaurants. Men tend to wear a jacket and tie to dinner most nights. Adding a distinct flair to the dining room is the common practice of staffing the restaurant with waiters of one nationality. Featured dishes may be prepared table side, and you often are able, with advance notice, to order a special diet, such as kosher, low salt, low cholesterol, sugar-free, or vegetarian (*see* Dining *in* On Board, *below*). There is a daily program of scheduled events, but there's time for more independent pursuits; passengers with similar interests are often encouraged to meet at appointed times for chess or checkers, deck games, and other friendly contests. Production-style shows are staged each evening, but the disco scene may not be too lively. Passenger-to-crew and space ratios assure good service and plenty of room for each passenger. Look for semiformal cruises aboard classic liners, cruise liners, megaships, and a few expedition ships on voyages of seven days or longer.

Casual Casual cruises are the most popular. Shipboard dress and lifestyle are informal. Meals in the dining room are served in two seatings on ocean liners and one seating on specialty ships; menus are usually not extensive, and the food is good but not extraordinary; your options may be limited if you have special dietetic requirements. Men dress in sport shirts and slacks for dinner most nights, in jackets and ties only two or three evenings of a typical seven-day sailing. Aboard casual ocean liners, activities are more diverse than on formal and semiformal ships, and there is almost always something going on, from bingo to beer-chugging contests. Las Vegas–style variety shows or Broadway revues headline the evening entertainment. Discos bop into the wee hours. Passenger-to-crew and space ratios are generally good, but service tends to be less personal. On specialty ships, activities on board will be limited as indicated in Types of Ships, *above*.

Look for casual cruises aboard classic liners, cruise liners, and megaships sailing three- to seven-day itineraries to fun-and-sun destinations; expedition ships; motor-sailing ships; riverboats; and coastal cruisers calling on more unusual ports.

Theme Cruises These increasingly popular sailings highlight a particular activity or topic. Onboard lectures and other events are coordinated with shoreside excursions. There are photography cruises, square-dancing cruises, sports cruises, financial-planning cruises, wine-tasting cruises, and more. The most popular destinations for theme cruises are Alaska and the Caribbean. To find out about theme cruises that might interest you, consult with the individual cruise lines or a travel agent. Lines that offer the greatest variety of theme cruises are **American Hawaii Cruises, Cunard Line, Dolphin Cruise Line, Holland America Line, Majesty Cruise Line, Norwegian Cruise Line, Premier Cruise Lines, and Royal Caribbean Cruise Line.**

How Long to Sail

After you choose the type of ship and cruise experience you prefer, you must decide on how long to sail: Do you want a two-day cruise to nowhere or a 100-day journey around the world? Two key factors to keep in mind are how much money you want to spend and how experienced are you at cruising—it probably wouldn't be a good idea to circumnavigate the globe your first time at sea.

Short cruises are ideal for first-time cruisers and families with children. In just two to five days you can get a quick taste of cruising. You'll have the chance to sail aboard some of the newest ships afloat, built exclusively for these runs. Short itineraries may include stops at one or two ports of call, or none at all. The most popular short cruises are three- and four-day sailings to the Bahamas or Key West and Cozumel out of Miami. From Los Angeles, three- and four-day cruises set sail for southern California and the Mexican Riviera.

After you have experienced a long weekend at sea, you may want to try a **weeklong cruise.** With seven days aboard ship, you get twice as much sailing time and a wider choice of destinations—as many as four to six ports, depending on whether you choose a loop or one-way itinerary (*see* Ship Itineraries, *below*). Since cruises are priced by a per-diem rate multiplied by the number of days aboard ship (*see* Cost, *below*), a weeklong cruise probably costs twice as much as a short cruise.

For some people, seven days is still too short—just when you learn your way around the ship, it's time to go home. On **10- or 11-day sailings,** you get more ports as well as more time at sea, but you won't pay as much as on **two-week sailings.** Many experienced cruisers feel it's just not worth the effort to board a ship for anything less than 14 days, so they opt for either a single 14-day itinerary or sign up for two seven-day trips back-to-back, combining sailings to eastern and western Caribbean ports of call, for example—and taking advantage of the discounts offered by some lines for consecutive sailings. Cruises that last longer than two weeks—**very long cruises**—require a lot of time and money and a love of cruising. If you have all these, then cruising can become more than a vacation—it can be a way of life.

Ship Itineraries

In choosing the best cruise for you, a ship's itinerary is another important factor. The length of the cruise will determine the variety and number of ports you visit, but so will the type of itinerary and the point of departure. Some cruises, known as **loop cruises,** start and end at the same point and usually explore ports close to one another; **one-way cruises** start at one port and end at another and range farther afield.

Most cruises to Bermuda, the Bahamas, the Mexican Riviera, and the Caribbean are loop cruises. On Caribbean itineraries, you often have a choice of departure points. Sailings out of San Juan, Puerto Rico, can visit up to six ports in seven days, while loop cruises out of Florida can reach up to four ports in the same time.

Cruises to Antarctica generally operate on one of two loop itineraries: most commonly from the tip of South America to the Antarctic Peninsula, but also from New Zealand or Australia to the Ross Sea. Because the latter itinerary covers much longer distances, you spend more time at sea and less on shore—though there is a stop at historic huts used by early Antarctic explorers.

The most common one-way itineraries are to Canada and New England or to South America. So-called Caribazon cruises combine a journey up or down the Amazon River with port calls in the Caribbean. Alaska sailings come as loop itineraries, generally only within the Inside Passage, and as one-way cruises, sailing across the Gulf of Alaska and giving you the chance to explore farther north on land before or after the cruise.

Many ships sailing the Caribbean or the Mexican Riviera in winter and spring move to Alaska or New England in summer and fall. Other ships spend part of the year in the Caribbean, part outside the Western Hemisphere. When a ship moves from one cruising area to another, it offers a **repositioning cruise,** which typically stops at less-visited ports and attracts fewer passengers. It often has a lower per diem than cruises to the most popular sailing destinations.

A handful of ships offer an annual one- to two-month **cruise around South America** or a three- to four-month **around-the-world cruise** that stops at dozens of fabulous ports. This continent-hopping itinerary typically costs from $20,000 per person for a small inside cabin to hundreds of thousands of dollars for a suite; partial segments, usually of 14 to 21 days, are also available.

Note: Cruise itineraries listed in Chapter 4 are for the late-1996 to mid-1997 cruise season but are subject to change. Contact your travel agent or the cruise line directly for up-to-the-minute itineraries.

Cost

For one price, a cruise gives you all your meals, accommodations, and onboard entertainment. The only extras are tips, shore excursions, shopping, bar bills, and other incidentals. The axiom "the more you pay, the more you get" doesn't always hold true: While higher fares do prevail for better ships, which have more comfortable cabins, more attractive decor, and better service, the passenger in the least-expensive inside cabin eats the same food, sees the same shows, and shares the same amenities as one paying more than $1,000 per day for the top suite on any given ship. (A notable exception is aboard the *Queen Elizabeth 2*, where your dining-room assignment is based on your cabin category.)

A handy way to compare costs of different ships is to look at the per diem—the price of a cruise on a daily basis per passenger, based on double occupancy. (For instance, the per diem is $100 for a seven-day cruise that costs $700 per person when two people share the same cabin.)

For each ship reviewed in Chapter 1, average per diems are listed in three cabin categories: suites, outside cabins, and inside cabins (*see* Accommodations, *below*). Rates are based on published brochure prices, in peak season, for itineraries as noted. Remember that these average per diems are meant for comparative purposes only—so you can see the relative costliness of one ship versus another. For actual cruise fares, which can vary wildly and are subject to widespread discounting, you'll need to contact your travel agent or cruise specialist. Of course, there will be additional expenses beyond your basic cruise fare. When you go to book a cruise, don't forget to consider these expenditures:

Pre- and post-cruise arrangements: If you plan to arrive a day or two early at the port of embarkation, or linger a few days for sightseeing after debarkation, estimate the cost of your hotel, meals, car rental, sightseeing, and other expenditures. Cruise lines sell packages for pre- and post-cruise stays that may or may not cost less than arrangements you make independently, so shop around.

Airfare: Be sure to check whether the price of your cruise includes air transportation to and from the ship. If it does not, you can purchase your airline tickets and transfers from the cruise line. This is known as an air-sea package. Air-sea packages generally are convenient and reasonably priced. However, the cruise line chooses your airline and flight. Lines sometimes give passengers who make their own arrangements an air transportation credit of $200 or more, depending on the destination. By arranging your own airfare, you may get a lower fare and a more convenient routing. If you have frequent-flyer miles, you may be able to get a free ticket.

Pre-trip incidentals: These may include trip or flight insurance, the cost of boarding your pets, airport or port parking, departure tax, visas, long-distance calls home, clothing, film or videotape, and other miscellaneous expenses.

Shore excursions and expenses: Costs for ship-organized shore excursions range from less than $20 for the cheapest city tour to almost $300 for the most expensive flightseeing packages. Review the descriptions of shore excursions in Chapter 3 to estimate how much you are likely to spend.

Amusement and gambling allowance: Video games, bingo, and gambling can set you back a bundle. If you plan to bet, budget for your losses—you'll almost certainly have them. You must be over 18 to gamble on a cruise ship.

Shopping: Include what you expect to spend for both inexpensive souvenirs and pricey duty-free purchases.

Onboard incidentals: Most cruise lines recommend that passengers tip their cabin steward, dining-room waiter, and assistant waiter a total of $8–$9 per person, per day. Tips for bartenders and others who have helped you will vary. Also figure in the bar tabs and the cost of wine with meals, laundry, beauty-parlor services, purchases in the gift shop, and other incidentals.

Accommodations

Cabins vary greatly depending upon the type of ship you choose. On every ship, though, there are different cabin categories priced according to their size, location, and amenities. Cruise brochures show the ship's layout deck by deck and the approximate location and shape of every cabin and suite. Use the deck plan to make sure the cabin you pick is not near public rooms, which may be noisy, or the ship's engines, which can vibrate at certain speeds, and make sure that you are near stairs or an elevator to avoid walking down long corridors every time you return to your cabin. Usually, the listing in the brochure of the ship's different cabin categories includes details on what kind of beds the cabin has, whether it has a window or a porthole, and what furnishings are provided. Brochures also usually show representative cabin layouts, but be aware that configurations within each category can differ. In Chapter 1, we have tried to indicate those outside cabins that may be partially obstructed by lifeboats or that overlook a public deck.

Cabin Size Compared with land-based accommodations, many standard ship cabins seem tiny. The higher you go in the ship, the larger the quarters tend to be; outside cabins are generally bigger than inside ones (*see* Location, *below*).

Suites are the roomiest and best-equipped accommodations, but even aboard the same ship, they may differ in size, facilities, and price. Steward service may be more attentive to passengers staying in suites; top suites on some ships are even assigned private butlers. Most suites have a sitting area with a sofa and chairs; some have two bathrooms, occasionally with a whirlpool bath. The most expensive suites may be priced without regard to the number of passengers occupying them.

Location On all ships, regardless of size or design, the bow (front) and stern (back) pitch up and down on the waves far more than the hull amidships (middle). Ships also experience a side-to-side motion known as roll. The closer your deck is to the true center of the ship—about halfway between the bottom of the hull and the highest deck and midway between the bow and the stern—the less you will feel the ship's movement. Some cruise lines charge more for cabins amidships; most charge more for the higher decks.

Outside cabins have portholes or windows (which cannot be opened); on the upper decks, the view from outside cabins may be partially obstructed by lifeboats or overlook a public deck. Because outside cabins are more desirable, newer ships are configured with mostly outside cabins or with outside cabins only. Increasingly, an outside cabin on an upper deck comes with a private veranda. Windows are mirrored in cabins that overlook an outdoor promenade so that passersby can't see in—at least by day; after dark, you need to draw your curtains.

Inside cabins on older vessels are often smaller and oddly shaped. On newer ships, the floor plans of inside cabins are virtually identical to those of outside cabins. Providing you don't feel claustrophobic without a window, inside cabins represent an excellent value.

Furnishings All ocean-liner cabins and most specialty ship cabins are equipped with individually controlled air-conditioning, limited closet space, and a private bathroom—usually closet-size, with a toilet, small shower, and washbasin. More expensive cabins, especially on newer ships, may have a bathtub. Most cabins also have a small desk or dresser, a reading light, and, on many ships, a TV and sometimes even a VCR. Except on some older ocean liners and smaller specialty ships, all cabins also come with a phone.

Depending upon the ship and category, a cabin may have beds or berths. The most expensive cabins usually have king- or queen-size beds. Cabins priced in the mid-range often have doubles or twins. In cabins with twins, the beds may be positioned side by side or at right angles. On most newer ships, the twin beds in many cabins can be pushed together to form a double. If this is what you want, get written confirmation that your specific cabin number has this capability. Less expensive cabins and cabins on smaller or older ships, especially those that accommodate three or four people, may have upper and lower bunks, or berths; these are folded into the wall by day to provide more living space. Sofa beds replace upper berths on some newer ships.

Sharing Most cabins are designed to accommodate two people. When more than two share a cabin, such as when parents cruise with their children, the third and fourth passengers are usually offered a discount, thereby lowering the per-person price for the room for the entire group.

Sailing Alone Some ships, mostly older ones, have a few single cabins. But on most ships, passengers traveling on their own must pay a single supplement, which usually ranges from 125% to 200% of the double-occupancy per-person rate. On request, many cruise lines will match up two strangers of the same sex in a cabin at the standard per-person double-occupancy rate.

Hints for Passengers with Children

Children aboard cruise ships are a common sight these days. To serve this growing market, a number of cruise lines have expanded their facilities and programs aimed at children. Many offer a discount for younger cruisers.

Discounts Discounted fares range from free passage on off-peak sailings to $400 per child during high season. Some cruise lines, such as Celebrity Cruises, Dolphin Cruise Line, Majesty Cruise Line, Norwegian Cruise Line, and Royal Olympic Cruises allow children under two to sail without charge; kids under 17 sail free on American Hawaii Cruises. Airfares and shore excursions also are frequently discounted. For single parents sailing with their children, Premier Cruise Lines offers a reduced single supplement of 25% (normally the charge is 100%).

Activities and Supervision Lines that frequently sail with children aboard may have costumed staff to entertain younger passengers. Premier Cruise Lines has Looney Tunes favorites, such as Bugs Bunny and Daffy Duck, running around its ships. Aboard Dolphin Cruise Line or Majesty

Luxury Suite/Apartment

The largest accommodations on board, luxury suites have sitting areas, queen-size beds, vanity desks, and walk-in closets (with safes).

1. Although televisions are common, luxury suites often have VCRs (and access to a video library) and stereos as well.
2. Private verandas, connected by sliding doors, are on some ships.
3. Most luxury suites have refrigerators, often with stocked bars. Butler service is provided on some ships.
4. Twin sinks and Jacuzzi bathtubs (with shower) are typical.
5. The sofa can usually unfold into a bed for additional passengers.

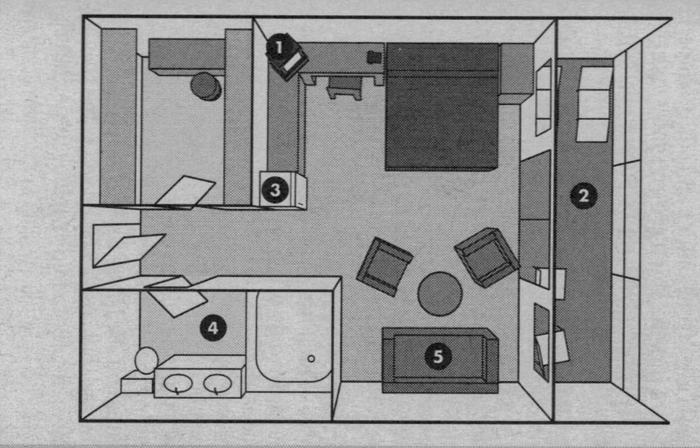

Suite

Though much more expensive than regular cabins, suites are also larger, featuring double beds, sitting areas, televisions, and comparatively large closets.

1. Bathrooms are likely to have single sinks and bathtubs (with showers).
2. Refrigerators are often included, although alcoholic beverages may not be complimentary.
3. Suites, which tend to be on upper decks, usually have large picture windows.
4. The sofa can be converted into a bed.

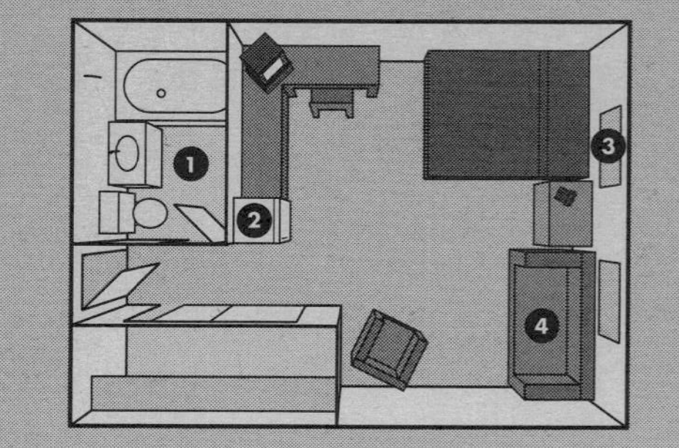

Outside Cabin

Outside cabins have showers rather than bathtubs and seldom have refrigerators. Most cabins have phones, and many have televisions.

1. Many cabins, especially those on lower decks, have portholes instead of picture windows. Cabins on newer ships, however, often have large windows.
2. Twin beds are common, although many ships now offer a double bed. Upper berths for additional passengers fold into the wall.

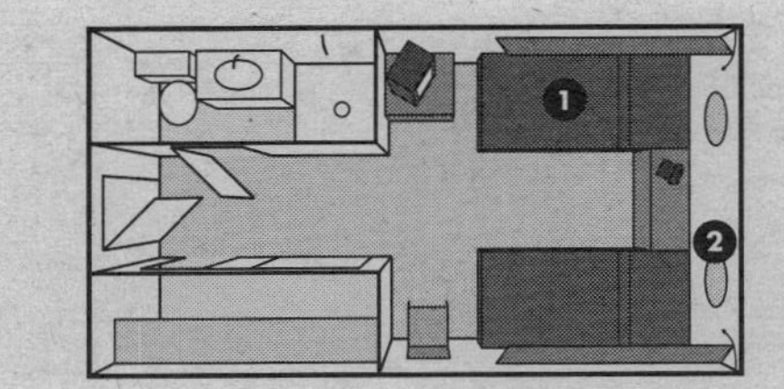

Inside Cabin

The least expensive accommodations, inside cabins have no portholes, tend to be tiny and oddly configured, have miniscule clothes closets, and bathrooms with showers only.

1. Almost all cabins have phones, but few have televisions.
2. Many inside cabins have upper and lower berths; the upper berth folds into the wall during the day, and the lower berth is made a couch.

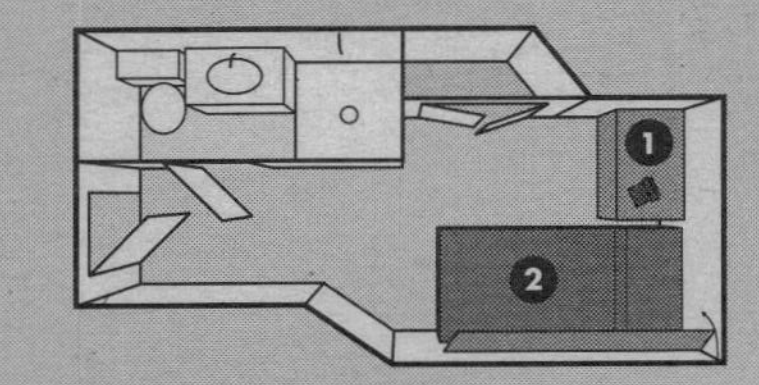

* Cruise lines offer a wide range of cabins, with a variety of names. This chart is intended as a general guide only.

Selecting a Cabin*

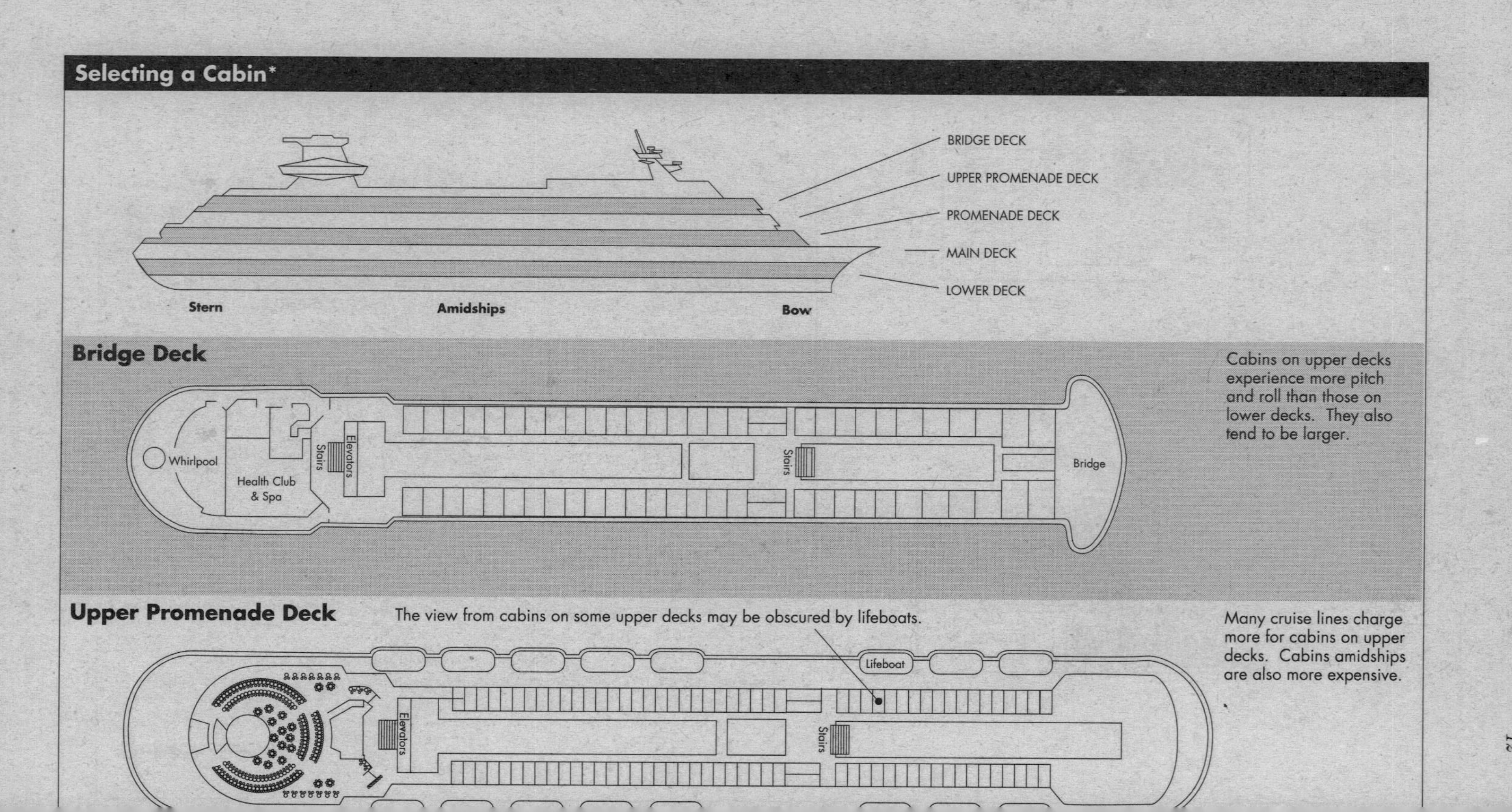

Cabins on upper decks experience more pitch and roll than those on lower decks. They also tend to be larger.

The view from cabins on some upper decks may be obscured by lifeboats.

Many cruise lines charge more for cabins on upper decks. Cabins amidships are also more expensive.

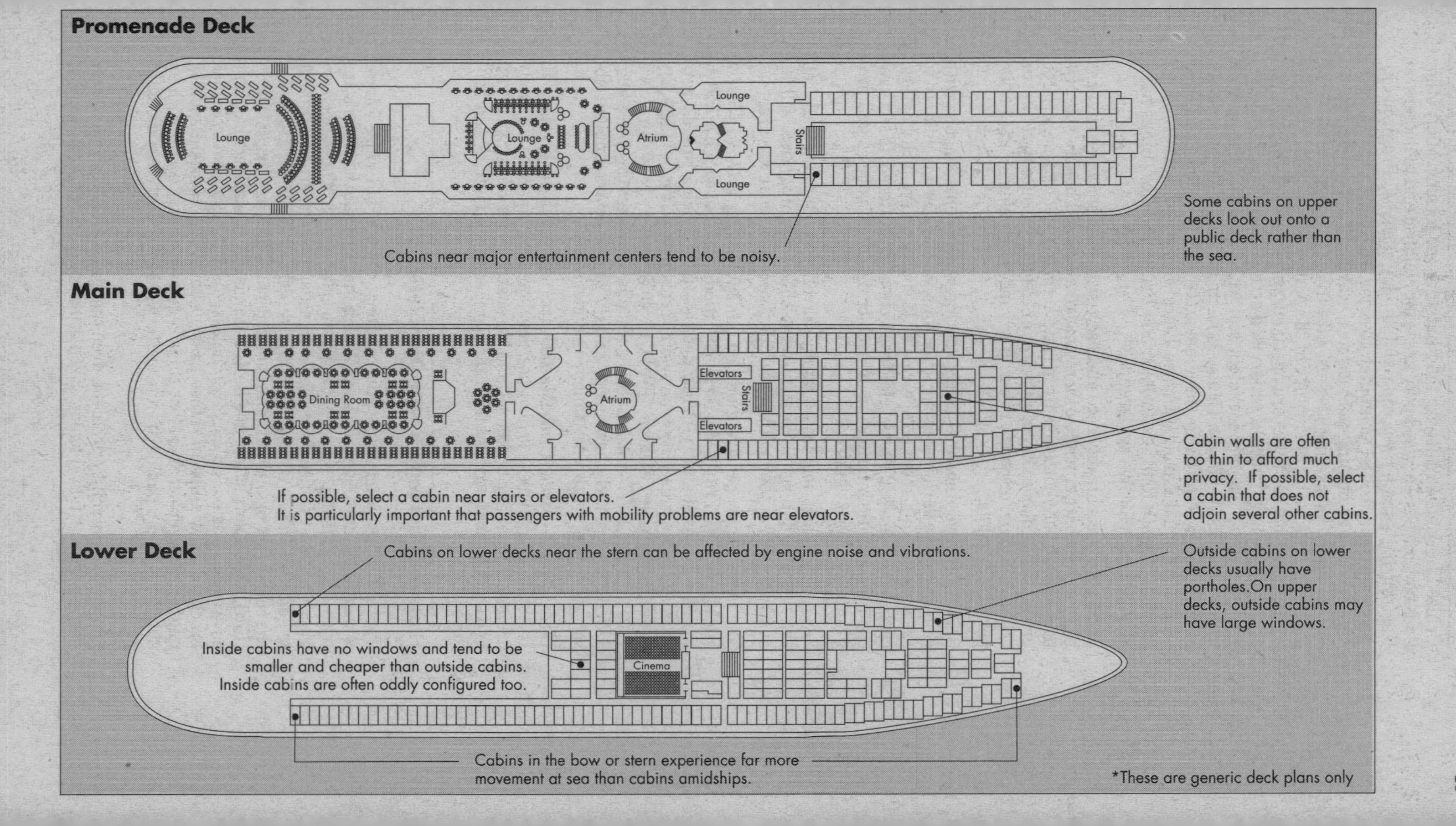
Promenade Deck
Lounge
Lounge
Atrium
Lounge
Stairs
Lounge
Some cabins on upper decks look out onto a public deck rather than the sea.
Cabins near major entertainment centers tend to be noisy.
Main Deck
Dining Room
Atrium
Elevators
Stairs
Elevators
Cabin walls are often too thin to afford much privacy. If possible, select a cabin that does not adjoin several other cabins.
If possible, select a cabin near stairs or elevators.
It is particularly important that passengers with mobility problems are near elevators.
Lower Deck
Cabins on lower decks near the stern can be affected by engine noise and vibrations.
Outside cabins on lower decks usually have portholes.On upper decks, outside cabins may have large windows.
Inside cabins have no windows and tend to be smaller and cheaper than outside cabins.
Inside cabins are often oddly configured too.
Cinema
Cabins in the bow or stern experience far more movement at sea than cabins amidships.
*These are generic deck plans only

Cruise Line you can sail with the Flintstones or Jetsons. Many other lines now have supervised play areas for children and teenagers, at least during summer vacation and holiday periods. Programs include arts and crafts, computer instruction, games and quizzes, kids' movies, swimming-pool parties, scavenger hunts, ship tours, magic shows, snorkeling lessons, kite flying, cooking classes, and teaching sessions on the history of the ports to be visited. Find out in advance whether there are special programs for your child's age group, how many hours of supervised activities are scheduled each day, whether meals are included, and what the counselor-to-child ratio is. Royal Caribbean Cruise Line and Celebrity Cruises have programs for children in three separate age groups; Norwegian Cruise Line and Carnival Cruise Lines' Camp Carnival programs are divided into four age groups; and Premier Cruise Lines has a kids' program for five age groups.

Some ships provide day care and baby-sitting for younger children at no extra charge, while others charge a nominal hourly rate. On many ships, baby-sitting is by private arrangement (at a negotiated price). If you plan to bring an infant or toddler, be sure to request a crib, high chair, or booster seat in advance and bring plenty of diapers and formula.

Ships with two dinner seatings routinely assign passengers with children to the earlier seating; some lines will not permit children to eat in the dining room on their own. If your kids are picky eaters, check ahead to see if special children's menus are offered. (*See* Chapter 1 for specific information on each cruise line's policies and programs regarding children.)

Publications Several excellent sources on family travel exist. But above all, call the line and determine exactly what children's programs will be available during your sailing, and talk it over with your travel agent.

The most comprehensive guide on family cruising is *Great Cruise Vacations With Your Kids*, formerly titled *Cruising with Children*, which contains the nitty-gritty details—from pricing to kids' programs to crib availability—on over 35 cruise lines. It is published by **Travel With Your Children** (TWYCH, 40 5th Ave., New York, NY 10011, tel. 212/477–5524) and is available in bookstores for $9.95. TWYCH's quarterly newsletter *Family Travel Times* (annual subscription $40), features a column on cruising.

Agencies to Contact Los Angeles–based **CruiseMasters** (*see* Agencies to Contact *in* Booking Your Cruise, *below*) has developed an expertise in family cruising and offers brochures and tip sheets about cruising, ports, and sightseeing, written from the perspective of families and children.

Hints for Passengers with Disabilities

The official position of the International Council of Cruise Lines, which represents cruise lines in Washington, is that the Americans with Disabilities Act does not apply to cruise ships. The council argues that most cruise ships, as foreign-flag vessels, are not subject to domestic U.S. laws governing construction and design. However, the council is working with the International Maritime Organization (IMO), which sets safety and design standards, to make cruise ships as accessible as possible. Nevertheless, disclaimers on every cruise brochure allow ships to refuse passage to anyone whose disability might endanger others. Most ships require that you travel with an able-bodied companion if you use a wheelchair or have mobility problems.

If you have a mobility problem, even though you do not use a wheelchair, tell your travel agent. Each cruise line sets its own policies;

choose the line that is most accommodating. Also be careful to select a ship that is easy to get around. Ships vary even within the fleet of the same line. (*See* Chapter 1 for specific recommendations on which ships are suitable for passengers with mobility problems.) Follow up by making sure that the cruise line is fully informed of your disabilities and any special needs, and ask if the ship has a full-time physician on board. (Virtually all major cruise ships have a doctor on call.) Get written confirmation of any promises that have been made to you about a special cabin or transfers to and from the airport. The line may request a letter from your doctor stating that you need neither a wheelchair nor a companion, or that you will not require special medical attention on board.

If you have any type of chronic health problem that may require medical attention, notify the ship's doctor soon after you board so he or she will be prepared to treat you appropriately, if necessary.

Passengers in Wheelchairs

The latest cruise ships have been built with accessibility in mind, and many older ships have been modified to accommodate passengers in wheelchairs. The key areas to be concerned about are public rooms, outer decks, and, of course, your cabin. If you need a specially equipped cabin, book as far in advance as possible and ask specific questions of your travel agent or a cruise-line representative. Specifically, ask how your cabin is configured and equipped. Is the entrance level or ramped? Are all doorways at least 30 inches wide (wider if your wheelchair is not standard size)? Are pathways to beds, closets, and bathrooms at least 36 inches wide and unobstructed? In the bathroom, is there 42 inches of clear space in front of the toilet and are there grab bars behind and on one side of it and in the bathtub or shower? Ask whether there is a three-prong outlet in the cabin, and whether the bathroom has a handheld showerhead, a bath bench, or roll-in shower or shower stall with fold-down seat, if you need them. For specific information about individual ships, *see* Accessibility *in* Chapter 1.

The best cruise ship for passengers who use wheelchairs is one that ties up right at the dock at every port, at which time a ramp or even an elevator is always made available. Unfortunately, it's hard to ascertain this in advance, for a ship may tie up at the dock at a particular port on one voyage and, on the next, anchor in the harbor and have passengers transported to shore via tender. Ask your travel agent to find out which ships are scheduled to dock on which cruises. If a tender is used, some ships will have crew members carry the wheelchair and passenger from the ship to the tender. Unfortunately, other ships point-blank refuse to take wheelchairs on tenders, especially if the water is choppy. At some ports, ships always tender because docking facilities are unavailable. For more information about where and whether ships dock or tender, *see* Coming Ashore for each port *in* Chapter 3.

Passengers with Vision Impairments

Some ships allow guide dogs to accompany passengers with vision impairments; however, if your cruise is scheduled to visit foreign ports (as most do), you may not be able to take a guide dog ashore, depending on the country. To avoid potential quarantine upon returning to the United States, guide dogs should have their shots updated within seven days of sailing, and owners should carry the dog's valid health and rabies certificates.

Hawaii is especially strict about importing animals. No dog, not even a guide dog, may step ashore without being quarantined for 120 days unless it arrives from an area recognized by the state as rabies-free. Guide dogs may remain aboard visiting ships during port calls for up to 48 hours. That period begins upon docking at the first Hawaiian port and includes all time spent in Hawaiian waters.

Pregnant Women

Considering advanced pregnancy a disability, cruise lines may refuse passage to pregnant women. "Advanced" usually refers to the third trimester. If you are pregnant, check on the cruise line's policy before you book passage.

Passengers with Diabetes Check with individual cruise lines to find out if a ship stocks insulin and other diabetic supplies and if a physician is on board. A good resource, chock-full of travel tips, is the quarterly newsletter ***The Diabetic Traveler*** (Box 8223 RW, Stamford, CT 06905, tel. 203/327–5832, $18.95 per yr). Back issues are available and include one dedicated to cruise vacations ($3, Autumn 1992).

Organizations Several organizations provide travel information for people with disabilities, usually for a membership fee, and some publish newsletters and bulletins. Among them are the **Information Center for Individuals with Disabilities** (29 Stanhope St., Box 256, Boston, MA 02217, tel. 617/450–9888; in MA, 800/462–5015; TTY 617/424–6855); **Mobility International USA** (Box 10767, Eugene, OR 97440, tel. and TTY 503/343–1284, fax 503/343–6812), the U.S. branch of an international organization based in Belgium (*see below*) that has affiliates in 30 countries; **MossRehab Hospital Travel Information Service** (tel. 215/456–9600, TTY 215/456–9602); **Society for the Advancement of Travel for the Handicapped** (SATH, 347 5th Ave., New York, NY 10016, tel. 212/447–7284; membership $35); and **Travelin' Talk** (Box 3534, Clarksville, TN 37043, tel. 615/552–6670, fax 615/552–1182).

In the United Kingdom Important information sources include the **Royal Association for Disability and Rehabilitation** (RADAR, 12 City Forum, 250 City Rd., London EC1V 8AF, tel. 0171/250–3222), which publishes travel information for people with disabilities in Britain, and **Mobility International** (Rue de Manchester 25, B1070 Brussels, Belgium, tel. 00–322–410–6297), an international clearinghouse of travel information for people with disabilities.

Travel Agencies and Tour Operators **Accessible Journeys** (35 W. Sellers Ave., Ridley Park, PA 19078, tel. 610/521–0339 or 800/846–4537, fax 610/521–6959) arranges escorted trips for travelers with disabilities and provides licensed health-care professionals to accompany those who require aid. **Flying Wheels Travel** (143 W. Bridge St., Box 382, Owatonna, MN 55060, tel. 507/451–5005 or 800/535–6790) is a travel agency specializing in domestic and worldwide cruises for people with mobility problems.

Publications *Wheels and Waves: A Cruise-Ferry Guide for the Physically Handicapped* ($13.95 plus $3 shipping, tel. 800/637–2256) describes more than 200 ships, including 100 with accessible cabins. It is a publication of Wheels Aweigh (17105 San Carlos Blvd., Fort Myers, FL 33931).

Several publications are available from the Consumer Information Center (Pueblo, CO 81009, tel. 719/948–3334): "Fly Smart" (include Dept. 575B in address), a free pocket-size brochure, details flight safety tips. "Fly-Rights" (Dept. 133B), is a booklet that includes a section on air-travel rights for passengers with disabilities ($1.75).

Travelin' Talk Directory (*see* Organizations, *above*) was published in 1993. This 500-page resource book ($35 check or money order with a money-back guarantee) is packed with information for travelers with disabilities. Twin Peaks Press (Box 129, Vancouver, WA 98666, tel. 360/694–2462 or 800/637–2256) publishes the *Directory of Travel Agencies for the Disabled* ($19.95), which lists more than 370 agencies worldwide, and *Wheelchair Vagabond* ($14.95), a collection of personal travel tips. Add $3 shipping for the first book, $1.50 for each additional. *Cruise Travel Magazine* published an in-depth article and chart on cruising for people with disabilities in its January 1996 issue. Back issues are available. "Cruising for the Physically Challenged" (tel. 800/882–9000) is a free booklet published by World Wide Cruises Inc., offering practical travel tips in a Q&A format.

Hints for Older Passengers

For older travelers, cruise vacations strike an excellent balance: They offer a tremendous variety of activities and destinations in one convenient package. You can do as much or as little as you want, meet new people, see new places, enjoy shows and bingo, learn to play bridge, or take up needlepoint—all within a safe, familiar environment. Cruises are *not* a good idea for those who are bedridden, have a serious medical condition that is likely to flare up on board, or are prone to periods of confusion or severe memory loss.

No particular rules apply to senior citizens on cruises, but certain freighter cruises do have an age limit (*see* Chapter 2). Those who want a leisurely, relaxed pace will probably be happiest on ships that attract a higher percentage of older passengers: luxury ocean liners, cruise yachts, and expedition ships on voyages of longer than seven days. Passengers who are less than spry should look for a ship where the public rooms are clustered on one deck and select a cabin near an elevator or stairway amidships. Do not book a cabin with upper and lower berths.

Only a couple of cruise lines, notably Royal Caribbean and Premier, have reduced rates for senior citizens, but senior citizens may be able to take advantage of local discounts ashore. When in port, showing proof of age often results in reduced admissions, half fares on public transportation, and special dining rates.

Several cruise lines employ "gentleman hosts," who act as dancing and bridge partners for single ladies traveling alone. Look into Cunard Line, Delta Queen Steamboat Company, Holland America Line, Royal Olympic Cruises, and Silversea Cruises.

Organizations The **National Council of Senior Citizens** (1331 F St. NW, Washington, DC 20004, tel. 202/347-8800; membership $12 annually) offers discounts on cruises, along with such nontravel perks as magazines and newsletters.

Tour Operators **Saga International Holidays** (222 Berkeley St., Boston, MA 02116, tel. 617/262-2262 or 800/343-0273) caters to those over age 50 who like to travel in groups. **SeniorTours** (508 Irvington Rd., Drexel Hill, PA 19026, tel. 800/227-1100) arranges cruises.

Publications "The Mature Traveler" (Box 50400, Reno, NV 89513, tel. 702/786-7419; $29.95), a monthly newsletter, lists discounts on cruises.

Hints for Gay and Lesbian Passengers

Organizations The **International Gay Travel Association** (Box 4974, Key West, FL 33041, tel. 800/448-8550, IGTA@aol.com), which has over 1,100 travel-industry members, will provide you with names of travel agents and cruise lines that specialize in gay travel.

Tour Operators and Travel Agencies Some of the largest agencies serving gay travelers are **Advance Damron Vacations** (10700 Northwest Fwy., #160, Houston, TX 77092, tel. 713/682-2650 or 800/695-0880), **Islanders/Kennedy Travel** (183 W. 10th St., New York, NY 10014, tel. 212/242-3222 or 800/988-1181), **Now Voyager** (4406 18th St., San Francisco, CA 94114, tel. 415/626-1169 or 800/255-6951), **Pied Piper** (tel. 212/239-2412 or 800/874-7312), and **Yellowbrick Road** (1500 W. Balmoral Ave., Chicago, IL 60640, tel. 312/561-1800 or 800/642-2488). **R.S.V.P. Travel Productions** (tel. 800/328-7787) operates many gay cruises, and **Olivia Cruises & Resorts** (tel. 800/631-6277) provides the same service for lesbian travelers.

Publications The premier international travel magazine for gays and lesbians is ***Our World*** (1104 N. Nova Rd., Suite 251, Daytona Beach, FL 32117, tel. 904/441-5367; $35 for 10 issues). **"Out & About"** (tel. 800/929-

2268; $49 for 10 issues) is a monthly newsletter that reports on gay-friendly cruise lines as well as other gay travel opportunities in a roundup-style format. A cruise, tour, and events calendar is published quarterly.

Booking Your Cruise

Using a Travel Agent

Since nearly all cruises are sold through travel agents, the agent you choose to work with can be just as important as the ship you sail on. So how do you know if an agent or agency is right for you? Talk to friends, family, and colleagues who have used an agency to book a cruise. The most qualified agents are members of CLIA (Cruise Lines International Association) and the NACOA (National Association of Cruise-Only Agencies), as well as ASTA (American Society of Travel Agents). Agents who are CLIA Accredited Cruise Counsellors or Master Cruise Counsellors have had extensive cruise and ship inspection experience; agents who are NACOA members are also experienced cruisers. If you're undecided about a ship or line, an agent's personal account of his or her own cruise can be invaluable. However, keep in mind that agencies often have partnerships with certain cruise lines. In some cases, the agency may actually block space on a ship; in other cases, the agency agrees to sell a certain amount of space. Either way, the agency gets a favorable rate from the cruise line; the agency can then afford to offer a "discounted" price to the public. But since agents often receive higher commissions on these cruises, they might steer you toward a cruise that might not be for you. *A good travel agent puts your needs first.*

Larger agencies often have more experienced cruisers on their staff and can provide the biggest discounts. Smaller agencies may compete with their personalized service. Whether you choose a large or small agency, a good agent takes the time to learn as much as possible about you and your cruise companion(s). An agent who asks a few cursory questions before handing you a brochure is a mere order taker; an agent who asks you to fill out a questionnaire about your personal interests is a professional. A travel agent might not know what ship is right for you; a good agent *will* know which ones are wrong.

Of course, you want the best price. When it comes down to it, the top agencies can more or less get you the same price on most cruises, because they'll guarantee that if the cruise line lowers the price in a promotion, you'll get the better deal. So look for an agency that offers this guarantee. But the overall value of your cruise depends on an agency's service, and agencies that are willing to go the extra mile for their clients by providing free cruise-discount newsletters, cabin upgrades, dollar-stretching advice, and 24-hour service in case of a problem are your best bet.

Cruise-Only Travel Agents As the name implies, "cruise-only" travel agencies specialize in selling cruises. However, these agencies can sell you air tickets and other travel arrangements, too, as part of your cruise package. Sometimes, your choice may be limited to a package put together by the cruise line. Increasingly, though, cruise-only agencies are putting together their own custom-designed cruise vacations.

Full-Service Travel Agents Full-service agents have broad travel experience, but may be less knowledgeable about cruise lines than their cruise-only counterparts. If you know exactly what line and ship you want to sail on and are more concerned about your pre- or post-cruise land arrangements, a full-service agent may be more helpful. (But keep in mind that full-service agencies may not have the same discounts as cruise-only agencies.) If you choose to use a full-service agency, look for one that has a cruise desk with agents who sell only cruises. Then, you get the best of both worlds.

Spotting Swindlers Always be on the lookout for a scam. Although reputable agencies far outnumber crooks, a handful of marketeers use deceptive and unethical tactics. The best way to avoid being fleeced is to pay for your cruise with a credit card, from deposit to full payment. That way, if an agency goes out of business before your cruise departs, you can cancel payment on services not rendered. Two tip-offs that an agency may be a bad apple: It doesn't accept credit cards and it asks for a deposit that is more than what the cruise line has requested (check the brochure). To avoid a disreputable agency, make sure the one you choose has been in business for at least five years. Check its reputation with the local Better Business Bureau or consumer protection agency *before* you pay any deposits. If a cruise price seems too good to be true, it could mean the agency is desperate to bring in money and may close its doors tomorrow, so don't be tempted by agencies that claim they can beat any price. Be wary of bait-and-switch tactics: If you're told that an advertised bargain cruise is sold out, don't be persuaded to book a more expensive substitute. Also, if you're told that your cruise reservation was canceled because of overbooking and that you must pay extra for a confirmed rescheduled sailing, demand a full refund. Finally, if ever you fail to receive a voucher or ticket on the promised date, place an inquiry immediately.

Getting the Best Cruise for Your Dollar

By selecting the right agent, you have the greatest chance of getting the best deal. But having a basic knowledge of how and why cruises are discounted can only benefit you in the end. Since your vacation experience can vary greatly depending on the ship and its ports of call, it's best to pick your vessel and itinerary first, and then try to get the best price. Remember, it's only a deal if the cruise you book, no matter what the price, meets your expectations.

Like everything in retail, each cruise has a brochure list price. But like the sticker price on a new car, nobody actually pays this amount. These days, if you asked any 10 cruise passengers on any given ship what they paid, they would give you 10 different answers. Discounts from cruise lines and agencies can range from 5% on a single fare to 50% on the second fare in a cabin.

Approach deep discounts with skepticism. Fewer than a dozen cabins may be offered at the discounted price, they may be inside cabins, and the fare may not include air transportation or transfers between the airport and the ship. Finally, do the math. A promotion might sound catchy, but if you divide the price by the number of days you'll be cruising and include the cost of air and accommodations, you might find that the deal of the century is really a dud.

Deals and Discounts

Seasonal Discounts Cruise-brochure prices are typically divided into three categories based on the popularity of sailing dates and weather: high season, shoulder season, and low-season. (Some lines divide their Alaska sailings into five seasons.) Obviously, prices will be higher for a Caribbean sailing in December than for the same sailing in August. Before you take advantage of a low-season rate, have your agent check on the specific weather conditions and on other factors (such as mosquitos) in your cruise destination.

Early-Bird Specials Almost all cruise lines provide a discount for passengers who book and put down a deposit far in advance; an additional discount may be provided if payment is made in full at the time of booking. These discounts, given to passengers who book at least six months before departure, range from 10% to 50% off the brochure rate. (Brochures are usually issued a year or more in advance of sailing dates.) Cruises to some of the more exotic destinations such as Southeast Asia are sometimes sold on a two-for-the-price-of-one basis from the outset. Most early-booking discounts in the Caribbean include round-trip airfare. Booking a popular cruise early is the best way to get the best price; there will likely be no last-minute deals on these sailings. The other advantage of booking far in advance is that you're more likely to get the cabin and meal seating you want. On most cruises, the cheapest and most expensive cabins sell out first.

Last-Minute Savings In recent years, cruise lines have provided fewer and fewer last-minute deals. However, if a particular cruise is not selling well, a cruise line may pick certain large cruise-only travel agencies to unload unsold cabins. These deals, sometimes referred to by agents as "distressed merchandise," are typically available three weeks to three months before the cruise departs. These specials are unadvertised, but may be listed in the agencies' newsletters and on their cruise telephone hot lines (*see* Agencies to Contact, *below*). Keep in mind that your choice of cabin and meal seating is limited for such last-minute deals. Distressed merchandise on older ships, those built before the 1980s, may be limited to smaller cabins in undesirable areas of the ship. Last-minute deals may only be available in certain regions.

Mixed Bag Besides the major discounts mentioned above, agencies and cruise lines might attract passengers with price promotions such as "Sail for 12 Days and Pay for Only 10," "Free Hotel Stay with Your Cruise," and "Two Sail for the Price of One." Read the fine print before you book. The offer may be a bargain—or just slick advertising. How can you tell? Compare the advertised price to the standard early-booking discount, and check if the promotion includes airfare. Free or discounted air on cruise-only prices are common for Caribbean sailings. Also check on senior-citizen discounts and "cruise dollars" accrued on participating credit cards. Cruise lines that target families sometimes take on a third or fourth cabin passenger for free. Some of the best cruise prices are available on repositioning cruises (*see* Ship Itineraries, *above*).

Payment

Once you have made a reservation for a cabin, you will be asked to put down a deposit. Handing money over to your travel agent constitutes a contract, so before you pay, review the cruise brochure to find out the provisions of the cruise contract. What is the payment schedule and cancellation policy? Will there be any additional charges before you can board your ship, such as transfers, port fees, or local taxes? If your air connection requires you to spend an evening in a hotel near the port before or after the cruise, is there an extra cost?

If possible, pay your deposit and balance with a credit card. This gives you some recourse if you need to cancel, and you can ask the credit-card company to intercede on your behalf in case of problems.

Deposit Most cruises must be reserved with a refundable deposit of $200–$500 per person, depending upon how expensive the cruise is; the balance is due 45–75 days before you sail. If the cruise is less than 60 days away, however, you may have to pay the entire amount immediately.

Cancellation Your entire deposit or payment may be refunded if you cancel your reservation between 45 and 75 days before departure; the grace period varies from line to line. If you cancel later than that, you will forfeit some or all of your deposit (*see* Protection, *below*). An average cancellation charge is $100 one month before sailing, $100 plus 50% of the ticket price between 15 and 30 days prior to departure, and $100 plus 75% of the ticket price between 14 days and 24 hours ahead of time. If you simply fail to show up when the ship sails, you will lose the entire amount. Many travel agents also assess a small cancellation fee. Check their policy.

Protection Cruise lines sell two types of policies that protect you in the event of cancellation or trip interruption. **Waivers** provide a full refund if you cancel your trip for any reason, usually up to 72 hours before sailing; the cost to cover a seven-day cruise is about $75. **Insurance,** sold by an insurance broker and through travel agencies, protects against cancellation for specified reasons plus trip delay, interruption, medical expenses, emergency evacuation, and lost, stolen, or damaged luggage; the cost to cover a seven-day cruise is about $99. The insurance does not cover cancellations, interruptions, or delays caused by a preexisting medical condition. Keep in mind that a waiver is only available at the time of booking; insurance policies are best purchased after you have paid a significant portion of your cruise, which you will lose in the case of cancellation. Neither insurance nor waivers protect you against cruise-line default. For that, you'll need special default insurance, sold only by a select number of companies, such as Travel Guard (*see* Insurance, *below*). These companies also cover preexisting medical conditions.

Agencies to Contact The agencies listed below specialize in booking cruises, have been in business at least five years, and emphasize customer service as well as price.

Cruise Only **Cruise Fairs of America** (2029 Century Park E, Suite 950, Los Angeles, CA 90067, tel. 310/556–2925 or 800/456–4386, fax 310/556–2254), established in 1987, has a fax-back service for information on the latest deals. The agency also publishes a free twice-yearly newsletter with tips on cruising.

Cruise Headquarters (4225 Executive Sq., #1600, La Jolla, CA 92037, tel. 619/453–1201 or 800/424–6111, fax 619/453–0653), established in 1988, specializes in luxury cruises and personalized shoreside arrangements.

Cruise Holidays of Kansas City (7000 N.W. Prairie View Rd., Kansas City, MO 64151, tel. 816/741–7417 or 800/869–6806, fax 816/741–7123), a franchisee of Cruise Holidays, a cruise-only agency with outlets throughout the United States, has been in business since 1988. The agency mails out a free newsletter to clients every other month with listings of cruise bargains.

Cruise Line, Inc. (150 N.W. 168th St., N. Miami Beach, FL 33169, tel. 305/653–6111 or 800/777–0707, fax 305/576–0073), established in 1983, publishes *World of Cruising* magazine three times a year and a number of free brochures, including "Guide to First Time Cruising," "Guide to Family Cruises," and "Guide to Cruise Ship Weddings and Honeymoons." The agency has a 24-hour hot line with prerecorded cruise deals that are updated weekly.

Cruise Pro (2527 E. Thousand Oaks Blvd., Thousand Oaks, CA 91362, tel. 805/371–9884 or 800/222–7447; in CA, 800/258–7447; fax 805/371–9084), established in 1983, has special discounts listed in its three-times-per-month mailings to members of its Voyager's Club ($15 to join).

Cruise Quarters of America (1241 E. Dyer Rd., Suite 110, Santa Ana, CA 92705, tel. 714/754–0280 or 800/648–2444, fax 714/850–1974), established in 1986, is a division of Associated Travel International, one of the country's largest travel companies, and has a VIP club (tel. 800/517–5391) for upscale cruise planning.

CruiseMasters (3415 Sepulveda Blvd., Suite 645, Los Angeles, CA 90034, tel. 310/397–7175 or 800/242–9000, fax 310/397–3568), established in 1987, gives each passenger a personalized, bound guide to their ship's ports of call. The guides provide money-saving tips and advice on whether to opt for a prepackaged port excursion or strike out on your own. The agency's Family Cruise Club serves parents cruising with their children. A World Cruise Desk is dedicated to booking very long cruises.

Cruises of Distinction (93 Dorsa Ave., Livingston, NJ 07039, tel. 201/716–0088 or 800/634–3445, fax 201/716–9893), established in 1984, publishes a free 80-page cruise catalog four times a year. For a fee of $39, which is credited to your first cruise booking, you can receive notification of unadvertised specials by mail or fax.

Don Ton Cruise Tours (3151 Airway Ave., E–1, Costa Mesa, CA 92626, tel. 714/545–3737 or 800/318–1818, fax 714/545–5275), established in 1972, features a variety of special-interest clubs, including a short-notice club, singles club, family cruise club, and adventure cruise club. The agency is also experienced in personalized pre- and post-cruise land arrangements.

Golden Bear Travel (16 Digital Dr., Novato, CA 94949, tel. 415/382–8900; outside CA, 800/551–1000; fax 415/382–9086) acts as general sales agent for a number of foreign cruise ships and specializes in longer, luxury cruises. Its Cruise Value club sends members free twice-a-month mailings with special prices on "distressed merchandise" cruises that are not selling well. The agency's Mariner Club runs escorted cruises for passengers who would like to travel as part of a group.

Kelly Cruises (1315 W. 22nd St., Suite 105, Oak Brook, IL 60521, tel. 708/990–1111 or 800/837–7447, fax 708/990–1147), established in 1986, publishes a quarterly newsletter highlighting new ships and special rates. Passengers can put their name on a free mailing list for last-minute deals.

Vacations at Sea (4919 Canal St., New Orleans, LA 70119, tel. 504/482–1572 or 800/749–4950, fax 504/486–8360), established in 1983, puts together its own pre- and post-cruise land packages and hosted tours, such as Caribbean golf cruises.

Full Service

Ambassador Tours (120 Montgomery St., Suite 400, San Francisco, CA 94104, tel. 415/981–5678 or 800/989–9000, fax 415/982–3490), established in 1955, does 80% of its business in cruises. Three times a year, the agency distributes a free 32-page catalog, which lists discounts on cruises and land packages.

Time to Travel (582 Market St., San Francisco, CA 94104, tel. 415/421–3333 or 800/524–3300, fax 415/421–4857), established in 1935, does 90% of its business in cruises. It mails a free listing of cruise discounts to its clients three to five times a month. Time to Travel specializes in pre- and post-cruise land arrangements and claims its staff of 19 has been nearly everywhere in the world.

Trips 'n Travels, (1024 Kane Concourse, Bay Harbor, FL 33154, tel. 305/864–2222 or 800/331–2745, fax 305/861–8809) does 80% of its business in cruises. The agency's concierge service arranges theater tickets and so forth in ports of call. Its free cruise-bargain newsletter is mailed out to clients six times per year.

White Travel Service (127 Park Rd., West Hartford, CT 06119, tel. 203/233–2648 or 800/547–4790, prerecorded cruise hot line with discount listings 203/236–6176, fax 203/236–6177), founded in 1972, does most of its business in cruises.

Before You Go

Tickets, Vouchers, and Other Travel Documents

After you make the final payment to your travel agent, the cruise line will issue your cruise tickets and vouchers for airport–ship transfers. Depending on the airline, and whether you have purchased an air-sea package, you may receive your plane tickets or charter-flight vouchers at the same time; you may also receive vouchers for any shore excursions, although most cruise lines issue these aboard ship. Should your travel documents not arrive when promised, contact your travel agent or call the cruise line directly. If you book late, tickets may be delivered directly to the ship.

Once aboard, you may be asked to turn over your passport for group immigration clearance (*see* Passports and Visas, *below*; Embarkation *in* Arriving and Departing, *below*) or to turn over your return plane ticket so the ship's staff may reconfirm your flight home. Otherwise, keep travel documents in a safe place, such as the safe in your cabin or at the purser's office.

Passports and Visas

U.S. Citizens American citizens boarding ships in the United States usually need neither a passport nor visas to call at ports in the Caribbean. However, carrying a passport is always a good idea, and entry requirements do change, so read your cruise documents carefully to see what you'll need for embarkation. (You don't want to be turned away at the pier!) If you are boarding a ship outside the United States, you'll need the appropriate entry requirements for that country.

On cruises to some countries, you may be required to obtain a visa in advance. Check with your travel agent or cruise line about specific requirements. If you do need a visa for your cruise, your travel agent should help you obtain it, through a visa service by mail or directly from the consulate or embassy. (There may be a charge of up to $25 for this service, added to the visa charge.)

Passport Renewal You can pick up new and renewal application forms at any of the 13 U.S. Passport Agency offices and at some post offices and courthouses. Although passports are usually mailed within four weeks of your application's receipt, allow five weeks or more from April through summer. Call the Department of State Office of Passport Services' information line (tel. 202/647–0518) for fees, documentation requirements, and other details.

If your passport is lost or stolen abroad, report the loss immediately to the nearest embassy or consulate and to the local police. If you can provide the consular officer with the information contained in the passport, he or she will usually be able to issue you a new passport promptly. For this reason, keep a photocopy of the data page of your passport separate from your money and traveler's checks. Also leave a photocopy with a relative or friend at home.

Non-U.S. Citizens If you plan to cruise from an American gateway, such as Miami or Los Angeles, and return to the United States at the end of the trip, you may need a passport from your own country, along with a B-2 visa, which allows multiple entries into the United States.

Canadians An identity card will be sufficient for entry and reentry into the United States. Passport application forms are available at 28 regional passport offices as well as post offices and travel agencies. Whether for a first or a subsequent passport, you must apply in person. Children under 16 may be included on a parent's passport but must have their own to travel alone. Passports are valid for five years and are usually mailed within two to three weeks of an application's receipt. For fees, documentation requirements, and other information, in English or French, call the passport office (tel. 819/994–3500 or 800/567–6868).

U.K. Citizens British citizens need a valid passport to enter the United States. However, if you will be boarding your ship within 90 days, you probably won't need a visa. You will need to fill out the Visa Waiver Form 1-94W, supplied by the airline. Applications for new and renewal passports are available from main post offices as well as at six passport offices, located in Belfast, Glasgow, Liverpool, London, Newport, and Peterborough. You may apply in person at all passport offices, or by mail to all except the London office. Children under 16 may travel on an accompanying parent's passport. All passports are valid for 10 years. Allow a month for processing.

Vaccinations and Inoculations

Unless you plan to cruise to exotic or out-of-the-way destinations, you probably will not need any shots. However, if you are middle-age or older or overweight or have high blood pressure, diabetes, or other chronic health problems, your doctor may wish to prescribe certain inoculations (such as a flu shot) not normally recommended.

If you intend to visit some of the more remote areas of Central America, South America, or Asia, you may wish to take antimalarial pills; depending on the prescription, you begin taking them a few days to three weeks in advance of your trip to build immunity. Hepatitis is another health concern in less-developed ports of call; a vaccination is available, but shots must be taken in advance of your trip. Boosters to consider taking before your departure include polio and tetanus.

Certain rarely given inoculations, such as that for yellow fever (necessary if you are going into the Amazon), are administered, at a nominal cost, only by U.S. Health Department clinics. Your physician or the local hospital can give you the address and hours of the nearest facility. After getting such a shot, you will be given an International Certificate of Vaccination to carry with your passport.

For up-to-date health advisories on the ports to which you will be sailing, contact the Centers for Disease Control's International Travelers Hotline (tel. 404/639–2572). This automated system provides vaccination requirements and recommendations by geographic area.

What to Pack

You will naturally pack differently for the tropics than for an Alaskan cruise, but even if you're heading for warmer climates, take along a sweater in case of cool evening ocean breezes or overactive air-conditioning. In Alaska, Asia, and the Caribbean, a rain slicker may come in handy. (To find out what to pack for cruises to Antarctica, *see* Chapter 3.) Make sure you take at least one pair of comfortable walking shoes for exploring port towns. Shorts or slacks are convenient for shore excursions, but remember that in Asia and Latin America women are expected to dress modestly and men to wear slacks. If you are going to Asia and plan to visit any holy places, both men and women will need a pair of slip-off shoes and garments that cover their knees (although these are usually available for rent at the site for a nominal charge). For European ports of call, pack as you would for any American city: casual clothes by day, dressier fashions for going out on the town at night. For visits to churches, cathedrals, and mosques, avoid shorts and other outfits that could be considered immodest. In Italy, women should cover their shoulders and arms (a shawl will do). In Turkey, women must have a head covering; a long-sleeve blouse and long skirt or slacks are also required.

In Chapter 1, we indicate how many formal evenings are typical on each ship—usually two per seven-day cruise. Men should pack a dark suit, a tuxedo, or a white dinner jacket. Women should pack one long gown or cocktail dress for every two or three formal evenings on board. Most ships have semiformal evenings, when men should wear a jacket and tie. On a few ships, men should wear a jacket and tie every evening (*see* The Cruise Experience *in* Choosing Your Cruise, *above*). A few lines have no dress codes or guidelines.

Generally speaking, plan on one outfit for every two days of cruising, especially if your wardrobe contains many interchangeable pieces. Ships often have convenient laundry facilities as well (*see* Shipboard Services *in* On Board, *below*). And don't overload your luggage with extra toiletries and sundry items; they are easily available in port and in the ship's gift shop (though usually at a premium price). Soaps, and sometimes shampoos and body lotion, are often placed in your cabin compliments of the cruise line.

Take an extra pair of eyeglasses or contact lenses in your carry-on luggage. If you have a health problem that requires a prescription drug, pack enough to last the duration of the trip or have your doctor write a prescription using the drug's generic name, because brand names vary from country to country. Always carry prescription drugs in their original packaging to avoid problems with customs officials. Don't pack them in luggage that you plan to check in case your bags go astray. Pack a list of the offices that supply refunds for lost or stolen traveler's checks.

Electricity Most cruise ships use U.S.-type 110V, 60-cycle electricity and grounded plugs, but others employ 220V, 50-cycle current and are fitted with European- or English-type outlets. In that case, to use U.S.-purchased electric appliances on board, you'll need an adapter plug. Unless the appliance is dual-voltage and made for travel, you'll also need a converter. (*See* Chapter 1 for details on each ship's voltage.) For a copy of the free brochure "Foreign Electricity is No Deep Dark Secret," send a stamped, self-addressed envelope to adapter-converter manufacturer Franzus Company (Customer Service, Dept. B50, Murtha Industrial Park, Box 142, Beacon Falls, CT 06403, tel. 203/723–6664).

Luggage

Allowances

On Board Ship Cruise passengers can bring aboard as much luggage as they like and are restricted only by the amount of closet space in their cabin. If you are flying to your point of embarkation, be aware of the airline's luggage policies. Because luggage is often tossed about and stacked as it is moved between ship and airport, take suitcases that can take abuse.

In Flight Free airline baggage allowances depend on the airline, the route, and the class of your ticket; ask in advance. In general, on domestic flights and on international flights between the United States and foreign destinations, you are entitled to check two bags. A third piece may be brought aboard, but it must fit easily under the seat in front of you or in the overhead compartment. In the United States, the Federal Aviation Administration gives airlines broad latitude to limit carry-on allowances and tailor them to different aircraft and operational conditions. Charges for excess, oversize, or overweight pieces vary.

If you are flying between two foreign destinations, note that baggage allowances may be determined not by piece but by weight; again, ask your airline about their specific restrictions. If your flight between two cities abroad *connects* with your transatlantic or transpacific flight, the piece method still applies.

Safeguarding Your Luggage When your cruise documents arrive, they will often include luggage tags bearing the name of your ship. Place one on each piece of luggage before leaving home: These tags will identify your luggage to cruise-line officials if there is an automatic luggage-pull service at the airport on arrival. Also tag your bags inside and out with your name, address, and phone number. (If you use your home address, cover it so that potential thieves can't see it.) Put a copy of your itinerary inside each bag, so you can easily be tracked, and itemize your bags' contents and their worth in case they go astray.

When you check in for your pre- or post-cruise flight, make sure that the tag attached by baggage handlers bears the correct three-letter code for your destination. If your bags do not arrive with you, or if you detect damage, immediately file a written report with the airline before you leave the airport.

Insurance

Travel insurance can protect your monetary investment, replace your luggage and its contents, or provide for medical coverage should you fall ill during your trip. Most travel agencies and many insurance agents sell specialized health-and-accident, flight, trip-cancellation, and luggage insurance, as well as comprehensive policies with some or all of these features. Comprehensive policies may also reimburse you for delays due to weather—an important consideration if you're traveling during the winter months. Some health-insurance policies do not cover preexisting conditions, but waivers may be available in specific cases. Coverage is sold by the companies listed below; these companies act as the policy's administrators. The actual insurance is usually underwritten by a well-known name, such as The Travelers or Continental Insurance.

Before you make any purchase, review your existing health and home-owner policies to find out whether they cover expenses incurred while traveling.

Baggage Insurance Airline liability for baggage is limited to $1,250 per person on domestic flights. On international flights, it amounts to $9.07 per pound or $20 per kilogram for checked baggage (roughly $640 per 70-pound bag) and $400 per passenger for unchecked baggage. Insurance for losses exceeding the terms of your airline ticket can be bought directly from the airline at check-in for about $10 per $1,000 of coverage; note that it excludes a rather extensive list of items, which is shown on your airline ticket.

Comprehensive Comprehensive insurance policies include all the coverages described above plus some that may not be available in more specific policies. If you have purchased an expensive vacation, especially one that involves travel abroad, comprehensive insurance is a must; look for policies that include trip-delay insurance, which will protect you in the event that weather problems cause you to miss your flight, tour, or cruise. A few insurers will also sell you a waiver for preexisting medical conditions. Some of the companies that offer both these features are Access America, Carefree Travel, Travel Insured International, and TravelGuard (*see below*).

Flight Insurance You should think twice before buying flight insurance. Often purchased as a last-minute impulse at the airport, it pays a lump sum when a plane crashes, either to a beneficiary if the insured dies or sometimes to a surviving passenger who loses his or her eyesight or a limb. Supplementing the airlines' coverage described in the limits-of-liability paragraphs on your ticket, it's expensive and basically unnecessary. Charging an airline ticket to a major credit card often automatically provides you with coverage that may also extend to travel by bus, train, and ship.

Health-and-Accident Insurance Medicare generally does not cover health-care costs outside the United States, nor do many privately issued policies. If your own health-insurance policy does not cover you outside the United States, consider buying supplemental medical coverage. It can reimburse you for $1,000–$150,000 worth of medical and/or dental expenses incurred as a result of an accident or illness during a trip. These policies also may include a personal-accident, or death-and-dismemberment, provision, which pays a lump sum ranging from $15,000 to $500,000 to your beneficiaries if you die or to you if you lose one or more limbs or your eyesight, and a medical-assistance provision, which may either reimburse you for the cost of referrals, evacuation, or repatriation and other services, or automatically enroll you as a member of a particular medical-assistance company.

Trip Insurance Without insurance, you will lose all or most of your money if you cancel your trip, regardless of the reason. Especially if your airline ticket, cruise, or package tour is nonrefundable and cannot be changed, it's essential that you buy trip-cancellation-and-interruption insurance. When considering how much coverage you need, look for a policy that will cover the cost of your trip plus the nondiscounted price of a one-way airline ticket should you need to return home early. Read the fine print carefully, especially sections that define "family member" and "preexisting medical conditions." Also consider default or bankruptcy insurance, which protects you against a supplier's failure to deliver. Be aware, however, that if you buy such a policy from a travel agency, tour operator, airline, or cruise line, it may not cover default by the firm in question. Another way to protect yourself is to buy a cruise packaged by one of the 33 members of the United States Tour Operators Association (USTOA, 211 E. 51st St., Suite 12B, New York, NY 10022, tel. 212/750–7371), which requires members to maintain $1 million each in an account to reimburse clients in case of default. Even better, pay for travel arrangements with a major credit card, so you can refuse to pay the bill if services have not been rendered—and let the card company fight your battles.

Companies to Contact Travel insurance covering baggage, health, and trip cancellation or interruption is available from **Access America, Inc.** (Box 90315, Richmond, VA 23286, tel. 804/285–3300 or 800/284–8300), **Carefree Travel Insurance** (Box 9366, 100 Garden City Plaza, Garden City, NY 11530, tel. 516/294–0220 or 800/323–3149), **Tele-Trip** (Mutual of Omaha Plaza, Box 31716, Omaha, NE 68131, tel. 800/228–9792), **Travel Guard International** (1145 Clark St., Stevens Point, WI 54481, tel. 715/345–0505 or 800/826–1300), **Travel Insured International** (Box 280568, East Hartford, CT 06128, tel. 203/528–7663 or 800/243–3174), and **Wallach & Company** (107 W. Federal St., Box 480, Middleburg, VA 22117, tel. 703/687–3166 or 800/237–6615).

U.K. Residents Most tour operators, travel agents, and insurance agents sell policies covering accidents, medical expenses, personal liability, trip cancellation, and loss or theft of personal property. You can also buy an annual travel-insurance policy valid for every trip (usually of less than 90 days) you make during the year in which it's purchased. Make sure you will be covered if you have a preexisting medical condition or are pregnant. The Association of British Insurers, a trade association representing 450 insurance companies, advises extra medical coverage for visitors to the United States.

For advice by phone or the free booklet "Holiday Insurance," which sets out what to expect from a holiday-insurance policy and gives price guidelines, contact the association (51 Gresham St., London

EC2V 7HQ, tel. 0171/600–3333; 30 Gordon St., Glasgow G1 3PU, tel. 0141/226–3905; Scottish Provident Bldg., Donegall Sq. W, Belfast BT1 6JE, tel. 01232/249176; call for other locations).

Planning for Expenses

Some ships will not cash personal checks or take certain credit cards. Consult your cruise documents to determine which forms of payment are accepted aboard ship. The purser's office usually cashes traveler's checks, and on some ships, you can even open an account there and get cash when you need it; it will be added to your bill along with onboard purchases, and you pay at the end of the cruise. Cashiers at onboard casinos also cash traveler's checks and dispense cash advances on your credit card, even to those who don't intend to gamble.

Foreign Currency U.S. dollars, traveler's checks, and credit cards are accepted in almost every port frequented by cruise ships. Many local businesses and vendors actually prefer receiving U.S. dollars. But there are always times when foreign currency will come in handy—for museum and theater admissions, public buses, telephones, vending machines, and small tips. When you change money, change only as much as you need (since it can be difficult to reconvert it to U.S. dollars), and do it at a bank or money-exchange booth, where you will probably get better rates than at hotels, restaurants, shops, or the ship's purser's office. If you do change too much, look for the box that several cruise lines keep somewhere near the purser's office or reception desk; passengers' leftover local bills and coins go to local charities or UNICEF.

Traveler's Checks The most widely recognized are **American Express, Citicorp, Thomas Cook,** and **Visa,** which are sold by major commercial banks. Both American Express and Thomas Cook issue checks that can be countersigned and used by you or your traveling companion. Typically, the issuing company or the bank at which you make your purchase charges 1% to 3% of the checks' face value as a fee. Also, there may be a charge for cashing the checks, so before leaving home, contact your issuer for information on where to cash your checks without incurring a transaction fee. Buy a few checks in small denominations to cash toward the end of your trip, so you won't be left with excess foreign currency. Record the numbers of checks as you spend them, and keep this list separate from the checks.

Cash Machines While there are many itineraries that never get near a port with automated-teller machines, ATMs are proliferating and can be found in most major tourist areas as well as aboard some ships; many are tied to international networks such as **Cirrus** and **Plus.** You can use your bank card at ATMs to withdraw money from an account and get cash advances on a credit-card account if your card has been programmed with a personal identification number, or PIN. Check in advance on limits on withdrawals and cash advances within specified periods. Ask whether your bank-card or credit-card PIN will need to be reprogrammed for use in the area you'll be visiting. Four digits are commonly used overseas. Note that Discover is accepted only in the United States. On cash advances you are charged interest from the day you receive the money from ATMs as well as from tellers. Within the United States, transaction fees for ATM withdrawals outside your local area may be higher than for withdrawals at home. Abroad, transaction fees may be even higher, but Cirrus and Plus exchange rates are excellent because they are based on wholesale rates only offered by major banks.

For specific Cirrus locations, call 800/424–7787. For U.S. Plus locations, call 800/843–7587 and press the area code and first three digits of the number you're calling from (or of the calling area where you want an ATM); for foreign Plus locations, consult the Plus directory at your local bank. Before traveling internationally, plan ahead: Obtain ATM locations and the names of affiliated cash-machine networks before departure.

Photography

Take with you all the film, tapes, and batteries that you will need. Such items are more expensive abroad or in the ship's commissary, and often the particular brand or size you want is not available. Never pack your film in your luggage and try to avoid X-ray machines by asking for hand inspection. Such a request is always granted at U.S. airports; it's up to the inspector abroad. Don't depend on a lead-lined bag to protect film in checked luggage—the airline or cruise line may increase the radiation to see what's inside. Call the Kodak Information Center (tel. 800/242–2424) for details.

Many long-distance shots cannot be captured with a normal lens, so take a telephoto if possible. An 81-series, amber-warming filter will remove excess blues that predominate at sea level and will protect your lens against sand and salt spray. Polarizing filters enhance bright skies and seas.

If you intend to charge video-camera batteries aboard ship, make certain that the ship supplies 110V–120V current or that you use the proper converter (*see* Electricity, *above*). Don't attempt to attach your camcorder to the television in your cabin in order to play back tapes—many ships' televisions use European broadcast standards, making them incompatible with U.S.-purchased video equipment.

Arriving and Departing

If you have purchased an air-sea package, you will be met by a cruise-company representative when your plane lands at the port city and then shuttled directly to the ship in buses or minivans. Some cruise lines arrange to transport your luggage between airport and ship—you don't have to hassle with baggage claim at the start of your cruise or with baggage check-in at the end. If you decide not to buy the air-sea package but still plan to fly, ask your travel agent if you can use the ship's transfer bus anyway; if you do, you may be required to purchase a round-trip transfer voucher ($5–$20). Otherwise, you will have to take a taxi to the ship.

If you live close to the port of embarkation, bus transportation may be available. If you are part of a group that has booked a cruise together, this transportation may be part of your package. Another option for those who live close to their point of departure is to drive to the ship. The major U.S. cruise ports all have parking facilities.

Embarkation

Check-In On arrival at the dock, you must check in before boarding your ship. (A handful of smaller cruise ships handle check-in at the airport.) An officer will collect or stamp your ticket, inspect or even retain your passport or other official identification, ask you to fill out a tourist card, check that you have the correct visas, and collect any unpaid port or departure tax. Seating assignments for the dining room are often handed out at this time, too. You may also register your credit card to open a shipboard account, although that may be done later at the purser's office (*see* Shipboard Accounts *in* On Board, *below*).

After this you may be required to go through a security check and to pass your hand baggage through an X-ray inspection. These are the same machines in use at airports, so ask to have your photographic film inspected visually.

Although it takes only five or 10 minutes per family to check in, lines are often long, so aim for off-peak hours. The worst time tends to be immediately after the ship begins boarding; the later it is, the less crowded. For example, if boarding begins at 2 PM and continues until 4:30, try to arrive after 3:30.

Boarding the Ship Before you walk up the gangway, the ship's photographer will probably take your picture; there's no charge unless you buy the picture (usually $6). On board, stewards may serve welcome drinks in souvenir glasses—for which you're usually charged between $3 and $5 cash.

You will either be escorted to your cabin by a steward or, on a smaller ship, given your key by a ship's officer and directed to your cabin. Some elevators are unavailable to passengers during boarding, since they are used to transport luggage. You may arrive to find your luggage outside your stateroom or just inside the door; if it doesn't arrive within a half hour before sailing, contact the purser. If you are among the unlucky few whose luggage doesn't make it to the ship in time, the purser will trace it and arrange to have it flown to the next port.

Visitors' Passes Some cruise ships permit passengers to invite guests on board prior to sailing, although most cruise lines prohibit all but paying passengers for reasons of security and insurance liability. Cruise companies that allow visitors usually require that you obtain passes several weeks in advance; call the lines for policies and procedures.

Most ships do not allow visitors while the ship is docked in a port of call. If you meet a friend on shore, you won't be able to invite him or her back to your stateroom.

Disembarkation

The last night of your cruise is full of business. On most ships you must place everything except your hand luggage outside your cabin door, ready to be picked up by midnight. Color-coded tags, distributed to your cabin in a debarkation packet, should be placed on your luggage before the crew collects it. Your designated color will later determine when you leave the ship and help you retrieve your luggage on the pier.

Your shipboard bill is left in your room during the last day; to pay the bill (if you haven't already put it on your credit card) or to settle any questions, you must stand in line at the purser's office. Tips to the cabin steward and dining staff are distributed on the last night.

The next morning, in-room breakfast service is usually not available because stewards are too busy. Most passengers clear out of their cabins as soon as possible, gather their hand luggage, and stake out a chair in one of the public lounges to await the ship's clearance through customs. Be patient—it takes a long time to unload and sort thousands of pieces of luggage. Passengers are disembarked by groups according to the color-coded tags placed on luggage the night before; those with the earliest flights get off first. If you have a tight connection, notify the purser before the last day, and he or she may be able to arrange faster preclearing and debarkation for you.

Customs and Duties

U.S. Customs Before your ship lands, each individual or family must fill out a customs declaration, regardless of whether anything was purchased abroad. If you have fewer than $1,400 worth of goods, you will not need to itemize purchases. Be prepared to pay whatever duties are owed directly to the customs inspector, with cash or check.

U.S. Customs now preclears a number of ships sailing in and out of Miami and other ports—it's done on the ship before you disembark. In other ports you must collect your luggage from the dock, then stand in line to pass through the inspection point. This can take up to an hour.

Allowances. You may bring home $400 worth of foreign goods duty-free if you've been out of the country for at least 48 hours and haven't already used the $400 exemption, or any part of it, in the past 30 days. Note that these are the *general* rules, applicable to most countries; if you're returning from a cruise that called in the U.S. Virgin Islands, the duty-free allowance is higher—$1,200.

Alcohol and Tobacco. Travelers 21 or older may bring back 1 liter of alcohol duty-free, provided the beverage laws of the state through which they reenter the United States allow it. In the case of the U.S. Virgin Islands, 5 liters are allowed. In addition, 100 non-Cuban cigars and 200 cigarettes are allowed, regardless of your age. From the U.S. Virgin Islands, 1,000 cigarettes are allowed, but only 200 of them may have been acquired elsewhere. Antiques and works of art more than 100 years old are duty-free.

Gifts. Duty-free, travelers may mail packages valued at up to $200 to themselves, up to $100 to others with a limit of one parcel per addressee per day (including alcohol or tobacco products or perfume valued at up to $5); mark the package "For Personal Use" or "Unsolicited Gift" and write the nature of the gift and its retail value on the outside.

For More Information. For a copy of "Know Before You Go," a free brochure detailing what you may and may not bring back to the United States, rates of duty, and other pointers, contact the **U.S. Customs Service** (Box 7407, Washington, DC 20044, tel. 202/927-6724).

Canadian Customs

Allowances. If you've been out of Canada for at least seven days, you may bring in C$500 worth of goods duty-free. If you've been away less than seven days but more than 48 hours, the duty-free exemption drops to C$200. You cannot pool exemptions with family members. Goods claimed under the C$500 exemption may follow you by mail; those claimed under the lesser exemption must accompany you.

Alcohol and Tobacco. Alcohol and tobacco products may be included in the seven-day and 48-hour exemption. If you meet the age requirements of the province or territory through which you reenter Canada, you may bring in, duty-free, 1.14 liters (40 imperial ounces) of wine or liquor *or* two dozen 12-ounce cans or bottles of beer or ale. If you are 16 or older, you may bring in, duty-free, 200 cigarettes, 50 cigars or cigarillos, and 400 tobacco sticks or 400 grams of manufactured tobacco. Alcohol and tobacco must accompany you on your return.

Gifts. An unlimited number of gifts valued up to C$60 each may be mailed to Canada duty-free. These do not count as part of your exemption. Label the package "Unsolicited Gift—Value Under $60." Alcohol and tobacco are excluded.

For More Information. For additional information, including details of duties on items that exceed your duty-free limit, contact Revenue Canada (2265 St. Laurent Blvd. S, Ottawa, Ontario K1G 4K3, tel. 613/993-0534) for a copy of the free brochure "I Declare/Je Déclare." For recorded information (within Canada only), call 800/461-9999.

U.K. Customs

Allowances. If your cruise was wholly within European Union (EU) countries, you no longer need to pass through customs when you return to the United Kingdom. If you plan to bring back large quantities of alcohol or tobacco, check in advance on EU limits. When returning from cruises that called at countries outside the European Union, you may import duty-free 200 cigarettes, 100 cigarillos, 50 cigars or 250 grams of tobacco; 1 liter of spirits or 2 liters of fortified or sparkling wine or liquer; 2 liters of still table wine; 60 milliliters of perfume; 250 milliliters of toilet water; plus £136 worth of other goods, including gifts and souvenirs.

For More Information. For further information or a copy of "A Guide for Travellers," which details standard customs procedures as well as what you may bring into the United Kingdom from abroad, contact HM Customs and Excise (Dorset House, Stamford St., London SE1 9NG, tel. 0171/202–4227).

U.S. Customs for Foreigners

If you hold a foreign passport and will be returning home within hours of docking, you may be exempt from all U.S. Customs duties. Everything you bring into the United States must leave with you when you return home. When you reach your own country, you will have to pay appropriate duties there.

On Board

Checking Out Your Cabin

The first thing to do upon arriving at your cabin or suite is to make sure that everything is in order. If there are two twin beds instead of the double bed you wanted, or other serious problems, ask to be moved *before* the ship departs. Unless the ship is full, you can usually persuade the chief housekeeper or hotel manager to allow you to change cabins. It is customary to tip the stewards who assist you in moving to another cabin.

Since your cabin is your home away from home for a few days or weeks, everything should be to your satisfaction. Take a good look around: Is the cabin clean and orderly? Do the toilet, shower, and faucets work? Check the telephone and television. Again, major problems should be addressed immediately. Minor concerns, such as not enough bath towels or pillows, can wait until the frenzy of embarkation has subsided.

Your dining-time and seating-assignment card may be in your cabin; now is the time to check it and immediately request any changes.

Shipboard Accounts

Virtually all cruise ships operate as cashless societies. Passengers charge onboard purchases and settle their accounts at the end of the cruise with a credit card, traveler's checks, or cash. You can sign for wine at dinner, drinks at the bar, shore excursions, gifts in the shop—virtually any expense you may incur aboard ship. On some lines, an imprint from a major credit card is necessary to open an account. Otherwise, a cash deposit may be required and a positive balance maintained to keep the shipboard account open. Either way, you will want to open a line of credit soon after settling into your cabin if an account was not opened for you at embarkation. This easily can be arranged by visiting the purser's office, located in the central atrium or main lobby.

Tipping

For better or worse, tipping is an integral part of the cruise experience. Most companies pay their cruise staff nominal wages and expect tips to make up the difference. Most cruise lines have recommended tipping guidelines (*see* Chapter 1), and on many ships "voluntary" tipping for beverage service has been replaced with a mandatory 15% service charge, which is added to every bar bill. On the other hand, the most expensive luxury lines include tipping in the cruise fare and may prohibit crew members from accepting any additional gratuities. On most small adventure ships, a collection box is placed in the dining room or lounge on the last full day of the cruise, and passengers are encouraged to contribute anonymously.

Dining

Ocean liners serve food nearly around the clock. There may be up to four breakfast options: early-morning coffee and pastries on deck, breakfast in bed via room service, buffet-style breakfast in the cafeteria, and breakfast in the dining room. There may also be two or three choices for lunch, mid-afternoon hors d'oeuvres, and midnight buffets. You can eat whatever is on the menu, in any quantity, at as many of these meals as you wish. Room service is traditionally, but not always, free (*see* Shipboard Services, *below*).

Restaurants The chief meals of the day are served in the main dining room, which on most ships can accommodate only half the passengers at once. So meals are usually served in two sittings—early (or main) and late (or second) seatings—usually from 1½ to 2½ hours apart. Early seating for dinner is generally between 6 and 6:30, late seating between 8 and 8:30.

Most cruise ships have a cafeteria-style restaurant, usually located near the swimming pool, where you can eat lunch and breakfast (dinner is usually served only in the dining room). Many ships provide self-serve coffee or tea in their cafeteria around the clock, as well as buffets at midnight.

Increasingly, ships also have alternative restaurants for ethnic cuisines, such as Italian, Chinese, or Japanese food. These are found mostly on newer vessels, although some older liners have been refitted for alternative dining. Other ships have pizzerias, ice-cream parlors, and caviar or cappuccino bars; there may be an extra charge at these facilities.

More and more lines are banning smoking in their main dining rooms. The policy of each line is noted in the individual cruise-line reviews in Chapter 1.

Seatings When it comes to your dining-table assignment, you should have options on four important points: early or late seating; smoking or no-smoking section (if smoking is allowed in the dining room); a table for two, four, six, or eight; and special dietary needs. When you receive your cruise documents, you will usually receive a card asking for your dining preferences. Fill this out and return it to the cruise line, but remember that you will not get your seating assignment until you board the ship. Check it out immediately, and if your request was not met, see the maître d'—usually there is a time and place set up for changes in dining assignments.

On some ships, seating times are strictly observed. Ten to 15 minutes after the scheduled mealtime, the dining-room doors are closed. On other ships, passengers may enter the dining room at their leisure, but they must be out by the end of the seating. When a ship has just one seating, passengers may enter at any time while the kitchen is open and are never rushed.

Seating assignments on some ships apply only for dinner. Several have open seating for breakfast or lunch, which means you may sit anywhere at any time. Smaller or more luxurious ships offer open seating for all meals.

Changing Tables Dining is a focal point of the cruise experience, and your companions at meals may become your best friends on the cruise. However, if you don't enjoy the company at your table, the maître d' can usually move you to another one if the dining room isn't completely full—a tip helps. He will probably be reluctant to comply with your request after the first full day at sea, however, because the waiters, busboys, and wine steward who have been serving you up to that point won't receive their tips at the end of the cruise. Be persistent if you are truly unhappy.

Cuisine Most ships sailing in the Western Hemisphere serve food geared to the American palate, but there are also theme dinners featuring the cuisine of a particular country. Some European ships, especially smaller vessels, may offer a particular cuisine throughout the cruise—Scandinavian, German, Italian, or Greek, perhaps—depending on the ship's or the crew's nationality. Aboard all cruise ships, the quality of the cooking is generally good, but even a skilled chef is hard put to serve 500 or more extraordinary dinners per hour. On the other hand, the presentation is often spectacular, especially at gala midnight buffets.

There is a direct relationship between the cost of a cruise and the quality of its cuisine. The food is very sophisticated on some (mostly expensive) lines, among them Crystal Cruises, Cunard Line, Seabourn Cruise Line, and Silversea Cruises. In the more moderate price range, Celebrity Cruises has gained renown for the culinary stylings of French chef Michel Roux, who acts as a consultant to the line.

Special Diets With notification well in advance, many ships can provide a kosher, low-salt, low-cholesterol, sugar-free, vegetarian, or other special menu. However, there's always a chance that the wrong dish will somehow be handed to you. Especially when it comes to soups and desserts, it's a good idea to ask about the ingredients.

Large ships usually offer an alternative "light" or "spa" menu based upon American Heart Association guidelines, using less fat, leaner cuts of meat, low-cholesterol or low-sodium preparations, smaller portions, salads, fresh-fruit desserts, and healthy garnishes. Some smaller ships may not be able to accommodate special dietary needs. Vegetarians generally have no trouble finding appropriate selections on ship menus.

Wine Wine at meals costs extra on most ships; the prices are usually comparable to those in shoreside restaurants and are charged to your shipboard account. A handful of luxury vessels include both wine and liquor.

The Captain's Table It is both a privilege and a marvelous experience to be invited to dine one evening at the captain's table. Although some seats are given to celebrities, repeat passengers, and passengers in the most expensive suites, other invitations are given at random to ordinary passengers. Any passenger can request an invitation from the chief steward or the hotel manager, although there is no guarantee you will be accommodated. The captain's guests always wear a suit and tie or a dress, even if the dress code for that evening is casual. On many ships, passengers may also be invited to dine at the other officers' special tables, or officers may visit a different passenger table each evening.

Bars

Ship's bars, whether adjacent to the pool or attached to one of the lounges, tend to be the social centers of a ship. Except on a handful of luxury-class ships where everything is included in the ticket price, bars operate on a pay-as-it's-poured basis. Rather than demand cash after every round, however, most ships allow passengers to charge drinks to their accounts. Prices are comparable to what you'd pay at home.

In international waters there are, technically, no laws against teenage drinking, but almost all ships require passengers to be over 18 or 21. Many cruise ships have chapters of Alcoholics Anonymous (a.k.a "Friends of Bill W") or will organize meetings on request. Look for meeting times and places in the daily program slipped under your cabin door each night.

Entertainment

Lounges and Nightclubs On ocean liners, the main entertainment lounge or showroom schedules nightly musical revues, magic acts, comedy performances and variety shows. Generally, the larger the ship, the bigger and more elaborate the productions. Newer ships—and some older ones as well—sometimes feature multitier seating balconies. During the rest of the day the room is used for group activities, such as shore-excursion talks or bingo games.

Many larger ships have a second showroom. Entertainment and ballroom dancing may go on here late into the night. Elsewhere you may find a disco, nightclub, or cabaret, usually built around a bar and dance floor. Music is provided by a piano player, a disc jockey, or by small performing ensembles such as country-and-western duos or jazz combos.

On smaller ships the entertainment options are more limited, sometimes consisting of no more than a piano around which passengers gather. There may be a main lounge where scaled-down revues are staged.

Library Most cruise ships have a library with anywhere from 500 to 1,500 volumes, including everything from the latest best-sellers to reference works. Many shipboard libraries also stock videotapes.

Movie Theaters All but the smallest vessels have a room for screening movies. On older ships and some newer ones, this is often a genuine cinema-style movie theater. On other ships, it may be just a multipurpose room. The films are frequently one or two months past their first release but not yet available on videotape or cable TV. Films rated "R" are edited to minimize sex and violence. On a weeklong voyage, a dozen different films may be screened, each one repeated at various times during the day. Theaters are also used for lectures, religious services, and private meetings.

With a few exceptions, ocean liners equip their cabins with closed-circuit TVs; these show movies (continuously on some newer ships), shipboard lectures, and regular programs (thanks to satellite reception). Ships with VCRs in the cabins usually provide a selection of movies on cassette at no charge (a deposit is sometimes required).

Casinos Once a ship is 12 miles off American shores, it is in international waters and gambling is permitted. (Some "cruises to nowhere," in fact, are little more than sailing casinos.) All ocean liners, as well as many cruise yachts and motor-sailing ships, have casinos. On larger vessels, they usually have poker, baccarat, blackjack, roulette, craps, and slot machines. House stakes are much more modest than those in Las Vegas or Atlantic City. On most ships the maximum bet is $200; some ships allow $500. Payouts on the slot machines (some of which take as little as a nickel) are generally much lower, too. Credit is never extended, but many casinos have handy credit-card machines that dispense cash for a hefty fee. Exceptions are the Caesars Palace at Sea casinos aboard the *Crystal Harmony* and *Crystal Symphony*, which are regulated by the Nevada Gaming Commission, offer the same gambling limits as in Las Vegas, and, by prior arrangement, will extend credit.

Children are officially barred from the casinos, but it's common to see them playing the slots rather than the adjacent video machines.

Most ships offer free individual instruction and even gambling classes in the off-hours. Casinos are usually open from early morning to late night, although you may find only unattended slot machines before evening. In adherence to local laws, casinos are always closed while in port.

Game Rooms Most ships have a game or card room with card tables and board games. These rooms are for serious players and are often the site of friendly round-robin competitions and tournaments. Most ships furnish everything for free (cards, chips, games, and so forth), but a few charge $1 or more for each deck of cards. Be aware that professional cardsharps and hustlers have been fleecing ship passengers almost as long as there have been ships.

There are small video arcades on most medium and large ships. Family-oriented ships often have a computer learning center as well.

Bingo and Other Games The daily high-stakes bingo games are even more popular than the casinos. You can play for as little as a dollar a card. Most ships have a snowball bingo game with a jackpot that grows throughout the cruise into hundreds or even thousands of dollars.

Another popular cruise pastime is the so-called "horse races": Fictional horses are auctioned off to "owners." Individual passengers can buy a horse or form "syndicates." Bids usually begin at around $25 and can top $1,000 per horse. Races are then "run" according to dice throws or computer-generated random numbers. Audience members bet on their favorites.

Sports and Fitness

Swimming Pools All but the smallest ships have at least one pool, some of them elaborate affairs with water slides or retractable roofs; hot tubs and whirlpools are quite common. Pools may be filled with fresh water or salt water; some ships have one of each. While in port or during rough weather, the pools are usually emptied or covered with canvas. Many are too narrow or too short to allow swimmers more than a few strokes in any direction; none have diving boards, and not all are heated. Often there are no lifeguards. Wading pools are sometimes provided for small children.

Sun Deck The top deck is usually called the Sun Deck or Sports Deck. On some ships this is where you'll find the pool or whirlpool; on others it is dedicated to volleyball, table tennis, shuffleboard, and other such sports. A number of ships have paddle-tennis courts, and a few have golf driving ranges. (Skeet shooting is usually offered at the stern of a lower deck.) Often, at twilight or after the sun goes down, the Sun Deck is used for dancing, barbecues, limbo contests, or other social activities.

Exercise and Fitness Rooms Most newer ships and some older ones have well-equipped fitness centers, many with massage, sauna, and whirlpools. An upper-deck fitness center often has an airy and sunny view of the sea; an inside, lower-deck health club is often dark and small unless it is equipped with an indoor pool or beauty salon. Many ships have full-service exercise rooms with bodybuilding equipment, stationary bicycles, rowing machines, treadmills, aerobics classes, and personal fitness instruction. Some ships even have structured, cruise-length physical-fitness programs, which may include lectures on weight loss or nutrition. These often are tied in with a spa menu in the dining room. Beauty salons adjacent to the health club may offer spa treatments such as facials and mud wraps. The more extensive programs are often sold on a daily or weekly basis.

Promenade Deck Many vessels designate certain decks for fitness walks and may post the number of laps per mile. Fitness instructors may lead daily walks around the Promenade Deck. A number of ships discourage jogging and running on the decks or ask that no one take fitness walks before 8 AM or after 10 PM, so as not to disturb passengers in cabins. With the advent of the megaship (*see* Types of Ships, *above*), walking and jogging have in many cases moved up top to tracks on the Sun or Sports deck.

Shipboard Services

Room Service A small number of ships have no room service at all, except when the ship's doctor orders it for an ailing passenger. Many offer only breakfast (Continental on some, full on others), while others provide no more than a limited menu at certain hours of the day. Most, however, have certain selections that you can order at any time. Some luxury ships have unlimited round-the-clock room service. There usually is no charge for room service, other than for beer, wine, or spirits.

Minibars An increasing number of ships equip their more expensive cabins with small refrigerators or minibars stocked with snacks, soft drinks, and liquors, which may or may not be free.

Laundry and Dry Cleaning All but the smallest ships and shortest cruises offer laundry services—full-service, self-service, or both. Use of machines is generally free, although some ships charge for detergent, use of the machines, or both. Valet laundry service includes cabin pickup and delivery and usually takes 24 hours. Most ships also offer dry-cleaning services.

Hairdressers Even the smallest ships have a hairdresser on staff. Larger ships have complete beauty parlors, and some have barbershops. Book hairdressers well in advance, especially before such popular events as the farewell dinner.

Film Processing Many cruise ships have color-film processing and printing equipment to develop film overnight. It's expensive but convenient.

Photographer The staff photographer, a near-universal fixture on cruise ships, records every memorable, photogenic moment. The thousands of photos snapped over the course of a cruise are displayed publicly in special cases every morning and are offered for sale, usually for $6 for a 5″ × 7″ color print or $12 for an 8″ × 10″. If you want a special photo or a portrait, the photographer is usually happy to oblige. Many passengers choose to have a formal portrait taken before the captain's farewell dinner—the dressiest evening of the cruise. The ship's photographer usually anticipates this demand by setting up a portable studio near the dining-room entrance.

Religious Services Most ships provide nondenominational religious services on Sundays and religious holidays, and a number offer daily Catholic masses and Friday-evening Jewish services. The kind of service held depends upon the clergy the cruise line invites on board. Usually religious services are held in the library, the theater, or one of the private lounges, although a few ships have actual chapels.

Communications
Shipboard Most cabins have loudspeakers and telephones. Generally, the loudspeakers cannot be switched off because they are needed to broadcast important notices. Telephones are used to call fellow passengers, order room service, summon a doctor, leave a wake-up call, or speak with any of the ship's officers or departments.

Ship to Shore Satellite facilities make it possible to call anywhere in the world from most ships. Most are also equipped with telex and fax machines, and some provide credit-card phones. It may take as long as a half hour to make a connection, but unless a storm is raging outside, conversation is clear and easy. On older ships, voice calls must be put through on short-wave wireless or via the one phone in the radio room. Newer ships are generally equipped with direct-dial phones in every cabin for calls to shore. Be warned: The cost of sending any message, regardless of the method, can be quite expensive—up to $15 a minute. If possible, wait until you go ashore to call home.

Health

Medical Care All but the tiniest ships carry at least one doctor, and larger ones have fully equipped infirmaries, staffed with doctors and nurses, most of whom have emergency-room experience and who are prepared to handle medical emergencies. Doctors have office hours and make cabin calls if you are bedridden. Fees for office visits are usually nominal—$20–$40 for a consultation, including any medicine you may need—but not always: The charge can run into the hundreds of dollars for broken bones or emergency surgery, for which you must pay in cash, by check, or with a credit card; you may then apply for reimbursement from your insurance company when you get home. In addition, most ships carry small quantities of the most frequently dispensed prescription drugs, from insulin to hypertension pills.

If you become seriously ill or injured and happen to be near a modern major city, you may be taken to a medical facility shoreside. But if you're farther afield, you may have to be airlifted off the ship by helicopter and flown either to the nearest American territory or to an airport where you can be taken by charter jet to the United States. If you have any reason to feel that you could have a medical emergency, ask your travel agent about buying trip or health insurance (*see* Insurance *in* Before You Go, *above*).

Seasickness Modern cruise ships, unlike their earlier transatlantic predecessors, are relatively motion-free vessels with computer-controlled stabilizers, and they usually sail in comparatively calm waters. If you have a history of seasickness, though, it's best to get treatment *before* you begin to feel ill. Two popular remedies are Bonine and Dramamine, both sold over the counter (in fact, many cruise ships hand out free packets of Dramamine at the purser's office or in the dining room); their one undesirable side effect is drowsiness. Some swear by wristbands (with an embedded plastic button) that employ acupressure to ward off seasickness; they're sold through travel-supply catalogs, at some travel agencies, and in some ships' shops. If you do feel seasick, don't talk about it; stay away from anybody complaining about seasickness, and go out on deck. Breathe in the fresh air. Look at the horizon rather than the waves. Get involved in fun activities. This is one problem that, when ignored, will often go away. Typically, seasickness does not last longer than 3 to 10 hours. In an emergency, ships' doctors can administer a shot that quickly relieves all symptoms of seasickness.

Potable Water Water and food on board any ship listed in Chapter 1 are as safe as at any stateside restaurant. Canada, Bermuda, Puerto Rico, the Virgin Islands, and other well-developed countries and islands are quite safe in terms of sanitation, but at many other ports, precautions are in order. Local water may taste good, but it can contain bacteria to which locals are immune but visitors are susceptible. Diarrhea and intestinal disorders can result.

As a rule, it is always safest to drink commercially bottled water in less developed ports of call (not tap water that has simply been poured into a bottle). Also drink beer or soda straight from the can or bottle, since the glass you use may have been washed in suspect water. Stay away from fruits or raw vegetables that you don't peel yourself.

Swimming Water Although swimming in the sea or salt water doesn't present any health hazard (unless the area is polluted, as in Acapulco), swimming in rivers, freshwater lakes, and streams in undeveloped countries may expose you to harmful microorganisms or aquatic parasites. So, unless you are on a ship-sponsored shore excursion or have been specifically told by the cruise director that the local creeks and lakes are safe, stick with the ocean or chlorinated swimming pools.

Lifeboats

By international law all ships must be equipped with lifeboats, and according to Coast Guard regulations and the SOLAS (Safety of Life at Sea) convention, every cruise ship must conduct at least one lifeboat drill, mandatory for all passengers, early in the voyage. Every passenger must correctly don a life preserver, which is usually found in the cabin under the bed or in the closet. On the back of the cabin door or nearby on the wall will be an instruction chart and possibly a map indicating how to get to your lifeboat mustering station. At the signal for abandoning ship—six long blasts of the ship's horn, followed by six short blasts—every passenger must proceed to a mustering station. All ships follow this drill with at least one full-fledged crew practice (usually while most passengers are ashore at one of the ports of call), and some ships have additional emergency drills during the cruise.

Make certain that the ship's purser knows if you or your spouse has some physical infirmity that may hamper a speedy exit from your cabin. In case of a real emergency, the purser can quickly dispatch a crew member to assist you. If you are traveling with children, be sure child-size life jackets are placed in your cabin.

World Time Zones

Numbers below vertical bands relate each zone to Greenwich Mean Time (0 hrs.). Local times frequently differ from these general indications, as indicated by light-face numbers on map.

Algiers, **29**
Anchorage, **3**
Athens, **41**
Auckland, **1**
Baghdad, **46**
Bangkok, **50**
Beijing, **54**

Berlin, **34**
Bogotá, **19**
Budapest, **37**
Buenos Aires, **24**
Caracas, **22**
Chicago, **9**
Copenhagen, **33**
Dallas, **10**

Delhi, **48**
Denver, **8**
Djakarta, **53**
Dublin, **26**
Edmonton, **7**
Hong Kong, **56**
Honolulu, **2**

Istanbul, **40**
Jerusalem, **42**
Johannesburg, **44**
Lima, **20**
Lisbon, **28**
London (Greenwich), **27**
Los Angeles, **6**
Madrid, **38**
Manila, **57**

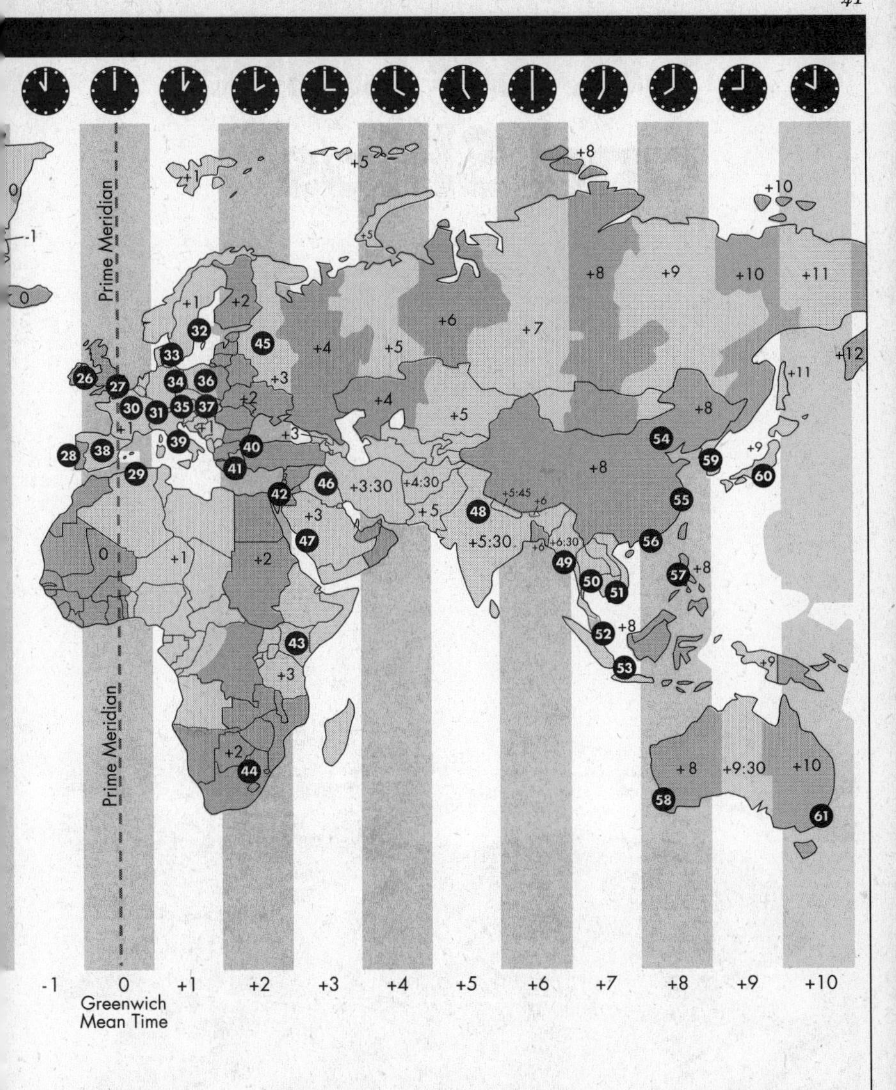

Mecca, **47**
Mexico City, **12**
Miami, **18**
Montréal, **15**
Moscow, **45**
Nairobi, **43**
New Orleans, **11**
New York City, **16**
Ottawa, **14**
Paris, **30**
Perth, **58**
Reykjavík, **25**
Rio de Janeiro, **23**
Rome, **39**
Saigon (Ho Chi Minh City), **51**
San Francisco, **5**
Santiago, **21**
Seoul, **59**
Shanghai, **55**
Singapore, **52**
Stockholm, **32**
Sydney, **61**
Tokyo, **60**
Toronto, **13**
Vancouver, **4**
Vienna, **35**
Warsaw, **36**
Washington, D.C., **17**
Yangon, **49**
Zürich, **31**

1 Cruise Lines and Ships

Abercrombie & Kent

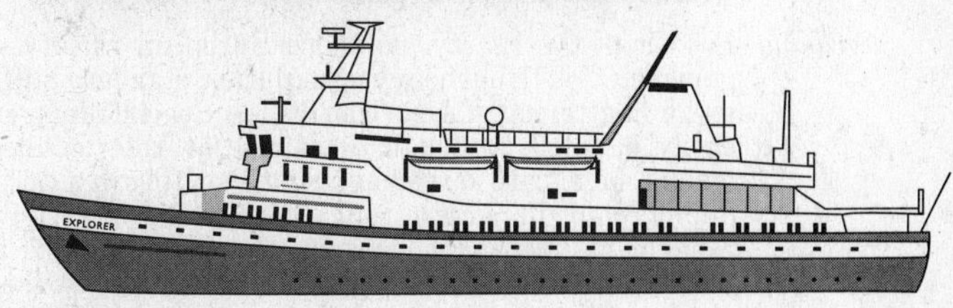

The Fleet MS *Explorer*

The *Explorer* has a long and illustrious history. In previous incarnations, it was the *Lindblad Explorer* and, later, the *Society Explorer*. When built in 1969, it incorporated many design features that set the standard for later expedition ships: It was the first to feature an ice-hardened hull, a relatively shallow draft, a small profile for entering otherwise inaccessible coves and harbors, and a fleet of Zodiacs. The *Explorer* was the first ship to offer adventure cruises to Antarctica and has sailed longer and farther than any other expedition ship.

Ship at a Glance

	Dining Rooms	Bars	Casino	Fitness Center	Pools	Average Per Diem
Explorer	1	1	○	●	1	$476

Cruise Experience Abercrombie & Kent (A&K) is better known for its luxury safaris and land tours, but the company also runs a diverse program of cruises. In addition to the *Explorer*, A&K represents barges in Europe, Nile riverboats, and other vessels in Australia and elsewhere (*see* Chapter 2). As one of the industry's foremost advocates of environmentally sensitive travel, or ecotourism, A&K appeals to well-educated, sophisticated travelers looking to expand their horizons. Its cruises aboard the *Explorer* underline this commitment to ecology by emphasizing an environmentally friendly philosophy during lectures, shore excursions, and Zodiac explorations. Lecturers and staff are familiar with ecological issues and urge passengers to avoid damaging the environment and not to disturb, harass, or interfere with the wildlife. Passengers tend to be couples 55–60 and above. Many are repeaters, and some may be aboard for their 10th time or more. There are few younger couples or single passengers.

Activities There is no daily program of organized events because most activity takes place off the ship. Once at anchor, the *Explorer* launches its fleet of Zodiacs, which can make landfall nearly anywhere as conditions allow. Naturalists lead these waterborne excursions, which frequently encounter penguins, seals, sea lions, humpback whales, and a host of other marine creatures and seabirds. There's no charge to participate, but passengers should be in reasonably good physical condition and have a sense of adventure: The unpredictable Antarctic climate sometimes means rough seas, and land outings can require long periods of hiking on icy, rugged terrain.

Landings are frequent, and many passengers try to be on every excursion. Those who choose to stay aboard can pass the time with a

Chart Symbols. Ships at a Glance. ●: *Fully equipped;* ◐: *Partially equipped;* ○: *Not equipped.* Cabins and Rates. **D:** *Double bed;* **K:** *King-size bed;* **Q:** *Queen-size bed;* **T:** *Twin bed;* **U/L:** *Upper and lower berths;* ●: *All cabins have this facility;* ○: *No cabins have this facility;* ◐: *Some cabins have this facility*

book from the ship's library or a visit to the captain on the bridge, which is always open to passengers.

Dining Food is of the hearty, northern European variety—not bad, not gourmet. You'll find heavy meat dishes, standard buffet breakfasts, and a smattering of American dishes. Special dietary needs are not easily handled, although there are low-calorie selections on the menus. Meals are served at a single seating in a rather diminutive dining room; dinner is at roughly 7:30. With no assigned seating arrangements, you can hop around from meal to meal, mingling with fellow travelers. This is no glamour cruise: The two semiformal evenings are frequently attended by casually dressed passengers who have wisely junked fancier duds to economize on packing space. There is no smoking in the dining room.

Other food service includes lunch and breakfast buffets, which are sometimes presented deck-side, weather permitting. Coffee and tea are available all day. Room service, too, is always available, but since there are no in-cabin phones, you must either find a steward or arrange delivery in advance.

Entertainment Except for enrichment talks and occasional screenings of documentary films or videos in the lecture hall, entertainment is a matter of making your own fun. There is a good selection of fiction and nonfiction books in the ship's library, along with magazines and board games. Before dinner every night, passengers are invited to meet with the naturalists for an informal recap of the day's events and to preview the next day's agenda. After dinner, passengers may gather around the piano for an impromptu sing-along. After-dinner drinks are served here, and members of the crew and staff often mingle with passengers in this informal setting.

Service and Tipping Instead of deferential white-glove service, you'll find naturalists and lecturers eating with and moving about among the passengers—like members of the family. A service charge is included in the cruise fare, and tips are not accepted.

Destinations The ship that originally launched cruising to the "White Continent" spends November through April sailing there from southern Chile. Other cruises aboard the *Explorer* call along the Amazon and in Europe. (For seasonal itineraries, *see* Chapter 4.)

For More Information Abercrombie & Kent (1520 Kensington Rd., Oak Brook, IL 60521, tel. 708/954–2944 or 800/323–7308).

MS Explorer

Specifications *Type of ship:* Expedition
Cruise experience: Casual
Size: 2,398 tons
Number of cabins: 51
Outside cabins: 100%
Passengers: 96
Crew: 67 (European, American, and Filipino)
Officers: German
Passenger/crew ratio: 1.4 to 1
Year built: 1969

Ship's Log Compared with the newest generation of expedition ships, such as the *Bremen* or *Hanseatic*, the *Explorer* is a bit small and spartan. The design is strictly practical, with narrow decks, exposed pipes, and cramped quarters. The *Explorer*'s compact size, however, enables all passengers to disembark onto Zodiacs in 15 minutes, allowing for several landings per day and additional time for shore excursions. Despite the *Explorer*'s age and size, the ship, with its red hull, continues to be a beacon to adventure cruisers, some of whom would never dream of sailing to Antarctica on any other ship.

Cabins and Rates

	Beds	Phone	TV	Sitting Area	Fridge	Tub	Average Per Diem*
Suite	T	○	○	●	●	○	$854
Outside	T	○	○	○	○	○	$476

**Rates are for Antarctica. Airfare and port taxes are extra.*

Cabins are tiny; each has a wooden desk and a view through a porthole or picture window. In the daytime, beds are converted into side-by-side sofas. Closet space is extremely limited; all accommodations have hair dryers. Cabins on the Boat Deck look onto the public promenade.

Outlet voltage: 220 AC.

Single supplement: 150%–200% of double-occupancy rate.

Discounts: You get a discount for booking early and for booking back-to-back cruises.

Sports and Fitness

Health club: Reclining bike, ski machines, free weights, sauna.

Recreation: Small pool (not filled on Antarctica cruises).

Facilities

Public rooms: Lounge, lecture hall; access to navigation bridge.

Shops: Small gift shop, beauty salon.

Health care: Doctor on call.

Child care: None.

Services: Laundry service.

Accessibility

Because there is no elevator aboard, this ship is not recommended for wheelchair users.

Alaska Sightseeing/ Cruise West

The Fleet MV *Spirit of Alaska*
MV *Spirit of Columbia*
MV *Spirit of Discovery*
MV *Spirit of Endeavour*
MV *Spirit of Glacier Bay*
MV *Spirit of '98*

Alaska Sightseeing's philosophy is that smaller is better: Each vessel measures less than 210 feet in length, weighs less than 100 tons, and carries no more than 107 passengers. Because they have shallow drafts, these small ships can hug the shoreline and explore narrow inlets, fjords, and rivers that bigger cruise ships must bypass. The *Spirit of Alaska*, *Spirit of Columbia*, and *Spirit of Discovery* have bow ramps that allow passengers to go ashore where docking or dropping anchor would otherwise be impossible.

Ships at a Glance

	Dining Rooms	Bars	Casino	Fitness Center	Pools	Average Per Diem
Spirit of Alaska	1	1	○	◐	0	$395
Spirit of Columbia	1	1	○	◐	0	$342
Spirit of Discovery	1	1	○	○	0	$439
Spirit of Endeavour	1	2	○	◐	0	NA
Spirit of Glacier Bay	1	1	○	◐	0	$388
Spirit of '98	1	2	○	◐	0	$457

Cruise Experience Alaska Sightseeing lets nature take center stage. Passengers are encouraged to spend their time out on deck, scanning the shore for wildlife. The captain may linger awhile when a foraging bear is sighted or a pod of whales is encountered. Guests may visit the wheelhouse anytime during daylight hours. Itineraries call for less time in port, and more time for shipboard touring, than is typical of cruises aboard large ocean liners. Passengers who sail this way are well-traveled nature lovers. Because there are so few people aboard, individual interests can be indulged, and sailing schedules are flexible enough to allow for extra time to watch a calving glacier or to photograph eagles. Upon request, crew members will awaken guests to view the northern lights.

Activities There are no showgirls, no midnight buffets, and no aerobics classes. Talks given by park naturalists or the cruise director are the only organized activities aboard ship. In addition to wildlife watch-

Chart Symbols. Ships at a Glance. ●: *Fully equipped;* ◐: *Partially equipped;* ○: *Not equipped.* Cabins and Rates. **D:** *Double bed;* **K:** *King-size bed;* **Q:** *Queen-size bed;* **T:** *Twin bed;* **U/L:** *Upper and lower berths;* ●: *All cabins have this facility;* ○: *No cabins have this facility;* ◐: *Some cabins have this facility*

ing, popular pastimes include checkers, cards, and comparing notes on the day's events.

Dining Food is plentiful and tasty; cuisine is classic American. Local catches and produce are often on the menu, as are home-baked breads and desserts. Meals are served in a single, open seating (dinner at 7 or 7:30). Passengers may choose from two entrées each evening. Like the rest of the Alaska Sightseeing cruise experience, dining is very informal, and food presentation is less important than the view outside. Leave all your dress clothes at home: No one dons anything resembling high fashion, even for the Captain's Dinner. Special dietary requests should be made at time of booking.

An early-riser Continental breakfast in the lounge is followed each morning by full breakfast in the dining room, where lunch also is served. Fresh fruit, coffee, tea, and other beverages are available throughout the day. Snacks are usually served around 4 and hors d'oeuvres at 6. There is no room service, except in the Owner's Suite on the *Spirit of '98*. However, since there is no cabin telephone, requests for in-suite meals must be made to the crew earlier in the day. Choices are limited to the day's menu.

Entertainment Most Alaska Sightseeing passengers would rather rise early than revel late into the night. Mingling in the lounge and discussing the day's wildlife sightseeing are the highlights of most evenings. On crew night, you'll learn why the ship's engineer is called a "mule." There's also movie night, a karaoke night, and a casino night, when the stakes are Alaska Sightseeing sweatshirts. Alaska Sightseeing's newest ship, the *Spirit of Endeavour*, was expected to introduce the line's first onboard pianist for evening and cocktail-hour entertainment.

Service and Tipping The all-American crew is enthusiastic and informative. Even with myriad ship duties, these young hosts find time to form close friendships with their guests. Recommended tipping is $5–$10 per person, per diem. Passengers place their tips in an envelope on the last evening of the cruise and leave them, anonymously, in the lounge.

Destinations Among the few American-flagged vessels sailing the Inside Passage, these are the only ships that have their home port in Seattle during the Alaska season. Spring and fall itineraries take in northern California's Napa Valley, Oregon's Columbia and Snake rivers, or the stretch of the Inside Passage that borders British Columbia. (For seasonal itineraries, *see* Chapter 4.)

For More Information Alaska Sightseeing/Cruise West (4th & Battery Bldg., Suite 700, Seattle, WA 98121, tel. 800/426–7702).

MV Spirit of Alaska

Specifications

Type of ship: Coastal cruiser	*Passengers:* 82
Cruise experience: Casual	*Crew:* 21 (American)
Size: 97 tons	*Officers:* American
Number of cabins: 39	*Passenger/crew ratio:* 3.9 to 1
Outside cabins: 70%	*Year built:* 1980

Ship's Log Alaska Sightseeing's original overnight vessel epitomizes the concept of small-ship cruising. You are never by yourself in the lounge, and meals in the homey dining room resemble a family affair soon after the cruise has begun. Sleek and small, the *Spirit of Alaska* feels like a real yacht. A bow ramp adds to the sense of adventure, allowing passengers to put ashore at tiny islands and beaches where few other cruise travelers ever visit.

Cabins and Rates

	Beds	Phone	TV	Sitting Area	Fridge	Tub	Average Per Diem*
Suite	D	○	●	●	○	○	$546
Outside	D, T	○	◐	◐	○	○	$395
Inside	T	○	○	○	○	○	$333

**Rates are for Alaska. Airfare and port taxes are extra.*

The *Spirit of Alaska* offers the widest variety of accommodations of any Alaska Sightseeing vessel, from top-deck suites with two picture windows to claustrophobic lower-deck cabins with a porthole. Most cabins are very small but tastefully decorated with colorful bedspreads and photographs of Alaskan wildlife. Toilets and showers are a combined unit.

Outlet voltage: 110 AC.

Single supplement: 175% of double-occupancy rate.

Discounts: Four cabins (two category AA, two category A) are available as triples at reduced per diems. You get a discount for booking early and for paying early.

Fitness **Health club:** StairMaster, exercise bike, rowing machine.

Recreation: Unobstructed circuit for jogging.

Facilities **Public rooms:** Lounge, access to navigation bridge.

Shops: Souvenir items available.

Accessibility Four main deck cabins, the aft dining room, and the forward lounge are located on a single level. There is no elevator.

MV Spirit of Columbia

Specifications

Type of ship: Coastal cruiser
Cruise experience: Casual
Size: 98 tons
Number of cabins: 38
Outside cabins: 64%
Passengers: 81
Crew: 21 (American)
Officers: American
Passenger/crew ratio: 3.8 to 1
Year built: 1979

Ship's Log Passengers who may have sailed aboard this ship during its days as ACCL's *New Shoreham II* will hardly recognize the vessel. After buying the ship in 1994, Alaska Sightseeing spent considerable money to gussy up its interiors, creating a more polished shipboard setting. At the same time, the vessel was renamed the *Spirit of Columbia* to reflect its positioning out of Portland on Columbia and Snake river cruises spring through fall. Although cut from the same mold as Alaska Sightseeing's *Spirit of Alaska*, it has one notable feature: a unique bow ramp design that allows passengers to walk directly from the forward lounge onto shore. The *Spirit of Columbia*'s interior design was inspired by the national-park lodges of the American West; colors are drawn from a muted palette of rust, evergreen, and sand.

Cabins and Rates

	Beds	Phone	TV	Sitting Area	Fridge	Tub	Average Per Diem*
Suite	Q or T	○	●	●	●	◐	$485
Outside	Q or T	○	◐	○	◐	○	$342
Inside	T	○	○	○	○	○	$256

**Rates are for the Columbia and Snake rivers. Airfare and port taxes are extra.*

After purchasing the *Spirit of Columbia*, Alaska Sightseeing built a new bridge deck with six suites. The Owner's Suite stretches the width of the vessel; located just under the bridge, its row of forward-facing windows gives a captain's-eye view of the ship's progress. All suites have a TV/VCR, a minirefrigerator, and an armchair and a desk. Deluxe cabins have a side table and chair. All cabins have modest-size closets and drawers between or under the beds. A watercolor print, depicting Pacific Northwest scenery, hangs in each cabin. Color schemes are similar to the shades found in the public rooms. Patterns were based on Native American designs from the desert Southwest.

Outlet voltage: 110 AC.

Single supplement: 175% of double-occupancy rate.

Discounts: You get a discount for booking early and for paying early.

Sports and Fitness

Health club: StairMaster, exercise bike, rowing machine.

Recreation: Unobstructed circuit (12 laps = 1 mile) for jogging.

Facilities

Public rooms: Lounge; access to navigation bridge.

Shops: Souvenir items available.

Accessibility

Four main-deck cabins, the aft dining room, and the forward lounge are located on a single level. There is no elevator.

MV Spirit of Discovery

Specifications

Type of ship: Coastal cruiser
Cruise experience: Casual
Size: 98 tons
Number of cabins: 27
Outside cabins: 52%
Passengers: 54
Crew: 16 (American)
Officers: American
Passenger/crew ratio: 3.4 to 1
Year built: 1971

Ship's Log

Alaska Sightseeing's smallest overnight cruise vessel is nearly identical to the line's *Spirit of Alaska*, and its public rooms are even cozier. Wraparound couches and small table-and-chair groupings in the lounge create a living-room feel.

Cabins and Rates

	Beds	Phone	TV	Sitting Area	Fridge	Tub	Average Per Diem*
Outside	D or T	○	○	○	○	○	$388
Inside	T	○	○	○	○	○	$306

**Rates are for Alaska. Airfare and port taxes are extra.*

The *Spirit of Discovery* has more inside cabins than any other Alaska Sightseeing ship. Furnishings are minimal, but soft cream- colored fabrics help brighten up the ship's tiny accommodations. All cabins have a hanging closet, minimal drawer space, and a combined toilet/shower/sink unit. Two outside cabins have a desk with a chair. Outside accommodations also have picture windows, and all have twin beds except two cabins, which instead have one double bed.

Outlet voltage: 110 AC.

Single supplement: 175% of double-occupancy rate.

Discounts: Two cabins (category AA) can be booked as triples at reduced per diems. You get a discount for booking early and for paying early.

Fitness

Health club: There are no exercise facilities aboard the *Spirit of Discovery*.

Recreation: Unobstructed circuit (12 laps = 1 mile) for jogging.

Facilities **Public rooms:** Bar/lounge; access to navigation bridge.

Shops: Souvenir items available.

Accessibility Four main deck cabins, the aft dining room, and the forward lounge are located on a single level. There is no elevator.

MV Spirit of Endeavour

Specifications

Type of ship: Coastal cruiser
Cruise experience: Casual
Size: 99 tons
Number of cabins: 48
Outside cabins: 100%
Passengers: 107
Crew: 30 (American)
Officers: American
Passenger/crew ratio: 3.5 to 1
Year built: 1983

Ship's Log Originally built by Clipper Cruise Line, the *Spirit of Endeavour* is Alaska Sightseeing's new flagship as well as its largest vessel. The *Endeavour*'s sleek lines and long, raked bow make it most similar in silhouette to the *Spirit of Glacier Bay*. The only Alaska Sightseeing ship that stretches longer than 200 feet, the *Endeavour* has open, airy public rooms, with higher ceilings and wider corridors than those aboard its fleetmates. It also is the only Alaska Sightseeing ship with a full-size bridge, like those found on oceangoing liners. The lounge opens directly onto the outdoor viewing area. Teak decks, maple cabinets, and a covered outdoor bar are other distinguishing features. From an engineering standpoint, the *Endeavour* is the quietest ship in the fleet because of its shrouded propellers. The *Endeavour* will also be the first to have phones for making cabin-to-cabin calls. At press time, Alaska Sightseeing was refurbishing the *Endeavour* and had not yet made final decisions on its decor and amenities.

Cabins and Rates

	Beds	Phone	TV	Sitting Area	Fridge	Tub	Average Per Diem*
Outside	T	●	●	NA	NA	NA	NA

**Rates are for Alaska. Airfare and port taxes are extra.*

The *Spirit of Endeavour*'s cabins have the largest picture windows in the Alaska Sightseeing fleet. Accommodations are comparable to those aboard the *Spirit of '98*—small but still the most spacious in the AS/CW fleet. Some cabins have connecting doors, which make them convenient for families traveling together. All have tiled bathrooms.

Outlet voltage: 110 AC.

Single supplement: 175% of double-occupancy rate.

Discounts: You get a discount for booking early and for paying early.

Fitness **Health club:** StairMaster, exercise bike, treadmill.

Recreation: Unobstructed circuit for jogging (12 laps = 1 mile).

Facilities **Public rooms:** Lounge; access to navigation bridge.

Shops: Souvenir items available.

Accessibility This ship is not recommended for wheelchair users.

MV Spirit of Glacier Bay

Specifications

Type of ship: Coastal cruiser
Cruise experience: Casual
Size: 94 tons
Number of cabins: 43
Outside cabins: 100%
Passengers: 84
Crew: 21 (American)
Officers: American
Passenger/crew ratio: 4 to 1
Year built: 1976

Ship's Log Floor-to-ceiling windows in the main lounge provide stunning views of glaciers, wildlife, and other passing scenery for passengers aboard this snazzy yacht. Blue-suede chairs, a wraparound bench sofa at the bow, and a mirrored ceiling make the chrome-filled lounge look extra swank. From here, passengers have direct access to a large outdoor viewing deck, one of two aboard. This is especially convenient for those who don't want to trudge upstairs every time a whale is spotted. Another advantage of the *Spirit of Glacier Bay* is its small workout room. In good weather, the equipment is moved to an outside deck under a protective canopy.

Cabins and Rates

	Beds	Phone	TV	Sitting Area	Fridge	Tub	Average Per Diem*
Outside	Q, D, or T	○	◐	○	○	○	$439

**Rates are for Alaska. Airfare and port taxes are extra.*

Although the cabins are small, their oversize picture windows keep the walls from closing in. Contemporary-style furnishings and Alaska wildlife photographs complement the ship's modern motif. All cabins have individual climate control and a vanity with a desk and chair. Deluxe cabins have minirefrigerators and minibars, plus TVs and VCRs. Two cabins are reserved for single travelers. The bathrooms' tight toilet/shower/sink configuration is the ship's most unappealing quality.

Outlet voltage: 110 AC.

Single supplement: 175% of double-occupancy rate. Two single cabins are available at no surcharge.

Discounts: You get a discount for booking early and for paying early.

Fitness **Health club:** StairMaster, exercise bike, rowing machine.

Facilities **Public rooms:** Bar/lounge; access to navigation bridge.

Shops: Souvenir items available.

Shops: Small gift shop.

Accessibility This ship is not recommended for wheelchair users.

MV Spirit of '98

Specifications

Type of ship: Coastal cruiser
Cruise experience: Casual
Size: 96 tons
Number of cabins: 49
Outside cabins: 100%

Passengers: 101
Crew: 24 (American)
Officers: American
Passenger/crew ratio: 4.2 to 1
Year built: 1984

Ship's Log With its rounded stern and wheelhouse, old-fashioned smokestack, and Victorian decor, the *Spirit of '98* evokes the feel of a turn-of-the-century steamship, even though it was built in 1984. Second in size only to the *Spirit of Endeavour,* the *Spirit of '98* remains the line's most elegant vessel. Inside and out, mahogany adorns this ship, including the sculptured sideboard in its main lounge, where massive floral curtains conjure up the days of the cancan and the player piano is in constant demand. Overstuffed chairs upholstered in crushed velvet complete the gold-rush-era motif. For private moments, there are plenty of nooks and crannies aboard ship, along with the cozy Soapy's Parlor at the stern, with a small bar (open only occasionally during each cruise) and a few tables and chairs.

Cabins and Rates

	Beds	Phone	TV	Sitting Area	Fridge	Tub	Average Per Diem*
Suite	K	○	●	●	●	●	$747
Outside	Q, D, or T	○	●	●	○	○	$457

**Rates are for Alaska. Airfare and port taxes are extra.*

The small but comfortable cabins are appointed with mahogany headboards and Audubon prints. Each has a picture window that may be opened. All cabins have individual climate control, separate showers and toilet in the bathrooms, and excellent light for bedtime reading. Most have both closet and drawer space for storage. In addition, Deluxe and Category 1 cabins have a sitting area, and the single Owner's Suite comes with a living room; game/meeting room; separate bedroom; TV; VCR; fully stocked, complimentary wet bar; and oversize bathroom.

Outlet voltage: 110 AC.

Single supplement: 175% of double-occupancy rate.

Discounts: Two category 1 cabins can be booked as triples at reduced per diems. You get a discount for booking early and for paying early.

Sports and Fitness

Health club: StairMaster, exercise bike, rowing machine.

Recreation: Unobstructed circuit (12 laps = 1 mile) for jogging.

Facilities

Public rooms: Bar/lounge; access to navigation bridge.

Shops: Souvenir items available.

Accessibility

Two cabins are accessible to wheelchair users. All public rooms and decks are accessible by elevator except the upper outdoor deck.

American Canadian Caribbean Line

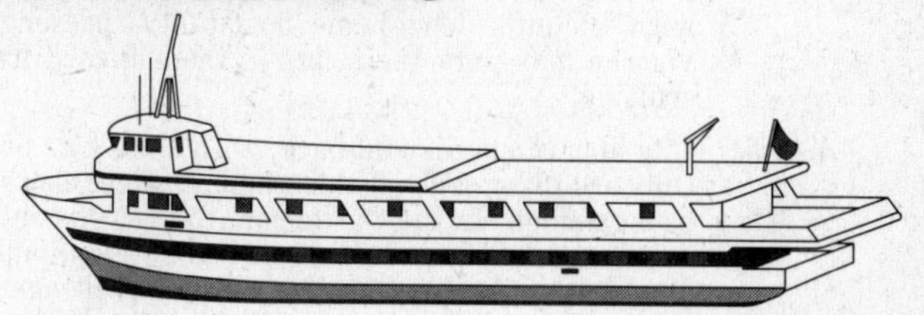

Caribbean Prince

The Fleet *Caribbean Prince*
Mayan Prince
Niagara Prince

ACCL's vessels are the personal creations of the line's owner, Luther H. Blount, who builds them in his Rhode Island shipyard. Their efficient layout and durability are the result of Blount's 45 years of shipbuilding experience—he has designed and constructed ferries, sightseeing boats, and small ships now operated by other cruise lines, such as Alaska Sightseeing/Cruise West. For ACCL, he has created a fleet of small, yachtlike vessels that are custom designed for cruising inland waterways and coastlines, with retractable pilothouses, shallow drafts, bow ramps, and rear swimming platforms.

Ships at a Glance

	Dining Rooms	Bars	Casino	Fitness Center	Pools	Average Per Diem
Caribbean Prince	1	0	○	○	1*	$190
Mayan Prince	1	0	○	○	1*	$198
Niagara Prince	1	0	○	○	1*	$190

**Rear swimming platform.*

Cruise Experience ACCL's passengers prefer a casual and simple shipboard environment to the glamour and luxury of pricier cruise lines. But some of the lowest rates in cruising mean that ACCL offers few traditional services and facilities—sheets and towels are changed every *other* day, and it's even suggested that you pack your own beach towel. These no-frills cruises are an excellent value, nevertheless. Everything is included in the base price except tips and certain shore excursions (*see* Activities, *below*). No alcohol is sold on board, although you are free to bring your own. At several ports, the crew can arrange to have liquor delivered directly to the ship. Mixers and other nonalcoholic drinks are available free from the bar at all hours.

New England charm and personal service make passengers feel like they're sailing on the family yacht. In a sense, they are, and Blount and his family personally send off every cruise that departs from the line's base in Warren, Rhode Island. Once underway, passengers find themselves on easy terms with one another as well as with the crew. The line is similar in its informal ambience and limited amenities to Alaska Sightseeing, but the latter's cabins and public spaces are decidedly more stylish. ACCL cruisers tend to be educated and older (63 on average), and children under 14 are not permitted.

Chart Symbols. Ships at a Glance. **●**: *Fully equipped;* **◐**: *Partially equipped;* ○: *Not equipped.* Cabins and Rates. **D**: *Double bed;* **K**: *King-size bed;* **Q**: *Queen-size bed;* **T**: *Twin bed;* **U/L**: *Upper and lower berths;* **●**: *All cabins have this facility;* ○: *No cabins have this facility;* **◐**: *Some cabins have this facility*

ACCL has inspired a loyal group of alumni passengers, and the number of repeaters aboard ship can be as high as 65 percent. On some Caribbean cruises you can board a day early and use the ship as a floating hotel for $50 per passenger, $100 per couple. In keeping with Blount's down-home hospitality, passengers embarking in Warren may park their cars in the shipyard free of charge while cruising.

Activities Life aboard ship is laid-back, with almost no organized activities. Onboard diversions include bingo, bridge, chess, golf putting, and backgammon. In the Caribbean, the focus is on beachcombing and water sports. Two Sailfish, snorkeling equipment, and a 21-seat glass-bottom boat are available free to passengers; you can swim or sail from the stern platform. Fishing from ship or beach is encouraged; bring your own tackle. Shore excursions tend to be informative and extremely worthwhile; if the local tour guides don't meet ACCL standards, the ship supplies a guide. Passengers are charged for shore excursions only when ACCL itself incurs a cost, and the line charges no markup. The average price for these excursions is only $12; the most expensive (in Belize) costs $25.

Dining ACCL is one of the few lines that reserves its full-meal service for dinner and serves just a light lunch at midday—a policy that many passengers prefer. Lunchtime selections may be sandwiches on fresh-baked bread and classic pastas, and are interspersed with such gourmet treats as chilled gazpacho and crab-stuffed pastry. Dinner menus are full-course meals of well-prepared, standard American cooking. Many dishes use fresh seafood and produce picked up in ports along the way. Breakfast is buffet, lunch is family style, and an open-seating dinner is served at 6. There is only one choice of dinner entrée; the chef will prepare a special dish for passengers who want another option, but special diets, including low fat, kosher, sugar-free, and low salt, must be requested at least two weeks before departure. Passengers can help themselves at any time to tea, coffee, lemonade, and snacks, such as fruit and homemade cookies. There are no formal nights and no room service.

Entertainment Local musicians frequently come aboard during port calls, and there's an electric piano for those who want to make their own music. Every evening, movies are shown on a VCR in the main lounge. Otherwise most passengers pass the time playing cards or reading.

Service and Tipping Service is quite casual. Tips are given anonymously via envelopes that you place in a basket in the lounge (tip $9–$12 per diem per passenger); the total is pooled among the crew.

Destinations Itineraries are as idiosyncratic as the line itself and take in offbeat islands in New England, the Caribbean, Central America, and the Bahamas; jungle rivers in Venezuela and Belize; the Panama Canal; the coastline of the Atlantic and the Gulf of Mexico; the Mississippi River system and the Great Lakes; and, in autumn, the Erie Canal and St. Lawrence Seaway. (For seasonal itineraries, *see* Chapter 4.)

For More Information American Canadian Caribbean Line (Box 368, Warren, RI 02885, tel. 401/247–0955 or 800/556–7450).

Caribbean Prince

Specifications

Type of ship: Coastal cruiser
Cruise experience: Casual
Size: 89.5 tons
Number of cabins: 39
Outside cabins: 84%

Passengers: 78
Crew: 17 (American)
Officers: American
Passenger/crew ratio: 4.6 to 1
Year built: 1983

Ship's Log The *Caribbean Prince*, one of the smallest cruise ships afloat, looks like a cross between an oversize yacht and a little ferry. It is Blount's most austere creation. The vessel's interior is made mostly of fiberglass and aluminum; a few Caribbean prints are the only hints of decor aboard. There are only two public rooms. The dining room, furnished with mahogany cabinets, tables for six, and pink-and blue-flowered curtains, doubles by day as a recreation room and lobby. On the same deck forward is a small lounge, where the bartender dispenses nonalcoholic drinks or will mix whatever concoctions you wish from liquor you bring aboard. Though the ship is tiny, there is ample room on deck for lounge chairs and a barbecue.

Cabins and Rates

	Beds	Phone	TV	Sitting Area	Fridge	Tub	Average Per Diem*
Outside	T or D	○	○	○	○	○	$190
Inside	T	○	○	○	○	○	$150

**Airfare and port taxes are extra.*

It doesn't get more no-frills than this—metal lockers, pale beige walls, and beds covered not with spreads but with blue velour blankets. The more expensive cabins have chairs, full-length closets, and mahogany trim. Take only the essentials on board; there is very little storage space. Reading lights and vanity mirrors are in every cabin, but you'll have to go outside your cabin to see yourself in a full-length mirror, found in the corridors. All cabins have picture windows except Cabins 20–22, which are inside and have one extra-wide bed (42 inches). Sun Deck cabins have partially obstructed views. There are no keys to the cabins, but valuables can be locked up in the ship's safe.

Outlet voltage: 110 AC.

Single supplement: 175% of double-occupancy rate (Cabins 20–22 only). The supplement is waived for passengers who agree to share with another single traveler, even if one is not found by the time of sailing.

Discounts: 15% per passenger when three passengers share a cabin. You get a 10% discount when booking consecutive cruises.

Sports and Fitness **Recreation:** Early-morning exercises, fishing, snorkeling, sailing, unobstructed circuit on Sun Deck (11 laps = 1 mile) for jogging, swimming platform.

Facilities **Public rooms:** Lounge.

Accessibility There are no facilities specifically equipped for wheelchair users. All public rooms are on one deck, though, along with a number of passenger cabins.

Mayan Prince

Specifications

Type of ship: Coastal cruiser
Cruise experience: Casual
Size: 92 tons
Number of cabins: 46
Outside cabins: 87%
Passengers: 92
Crew: 17 (American)
Officers: American
Passenger/crew ratio: 5.4 to 1
Year built: 1992

Ship's Log The *Mayan Prince* was inspired by passenger feedback collected with questionnaires on the *Caribbean Prince*. Well designed and modern in both layout and convenience, the *Mayan Prince* has individual cabin temperature controls and 20% more deck space than its predecessor. Slightly bigger than the *Caribbean Prince*, it also carries 14 more passengers. There is still a noticeable lack of artwork, except for the few Mayan prints that dot the public areas, Mayan-inspired designs on the curtains, and a small display of Mayan artifact replicas. There is little use of decorative wood; instead, most of the ship's interior is made of painted aluminum and other metal.

As on the *Caribbean Prince*, there are two public rooms. The dining room seats passengers in groups of six or eight. The galley faces the dining area, so passengers can chat easily with the chef. After dinner, travelers can walk directly into the forward lounge and relax on a blue vinyl wraparound couch or in armchairs upholstered in a bright rainbow tweed, watch a movie on one of the two televisions, or select a paperback from the bookshelves. During the day, passengers gather here to disembark by a ramp when the ship makes bow landings.

Cabins and Rates

	Beds	Phone	TV	Sitting Area	Fridge	Tub	Average Per Diem*
Outside	T or D	○	○	◐	○	○	$198
Inside	T or D	○	○	○	○	○	$158

**Airfare and port taxes are extra.*

Like the *Caribbean Prince*, the *Mayan Prince*'s cabins are tiny and spartan, appointed in beige and blue and equipped with a reading light and vanity mirror; you must leave your cabin to see yourself in a full-length mirror. Floral curtains have the same Mayan pattern as those in the public rooms. Bathrooms have a state-of-the-art silent commode—not the roaring vacuum-type systems found on other ships. Cabins with numbers in the 50s and 60s have full-length wooden closets; others have small metal lockers. In contrast to the *Caribbean Prince*, all cabins have drawers, but you should pack lightly just the same. Top-level cabins open directly onto an outdoor deck. All cabins have picture windows except cabins 20–22, which are inside. There are no keys to the cabins, but valuables can be locked up in the ship's safe.

Outlet voltage: 110 AC.

Single supplement: 175% of double-occupancy rate (Cabins 20–22 only). The supplement is waived for passengers who agree to share with another single traveler, even if one is not found by the time of sailing.

Discounts: 15% per passenger when three passengers share a cabin. You get a 10% discount when booking consecutive cruises.

Sports and Fitness **Recreation:** Informal workouts, fishing, snorkeling, unobstructed circuit on Sun Deck for jogging, swimming platform.

Facilities **Public rooms:** Lounge.

Accessibility There are no facilities specifically equipped for wheelchair users. All public areas are on one deck, though, along with a number of passenger cabins.

Niagara Prince

Specifications

Type of ship: Coastal cruiser
Cruise experience: Casual
Size: 99 tons
Number of cabins: 42
Outside cabins: 95%
Passengers: 84
Crew: 17 (American)
Officers: American
Passenger/crew ratio: 5 to 1
Year built: 1994

Ship's Log The newest ACCL ship is also the line's largest and spiffiest. Slightly sleeker than its sisters, the *Niagara* was built for both canal and ocean cruising. Along with the retractable wheelhouses found on the other two ships, it employs a unique ballasting system that submerges the vessel 10 inches so it can pass under the bridges of the Erie Canal. The *Niagara* has the widest swimming platform of any ACCL vessel and is one of the only cruise ships that can launch or pick up a tender without stopping.

Although dining room and lounge are laid out almost identically to those aboard the line's other ships, they are located on a higher deck for easier access to the outside. Wide wraparound windows give better viewing, too. Both rooms are appointed in the standard ACCL furnishings—round tables in the dining room, wraparound couch and overstuffed armchairs in the lounge—but the upholstery and carpeting, with mauve and teal accents, are brighter and more sumptuous than on the *Caribbean* or *Mayan Prince*. Similarly, Caribbean watercolors and pastel prints brighten up the public rooms and corridors.

Cabins and Rates

	Beds	Phone	TV	Sitting Area	Fridge	Tub	Average Per Diem*
Outside	T or D	○	○	◐	○	○	$190
Inside	T or D	○	○	○	○	○	$137

**Airfare and port taxes are extra.*

Cabins remain small but storage space has been improved with roomier metal lockers and drawers. The *Niagara* is Blount's first attempt at interior decorating—tweed teal carpeting and vibrant green and mauve trim are considerable improvements from the stark staterooms of his previous ships. Prints and treasure maps depicting ports visited by ACCL add a nice finishing touch. In another plus, most staterooms have a chair and table. Along with quiet commodes, cabins have individual climate controls. Cabins with numbers in the 50s, 60s, and 70s have sliding picture windows. A few cabins have portholes. Beds in most cabins can be converted to doubles upon request. There are two inside cabins. There are no keys to the cabins, but valuables can be locked up in the ship's safe.

Outlet voltage: 110 AC.

Single supplement: 175% of double-occupancy rate (Cabins 20–22 only). The supplement is waived for passengers who agree to share with another single traveler, even if one is not found by the time of sailing.

Discounts: 15% per passenger when three passengers share a cabin. You get a 10% discount when booking consecutive cruises.

Sports and Fitness

Recreation: Informal workouts, fishing, snorkeling, unobstructed circuit on Sun Deck for jogging, swimming platform.

Facilities

Public rooms: Lounge.

Accessibility

There is a stair lift for each deck, and all public areas are accessible to wheelchair users. Two cabins are accessible to wheelchair users as well.

American Hawaii Cruises

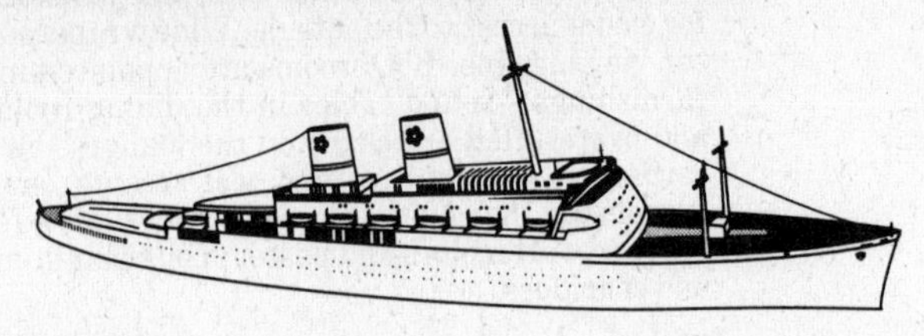

The Fleet SS *Independence*

Built in 1951, the *Independence* and its now departed sister, the *Constitution*, were the first modern liners to sail between New York and the Mediterranean; it was the *Constitution* that brought Grace Kelly and her wedding party to Monaco for her marriage to Prince Rainier in 1956. Other famous passengers have included Ernest Hemingway and Ronald Reagan. After 45 years at sea, the *Independence* shows its age, although a $30 million makeover in late 1994 did much to reverse the wear and added a tasteful Hawaiian motif to the cabins and many public rooms.

Ship at a Glance

	Dining Rooms	Bars	Casino	Fitness Center	Pools	Average Per Diem
Independence	2	3	○	◐	2	$278

Cruise Experience Travel on the *Independence* is really two cruise experiences in one. Fans of classic liners built for transatlantic travel will appreciate the finer points of this ship's design. Particularly noteworthy are the enclosed promenades, whose huge brass and glass doors open to the sea, letting in cool ocean breezes when the ship is docked or at anchor. Other "they don't make them like that anymore" qualities include heavy wooden doors with brass-rimmed portholes, which lead between inside and outside decks. Original cabin furnishings include light fixtures, medicine cabinets, bureaus, and Pullman-style folding beds.

For many other passengers, the attraction of this line is the chance to see Hawaii's major islands at an affordable price. In all, the ship visits five ports on four islands in seven days, without the need to change hotels and to make intra-island plane connections. Because the ship sails solely within Hawaii, the emphasis of the cruise, both aboard ship and ashore, is on the islands. The daily program of activities includes a full slate of Hawaii crafts classes, storytelling, and other island traditions. You can learn to make jewelry from seashells or to play the ukulele. Whale watching, too, is a big event, and local environmental representatives come aboard ship to lecture and point out the huge creatures. The line's shore-excursion booklet lists more than 50 choices, ranging from bus tours to rain-forest hikes.

Whether it's the classic style or the island ambience that appeals to you, make no mistake—this is not a luxury cruise. It is, however, a very good value. In fact, you'll find a number of nice touches aboard, such as complimentary bon-voyage mai-tais, free soft drinks, and no-charge laundry machines. Dramamine, aspirin, and acetaminophen are always available for free at the purser's office. On some

Chart Symbols. Ships at a Glance. ●: *Fully equipped;* ◐: *Partially equipped;* ○: *Not equipped.* Cabins and Rates. **D:** *Double bed;* **K:** *King-size bed;* **Q:** *Queen-size bed;* **T:** *Twin bed;* **U/L:** *Upper and lower berths;* ●: *All cabins have this facility;* ○: *No cabins have this facility;* ◐: *Some cabins have this facility*

higher priced lines, there's often a charge for all of these. Another appealing quality is the ship's casual atmosphere, which emphasizes comfort and relaxation over pomp and circumstance.

This combination of convenience and value attracts passengers in all age ranges. Aboard this liner you'll find everyone except younger couples. A typical mix includes families with younger children, middle-age couples, and older passengers celebrating their 50th wedding anniversary.

Activities Shoreside activities are emphasized, and there are more than 50 excursions to choose from, including flightseeing by helicopter over an active volcano, bicycling down the slopes of a dormant volcano, or visiting Hawaii Volcanoes National Park—you should be detecting a theme here. Also big are whale watching, snorkeling, and kayaking.

Passengers who stay aboard by day will find plenty to do, from the usual cruise activities to ukulele, hula, lei making, palm weaving, and Hawaiian-language lessons. There are also such typical cruise diversions as line-dancing classes and, of course, bingo. Movies are screened daily in the ship's cinema-style theater. Be sure to see *An Affair to Remember*—the shipboard shots were filmed aboard the *Constitution.*

Dining American cuisine—steaks, seafood, and lamb—dominates the daily menus, and although food is well prepared, dishes tend to be bland. An effort is made whenever possible to use local ingredients. The Kona coffee and Hawaiian pineapple are particularly noteworthy. Traditional Hawaiian "plate lunches" (combination platters of fish, meat, rice, and poi) top the menu in the dining room at the midday meal, and fresh local fish is always a selection at dinner. A Pu'uwai (Healthy Heart) program is available for low-fat, low-cholesterol entrées. The extensive wine list offers Californian, French, and German vintages.

On the *Independence*, passengers are assigned to one of two dining rooms at random. Although the dining rooms are below decks and lack panoramic windows, they are bright and colorful. There are two open seatings for dinner (6 and 8); breakfast and lunch are open seating. There is one semiformal/formal evening each cruise; otherwise, all dress is casual. On the first evening, dinner is a grand buffet. Passengers don Hawaiian fashions for the Polynesian dinner.

Breakfast and lunch are also served in a midships buffet. These are just as good as meals in the dining room, and taking your lunch or breakfast here has the added benefit of allowing you to sit outside on deck or in an enclosed promenade. Service also can be slow in the dining room for breakfast and lunch.

Other food service includes Continental breakfast of coffee, pastries, and fruit in one of the bars; afternoon hors d'oeuvres in the lounges; and complimentary brown-bag lunches for those going ashore for the day. A midnight buffet rounds out the day's food service. Coffee, soft drinks, and juices are available 24 hours, as is room service.

Entertainment Passengers looking for a throbbing disco or casino will not find it here. (Because the *Independence* never leaves American waters, there is no gambling aboard.) Instead, you'll find pajama parties, 1950s sock hops, and karaoke nights, as well as traditional cruise-ship musical reviews in the main showroom and a piano player who takes requests in another lounge. There's also an orchestra for big-band dancing. All the entertainers, from the singers to the orchestra members, are accomplished musicians.

Service and Tipping The American crew is this line's great strength. Each member of the hotel staff—cabin stewards, waiters, waitresses, and bartenders—

wears a badge identifying his or her name and home state, making for instant and easy conversation. Recommended tips per passenger, per diem are: dining-room waiter, $3.50; assistant waiter, $1.75; cabin steward, $3.50. A 15% gratuity is automatically added to bar and wine service.

Destinations As the name says, American Hawaii sails only in the Aloha state. (For year-round itineraries, *see* Chapter 4.)

For More Information American Hawaii Cruises (2 N. Riverside Plaza, Chicago, IL 60606, tel. 312/466-6000 or 800/765-7000).

SS Independence

Specifications

Type of ship: Classic liner
Cruise experience: Casual
Size: 30,090 tons
Number of cabins: 414
Outside cabins: 43%

Passengers: 828
Crew: 315 (American)
Officers: American
Passenger/crew ratio: 2.5 to 1
Year built: 1951

Ship's Log Age has its virtues, such as spacious cabins and enclosed, teak-lined promenades. A $30 million refit of the *Independence* in late 1994 created several new public rooms. The main lounge, often referred to as the ship's "living room," is a study in polished teak and rattan, with French doors that open onto the enclosed promenades. The adjoining bar is just as stylish, highlighted by an old-fashioned jukebox and Tiffany-style lamps. Not everything has been rejuvenated, though. There is still a fair amount of rot and rust on the outside decks—about what you'd expect on a ship that's been at sea for four decades. But there is another reason for the decay: You rarely see anybody painting and scraping as they should be. On the other hand, the improvements made during dry dock were expertly executed. Most impressive is a grand, outdoor staircase, which links the two pool decks and promenade deck for easy access.

Cabins and Rates

	Beds	Phone	TV	Sitting Area	Fridge	Tub	Average Per Diem*
Suite	K, Q, or T	●	●	●	●	●	$379
Outside	K, Q, D, T, or U/L	●	○	◐	●	◐	$278
Inside	D, T, or U/L	●	○	◐	●	◐	$221

**Rates are for Hawaii. Airfare and port taxes are extra.*

Cabins come in 50 different configurations priced in 13 categories. Spaciousness can differ significantly even within the same category, so if roominess is most important to you, ask for a cabin configured to hold third and fourth passengers. If a double or queen-size bed is most important, emphasize that when booking.

Forty cabins, including six solarium suites on the Bridge Deck, were added to the *Independence* during the recent refit. The new suites are roomy and feature high ceilings and skylights, but they lack the traditional charm of these ships' original accommodations, which incorporate such classic hallmarks as in-the-round tiled showers and built-in half-moon sinks in the bathrooms. Decor in all cabins uses a kaleidoscope of colorful Hawaiian motifs. Patterns evoke a range of island imagery, from local flora to aloha shirts. Each cabin also has been given its own Hawaiian name.

Outlet voltage: 110 AC.

Single supplement: 200% of double-occupancy rate for suites, 160% for most other categories. Some inside cabins are available as singles for a $100 surcharge over the double-occupancy per diem.

Discounts: A third or fourth passenger in a cabin pays reduced per diems. Children under 17 sail free.

Sports and Fitness

Health club: Exercise equipment including Lifecycles and StairMasters, saunas, massage (extra charge).

Recreation: Aerobics and stretch-and-tone classes, two freshwater pools, unobstructed circuit on wraparound promenade (7 laps = 1 mile) for jogging.

Facilities

Public rooms: Three bars, main lounge, showroom, study, conference room, cinema.

Shops: Shopping arcade, beauty parlor/barber, photo gallery.

Health care: Doctor and nurse on call.

Child care: Supervised activities for children ages 5–16 during summer and holidays, youth recreation center, baby-sitting arranged privately with staff members.

Services: Self-service laundry, dry cleaning arranged off-ship, film processing.

Accessibility

Although these ships do not have designated cabins for wheelchair users, the line makes an effort to assign passengers with mobility problems to larger cabins off a main hallway on the Main Deck or on the decks above. Elevators are accessible to passengers using folding wheelchairs.

Carnival Cruise Lines

Jubilee

The Fleet MS *Celebration*
MS *Destiny*
MS *Ecstasy*
MS *Fantasy*
MS *Fascination*
MS *Holiday*
MS *Imagination*
MS *Inspiration*
MS *Jubilee*
MS *Sensation*
MS *Tropicale*

Carnival ships are like floating theme parks, and all the line's vessels share this fun-house aura to some degree. A real automobile, bus, or trolley car may be parked in one of the bars just as part of the decor. The effect is most exaggerated on the newer, bigger ships, but even the older, smaller ones have their share of whimsy. No Carnival vessel carries less than 1,000 passengers, and the line continues to build ever-bigger megaships. Its latest project, which was scheduled to be launched in late 1996, is a 100,000-ton behemoth capable of holding more than 3,000 passengers when fully loaded. A sister will follow in 1998, as well as two more 70,000-ton vessels.

Ships at a Glance

	Dining Rooms	Bars	Casino	Fitness Center	Pools	Average Per Diem
Celebration/Jubilee	2	7	●	●	2	$211
Destiny	2	11	●	●	4	$215
Ecstasy/Fantasy *Fascination/Imagination* *Inspiration/Sensation*	2	9	●	●	2	$220 $215
Holiday	2	7	●	●	2	$213
Tropicale	1	6	●	●	2	$211

Cruise Experience Due to its success, Carnival is the standard by which all lower-priced cruise lines are measured. Advertising hype aside, not even its critics can deny that the line delivers what it promises: Activities and entertainment are nonstop, food is plentiful, and cabins are spacious and comfortable. Though there's nothing exotic about it, and it has none of the gentility or grace of some other lines, brash and sometimes crass Carnival does throw a great party. If you're looking for a good tan, an island-hopping itinerary, and pulsating nightlife, Carnival delivers a fun time at a reasonable price.

Chart Symbols. Ships at a Glance. ●: *Fully equipped;* ◐: *Partially equipped;* ○: *Not equipped.* Cabins and Rates. **D:** *Double bed;* **K:** *King-size bed;* **Q:** *Queen-size bed;* **T:** *Twin bed;* **U/L:** *Upper and lower berths;* ●: *All cabins have this facility;* ○: *No cabins have this facility;* ◐: *Some cabins have this facility*

Passengers are young, or at least young at heart. More singles cruise on Carnival than on any other line, although the average passenger's age is 42, and you'll still find many cruisers older than 55. In many ways, Carnival is perfect for families, and the line continues to attract an ever-increasing number of parents who are cruising with their children. If you're lucky, your kids will develop friendships with children from all around the country, which sometimes last long after the cruise is over. However, parents should keep in mind that taking the kids on any mass-appeal cruise line is somewhat akin to taking them to Las Vegas. They'll love the glitz and glitter and nonstop fun of a Carnival cruise, but occasionally, the banter by cruise directors and passengers can get a little racy, and the scene at poolside can, at times, be described as a ruckus. Carnival has, however, taken steps to eliminate underage drinking and to discourage the "spring break" crowd. The line has, for example, raised its minimum drinking age from 18 to 21. To enforce the rule, all minors are issued a specially marked on-board charge card—so they can't use the card to charge drinks to their parents' room.

Activities Carnival vessels offer every activity that a cruise ship can, including beer-drinking contests, greased-pole pillow fights, bingo, masquerade parties, pool games, water-balloon tosses, and trivia contests. No one can do it all, but many passengers try. Activity is centered around movement—from room to room and deck to deck. There are no lounges for curling up with a good book, except for the small libraries.

Dining The line has worked hard in recent years to shed its image as the McDonald's of the cruise industry, and current menus are healthier and more diverse. Seafood and poultry are served in light sauces, and specialties may include fajitas or blackened swordfish. Vegetarian dishes are available on all lunch and dinner menus, too.

Carnival's "Nautica Spa Selections" offer fare that is lighter in calories and lower in sodium, cholesterol, and fat. Salad bars serving an array of fruits, salads, and vegetables can be found in the indoor/outdoor bar and grille areas on all of the line's ships. Frozen yogurt is an alternative at the afternoon ice-cream bar and on dessert menus. Children's lunch and dinner menus offer favorites such as ravioli, hamburgers, and fish-and-chips. Meals are nothing less than feasts, with oversize but attractively arranged portions, noisy conversation, overly friendly waiters, and strolling musicians. French night, Spanish night, and other theme dinners feature special dishes and costumed waiters. The food quality is average, but the quantity and hoopla associated with its presentation make it seem better than it is.

The dining room has two seatings per meal (dinner at 6 and 8). Tables are assigned, though you may ask to be placed at a table of your peers or with families traveling with children. Two formal evenings are held on cruises of four days or longer, one on three-day cruises. Requests for special diets should be made at the time of booking. Kosher food is not available. There is no smoking in the dining room.

Breakfast and lunch buffets are served on the Lido Deck, as are mid-morning snacks and afternoon tea. Coffee is on 24 hours a day; specialty coffees are available (at extra cost) on the newer ships. Every night there's a midnight buffet; some ships even offer a still-later buffet for those who party into the wee hours. All ships feature 24-hour room service from a limited menu.

Entertainment The action begins just after sunrise and continues well into the night. Disco music begins throbbing by mid-afternoon on deck and around the pool. At any given time you can choose from an abundance of contests, parties, classes, games, bar and lounge entertainers, and bands. In-cabin movies are limited to one film run several times a day. Carnival wants its passengers out and about its ships.

Carnival's performers are among the most diverse group at sea. There are musicians, magicians, dancers, comedians, jugglers, and other specialty acts. On the larger ships it's not unusual to have a country-and-western duo, a full-size dance band, a rock-and-roll group, a '40s swing band, a song stylist, a cocktail pianist, *and* a classical-music quartet, all performing simultaneously—in addition to the action in the disco and the teenage dance club. Even the smaller Carnival ships have more entertainment options than most cruise lines' largest. Carnival's casinos are the largest afloat, and heavy emphasis is placed on gambling. Main lounge shows can be high-tech extravaganzas. On the newest ships, Carnival has taken these productions light-years ahead of what used to be standard revues, with laser lighting, superior sound systems, and state-of-the-art stages.

Year-round children's programs include "Coketail" parties, kite-flying contests, arts and crafts, bridge tours, and bingo. Baby-sitting is available in the playroom for a nominal charge. The newer ships have teen clubs with video games and music.

Service and Tipping In the past, the pressure to tip on Carnival ships has been considerable. Here, too, the line is working to bring a little more grace to its cruises. Tip the room steward and the waiter $3 each per passenger per diem; the busboy, $1.50. Bellboys, deck stewards, and room-service waiters expect to be tipped at the time of service; 15% is customary. Tip the maître d' and the head waiter at your own discretion and whenever you request a special service, such as a change in your table assignment. A 15% service charge is automatically added to all bar bills.

Destinations True to its festive reputation, Carnival's ships call on sun-and-fun ports throughout the Caribbean, the Bahamas, and the Mexican Riviera, with one ship spending the summer in Alaska. Occasional cruises to Hawaii and the Panama Canal are also scheduled. Land/sea packages combine a stay at Walt Disney World or Disneyland with a cruise. Itineraries run from 3 to 11 days. (For seasonal itineraries, *see* Chapter 4.)

For More Information Carnival Cruise Lines (Carnival Pl., 3655 N.W. 87th Ave., Miami, FL 33178, tel. 305/599–2600).

MS Celebration and MS Jubilee

Specifications

Type of ship: Cruise liner
Cruise experience: Casual
Size: 47,262 tons
Number of cabins: 743
Outside cabins: 61%
Passengers: 1,486
Crew: 670 (international)
Officers: Italian
Passenger/crew ratio: 2.2 to 1
Year built: 1987/1986

Ship's Log Showy, brassy art; brightly colored walls; neon lights; spectacularly lighted ceilings and floors—when it comes to design and decor, there is nothing subtle about these vessels. Just about every decorative material imaginable—wrought iron, stained glass, wood paneling, padded leather, Plexiglas—has been used to startling effect. Scattered throughout the two ships are a trolley car, a Wizard of Oz–theme disco, a '20s Speakeasy Café, and other imaginative touches. The result is overwhelming and is guaranteed to keep your adrenaline flowing from the moment you get up until you collapse into bed. Both ships have an arcade of lounges and bars, each with its own motif, several dance floors, and a number of small nooks. The large bars are awfully rowdy. The main entertainment lounges are spacious steel-and-marble extravaganzas, as flashy and tacky as anything aglow in Las Vegas. Discos on both ships have a futuristic, sci-fi look.

Cabins and Rates

	Beds	Phone	TV	Sitting Area	Fridge	Tub	Average Per Diem*
Suite	T or K	●	●	●	●	●	$312
Outside	T, K, or U/L	●	●	○	●	○	$211
Inside	T, K, or U/L	●	●	○	●	○	$197

**Rates are for seven-day cruises. Airfare and port taxes are extra.*

Cabins are of similar size, shape, and appearance, decorated in bright colors and wood tones. The Veranda Suite, however, has a whirlpool and a private balcony. Closed-circuit TV plays films all day and most of the night.

Outlet voltage: 110 AC.

Single supplement: 150%–200% of double-occupancy rate. Carnival can match up to four same-sex adults in a cabin for $650 each on seven-day cruises.

Discounts: A third or fourth passenger in a cabin pays reduced per diems. You get a discount for booking early.

Sports and Fitness

Health club: Gym with exercise equipment; men's and women's spas with whirlpools, saunas, facial- and body-treatment center.

Recreation: Aerobics classes, shuffleboard, table tennis, trapshooting, two pools, children's wading pool, unobstructed circuit for jogging.

Facilities

Public rooms: Seven bars, six entertainment lounges, casino, disco, library, card room, video-game room.

Shops: Gift shops, beauty salon/barber.

Health care: Doctor and nurse on call.

Child care: Playroom, youth programs in four age groups run by counselors, baby-sitting arranged privately with youth counselor.

Services: Full- and self-service laundry, photographer.

Accessibility

Fourteen cabins on each ship are accessible to wheelchair users.

MS Destiny

Specifications

Type of ship: Megaship
Cruise experience: Casual
Size: 101,000 tons
Number of cabins: 1,321
Outside cabins: 60%
Passengers: 2,642
Crew: 1,000
Officers: Italian
Passenger/crew ratio: 2.6 to 1
Year built: 1996

Ship's Log

The Carnival *Destiny*, for now the only 100,000-ton cruise ship in the world, carries 2,642 people based on double occupancy, but when all its third and fourth berths are filled, that number can balloon to 3,400. In keeping with its size, everything on the Carnival Destiny is big: The spa spans two decks, an outdoor water slide stretches 200 feet, and the casino covers 9,000 square feet. There's a two-level dance floor and a three-story theater for Las Vegas–style shows. In fact, among cruise ships in service or under construction today, only Princess Cruises' Grand Princess is larger. This is a ship with all the bells and whistles—and then some.

The *Destiny*'s incredible deck area has four swimming pools and seven whirlpools. Two pools have swim-up bars; one has a retractable roof—a great advantage during the inevitable Caribbean rain showers. Inside, there are multiple venues for dining. In addition to the main dining rooms, serving breakfast, lunch, and dinner, and the standard Lido grille for casual fare, such as hamburgers and hot dogs, Carnival has embraced the trend toward alternative restaurants. Specialty foods available aboard the ship include Italian cuisine, served in the Trattoria; Chinese food, served in the Happy Valley restaurant; and a 24-hour pizzeria and patisserie.

The *Destiny* is designed to keep children busy, too. Besides the above-mentioned water slide, a Carnival trademark enjoyed by kids of all ages, there is a two-story indoor/outdoor children's play area with its own swimming pool. An arcade has the latest in virtual-reality and electronic games.

Cabins and Rates

	Beds	Phone	TV	Sitting Area	Fridge	Tub	Average Per Diem*
Suite	T or K	●	●	●	●	●	$312
Outside	T, K, or U/L	●	●	○	●	○	$215
Inside	T, K, or U/L	●	●	○	●	○	$197

**Rates are for seven-day cruises. Airfare and port taxes are extra.*

More than 60 percent of the cabins on the *Destiny* have ocean views. Sixty percent of the standard outside cabins and all suites have private balconies. All outside cabins have a sitting area with a sofa and coffee table. Specially designed family staterooms, some with connecting cabins, are conveniently located near the ship's children's facilities.

Outlet voltage: 110 AC.

Single supplement: 150%–200% of double-occupancy rate. Carnival can match up to four same-sex adults in a cabin for $650 each on seven-day cruises.

Discounts: A third or fourth passenger in a cabin pays reduced per diems. You get a discount for booking early.

Sports and Fitness

Health club: 15,000-square-foot fitness center with gym, aerobics, massage, men's and women's steam rooms and saunas, fitness machines, two whirlpools, facial and body treatments, juice bar.

Recreation: Aerobics classes, shuffleboard, table tennis, trapshooting, four pools (one with water slide, one with retractable dome, and one children's pool), seven whirlpools, jogging track.

Facilities

Public rooms: Eleven bars and lounges, casino, disco, library.

Shops: Boutiques, drugstore, beauty salon/barber.

Health care: Doctor and nurse on call.

Child care: Two-level indoor/outdoor children's play area with children's pool. Youth programs in four age groups run by counselors, baby-sitting arranged privately with youth counselor. Video arcade with virtual-reality electronic games.

Services: Full- and self-service laundry, photographer, photo studio for portraits.

Accessibility

Twenty-three cabins, on Upper, Empress, and Lido decks, are accessible to wheelchair users.

MS Ecstasy, MS Fantasy, MS Fascination, MS Imagination, MS Inspiration, and MS Sensation

Specifications

Type of ship: Megaship
Cruise experience: Casual
Size: 70,367 tons
Number of cabins: 1,020/1,022 (Fantasy)
Outside cabins: 60.7%
Passengers: 2,040/2,044 (Fantasy)
Crew: 920 (international)
Officers: Italian
Passenger/crew ratio: 2.2 to 1
Years built: 1990–1996

Ship's Log

These six $225 million ships, the newest in the Carnival fleet, appeal to the kind of crowd that loves Atlantic City and Las Vegas. They are identical in all but decor, although all share the marble, brass, mirrors, and electric lights that heighten Carnival's now-notorious hyperactivity. In addition to Olympic-size pools, the ships also have unique banked and padded jogging tracks with a special surface; their casinos and fitness centers are among the largest afloat. Each is built around a central, seven-story atrium.

Big, bright, bold, and brassy, the *Fantasy* lives up to its name, resembling a series of fantastic Hollywood sets rather than a cruise ship. Fifteen miles of bright neon tubing snake through the ship. The public rooms are lavishly decorated in elaborate motifs; the Cats Lounge, for example, was inspired by the famous musical, and Cleopatra's Bar re-creates the interior of an Egyptian tomb.

The *Ecstasy* and *Sensation* are less futuristic and more elegant. The *Ecstasy*'s cityscape motif links the public areas: City Lights Boulevard evokes an urban street scene, the Rolls Royce Café is built around an antique Rolls, the Metropolis Bar is home to a skyscraper-like neon sculpture, and the entrance to the Chinatown lounge is guarded by twin lion-head foo dog sculptures reminiscent of ancient China. The *Sensation* takes a more subtle approach. Public rooms indulge the senses with lush greenery and carved wood in the Oak Room or a copy of the sculpture *David* in the Michelangelo Lounge. A portal of arched hands invites passengers to enter the Touch of Class piano bar, where passengers sit in the palms of still more hands.

The *Fascination* takes the movie-set theme quite literally: Public rooms evoke a Hollywood motif, and likenesses of tinsel-town legends populate its salons and lounges. Life-size figures portray Marilyn Monroe, James Dean, Bette Davis, Gary Cooper, John Wayne, and Humphrey Bogart—just to name a few.

The *Imagination*'s interior reaches deep into the past and peeks far into the future for its imagery. Symbols of antiquity—sphinxes, Medusas, and winged Mercury figures—evoke a classical ambience, while spaceships represent the dawn of the computer age. The casino is equipped with vintage slot machines from the 1930s and 1940s, while the library creates a Victorian feel with its 19th-century European antiques. In the Candlelight Lounge, hundreds of electric candlesticks create a moody ambience for the room's late-night entertainment.

The *Inspiration* draws its decor from muses of the past, too. An avant-garde interpretation of the Mona Lisa and quotes from Shakespeare, painted on the library ceiling, are among the ship's more noteworthy design flourishes. Both the *Imagination* and the *Inspiration* have 24-hour pizzerias serving pizza, calzone, and a range of domestic and imported beers—so you can ponder the questions of the ages.

Cabins and Rates

	Beds	Phone	TV	Sitting Area	Fridge	Tub	Average Per Diem*
Suite	T, K, or Q	●	●	●	●	◐	$300–$310
Outside	T or K	●	●	●	●	○	$215–$220
Inside	T, K, or U/L	●	●	○	○	○	$196–$197

**Higher rates are for three-day cruises; lower rates are for seven-day cruises. Airfare and port taxes are extra.*

Cabins are decorated in bright colors and wood tones. Each is quite spacious, with closed-circuit TV and private safes. Veranda Suites and Demi Suites have private balconies, wet bars, and VCRs. Veranda Suites have tubs with whirlpool jets. Some outside cabins on the Veranda Deck have partially obstructed views.

Outlet voltage: 110 AC.

Single supplement: 150%–200% of double-occupancy rate. Carnival can match up to four same-sex adults in a cabin for $275 (three-day cruises) or $395 (four-day cruises) each.

Discounts: A third or fourth passenger in a cabin pays reduced per diems. You get a discount for booking early.

Sports and Fitness

Health club: Gym, aerobics room, massage room, women's and men's locker rooms with steam rooms and saunas, fitness machines, two whirlpools, facial and body treatments.

Recreation: Aerobics classes, shuffleboard, table tennis, trapshooting, two outdoor pools (one with slide), children's wading pool, four outdoor whirlpools, banked jogging track (11 laps = 1 mile).

Facilities

Public rooms: Nine bars and lounges, casino, disco, card room, library.

Shops: Boutiques, drugstore, beauty salon/barber.

Health care: Doctor and nurse on call.

Child care: Playroom, teen center (with video games), youth programs in four age groups run by counselors, baby-sitting arranged privately with youth counselor.

Services: Full- and self-service laundry, photographer.

Accessibility

Twenty cabins, all on the Empress Deck of each ship, are accessible to wheelchair users.

MS Holiday

Specifications

Type of ship: Cruise liner
Cruise experience: Casual
Size: 46,052 tons
Number of cabins: 726
Outside cabins: 62%
Passengers: 1,452
Crew: 660 (international)
Officers: Italian
Passenger/crew ratio: 2.2 to 1
Year built: 1985

Ship's Log

One of the first generation of "superliners" built for Carnival, the *Holiday* was the forerunner of the line's megaships. On the outside, it ushered in the age of boxy hulls and superstructures that rise straight out of the water. Inside, it took Carnival's palatial, theme-park atmosphere to new extremes. A bar called the Bus Stop has red-top luncheonette stools, traffic signs, and an actual red-and-white bus from the 1930s. Another bar, Carnegie's, has the luxurious look of a private club, with overstuffed leather chairs and sofas and glass-door library shelves. Rick's American Café is straight from *Casablanca*. The *Holiday* ushered in Carnival's first extra-wide, enclosed walkway that runs along the port side of the Promenade Deck. The teak passageway called Broadway connects the casino and all the bars and lounges on the deck. The main entertainment lounge, the Americana, is a six-level, curved room that accommodates more than 900 passengers. The Gaming Club Casino has more than 100 slot machines and 250 seats. A recent addition to the ship is a $1 million entertainment center, complete with the latest virtual-reality and video games.

Cabins and Rates

	Beds	Phone	TV	Sitting Area	Fridge	Tub	Average Per Diem*
Suite	T/K	●	●	●	●	●	$310
Outside	T, K, or U/L	●	●	○	○	○	$213
Inside	T or K	●	●	○	○	○	$197

**Lower rates are for three-day cruises. Airfare and port taxes are extra.*

The slightly larger-than-average cabins are appointed in bright colors and wood tones. The Veranda Suites have a sitting room, private balcony, and whirlpool. All cabins have wall safes.

Outlet voltage: 110 AC.

Single supplement: 150%–200% of double-occupancy rate. Carnival can match up to four same-sex adults in a cabin for $650 each.

Discounts: A third or fourth passenger in a cabin pays reduced per diems. You get a discount for booking early.

Sports and Fitness

Health club: Exercise equipment, spas with whirlpools, sauna, massage room, facial- and body-treatment center.

Recreation: Aerobics, shuffleboard, table tennis, trapshooting, two outdoor pools, wading pool, unobstructed circuit for jogging.

Facilities

Public rooms: Seven bars, three entertainment lounges, casino, disco, library, virtual-reality and video-game room.

Shops: Boutique, gift shop, beauty salon/barber.

Health care: Doctor and nurse on call.

Child care: Playroom, youth programs in four age groups run by counselors, baby-sitting arranged privately with youth counselor.

Services: Full- and self-service laundry, photographer.

Accessibility

Fifteen cabins are accessible to wheelchair users.

MS Tropicale

Specifications

Type of ship: Cruise liner
Cruise experience: Casual
Size: 36,674 tons
Number of cabins: 511
Outside cabins: 63%
Passengers: 1,022
Crew: 550 (international)
Officers: Italian
Passenger/crew ratio: 1.9 to 1
Year built: 1981

Ship's Log

The *Tropicale* has been a very influential ship because of its resortlike qualities. Responding to passenger suggestions, Carnival created a vessel ideal for cruising, with plenty of open space; a good choice of bars, lounges, and play areas; and a spectacular swimming pool. From the outside, the *Tropicale* is recognizable by its clean lines; sloping superstructure; oversize portholes; and the raked, double-winged funnel near the stern. The interior is ultramodern and spans the entire spectrum of colors. The Exta-Z Disco's dance floor, for instance, is alive with red and yellow lights, the elaborate ceiling with blue, green, and red neon lights. Indirect lighting sets a more appetizing mood in the Riviera Restaurant, which, with its rattan furniture, resembles a tropical grand hotel.

Cabins and Rates

	Beds	Phone	TV	Sitting Area	Fridge	Tub	Average Per Diem*
Suite	T/K	●	●	●	●	●	$312
Outside	T, K, or U/L	●	●	○	○	○	$211
Inside	T, K, or U/L	●	●	○	○	○	$197

**Rates are for seven-day cruises. Airfare and port taxes are extra.*

Cabins are of similar size and appearance, comfortable and larger than average; the majority have twin beds that can be made into a king. Decor is a mix of bright colors and wood tones. Veranda Suites have private balconies. Most outside cabins have large square windows rather than portholes.

Outlet voltage: 110 AC.

Single supplement: 150%–200% of double-occupancy rate. Carnival can match up to four same-sex adults in a cabin for $650 each.

Discounts: A third or fourth passenger in a cabin pays reduced per diems. You get a discount for booking early.

Sports and Fitness

Health club: Exercise equipment, men's and women's saunas and massage rooms, facial- and body-treatment center.

Recreation: Aerobics classes, shuffleboard, table tennis, trapshooting, two pools, wading pool, small but unobstructed circuit for jogging.

Facilities

Public rooms: Six bars and lounges, casino, disco, card room, library, video-game room.

Shops: Gift shops, beauty salon/barber.

Health care: Doctor and nurse on call.

Child care: Playroom, youth programs in three age groups run by counselors, baby-sitting arranged privately with youth counselor.

Services: Full- and self-service laundry, photographer.

Accessibility

Eleven cabins are accessible to wheelchair users.

Celebrity Cruises

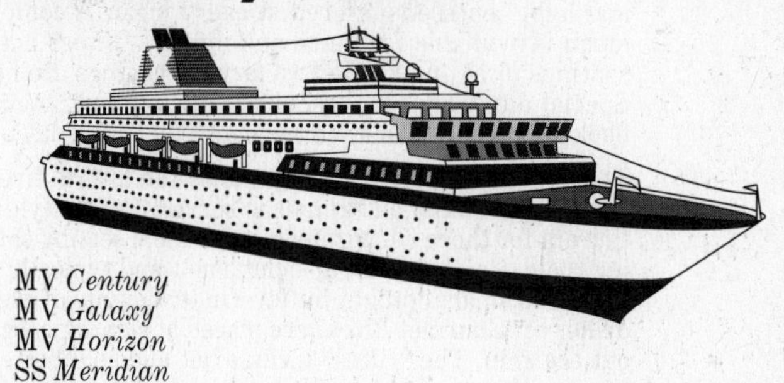

The Fleet MV *Century*
MV *Galaxy*
MV *Horizon*
SS *Meridian*
MV *Zenith*

Since its inception in 1990, Celebrity has been in the vanguard. Even the classic Meridian, when refitted in 1990, met the latest fire-safety codes seven years ahead of schedule. All of the line's vessels combine the best of traditional cruise-ship design with the latest trends in dining and decor. As a result, Celebrity's liners feel like all-inclusive Caribbean resorts, yet with a warmth and intimacy often missing on many other late-model big ships.

Ships at a Glance

	Dining Rooms	Bars	Casino	Fitness Center	Pools	Average Per Diem
Century/Galaxy	2*	11	●	●	2	$335
Horizon/Zenith	2*	9/7	●	●	2	$335
Meridian	2*	7	●	●	1	$334

**includes alternative dining in the casual restaurant*

Cruise Experience Celebrity Cruises has made a name for itself based on sleek ships and superior food (*see* Dining, *below*). If cruising were a soup, Celebrity would be made from a recipe for success. In terms of size and amenities, Celebrity's ships rival almost any in cruising, but with a level of refinement rare on bigger ships.

Celebrity attracts everyone from older couples to honeymooners for its Bermuda and repositioning cruises. Passengers are decidedly older, averaging in their mid-fifties, on the 10- and 11-day Caribbean sailings. Aboard the *Meridian* and the *Zenith*, the summertime children's programs are among the best on board any upscale cruise line.

Activities Though not party ships, Celebrity packs plenty of fun. Activities include pool and card games, shuffleboard, snorkeling instruction, "horse racing," skeet shooting, and golf putting. Passengers are not pressured to participate, and many choose to read or relax on their own in a lounge chair.

Dining Celebrity has risen nicely above typical cruise cuisine by hiring chef Michel Roux, proprietor of two of Britain's finest restaurants, as a consultant. Roux's experience in creating and cooking for large numbers of discriminating diners has been put to wonderful use. Food is truly outstanding; both familiar and exotic dishes have been

Chart Symbols. Ships at a Glance. ●: *Fully equipped;* ◐: *Partially equipped;* ○: *Not equipped.* Cabins and Rates. **D:** *Double bed;* **K:** *King-size bed;* **Q:** *Queen-size bed;* **T:** *Twin bed;* **U/L:** *Upper and lower berths;* ●: *All cabins have this facility;* ○: *No cabins have this facility;* ◐: *Some cabins have this facility*

customized to appeal to the mellow palate of American cruisers. To keep things fresh, the menus change constantly. At least one "lean and light" entrée is offered at every meal. A complete vegetarian menu is available for lunch and dinner. Dinner is at two assigned seatings (6:15 and 8:30). Two formal evenings are held each cruise. Special diets, such as kosher or salt-free, can be catered to when booked in advance or with the maître d' on the day of sailing.

There are no specialty restaurants for alternative dining aboard Celebrity's ships, but dinner is served buffet-style in a casual restaurant for those who prefer a less formal setting than the main dining room. Celebrity has also put a new and typically stylish twist on the traditional midnight buffet. On two nights of every week at sea, dishes of "Gourmet Bites" are placed at strategic locations throughout the ship. The "Bites" include hot and cold buffets, carving stations, and pastry tables. White-gloved waiters circulate through the public rooms, serving from trays of selected delicacies. Limited room service is available 24 hours.

Entertainment Celebrity's ships present lavish, if predictable, variety shows, enlivened by the occasional surprise guest (e.g., performers from a Russian circus). Smaller lounges offer low-key jazz and big-band music. Karaoke parties are popular, and the discos rock until 3 AM.

Service and Tipping Service is friendly and first class—rapid and accurate in the dining room, but sometimes slower and uneven in the bars. Waiters, stewards, and bartenders are enthusiastic, take pride in their work, and try to please. Tip your room steward and your waiter $3 each per passenger per diem, the busboy $1.50. Celebrity also recommends tipping the chief housekeeper $5 per passenger per cruise and the maître d' $7.50 per passenger per cruise. Bar stewards should be tipped 15% of the bill at the time of service.

Destinations During the summer, Celebrity offers Bermuda cruises out of New York and Alaska cruises from Vancouver. During winter it operates 10- and 11-day Caribbean cruises out of San Juan that visit up to eight ports. Year-round sailings from Fort Lauderdale cruise the Caribbean for seven days. (For seasonal itineraries, *see* Chapter 4.)

For More Information Celebrity Cruises (5201 Blue Lagoon Dr., Miami, FL 33126; tel. 800/437–3111).

MV Century and MV Galaxy

Specifications
Type of ship: Megaship
Cruise experience: Semi-formal
Size: 70,606 tons/73,000 tons
Number of cabins: 875/935
Outside cabins: 65%/68%
Passengers: 1,750/1,870
Crew: 858/909 (international)
Officers: Greek
Passenger/crew ratio: 2.1 to 1
Year built: 1995/1996

Ship's Log The *Century* is designed to appeal to both present-day and 21st-century cruisers. It has public rooms to satisfy virtually every taste: There's the cozy Michael's Club, a British-style pub appointed in wood paneling and overstuffed leather chairs, and the high-tech Images video bar—as colorful as it sounds. Unlike its predecessors in the Celebrity fleet, the *Century* has a glass-domed, three-story atrium at its center. Other departures from the design of its fleetmates are a single-level dining room whose ceilings rise two stories high and a two-deck theater with a stage large enough for full-scale musical productions.

Passengers who have sailed aboard the *Horizon* or the *Zenith* will nevertheless find themselves in familiar surroundings. The main public lounges—the forward observation lounge/disco, cocktail lounge amidships, and cabaret lounge at the stern—are all based on similar rooms aboard the line's earlier ships.

The centerpiece of the ship's hardware, however, is not the public rooms but a high-tech interactive video system, developed jointly with Sony. The system allows passengers unprecedented in-cabin choices—for ordering room service or shore excursion tickets, for example. Throughout the ship, video screens and "video wallpaper" present passengers with a constant array of visual images. An arcade has 34 video games for kids of all ages. Monitors in the elevators tell passengers the time, date, and next stop. The Sony connection, as impressive as it is, gets a bit tacky when it comes to the department-store-style displays of Sony consumer electronics and the Sony retail store, selling Sony entertainment videos and compact discs. There's even a copy of *Sony Style* magazine placed in each cabin so passengers can order Sony products.

The *Galaxy*, second in the series, was expected to be even more extravagant when launched in fall of 1996. There will be two atrium lobbies (one three stories and the other four), three swimming pools (one with a retractable glass roof), plus a multilevel observation lounge in a "futuristic setting." A third sister, the 74,000-ton *Mercury*, will be introduced late 1997, also with two atriums plus a sliding glass roof over one of the ship's three pools.

Cabins and Rates

	Beds	Phone	TV	Sitting Area	Fridge	Tub	Average Per Diem*
Suite	T/K	●	●	●	○	●	$471
Outside	D or T/K	●	●	●	○	○	$335
Inside	T/K	●	●	○	○	○	$278

**Airfare and port taxes are extra.*

Standard cabins are intelligently appointed and apportioned. Space is well used, making for maximum elbow room in the bathrooms and good storage space in the closets. All categories have a built-in minibar and a recessed nook for a 20-inch TV. All outside cabins also have a small sitting area. The decor is somewhat sparse, dispensing with fluff and frills. Each deck has been given its own color theme, and every cabin is decorated in corresponding colors. Bathtubs in the Royal and Penthouse suites have whirlpool jets and verandas.

Outlet voltage: 110/220 AC.

Single supplement: 150%–200% of double-occupancy rate.

Discounts: A third or fourth passenger in a cabin pays reduced per diems. Children 2–12 traveling with two full-paying adults pay reduced per diems. Children under two travel free. You get a discount for booking early.

Sports and Fitness

Health club: Aerobics, stationary bikes, weight machines, free weights, treadmills, rowing machines, saunas, massage rooms, steam rooms, spa treatments.

Recreation: Electronic golf simulator, shuffleboard, table tennis, trapshooting, swimming, volleyball, basketball, darts, snorkeling, exercise classes, jogging track, two pools (three on *Galaxy* and *Mercury*).

Facilities

Public rooms: Eleven bars, four entertainment lounges, casino, cinema, card room, library, video-game room, conference center.

Shops: Atrium boutiques.

Health care: Doctor on call.

Child care: Playroom with interactive computer center; baby-sitting arranged with crew member.

Services: Photographer, full- and self-service laundry, beauty shop/barber.

Accessibility Eight cabins are accessible to wheelchair users.

MV Horizon and MV Zenith

Specifications *Type of ship:* Cruise liner
Cruise experience: Semi-formal
Size: 46,811/47,255 tons
Number of cabins: 677/687
Outside cabins: 79%/84%
Passengers: 1,354/1,374
Crew: 642/657 (international)
Officers: Greek
Passenger/crew ratio: 2.1 to 1
Year built: 1990/1992

Ship's Log With a navy-blue band of paint encircling their otherwise white hulls, these ships cut a sharp profile at sea. The interiors are indisputably gracious, airy, and comfortable. The design makes the most of natural light through strategically placed oversize windows. The nine passenger decks sport several bars and entertainment lounges, and ample deck space. Wide corridors, broad staircases, seven elevators, and well-placed signs make it easy to get around. Decor is contemporary and attractive, and the artwork is pleasant rather than memorable. The Zenith has a slightly different layout from that of its sister ship: There are two fewer bars—though some have been enlarged—more suites, a larger health club, more deck space, and a meeting room.

Cabins and Rates

	Beds	Phone	TV	Sitting Area	Fridge	Tub	Average Per Diem*
Suite	D or T/K	●	●	●	○	●	$456
Outside	D or T/K	●	●	●	○	○	$335
Inside	D or T/K	●	●	○	○	○	$278

**Airfare and port taxes are extra.*

The cabins are modern and quite roomy. Furnishings include a nightstand, a desk, and a small glass-top coffee table. Closets are reasonably large, as are bathrooms. Bedtime readers will find the lone lamp on the nightstand insufficient, especially in rooms with double beds. Every cabin is equipped with a television showing CNN and other broadcasts. The suites are enormous. They have large sitting areas, tubs with whirlpool jets, 24-hour room service, and a private butler. The view from many outside cabins on the Bermuda Deck is partially obstructed by lifeboats.

Outlet voltage: 110/220 AC.

Single supplement: 150%–200% of double-occupancy rate.

Discounts: A third or fourth passenger in a cabin pays reduced per diems. Children 2–12 traveling with two full-paying adults pay reduced per diems. Children under two travel free. You get a discount for booking early.

Sports and Fitness **Health club:** Bright, sunny upper-deck spa with sauna, massage, weight machines, stationary bicycles, rowing machine, stair climber, treadmill, separate mirrored aerobics area, massage, facial/body treatments.

Recreation: Exercise classes, putting green, shuffleboard, snorkeling, trapshooting, table tennis, two pools, three whirlpools, unobstructed circuit (5 laps = 1 mile) for jogging.

Facilities **Public rooms:** Nine bars and lounges (*Horizon*) or seven bars and lounges (*Zenith*), showroom, casino, disco, card room, library/reading room, video-game room.

Shops: Gift shop, boutique, perfume shop, cigarette/liquor store, photo shop.

Health care: Doctor and nurse on call.

Child care: Playroom, teen room on Sun Deck, youth programs in three age groups supervised by counselors in summer (*Zenith*), baby-sitting arranged with crew member.

Services: Photographer, laundry service, beauty shop/barber.

Accessibility Four cabins with 39½-inch doorways are accessible to wheelchair users. Specially equipped public elevators are 35½ inches wide, but certain public areas may not be wide enough for wheelchairs.

SS Meridian

Specifications *Type of ship:* Classic liner
Cruise experience: Semi-formal
Size: 30,440 tons
Number of cabins: 553
Outside cabins: 53%
Passengers: 1,106
Crew: 580 (international)
Officers: Greek
Passenger/crew ratio: 1.9 to 1
Year built: 1963

Ship's Log The *Meridian* radiates a relaxed, personable charm—it's like staying in someone's home. The dining-room food is even better than that on its fleetmates, although the same cannot be said about the lunch and breakfast buffets. Two crowds seem to prefer this ship: Families take advantage of the children's program, which is broken down into three age groups. Older passengers appreciate the ship's lineage, its traditional design, and intimate public areas—most of which are on the same deck, allowing easy access. But there are drawbacks that discourage singles and young couples: The health club is neither as large nor as bright as aboard the newer ships, and the Marina Cafe doubles as a dreary disco at night.

Cabins and Rates

	Beds	Phone	TV	Sitting Area	Fridge	Tub	Average Per Diem*
Suite	T	●	●	●	○	●	$449
Outside	T or D	●	○	◐	○	○	$334
Inside	T, D, or U/L	●	○	○	○	○	$240

**Airfare and port taxes are extra.*

Cabins are similar in size and amenities to those aboard the *Horizon* and *Zenith*; however, they are decorated in a somewhat jarring scheme of orange, red, and purple sunset hues. Bathtubs in the Presidential, Starlight, and Deluxe suites have whirlpool jets. Outside cabins on the Horizon Deck have floor-to-ceiling windows. Many outside cabins on the Atlantic Deck have obstructed or partially obstructed views.

Outlet voltage: 110/220 AC.

Single supplement: 150%–200% of double-occupancy rate.

Discounts: A third or fourth passenger in a cabin pays reduced per diems. Children 2–12 sharing a cabin with two full-paying adults pay reduced per diems. Children under two travel free. You get a discount for booking early.

Sports and Fitness **Health club:** Stationary bikes, weight machines, treadmills, rowing machines, sauna, massage, facial/body treatment.

Recreation: Exercise classes, putting green, golf driving, shuffleboard, snorkeling, trapshooting, table tennis, pool, children's pool, three outdoor whirlpools, unobstructed circuit on Captain's Deck (8 laps = 1 mile).

Facilities **Public rooms:** Seven bars, four entertainment lounges (including main showroom), casino, disco, cinema, card room/library, video-game room, chapel/synagogue.

Shops: Boutique, perfumery, drugstore, photo shop, beauty salon/barber.

Health care: Doctor on call.

Child care: Playroom with large windows, patio, and wading pool; youth programs in three age groups with counselors in summer; baby-sitting arranged privately with crew members.

Services: Photographer, laundry service, beauty shop/barber.

Accessibility Two cabins are accessible to wheelchair users.

Clipper Cruise Line

Yorktown Clipper

The Fleet MV *Nantucket Clipper*
MV *Yorktown Clipper*

The yachtlike *Nantucket Clipper* and *Yorktown Clipper* are small, stylish coastal cruisers with a casual sophistication. With their shallow drafts and Zodiac landing craft, they are well suited to exploring remote and otherwise inaccessible waters.

Ships at a Glance

	Dining Rooms	Bars	Casino	Fitness Center	Pools	Average Per Diem
Nantucket Clipper *Yorktown Clipper*	1	1/2	○	○	0	$330

Cruise Experience Clipper Cruise Line's sailings come under the general category of "soft adventure," but these are adventures that don't sacrifice aesthetics. The vessels are nicely appointed, and the line emphasizes such shipboard refinements as fine dining.

Compared with other small ship lines, Clipper's Caribbean and East Coast experience is more sophisticated and service-oriented than life aboard an American Canadian Caribbean Line vessel. In Alaska, Clipper combines the creature comforts of Alaska Sightseeing with the educational emphasis of Special Expeditions. Passengers are older (typically in their mid-sixties), wealthier, and better educated than the average cruise passenger.

Activities Clipper is noted for its cultural bent, and on each cruise a naturalist, historian, or other expert leads lectures and field trips. Apart from these occasional talks and excursions, organized activities are few. Board games and card games are popular, but reading and socializing are the main onboard activities. In the Caribbean, snorkeling off the side of the ship is popular.

Dining Clipper's American cuisine is quite good, with regional and vegetarian specialties. There is also a pastry chef aboard. Dinner (at 7:30) is served at one open seating. There are two "dressy" evenings per cruise, but formal attire is not necessary. Special dietary requests should be made in writing three weeks before departure; no kosher meals are available. Other food service includes a Continental breakfast served in the Observation Lounge and fresh chocolate-chip cookies available in the afternoon. Cappuccino, coffee, tea, juice, and fresh fruit can be had at any time, but there is no room service.

Entertainment There are no discos, casinos, or musical revues aboard Clipper's ships. Though local entertainers sometimes perform on board and movies may be shown, evenings are low-key; socializing in the

Chart Symbols. Ships at a Glance. ●: *Fully equipped;* ◐: *Partially equipped;* ○: *Not equipped.* Cabins and Rates. **D:** *Double bed;* **K:** *King-size bed;* **Q:** *Queen-size bed;* **T:** *Twin bed;* **U/L:** *Upper and lower berths;* ●: *All cabins have this facility;* ○: *No cabins have this facility;* ◐: *Some cabins have this facility*

lounge over drinks is about as rowdy as this crowd usually gets. Many passengers venture ashore to enjoy the nightlife or take evening strolls.

Service and Tipping Though small, the American staff is young, energetic, and capable, working nicely together to provide good service without lobbying for tips. On the last evening passengers may leave tips in an envelope on the purser's desk (tip $9 per passenger per diem); these are pooled and distributed.

Destinations Clipper sails throughout the Americas. On the Atlantic coast, its programs stretch the length of the Eastern Seaboard from New England and Canada to the Southeast's Intracoastal Waterway. Some sailings venture as far as the Caribbean or Central and South America. Mid-continental cruises explore the Great Lakes on both sides of the border. In western North America, the line has sailings from the Baja Peninsula to the California wine country and north to Alaska. (For seasonal itineraries, *see* Chapter 4.)

For More Information Clipper Cruise Line (7711 Bonhomme Ave., St. Louis, MO 63105, tel. 800/325–0010).

MV Nantucket Clipper and MV Yorktown Clipper

Specifications
Type of ship: Coastal cruiser
Cruise experience: Casual
Size: 95 tons/97 tons
Number of cabins: 51/69
Outside cabins: 100%
Year built: 1984/1988
Passengers: 102/138
Crew: 32/40 (American)
Officers: American
Passenger/crew ratio: 3.2 to 1/3.5 to 1

Ship's Log The *Clippers* look more like boxy yachts than cruise ships. Their signature design is dominated by a large bridge and large picture windows that ensure bright interior public spaces. As with all small ships, there are only a few public rooms and deck space is limited. However, the cozy quarters engender a camaraderie and familiarity among passengers that you're unlikely to find on a big liner. The glass-walled Observation Lounge, for example, is small enough to foster conversation that can be heard anywhere in the room. Such close quarters can also seem claustrophopic at times, due to some very low ceilings. A knowledgeable crew offers advice as to what and what not to see in port.

Cabins and Rates

	Beds	Phone	TV	Sitting Area	Fridge	Tub	Average Per Diem*
Outside	T	○	○	○	○	○	$330

**Airfare and port taxes are extra.*

The all-outside cabins are small. How the designers stuffed two beds, a dresser, a desk, a bathroom, and a closet into such a tiny space is a great mystery. Nicely finished in pastel fabrics and accented with blond woods and prints on the walls, they make a comfortable home at sea. Most cabins have a picture-window view; a few have portholes. Category Two cabins open onto the public promenade.

Outlet voltage: 110 AC.

Single supplement: Single-occupancy cabins are available at $420–$450 per diem, depending on the itinerary.

Discounts:A third passenger in a cabin pays reduced per diems.

Sports and Fitness **Recreation:** Snorkeling equipment and instruction, unobstructed circuit for jogging; no organized deck sports or facilities.

Facilities **Public rooms:** Small lounge serves as living room, bar, outdoor deck bar (*Yorktown* only), card room, and entertainment center; there are TVs in the dining room and lounge.

Shops: Souvenir items available.

Health care: None.

Accessibility There are no facilities specifically equipped for wheelchair users.

Club Med

The Fleet *Club Med 1*
Club Med 2

The huge Club Med ships are like small ocean liners with sails. In fact, they are the largest passenger sailing ships afloat. Built by the French shipyard that produced the graceful *Windstar* ships (*see below*), the *Club Med 1* and *Club Med 2* are distinctive, sleek, white vessels that combine traditional sail power with cutting-edge technology.

Ships at a Glance

	Dining Rooms	Bars	Casino	Fitness Center	Pools	Average Per Diem
Club Med 1 *Club Med 2*	2	5	●	◐	2	$330

Cruise Experience Club Med, known for fun-in-the-sun villages, has taken its activity-packed vacations and sent them to sea. There's always something to do, and the ship's team of cruise directors (known as G.O.s or *gentils organisateurs*) makes sure that everybody has a good time. There's no pressure to join in, though, and a laid-back atmosphere prevails.

A Club Med cruise is international— only 20% to 30% of the passengers may be American. The majority come from Europe, particularly from France. Shipboard announcements are made in English, French, and German, and all the G.O.s speak English. Because a Club Med cruise costs more than its land-based vacations, passengers tend to be more affluent. Most are couples in their mid-thirties to sixties who have never been to a Club Med village before.

Despite the impressiveness of the ships and Club Med's exceptional reputation, these cruises are not especially sophisticated. In fact, for the rather pricey $300 per person per diem, you're probably better off aboard one of Star Clipper's authentic sailing vessels.

Activities On a typical day, the ship drops anchor in a protected bay. For those who want to go ashore, there's tender service. For those who stay aboard, the most popular activities are water sports, such as sailing, snorkeling, and scuba diving (for certified divers only). Every day, weather permitting, a large platform is lowered from the stern, creating a diving and sunning deck at water level. The G.O.s are always on hand to provide instruction on using the ship's water-sports equipment, as well as to lead traditional cruise diversions, such as bridge lessons. Calisthenics and aerobics are conducted on deck and in the pool.

Dining Just as in France, dinner is a big event, and it lasts longer than many Americans may be accustomed to. Cuisine is mainly French and

Chart Symbols. Ships at a Glance. **●**: *Fully equipped;* **◐**: *Partially equipped;* ○: *Not equipped.* Cabins and Rates. **D:** *Double bed;* **K:** *King-size bed;* **Q:** *Queen-size bed;* **T:** *Twin bed;* **U/L:** *Upper and lower berths;* **●**: *All cabins have this facility;* ○: *No cabins have this facility;* **◐**: *Some cabins have this facility*

Continental, with low-calorie, nonfat, and vegetarian dishes available upon request. However, the fare is geared toward European tastes—sauces in particular can be rather heavy.

Dinner is served from 7:30 to 9:30 in two restaurants—the main dining room, where seating is open, and an indoor-outdoor café, where reservations are required. Twice a week, passengers dress for dinner, but neither jackets nor ties are required for men on any evening. Women dress "casually elegant," nothing fancier than a basic black dress or a smart pantsuit. Beer and Club Med's private-label wines are complimentary at lunch and dinner; other wines may be ordered at an additional charge.

Breakfast and lunch are served in the indoor-outdoor café; lunch is also served in the main dining room. Except for the complimentary Continental breakfast, there is a charge for 24-hour room service. A limited in-cabin menu ranges from $3 cheese sandwiches to $25 caviar platters.

Entertainment A piano bar, a disco, and a cabaret lounge with performances by G.O.s and local bands constitute the entertainment. Don't look for the Las Vegas–style shows you see on some ships; Club Med's entertainment is amateurish in comparison. A favorite on every cruise is "Carnival Night," when passengers masquerade in elaborate costumes and stage makeup provided by the crew.

Service and Tipping The G.O.s are neither servile nor condescending. The friendly and informal staff seems genuinely enthused and eager to help passengers. No tips are accepted.

Destinations Thanks to its shallow draft, *Club Med 1* can sail into small Caribbean harbors in such places as Les Saintes, Mayreau, Carriacou, and Tintamarre. In summer, the ship sails the Mediterranean. The *Club Med 2* sails year-round from New Caledonia and through the islands of French Polynesia. (For seasonal itineraries, *see* Chapter 4.)

For More Information Club Med (40 W. 57th St., New York, NY 10019, tel. 800/258–2633 or 800/453–7447).

Club Med 1 and Club Med 2

Specifications
Type of ship: Motor-sail
Cruise experience: Casual
Size: 14,745 tons/14,983 tons
Number of cabins: 186/191
Outside cabins: 100%
Passengers: 376/386
Crew: 214 (international)
Officers: French
Passenger/crew ratio: 1.8 to 1
Year built: 1990/1992

Ship's Log There's no mistaking one of these Club Med ships when all seven white sails are unfurled. They are vessels of beauty and grace, reminiscent of the great clipper ships of old. But unlike those ships—or Star Clippers' modern-day re-creations—the sails are really for show, and the ships' main power comes from electric diesel engines. A draft of only 15 feet allows the ship to sail safely into small, off-the-beaten-path harbors.

Eschewing the chrome, neon, and plastic decor of today's glitzy megaships, Club Med wisely opted instead for a yachtlike ambience achieved through rich teak and mahogany decks and paneling. The public rooms are nautical in style, with muted blue and beige fabrics, and are wrapped in large windows that make you feel very much at one with the sea.

Cabins and Rates

	Beds	Phone	TV	Sitting Area	Fridge	Tub	Average Per Diem*
Suite	T/K	●	●	●	●	○	$440

Outside	T/K	●	●	●	●	○	$330

**Rates are for the Caribbean. Airfare and port taxes are extra.*

Cabins are all outside, not huge but roomy, and sharply appointed in a modern yet nautical style, with mahogany furnishings, twin brass-trimmed portholes, and stark white walls. Each is equipped with local and closed-circuit TV, a telephone, a radio, an honor bar, two minisafes, a hair dryer, and terry robes.

Outlet voltage: 110/220 AC.

Single supplement: 130% of double-occupancy rates.

Discounts: A third passenger in a cabin pays reduced per diems.

Sports and Fitness

Health club: Spacious top-deck fitness center with sea-view windows and modern weight-training machines, stationary bikes, rowing machines, and treadmill (*Club Med 1* only); massage, tanning, sauna, facials, manicures, and hairstyling.

Recreation: Aerobics and other exercise classes, Windsurfers, Sunfish sailboats, scuba equipment (for certified divers), waterskiing off swimming platform, two pools, two Zodiac dive boats, unobstructed circuit for jogging, golf simulator (*Club Med 2* only).

Facilities

Public rooms: Five bars, showroom, disco, casino.

Shops: Gift shop, beauty salon.

Health care: Doctor and nurse on call.

Child care: Children under 10 not allowed; G.O.s supervise daytime activities for teenagers.

Services: Bank, laundry service, pressing service.

Accessibility

There are no facilities specifically equipped for wheelchair users.

Commodore Cruise Line

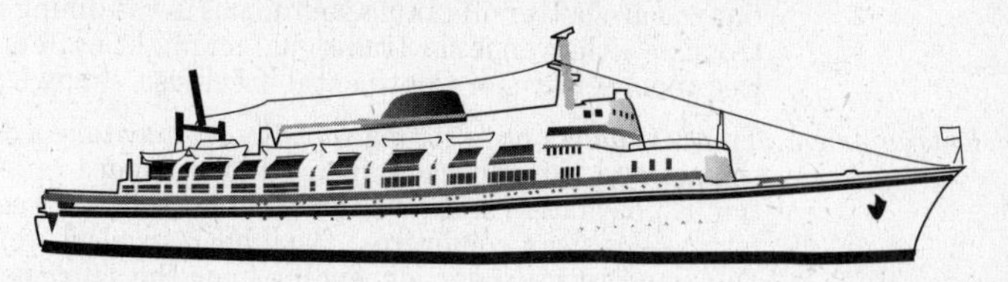

The Fleet SS *Enchanted Isle*

Built in 1958, the *Enchanted Isle* was originally named the *Brasil* and designed for all-first-class passenger service between New York and South America. Over the years, the ship was re-christened with many names, and saw service with Holland America Line and later Bermuda Star Line as the *Bermuda Star*. Unfortunately, the *Enchanted Isle* has not aged gracefully. Signs of its many years at sea include corroded brass, thick layers of paint, and scarred and pitted wood. On the other hand, if you look closely, you can still see touches of the *Brasil*'s original art deco design.

The *Enchanted Isle* was recently separated from its sister and former fleetmate, the *Enchanted Seas*. The latter now sails with World Explorer Cruises (*see below*), and shares a similar history and classic appeal.

Ship at a Glance

	Dining Rooms	Bars	Casino	Fitness Center	Pools	Average Per Diem
Enchanted Isle	1	6	●	◐	1	$162

Cruise Experience A casual onboard atmosphere, low prices, and the chance to sail on a classic-style liner are this line's chief attractions. Commodore draws its passengers mostly from the South; 80% come from Alabama, Georgia, Louisiana, Mississippi, or Texas. Agewise, passengers span the range, from couples in their twenties to those in their seventies. Many are aboard ship to celebrate a special birthday or anniversary. Families with children will appreciate being able to fit three or four passengers in many of the staterooms at greatly reduced rates. In all, the line makes up for what it lacks in elegance and amenities with value and passenger satisfaction, which is why many consider the line one of cruising's best buys.

Activities Daily events run the gamut of typical ocean-liner activities. Choices include bingo, scavenger hunts, wine-and-cheese tastings, ice-carving demonstrations, and poolside games. Theme cruises include a country-and-western cruise, jazz cruise, and blues cruise, plus a "Great Chefs" cruise.

Dining Commodore's strictly American fare is what one would expect from an economy cruise line: adequate, correctly prepared, but far from memorable. Lunch and dinner in the main dining room are served at two assigned seatings (6 and 8:30 for dinner); there is a single open seating for breakfast. There are two formal evenings. Low-fat, no-sugar, low-salt, vegetarian, and low-calorie diets are available, but kosher meals are not. There is no smoking in the dining room. Sub-

Chart Symbols. Ships at a Glance. ●: *Fully equipped;* ◐: *Partially equipped;* ○: *Not equipped.* Cabins and Rates. **D:** *Double bed;* **K:** *King-size bed;* **Q:** *Queen-size bed;* **T:** *Twin bed;* **U/L:** *Upper and lower berths;* ●: *All cabins have this facility;* ○: *No cabins have this facility;* ◐: *Some cabins have this facility*

stantial buffet breakfasts and lunches are served daily in the Promenade Deck's Bistro, as are ice cream, cakes, and cookies at teatime, but you are better off taking your meals in the dining room. The Bistro also is the venue for traditional midnight buffets. There is limited room service for Continental breakfast, sandwiches, and cake.

Entertainment This is Commodore's strong suit. Shows may take a destination as a theme, and the general shipboard atmosphere reflects the ports, too: Embarkation staff, waiters, and bartenders wear colorful uniforms—Mexican sombreros, Caribbean tropical wear, or perhaps Dixieland jazz tuxedos, depending upon the ship's next port of call. A disco and piano bar continue the party well into the wee hours.

Service and Tipping Tip the room steward and waiter $3 each per passenger per diem; the busboy, $2. A 15% service charge is automatically added to beverage purchases.

Destinations The *Enchanted Isle* departs every Saturday from New Orleans on seven-day cruises to the western Caribbean. (For year-round itineraries, *see* Chapter 4.)

For More Information Commodore Cruise Lines (4000 Hollywood Blvd., South Tower, Suite 2385, Hollywood, FL 33021, tel. 954/967–2100 or 800/832–1122).

SS Enchanted Isle

Specifications

Type of ship: Classic liner
Cruise experience: Casual
Size: 23,395 tons
Number of cabins: 367
Outside cabins: 77%
Passengers: 726
Crew: 350 (international)
Officers: European and American
Passenger/crew ratio: 2.1 to 1
Year built: 1958

Ship's Log This is a very handsome ship from the outside but less thoughtfully designed inside. Public rooms are fairly small and irregularly shaped. The lack of bright, open spaces can make them feel cramped at times; the gym in particular is windowless and poorly equipped, especially compared with fitness centers on other ships. These minuses are balanced, however, by the fact that the passenger capacity is relatively low and cabins are quite large.

Cabins and Rates

	Beds	Phone	TV	Sitting Area	Fridge	Tub	Average Per Diem*
Suite	D or T	●	●	●	○	●	$224
Outside	D, T, or U/L	●	●	◐	○	◐	$162
Inside	D, T, or U/L	●	●	◐	○	○	$136

**Rates are for the Caribbean. Airfare and port taxes are extra.*

Cabins are large, with plentiful closet space. The top three categories have additional amenities such as sitting areas, desks, bidets, and bathtubs. Recent redecorations have helped spruce things up, but the age of this ship is still apparent in such things as cracked bathroom tiles, dented doors, and worn bathroom fixtures. The view from outside cabins on the Navigation Deck is partially obstructed, except cabins 222–224. Outside cabins on the Boat Deck look onto a public promenade.

Outlet voltage: 110 AC.

Single supplement: There are a limited number of outside single cabins available in Category 7. Otherwise, passengers pay 150%–200%

of double-occupancy rate. Commodore will match two same-sex adults in a cabin at the double-occupancy rate.

Discounts: A third or fourth passenger in a cabin pays reduced per diems. A child under 17 sharing with two adults pays reduced per diems. You get a discount for booking early

Sports and Fitness

Health club: Small inside exercise room, massage.

Recreation: Aerobics, golf driving, table tennis, shuffleboard, skeet shooting, pool.

Facilities

Public rooms: Six bars, two entertainment lounges, casino, disco, cinema, card/writing room, library.

Shops: Duty-free boutique, gift shop, beauty salon/barber.

Health care: Doctor on call.

Child care: Playroom, baby-sitting, youth programs for children 12 and under and teens 13 to 17 run by counselors during holidays and in summer.

Services: Full-service laundry, photographer, film processing.

Accessibility

Elevators are accessible to wheelchair users, and public doorways with ledges are fitted with ramps. However, cabin bathrooms have a step, and there is no elevator service to the lowest passenger deck.

Costa Cruise Lines

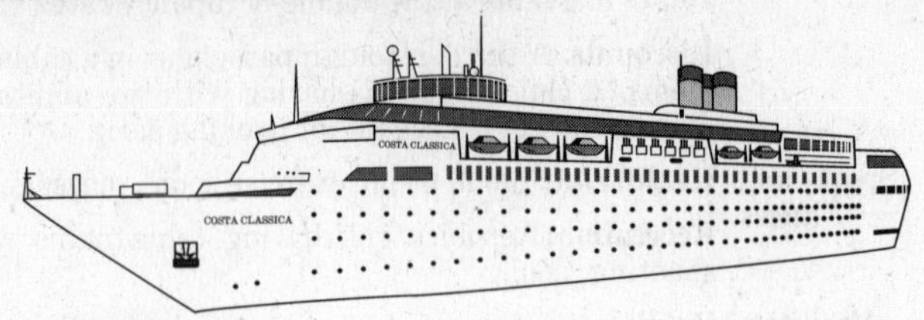

Costa Classica

The Fleet MV *CostaAllegra*
MV *CostaClassica*
MS *CostaMarina*
SS *CostaRiviera*
MV *CostaRomantica*
MV *CostaVictoria*
MTS *Daphne*
TS *EugenioCosta*

Costa's ships completely span the range, from gleaming new megaships to decades-old liners. A couple of Costa vessels are rebuilt freighters—completely reconstructed from the hull up. The newer vessels carry primarily American passengers, while the older liners have mostly European passengers aboard (*see* On Board European Liners *in* Chapter 2). With such diversity comes great variation in onboard atmosphere and amenities.

Ships at a Glance

	Dining Rooms	Bars	Casino	Fitness Center	Pools	Average Per Diem
Allegra	1	4	●	●	1	$400
CostaClassica *CostaRomantica*	1	2	●	●	2	$378
CostaMarina	1	4	●	●	1	$380
CostaRiviera	1	2	●	●	1	$275
CostaVictoria	2	8	●	●	4	$387
Daphne	1	2	●	●	1	$272
EugenioCosta	1	4	●	●	2	$313

Cruise Experience Costa emphasizes what it calls "cruising Italian style": Italian cooking demonstrations, language classes, and competitions that pit pizza-dough-throwing passengers against one another. Dining-room menus emphasize Italian cuisine, and on some ships, you'll find pizzerias, bistros, patisseries, and geleterias. Don't, however, expect an Italian crew—most of the staff is international, much like any other cruise line.

Along with Cunard and Holland America, Costa is one of the oldest names in passenger-ship travel. The line traces its history back to 1860, as a freight company transporting olive oil; passenger service began in early 1948, when the *Anna "C"* sailed between Genoa, Italy, and South America. At press time, the line's oldest ships were up

Chart Symbols. Ships at a Glance. ●: *Fully equipped;* ◐: *Partially equipped;* ○: *Not equipped.* Cabins and Rates. **D:** *Double bed;* **K:** *King-size bed;* **Q:** *Queen-size bed;* **T:** *Twin bed;* **U/L:** *Upper and lower berths;* ●: *All cabins have this facility;* ○: *No cabins have this facility;* ◐: *Some cabins have this facility*

for sale. The *EugenioCosta* had already been sold, and was scheduled to leave service after its 1997 season in the Canary Islands.

Activities Costa offers the usual bag of merriment—bingo, skeet shooting, and myriad get-togethers—along with more unusual offerings: lectures on wine, astrology, and Italian history, for instance. In keeping with the Italian flair for romance, Costa's captains invite married couples to renew their vows in a special ceremony—after which they'll happily sell you champagne. The ships' spas are more elaborate than most.

Dining Costa's "Italian style" of cruising is most evident in the dining room. Menus feature regional Italian cooking, including specialty pastas and other dishes such as osso bucco, risotto alla funghi, and veal scallopine. Continental entrées range from beef and chicken to seafood. Vegetarian and low calorie spa dishes are also available. Dining-room meals are served at two assigned seatings (dinner at 6:15 and 8:30). Breakfast and lunch are sometimes open when in port. Two formal nights are scheduled on each seven-day cruise. Special dietary requests, as well as arrangements for birthday and anniversary celebrations, should be made in writing at least four weeks in advance.

Each vessel also has a casual restaurant serving buffet breakfasts and lunches. Many Costa ships have a specialty restaurant for daytime snacks as well. On the *CostaAllegra*, you'll find a patisserie in the Piazzetta Allegra shopping center. On the *CostaClassica*, Il Dolce Amore is styled like a Viennese café; on the *CostaRomantica* there's a pizzeria and a patisserie. The *CostaRiviera* and *Daphne* also have pizzerias.

Room service is available around the clock but is limited to sandwiches and Continental breakfast. (Passengers who book suites, however, are entitled to order in-room dinners from the dining-room menu, complete with linens and china.)

Entertainment The festive atmosphere aboard ship includes theme nights: Most popular are the Italian *Festa* and the Roman Bacchanal, for which passengers fashion togas out of bedsheets. Otherwise, entertainment is fairly typical, from cabaret shows to dancing to sing-alongs in the piano bar. None of the line's oldest ships—the *Daphne*, *Eugenio*, and *Riviera*—have in-cabin televisions; instead, they have cinema-style theaters for showing movies.

Service and Tipping Service can be nonchalent—pleasant but not especially fast. Overall, the ambience is relaxed and friendly. Tip the room steward and waiter $3 each per passenger per diem, the head waiter $1, the busboy $1.50.

Destinations Costa ships sail throughout the Caribbean in winter, returning to their home waters each summer for a variety of European and Mediterranean cruises. Some European and transatlantic cruises include land packages from Perillo Tours. (For seasonal itineraries, *see* Chapter 4.)

For More Information Costa Cruise Lines (World Trade Center, 80 S.W. 8th St., Miami, FL 33130, tel. 800/462–6782).

MV CostaAllegra

Specifications

Type of ship: Cruise liner
Cruise experience: Semi-formal
Size: 30,000 tons
Number of cabins: 405
Outside cabins: 60%

Passengers: 800
Crew: 400 (international)
Officers: Italian
Passenger/crew ratio: 2 to 1
Year built: 1969, rebuilt 1992

Ship's Log The *Allegra* is one of Costa's rebuilt freighters that has been impressively reincarnated as a cruise ship. The designers made wonderful use of sunlight and sea in the public areas: A stunning plant-filled atrium caps the health club, and the boxy aft of the ship allows high windows in the dining room, with a splendid view of the ocean. An open deck area off the Yacht Club Buffet lets you enjoy seaside dining for breakfast or lunch. The Monte Carlo Casino, on the other hand, is rather small by modern cruise-ship standards.

Each deck is named after a modern painter—Gaugin, Rousseau, van Gogh—and follows a bright color scheme meant to evoke that artist's work. In contrast to the warm tones of the ship's corridors, public rooms project a cooler mood: the Murano Bar, a popular nighttime spot for jazz and piano music, is decorated in blue fabrics, with chrome accents and halogen lighting.

Cabins and Rates

	Beds	Phone	TV	Sitting Area	Fridge	Tub	Average Per Diem*
Suite	Q, T	●	●	●	●	●	$471
Outside	Q, T	●	●	○	○	○	$400
Inside	Q, T, or U/L	●	●	○	○	○	$357

**Rates are for the Mediterranean. Airfare and port taxes are extra.*

Inside and outside cabins are equally spacious and stylish, all exceptionally decorated with modern Italian furnishings accented in burnished wood and woven fabrics. Some cabins have twins that convert to a queen, and all have built-in hair dryers and safes. The Grand Suite, on the bow, has large windows on two sides but no balcony. Like the Grand Suite, standard suites have whirlpool bathtubs and walk-in closets, but they also have private balconies. Suites receive flowers and fruit baskets replenished daily.

Outlet voltage: 110/220 AC.

Single supplement: 200% of double-occupancy rate for suites, 150% for other cabins.

Discounts: A third or fourth passenger in a cabin pays reduced per diems. You get a discount for booking early

Sports and Fitness **Health club:** Stair climbers, Lifecycles, treadmills, rowing machines, free weights, aerobic and stretch classes, massage and facial-treatment center.

Recreation: Pool, three hot tubs, jogging track.

Facilities **Public rooms:** Four bars, two entertainment lounges, casino, disco, card room, library, meeting room, chapel.

Shops: Boutique, perfume and jewelry shop, photo shop, beauty salon/barber.

Health care: Doctor on call.

Child care: Youth center, supervised children's program in three age groups, baby-sitting.

Services: Laundry service, photographer.

Accessibility Elevators and public lavatories are accessible to wheelchair users, as are eight cabins.

MV CostaClassica and MV CostaRomantica

Specifications

Type of ship: Cruise liner
Cruise experience: Semi-formal
Size: 53,000 tons/54,000 tons
Number of cabins: 654
Outside cabins: 67%

Passengers: 1,300
Crew: 650 (international)
Officers: Italian
Passenger/crew ratio: 2 to 1
Year built: 1991/1993

Ship's Log

At $325 million each, the *CostaClassica* and *CostaRomantica* are among the world's most expensively built cruise ships per passenger. They have the regal bearing of a fine European hotel—with plenty of cool Italian marble and handmade ceramic tile—but a sassy, charged Italian spirit. Despite their size, an intimate, yachtlike ambience can be found aboard both ships. The second pool, for instance, is an often uncrowded place to be alone with a good book. On the *Romantica,* the wicker cabanas forward on the top deck are ideal for a private moment with a sunset.

On both ships, dining is a grand affair amid Italian marble floors, Louis XIV–style chairs, and murals. Fare is northern Italian, plus classic crowd pleasers such as lobster and beef Wellington. Two theme dinners highlight foods of the Renaissance and Roman eras. By contrast, early breakfasts and buffet lunches are served in a contemporary-style Italian café with hand-painted tiles and marble tables. You can also eat lightly at the salad bar or build your own sandwich at Leonardo's deli. Rounding out the classical suggestions of these ships are the main showrooms, where typical Las Vegas–style revues are staged in a faithful reproduction of a Renaissance theater, with tiered seating for excellent views all around.

Only differences in interior design distinguish these otherwise identical sister ships. The *Classica* sports a decidedly modern, minimalist edge—some consider it too severe. The *Romantica* is softer, with more use of wood and pastel colors. In the *Romantica*'s main dining room, a noise-absorbing ceiling mutes the din reflected off the Italian marble floors. The design of the lunch buffet on the *Romantica* provides for a smoother flow of traffic.

Cabins and Rates

	Beds	Phone	TV	Sitting Area	Fridge	Tub	Average Per Diem*
Suite	Q	●	●	●	●	●	$492
outside	Q or T	●	●	●	○	○	$378
Inside	T or U/L	●	●	●	○	○	$335

**Rates are for the Mediterranean. Airfare and port taxes are extra.*

Cherry-wood furniture, designer fabrics, watercolor prints of European cities on the walls, and roomy bathrooms highlight the large cabins. Light sleepers may grumble, however, about the thin walls. Current movies are shown continuously on cabin TVs. Some twins convert to a queen. Staterooms that accommodate three passengers offer upper and lower berths. Suites sleep up to four, using a twin sofa bed and a twin Murphy bed along with the queen-size bed; in addition to a sitting area, the suites have a graceful, wood-rimmed balcony large enough to accommodate two chaise longues with room to spare. On the *Romantica,* some suites also come with floor-to-ceiling windows.

Outlet voltage: 110/220 AC.

Single supplement: 200% of double-occupancy rate for suites, 150% for other cabins.

Discounts: A third or fourth passenger in a cabin pays reduced per diems. You get a discount for booking early.

Sports and Fitness

Health club: Aerobics studio; exercise room with free weights, Lifecycles, treadmills, stair climbers, circuit weight-training system; whirlpool spas, roman bath, steam and sauna rooms; massage and facial-treatment center; juice bar.

Recreation: Two pools, jogging track.

Facilities

Public rooms: Two bars, two entertainment lounges, casino, disco, card room, library, conference center/chapel.

Shops: Boutique, perfume shop, jewelry/gift shop, photo shop, sports-clothing shop, gourmet deli, beauty salon/barber.

Health care: Doctor on call.

Child care: Youth center, supervised children's program in three age groups, baby-sitting.

Services: Laundry service, photographer.

Accessibility

Elevators and public lavatories are accessible to wheelchair users, as are six cabins.

MS CostaMarina

Specifications

Type of ship: Cruise liner
Cruise experience: Semi-formal
Size: 25,000 tons
Number of cabins: 353
Outside cabins: 51%
Passengers: 770
Crew: 385 (international)
Officers: Italian
Passenger/crew ratio: 2 to 1
Year built: 1969; rebuilt 1990

Ship's Log

Another of Costa's cruise liners that was created from the hull of a freighter, the *CostaMarina* is small by today's cruise-ship standards and has relatively few public rooms compared with most modern-day vessels. However, the ship's designers did incorporate a number of up-to-date amenities when reconfiguring the ship to carry passengers instead of freight. The centerpiece of the vessel is a three-deck atrium lobby topped with a glass roof. On the sports deck, a two-level spa is state of the art and equipped with the latest workout machines, Jacuzzis, and steam, sauna, and massage rooms. There is also a business center, shopping arcade, and high-tech nightclub aboard.

Cabins and Rates

	Beds	Phone	TV	Sitting Area	Fridge	Tub	Average Per Diem*
Suite	Q, T	●	●	●	○	●	$494
Outside	Q, T	●	●	○	○	○	$380
Inside	Q, T	●	●	○	○	○	$337

**Rates are for Europe. Airfare and port taxes are extra.*

Cabins—nearly half of them inside accommodations—are appointed in a nautical style, with colorful fabrics and teak furnishings. All have televisions, telephones, and hair dryers. Eight suites have private verandas, sitting areas, whirlpool baths, and queen-size beds.

Outlet voltage: 110 AC.

Single supplement: 200% of double-occupancy rate for suites, 150% for other cabins.

Discounts: A third or fourth passenger in a cabin pays reduced per diems. You get a discount for booking early.

Sports and Fitness **Health club:** Stair climbers, Lifecycles, free weights, aerobics, steam and sauna, massage and facial treatments.

Recreation: Pool, three hot tubs, jogging track.

Facilities **Public rooms:** Three bars, two entertainment lounges, casino, disco, card room, library, business center, chapel.

Shops: Shopping arcade, beauty salon/barber.

Health care: Doctor on call.

Child care: Youth center, supervised children's program in three age groups, baby-sitting.

Services: Laundry service, photographer.

Accessibility No cabins are specially equipped for wheelchair users.

SS CostaRiviera

Specifications *Type of ship:* Cruise liner
Cruise experience: Semi-formal
Size: 31,500 tons
Number of cabins: 487
Outside cabins: 62%
Passengers: 974
Crew: 500 (international)
Officers: Italian
Passenger/crew ratio: 1.9 to 1
Year built: 1963, rebuilt 1993

Ship's Log As one of Costa's older ships, the *CostaRiviera* lacks the walls of glass and picture windows that fill the line's newer ships with light. The fitness center, for example, while located on the top deck, hasn't the brightness of the same facility on some of the line's other vessels. The ship does, however, have such classic features as a traditional, balconied cinema for screening movies and a traditional foyer lobby. The availability of cabins that hold up to six passengers make this ship a good choice for families.

Cabins and Rates

	Beds	Phone	TV	Sitting Area	Fridge	Tub	Average Per Diem*
Outside	Q, T	●	○	○	○	○	$332
Inside	Q, T, U/L	●	○	○	○	○	$275

**Rates are for the Mediterranean. Airfare and port taxes are extra.*

All outside cabins have portholes. Many cabins can hold three, four, five, or even six passengers.

Outlet voltage: 110 AC.

Single supplement: 200% of double-occupancy rate for suites, 150% for other cabins.

Discounts: A third or fourth passenger in a cabin pays reduced per diems. You get a discount for booking early.

Sports and Fitness **Health club:** Exercise room with rowing machines, Lifecycles, weight machine, free weights.

Recreation: Pool, three hot tubs, basketball half-court, jogging track.

Facilities **Public rooms:** Three bars, two entertainment lounges, casino, disco, cinema, computer center.

Shops: Shopping arcade, beauty salon/barber.

Health care: Doctor on call.

Child care: Youth center, supervised children's program in three age groups, baby-sitting.

Services: Laundry service, photographer.

Accessibility No cabins are specially equipped for wheelchair users.

MV CostaVictoria

Specifications
Type of ship: Megaship
Cruise experience: Semi-formal
Size: 75,000 tons
Number of cabins: 964
Outside cabins: 60%
Passengers: 1,928
Crew: 800 (international)
Officers: Italian
Passenger/crew ratio: 2.4
Year built: 1996

Ship's Log Costa's biggest ship to date, the *CostaVictoria*, was scheduled to be launched in June 1996. At press time, only a few details were available on the vessel. Among its notable design features will be two atriums (one a seven-deck lobby and the other a four-deck forward observation lounge), two main dining rooms, four swimming pools (two outside, one inside, and one "splash pool"), and a tennis court. A sister ship, still unnamed, is expected to be even bigger at 78,000 tons and will carry 2,100 passengers.

Cabins and Rates

	Beds	Phone	TV	Sitting Area	Fridge	Tub	Average Per Diem*
Suite	Q,T	●	●	●	●	●	$478
Outside	Q,T	●	●	○	○	○	$387
Inside	Q,T	●	●	○	○	○	$321

**Rates are for the Mediterranean. Airfare and port taxes are extra.*

All standard cabins come equipped with a television, minibar, and safe. Minisuites add a sitting area; top-category suites are finished in pearwood and Laura Ashley fabrics.

Outlet voltage: 110/220 AC.

Single supplement: 200% of the double-occupancy rate for suites, 150% for other cabins.

Discounts: A third or fourth passenger in a cabin pays reduced per diems. You get a discount for booking early.

Sports and Fitness **Health club:** Fitness center with exercise equipment, aerobics, sauna, Turkish bath, indoor pool, Thalassic therapy and hydrotherapy.

Recreation: Deck games including tennis, basketball, volleyball, and shuffleboard; two outdoor pools; four hot tubs; splash pool; unobstructed circuit for jogging.

Facilities **Public rooms:** Eight bars, two entertainment lounges, casino/piano bar, card room, library, chapel, conference center.

Shops: Arcade with various boutiques.

Health care: Doctor on call

Child care: Teen center, supervised children's program in three age groups, baby-sitting.

Services: Laundry service, photographer.

Accessibility Six cabins are specially equipped for wheelchair users.

MTS Daphne

Specifications

Type of ship: Cruise liner
Cruise experience: Semi-formal
Size: 17,000 tons
Number of cabins: 211
Outside cabins: 90%
Passengers: 422
Crew: 250 (international)
Officers: Italian
Passenger/crew ratio: 1.6 to 1
Year built: 1955

Ship's Log The *Daphne* is an unusually small ship for one that specializes in yearly world cruises and other long, exotic itineraries. But what it lacks in size, the ship makes up for in spaciousness, given the relatively small number of passengers aboard. In fact, its passenger-to-crew ratio of 1.6 compares favorably with many higher priced ships. And of the ship's 211 cabins, only 22 are inside accommodations. However, passengers signing aboard for one of the *Daphne*'s extended cruises should keep in mind the limited number of public rooms aboard ship.

Cabins and Rates

	Beds	Phone	TV	Sitting Area	Fridge	Tub	Average Per Diem*
Suite	T	●	○	●	●	●	$395
Outside	T	●	○	○	○	●	$272
Inside	T	●	○	○	○	●	$230

**Rates are for the Mediterranean. Airfare and port taxes are extra.*

Cabins, virtually all of them outside, are generously apportioned. Most have sea views and a real tub. Suites have minirefrigerators and sitting rooms. Some also have private verandas.

Outlet voltage: 220 AC.

Single supplement: 200% of double-occupancy rate for suites, 150% for other cabins.

Discounts: A third or fourth passenger in a cabin pays reduced per diems. You get a discount for booking early.

Sports and Fitness

Health club: Exercise room, sauna, massage.

Recreation: Pool, two hot tubs, unobstructed circuit for jogging.

Facilities

Public rooms: Two bars, two entertainment lounges, casino, disco, cinema, card room, library.

Shops: Shopping arcade, beauty salon/barber.

Health care: Doctor on call.

Child care: Supervised children's program in three age groups.

Services: Laundry service, photographer.

Accessibility No cabins are specially equipped for wheelchair users.

TS EugenioCosta

Specifications

Type of ship: Cruise liner
Cruise experience: Semi-formal
Size: 30,000 tons
Number of cabins: 498
Outside cabins: 53%
Passengers: 996
Crew: 475 (international)
Officers: Italian
Passenger/crew ratio: 2.3 to 1
Year built: 1966

Ship's Log The *EugenioCosta* is a handsome and distinctive vessel. Outwardly, its most distinguishing characteristic is two side-by-side funnels, painted yellow with a big "C" on each side. Long rows of windows, just above the hull, indicate the presence of an enclosed promenade, 96another noteworthy aspect of this ship.

Cabins and Rates

	Beds	Phone	TV	Sitting Area	Fridge	Tub	Average Per Diem*
Suite	Q, T	●	○	●	●	●	$493
Outside	Q, T or U/L	●	○	○	○	◐	$313
Inside	T or U/L	●	○	○	○	○	$293

**Rates are for the Mediterranean. Airfare and Port taxes are extra.*

As is common for an older ship, the EugenioCosta has a very wide range of cabin configurations. Nearly half are inside.

Outlet voltage: 110/220 AC.

Single supplement: 200% of double-occupancy rate for suites, 150% for other cabins.

Discounts: A third or fourth passenger in a cabin pays reduced per diems. You get a discount for booking early.

Sports and Fitness

Health club: Small gym, sauna and massage rooms.

Recreation: Two pools, hot tub, sports tournament center.

Facilities

Public rooms: 4 bars, 3 entertainment lounges, casino, disco, cinema, card room, library, meeting rooms.

Shops: Shopping arcade, beauty salon/barber, photo shop.

Health care: Doctor on call.

Child care: Youth center, supervised children's program in three age groups, baby-sitting.

Services: Laundry service, photographer.

Accessibility

No cabins are specially equipped for wheelchair users.

Crystal Cruises

The Fleet *Crystal Harmony*
Crystal Symphony

Counted among the world's most luxurious ocean liners, the Crystal fleet stands out for its modern design and amenities. The vessels were built to deliver the first-rate service of a luxury small ship with the onboard facilities of a big ship. As a result, the *Harmony* and *Symphony* feel much like all-inclusive land-based resorts catering to an upscale clientele.

Ships at a Glance

	Dining Rooms	Bars	Casino	Fitness Center	Pools	Average Per Diem
Crystal Harmony	3*	7	●	●	2	$434
Crystal Symphony	3*	6	●	●	2	$456

**includes two alternative restaurants*

Cruise Experience Crystal likes to refer to its passengers as "guests," and this is a reflection of the line's accommodating approach to cruising. The ships carry relatively few passengers for their size, which means that passengers can expect to find a level of service and refinement befitting the premium price they will be asked to pay.

Crystal combines the best of computer-age know-how with an Old World flair for service and attention. Engines, radar, and navigational equipment are state of the art. Business services for the high-powered executive include audiovisual, translation, and satellite telecommunications equipment, as well as fax machines, computers, and secretarial services. And the spacious fitness centers are arguably the seagoing world's most advanced. White-glove service, stellar cuisine, air-conditioned tenders with toilets, and a contemporary interior complete the effect of total luxury and comfort. About the only flaw in Crystal's finely conceived and executed concept lies in its dining-room arrangements (*see* Dining, *below*) and its tipping policy (*see* Service and Tipping, *below*).

Activities To the typical litany of ocean-liner diversions, Crystal adds high-powered intellectual and cultural debates and destination-oriented lectures by scholars, political figures, and diplomats. The ships also carry fully equipped fitness centers and casinos, another advantage over Crystal's small-ship competitors. The casinos are the only ones at sea operated under the auspices of Caesars Palace.

Dining A gourmet aesthetic is evident in Crystal's lavish, distinctive food presentations. To complement dinner, each ship has an extensive wine cellar. Three formal nights are scheduled every 7 to 10 days, but men wear a jacket and tie to dinner virtually every night.

Chart Symbols. Ships at a Glance. ●: *Fully equipped;* ◐: *Partially equipped;* ○: *Not equipped.* Cabins and Rates. **D:** *Double bed;* **K:** *King-size bed;* **Q:** *Queen-size bed;* **T:** *Twin bed;* **U/L:** *Upper and lower berths;* ●: *All cabins have this facility;* ○: *No cabins have this facility;* ◐: *Some cabins have this facility*

Unlike other lines in this price category, Crystal seats passengers for dinner in two seatings (6:30 and 8:30). On any night passengers may also choose to dine in a Japanese restaurant on the *Harmony* or in a Chinese restaurant aboard the *Symphony*. A third choice, the Prego Italian restaurant, is found on both ships. Although the line promotes these restaurants as alternatives to dinner in the main dining room, in reality only abut 300 passengers per ship can be accommodated on any given night. And while there is officially no extra charge for dining in one of the alternative restaurants, passengers do receive a tab of $5 per person to cover at the end of the meal "gratuities".

Other food-service options include the canopy-covered, indoor-outdoor Lido Cafe, which serves breakfast, mid-morning bouillon, and lunch. The Trident Bar and Grill serves hot dogs, hamburgers, sandwiches, and pizza. The Bistro sells specialty coffees and wine and serves international cheeses. Room service is available 24 hours a day. Passengers can order from the full dining-room menu at lunch and dinner; a limited menu is served in-cabin at non-meal times.

Entertainment There are pre- and post-dinner cabarets, Broadway-style shows in the main lounge, a piano bar, before- and after-dinner dancing, a harpist, a trio (sometimes classical), and the casinos. Local entertainers are sometimes brought on board to entertain during the ships' frequent parties.

Service and Tipping Crystal's staff members are well trained, highly motivated, and thoroughly professional. However, tips are not included in the cruise fare, and the crew can be noticeably solicitous of gratuities. Recommended amounts are: Tip the steward and the waiter $3.50 each per passenger per diem, the assistant waiter $2.

Destinations Crystal brings its refined level of cruising to all of the world's top cruising destinations, including the Caribbean, Europe, Alaska, Mexico, Asia, and the Panama Canal. (For seasonal itineraries, *see* Chapter 4.)

For More Information Crystal Cruises (2121 Ave. of the Stars, Los Angeles, CA 90067, tel. 800/446–6620).

Crystal Harmony and Crystal Symphony

Specifications

Type of ship: Cruise liner
Cruise experience: Formal
Size: 49,400 tons/50,000 tons
Number of cabins: 480
Outside cabins: 96%/100%
Year built: 1990/1995

Passengers: 960
Crew: 545/530 (European)
Officers: Norwegian and Japanese
Passenger/crew ratio: 1.7 to 1/1.8 to 1

Ship's Log The *Crystal Harmony*, exceptionally sleek and sophisticated, contradicts the conventional wisdom that all new state-of-the-art ships must look like high-rise, barge-bound hotels. Technologically advanced and superbly equipped, it is tastefully decorated as well. Harmonious colors, lots of plants and neoclassical sculptures, and a light-and-airy design give a sense of both luxury and simplicity. At the center is a multilevel atrium, Crystal Plaza—a study in glass stairways and railings, brass fixtures, and dazzling white walls. The Vista Lounge is a beautiful wedding-white room with oversize observation windows. A portion of the Lido Deck is covered by a retractable canopy. With one of the highest space ratios afloat, there's never a feeling of claustrophobia, in either the public rooms or the hallways.

The *Crystal Symphony* is the biggest ship to be built with all outside cabins since the *Royal Princess* (*see* Princess Cruises). Inside, it differs from its sibling in a lighter color scheme for the decor and several larger public rooms. Repeat Crystal passengers will find that their favorite rooms, such as the Palm Court, alternative restaurants, casino, bistro, and Lido Cafe, have been expanded. The *Symphony*'s two-story atrium is twice the size of the same space aboard the *Harmony*.

Cabins and Rates

	Beds	Phone	TV	Sitting Area	Fridge	Tub	Average Per Diem*
Suite	T/K	●	●	●	●	●	$719/ $722
Outside	T/Q	●	●	●	●	●	$434/ $456
Inside	T/Q	●	●	●	●	●	$327

**Rates are for the Panama Canal. Higher rates are for the Symphony. Lower rates are for the Harmony. Inside cabins are on the Harmony only. Airfare and port taxes are extra.*

Thanks to the skillful use of paneling and mirrors, the large accommodations appear even larger. Cabins are appointed similarly on both ships, although standard cabins on the newer *Symphony* are more conveniently arranged and have better storage space. Cabins in every category are beautifully decorated and equipped with 14-channel TVs (including CNN and ESPN), VCRs, hair dryers, and robes. Other standard amenities and creature comforts include voice mail, goose-down pillows, fine linens, thick bath towels, and in-cabin safes. Penthouses have verandas and Jacuzzis (butler service is available); certain standard cabins have verandas as well. Some cabins on the Horizon and Promenade decks have obstructed views (Crystal's brochures clearly identify rooms with limited views). Cabins on the Promenade Deck look out onto a public walkway.

Outlet voltage: 110/220 AC.

Single supplement: 110%–200% of double-occupancy rate.

Discounts: A third passenger in a cabin pays the minimum per-person fare for that cruise. Children under 12 with two full-paying adults pay half the minimum per-person fare. You get a discount for booking early, paying early, and for booking a future cruise while on board. Repeat passengers get a 5% discount.

Sports and Fitness

Health club: Spa with state-of-the-art equipment (stationary bikes, rowing machines, stair climbers, treadmills), free weights, saunas, steam rooms, massage, exercise classes, personal fitness trainers, weight-reduction regimens, body and facial care, makeup services.

Recreation: Aerobics, jazz-dance, exercise classes, paddle tennis, shuffleboard, skeet shooting, table tennis, two pools (one for laps), two whirlpools, unobstructed circuit for jogging.

Facilities

Public rooms: Seven bars (*Harmony*), six bars (*Symphony*), six entertainment lounges, casino, disco, cinema, card room, library (books and videotapes), video-game room, smoking room.

Shops: Shopping arcade of boutiques, beauty salon/barber.

Health care: Doctors and nurses on call.

Child care: Youth programs with counselors during holidays or whenever a large number of children are on board, baby-sitting arranged privately with crew members.

Services: Concierge service, full- and self-service laundry, dry cleaning, photographer, video-camera rentals, film processing, secretarial and photocopying services, translation equipment for meetings.

Accessibility Two standard cabins on the *Harmony* and five standard cabins on the *Symphony* are accessible to wheelchair users. Two penthouses on both ships are also designed for travelers with disabilities.

Cunard Line Limited

The Fleet MV *Cunard Countess*
SS *Cunard Dynasty*
MS *Cunard Royal Viking Sun*
RMS *Queen Elizabeth 2*
MV *Sea Goddess I and II*
MS *Vistafjord*

Unlike many other major cruise lines, Cunard has assembled its fleet mostly through acquisition rather than by building new ships. In fact, the last time the line commissioned a new vessel was in the 1970s. Nevertheless, Cunard is heir to the tradition of luxury ocean-liner cruising, and some of its ships are among the finest afloat.

Ships at a Glance

	Dining Rooms	Bars	Casino	Fitness Center	Pools	Average Per Diem
Countess	1	4	●	●	1	$175
Dynasty	1	4	●	●	1	$323
QE 2	5	6	●	●	4	$692
Royal Viking Sun	2*	5	●	●	2	$561
Sea Goddess	1	3	●	●	1	$571
Vistafjord	2*	4	●	●	2	$457

**includes alternative restaurant*

Cruise Experience Cunard has a knack for aggravating its passengers. Over the years, complaints against the line have ranged from bad plumbing to mishandled baggage. Cunard's problems reached a peak with the bungled launch of the refurbished *Queen Elizabeth 2*. The ship, which sailed before it was ready, attracted the ire of passengers and the press alike. News reports quoted passenger complaints about a construction-zone-like atmosphere and "exploding toilets" aboard ship. One group of disgruntled customers even filed a $10 million legal action. The lawsuit was settled, and in the wake of the debacle, the line subsequently hired a new chief executive officer, who has talked about "changing the mistakes of the past." Cunard sailed into more choppy waters when the line's parent company, Trafalgar House, was sold in early 1996. At press time, the new owners' plans for the line were unclear, but uncertainty is definitely not the medicine that Cunard needs.

Despite its deficiencies, Cunard does do some things exceptionally well. Dining-room and cabin service is often flawless, and the restaurants on its more expensive ships, such as the *QE2*, *Royal*

Chart Symbols. Ships at a Glance. ●: *Fully equipped;* ◐: *Partially equipped;* ○: *Not equipped.* Cabins and Rates. **D:** *Double bed;* **K:** *King-size bed;* **Q:** *Queen-size bed;* **T:** *Twin bed;* **U/L:** *Upper and lower berths;* ●: *All cabins have this facility;* ○: *No cabins have this facility;* ◐: *Some cabins have this facility*

Viking Sun, *Sea Goddesses*, and *Vistafjord* are as good as any at sea.

Destinations The sun never sets on the Cunard fleet, as the line sails to every major destination from Alaska to Australia. (For seasonal itineraries, *see* Chapter 4.)

For More Information Cunard Line Limited (555 5th Ave., New York, NY 10017, tel. 800/528–6273).

MV Cunard Countess

Specifications

Type of ship: Cruise liner
Cruise experience: Casual
Size: 17,593 tons
Number of cabins: 398
Outside cabins: 65%
Passengers: 796
Crew: 350 (international)
Officers: British
Passenger/crew ratio: 2.3 to 1
Year built: 1976

Ship's Log The *Cunard Countess* is an affordable ship that caters to a relaxed, informal, and mostly European crowd. The vessel's Caribbean itinerary, which calls at six different ports in seven days, is especially good for first-time cruisers looking for something a little more sophisticated than a Carnival cruise. But since these are among the least expensive cruises available, don't mistake the Cunard name for an automatic stamp of luxury. The ship is compact, cabins are small, but public rooms are spacious; the Showtime Lounge, for example, features a 40-square-foot, black-marble dance floor. The Starlight Lounge, a card and entertainment room, is one of the ship's highlights; furnished in art nouveau style, it commands a magnificent view of the sea. Public areas and cabins were refurbished in the fall of 1992—furniture was reupholstered, and new navy-and-gold carpeting was installed.

Activities In addition to typical ocean-liner activities, the ship has a 24-hour health club. Exercise options continue ashore in the form of hikes, sports programs, and competitive runs—the *Countess* is known for its extensive shore excursion program.

Dining Food is above average, and the service is usually excellent. The dining room has two assigned seatings per meal (dinner at 6:30 and 8:30) and a midnight buffet. There are two formal evenings per week. A special fitness diet is available, though special dietary requests should be made two weeks before sailing. The Lido serves early-morning coffee and pastries, light breakfast, mid-morning bouillon, and light lunch. Help-yourself coffee and tea are available all day, and afternoon tea is served. Room service may be ordered 24 hours a day from a limited menu.

Entertainment Variety shows in the main lounge are the main event of evening entertainment, and there's an indoor-outdoor nightclub and a piano bar. You can ballroom dance, disco dance, or, on certain evenings, dress up for the Masquerade Ball. The *Countess*'s music theme cruises are especially popular, so be sure to book well in advance if you're interested.

Service and Tipping Service is excellent. Tip the room steward and the waiter $3 each per passenger per diem, the busboy $1.50; the wine steward gets 15% of the wine bill.

Cabins and Rates

	Beds	Phone	TV	Sitting Area	Fridge	Tub	Average Per Diem*
Suite	T	●	●	●	●	●	$239
Outside	T	●	○	○	○	○	$175

Inside	T or U/L	●	○	○	○	○	$159

**Rates are for the Caribbean. Airfare and port taxes are extra.*

Cabins are small but convert into sitting rooms during the day. Recent renovations include thicker mattresses, beds set in an L-shape arrangement, and more luggage space. Cabinetwork consists of colorfully laminated desks and dressers.

Outlet voltage: 110 AC.

Single supplement: 150% of double-occupancy rate; if a confirmed reservation is made at least 30 days prior to sailing, the single supplement may be waived. Cunard will match two same-sex adults in a cabin for the double-occupancy rate.

Discounts: A third or fourth passenger in a cabin pays $127–$142 per diem. You get a 20% discount for booking early.

Sports and Fitness

Health club: 24-hour gym with free weights, computerized weight machines, rowing machines, stationary bikes, ballet barre, sauna, massage; aerobics, stretch, yoga, and other exercise classes.

Recreation: Basketball, golf driving, paddle tennis, table tennis, shuffleboard, pool, two outdoor whirlpools.

Facilities

Public rooms: Four bars, three entertainment lounges, casino, disco, cinema, card room, library/writing room.

Shops: Small arcade of boutiques and gift shops, beauty salon/barber.

Health care: Doctor on call.

Child care: Wading pool, baby-sitting, youth programs run by counselors during holidays or in summer.

Services: Laundry service, photographer.

Accessibility

Not all public areas are accessible to wheelchair users, and wheelchairs are not permitted on tenders.

SS Cunard Dynasty

Specifications

Type of ship: Cruise liner
Cruise experience: Semi-formal
Size: 20,000 tons
Number of cabins: 400
Outside cabins: 63%
Passengers: 800
Crew: 320 (international)
Officers: British
Passenger/crew ratio: 2.5 to 1
Years built: 1993

Ship's Log

The *Dynasty* is impressive in its shipboard appointments, especially for a ship of this size. Clever use of glass yields an especially spacious result. Other design touches are at once elegant and dramatic: A skylight and three window walls brighten the Bon Vivant dining room, where tiered seating allows unobstructed sea views. In the Crown Plaza atrium, a five-story wall of glass offers a spectacular view as well, and a grand staircase completes the space.

The one flaw in this otherwise finely conceived vessel has been passenger complaints about the service. Otherwise, everything about the *Dynasty* is first-rate.

Activities

The *Dynasty* offers "low density, low impact" activities, such as bingo, pool games, "horse racing," wine tasting, "whodunit" evenings, and crafts classes. The "Seafit" health-and-fitness program combines aerobics, water exercises, toning classes, and low-calorie, low-cholesterol, low-sodium cuisine.

Dining

The American and Continental cuisine is rich and varied, and there are always light and healthy offerings. Desserts are good but not excessively rich. The Bon Vivant dining room's innovative, tiered design affords unobstructed sea views from nearly every table. Dinner is served at two assigned seatings (6 and 8:15); breakfast and lunch have open seating. Two formal nights are scheduled on each weeklong cruise. Special dietary requests must be made in writing at least two weeks before sailing.

The Marco Polo Café, a bright indoor-outdoor facility, serves breakfast, lunch, snacks, and outdoor grill selections, but the fare isn't of the quality found in the dining room. Afternoon tea and midnight buffets are offered. Room service is available 24 hours a day but is limited to sandwiches and Continental breakfast.

Entertainment

Entertainment is not dazzling, but it seems to suit passengers just fine. Broadway-style shows, cabarets, and dancing take place in the Rhapsody Lounge, which has large windows that are great for sea viewing by day. Jazz combos and dance music are featured in the aft lounge, Valentino's, while music videos and disco pound out until the wee hours of the morning in the Kit Kat Club. Those who would rather stay in their cabins at night can enjoy in-room movies.

Service and Tipping

Service on the *Dynasty* is erratic: Sometimes it is very good, other times less so. Dining-room service in particular ranges from excessively slow to rushed. Tip the steward and the waiter $2.50 each per passenger per diem, the busboy $1.50. A 15% service charge is added to bar bills.

Cabins and Rates

	Beds	Phone	TV	Sitting Area	Fridge	Tub	Average Per Diem*
Suites	D	●	●	●	●	○	$458
Outside	T/D	●	●	◐	◐	○	$323
Inside	T/D	●	●	○	○	○	$235

**Rates are for the Panama Canal. Airfare amd port taxes are extra.*

Light wood, brass accents, and pastel colors combine to create very pleasant and airy cabins. Standard staterooms are furnished with two lower beds that convert to a double, remote-control TVs (including CNN), ample storage, and a safe. Each Deluxe Suite has a double bed, a sitting area, an extra closet, and a refrigerator. Ten suites have private balconies. Two larger suites have bay windows.

Outlet voltage: 110 AC.

Single supplement: No surcharge, subject to confirmation 30 days prior to sailing; earlier confirmation at 150% of double-occupancy rate.

Discounts: A third passenger in a cabin pays $64 per diem, as does a child under 15 sailing with a single parent. You get a discount for arranging your own airfare and 20% off for booking early.

Sports and Fitness

Health club: Nautilus equipment, aerobics, sauna, steam room, massage, facials, manicures, pedicures.

Recreation: Pool, indoor and outdoor hot tubs, shuffleboard, table tennis, unobstructed circuit for jogging.

Facilities

Public rooms: Four lounges, casino, disco, library, meeting room.

Shops: Boutiques, beauty salon.

Child care: Youth center.

Accessibility

Four cabins (two inside, two outside) and the elevators are accessible to wheelchair users.

MS Cunard Royal Viking Sun

Specifications

Type of ship: Cruise liner
Cruise experience: Formal
Size: 38,000 tons
Number of cabins: 380
Outside cabins: 93%
Passengers: 758
Crew: 450 (international)
Officers: Norwegian
Passenger/crew ratio: 1.6 to 1
Year built: 1988

Ship's Log

The former flagship of Royal Viking Line is arguably Cunard's most elegant ship. When built in 1988, no expense was spared in outfitting the *Sun*, but since that time the ship's former owners had let the vessel slip into a tired appearance, with faded upholstery and paint-chipped furniture. To reverse the wear, Cunard spent $11 million in May 1995 to refurbish the *Sun*'s public rooms. New carpeting was installed and furnishings received new coverings, which gave the ship a fresh and colorful look.

This is the last ship to carry the Royal Viking name and to carry on a 25-year tradition of ceremonial cruising. There are other former Royal Viking ships still in service, but aboard none do the passengers sing, "Skald! Skald! Skald!" as they raise a toast with aquavit that has traveled around the world.

First and foremost of the Royal Viking traditions is fine dining in a single seating for dinner. The *Sun's* dining room may not be the prettiest or most elaborate afloat, but the food and service are among the best. In addition, a new bistro option has been introduced for more casual, alternative dining.

As with all of the former Royal Viking Line ships, the *Sun* was built for long-distance cruising. Its interior is spacious and designed for maximum comfort. A feeling of light and space is created by the use of floor-to-ceiling windows and two glass-walled elevators. The vessel also has its share of small lounges. Best is the Oak Room, an old-world retreat of leather chairs, nautical paintings, and a simulated fireplace. Unfortunately, these attractive rooms are little-used, creating a dead space in the middle of the ship. At the bow is the Stella Polaris Room, a handsome observation lounge with 180° views. However, outdoor deck spaces are less attractive—little has been done to dress them up and make them welcoming.

Despite its quirks, the *Sun* has a very loyal following. Its passenger repeat rate is 66%, so many passengers know the ship, the staff, and, often, fellow passengers well. The clientele tends to be older (fifties to mid-seventies), experienced, and sophisticated, with enough time and money to take long voyages. Foreign travelers make up about 20% of Royal Viking's clientele and are assisted by an international staff. Life on board tends toward the formal, and neat attire is required at all times.

Activities

Fun on the *Sun* is decidedly low-key, and passengers tend to pursue their individual interests. Those concerned with keeping their minds and bodies in shape can sign up for as many as seven daily classes from the ship's Golden Door Spa at Sea program, conducted by staff from the famous spa in California, and enrich themselves by attending the World Affairs Program lecture series. Talks cover a diverse range of topics and are designed to give passengers greater insight into the ship's ports of call. You may learn, for example, that Samuel Cunard founded Cunard Line in Halifax, Nova Scotia (*see* Chapter 3).

For many passengers, afternoon tea in the ship's observation lounge is the highlight of the day's activities. On all cruises there's a Goren bridge program and a staff golf pro who conducts clinics. Gentlemen hosts also sail aboard the *Sun* to act as social partners for single women traveling alone.

Dining The *Royal Viking Sun*'s cuisine has long been touted as some of cruising's best, and that's not an idle boast. Chefs from highly acclaimed restaurants frequently sail on board to prepare meals for passengers. Healthful menu selections at each meal are tied in with the ship's Golden Door Spa at Sea program.

All meals in the dining room are served in a single, assigned seating. Dinner is served from 7:30 to 9:00. On a Royal Viking ship, virtually every night is a formal night, and passengers are expected to dress smartly even on informal evenings. The dress code is in effect from 6 PM onward, enforced by the passengers themselves, who revel in showing off their finest.

Befitting such elaborate ceremony, much care and attention is devoted to food preparation, and passengers never see the same menu twice. Caviar may be ordered at any dinner, even when it isn't on the menu, and just about any special order can be prepared with 24 hours' notice. However, special dietary requests (such as for diabetics or vegetarians) should be made in writing at least four weeks before sailing.

More casual dining is also available. The Garden Café serves early-morning coffee and an extensive buffet lunch. On occasional evenings the Garden Café serves as the ship's alternative restaurant for dinner. The outdoor Pool Bar serves hamburgers, hot dogs, and sandwiches during the day. Other food service on the *Sun* includes mid-morning bouillon, afternoon snacks, elegant afternoon teas, evening sandwiches, and a midnight buffet. On Norwegian Day, passengers feast on a midday Norwegian Grand Buffet and enjoy Norwegian folk entertainment in the evening. Room service is always available, from a full menu at mealtimes and limited service at other times.

Entertainment Shipboard performances on the *Sun*, which cater to an older audience, have improved under Cunard. Hollywood celebrities and big-name entertainers are occasional headliners. In addition to the main showroom productions, there are occasional cabarets or game shows. Classical-music recitals and performances by solo harpists and pianists are common. Two movies are shown daily, and the library is stocked with 700 videotapes for cabin VCRs.

Service and Tipping Royal Viking has set the standard of service for every other luxury cruise line, and the *Sun*'s passenger-to-crew ratio is just about the best among cruise ships. Concierges handle special requests, whether you want to make a restaurant reservation ashore or hire a baby-sitter. Gratuities for cabin stewards and waiters are included in the cruise fare. Maître d's, butlers, and night stewards may be tipped for unusual service, but they never solicit a gratuity. A 15% service charge is automatically added to bar and wine purchases.

Cabins and Rates

	Beds	Phone	TV	Sitting Area	Fridge	Tub	Average Per Diem*
Suite	T/K	●	●	●	●	●	$846
Outside	T/K	●	●	●	●	◐	$561
Inside	T	●	●	○	●	◐	$340

**Rates are for a South America/Caribbean cruise. Airfare and port taxes are extra.*

Cabins are oversize, beautifully furnished, and equipped with all the amenities, including walk-in closets, bathrobes, lockable drawers, TVs (including CNN), and VCRs. Penthouses, deluxe bedrooms, and 40% of the outside cabins have verandas. Only 25 of the ship's 380 cabins are inside. The remarkable Owner's Suite features a large veranda and two bathrooms, one with a whirlpool in a glassed-in alcove looking out at the ocean. Penthouses and the

Owner's Suite also come with butler service. Cabins on the Promenade Deck look onto a public area.

Outlet voltage: 110/220 AC.

Single supplement: 125%–200% of double-occupancy rate.

Discounts: A third passenger in a cabin pays the minimum fare. A child under 12 sharing a cabin with two adults pays half the minimum. Various discounts are offered for repeaters and first-time cruisers. You get a discount for arranging your own airfare and 20% off for booking early.

Sports and Fitness

Health club: Golden Door Spa at Sea with fitness classes, exercise equipment, free weights, aerobics floor, saunas, and massage.

Recreation: Aerobics and other exercise classes, croquet, putting course, computerized golf simulator, table tennis, paddle tennis, shuffleboard, quoits, trapshooting, two pools (one with swim-up bar), whirlpool, unobstructed circuit (4 laps = 1 mile) for jogging.

Facilities

Public rooms: Five bars, four entertainment lounges, casino, disco, cinema, card room, library (books and videotapes), photo gallery.

Shops: Gift shops, beauty salon (with facials and massages).

Health care: Doctor and two nurses on call.

Child care: Children's programs only during Christmas cruises, baby-sitting arranged through concierge.

Services: Concierge, laundry service, dry cleaning and pressing, two launderettes, ironing room, photographer, film processing.

Accessibility

Four staterooms have L-shape bed configurations for greater wheelchair maneuverability and are specially equipped.

RMS Queen Elizabeth 2

Specifications

Type of ship: Classic liner
Cruise experience: Semi-formal/Formal
Size: 70,327 tons
Number of cabins: 936
Outside cabins: 70%
Year built: 1969

Passengers: 1,750
Crew: 1,015 (international)
Officers: British and European
Passenger/crew ratio: 1.7 to 1 (varies according to cabin category)

Ship's Log

The *Queen Elizabeth 2* is the last of its kind: Put into service in 1969 as a transatlantic liner, the *QE2* is the only cruise ship that still makes regularly scheduled crossings of the Atlantic between New York and England and the only one that assigns passengers to dine according to their cabin class in one of five restaurants.

The ship has undergone numerous refits, including one that transformed it into a military carrier during the Falklands War. Most recently, Cunard spent $45 million to upgrade many of the cabins and create several new public rooms. Among the most noteworthy are the Golden Lion, styled after a traditional English pub and a new Lido, which, with its generous use of blond woods, floor-to-ceiling glass, and brass finishings, brings a contemporary touch to this very traditional ship. Celebrating that tradition is a new "Heritage Trail" exhibit, which showcases Cunard memorabilia and artifacts. New works of art were also commissioned, depicting Cunard ships throughout the ages. All told, the renovation consumed 8,000 gallons of paint, 40,000 square yards of carpeting were laid, and 2,000 new lighting fixtures were installed.

Despite this major investment, the *Queen Elizabeth 2* continues to show its age. Many of the problems evident before the last refurbishment were still apparent after the ship came out of dry dock. Dented and corroded ceiling panels, cracked banisters repaired with plastic packing tape, and bathroom grouting stained with mold were among the details left unimproved.

Yet, for a traditional crossing of the Atlantic, this remains the purist's choice and therein lies the ship's continuing appeal: It's the sole survivor of a bygone era. And as perhaps the most famous ship in cruising, the *QE2* has the name recognition to overcome many of its disadvantages. Transatlantic sailings, in particular, attract ship aficionados who are as interested in the ship's history and legacy as they are in its fine dining. Many are repeat passengers, who share stories about their many previous crossings.

At press time Cunard announced another $18 million refurbishment of the *QE2*. Passenger capacity was to be reduced to 1,500, and the Mauretania restaurant was to become a single-seating dining room.

Activities Without diverging from the traditional fare of bingo, "horse racing," and similar get-togethers, the *QE2* also serves up a sophisticated agenda of daily activities. These include numerous lectures and seminars, classical-music concerts, fashion shows, computer courses, and an extensive fitness program. Art-history buffs will appreciate the "Heritage Trail" displays found throughout the ship. The ship's library is one of the most impressive at sea.

Dining In terms of dining, the *QE2* is a four-class ship, and passengers are assigned to one of five dining rooms according to their cabin category. The best is the Queen's Grill, a celebrated gourmet restaurant featuring table-side cooking and roast carving, where you can order virtually anything, even if it's not on the menu. Below this room are the Princess Grill and Britannia Grill, top-notch restaurants where you can also order off the menu. Next, in descending order, is the Caronia, the final of the *QE2*'s single-seating restaurants. (Past passengers should note that this restaurant is now located where the Mauretania used to be, to the displeasure of some longtime cruisers.) The present Mauretania room is a spacious restaurant for all other passengers, and dinner is served in two seatings (6:30 and 8:30). Two or three formal evenings are held each week in all the restaurants, though dinners in the Queen's Grill, Britannia Grill, and Princess Grill are rarely casual. Spa meals are available, but other dietary requests should be made at least three weeks ahead. The ship's wine cellar stocks more than 20,000 bottles.

Early-morning coffee and pastries, a buffet breakfast and lunch, and hamburgers and hot dogs are served in the new Lido. Health-conscious passengers may opt for the breakfast (and sometimes lunch) spa buffets. Other food service includes mid-morning bouillon, a traditional high tea, and a midnight buffet; 24-hour room service from a limited menu is available.

Entertainment Foremost among the *QE2*'s new public rooms are its rebuilt public lounges. The main showroom, the Grand Lounge, has been outfitted with a new stage, a dance floor, carpeting, and an upgraded sound-and-light system. The former Midships Bar has been reincarnated as the Chart Room Bar; its centerpiece is the piano from the *Queen Mary*, and before dinner the truly nostalgic can listen to cocktail music here and reminisce. In these rooms and others, the "City at Sea" comes alive at night with variety shows, cabaret, classical-music concerts, disco parties, and more. A highlight of *QE2* entertainment is a series of talks given by such celebrities as Jeremy Irons, Meryl Streep, Jason Robards, Art Buchwald, and Barbara Walters. Dance and talent contests and costume parties are also held. The liner has its own 20-station TV network. A daily newspaper is published on board.

Service and Tipping Service in the grill-class staterooms and restaurants is impeccable because that's where the most—and the best—staff members work. The service at all levels of the ship, however, is above average.

Unfortunately, Cunard suffers from occasional labor problems, and there have been a few incidents of work slowdowns or stoppages. Also, some passengers find the British attitude a bit stuffy and unspontaneous. In the Mauretania Restaurant, tip the cabin steward and waiter $3 each per passenger per diem; in the Columbia Restaurant, $4; in the Queen's and Princess grills, $5. A 10% service charge is added to bar bills.

Cabins and Rates

	Beds	Phone	TV	Sitting Area	Fridge	Tub	Average Per Diem*
Queen's Grill	T/K	●	●	●	●	●	$1,232
Britannia or Princess Grill	Q or T/D	●	●	●	●	●	$1,016
Caronia	Q or T	●	●	◐	◐	◐	$692
Mauretania	T or U/L	●	●	○	○	○	$399

**Rates are for transatlantic crossings. Airfare and port taxes are extra.*

During the most recent refit, it seems that the lower-category cabins got the most attention. Lower-deck accommodations revealed brand-new bathrooms upon inspection, but some upper-category cabins had old facilities that needed a good cleaning. Before booking, check carefully that your particular cabin number has been renovated, and get it in writing.

Suites accommodate up to four passengers, at no extra charge per passenger, making them more economical for a family of four than two luxury cabins. Penthouse Suites, with verandas and whirlpools, are the largest, most luxurious accommodations afloat; first-class cabins (all with VCRs) also are spacious. Luxury cabins, except No. 8184, have private verandas. Lifeboats partially obstruct the view from some cabins on the Sports Deck, and Boat Deck cabins look onto a public promenade.

Outlet voltage: 110 AC.

Single supplement: 175%–200% of double-occupancy rate; several single cabins are available at $179–$726 per diem.

Discounts: A third or fourth passenger in a cabin pays half the minimum fare in the cabin's restaurant grade. Except on transatlantic crossings, you get 20% off for booking early.

Sports and Fitness

Health club: Thalassotherapy pool, inhalation room, French hydrotherapy bath treatment, computerized nutritional and lifestyle evaluation, aerobics and exercise classes, weight machines, Lifecycles, rowers, StairMasters, treadmills, sauna, whirlpools, hydrocalisthenics, massage.

Recreation: Putting green, golf driving range, paddle tennis, table tennis, shuffleboard, tetherball, trapshooting, volleyball, two outdoor and two indoor pools, four whirlpools, sports area with separate clubhouses for adults and teens.

Facilities

Public rooms: Six bars, five entertainment lounges, casino, disco, cinema, card room, library/reading room, video-game room, executive boardroom, Epson computer center, chapel/synagogue, art gallery.

Shops: Arcade with men's formal rental shop, Harrods, designer boutiques (Burberry, Pringle, Wedgwood), florist, beauty center, barbershop.

Health care: Extensive hospital with full staff of doctors and nurses.

Child care: A nursery is staffed by two British nannies, who watch over children age two to eight. Counselors supervise children 8 to 12. At breakfast and lunch, children can eat by themselves in the Lido or Pavilion cafés.

Services: Laundry service, dry cleaning, valet service, ironing room, photographer, film processing.

Accessibility Ramps were installed in public corridors during the most recent refit, but many public rooms still have a step or two up or down. Four cabins have been refitted to accommodate wheelchair users.

MV Sea Goddess I and Sea Goddess II

Specifications

Type of ship: Cruise yacht
Cruise experience: Formal
Size: 4,250 tons
Number of cabins: 58
Outside cabins: 100%
Passengers: 116
Crew: 89 (American and European)
Officers: Norwegian
Passenger/crew ratio: 1.3 to 1
Year built: 1984

Ship's Log The *Sea Goddess*es were designed to raise the level of cruise luxury (and prices) to new heights, and largely, they have succeeded. Life aboard ship is unstructured, elegant, and unforgettable. Once you've paid the exorbitant fare, there are no more out-of-pocket expenses. Cruise fares really do include everything imaginable, from drinks to caviar any time of day or night. Inside and out, the *Sea Goddess* ships look like royal yachts—from their dramatic profile and upswept twin funnels to the marble dance floors in the Main Salon and fine Oriental rugs in the lobbies. A shallow draft allows the ships to anchor in out-of-the-way coves and unfrequented ports, where the stern's water-sports platform can be lowered for snorkeling, sailing, windsurfing, and swimming (weather permitting). Though small, these intimate, romantic vessels offer ample room for 59 couples to enjoy what, in many ways, still sets the standard for luxurious vacations afloat.

Activities No structured shipboard activities are offered; passengers set their own pace. Special-interest cruises include lectures and seminars; epicurean cruises, for example, feature guest chefs and talks by California vintners. A Golden Door Spa fitness trainer offers exercise classes and designs personal programs. At port, the accommodating staff can arrange entry to exclusive onshore clubs for tennis, golf, gambling, and dancing. The ship-organized beach parties are renowned for endless quantities of champagne and caviar.

Dining In the tradition of the finest restaurants, the kitchen caters to special requests, preparing dishes individually as they are ordered. The quality of the food is excellent but, given the limited kitchen space, not as good as that in the *QE2*'s Queen's Grill. Fine wines and after-dinner drinks are served, and Beluga caviar is dispensed as freely as the champagne. Meals are served in a single, open seating (dinner from 8 to 10). Two formal evenings are held each week, but passengers tend to dress elegantly every night. The Outdoor Café serves coffee, breakfast, and lunch, but full service is available any time. Room service will provide anything day or night, including full-course meals—all served on china and linen.

Entertainment Entertainment is understated, featuring perhaps a pianist or a dance trio in the piano bar or local entertainment from the day's port of call. Since there is no showroom aboard, no production-style shows are staged. Many passengers visit the casinos or nightclubs in town while in port.

Service and Tipping With one of the best passenger-to-crew ratios, the ship offers attentive and personal service. The aim is to make you feel that all your needs, wishes, and perhaps even fantasies will be fulfilled. An elegant black-tie midnight dinner for two on the deck? No problem. Chilled champagne and caviar brought ashore to you while you sunbathe in a quiet, white-sand cove? You have but to ask. No tipping is allowed.

Cabins and Rates

	Beds	Phone	TV	Sitting Area	Fridge	Tub	Average Per Diem*
Suite	Q or T	●	●	●	●	●	$571

**Rates are for the Caribbean. Airfare and port taxes are extra.*

Cabins on the *Sea Goddess*es set the standard for modern seafaring comfort. Oversize picture windows overlooking the sea top the list of amenities in the all-outside, all-suite accommodations. Each has an electronic safe, a stereo, a remote-control color TV (including CNN) and VCR, and a minibar. The refrigerator can be stocked with any food from the kitchen or any liquor, wine, or beverage you'd like, at no charge; a personal-preference form is mailed to every passenger before sailing, so the crew can stock the cabin and the kitchen accordingly. A few suites have removable adjoining walls for those who want even more space and a second bathroom; the cost is about 150% of the single-cabin rate. Cabins on Deck 5 look onto the Promenade. Cabin 315 is a larger suite that doesn't cost more.

Outlet voltage: 110 AC.

Single supplement: 150%–175% of double-occupancy rate.

Discounts: You get a 50% discount for booking consecutive cruises and a discount for arranging your own airfare.

Sports and Fitness

Health club: Gym, sauna, massage, showers. Golden Door Spa personnel will develop individualized fitness programs.

Recreation: Skeet shooting, water sports (windsurfing, snorkeling, sailing, waterskiing off the stern swimming platform), pool, unobstructed circuit for jogging.

Facilities

Public rooms: Three bars, two entertainment lounges, casino, library (books and videotapes).

Shops: Gift shop, beauty salon/barber.

Health care: Doctor on call.

Child care: Baby-sitting can be arranged privately.

Services: Laundry service, dry cleaning.

Accessibility

Cabin doorways and rest rooms are not large enough for wheelchairs. Wheelchairs may not be taken on launches at ports where the ship must anchor offshore, preventing wheelchair users from going ashore.

MS Vistafjord

Specifications

Type of ship: Cruise liner
Cruise experience: Formal
Size: 24,492 tons
Number of cabins: 375
Outside cabins: 86%
Passengers: 677
Crew: 379 (European)
Officers: Norwegian
Passenger/crew ratio: 1.8 to 1
Year built: 1973

Ship's Log

The *Vistafjord* is revered by a loyal core of repeat passengers who cherish the ship as a treasure. Most of its followers hail from North America, Britain, and Germany—a mix quite different from the complement found aboard the now departed *Sagafjord* (*Vistafjord's* sister and former fleetmate), which left Cunard in October 1996. All announcements and printed information are in English and German, and the ship's menus, activities, and entertainment reflect the tastes and interests of its sophisticated, international clientele.

A major 1994 refit put the *Vistafjord* in tip-top shape, and few ships exude such a warmth. The latest renovation gave the *Vistafjord* such up-to-date facilities as an alternative restaurant and balconied suites, but the ship's wood paneling, soft fabric colors, and pervasive Scandinavian atmosphere have changed little since the vessel entered service in 1973.

Spaciousness is evident throughout the ship, especially in the high-ceiling grand ballroom and in the circular, forward Garden Lounge, which is bathed in natural light during the day and takes on a warm glow in the evening. An intimacy prevails in the port-side North Cape Bar, the wood-paneled library, and the aft Club Viking, with its view over the Lido and outdoor pool. The varnished teak promenade deck is ideal for reading and relaxing in recessed alcoves and for circular constitutional walks.

Activities Shipboard diversions reflect the sophisticated tastes of the ship's clientele—among them dance, card and craft classes, indoor and outdoor aerobics, and lectures in the theater by literary, political, stage, and screen personalities. On the Bridge Deck, there is shuffleboard and a golf driving net, and table tennis is available aft on a sheltered deck.

Dining Catering to an international clientele, the *Vistafjord*'s cuisine offers the best of standard American and classic European cooking. A different menu is served every day of the month, and if you don't see something you like, you can order off the menu as well. Meals are served in a single seating between 7 and 9 in an elegant, windowed dining room with many tables available for two. Nearly all evenings are formal or semiformal. Healthy selections are featured at every meal, but special dietary requests should be made in advance.

A second option for dining is the 40-seat Tivoli Restaurant, with its own galley and a set Italian menu also featuring daily specials. The wine list is different from and more pricey than that in the main dining room. The staff speaks fluent Italian and provides personal if sometimes slow service. Reservations, which must be made daily between 11 and 1, are staggered between 6:45 and 8:30. Diners arriving before 7:30 benefit from the entertainment below, and the view is aft through two levels of glass.

The Lido Cafe offers seating inside and out, and when the weather discourages outdoor dining, the adjacent ballroom takes the overflow. The serving areas are separated to minimize lines and, at breakfast, include a hot and cold buffet (special orders can be placed here) and stations for fresh fruit, juice, and freshly brewed coffee. For lunch, there are pasta and dessert counters, a carvery, and an outdoor ice-cream stand.

Room service is available 24 hours from the full dining-room menu.

Entertainment Entertainment is sophisticated and low-key, as the ship is not equipped for elaborate stage productions. Before dinner, there is dancing in the Garden Lounge and light entertainment in the Club Viking. After dinner, the Garden Lounge becomes an elegant setting for a musical concert or operatic or show singers. The main ballroom offers dancing to an excellent band and then an evening show, which may include a simple revue, singers, a comedian or magician, and special theme evenings. A gentleman-host program provides dancing partners for single ladies traveling alone.

Service and Tipping The mainly European staff is highly professional, providing unobtrusive service with a personal touch. Tip the cabin steward or stewardess $4 per person per diem and the waiter $5 per person per diem. A 15% service charge is automatically added to all bar bills.

Cabins and Rates

	Beds	Phone	TV	Sitting Area	Fridge	Tub	Average Per Diem*
Suite	Q or T/D	●	●	●	●	●	$1,177
Outside	Q or T	●	●	◐	●	◐	$457
Inside	T	●	●	◐	●	◐	$381

**Rates are for the Caribbean. Airfare and port taxes are extra.*

The recently refurbished cabins and remodeled bathrooms (some with smallish tubs) are in excellent shape and well insulated. However, small blocks of cabins amidships on Main and A decks are susceptible to engine-room noise. The wood-and-fabric furnishings are light in color and reflect the natural light coming in through the windows. All cabins have refrigerators, safes, TVs with VCR, hair dryers, robes, slippers, daily baskets of fresh fruit, and bottles of sparkling wine at embarkation. The onboard newspaper, delivered to the cabins, comes in U.S., British, and German editions. Seventy-three cabins are sold as singles. Eleven brand- new luxury suites with balconies have been added to the Bridge Deck. Two Hollywood-style suites are 880-square-foot duplexes with bedroom downstairs, bar, exercise equipment, indoor and outdoor jacuzzis, sauna, and private decks. A number of higher-priced cabins on the Promenade and Sun decks have obstructed views, as indicated in the Vistafjord's brochure.

Outlet voltage: 110 AC.

Single supplement: Seventy-three cabins are available as designated singles.

Discounts: A third or fourth passenger in a cabin pays reduced per diems. You get a discount for arranging your own airfare and 20% off for booking early.

Sports and Fitness

Health club: Well-equipped below-decks facility with rowing machines, stationary bikes, and Stair Masters, thalassotherapy, sauna, steam bath, massage, indoor pool.

Recreation: Aerobics, aqua-aerobics, driving range, shuffleboard, table tennis, whirlpools, indoor pool, outdoor pool, unobstructed circuit for jogging (7 laps = 1 mile).

Facilities

Public rooms: Four bars, observation/show lounge, ballroom with stage, cinema, casino, card room, library.

Shops: Two gift shops, beauty salon/barber.

Health care: Doctor on call.

Child care: Baby-sitting can be arranged with crew member.

Services: Full- and self-service laundry, dry cleaning, photographer, film processing.

Accessibility

Four cabins are designed for wheelchair users.

Delta Queen Steamboat Company

The Fleet *American Queen*
Delta Queen
Mississippi Queen

Evocative of the great floating palaces about which Mark Twain lovingly wrote, these boats (they're *not* ships) are among the few remaining overnight paddle-wheel riverboats in the country. Nostalgia is the name of the game: They ply the Mississippi River System at a leisurely 6–7 miles per hour. The intimate, wooden *Delta Queen* is like a homey bed-and-breakfast. The *American Queen* and *Mississippi Queen* are steamboating's answer to megaships. The largest paddle wheelers ever built, they dwarf the size of the *Delta Queen*.

Ships at a Glance

	Dining Rooms	Bars	Casino	Fitness Center	Pools	Average Per Diem
American Queen	1	4	○	●	1	$397
Delta Queen	1	3	○	◐	0	$397
Mississippi Queen	1	3	○	●	0	$397

Cruise Experience Delta Queen preserves "Life on the Mississippi" with 19th-century charm, plus 20th-century air-conditioning and other newfangled doodads. These floating wedding cakes are outfitted in Victorian-style gingerbread trim, Tiffany-type stained glass, polished brass, crystal chandeliers, plush carpeting, and warm wood paneling. Public areas have cushy leather wing chairs and handsomely upholstered Chesterfield sofas. On deck, you can watch the country go by from oversize wooden rocking chairs, old-fashioned porch swings, and white-iron patio furniture—and you can do so while munching freshly made popcorn or a hot dog. Most passengers are well-heeled retirees, many of whom return time and again—the Paddlewheel Steamboatin' Society of America hosts a champagne-and-punch reception for repeat passengers. For single women passengers sailing alone, senior gentlemen act as hosts and social partners.

A "Riverlorian" (the steamboat company's term for river historian) gives lively talks about the river, explains how to find mile markers and read the river charts, answers questions, lends books, and provides free binoculars. The captain's lecture is a not-to-be-missed event. Passengers can try their hands at playing the calliopes. There's little pressure to participate in anything; you can do as little or as much as you like. The size of the boats governs the scope of the

Chart Symbols. Ships at a Glance. **●**: *Fully equipped;* **◐**: *Partially equipped;* ○: *Not equipped*. Cabins and Rates. **D:** *Double bed;* **K:** *King-size bed;* **Q:** *Queen-size bed;* **T:** *Twin bed;* **U/L:** *Upper and lower berths;* **●**: *All cabins have this facility;* ○: *No cabins have this facility;* **◐**: *Some cabins have this facility*

onboard activities and entertainment; these are covered individually under Ship's Log. Although Louisiana allows riverboat gambling, there are no casinos aboard.

Theme cruises are often scheduled. Topics may include sports, like the Kentucky Derby; American history, such as the Civil War; and various music cruises. Seasonal sailings highlight southern gardens in spring or the colors of fall foliage. Two special events should be noted: One is the annual Great Steamboat Race, an 11-night cruise from New Orleans to St. Louis that steams toward the finish line on the Fourth of July. It replicates a famous 19th-century race between the *Natchez* and the *Robert E. Lee*. This is a wildly popular cruise: Crews challenge each other to tests of speed and maneuverability, pitting the *DQ* against the *MQ*, and passengers gussy up for the annual Floozy Contest. With their flags flying and calliopes whistling away, the boats race at a dizzying 12 miles per hour or so, while landlubbers line the shore and cheer them on. At Christmas, the bonfire cruises are also enormously popular. Replicating an age-old Cajun custom (the bonfires light the way for Papa Noel), a huge bonfire is lit along the levee, and there is a spectacular fireworks display. Shores and boat decks are lined with folks shouting Christmas greetings back and forth—and Papa Noel does pay a visit.

Dining If bigger is better, then it shows most in *Delta Queen's* food: The food on the larger *AQ* and *MQ* is superior to that aboard the *DQ*, and the presentation on the bigger boats is more spectacular than on the *DQ* as well. Dinner on the *AQ* and *MQ* is a bit dressier than on the *DQ*, but formal wear is never required. Dining rooms on the big twins offer better views; the only good river view in the low-lying *DQ* dining room is from a window seat.

Aboard all three boats, five meals are served daily. Dinner is scheduled in two seatings (5:30 and 8 on the *MQ* and *AQ*, 5:30 and 7 on the *DQ)*. Menus mix American standards, southern dishes, and a hint of Cajun cooking. Every meal includes at least one "Heart Smart" selection. "Theme" meals include an old-fashioned family-style picnic, with waiters in jeans passing around huge platters of fried chicken, barbecue ribs, corn bread, corn on the cob, potato salad, and such. Passengers with special dietary needs should notify the company a month in advance. The only room service is for Continental breakfast.

Destinations and Ports of Call Because the Delta Queen Steamboat Company's ports are not covered in Chapter 3, we've tried to give you a general idea of how time is spent ashore on a typical riverboat cruise. (For year-round itineraries, *see* Chapter 4.)

The boats never paddle for more than two days without putting into port, where they are usually docked for at least a half day. Shore excursions visit plantation homes, historic towns and Civil War battlefields, sleepy villages, and major metropolises. Tours are either by bus or on foot, and since there are scores of ports, there is a wide range available.

Shore excursions range from tours of riverside plantations to bus tours of Civil War military sites. About the most expensive is the Cajun Heritage tour from Baton Rouge (3 1/2 hrs., $35). Casino boats are docked in several ports—but beware of boats that leave the pier, lest you gamble on missing your own.

In some ports the steamboat company provides a free shuttle into town. This is fine if you want to poke around on your own; however, the shore excursions are narrated and take you to plantation homes that you can't always reach on foot. In other ports, you can simply amble down the gangplank and walk to the sights.

Service and Tipping The staff and crew are extraordinarily friendly and helpful, and not at all intrusive. Dining-room service is superb. The night before debarkation, instructions and envelopes for tips are left in each stateroom. Tip waiters, waitresses, and cabin attendants $3.50 per person per diem; busboys $2.25 per person per diem; maître d's $5 per couple per cruise; porters $1.50 per bag. An automatic 15% is added to wine and bar purchases.

For More Information Delta Queen Steamboat Co. (30 Robin St. Wharf, New Orleans, LA 70130, tel. 504/586-0631 or 800/543-1949).

American Queen

Specifications

Type of boat: Riverboat
Cruise experience: Casual
Size: 4,700 tons
Number of cabins: 222
Outside cabins: 75%
Passengers: 436
Crew: 165 (American)
Officers: American
Passenger/crew ratio: 2.6 to 1
Year built: 1995

Ship's Log The largest steamboat ever built for the Mississippi River system, the *American Queen* is based on the great paddle wheelers of the past. The *AQ*'s designers studied such famous river giants as the *J.M. White*, the *Robert E. Lee*, and the *New Orleans*. At the *AQ*'s stern, a huge, red paddle wheel is not just for show—its 60 tons churn the muddy Mississippi, propelling the boat forward. Two immense, black, fluted smokestacks signify the presence of authentic steam engines salvaged from a 1930s river dredge. The retractable pilothouse was modeled after the one on the turn-of-the-century *Charles Rebstock*, another famous riverboat; on its roof stands a 6-foot-high, rooster-shaped weather vane. Inside, the nostalgia continues. At the bow, a sweeping grand staircase is based on the one once found aboard the *J.M. White*. Bookcases in the gentlemen's card room and ladies' parlor are stocked with firsthand accounts of exploration, how-to books, and novels from a century ago. More Victoriana can be found in the Mark Twain Gallery, a long, narrow room overlooking the dining salon. Scattered throughout the boat's various public rooms are more than 200 pieces of artwork, most in their original frames, from the 1860s to 1890s.

Activities On the *AQ*, you can be as active or as relaxed as you want. On the leisurely side, you can do nothing more strenuous than write a letter in the card room or ladies' parlor, or sip a mint julep outside your cabin, by the railing. You can learn to read navigational charts and maps in the chart room, with help from the Riverlorian, or watch the world go by from a swing in the glass-enclosed Porch of America, where there's a soda fountain and a player piano. More active types can join their fellow passengers at bingo, bridge, and board games, plus dance lessons and sing-alongs.

Entertainment The evening's entertainment begins at dinner, when passengers are serenaded by a band playing antique musical instruments. The Grand Saloon is the main showroom for floor shows by night and lectures by day, and it's the venue for dancing to a big band, cabarets, and vaudeville shows. The saloon's design is especially noteworthy: It was conceived as a miniature opera house, like the ones commonly found in small river towns during the 1880s. In the Engine Room Bar, entertainment on a smaller scale includes sing-alongs and recitals evocative of the Victorian era.

Cabins and Rates

	Beds	Phone	TV	Sitting Area	Fridge	Tub	Average Per Diem*
Suite	Q or T	●	○	●	○	●	$497
Outside	T	●	○	●	○	◐	$397

Inside	T	●	○	○	○	○	$227

**Rates are for a seven-night river cruise. Airfare and port taxes are extra.*

Cabins continue the Victorian theme with reproduction wallpaper, floral carpeting, artwork, lighting fixtures, and period furnishings—some have authentic antique bureaus. Outside accommodations have private verandas, bay windows for panoramic views of the river, or direct access to an outdoor promenade through windowed French doors. Top-category suites are furnished with antique queen-size beds. Complimentary champagne, fresh fruit, and cheese are provided to passengers in suites and upper-category outside staterooms. Twenty-seven cabins have private verandas, while six cabins have partially obstructed views due to exterior staircases, which are shown clearly on the brochure deck plans.

Outlet voltage: 110 AC.

Single supplement: 150%–175% of double-occupancy rate.

Discounts: A third passenger in a cabin pays reduced per diems. One child 16 or younger cruises free in some staterooms, when sharing a cabin with two full-fare adults. You get a discount for booking early.

Sports and Fitness

Health club: StairMaster, stationary bikes, treadmills.

Recreation: Small swimming pool.

Facilities

Public rooms: Four bars, showroom/lecture hall, theater, card room, ladies' parlor, observation deck.

Shops: Victorian gift shop, beauty/barber shop.

Health care: None.

Child care: Passengers may make private baby-sitting arrangements with a staff or crew member.

Accessibility

Nine cabins, as well as elevators and wide hallways, are accessible to wheelchair users.

Delta Queen

Specifications

Type of boat: Riverboat
Cruise experience: Casual
Size: 3,360 tons
Number of cabins: 87
Outside cabins: 100%
Passengers: 174
Crew: 75 (American)
Officers: American
Passenger/crew ratio: 2.3 to 1
Year built: 1926

Ship's Log

If the *Delta Queen* were a song, she'd be *Up the Lazy River.* This grande dame of America's most famous river first sailed the waters of the Sacramento River and served her country during World War II as a U.S. Navy ferry on San Francisco Bay. She began cruising the Mississippi River system after World War II. In the late '60s, due to federal legislation banning boats with wooden superstructures, she seemed doomed for demolition, but the hue and cry raised by preservationists and nostalgia buffs resulted in a congressional exemption, under which she still sails. This four-decker time capsule is now a designated National Historic Landmark and is listed on the National Register of Historic Places. Because the boat is made of wood, smoking is restricted to designated areas and forbidden in the cabins.

Activities

A person can while away a fair amount of time just sitting on deck in a rocking chair or a swing. The *DQ* is really not for type-A personalities. Bingo and bridge, quilting and hatmaking, trivia and kite-flying contests are about as hectic as things get. Tours of the pilothouse are conducted and passengers are encouraged to visit the engine room and have a cup of coffee with the crew, who will cheerfully show you how the engines and the 44-ton paddle operate.

Entertainment Because the boat is small, the dining room has to do extra duty as a lecture and concert hall, a movie theater, and a nightclub. As a result, there is a great deal of moving about of chairs and tables between meals and during various functions. The nightly floor shows range from outstanding classical ragtime concerts to corny country hoedowns. Jokes and music are geared toward the older crowd. After the show, the orchestra plays music for dancing, while up in the Texas Lounge a pianist/vocalist entertains with standards and show tunes, mostly from the '40s and '50s, as she does during the cocktail hour. Sing-alongs are also popular, and the Texas Lounge features a great Dixieland band.

Cabins and Rates

	Beds	Phone	TV	Sitting Area	Fridge	Tub	Average Per Diem*
Suite	Q or T	○	○	●	○	●	$497
Outside	Q	○	○	●	○	○	$397

**Rates are for a seven-night river cruise. Airfare and port taxes are extra.*

One of the standard jokes aboard the *DQ* is, "You didn't realize that the brochure picture of your cabin was actual size, did you?" Most *are* quite small (baths are minuscule), but all cabins are outside. A slight disadvantage here is that in order to have any privacy it's necessary to keep your shades or shutters closed: There is a lot of activity on the wraparound decks. Accommodations on the Cabin Deck have inside entrances, while those on the Sun and Texas decks have outside entrances. The most charming aspect of these small accommodations is their original wood paneling. All also come with complimentary soap, shampoo, and body lotion, wall- to-wall carpeting, and limited closet and storage space. Suites 307 and 308 are up front, on either side of the pilothouse. Superior Staterooms 117, 118, 121, and 122 on the Cabin Deck, and Staterooms 207, 208, 227, 228, and 230 on the Texas Deck have partially obstructed river views. Complimentary champagne, fresh fruit, and cheese are provided to passengers in suites and superior staterooms.

Outlet voltage: 110 AC.

Single supplement: 150%–175% of double-occupancy rate.

Discounts: No cabins accommodate third or fourth passengers. You get a discount for booking early.

Sports and Fitness **Health club:** Stationary bike, rowing machine.

Recreation: Unobstructed circuits for jogging.

Facilities **Public rooms:** Three lounges.

Shops: Gift shop.

Health care: None.

Child care: Passengers may make private baby-sitting arrangements with a crew member.

Accessibility The *Delta Queen* has no facilities for wheelchair users. However, passengers with mobility problems can travel aboard the boat provided they can traverse stairways.

Mississippi Queen

Specifications *Type of boat:* Riverboat *Passengers:* 420
Cruise experience: Casual *Crew:* 165 (American)

Size: 3,364 tons
Number of cabins: 207
Outside cabins: 64%
Officers: American
Passenger/crew ratio: 2.5 to 1
Year built: 1976

Ship's Log The seven-deck *Mississippi Queen* combines the traditions of steamboating with resort-style facilities. She was built in 1976 at a cost of $27 million and refurbished in 1996 in a pleasing Victorian style. There is infinitely more space, in public areas, on decks, and in the cabins, than aboard the *DQ*. Her huge calliope is the world's largest.

Activities In addition to bingo, bridge, masquerades, lectures, and contests, the *MQ* offers a cavelike gym with exercise machines, classes, and a whirlpool; shuffleboard; a full-service beauty shop (perms, cuts, facials, manicures); a first-run movie theater (*Showboat* is also frequently screened); a library; and a conference center with audiovisual equipment.

Entertainment As on the *AQ*, evening entertainment centers on floor shows in the Grand Saloon, celebrating American music. There are cabarets with Dixieland bands, ragtime and rinky-dink piano sessions, banjo players, and singers and dancers; the *MQ*'s renditions of the Andrews Sisters, Sophie Tucker, and Al Jolson; Mardi Gras bashes; Broadway-style show revues; and barbershop quartets. The ship employs two "dance hosts," who dance with single female passengers. The bars and lounges are large and lively—the Paddlewheel Lounge is a glitzy, two-tier affair on the Observation and Texas decks.

Cabins and Rates

	Beds	Phone	TV	Sitting Area	Fridge	Tub	Average Per Diem*
Suite	Q or T	●	○	●	○	●	$497
Outside	T	●	○	●	○	●	$397
Inside	T	●	○	●	○	●	$227

**Rates are for a seven-night river cruise. Airfare and port taxes are extra.*

While none of the staterooms is huge, and some are quite small, they're great places to settle in and contemplate the river in peace and quiet. Recent redecoration has added some Victorian character through the use of period wallcoverings, fabrics, and artwork. But closet and storage space, while not vast, is more generous than the *DQ's* limited hooks and rods. Of the outside cabins, 94 have private verandas. Inside cabins, however, are not for the claustrophobic. The four Victorian-style suites are another story entirely. Two are adjacent to the pilothouse, with windows facing forward and to the side for a captain's-eye view of the river; two are adjacent to the paddle wheel, with its lulling, sleep-inducing sounds. Staterooms 131, 132, 141, 220, 221, 327, and 328 have partially obstructed river views. Suites, and some outside and inside staterooms, can accommodate more than two passengers. Complimentary champagne, fresh fruit, and cheese are provided to passengers in suites and superior staterooms.

Outlet voltage: 110 AC.

Single supplement: 150%–175% of double-occupancy rate.

Discounts: A third passenger in a cabin pays reduced per diem. One child 16 or younger cruises free in some staterooms when sharing a cabin with two full-fare adults. You get a discount for booking early.

Sports and Fitness **Health club:** Stationary bike, treadmill, exercise classes, stair climber.

Recreation: Shuffleboard, sauna, whirlpool spa, pool.

Facilities **Public rooms:** Three bars, two lounges, showroom, lecture hall, theater/conference center, library, game room, activity center.

Shops: Gift shop, beauty/barbershop.

Health care: None.

Child care: Passengers may make private baby-sitting arrangements with a staff or crew member.

Accessibility Elevators, wide hallways, and one cabin are accessible to wheelchair users.

Dolphin Cruise Line

The Fleet SS *IslandBreeze*
SS *OceanBreeze*
SS *SeaBreeze*

Under the Dolphin banner sails a collection of steam-powered, vintage vessels. All are 35–40 years old, but they have been well maintained and periodically refurbished during their many years of service.

Ships at a Glance

	Dining Rooms	Bars	Casino	Fitness Center	Pools	Average Per Diem
IslandBreeze	1	5	●	●	3	$249
OceanBreeze	1	3	●	●	1	$132
SeaBreeze	1	5	●	◐	1	$134

Cruise Experience While there never has been anything fancy about a Dolphin cruise, passengers get their money's worth, and perhaps a bit more. Despite its fleet of older vessels, the line has established a reputation for caring about its passengers. Value is the word most often associated with Dolphin—which keeps a loyal following coming back again and again.

Activities For adults, Dolphin includes all the typical ocean-liner diversions, such as bingo, pool games, dance classes, and trivia contests. As the official cruise line of Hanna-Barbera, Dolphin's children's program features youth counselors dressed as Yogi Bear, Fred Flintstone, and other cartoon characters, who frolic with kids and lead such daily events as scavenger hunts, teen parties, and talent shows. The tiny island that the *OceanBreeze* visits for its private beach parties is one of the most picturesque.

Dining Menus are extensive and innovative, and food quality is well above average. Children's menus reflect the Hanna-Barbera theme, with such specialties as the "Astro Dog" and the "Zoinks Sundae." Waiters hustle and go out of their way to please; what's more, they're genuinely friendly, not just tip-hungry. There are two assigned seatings per meal. A pianist entertains at dinner (6 and 8). Formal nights are scheduled twice on every weeklong cruise and once on every three- or four-day sailing. Make special dietary requests in writing seven days before sailing. A small section of the dining room is set aside for smoking.

Breakfast and lunch buffets in the open-air cafés are excellent, by any standard. Other food service includes 24-hour self-serve coffee

Chart Symbols. Ships at a Glance. ●: *Fully equipped;* ◐: *Partially equipped;* ○: *Not equipped.* Cabins and Rates. **D:** *Double bed;* **K:** *King-size bed;* **Q:** *Queen-size bed;* **T:** *Twin bed;* **U/L:** *Upper and lower berths;* ●: *All cabins have this facility;* ○: *No cabins have this facility;* ◐: *Some cabins have this facility*

and tea, afternoon cookies and cake, a midnight buffet, and 24-hour room service from a limited menu.

Entertainment Shows in the main lounge feature the usual variety of singers, comedians, and jugglers. An orchestra performs nightly for dancing.

Service and Tipping Staff members are energetic, thorough, and unusually personable. Tip the room steward $3.50 per passenger per diem, the waiter $3, the busboy $1.50. The maître d' should get $4 per passenger per cruise, the wine steward or bartender 15% of your final tab.

Destinations The *IslandBreeze* sails seasonally from New York on cruises to nowhere or to New England and Canada. In winter, it repositions to Montego Bay, Jamaica, for Panama Canal cruises. The *SeaBreeze* and *OceanBreeze* sail year-round from Miami to the Bahamas and the Caribbean. (For seasonal itineraries, *see* Chapter 4.)

For More Information Dolphin Cruise Line (901 South America Way, Miami, FL 33132, tel. 800/992–4299).

SS IslandBreeze

Specifications

Type of ship: Classic liner
Cruise experience: Casual
Size: 38,175 tons
Number of cabins: 580
Outside cabins: 53%

Passengers: 1,146
Crew: 580 (international)
Officers: Greek
Passenger/crew ratio: 2 to 1
Year built: 1961

Ship's Log The *IslandBreeze* was scheduled to join the Dolphin fleet in spring 1996 as a replacement for the *Dolphin IV*, which was sold to fledgling Canaveral Cruise Line (*see* What's New *in* At Sea with Fodor's). The ship was built in 1961 as the *Transvaal Castle* and later became Carnival Cruise Line's *Festivale* in 1978. The vessel's transatlantic heritage is evident in its classic lines, winged bridge, and single smokestack. Public areas, too, retain much of the original wood paneling and have polished brass railings and doors. The decor features muted colors, classic etched glass, and a fabulous art deco steel stairway.

As the *Festivale*, the ship was starting to show its age, and although Dolphin planned to spend $1.8 million to spruce up the liner before putting it into service, the project did not include any redecoration, so the *IslandBreeze* still incorporates a taste of Carnival's signature whimsy: The Tradewinds and Copa Cabana lounges are reminiscent of 1930s film sets. The Gaslight Café looks like a mishmash of every B movie ever made, mixing teak paneling with a mirrored ceiling, petite pink tables, and overstuffed purple chairs.

Cabins and Rates

	Beds	Phone	TV	Sitting Area	Fridge	Tub	Average Per Diem*
Suite	K or T	○	○	●	○	●	$306
Outside	Q, T, or U/L	○	○	○	○	●	$249
Inside	Q, T, or U/L	○	○	○	○	○	$227

**Rates are for seven-day Panama Canal cruises. Airfare and port taxes are extra.*

Recalling the ship's heyday as an ocean liner, some suites have wooden headboards, full-length mirrors, and separate sitting rooms. Demi Suite V55 does not have a bathtub. Some outside cabins on the Veranda Deck have partially obstructed views.

Outlet voltage: 110 AC.

Single supplement: 150% of double-occupancy rate.

Discounts: A third or fourth passenger in a cabin pays reduced per diems. You get a discount for booking early.

Sports and Fitness

Health club: Exercise equipment, sauna, massage room.

Recreation: Aerobics classes, shuffleboard, table tennis, trapshooting, two pools, wading pool, unobstructed circuit (7½ laps = 1 mile) for jogging.

Facilities

Public rooms: Five bars, four entertainment lounges, casino, disco, cinema, library, video-game room.

Shops: Boutique, gift shop, liquor/sundries shop, beauty salon/barber.

Health care: Doctor on call.

Child care: Playroom, play deck, baby-sitting, youth programs with counselors year-round.

Services: Laundry service, photographer.

Accessibility

There are no cabins specifically equipped for wheelchair users.

SS OceanBreeze

Specifications

Type of ship: Classic liner
Cruise experience: Casual
Size: 21,667 tons
Number of cabins: 384
Outside cabins: 61.3%
Passengers: 776
Crew: 310 (international)
Officers: Greek
Passenger/crew ratio: 2.5 to 1
Year built: 1955

Ship's Log

The *OceanBreeze* is Dolphin's most elegant ship, although it's still far more casual than a Princess or even a Royal Caribbean vessel. Fans of the now-defunct Admiral Cruise Lines may remember the *OceanBreeze* in its former life as the *Azure Seas*. After joining the line in 1992, it underwent extensive renovations. Though still no luxury ship, Dolphin has brightened the decor, remodeled cabins, and added a children's room. Probably the ship's most stunning feature is the huge two-level casino on the Boat and Promenade decks, where you can chance it on 123 slot machines or try your luck in every other kind of gambling endeavor imaginable. The atmosphere is decidedly festive and upbeat. Passengers are welcomed aboard with an introductory show and verbal tour of the ship in the Rendezvous Lounge. The evening entertainment is lively and professional; rollicking theme nights include country-and-western and rock-and-roll parties.

Cabins and Rates

	Beds	Phone	TV	Sitting Area	Fridge	Tub	Average Per Diem*
Suite	K, Q, D, or U/L	●	●	●	●	●	$149
Outside	D, T, or U/L	●	○	○	○	○	$139
Inside	D, T, or U/L	●	○	○	○	○	$108

**Airfare and port taxes are extra.*

Because this is an older vessel, cabins are fairly large. The new decor is a tasteful array of muted blues, pinks, and greens. All cabins have a double or two lower beds, plenty of closet and dresser space, and carpeting, and are minimally equipped with climate control and a radio. The plush Owner's Suite is a two-bedroom pad with all the usual amenities plus a minibar. Outside cabins on the Atlantis Deck look out onto a public promenade.

Outlet voltage: 110/220 AC.

Single supplement: 150% of double-occupancy rate.

Discounts: A third or fourth passenger in a cabin pays reduced per diems. You get a discount for booking early.

Sports and Fitness

Health club: Exercise equipment, whirlpool, sauna.

Recreation: Table tennis, heated pool.

Facilities

Public rooms: Three bars and lounges, casino, disco, cinema, card room/library, video-game room, meeting room.

Shops: Gift shop, beauty salon/barber.

Health care: Doctor on call.

Child care: Playroom, baby-sitting, youth programs with counselors year-round.

Services: Laundry service, dry cleaning, photographer, film processing.

Accessibility

No cabins are specially equipped for wheelchair users.

SS SeaBreeze

Specifications

Type of ship: Classic liner
Cruise experience: Casual
Size: 21,010 tons
Number of cabins: 421
Outside cabins: 62.5%
Passengers: 840
Crew: 400 (international)
Officers: Greek
Passenger/crew ratio: 2.1 to 1
Year built: 1958

Ship's Log

The *SeaBreeze* was completely refurbished when it joined the Dolphin fleet in 1989, having previously seen service as Premier's *Royale* and Costa's *Federico 'C*. The exterior is not beautiful, with twin cargo booms on the fo'c'sle, a bulky superstructure, and a large, squarish stack amidships. But the *SeaBreeze* does offer plenty of deck space, easily accommodating the small swimming pool and three honeycomb-shape whirlpools—maybe the most popular attractions on board. The interior is appointed in shades of blue, lavender, and peach, and the ship retains many of its original brass fixtures.

Cabins and Rates

	Beds	Phone	TV	Sitting Area	Fridge	Tub	Average Per Diem*
Suite	Q or T	●	○	●	○	●	$151
Outside	D, T, or U/L	●	○	○	○	◐	$134
Inside	D, T, or U/L	●	○	○	○	○	$109

**Airfare and port taxes are extra.*

Cabins are small and simply furnished in a melánge of blues, greens, and yellows. Mirrors are employed generously. Furniture is minimal. Only suites have desks; standard cabins have pullout writing tables. Outside cabins on the Daphne Deck look onto a public promenade, and the view from most outside cabins on La Bohème Deck is obstructed by lifeboats.

Outlet voltage: 110/220 AC.

Single supplement: 150% of double-occupancy rate.

Discounts: A third or fourth passenger in a cabin pays reduced per diems. You get a discount for booking early.

Sports and Fitness

Health club: Exercise equipment, two whirlpools, massage.

Recreation: Aerobics, basketball, golf driving, table tennis, scuba and snorkeling lessons, shuffleboard, skeet shooting, pool, unobstructed circuit for jogging.

Facilities

Public rooms: Five bars, four entertainment lounges, casino, disco, cinema, video-game room.

Shops: Gift shop, beauty salon/barber.

Health care: Doctor on call.

Child care: Playroom, baby-sitting, youth programs with counselors year-round.

Services: Laundry service, dry cleaning, photographer, film processing.

Accessibility

Public areas are accessible to wheelchair users, although bathroom and cabin entrances have doorsills. Cabin bathroom doorways are 20 inches wide.

Holland America Line

Rotterdam

The Fleet MS *Maasdam*
MS *Nieuw Amsterdam*
MS *Noordam*
SS *Rotterdam*
MS *Ryndam*
MS *Statendam*
MS *Veendam*
MS *Westerdam*

Holland America emphasizes its nautical history more than any other line, except perhaps Cunard, one of the only other lines that dates back to the beginning of passenger-ship travel. Nautical antiques and memorabilia, from historic artifacts to nostalgic soap boxes, reflect the line's 100-year-plus seafaring heritage. All the line's vessels were originally built for Holland America except the *Westerdam*, which was purchased as the *Homeric* from Home Lines, stretched, and rechristened. Four new sister ships, the *Statendam*, *Maasdam*, *Ryndam*, and *Veendam* are the biggest and most spacious the line has ever built.

Ships at a Glance

	Dining Rooms	Bars	Casino	Fitness Center	Pools	Average Per Diem
Maasdam/Ryndam Statendam/Veendam	1	7	●	●	2	$298
Nieuw Amsterdam Noordam	1	8	●	●	2	$280
Rotterdam	1	7	●	●	2	$402
Westerdam	1	7	●	●	2	$280

Cruise Experience Founded in 1873, Holland America is one of the oldest names in cruising. Steeped in the traditions of the transatlantic crossing, its cruises are conservative affairs renowned for their grace and gentility. No money changes hands (you sign for everything), and loudspeaker announcements are kept to a minimum. A noteworthy feature is the Passport to Fitness program, combining fitness activities and spa cuisine. Participation in shore excursions and special activities is emphasized, but passengers are otherwise left to their own devices.

Holland America passengers tend to be better educated, older, and less active than those traveling on sister line Carnival's ships, but younger and less affluent than those on a ship like Cunard's Royal *Viking Sun*. Passenger satisfaction is high, as is the percentage of repeat passengers. Holland America is known throughout the in-

Chart Symbols. Ships at a Glance. ●: *Fully equipped;* ◐: *Partially equipped;* ○: *Not equipped.* Cabins and Rates. **D:** *Double bed;* **K:** *King-size bed;* **Q:** *Queen-size bed;* **T:** *Twin bed;* **U/L:** *Upper and lower berths;* ●: *All cabins have this facility;* ○: *No cabins have this facility;* ◐: *Some cabins have this facility*

dustry for its almost fanatical devotion to safety and sanitation. All ships exceed every international safety standard, and kitchens and dining rooms are exceptionally clean. Like only a few other lines, it maintains its own school (in Indonesia) to train staff members, rather than hiring them out of a union hall.

If you're looking for a refined and relaxing cruise, you'll never go wrong taking one of Holland America's ships or shore excursions. If, however, you like dawn-to-midnight entertainment, nonstop partying, or lots of young families on board, you should probably choose another cruise line.

Activities Holland America offers the full complement of organized group activities, such as poolside games, dance classes, trivia contests, and bingo, as well as the more offbeat karaoke machines, which allow passengers to sing along with orchestrated recordings. Nevertheless, relaxing in a deck chair and letting the world take care of itself while the ship's staff takes care of you is the prime attraction of a Holland America cruise.

Dining Food is good by cruise-ship standards, served on Rosenthal china. In January of 1995, Holland America went "nouvelle" and introduced more than 350 new recipes to its menu, including many pastas and "heart-healthy dishes," as well as fresh fish from local markets. (However, it's sometimes hard to tell exactly what is lighter or healthier about some of these dishes.)At the same time, the line placed additional emphasis on "American-style dishes" to complement its trendy fare. In keeping with its ethnic traditions, the line continues to offer an occasional Dutch or Indonesian dish for variety. Special dinner menus are available for children. Breakfast and lunch are open seating; dinner is served at two assigned seatings (6:15 and 8:15). There are two formal evenings each week, three during a 10-day cruise. Special diets are catered to if requests are made one month in advance.

The menus for Holland America's breakfast and lunch buffets, served in the Lido, often outdo its dining-room selections. Once during each cruise there's an Indonesian lunch and an outdoor barbecue dinner. Every day there's a deck lunch of barbecued hot dogs and hamburgers, pasta, stir-fries, or make-your-own tacos. The Lido also features a self-serve ice-cream/frozen-yogurt parlor. Other food service includes mid-morning bouillon or iced tea, traditional afternoon tea served in an inside lounge, and hot hors d'oeuvres served during the cocktail hour. Passengers can help themselves to tea and coffee at any time; 24-hour room service is available from a limited menu.

Entertainment Holland America's entertainment tends to be more subdued than on lines known for Las Vegas–style productions, but on the newer ships it has been infused with higher-tech sets, flashier costumes, and jazzier music. Apart from a disco, the entertainment is slanted toward an older audience. Main lounge shows, offered twice nightly, feature big-band sounds, comedy, magic and dance acts, and revues. You'll also find dance orchestras, a piano bar, string trios, and dance quartets. The Filipino members of the crew put on a show once during each cruise, and there also is a passenger talent show one evening. Cabin TVs, standard on all ships, have superb closed-circuit service, including CNN broadcasts. Rare appearances are made by big-name performers and guest lecturers.

Service and Tipping In the 1970s Holland America adopted a no-tips-required policy. Staff members perform their duties with great pride and professionalism. In turn, passengers don't feel the pressure or the discomfort of having crew members solicit tips. As it happens, about 80% of Holland passengers give tips comparable to those recommended on other lines—but entirely at their own discretion. Perhaps that's because the crew seems to take a genuine, personal interest in passengers, learning not only their names but habits and personal preferences.

As Holland America absorbs its new ships, service has been spotty at times. Passengers may experience some momentary lapses, but they will also find the finer moments that Holland America has become known for—bartenders who make personalized bookmarks for guests and roll napkins into flowers for the ladies, for example.

Destinations Holland America offers Caribbean itineraries year-round from Fort Lauderdale, Tampa, and New Orleans. Seasonal sailings visit Alaska, Europe, and the Panama Canal. A world cruise is scheduled every year. (For seasonal itineraries, *see* Chapter 4.)

For More Information Holland America Line (300 Elliott Ave. W, Seattle, WA 98119, tel. 800/426–0327).

MS Maasdam, MS Ryndam, MS Statendam, and MS Veendam

Specifications
Type of ship: Cruise liner
Cruise experience: Semi-formal
Size: 55,451 tons
Number of cabins: 633
Outside cabins: 77%
Passengers: 1,266
Crew: 571 (Indonesian and Filipino)
Officers: Dutch
Passenger/crew ratio: 2.2 to 1
Years built: 1993–1996

Ship's Log These ships can best be described as classic-revival, combining the old and new in one neat package. From the outside, they look bigger than their 55,000 tons, thanks to their megaship profile. Inside, they dramatically express Holland America's past in a two-tier dining room, replete with dual grand staircases framing an orchestra balcony—the latter first introduced on the *Nieuw Amsterdam* of 1938.

Although these four ships are structurally identical, Holland America has given each its own distinct personality. Layout and decor of the public rooms differ from ship to ship; it is here that parent company Carnival's influence shows. For the first time, public rooms have whimsical themes. The Crow's Nest on the *Statendam* draws its inspiration from *Composition with Red, Blue and Yellow* by Dutch abstract painter Piet Mondrian. The same room on the *Maasdam* evokes Alaska's northern lights; the theme on the *Ryndam* is the glaciers of Alaska. Aboard the *Veendam*, the Crow's Nest has not one but three different themes: a "Captain's Area," "Tea Area," and an unnamed bar area, decorated with various artifacts and nautical antiques.

The *Statendam* and *Ryndam* are more typical of Holland America than the *Maasdam* or *Veendam*. In a central three-story atrium, a fountain of bronze mermaids or fish, respectively, states the ships' connection to the sea. On the *Maasdam*, this space is occupied by a modern, green glass sculpture of no nautical significance. Similarly, a wall of televisions on the *Maasdam* displays computer-generated video art. The *Veendam's* atrium has *Jacob's Staircase* at its center—a blue and gold spiraling pillar made of steel and glass.

A big improvement on these ships over some previous Holland America cruise liners is the tiered showroom, where terraced seating creates good lines of sight all around. Aboard the *Maasdam*, notice the depictions of Henry Hudson's ship, the *Half Moon*, on the showroom light fixtures—a fitting reminder of Holland America's maritime heritage.

Cabins and Rates

	Beds	Phone	TV	Sitting Area	Fridge	Tub	Average Per Diem*
Suite	T, K, or Q	●	●	●	○	●	$461
Outside	T/Q	●	●	●	○	●	$298
Inside	T/Q	●	●	●	○	●	$233

**Rates are for the Caribbean. Airfare and port taxes are extra.*

Every standard cabin comes with a small sitting area with a sofa; outside cabins have tubs in the bath, inside cabins have just showers. All have wall-mounted hair dryers. Closet space is excellent, but drawer space is limited. Color schemes are in muted blues, peaches, and grays, with plenty of wood paneling. A fruit basket is refilled each day, and every passenger gets a canvas tote bag. Of the 633 cabins, 148 have private verandas. Suites also have verandas, whirlpool tubs, VCRs, and minibars.

Outlet voltage: 110 AC.

Single supplement: 200% of double-occupancy rates in suites and deluxe staterooms, 150% elsewhere.

Discounts: A third or fourth passenger pays reduced per diems. You get a discount for booking early.

Sports and Fitness

Health club: Top-deck, ocean-view facility with exercise equipment, massage, aerobics studio, saunas, steam rooms.

Recreation: Fitness programs and classes, shuffleboard, skeet shooting, two whirlpools, two pools (one with retractable glass roof), practice tennis courts (*Maasdam* and *Ryndam*), unobstructed circuit on wraparound promenade (4 laps = 1 mile) for jogging, cushioned jogging track (14.5 laps = 1 mile; *Statendam* only).

Facilities

Public rooms: Seven bars, five lounges, showroom, casino, disco, cinema, card and puzzle room, video-game room, meeting rooms.

Shops: Several boutiques and gift shops, beauty salon/barber.

Health care: Doctors and nurses on board.

Child care: Youth programs with counselors offered when demand warrants it; baby-sitting arranged privately with crew members.

Services: Full- and self-service laundry, dry cleaning, photographer, film processing.

Accessibility

Six cabins are specially equipped for wheelchair users. Corridors are wide; elevators and public lavatories are accessible.

MS Nieuw Amsterdam and MS Noordam

Specifications

Type of ship: Cruise liner
Cruise experience: Semi-formal
Size: 33,930 tons
Number of cabins: 607
Outside cabins: 68%
Passengers: 1,214
Crew: 542 (Indonesian and Filipino)
Officers: Dutch
Passenger/crew ratio: 2.2 to 1
Year built: 1983/1984

Ship's Log

The N-ships, as they are sometimes called, evoke the days of Dutch exploration, from early New York to India. Dutch nautical antiques, scattered liberally throughout, give the vessels a sense of identity and history. Passengers will be struck by how conveniently laid out and comfortable the liners are. Although these ships are not particularly large, their designers managed to capture a sense of space with extra-wide teak promenades, oversize public rooms, and wide corridors. It's hard to pick a favorite room from among the many bars and lounges; however, with their polished hardwood floors and twin balconies, the Admiral's Lounge on the *Noordam* and the Stuyvesant Lounge on the *Nieuw Amsterdam* are always popular.

Cabins and Rates

	Beds	Phone	TV	Sitting Area	Fridge	Tub	Average Per Diem*
Suite	K	●	●	●	●	●	$316
Outside	T, K, or Q	●	●	○	○	◐	$280
Inside	T	●	●	○	○	○	$218

**Rates are for the Caribbean. Airfare and port taxes are extra.*

Cabins are spotless, comfortable, and relatively large. The art deco–inspired northern European furnishings are among the most handsome to be found aboard any cruise ship. A fruit basket is refilled each day, and every passenger gets a canvas tote bag. Views from most cabins on the Boat and Navigation decks (including the Staterooms Deluxe) are partially obstructed.

Outlet voltage: 110/220 AC.

Single supplement: 200% of double-occupancy rate in Staterooms Deluxe, 150% elsewhere. Holland America can arrange for two same-sex adults to share a cabin at the double-occupancy rate.

Discounts: A third or fourth passenger in a cabin pays reduced per diems. You get a discount for booking early.

Sports and Fitness

Health club: Jogging and rowing machines, stationary bicycles, barbells, isometric pulleys, massage, dual saunas, loofah scrubs, Kerstin facials, health-care program.

Recreation: Exercise classes, golf putting, paddle and deck tennis, shuffleboard, trapshooting, two pools, whirlpool, unobstructed circuit (5 laps = 1 mile) for jogging.

Facilities

Public rooms: Eight bars, three entertainment lounges, casino, disco, cinema, card room, library, video-game room, computer room.

Shops: Boutiques, gift shop, beauty salon/barber.

Health care: Doctor on call.

Child care: Youth programs with counselors offered when demand warrants it; baby-sitting arranged privately with crew member.

Services: Full- and self-service laundry, dry cleaning, photographer, film processing.

Accessibility

Elevators and four staterooms on each ship are accessible to wheelchair users. They are Category-B cabins, which are Deluxe Outside Double rooms on the Navigation Deck.

SS Rotterdam

Specifications

Type of ship: Classic liner
Cruise experience: Semi-formal
Size: 38,645 tons
Number of cabins: 575
Outside cabins: 53%
Passengers: 1,075
Crew: 603 (Indonesian and Filipino)
Officers: Dutch
Passenger/crew ratio: 1.8 to 1
Year built: 1959

Ship's Log

The *Rotterdam*, the flagship of the line, carries the name of four previous Holland America ships, including the line's very first vessel. The current *Rotterdam* was launched in 1959 as a transatlantic liner, rebuilt in 1969 for cruising, and last refurbished in 1989. At that time the ship was given a brighter look, including new carpets and upholstery throughout and new tile for the pool. However, the beautiful wood floors, decks, and paneling have been retained, as have the shopping arcade and one of the largest double-decker movie theaters afloat. Although significantly larger than the N-ships, the *Rotterdam* carries fewer passengers. On the upper promenade deck is the impressive Ritz-Carlton ballroom, with two levels connected by a curved grand staircase. The ceiling lighting in the ballroom is dazzling.

The *Rotterdam* will leave Holland America's fleet at the end of September 1997 and will be replaced by a new ship bearing the same name.

Cabins and Rates

	Beds	Phone	TV	Sitting Area	Fridge	Tub	Average Per Diem*
Suite	Q	●	●	●	●	●	$670
Outside	D, T, K or U/L	●	●	◐	○	◐	$402
Inside	D, T, or U/L	●	●	○	○	◐	$233

**Rates are for a world cruise. Airfare and port taxes are extra.*

Views from most cabins on the Sun and Boat decks are partially obstructed. Passengers on B Deck use the upper decks to go from one end of the ship to the other because the dining room blocks passage. A fruit basket is refilled each day, and every passenger gets a canvas tote bag.

Outlet voltage: 110 AC.

Single supplement: 200% of double-occupancy rate for Staterooms Deluxe, 150% elsewhere. There are several single cabins. Holland America can arrange for two same-sex adults to share a cabin at the double-occupancy rate.

Discounts: A third or fourth passenger in a cabin pays reduced per diems. You get a discount for booking early.

Sports and Fitness

Health club: Stationary bicycles, weight machine, exercise board, indoor pool, sauna, massage.

Recreation: Exercise classes, golf driving, paddle and deck tennis, shuffleboard, trapshooting, indoor pool, outdoor pool, partially enclosed circuit for jogging.

Facilities

Public rooms: Seven bars, five entertainment lounges, casino, disco, cinema, card room, library/writing room, smoking lounge, videogame room, computer center.

Shops: Boutique, drugstore, newsstand, gift shop, beauty salon/barber.

Health care: Doctor on call.

Child care: Youth programs with counselors during holidays and in summer; baby-sitting arranged privately with crew member.

Services: Full- and self-service laundry, dry cleaning, photographer, film processing.

Accessibility

Although some entranceways have doorsills, ramps have been placed over the key ones to improve access for wheelchair users. All public rooms, except the dining room, are located on a single deck. All public areas are accessible. No cabins are specifically equipped for passengers with mobility problems.

MS Westerdam

Specifications

Type of ship: Cruise liner
Cruise experience: Semi-formal
Size: 53,872 tons
Number of cabins: 747
Outside cabins: 66%
Passengers: 1,494
Crew: 620 (Indonesian and Filipino)
Officers: Dutch
Passenger/crew ratio: 2.4 to 1
Year built: 1986

Ship's Log

Holland America set a record with this ship in 1989, when the line installed a 130-foot section into the midsection of the Westerdam—accomplishing the biggest stretch job in the history of cruising. This $84 million investment made the *Westerdam* into a bigger version of the *Nieuw Amsterdam* and *Noordam* and created a spacious, well-apportioned ship. Like its smaller siblings, the *Westerdam* carries a multimillion-dollar art collection that evokes Holland America's storied history. Perhaps most impressive is an antique bronze cannon, cast in Rotterdam, which is strategically positioned in the center of the ship. Also worthy of special note is the dining room. Unlike on many newer ships, where the restaurant occupies a strategic perch with expansive views, on the *Westerdam* it is located below decks. But Holland America has turned a negative into a positive and created a venue that is a rich and inviting. The room is accented in wood and brass, and traditional portholes rather than picture windows line the walls.

Cabins and Rates

	Beds	Phone	TV	Sitting Area	Fridge	Tub	Average Per Diem*
Suite	T or K	●	●	●	○	●	$459
Outside	Q/T, D or U/L	●	●	◐	○	◐	$280
Inside	T	●	●	○	○	○	$218

**Rates are for the Caribbean. Airfare and port taxes are extra.*

Cabins are large, with plenty of storage space; all but the least expensive feature a sitting area with a convertible couch. The use of blond wood and ivory tones adds to the overall sense of airiness. A fruit basket is refilled each day, and every passenger gets a canvas tote bag.

Outlet voltage: 110 AC.

Single supplement: 200% of double-occupancy rate for suites or staterooms deluxe, 150% elsewhere. Holland America will arrange for two same-sex adults to share a cabin at the double-occupancy rate.

Discounts: A third or fourth passenger in a cabin pays reduced per diems. You get a discount for booking early.

Sports and Fitness

Health club: Hydro-fitness exercise equipment, dual saunas, massage, loofah scrubs, facials, health-care program.

Recreation: Exercise classes, golf putting, paddle and deck tennis, shuffleboard, skeet shooting (Caribbean), basketball, two pools (one with retractable glass roof), three whirlpools, unobstructed circuit (4 laps = 1 mile) for jogging.

Facilities

Public rooms: Seven bars, two entertainment lounges, casino, disco, cinema, card room, library, video-game room, meeting room.

Shops: Boutiques, drugstore, beauty salon/barber.

Health care: Doctor on call.

Child care: Youth programs with counselors when demand warrants it; baby-sitting arranged privately with crew member.

Services: Full- and self-service laundry, dry cleaning, photographer, film processing.

Accessibility Elevators and four cabins are accessible to wheelchair users.

Majesty Cruise Line

The Fleet MV *Royal Majesty*

The sole ship in the fleet of Majesty Cruise Line was built specifically to sail on three- and four-day cruises, and it's one of the few upscale cruise liners sailing these short itineraries (although it also does weeklong cruises to Bermuda in summer). Thoroughly modern in its appointments, the *Royal Majesty* was designed to attract passengers who might otherwise sail aboard Holland America or Celebrity. To that end, it combines the best qualities of both these lines, and the result is a contemporary vessel with burnished woods and polished brass bathed in warm, natural light.

Ship at a Glance

	Dining Rooms	Bars	Casino	Fitness Center	Pools	Average Per Diem
Royal Majesty	1	3	●	●	1	$270

Cruise Experience The *Royal Majesty* delivers a level of sophistication rarely found on three- and four-day cruises. The ship excels in its onboard appointments, activities, and innovative entertainment. Passengers looking for action amid their refinement will like the ship's Regal Bodies fitness program of aerobics and weight lifting and the Club Nautica program of snorkeling and diving. There's also a full-service spa for more relaxed rejuvenation.

Activities Majesty mixes standard cruise activities—pool games, trivia contests, bingo, dance classes—with a daily program of more offbeat options, such as early-morning tai-chi classes and wine-tasting seminars. The Club Nautica water-sports program takes passengers off the ship in each port for snorkeling and dive safaris, led by an expert-in-residence. You can't earn certification, but you can get your flippers wet during scuba classes for beginners, too. Activities for younger passengers include scavenger hunts and talent shows, led by youth counselors dressed as Yogi Bear and Fred Flintstone. Majesty, along with sister line Dolphin, is the official cruise line of Hanna-Barbera, which is good for families cruising together but can seem somewhat incongruous in the elegantly appointed dining room.

Dining Dining aboard Majesty is good basic cruise fare, but not as impressive as other aspects of the ship. Menus lack imagination, from the presentation to the flavoring, but they are extensive, with choices to suit every taste. Dinner always includes five entrées plus a vegetarian and "light" selection. Service is sophisticated, though, and there's piano music to dine by. Kids get their own menus, featuring fun foods such as "Yummy Yogi Pizza" and "Bam-Bam's Chilly-Willy Hot Dog." Formal nights are scheduled once on every three- or four-

Chart Symbols. Ships at a Glance. ●: *Fully equipped;* ◐: *Partially equipped;* ○: *Not equipped.* Cabins and Rates. **D:** *Double bed;* **K:** *King-size bed;* **Q:** *Queen-size bed;* **T:** *Twin bed;* **U/L:** *Upper and lower berths;* ●: *All cabins have this facility;* ○: *No cabins have this facility;* ◐: *Some cabins have this facility*

day cruise and twice on every weeklong sailing to Bermuda. Make special dietary requests in writing seven days before sailing. There is no smoking in the dining room.

The buffets are a better choice than the dining room for lunch or breakfast—the spreads are impressive and the food quite tasty. Other food service includes pizza and ice cream twice a day; afternoon tea with sandwiches, cookies, and cake; and a midnight buffet. Coffee and tea are available 24 hours a day, as is room service from a limited menu.

Entertainment As with its daily schedule of activities, the *Royal Majesty*'s nightly program of entertainment features typical cruise-ship song-and-dance productions, plus some novel alternatives: one-act plays, classical guitar recitals, and an elaborate medieval-style festival. There are also masquerade parties and karaoke nights.

Service and Tipping Tip the room steward $3.50 per passenger per diem, the waiter $3, the busboy $1.50. The maître d' should get $5 per passenger per cruise, the wine steward or bartender 15% of your final tab.

Destinations During fall, winter, and spring, the *Royal Majesty* sails from Miami on three- and four-day cruises to the Bahamas or Mexico's Yucatán. In summer, it repositions to Boston for weeklong cruises to Bermuda. (For seasonal itineraries, *see* Chapter 4.)

For More Information Majesty Cruise Lines (901 South America Way, Miami, FL 33132, tel. 800/645–8111).

MV Royal Majesty

Specifications *Type of ship:* Cruise liner
Cruise experience: Semi-formal
Size: 32,400 tons
Number of cabins: 528
Outside cabins: 65%
Passengers: 1,056
Crew: 500 (international)
Officers: Greek
Passenger/crew ratio: 2.1 to 1
Year built: 1992

Ship's Log The "royal" theme reigns throughout the ship, from the Queen of Hearts Card Room to the House of Lords Executive Conference Room to the Royal Fireworks Lounge. Excellent use of light and space creates bright, inviting public areas from which passengers can enjoy fine sea views. The Royal Observatory Panorama Bar is a favorite perch from which to watch the ship pull into and out of ports of call. The Cafe Royale is where you'll want to be for breakfast and lunch; its perch just above the bridge makes for panoramic views forward. At the other end of the ship, the Piazza San Marco serves pizza and ice cream twice a day amid sweeping views aft.

Cabins and Rates

	Beds	Phone	TV	Sitting Area	Fridge	Tub	Average Per Diem*
Suite	Q or T	●	●	●	●	○	$356
Outside	Q, D, or T	●	●	○	○	○	$270
Inside	Q, D, or T	●	●	○	○	○	$196

**Rates are for three-night Bahamas cruises. Airfare and port taxes are extra.*

Like the rest of the ship, cabin decor is tasteful and classy. Color schemes are understated earth tones complemented with wood furnishings and moldings. Each stateroom comes with robes, color TV (including CNN), five channels of music, direct-dial ship-to-shore telephones, hair dryers, security safes, and ironing boards. Suites and some outside cabins have a minibar, a queen-size bed, and an enormous ocean-view picture window. Views from many cabins on Queen's Deck are obstructed by lifeboats; cabins on Princess Deck look out onto a public promenade.

Outlet voltage: 110 AC.

Single supplement: 150% of double-occupancy rate.

Discounts: A third or fourth passenger in a cabin pays reduced per diems. You get a discount for booking early.

Sports and Fitness

Health club: Fitness center with LifeCircuit, weights, stair climber, stationary bikes, rowing machines, and treadmills; aerobics studio with exercise and dance classes; spa with body and facial treatments.

Recreation: Pool, two whirlpools, jogging track.

Facilities

Public rooms: Three bars, showroom, casino, disco, card room, library, meeting rooms, boardroom.

Shops: Gift shop, beauty salon.

Child care: Playroom, splash pool, baby-sitting, youth program with counselors year-round.

Services: Photographer.

Accessibility

The ship is fully accessible to wheelchair users, including four elevators, rest rooms on various decks, and four specially equipped staterooms.

Norwegian Cruise Line

The Fleet MS *Dreamward*
MS *Leeward*
SS *Norway*
MS *Norwegian Crown*
MS *Seaward*
MS *Windward*

NCL has a hodgepodge of big ships and small ships, old ships and new ships. The *Norway*, formerly the *France*, was built in 1962 and is still the longest cruise ship afloat. NCL's newest ships, the *Dreamward* and *Windward*, are state-of-the-art vessels, with mostly outside cabins (some with private balconies), picture windows, multiple restaurants, and tiered public rooms.

Ships at a Glance

	Dining Rooms	Bars	Casino	Fitness Center	Pools	Average Per Diem
Dreamward *Windward*	4*	8	●	●	2	$292 $321
Leeward	3*	5	●	●	1	$279
Norway	3*	5	●	●	2	$306
Norwegian Crown	2*	6	●	●	3	$299
Seaward	3*	8	●	●	2	$292

**includes alternative Italian restaurant*

Cruise Experience NCL was the originator of the modern formula for cruising: Its ships offer a full schedule of activities and entertainment, generous portions of American-style food, and a wide range of popular ports. NCL tries to be everything to everyone, so its passengers tend to span generations, economic brackets, and lifestyles. The newer ships, however, attract a younger, partying crowd, while the *Norway* and *Seaward* appeal to an older, more affluent group.

In years past, the line's onboard experience lacked the polish found aboard its competitors. Recently, that has begun to change. Refinements include traditional afternoon high tea served by white-gloved waiters to the accompaniment of classical music, an out-of-this-world Chocoholic Bar, and specialty coffees served in the main dining rooms. Around the pools, passengers will notice more attendants at the ready with towels and spritzers upon request.

Activities NCL doesn't skimp here. It's not unusual to see 30 different classes, contests, games, demonstrations, lectures, and performances scheduled for a single day. The line keeps in step with America's changing lifestyles: Fitness programs have been beefed up con-

Chart Symbols. Ships at a Glance. ●: *Fully equipped;* ◐: *Partially equipped;* ○: *Not equipped.* Cabins and Rates. **D:** *Double bed;* **K:** *King-size bed;* **Q:** *Queen-size bed;* **T:** *Twin bed;* **U/L:** *Upper and lower berths;* ●: *All cabins have this facility;* ○: *No cabins have this facility;* ◐: *Some cabins have this facility*

siderably, and children's programs have been instituted. New adventure-oriented excursions appeal to sporting types. In the Caribbean, a limited number of passengers can sign up for snorkeling or scuba-diving tours, and in Alaska, they can go mountain biking, sea kayaking, or glacier hiking.

An extensive schedule of theme cruises enlivens the usual offerings of bingo, trivia contests, dance classes, wine tastings, and vegetable-carving demonstrations. Most popular is the sports series aboard the *Norway* and *Dreamward,* when famous football, basketball, hockey, and baseball players—just to name a few—meet and play with passengers. Other theme cruises frequently highlight music, from country music to jazz to '50s and '60s pop (all on the *Norway*). Most upper Caribbean itineraries include an all-day beach party on NCL's own Bahamian island, Great Stirrup Cay, with snorkeling, beach games, and a barbecue.

Dining The food is plentiful but average; standards are highest on the *Norway*. Cuisine is a combination of American and Continental, usually with at least one Norwegian fish appetizer or entrée at lunch or dinner. (Caviar is served at an extra charge.) "Light entrée" options are available, but special dietary requests should be made one month prior to sailing. There are two assigned seatings for dinner (6 and 8:30); breakfast and lunch are open seating when ships are in port. Two formal evenings are held each week.

The *Leeward*, *Norway*, and *Seaward* each have two dining rooms to which passengers are assigned according to the location of their cabin; on the *Dreamward* and *Windward*, passengers are assigned to one of three dining rooms at random. The *Norwegian Crown* has a single dining room.

On all the ships, a small alternative restaurant, called Le Bistro, serves Italian cuisine à la carte at no additional cost. Passengers are served on a first-come, first-served basis (no reservations accepted). Because only a small number of passengers are served at one time, the food tends to be better prepared than that in the main dining rooms.

Lidos on all NCL ships serve a buffet breakfast and lunch (the *Seaward*'s Lido also serves dinner). There's also an ice-cream parlor aboard each vessel except the *Leeward*. Midnight buffets are served every evening. Room service is available 24 hours a day from a limited menu.

Entertainment Everything one would expect from a cruise is available in full measure on NCL ships, including Las Vegas–style variety shows, dance orchestras, piano bars, and discos. The *Norway*, *Seaward*, *Dreamward*, and *Windward* go so far as to feature scaled-down Broadway shows and revues, although the productions don't approach the elaborate, high-tech shows aboard Carnival's newest ships. The *Norway*'s music cruises have headlined such celebrities as Ricky Skaggs, the Bellamy Brothers, Tanya Tucker, the Tommy Dorsey Orchestra, Mary Wilson, and Paul Revere and the Raiders. In-cabin TVs on all ships show CNN broadcasts and movies all day.

Service and Tipping The general level of service on NCL ships is very good; the *Norway* has established the best reputation. Tip the room steward and the waiter each $3 per passenger per diem, the busboy $1.50. A 15% service charge is added to the bar tab, and a tip of 50¢ or $1 is expected each time room service is ordered.

Destinations NCL's itineraries are as varied as its fleet, sailing to well-traveled and off-the-beaten-path ports in the Caribbean, plus the Bahamas, Bermuda, southern California, the Mexican Riviera, and Alaska. (For seasonal itineraries, *see* Chapter 4.)

For More Information Norwegian Cruise Line (95 Merrick Way, Coral Gables, FL 33134, tel. 800/327–7030).

MS Dreamward and MS Windward

Specifications

Type of ship: Cruise liner
Cruise experience: Casual
Size: 41,000 tons
Number of cabins: 623
Outside cabins: 85%
Passengers: 1,242/1,246
Crew: 483 (international)
Officers: Norwegian
Passenger/crew ratio: 2.6 to 1
Year built: 1992/1993

Ship's Log Like most sister ships, these identical twins differ only in decor. Public rooms even have the same names, making it a breeze to get around on one if you have already sailed on the other. Terraced decks give panoramic views forward and aft, and walls of glass line the length of the ship. Multilevel public rooms include the Terrace dining room, the Stardust show lounge, and the two-deck-high Casino Royale, where the action includes roulette, craps, blackjack, and slot machines. Instead of one, big dining room, four smaller restaurants create a more intimate ambience. Even the biggest, the Terrace, seats only 282, on several levels, and has windows on three sides. Matching these two ships' variety of eateries is a variety of special menus, theme meals, and children's menus. Dinner has two assigned seatings, but breakfast and lunch are open, so you can try the other restaurants or opt for hamburgers and hot dogs at the casual Sports Bar & Grill.

Showroom productions are the usual festive affairs, including the full-length Broadway-style shows that NCL is famous for. A proscenium stage makes these productions NCL's most elaborate yet, although the line's productions lag behind Carnival's, whose newest ships feature even more high-tech stage equipment, and, consequently, more elaborate shows. After the show, the lounge metamorphoses into a late-night disco. The Sports Bar & Grill transmits live ESPN and NFL broadcasts on multiple screens. There's plenty of space for relaxing on the five-tier Sun Deck, and the especially broad Promenade Deck is good for walking and jogging.

Cabins and Rates

	Beds	Phone	TV	Sitting Area	Fridge	Tub	Average Per Diem*
Suite	T/Q	●	●	●	●	◐	$342/ $371
Outside	T/Q	●	●	●	○	○	$292/ $321
Inside	T/Q	●	●	○	○	○	$242/ $271

**Rates are for the Caribbean. Higher rates are for the Windward. Lower rates are for the Dreamward. Airfare and port taxes are extra.*

The *Dreamward* and *Windward* have an unusually high percentage of outside cabins, most with picture windows. Standard cabins, with their Caribbean villa look and feel, are among the prettiest at sea. The suites have floor-to-ceiling windows; some have private balconies and special amenities that include daily fruit baskets, champagne, trays of hors d'oeuvres, and concierge service. Adjoining suites are available on the Norway, International, and Star decks. Outside cabins have couches that convert into beds. Deluxe suites can accommodate up to four people, and adjoining U-shape suites work well for families of up to six. Some cabins on the Norway Deck have obstructed views.

Outlet voltage: 110 AC.

Single supplement: 150%–200% of double-occupancy rate.

Discounts: A third or fourth passenger in a cabin pays reduced per diems. You get a discount for booking early.

Sports and Fitness

Health club: Lifecycles, Lifesteps, exercise equipment, Jacuzzis, a variety of massage treatments.

Recreation: Basketball court, exercise course, two pools, golf range, unobstructed cushioned circuit for jogging.

Facilities

Public rooms: Eight bars, entertainment lounge/theater, observation lounge/nightclub, casino, library, video-game room, conference center.

Shops: Gift shops and boutiques, beauty salon/barber.

Health care: Doctor on call.

Child care: Playroom; youth counselors; children's programs in three age groups year-round, four age groups during holidays and in summer; guaranteed baby-sitting.

Accessibility

All decks and activities are accessible to wheelchair users, except the Sky Deck and public lavatories. Six specially equipped cabins are accessible to wheelchair users, 28 are for passengers with hearing impairments.

MS Leeward

Specifications

Type of ship: Cruise liner
Cruise experience: Casual
Size: 25,000 tons
Number of cabins: 475
Outside cabins: 67%
Passengers: 950
Crew: 400 (international)
Officers: Norwegian
Passenger/crew ratio: 2.4 to 1
Year built: 1980

Ship's Log

The sleek *Leeward* joined Norwegian Cruise Line in 1995, after seeing service as the *Viking Saga*, a cruise ferry on the Baltic Sea. And although from the outside it looks like a ferry, after a $60 million refit, the interior is all cruise ship. The new decor makes use of liberal use of wood and stone accents throughout the ship. A sports bar and grill, a NCL first on the *Dreamward* and *Windward*, has been put aboard the *Leeward* as well. Passengers are assigned to one of two main dining rooms for dinner, and they can always choose to eat in the 80-seat alternative restaurant, Le Bistro. In all, this is one of the most elegant—and intimate—vessels operating on short three- and four-day cruises to the Bahamas.

Cabins and Rates

	Beds	Phone	TV	Sitting Area	Fridge	Tub	Average Per Diem*
Suite	Q or T	●	●	●	●	○	$326
Outside	Q, T, or U/L	●	●	◐	○	○	$279
Inside	Q, T, or U/L	●	●	○	○	○	$189

**Rates are for three-night Bahamas cruises. Airfare and port taxes are extra.*

Cabins are decorated in an art deco style; color schemes incorporate hues of dusty rose and gray. All have televisions; none, not even the suites, have tubs. Two owner's suites have large private balconies and Jacuzzis; eight penthouses have balconies and a separate bedroom and living room.

Outlet voltage: 110 AC.

Single supplement: Single-occupancy cabins are bookable at no surcharge, subject to availability.

Discounts: A third or fourth passenger in a cabin pays reduced per diems. You get a discount for booking early.

Sports and Fitness

Health club: Exercise equipment, full-service spa.

Recreation: Aerobics and other exercise classes, table tennis, skeet shooting, snorkeling lessons and excursions, pool, Jacuzzis, unobstructed circuit for jogging.

Facilities

Public rooms: Five bars and lounges, casino, disco, library, meeting rooms.

Shops: Duty-free shops and gift boutique, barber/beauty salon.

Health care: Doctor on call.

Child care: Playroom; youth counselors; children's programs year-round, four age groups during holidays and in summer; guaranteed baby-sitting.

Services: Laundry service, photographer, film processing.

Accessibility

Six cabins and five elevators are accessible to wheelchair users. All decks and public rooms are accessible, except for the beauty salon. No public rest rooms are accessible.

SS Norway

Specifications

Type of ship: Classic liner
Cruise experience: Semi-formal
Size: 76,049 tons
Number of cabins: 1,016
Outside cabins: 56.9%
Passengers: 2,032
Crew: 900 (international)
Officers: Norwegian
Passenger/crew ratio: 2.3 to 1
Year built: 1962

Ship's Log

Deep within the huge hull of the *Norway* beats a Gallic heart. The ship began life in 1962 as the *France*, built with French government subsidies to be the biggest, most beautiful transatlantic liner afloat—a symbol for a country impressed with its own style and stature. And while the ship was one of the most popular of its time, the subsidies were less popular with the French government. The ship was sold to Norwegian Cruise Line in 1979 and extensively refitted for vacation cruises.

One of the best-looking ocean liners ever built, the *Norway* has an incredible amount of deck space, as well as a cavernous interior. The enclosed International Deck is so large and wide that its tree-edged walkways, lined with sidewalk cafés, bars, shops, and boutiques, resemble an upscale shopping mall. The port walkway is named Fifth Avenue, and the starboard side, Champs-Elysées.

The *Norway* has undergone two major refurbishments in the past several years. The first added almost 3,000 tons to its gross tonnage, making it the largest ship afloat—although it will soon lose that title. Among the additions were two new decks, a 6,000-square-foot spa (spa packages include calorie-controlled lunches), a new restaurant, and 124 luxury staterooms (54 with private balconies). The second and most recent restored the ship to its former art deco glory. Much of the original *France* is still visible in the wood decks, slate floors, magnificent artwork, sweeping staircases, and sparkling chandeliers. The Windward and Leeward dining rooms are as large as hotel banquet halls. It's easy to get lost among the plethora of bars and lounges; many passengers never see all the public rooms.

Cabins and Rates

	Beds	Phone	TV	Sitting Area	Fridge	Tub	Average Per Diem*
Suite	K, Q, T, or U/L	●	●	●	●	●	$364
Outside	D, T, or U/L	●	●	○	◐	◐	$306
Inside	D, T, or U/L	●	●	○	○	◐	$225

**Rates are for the Caribbean. Airfare and port taxes are extra.*

Most suites and cabins are larger than those of comparably priced ships. Standard cabins have portholes; upper categories have picture windows. Suites offer concierge service. Each Owner's Suite has a private wraparound balcony, a living room, a master bedroom and second bedroom, a dressing room, a bathroom, and a whirlpool. Some Grand Deluxe Suites have a separate living room and a second bedroom, a whirlpool, and a powder room. Most Penthouse Suites have private balconies. Olympic Deck cabins look onto the jogging track. Most cabins on the Fjord and Olympic decks have obstructed or partially obstructed views.

Outlet voltage: 110 AC.

Single supplement: Single-occupancy cabins are bookable at no surcharge, subject to availability.

Discounts: A third or fourth passenger in a cabin pays reduced per diems. You get a discount for booking early.

Sports and Fitness

Health club: Fitness center with 16 treatment rooms (for massage, reflexology, herbal treatment, hydrotherapy, thermal body wraps, and more), two saunas, two steam rooms, body-jet showers, Cybex Eagle strength-training equipment, Lifecycles and Lifesteps, whirlpool, indoor pool for water exercise. The spa's beauty salon (separate from the ship's main salon) offers facials and other beauty treatments.

Recreation: Aerobics and other exercise classes, basketball, deck Olympics, golf driving and putting, paddleball, table tennis, shuffleboard, skeet shooting, snorkeling classes and excursions, volleyball, two outdoor pools, unobstructed cushioned circuit for jogging.

Facilities

Public rooms: Five bars and lounges, cabaret, casino, disco, theater, library, video-game room, two meeting rooms.

Shops: Arcade of gift shops and boutiques, beauty salon/barber.

Health care: Doctor on call.

Child care: Playroom; youth counselors; children's programs in three age groups year-round, four age groups during holidays and in summer; guaranteed baby-sitting.

Services: Concierge service in suites, laundry service, dry cleaning, photographer, film processing.

Accessibility

The *Norway* has 11 cabins accessible to wheelchair users. All public areas except the Sun Deck pool are accessible. The ship's size forces it to anchor offshore at most ports; boarding the tenders can pose a difficulty for passengers with mobility problems.

MS Norwegian Crown

Specifications

Type of ship: Cruise liner
Cruise experience: Casual
Size: 34,250 tons
Passengers: 1,052
Crew: 470 (Greek)
Officers: Greek

Number of cabins: 526 *Passenger/crew ratio:* 2.2 to 1
Outside cabins: 78% *Year built:* 1988

Ship's Log The *Norwegian Crown*, formerly the *Crown Odyssey*, joined NCL in May 1996 after Royal Cruise Line ceased operations. Size-wise, the *Crown* fits right in the middle of NCL's fleet—about half the size of the giant *Norway* but bigger than the relatively tiny *Leeward*. From top to bottom, the *Norwegian Crown* facilities are impressive for a smaller liner. Far below decks lies one of the *Crown*'s jewels: a Roman-style health center with an indoor pool, whirlpools, saunas, and other spa treatments. On the ship's top deck, passengers will find the Top of the Crown Lounge, a multipurpose room surrounded by glass and topped by two glass domes. During the day it's an observation lounge and at night it becomes the ship's disco. At press time, NCL planned to add its signature sports bar and Le Bistro alternative restaurant in 1997.

Cabins and Rates

	Beds	Phone	TV	Sitting Area	Fridge	Tub	Average Per Diem*
Suite	T/D	●	●	●	●	●	$342
Outside	T	●	●	○	○	◐	$292
Inside	T/D	●	●	○	○	◐	$242

**Rates are for the Caribbean. Airfare and port taxes are extra.*

Suites are spacious and comfortable. Wood paneling and trim are used extensively. The top accommodations have private balconies, marble bathrooms, walk-in closets, whirlpool baths, and butler service. Some suites can be combined with an adjoining cabin to provide 1,000 square feet of space. Suites located on the Riviera Deck have bay windows with panoramic views. All cabins have televisions, hardwood furniture and cabinetry, full vanities, two mirrored closets with tie and shoe racks, and European-style fixtures in the bathrooms. Many outside cabins have extra-large picture windows. Views from most cabins on the Lido Deck are partially or fully obstructed by lifeboats.

Outlet voltage: 110/220 AC.

Single supplement: Single-occupancy cabins are bookable at no surcharge, subject to availability.

Discounts: A third or fourth passenger in a cabin pays reduced per diems. You get a discount for booking early.

Sports and Fitness **Health club:** Eight-station Universal gym with full-time fitness instructor, four Lifecycles, treadmill, rower, free weights, ballet barre, indoor pool, two whirlpools, massage, health bar, men's and women's saunas, full-service beauty center (herbal wraps, facials, and more).

Recreation: Table tennis, shuffleboard, exercise classes, outdoor pool, children's pool, two outdoor whirlpools, unobstructed circuits for jogging.

Facilities **Public rooms:** Six bars, five entertainment lounges, casino, disco, cinema, card room, library.

Shops: Two boutiques, sundries shop, beauty salon/barber.

Health care: Doctor on call.

Child care: Organized youth programs with counselors during selected holidays only.

Services: Laundry service, pressing, dry cleaning, 24-hour information desk, photographer, film processing.

Accessibility Four cabins are equipped with sit-down showers, grip bars around the shower and toilet areas, and tilting mirrors.

MS Seaward

Specifications
Type of ship: Cruise liner
Cruise experience: Casual
Size: 42,000 tons
Number of cabins: 752
Outside cabins: 67.7%
Passengers: 1,504
Crew: 630 (international)
Officers: Norwegian
Passenger/crew ratio: 2.4 to 1
Year built: 1988

Ship's Log Compared with other ships built in the late 1980s, the *Seaward* is surprisingly spartan. A spacious pool deck is well equipped with back-to-back swimming pools and twin Jacuzzis, but there's more all-weather carpeting than teak decking. The Crystal Court, a two-story lobby, is also disappointingly modest for a ship of such recent vintage.

On the positive side, the *Seaward*'s two large dining rooms are gracious and welcoming, their many tables set with white linens and formal stemware. The newest addition to the ship, the Le Bistro Italian restaurant, is a more casual alternative for dinner. The bars and lounges are inviting and plushly appointed, and there are two showrooms—one for small-scale shows by bands and comedians and another for full-scale musical productions. (Be sure to get to the Cabaret Lounge early; its single-level construction makes viewing difficult for those at the back and sides of the room.)

The *Seaward* was recently refreshed with new carpeting, curtains, and furnishings in various public rooms. Among the spaces to get the new treatments were the wine bar (new fabrics and upholstery), the observatory lounge (new white-marble floor at the entryway), and the main dining rooms (new mirrors and artwork). Other areas were equipped with new tables and chairs.

Cabins and Rates

	Beds	Phone	TV	Sitting Area	Fridge	Tub	Average Per Diem*
Suite	T/D	●	●	●	●	●	$342
Outside	T/D	●	●	◐	○	○	$299
Inside	T/D or U/L	●	●	○	○	○	$256

**Airfare and port taxes are extra.*

Cabins were recently redecorated with new carpeting, curtains, and bedding. Rounded picture windows in outside cabins look like elongated portholes. Some cabins on the Norway and Star decks have obstructed or partially obstructed views.

Outlet voltage: 110 AC.

Single supplement: Single-occupancy cabins are bookable at no surcharge, subject to availability.

Discounts: A third or fourth passenger in a cabin pays reduced per diems. You get a discount for booking early.

Sports and Fitness **Health club:** Exercise equipment, massage, sauna.

Recreation: Aerobics and other exercise classes, basketball, golf driving, table tennis, shuffleboard, skeet shooting, snorkeling lessons and excursions, volleyball, two pools, two Jacuzzis, unobstructed cushioned circuit (4 laps = 1 mile) for jogging.

Facilities **Public rooms:** Eight bars and lounges, casino, disco, cabaret, card room/library.

Shops: Several boutiques, beauty salon/barber.

Health care: Doctor on call.

Child care: Playroom; youth counselors; children's programs in three age groups year-round, four age groups during holidays and in summer; guaranteed baby-sitting.

Services: Laundry service, dry cleaning, photographer, film processing.

Accessibility The *Seaward* has excellent facilities for wheelchair users. Four cabins are specially equipped, and no area of the ship is inaccessible to passengers with mobility problems.

Orient Lines

The Fleet *MS Marco Polo*

Like its namesake, the *Marco Polo* visits faraway lands on extended journeys. The vessel will appeal to ship buffs and world travelers alike. A former transatlantic liner, it first set sail as the *Alexandr Pushkin* in 1965 for the Soviet-flag Baltic Shipping Company. Completely rebuilt over a two-year period, the 850-passenger *Marco Polo* retains an ice-strengthened hull, a handsome profile, and smooth-running twin Sulzer diesel engines. The cabin accommodations and public rooms are completely new and decorated in understated good taste, and the deck spaces are generously proportioned.

Ship at a Glance

	Dining Rooms	Bars	Casino	Fitness Center	Pools	Average Per Diem
Marco Polo	2*	5	●	●	1	$224

**includes alternative restaurant*

Cruise Experience Since its inception in late 1993, Orient Lines has quickly established a reputation for its destination-intensive cruises. Moderate rates that include pre- or post-cruise land packages and exotic ports of call on six continents put this line in a niche with few competitors. The line already has its share of loyal repeaters, mostly 55 and older. American passengers predominate, but there is usually a sizable contingent of British passengers aboard and, to a lesser extent, Europeans and Australians.

Activities During days at sea, enrichment lectures are the most well-attended events. The daily program also lists bingo, "horse racing," bridge tournaments, fashion shows, food demonstrations, deck games, and exercise classes.

Dining Menus were developed by Wolfgang Puck, a southern California chef and restaurateur, but the menu selection goes far beyond this one region to please the ship's varied American and international clientele. There are four choices of entrées at dinner, plus healthy and vegetarian selections. From preparation to presentation, the quality is consistently good to excellent—above the standard expected from a mid-price ship.

Dinner is served in two seatings (6:30 and 8:30) at assigned tables. Breakfast and lunch are open seating. Two formals are scheduled each week. Raffles, an attractive buffet restaurant, also serves a varied menu at breakfast and lunch. There's also an outdoor barbecue by the pool. On several nights, Raffles is transformed into a tranquil, reservations-only dining room. You'll pay an extra $5 service

Chart Symbols. Ships at a Glance. **●:** *Fully equipped;* **◐:** *Partially equipped;* ○: *Not equipped.* Cabins and Rates. **D:** *Double bed;* **K:** *King-size bed;* **Q:** *Queen-size bed;* **T:** *Twin bed;* **U/L:** *Upper and lower berths;* **●:** *All cabins have this facility;* ○: *No cabins have this facility;* **◐:** *Some cabins have this facility*

charge to eat from the Asian menu. Room service is limited to breakfast.

Entertainment Two shows (one for each dining-room seating) are offered every night, featuring singers, dancers, and perhaps a magician or comedian. A small band provides dance music; in good weather, the band may play on deck. Local folkloric performers come aboard in some ports. A late-night disco generally attracts more officers and staff than passengers.

Service and Tipping The friendly and efficient hotel staff is Filipino. Tip the dining-room waiter $3.75 per person per day, $1.25 to the busboy, and $4 to the cabin steward. A 15% service charge is automatically added to your bar bill and to drinks in the dining rooms.

Destinations Cruise-tours of 8 to 25 days call at ports on six continents, including Antarctica, Asia, Australia, Africa, Europe, and South America—everywhere but North America. Antarctic expeditions, limited to 400 passengers, are made in alternate years, with the next program scheduled for 1997–1998. (For seasonal itineraries, *see* Chapter 4.)

For More Information Orient Lines (1510 S.E. 17th St., Suite 400, Fort Lauderdale, FL 33316, tel. 954/527–6660 or 800/333–7300).

MS Marco Polo

Specifications *Type of ship:* Classic liner
Cruise experience: Semiformal
Size: 22,080 tons
Number of cabins: 425
Outside cabins: 70%
Passengers: 850
Crew: 350 (Filipino)
Officers: European
Passenger/crew ratio: 2.4 to 1
Year built: 1965; rebuilt 1993

Ship's Log A handsome vessel with a raked profile, the Marco Polo is well suited to passengers who enjoy relaxing days at sea in preparation for an intensive itinerary of popular and exotic ports. Nearly all the cheerfully decorated public rooms are located on one deck with an easy flow from the forward show lounge to the outdoor Lido surrounding the pool. The teak Promenade Deck offers wooden deck chairs and a wide, but not quite circular, walking track. The Upper Deck has a wraparound promenade but with narrow stretches alongside the lifeboats. The forward observation deck and tiered afterdecks are well designed for lounging and sightseeing. A helipad is used for reconnaissance and passenger flights in Antarctica.

Cabins and Rates

	Beds	Phone	TV	Sitting Area	Fridge	Tub	Average Per Diem*
Suite	D, Q, or T	●	●	●	●	●	$328
Outside	D or T	●	●	◐	○	◐	$224
Inside	D or T	●	●	○	○	○	$161

**Rates are for cruise-tours and include pre- or post-cruise land stays. Airfare and port charges are extra.*

Cabins are new, with light-wood furniture trim and wainscoting, and those facing open decks have one-way glass for privacy. Furnishings include one or two chairs, a bedside table, and a chest of drawers—some doubling as writing desks. Closet space is adequate and suitcases may be stored under the beds. Bathrooms have hair dryers, complimentary toiletries, and a clothesline. Some cabins can accommodate a third and fourth person. Two deluxe and four junior suites have sitting areas and small refrigerators. TVs show feature films (some related to the destinations on your itinerary), documentaries, CNN, and taped lectures. Radios have two music channels. Cabins on Sky Deck and Cabins 712–727 have views partially obstructed by lifeboats.

Outlet voltage: 110/220 AC

Single supplement: 125%–200% of double-occupancy rate. The supplement is waived for passengers who agree to share with another single traveler, even if one is not found by the time of sailing.

Discounts: A third or fourth passenger in a cabin pays the minimum fare. You get a discount for booking early and for booking back-to-back cruises. Repeat passengers get an additional discount.

Sports and Fitness

Health Club: Fitness equipment, sauna, massage.

Recreation: Aerobics, table tennis, shuffleboard, pool, three Jacuzzis, two circuits (one unobstructed, one unobstructed) for jogging.

Facilities

Public rooms: Five bars, two entertainment lounges, casino, disco, library, card room.

Shops: Two gift shops, beauty center/barber.

Health care: Doctor and nurse on call.

Child care: None.

Services: Laundry service, dry cleaning, photographer, film processing, post office and currency exchange in some ports.

Accessibility

Two cabins have wheelchair-accessible bathrooms; all others have 2- to 12-inch raised thresholds. Accessibility aboard local transportation and other facilities ashore varies greatly in the ports visited.

Premier Cruise Lines

Starship Oceanic

The Fleet *Star/Ship Atlantic*
Star/Ship Oceanic

These two ships, known collectively as the Big Red Boat, are instantly recognizable by their cherry-color hulls. Premier has acquired its fleet from a venerable name of cruising past: The *Atlantic* and *Oceanic* both sailed under the same names for now-defunct Home Lines. The ships were refitted to suit the family cruise market. A recreation center for children ages two and older has its own wading pool and sundeck, teenagers have their own recreation room, and many cabins can accommodate three, four, or even five passengers.

Ships at a Glance

	Dining Rooms	Bars	Casino	Fitness Center	Pools	Average Per Diem
Atlantic	1	5	●	●	3	$222
Oceanic	1	4	●	●	3	$222

Cruise Experience Premier invented family cruising in 1984 and still runs one of the best child-care and youth programs on the high seas. Formerly the official cruise line of Walt Disney World, the line now carries Looney Tunes characters, such as Bugs Bunny and Daffy Duck, on every sailing. If you don't like children, don't sail with Premier—but you don't have to have a family to enjoy these lively, unpretentious cruises. Increasingly, they are popular with honeymooners who want to combine a cruise with a visit to Florida. For senior citizens, the line offers a 10%–15% discount. The line also has special rates for single parents staying in the same cabin with one or more children and for family reunions.

Premier operates three- and four-day cruises exclusively. These may be bought cruise-only or combined with a land package to Orlando-area theme parks for seven-day vacations. Choices include Walt Disney World, Universal Studios, Sea World, Kennedy Space Center's Spaceport USA, and the Major League Baseball Players' Alumni Fantasy Camp.

Activities For adults, Premier offers traditional cruise activities—"horse racing," bingo, pool games, trivia contests, bridge tournaments—as well as extensive fitness programs and facilities. Golfers will appreciate the Premier Cruise Line Golf Academy. A golf pro sails aboard each ship, providing instruction and videotape analysis of your swing. Golf excursions off the ship can be arranged in port.

Young children and teenagers have their own activities centers, video-game room, and counselor-supervised programs. In keeping

Chart Symbols. Ships at a Glance. ●: *Fully equipped;* ◐: *Partially equipped;* ○: *Not equipped.* Cabins and Rates. **D:** *Double bed;* **K:** *King-size bed;* **Q:** *Queen-size bed;* **T:** *Twin bed;* **U/L:** *Upper and lower berths;* ●: *All cabins have this facility;* ○: *No cabins have this facility;* ◐: *Some cabins have this facility*

with recent trends both at sea and ashore, both ships have computer learning centers.

Dining Food is good basic fare. The waiters are exceptionally good with children, but don't look for elegance or snappy service, especially with the high number of children served. The menu, decor, and waiters' costumes change nightly to reflect a theme—French, Italian, Caribbean, American. A children's menu is available, with such favorites as hamburgers, hot dogs, and macaroni and cheese. Meals are served at two assigned seatings (6 and 8:15 for dinner). If you are traveling with small children, it's smart to sign up for the first seating. If you wish a more sedate environment, you would be wise to select the late seating. There is one semiformal evening on each cruise. Special dietary requests should be made in writing at least four weeks prior to sailing. There is no smoking in the dining rooms.

Early-morning coffee is served on the Pool Deck, as are extensive breakfast and lunch buffets. Other food service includes a make-your-own sundae bar, afternoon tea, a midnight buffet, and a late-night omelet bar. Room service is available 24 hours from a limited menu.

Entertainment Looney Tunes characters roam the decks to play with children (and adults, who seem to get into the act when no one is looking). You can even arrange for your child to be tucked into bed at night by his or her favorite character or to have breakfast with the Looney Tunes. Otherwise, entertainment is traditional, featuring variety shows, magicians, films, and theme parties. After the sun goes down, Premier presents Las Vegas–style revues, cabaret acts, piano playing, and other adult forms of entertainment. (The comedy, however, is strictly PG-13, instead of the R-rated material most ships offer late-night passengers.) Premier also features large casinos with row upon row of slot machines. In-cabin TVs show CNN broadcasts.

Service and Tipping Generally, the crew is superb at handling children and all their wants. They're patient, always smiling, and ready to give a helping hand. On three-night cruises, tip the room steward and the waiter each $10 per passenger, the busboy $5. On four-night cruises, tip the room steward and the waiter each $12 per passenger, the busboy $6. When you sign for bar and wine bills, a 15% service charge is automatically added.

Destinations The *Atlantic* and *Oceanic* sail on three- and four-night cruises to the Bahamas. (For year-round itineraries, *see* Chapter 4.)

For More Information Premier Cruise Lines (Box 517, Cape Canaveral, FL 32920, tel. 800/327–7113).

Star/Ship Atlantic

Specifications

Type of ship: Cruise liner
Cruise experience: Casual
Size: 36,500 tons
Number of cabins: 549
Outside cabins: 73%
Passengers: 1,098
Crew: 500 (international)
Officers: Greek
Passenger/crew ratio: 3.1 to 1
Year built: 1982

Ship's Log The *Atlantic* is a generic-looking cruise ship that has the appearance of a freighter—although it never served as one. During a major refurbishment in 1989, the public rooms and casino were enlarged, extra cabins were added, and more facilities for children were installed. So although the ship's capacity, based on two to a cabin, is 1,098, that number can balloon to 1,550 if every bed is filled. Like its fleetmate the *Oceanic*, it features a retractable, transparent roof over the Riviera Pool. Most daytime activities are centered on the Promenade Deck, which has an ice-cream parlor, a well-equipped sports-and-fitness center, and two pools with adjacent sun areas.

Youngsters age two or older can enjoy Pluto's Playhouse in the children's recreation center (the largest of any ship sailing the Bahamas), as well as a shallow children's pool. For older children, the Space Station Teen Center has a jukebox and a dance floor, and the Star Fighter Arcade is packed with state-of-the-art video games.

Cabins and Rates

	Beds	Phone	TV	Sitting Area	Fridge	Tub	Average Per Diem*
Suite	Q or T	●	●	●	○	●	$247
Outside	Q, T, or U/L	●	●	●	○	●	$222
Inside	D, T, or U/L	●	●	○	○	◐	$165

**Rates are for four-night Bahamas cruises. Airfare and port taxes are extra.*

Cabins are simply furnished, but many can accommodate three, four, or five passengers.

Outlet voltage: 110 AC.

Single supplement: 200% of double-occupancy rate. Single parents traveling with children under 17 pay 125% on selected cabin categories.

Discounts: A third, fourth, or fifth passenger in a cabin pays reduced per diems. You get a discount for booking early. Senior citizens receive a 10% discount on peak sailings, 15% on shoulder-season sailings, and 20% on off-peak sailings on selected cabin categories.

Sports and Fitness

Health club: Lifecycles, Universal weights, minitrampolines, sit-up boards, massage.

Recreation: Aerobics and other exercise classes, table tennis, snorkeling lessons, shuffleboard, skeet shooting, volleyball, whirlpools, three pools, wading pool, jogging track.

Facilities

Public rooms: Five bars, three entertainment lounges, casino, disco, cinema, video-game room.

Shops: Three gift shops, beauty salon/barber.

Health care: Doctor on call.

Child care: Children's recreation center (age two and up), with wading pool, sundeck, supervised programs aboard ship and ashore; teen centers and programs; 24-hour baby-sitting for children ages 2 to 12.

Services: Laundry service, photographer.

Accessibility

Accessibility aboard ship for wheelchair users is limited. Passengers with mobility problems may have difficulty boarding the tenders that ferry passengers to Port Lucaya and Salt Cay.

Star/Ship Oceanic

Specifications

Type of ship: Classic liner
Cruise experience: Casual
Size: 40,000 tons
Number of cabins: 590
Outside cabins: 44%
Passengers: 1,609
Crew: 530 (international)
Officers: Greek
Passenger/crew ratio: 3 to 1
Year built: 1965

Ship's Log

In the tradition of having prominent women christen ships, Minnie Mouse was the celebrity wielding the champagne bottle when the *Oceanic* was inaugurated as a Premier ship in 1986. The exterior is stunning, with the classic lines of a transatlantic liner. The ship boasts two pools that can be covered by a retractable, transparent dome in the event of rain. The Seven Continents Restaurant is huge and well lighted, with wide aisles and ample space between the tables, but it tends to become noisy. The casino is one of the largest on any cruise ship; children under 18 are forbidden to play the slot machines, but a video arcade is nearby.

Cabins and Rates

	Beds	Phone	TV	Sitting Area	Fridge	Tub	Average Per Diem*
Suite	Q, D, or T	●	●	●	○	●	$247
Outside	D, T, or U/L	●	●	◐	○	●	$222
Inside	D, T, or U/L	●	●	○	○	◐	$165

**Rates are for four-night Bahamas cruises. Airfare and port taxes are extra.*

Cabins are simply furnished; many accommodate three, four, or five passengers.

Outlet voltage: 110 AC.

Single supplement: 200% of double-occupancy rate. Single parents traveling with children under 17 pay 125% on selected cabin categories.

Discounts: A third, fourth, or fifth passenger in a cabin pays reduced per diems. You get a discount for booking early. Senior citizens receive a 10% discount on peak sailings, 15% on shoulder-season sailings, and 20% on off-peak sailings on selected cabin categories

Sports and Fitness

Health club: Lifecycles, Universal weight equipment, minitrampolines, sit-up boards, massage.

Recreation: Aerobics and other exercise classes, basketball, table tennis, pool volleyball, snorkeling lessons, shuffleboard, skeet shooting, tennis practice, volleyball, two adjacent swimming pools, wading pool, three whirlpools, jogging track.

Facilities

Public rooms: Four bars, four entertainment lounges, casino, disco, cinema, reading room, video-game room.

Shops: Two gift shops, beauty salon/barber.

Health care: Doctor on call.

Child care: Children's recreation center (age two and up), with wading pool, sundeck, supervised programs aboard ship and ashore; teen centers and programs; 24-hour baby-sitting for children ages two to 12.

Services: Laundry service, photographer.

Accessibility

Accessibility aboard ship for wheelchair users is limited. Passengers with mobility problems may have difficulty boarding the tenders that ferry passengers to Port Lucaya and Salt Cay.

Princess Cruises

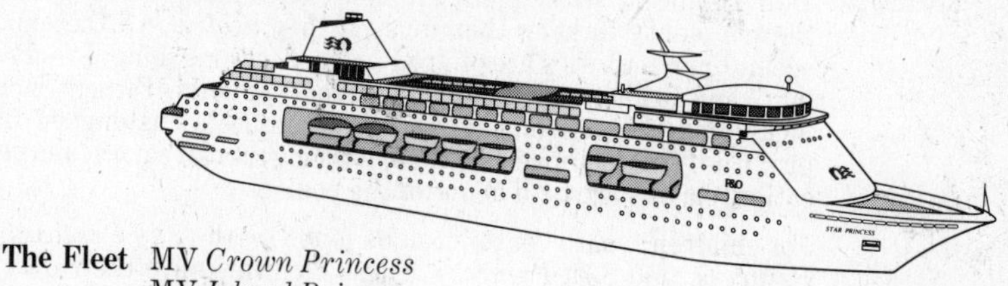

Star Princess

The Fleet MV *Crown Princess*
MV *Island Princess*
MV *Pacific Princess*
MV *Regal Princess*
MV *Royal Princess*
TSS *Sky Princess*
MV *Star Princess*
MV *Sun Princess*

Princess proves that big can be classy aboard its increasingly huge, upscale megaships. Most of the ships in the Princess fleet are bigger than 70,000 tons but carry fewer than 2,000 passengers, a small complement for ships this size. And Princess is looking at an even bigger future: In early 1998, the line expects delivery of the *Grand Princess*, a 105,000-ton giant too big to fit through the Panama Canal. It will be the biggest of all cruise ships and is expected to have two atrium lobbies, three main showrooms, three main dining rooms, and a disco suspended high above the stern of the ship—like a spoiler on a race car.

Ships at a Glance

	Dining Rooms	Bars	Casino	Fitness Center	Pools	Average Per Diem
Crown Princess *Regal Princess*	1	9	●	●	2	$275 $328
Island Princess *Pacific Princess*	1	6	●	●	2	$356
Royal Princess	1	7	●	●	3	$348
Sky Princess	1	7	●	●	2	$356
Star Princess	1	7	●	●	3	$250
Sun Princess	2	7	●	●	5	$285

Cruise Experience Most of us remember Princess ships from the cheerful TV series *The Love Boat*. In the real world, Princess Cruises is the refined North American arm of British shipping giant P&O (see Chapter 2). Nearly everything about Princess is big, but the line doesn't sacrifice quality for quantity. Decor and materials used to build the ships are top-notch, and service, especially in the dining rooms, is of a high standard. In short, Princess is refined without being pretentious.

From Caribbean getaways to Asian adventures, the Princess fleet has global reach. Due to the great variety of its itineraries, the line attracts an equally diverse range of passengers. On exotic sailings,

Chart Symbols. Ships at a Glance. **●**: *Fully equipped;* **◐**: *Partially equipped;* ○: *Not equipped.* Cabins and Rates. **D:** *Double bed;* **K:** *King-size bed;* **Q:** *Queen-size bed;* **T:** *Twin bed;* **U/L:** *Upper and lower berths;* **●**: *All cabins have this facility;* ○: *No cabins have this facility;* **◐**: *Some cabins have this facility*

you're likely to find more retirees, but in the Caribbean, families and an increasing mix of couples prevail.

Activities Many Princess passengers are content to take it easy, although there's plenty to keep them busy if they prefer. All the expected ocean-liner activities are offered—dance lessons, bingo, "horse racing," and bridge and backgammon tournaments. Fitness facilities include an exercise manager who can create a customized fitness program. On Caribbean sailings, passengers can earn scuba certification; classes are held in one of the pools.

For children, youth centers can be found on the *Sky Princess*, *Star Princess*, and *Sun Princess*. These facilities have their own kids' pool and sundeck, and provide daily supervised activities year-round; children's programs are available on the other ships when the numbers warrant it.

Dining The mostly Italian dining-room staff supervises meals with élan and pride. Each night at dinner the headwaiter prepares a fresh pasta dish table-side. Continental cuisine is presented with flair and fanfare—the baked Alaska, in particular, is reason for a grand parade—but sometimes it is a bit disappointing to the palate. Alternative vegetarian, low-fat, low-cholesterol, and low-sodium selections are offered at every meal. Meals are served at two assigned seatings (dinner at 6:15 and 8:15); breakfast and lunch may be open seating when the ship is in port. Two formal evenings are held on seven-day cruises, three on 9- to 16-day cruises. Special dietary requests are well handled, but they should be made in writing three weeks before sailing. There is no smoking in the dining room.

The Lido serves breakfast and lunch buffets, but the food is usually better in the dining room. (On the *Sun Princess*, the Lido is open around the clock.) Other food service includes mid-morning bouillon, afternoon tea, and a midnight buffet; 24-hour room service is limited to sandwiches and beverages except during dinner, when a full menu is served. The *Crown*, *Regal*, *Royal*, *Sky*, *Star*, and *Sun* have free pizza parlors open throughout the afternoon and evening. On the *Crown*, *Regal*, *Royal*, *Star*, and *Sun* a patisserie serves complimentary desserts and specialty coffees for an extra charge.

Entertainment Princess emphasizes entertainment suitable for the entire family, with a little more flair and flash than its chief rivals. Evening diversions include musical revues, variety shows, cabarets, a piano bar, a dance orchestra and combo, and a disco. Local musicians sometimes come aboard to perform. In-cabin TV programming is among the most extensive you'll find on any ship; choices include movies, CNN, ESPN, the Discovery Channel, and the Learning Channel.

Service and Tipping Princess places heavy emphasis on keeping passengers happy and satisfied. Generally, the service is excellent and unobtrusive, though passengers occasionally complain of stuffiness among British crew members. The Italian dining-room staff is a great deal of fun, however, and the room service is exceptional. Tip the room steward and waiter $3 each per passenger per diem, the waiter's assistant $1.75. The maître d' and the headwaiter may be tipped at the passenger's discretion for a job well done. A 15% gratuity is automatically added to bar and wine charges.

Destinations The Princess fleet is like a small navy, sailing to virtually every cruise destination. Itineraries cover Alaska, Asia, the Caribbean, Europe, Hawaii, the Mexican Riviera, New England and Canada, South America, and the Panama Canal. (For seasonal itineraries, *see* Chapter 4.)

For More Information Princess Cruises (10100 Santa Monica Blvd., Los Angeles, CA 90067, tel. 310/553–1770).

MV Crown Princess and MV Regal Princess

Specifications *Type of ship:* Megaship
Cruise experience: Semi-formal
Size: 70,000 tons
Number of cabins: 795
Outside cabins: 80%
Passengers: 1,590
Crew: 696 (international)
Officers: Italian
Passenger/crew ratio: 2.2 to 1
Year built: 1990/1991

Ship's Log Supposedly modeled on the curves of a dolphin, these sister ships look more like oversize, seafaring versions of the Japanese bullet train. (A picture of the *Crown* is shown on the cover of this book.) The unusual exteriors are a blend of the traditional (note the single, upright funnel) and the avant-garde. The ships are instantly recognizable for their most dramatic feature: a domed observation lounge/casino/entertainment area that sits atop the bridge. Other highlights include a million-dollar art collection and a three-story atrium foyer. And although the *Crown* and *Regal* are almost as large as Royal Caribbean Cruise Line's 74,000-ton megaship, *Majesty of the Seas,* they hold about 1,200 fewer passengers (counting upper and lower berths). The ships also have a high percentage of outside cabins, many of which have private verandas. These comfortable ships manage to avoid overwhelming passengers with their sheer size by creating a soft, warm interior, appointed with cozy couches and armchairs; art deco furnishings; light-wood panels; polished metals; and muted coral, blue, and aqua tones.

Cabins and Rates

	Beds	Phone	TV	Sitting Area	Fridge	Tub	Average Per Diem*
Suite	T/Q	●	●	●	●	●	$375/ $566
Outside	T/Q or U/L	●	●	●	●	○	$275/ $328
Inside	T/Q	●	●	●	●	○	$220/ $262

**Higher rates are for the Panama Canal. Lower rates are for the Caribbean. Airfare and port taxes are extra.*

Cabins are pleasantly appointed in contemporary wood and upholstered furnishings with framed prints on the walls. Each has a walk-in closet, a refrigerator, a separate dressing area, and a safe. Terry robes and fresh-fruit baskets are also found in each stateroom. Outside cabins have large picture windows. Most outside cabins on the Aloha and Baja decks (including all suites and minisuites) have private verandas. The view from the F-category outside cabins on the Dolphin Deck is obstructed.

Outlet voltage: 110 AC.

Single supplement: 150%–200% of double-occupancy rate.

Discounts: A third or fourth passenger in a cabin pays half the double-occupancy rate. You get a discount for booking early.

Sports and Fitness **Health club:** Sizable below-decks facility with aerobics room, steam room, sauna, weight machines, stationary bikes, other exercise equipment, massage, beauty parlor.

Recreation: Exercise classes, golf driving, table tennis, scuba and snorkeling lessons (scuba certification available), shuffleboard, skeet shooting, two pools (one with a waterfall, the other with a swim-up bar), two whirlpools, unobstructed jogging track (6 laps = 1 mile).

Facilities **Public rooms:** Nine bars, five entertainment lounges, domed observation lounge, casino, disco, cinema/conference center, card room, library.

Shops: Two-level arcade of boutiques, gift shops, drugstore, hairdresser.

Health care: Two doctors and two nurses on call.

Child care: Children's program with youth counselor year-round.

Services: Laundry service, dry cleaning, photographer, film processing.

Accessibility Ten cabins are accessible to wheelchair users.

MV Island Princess and MV Pacific Princess

Specifications *Type of ship:* Cruise liner
Cruise experience: Semi-formal
Size: 20,000 tons
Cabins: 305
Outside cabins: 77.5%
Passengers: 640
Crew: 350 (international)
Officers: British
Passenger/crew ratio: 1.8 to 1
Year built: 1972/1971

Ship's Log The *Pacific Princess*, star of *The Love Boat* television series, and her twin sister, the *Island Princess*, were among the grandest ships at sea when they set sail in the early 1970s. Dwarfed in size by Princess's newest ships, they nevertheless remain impressive in other ways. They are intimate vessels, ideally suited to the exotic and longer itineraries on which they sail with a crew that has a distinctly familial style.

Unlike the expansive open deck spaces aboard their newer fleetmates, the *Island* and *Pacific* are given to lots of nooks and crannies for private repose. In a short time you'll find some of the perennial hiding spaces—a few yards of deck just behind the bridge with half-a-dozen lounge chairs, a spot near the card room where two cozy chairs are framed by high windows, or the quieter second story of the Carib/Pacific Lounge, with a panoramic view aft through a two-deck window.

Recent $40 million makeovers modernized both ships and updated patterns and fabrics throughout. Color schemes now bathe the public spaces in rich tones of blue and burgundy. One frustrating aspect that was left untouched (and apparently overlooked) is the Princess Theater, which, despite its use for showing films, still has lounge-style seating with groupings of couches and cocktail tables.

Cabins and Rates

	Beds	Phone	TV	Sitting Area	Fridge	Tub	Average Per Diem*
Suite	D/T	●	●	●	●	●	$587
Outside	T	●	●	◐	◐	○	$356
Inside	T	●	●	◐	◐	○	$308

**Rates are for Southeast Asia (Island Princess) or South America/Amazon cruises* (Pacific Princess). *Airfare and port taxes are extra.*

The new cabin decor on both ships features textured and woven fabrics. On the *Island Princess*, it's a blend of soft blues, pinks, and greens; on the *Pacific Princess*, the palette draws from a mix of earth tones and blues. All staterooms are outfitted with a color television, terry robes, and fresh-fruit baskets; deluxe outside cabins and suites also have a refrigerator. No cabins have private balconies. Some cabins on the Promenade Deck look onto a public area.

Outlet voltage: 110 AC.

Single supplement: 160%–200% of double-occupancy rate.

Discounts: A third or fourth passenger in a cabin pays half the double-occupancy rate. You get a discount for booking early.

Sports and Fitness

Health club: Lifecycles, rowing machines, weights, weight machines, saunas, massage.

Recreation: Aerobics and other exercise classes, golf driving, table tennis, shuffleboard, skeet shooting, two pools, unobstructed circuit (18 laps = 1 mile) for jogging.

Facilities

Public rooms: Six bars, four entertainment lounges, casino, disco, cinema, card room, library/writing room.

Shops: Gift shop, beauty salon/barber.

Health care: Doctor and two nurses on call.

Child care: Daytime youth programs with counselors when 15 or more children on board.

Services: Laundry service, dry cleaning, photographer.

Accessibility

Public lavatories and four cabins on each ship are equipped with wide toilet stalls and hand bars to accommodate passengers with mobility problems. All four elevators are accessible.

MV Royal Princess

Specifications

Type of ship: Cruise liner
Cruise experience: Semi-formal
Size: 45,000 tons
Cabins: 600
Outside cabins: 100%
Passengers: 1,200
Crew: 520 (international)
Officers: British
Passenger/crew ratio: 2.4 to 1
Year built: 1984

Ship's Log

Among big ships, the *Royal Princess* is one of only two that offers all outside staterooms (the other is the *Crystal Symphony*). Add to this 2 acres of open deck space forward, aft, and amidships, including a wraparound promenade, and you see why this is one of the most acclaimed cruise liners ever built.

The Horizon Lounge and Bar offers a breathtaking, 360° view of the sea from its position atop the ship. Lovely as it is, the lounge is rarely crowded. Most other public rooms are clustered on the Riviera Deck. The two main showrooms—the circular International Lounge and the plush and frilly cabaret-style Riviera Club—boast excellent acoustics. The Continental dining room has a bright, airy feel, thanks to its pastel color scheme, a touch of art deco brass, and walls of windows to let in the sunlight. Recent upgrades to the ship include a fully rebuilt Lido Cafe and a new pizzeria.

Cabins and Rates

	Beds	Phone	TV	Sitting Area	Fridge	Tub	Average Per Diem*
Suite	Q	●	●	●	●	●	$605
Outside	T/Q	●	●	◐	●	●	$348

**Airfare included. Port taxes are extra.*

Cabins are all outside, and all standard staterooms are the same size. Each is finished in a different wood by category: oak veneers in the penthouses, teak in the suites, mahogany in the minisuites, and teak again in the standard cabins. Penthouses, suites, minisuites, and Aloha Deck outside cabins have private verandas. Even the smallest cabins are well equipped, with details and amenities not found in standard accommodations aboard many other ships, such as double sinks, shower/bathtubs, refrigerators, and large windows. Higher-priced cabins have wall safes, and penthouses have whirlpools. Terry robes and fresh-fruit baskets are found in each stateroom. Categories H, HH, I, J, JJ, and K are outside cabins with partially or entirely obstructed views.

Outlet voltage: 110 AC.

Single supplement: 200% of double-occupancy rate for suites or outside cabins with verandas, 150%–160% for other cabins.

Discounts: A third or fourth passenger in a cabin pays $132–$150 per diem. You get a discount for early booking and for arranging your own airfare.

Sports and Fitness

Health club: Five high-tech stationary bikes, rowing machines, whirlpool; adjacent beauty center with two saunas, two massage rooms, spa treatments.

Recreation: Aerobics and other exercise classes, golf driving, table tennis, pool sports, shuffleboard, skeet shooting, three pools (one for laps, a circular one surrounded by dipping pools, and another wading pool, all on Lido Deck), Jacuzzi, unobstructed circuit (3.5 laps = 1 mile) for jogging.

Facilities

Public rooms: Seven bars, four entertainment lounges, casino, disco, cinema, card room, library, video-game room.

Shops: Gift shop, beauty salon/barber.

Health care: Two doctors and two nurses on call.

Child care: Daytime youth programs with counselors when 15 or more children on board.

Services: Full- and self-service laundry, dry cleaning, photographer, film processing.

Accessibility

Four cabins and all public areas, except the self-service laundry room, are accessible to wheelchair users. Several public lavatories are grab bar–equipped. Raised thresholds leading to outside decks are especially high, but ramps are located at selected entrances.

TSS Sky Princess

Specifications

Type of ship: Cruise liner
Cruise experience: Semi-formal
Size: 46,000 tons
Number of cabins: 600
Outside cabins: 64%
Passengers: 1,200
Crew: 535 (international)
Officers: British
Passenger/crew ratio: 2.2 to 1
Year built: 1984

Ship's Log

Formerly Sitmar's *Fairsky*, the *Sky Princess* underwent a major refurbishment in 1992. A huge showroom—with a tiered floor, a large stage, and new light and sound systems—was installed. In addition to redecorating the entire ship, Princess expanded the shopping area. Three swimming pools are on deck, along with plenty of space for sunning.

Cabins and Rates

	Beds	Phone	TV	Sitting Area	Fridge	Tub	Average Per Diem*
Suite	T/D	●	●	●	●	◐	$587
Outside	T	●	●	○	○	○	$356

Inside	T	●	●	○	○	○	$316

**Rates are for Southeast Asia. Airfare and port taxes are extra.*

Suites have verandas. Many cabins have two upper berths to accommodate third and fourth passengers. Terry robes and fresh-fruit baskets are found in each stateroom.

Outlet voltage: 110 AC.

Single supplement: 160%–200% of double-occupancy rate.

Discounts: A third or fourth passenger in a cabin pays half the double-occupancy rate. You get a discount for booking early.

Sports and Fitness

Health club: Nautilus machines, sit-up board, three Lifecycles, two stationary bikes, ballet barre, sauna, massage room, large whirlpool.

Recreation: Aerobics and other exercise classes, paddle and table tennis, pool games, shuffleboard, skeet shooting, volleyball, three pools (one for children), scuba certification, jogging track (15 laps = 1 mile).

Facilities

Public rooms: Seven bars, five entertainment lounges, casino, disco, card room, library, video-game room.

Shops: Four boutiques/gift shops, beauty salon/barber.

Health care: Doctor and two nurses on call.

Child care: Youth center (open 9 AM–midnight) with separate rooms for teens and younger children (older than six months), games, video games, wide-screen TV, children's pool, sundeck, programs supervised by counselors year-round.

Services: Full- and self-service laundry, dry cleaning, photographer, film processing.

Accessibility

Six cabins and all six elevators are accessible to wheelchair users.

MV Star Princess

Specifications

Type of ship: Megaship
Cruise experience: Semi-formal
Size: 63,500 tons
Number of cabins: 736
Outside cabins: 77.6%
Passengers: 1,494
Crew: 600 (international)
Officers: Italian
Passenger/crew ratio: 2.5 to 1
Year built: 1989

Ship's Log

The *Star Princess*, the first new ship to be built after Sitmar and Princess merged, is striking for its size alone: It has 12 public decks. Princess resisted the temptation to cram in as many cabins and staterooms as possible, and as a result, the ship is extremely spacious. Its centerpiece is the Plaza, a dramatic three-deck-high atrium topped by a dome. Perhaps the most engaging public room is the Windows on the World Lounge, with its 360° view of the sea. A million-dollar collection of contemporary art is placed throughout the ship, both in the public rooms and in individual cabins. Daytime activities revolve around the Pool Deck, where two swimming pools and four whirlpools are connected by a walkway and waterfalls, and passengers can swim to the splash bar.

Cabins and Rates

	Beds	Phone	TV	Sitting Area	Fridge	Tub	Average Per Diem*
Suite	T/Q	●	●	●	●	●	$414
Outside	T/Q	●	●	○	●	○	$250

Inside	T/Q	●	●	○	●	○	$200

**Rates are for the Caribbean. Airfare and port taxes are extra.*

Standard cabins are spacious, with twin beds that convert to queen-size, a built-in safe, minirefrigerators, and remote-control color TVs. Terry robes and fresh-fruit baskets are also found in each stateroom. The suites have separate sitting areas, marble baths, and king-size beds. Outside cabins have large picture windows; the suites and minisuites have verandas with sliding glass doors. Some outside cabins have obstructed views. Most cabins have upper berths to accommodate a third or fourth passenger.

Outlet voltage: 110 AC.

Single supplement: 150%–200% of double-occupancy rate.

Discounts: A third or fourth passenger in a cabin pays half the double-occupancy rate. You get a discount for booking early.

Sports and Fitness

Health club: Nautilus equipment, aerobics area, sauna, steam room, massage, beauty treatments.

Recreation: Exercise classes, shuffleboard, skeet shooting, volleyball, three pools, four whirlpools, scuba certification, jogging track (5 laps = 1 mile).

Facilities

Public rooms: Seven bars, seven lounges, casino, disco, cinema, card room, library.

Shops: Four boutiques/gift shops, beauty salon/barber.

Health care: Two doctors and two nurses on call.

Child care: Youth center (open 9 AM–midnight) for children ages 2 to 17, with games, video games, wide-screen TV, children's pool and sundeck, programs supervised by counselors year-round.

Services: Full- and self-service laundry, dry cleaning, photographer, film processing.

Accessibility

Ten cabins and all nine elevators are accessible to wheelchair users.

MV Sun Princess

Specifications

Type of ship: Megaship
Cruise experience: Semi-formal
Size: 76,500 tons
Number of cabins: 975
Outside cabins: 61.8%
Passengers: 1,950
Crew: 900 (international)
Officers: Italian
Passenger/crew ratio: 2 to 1
Year built: 1973

Ship's Log

When the *Sun Princess* made its debut in December 1995, it was—for the time being—the largest cruise ship afloat. Yet despite its undeniable hugeness, the *Sun* avoids the cumbersome lines and cavernous feeling that accompany many other megaships. Public areas have an intimacy that is unexpected on such a huge vessel. The main pool area, with its hundreds of deck chairs, seems more like a private country club. The ship has two main dining rooms rather than one massive one, and again, the atmosphere is remarkably cozy, with clusters of two to four tables set between dividers of etched glass and arranged on three levels. Adding to the sense of privacy is the decor, which uses generous amounts of burnished woods, leather, and paintings framed in brass.

As the first entry in Princess' new "Grand Class" of ships, the *Sun* is an innovative vessel. On many newer ships, only the more expensive categories of cabins have private verandas, but on the *Sun*, nearly 70% of all outside accommodations have their own balcony. Food service has been expanded to new dimensions as well. The Lido is open 24 hours a day: Continental breakfast begins at 4 in the morning, full breakfast at 6, lunch at 11, and snacks are served from 7:30 in the evening until Continental breakfast begins again. And if that's not enough, there is a wine and caviar bar, pizzeria, patisserie for coffee and fresh pastries, an outdoor hamburger and hot-dog grill, an ice-cream bar, and 24-hour room service.

Because of its size, the *Sun Princess* can offer an enormous variety of activities and entertainment. Various small lounges present different acts, and two large showrooms stage a production every evening. One mounts elaborate performances, while the other serves as a cabaret. An open-air sports deck has courts for volleyball, basketball, badminton, and paddle tennis. A computerized golf center simulates play on many of the world's top golf courses, and the glass-enclosed fitness center surrounds a pool suspended between two decks. The ship's extensive array of facilities extends to younger cruisers as well. Princess has always welcomed children, but on the *Sun*, teens and youths now have their own splash pool, theater, video disco, arcade, and refreshment bar.

Cabins and Rates

	Beds	Phone	TV	Sitting Area	Fridge	Tub	Average Per Diem*
Suite	Q	●	●	●	●	●	$414
Outside	Q/T	●	●	◐	●	○	$285
Inside	Q/T	●	●	○	●	○	$221

**Rates are for the Caribbean. Airfare and port taxes are extra.*

All suites and minisuites and 372 outside cabins have a private balcony. All cabins have refrigerators. Suite and minisuites have two televisions and bathrooms with separate glass-enclosed shower and tub with Jacuzzi jets. Some cabins on the Dolphin Deck have obstructed views. Cabins designed for families have upper berths.

Outlet voltage: 110 AC.

Single supplement: 150%–200% of double-occupancy rate.

Discounts: A third or fourth passenger in a cabin pays half the double-occupancy rate. You get a discount for booking early.

Sports and Fitness

Health club: Top-deck facility with StairMasters, Lifecycles, treadmills, rowing machines, free weights, weight stations, saunas, massage, facial and body treatments.

Recreation: Aerobics and other exercise classes; four adult swimming pools and one children's splash pool; five whirlpool spas; sports deck with volleyball, basketball, badminton, and paddle tennis; computerized golf center; unobstructed circuit for jogging (6 laps = 1 mile).

Facilities

Public rooms: Seven bars and lounges, two showrooms, casino, disco, library, business center with phone, fax, and computers.

Shops: Seven duty-free shops.

Health care: Two doctors and two nurses on call.

Child care: Youth center and programs with counselors offered year-round.

Services: Full- and self-service laundry, dry cleaning, photographer, film processing.

Accessibility The *Sun Princess* is well suited to wheelchair users and has been designed with accessible elevators, wide corridors, and specially equipped public lavatories. Nineteen cabins meet the standards of the Americans with Disabilities Act.

Radisson Seven Seas Cruises

The Fleet MS *Hanseatic*
SSC *Radisson Diamond*
MS *Song of Flower*

An expedition ship, a catamaran, and a cruise yacht: This odd collection of ships couldn't be more different by design, but what they share in common is a similar level of luxury. The *Radisson Diamond* is the largest twin-hull ship ever built for cruising, while the *Hanseatic* claims the title of biggest expedition ship afloat. Both were built by the same Finnish shipyard and have space and passenger-to-crew ratios as good as any ship afloat. All three ships also offer all outside cabins. A fourth ship, the *Paul Gaugin,* was expected to join the line in late 1997.

Ships at a Glance

	Dining Rooms	Bars	Casino	Fitness Center	Pools	Average Per Diem
Hanseatic	1	1	○	●	1	$605
Radisson Diamond	2	4	●	●	1	$521
Song of Flower	1	4	●	●	1	$468

Cruise Experience The *Diamond* and the *Hanseatic* were built to cruise the Caribbean and Antarctica, respectively, while the *Song of Flower* concentrates mainly on Asia and Europe. Each ship delivers a different cruise experience. For that reason, details on dining, activities, entertainment, and service are covered individually under each Ship's Log.

For More Information Radisson Seven Seas Cruises (600 Corporate Dr., Suite 410, Fort Lauderdale, FL 33334, tel. 800/333–3333).

MS Hanseatic

Type of ship: Expedition
Cruise experience: Casual
Size: 9,000 tons
Number of cabins: 94
Outside cabins: 100%
Passengers: 188
Crew: 125 (international)
Officers: European
Passenger/crew ratio: 1.5 to 1
Year built: 1993

Ship's Log The Hanseatic is the world's newest, biggest, and most luxurious expedition ship. It carries all the standard expedition features—a hardened hull for plowing through Antarctic ice and 14 Zodiac landing craft for exploring otherwise inaccessible shores—in a level of comfort unusual for an adventure ship. There's a small fitness center and spa, for instance, with a whirlpool, swimming pool, sauna, and massage therapy. The ship's passenger-to-crew ratio rivals the standards of the cruise world's most expensive ships. Because of its

Chart Symbols. Ships at a Glance. ●: *Fully equipped;* ◐: *Partially equipped;* ○: *Not equipped.* Cabins and Rates. **D:** *Double bed;* **K:** *King-size bed;* **Q:** *Queen-size bed;* **T:** *Twin bed;* **U/L:** *Upper and lower berths;* ●: *All cabins have this facility;* ○: *No cabins have this facility;* ◐: *Some cabins have this facility*

relatively large size, the *Hanseatic* is equipped with a more varied selection of public rooms than most expedition ships. There's a cruise-ship-style lounge for evening entertainment; a full-size lecture hall, which doubles as a cinema; and a top-deck observation lounge with 180° views of the sea. You can always visit the captain on the navigation bridge between the enrichment lectures and Zodiac excursions that are the hallmark of the expedition experience.

The *Hanseatic*'s very high standards of comfort, especially as compared with the earlier generation of expedition ships, attract people who might not otherwise take such a cruise. It also means that the hard-core adventure traveler with special interests will be sharing the experience with more mainstream, general-interest passengers. Increasingly, these passengers are Americans, especially on Antarctica cruises, but at other times the passenger list may be mostly German, as the ship is marketed extensively in Europe as well.

Activities Zodiac explorations are the primary daytime event aboard the *Hanseatic*. In preparation for these shoreside explorations, a team of experts, such as naturalists, marine biologists, geologists, or anthropologists, brief passengers in the Darwin Lounge, a state-of-the-art facility with video and sound systems. The experts then accompany passengers ashore. Hitting the beach in a Zodiac usually means a wet landing, but the *Hanseatic* also carries two cruise ship–style enclosed tenders.

Dining Menus are distinctly European, with an emphasis on central European cooking rather than the Continental cuisine more familiar to American cruise-ship passengers. This means excellent cream soups, very good salads, a game dish every night, and rich desserts—Americans may find the diet somewhat heavy-handed. A "light" menu is always available at dinnertime, though. The food is expertly presented, but portions are generally small by American standards.

The main restaurant is a spacious room, surrounded on three sides by windows. Meals are served in a single, open seating (dinner from 7 to 9:30). Breakfasts and lunches are hot and cold buffets or from a menu, while dinners are served from a menu only. The captain hosts a table several times during the cruise. A jacket and tie is standard attire for the welcome and farewell dinners, but otherwise, dress is "smart casual."

A second restaurant, the informal café, also serves a light breakfast and lunch. Menus are the standard buffets of salads, hot dogs, hamburgers, hot pastas, and soups, but the main dining room is so attractive that meals here become an afterthought. There are outside tables, though, for warm-weather alfresco dining.

Entertainment Cabaret shows, orchestras, and dancing are nighttime staples in the Explorer Lounge. Throughout the day, documentary and feature films are shown in the Darwin Hall, as well as over closed-circuit television in the cabins. A four-piece band plays at afternoon tea and for before- and after-dinner dancing. A resident pianist also performs pre- and post-dinner music in the Observation Lounge and may hold a classical-music evening.

Service and Tipping Service is excellent and the standard of English spoken by the crew is very high. The cabin staff is female, and the dining-room staff is male and female—all young, energetic Germans or northern Europeans. Tips are included in the *Hanseatic*'s cruise fares, but gratuities are allowed for special service. Still, additional tipping is not expected and is never solicited.

Destinations The *Hanseatic* sails from the Arctic to Antarctica, and along both coasts of North and South America. You're not likely to find a more comfortable ship going to these remote destinations. (For seasonal itineraries, *see* Chapter 4.)

Cabins and Rates

	Beds	Phone	TV	Sitting Area	Fridge	Tub	Average Per Diem*
Suite	Q or T	●	●	●	●	●	$935
Outside	Q	●	●	●	●	●	$605

**Rates are for Antarctica. Airfare is extra.*

Standard cabins are unusually spacious for an expedition ship. All are outside with ocean views, and come with a sitting area, marble bathroom, color television/VCR and refrigerator stocked with complimentary nonalcoholic drinks. Private butler service is available for suites and some upper-category double staterooms.

Outlet voltage: 220 AC.

Single supplement: 150%–200% of the double-occupancy rate.

Discounts: A third passenger in a cabin pays 50% of the double-occupancy rate. You get a discount for booking early and for booking back-to-back cruises.

Sports and Fitness

Health club: Top-deck facility with exercise equipment, free weights, sauna, massage, and glass-enclosed whirlpool.

Recreation: Swimming pool.

Facilities

Public rooms: Main lounge with dance floor and bar, observation lounge with bar, library (books and videos), cinema.

Shops: Boutique, beauty salon.

Health care: Doctor and nurse on call.

Child care: Baby-sitting arranged privately with crew member.

Services: Laundry service, dry cleaning, photographer, film processing.

Accessibility

Two cabins are accessible to wheelchair users, as are all elevators and decks except Cinema Deck. Many voyages require Zodiac landings at all or most ports, which may make it difficult for passengers with mobility impairments to go ashore.

SSC Radisson Diamond

Type of ship: Cruise liner
Cruise experience: Semi-formal
Size: 20,000 tons
Number of cabins: 177
Outside cabins: 100%

Passengers: 350
Crew: 192 (international)
Officers: Finnish
Passenger/crew ratio: 1.8 to 1
Year built: 1992

Ship's Log

As wide as an ocean liner but only as long as a yacht, the *Diamond* is the only cruise ship ever to receive a *Popular Mechanics* design and engineering award. The futuristic catamaran resembles a spider perched over the sea. While the twin-hull design actually does make the ship more stable and reduce the chance of getting seasick, the difference in motion takes some getting used to. During a storm there is none of the normal pitch and roll, but stabilizers cause a very slight side-to-side jerking motion—which only becomes an issue if you are wearing high heels and trying to keep your balance. The *Diamond* was specifically built to stage meetings and conventions at sea, so in addition to being one of the most stable cruise ships afloat, it is also especially spacious.

A cruise aboard *Diamond* is pure class all the way, catering to the passenger who has seen many ships and has specific demands of a cruise ship. Impeccable service and attention to detail, combined with some of the most extensive business facilities afloat, give the

Diamond the feel of a seagoing Radisson hotel, the company that handles all the ship's hotel operations. Whether passengers travel on this ship for business or pleasure, the *Diamond* and Radisson ensure that everyone is treated like a guest at a fine luxury resort.

Activities In keeping with the ship's relaxed mood, there are few organized events on board. People gather at their leisure for such activities as dancing lessons, card games, backgammon, and shuffleboard. The *Diamond* also has an extensive book and videotape library. At least once a cruise (weather permitting), water activities are held off the large marina platform, which is built into the stern of the ship and lowers into the water. Passengers can swim in a small netted pool, ride on a Jet Ski, or snorkel.

A number of theme cruises are scheduled each year; the most popular are culinary and literary. The ship's lecture series headlines speakers on a wide range of topics from banking to Broadway musicals. Ashore, the *Diamond* offers some interesting alternatives to the usual shore excursions: In St. Maarten you can race on an "America's Cup" 12-meter sailboat.

Dining Dining aboard the *Diamond* reflects its elegant and exclusive demeanor. International cuisine is served in the Grand Dining Room—one of the prettiest dining rooms afloat—in one open seating, so you dine when and with whomever you want (dinner is served 7:30–10). Wine is complimentary at dinner. There's one formal night per seven-night cruise, with elegant casual attire the norm other evenings—a little more relaxed than on other ships in this price category.

A second dinner option is the intimate gourmet Italian restaurant, also with one seating at 8. Six wonderful courses are served from a fixed menu in a festive atmosphere. Reservations should be made as soon as you board, because the restaurant is very popular.

Breakfast and lunch buffets are served in the Grill (at night this is the Italian restaurant). Early-riser coffee is served daily beginning at 6:30 AM, and afternoon tea is served with rich pastries in the Windows Lounge or the Grill. Room service is available 24 hours a day from an extensive menu; in-room dinners are served complete with linen napery, crystal, china, and flowers.

Entertainment Evening entertainment is generally mellow and consists of cabaret-style shows, a pianist, a small musical combo, and comedians. Partyers can stay as late as they like in the disco and the casino.

Service and Tipping Cabin service is expertly provided by female Austrian, Swiss, and Scandinavian cabin stewardesses; the dining-room staff is mostly female as well. The *Radisson Diamond* has a no-tipping policy.

Destinations The *Diamond* gives passengers a choice of wintertime Caribbean itineraries lasting 3, 4, 7, or 10 days, as well as Panama Canal transits. Summer and fall are spent cruising the Mediterranean. (For seasonal itineraries, *see* Chapter 4.)

Cabins and Rates

	Beds	Phone	TV	Sitting Area	Fridge	Tub	Average Per Diem*
Suite	Q or T	●	●	●	●	●	$521

* *Rates are for the Mediterranean. Airfare and port taxes are extra.*

Cabins are all outside on three upper decks; most have a private balcony, others have a large bay window. None have obstructed views. Soothing mauve, sky-blue, or sea-green fabrics are accented by birch wood, and each cabin has a stocked minibar and refrigerator. (Your initial allotment of drinks is free; refills are provided for a fee.)

Bathrooms are spacious, with marble vanities, tubs, and hair dryers. In-cabin TVs show CNN and feature films. No third or fourth berths are available.

Outlet voltage: 110 AC.

Single supplement: 125% of double-occupancy rate.

Discounts: You get a discount for booking early and for booking back-to-back cruises on selected itineraries.

Sports and Fitness **Health club:** Aerobics studio, weight room, Lifecycles, Lifesteps, Liferowers, Jacuzzi, and body-toning spa with massage and herbal-wrap treatments.

Recreation: Golf driving range with nets, putting green, minigolf; shuffleboard; water sports, including snorkeling, windsurfing, jet skiing, and swimming; jogging track.

Facilities **Public rooms:** Four bars, entertainment lounge/disco, casino, library, conference center and boardroom.

Shops: Boutique, drugstore, beauty salon/barber.

Health care: Doctor and nurse on call.

Child care: None.

Services: Laundry service, photographer, film-developing service, business center with software library, fax, publishing facilities, personal computer hookups.

Accessibility Elevators, public lavatories, and two cabins are accessible to wheelchair users.

MS Song of Flower

Type of ship: Cruise yacht
Cruise experience: Semi-formal
Size: 8,282 tons
Number of cabins: 100
Outside cabins: 100%

Passengers: 172
Crew: 144 (international)
Officers: Norwegian
Passenger/crew ratio: 1.2 to 1
Year built: 1986

Ship's Log Like its fleetmates, the *Song of Flower* is designed to appeal to upscale cruisers. Although the ship is luxurious, it is also quite small, with limited public space. The main purpose of this vessel is to provide a stylish home base for visiting exotic ports of call.

Activities There are few of the usual cruise games and demonstrations on the *Song of Flower*'s daily schedule. Other than exploring in port, the main activities are lectures given by an expert speaker who accompanies every cruise. Topics may include art, history, and local culture.

Dining The Galaxy Dining Room accommodates all passengers in one seating, with dinner served from 7 to 9:30. An outdoor café and grill on the Sun Deck serves buffet breakfast and lunch, but cook-to-order entrées are available, too. Room service is available 24 hours a day.

Entertainment Entertainment is low-key. There are nightly cabaret shows, a five-piece orchestra for dancing, a small disco, and a pianist, who plays during afternoon tea and dinner. The ship's library stocks 2,000 books and 400 videos for use on in-cabin VCRs.

Service and Tipping Scandinavian stewardesses keep staterooms stocked with fresh flowers and fruit. All beverages, alcoholic and otherwise, are complimentary throughout the ship—in the bars, dining room, and suites. The *Song of Flower* has a no-tipping policy.

Destinations *Song of Flower* sails to Europe, India, Arabia and the Far East. (For seasonal itineraries, *see* Chapter 4.)

Cabins and Rates

	Beds	Phone	TV	Sitting Area	Fridge	Tub	Average Per Diem*
Suite	Q or T	●	●	●	●	●	$735
Outside	Q or T	●	●	●	●	◐	$468

**Airfare and port taxes are extra.*

Cabins are all outside. Each is equipped with a TV/VCR, hair dryer, and stocked minibar. Two-room suites have private balconies.

Outlet voltage: 110/220 AC.

Single supplement: 125% of double-occupancy rate.

Discounts: You get a discount for booking early and for booking back-to-back cruises on selected itineraries.

Sports and Fitness

Health club: Lifecycles, StairMaster, free weights, Jacuzzi, sauna, and massage.

Recreation: Swimming pool; Windsurfers and snorkeling equipment available when in port.

Facilities

Public rooms: Four bars, observation lounge, showroom, casino, disco, library.

Shops: Gift shop, beauty salon/barber.

Health care: Doctor and nurse on call.

Child care: None.

Services: Laundry and dry-cleaning service, photographer, business center, concierge.

Accessibility

Elevators, public lavatories, and two cabins are accessible to wheelchair users.

Renaissance Cruises

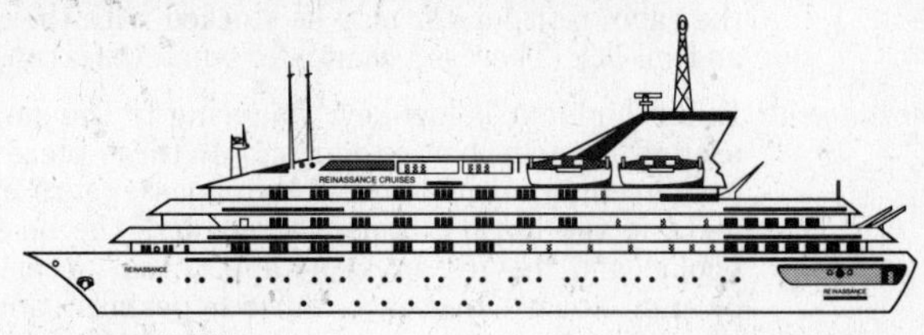

The Fleet *Renaissance I–IV*
Renaissance V–VIII

Renaissance's cruising yachts are incredibly tiny by today's cruise-ship standards—they carry about as many passengers as a big ship's tenders. But what they lack in size and facilities they make up for with handsome surroundings and some of the lowest rates in the luxury small-ship category.

Ship at a Glance

	Dining Rooms	Bars	Casino	Fitness Center	Pools	Average Per Diem
Renaissance III–VIII	1	1	◐	◐	1	$326

Cruise Experience Though outwardly similar to Cunard's *Sea Goddess*, the lifestyle aboard these Renaissance yachts places less emphasis on elegance. Although men dress for dinner most nights, it's not quite the tuxedo crowd found aboard the line's pricier competitors. Culture, not couture, accounts for Renaissance's appeal. There are, however, certain similarities between Renaissance and such lines as Seabourn or Silversea. All accommodations are outside suites, and meals are served in a single, open seating.

Passengers are typically intellectual, culturally minded individuals. They are experienced cruisers, in their late sixties or early seventies, who want to learn about the world as they travel in supreme comfort that is priced less than other luxury yachts. Many are repeat passengers who move from ship to ship on various cruises around the world. A number of special-interest tour operators, such as the Smithsonian Institution, charter Renaissance vessels for educational tours.

Activities Aside from an occasional trivia contest, don't look for pool games or other traditional cruise pastimes. Renaissance passengers prefer more introspective activities, such as enjoying a reading selection from the ship's library or viewing a first-run video on their in-suite VCR.

Dining The cuisine is international, with a focus on nouvelle light dishes with fresh ingredients. Cooking has its exceptional moments, but otherwise, Renaissance serves standard cruise fare in a better-than-average way. The dining-room staff is particularly adept at remembering passengers' likes and dislikes. Meals in the restaurant are at a single open seating (dinner at 7:30). Men are expected to wear a jacket and tie to dinner. The extensive wine cellar is moderately priced. There is no smoking in the dining room. Early-morning coffee, breakfast, and lunch are available on deck, weather permit-

Chart Symbols. Ships at a Glance. ●: *Fully equipped;* ◐: *Partially equipped;* ○: *Not equipped.* Cabins and Rates. **D:** *Double bed;* **K:** *King-size bed;* **Q:** *Queen-size bed;* **T:** *Twin bed;* **U/L:** *Upper and lower berths;* ●: *All cabins have this facility;* ○: *No cabins have this facility;* ◐: *Some cabins have this facility*

ting. Room service from a limited menu begins at 7 AM and ends at 11 PM. A questionnaire is mailed to passengers before their trip so that the cabin refrigerator may be stocked with their favorite beverages and snacks. (There is a charge for whatever is consumed.)

Entertainment Entertainment is low-key: wagering in the small casino, relaxing around the piano bar, or dancing to a three-piece band that performs each evening in the lounge. Many passengers find their entertainment in the library, well stocked with the best-sellers, reference books, and movies on videotape. Local entertainers are usually brought aboard once each cruise to perform, and toward the end of the cruise, passengers and crew join together for a talent show that for many is the highlight of their vacation.

Service and Tipping Service is elegant, unobtrusive, and omnipresent, though a bit short of flawless. Tip the stewardess $3 per passenger per diem, the dining-room staff $5 (dining-room tips are pooled). A 15% gratuity is automatically added to the bar bill. All tips may be charged to your shipboard account, if you'd rather not use cash.

Destinations Renaissance sails to off-the-beaten-track destinations the world over. (For seasonal itineraries, *see* Chapter 4.)

For More Information Renaissance Cruises (1800 Eller Dr., Suite 300, Box 350307, Fort Lauderdale, FL 33335, tel. 800/525–2450).

Renaissance III–IV and Renaissance V–VIII

Specifications

Type of ship: Cruise yacht
Cruise experience: Semi-formal
Size: 4,077 tons/4,280 tons
Number of cabins: 50/57
Outside cabins: 100%
Passengers: 100/114
Crew: 67/72 (European)
Officers: Italian
Passenger/crew ratio: 1.6 to 1
Year built: 1990–1992

Ship's Log The atmosphere aboard these ships is refined and warm, and (because the ships are so small) friendly—like a private club. By the end of your cruise, you'll probably have met all your fellow passengers. The decor adds to the yachtlike ambience. You'll find polished teak, marble, and tasteful modern art.

Cabins and Rates

	Beds	Phone	TV	Sitting Area	Fridge	Tub	Average Per Diem*
Suite	T/Q	●	●	●	●	○	$326

**Rates are for the Greek Islands and include airfare. Port taxes are extra.*

Every cabin on a Renaissance ship is an outside suite, but cabins come in eight different categories. All are large compared with those on other small upscale cruise ships and are appointed in dark woods and gleaming brass. Bathrooms have teak floors and built-in hair dryers; none have bathtubs, however—an unusual omission for this type of ship. Beds can be configured as either twins or queen size. All cabins have VCRs, refrigerators, and a lockable drawer.

Outlet voltage: 110 AC.

Single supplement: Single-occupancy cabins and guaranteed-share rates are available at no surcharge.

Discounts: A third or fourth passenger in a cabin pays reduced per diems.

Sports and Fitness

Health club: Massage, sauna.

Recreation: Zodiacs, Sailfish, snorkeling, pool, whirlpool, unobstructed circuits for jogging.

Facilities **Public rooms:** Piano bar, lounge, small casino, library.

Shops: Gift shop, hairdresser.

Health care: Doctor on call.

Child care: None.

Services: Laundry service.

Accessibility There are ledges at the entrance to cabin bathrooms and at the doors that lead from the outer decks to the inside of the ship.

Royal Caribbean Cruise Line

Sovereign of the Seas

The Fleet MS *Grandeur of the Seas*
MS *Legend of the Seas*
MS *Majesty of the Seas*
MS *Monarch of the Seas*
MS *Nordic Empress*
MS *Song of America*
MS *Song of Norway*
MS *Sovereign of the Seas*
MS *Splendour of the Seas*
MS *Sun Viking*
MS *Viking Serenade*

Imagine if they took the Mall of America and sent it to sea. Then you have a pretty good idea of what Royal Caribbean's huge megaships are all about. These giant vessels are indoor/outdoor wonders, with atrium lobbies, shopping arcades, elaborate spas, and expansive sundecks. Two RCCL ships have 18-hole miniature-golf courses; another vessel has two movie theaters. And as the year 2000 approaches, these mammoth ships are fast replacing the smaller vessels in Royal Caribbean's fleet. RCCL is currently engaged in the industry's most ambitious shipbuilding program, making cruising's biggest fleet even bigger. Scheduled to debut in the coming months and years are the *Rhapsody of the Seas* (April 1997), *Enchanted Seas* (September 1997), and *Vision of the Seas* (1998).

Ships at a Glance

	Dining Rooms	Bars	Casino	Fitness Center	Pools	Average Per Diem
Grandeur of the Seas	1	8	●	●	2	$285
Legend of the Seas *Splendour of the Seas*	1	7	●	●	2	$309 $292
Majesty of the Seas *Monarch of the Seas*	2	8	●	●	2	$271 $285
Nordic Empress	1	5	●	●	1	$310
Song of Norway	1	4	●	●	1	$254
Song of America	1	6	●	●	2	$278
Sovereign of the Seas	2	8	●	●	2	$266
Sun Viking	1	5	●	●	1	$264
Viking Serenade	2	4	●	●	1	$293

Cruise Experience RCCL is one of the best-run and most popular cruise lines. While the fleet comprises ships both big and small, the company's philosophy

Chart Symbols. Ships at a Glance. **●:** *Fully equipped;* **◐:** *Partially equipped;* **○:** *Not equipped.* Cabins and Rates. **D:** *Double bed;* **K:** *King-size bed;* **Q:** *Queen-size bed;* **T:** *Twin bed;* **U/L:** *Upper and lower berths;* **●:** *All cabins have this facility;* **○:** *No cabins have this facility;* **◐:** *Some cabins have this facility*

remains consistent: Offer every imaginable activity in a resortlike atmosphere between port calls at a variety of destinations. RCCL draws customers from every age group and economic bracket, all lured by the prospect of a cruise experience that is well executed in every respect.

Activities Life on board is similar to that on the party ships run by Carnival, but slightly more sophisticated and conservative. Among the many activities offered are cash bingo (plus free poolside bingo for prizes), board and card games, arts and crafts, pool games, dance classes, golf driving and putting, and "horse racing." Following current fitness trends, the ships also feature numerous exercise activities and well-equipped gyms. Most Caribbean cruises have daylong beach parties at Labadee, Haiti, or CocoCay, a private Bahamian island. The line's Golf Ahoy program includes greens time at private courses in Florida, the Caribbean, Bermuda, the Bahamas, and Baja Mexico.

Dining Food is above-average Continental fare, served at two assigned seatings per meal (dinner at 6:15 and 8:30). Two formal evenings are held on each seven-day cruise, one on three- and four-day cruises. The line's *Monarch* and *Majesty* sisters have two dining rooms—the closest you get to intimate aboard these huge vessels. Health-conscious eaters or those just watching their diet can order menu selections that conform to American Heart Association guidelines, but RCCL is not equipped to handle special dietary requests, other than providing an extensive vegetarian menu and children's dishes at all meals.

The Lido-style indoor-outdoor café serves early-morning coffee, a buffet breakfast, and lunch. Other food service includes afternoon tea (with a make-your-own sundae bar), a midnight buffet, and late-night sandwich service in the lounges. Room service is available 24 hours from a limited menu. In-cabin multicourse dinners can be ordered from a selection of dishes off the evening's dining-room menu.

Entertainment This is one of RCCL's strong suits. The company follows the established formula for cruise-ship entertainment, but with a dash of pizzazz and professionalism. Nightly variety shows, late-night comedy and solo cabaret acts, steel-drum combos, passenger talent shows, and theme parties are staged on each cruise.

Service and Tipping The crew is generally enthusiastic and personable, although service can be slow—not surprising given the number of passengers that must be served on the larger ships. Tip the room steward and the waiter each $3 per passenger per diem, the busboy $1.50; the headwaiter gets $2.50 per passenger per cruise (for excellent service only). Tips for bar staff should be given at the time of service.

Destinations Royal Caribbean still calls its namesake home, but the line also sails to Alaska, Asia, Bermuda, Europe, Hawaii, Mexico, and the Panama Canal. (For seasonal itineraries, *see* Chapter 3.)

For More Information Royal Caribbean Cruise Line (1050 Caribbean Way, Miami, FL 33132, tel. 305/539–6000).

MS Grandeur of the Seas

Specifications

Type of ship: Megaship
Cruise experience: Casual
Size: 74,000 tons
Number of cabins: 975
Outside cabins: 58%
Passengers: 1,950
Crew: 760 (international)
Officers: International
Passenger/crew ratio: 2.5 to 1
Year built: 1996

Ship's Log The *Grandeur of the Seas* was scheduled to enter service in December 1996. At press time, a few differences between the *Grandeur* (which represents RCCL's third generation of megaships) and previous RCCL big boats were apparent. Fifty feet longer than the *Legend of the Seas* and *Splendour of the Seas*, the *Grandeur* will have a larger casino, a two-level health club, and a balconied showroom (rather than amphitheater seating), but no miniature-golf course. The ship is designed to be fast, which the line says will allow the vessel to spend four full days in port during its weeklong Caribbean itineraries. Of course, it will have RCCL's signature design features, including a seven-story Centrum atrium, a Viking Crown observation lounge, and an array of public rooms and other facilities.

Cabins and Rates

	Beds	Phone	TV	Sitting Area	Fridge	Tub	Average Per Diem*
Suite	T/Q	●	●	●	●	●	$392
Outside	T/Q	●	●	●	○	○	$285
Inside	T/Q	●	●	●	○	○	$242

**Rates are for the Caribbean. Airfare and port taxes are extra.*

The *Grandeur*, like the earlier *Legend* and *Splendour*, will have relatively large cabins and more balconies than RCCL's previous megaships. Of the 975 total cabins aboard, 212 have private verandas. The ship also will have specially designed family suites with separate bedrooms for parents and children.

Outlet voltage: 110/220 AC.

Single supplement: 150% of double-occupancy rate; however, less expensive singles are available if you are willing to wait until embarkation time for your cabin assignment.

Discounts: A third or fourth passenger in a cabin pays reduced per diems. You get a discount for booking early.

Sports and Fitness

Health club: Two-level spa with Lifecycles, Lifesteps, exercise equipment, Jacuzzis, sauna, and massage.

Recreation: Two pools, shuffleboard, table tennis, unobstructed circuit for jogging.

Facilities

Public rooms: Eight bars, three entertainment lounges, casino, disco, library, card room, video-game room, conference center.

Shops: Gift shop and boutiques, beauty salon/barber.

Health care: Doctor and three nurses on call.

Child care: Playroom; teen center; youth counselors, children's programs in three age groups year-round; baby-sitting arranged privately with crew member; cribs available but must be requested at time of booking.

Services: Laundry service, dry cleaning, photographer.

Accessibility

Fourteen staterooms will be designed to meet the standards of the Americans with Disabilities Act. Elevators, extra-wide corridors, and public lavatories are also designed to be accessible to wheelchair users. Crew members will carry passengers and their wheelchairs onto the ship's tenders if conditions permit.

MS Legend of the Seas and MS Splendour of the Seas

Specifications

Type of ship: Megaship
Cruise experience: Casual
Size: 69,130 tons
Number of cabins: 902/900
Outside cabins: 65%
Passengers: 1,804/1,800
Crew: 732 (international)
Officers: International
Passenger/crew ratio: 2.4 to 1
Year built: 1995/1996

Ship's Log These may not be the biggest ships afloat, but they are state of the art in every other respect. Aboard the *Legend* and *Splendour* you'll find everything one would expect on a cruise ship and more: There's a indoor/outdoor spa reminiscent of a Roman bath, and the cruise world's first 18-hole miniature-golf courses, landscaped to imitate real links with greens, sand traps, and water hazards. The Solarium, an indoor-outdoor public space set around the pool, uses a new design that increases the amount of glass in the retractable roof and minimizes the need for steel supports. The Solarium's Roman-inspired decor uses lightweight plastics and plaster to simulate a setting of marble and stone. Each ship also has a stargazing platform on the highest forward deck.

The dining rooms aboard the *Legend* and *Splendour* are two-level extravaganzas, flanked on either side by 20-foot walls of glass. In the center, a revolving platform supports a grand piano. A grand staircase connects the upper and lower dining levels. Main showrooms span two decks as well, but rather than a balconied design, there is a single, sloping, amphitheater-style floor. At the stage, a real orchestra pit can be raised and lowered. Unlike many other showrooms, passengers sit in real theater seats rather than in groupings of lounge chairs and couches.

Cabins and Rates

	Beds	Phone	TV	Sitting Area	Fridge	Tub	Average Per Diem*
Suite	T/Q	●	●	●	●	●	$499/ $435
Outside	T/Q	●	●	●	○	○	$309/ $292
Inside	T/Q	●	●	●	○	○	$281/ $242

**Airfare included. Port taxes are extra.*

The *Legend* and *Splendour* have larger cabins than RCCL's earlier megaships and more have balconies (231 compared with 60). All cabins have a sitting area—even inside cabins—and are appointed in pretty pastels, with brass accents and wood moldings. Many have upper berths for a third or fourth person in a cabin; this is good for families. Bathrooms lack hair dryers, an odd omission on a ship otherwise so well equipped. The Royal Suite, largest on the ship, has a bedroom, a dining room, and a living room with a baby grand piano. Other suites have separate sleeping and living quarters, too, but no piano. Standard equipment does include refrigerators, bars, and real bathtubs.

Outlet voltage: 110/220 AC.

Single supplement: 150% of double-occupancy rate; however, less expensive singles can be had if you're willing to wait until embarkation time for your cabin assignment.

Discounts: A third or fourth passenger in a cabin pays reduced per diems. You get a discount for booking early.

Sports and Fitness **Health club:** Rowing machines, treadmills, stationary bikes, massage, men's and women's saunas, outdoor whirlpools.

Recreation: Aerobics and fitness program, miniature golf, table tennis, shuffleboard, skeet shooting, snorkeling lessons, two pools, jogging track.

Facilities **Public rooms:** Seven bars, four entertainment lounges, casino, disco, theater, card room, library, video-game room.

Shops: Five boutiques and gift shops, beauty salon/barber.

Health care: Two doctors and three nurses on call.

Child care: Teen center, children's playroom, year-round supervised youth programs in three age groups, baby-sitting privately arranged with crew member, cribs available but must be requested at time of booking. Two family cabins with a parent's bedroom, children's bedroom, two bathrooms, living area, and private balcony.

Services: Laundry service, dry cleaning, photographer, film processing.

Accessibility These ships are well suited to wheelchair users, with accessible elevators, wide corridors, and specially equipped public lavatories. Seventeen cabins are designed for passengers with mobility problems. Crew members will carry passengers and their wheelchairs onto the tenders if conditions permit.

MS Majesty of the Seas and MS Monarch of the Seas

Specifications

Type of ship: Megaship
Cruise experience: Casual
Size: 73,941 tons
Number of cabins: 1,177
Outside cabins: 63%
Passengers: 2,354
Crew: 822 (international)
Officers: Norwegian
Passenger/crew ratio: 2.8 to 1
Year built: 1992/1991

Ship's Log *Majesty of the Seas* and *Monarch of the Seas*, identical sister ships, are two of the largest vessels built specifically for cruising. Each is as tall as the Statue of Liberty and three football fields long. The glass-enclosed Viking Crown Lounge is 14 stories above sea level. Given such enormous dimensions, these ships are often described in superlatives. Their immense size, however, also means that you can spend seven days on board and never feel that you're really at sea. Lines, too, can be long, and the service, although efficient, sometimes lacks a personal touch. Nevertheless, these are excellent ships for first-time passengers because they have everything a cruise was ever meant to have.

The heart of each ship is a dramatic five-story atrium accented with brass railings and curving stairways as well as signature glass elevators. An arcade with 10 shops sells everything from fur coats to jewelry. During mealtimes and in the afternoon, passengers are serenaded with music. The dining room serves a different international menu each evening; waiters dress accordingly, and musicians stroll among the tables playing music to match the cuisine.

Cabins and Rates

	Beds	Phone	TV	Sitting Area	Fridge	Tub	Average Per Diem*
Suite	T/Q	●	●	●	◐	●	$378/ $392
Outside	T/Q	●	●	◐	○	◐	$271/ $285
Inside	T/Q	●	●	○	○	○	$228/ $242

* *Rates are for the Caribbean. Higher rates are for the Monarch. Lower rates are for the Majesty. Airfare and port taxes are extra.*

Standard cabins on the *Majesty* and *Monarch* are appointed in either nautical blues or shades of pink. Cabins on the Promenade Deck look onto a public area. Concierge service is provided for passengers in suites. Many cabins have one or two upper berths in addition to beds. In-cabin TVs show CNN broadcasts.

Outlet voltage: 110/220 AC.

Single supplement: 150% of double-occupancy rate; however, less expensive singles can be had if you're willing to wait until embarkation time for your cabin assignment.

Discounts: A third or fourth passenger in a cabin pays reduced per diems. You get a discount for booking early.

Sports and Fitness

Health club: Rowing machines, treadmills, stationary bikes, massage, men's and women's saunas, outdoor whirlpool.

Recreation: Aerobics and fitness program, basketball, table tennis, shuffleboard, skeet shooting, snorkeling lessons, two pools, unobstructed circuits for jogging.

Facilities

Public rooms: Eight bars, seven entertainment lounges, casino, disco, cinema, card room, library, video-game room.

Shops: Ten boutiques and gift shops, beauty salon/barber.

Health care: Two doctors and three nurses on call.

Child care: Playroom, teen centers; youth counselors, children's programs in three age groups year-round, baby-sitting privately arranged with crew member, cribs available but must be requested at time of booking. Each ship has a family cabin (No. 1549) with a parent's bedroom, children's bedroom, two bathrooms, living area, and private balcony.

Services: Laundry service, dry cleaning, photographer, film processing.

Accessibility

These ships are well suited to wheelchair users, with 18 accessible elevators, wide corridors, and specially equipped public lavatories. Four cabins, two inside and two outside, are designed for passengers with mobility problems. Crew members will carry passengers and their wheelchairs onto the ship's tenders if conditions permit; CocoCay is all sand, however, which makes moving about in a wheelchair difficult.

MS Nordic Empress

Specifications

Type of ship: Cruise liner
Cruise experience: Casual
Size: 48,563 tons
Number of cabins: 800
Outside cabins: 60%
Passengers: 1,600
Crew: 671 (international)
Officers: International
Passenger/crew ratio: 2.3 to 1
Year built: 1990

Ship's Log

The *Nordic Empress*—a distinctive-looking ship with huge rear bay windows—was specifically designed for the three- and four-day cruise market. Much thought was put into making it easy for passengers to learn their way about the ship on such a short voyage. The result includes the innovative idea of a single main corridor running down only one side of the ship, on the decks where the public rooms are located.

The interior, filled with large and festive public rooms, is a glittering combination of art deco and futuristic designs. At the center of the ship is an incredible nine-story atrium, which dazzles with light, glass, chrome, and even cascading waterfalls. Vying for attention is cruising's only triple-level casino and a spacious double-decker dining room with a sensational view of the sea. The commodious showroom and the disco also rise two decks. Because of the stern windows, the *Empress*'s Windjammer Café is forward rather than aft, where most Lidos are traditionally situated. The unusually configured and decorated Sun Deck is more like a private club, with its sail-like canopies, gazebos, and fountains.

Cabins and Rates

	Beds	Phone	TV	Sitting Area	Fridge	Tub	Average Per Diem*
Suite	T/Q	●	●	●	●	●	$483
Outside	T/Q	●	●	○	○	◐	$310
Inside	T/Q	●	●	○	○	○	$233

* *Rates are for three-night Caribbean cruises. Airfare and port taxes are extra.*

Cabins are average in size but have spacious closets. Interiors are in Scandinavian blond woods and white trim with light pastels and contemporary furnishings. Bathrooms are bright, compact, and intelligently laid out. In-cabin TVs show CNN broadcasts. Some cabins are not well insulated against noise. Views from some cabins on the Mariner Deck are obstructed by lifeboats. Suites have private verandas.

Outlet voltage: 110/220 AC.

Single supplement: 150% of double-occupancy rate; however, less expensive singles can be had if you're willing to wait until embarkation time for your cabin assignment.

Discounts: A third or fourth passenger in a cabin pays reduced per diems. You get a discount for booking early.

Sports and Fitness

Health club: Gym with aerobics area, rowing machine, stationary bicycles, free weights, sauna, steam room, and massage.

Recreation: Aerobics and other exercise classes, skeet shooting, table tennis, shuffleboard, pool, children's pool, four whirlpools, unobstructed circuit (5 laps = 1 mile) for jogging.

Facilities

Public rooms: Five bars, three entertainment lounges, casino, disco, video-game room, conference center.

Shops: Gift shop, beauty salon/barber.

Health care: Doctor and two nurses on call.

Child care: Kid/Teen Center playroom on Sun Deck has supervised programs in three age groups year-round; baby-sitting arranged privately with crew member; cribs available but must be requested at time of booking.

Services: Laundry service, photographer.

Accessibility

The *Nordic Empress* is well suited to wheelchair users, although official company policy requires that an able-bodied traveling companion accompany wheelchair users. Four cabins are accessible, with wide doors, level floors, and oversize bathrooms with rails. Most elevators accommodate standard-size wheelchairs. Crew members will carry passengers and their wheelchairs onto the ship's tenders if conditions permit.

MS Song of America

Specifications

Type of ship: Cruise liner
Cruise experience: Casual
Size: 37,584 tons
Number of cabins: 701
Outside cabins: 57%
Passengers: 1,402
Crew: 535 (international)
Officers: Norwegian
Passenger/crew ratio: 2.6 to 1
Year built: 1982

Ship's Log

The *Song of America* is unusually handsome. Despite its size, it looks more like a yacht than a cruise ship, though its width gives it space and stability that a yacht could never manage. Plentiful chrome, mirrors, and overhead lights give the ship a flashy look, but the overall effect is clean, crisp, and airy. A refurbishment finished in 1994 ensured that the *Song of America* kept its youthful appearance.

Cabins and Rates

	Beds	Phone	TV	Sitting Area	Fridge	Tub	Average Per Diem*
Suite	T or T/Q	●	●	●	●	●	$371
Outside	T or T/Q	●	●	○	○	○	$278
Inside	T or T/Q	●	●	○	○	○	$235

**Rates are for the Caribbean. Airfare and port taxes are extra.*

Standard outside cabins are done in a soft blue; inside cabins are finished in peach. In-cabin TVs show CNN broadcasts. Suites on the Promenade Deck look onto a public area.

Outlet voltage: 110/220 AC.

Single supplement: 150% of double-occupancy rate; however, less expensive singles are available if you are willing to wait until embarkation time for your cabin assignment.

Discounts: A third or fourth passenger in a cabin pays reduced per diems. You get a discount for booking early.

Sports and Fitness

Health club: Rowing machines, treadmills, stationary bikes, massage, men's and women's saunas.

Recreation: Aerobics, table tennis, ring toss, snorkeling lessons, shuffleboard, skeet shooting, two pools, unobstructed circuits for jogging.

Facilities

Public rooms: Six bars, four entertainment lounges, casino, disco, cinema, card room.

Shops: Gift shop, drugstore, beauty salon/barber.

Health care: Doctor and two nurses on call.

Child care: Youth counselors, children's programs in three age groups during holidays and in summer, baby-sitting arranged privately with crew member, cribs available but must be requested at time of booking.

Services: Laundry service, dry cleaning, photographer, film processing.

Accessibility

Accessibility aboard this ship is limited. Doorways have lips, and public bathrooms are not specially equipped. Crew members will carry passengers and their wheelchairs onto the ship's tenders if conditions permit.

MS Song of Norway

Specifications

Type of ship: Cruise liner
Cruise experience: Casual
Size: 22,945 tons
Number of cabins: 502
Outside cabins: 65.2%
Passengers: 1,004
Crew: 423 (international)
Officers: Norwegian
Passenger/crew ratio: 2.4 to 1
Year built: 1970

Ship's Log

This is a historic if unheralded ship. The *Song of Norway* was the first ship of fledgling Royal Caribbean Cruise Line when it was launched in 1970. Eight years later, it became one of the first cruise ships to be split and stretched. In what later became a common procedure, the ship was cut in two, fitted with a new midsection, and then reassembled. The lengthening increased passenger capacity by 300 and added new deck space and public rooms. As a result, the *Song of Norway* has a superb Sun Deck with an unusually large pool for swimming laps. The lobby, while not the soaring atriums of later RCCL ships, is handsomely accented in wood paneling and marble.

Cabins and Rates

	Beds	Phone	TV	Sitting Area	Fridge	Tub	Average Per Diem*
Suite	D or T/Q	●	●	●	●	●	$375
Outside	D or T/Q	●	○	○	○	○	$254
Inside	T	●	○	○	○		$230

**Rates are for the Caribbean. Airfare and port taxes are extra.*

Decorative touches in standard cabins include brass-accented wall sconces. Cabins on the Promenade Deck look onto a public area.

Outlet voltage: 110 AC.

Single supplement: 150% of double-occupancy rate; however, less expensive singles are available if you are willing to wait until embarkation time for your cabin assignment.

Discounts: A third or fourth passenger in a cabin pays reduced per diems. You get a discount for booking early.

Sports and Fitness

Health club: Stationary bikes, rowing machines, treadmills, separate men's and women's saunas and massage rooms.

Recreation: Aerobics, basketball, dancercise, table tennis, shuffleboard, skeet shooting, yoga, snorkeling lessons, pool, unobstructed circuit for jogging.

Facilities

Public rooms: Four bars, three entertainment lounges, casino, disco.

Shops: Gift shop, beauty salon/barber.

Child care: Youth counselors, children's programs in three age groups during holidays or in summer, baby-sitting arranged privately with crew member, cribs available but must be requested at time of booking.

Health care: Doctor and two nurses on call.

Services: Laundry service, dry cleaning, photographer, film processing.

Accessibility

Accessibility aboard these ships is limited. The Viking Crown Lounge is inaccessible to wheelchair users. Doorways throughout the ship have lips, and public bathrooms are not specially equipped. Crew members will carry passengers and their wheelchairs onto the ship's tenders if conditions permit.

MS Sovereign of the Seas

Specifications

Type of ship: Megaship
Cruise experience: Casual
Size: 73,192 tons
Number of cabins: 1,138
Outside cabins: 63%

Passengers: 2,276
Crew: 808 (international)
Officers: Norwegian
Passenger/crew ratio: 2.8 to 1
Year built: 1988

Ship's Log

It seems like decades ago, but when the brand-new *Sovereign of the Seas* sailed into the Port of Miami in 1988, it dwarfed the ships around it. The *Sovereign* was the first of RCCL's ships to have an atrium, which the line called "The Centrum." An architectural tour de force, this five-deck lobby featured a dazzling display of glass elevators, curving stairways, and boutiques for shopping. The Viking

Crown Lounge, a standard on every RCCL ship, was perched an amazing 14 stories above sea level.

It's still big by today's standards, but no longer the giant it once seemed, as other ships have surpassed the *Sovereign* in size (with even bigger vessels yet to come). Still, the *Sovereign* was definitely a trendsetter. It established the standards for big-ship design, and ushered in some of the facilities that are now commonplace.

Cabins and Rates

	Beds	Phone	TV	Sitting Area	Fridge	Tub	Average Per Diem*
Suite	T or T/Q	●	●	●	◐	●	$450
Outside	T or T/Q	●	●	◐	○	◐	$266
Inside	T or T/Q	●	●	○	○	○	$200

**Airfare included. Port taxes are extra.*

Cabins on the *Sovereign* are decorated in shades of nautical blues and pink. Cabins on the Promenade Deck look onto a public area. Many cabins have one or two upper berths in addition to beds. Concierge service is provided for passengers in suites.

Outlet voltage: 110/220 AC.

Single supplement: 150% of double-occupancy rate; however, less expensive singles are available if you are willing to wait until embarkation time for your cabin assignment.

Discounts: A third or fourth passenger in a cabin pays reduced per diems. You get a discount for booking early.

Sports and Fitness

Health club: Rowing machines, stationary bikes, treadmills, sauna, massage, outdoor whirlpool.

Recreation: Aerobics and other exercise classes, table tennis, shuffleboard, skeet shooting, basketball, snorkeling lessons, two pools, unobstructed circuit (8 laps = 1 mile) for jogging.

Facilities

Public rooms: Eight bars, seven entertainment lounges, casino, disco, two cinemas, card room, library, video-game room.

Shops: Ten boutiques and gift shops, beauty salon/barber.

Health care: Doctor and three nurses on call.

Child care: Playroom; youth counselors, children's programs in three age groups year-round, baby-sitting arranged privately with crew member, cribs available but must be requested at time of booking.

Services: Laundry service, dry cleaning, photographer, film processing.

Accessibility

The *Sovereign* doesn't have any cabins specifically equipped for wheelchair users, but 10 cabins have extra-wide doors. Crew members will carry passengers and their wheelchairs onto the ship's tenders if conditions permit.

MS Sun Viking

Specifications

Type of ship: Cruise liner
Cruise experience: Casual
Size: 18,455 tons
Number of cabins: 357
Outside cabins: 68.9%

Passengers: 714
Crew: 341 (international)
Officers: Norwegian
Passenger/crew ratio: 2.1 to 1
Year built: 1972

Ship's Log

The *Sun Viking* is RCCL's smallest ship and, in a way, its most exclusive. The *Sun Viking*'s Asian itineraries are among RCCL's longest and most expensive sailings, so they attract an older and more affluent crowd. Exotic destinations are only one reason why passengers may choose to book this vessel rather than one of RCCL's megaships. Many passengers feel more in touch with the sea here than on the larger vessels. Certainly, passengers and crew get to know one another better. Don't expect to find a busy, partying atmosphere on this ship. One important feature is the swimming pool, which has a shallow area around the perimeter for wading.

Cabins and Rates

	Beds	Phone	TV	Sitting Area	Fridge	Tub	Average Per Diem*
Suite	T or T/Q	●	○	●	●	●	$414
Outside	T, D, or T/Q	●	○	○	◐	○	$264
Inside	T	●	○	○	○	○	$235

**Rates are for Southeast Asia. Airfare and port taxes are extra.*

Cabins are significantly smaller than on comparable ships. Decorative touches include brass-accented wall sconces. Suites and cabins on the Promenade Deck look onto a public area.

Outlet voltage: 110 AC.

Single supplement: 150% of double-occupancy rate; however, less expensive singles are available if you're willing to wait until embarkation for your cabin assignment.

Discounts: A third or fourth passenger in a cabin pays reduced per diems. You get a discount for booking early.

Sports and Fitness

Health club: Exercise equipment, men's and women's saunas.

Recreation: Aerobics and other exercise classes, basketball, table tennis, ring toss, shuffleboard, skeet shooting, pool, unobstructed circuits for jogging.

Facilities

Public rooms: Five bars, three entertainment lounges, small casino (slot machines), disco.

Shops: Boutique, gift shop, beauty salon/barber.

Health care: Doctor and two nurses on call.

Child care: Youth counselors, children's programs in three age groups during holidays and in summer, baby-sitting arranged privately with crew member, cribs available but must be requested at time of booking.

Accessibility

Accessibility aboard this ship is limited. Doorways have lips, and public bathrooms are not specially equipped. The Viking Crown Lounge is inaccessible to wheelchair users. Crew members will carry passengers and their wheelchairs onto the ship's tenders if conditions permit.

MS Viking Serenade

Specifications

Type of ship: Cruise liner
Cruise experience: Casual
Size: 40,132 tons
Number of cabins: 756
Outside cabins: 63%
Passengers: 1,512
Crew: 612 (international)
Officers: International
Passenger/crew ratio: 2.4 to 1
Year built: 1982; rebuilt 1991

Ship's Log Formerly Admiral Cruises' *Stardancer*, the *Viking Serenade* was originally designed as the world's only cruise ship/car ferry, which explains why it looks more like a barge than a cruise ship. However, RCCL spent $75 million to convert the car deck into cabins, add a three-story atrium, renovate the existing cabins and public rooms, and add the company's signature observation deck, the glass-enclosed Viking Crown Lounge. Other features are a much-enlarged casino, a shopping arcade, a teen disco, and a state-of-the-art fitness center. Designs and furnishings are bright and contemporary. Brass, glass, mirrors, and stainless steel are used extensively.

Cabins and Rates

	Beds	Phone	TV	Sitting Area	Fridge	Tub	Average Per Diem*
Suite	T or T/Q	●	●	●	●	●	$443
Outside	T or T/Q	●	●	◐	◐	◐	$293
Inside	T or T/Q	●	●	○	○	○	$226

**Airfare included. Port taxes are extra.*

Standard outside cabins are pretty, with frilly window treatments; standard inside cabins feature murals in the window's place. In-cabin TVs show CNN broadcasts. The larger outside staterooms on Club Deck have partially obstructed views.

Outlet voltage: 110/220 AC.

Single supplement: 150% of double-occupancy rate; however, less expensive singles are available if you are willing to wait until embarkation time for your cabin assignment.

Discounts: A third or fourth passenger in a cabin pays reduced per diems. You get a discount for booking early.

Sports and Fitness **Health club:** Top-deck spa with rowing machines, stationary bikes, free weights, sauna.

Recreation: Aerobics and other exercise classes, table tennis, shuffleboard, trapshooting, pool with retractable dome, unobstructed circuit (8 laps = 1 mile) for jogging.

Facilities **Public rooms:** Four bars, four entertainment lounges, casino, disco, card room/library.

Shops: Gift shop, beauty salon/barber.

Health care: Doctor and two nurses on call.

Child care: Playroom; teen club with soda bar, video games, and dance floor; youth counselors, children's programs in three age groups year-round, cribs available but must be requested at time of booking.

Services: Laundry service, dry cleaning, photographer.

Accessibility Four cabins and all public areas are accessible to wheelchair users. Crew members will carry passengers and their wheelchairs onto the ship's tenders if conditions permit.

Royal Olympic Cruises

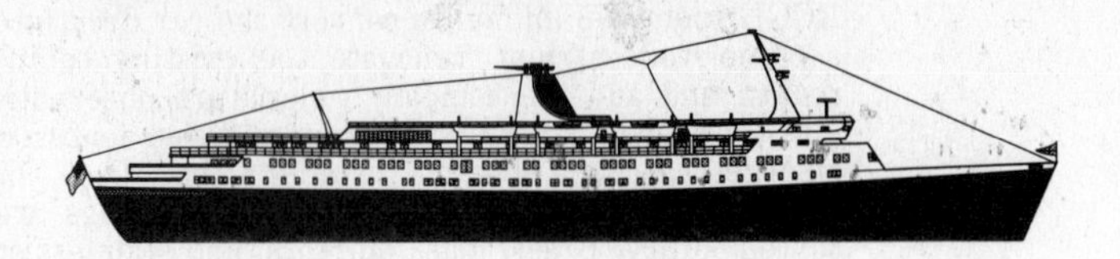

The Fleet
The Blue Fleet *MS Odysseus*
MS Stella Oceanis
TSS Stella Solaris

The White Fleet *TSS Olympic*
MS Orpheus
MS Triton

Royal Olympic Cruises is the name adopted by two well-known Greek cruise lines, Sun Line Cruises (the blue fleet) and Epirotiki (the white fleet). While the ships in both fleets are nearly identically priced, each line sails with a distictly different style—so choose your ship carefully.

Ships at a Glance

	Dining Rooms	Bars	Casino	Fitness Center	Pools	Average Per Diem
Odysseus	1	4	●	●	1	$270
Stella Oceanis	1	3	◐	○	1	$260
Stella Solaris	1	4	●	●	1	$295
Olympic	1	5	●	●	3	$260
Orpheus	1	2	●	○	1	$295
Triton	1	5	●	●	1	$289

The individual review of each ship is organized according to the table above. Sun Line's blue-fleet ships come first, in alphabetical order, followed by Epirotiki's white-fleet ships, also in alphabetical order.

Cruise Experience Although both lines offer a distinctive Greek flavor, Sun Line remains more elegant, traditional, and low-key, while Epirotiki has more activities and entertainment and is less formal. Historically, Sun Line has largely catered to Americans. Some Europeans join the line's Mediterranean cruises, but U.S. passengers are in the great majority during winter sailings to the Caribbean and Amazon. Epirotiki's individual passengers are mostly European, although tour groups, a large part of the line's business, come from both North America and Europe.

Mediterranean itineraries on both lines are port-intensive, and these Greek ships are completely at home there, providing comfortable and convenient conveyance. The *Stella Solaris* is equally well suited to an oceangoing experience on its twice-yearly transatlantic crossings and long "Caribazon" cruises.

Chart Symbols. Ships at a Glance. ●: *Fully equipped;* ◐: *Partially equipped;* ○: *Not equipped.* Cabins and Rates. **D:** *Double bed;* **K:** *King-size bed;* **Q:** *Queen-size bed;* **T:** *Twin bed;* **U/L:** *Upper and lower berths;* ●: *All cabins have this facility;* ○: *No cabins have this facility;* ◐: *Some cabins have this facility*

Activities Lectures, to prepare passengers for the trips ashore to ancient sites, are key elements of the cruise. Of particular note for the *Stella Solaris'* Amazon itineraries are talks by Captain Loren McIntyre, who is credited with discovering the source of the Amazon and who helped Sun Line pioneer Amazon cruising in 1983.

Traditional cruise activities, such as bingo, card tournaments, board games, and trivia contests, are scheduled, as are classes in bridge, arts and crafts, and ballroom and Greek dancing.

Dining Cuisine is essentially Continental, with Greek specialties featured at lunch and on Greek Night. Expect more careful preparation and presentation from Sun Line ships. The wine lists feature inexpensive Greek and Italian choices as well as more pricey French selections. Dinner is served in two seatings (6:30 and 8:30) with assigned tables. Sun Line passengers dress more formally on the longer cruises, and men tend to wear a jacket and tie on most nights, while Epirotiki is more casual—with a jacket and tie requested on two nights a week.

All Royal Olympic ships offer buffet dining at breakfast and lunch, formal afternoon tea, and 24-hour room service from a limited menu. Special dietary requests can be accommodated if furnished in writing two weeks prior to sailing.

Entertainment Epirotiki passengers tend to stay up later, so the line offers more elaborate after-dinner shows, while Sun Line emphasizes cabaret acts such as a singer, comedian, or magician. All the ships have late-night discos and bands for dancing, and Greek Night is an exuberant affair on every vessel.

Gentlemen hosts, who act as dancing and card partners for single women traveling along, are aboard the *Stella Solaris*. Both the *Olympic* and *Stella Solaris* have cinemas for showing documentaries and feature films.

Service and Tipping Longevity of employment is the norm, and it is not unusual to find cabin and dining stewards who have 20 or more years of service with the line. Tips of $8–$9 per person per day are pooled among the crew according to the Greek Stewards' Union, and individual tipping is discouraged.

Destinations The Mediterranean is home water for both these lines, and from spring through fall up to six ships sail to the Greek Islands, Turkish coast, Egypt, Israel, and elsewhere. The rest of the year, the *Stella Oceanis* offers Red Sea cruises to Egypt, Israel, and Jordan and two positioning cruises to and from Greece at the beginning and end of the season. The *Stella Solaris* crosses the Atlantic before Christmas to spend the winter on long Amazon-Caribbean voyages and shorter Panama Canal and Caribbean cruises. The *Odysseus* sails along the coasts of South America during the winter months. (For seasonal itineraries, *see* Chapter 4.)

For More Information Royal Olympic Cruises (1 Rockefeller Plaza, Suite 325, New York, NY 10020, tel. 212/397–6400 or 800/872–6400; in Canada, 800/368–3888).

MS Odysseus

Specifications

Type of ship: Cruise liner
Cruise experience: Semi-formal
Size: 12,000 tons
Number of cabins: 226
Outside cabins: 81%
Passengers: 400
Crew: 190 (mostly Greek)
Officers: Greek
Passenger/crew ratio: 2.1 to 1
Year built: 1962; rebuilt 1988

Ship's Log A transfer from the Epirotiki fleet, the Odysseus has a most pleasing profile and once sailed as a Brazilian coastal liner. Its airy and bright public rooms run the length of the Jupiter Deck, then open onto a spacious Lido. Four decks offer open side promenades for constitutional walks or for watching as the ship arrives in port and departs. The dining room, located on a lower deck, is a bit crowded. Apart from short, standard eastern Mediterranean cruises, the Odysseus offers a unique winter Red Sea itinerary.

Cabins and Rates

	Beds	Phone	TV	Sitting Area	Fridge	Tub	Average Per Diem*
Suite	D or T	●	○	●	○	◐	$338
Outside	D, T, or U/L	●	○	○	○	○	$270
Inside	T or U/L	○	○	○	○	○	$201

**Rates are for the Greek Islands. Airfare and port taxes are extra.*

The great majority of cabins are outside, with double, parallel, or L-shape bed configurations, and are attractively furnished with wood and cane chairs. Some have third and fourth upper berths. All, apart from the two top suites, have showers only. Every cabin has a radio and phones, but none have televisions.

Outlet voltage: 110 AC.

Single supplement: 150% of double-occupancy rate; 200% for suites. Guaranteed share rates are available at no surcharge.

Discounts: First through fourth passengers in a cabin pay 15% less than the double-occupancy rate. Passengers who book early get a 10% discount on Mediterranean cruises. Children pay reduced per diems; Kids under two sail free.

Sports and Fitness

Health Club: Gym, sauna, massage.

Recreation: Pool, four whirlpools, shuffleboard, table tennis, partially obstructed circuits for jogging.

Facilities

Public rooms: Four bars, entertainment lounge, casino, disco, card room, library/reading room, solarium.

Shops: Two shops, beauty salon/barber.

Health care: Doctor and nurse on call.

Child care: Children's playroom.

Services: Laundry service, pressing service, photographer, film processing.

Accessibility: No cabins are designed for wheelchair users.

MS Stella Oceanis

Specifications

Type of ship: Cruise liner
Cruise experience: Semi-formal
Size: 5,500 tons
Number of cabins: 150
Outside cabins: 75%
Passengers: 300
Crew: 140 (mostly Greek)
Officers: Greek
Passenger/crew ratio: 1.9 to 1
Year built: 1965

Ship's Log

With its Mediterranean-style atmosphere, the *Stella Oceanis* is a professionally run veteran of Greek Island cruising. Public rooms are few, limited to a large lounge for lectures and entertainment, a small annex, and a dark tavern bar forward on the deck above. By contrast, the attractive restaurant has windows on three sides and offers a very good Continental menu. A variety of Greek specialty dishes are available at the luncheon buffet. During days at sea, the deck chairs are in limited supply. To avoid the crowded Lido, many passengers retreat to the open promenade below.

Cabins and Rates

	Beds	Phone	TV	Sitting Area	Fridge	Tub	Average Per Diem*
Suite	T	●	○	●	○	●	$321
Outside	T	●	○	○	○	◐	$260
Inside	T or U/L	●	○	○	○	○	$192

**Rates are for the Greek Islands. Airfare and port taxes are extra.*

The average-size cabins are plainly furnished and come with limited storage space, but these warm-weather cruises do not require an elaborate wardrobe. Cabins in the top three categories have twin portholes and bathtubs, and except for the 10 suites, they are located on a lower, but stable, passenger deck. The largest cabins are on a higher deck. These accommodations have windows rather than portholes; some face an open promenade deck through one-way glass.

Outlet voltage: 220 AC (razors only).

Single supplement: 150% of double-occupancy rates; 200% for suites. Guaranteed share rates are available at no surcharge.

Discounts: First through fourth passengers in a cabin pay 15% less than the double-occupancy rate. Passengers who book early get a 10% discount on Mediterranean cruises. Children pay reduced per diems; kids under two sail free.

Sports and Fitness

Health Club: None.

Recreation: Outdoor pool, partially obstructed circuit for jogging.

Facilities

Public rooms: Three bars, entertainment lounge, casino (slot machines only).

Shops: Boutique.

Health care: Doctor and nurse.

Child care: None.

Services: Laundry service, pressing service, photographer, film processing.

Accessibility: No cabins are designed for wheelchair users.

TSS Stella Solaris

Specifications

Type of ship: Cruise liner
Cruise experience: Semi-formal
Size: 18,000 tons
Number of cabins: 329
Outside cabins: 76%
Passengers: 620
Crew: 310 (Greek and Filipino)
Officers: Greek
Passenger/crew ratio: 2 to 1
Year built: 1953; rebuilt 1973

Ship's Log

This former French passenger liner once sailed as the *Cambodge* on long ocean voyages between France, Indochina, and the Far East. It was completely rebuilt in 1973 as a cruise liner, so that only the graceful hull and quiet steam engines remain from the original ship. An attractive vessel with curving lines, teak decks, and hardwood railings, the *Solaris* today is a homey ship with a friendly atmosphere. Spacious, with relatively few passengers aboard, it's designed for easy mixing. The centrally located foyer serves as a village green of sorts, where several times a day, everyone pauses or passes through on their way to the restaurant, one of the lounges, a favorite bar, or the completely new spa that was added during a 1995 refurbishment. The boat deck, the prime outdoor gathering area, attracts sizable numbers of early-morning walkers (not many joggers on this ship) doing their constitutional rounds. As the day wears on, many take to the sheltered deck chairs that line both sides of the wide promenade.

Cabins and Rates

	Beds	Phone	TV	Sitting Area	Fridge	Tub	Average Per Diem*
Suite	D or T	●	●	●	○	●	$379
Outside	T	●	●	○	○	◐	$295
Inside	T	●	●	○	○	○	$252

**Rates are for the Greek Islands. Airfare and port taxes are extra.*

Cabins come in either green, salmon, or gold, and most are well apportioned; storage space is especially generous. Many can be connected as adjoining staterooms. Each is equipped with a lockable drawer for valuables. Suites on the Boat Deck (category 1) look out onto a public promenade through one-way glass and have a large walk-in closet and a sitting area with coffee table, sofa, and chairs. Superior inside and standard outside cabins have upper berths for third and fourth passengers. A third passenger may also be accommodated in a sofa bed in the deluxe suites.

Outlet voltage: 110/220 AC.

Single supplement: 150%–200% of double-occupancy rate. Guaranteed share rates are available at no surcharge.

Discounts: First through fourth passengers in a cabin pay 15% less than the double-occupancy rate. Passengers who book early get a 10%–35% discount. Children pay reduced per diems; kids under two sail free.

Sports and Fitness

Health club: Fitness equipment, sauna, massage.

Recreation: Aerobics, table tennis, shuffleboard, pool, unobstructed circuit (7 laps = 1 mile) for jogging.

Facilities

Public rooms: Four bars, three entertainment lounges, casino, disco, cinema, card room, library/writing room.

Shops: Gift shop, beauty salon/barber.

Health care: Doctor and two nurses on call.

Child care: Playroom, youth programs with counselors when demand warrants it, baby-sitting arranged privately with crew member.

Services: Laundry service, pressing service, photographer, film processing, shoe shines.

Accessibility

All public areas except the disco are accessible to wheelchair users. No cabin is specially equipped, and cabin and bathroom entrances have raised thresholds. Bathroom entries are 21½ inches wide.

TSS Olympic

Specifications

Type of ship: Classic liner
Cruise experience: Casual
Size: 31,500 tons
Number of cabins: 472
Outside cabins: 47%
Passengers: 900
Crew: 440 (mostly Greek)
Officers: Greek
Passenger/crew ratio: 2 to 1
Year built: 1956

Ship's Log By far the largest ship in the Royal Olympic fleet, the *Olympic* sailed for two decades for Carnival Cruise Lines as the *Carnivale.* Her size results in a very wide range of facilities for a ship making three- and four-day cruises. Public rooms occupy an entire deck and above that, open deck space runs fore and aft on three levels. Originally built as a transatlantic liner, there is an enclosed promenade deck, some wood paneling, brass decorative features, and an indoor pool deep in the hull.

Cabins and Rates

	Beds	Phone	TV	Sitting Area	Fridge	Tub	Average Per Diem*
Suites	D	●	○	●	○	●	$321
Outside	D, T, or U/L	●	○	○	○	◐	$260
Inside	D, T, or U/L	●	○	○	○	○	$182

**Rates are for the Greek Islands. Airfare and port taxes are extra.*

Cabins come in a wide range of configurations even within a specific category, reflecting the ship's classic liner origins. More than half are inside, and many have extra sofa beds and upper berths, which make the ship especially popular with families. Suites and deluxe cabins are all located amidships on the highest cabin deck—one deck below the public rooms.

Outlet voltage: 110 AC.

Single supplement: 150% of the double occupancy rate. 200% for suites. Guaranteed share rates are available at no surcharge.

Discounts: First through fourth passengers in a cabin pay 15% less than the double-occupancy rate. On Mediterranean cruises, passengers who book early get a 10% discount. Children pay reduced per diems; kids under two sail free.

Sports and Fitness **Health Club:** Gym, massage, sauna.

Recreation: Two pools (one for children), whirlpool, shuffleboard, table tennis, partially obstructed circuit for jogging.

Facilities **Public rooms:** Five bars, three entertainment lounges, piano bar, nightclub, cinema, casino, card room.

Shops: Two gift shops, drugstore, beauty salon/barber.

Health care: Doctor and nurse on call.

Child care: Children's playroom, outdoor play area, children's pool.

Services: Laundry service, pressing service, photographer, film processing.

Accessibility No cabins are designed for wheelchair users.

MS Orpheus

Specifications

Type of ship: Cruise liner
Cruise experience: Casual
Size: 6,000 tons
Number of cabins: 152
Outside cabins: 77%
Passengers: 290
Crew: 110 (mostly Greek)
Officers: Greek
Passenger/crew ratio: 2.6 to 1
Year built: 1948; rebuilt 1969

Ship's Log For 26 years, the *Orpheus* did yeoman charter service for the British firm Swan Hellenic, sailing on intensive enrichment cruises of the Mediterranean and northern Europe. Rebuilt from an Irish Sea overnight ferry, the *Orpheus* has been well maintained, although the ship is now considered rather elderly and lacks a variety of on-board amenities; it has, for example, just two bars. Mediterranean decor and Greek artifacts enhance the large, functional multipurpose lounge and the much more attractive lounge and adjacent bar one deck above. Although the deck space around the aft pool is limited, the parallel boat deck promenades are spacious and attractive for lounging and walking.

Cabins and Rates

	Beds	Phone	TV	Sitting Area	Fridge	Tub	Average Per Diem*
Outside	T	●	○	◐	○	◐	$295
Inside	T or U/L	●	○	○	○	○	$222

**Rates are for the Greek Islands. Airfare and port taxes are extra.*

Cabins are plain and functional with adequate storage space. Most have parallel beds and private facilities with showers. Eight suites are located toward the front of the ship, on the same deck as the main lounge. Perhaps the most desirable cabin location on the ship is the small cluster of doubles that face the promenade deck, affording easy access to the open deck.

Outlet voltage: 220 AC.

Single supplement: 150% of double-occupancy rates. Guaranteed share rates are available at no surcharge.

Discounts: First through fourth passengers in a cabin pay 15% less than the double-occupancy rate. Children pay reduced per diems; kids under two sail free.

Sports and Fitness **Recreation:** Outdoor pool, shuffleboard, table tennis, unobstructed circuit for jogging.

Facilities **Public rooms:** Two bars, two entertainment lounges, casino, library.

Shops: Gift shop, beauty salon/barber.

Health care: Doctor and nurse.

Child Care: None.

Services: Laundry service, pressing service, photographer, film processing.

Accessibility No cabins are designed for wheelchair users, and this ship has no elevator.

MS Triton

Specifications

Type of ship: Cruise liner
Cruise experience: Casual
Size: 14,110 tons
Number of cabins: 377
Outside cabins: 67%
Passengers: 620
Crew: 285 (mostly Greek)
Officers: Greek
Passenger/crew ratio: 2.2 to 1
Year built: 1971

Ship's Log First serving Cunard (as the *Cunard Adventurer*), then Norwegian Cruise Line (*Sunward II*), the *Triton* is well equipped for warm-weather Greek Island cruises. A variety of public rooms are located on three consecutive decks, each one offering a special atmosphere or activity. After dark, an outdoor disco is very popular. Deck space becomes crowded during the few half days at sea.

Cabins and Rates

	Beds	Phone	TV	Sitting Area	Fridge	Tub	Average Per Diem*
Outside	D or T	●	○	◐	○	◐	$289
Inside	T or U/L	●	○	○	○	○	$222

**Rates are for the Greek Islands. Airfare and port taxes are extra.*

The great majority of cabins are small outside rooms with decent storage capacity for a casual cruise. Deluxe cabins are on the same deck as the dining room. Many cabins have third and fourth upper berths.

Outlet voltage: 110/220 AC.

Single supplement: 150% of the double-occupancy fare. Guaranteed share rates are available at no surcharge.

Discounts: First through fourth passengers in a cabin pay 15% less than the double-occupancy rate. Children pay reduced per diems; kids under two sail free.

Sports and Fitness

Health club: Gym, massage.

Recreation: Outdoor pool, shuffleboard, table tennis, unobstructed circuit for jogging.

Facilities

Public rooms: Five bars, two entertainment lounges, observation lounge/disco, casino, cinema.

Shops: Gift shop, beauty salon/barber.

Health care: Doctor and nurse on call.

Child care: None.

Services: Laundry and pressing service, photographer, film processing.

Accessibility

No cabins are designed for wheelchair users.

Seabourn Cruise Line

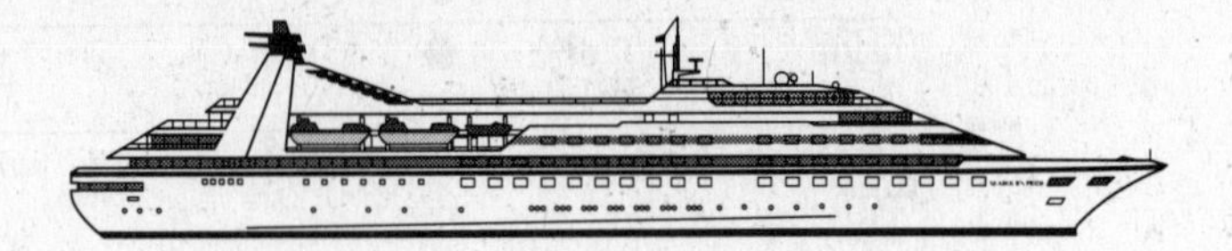

The Fleet *Seabourn Legend*
Seabourn Pride
Seabourn Spirit

The streamlined Seabourn ships always attract attention when they pull into port. Inside and out these vessels exude luxury. As on all cruise yachts, every cabin is an outside suite. A platform at the stern lowers for water sports, but it is used sparingly and only in the calmest waters.

Ships at a Glance

	Dining Rooms	Bars	Casino	Fitness Center	Pools	Average Per Diem
Seabourn Legend *Seabourn Pride* *Seabourn Spirit*	1	3	●	●	1	$885

Cruise Experience Seabourn sells snob appeal: The line has the highest rates in cruising and is proud of it. Seabourn officially does not discount its cruises; there are, however, programs that reward frequent cruisers and passengers who book in advance, take back-to-back cruises, book with a friend, and book repositioning cruises.

No expense was spared in the construction and decoration of the *Seabourn Pride* and *Seabourn Spirit*. From the crystal glassware in the staterooms to the huge expanse of marble in the circular atrium, Seabourn represents the pinnacle of cruising elegance. These ships are among the most spacious ships afloat, too, and notably so in the all-suite accommodations, which are the highlight of the ship. Passengers get a complimentary allotment of their favorite wines, spirits, or other alcoholic beverages in their cabin. If you want refills, there's a fee. In the bars and in the dining rooms, drinks are sold on a pay-as-you go basis.

Passengers pay an extremely high price for such luxury. As a result, the majority are middle-age or older. While this is reflected in the generally low-key activities and entertainment, there is plenty in the way of water sports to keep even passengers in their thirties busy.

Activities Seabourn lets passengers enjoy the ship's facilities at their own pace, and there are few organized activities. There's a small casino, a library with a good selection of books and videos, and a card room. Water sports are popular on cruises to warm-weather destinations. Anchored in the calm waters of a cove or bay, the ship can lower its stern to create a platform with a central swimming area protected by wire netting; from this platform passengers can swim, sail, water-

Chart Symbols. Ships at a Glance. ●: *Fully equipped;* ◐: *Partially equipped;* ○: *Not equipped.* Cabins and Rates. **D:** *Double bed;* **K:** *King-size bed;* **Q:** *Queen-size bed;* **T:** *Twin bed;* **U/L:** *Upper and lower berths;* ●: *All cabins have this facility;* ○: *No cabins have this facility;* ◐: *Some cabins have this facility*

ski, or ride banana boats—weather permitting. For more sedate explorations, the ship also carries paddleboats and a glass-bottom boat.

The few scheduled events include a diverse series of enrichment lectures. Well-known personalities talk about everything from cruising to cuisine. Speakers include renowned chefs, editors of major travel and lifestyle publications, and celebrities. Headliners during the past year included Walter Cronkite, Marvin Hamlisch, talk-show host Dick Cavett, astronaut Wally Schirra, and humorist Art Buchwald. The line's "Signature Series" of shore excursions include invitations to private golf clubs of championship caliber. Other unique excursions on past cruises have included a reception with an Ottoman princess and a visit to a family-run château and winery.

Dining The outstanding cuisine has a French accent and is strongly nouvelle-influenced in presentation and portions. Meals are prepared to order, and passengers are free to ask for dishes not on the menu. The fine food is complemented by a superb wine list. The dining room is formal and large, with tables spaced so far apart it would make a New York restaurateur swoon. Tables are unassigned, and passengers may dine at any time during meal hours (dinner is from 7:30 to 10). Typically, passengers line up fellow tablemates in the afternoon, perhaps meeting before dinner for drinks at the bar—it can be a bit like arranging a new dinner party every day. Two formal evenings are held each week, but gentlemen are expected to wear a jacket and tie virtually every night. The formality of the dining room, which works so successfully for dinner, seems stuffy at breakfast and lunch.

For more informal meals, the Veranda Café is a delightful spot. With its rattan furniture and tightly packed tables, it is the ship's cheeriest room. Located on the same deck as the pool, the café serves opulent buffet breakfasts and lunches, as well as a few items cooked to order, such as eggs, hot dogs, hamburgers, and fresh pastas. The Veranda Café is also the venue for theme dinners. Served one or two nights per cruise, these informal events are very popular; a table must be reserved in advance.

Room service is superb and available 24 hours. At least once during your cruise, be sure to have dinner in your cabin; it's a romantic affair, with personal service and beautifully prepared cuisine served course by course. Breakfast in the cabin is also presented with grace and panache.

Entertainment In the small show lounge, solo artists give nightly performances, and there's a cabaret-style show twice a week. In warm-weather cruising areas, films are screened on deck under the stars. Nightly dancing and piano music round out the low-key evening entertainment.

Service and Tipping The passenger-to-crew ratio is among the lowest of any ship. No tipping is allowed, yet the European service crew is professional, personable, and eager to accommodate virtually any personal request.

Destinations Seabourn ships call at nearly 300 ports of call in 78 countries. The line's cruising regions include Alaska, the Caribbean, Europe and the Mediterranean, Asia, and elsewhere. (For seasonal itineraries, *see* Chapter 4.)

For More Information Seabourn Cruise Line (55 Francisco St., San Francisco, CA 94133, tel. 415/391–7444 or 800/929–9595).

Seabourn Legend, Seabourn Pride, and Seabourn Spirit

Specifications *Type of ship:* Cruise yacht
Cruise experience: Formal
Size: 10,000 tons
Passengers: 204 (212 *Legend*)
Crew: 140 (international)
Officers: Norwegian

Number of cabins: 106 *Passenger/crew ratio:* 1.5 to 1
Outside cabins: 100% *Year built:* 1992/1988/1989

Ship's Log Aesthetically, the Seabourn ships may be the most striking small ships afloat. With their sleek lines and twin funnels that resemble airfoils, they are streamlined and futuristic. Generous use of glass, brass, and marble inside is subtle and sophisticated, a sensation heightened by the ship's spaciousness. The refined color schemes of peach, blue, and soft beige add to the light and airy feel aboard ship. From morning until sunset, passengers take a break from sunbathing around the Sky Bar—a simple outdoor gathering spot that is the premier daytime attraction.

The other most popular spot is the Club/Casino, with its piano bar and the sloping picture windows that form the stern wall. Spotlights, potted plants, and glass partitions make this an attractive room for preprandial cocktails and after-dinner dancing. The darker Magellan Lounge on the deck below has none of the Club/Casino's charm, but its gently tiered floor makes it ideal for musical revues and lectures. Two decks up is the magnificent Constellation Lounge; from its position above the bridge it has a commanding view of the sea through a semicircle of large picture windows.

The *Legend*, last of the Seabourn sisters, is like a wayward child come home. It was originally designed to be the third ship in Seabourn's fleet. However, the line didn't have the money at the time to construct the vessel. Instead, Royal Viking Line built the ship and commissioned it as the *Royal Viking Queen*. When RVL was disbanded, the ship was transferred to Royal Cruise Line and operated as the *Queen Odyssey*. In January of 1996, Royal announced that it, too, would close its doors, and the ship finally assumed its rightful place alongside its sisters. Other than minor differences in detail and decor, the *Legend* is structurally identical to the *Pride* and *Spirit*.

Cabins and Rates

	Beds	Phone	TV	Sitting Area	Fridge	Tub	Average Per Diem*
Suite	Q or T	●	●	●	●	●	$885

**Lower rates are for the Caribbean. Higher rates are for Alaska. Airfare included. Port taxes are extra.*

Five-foot-high picture windows, a sitting area, stocked bar and refrigerator, TV (including CNN) and VCR, large marble bath with twin sinks and tub/shower, and walk-in closets are among the creature comforts of every suite. Here, as in the rest of the ship, glass, blond woods, and mirrors are used to great effect. Refrigerators/bars are stocked with a large selection of liquors, beer, and soft drinks; there's a charge for liquor refills. Unlimited soft drinks are complimentary here, as they are throughout the ship. All cabins have coffee tables that convert to dining tables, and safes. The Owner's Suites at the front of the ship have curved bow windows that make you feel as though you're on your own yacht, but midship Owner's Suites are larger.

Outlet voltage: 110/220 AC.

Single supplement: 110%–150% of double-occupancy rate; 200% for Owner's and Regal suites.

Discounts: A third passenger in a suite pays reduced per diems. You get a discount for paying early and—on selected cruises—for booking more than one cabin with family or friends. A frequent-cruiser program offers reduced rates to passengers who sail 45–120 days in a 36-month period.

Sports and Fitness **Health club:** Aerobics rooms, exercise equipment (including Nautilus), weight-training classes, massage, steam room, sauna, health and beauty treatments (herbal wraps, facials, dietary counseling, personalized fitness programs).

Recreation: Aerobics and other exercise classes, shuffleboard, skeet shooting, small pool, three whirlpools, sailing, windsurfing, waterskiing, snorkeling, unobstructed circuit for jogging.

Facilities **Public rooms:** Three bars, two lounges, casino, card room, library (books and videos), business center.

Shops: Clothing boutique, gift shop, beauty salon/barber.

Health care: Doctor on call.

Child care: Baby-sitting arranged with purser's office.

Services: Full- and self-service laundry, dry cleaning, overnight shoe-shine service, photographer, film processing.

Accessibility Three Seabourn Suites (Type A) are laid out for easier access by wheelchair users. All elevators and public areas are accessible, and public lavatories are specially equipped. In small ports to which passengers must be ferried by tender, wheelchair users may have trouble getting ashore.

Seawind Cruise Line

The Fleet TSS *Seawind Crown*

The Portuguese *Seawind Crown* was built in 1961 as the *Infante Dom Henrique* and became the sole ship of Seawind Cruise Line 30 years later. One of the last remaining ships powered by steam turbines, the look of this venerable midsize vessel is a far cry from today's glitzy megaships. Built along classic lines, the *Seawind Crown*'s Old World interior is appointed with dark woods and polished brass instead of neon atriums and synthetic waterfalls. However, the ship is not being maintained to the same standards as those employed on more upscale lines, where vessels are sanded, scraped, and painted on a daily basis. A $4 million renovation in late 1994 added 50 new cabins and furnishings, but the ship could use additional work. Carpets in some of the public rooms and corridors are worn and stained, while curtains are drab and threadbare. In certain cabins, there are visible dents and chips in the metal and wood. Outside the ship, the wraparound teak decking is buckled and cracked in many places.

Ship at a Glance

	Dining Rooms	Bars	Casino	Fitness Center	Pools	Average Per Diem
Seawind Crown	1	5	●	●	2	$278

Cruise Experience Relatively low prices, including free airfare from 43 U.S. gateways and early booking discounts of up to $500 per person, have made this one-ship line popular among cost-conscious cruisers. An unusual southern-Caribbean itinerary, sailing round-trip from Aruba and calling at less-visited islands, is another attractive quality for many.

Originally built for Scandinavian and German passengers, the ship still draws an international mix of Europeans, South Americans, and North Americans. On average, passengers are younger than on most cruise ships, with a substantial number of South American couples in their twenties and thirties. Americans tend to range in age from 30-year-olds to 50-year-olds. Few senior passengers are aboard. On the other hand, the *Seawind Crown* is popular with honeymooners and couples celebrating their wedding anniversary. A smattering of families and singles rounds out the typical passenger manifest. With so many different nationalities aboard, passengers tend to socialize according to common languages. For assigned seatings at meals, Americans are placed at tables with other Americans.

Activities Though English is the ship's first language, activities are conducted in English, Spanish, Portuguese, and German to accommodate the large number of European and South American passengers. While

Chart Symbols. Ships at a Glance. ●: *Fully equipped;* ◐: *Partially equipped;* ○: *Not equipped.* Cabins and Rates. **D:** *Double bed;* **K:** *King-size bed;* **Q:** *Queen-size bed;* **T:** *Twin bed;* **U/L:** *Upper and lower berths;* ●: *All cabins have this facility;* ○: *No cabins have this facility;* ◐: *Some cabins have this facility*

in port, there are few activities scheduled, as most passengers are off the ship on shore excursions or exploring on their own. The destination-intensive itinerary does, however, have two days at sea for such on-board activities as wine-and-cheese seminars, bridge get-togethers, and table-tennis tournaments. Traditional cruise pastimes, such as bingo, are also scheduled. The casino, which is not as loud and crowded as on some other ships, has 60 slot machines along with blackjack and roulette tables.

Dining The food is good but unspectacular, with Portuguese, Greek, and Italian influences. Menus typically are built around a culinary theme—South American, French, or Caribbean, for example. Portions are plentiful; preparation is average. Some dishes are served in heavy sauces. Lunch and dinner are presented at two assigned seatings (dinner at 6:30 and 8:30) in the nicely appointed Vasco da Gama Dining Room. Two formal evenings are scheduled during each week-long cruise.

For breakfast and lunch, the ship has a second, smaller dining room, the Madeira. Many passengers prefer this room's buffets to the sit-down meals in the main dining room. Both dining rooms are divided into smoking and no-smoking sections. Special diets must be requested in writing at least two weeks prior to the date of sailing.

During the ship's two days at sea, lunch buffets are served in the Taverna near the pool, where passengers can eat outside. The Taverna also has a daily early riser's coffee and danish, while the Madeira is the setting for afternoon tea. A midnight buffet rounds out the *Seawind Crown*'s daily food service. There is limited room service for Continental breakfast or for snacks and beverages.

Entertainment Although there are no lavish productions, entertainment on the *Seawind Crown* is commendable for its variety and quality. Performances may be a cabaret act, an international vocalist, a comedian, or a magician. Four dancers stage various musical revues, too, in the compact Seawind Show Lounge. A very good Brazilian band plays nightly in the small Panorama Lounge (capacity 140 passengers). A lively Caribbean steel band entertains frequently at poolside, while an orchestra plays ballroom dance music before dinner in the Seawind Lounge.

Service and Tipping Service is adequate but far from pampering. Transfer of your luggage to your cabins from arriving flights may be delayed by several hours, but eventually it gets there. Tip your waiter $3 per diem per passenger, the busboy $1.50, the cabin steward $3; the headwaiter gets $5 per week per passenger. A 15% service charge is automatically added to the bar bill.

Destinations From its home port in Aruba, the *Seawind Crown* sails two different itineraries throughout the southern Caribbean. A land-sea program includes three to seven nights at the La Cabana resort in Aruba. (For year-round itineraries, *see* Chapter 4.)

For More Information Seawind Cruise Line (1750 Coral Way, Miami, FL 33145, tel. 305/854–7800).

TSS Seawind Crown

Specifications
Type of ship: Classic liner
Cruise experience: Semi-formal
Size: 24,000 tons
Number of cabins: 362
Outside cabins: 68%
Passengers: 728
Crew: 320 (international)
Officers: International
Passenger/crew ratio: 2.3 to 1
Year built: 1961

Ship's Log This ship's most outstanding feature is its proportions: more than 43,000 square feet of deck space and suites that measure 500 square feet—more than double what you find on many ships. Among the ship's facilities are an array of bars and lounges, a shopping gallery, an exercise room, and two swimming pools. An asset for southern Caribbean enthusiasts is that the *Crown* spends several more hours in Curaçao and Grenada than do most ships.

Cabins and Rates

	Beds	Phone	TV	Sitting Area	Fridge	Tub	Average Per Diem*
Suite	K or D	●	●	●	●	○	$366
Outside	Q, D, T, or U/L	●	●	○	●	◐	$278
Inside	D, T, or U/L	●	●	○	●	○	$222

**Rates are for the Caribbean and include airfare.*

Cabins are large but oddly configured, appointed in pastel hues, and outfitted with a telephone, minirefrigerator, and closed-circuit TV. Bathrooms are spacious but equipped with European-style hand-held shower nozzles. Many cabins overlook a public promenade.

Outlet voltage: 220 AC.

Single supplement: 150%–200% of double-occupancy rate for all categories except the smallest inside cabins (Category M), for which single passengers pay no extra charge.

Discounts: A third or fourth passenger in a cabin pays reduced per diems. You get a discount for booking early.

Sports and Fitness

Health club: Exercise equipment including rowing machines, stationary bikes, StairMaster, sauna, massage.

Recreation: Two pools, volleyball, shuffleboard, table tennis, unobstructed circuits for jogging.

Facilities

Public rooms: Five bars and lounges, showroom, casino, disco, cinema, card room, library, chapel.

Shops: Boutiques gallery, beauty salon/barber.

Health care: A doctor and a nurse are on call.

Child care: Playroom, daily chaperoned children's activities.

Services: Photo service, photo shop.

Accessibility

There two cabins accessible to wheelchair users. There are four elevators, but they are old and somewhat difficult to use.

Silversea Cruises

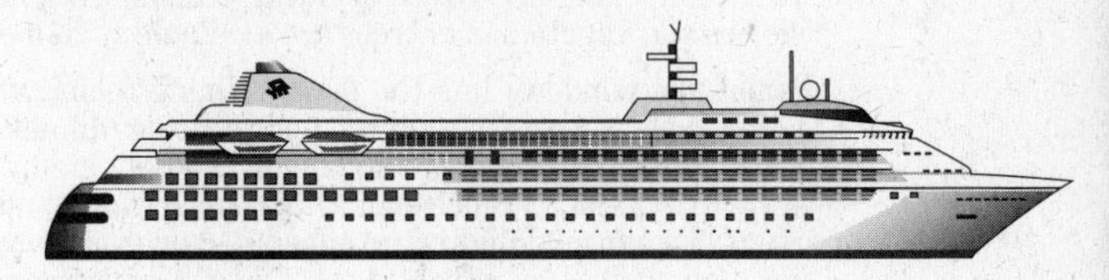

The Fleet MV *Silver Cloud*
MV *Silver Wind*

Silversea straddles the line that separates ocean-liner and small-ship cruising. On the one hand, its ships have full-size showrooms, domed dining rooms, and a selection of bars and shops. On the other hand, accommodations are all outside suites, and space and passenger-to-crew ratios are among the best at sea. Two new ships, on order through 1997 and 1998, will be even bigger than the *Silver Cloud* and *Silver Wind*, but they will preserve the spaciousness that has made Silversea one of cruising's most luxurious lines.

Ships at a Glance

	Dining Rooms	Bars	Casino	Fitness Center	Pools	Average Per Diem
Silver Cloud *Silver Wind*	1	3	●	●	1	$550

Cruise Experience Larger ships mean more facilities and room for passengers. For example, the Silversea ships have larger swimming pools and more deck space than other cruise yachts. Most of the all-suite cabins have private verandas—an important consideration if you're deciding among Silversea, Seabourn, and Cunard's *Sea Goddess*. Another of the line's selling points is its all-inclusive packaging, which includes gratuities, port charges, transfers, selected shore excursions, and all beverages aboard ship. These complimentary drinks include alcoholic and non-alcoholic beverages—in suites, in the dining room, and in the public lounges. A full list of wines is available at lunch and dinner. Not included are some special-vintage wines, champagnes, and spirits. Each air-sea package comes with round-trip economy airfare and a complimentary pre-cruise hotel room for passengers who arrive early. But, depending on the itinerary, Silversea may still cost hundreds of dollars a day less than its competitors.

Activities With its more extensive facilities, Silversea offers passengers a little more to do aboard ship than does Seabourn or the *Sea Goddess*. Passengers can join the morning aerobics classes, work out in small exercise rooms, swim in the tile-lined pool, or jog on the promenade deck. For the less athletically inclined, there are card and board games, celebrity speakers, foreign-language classes, chess and bridge competitions, and a large library stocked with books, videotapes, and compact discs. The library has an IBM-compatible computer with CD-ROM drive.

Dining Continental, American, and regional specialties tied to the itinerary top Silversea's wide-ranging menus. The line's executive chef has been trained at Le Cordon Bleu cooking school in Paris. A dish

Chart Symbols. Ships at a Glance. **●**: *Fully equipped;* **◐**: *Partially equipped;* ○: *Not equipped.* Cabins and Rates. **D**: *Double bed;* **K**: *King-size bed;* **Q**: *Queen-size bed;* **T**: *Twin bed;* **U/L**: *Upper and lower berths;* **●**: *All cabins have this facility;* ○: *No cabins have this facility;* **◐**: *Some cabins have this facility*

from an original Le Cordon Bleu recipe is featured at every meal, and there are specially highlighted Le Cordon Bleu theme cruises as well. In keeping with recent eating trends, "Light and Healthy" choices and vegetarian entrées are available at all meals.

Panoramic windows line the domed dining room, which accommodates all passengers in a single, open seating (dinner is from 7:30 to 9:30). Meals are served in a setting of candlelight and fresh flowers, German crystal, French china and silverware, and Italian table linens. Two formal nights are scheduled on every seven-day cruise; three on cruises of 8 to 14 days. Longer cruise combinations will have additional formal nights, depending on the itinerary and number of days at sea. However, passengers tend to primp for dinner every evening. Most special dietary requests should be submitted well in advance.

Another room with a view for dining is the Terrace Cafe, which overlooks an open deck. Breakfast, lunch, and occasional theme dinners are served in this more casual setting. Seating is mostly indoors, with a few outdoor tables. Although the Terrace Cafe is designed for buffet meals, the tables are nevertheless set with china, silver, and crystal, as they are in the main dining room. Waiters take orders for drinks and hot entrées. Certain dishes, such as eggs and pizzas, may be prepared to order.

Room service is available 24 hours from a special menu, and passengers may choose to have lunch and dinner served course-by-course in their suites. Appetizers are delivered to each suite in the early evening.

Entertainment Production-style shows are staged a few nights a week in the Venetian Lounge showroom, featuring resident performers as well as local talent. A variety of other acts and entertainers take the stage on other evenings. Films and lectures are presented in the main showroom as well.

However, in the tradition of small-ship cruising, many passengers bypass the main show for more intimate socializing in one of the convivial bars. There's also a small casino for gaming. For in-cabin entertainment, films are broadcast over the ship's closed-circuit television system, and an array of videotapes is available in the library.

Service and Tipping Silversea's staff has been recruited from some of the finest lines in cruising, such as Crystal and Seabourn. Service is highly personalized, attentive, and friendly throughout the ship. Tipping is included in the cruise fare, and no additional gratuities are accepted.

Destinations Silversea cruises throughout the world on itineraries of 7 to 14 days. Itineraries can be combined for longer cruises. (For seasonal itineraries, *see* Chapter 4.)

For More Information Silversea Cruises (110 E. Broward Blvd., Fort Lauderdale, FL 33301, tel. 954/522–4477 or 800/722–9955).

MV Silver Cloud and MV Silver Wind

Specifications

Type of ship: Cruise yacht
Cruise experience: Formal
Size: 16,800 tons
Number of cabins: 148
Outside cabins: 100%
Passengers: 296
Crew: 196 (European)
Officers: Italian
Passenger/crew ratio: 1.5 to 1
Year built: 1994

Ship's Log The *Silver Cloud* and *Silver Wind* have taken the cruise-yacht category to new extremes of size and spaciousness. The additional space their tonnage allows has been put to use in the public rooms, particularly in the two-tier showroom, where a movable stage makes full-scale productions possible. Unlike the *Sea Goddess* and Seabourn ships, there is no retractable marina at the stern for water sports. They do, however, have larger pools, more open deck space, and private verandas in 75% of the all-suite cabins.

The decor aboard the Silversea ships is subtle yet distinctive and meant to evoke the great steamships of the past. Brass sconces, wood paneling, and brass-ringed portholes in the dining room deliver the desired effect. Throughout the ship, there is an obvious attention to detail. Note, for instance, the inlaid designs in the dining room's hardwood floor.

Public rooms on the *Silver Wind* and *Silver Cloud* are well designed, and, except for the forward observation lounge, are congregated at the rear of the ship. Cut off from the ship's passenger flow, the forward lounge seems more like an afterthought than an integrated part of the design. Passengers must go outside to reach the lounge, which is sparsely furnished—just some simple tables, chairs, plants, and an array of navigation equipment that gives passengers a captain's-eye view of the ship's course. However, this room is one of the few flaws in these otherwise well-executed vessels.

Cabins and Rates

	Beds	Phone	TV	Sitting Area	Fridge	Tub	Average Per Diem*
Suite	Q, T	●	●	●	●	●	$550

**Rates are for New England and Canada and include airfare and port taxes.*

As with every luxury cruise yacht, every warmly appointed cabin is an outside suite. Large picture windows, walk-in closets, and marble bathrooms with robes, slippers, make-up mirrors, and a wall-mounted hair dryer are among the many amenities, along with a writing table stocked with personalized stationery, a basket of fresh fruit replenished daily, and flowers and champagne upon arrival. The creature comforts extend to bedding (pure-cotton Frette linens and down pillows); the large umbrellas placed in each room and the complimentary shoe-shine service are evidence of the attention to detail. Other standard equipment includes remote-controlled television with closed-circuit and satellite broadcasts (including CNN), a VCR, refrigerator (stocked with complimentary beverages of your choice), and wall safe. Except for Vista Suites, all accommodations open onto a teak veranda with floor-to-ceiling glass doors.

Outlet voltage: 110/220 AC.

Single supplement: 110%–150% of the double-occupancy rate.

Discounts: A third or fourth passenger in the Vista pays reduced per diems. You get a discount for booking early and for booking back-to-back cruises.

Sports and Fitness

Health club: Fitness center with exercise equipment, spa treatments, sauna, and massage rooms.

Recreation: Pool, two whirlpools, unobstructed circuit for jogging.

Facilities

Public rooms: Three bars, observation area, showroom, casino, library/computer center, card/conference room.

Shops: Boutique, beauty salon/barber, photo shop.

Health care: Doctor and nurse on call.

Child care: None.

Services: Laundry service, dry cleaning, photographer, film processing, fax.

Accessibility

Two cabins are accessible to wheelchair users on the *Silver Wind*.

Society Expeditions

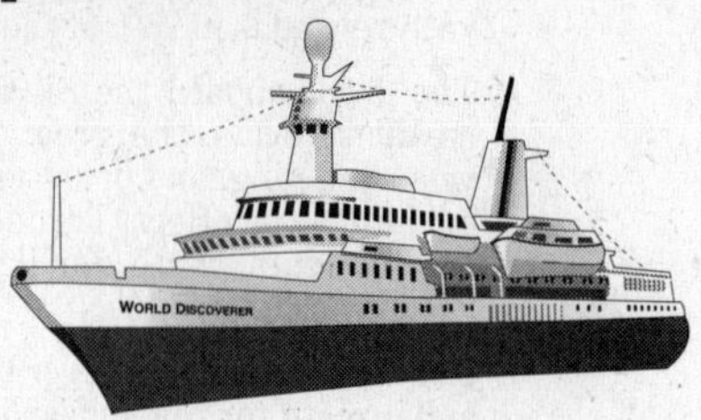

The Fleet MS *World Discoverer*

The *World Discoverer* conforms to exacting standards for adventure cruises, including a hardened hull to plow through ice-choked channels and a fleet of Zodiac landing craft, which allow passengers to make landfall virtually anywhere. Equipped to explore, this ship makes good use of its capabilities and has on a number of occasions made a name for itself in the annals of cruising. In 1985 it made the first Northwest Passage crossing by a passenger ship, and it later made headlines again with an unscheduled excursion across the Bering Strait during an Alaskan cruise. The U.S. government fined the line for this historic bold stroke; these days, a crossing to the Russian Far East is part of its regular itineraries.

Ship at a Glance

	Dining Rooms	Bars	Casino	Fitness Center	Pools	Average Per Diem
World Discoverer	1	3	○	◐	●	$475

Cruise Experience The *World Discoverer* draws well-traveled cruisers, largely retired professionals. About 80% come from the United States and the remaining 20% from countries in Europe. Many have sailed aboard the *World Discoverer* before. A spirit of camaraderie usually develops among everyone on board, as passengers mingle with one another and the ship's officers and crew. Central to this shared experience are the Zodiac excursions off the ship. Together, small bands of passengers search for wildlife and explore little-visited shorelines from Antarctica to the Arctic.

Activities These are active cruises. Two or three excursions daily may include shoreside walks or hikes over rough terrain. Away teams are led by naturalists, anthropologists, historians, and botanists, who also lecture aboard ship to enrich passengers' appreciation of the creatures they see and the places they visit. Those who stay aboard will also find an assortment of pastimes, whether it be checking out a good book from the library or working out in the modest gym.

Dining Food is basic, no-frills fare, served in a single, open seating in the Marco Polo dining room. Portions for all meals are hearty, from the American-style breakfasts to the Continental cuisine served at dinner. Considering the remote regions visited and the inability to frequently stock the ship, the produce is surprisingly fresh at all times.

Entertainment Enrichment talks conducted by the staff scientists are a daily event in the lecture hall, which also doubles as the ship's theater for the occasional film or video screening. For those who just want to watch

Chart Symbols. Ships at a Glance. ●: *Fully equipped;* ◐: *Partially equipped;* ○: *Not equipped.* Cabins and Rates. **D:** *Double bed;* **K:** *King-size bed;* **Q:** *Queen-size bed;* **T:** *Twin bed;* **U/L:** *Upper and lower berths;* ●: *All cabins have this facility;* ○: *No cabins have this facility;* ◐: *Some cabins have this facility*

the passing scenery, there are 180° panoramic views through the windows of the observation lounge.

Service and Tipping The amiable European and Filipino dining-room staff and cabin attendants perform their duties quickly and efficiently. Recommended tipping is $8–$9 per person per day.

Destinations From Alaska to Antarctica, the *World Discoverer* sails some of the most interesting itineraries to be found anywhere. Of special note are its Bering Sea and Arctic Ocean cruises. (For seasonal itineraries, *see* Chapter 4.)

For More Information Society Expeditions (2001 Western Ave., Suite 300, Seattle, WA 98121, tel. 800/548–8669).

MS World Discoverer

Specifications

Type of ship: Expedition
Cruise experience: Casual
Size: 3,153 tons
Number of cabins: 71
Outside cabins: 100%
Passengers: 138
Crew: 75 (international)
Officers: German
Passenger/crew ratio: 1.8 to 1
Year built: 1974

Ship's Log With its blue hull, white funnel, and picture windows lining the ship, the *World Discoverer* strikes a dramatic pose wherever it drops anchor. Although not the largest or most luxurious expedition ship afloat, it delivers adventure in a warm and comfortable environment, with a touch of cruise-ship amenities. Onboard facilities include an observation lounge, cocktail lounge, library, lecture hall, a small fitness center with a sauna, and a swimming pool—the ship even carries water-sports equipment.

Cabins and Rates

	Beds	Phone	TV	Sitting Area	Fridge	Tub	Average Per Diem*
Suite	T	●	○	●	○	●	$628
Outside	T or U/L	●	○	○	○	○	$475

**Rates are for Antarctica. Airfare and port taxes are extra.*

A European minimalism is softened by pastel colors in the small, spartan, all-outside cabins. Stainless-steel accents and molded contours lend a modern edge to the decor. The otherwise simple appointments are more than adequate for the typical adventure passenger, who tends to be active and use the cabin for little besides sleep. There are three suites aboard, as well as five single cabins. All accommodations come with individual climate control, ample storage space, and hair dryers in the bathrooms. Cabins 100–103 and 110–113 have picture windows.

Outlet voltage: 220 AC.

Single supplement: Five single outside cabins are available at no surcharge.

Discounts: A third or fourth passenger in a cabin pays $1,750–$3,450 per cruise, depending upon the itinerary.

Sports and Fitness **Health club:** Tiny gym, sauna, solarium, massage (sometimes).

Recreation: Pool, equipment for diving, fishing, snorkeling, waterskiing, windsurfing.

Facilities **Public rooms:** Three bars, two lounges, observation lounge, cinema/lecture hall, library/card room; navigation bridge open to passengers.

Shops: Gift shop, beauty salon/barber.

Health care: Doctor on call.

Accessibility There are no facilities specifically equipped for wheelchair users.

Special Expeditions

The Fleet MS *Polaris*
MV *Sea Bird*
MV *Sea Lion*

Like other small-ship lines, Special Expeditions operates a collection of shallow-draft vessels designed to explore nature and visit remote ports. The yachtlike *Sea Bird* and *Sea Lion* are tiny, and even the *Polaris* is among the smallest of expedition ships. While all carry Zodiacs for wet landings almost anywhere, none of these vessels—not even the *Polaris*—has an ice-hardened hull.

Ships at a Glance

	Dining Rooms	Bars	Casino	Fitness Center	Pools	Average Per Diem
Polaris	1	1	○	○	○	$490
Sea Bird/Sea Lion	1	1	○	○	○	$445

Cruise Experience Special Expeditions cruises attract a slightly younger, less affluent, more easygoing crowd than other adventure lines. Unlike guest experts on some ships, who are treated either as employees or celebrities, specialists on Special Expeditions cruises eat and socialize with passengers. You'll feel less like a paying spectator and more like part of a grand adventure. Because all shore excursions, snorkeling, entrance fees, and lectures are included in the fare, few financial surprises await you.

Special Expeditions' primary vessels, the *Sea Bird* and *Sea Lion*, are neither as plushly appointed as Clipper's similar ships nor as roomy as Alaska Sightseeing's larger vessels. Where Special Expeditions excels is in its staff, especially the lecturers. In fact, Special Expeditions sails with more top experts aboard than any other small-ship line.

Activities These are truly active cruises. Most passengers have come to explore off the ship as much as possible, and the daily schedule of events is centered around one or two Zodiac excursions. More may be arranged if time, weather, and sea conditions permit. The captain and expedition leader work closely together, occasionally diverting from the planned route to get a closer look at wildlife or some natural phenomenon. As with any cruise, certain activities, such as lectures, are run according to a published schedule. But spontaneity and unpredictability are important elements of any Special Expeditions cruise, and the anticipation of unexpected wildlife sightings are a key part of the expedition experience.

Shipboard activities consist mainly of numerous lectures given by the staff of naturalists and historians. Topics usually examine the

Chart Symbols. Ships at a Glance. ●: *Fully equipped;* ◐: *Partially equipped;* ○: *Not equipped.* Cabins and Rates. **D:** *Double bed;* **K:** *King-size bed;* **Q:** *Queen-size bed;* **T:** *Twin bed;* **U/L:** *Upper and lower berths;* ●: *All cabins have this facility;* ○: *No cabins have this facility;* ◐: *Some cabins have this facility*

wildlife or culture in the next port of call. In keeping with similar programs on other expedition lines, there are recap sessions in the lounge just before dinner. During these nightly get-togethers, passengers can ask questions of the naturalists and other experts and compare notes on the day's events. In tropical waters, more emphasis is placed upon individual leisure activities, such as snorkeling and sailing.

Dining Hearty meals draw on fresh ingredients available in ports along the way and are influenced by North American and European cooking traditions. The diet, more homey than gourmet, is somewhat heavy (especially if you help yourself to seconds), but with all the adventure activity you will quickly burn off the calories. Meals are served in a single, open seating (dinner from about 7 to 8:30). There is no smoking in the dining room.

Mealtimes on Special Expeditions' ships are more social than ceremonial. There are no dress-up nights, and passengers can help themselves to coffee and cookies at any time. Special dietary requests are not easily handled. Room service is available only if you are ill.

Entertainment Although there is no organized entertainment, the captain will occasionally invite local performers to dinner and have them play or sing in the lounge afterward. Otherwise, passengers play cards or board games at night or read. Most passengers hit the sack early to rest up for the next day's adventures.

Service and Tipping Besides the sheer adventure of a Special Expeditions cruise, it is the warmth, competence, and intelligence of the crew that passengers remember. Crew members are very special; they engender trust, respect, and friendship. Tips are given anonymously by placing cash (or not-so-anonymous personal checks) in an envelope at the purser's office, where they're then pooled and divided among the crew. Tip $7 per passenger per diem.

Destinations The line's special expeditions are concentrated primarily along the West Coast of the Americas, from Alaska to Baja California. The Polaris also sails to Belize and Costa Rica, up the Amazon, and to Europe every summer. (For seasonal itineraries, *see* Chapter 4.) Special Expeditions also represents ships in such destinations as the Nile and the Galápagos (*see* Chapter 2).

For More Information Special Expeditions (720 5th Ave., New York, NY 10019, tel. 212/265–7740 or 800/762–0003).

MS Polaris

Specifications

Type of ship: Expedition
Cruise experience: Casual
Size: 2,214 tons
Number of cabins: 41
Outside cabins: 100%
Year built: 1960

Passengers: 80
Crew: 44 (Filipino and Swedish)
Officers: Swedish
Passenger/crew ratio: 1.8 to 1

Ship's Log The *Polaris* began its life as a Scandinavian ferry and was later converted for expedition service. It lacks a wealth of amenities, but is well suited for adventure cruises. The main public room is more like an oversize living room than a cruise-ship lounge. Before dinner, passengers gather here to recap the day's events and hear informal talks by the naturalists. After dinner, videos are shown. Serving as the ship's library is an even smaller room at the stern—well stocked with reference books, best-sellers, and atlases. The dining room commands a magnificent view of the sea. For views below the waterline, the vessel is stocked with snorkeling equipment and carries a glass-bottom boat.

Cabins and Rates

	Beds	Phone	TV	Sitting Area	Fridge	Tub	Average Per Diem*
Outside	T	○	○	◐	○	○	$490

** Rates are for the Amazon. Airfare and port taxes are extra.*

Cabins are tiny, narrow, and poorly lighted, but they all have sea views. Stylistically speaking, the furnishings are purely practical.

Outlet voltage: 220 AC (bathrooms 110 AC).

Single supplement: 150% of double-occupancy rate. Guaranteed share rates are available at no surcharge.

Discounts: A third passenger in a cabin pays half the double-occupancy rate.

Facilities **Public rooms:** Lounge/bar, library; navigation bridge open to passengers.

Shops: Small gift shop, beauty salon/barber.

Health care: Doctor on call.

Services: Laundry service.

Accessibility This ship is not recommended for passengers with mobility problems.

MV Sea Bird and MV Sea Lion

Specifications

Type of ship: Coastal cruiser
Cruise experience: Casual
Size: 99.7 tons
Number of cabins: 37
Outside cabins: 100%
Passengers: 70
Crew: 21 (American)
Officers: American
Passenger/crew ratio: 3.3 to 1
Year built: 1982/1981

Ship's Log The lilliputian *Sea Lion* and *Sea Bird* look like hybrids of ferries and riverboats. While technically oceangoing vessels, they mostly sail on rivers and protected waterways. Their shallow drafts allow them to enter waters that would ground larger ships, even the *Polaris*.

Homey and very friendly, the *Sea Lion* and the *Sea Bird* carry almost the same number of passengers as the *Polaris*, despite their smaller size. The ships' storage capacity, the size of the crews, and the number of public areas have been cut back as a result. Lectures, films, and other entertainment are held in the single lounge/bar, which also holds the ship's small reference library. While cruising, the partially covered Sun Deck is the most comfortable public space for watching the passing scenery. Another favorite perch is the bow area on the upper deck, which is an excellent vantage point for whale watching. However, these ships are not for claustrophobics, or for those who easily become seasick. They rock noticeably in rough waters. Packets of Dramamine are available from the purser's office.

Cabins and Rates

	Beds	Phone	TV	Sitting Area	Fridge	Tub	Average Per Diem*
Outside	T/D	○	○	◐	○	○	$445

**Rates are for Alaska. Airfare and port taxes are extra.*

The cabins are among the smallest afloat, so form follows function to maximize space and minimize waste. The majority of cabins are in Category 2 and come with twin lower beds and large picture windows. Although all cabins are outside with sea views, the lower deck accommodations (Numbers 400–404 in Category 1) have portlights (very small portholes) rather than windows. Category 1 cabins are equipped with one double bed and one single, which converts to a day couch. Categories 3 and 4 have writing desks; Category 4 has a sitting area with a table, too.

Outlet voltage: 110 AC.

Single supplement: 150% of double-occupancy rate subject to availability.

Discounts: No cabins are available for third or fourth passengers.

Facilities **Public rooms:** Lounge/bar, library; navigation bridge open to passengers.

Shops: Gift shop.

Health care: Doctor on board only on Baja California cruises; otherwise, the ship, never far from land, will dock in a U.S. or Canadian port if care is required.

Services: Laundry service.

Accessibility These ships are not recommended for passengers with mobility problems.

Star Clippers

The Fleet *Star Clipper*
Star Flyer

Taller, faster, and bigger than the original clippers, these sister ships re-create the 19th-century vessels that supplied the California gold rush. First-time sailors and seasoned yachtsmen alike will appreciate Star Clippers' attention to sailing's finer details. The ships rely chiefly on sail power, with a single engine used to augment the wind and to maneuver in tight harbors. Some concessions have been made to modern technology: The ships are equipped with anti-rolling systems that keep them upright at high speeds and prevent rocking while at anchor.

Ships at a Glance

	Dining Rooms	Bars	Casino	Fitness Center	Pools	Average Per Diem
Star Clipper *Star Flyer*	1	2	○	○	2	$263

Cruise Experience Old-fashioned sailing is the key to Star Clippers' appeal. Guests can pitch the sails, help steer the ship, and learn about navigational techniques from the captain. Most, however, opt to take in the nautical ambience as they lounge on the upper deck. While Star Clippers' sailing philosophy is similar to a windjammer cruise (*see* Chapter 2), the vessels' facilities were designed with a more upscale passenger in mind: They have greater public space and larger cabins, with hair dryers, televisions, and telephones, plus two swimming pools aboard. As cruise ships, their amenities fall somewhere in between Special Expedition's authentic *Sea Cloud* and the high-tech, computer-controlled vessels of Club Med and Windstar, but at a more affordable price. However, the differences are more than a matter of creature comforts: The Star Clippers are true sailing vessels, albeit with motors, while Club Med and Windstar vessels are ocean liners with masts and sails.

Star Clippers' crowd is an international one: About half the 170 passengers are European (French, German, and Swedish). Nearly all are couples, ranging from honeymooners to well-traveled retirees. The ships' officers mix socially with passengers and eat with passengers during dinner.

Activities Passengers do their own thing. The only organized activities are daily exercise classes, scuba-diving excursions, talks on ports of call, knot-tying lessons, and afternoon captain's tales. Scrabble, checkers, and other board games are played in the library. Snorkeling, windsurfing, waterskiing, and sailing are available whenever the ship is at anchor; the ship carries its own banana boat and four Zodi-

Chart Symbols. Ships at a Glance. ●: *Fully equipped;* ◐: *Partially equipped;* ○: *Not equipped.* Cabins and Rates. **D:** *Double bed;* **K:** *King-size bed;* **Q:** *Queen-size bed;* **T:** *Twin bed;* **U/L:** *Upper and lower berths;* ●: *All cabins have this facility;* ○: *No cabins have this facility;* ◐: *Some cabins have this facility*

acs, two for divers and two for water-skiers. Night dives are particularly popular. Divers must be certified, but pool instruction is given to beginners who are interested.

Dining Star Clippers has hired a new executive chef and created new menus in a continuing effort to improve what is a weakness. The wine list is excellent. Passengers are charged for all nonalcoholic drinks except during breakfast, dinner, and some lunches. Tables and booths seat 8 to 10, so dining tends to be a family-style event. Dinner is served at an open seating from 7:30 to 10. Formal attire is never required in the dining room; collared shirts for men is about as dressy as it gets. Special dietary requests, with the exception of vegetarian meals, are not easily accommodated.

Other food service includes Continental breakfast in the piano bar and a buffet breakfast, with omelets cooked to order, served in the dining room. Lunchtime beach barbecues are a favorite among passengers. Lunch buffets are also served on deck or in the dining room, followed by hors d'oeuvres in the afternoon. Midnight sandwiches in the piano bar conclude the eating day. There is no room service.

Entertainment The piano bar, with its friendly piano player/singer, and a covered outdoor bar are the main gathering spots for low-key evening diversion. Passengers often request songs and join the show, especially on crew-passenger talent night. Local musical groups board the ship at happy hours for short but colorful performances. Two disco nights are held each cruise on a semi-enclosed upper deck. Traditional crab races, as practiced by the sailors of yesteryear, are another evening highlight. Several movies play throughout the night on in-cabin televisions.

Service and Tipping Cabin service is excellent; dining-room service is a bit harried. The genial international crew works well together and is generally helpful, if not overly attentive. Tip the room steward $3 per diem and dining-room staff $5 per diem.

Destinations Stopping at ports rarely visited by larger ships, the *Star Flyer* and *Star Clipper* cruise the Caribbean, Mediterranean, and Southeast Asia. Transatlantic crossings are also available. (For seasonal itineraries, *see* Chapter 4.)

For More Information Star Clippers (4101 Salzedo Ave., Coral Gables, FL 33146, tel. 800/442–0551).

Star Clipper and Star Flyer

Specifications

Type of ship: Motor-sail
Cruise experience: Casual
Size: 3,025 tons
Number of cabins: 85
Outside cabins: 83%
Passengers: 180
Crew: 72 (international)
Officers: International
Passenger/crew ratio: 2.3 to 1
Year built: 1992/1991

Ship's Log These long, slender white ships have sharp, pointed bows to cut quickly through the water, narrowly curved steel hulls, teak decks and trim, and four tapered steel masts rigged with 16 sails. Two small, saltwater swimming pools are surrounded by sunning areas on the aft and sundecks. The pool on the latter has a glass bottom, so patrons of the piano bar can view swimmers from below. Deck-chair mats can be used as floats in the pool or in the ocean. Most social activity takes place on the Tropical Deck, either outside at the bar or inside the chrome-finished piano bar. Here, passengers gather to chat and relax on leather, semicircular booths. Navy blue and beige lend a nautical air to the room. A winding grand stairway leads from the bar to the dining room, appointed in the same blue/beige decor, teak-and-marble trim, and handsome nautical art.

Cabins and Rates

	Beds	Phone	TV	Sitting Area	Fridge	Tub	Average Per Diem*
Outside	T	●	●	●	○	○	$263
Inside	T	●	●	●	○	○	$227

**Rates are for the Mediterranean. Airfare and port taxes are extra.*

Accommodations are somewhat small but closets are adequately roomy. Each cabin has a vanity and a tiny corner sitting area with a built-in seat and an upholstered stool. Outside cabins have portholes; only a very few have picture windows. Showers and sink faucets are the push type and require constant pressing to maintain water flow. Ten cabins have an additional berth that folds out of the wall for a third passenger. A hardcover illustrated history of Star Clippers is placed in each cabin prior to embarkation.

Outlet voltage: 110/220 AC.

Single supplement: 150% of double-occupancy rate.

Discounts: A third passenger in a cabin pays reduced per diems. You get a discount for booking early and for booking back-to-back cruises.

Sports and Fitness

Recreation: Four fitness instructors, water-sports equipment, scuba gear for certified divers.

Facilities

Public rooms: Two bars, one lounge, library.

Shops: Gift shop.

Health care: Nurse on call.

Child care: There are no organized children's programs or provisions for young children, but older children are welcome.

Accessibility

These ships are not recommended for passengers with mobility problems.

Windstar Cruises

The Fleet *Wind Song*
Wind Spirit
Wind Star

In creating Windstar's vessels, the designers crossed a 19th-century sailing ship with an ultramodern yacht. They took the latest in hull technology and put four masts on top, then added computers to control the six sails. At the touch of a button, 22,000 feet of canvas unfurl in two minutes—a spectacular sight to see. Diesel engines help to propel the ships when the wind does not provide enough sail power. Inspired as much by today's luxury cruise liners as yesterday's clippers, Windstar celebrates the new as well as the old.

Ships at a Glance

	Dining Rooms	Bars	Casino	Fitness Center	Pools	Average Per Diem
Wind Song *Wind Spirit* *Wind Star*	1	2	◐	◐	1	$456

Cruise Experience Few modern vessels capture the feeling of being at sea the way a Windstar ship does. But although the ship's design may be reminiscent of sailing vessels of yore, the amenities and shipboard service are among the best at sea. Life on board is unabashedly sybaritic, attracting a sophisticated crowd happy to sacrifice bingo and masquerade parties for the attractions of remote islands and water sports. While the cruise experience is casual, the daily rates aren't cheap: Average per diems put these sailings in the upper echelon of cruising.

Due to the romantic nature of the Windstar cruise experience, these ships are especially popular with honeymooners, and there are usually several newlyweds aboard. On the other hand, you won't find many singles or children aboard. Most passengers tend to be well-heeled couples in their thirties to fifties. Windstar inspires a loyal following of alumni passengers, and it's likely that up to a third of those aboard any given cruise may be repeaters.

Activities Shipboard life is unregimented and unstructured. No group activities are held; passengers pursue their own interests. Chief among these is water sports. In calm waters, the ship lowers a platform built into the stern, creating a water-level deck for swimming and sunning. Snorkels, masks, and fins are distributed to passengers, free of charge, at the beginning of the week and are theirs to use for the duration of the cruise. Other water sports include waterskiing, kayaking, windsurfing, sailing, and even fishing. Banana-boat rides

Chart Symbols. Ships at a Glance. ●: *Fully equipped;* ◐: *Partially equipped;* ○: *Not equipped.* Cabins and Rates. **D:** *Double bed;* **K:** *King-size bed;* **Q:** *Queen-size bed;* **T:** *Twin bed;* **U/L:** *Upper and lower berths;* ●: *All cabins have this facility;* ○: *No cabins have this facility;* ◐: *Some cabins have this facility*

are always popular (the banana boat is a large, yellow inflatable that sits up to five people as it's pulled at a rapid rate of speed by another boat). There is a small casino on board, but gambling is not a priority for most Windstar passengers.

Dining Windstar's food is among the best served by any cruise line. The menus have been created by award-winning chef Joachim Slichal of Los Angeles. Dinner is open seating, and passengers can wander in any time between 7:30 and 9:30. Elaborate formal wear is not considered appropriate; men generally do not wear a tie or jacket to dinner. The one exception is the weekly barbecue dinner, which is held on deck (weather permitting) to the accompaniment of a local band.

Breakfast and lunch are served in the glass-enclosed Veranda Lounge, or on an outside deck, weather permitting. Other food service includes early-morning coffee and croissants, plus afternoon tea. Limited room service, available 24 hours a day, features selections from the ship's regular dining-room menu. Special dietary requests should be made four weeks before sailing.

Entertainment The little entertainment that is planned is strictly low-key. Every evening the ship's band or local musicians play in the lounge; there is also a piano bar and nightly dancing. The library has a selection of videotapes for use in the cabins. When the ship is in port, many passengers go ashore to sample the local nightlife. A new enrichment series, introduced in 1996, brings experts aboard to talk about wine tasting, cooking, art appreciation, and other lifestyle topics.

Service and Tipping Service is comprehensive, competent, and designed to create an elite and privileged ambience. Tipping is not expected.

Destinations The *Wind Spirit* and *Wind Star* spend late autumn, winter, and spring in the Caribbean. In summer, both ships sail to ports of call in the Mediterranean. The *Wind Song* is based year-round in Tahiti. (For seasonal itineraries, *see* Chapter 4.)

For More Information Windstar Cruises (300 Elliott Ave. W, Seattle, WA 98119, tel. 800/258–7245).

Wind Song, Wind Spirit, and Wind Star

Specifications *Type of ship:* Motor-sail
Cruise experience: Casual
Size: 5,350
Number of cabins: 74
Outside cabins: 100%
Passengers: 148
Crew: 88 (Indonesian and Filipino)
Officers: British
Passenger/crew ratio: 1.6 to 1
Year built: 1987/1988/1986

Ship's Log Inspired by the great sailing ships of a bygone era, the Windstar ships are white, long, and lean, with bow masts and brass-rimmed portholes. To satisfy international safety regulations, the hulls are steel, not wood; the interiors, however, glow with wood paneling and teak trim—a look rare among modern cruise ships. Instead of the chrome-and-glass banisters so popular on other ships, Windstar vessels feature white-painted iron ones with teak handrails. Although the ships are narrow—a necessity for sail-powered vessels—the interiors are unusually spacious, mainly because there are so few passengers. The sense of space is heightened by huge glass windows that allow plenty of light into the public rooms.

Cabins and Rates

	Beds	Phone	TV	Sitting Area	Fridge	Tub	Average Per Diem*
Suite	T/Q	●	●	●	●	○	$456

**Rates are for the Caribbean. Airfare and port taxes are extra.*

Windstar cabins represent the height of sailing luxury. Every cabin is an outside suite, appointed in burled maple veneer and outfitted with plentiful closet space and mirrors. Portholes are trimmed in brass, the white laminated cabinetwork is accented with rich wood moldings, and bathroom floors are made of teak. All are outside suites with stocked refrigerators, sitting areas, safes, CD players, and VCRs. In-cabin TVs show CNN broadcasts. The larger Owner's Suite costs 30% more. Some cabins can accommodate a third passenger.

Outlet voltage: 110 AC.

Single supplement: 150% of double-occupancy rate; 200% for Owner's Suite.

Discounts: A third passenger in a cabin pays 50% of the double- occupancy rate. You get a discount for booking early.

Sports and Fitness

Health club: Exercise equipment, sauna, massage, hot tub.

Recreation: Exercise classes, sailing, scuba diving (for certified divers), snorkeling, waterskiing, windsurfing, swimming platform, pool, scheduled morning walks on unobstructed circuit.

Facilities

Public rooms: Two bars, entertainment lounge, small casino (slots and blackjack), disco, library (books and videotapes).

Shops: Boutique, sports shop, hairstylist.

Health care: Doctor on call.

Child care: Bringing children on board is discouraged; no provisions are made for them.

Services: Laundry service.

Accessibility

The lack of an elevator makes moving through the ship almost impossible for wheelchair users. Tenders are used to transport passengers from ship to shore in most ports.

World Explorer Cruises

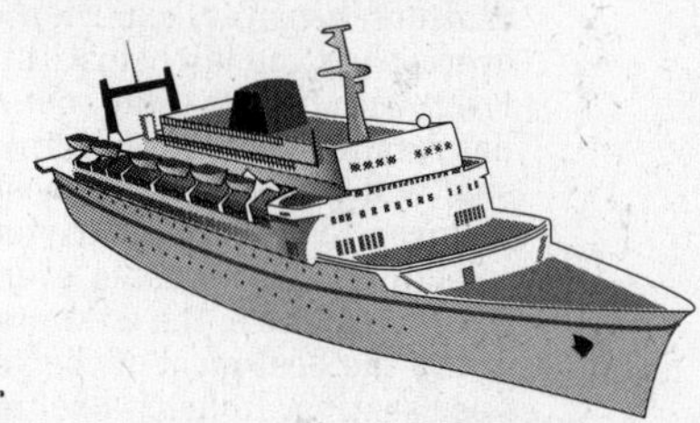

The Fleet SS *Universe Explorer*

World Explorer's ship, the *Universe Explorer* (formerly Commodore Cruise Line's *Enchanted Seas*), was built in 1957 as a atlantic liner, but World Explorer has modified the vessel to serve as a floating classroom. Rather than the disco and casino typically found on a cruise ship, the *Universe Explorer* has an onboard herbarium and a 15,000-volume library—the largest at sea. Repeat passengers should note that the *Universe Explorer* has replaced the old *Universe*.

Ship at a Glance

	Dining Rooms	Bars	Casino	Fitness Center	Pools	Average Per Diem
Universe Explorer	1	6	○	●	0	$235

Cruise Experience World Explorer's strong suit is education, and passengers should not expect the glitz and glamour of some newer ships sailing in Alaska. Instead, the line emphasizes an onboard enrichment program that is one of cruising's best. So extensive is the program by experts in history, art, geology, marine life, music, and geography that college credit can be earned during the cruise. The *Universe Explorer*'s itinerary incorporates long port stays and an excellent array of shore excursions. Evening entertainment is by noted classical artists. Gentlemen hosts sail on certain cruises. Cabins are spacious and there are several public rooms, including a forward observation lounge, for watching the passing scenery. If you want to learn about Alaska, and don't need the amenities associated with a luxury cruise, this ship is comfortable and a good value.

Activities Days at sea and mornings en route to a port are packed with classes, slide shows, video presentations, and educational films. Four or five experts give a series of lectures on subjects ranging from Alaskan anthropology to history, geology, glaciers, whales, and oceanography. Much time is spent observing passing scenery and wildlife, but bridge, table tennis, board games, and jigsaw puzzles are popular pastimes, too. Typical cruise-ship activities include bingo, trivia contests, and other competitions. Feature films are occasionally screened in the ship's theater.

In previous seasons, World Explorer has offered a special bike-touring option on selected departures. Passengers who choose this program, which costs extra, go on 12- to 15-mile rides in each port of call. On all cruises, World Explorer offers a wide-ranging choice of more than 40 shore excursions.

Chart Symbols. Ships at a Glance. ●: *Fully equipped;* ◐: *Partially equipped;* ○: *Not equipped.* Cabins and Rates. **D:** *Double bed;* **K:** *King-size bed;* **Q:** *Queen-size bed;* **T:** *Twin bed;* **U/L:** *Upper and lower berths;* ●: *All cabins have this facility;* ○: *No cabins have this facility;* ◐: *Some cabins have this facility*

Dining In years past, World Explorer's food and dining-room service got moderate to high marks from passengers, especially first-time cruisers; however, experienced cruisers often found the food to be overcooked and fairly institutional when compared with other lines. Even with the new ship, not much is expected to change, as the line has retained its best waiters and its chef from the old *Universe*. Cuisine will continue to be mostly American, with Asian, Italian, or Mexican dishes frequently on the menu. Low-salt and vegetarian selections are available every evening as well. Once during each two-week cruise, the crew prepares an Asian theme dinner. It's generally the best meal of the voyage. Breakfast is served in a single, open seating. Lunch is open seating when the ship is in port, at your assigned table during days at sea. Dinner is served at two assigned seatings (6 and 7:45), and a classical guitarist or string quartet may play during the meal. Two semiformal evenings are held each cruise. Make special diet requests in writing 30 days prior to sailing (no kosher available).

Continental breakfast, afternoon tea, and late-night snacks are served buffet style. The food selection tends to be skimpy, however. Self-serve coffee, hot chocolate, and tea are available at all times, but there is no room service.

Entertainment Lecturers become the daytime entertainment on these cruises. In the evening, you'll find outstanding classical and folk performances by singers, string quartets, a pianist or violinist, a harp-and-dulcimer duo, or perhaps a flamenco guitarist. There's also a smattering of more traditional cruise fun: dancing, passenger talent competitions, and costume shows.

Service and Tipping Crew members are friendly, but service is not of the pampering kind usually associated with cruise ships. The ship's waiters, bartenders, and cabin stewards receive consistently high marks from passengers. Other staff members may be college students aboard just for the summer. There is no room service, not even coffee in the morning. Tip the room steward and the waiter $3 each per passenger per diem and the assistant waiter $2 per passenger per diem.

Destinations Two-week summer cruises to Alaska and winter cruises to Latin America are the only sailings aboard the *Universe Explorer* sold to the general public through World Explorer Cruises. (For seasonal itineraries, *see* Chapter 4.) From September to May, the ship operates as a floating university, taking university students, and a few leisure passengers, around the world (*see* Educational Cruises *in* Chapter 2).

For More Information World Explorer Cruises (555 Montgomery St., San Francisco, CA 94111, tel. 800/854-3835).

SS Universe Explorer

Specifications
Type of ship: Cruise liner
Cruise experience: Casual
Size: 23,500
Number of cabins: 370
Outside cabins: 79%
Passengers: 739
Crew: 350 (international)
Officers: International
Passenger/crew ratio: 2.2 to 1
Year built: 1958

Ship's Log The *Universe Explorer*, with its emphasis on learning, is noteworthy mostly for its facilities that contribute to the Alaskan experience: the herbarium, library, artwork, and large picture windows along the enclosed promenade that provide wonderful views of the Alaskan landscape and wildlife.

The library is well used, probably much more so than on other cruise ships. It's packed with reference books, field guides, and clippings of magazine and newspaper articles on the ports of call. In fact, you'll sometimes have to wait your turn to get a look at the files. The expert speakers are available to passengers outside of scheduled lecture times. When not delivering formal talks, they're just fellow passengers watching the world go by from the rail.

The educational nature of a World Explorer cruise tends to attract like-minded people, many of whom are repeaters. So you'll probably get to know your fellow passengers well during the course of your two weeks in Alaska, and maybe even get a Christmas card or two.

Cabins and Rates

	Beds	Phone	TV	Sitting Area	Fridge	Tub	Average Per Diem*
Suite	D, T, or U/L	●	●	●	○	◐	$285
Outside	D, T, or U/L	●	●	○	○	◐	$235
Inside	D, T, or U/L	●	●	○	○	◐	$200

**Rates are for Alaska. Airfare and port taxes are extra.*

As with most ships built for transatlantic travel, cabins are larger than average. All accommodations have television and telephones, but few other amenities.

Outlet voltage: 110 AC.

Single supplement: 130% of double-occupancy rate.

Discounts: A third or fourth passenger in a cabin pays reduced per diems.

Sports and Fitness

Health club: Exercise equipment, aerobics classes, massage.

Recreation: Table tennis, unobstructed circuit for jogging.

Facilities

Public rooms: Six bars, five lounges, cinema, card room, library.

Shops: Gift shops, beauty salon/barber.

Health care: Doctor on call.

Child care: Youth center, supervised children's programs.

Services: Self-service laundry.

Accessibility

Several cabins are accessible to wheelchair users and should be requested at the time of booking.

2 Special-Interest Cruises

Special-Interest Cruises

We call the cruises in this chapter "special interest" because they appeal to a certain type of person. Perhaps it's someone looking for an international experience. Maybe it's an explorer type, looking for a tour of hidden towns and coastlines. Or it could be a cerebral sort of person, who wants as much to learn as to cruise.

Destinations are worldwide, and the types of ships are as varied as the ports they call on. Icebreakers sail to the Canadian Arctic and Antarctica. Tall ships visit secluded harbors and idyllic islands. Old-fashioned steamboats ply the Columbia River and St. Lawrence Seaway. Riverboats explore deep up the Amazon, the Irrawaddy, and the Nile. Barges travel a network of inland canals and rivers in France, Belgium, and Holland, while ferries crisscross the waterways of coastal Europe.

Many of the cruises described below fall under the broad and often-used label of "educational cruises." The term refers not to formal education, but to the tradition of expanding your horizon as part of the cruise experience. Most of the education that takes place on or off ship is relatively casual—nothing more than a scheduled lecture or slide show. Remember, however, that although many cruise lines carry lecturers who speak on a wide variety of subjects, putting one expert aboard a 1,000-passenger ship does not make a learning experience. The most highly regarded educational cruises limit their passenger capacity to 150 or less, and their experts are available not just during scheduled enrichment talks but on deck, at meals, and during trips ashore.

Along America's Waterways

Cruises in sheltered American and Canadian waters have become increasingly popular in recent years. The Inside Passage from Vancouver or Seattle north to Alaska remains the most popular and best-known protected North American waterway. Lesser-known choices include Oregon's Columbia and Snake rivers, California's Sacramento Delta, and the East Coast's Intracoastal Waterway.

Cruise Experience Ever since Robert Fulton invented the steamboat, traveling up and down America's inland waters and along its coastline has been fashionable. In many respects, that tradition remains unchanged. Ships stop at historic ports—although not to board passengers but to disembark those already aboard for shore excursions. Cuisine may also capture the flavor of America and be geared to take advantage of local specialties—such as Cajun in the South, fresh seafood in the Pacific Northwest, and local wines in the Napa Valley.

The Fleet Some of the local ships specializing in regional cruises replicate the steamships of more than a century ago. Others are more yachtlike in their design, while a few are typical but comfortable ferries, capable of carrying both passengers and motor vehicles.

Down the St. Lawrence Seaway

When to Go Cruises run along the St. Lawrence River and Seaway from May to October. Spring is warm but relatively uncrowded. Summer means long hours of daylight and warm temperatures. Fall is especially popular for its colorful foliage.

Operators and Itineraries **St. Lawrence Cruise Lines** (253 Ontario St., Kingston, Ontario, Canada K7L 2Z4, tel. 613/549–8091 or 800/276–7868, fax 613/549–8410) operates the 64-passenger *Canadian Empress* on five-, six-, and seven-day cruises. Voyages are one way by ship and the other way by VIA Rail express train. The ship attracts mainly older Americans and Canadians, who come for relaxed sightseeing on the river and to learn about Canadian history. The compact cabins are all outside, and the one public room serves as the restaurant, lounge, and bar. This is a very personal, well-organized, family-owned operation aimed at middle-income North Americans. Ports of call include Kingston, Montreal, Ottawa, and Quebec City, depending on your itinerary. Scenic cruising areas include the locks of the international seaway, the 1,000 islands region, and the Ottawa River.

American Canadian Caribbean Line and Clipper Cruise Line both pass through the St. Lawrence on their way to and from the Sageunay Fjord and the Great Lakes. For detailed descriptions of both lines, see Chapter 1.

In the California Wine Country

When to Go Wine country cruises have a very short season. Springtime cruises are scheduled mostly in March, with a few in April and May. Fall departures are available in October.

Operators and Itineraries Alaska Sightseeing/Cruise West and Clipper Cruise Line both have itineraries that visit Sonoma and Napa valleys. For detailed descriptions of both lines, *see* Chapter 1.

North to Alaska

When to Go June through August are the most popular months to cruise Alaska. Spring, especially May, is less crowded and drier than the summer, which gets rainier as fall approaches. Autumn is a fleeting time of colorful foliage and cooler temperatures in Alaska, where fall reaches its peak in early to late September along the Inside Passage. The state ferry system runs year-round, but other boat operators may sail only during the warm-weather months.

Operators and Itineraries The **Alaska Marine Highway** (Box 25535, Juneau, AK 99802, tel. 800/642–0066, fax 907/277–4829) has cabins aboard several ferries that serve the communities of southeast and south-central Alaska. Dining is cafeteria-style with good American-style food. Public rooms include an observation lounge, a bar, and a solarium. Many passengers are RV travelers transporting their vehicles (no roads connect the towns within the Inside Passage). Time spent in port is short—often just long enough to load and unload the ship. A weekly departure leaves from Bellingham, Washington, north of Seattle. Service to Alaska is also available from Prince Rupert, British Columbia, where the marine highway system connects with Canada's **BC Ferries.** Cabins on the Alaskan ferries book up as soon they become available, but a number of tour operators sell packages that include accommodations. One of the oldest and largest is **Knightly Tours** (Box 16366, Seattle, WA 98116, tel. 206/938–8567 or 800/426–2123).

Discovery Voyages (tel. 907/424–7602) sails solely within Prince William Sound on the 12-passenger, 65-foot *Discovery*, which was built in the 1950s as a Presbyterian mission boat. To carry guests, the vessel has been completely renovated by owners Dean and Rose Rand, who live aboard the ship year-round. Passenger facilities include six cabins with shared baths and a main lounge/dining room. The ship is also equipped with inflatable skiffs and kayaks for off-ship excursions. Sailings are round-trip from Whittier.

Another option for cruising Prince William Sound is the four-passenger *Arctic Tern III*, which is one of the smallest overnight vessels sailing in Alaska. Longtime Sound residents Jim and Nancy Lethcoe operate the boat under the name **Alaska Wilderness Sailing**

Safaris (tel. or fax 907/835–5175, lethcoe@aol.com) and charter the 40-foot sloop to small parties of two to four passengers, generally for three days of sailing and kayaking.

A number of interesting and unorthodox cruise vessels travel the Inside Passage, too. **Marine Expeditions** (tel. 800/263–9147) books an ice-rated Russian research vessel equipped with Zodiac landing craft and onboard laboratories. The exact vessel used varies each year, but none carries more than 82 passengers. (For more information about Marine Expeditions and other icebreaker cruises, *see* On Board Research Vessels, *below.*)

For a cruise of the Inside Passage aboard a former minesweeper, contact **The Boat Company** (tel. 407/832–8845). The 12-passenger *Observer* and 20-passenger *Liseron* were commissioned by the Navy in the 1940s and 1950s, but are now in service to the conservation movement. In the past, groups such as the Sierra Club have brought groups aboard, and all sailings are designed to raise awareness of environmental issues. The vessels themselves are constructed of wood and finished with accents of brass and bronze, so dismiss any thoughts of boats painted battleship gray.

Similar environmentally oriented programs can be found aboard the 16-passenger *Island Roamer*, a 68-foot sailboat operated by **Bluewater Adventures** (tel. 604/980–3800), which has been in business for more than 20 years. The vessel is sometimes chartered by Oceanic Society Expeditions, an affiliate of Friends of the Earth. Bluewater Adventures recently added a second ship to its Alaska roster, the 12-passenger *Snow Goose*, a 65-foot, steel-hulled motor yacht. Built in 1973, it too has served time as a research vessel. For leisure cruising, the *Snow Goose* has a Zodiac, two kayaks, and a natural-history library.

For something even smaller, **Dolphin Charters** (tel. 510/527–9622) uses the *Delphinus* (eight passengers), a 50-foot motor yacht, to explore uncharted coves in Glacier Bay. This vessel is popular with professional photographers, who often hire it for their photographic workshops.

Equally intimate is the eight-passenger *Steller* from **Glacier Bay Adventures** (tel. 907/697–2442). The vessel was built as a research vessel for the Alaska Department of Fish and Game and is staffed by a crew of trained naturalists.

Outside of Glacier Bay, another cozy cruise for just six passengers at a time can be booked from **All Aboard Yacht Charters** (tel. 360/898–7300). Cruises sail from Seattle to Ketchikan, from Ketchikan to Juneau, and on loops round-trip from Juneau.

Alaska Sea Adventures (tel. 206/284–7648) caters to sportfishing enthusiasts, photography buffs, and amateur naturalists aboard the *Alaska Adventurer*. The ship holds up to 10 passengers and was built in 1980 specifically for cruising the Inside Passage.

Stopping on the Labrador Coast

When to Go Cruises of coastal Labrador operate seasonally between early July and late October from a port in Newfoundland.

Operators and Itineraries **Marine Atlantic** (100 Cameron St., Moncton, New Brunswick E1C 5Y6, Canada, tel. 506/851–3600, fax 506/851–3615) runs the *Northern Ranger* along the coast of Labrador on one of the most unusual cruise-ferry experiences in North America. It's similar to that of the Alaska Marine Highway or the Norwegian Coastal Voyage, but much less traveled. The ship sails northward, making dozens of passenger and cargo calls on its 2,500-mile round-trip route. The *Northern Ranger* was built in 1986 and accommodates 131 passengers in standard cabins with facilities or economy berths with shared showers. Meals are taken in a cafeteria, and a cruise director of sorts arranges activities and shore excursions. TravLtips (*see* On Board Freighters, *below*) also handles bookings.

Up the Columbia and Snake Rivers

When to Go Ships ply the Columbia and Snake rivers in the spring, summer, and fall.

Operators and Itineraries The **American West Steamboat Company** (520 Pike St., Suite 1400, Seattle, WA 98101, tel. 206/292–9606 or 800/434–1232, fax 206/623–7809) is the latest entry on the Columbia and Snake rivers. The company's sole ship is the 165-passenger stern-wheeler *Queen of the West*, which was built in 1995 to modern standards of accommodations but has a turn-of-the-century decor. These cruises sail the full navigable length of the river—1,000 miles round-trip.

Among the major lines (reviewed in Chapter 1) that offer these itineraries are Alaska Sightseeing/Cruise West, and Special Expeditions.

Along the Belize and Costa Rica Coasts

The longest barrier reef in the Western Hemisphere parallels the coast of Belize, while nearby Costa Rica offers two coasts with awesome rain forests and national parks, some only accessible by sea.

When to Go High season for cruises along the Belize and Costa Rica coasts is late November to March, but one line offers departures year-round.

Cruise Experience Cruising the coast, the ships are never out of sight of beaches, the rain forest, or the mountains. Passengers go ashore in small groups aboard inflatable landing craft, accompanied by naturalists. Excursions include jaunts up the coastal rivers and other natural waterways and walks on deserted beaches and jungle paths in search of birds, wildlife, and unusual plants and flowers. Dress aboard ship is always casual, and most activities take place during the day. An international crowd is found aboard the ships run by Temptress Voyages (*see* Operators and Itineraries, *below*), while the other seasonal operators attract mainly North Americans.

The Fleet The group of ships that sail along the coastlines of Belize and Costa Rica is small but nonetheless diverse: You can choose from among motor yachts, coastal cruisers, or a tall ship.

Operators and Itineraries **Temptress Voyages** (Cruise Company of Greenwich, 31 Brookside Dr., Greenwich, CT 06830, tel. 203/622–0203 or 800/825–0826, fax 203/622–4036) has two ships exploring these pristine cruising areas. The 63-passenger *Temptress Voyager* makes three- and six-night cruises to the barrier reef, islands, rain forests, and Mayan temples of Belize, while the new and larger 99-passenger *Temptress Explorer* cruises the Pacific coast's national seashore, islands, and ports for three or six nights.

For a luxury motor-yacht experience, **Tauck Tours** (Box 5027, Westport, CT 06881, tel. 203/226–6911 or 800/468–2825, fax 203/221–6828) operates the sleek new 48-passenger *Lady Caterina* along the Belize coast. Four-night cruises are combined with a land-and-air package to Guatemala. Departures are scheduled from December to March.

Also from Tauck Tours is the tall ship *Le Ponant* (*see* On Board Tall Ships, *below*), which cruises the Pacific coast between Costa Rica and Panama, including the Panama Canal and San Blas Islands. These six-day voyages are scheduled from January through March.

Special Expeditions (*see* Chapter 1) also sends its 80-passenger *Polaris* and a staff of naturalists to the Belize and Costa Rica coasts on 8- or 13-day cruises. The enrichment programs on these cruises, scheduled from January to March, is tops.

Clipper Cruise Line (*see* Chapter 1) sends its 138-passenger *Yorktown Clipper* on several voyages along the coasts of Costa Rica and Panama and through the canal to the Darien Jungle and San Blas Islands. These 13-day, one-way cruises sail in March and April.

Along the Great Barrier Reef

Cruising Australia's Great Barrier Reef, the world's longest, puts you on the water's surface for some of the best snorkeling and scuba diving anywhere. Shoreside excursions visit resort islands, national parks, and the Queensland coast.

When to Go Great Barrier Reef cruises operate year-round, and the waters are always warm enough for swimming and snorkeling. Queensland's weather gets very hot in the Australian summer (December through March), although it's more uncomfortable ashore than afloat.

Cruise Experience Although most people visit the Barrier Reef on a day trip from the mainland, a longer cruise gives you the opportunity to truly appreciate this unique environment. On one side lies the Pacific ocean, separated from the calm waters sheltered by the reef. Days are spent exploring the marine life on diving and snorkeling excursions—some operators organize fishing and sailing for passengers, too. And menus aboard ship offer some of the best seafood in the world, featuring barramundi, tuna, oysters, shrimp, and crayfish.

The Fleet Several Australian operators use small catamarans or single-hull vessels to explore the reef. These boats provide an intimate experience for an international clientele in a thoroughly relaxed Aussie setting.

Operators and Itineraries **Captain Cook Cruises** (Qantas Vacations, tel. 800/641–8772) operates the largest of the local vessels: the 168-passenger *Reef Endeavour.* The ship departs from Cairns on three-, four-, and seven-day trips. Cruises are comparable to a sailing aboard Clipper Cruise Line (*see* Chapter 1), with excellent seafood meals, a friendly young staff, all outside cabins, a lounge, a bar, and good open and covered deck space.

The 116-foot, 54-passenger *Coral Princess* from **Melanesian Tourist Services** (302 W. Grand Ave., Suite 10B, El Segundo, CA 90245, tel. 800/441–6880) is an upscale catamaran making four-day, one-way coastal voyages between Cairns and Townsville. **Abercrombie and Kent** (1520 Kensington Rd., Oak Brook, IL 60521, tel. 708/954–2944 or 800/323–7308, fax 708/954–3324) also includes a Barrier Reef cruise aboard the *Coral Princess* as part of its Wonders of Australia tour.

The most unusual itinerary along the reef is undertaken by the tiny 82-foot, 40-passenger *Kangaroo Explorer*, bookable through **ATS Tours** (2381 Rosecrans Ave., Suite 325, El Segundo, CA 90245, tel. 800/423–2880) or **Newmans** (6033 W. Century Blvd., #1270, Los Angeles, CA 90045, tel. 310/348–8282 or 800/421–3326, fax 310/215–9705). This little vessel sails between Cairns and Far North Queensland on six-day, one-way trips that visit the remote Cape York Peninsula and Thursday Island in the Torres Strait.

Roylen Cruises, which can be booked through **ATS Tours,** uses a pair of catamarans, the *Royal Endeavor* and *Royal Endeavor II*, on Barrier Reef cruises from Mackay. This company has been in business longer than any of the companies operating along the Great Barrier Reef. Another advantage is the ships' southerly departure point, which is closer to international resort islands.

For a Semester at Sea

As noted above, many cruises in this chapter can legitimately be considered educational cruises, but aboard only one cruise can you actually earn college credits. The **Semester at Sea** (University of Pittsburgh, 811 William Pitt Union, Pittsburgh, PA 15260, tel. 412/648–7490 or 800/854–0195, fax 412/648–2298) is a bona fide educational experience, sponsored by the University of Pittsburgh, for undergraduate students to gain college credit while seeing the world and for a small number of adults who would like to share this experience on a more informal basis. Sailings are aboard the *Universe Explorer* (formerly Commodore Cruise Line's *Enchanted Seas*); "semesters" last 100 days, but shorter eight-week summer programs are also available. Destinations include the Pacific Rim, the coast of Africa, and South America. The staff, students, and adults mix freely aboard ship and on visits ashore to hosting universities, cultural venues, cities, and villages.

In the Galápagos

Ecuador's "Enchanted Isles," the Galápagos archipelago, include 13 major islands and dozens of islets. This 3-million-year-old cluster of volcanic islands is home to giant tortoises (after which the Galápagos Islands are named); marine iguanas; sea lions; and such rare birds as cormorants, albatross, and blue-footed boobies. The islands, while no longer pristine, still captivate amateur naturalists, who come to see species described by Charles Darwin—some of which exist nowhere else in the world.

When to Go The Galápagos climate is subtropical, and cruises operate throughout the year. December to May is warm and sunny; June to November is cool and breezy. Most birds nest year-round.

Cruise Experience Passengers go ashore in groups of 20. For a more personal experience, there are a number of converted motor sailers and yachts that take only a score of people.

The Fleet The government of Ecuador (which governs the Galápagos) has banned foreign cruise ships from calling directly at the islands. All visitors, therefore—even ones sailing on foreign-ship itineraries billed as Galápagos sailings—must arrive aboard a local boat that carries no more than 100 passengers. These are the *Galapagos Explorer* (100 passengers) and the *Ambassador I* (86 passengers), both spacious but older ships. Newer is the *Santa Cruz* (90 passengers), built in 1979 specifically to cruise the Galápagos. Smaller are the *Corinthian* (48 passengers) and the *Isabella II* (38 passengers).

Operators and Itineraries Local Galápagos cruises are available in three-, four-, and seven-day packages. Many operators sell these vacations, and many ships are sold by more than one operator. Shop around for the best air, land, and cruise combination. Among the companies to contact are:

Adventure Associates (Metropolitan Touring, 13150 Coit Rd., Suite 110, Dallas, TX 75240, tel. 214/907–0414 or 800/527–2500, fax 214/783–1286).

Cruise Company of Greenwich (31 Brookside Dr., Greenwich, CT 06830, tel. 203/622–0203 or 800/825–0826, fax 203/622–4036).

Galapagos Network (7200 Corporate Center Dr., Miami, FL 33126, tel. 305/592–2294 or 800/633–7972, fax 305/592–6394).

Galapagos Yacht Cruises (7800 Red Rd., Suite 112, South Miami, FL 33143, tel. 305/665–0841 or 800/327–9854, fax 305/661–1457).

Marco Polo Vacations (16776 Bernardo Center Dr., San Diego, CA 92128, tel. 619/451–8406 or 800/421–5276, fax 619/451–8472).

Mountain Travel-Sobek (6420 Fairmount Ave., El Cerrito, CA 94530, tel. 800/227–2384, fax 510/525–7710).

OdessAmerica Cruises (170 Old Country Rd., Suite 608, Mineola, NY 11501, tel. 516/747–8880 or 800/221–3254, fax 516/747–8367).

In Southeast Asia

Southeast Asia has long been regarded as the next big destination in cruising. Slowly, the large cruise lines are offering more and more itineraries. In the meantime, you can book a cruise with a local operator that specializes in a specific area, such as Singapore and Malaysia, the Indonesian archipelago, and New Guinea.

When to Go The waters of Southeast Asia straddle the equator, so temperatures change very little from month to month; it's generally hot and humid.

Cruise Experience Due to the wide range of ships in service in this region (*see* The Fleet, *below*), there is a great range of onboard amenities. Big ships may have ocean-liner-type facilities, while the smallest vessels emphasize the destinations, offering intimate quarters and little in the way of shipboard diversions. Ashore, the region offers large cities and international resorts in Malaysia and Thailand, as well as more remote and less-visited landfalls in the Indonesian Islands and along the coast of New Guinea. Most people combine a Southeast Asia cruise with a land itinerary.

The Fleet Ships in service in Southeast Asia can be small or huge, and they range from a catamaran to ferries that once operated on the Baltic Sea.

Operators and Itineraries By far the largest local operator is **Star Cruise** (391B Orchard Rd., #13-01, Ngee Ann City, Tower B Singapore 0923, tel. 011/65–733–6988, fax 011/65–733–3622), with five ships based in Singapore plus additional cruises from Hong Kong. Most interesting are two huge ships, the 1,900-passenger *Star Aquarius* and the 1,900-passenger *Star Pisces*, both former Baltic cruise ferries.

The 330-passenger *Andaman Princess* of **Siam Cruise Line** (33/10-11 Chaiyod Arcade, Sukhumvit Soi 11, Sukhumvit Rd., Bangkok 10110 Thailand, tel. 011/66–2–255–4563, fax 011/66–2–255–8961) operates from Thai ports along both coasts depending on the season. The food and most of the passengers are Thai, so it's a true ethnic experience on a very handsome, older ship, built in 1960 for Baltic service.

For a short Indonesian cruise from Bali that includes Komodo Island, home of the famous dragons, the *Bali Sea Dancer* (formerly Classical Cruises' *Illiria*) offers a very high standard of accommodations for 150 passengers. The ship is represented in the United States by **Esplanade Tours** (581 Boylston St., Boston, MA 02116, tel. 617/266–7465 or 800/426–5492, fax 617/262–9829).

Farther east, the *Melanesian Discoverer*, a 42-passenger catamaran, operates four-, five-, and seven-night cruises calling at the coastal villages and islands of Papua New Guinea. The ship can be booked in the United States through **Melanesian Tourist Services** (302 W. Grand Ave., El Segundo, CA 90245, tel. 310/785–0370 or 800/776–0370, fax 310/785–0314).

On Board Barges

In Britain and Europe, rivers have served as arteries of commercial transportation for centuries, while canals have been in service for the past 200 years. For cruise passengers, this network of waterborne transportation offers literally thousands of boats for hire, at many different price levels, in the United Kingdom, Ireland, France, Belgium, and the Netherlands.

Cruise Experience

Boat and barge travel is about as far removed from deep-sea cruising as you can get. About the only shared factor is the water flowing beneath the hull as you cruise along at the pace of a fast walk. Smaller boats and barges may be available only on a charter basis—your party of six to eight will have the whole vessel to itself. Larger barges are usually booked on an individual basis, meaning that you'll be traveling in the company of other passengers, just as you would on any other cruise.

In England, an active 2,000-mile canal system stretches from London to Yorkshire. The canals, 18th- and 19th-century equivalents of automobile freeways, cut right through city centers, cross valleys on aqueducts, and climb hills using a stepladder of locks. Today, the network is used almost exclusively by pleasure craft, and in many places, the lock operations are self-service. Popular rivers are the Thames between London, Windsor, and Oxford, and the Shannon in Ireland.

Across the English Channel in France, Belgium, and the Netherlands, the canals and rivers are broader and the barges are larger. As most waterways still see commercial traffic, self-hire boats are few.

The most popular barges feature beautifully decorated, wood-paneled accommodations, gourmet food and wines, and a shared social experience for three to six nights. Besides the chance to drift leisurely through the countryside, canal and barge cruises may offer the opportunity for excursions by van, bike, foot, and hot-air balloon to medieval villages, châteaus, and wineries.

Least expensive are the self-driven English boats, which may cost as little as $250 per person for a week's charter. Hotel boats, with crew and food provided, are mid-priced at about $650 per person for a week. At the top of the scale are luxury barges. Six nights, including a crew and all food and drinks, will range from about $1,400 to $3,300 per person.

The Fleet

Within this varied fleet, there are substantial differences in accommodations.

Luxury barges, stretching from 100 to 200 feet in length and carrying up to 50 people, may have one or two decks of interior space that includes roomy outside cabins and suites with private facilities, a dining room, and a separate lounge with a bar. The sundeck is usually open with lounge seating, umbrellas for shade, and space to store bicycles. Some are air-conditioned, and all have central heating. Charter barges are usually smaller than hotel barges, but they share the great emphasis on food and wines.

English narrow boats have more basic accommodations for 2 to 12, with small cabins, shared facilities, and a combination lounge and dining area. The operator supplies the bedding, linens, and galley equipment, and passengers bring their food or eat out en route. Learning to drive a narrow boat is quite easy, but considerable patience is required during multiple locking operations and frequent waits for opposing traffic on one-way stretches.

In Britain and Ireland

When to Go Most narrow boats and hotel barges operate between the end of April and the beginning of October. However, the weather is highly unpredictable, so be prepared to spend at least some time cooped up inside. Boats are not air-conditioned—not normally a problem—but cabins do get stuffy in persistent hot weather.

Operators and Itineraries **Abercrombie & Kent** (1520 Kensington Rd., Oak Brook, IL 60521, tel. 708/954–2944 or 800/323–7308, fax 708/954–3324) represents the 100-foot, 12-passenger *Actief* on three- and six-night cruises between Windsor and Oxford in the Upper Thames Valley. This barge has two suites, three twins, and two singles. All are outside accommodations with private facilities.

The Cruise Company of Greenwich (31 Brookside Dr., Greenwich, CT 06830, tel. 203/622–0203 or 800/825–0826, fax 203/622–4036) represents the 80-foot, eight-passenger barge *Merganser*, which sails on three- to six-night trips along the Thames between London and Oxford. Stops are made at Kew Gardens, Hampton Court, Windsor Castle, Eton, and Henley. Three twins and two singles have private facilities.

Also from the Cruise Company are the twin, 10-passenger barges *Barkis* and *Peggotty*, which both operate six-night cruises in Cambridgeshire along the River Great Ouse, visiting picturesque villages, inns, country gardens, and churches.

This same agent sells the 105-foot, 12-passenger *Shannon Princess*, which cruises along the 130-mile River Shannon in Ireland. The Dutch-style barge has cabins with windows that open and private facilities. Golfing and fishing are popular activities, in addition to viewing scenery and visiting villages, castles, estates, and pubs.

Highland Steamboat Holidays (c/o Nick Walker, The Change House, Lochgilphead, Argyll, Scotland PA31 8QH, tel. 011/44–1546–5232, fax 011/44–1546–5249) operates a unique 12-passenger, coal-fired coastal steamboat on five- and six-day cruises in the sheltered waters off the west coast of Scotland and along the Caledonian Canal. Known as a Clyde Puffer, the former cargo carrier was built in 1943 and, for the last 20 years, has operated passenger cruises. Cabin bunks are tiny—basic twins or doubles with shared shower and toilet facilities—and there's a small dining lounge.

For More Information The **British Tourist Authority** (551 5th Ave., New York, NY 10176, tel. 800/462–2748) has information on individual operators as well as the booklet "Inland Waterways."

On the Continent

When to Go In France, Belgium, and the Netherlands, the barging season stretches from early March into December, though the best chance of warm weather begins in late April and ends in the early autumn. Some itineraries highlight tulip time in Holland, gardens in flower in England, and the grape harvest in France.

Operators and Itineraries **Abercrombie & Kent** (*see* In Britain and Ireland, *above*) has no less than nine barges in France, plus two in Holland and Belgium and one in Austria. The barges in this top-of-the-line fleet accommodate from 6 to 51 passengers; all cabins have private facilities. Three- to six-night cruises travel the Loire, Soane, Seine, and Rhone rivers and the canals of Belgium and Holland.

The **Cruise Company of Greenwich** (*see* In Britain and Ireland, *above*) represents seven hotel barges in France that carry between 6 and 12 passengers. Destinations include the Upper Loire, Burgundy, Alsace-Lorraine, Provence, Canal du Midi, and Gascogny. Additional barges cruise the waterways of Belgium and Holland, the

River Thames in England, the Upper Shannon in Ireland, and the Caledonian Canal and Loch Ness in Scotland.

French Country Waterways (Box 2195, Duxbury, MA 02331, tel. 617/934–2454 or 800/222–1236, fax 617/934–9048) operates four 8- to 18-passenger luxury barges on six-night trips through Burgundy. Cabins have twin or double beds with private facilities. All cruises include a dinner at a Michelin three-star restaurant.

On Board European Ferries

Combining the amenities and comforts of an ocean liner with the point-to-point service of a bus or train, a trip on a European ferry makes for a very attractive short cruise. In northern and southern Europe, these ferries form major links with the highway and railway system. In fact, a ferry cruise can be combined with a driving or Eurailpass itinerary.

Some routes, especially in Scandinavia, thread through forested archipelagos and sail into scenic fjords, and the relaxing onboard ambience encourages visitors to meet local people. In the Mediterranean, large ferry liners link Italy with Greece. Feeder routes continue on to the Greek Islands, Turkey, Cyprus, and Israel.

Along the Coast of Norway

Like Alaska's Inside Passage, the Norwegian coastline boasts spectacular scenery and the advantage of cruising in calm waters. And as in southeast Alaska, the coastal waters serve as a "marine highway," where a network of mail ferries provides transportation for local travelers and visitors alike.

When to Go Again like Alaska, Norway has its period of nearly continuous daylight from mid-May to July, and this is, of course, the most popular time to travel. Although the summer season books up early, space may nevertheless be available at short notice. Cabins may be easier to find during the less-traveled spring and fall.

Cruise Experience Most of the route is protected from the open sea, but short open-water stretches can be rough. Passengers may elect to take the entire 11-day, 2,500-mile round-trip journey or get on and off at any one of 35 stops in between. Time in port ranges from 15 minutes to several hours. Optional overland shore excursions leave the ship in one port and rejoin it in another.

Travelers hail from the United States, Britain, and the rest of Europe, particularly Germany and, of course, Norway. As a result, menus aboard ship are mainly Continental, with Norwegian specialties. Breakfast and lunch are served buffet style, while dinner is a sit-down affair at reserved tables. Daily activities include watching the scenery pass by, watching the ship's cargo operations, and socializing with fellow passengers. Newer ships may have a band aboard during summer sailings.

The Fleet Three generations of vessels operate on Norwegian coastal cruises. The newest, built since 1993, have modern cruise-ship amenities such as cocktail lounges, library/card rooms, a restaurant, a cafeteria, a sauna, and an observation lounge. They carry 490 passengers and register about 11,000 tons.

A little older are the ferries built in 1982–83. These ships, which were enlarged in 1988–89, carry 325 passengers. Cabins are smaller than in the newest ships, but the vessels have restaurant facilities and two observation lounges—one of which is glass-enclosed.

The oldest ships in the Norwegian coastal fleet were built in the 1960s. They carry 170 to 225 passengers in small cabins—some without private facilities. What they lack in amenities they make up for in historical appeal. Their onboard ambience reflects Norway's maritime heritage, with wood-paneled lounges, local artwork, and teak decks. Public rooms are limited to two forward-facing lounges, a restaurant, and a cafeteria used by deck passengers.

Operators and Itineraries Cruises of Norway travel nearly the entire length of the coastline from the North Sea to the Arctic Ocean. In the south, the terminus is Bergen, Norway's second-largest city and most important seaport. In the north, Kirkenes, near the border with Finland and Russia, is the end of the line. Eleven ships, marketed by **Bergen Line** (405 Park Ave., New York, NY 10022, tel. 212/319–1300 or 800/323–7436, fax 212/319–1390) depart daily.

Elsewhere in Scandinavia and the North Sea

Like a spider's web connecting the cities of Scandinavia and its offshore islands, overnight ferry routes crisscross the Baltic and North seas. Many routes are designed to feed into the well-developed northern European rail system, allowing passengers to create their own rail-sea itineraries.

When to Go Most of these ferry services operate on a year-round basis. Ships may shift from route to route depending on the season.

Cruise Experience Most passengers are British, German, and Scandinavian. Dining varies by the size of the ship (*see* The Fleet, *below*). Meals may be served by waiters in sit-down restaurants, at elaborate buffet-style smorgasbords, or in inexpensive cafeterias. One ship even has a McDonald's franchise. Cruise-ship-style entertainment is equally varied: There may be cabarets, dancing, and gambling, again, depending upon the size of the ship.

The Fleet The largest ships resemble oceangoing cruise liners. Some are bigger than 30,000 tons and have such onboard facilities as theaters, saunas, and duty-free shops. There may also be playrooms and video arcades for children. Cabins range from outside accommodations with picture windows to inside cabins designed for families.

Operators and Itineraries The following lines operate some of the most popular northern European ferry routes:

The Norwegian-based **Color Line** sails across the North Sea, connecting Norway, Germany, Denmark, and England. Routes include Bergen–Newcastle, Stavanger–Newcastle, Oslo–Kiel; Oslo–Kristiansand, and Oslo–Hirtshals.

Danish-owned **Scandinavian Seaways** operates between England and Denmark, Sweden and Germany, and Norway and Denmark and the Netherlands. Routes include Copenhagen–Oslo and Harwich (England)–Esbjerg (Denmark).

Silja Line operates the world's largest cruise ferries, registering up to 60,000 tons and carrying almost 3,000 passengers. Routes include Stockholm–Helsinki and Stockholm–Turku (Finland).

Silja Line's main competitor is **Viking Line,** which offers similarly large ships. Routes include Stockholm–Helsinki or Stockholm–Turku.

Two principal U.S. agencies can book passages and combination tours with the lines described above and others not specifically listed here, such as short-duration Baltic Sea cruises from Scandinavian ports to Russia, Estonia, and Latvia and longer sea routes to the Shetland Islands, Faroes, Iceland, and Spitzbergen.

Bergen Line (405 Park Ave., New York, NY 10022, tel. 212/319–1300 or 800/323–7436, fax 212/319–1390) books one-way and round-trip cruises and cruise-tour packages for more than a half-dozen lines.

EuroCruises (303 W. 13th St., New York, NY 10014, tel. 212/691–2099 or 800/688–3876) represents more than 20 European-based cruise lines and 60 ships, sailing throughout Scandinavia, the Baltic states, and Russia.

For More Information National tourist offices can supply connecting rail and ferry schedules. Rail Europe (tel. 800/438–7245) is the main source of rail passes; some are valid for certain ferry routes at no extra cost or at a discount. None, however, include cabin accommodations.

Through Southern Europe

Like the northern European ferry system described above, the Mediterranean abounds with unusual cruise options. Unlike the northern European ferry routes, which link mainly coastal cities, southern European ferries principally connect vacation islands with the Continent.

Italy is the main gateway for ferry cruises to points in Greece, Turkey, Cyprus, Israel, and Egypt. Ports of embarkation include Venice, Ancona, Bari, and Brindisi. Most runs to Greece take about 24 hours, but longer one-way and round-trip voyages are available to the eastern Mediterranean ports of İzmir (Turkey), Limassol (Cyprus), Haifa (Israel), and Alexandria (Egypt).

To island-hop through Greece, ferry travel is not only affordable but it may be the only way to go. Once in Aegean waters, a short crossing to the Turkish coast—or beyond—becomes a natural extension to a Greek-island itinerary.

When to Go Although some of the most popular routes have frequent service and schedules that change little from year to year, other destinations may see only seasonal access. Summertime travel can be crowded with backpackers. Determining specific departure times for Greek-island ferries has always been problematic, but there are some reliable and fairly comprehensive sources for those who like to plan ahead.

Cruise Experience From the deck of your ferry, anticipation runs high at the first sighting of Corsica's rugged north coast, the swirling waters known as Charybdis off Sicily, the Grand Harbor at Malta, or the white-washed towns of the Aegean Islands.

Operators and Itineraries From Spanish ports, the state-owned **Trasmediterranea Line** operates high-standard ferries on overnight runs. Routes include Cadiz–Canary Islands, Barcelona–Balearic Islands (Palma de Majorca, Ibiza, and Mahon), and Valencia–Balearic Islands. Shorter day ferries run from southern Spain to North Africa.

From French ports, **SNCM** uses the embarkation points of Toulon, Marseille, and Nice for day and overnight cruises. Routes include service to Corsica, Sardinia, and North Africa.

From Italian ports, there are dozens of state-run and privately owned lines sailing from points on Italy's west coast. Routes service Corsica, Sardinia, Sicily, Malta, Tunisia, and coastal islands such as Elba, Ischia, and Capri. From Italy's east-coast ports of Venice, Ancona, Bari, and Brindisi, passengers can sail to the Greek island of Corfu and the coastal ports of Igoumentisa and Patras, the principal entry point for connecting buses to Athens and the port of Piraeus. Major lines sailing on these routes include **Adriatica** (also service to Alexandria), **Hellenic Mediterranean, Marlines** (also to Crete and Cesme, Turkey), **Minoan** (also to Crete and Cesme, Turkey), **Poseidon** (also to Limassol and Haifa), **Strintzis, SuperFast Ferries,** and **Vergina Cruises** (also to Limassol and Haifa). **Turkish Maritime Lines** uses Venice, but bypasses Greek ports for Antalya, Cesme, and İzmir.

From Greek ports, many ships that originated in Italy may be boarded en route to destinations on the Turkish coast, Cyprus, Israel, and Egypt. Most domestic services leave from Piraeus, the port of Athens, and northern routes depart from Thessaloniki.

From Turkish ports, **Turkish Maritime Lines** operates summer sailings of several days' duration that make an inexpensive cruise along the Black Sea coast. The route sails from Istanbul to Samsun and Trabzon. Other routes include an overnight run from southern Turkey to Cyprus and service between İzmir and Istanbul.

For More Information Unlike Scandinavian operators, most Mediterranean ferry services do not have representatives in the United States, and unfortunately some lines do not think it worthwhile to answer queries. However, national tourist offices for Spain, France, Italy, Greece, Turkey, Cyprus, Israel, and Egypt can often supply ferry information, along with handy timetables (sometimes photocopies only) and overseas addresses, telephone numbers, and fax numbers for specific lines. Some Italy–Greece ferry operators are participants in the Eurailpass. Fares are included, but cabin accommodations are always extra.

Another excellent source of information is the Thomas Cook European Timetable (Forsythe Travel Library, 9154 W. 57th St., Box 2975, Shawnee Mission, KS 66201, tel. 913/384–3440 or 800/367–7984), a monthly guide to major rail and ferry schedules that includes a section of useful route maps.

On Board European Liners

The cruise ships detailed in Chapter 1 carry primarily North American passengers. Other liners serve mostly British, German, or Italian passengers. Generally speaking, these ships are for experienced cruisers. If the idea of cruising with people from other countries sounds appealing, you may find the experience extremely satisfying.

Cruise Experience The experience of sailing on a European ship can be quite different from that encountered on the American lines. Cuisine and entertainment are geared for European tastes. Ethnic dishes in the dining room and folkloric dancing in the showroom frequently reflect the origin of the ship's crew and passengers. There's often a single seating for meals, with passengers divided between two restaurants, and wine may be complimentary at dinner. Announcements may be made in a language other than English, and shipboard performers may entertain in their native language as well. Also, many Europeans have very different ideas about smoking and there are fewer restrictions.

The Fleet European ships tend to be smaller and older than those sold primarily to North American passengers. Most ships listed here will have English-language information and English-speaking personnel. However, the mother tongue aboard ship will reflect the line's country of origin.

Operators and Itineraries **Classical Cruises** (132 E. 70th St., New York, NY 10021, tel. 212/794–3200 or 800/252–7745, fax 212/774–1545) can put you aboard the 16,107-ton, 758-passenger *Bolero* (formerly Norwegian Cruise Line's *Starward*) for a variety of 10- or 11-day cruises from Venice to the eastern Mediterranean. The chefs are Italian, the food Continental, and the ship a good value for the money. Packages include hotels, air, and transfers.

Italian **Costa Cruise Lines** is reviewed in Chapter 1 for its ships that cater to North Americans, but the line is also one of the best-known names in Europe for cruising. The ships sail in European waters in summer and in South America or the Caribbean in winter. One vessel, the *Daphne,* makes one of the longest and most interesting world cruises departing from Genoa in December. The *Eugenio-Costa* makes a transatlantic trip to South America for the winter. These Costa ships may be booked through the line's U.S. headquarters (tel. 800/462–6782). The line also operates the *CostaPlaya* (formerly Ocean Cruise Line's *Pearl*) on itineraries to Cuba and other Caribbean ports, although this cruise is not available to U.S. citizens.

New York–based **EuroCruises** (303 W. 13th St., New York, NY 10014, tel. 212/691–2099 or 800/688–3876, fax 212/366–4747) represents several European cruise ships, such as the 15,000-ton, 750-passenger *Azur*; the 16,107-ton, 758-passenger *Bolero* (also represented by Classical Cruises, *see above*); and the 9,846-ton, 406-passenger *Funchal* on a wide variety of cruises in northern and southern Europe. One of the agency's specialties is summer Baltic cruises aboard the *Anna Karenina, Ilich, Konstantin Simonov,* and *Kristina Regina.*

Fantasy (Chandris) Cruises (TravLtips, Box 580188, Flushing, NY 11358, tel. 717/939–2400 or 800/872–8584) was once a popular name among American cruisers, who sailed aboard the *Amerikanis* for a quarter century. Now carrying primarily European passengers, the 20,000-ton, 617-passenger *Amerikanis* undertakes inexpensive 7- to 14-day Mediterranean and northern European cruises from April to November. The *Amerikanis,* a traditional ship with Greek officers and an international crew, is well maintained and old-fashioned. The few Americans aboard are usually traveling in a group.

Fred Olsen Cruise Lines' 450-passenger *Black Prince* is Norwegian-owned with a Filipino crew. The vessel caters to middle-income British passengers with year-round cruises from southern England to Iberia, Madeira, the Canary Islands, Morocco, the western Mediterranean, the Caribbean, and, in summer, northern Europe. Built in 1966, this well-maintained, professionally run ship has built a very loyal following over many years. This ship is represented in the United States by EuroCruises (*see above*). In fall 1996, Fred Olsen was scheduled to take delivery of the *Star Odyssey,* formerly of Royal Cruise Line, and rename it the *Black Watch.* At press time, the ship was expected to sail on cruises to Europe and Africa.

The 49-passenger *Hebridean Princess,* from **Hebridean Island Cruises** (Acorn Park, Skipton, North Yorkshire, DB23 2UE, England, tel. 011/44–1756–701338, fax 011/44–1756–701455), is comparable to a five-star country hotel and quite unlike any other ship afloat. It puts to sea mostly from Oban and other Scottish ports, sailing to the Inner and Outer Hebrides, Orkney and Shetland islands, Ireland, and the coast of Norway. Each day includes one or two calls, and the ship anchors or docks at night. Cabins and lounges are beautifully decorated; the restaurant is outstanding. The *Hebridian Princess* caters to an upper-income British clientele. An increasing number of Americans have discovered this gem, but generally no more than four to six are aboard at any one time.

The Italian-based company **Mediterranean Shipping Cruises** (420 5th Ave., New York, NY 10018, tel. 212/764–4800 or 800/666–9333, fax 212/764–8592) caters to Europeans on northern European, Mediterranean, and Caribbean cruises and to South Africans during the Southern Hemisphere winter. The fleet consists of the American-built, 21,051-ton, 600-passenger *Monterey*; the 17,495-ton, 800-passenger *Rhapsody* (formerly the *Cunard Princess*); and the 16,495-ton, 775-passenger *Symphony* (formerly Costa Cruise Lines' *EnricoCosta*).

Another English firm that caters to a British clientele, **Noble Caledonia** (Esplanade Tours, 581 Boylston St., Boston, MA 02116, tel.

617/266–7465 or 800/426–5492, fax 617/262–9829) operates expedition-style cruises aboard the 3,095-ton, 144-passenger *Caledonian Star*. Itineraries are worldwide; sailings are accompanied by guest lecturers. Noble Caledonia also books the expedition ships *Explorer* (*see* Abercrombie & Kent *in* Chapter 1) and *World Discoverer* (*see* Society Expeditions *in* Chapter 1) or Russian icebreakers for voyages up the Amazon and to Antarctica. Other possibilities include riverboats in Europe, Russia, and Burma.

The 17,270-ton, 750-passenger **Southern Cross** (formerly Premier's *Star/Ship Majestic*) now sails for British-based CTC Cruise Lines (OdessAmerica Cruise, 170 Old Country Rd., Suite 608, Mineola, NY 11501, tel. 516/747–8880 or 800/221–3254, fax 516/747–8367). Considered a good value but hardly luxurious, the ship sails to and from Australia, in the Caribbean, and on cruises closer to the home of its mainly British clientele.

Paquet French Cruises (1510 S.E. 17th St., Fort Lauderdale, FL 33316, tel. 305/764–3500 or 800/556–8850, fax 305/764–2888) is another name that longtime American cruisers may remember well. The line's sole ship, the 13,691-ton, 533-passenger *Mermoz* offers a sophisticated classic-ship experience on cruises in northern and southern Europe in the summer and in the Caribbean and along the South American coast in winter. These cruises draw mostly French passengers, along with others who speak French or are Francophiles.

British **P&O,** the parent company of Los Angeles–based Princess Cruises (tel. 310/553–1770), has one of the few brand-new ships built specifically for British passengers. This vessel, the 67,000-ton, 1,760-passenger *Oriana*, is also one of the biggest of the European ships. It carries mostly British passengers on cruises from England to northern Europe, the Atlantic Islands, the Mediterranean, and the Caribbean. Many more Americans (and Australians) are aboard for the round-the-world cruises, which call at U.S. ports, such as Los Angeles and San Francisco. Other ships in P&O's fleet include the 35-year-old, 1,600-passenger *Canberra*, an aging liner with a very loyal British clientele. P&O's smallest ship is the 714-passenger *Sea Princess*, another classic liner with a lovely wood-paneled Scandinavian interior. The trio operates with British officers and a British and Goan (Indian) hotel staff.

Another venerable British institution, **Swan Hellenic Cruises** (Classical Cruises, 132 E. 70th St., New York, NY 10021, tel. 212/794–3200 or 800/252–7745, fax 212/774–1545) has offered educationally oriented cruises for more than 40 years. Professors from British universities accompany every cruise, giving 45-minute lectures and providing leadership ashore. As educational cruises have become more popular, the line's long-standing reputation has attracted an increasing number of Americans. Many are aboard as part of an alumni or museum group. In 1996, the line, owned by P&O (*see above*), introduced a new ship, the 300-passenger *Minerva*, built specifically for enrichment cruises and far more spacious than its previous vessel, *Orpheus*, which now sails for Royal Olympic Cruises (*see* Chapter 1). The *Minerva*'s summer destinations include ports in Europe and the Mediterranean; winter voyages sail to destinations in the Indian Ocean and Southeast Asia. Swan Hellenic also charters a riverboat in Europe and another on the Nile (*see below*).

On Board Freighters

To embark on a freighter cruise is to join a tiny floating community that roams the high seas in a world of its own. Freighter travelers are a special breed; most are retired yet active people who like a leisurely pace, lots of time at sea, considerable comfort, and moderate rates averaging about $100 per day.

Cruise Experience

Unlike most cruise ships, which have precisely scheduled port calls, freighters stay in port as long as it takes to load or unload their cargo. This can be measured in hours or in days—depending upon how modern the ship is. Itineraries, too, are sometimes subject to change. Flexibility is the key word as there may be delays.

Passengers tend to be older than the typical cruiser, and the complement of passengers aboard a freighter is considerably smaller than that aboard a standard cruise ship. Cargo ships that take from 2 to 12 passengers do not carry a doctor and have age limits that vary from 75 to 82. Larger passenger freighters have no age restrictions and may employ a physician.

The Fleet

Most cargo liners carry up to 12 passengers, although the biggest accommodates 88. Because most of the space aboard ship is devoted to freight, passenger facilities are more limited than they are on ocean liners and usually consist of a dining room, small lounge, and exercise room. Outdoor deck space for passengers is provided at the stern, where there may be a small pool and a whirlpool. Often, passengers share these facilities with the ship's officers. Cabins are larger than those on a typical cruise ship, but they're much more modestly decorated. There usually is no room service.

Operators and Itineraries

Passenger-carrying cargo ships depart the United States from ports on the East Coast, West Coast, and Gulf Coast. Some also travel the St. Lawrence River from ports on the Great Lakes and in Canada. Round-trip journeys last from four weeks to four months. Shorter one-way passages may also be available.

The list of passenger-carrying freighter companies included below is a small but varied selection of ships sailing from North America and elsewhere. Some lines have years of service while others, dependent on sufficient cargo inducement, may appear and disappear at fairly short notice. A few of these operators may be contacted directly, as noted; otherwise, contact one of the two freighter-cruise agencies listed under For More Information, *below*.

Bank Line (British and Indian officers) operates the eight-passenger semicontainer ship *Olivebank* from Savannah, Georgia, on a 78- to 80-day round-trip voyage to the Canary Islands, Africa, and South America. From Hull, England, this venerable British company also runs 110- to 115-day around-the-world freighter cruises, which depart on a monthly basis.

Blue Star runs two services with high standards, using six ships (British officers) that take 10 to 12 passengers. The East Coast Service, a 70-day round-trip, embarks in Jacksonville, Florida, for ports in Australia and New Zealand and returns to Philadelphia. The West Coast Service, 42–45 days round-trip, departs Los Angeles, also bound for Australia and New Zealand, and returns via Fiji to Seattle, Oakland, and Los Angeles.

Chilean Line has two popular 12-passenger ships sailing from the Gulf Coast of the United States to the west coast of South America. The *Laja* and the *Lircay*, built in 1978, operate voyages of about 48 days through the Panama Canal to Ecuador, Peru, Chile, and Colombia.

Columbus Line operates two top-notch services on ships carrying 8 to 12 passengers (German officers). The East Coast (Boomerang

Service) sails from Jacksonville, Florida, and usually Houston, Texas, by way of the Panama Canal to Australia and New Zealand, and returns to Philadelphia. The round-trip voyage takes 68 to 70 days. The West Coast (Kiwi Service) departs Los Angeles for Australia and New Zealand and returns to Seattle. This round-trip lasts 42 to 45 days.

Compagnie Polynesienne de Transport Maritime (Box 22, Papeete, Tahiti, tel. 011/689–426240) provides the lifeline for French Polynesia with the 77-passenger cargo ship *Aranui II* on a 16-day round-trip voyage from Papeete, Tahiti, to the Society Islands and Marquesas, calling at Ua Pou, Nuku Hiva, Hiva Oa (where French painter Gauguin lived), Fatu Hiva, Ua Huka, and Rangiroa. The ship carries local passengers on deck and international passengers in cabins. The accommodations are simple, and some do not have private facilities. Tours, included in the fare, are organized in each port, and although there is no age limit, clambering into small boats and landing through the surf requires some agility.

Curnow Shipping Ltd. (The Shipyard, Porthleven, Helston, Cornwall TR13 9JA, England, tel. 011/44–1326–563434) of Cornwall, England, operates the world's most remote passenger and cargo service with the Royal Mail Ship *St. Helena*, sailing from Cardiff in South Wales to the beautiful South Atlantic island of St. Helena, a British dependency that does not have an airport. The ship carries up to 132 islanders and adventure-seeking tourists in a wide variety of cabins. Most trips call at Tenerife and Ascension. Passengers continuing on to Cape Town, South Africa, enjoy a week ashore on St. Helena and a warm welcome at a small hotel or guest house while the ship unloads cargo and makes a shuttle run to Ascension and back. The one-way passage between Britain and South Africa takes about four weeks. Passengers have the option of sailing or flying back. Once a year, the *St. Helena* departs from Cape Town on a two-week round-trip voyage, always a sellout, to even more remote Tristan da Cunha.

Ivaran Lines (111 Pavonia Ave., Jersey City, NJ 07310, tel. 201/798–5656 or 800/451–1639, fax 201/798–2233) has the distinction of operating the world's largest and most luxurious container ship, the *Americana*, carrying 88 passengers in cruise-ship-style accommodations. Cabins consist of singles, doubles, and suites, some with sitting areas and private verandas. Passenger facilities include a piano bar and lounge, library/card room, dining room, exercise room, sauna, outdoor pool, ample deck space, and a hospital with a Scandinavian doctor and nurse. The service, by a South American staff, and the food, which includes Norwegian delicacies, are both excellent. A purser/cruise director arranges excursions ashore. A 51- or 52-day round-trip voyage departs New Orleans and Houston, setting sail for Venezuela, Brazil, Argentina, the Caribbean, and Mexico. Ivaran also operates a smaller ship, the 12-passenger *San Antonio*. Built in 1994, this 12-passenger ship embarks at Port Elizabeth, New Jersey, and makes calls in Baltimore, Norfolk, Savannah, and Miami before heading for South America. The round-trip from New Jersey takes 44 days.

Mineral Shipping operates two 7- to 12-passenger ships (Croatian officers) from Savannah, Georgia, to Dutch ports, with several days' stay ashore, before returning to the U.S. East Coast. Voyages last 32 to 40 days round-trip. Sailings from Savannah to the Mediterranean are also available aboard 12-passenger ships. The round-trip voyages take about 70 days and ports change at short notice.

Windjammer Barefoot Cruises (Box 120, Miami Beach, FL 33119, tel. 800/327–2601), best known for its fleet of tall ships (*see* On Board Tall Ships, *below*), operates the 100-passenger *Amazing Grace* as a supply vessel for its Caribbean ships. Built in 1955 as a Scottish lighthouse tender, the ship has wood-paneled accommodations, including original cabins with shared facilities and more recently added rooms with private showers. The onboard atmosphere is low-key, and the food is thoroughly American. Sailing from Freeport, the Bahamas, the ship makes 13-day one-way and 26-day round-trips to 20 islands as far south as Grenada.

For More Information The following agencies have been booking freighter travel for many years, and they may act as general sales agents (GSA) for individual lines. Both agencies offer useful though very different publications.

Freighter World Cruises (180 S. Lake Ave., Suite 335, Pasadena, CA 91101, tel. 818/449–3106, fax 818/449–9573) publishes the "Freighter Space Advisory" every two weeks. This is the bible of freighter cruises, listing itineraries, cabin availability, and special fares. Brief descriptions detail the accommodations aboard the various ships. Most of the freighters listed have been inspected by the agency's staff.

TravLtips (Box 580188, Flushing, NY 11358, tel. 718/939–2400 or 800/872–8584) publishes a bimonthly magazine ($20 a year) with black-and-white photos and reports on freighter trips by passengers. The magazine also lists special offers.

On Board Research Vessels

Perhaps the most adventurous endeavor in cruising is to book yourself aboard an icebreaker on a scientific research mission.

When to Go Cruises aboard research vessels sail to the Arctic and Antarctic in the summer—June through September in the Northern Hemisphere and December through March in the Southern Hemisphere. At these times of year, days are generally sunny and temperatures are relatively warm (at least above freezing), but wind and cloud cover can create bundle-up conditions.

The Fleet Most passenger-carrying research vessels are Russian, Ukrainian, or Estonian, under charter to tour agencies. They usually accommodate up to 100 passengers, sometimes less. Cabins are typically all outside with private facilities, although some may have shared baths. Shipboard amenities can be surprisingly good, as some of these vessels were designed to spend extended time at sea. One icebreaker even has an indoor swimming pool.

Cruise Experience Sailing to the polar regions and elsewhere, the "shore excursions" aboard these ships may include standing beside the ship on the Arctic pack ice or taking a helicopter flight to scout the route ahead. The research opportunities that these unique vessels present attract top-echelon lecturers, too.

Operators and Itineraries Canadian-based **Marine Expeditions** (13 Hazelton Ave., Toronto, Ontario M5R 2EI, tel. 416/964–9069 or 800/263–9147, fax 416/454–8712) charters five research vessels for expedition cruises in Antarctica and the Arctic, plus the coast of Norway, and positioning trips that call at mid-Atlantic islands from the Falklands northward. Although officially the five ships are Russian- and Estonian-owned, they carry "marine" aliases such as *Marine Adventurer* and *Marine Challenger*. The vessels vary in size, carrying from 38 to 82 passengers.

Mountain Travel-Sobek (6429 Fairmount Ave., El Cerrito, CA 94530, tel. 510/527–8100 or 800/227–2384, fax 510/525–7710), one of the oldest adventure-travel companies, charters the 38-passenger ice-class *Livonia* for a December to February Antarctic program.

Noble Caledonia (*see* On Board European Liners, *above*) uses the 36-passenger research vessel *Professor Khromov*, with one of the smallest passenger complements, on 11-night cruises from the tip of

South America to Antarctica. The company also books space on other research ships to the North Pole, the Northeast Passage, and the Spitsbergen and Arctic islands.

Quark Expeditions (980 Post Rd., Darien, CT 06820, tel. 203/656–0499 or 800/356–5699, fax 203/655–6623) travels from the top to the bottom of the world on one of the most extensive and innovative research-vessel programs available. In the Arctic region, the 98-passenger icebreaker *Yamal* crashes through the Russian ice to the North Pole, while the 106-passenger *Kapitan Dranitsyn* pounds its way along the Northeast Passage above Siberia to Greenland, Spitzbergen, and remote islands within the Arctic Circle. At the other end of the world, the 108-passenger *Kapitan Khlebnikov* was scheduled to undertake a pioneering, passenger-carrying, 65-day complete circumnavigation of Antarctica round-trip from Port Stanley, Falkland Islands, in November 1996. Additional cruises to the Antarctic Peninsula, the Falklands, and South Georgia use the 79-passenger *Akademik Ioffe* and other research ships. Quark has also experimented with expedition voyages to the more remote regions of the Indian Ocean and the South Pacific.

TCS Expeditions (2025 1st Ave., Seattle, WA 98121, tel. 206/727–7300 or 800/727–7477, fax 206/727–7309) also charters the *Yamal* for voyages to the North Pole. The icebreaker, originally designed to spend months away from its home base, offers such luxuries as an indoor swimming pool, a sauna, a gym, and a basketball/volleyball court.

Any one ship may be sold by more than one operator. Rates vary enormously, depending on the itinerary's remoteness and the degree of competition. When comparing different packages, look carefully at what's included and what's not.

On Board Riverboats

Cruises on the rivers of the world are as varied as the rivers themselves. The Rhine's castles and cathedrals look down onto a busy commercial waterway, while the mighty Amazon surges through the rain forest, and the Nile forms a green ribbon in the desert. The Yangtze is best known for the Three Gorges and Australia's Murray River is hardly known at all. In Russia, the Volga leads to small villages closed to the outside world less than a decade ago. Burma's Irrawaddy, Kipling's "Road to Mandalay," has become the newest river-cruise destination.

Cruise Experience Some waterways are high on scenery, while others offer more in the way of cultural interest. All explore deep inland at a leisurely pace, visiting remote villages and attractions both natural and man-made.

The Fleet Riverboats may be plain or fancy, and the leisurely pace might suit some and bore others. Most have all outside cabins, private facilities, a restaurant for dining, and perhaps a single lounge/bar for entertainment. Some rivers, such as the Amazon, the Niger in West Africa, the Upper Nile in the Sudan, and the Congo, maintain scheduled daily or weekly services, but these boats are only suitable for the hardy. The boats and river trips listed here meet international standards for comfort, safety, and expert guidance.

In Europe

When to Go European river cruises generally operate from April through October, but the best times to go are late spring and early fall, when the Continent is less crowded. Discounts are often available at the very beginning and very end of the season.

Operators and Itineraries

KD River Cruises of Europe (2500 Westchester Ave., Purchase, NY 10577, tel. 914/696–3600 or 800/346–6525, fax 914/696–0833) is the largest and oldest passenger line in Europe; its Rhine River voyages date from 1827. The modern era began in 1960, with the first cruise vessel sailing between Rotterdam and Basel, Switzerland. Now, 450 annual departures, mostly three to seven days, operate on the Rhine, Main, Moselle, Neckar, Elbe, Danube, Seine, Soane, and Rhone rivers in Germany, Holland, France, Switzerland, Austria, Hungary, and the Czech Republic. The riverboats carry between 104 and 184 passengers, generally in windowed cabins with twin beds (one converting to a daytime sofa) and private facilities.

Peter Deilmann/EuropAmerica Cruises (1800 Diagonal Rd., Suite 170, Alexandria, VA 22314, tel. 703/549–1741 or 800/348–8287, fax 703/549–7924) markets five high-standard riverboats that carry 110 to 207 passengers on mostly seven-day cruises of the Danube, Elbe, Rhine, Main, Moselle, Rhone, and Soane.

EuroCruises (303 W. 13th St., New York, NY 10014, tel. 212/691–2099 or 800/688–3876, fax 212/366–4747) represents the 148-passenger *Rhine Princess*, with twin- or double-bedded outside cabins, making eight-day cruises between Amsterdam and Basel via a beautiful section of the Moselle. The 120-passenger *Blue Danube* sails between Berching near Nuremburg and Budapest via the Main-Danube Canal, an eight-day cruise making stops at Regensburg, Passau, Linz, Vienna, and Bratislava.

Sea Air Holidays (733 Summer St., Stamford, CT 06901, tel. 800/732–6247, fax 203/358–2333) offers one of the most ambitious riverboat itineraries in Europe: a 15-day river and canal cruise from Amsterdam along Dutch waterways, the Rhine, Main, and Danube rivers, and the Main-Danube Canal to Vienna. Stops are made at the cathedral city of Cologne; Rudesheim for wine production; at the medieval towns of Miltenburg, Rothenburg, Bamburg, and Regensburg; and in large cities such Frankfurt, Nuremburg, and Munich. Passage is aboard the 146-passenger *Queen of Holland*, which has all outside double cabins with private facilities. Also from Sea Air Holidays is an eight-day cruise on the Elbe between Berlin, Potsdam, Meissen, Dresden, and Prague aboard the 62-passenger *Konigstein*. Cabins are also all outside with private facilities.

Both **Bergen Line** (405 Park Ave., New York, NY 10022, tel. 212/319–1300 or 800/323–7436, fax 212/319–1390) and **EuroCruises** (*see above*) market three classic 60-passenger riverboats, the *Diana* (1931), *Wilhelm Tham* (1912), and *Juno* (1874), which sail on four- and six-day voyages along Sweden's Gota Canal between Stockholm and Gothenburg. The sheltered and sometimes forested route passes islands, forts, palaces, churches, villages, and 65 locks. These are not luxury vessels, and the compact cabins have upper and lower berths, while toilets and showers are in the hallways. The smorgasbord, however, is among the best in Sweden.

In Russia and the Ukraine

When to Go Cruising in Russia is a summer pastime, while the season in the more southerly Ukraine extends into the spring and fall.

Operators and Itineraries **EuroCruises** (*see above*) uses the large 424-foot, 250-passenger *Sergei Kirov* for its 12- and 13-day program of cruises between Moscow and St. Petersburg. The five-deck vessel is Swiss-managed, ensuring high standards, and it acts as a hotel for two nights in both terminal cities. The Svir and Volga River route crosses lakes and reservoirs and calls at cities, towns, cathedrals, and monasteries. One of the most remote inland cruises in the world takes place on the

Yenisey River in Siberia aboard the 184-passenger *Anton Chekhov*. The 9- or 10-day cruise operates, at the north end, above the Arctic Circle.

The **Cruise Company Greenwich** (31 Brookside Dr., Greenwich, CT 06830, tel. 203/622–0203 or 800/825–0826, fax 203/622–4036) also markets the *Sergei Kirov* on the route between Moscow and St. Petersburg, but the Cruise Company's itinerary includes the Golden Ring of ancient cities outside Moscow.

OdessAmerica Cruise Line (170 Old Country Rd., Suite 608, Mineola, NY 11501, tel. 516/747–8880 or 800/221–3254, fax 516/747–8367) is another source of 15-day Moscow–St. Petersburg cruises, but its vessels—the 270-passenger *Andropov*, *Lenin*, and *Litvinov*—are not Western-managed. Accommodations on all three riverboats are outside, with picture windows and private facilities. A wide variety of configurations are available, including cabins designed for two passengers, four passengers, and even 12 single cabins for passengers traveling alone. There are two suites as well.

In the Ukraine, OdessAmerica has 11- and 12-day cruises on board the 270-passenger *Glushkov*. The boat sails the Dnieper River and the Black Sea between Kiev and Odessa, visiting the Cossack region as well as Sevastopol and Yalta in the Crimea.

On the Amazon

It's nearly impossible to comprehend the Amazon Basin without taking a river cruise of at least several days. Oceangoing cruise ships sail the Amazon, but just the lower portion—from the mouth of the river to Manaus, Brazil—is a mere 1,000 miles upriver. For the real flavor of the steamy jungle, head for the Upper Amazon or the Solimoes (a tributary of the Amazon that meets the river at Manaus).

When to Go

Oceangoing ships visit the Amazon during the dry season (which coincides with the northern winter months between December and March), but local cruises run year-round. Even during the dry season, it's hot ashore in villages and during rain-forest walks, but quite pleasant when underway on the river.

Operators and Itineraries

Amazon Tours & Cruises (8700 W. Flagler St., Miami, FL 33174, tel. 305/227–2266 or 800/423–2791, fax 305/227–1880) will bring you up the river and into the jungle for a true taste of the rain forest. Three- to six-night trips operate between Iquitos, Peru, and Leticia, Colombia, or Tabatinga, Brazil. Aboard these small riverboats, which aren't always air-conditioned, you can scan the water for pink dolphins and watch for birds from a deck chair. Excursions off the boat include jungle walks and visits to Indian villages.

The *Rio Amazonas* is the largest of ATC's fleet, carrying 44 passengers in 21 air-conditioned cabins with private baths. The dining room is air-conditioned, too. The *Arca* has 16 air-conditioned cabins (upper and lower berths) with private baths. The non-air-conditioned dining room and lounge are screened in. The *Explorer* (not to be confused with A&K's ship) has 16 air-conditioned cabins with private facilities and an air-conditioned lounge. For really roughing it, the *Delfin* (20 passengers) and *Amazon Discoverer* (16 passengers) have non-air-conditioned cabins with shared facilities.

Among the major cruise ships with upper Amazon sailings are Abercrombie & Kent's *Explorer* and Special Expeditions' *Polaris* (*see* Chapter 1).

On the Irrawaddy

In a country now called Myanmar but formerly known as Burma, a relatively new riverboat links Pagan and its field of 5,000 temples with the northern river city of Mandalay. The boat, originally from the Rhine, has been renamed *The Road to Mandalay* and accommodates 139 passengers and a crew of 70. Beyond Mandalay, another riverboat, the *Irrawaddy Princess*, sails even farther north—well beyond the tourist circuit to the start of navigation in upper Burma. River travel does not get more exotic than this.

When to Go Myanmar is a year-round destination with high temperatures and humidity that vary little from month to month.

Operators and Itineraries Cruises on *The Road to Mandalay* last three days and include a stay in Yangon (Rangoon), with optional extensions to Thailand, Laos, and Cambodia and a two-night ride on the Eastern & Oriental Express, a luxury train operating between Bangkok, Penang, Kuala Lumpur, and Singapore. **Abercrombie & Kent** (1520 Kensington Rd., Oak Brook, IL 60521, tel. 708/954–2944 or 800/323–7308, fax 708/954–3324) offers complete tours. The riverboat agent is **Venice-Simplon Orient-Express** (tel. 800/524–2420).

Cruises on the new *Myat Thanda,* built in 1995, offer a more comprehensive tour and spend more time on the river. The complete trip is ten nights, including overnights in Rangoon. The *Myat Thanda* can be booked through **Esplanade Tours** (581 Boylston St., Boston, MA 02116, tel. 617/266–7465 or 800/426–5492, fax 617/262–9829).

On the Murray

Cruising Australia's Murray River closely parallels a lazy trip on the Mississippi, if on a much more intimate scale. The 1,609-mile Murray divides New South Wales and Victoria, and exits through South Australia into the sea. In the 19th century it served as an important water highway for the farms and mines in the developing interior.

When to Go The austral spring and fall are the most pleasant seasons. Summers can be quite hot and dry in the river valley. Victorian winters are mild compared with those of the northeastern United States, but they can still be damp and rainy.

Operators and Itineraries Two- to five-night cruises embark year-round from Murray Bridge, Mannum, and Blanchetown. The *Murray Princess* is operated by Captain Cook Cruises (International Cruise Connections., tel. 800/433–8747), which runs the *Reef Endeavor* and *Reef Escape* (*see* Along the Great Barrier Reef, *above*).

Also contact the *Proud Mary* (Proud Australia Cruises, 33 Pirie St., Adelaide, SA 5000 Australia, tel. 011/61–8–231–9472, fax 011/61–8–212–1520).

On the Nile

Without the Nile, there would be no Egypt—no Aswan, Luxor, Thebes, Valley of the Kings, or Valley of the Queens—all stops on most Nile cruises. The Nile River fleet numbers over 200, and with each flotilla catering to a special market, the quality of onboard enrichment programs, facilities, and service varies enormously. Although the cruising portion will be relaxing, shore excursions can get very crowded, especially in the cooler high-season months. The best operators get you up early to be among the first at the tomb entrance and to have everyone back on the boat during the midday heat.

When to Go Boats sail the Nile year-round, but late fall, winter, and spring are the most comfortable times. The Nile Valley gets extremely hot in summer, when nothing much takes place in the middle of the day.

Operators and Itineraries Nearly all Nile cruises are three to seven days long and are packaged with hotel stays in Cairo, Luxor, or Aswan. Group travel in Egypt is almost de rigueur, but the numbers need not be large. The Nile operators listed here run boats that have all outside cabins and private facilities, open and covered top-deck seating, a tiny pool, a lounge, a bar, a dining room with Western and Middle Eastern menus, and a comprehensive lecture program.

Abercrombie & Kent (1520 Kensington Rd., Oak Brook, IL 60521, tel. 708/954–2944 or 800/323–7308, fax 708/954–3324) has two boats, the 64-passenger *Sun Boat II* and the 40-passenger *Sun Boat III*, which are among the most spacious on the Nile. Upper Nile cruises of five to eight days are part of an Egyptian tour package, with a limit of 24 passengers.

Hilton International Nile Cruises (c/o Misr Travel, 630 5th Ave., New York, NY 10111, tel. 212/582–9210 or 800/223–4978) uses the *Isis* and *Osiris*, each carrying 96 passengers, and the 120-passenger *Nephtis* on four- and six-day cruises between Luxor and Aswan.

Nabila Nile Cruises (605 Market St., Suite 1310, San Francisco, CA 94105, tel. 415/979–0160 or 800/443–6453) operates a fleet of five boats—*Queen Nabila I, Queen Nabila III, Queen of Sheba, Ramses of Egypt*, and *Ramses King of the Nile*. The boats carry 72 to 156 passengers on four- and six-day trips between Luxor and Aswan.

Special Expeditions (720 5th Ave., New York, NY 10019, tel. 212/765–7740 or 800/762–0003) puts only 30 passengers aboard its Nile boat, the *Hapi*, for seven-day cruises between Luxor and Aswan. These cruises are part of longer land-and-air tour packages from the United States.

Swan Hellenic (Classical Cruises & Tours, 132 E. 70th St., New York, NY 10021, tel. 212/794–3200 or 800/252–7745), a British operator with top lecturers (*see* On Board European Liners, *above*), charters the *Nubian Princess*, one of the best boats on the river, for seven-day cruises between Luxor and Aswan as part of a 14-day tour from the United States.

On the Yangtze

The Yangtze is 4,000 miles long and with much of it navigable, the river is central China's main artery for moving freight, produce, and passengers. Travelers may embark in Shanghai on scheduled boats and travel upriver to Chongqing and beyond, but most visitors come to experience the magnificent Three Gorges and village life between Chongqing and Wuhan.

When to Go Cruises operate April through November, but spring and fall are best. Summer months are very hot. Winter is very cold, and fog may prevent navigation during the season. In 1998 rising waters behind the Three Gorges Dam, now under construction, will begin to submerge some of the archaeological sites and diminish the natural grandeur of the region.

Operators and Itineraries The two operators listed below, both Sino-American joint ventures, are the largest operators on the Yangtze River. Both aim for international standards of accommodations, service, and Chinese and Western food. Their riverboats have all outside cabins and river views, restaurants with a single seating for dinner, several lounges and bars, a gift shop, a beauty salon, and a fitness center. Cruises to the Three Gorges are four, five, or six days.

Regal China Cruises (57 W. 38th St., New York, NY 10018, tel. 212/768–3388 or 800/808–3388, fax 212/768–4939) operates three German-built boats: *Princess Jeannie, Princess Elaine,* and *Princess Sheena.* Each carries 258 passengers.

Victoria Cruises (57-08 39th Ave., Woodside, NY 11377, tel. 212/818–1680 or 800/348–8084, fax 212/818–9889) operates three Chinese-built boats, *Victoria I* through *III,* each carrying 154 passengers, and charters two other vessels, the 160-passenger *President I* and the *Baidou.*

Several other tour operators, such as **Abercrombie & Kent, General Tours, Maupintour,** and **Uniworld,** include these riverboats in their China packages.

On Board Tall Ships

Unfurling their sails for part of each day and night (and motor powered the rest of the time), windjammers differ only in size and amenities from the big motor-sailing cruise ships reviewed in Chapter 1, such as those of Star Clippers, Club Med, or Windstar. What these windjammers lack in terms of swimming pools or in-room televisions, they make up for in romance and intimacy. People come aboard for the genuine experience of sailing before the wind and to join an informal seagoing community where handling the lines is entirely optional.

When to Go Tall-ship cruises operate year-round in the Caribbean, although some vessels are redeployed to the Mediterranean for the late spring, summer, and early fall. Summer in the Caribbean and the Mediterranean is very pleasant, but the south coast of Turkey can be beastly hot in July and August. Between seasons, transatlantic positioning cruises are available. Maine windjammers operate only in the summer, and even then, expect some rain and somewhat cool water temperatures.

Cruise Experience Most tall ships cruise between nearby ports, then anchor so that passengers can swim, snorkel, scuba dive, sun, or even take the rudder of something smaller, such as a Sunfish. Itineraries include part of the day under sail, but for those desirous of ocean cruising, a positioning voyage between the Caribbean and the Mediterranean offers the truest experience under sail.

The Fleet The tall-ship cruises listed here come under the broad term of windjammers, which includes historic ships plus a new breed of sleek, boutique sailing yachts. Windjammer cruises appeal to nature lovers, photographers, sailors, and those who just want to get away from it all. Some are family oriented, while others are designed for adults or for singles. Bunk accommodations are simple, and don't expect private facilities—the rates are moderate.

Operators and Itineraries

Historic Ships

The four-masted *Sea Cloud* (Sea Cloud Cruises, Ballindamm 17, D-20095 Hamburg, Germany, tel. 49–40–3690272, fax 49–40–373047), perhaps the most beautiful barque afloat, is a vision of maritime grace and elegance. Every inch of this classic sailing yacht is finely polished and crafted. It's truly a sight to watch crew members scamper up the 20-story masts to unfurl the ship's 30 billowing sails (which cover 32,000 square feet). When it was built, as the *Hussar V,* for the heiress Marjorie Merriweather Post and financier E. F. Hutton, it was the world's largest privately owned yacht. It has led a colorful life since then: as a naval weather station during World War II, as the yacht of Dominican dictator Molina Trujillo, and as the carrier of numerous Hollywood stars and even the Duke and Duchess of Windsor. Every attempt has been made to keep the *Sea Cloud* true to its origins, an artifact of a grander, more glamorous era. Many of the original wood panels, desks, antiques, and other furnishings have been meticulously restored. From its companionways to its salons, the ship evokes the air of a millionaire's mansion.

The **Maine Windjammer Association** (Box 1144P, Blue Hill, ME 04614, tel. 207/374–2955 or 800/807–9463) represents 10 vessels, many with interesting former lives as private yachts, lighthouse tenders, or cargo carriers. In their present incarnations, they sail the coast and islands of Maine, departing from Camden, Rockport, and Rockland. Other windjammer fleets are based at Mystic, Connecticut, and Greenport, Long Island, New York. Authenticity often means tight cabins with shared, even cold-water, showers, but those who come prepared enjoy a unique sailing experience.

Tall Ship Adventures (1389 S. Havana St., Aurora, CO 80012, tel. 303/755–7983 or 800/662–0090, fax 303/755–9007) operates the 39-passenger *Sir Francis Drake*, a three-masted schooner with an 80-year history and a good standard of accommodations. The ship sails on short Caribbean itineraries, which may be combined for a longer cruise.

Windjammer Barefoot Cruises (Box 190120, Miami Beach, FL 33119, tel. 800/327–2601, fax 305/674–1219) has the largest single fleet and a name that says it all about informality. Based in the Caribbean since 1947, the five vessels, with between 64 and 128 berths, possess intriguing histories equal to those of the Maine windjammers. Although the standard of accommodations varies from ship to ship, most cabins have a private head and shower. Island-hopping cruises last from 6 to 13 days. For information on the company's supply ship, the *Amazing Grace*, *see* On Board Freighters, *above*.

Newly Built Tall Ships

In addition to the restored vessels described above, a new class of modern-day tall ships has recently hit the scene. These vessels offer a uniformly high standard of accommodations, food, and service, and they have smaller passenger capacities.

For a private yacht experience, **Classical Cruises** (132 E. 70th St., New York, NY 10021, tel. 212/794–3200 or 800/252–7745, fax 212/774–1545) operates the three-masted *Panorama* on Red Sea itineraries in winter and Greek island and Turkish coastal voyages in summer. Built in Greece in 1994, the 175-foot ship carries up to 45 passengers in 23 well-appointed outside cabins. Seven-day sailings are combined with pre- or post-cruise hotel stays on land for an in-depth travel experience.

The **Cruise Company of Greenwich** represents the stylish *Lili Marleen*, a three-masted barkentine making 7- to 12-day Caribbean winter cruises, then sailing transatlantic to cruise the Baltic, western Europe, the Canary Islands, and the Mediterranean in summer. This technically advanced 250-foot ship entered service in 1994 and takes on 50 passengers in considerable comfort; cabins have private facilities. The *Lili Marleen* was built in Germany, and the officers and most of the crew are German. The ship can also be booked directly through its owner, Peter Deilmann (1800 Diagonal Rd., Suite 170, Alexandria, VA 22314, tel. 703/549–1741 or 800/348–8287, fax 703/549–7924).

The 64-passenger *Le Ponant*, a three-master with a French flavor built in 1991, is now mostly under charter to tour operators such as Tauck Tours (*see* Along the Belize and Costa Rica Coasts, *above*).

Through the Chilean Fjords

The waterways and fjords that line the coast of Chile are more remote and much less traveled than the fjords of Norway. Large cruise ships—which frequent the more famous Norwegian fjords—can only duck in and out, while small expedition ships can make the full voyage from Puerto Montt south to the Strait of Magellan.

When to Go Cruises of coastal Chile operate in the Southern Hemisphere's spring, summer, and fall. The farther south you sail, the colder and windier it's likely to get. Unexpected gusts may come racing down the mountains and glaciers, quickly depressing temperatures—but the scenic rewards are unparalleled.

Cruise Experience Passengers will probably be an international mix, drawn from all over the world to see the stunning scenery of rugged mountains, massive glaciers, uninhabited islands, and deep fjords. The short stretches of open sea can get rough. Shore excursions tend to emphasize the area's natural beauty, and apart from the embarkation ports, towns and villages are minor and secondary.

The Fleet With the exception of a few oceangoing expedition ships, which make seasonal calls in the Chilean fjords, local vessels are relatively small but adequately comfortable.

Operators and Itineraries Two Chilean-based companies specialize in these cruises.

The 100-passenger *Terra Australis* (formerly an American coastal ship known as the *Savannah*) makes weekly cruises into the Beagle Channel and along the coast of Tierra del Fuego. The ship has all outside cabins, two lounges, and good food in a noisy dining room. Departures are scheduled about seven months of the year. The ship can be booked in the United States through **OdessAmerica** (Cruceros Australis, c/o OdessAmerica, 170 Old Country Rd., Suite 608, Mineola, NY 11501, tel. 516/747–8880 or 800/221–3254, fax 516/747–8367).

OdessAmerica also represents the 160-passenger *Skorpios II*, which includes the spectacular San Rafael Lagoon and Glacier on its Chilean fjord cruises.

The *Terra Australis*, *Skorpios II*, and the smaller and older 74-passenger *Skorpios I* may also be booked through **Meg Tours** (tel. 800/579–9731) and **Ladeco Chilean Airlines** (tel. 800/825–2332).

Abercrombie & Kent's *Explorer* and Society Expedition's *World Discoverer* (*see* Chapter 1), and other major expedition ships heading to Antarctica often make several voyages that thread through Chilean coastal waters as well.

3 Ports of Call

Going Ashore

Traveling by cruise ship presents an opportunity to visit many different places in a short time. The flip side is that your stay will be limited in each port of call. For that reason, cruise lines invented shore excursions, which maximize passengers' time by organizing their touring for them. There are a number of advantages to shore excursions: In some destinations, transportation may be unreliable, and a ship-packaged tour is the best way to see distant sights. Also, you don't have to worry about being stranded or missing the ship. The disadvantage is that you will pay more for the convenience of having the ship do the legwork for you. Of course, you can always book a tour independently, hire a taxi, or use foot power to explore on your own.

Disembarking

When your ship arrives in a port, it either ties up alongside a dock or anchors out in a harbor. If the ship is docked, passengers just walk down the gangway to go ashore. Docking makes it easy to go back and forth between the shore and the ship.

Tendering If your ship anchors in the harbor, however, you will have to take a small boat—called a launch or tender—to get ashore. Tendering is a nuisance. When your ship first arrives in port, everyone wants to go ashore. Often, in order to avoid a stampede at the tenders, you must gather in a public room, get a boarding pass, and wait until your number is called. This continues until everybody has disembarked. Even then, it may take 15–20 minutes to get ashore if your ship is anchored far offshore. Because tenders can be difficult to board, passengers with mobility problems may not be able to visit certain ports. The larger the ship, the more likely it will use tenders. It is usually possible to learn before booking a cruise whether the ship will dock or anchor at its ports of call. (For more information about where and whether ships dock, tender, or both, *see* Coming Ashore for each port, *below*.)

Before anyone is allowed to walk down the gangway or board a tender, the ship must first be cleared for landing. Immigration and customs officials board the vessel to examine passports and sort through red tape. It may be more than an hour before you're actually allowed ashore. You will be issued a «boarding pass, which you must have with you to get back on board.

Returning to the Ship

Cruise lines are strict about sailing times, which are posted at the gangway and elsewhere as well as announced in the daily schedule of activities. Be certain to be back on board at least a half hour before the announced sailing time or you may be stranded. If you are on a shore excursion that was sold by the cruise line, however, the captain will wait for your group before casting off. If the ship must leave without you, the cruise company will fly you, at its expense, to the next port. That is one reason many passengers prefer ship-packaged tours.

If you are not on one of the ship's tours and the ship does sail without you, immediately contact the cruise line's port representative, whose name and phone number are often listed on the daily schedule of activities. You may be able to hitch a ride on a pilot boat, though that is unlikely. Passengers who miss the boat must pay their own way to the next port of call.

Alaska

Alaska, it would seem, was made for cruising. The traditional route to the state is by sea, through a 1,000-mile-long protected waterway known as the Inside Passage. From Vancouver in the south to Skagway in the north, the Inside Passage winds around islands large and small, past glacier-carved fjords, and along hemlock-blanketed mountains. This great land is home to breaching whales, nesting eagles, spawning salmon, and calving glaciers. Most towns here can be reached only by air or sea; there are no roads. Juneau, in fact, is the only water-locked state capital in the United States. Beyond the Inside Passage, the Gulf of Alaska leads to Prince William Sound—famous for its marine life and more fjords and glaciers—and Anchorage, Alaska's largest city.

An Alaska cruise is no longer the exclusive domain of retirees. Following the latest trend in cruising, more and more families are setting sail for Alaska. The peak season falls during summer school vacation, so kids are now a common sight aboard ship. Cruise lines have responded with programs designed specifically for children, and some discount shore excursions for kids under 12.

For adults, too, the cruise lines now offer more than ever before. Alaska is one of cruising's hottest destinations, so the lines are putting their newest, biggest ships up here. These gleaming vessels have the best facilities at sea. Fully equipped, top-deck health spas give panoramic views of the passing scenery. Some ships feature onboard broadcasts of CNN and ESPN—one vessel even has a sports bar showing live televised events. New itineraries give passengers more choices than ever before, too—from Bering Strait cruises, which include a crossing to the Russian Far East, to 10-, 11-, and 14-day loop cruises of the Inside Passage, round-trip from Vancouver.

You will still find all the time-honored diversions of a vacation at sea aboard Alaska-bound ships. Daily programs schedule bingo and bridge tournaments, deck games, and various contests, demonstrations, and lectures. You'll also find trendier pursuits: computer classes, stress-management seminars, and talks on financial planning. Theme cruises, from photography to square dancing, are becoming increasingly popular on Alaska cruises.

Food remains a major reason to visit Alaska aboard a cruise ship. On the big ocean liners, you can eat practically all day and night. Along with prime rib now comes a selection of healthy choices for nutrition-conscious eaters. Some ships offer a "spa menu," which ties your dining-room meals together with your exercise program in the health club.

Nearly every day, your ship will make a port call. Alaskan port cities are small and easily explored by foot. For those who prefer to be shown the sights, ship-organized shore excursions are available. These range from typical city bus tours to Alaska's most exciting excursion adventure: helicopter flightseeing with a landing on a glacier. Other choices include charter fishing, river rafting, and visits to Native American communities. To satisfy the interest of their ever-younger and more active passengers, Alaska's cruise lines constantly refine their shore-excursion programs, adding new educational and adventure-oriented choices. The programs change annually, as the lines search for just the right mix of leisure and learning (*see* Shore Excursions, *below*).

Itineraries About a dozen major cruise lines deploy ships in Alaska. Sailings come chiefly in two varieties: round-trip southeastern sailings and one-way cruises that also visit the south-central part of the state. The first, weeklong loops from Vancouver, are cruise-only and sail en-

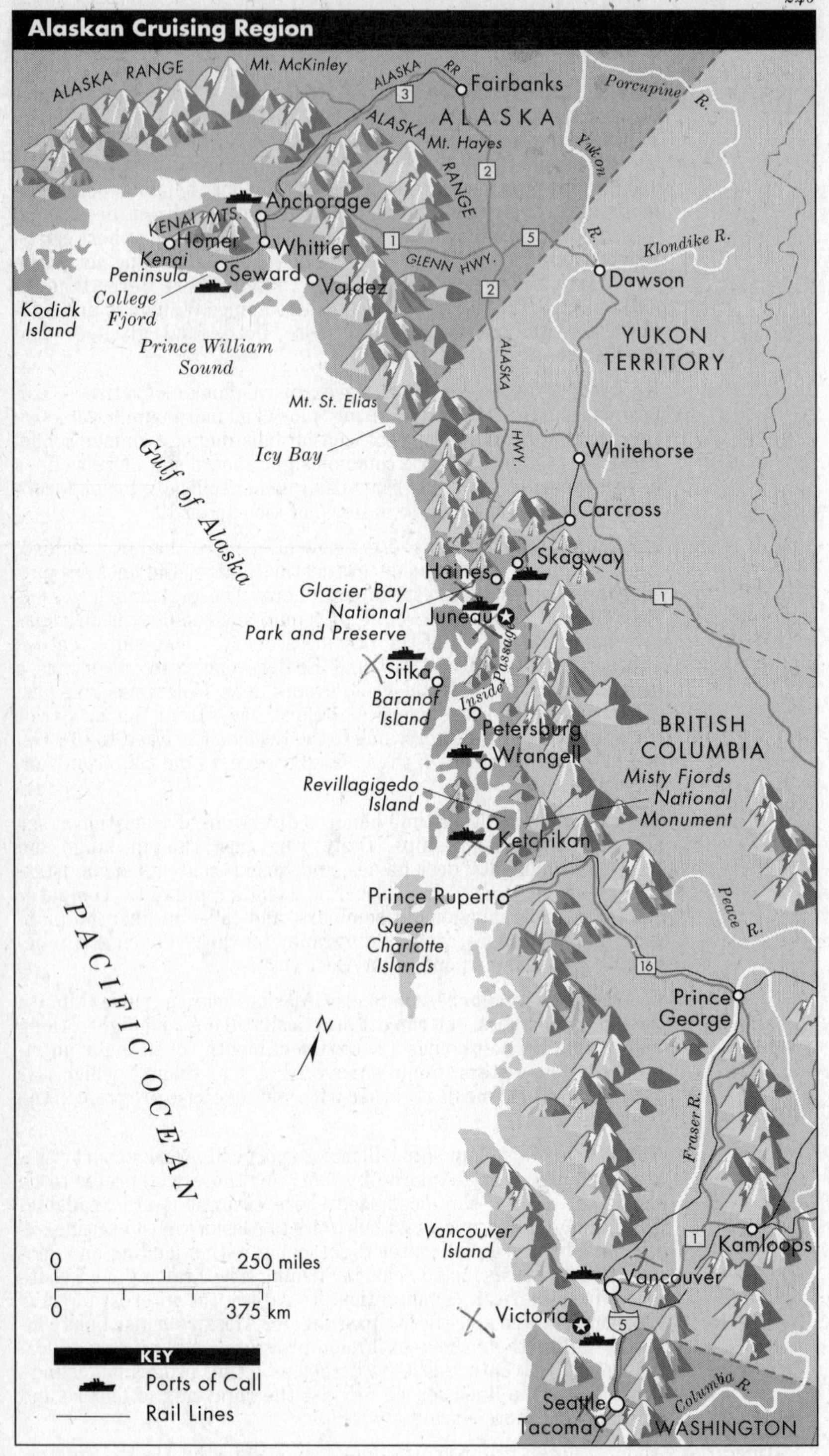
Alaskan Cruising Region
ALASKA RANGE
Mt. McKinley
ALASKA RR
Fairbanks
3
ALASKA
ALASKA RANGE
Mt. Hayes
2
Porcupine R.
Yukon R.
Anchorage
KENAI MTS.
Homer
Whittier
Kenai Peninsula
Seward
Valdez
College Fjord
1
5
GLENN HWY.
2
Klondike R.
Dawson
Kodiak Island
Prince William Sound
YUKON TERRITORY
ALASKA HWY.
Mt. St. Elias
Icy Bay
Whitehorse
Gulf of Alaska
Carcross
Skagway
Haines
1
Glacier Bay National Park and Preserve
Juneau
Inside Passage
Sitka
Baranof Island
Petersburg
Wrangell
BRITISH COLUMBIA
Revillagigedo Island
Misty Fjords National Monument
Ketchikan
Prince Rupert
Queen Charlotte Islands
Peace R.
16
PACIFIC OCEAN
N
Prince George
Fraser R.
Vancouver Island
1
Kamloops
0
250 miles
0
375 km
Vancouver
Victoria
5
KEY
Ports of Call
Rail Lines
Columbia R.
Seattle
Tacoma
WASHINGTON

tirely within the Inside Passage. (Three- or four-day segments are one-way and allow the option of exploring further inland.) The second—one-way, seven-day cruises to or from Vancouver—adds the Gulf of Alaska to the Inside Passage, visiting the communities and glaciers of Prince William Sound. With an optional land tour, passengers can explore farther north and still spend a full week at sea. A few lines schedule longer one-way or round-trip sailings from Vancouver or San Francisco. (For detailed itineraries, *see* Chapter 4.)

Cruise Tours Most cruise lines give you the option of a land tour before or after your cruise. Modes of tour transportation range from plane to bus, rail to day boat. Most cruise-tour itineraries include a ride aboard the Alaska Railroad in a private, glass-domed railcar. Running between Anchorage, Denali National Park, and Fairbanks, Holland America's *McKinley Explorer* and Princess's *Midnight Sun Express Ultra Dome* offer unobstructed views of the passing land and wildlife.

In addition to full-length cruise-tours, cruise lines usually sell pre- or post-cruise packages lasting one to three days. Hotel accommodations and some sightseeing in port cities are generally included.

When to Go The Alaska cruise season runs from spring through fall, but midsummer departures are the most popular. Cruise lines schedule first sailings in mid-May and final sailings in late September. May and June are the driest cruise months. At least two cruise lines price sailings by five "seasons," with spring and fall departures the least expensive and midsummer sailings the most costly. Virtually every line offers early-booking discounts to passengers for deposits in advance.

Shore Excursions Shore excursions in Alaska give cruise passengers a chance to get closer to the state's natural beauty. For this reason, active or adventure-oriented tours are usually the best choices. Not all shore excursions are offered by every ship. However, you can book any excursion directly; try calling one of the ground operators listed below (*see* Independent Touring, *below*).

Aerial Tours Anyone unwilling to hike or boat in the backcountry should take at least one helicopter or small-plane tour to see the state in its full glory. The aircraft fly over glaciers and waterways; the best helicopter tours actually land on a glacier and let passengers out for a walk.

Fishing The prospect of bringing a trophy king salmon or a rainbow trout to net is the reason many people choose an Alaskan cruise. Every ship offers optional fishing excursions on charter boats.

Hiking Trekking through woods and mountains and along the beaches is southeastern Alaska's unofficial pastime. Some trails are abandoned mining roads; others are natural routes or game trails that meander over ridges, through forests, and alongside streams and glaciers. Many ships offer hiking excursions, but every port is within easy access of at least some hiking. Trails go through real wilderness, so check with local park rangers or tourist offices for current conditions, and leave your intended itinerary with someone on the ship. Look under the hiking section for each port to find trails and paths convenient to cruise passengers.

Salmon Bake Alaska is famous for outdoor salmon barbecues, called salmon bakes. Fresh fish is grilled on an open fire and served with plenty of fixings. Quality varies, so ask locals for advice on which bake to attend. Juneau's Gold Creek salmon bake is a good choice.

Whale Watching Whales are plentiful in these waters, and several small-boat excursions offer excellent opportunities to see them up close. The captains of these craft keep in contact and let one another know when a whale pod is near.

Independent Touring In Haines: For flightseeing contact L.A.B. Flying Service (tel. 907/766–2222) or Haines Airway (tel. 907/766–2646). For local sightseeing contact Fort Seward Tours (tel. 907/766–2000). For soft-adventure tours contact River Adventures (tel. 907/766–2050).

In Homer: For flightseeing contact Homer Air (tel. 907/235–8591), Southcentral Air (tel. 907/235–6172), or Bald Mountain Air Service (tel. 800/478–7969). For local sightseeing contact Homer Tours (tel. 907/235–8687). For wildlife watching contact Rainbow Tours (tel. 907/235–7272) or the m/v Denaina (tel. 907/235–2490).

In Juneau: For flightseeing contact L.A.B. Flying Service (tel. 907/766–2222) or Temsco Helicopters (tel. 907/789–9501). For local sightseeing contact Alaska Native Tours (907/463–3231). For soft adventure contact Alaska Travel Adventures (tel. 907/789–0052).

In Ketchikan: For soft adventure contact Alaska Travel Adventures (tel. 907/789–0052). For native culture contact Saxman Native Village (tel. 907/225–5163, ext. 301) or Ketchikan Indian Corporation (800/252–5158).

In Petersburg: For flightseeing contact Temsco Helicopters (tel. 907/772–4780), Pacific Wing (tel. 907/772–4258), or Kupreanof Flying Service (tel. 907/772–3396). For soft adventure contact Far Country Adventures (tel. 907/772–4400), Hook & Eye Adventures (tel. 907/772–3400) or Hindman Charters (tel. 907/772–4478). For charter fishing, contact the Petersburg Visitors Center (tel. 907/772–4636).

In Sitka: For local sightseeing, contact Tribal Tours (800/746–3207). For soft adventure, contact Baidarka Boats (tel. 907/747–8996).

In Skagway: For flightseeing contact L.A.B. Flying Service (tel. 907/766–2222) or Temsco Helicopters (tel. 907/789–9501). For local sightseeing contact Skagway Street Car Company (tel. 907/983–2908).

In Valdez: For local sightseeing contact Valdez Tours (tel. 907/835-4402) or Sentimental Journeys (tel. 907/835-2075). For soft-adventure tours contact Anadyr Seakayaking Adventures (tel. 907/835–2814), Northern Magic Charters (tel. 800/443–3543), or Stan Stephens Charters (tel. 800/992–1297).

Saloons Socializing at a bar or "saloon" is an old Alaska custom, and the towns and cities of the Southeast Panhandle are no exception. Listed under the individual ports of call are some of the favorite gathering places in these parts.

Scuba Diving Although the visibility is not very good in most southeast waters, there's still a lot of scuba and skin-diving activity throughout the region. Quarter-inch wet suits are a must. So is a buddy; stay close together. Local dive shops can steer you to the best places to dive for abalone, scallops, and crabs and advise you on the delights and dangers of underwater wrecks.

Shopping Alaskan Native American handicrafts range from Tlingit totem poles—a few inches high to several feet tall—to Athabascan beaded slippers. Tlingit, Inuit, and Aleut wall masks, dance rattles, baskets, and beaded items in traditional designs can be found at gift shops up and down the coast. To ensure authenticity, buy items tagged with the state-approved AUTHENTIC NATIVE HANDCRAFT FROM ALASKA "Silverhand" label. Or buy at Saxman Village outside Ketchikan or at similar Native American–run shops. Better prices are found the farther you go to the north and away from the coast.

Salmon—smoked, canned, or fresh—is another popular item. Most towns have a local company that packs and ships local seafood.

Dining Not surprisingly, seafood dominates most menus. In summer, king salmon, halibut, king crab, cod, and prawns are usually fresh. Restaurants are uniformly informal; clean jeans and windbreakers are the norm.

Category	Cost*
$$$	over $40
$$	$20–$40
$	under $20

**per person for a three-course meal, excluding drinks, service, and sales tax*

Anchorage

A local newspaper columnist once dubbed Anchorage "a city too obviously on the make to ever be accepted in polite society." And for all its cosmopolitan trappings, this city of 225,000 does maintain something of an opportunistic, pioneer spirit. Its inhabitants, whose average age is just 28, hustle for their living in the banking, transportation, and communications fields.

Superficially, Anchorage looks like any other western American city, but sled-dog races are as popular here as surfing is in California, and moose occasionally roam along city bike trails. This is basically a modern, relatively unattractive city, but the Chugach Mountains form a striking backdrop, and spectacular Alaskan wilderness is found just outside the back door.

Anchorage took shape with the construction of the federally built Alaska Railroad (completed in 1923), and traces of the city's railroad heritage remain. With the tracks laid, the town's pioneer forefathers actively sought expansion by hook and—not infrequently—by crook. City fathers, many of whom are still alive, delight in telling how they tricked a visiting U.S. congressman into dedicating the site for a federal hospital that had not yet been approved.

Boom and bust periods followed major events: an influx of military bases during World War II; a massive buildup of Arctic missile-warning stations during the Cold War; and most recently, the discovery of oil at Prudhoe Bay and the construction of the trans-Alaska pipeline.

Anchorage today is the only true metropolis among Alaskan port cities. There's a performing-arts center, a diversity of museums, and a variety of ethnic eateries for cruise passengers to sample.

Shore Excursions Other than a typical city bus tour, few shore excursions are scheduled in Anchorage. Most cruise passengers are only passing through the city as they transfer between the airport and the ship or a land tour and their cruise. For passengers who arrive early or stay later, independently or on a pre- or post-cruise package, there is much to see and do (*see* Exploring Anchorage, *below*).

Coming Ashore Cruise ships visiting Anchorage most often dock at the port city of Seward, 125 miles away on the east coast of the Kenai Peninsula; from here passengers must travel by bus or train to Anchorage. Ships that do sail directly to the city dock just beyond downtown. A tourist information booth is located right on the pier. The major attractions are a 15- or 20-minute walk away; turn right when you disembark and head south on Ocean Dock Road.

Alaska Public Lands Information Center, **4**
Anchorage Museum of History and Art, **7**
Fourth Avenue Theater, **3**
Imaginarium, **6**
Log Cabin Visitor Information Center, **1**
Old City Hall, **2**
Oscar Anderson House, **5**

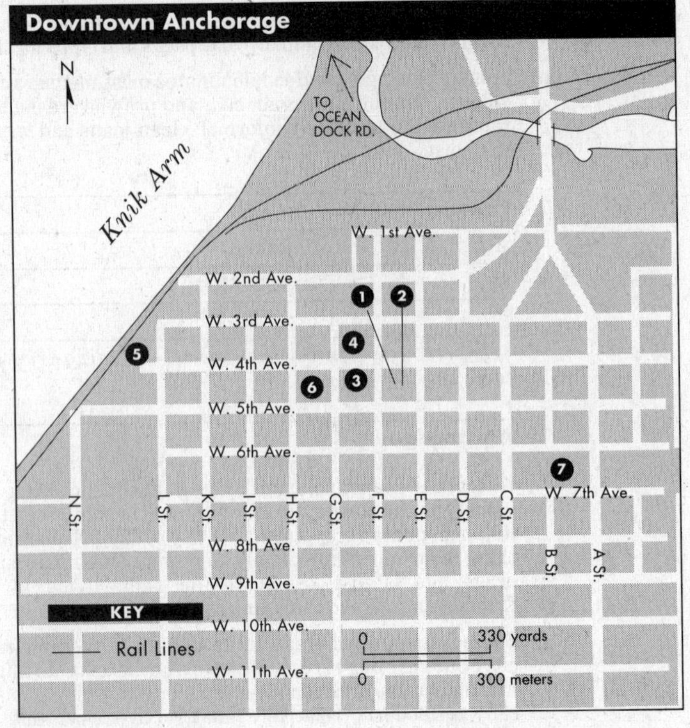

Getting Around

By Bus

The municipal **People Mover** (tel. 907/343–6543) bus system covers the whole Anchorage bowl. It's not convenient for short downtown trips but can be used for visits to outlying areas. The central depot is at 6th Avenue and G Street. The fare is $1, plus an additional 10¢ for transfers.

By Taxi

Prices for taxis start at $2 for pickup and $1.50 for each mile. Most people in Anchorage telephone for a cab, although it is not uncommon to hail one. Contact **Alaska Cab** (tel. 907/563–5353), **Checker Cab** (tel. 907/276–1234), or **Yellow Cab** (tel. 907/272–2422).

Exploring Anchorage

Numbers in the margin correspond to points of interest on the Downtown Anchorage map.

❶ A marker in front of the **Log Cabin Visitor Information Center** (corner of 4th Ave. and F St.) shows the mileage to various world cities. Fourth Avenue sustained heavy damage in the 1964 earthquake. The businesses on this block withstood the destruction, but those a block east, where the McDonald's now stands, fell into the ground as the earth under them slid toward Ship Creek. Most of these buildings have since been rebuilt.

❷ **Old City Hall** was built in 1936. The marble sculpture out front is a monument to William Seward, the secretary of state who engineered the purchase of Alaska from Russia in 1867.

❸ The Art Deco **Fourth Avenue Theater** (4th Ave., between F and G Sts.) has been restored and put to new use as a museum and gift shop. Historic photos and the theater's original bronze murals tell the story of Alaska's past. Note the lighted stars in the ceiling that form the Big Dipper against a field of blue—it's the Alaska state flag.

❹ Displays about Alaska's national parks, forests, and wildlife refuges can be seen at the **Alaska Public Lands Information Center** (4th Ave.

and F St.). The center also shows films highlighting different regions of the state.

The paved walking and cycling **coastal trail,** which runs along the water for about 12 miles, can be reached by returning to 2nd Avenue and heading west three blocks to the marked entrance. Mt. Susitna (known as the Sleeping Lady) is the prominent low mountain to the northwest. To her north, Mt. McKinley is often visible. On the left is Resolution Park, a cantilevered viewing platform above the trail, dominated by the Captain Cook monument.

5 The **Oscar Anderson House** is next to the trail at the north end of Elderberry Park, near 5th Avenue between L and N streets. It was Anchorage's first permanent frame house, built in 1915. Tours are free. The park is also a good place to watch for whales off the coast.

6 A fun stop for kids and adults alike is the **Imaginarium,** an interactive science museum with a great shop. *725 W. 5th Ave., tel. 907/276–3179. Admission: $4. Open Mon.–Sat. 10–6, Sun. noon–5.*

7 The **Anchorage Museum of History and Art** occupies the whole block at 6th Avenue and A Street. The entrance is on 7th Avenue. It houses a fine collection of historical and contemporary Alaskan art, displays on Alaskan history, and a special section for children. One gallery is devoted to views of Alaska, as seen by early explorers, resident painters, and contemporary artists. *121 W. 7th Ave., tel. 907/343–4326. Admission: $4. Open daily 9–6.*

If you have the time, take a taxi to the **Lake Hood floatplane base,** where colorful aircraft come and go hourly. A good place to watch the planes take off and land is from the Fancy Moose lounge inside the Regal Alaskan Hotel. *4800 Spenard Rd., tel. 907/243–2300.*

Shopping The **Alaska Native Arts and Crafts Association** (333 W. 4th Ave., tel. 907/274–2932; open weekdays 10–6, Sat. 10–5) sells items from all Alaskan Native American groups and carries the work of the best-known carvers, silversmiths, and bead workers, as well as the work of unknown artists. The best buys on native Alaskan artists' work are found at the **Alaska Native Medical Center** gift shop (3rd Ave. and Gambell St., tel. 907/257–1150; open weekdays 10–2, also 11–2 on 1st Sat. of month). The **Stonington Gallery** (737 W. 5th Ave., tel. 907/272–1489) carries the work of better-known Alaskan artists, both Native and non-Native.

Jogging/Walking The coastal trail (*see* Exploring Anchorage, *above*) and other trails in Anchorage are used by cyclists, runners, and walkers. The trail from Westchester Lagoon at the end of 15th Avenue runs 2 miles to Earthquake Park and, beyond that, 8 miles out to Kincaid Park. For bike rentals, contact **Adventures and Delights** (K St. between 4th and 5th Aves., tel. 907/276–8282) or **Downtown Bicycle Rental** (corner of 6th Ave. and B St., tel. 907/279–5293).

Dining

$$–$$$ **Simon & Seaforts Saloon and Grill.** This is the place to enjoy a great view while dining on fresh Alaska seafood or rock-roasted prime rib. The bar is a popular spot for appetizers (some regular menu items can also be ordered in the lounge). *Corner of 4th Ave. and L St., tel. 907/274–3502. AE, MC, V.*

$$ **Aladdin's.** In a strip-mall setting on the south side of Anchorage, the former director of catering for the Anchorage Hilton has created one of the city's most interesting dining experiences. The menu features dishes from virtually every country that rings the Mediterranean. The wine selection is equally diverse. *4240 Old Seward Hwy., tel. 907/561–2373. AE, D, DC, MC, V. Closed Sun. No lunch Sat.*

$$ **Club Paris.** It's dark and smoky up front in the bar, where for decades old-time Anchorage folks have met to drink and chat. Halibut and fried prawns are available, but the star attractions are the big, tender, flavorful steaks. If you forget to make a reservation, have a drink at the bar and order the hors d'oeuvres tray—a sampler of

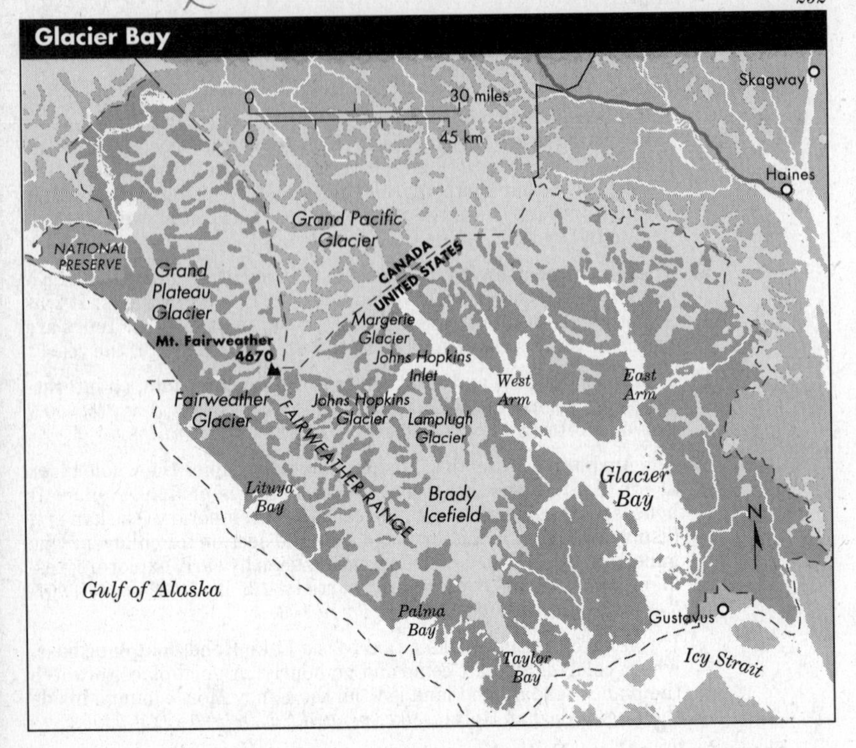

steak, cheese, and prawns that could be a meal for two people. *417 W. 5th Ave., tel. 907/277–6332. Reserve early that day. AE, D, DC, MC, V.*

$ **Lucky Wishbone.** At this old Anchorage eatery, where old-timers sit around the brightly lit Formica tables and waitresses never seem to have a bad day, great fried chicken is the fare. Order all white meat, with just the wishbone and no ribs, or try the livers or gizzards. *1033 E. 5th Ave., tel. 907/272–3454. No credit cards. Closed Sun.*

Glacier Bay National Park and Preserve

Cruising Glacier Bay is like revisiting the Little Ice Age, when glaciers covered much of the Northern Hemisphere. It is one of the few places in the world where you can get within a quarter mile of tidewater glaciers, which have their base at the water's edge. Sixteen of them line the 60 miles of narrow fjords at the northern end of the Inside Passage, rising up to 7,000 feet above the bay. Huge chunks of ice break off the glaciers and crash into the water, producing a dazzling show known as calving.

Although the Tlingit Indians have lived in the area for 10,000 years, the bay was first popularized by naturalist John Muir, who visited in 1879. Just 100 years before, the bay was completely choked with ice. By 1916, though, the ice had retreated 62 miles—the most rapid glacial retreat ever recorded. To preserve its clues to the world's geological history, the bay was declared a national monument in 1925. It became a national park in 1980. Today, a few of the glaciers are advancing again, but very slowly.

Competition is fierce among cruise ships for entry permits into Glacier Bay. To protect the humpback whale, which feeds here in summer, the park service limits the number of ships that can call. Check your cruise brochure to make sure that Glacier Bay is included in your sailing. Most ships that do visit spend at least one full day exploring the park. There are no shore excursions or landings in the bay, but a park-service naturalist boards every cruise ship to provide narration on its history and scientific importance. It is often misty or rainy, so rain gear is essential. The average summer temperature is 50°F. As always in Alaska, be prepared for the cold. Also, be sure to bring binoculars, extra film, and a telephoto lens.

The glaciers that most cruise passengers see are located in the west arm of Glacier Bay. Ships linger in front of four glaciers so passengers may view their stunning appearance. **Lamplugh,** one of the bluest in the park, is at the mouth of Johns Hopkins Inlet and is often the first stop on the glacier tour. Next is **Johns Hopkins Glacier** at the end of the inlet, where cruise passengers are likely to see a continuous shower of calving ice. Sometimes there are so many icebergs in the inlet that ships must avoid the area. Moving farther north, to the end of the western arm, **Margerie Glacier** is also quite active. Adjacent is **Grand Pacific Glacier,** the largest glacier in the park.

Your experience in Glacier Bay will depend partly on the size of your ship. Ocean liners tend to stay mid-channel, while small yachtlike ships spend more time closer to shore. Passengers on smaller ships may get a better view of the calving ice and wildlife—such as brown and black bears, mountain goats, moose, and seals with their pups—but big-ship passengers, on vessels with much higher decks, get a loftier perspective.

Haines

Unlike most other cities in southeast Alaska, Haines can be reached by road (the 152-mile Haines Highway connects at Haines Junction with the Alaska Highway). Missionary S. Hall Young and famed naturalist John Muir picked the site for this town in 1879 as a place to bring Christianity and education to the natives. They could hardly have picked a more beautiful spot. The town sits on a heavily wooded peninsula with magnificent views of Portage Cove and the Coastal Mountain Range. It lies 80 miles north of Juneau via fjordlike Lynn Canal.

The town has two distinct personalities. On the northern side of the Haines Highway is the portion of Haines founded by Young and Muir. After its missionary beginnings the town served as the trailhead for the Jack Dalton Trail to the Yukon during the 1897 gold rush to the Klondike. The following year, when gold was discovered in nearby Porcupine (now deserted), the booming community served as a supply center and jumping-off place for those goldfields as well. Today things are quieter; the town's streets are orderly, its homes are well kept, and for the most part it looks a great deal like any other Alaska seacoast community.

South of the highway, the town looks like a military post, which is what it was for nearly half a century. In 1903 the U.S. Army established a post—Ft. William Henry Seward—at Portage Cove just south of town. For 17 years (1922–39) the post (renamed Chilkoot Barracks to avoid confusion with the city of Seward, farther north in the south-central part of the state) was the only military base in the territory. That changed with World War II. Following the war the post closed down.

Right after the war a group of veterans purchased the property from the government. They changed its name to Port Chilkoot and created residences, businesses, and a Native American arts center out of the officers' houses and military buildings that surrounded the old fort's parade ground. Eventually Port Chilkoot merged with the city of Haines. Although the two areas are now officially one municipality, the old military post with its still-existing grass parade ground is referred to as Ft. Seward.

The Haines–Ft. Seward community today is recognized for the enormously successful Native American dance and culture center at Ft. Seward, as well as for the superb fishing, camping, and outdoor recreation to be found at Chilkoot Lake, Portage Cove, Mosquito Lake, and Chilkat State Park on the shores of Chilkat Inlet. The last locale, one of the small treasures of the Alaska state park system, features views of the Davidson and Rainbow glaciers across the water.

Shore Excursions The following are good choices in Haines. They may not be offered by all cruise lines. All times and prices are approximate.

Adventure **Glacier Bay Flightseeing.** If your cruise doesn't include a visit to Glacier Bay, here's a chance to see several of its tidewater glaciers during a low-altitude flight. *1-hr flight plus transfers. Cost: $113.*

City Sights **Haines Cultural and Natural Wonders Tour.** This excursion tours Ft. Seward, the Sheldon Museum and Cultural Center, and the Alaskan Indian Arts Center and includes time to browse through the downtown galleries. *2½–3 hrs. Cost: $25–$32.*

Native Cultural **The Chilkat Dancers.** A drive through Ft. William Henry Seward includes a dance performance by the Chilkat Dancers, noted for their vivid tribal masks. Some lines combine this tour with a salmon bake (*see below*). *1-hr performance. Cost: $32.*

Salmon Bake **Chilkat Dancers and Salmon Bake.** The narrated tour of Haines and Ft. Seward and a Chilkat Dancers' performance are combined with a dinner of salmon grilled over an open fire. *2½–3 hrs. Cost: $49.*

Wildlife Up Close **Chilkat River by Jet Boat.** A cruise through the Chilkat Bald Eagle Preserve reveals some eagles and—if you're lucky—perhaps a moose or a bear. It is a smooth, rather scenic trip, but in summer, you'll see little wildlife. Come October, though, imagine the trees filled with up to 4,000 bald eagles. *3½ hrs. Cost: $70.*

Coming Ashore Cruise ships dock in front of Fort Seward and downtown Haines is just a short walk away (about ¾ mile). Taxis are always standing by, although most cruises provide a shuttle service to downtown. You can pick up walking-tour maps of both Haines and Ft. Seward at the visitor center on 2nd Avenue (tel. 907/766–2234).

Getting Around Hour-long taxi tours of the town cost $10 per person. A one-way trip between the pier and town costs $5. If you need to call for a pickup, contact **The Other Guys Taxi** (tel. 907/766–3257) or **Haines Taxi** (tel. 907/766–3138).

Exploring Haines *Numbers in the margin correspond to points of interest on the Haines map.*

❶ The **Sheldon Museum and Cultural Center,** near the foot of Main Street, houses an Alaskan family's personal collection of Native American artifacts, Russian items, and gold-rush memorabilia, such as Jack Dalton's sawed-off shotgun. *25 Main St., tel. 907/766–2366. Admission: $3. Open summer, daily 1–5; winter, Sun., Mon., and Wed. 1–4 and Tues., Thurs., and Fri. 3–5.*

❷ The building that houses the **Chilkat Center for the Arts** was once the army post's recreation hall, but now it's the space for Chilkat Indian dancing. Some performances may be at the tribal house next door; check posted notices for performance times.

At **Alaska Indian Arts,** a nonprofit organization dedicated to the revival of Tlingit Indian art forms, you'll see Native carvers making totems, metalsmiths working in silver, and weavers making blankets. *Between the Chilkat Center for the Arts and the Haines parade ground, tel. 907/766–2160. Admission free. Open weekdays 9–noon and 1–5.*

Chilkat Center for the Arts, **2**
Sheldon Museum and Cultural Center, **1**

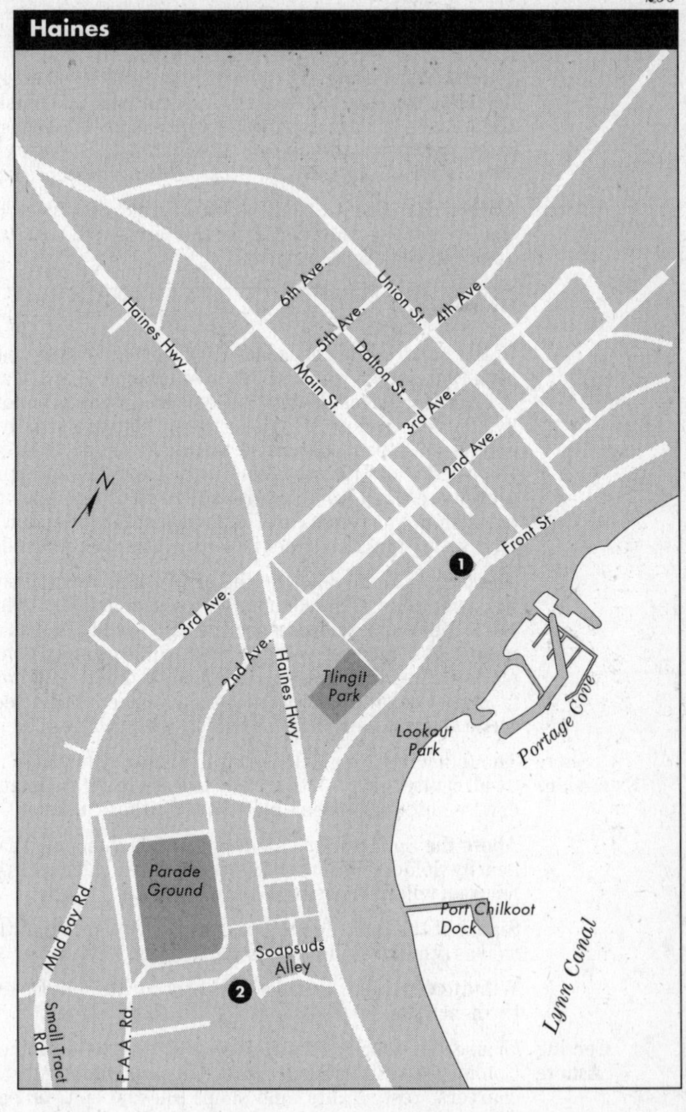

Sports *Hiking* One of the most rewarding hikes in the area is to the north summit of **Mt. Ripinsky,** the prominent peak that rises 3,610 feet behind the town. Be warned: It's a strenuous trek and requires a full day, so most cruise passengers will want to only try a partial summit. (Make sure you leave plenty of time to get back to your ship.) The trailhead lies at the top of Young Street, along a pipeline right-of-way. For other hikes, pick up a copy of "Haines Is for Hikers" at the visitor center.

Dining *$$* **Lighthouse Restaurant.** At the foot of Main Street next to the boat harbor, the Lighthouse offers a great view of Lynn Canal, boats, and boaters, along with fine steaks, seafood, and barbecued ribs. Its Harbor Bar is a popular watering hole for commercial fishermen. It's colorful but can get a little loud at night. *Front St. on the harbor, tel. 907/766–2442. AE, MC, V.*

$ **Bamboo Room.** This unassuming coffee shop is popular for sandwiches, burgers, fried chicken, seafood, and, of course, break-

fast. Diners have views of the mountains beyond. *2nd Ave. near Main St., tel. 907/766–2800. AE, D, DC, MC, V.*

$ **Chilkat Restaurant and Bakery.** Family-style cooking is served in a homelike, no-smoking setting. Lace curtains and plush green carpet add a touch of class. Seafood, steaks, and sandwiches are cooked to order; Friday is all-you-can-eat night. *5th Ave. near Main St., tel. 907/766–2920. AE, MC, V. Closed Sun., winter hrs vary.*

Saloons **Harbor Bar** (Front St. at the Harbor, tel. 907/766–2444). Commercial fisherfolk gather nightly at this circa (1907) bar and restaurant. Sometimes there is live music.

Homer

Of the hundreds of thousands of cruise passengers that visit Alaska each year, only a very few get to see Homer. It's a shame. In a state of beautiful places, Homer has emerged as its premier artists' colony. Those travelers who do arrive by ship are usually beginning or ending an expedition cruise to the Arctic or traveling aboard an Alaska Marine Highway ferry (*see* Chapter 2). Fortunately, Homer is easily reached from Seward, where all Gulf of Alaska cruises start or finish. If you rent a car, Homer is just 173 miles down the Sterling Highway—practically next door by Alaskan standards.

The city of Homer lies at the end of a narrow spit that juts into Kachemak Bay. This community was founded just before the turn of the century as a gold-prospecting camp and later was used as a coal-mining headquarters. Today the town is a funky fishing port with picturesque buildings, good seafood, and beautiful bay views. It's a favorite weekend spot of Anchorage residents who need a change of scene and weather. Halibut fishing is especially good in this area.

Shore Excursions The following are good choices in Homer. They may not be offered by all cruise lines. All times and prices are approximate. Unless otherwise noted, children's prices are for those under 13.

Above the Spit. See the sights from a flightseeing plane, including nearby Seldovia. Longer flights visit area glaciers; other tours may focus on wildlife spotting. *1 hr. Cost: $145.*

Sights of the Spit. See the unique Homer Spit from the ground, as well as other area sights and attractions. *3 hrs. Cost: $45.*

Wildlife Watching. Board a local boat for Halibut Cove, Seldovia, or the nearby seabird colonies. *1½ hrs. Cost: $35–$45.*

Coming Ashore Cruise ships dock at the Homer Spit, where the Homer Chamber of Commerce Visitor Center is within easy walking distance. Fishing charters, restaurants, and shops line the spit, or passengers can take a taxi to town, where local galleries and additional dining are found.

Getting Around Call **Chuck's Cab** (tel. 907/235–2489) for transportation into town. A ride from the spit into town costs $8 one-way or $15 round-trip for the first person and 50¢ for each additional passenger. Taxi tours of Homer are available for $35 an hour.

Exploring Homer For an introduction to Homer's history, the **Pratt Museum** offers pioneer, Russian, and Indian displays, a saltwater aquarium, an exhibit on the 1989 Prince William Sound oil spill, a wildflower garden, and a gift shop. *Bartlett St., just off Pioneer Ave., tel. 907/235–8635. Admission: $4. Open daily 10–6.*

Kachemak Bay abounds in wildlife. Shore excursions or local tour operators take visitors to bird rookeries in the bay or across the bay to gravel beaches for clam digging. Most fishing charters will include an opportunity to view whales, seals, porpoises, and birds close-up. A walk along the docks on Homer Spit at the end of the day is a pleasant chance to watch commercial fishing boats and charter boats unload their catch. The bay supports a large population of puffins and eagles.

Directly across from the end of the Homer spit, **Halibut Cove** is a small community of people who make their living on the bay or by selling handicrafts. The Central Charter (tel. 907/235–7847) booking agency runs frequent boats to there from Homer. Halibut Cove has an art gallery and a sushi restaurant that serves local seafood. The cove itself is lovely, especially during salmon runs, when fish leap and splash in the clear water. There are also several lodges on this side of the bay, on pristine coves away from summer crowds.

Seldovia, isolated across the bay from Homer, retains the charm of an earlier Alaska. The town's Russian bloodline shows through in its onion-domed church and its name, derived from a Russian place-name meaning "herring bay." Those who fish use plenty of herring for bait, catching record-size salmon, halibut, and king or Dungeness crab. You'll find excellent fishing whether you drop your line into the deep waters of Kachemak Bay or cast into the surf for silver salmon on the shore of Outside Beach, near town. Self-guided hiking or berry picking in late July are other options. Seldovia can be reached from Homer by boat, and the dock of the small boat harbor is in the center of town—allowing for easy exploration. For a guided tour, contact Southshore Tours (tel. 907/234–8500).

Shopping The galleries on and around Pioneer Avenue, including **Ptarmigan Arts** (471 Pioneer Ave., tel. 907/235–5345), a local cooperative, are good places to find works by the town's residents.

Dining

$–$$$$ **Land's End.** The restaurant in this popular motel at the end of Homer Spit specializes in local seafood, including crab, scallops, halibut, and salmon. Burgers and steaks are also available. *4786 Homer Spit Rd., 99603, tel. 907/235–2500. AE, DC, MC, V.*

$–$$ **Saltry in Halibut Cove.** Exotically prepared local seafood dishes, including curries and pastas, and a wide selection of imported beers are available here. The deck overlooks the boat dock and the cove. It's a good place to while away the afternoon or evening, meandering along the boardwalk and visiting galleries. Dinner seatings are at 6 and 7:30. *Take the* Danny J *ferry ($17.50 round-trip) from the Homer harbor; tel. 907/235–7847. Reservations essential. AE, MC, V.*

$–$$ **Sportsman's Grill in the Bidarka Inn.** The proprietor here specializes in locally caught seafood, including fresh halibut that will melt in your mouth. Menu selections also include steaks and sandwiches, and there's an appetizing array of daily specials. *575 Sterling Hwy., tel. 907/235–8148. AE, MC, V.*

$ **Café Cups.** With microbrewery beer on tap and local artists' works on the walls, this renovated house offers more than just great food, fresh-baked breads, and desserts. Locals and visitors alike crowd into the cozy dining room for coffee and conversation in the morning or later in the day for fresh pasta, local seafood, and an eclectic but reasonably priced wine selection. Desserts include a triple decadent cheesecake and black-bottom almond cream pie. *162 W. Pioneer Ave., tel. 907/235–8330. MC, V.*

$ **Red Pepper Kitchen.** You know a place must be good when other restaurant owners list it among their favorites. So it goes with this place, where wholesome, inexpensive dishes are the order of the day. Try the vegetarian curried tofu burrito, enchiladas, or a pesto–mushroom–Parmesan cheese pizza. There's also pasta and a kids' playroom. Smoking is not allowed. *475 E. Pioneer Ave., tel. 907/235–8362. MC, V.*

Tastes of Alaska **Alaska Wild Berry Products** (528 Pioneer Ave., tel. 907/235–8858) manufactures jams, jellies, sauces, syrups, chocolate-covered candies, and juices made from wild berries handpicked on the Kenai Peninsula; shipping is available.

Juneau

Juneau owes its origins to a trio of colorful characters: two pioneers, Joe Juneau and Dick Harris, and a Tlingit chief named Kowee, who discovered rich reserves of gold in the stream that now runs through the middle of town. That was in 1880, and shortly after the discovery a modest stampede led first to the formation of a camp, then a town, then the Alaska district (now state) capital.

For nearly 60 years after Juneau's founding, gold remained the mainstay of the economy. In its heyday, the Alaska Juneau gold mine was the biggest low-grade-ore mine in the world. Then, during World War II, the government decided it needed Juneau's manpower for the war effort, and the mines ceased operations. After the war, mining failed to start up again, and the government became the city's principal employer.

Juneau is a charming, cosmopolitan frontier town. It's easy to navigate, has one of the best museums in Alaska, is surrounded by beautiful wilderness, and has a glacier in its backyard. To capture the true frontier ambience, stop by the Red Dog Saloon and the Alaskan Hotel. Both are on the main shopping drag, just a quick walk from the cruise-ship pier.

Shore Excursions The following are good choices in Juneau. They may not be offered by all cruise lines. All times and prices are approximate.

Adventure **Mendenhall Glacier Helicopter Ride.** One of the best helicopter glacier tours, including a landing on an ice field for a walk on the glacier. Boots and rain gear provided. *2 hrs. Cost: $140–$154.*

Mendenhall River Float Trip. A rafting trip down the Mendenhall River passes through some stretches of gentle rapids. Experienced oarsmen row the rafts; rubber boots, ponchos, and life jackets are provided. The minimum age is six. An excellent first rafting experience for those in good health, it's great fun. *3½ hrs. Cost: $83–$95.*

Salmon Bakes **Gold Creek Salmon Bake.** This all-you-can-eat outdoor meal features Alaskan king salmon barbecued over an open alder-wood fire. After dinner, walk in the woods, explore the abandoned mine area, or pan for gold. *1½–2 hrs. Cost: $22–$25.*

Taku Glacier Lodge Wilderness Salmon Bake. Fly over the Juneau Ice Field to Taku Glacier Lodge. Dine on barbecued salmon, then explore the virgin rain forest or enjoy the lodge. It's expensive, but this trip consistently gets rave reviews. *2½–3 hrs. Cost: $152–$173.*

Coming Ashore Cruise ships dock or tender passengers ashore at **Marine Park,** or at the old **Ferry Terminal,** nearby. A small visitor kiosk on the pier at Marine Park is filled with tour brochures, bus schedules, and maps (staffed according to cruise-ship arrivals). There is a tourist information center at the old ferry terminal as well. The downtown shops along South Franklin Street are just minutes away. The **Davis Log Cabin** (3rd and Seward Sts., tel. 907/586–2201) also dispenses information.

Getting Around
By Taxi Taxis wait for cruise-ship passengers at Marine Park. There are no standard rates; they must be negotiated. Elsewhere in town, call **Taku Glacier Cab Co.** (tel. 907/586–2121); rates begin at $1.85 for pickup, and $1.80 per mile.

Exploring Juneau *Numbers in the margin correspond to points of interest on the Juneau map.*

❶ A block east of the cruise-ship docks at Marine Park is **South Franklin Street.** The buildings here and on Front Street, which intersects South Franklin several blocks north, are among the oldest and most interesting in the city. Many reflect the architecture of the '20s and '30s; some are even older.

Alaska State Capitol, **2**
Alaska State Museum, **7**
City Museum, **5**
Evergreen Cemetery, **6**
House of Wickersham, **4**
St. Nicholas Russian Orthodox Church, **3**
South Franklin Street, **1**

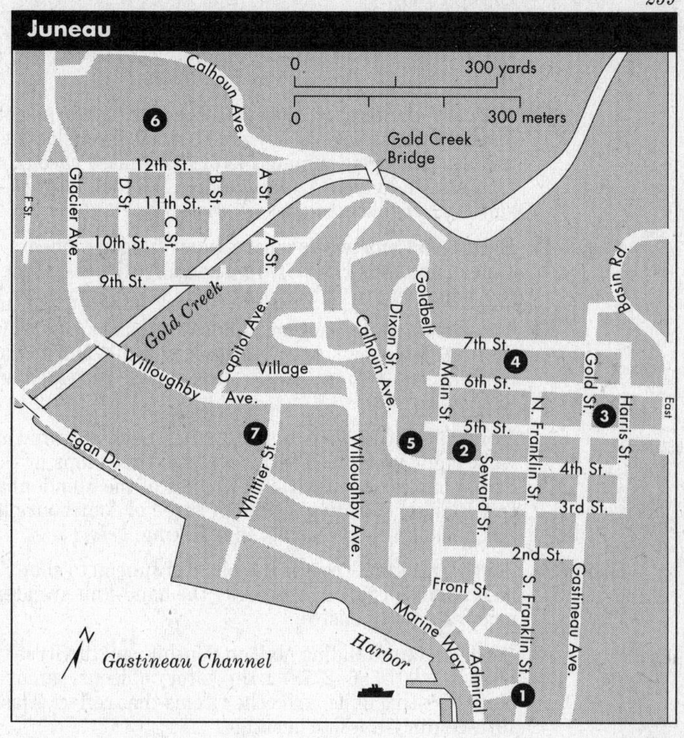

At No. 278 South Franklin Street is the **Red Dog Saloon.** With a sawdust-covered floor, a stuffed bear, and big-game heads mounted on the walls, this is Alaska's most famous saloon.

Just down the street from the Red Dog Saloon is the small **Alaskan Hotel** (167 S. Franklin St.), which was called "a pocket edition of the best hotels on the Pacific Coast" when it opened in 1913. Owners Mike and Betty Adams have restored the building with period trappings. The barroom's massive, mirrored oak bar, accented by Tiffany lamps and panels, is a particular delight.

Also on South Franklin Street is the **Alaska Steam Laundry Building,** a 1901 structure with a windowed turret. It now houses a great collection of photos from Juneau's past, a coffeehouse, and several stores.

Across the street from the Steam Laundry Building, the equally venerable **Senate Building Mall** (175 S. Franklin St.) contains one of the two Juneau Christmas Stores, a fine jewelry shop, a Native arts-and-crafts store, and a place to buy Russian icons.

2 At the corner of Seward Street is the **Alaska State Capitol,** constructed in 1930, with pillars of southeastern-Alaska marble. The structure now houses the governor's offices and other state agencies, and the state legislature meets here for four months each year. *Tel. 907/465–2479. Tours daily 8:30–5.*

3 At the top of the hill on 5th Street is little **St. Nicholas Russian Orthodox Church,** built in 1894 and the oldest original Russian church in Alaska. *326 5th St., off N. Franklin St. Donation requested. Open daily in summer, but hrs vary. Check at visitor kiosk.*

4 The **House of Wickersham,** the 1899 residence of James Wickersham, a pioneer judge and delegate to Congress, houses memorabilia from the judge's travels, ranging from rare Native American basketry and ivory carvings to historic photos, 47 diaries, and a

Chickering grand piano that came "round the horn" to Alaska when the Russians still ruled the region. *213 7th St., tel. 907/586-9001. Admission: $2. Tours Sun.–Fri. noon–5.*

5 In front of the **City Museum** stands a totem pole that is one of Juneau's finest; it tells a symbolic story of Alaska. Inside the museum, Juneau's gold-mining history is related through memorabilia, exhibits, and videos. *4th and Main Sts., tel. 907/586–3572. Admission: $2. Open weekdays 9–6, weekends 10–6.*

6 **Evergreen Cemetery** is where many Juneau pioneers (including Joe Juneau and Dick Harris) are buried. At the end of the gravel lane is the monument to Chief Kowee, who was cremated on this spot.

7 The **Alaska State Museum** is one of Alaska's best, with exhibits on the state's history, native cultures, wildlife, and industry. *395 Whittier St., tel. 907/465–2901. Admission: $3. Open weekdays 9–6, weekends 10–6.*

Mendenhall Glacier is only 13 miles from downtown, and you can walk right up to it. The bus ($1.25) that stops at South Franklin Street can take you within 1¼ miles of the Mendenhall visitor center. Plan on spending a total of three or four hours if you take the bus, including sightseeing. (*See* Hiking, *below.*)

Shopping

South Franklin Street is the place in Juneau to shop. The variety of merchandise is good (especially the hand-knit sweaters); prices are moderate to expensive.

In the Senate Building Mall on South Franklin Street is the **Russian Shop** (tel. 907/586–2778), a repository of icons, samovars, lacquered boxes, nesting dolls, and other items that reflect Alaska's 18th- and 19th-century Russian heritage.

For a souvenir from one of Alaska's most famous saloons, stop by the gift shop at the **Red Dog Saloon** (*see* Exploring Juneau, *above*).

Knowledgeable locals frequent the **Rie Munoz Gallery** (2101 N. Jordon Ave., tel. 907/789–7411) for fine art. Munoz is one of Alaska's favorite artists, and her stylized, colorful design technique is much copied. Other artists' works are also on sale, including wood-block prints by nationally known artist Dale DeArmond.

Sports

Fishing

Contact **Beartrack Charters** (tel. 907/586–6945) or **Juneau Sportfishing** (tel. 907/586–1887).

Hiking

Surrounded by the **Tongass National Forest,** Juneau is a hiker's paradise. For trail maps, information, and advice, stop by Centennial Hall on Willoughby at Egan Drive.

The Davis Log Cabin (3rd and Seward Sts., tel. 907/586–2201) sells two useful booklets, "90 Short Walks Around Juneau" ($5) and "Juneau Trails" ($4). Good trails for cruise passengers begin just behind the **Mendenhall Glacier** Visitor Center (*see* Exploring Juneau, *above*).

For guided walks, **Parks and Recreation/Juneau** (tel. 907/586–5226 or 907/586–2635) sponsors open Wednesday- and Saturday-morning group hikes. On Saturday, there's free car-pool pickup at the docks.

Alaska Rainforest Treks (tel. 907/463–3466) offers guided day hikes through Tongass National Forest. Day packs and rain gear are provided. Tours are limited in size, so call before leaving home. Departure times can be customized according to your ship's schedule. The price of $95 includes lunch.

Kayaking

Alaska Discovery (tel. 907/780–6226) offers escorted day tours for $95 per person plus $10 round-trip transportation. Lunch and rain gear are included. Trips leave around mid-morning and return about dinnertime, so participation is practical only for passengers whose ships make daylong calls.

Dining

$$ **Silver Bow Inn.** The ground floor of this little hotel houses one of Juneau's best restaurants. The dining room is furnished with mismatched antiques from the city's early days, and there's limited seating outdoors. Local fish is a specialty. Try the halibut in berries and port sauce or the mixed seafood grill in lemon-garlic sauce. The rich dessert menu features homemade ice cream. The wine list is extensive. *120 2nd St., tel. 907/586–4146. AE, D, DC, MC, V.*

$–$$ **Fiddlehead.** This is probably the favorite restaurant of Juneau locals, a delightful place of light wood, softly patterned wallpaper, stained glass, and historic photos. Food is healthy, generously served, and *different*. How about a light dinner of black beans and rice? Or pasta Greta Garbo (locally smoked salmon tossed with fettuccine in cream sauce). The homemade bread is laudable. *429 W. Willoughby Ave., tel. 907/586–3150. AE, D, DC, MC, V.*

Saloons

Juneau is one of the best saloon towns in all of Alaska. Try stopping in one of the following:

Alaskan Hotel Bar (167 S. Franklin St., tel. 907/586–1000). This spot is popular with locals and distinctly less touristy. If live music isn't playing, an old-fashioned player piano usually is.

Bubble Room (127 N. Franklin St., tel. 907/586–2660). This comfortable lounge off the lobby in the Baranof Hotel is quiet—and the site (so it is said) of more legislative lobbying and decision making than in the nearby state capitol building. The music from the piano bar is soft.

Galleon Bar (544 S. Franklin St., tel. 907/586–4700). On the pier adjacent to Giorgio's restaurant, the Galleon has a seafaring motif. Teakwood and portholes adorn the room; booths are designed as ship cabins; and the central bar is a model of a 15th-century galleon, complete with a two-story mast. There's live music nightly and a well-rounded snack menu you can build a meal on.

Red Dog Saloon (278 S. Franklin St., tel. 907/463–3777). This pub carries on the sawdust-on-the-floor tradition, with a mounted bear and other game animal trophies on the walls and lots of historic photos. There's live music and the crowd is lively, particularly when the cruise ships are in port.

Tastes of Alaska

You can't take it with you because of its limited shelf life, but when you're "shopping" the bars and watering holes of southeast Alaska, ask for Alaskan Beer, an amber beer brewed and bottled in Juneau. Visitors are welcome at the **minibrewery's plant** and can sample the product during the bottling operation on Tuesday and Thursday 11–4. *5429 Shaune Dr., Juneau, tel. 907/780–5866.*

Kenai Peninsula

The Kenai Peninsula, thrusting into the Gulf of Alaska south of Anchorage, offers salmon fishing, scenery, and wildlife. Commercial fishing is important to the area's economy, and the city of Kenai, on the peninsula's northwest coast, is the base for the Cook Inlet offshore oil fields.

The area is dotted with roadside campgrounds, and you can explore three major federal holdings on the peninsula—the western end of the sprawling **Chugach National Forest, Kenai National Wildlife Refuge,** and **Kenai Fjords National Park.**

Portage Glacier, located 50 miles southeast of Anchorage, is one of Alaska's most frequently visited tourist destinations. A 6-mile side road off the Seward Highway leads to the Begich-Boggs Visitor Center on the shore of Portage Lake. Boat tours of the face of the glacier are conducted aboard the 200-passenger *Ptarmigan*. Unfortunately, the glacier is receding rapidly, so the view across the lake is not as good as it used to be.

The mountains surrounding Portage Glacier are covered with smaller glaciers. A short hike to Byron Glacier Overlook, about 1 mile west, is popular in the spring and summer. In summer, naturalists lead free weekly treks in search of microscopic ice worms. Keep an eye out for black bears in all the Portage side valleys in the summer.

Ketchikan

Ketchikan sits at the base of 3,000-foot Deer Mountain. Until miners and fishermen settled here in the 1880s, the mouth of Ketchikan Creek was a summer fishing camp for Tlingit Indians. Today, commercial and recreational fishing are still important to the area.

Ketchikan is Alaska's totem-pole port: At the nearby Tlingit village of Saxman, 2½ miles south of downtown, there is a major totem park, and residents still practice traditional carving techniques. The Ketchikan Visitors Bureau on the dock can supply information on getting to Saxman on your own, or you can take a ship-organized tour. Another outdoor totem display is at Totem Bight State Historical Park, a coastal rain forest 10 miles north of town. The Totem Heritage Center preserves historic poles, some nearly 200 years old.

Ketchikan is easy to explore, with walking-tour signs to lead you around the city. It is not advisable to walk to outlying areas, such as Saxman, because there are no sidewalks en route. Expect rain at some time during the day, even if the sun is shining when you dock: average annual precipitation is more than 150 inches.

Shore Excursions The following are good choices in Ketchikan. They may not be offered by all cruise lines. All times and prices are approximate.

Adventure **Misty Fjords Flightseeing.** Aerial views of granite cliffs rising 4,000 feet from the sea, waterfalls, rain forests, and wildlife lead to a landing on a high wilderness lake. *1½–2 hrs. Cost: $140–$159.*

Sportfishing. You're almost sure to get a bite in the "Salmon Capital of the World." Charter boats hold from four to six passengers; fish can be butchered and shipped home for an additional charge. *4–5 hrs, including 3–4 hrs of fishing. Cost: $135–$150.*

Native Culture **Saxman Village.** See 27 totem poles and totem carvers at work at this Native Community. The gift shop is among the best for Alaska native crafts. *2½ hrs. Cost: $39–$42.*

Totem Bight Tour. This look at Ketchikan's native culture focuses on Tlingit totem poles in Totem Bight State Historical Park. Guides interpret the myths and symbols in the traditional carvings. *1¾–2 hrs. Cost: $29–$31.*

Coming Ashore Ships dock or tender passengers ashore directly across from the Ketchikan Visitors Bureau on Front and Mission streets, in the center of downtown. Here you can pick up brochures and maps. Most of the town's sights are within easy walking distance.

Getting Around
By Taxi To reach the sights outside downtown on your own, you'll want to hire a cab. Metered taxis meet the ships right on the docks and also wait across the street. Rates are $2.10 for pickup, 23¢ each ⅒ mile.

Exploring Ketchikan *Numbers in the margin correspond to points of interest on the Ketchikan map.*

❶ You can learn about Ketchikan's early days of fishing, mining, and logging at the **Tongass Historical Museum and Totem Pole.** *Dock and Bawden Sts., tel. 907/225-5600. Admission: $2. Open daily 8–5 during cruise season.*

❷ For a great view of the harbor, take curving Venetia Avenue to the **Westmark Cape Fox Lodge.** Aside from providing stunning views and

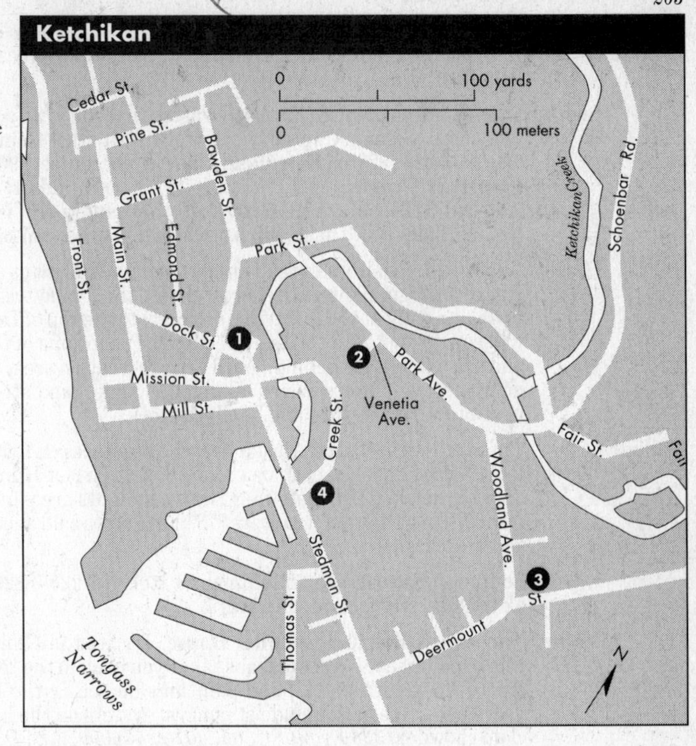

fine dining, the lodge also runs tramway rides ($1) down the mountainside to popular Creek Street (*see below*).

❸ Every visitor to Ketchikan should stop by the **Totem Heritage Center and Nature Park,** which houses a fascinating display of weathered, original totem carvings. *Woodland Ave. at corner of Deermont St., tel. 907/225–5900. Admission: $3. Open daily 8–5 during cruise season.*

❹ **Creek Street,** formerly Ketchikan's infamous red-light district remains the centerpiece of town. Its small houses, built on stilts over the creek, have been restored as trendy shops. The street's most famous brothel, Dolly's House (admission $3), has been preserved as a museum, complete with furnishings and a short history of the life and times of Ketchikan's best-known madam. There's good salmon viewing in season at the Creek Street Footbridge. You can catch the tram here for a ride up to the Westmark Cape Fox Lodge, if you missed it before (*see above*).

Scuba Diving

A shop that rents tanks and equipment to qualified divers is **Alaska Diving Service** (4845 N. Tongass Ave., tel. 907/225–4667).

Shopping

The **Saxman Village** gift shop has some superb handcrafted Tlingit merchandise, along with cheaper mass-produced souvenirs. Because artists are local, prices for Native American crafts are better here than at most other ports.

Creek Street has several attractive boutiques. At **Parnassus Bookstore** (5 Creek St., tel. 907/225–7690), you can browse through an eclectic collection of books. Try **Soho Coho** (5 Creek St., tel. 907/225–5954) for contemporary art and various crafts.

Scanlon Gallery (318 Mission St., tel. 907/225–4730) handles not only major Alaskan artists and local talent but also traditional and contemporary Native art, soapstone, bronze, and walrus ivory.

Salmon, Etc. (322 Mission St., tel. 907/225–6008) sells every variety of Alaskan salmon, which can be sent, frozen and processed, to your home.

Sports *Fishing* Salmon are so plentiful in these waters that the town has earned the nickname "Salmon Capital of the World." Contact **Chinook Charters** (tel. 907/225–9225), **Ketchikan Charter Boats** (tel. 907/225–7291), **Chip Port Charters** (tel. 907/225–2447), or **Knudson Cove Marina** (tel. 907/247–8500). The **Ketchikan Convention & Visitors Bureau** (tel. 907/225–6166) has a full list of other charter companies.

Hiking Check at the visitors bureau on the dock for trail maps and advice. If you're a tough hiker with sturdy shoes, the 3-mile trail from downtown (starting at the end of Fair Street) to the top of **Deer Mountain** will repay your effort with a spectacular panorama of the city below and the wilderness behind. **Ward Cove** recreation area, about 6 miles north of town, offers easier hiking along lakes and streams and beneath towering spruce and hemlock trees.

Kayaking and Canoeing Contact Juneau-based **Alaska Travel Adventures** (tel. 907/789–0052) for a Native American canoe excursion on Harriet Hunt Lake north of town; smoked fish and other Native delights are part of the experience. This 3½-hour trip costs $73 and is often sold aboard ships as a shore excursion.

Southeast Exposure (507 Stedman St.,tel. 907/225–8829) offers kayak rentals, instruction, and tours.

Dining *$$–$$$* **Annabelle's Keg and Chowder House.** Located in Gilmore's Hotel, this popular seafood restaurant takes you back to the '20s. The walls are covered with photos and paintings depicting the Ketchikan of years past. Specials include steamers, oysters on the half shell, and clam chowder. *326 Front St., tel. 907/225–6009. AE, D, DC, MC, V.*

Saloons **Annabelle's Keg and Chowder House** (326 Front St., tel. 907/225–6009). This restaurant-lounge with a jukebox in the Gilmore Hotel blends old and new Alaska in a semiformal atmosphere.

Misty Fjords National Monument

In the past, cruise ships used to bypass Misty Fjords on their way up and down the Inside Passage. But today this national monument has become a favorite on Alaska itineraries. Ships big and small, from the yachtlike vessels of Alaska Sightseeing to the liners of Crystal, Cunard, Norwegian Cruise Line, and others, now feature a day of scenic cruising through this protected wilderness. At the southern end of the Inside Passage, Misty Fjords usually lies just before or after a call at Ketchikan. The attraction here is the wilderness—3,500 square miles of it—highlighted by waterfalls and cliffs that rise 3,000 feet.

Petersburg

Getting to Petersburg is an experience. Only ferries and the smallest cruise ships can squeak through Wrangell Narrows with the aid of more than 50 buoys and range markers along the 22-mile crossing. At times the channel seems too narrow for ships to pass through, making for a nail-biting—though safe—trip.

The inaccessibility of Petersburg is part of its off-the-beaten-path charm. Unlike at several other southeast communities, you'll never be overwhelmed by the hordes of cruise passengers here.

At first sight of Petersburg you may think you're in the old country. Neat, white, Scandinavian-style homes and storefronts with steep roofs and bright-colored swirls of leaf and flower designs (called rosemaling) and row upon row of sturdy fishing vessels in the harbor invoke the spirit of Norway. No wonder. This prosperous fishing community was founded by Norwegian Peter Buschmann in 1897.

The Little Norway Festival is held here each year on the third full weekend in May. If you're in town during the festival, be sure to partake in one of the fish feeds that highlight the Norwegian Independence Day celebration. You won't find better beer-batter halibut and folk dancing outside of Norway.

Shore Excursions The following are good choices in Petersburg. They may not be offered by all cruise lines. All times and prices are approximate.

Adventure **LeConte Flightseeing.** One of the best flightseeing tours in Alaska takes you to the southernmost calving glacier in North America. *45 min–1 hr. Cost: $123–$165.*

Petersburg by Bus. Here's a chance to get outside of town and see the scenery. The tour ends with Norwegian refreshments and a performance of Norwegian dance. *1½ hrs. Cost: $25.*

Walking Tour. A guide will relate the history and fishing heritage of Petersburg as you explore the old part of town on foot. *1 hr. Cost: $10.*

Coming Ashore Ships small enough to visit Petersburg dock in the South Harbor, which is about a half-mile walk to downtown. Taxis are usually available dockside, or call **Chris Cab** (tel. 907/772–2222) or **City Cab** (tel. 907/772–3003). A ride into town costs $4 per person. Petersburg tours are priced at $35 to $55 per hour.

Getting Around Everything in Petersburg is within easy walking distance of the harbor. Renting a bicycle is an especially pleasant way to see the sights. A good route is to ride along the coast on Nordic Drive, past the lovely homes, to the boardwalk and the city dump, where you might spot some bears. Coming back to town, take the interior route and you'll pass the airport and some pretty churches before returning to the waterfront. Bicycles are available for rent from Northern Bikes at the Scandia House Hotel.

Passengers who want to learn about the local history, the commercial fishing industry, and the natural history of the Tongass National Forest can book a guided van tour. Contact Alaska Tours and Charters (tel. 907/772–4656).

Exploring Petersburg *Numbers in the margin correspond to points of interest on the Petersburg map.*

One of the most pleasant things to do in Petersburg is to roam among the fishing vessels tied up at dockside. This is one of Alaska's busiest, most prosperous fishing communities, and the variety of seacraft is enormous. You'll see small trollers, big halibut vessels, and sleek pleasure craft as well. Wander, too, around the fish-processing structures (though beware of the pungent aroma). Just by watching shrimp, salmon, or halibut catches being brought ashore, you can get a real appreciation for this industry and the people who engage in it.

Overlooking the city harbor there are great viewing and picture-taking vantage points. For a scenic hike, go north on Nordic Drive to ❶ get to **Sandy Beach,** where there's frequently good eagle viewing and access to one of Petersburg's favorite picnic and recreation locales.

❷ Still another photo opportunity lies in the center of town at **Hammer Slough.** The houses built on stilts make for a postcard-perfect picture.

Those wanting to do some sightseeing in town should head northeast ❸ up the hill from the visitor center to the **Clausen Museum** and the bronze *Fisk* (Norwegian for "fish") sculpture at 2nd and Fram

Clausen Museum, **3**
Hammer Slough, **2**
Sandy Beach, **1**
Sons of Norway Hall, **4**

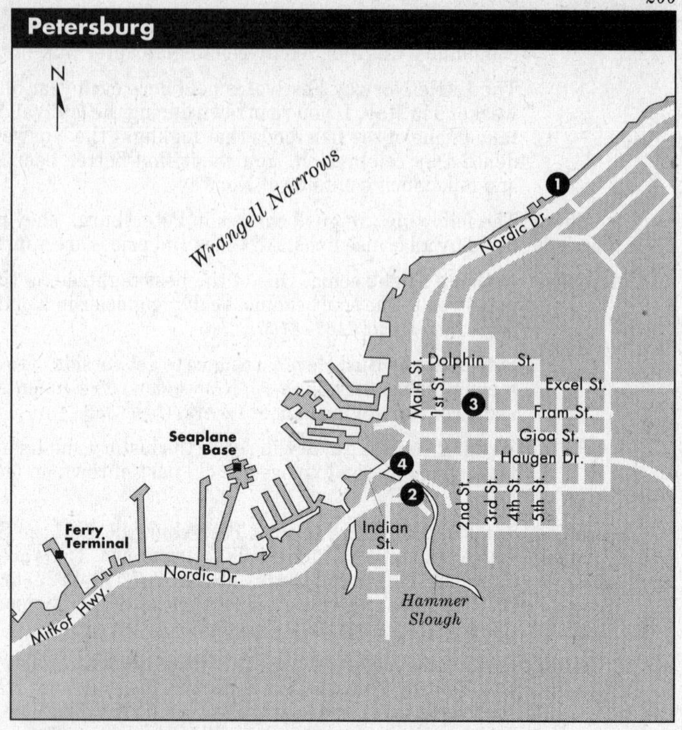

streets. The monument, featuring scores of separately sculpted salmon, halibut, and herring, celebrates the bounty of the sea. It was created in 1967 as part of Petersburg's celebration of the 100th anniversary of the Alaska Purchase from Russia. The museum—not surprisingly—devotes a lot of its space to fishing and processing. There's an old "iron chink," used in the early days for gutting and cleaning fish, as well as displays that illustrate the workings of several types of fishing boats. A 126½-pound king salmon, the largest ever caught, came out of a fish trap on Prince of Wales Island in 1939 and is on exhibit, as is the world's largest chum salmon—a 36-pounder. There are also displays of Native artifacts. *203 Fram St., tel. 907/772–3598. Admission: $2. Open May 13–Sept. 25, Mon.–Sat. 10–4, Sun. 1–4.*

Three **pioneer churches**—Catholic, Lutheran, and Presbyterian—are located nearby at Dolphin and 3rd streets, Excel and 5th streets, and on Haugen Street between 2nd and 3rd streets, respectively. Of the three, the 50-year-old Lutheran edifice is the oldest. It is said that boys wheelbarrowed fill from elsewhere in the city for landscaping around the foundation. Their compensation? Ice-cream cones. The enticement was so successful that, after three years of ice-cream rewards, it was necessary to bring in a bulldozer to scrape off the excess dirt.

4 The large, white, barnlike structure on stilts that stands in Hammer Slough off Indian Street is the **Sons of Norway Hall,** the headquarters of an organization devoted to keeping alive the traditions and culture of the old country.

Petersburg's biggest draw actually lies about 25 miles east of town and is accessible only by water or air. **LeConte Glacier** is the continent's southernmost tidewater glacier and one of its most active, often calving off so many icebergs that the bay at its face is carpeted bank-to-bank with floating bergs. Ferries and cruise ships pass it at a distance.

Dining

$ **Helse.** Natural foods, including enormous vegetable-laden sandwiches, are a specialty in this homey cross between a diner and a restaurant. Helse, a favorite lunchtime spot with locals, is filled with plenty of plants and works by local artists. The menu features soups, chowders, home-baked breads, and salads. Espresso makes a nice ending to a meal. Breakfast is not served, excepting raisin-bran muffins. *Sing Lee Alley and Harbor Way, tel. 907/772–3444. No credit cards.*

$ **The Homestead.** There's nothing fancy here, just basic American fare: steaks, local prawns and halibut, a salad bar, and especially generous breakfasts. Rhubarb pie is the fastest-selling item on the menu. It's a popular place with locals. *217 Main St., tel. 907/772–3900. DC, MC, V.*

$ **Pellerito's Pizza.** Recommended pizza toppings here include Canadian bacon and pineapple or local shrimp. *Across from ferry terminal, tel. 907/772–3727. No credit cards.*

Saloons

Harbor Bar (Nordic Dr. near Dolphin St., tel. 907/772–4526). The name suggests the decor here—ship's wheels, ship pictures, and a mounted red snapper.

Tastes of Alaska

One of the southeast's gourmet delicacies is "Petersburg shrimp." Small (they're seldom larger than half your pinky finger), tender, and succulent, they're much treasured by Alaskans, who often send them "outside" as thank-you gifts. You'll find the little critters fresh in meat departments and canned in gift sections at food stores throughout the Panhandle. You can buy fresh vacuum-packed Petersburg shrimp in Petersburg at Coastal Cold Storage, downtown on Main Street, or mail-order them (Box 307, Petersburg 99833, tel. 907/772–4177).

Prince William Sound

Every Gulf of Alaska cruise visits Prince William Sound. The sound made headlines in 1989, when the *Exxon Valdez* hit a reef and spilled 11 million gallons of North Slope crude. The oil has sunk into the beaches below the surface, however, and vast parts of the sound appear pristine, with abundant wildlife. What lasting effect this lurking oil—which is sometimes uncovered after storms and high tides—will have on the area is still being studied.

Numbers in the margin correspond to points of interest on the South Central Alaska map.

❶ A visit to **Columbia Glacier,** which flows from the surrounding Chugach Mountain range, is included on many Gulf of Alaska cruises. Its deep aquamarine face is 5 miles across, and it calves new icebergs with resounding cannonades. This glacier is one of the largest and most readily accessible of Alaska's coastal glaciers.

❷ The major attraction in Prince William Sound on most Gulf of Alaska cruises is the day spent in **College Fjord.** Dubbed "Alaska's newest Glacier Bay" by one cruise line, this deep finger of water is ringed by 16 glaciers, each one named after one of the colleges that sponsored early exploration of the fjord.

❸ Of the three major Prince William Sound communities—Valdez, Whittier, and Cordova—only **Valdez** (pronounced val-*deez*) is a major port of call for cruise ships. For more information on visiting Valdez, *see below.*

Seward

On the southeastern coast of the Kenai Peninsula, Seward is surrounded by four major federal landholdings—**Chugach National Forest, Kenai Wildlife Refuge, Kenai Fjords National Park,** and the

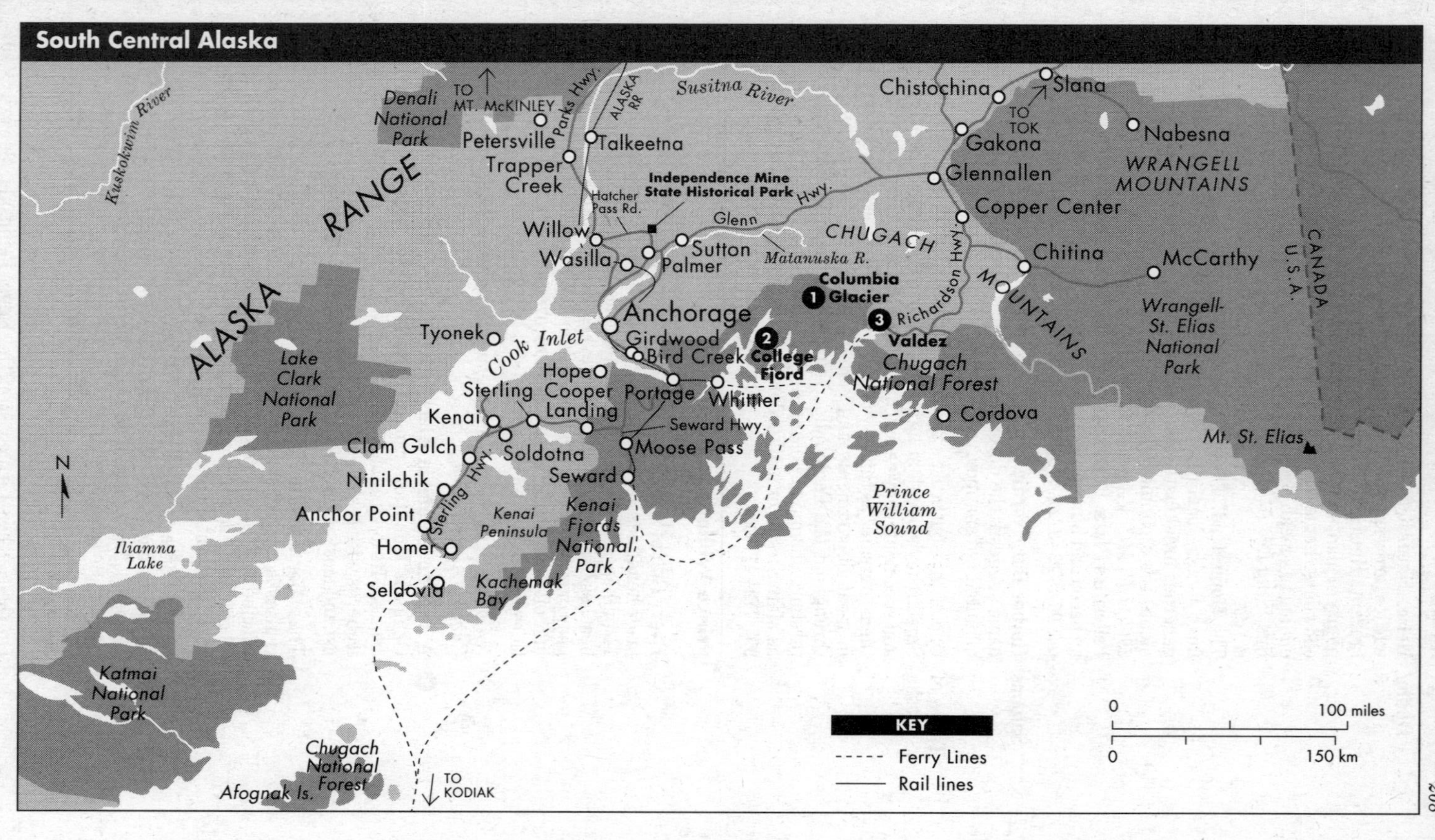
South Central Alaska
Denali National Park
TO MT. McKINLEY
Petersville
Parks Hwy.
ALASKA RR
Talkeetna
Trapper Creek
Susitna River
Kuskokwim River
ALASKA RANGE
Independence Mine State Historical Park
Hatcher Pass Rd.
Glenn Hwy.
Willow
Wasilla
Sutton
Palmer
Matanuska R.
CHUGACH MOUNTAINS
Chistochina
Slana
TO TOK
Gakona
Glennallen
Copper Center
Chitina
Nabesna
WRANGELL MOUNTAINS
McCarthy
Wrangell-St. Elias National Park
CANADA
U.S.A.
Mt. St. Elias
Columbia Glacier
College Fjord
Anchorage
Girdwood
Bird Creek
Richardson Hwy.
Valdez
Chugach National Forest
Cordova
Prince William Sound
Tyonek
Cook Inlet
Lake Clark National Park
Hope
Sterling
Cooper Landing
Portage
Whittier
Kenai
Seward Hwy.
Moose Pass
Clam Gulch
Soldotna
Seward
Ninilchik
Sterling Hwy.
Kenai Peninsula
Kenai Fjords National Park
Anchor Point
Homer
Iliamna Lake
Seldovia
Kachemak Bay
Katmai National Park
Chugach National Forest
Afognak Is.
TO KODIAK
N
KEY
Ferry Lines
Rail lines
0
100 miles
0
150 km

Alaska Maritime National Refuge. The entire area is breathtaking, and you should not miss it in your haste to get to Anchorage.

Seward was founded in 1903, at the time that planning for the railroad to Alaska's interior began. The tidal wave that followed the 1964 earthquake devastated the town but, fortunately, most residents saw the harbor drain almost entirely, knew the wave would follow, and ran to high ground. Since then the town has relied heavily on commercial fishing, and its harbor is important for shipping coal to the Orient.

If you're in Seward on the Fourth of July, stick around for the insane Mt. Marathon foot race, 3,000 feet straight uphill from downtown. (*See* Hiking, *below.*)

Shore Excursions Like Anchorage, Seward is mainly a transfer point for embarking and disembarking cruise passengers. If your ship is one that calls here for the day, though, the following excursion is a good choice.

Adventure **Mt. McKinley Flightseeing.** From Anchorage, fly to Denali National Park (filled with bears, wolves, caribou, and moose) to see North America's highest peak. The trip is often canceled due to cloudiness. *3 hrs, 2 hrs flying time. Cost: $288.*

Coming Ashore Cruise ships dock within a half mile of downtown. The Kenai Fjords National Park visitor center is within walking distance: Turn left as you leave the pier, then left again onto 4th Avenue; the center is two blocks ahead. The Chugach National Forest Ranger District Information Center is at 334 Fourth Avenue.

Getting Around Public bus routes include stops timed to meet ships. For a taxi call 907/224–5000 or 907/224–5555 from the pay phones at the dock. Rates are $2 for pickup, $1.50 per mile.

Exploring Seward Seward offers little to compare with the splendor of its surroundings: Most passengers head into Anchorage or explore the federal parks of the Kenai Peninsula. Don't miss the fjords in Resurrection Bay, with their bird rookeries and sea-lion colonies.

Shopping The **Alaska Shop** (210 4th Ave., tel. 907/224–5420) has a variety of souvenirs, from T-shirts to jewelry to Alaska books.

The **Treasure Chest** (Small Boat Harbor, tel. 907/224–8087) has T-shirts and sweatshirts, plus a wide selection of Alaskan gifts.

Ranting Raven Bakery (228 4th Ave., tel. 907/224–2228) has a gift shop stocked with Russian and Ukrainian imports. Don't forget to try the home-baked breads, pastries, and cakes.

Bardarson Studio (Small Boat Harbor, tel. 907/224–5448) has local Alaskan art—originals and reproductions—as well as imported goods.

Sports

Fishing The Seward Jackpot Halibut Tournament runs through July, and the Seward Silver Salmon Derby is in August. For fishing, sightseeing, and drop-off/pickup tours, contact **Fish House** (tel. 800/257–7760; in AK, 907/224–3674), Seward's oldest operator, or **Kenai Fjords Tours** (tel. 907/224–8068 or 800/478–8068).

For Kenai Fjords National Park wildlife and glacier tours, call Anchorage-based **Mariah Charters** (tel. 907/243–1238 or 800/270–1238).

Hiking The **Mt. Marathon** trail starts at the west end of Lowell Street and runs practically straight uphill. An easier and more convenient hike for cruise passengers is the **Two Lakes Trail,** a loop of footpaths and bridges on the edge of town. A map is available from the Seward Chamber of Commerce (Box 749, Seward 99664, tel. 907/224–8051).

Dining

$–$$ **Harbor Dinner Club & Lounge.** At this house downtown, the lounge is decorated with hand-painted murals depicting Alaskan wildlife,

and the halibut is great. Try a halibut burger with homemade french fries. *220 5th Ave., tel. 907/224–3012. AE, D, DC, MC, V.*

Sitka

For hundreds of years before the 18th-century arrival of the Russians, Sitka was the home of the Tlingit nation. But Sitka's beauty, mild climate, and economic potential caught the attention of outsiders. Russian Territorial Governor Alexander Baranof saw in the island's massive timbered forests raw materials for shipbuilding, and its location suited trading routes to California, Hawaii, and the Orient. In 1799 Baranof established an outpost that he called Redoubt St. Michael, 6 miles north of the present town, and moved a large number of his Russian and Aleut fur hunters there from Kodiak Island.

The Tlingits attacked Baranof's people and burned his buildings in 1802, but Baranof returned in 1804 with a formidable force, including shipboard cannons. He attacked the Tlingits at their fort near Indian River (site of the present-day, 105-acre Sitka National Historical Park) and drove them to the other side of the island. The Tlingits and Russians made peace in 1821, and, eventually, the capital of Russian America was shifted to Sitka from Kodiak.

Sitka today is known primarily for its onion-domed Russian Orthodox church, one of southeast Alaska's most famous landmarks, and the Raptor Rehabilitation Center, a hospital for injured bald eagles and other birds of prey. Don't miss the 15 totem poles scattered throughout the grounds of the historical park.

Shore Excursions The following is a good choice in Sitka. It may not be offered by all cruise lines. All times and prices are approximate.

Adventure **Kayak Adventure.** Get down to sea level to search for marine and land wildlife in two-person sea kayaks. Sightings of eagles, seals, bears, and deer are likely. If your ship doesn't offer this excursion, contact Baidarka Boats (*see* Kayaking, *below*). *3 hrs, includes 1½ hrs of kayaking. Cost: $65–$75.*

Coming Ashore Only the smallest excursion vessels can dock at Sitka. Ocean liners must drop anchor in the harbor and tender passengers ashore near the Centennial Building, with its big Tlingit war canoe. Inside is the Sitka Visitors Bureau, which provides maps and brochures. A taxi ride downtown costs about $3, though the distance can easily be walked.

Getting Around

By Taxi Taxis meet the cruise ships, but if none is around, call 907/747–8888 or 907/747–5001. A 30-minute taxi tour costs $20 per carload; an hour tour costs $40. Pay phones are in the Centennial Building and across the way in the Bayview Trading Company.

Exploring Sitka *Numbers in the margin correspond to points of interest on the Sitka map.*

To get one of the best views in town, turn left on Harbor Drive and

❶ head for **Castle Hill,** where Alaska was handed over to the United States on October 18, 1867, and where the first 49-star U.S. flag was flown on January 3, 1959, signifying the spirit of Alaska's statehood. Take the first right off Harbor Drive, then look for the entrance to Baranof Castle Hill State Historic Site. Make a left on the gravel path that takes you to the top of the hill overlooking Crescent Harbor.

❷ The **Sitka State Pioneers' Home** was built in 1934 as the first of several state-run retirement homes and medical-care facilities. The statue, symbolizing the spirit of Alaska's frontier sourdough (as the locals are nicknamed), was modeled after an authentic pioneer, Wil-

Alaska Raptor Rehabilitation Center, **8**
Castle Hill, **1**
Russian Bishop's House, **5**
Russian and Lutheran cemeteries, **3**
St. Michael's Cathedral, **4**
Sheldon Jackson Museum, **6**
Sitka National Historical Park Visitor Center, **7**
Sitka State Pioneers' Home, **2**

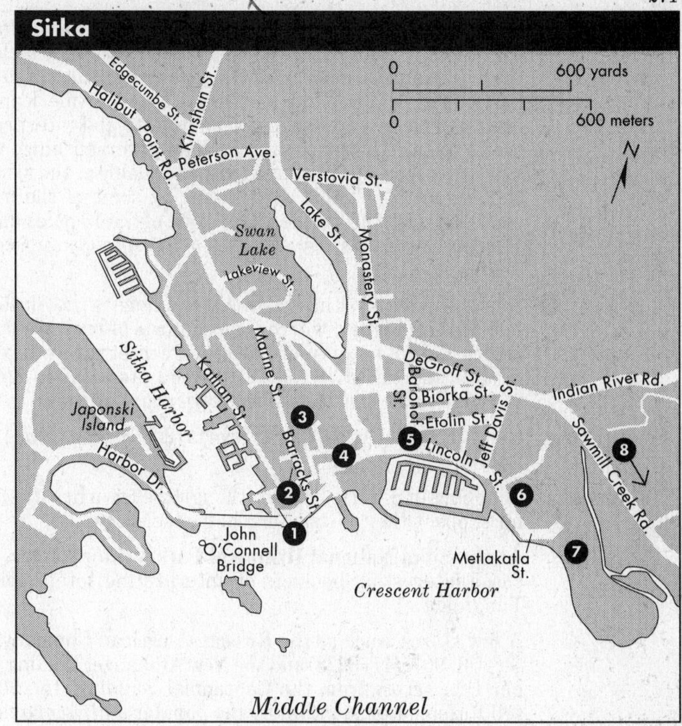

liam "Skagway Bill" Fonda. It portrays a determined prospector with pack, pick, rifle, and supplies, headed for gold country.

Three old anchors, believed to be from 19th-century British ships, mark **Totem Square.** Notice the double-headed eagle of czarist Russia on the park's totem pole.

❸ The most distinctive grave in the **Russian and Lutheran cemeteries** marks the final resting place of Princess Maksutoff, one of the most famous members of the Russian royal family buried on Alaskan soil.

❹ Sitka's most famous and most photographed sight, **St. Michael's Cathedral** had its origins in a frame-covered log structure built in the 1840s. In 1966 the church burned in a fire that swept through the business district. Using original blueprints, an almost-exact replica of St. Michael's was built and dedicated in 1976. *Lincoln St., tel. 907/747–8120. $1 donation requested. Open daily 1:30–5:30 and to accommodate cruise passengers when in port.*

❺ Several blocks past St. Michael's Cathedral on Lincoln Street and facing the harbor is the **Russian Bishop's House.** Constructed in 1842, this is one of the few remaining Russian log homes in Alaska. Inside are exhibits on the history of Russian America and the Room Revealed, where a portion of the house's structure is peeled away to expose Russian building techniques. *Admission free. Call 907/747–6281 for hrs.*

❻ The octagonal **Sheldon Jackson Museum,** built in 1895, contains priceless Native American items collected by Dr. Sheldon Jackson from the remote regions of Alaska. Carved masks, Chilkat Indian blankets, dogsleds, kayaks—even the helmet worn by Chief Katlean during the 1804 battle between the Sitka Tlingits and the Russians—are displayed here. *Lincoln St., tel. 907/747–8981. Admission: $3. Open daily 8–5.*

7 **Sitka National Historical Park Visitor Center** is at the far end of Lincoln Street. Audiovisual programs and exhibits, including Native American and Russian artifacts, give an overview of southeast Alaskan cultures, both old and new. Native American artists and craftspeople are on hand to demonstrate and interpret traditional crafts of the Tlingit people, such as silversmithing, weaving, and basketry. A self-guided trail (maps available at the visitor center) to the site of the Tlingit Fort passes by some of the most skillfully carved totem poles in the state; some of the 15 poles date back more than eight decades. *Tel. 907/747–6281. Admission free. Open daily 8–5.*

8 One of Sitka's most interesting attractions is the **Alaska Raptor Rehabilitation Center,** where injured birds of prey are nursed back to health. A visit to this unusual nature center rarely disappoints. *1101 Sawmill Creek Rd., tel. 907/747–8662. Admission: $10. Open daily 8–5, and when cruise-ship passengers are in port.*

Scuba Diving Contact **Southeast Diving & Sports** (203 Lincoln Ave., tel. 907/747–8279).

Shopping Shopping in Sitka is limited, though the town has its share of souvenir shops. Other ports offer a better selection.

At the **Sitka National Historical Park Visitor Center,** you can purchase interesting booklets on interpreting totem poles and other Tlingit art.

A few stores, such as the **Russian-American Company** (407 Lincoln St., tel. 907/747–6228) and the **New Archangel Trading Co.** (335 Harbor Dr., across from the Centennial Building, tel. 907/747–8181), sell Russian items, including the popular *matruchka* nesting dolls.

For books on Alaska, stop by **Old Harbor Books** (201 Lincoln St., tel. 907/747–8808).

Sports
Fishing Fishing is excellent here. Contact **Steller Charters** (tel. 907/747–6711) or see the information desk in the Centennial Building for a list of other charter operators.

Hiking Sitka's best hiking can be done along the 2 miles of trails in **Sitka National Historical Park.** Here you can find some of the most dramatic totem poles in Alaska, relax in the picnic areas, and see spawning salmon during the seasonal runs on the Indian River.

Kayaking **Baidarka Boats** (tel. 907/747–8996) rents sea kayaks ($25–$45) and offers guided trips in the island-strewn waters around Sitka ($85 minimum plus rental fee). Be sure to make arrangements in advance so that your guide and/or kayak is waiting for you at the harbor.

Dining
$$–$$$ **Channel Club.** This is Sitka's best gourmet restaurant—a five-time winner of the Silver Spoon award from the Gourmet Club of America. Halibut cheeks are a favorite, and the recipe for the steak's delicious seasoning is a closely held secret. Decor is nautical, with glass fishing balls, whale baleen, and Alaska pictures on the walls. *Mile 3.5 on Halibut Point Rd., tel. 907/747–9916. AE, DC, MC, V.*

Saloons **Pilot House** (713 Katlean St., tel. 907/747–4707) is a new dance spot with a waterfront view.

Pioneer Bar (212 Katlean St., tel. 907/747–3456), across from the harbor, is a hangout for local fishermen. Tourists get a kick out of its authentic Alaskan ambience; the walls are lined with pictures of ships.

Rockies (1617 Sawmill Creek Rd., tel. 907/747–3285) is a sports bar with pool, air hockey, darts, and plenty of munchies. A DJ plays dance music.

Skagway

The early gold-rush days of Alaska, when dreamers and hooligans descended on the Yukon via the murderous White Pass, are preserved in Skagway. Now a part of the Klondike Gold Rush National Historical Park, downtown Skagway was once the picturesque but sometimes lawless gateway for the frenzied stampede to the interior goldfields.

Local park rangers and residents now interpret and re-create that remarkable era for visitors. Old false-front stores, saloons, brothels, and wood sidewalks have been completely restored. You'll be regaled with tall tales of con artists, golden-hearted "ladies," stampeders, and newsmen. Such colorful characters as outlaw Jefferson "Soapy" Smith and his gang earned the town a reputation so bad that, by the spring of 1898, the superintendent of the Northwest Royal Mounted Police had labeled Skagway "little better than a hell on earth." But Soapy was killed in a duel with surveyor Frank Reid, and soon a civilizing influence, in the form of churches and family life, prevailed. When the gold played out just a few years later, the town of 20,000 dwindled to its current population of 811.

Shore Excursions The following are good choices in Skagway. They may not be offered by all cruise lines. All times and prices are approximate.

Adventure **Glacier Bay Flightseeing.** If your ship doesn't sail through Glacier Bay—or even if it does—here's your chance to see it from above. *1¼–1¾ hrs, includes 75-min flight. Cost: $112–$124.*

Gold Rush Helicopter Tour. Fly over the Chilkoot Gold Rush Trail into a remote mountain valley for a landing on a glacier. Special boots are provided for walking on the glacier. *1½ hrs. Cost: $135–$159.*

Gold-Rush History **White Pass and Yukon Railroad.** The 20-mile trip in vintage railroad cars, on narrow-gauge tracks built to serve the Yukon goldfields, runs past the infamous White Pass, skims along the edge of granite cliffs, crosses a 215-foot-high steel cantilever bridge over Dead Horse Gulch, climbs to a 2,865-foot elevation at White Pass Summit, and zigzags through dramatic scenery—including the actual Trail of '98, worn into the mountainside a century ago. A must for railroad buffs; great for children. *3 hrs. Cost: $75.*

Coming Ashore Cruise ships dock just a short stroll from downtown Skagway. From the pier you can see the large yellow-and-red White Pass & Yukon Railroad Depot, now the National Park Service Visitor Center. Inside is an excellent photographic exhibit and a superb documentary film. Ask the rangers about where to find the nearby hiking trails and a brochure on exploring the gold-rush cemetery.

Getting Around Virtually all the shops and gold-rush sights are along Broadway, the main strip that leads from the visitor center through the middle of town, so you really don't need a taxi. Horse-drawn surreys, antique limousines, and modern vans pick up passengers at the pier and along Broadway for tours. The tracks of the White Pass and Yukon Railway run right along the pier; train departures are coordinated with cruise-ship arrivals.

Exploring Skagway *Numbers in the margin correspond to points of interest on the Skagway map.*

Skagway is perhaps the easiest port in Alaska to explore on foot. Just walk up and down Broadway, detouring here and there into the side streets. Keep an eye out for the humorous architectural details and advertising irreverence that mark the Skagway spirit.

❶ From the cruise-ship dock, follow the road into town to the **Red Onion Saloon** (Broadway and 2nd Ave.), where a lady-of-the-evening

Arctic Brotherhood Hall/Trail of '98 Museum, **2**
Eagles Hall, **4**
Soapy's Parlor, **3**
Red Onion Saloon, **1**

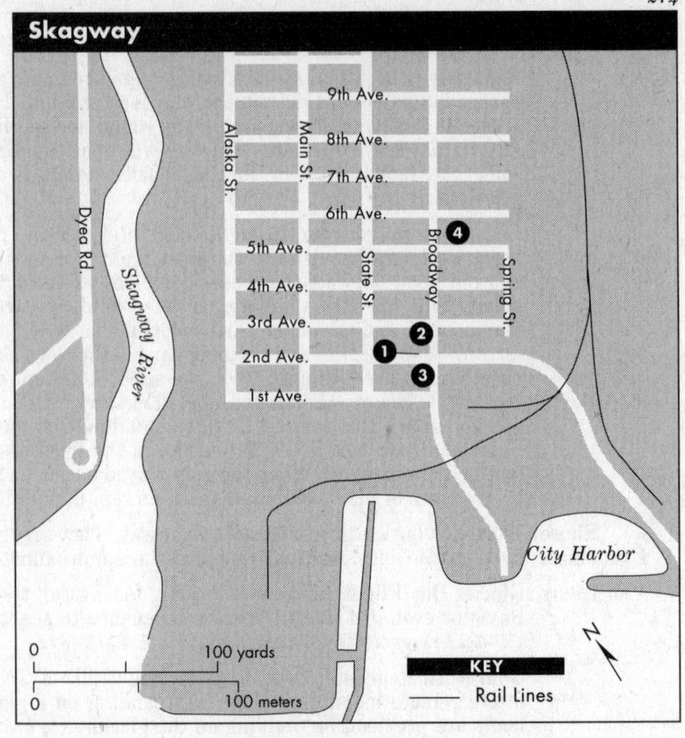

mannequin peers down from the former second-floor brothel, and drinks are still served on the original mahogany bar.

2 You can't help but notice the **Arctic Brotherhood Hall/Trail of '98 Museum,** with its curious driftwood-mosaic facade.

3 A small, almost inconsequential shack on 2nd Avenue was **Soapy's Parlor,** but it is rarely open to tourists.

You'll find down-home sourdough cooking at the **Golden North Hotel** (Broadway and 3rd Ave.).

4 A rip-roaring revue, "Skagway in the Days of '98," is staged at the **Eagles Hall** (Broadway and 6th Ave.).

Shopping Broadway is filled with numerous curio shops selling unusual merchandise. Although prices tend to be high as a general rule, good deals can be found, so shop around and don't buy the first thing you see.

David Present's Gallery (tel. 907/983–2873) has outstanding but pricey art by Alaskan artists.

Dedman's Photo Shop (tel. 907/983–2353) has been a Skagway institution since the early days; here you'll find unusual historical photos, guidebooks, and old-fashioned newspapers.

Kirmse's (tel. 907/983–2822) has a large selection of expensive, inexpensive, and downright tacky souvenirs. On display is the world's largest, heaviest, and most valuable gold-nugget watch chain.

Sports
Hiking Real wilderness is within a stone's throw of the docks, which makes this an excellent hiking port. Try the short jaunt to beautiful **Lower Dewey Lake.** Start at the corner of 4th Avenue and Spring Street, go toward the mountain, cross the footbridge over Pullen Creek, and follow the trail.

A less strenuous hike is the trip through **Gold Rush Cemetery,** where the epitaphs offer strange but lively bits of social commentary. To get there, keep walking up Broadway, turn left onto 8th Avenue, then right onto State Street. Go through the railroad yards and follow the signs to the cemetery, which is 1½ miles, or a 30- to 45-minute walk, from town. To reach 300-foot-high **Reid Falls,** continue through the cemetery for a quarter mile. The National Park Service Visitor Center offers trail maps, advice, and the helpful brochure, *Skagway Gold Rush Cemetery Guide.*

Dining
$–$$ **Golden North Restaurant.** To eat in the Golden North Hotel's dining room is to return to the days of gold-rush con man Soapy Smith, heroic Frank Reid, and scores of pioneers, stampeders, and dance-hall girls. The decor is authentic and has been tastefully restored. Popular choices include sourdough pancakes for breakfast; soup, salad bar, and sandwiches for lunch; and salmon or other seafood for dinner. *3rd Ave. and Broadway, tel. 907/983–2294. AE, DC, MC, V.*

$ **Prospector's Sourdough Restaurant.** "Sourdough" is the nickname for locals, who often outnumber the tourists here. Breakfast specialties are hotcakes and snow-crab omelets. *4th Ave. and Broadway, tel. 907/983–2865. AE, DC, MC, V.*

Saloons
Moe's Frontier Bar (Broadway between 4th and 5th Sts., tel. 907/983–2238). A longtime fixture on the Skagway scene, Moe's is a bar much frequented by the local folk.

Red Onion (Broadway at 2nd St., tel. 907/983–2222). You'll meet at least as many Skagway people here as you will visitors. There's live music on Thursday nights, ranging from rock and jazz to folk and acoustic. The upstairs was a gold-rush brothel.

Tracy Arm

Like Misty Fjords (*see above*), Tracy Arm and its sister fjord, Endicott Arm, have become staples on many Inside Passage cruises. Ships sail into the arm just before or after a visit to Juneau, the state capital, located 50 miles to the north. A day of scenic cruising in Tracy Arm is a lesson in geography and the forces that shaped Alaska. The fjord was carved by a glacier eons ago, leaving behind sheer granite cliffs. Waterfalls continue the process of erosion that the glaciers began. Very small ships may nudge their bows under the waterfalls, so crew members can fill pitchers full of glacial runoff. It's a uniquely Alaskan refreshment. Tracy Arm's glaciers haven't disappeared, though, they've just receded, and at the very end of Tracy Arm you'll come to two of them, known collectively as the twin Sawyer Glaciers.

Valdez

Valdez, with its year-round ice-free port, was an entry point for people and goods going to the interior during the gold rush. Today that flow has been reversed, and Valdez Harbor is the southern terminus of the trans-Alaska pipeline, which carries crude oil from Prudhoe Bay and surrounding oil fields nearly 800 miles to the north.

Much of Valdez looks new because the business area was relocated and rebuilt after being destroyed by the devastating Good Friday earthquake in 1964. A few of the old buildings were moved to the new town site.

Many Alaskan communities have summer fishing derbies, but Valdez may hold the record for the number of such contests, stretching from late May into September for halibut and various runs of salmon. The Valdez Silver Salmon Derby begins in late July and runs the entire month of August. Fishing charters abound in this area of

Prince William Sound, and for a good reason, too: These fertile waters provide some of the best saltwater sportfishing in all of Alaska.

Shore Excursions

The following are good choices in Valdez. They may not be offered by all cruise lines. All times and prices are approximate.

Adventure

Columbia Glacier Helicopter Flightseeing. The flight over the huge Columbia Glacier includes a landing near the face of Shoup Glacier and aerial views of Valdez Bay, the pipeline terminus, and the old Valdez site. *2 hrs. Cost: $168.*

Columbia Glacier Floatplane Sightseeing. Enjoy aerial views of Valdez and Shoup Glacier, a section of the pipeline, and its terminus. The highlight is touching down in the water for a close-up view of the massive Columbia Glacier. *2 hrs. Cost: $139.*

Keystone River Rafting. This 1½-hour raft trip goes down the Lowe River, through a scenic canyon, and past the spectacular Bridal Veil Falls, which cascades 900 feet down the canyon wall. The bus trip from the ship is narrated. *2¼ hrs. Cost: $55–$65.*

Sea-kayaking Adventures. Get down on the water's surface for a guided tour of the port of Valdez or Robe Lake. See a seabird rookery and seals up close or float across the mirrorlike surface of a freshwater lake tucked against the bottom of the Chugach Mountains. *4–6 hrs. Cost: $52–$185.*

Trans-Alaska Pipeline

Pipeline Story. Tour the pipeline terminus and hear tales of how the pipeline was built. This is the only way to get into this high-security area. *1 hr. Cost: $24–$28.*

Coming Ashore

Ships tie up at the world's largest floating container dock. Located about three miles from the heart of town, the dock is used not only for cruise ships, but also for loading cargo ships with timber and other products bound for markets "outside" (that's what Alaskans call the rest of the world).

Ship-organized motor coaches meet passengers on the pier and provide transportation into town. Cabs and car-rental services will also provide transportation from the pier. Several local ground and adventure-tour operators meet passengers as well.

Getting Around

Valdez is a very compact community. Almost everything is within easy walking distance of the Valdez Convention and Visitors Bureau in the heart of town. Motor coaches drop passengers at the Visitor Information Center. Taxi service is available and individualized tours of the area can be arranged with the cab dispatcher.

Exploring Valdez

Other than visiting the oil-pipeline terminal, which must be done on a tour, sightseeing in Valdez is mostly limited to gazing at the 5,000-foot mountain peaks surrounding the town or visiting the **Valdez Museum.** It depicts the lives, livelihoods, and events significant to Valdez and surrounding regions. Exhibits include a 1907 steam fire engine, a 19th-century saloon, and a model of the pipeline terminus. *217 Egan Ave., tel. 907/835–2764. Admission: $2. Open June–early Aug., daily 9–7; early Aug.–May, Tues.–Sat. noon–5.*

Dining

$$$$ **Westmark Valdez Hotel.** Located next to the small-boat harbor, the hotel restaurant overlooks the water and serves fare worthy of an upscale steak-and-seafood house. *100 Fidalgo Dr., 99686, tel. 907/835–4391 or 800/544–0970, fax 907/835–2308. AE, DC, MC, V.*

$ **Mike's Palace.** This busy restaurant with typical Italian-diner decor is popular with locals. The menu includes veal, the best pizza in Alaska, beer-battered halibut, and Greek specialties, including gyros. *On the harbor, 201 N. Harbor Dr., tel. 907/835–2365. MC, V.*

Victoria, British Columbia

Though Victoria is not in Alaska, it is a port of call for many ships cruising the Inside Passage. Just like the communities of southeast Alaska, Victoria had its own gold-rush stampede in the 1800s, when 25,000 miners flocked to British Columbia's Cariboo country. Today the city is a mix of stately buildings and English traditions. Flower baskets hang from lampposts, shops sell Harris tweed and Irish linen, locals play cricket and croquet, and visitors sightsee aboard red double-decker buses or horse-drawn carriages. Afternoon tea is still held daily at the city's elegant Empress Hotel. No visit to Victoria is complete without a stroll through Butchart Gardens, a short drive outside the city.

Shore Excursions The following are good choices in Victoria. They may not be offered by all cruise lines. All times and prices are approximate.

Grand City Drive and Afternoon High Tea. This drive through downtown, past Craigdarroch Castle and residential areas, finishes with a British-style high tea at a hotel. A variation of this excursion takes visitors on a tour of the castle in lieu of high tea. *2½ hrs. Cost: $18–$30.*

Short City Tour and Butchart Gardens. Drive through key places of interest, such as the city center and residential areas, on the way to Butchart Gardens—a must for garden aficionados. *3½ hrs. Cost: $30–$38.*

Coming Ashore Only the smallest excursion vessels can dock downtown in the Inner Harbour. Ocean liners must tie up at the Ogden Point Cruise Ship Terminal, a C$4–C$5 cab ride from downtown. Metered taxis meet the ship. The tourist information office (812 Wharf St., tel. 604/953–2033 for information, 800/663–3883 for reservations only) is in front of the Empress Hotel, midway along the Inner Harbour.

Getting Around Most points of interest are within walking distance of the Empress Hotel. For those that aren't, public and private transportation is readily available from the Inner Harbour.

By Bus The public bus system is excellent. Pick up route maps and schedules at the tourist information office.

By Taxi Rates are C$2.15 for pickup, C$1.30 per kilometer. Contact **Bluebird** (tel. 604/382–3611) or **Victoria Taxi** (604/383–7111).

Exploring Victoria *Numbers in the margin correspond to points of interest on the Inner Harbour, Victoria, map. Prices are in Canadian dollars.*

❶ Victoria's heart is the **Inner Harbour,** always bustling with ferries, seaplanes, and yachts from all over the world. The ivy-covered Empress Hotel (721 Government St., tel. 604/384–8111), with its well-groomed gardens, is the dowager of Victoria. High tea in this little patch of England is a local ritual: Recline in deep armchairs and nibble on scones or crumpets with honey, butter, jam, and clotted cream while sipping blended tea.

❷ The **Crystal Gardens** (on Douglas St. behind the Empress Hotel) were built in 1925 under a glass roof as a public saltwater swimming pool. They have been renovated into a tropical conservatory and aviary, with flamingos, parrots, fountains, and waterfalls.

❸ **Thunderbird Park** (on Belleville Street) displays a ceremonial longhouse (a communal dwelling) and the finest collection of replicated totem poles outside Alaska.

❹ Next to Thunderbird Park is **Helmcken House,** the province's oldest residence, which has a display of antique medical instruments. *10 Elliot St. Sq., tel. 604/361–0021. Admission: $4. Open daily 10–5.*

Bastion Square, **9**
British Columbia Parliament Buildings, **6**
Crystal Gardens, **2**
Emily Carr House, **7**
Helmcken House, **4**
Inner Harbour, **1**
Maritime Museum of B.C., **10**
Pacific Underseas Gardens, **8**
Royal British Columbia Museum, **5**
Thunderbird Park, **3**

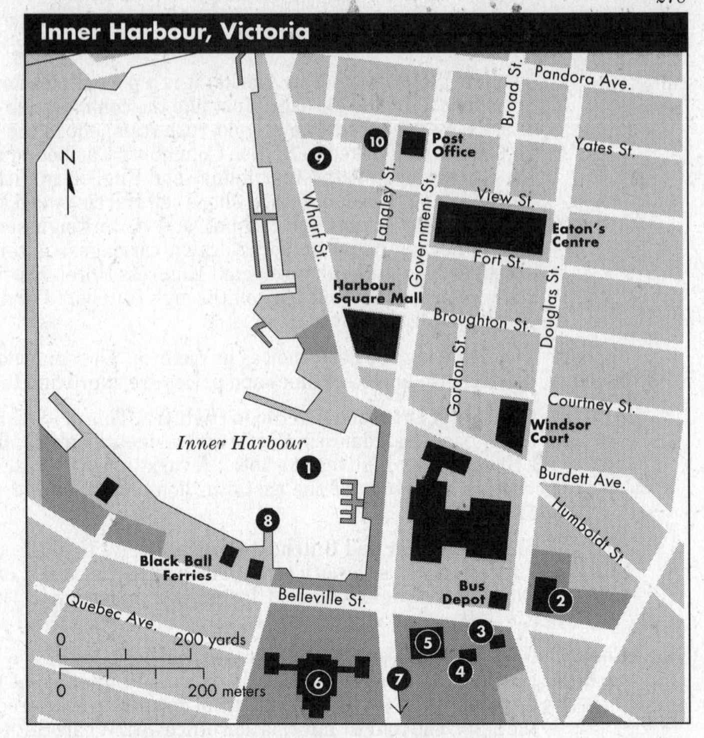

5 The superb **Royal British Columbia Museum** will require at least an hour of your time: Its exhibits encompass 12,000 years of natural and human history. *675 Belleville St., tel. 604/387-3014. Admission: $5. Open summer, daily 9:30–7.*

6 The stately, neo-Gothic **British Columbia Parliament Buildings** (501 Belleville St.) were constructed of local stone and wood and opened in 1898. Atop the central dome is a gilded statue of Captain George Vancouver, for whom Vancouver Island is named.

7 Prints by Emily Carr, who was a member of the "Canadian Group of Seven," adorn the walls at the **Emily Carr House,** the beautifully restored residence of the famous early 20th-century painter. *207 Government St., tel. 604/383-5843. Admission: $4. Open May–Oct., daily 10–5.*

8 You can descend beneath the water for a live scuba show with Armstrong, the Pacific octopus, at the **Pacific Underseas Gardens,** a natural aquarium with more than 5,000 species from the area. *490 Belleville St., tel. 604/382-5717. Admission: $6.75. Open summer, daily 10–9.*

9 Just a short walk from the Inner Harbour is **Bastion Square.** Follow Government Street to Humboldt Street. With the water to your left, bear left onto Wharf Street, and look for the square on your right. Established in 1843 as the original site of Ft. Victoria, it now boasts several restored buildings open for viewing.

10 On the far side of Bastion Square, the old courthouse is now the **Maritime Museum of British Columbia.** It has a collection of artifacts—including a 38-foot Native American dugout canoe and the 20-foot ketch *Trekka,* which has sailed around the world. In the Captain Cook gallery, nautical maps and other tools of 17th-century exploration are on display. *28 Bastion Sq., tel. 604/385-4222. Admission: $5. Open daily 9:30–4:30.*

Take a taxi (or a shore excursion) to **Butchart Gardens.** In a city of gardens, these 50 acres rank among the most beautiful in the world. In July and August, a fireworks display is held every Saturday evening. *14 mi north of Victoria on Hwy. 17, tel. 604/652–4422. Admission: $14. Open daily at 9, call for closing hrs.*

Shopping Save your receipts to receive a 7% GST tax refund from the Canadian government when you leave Canada; ask for a form at customs. Victoria stores specializing in English imports are plentiful, though Canadian-made goods are usually a better buy for foreigners. Look for Hudson's Bay Co. blankets and other woolens. From the Empress Hotel walk along Government Street to reach **Piccadilly Shoppe British Woolens** and **Sasquatch Trading Company,** both of which sell high-quality woolen clothing.

Turn right onto Fort Street and walk four blocks to **Antique Row,** between Blanshard and Cook streets. The **Connoisseurs Shop** and **David Robinson, Ltd.** offer a wide variety of 18th-century pieces.

Dining

$$ **Bengal Lounge.** Buffet lunches in the elegant Empress Hotel include curries with extensive condiment trays of coconut, nuts, cool *raita* (yogurt with mint or cucumber), and chutney. Popular with cabinet ministers and bureaucrats, the Bengal Lounge offers splendid garden views. *721 Government St., tel. 604/384–8111. AE, D, DC, MC, V.*

$$ **La Ville d'Is.** This cozy and friendly seafood house, run by Brittany native Michel Duteau, is one of the best bargains in Victoria. Although seafood, such as *perche de la Nouvelle Aelande* (orange roughie in Muscadet with herbs), is the chef's strong suit, rabbit, lamb, and beef tenderloin are also available. The wine list is limited but imaginative. On warm days there's seating outside. *26 Bastion Sq., tel. 604/388–9414. AE, DC, MC, V. Closed Sun.*

Wrangell

Between Ketchikan and Petersburg lies Wrangell, on an island near the mouth of the fast-flowing Stikine River. The town is off the typical cruise-ship track and is visited mostly by lines with an environmental or educational emphasis, such as Alaska Sightseeing or World Explorer Cruises. A small, unassuming timber and fishing community, it has lived under three flags since the arrival of the Russian traders. Known as Redoubt St. Dionysius when it was part of Russian America, the town was renamed Fort Stikine after the British took it over. The name was changed to Wrangell when the Americans bought it.

Shore Excursions The following are good choices in Wrangell. They may not be offered by all cruise lines. All times and prices are approximate.

Island Sights **City Tour.** Explore Native history at Shakes Island, the Wrangell Museum, and Petroglyph Beach. *1½ hrs. Cost: $19.*

Stikine River Tour. Experience a thrilling jet-boat ride to the Stikine River. Visit Shakes Glacier, sit and relax in the natural hot tubs surrounded by snowcapped mountains, and listen to tales of gold-mining and fur trapping. *4–8 hrs. Cost: $140.*

Coming Ashore Cruise ships calling in Wrangell dock downtown, within walking distance of the museum and gift stores. There is a U.S. Forest Service mobile information service stand on the dock; Senior Citizen Greeters welcome passengers and are available to answer questions. The Chamber of Commerce office is at the very end of the dock in the Stikine Inn, or you can visit the Chamber of Commerce Visitor Center in the A-frame one block away (on the waterfront next to city hall).

Getting Around Many attractions are within walking distance of the dock. For island tours, there are two cab companies. Call **Porky's Cab Co.** (tel. 907/

Boat harbor, **5**
Chief Shakes's grave site, **2**
Chief Shakes Island, **3**
KikSadi Totem Park, **1**
"Our Collections", **8**
Petroglyph Beach, **9**
Public library, **7**
Seaplane float, **4**
Wrangell City Museum, **6**

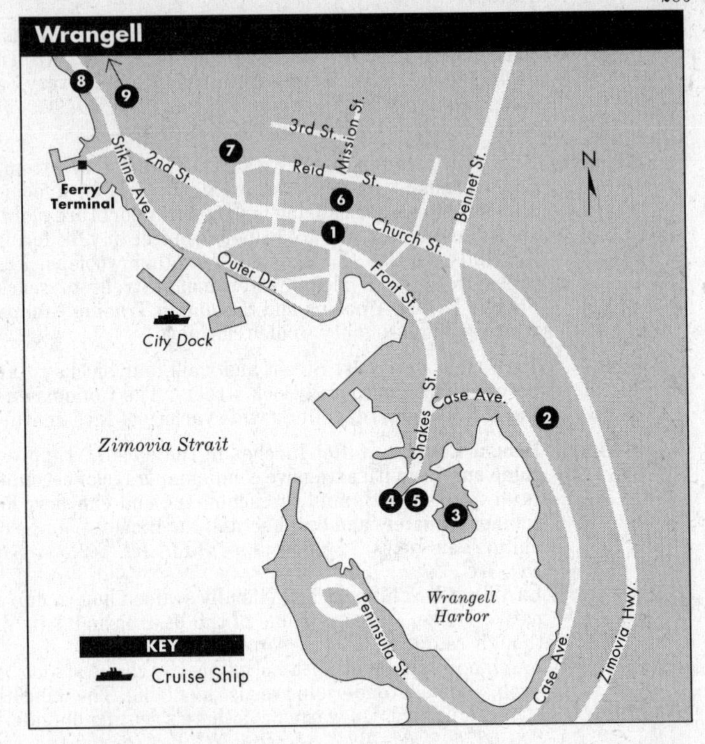

874–3603) or **Star Cab** (tel. 907/874–3622). The **Island Tour Company** (same phone as Porky's) has vans to accommodate larger groups.

Exploring Wrangell *Numbers in the margin correspond to points of interest on the Wrangell map.*

❶ Walking up Front Street will bring you to **KikSadi Totem Park,** a pocket park of Alaska greenery and impressive totem poles. This is the spot for a pleasant stroll.

❷ On your way to Wrangell's number-one attraction—Chief Shakes Island—stop at **Chief Shakes's grave site,** uphill from the Wrangell shipyard on Case Avenue. Buried here is Shakes V, one of a number of local chiefs to bear that name. He led the local Tlingits during the first half of the 19th century. Two killer-whale totems mark the chief's burial place.

❸ On **Chief Shakes Island,** reached by a footbridge off the harbor dock, you can see some of the finest totem poles in Alaska, as well as a tribal house constructed in the 1930s as a replica of one that was home to many of the various Shakes and their peoples. You'll see six totems on the island, two of them more than 100 years old. The original corner posts of the tribal house are located in the museum. The house is opened for passengers when ships are in port. *Tel. 907/874–2023 or 907/874–3747. Admission: $1 donation requested.*

❹ ❺ After your visit to Chief Shakes Island, wander out to the end of the dock for the view and for picture taking at the **seaplane float** and **boat harbor.**

❻ The **Wrangell City Museum** contains a historical collection that includes totem fragments, petroglyphs, and other Native artifacts; a bootlegger's still; a vintage 1800s Linotype and presses; and a cedar-bark basket collection. *318 Church St., tel. 907/874–3770. Admission: $2. Open summer, weekdays 10–5, Sat. 1–5, and, when* *cruise ships are in port, Sun. 8–6; winter, Mon. and Wed.–Fri. 10–4.*

7. The **public library** (124 2nd Ave., tel. 907/874–3535) has a small collection of ancient petroglyphs. It's worth seeing if you don't plan to make the trip to Petroglyph Beach (*see below*).

8. To some, the artifacts that make up **"Our Collections"** by owner Elva Bigelow constitute less a museum than a garage sale waiting to happen. Still, large numbers of viewers seem quite taken by the literally thousands of unrelated collectibles (clocks, animal traps, waffle irons, tools, etc.) that the Bigelows have gathered in a half century of Alaska living. *Evergreen Ave., tel. 907/874–3646. Call before setting out to visit. Admission: Donations accepted.*

9. **Petroglyph Beach** is undoubtedly one of the more curious sights in southeast Alaska. Here, scattered among other rocks, are three dozen or more large stones bearing designs and pictures chiseled by unknown ancient artists. No one knows why the rocks were etched the way they were. Perhaps they were boundary markers or messages; possibly they were just primitive doodling. Because the petroglyphs can be damaged by physical contact, the state discourages visitors from creating a "rubbing" off the rocks with rice paper and crayons. Instead, you can photograph the petroglyphs or purchase a rubber-stamp duplicate of selected petroglyphs from the city museum. Do not, of course, attempt to move any of the petroglyph stones.

Shopping A unique souvenir from Wrangell is a natural garnet, gathered at Garnet Ledge, facing the Stikine River. The semiprecious gems are sold on the streets by the children of Wrangell for 50¢ to $50, depending on their size and quality.

Dining

$–$$ **Roadhouse Lodge.** The walls here are practically a museum of early Alaska. The food is wholesome, tasty, and ample. Specialties include local prawns (sautéed, deep-fried, or boiled in the shell) and deep-fried Native American fry bread. The lodge is 3½ miles from downtown. *Mile 4, Zimovia Hwy., tel. 907/874–2335. MC, V.*

$–$$ **Stikine Inn.** On the dock in the main part of town, this inn offers great views of Wrangell's cruise-ship dock and Zimovia Straits from the Dock Side Restaurant, a coffee shop and dining room. Seafood and steaks are staples. *1 block from ferry terminal; 107 Front St., 99929, tel. 907/874–3388. AE, DC, MC, V.*

Antarctica

Antarctica is bigger than the continental United States, drier than the Sahara, colder than Siberia, and less populated than the Arabian Empty Quarter. Of all the fresh water in the world, 60% is locked in Antarctica's ice, which in places is more than 10 times thicker than the Empire State Building is tall.

First visited by only a handful of hearty whalers and intrepid explorers, Antarctica has been almost exclusively the domain of research scientists. Its purity and distance from civilization make it an ideal laboratory in which to study many problems that plague the rest of the planet.

In the late 1950s, a small company that specialized in adventure vacations began offering cruises to Antarctica. Although only a few ships followed over the next quarter century, a sudden, recent surge of interest in travel to the "White Continent" has produced a flood of inquiries and bookings. This year an estimated 9,000 visitors will make landfall on Antarctica. Among the major cruise ships with voyages scheduled are Abercrombie & Kent's *Explorer*, Orient Lines' *Marco Polo*, Radisson Seven Seas Cruises' *Hanseatic*, and Society Expeditions' *World Discoverer*. (For seasonal itineraries, *see* Chapter 4.) Cruises to the White Continent are also available aboard chartered Russian or Ukrainian research ships (*see* Chapter 2).

Now is a particularly good time to visit Antarctica, because there are still no limitations on tourists or cruise ships. Sentiment is building, however, to restrict visitors. Some environmentalists want to ban them entirely. Still, many scientists and ecologists are delighted that cruise passengers want to see Antarctica, because passengers return home among the most ardent supporters and lobbyists for protecting and preserving this as-yet-unspoiled continent.

Cruising to Antarctica requires a certain temperament and a moderate level of physical fitness. It involves a small degree of inconvenience, discomfort, and even risk. Ships leaving from South America must navigate the Drake Passage, one of the roughest stretches of ocean in the world. Because there are no landing wharfs or tour buses on the continent, getting from the ship to land means bundling up in bulky jackets and life preservers, climbing into small rubberized craft called Zodiacs, maneuvering in as close to the shore as possible, and, quite often, wading through the shallow surf. Then the only way to get inland to the research stations or penguin rookeries is by walking up rocky beaches or uneven ice surfaces. Although all ships carry doctors and nurses, the nearest hospital is several thousand miles away.

Since the weather conditions in Antarctica are so unpredictable, itineraries are extremely flexible and are more commonly subject to last-minute changes. Heavy seas may prevent your ship from landing at a particular research station, and floating ice may cut a half-day tour down to an hour-long stop.

Catching your ship entails flying great distances to ports in either South America, New Zealand, or Australia. Flights are expensive and often arduous; it can take more than 24 hours to get to your initial departure point. For a cruise to the Antarctic Peninsula, you must fly first to either Santiago, Chile, or Buenos Aires, Argentina, and you'll usually be put up in a hotel overnight. The next day, you'll fly to Ushuaia on Tierra del Fuego or, less often, Port Stanley in the Falkland Islands, to meet your ship. If your cruise leaves from Christchurch, New Zealand, or Hobart in Tasmania, Australia, your route to the ship will be more direct, if no less time consuming.

When to Go Cruise ships visit Antarctica only from early December to February—the austral summer. The best time is between mid-December and mid-January, when the weather is mildest and the wildlife most active.

What to Take Packing for Antarctica is quite different from preparing for any other cruise. Forget about elegance and formality, although you may wish to take a sports jacket and tie or a simple all-purpose dress for the captain's informal get-together.

The most common mistake in packing for an Antarctic cruise is taking gear designed for subzero temperatures. Although it gets as cold as −100°F in the dead of winter (July and August), the median coastal temperatures in December and January average 35°F–55°F. The cruise lines supply recommended packing lists, as well as the bulky red parka that will provide your primary protection. Waterproof pullover pants and waterproof boots at least 12 inches high are necessities (check whether your line provides these or if you must supply your own). You'll also want a good pair of binoculars, a 35mm camera with telephoto and wide-angle lenses, and lots of color film—remember, it's illegal to take a single stone, bone, feather, or artifact as a souvenir.

It's a nice idea to bring small gifts for the scientists and other workers in the research stations: recent magazines, books, candy, and fresh fruit.

Currency Since there are practically no stores or shops in Antarctica, you won't need much money here. Some of the research stations sell sweatshirts and T-shirts with Antarctica logos, decorative patches that can be sewn or ironed onto your parka, and postcards with Antarctic postmarks that you can mail to friends or relatives (the mail goes out with your ship and can take days, weeks, or months to be delivered). You can pay for these in U.S. dollars. In some places the merchandise is available only to station personnel, who will sometimes barter with you for books, magazines, and patches.

Passports and Visas No one visiting or living in Antarctica needs any kind of documents, but to get there, you will have to fly through Argentina, Chile, Australia, or New Zealand, all of which require passports and visas from U.S., Canadian, and British citizens.

Shore Excursions The only stops in Antarctica are at the research stations of various nations, historic huts built by explorers from the heroic era early in the century, and the penguin and seal rookeries and other places of interest to naturalists. Weather conditions as well as the needs and wishes of the research station personnel will dictate your itinerary.

Research Stations If you do visit a research station, you may or may not be invited into the common room, may or may not be able to buy a souvenir postcard or patch, and may or may not meet with scientists who speak English. Also, because of the dramatic increase in tourists, many stations have cut back, not only on the number of cruise ships permitted to visit, but on the areas open to visitors.

If you come from South America, you'll explore the area known as the Antarctic Peninsula, home to **Palmer Station,** a U.S. base with a PX; **Gonzalez Videla Station,** or **Esperanza**; and the nine bases on King George Island, including the Polish **Arctowski.** Your ship may also stop at **Deception Island, Nelson Island,** the **South Georgia Islands,** or the **South Orkney Islands.** Some adventure ships stop at the **Falkland Islands,** one of the most remote and forbidding inhabited places on earth. Argentina calls these islands the Malvinas and went to war with Britain in 1982 in an unsuccessful attempt to seize sovereignty; who owns them is still a hot issue in this part of the world. You may visit **Port Stanley,** the Falklands' picturesque capital, which seems like a transplanted northern Scotland village; or **New**

Antarctica

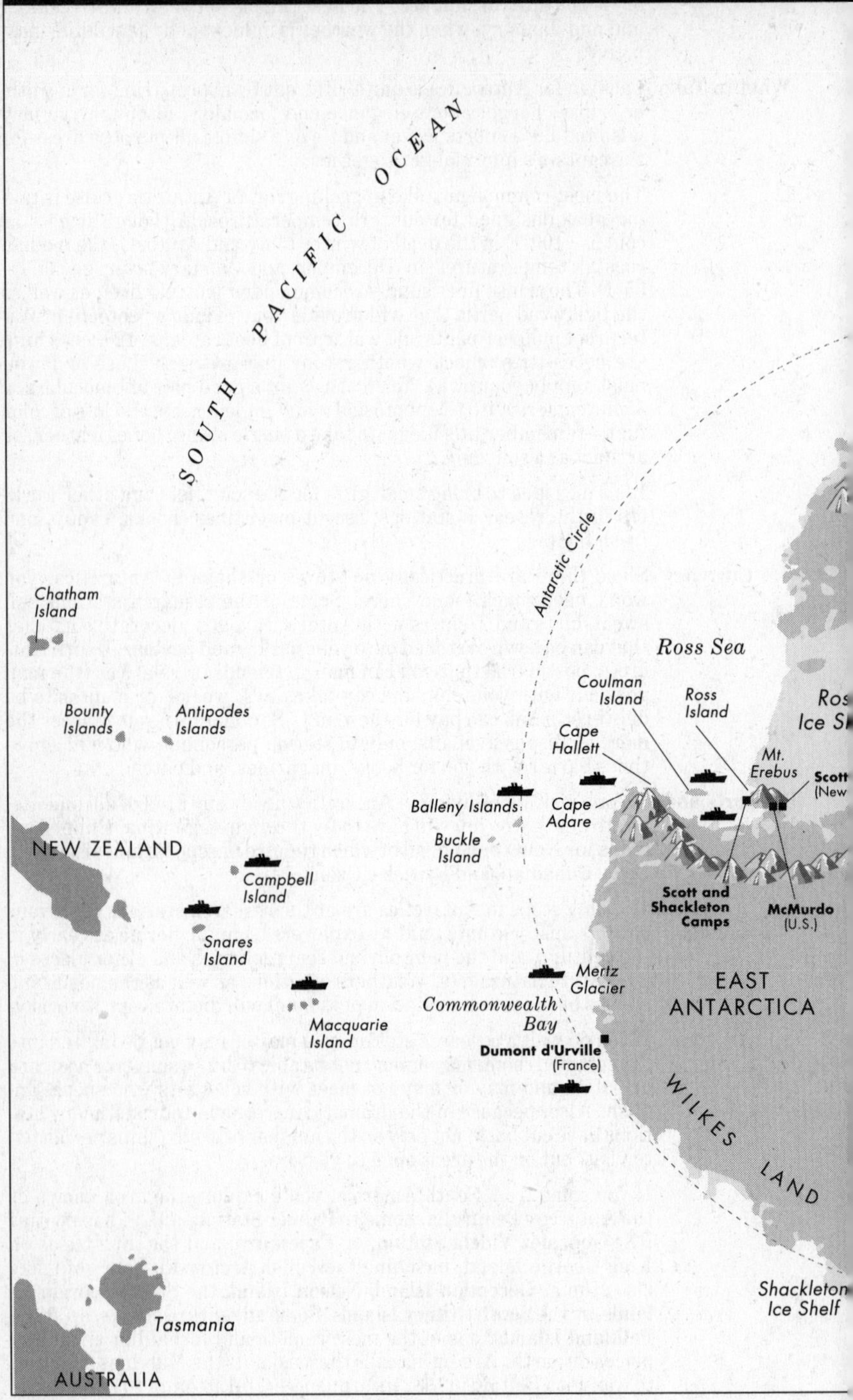

SOUTH PACIFIC OCEAN
Chatham Island
Bounty Islands
Antipodes Islands
NEW ZEALAND
Campbell Island
Snares Island
Macquarie Island
Tasmania
AUSTRALIA
Antarctic Circle
Ross Sea
Balleny Islands
Buckle Island
Coulman Island
Cape Hallett
Cape Adare
Ross Island
Mt. Erebus
Ross Ice S
Scott (New
Scott and Shackleton Camps
McMurdo (U.S.)
Mertz Glacier
Commonwealth Bay
Dumont d'Urville (France)
EAST ANTARCTICA
WILKES LAND
Shackleton Ice Shelf

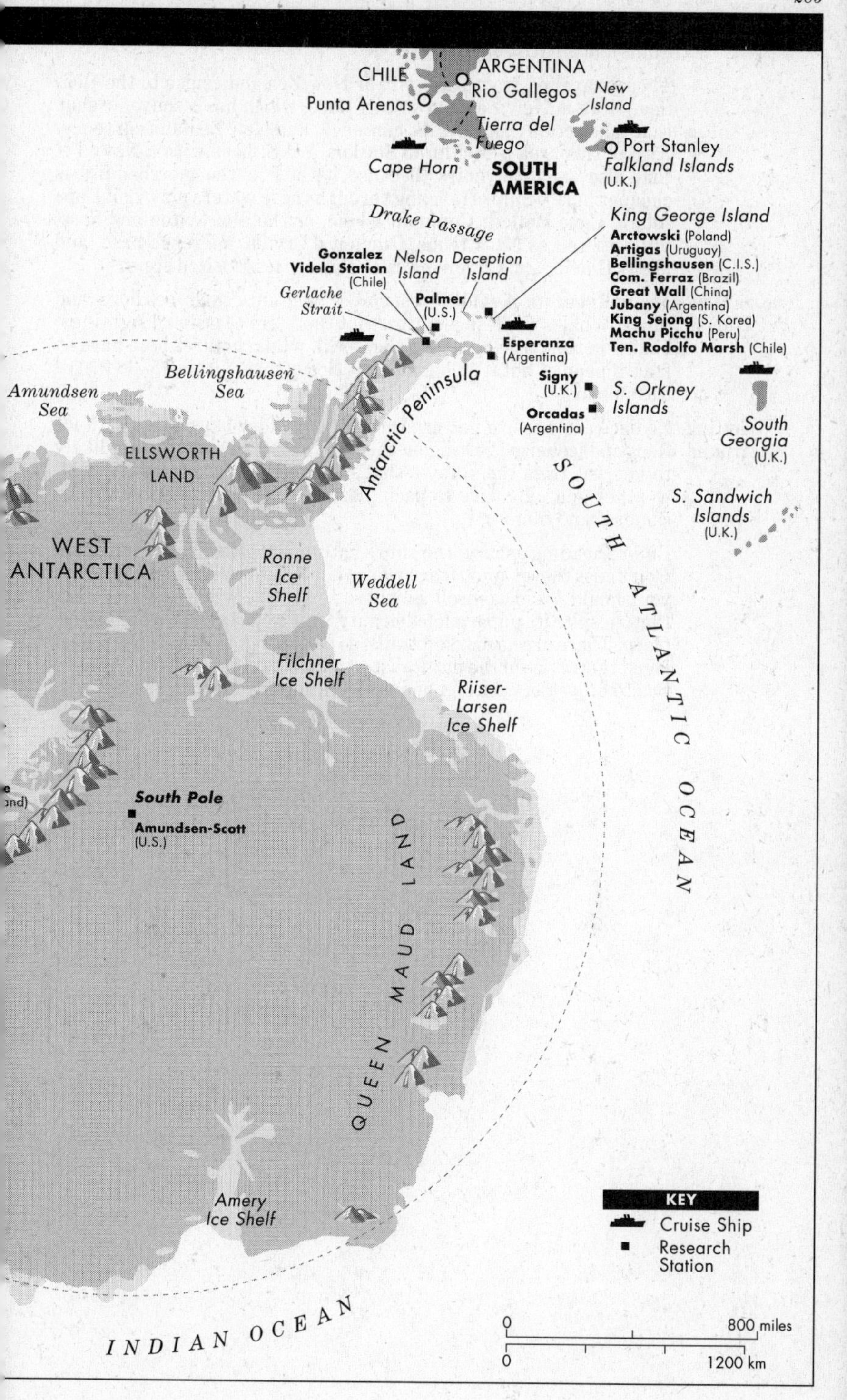
CHILE
ARGENTINA
Rio Gallegos
Punta Arenas
New Island
Tierra del Fuego
Port Stanley
Falkland Islands (U.K.)
Cape Horn
SOUTH AMERICA
Drake Passage
King George Island
Arctowski (Poland)
Artigas (Uruguay)
Bellingshausen (C.I.S.)
Com. Ferraz (Brazil)
Great Wall (China)
Jubany (Argentina)
King Sejong (S. Korea)
Machu Picchu (Peru)
Ten. Rodolfo Marsh (Chile)
Gonzalez Videla Station (Chile)
Nelson Island
Deception Island
Gerlache Strait
Palmer (U.S.)
Esperanza (Argentina)
Signy (U.K.)
Orcadas (Argentina)
S. Orkney Islands
South Georgia (U.K.)
S. Sandwich Islands (U.K.)
Amundsen Sea
Bellingshausen Sea
Antarctic Peninsula
ELLSWORTH LAND
WEST ANTARCTICA
Ronne Ice Shelf
Weddell Sea
Filchner Ice Shelf
Riiser-Larsen Ice Shelf
SOUTH ATLANTIC OCEAN
South Pole
Amundsen-Scott (U.S.)
QUEEN MAUD LAND
Amery Ice Shelf
INDIAN OCEAN
KEY
Cruise Ship
Research Station
0
800 miles
0
1200 km

Island, a 5-square-mile rock that is home to several species of penguins and albatross.

Those traveling from Australia or New Zealand cruise to the Ross Sea. Here is New Zealand's **Scott Base,** which has a souvenir shop that takes credit cards, U.S. currency, and New Zealand currency. Also in this area is **McMurdo Station,** a U.S. base with a Navy PX that also sells souvenirs (because it's a PX, the merchandise is cheaper here). Ships traveling through these waters may visit **Cape Adare, Cape Hallett, Coulman Island,** or the **Shackelton and Scott huts,** as well as **Mt. Erebus. Dumont d'Urville,** a French base, and **Mertz Glacier** and **Commonwealth Bay** are less-visited stops.

Penguins and Other Wildlife

You will see lots of wildlife, especially penguins, seals, sea lions, and birds. Whales are less plentiful, but there are occasional sightings. Unlike in most other parts of the world, wild creatures here have no fear of people, but it's illegal to get closer than within 15–30 feet of the animals.

Getting Around

Zodiacs are used to get ashore and to explore bays filled with ice floes and icebergs. Sitting on the edge of these craft, you are likely to get wet from the spray—that's one of the reasons for the foul-weather gear. Be sure to pack plastic Ziploc bags to protect your cameras and film.

Before heading ashore, the ship's naturalists give orientation talks. Don't miss these: You'll learn where it is safe to walk and which areas you should avoid, as well as where to see the wildlife. Remember that, despite its unparalleled beauty, Antarctica can be a dangerous place. There are no marked trails, so be sure not to wander off alone. Heed the advice of the naturalists, though, and you will find Antarctica to be a safe, exciting, and invigorating adventure.

The Bahamas

The Bahamas is an archipelago of more than 700 islands that begins in the Atlantic Ocean off the coast of Florida and stretches in a great southeasterly arc for more than 750 miles to the Caribbean Sea. Each island is bordered by soft, white-sand beaches lined with whispering casuarinas and swaying palms. Offshore, the islands are fringed by coral reefs and surrounded by a palette of blue and green waters of unbelievable clarity.

Fewer than 250,000 people live in the Bahamas, most of them in the two major urban resort centers of Nassau and Freeport. The Bahamas are one of cruising's most popular destinations. Three- and four-day cruises from Florida to Nassau and Freeport are a big hit among young and budget-conscious travelers. Many cruise lines also include a port call in the Bahamas as part of a longer sailing, sometimes for a beach party or barbecue at one of several isolated Bahamian islands. For some passengers, these excursions are the highlight of a cruise. One of the best such destinations is Blue Lagoon Island (also called Sale Cay). It is used by Dolphin and Premier. (For seasonal itineraries, *see* Chapter 4.)

A cruise to the Bahamas is ideal for first-time cruisers, shopping fanatics, beach bums, and party goers. You can sail and scuba dive all day and, if your ship ties up overnight, gamble and dance well into the evening. But don't expect an unspoiled paradise: Nassau and Freeport/Lucaya are crowded and far less scenic than most Caribbean islands.

When to Go Winter, from mid-December through April, is the traditional high season. However, Bahamas cruises are offered all year, and the weather remains consistently mild, in the 70s and 80s. The Goombay Summer, from June through August, is filled with social, cultural, and sporting events. June through October is the rainy season, and humidity is high.

Currency The Bahamian dollar is held at a par with the U.S. dollar, and the two currencies are used interchangeably. Be sure to request U.S. dollars and coins when you receive change, however. Traveler's checks and major credit cards are accepted by most fine restaurants and stores.

Passports and Visas U.S., Canadian, and British citizens do not need passports or visas if they have proof of citizenship; however, a passport is preferable.

Telephones and Mail Long-distance credit-card and collect calls can be made from most public phones. Airmail rates to the United States and Canada are 55¢ for first-class letters and 40¢ for postcards.

Shore Excursions Many ships offer excursions to a casino for round-the-clock gaming action and various other forms of entertainment, including elaborate floor shows and topless revues. Some ships stay overnight in Freeport or Nassau.

In addition, many ships offer shopping excursions. Both Freeport and Nassau have a host of malls and stores (*see below*). Water sports are a major draw, and most ships offer snorkeling or boat trips to outlying islands, as well as fishing.

Shopping Duty-free bargains in the Bahamas include imported china, crystal, leather, electronics, sweaters, liquor, watches, and perfume. Figure a 25% savings on most goods and a 35%–60% savings on liquor. Though no store will deliver to your ship, most shopping is within a 10-minute walk of the pier. Most stores are open Monday–Saturday 9–5; some close at noon on Thursday.

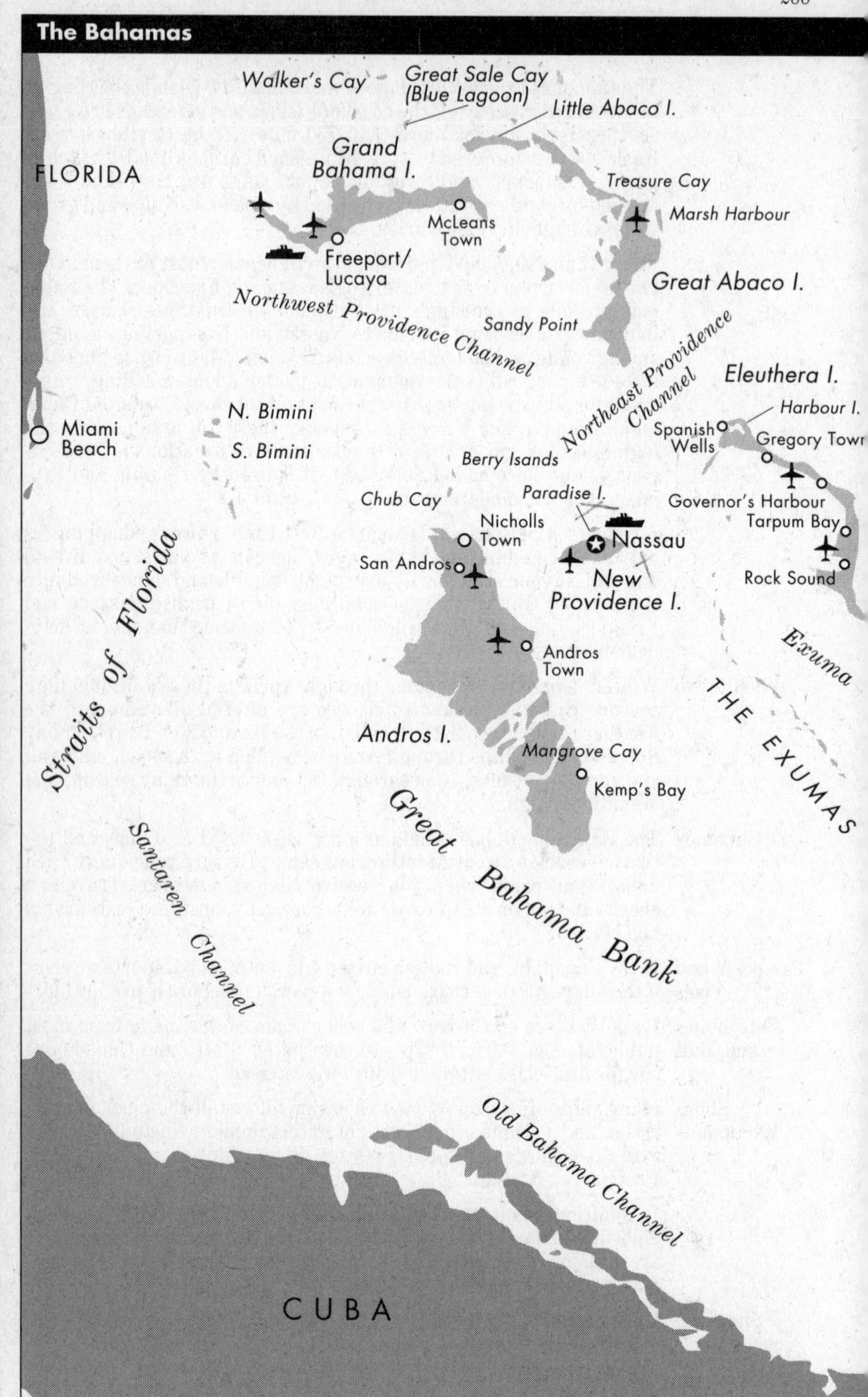
The Bahamas
Walker's Cay
Great Sale Cay
(Blue Lagoon)
Little Abaco I.
Grand
Bahama I.
FLORIDA
Treasure Cay
Marsh Harbour
McLeans
Town
Freeport/
Lucaya
Great Abaco I.
Northwest Providence Channel
Sandy Point
Northeast Providence
Channel
Eleuthera I.
Harbour I.
N. Bimini
Miami
Beach
S. Bimini
Spanish
Wells
Gregory Town
Berry Isands
Paradise I.
Chub Cay
Governor's Harbour
Nicholls
Town
Tarpum Bay
Nassau
San Andros
New
Providence I.
Rock Sound
Straits of Florida
Andros
Town
Exuma
THE EXUMAS
Andros I.
Mangrove Cay
Kemp's Bay
Great Bahama Bank
Santaren
Channel
Old Bahama Channel
CUBA

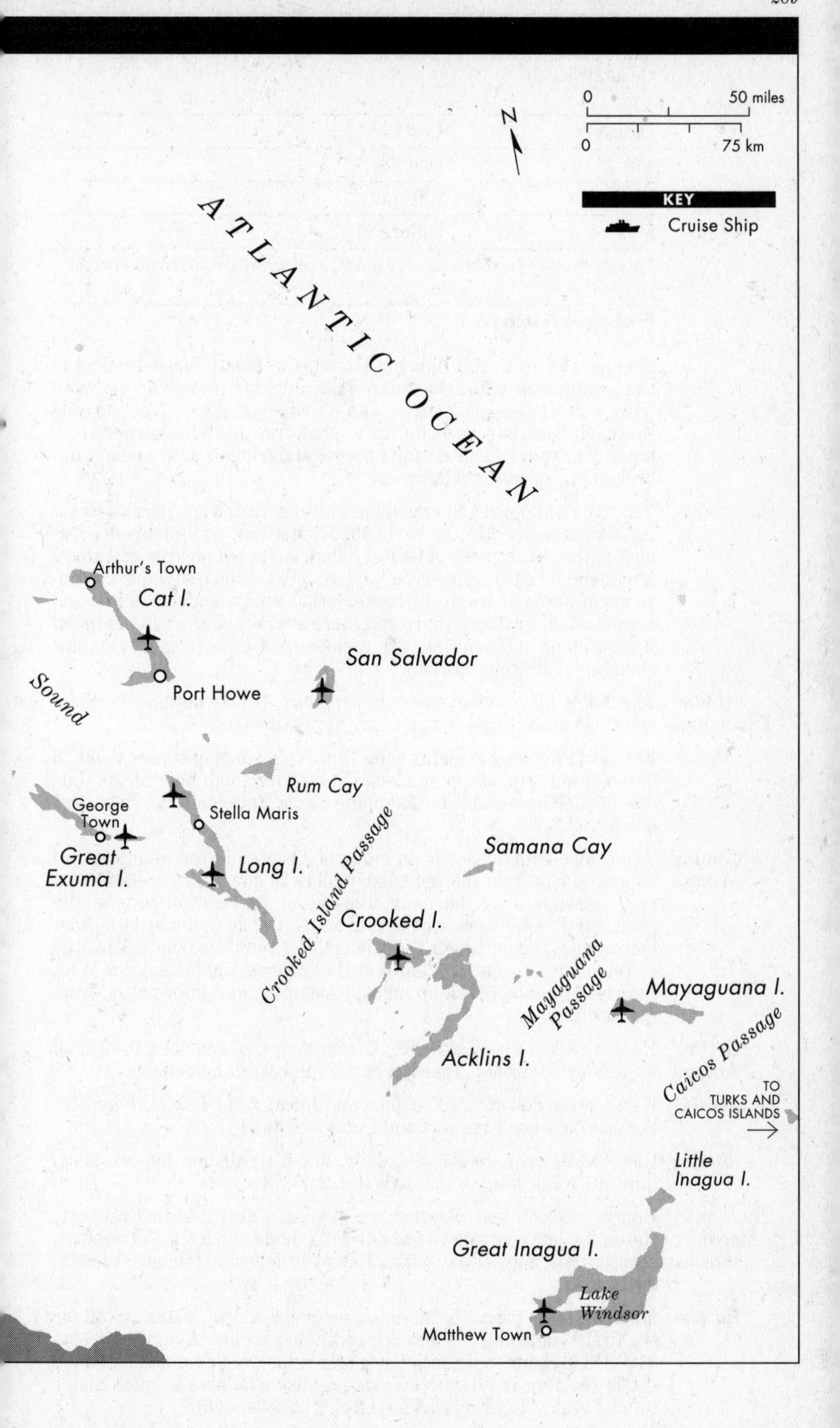
0
50 miles
0
75 km
N
KEY
Cruise Ship
ATLANTIC OCEAN
Arthur's Town
Cat I.
Sound
Port Howe
San Salvador
Rum Cay
George Town
Stella Maris
Great Exuma I.
Long I.
Crooked Island Passage
Samana Cay
Crooked I.
Mayaguana Passage
Mayaguana I.
Acklins I.
Caicos Passage
TO TURKS AND CAICOS ISLANDS
Little Inagua I.
Great Inagua I.
Lake Windsor
Matthew Town

Dining Most Bahamian restaurants have adopted the European custom of adding a service charge to your bill—usually 15%, sometimes as little as 10%.

Category	Cost*
$$$	over $30
$$	$20–$30
$	under $20

per person for a three-course meal, excluding drinks and service

Freeport/Lucaya

Freeport is on Grand Bahama Island, the fourth-largest island in the archipelago. Its 530-square-mile interior is heavily forested with palmettos, casuarinas, and Caribbean pines. The 96-mile southern coastline is made up of sheltered harbors bordered by miles of unspoiled white-sand beaches and fringed with a nearly unbroken line of spectacular reefs.

Virtually unknown and unpopulated a generation ago, Grand Bahama was developed in the early 1950s. Modern, well-planned Freeport is the centerpiece of Grand Bahama. Its boulevards and shops are linked by a palm-lined road to Lucaya, a suburb set among thousands of acres of tropical greenery that sprawls along canals and ocean beach. Scattered here and there are hotels, the International Bazaar, four golf courses, two casinos, and Port Lucaya, the new shopping mall/tourist area.

Shore Excursions The following is a good choice in Freeport. It may not be offered by all cruise lines. Time and price are approximate.

Freeport Shopping & Sightseeing Tour. This bus trip covers about 26 miles round-trip, stopping along the way for a half hour at the Garden of the Groves and for shopping at the International Bazaar. *3 hrs. Cost: $12.*

Coming Ashore The cruise-ship harbor is an industrial center in the middle of nowhere. A cab from the cruise-ship piers to downtown costs $10 for two passengers. A Bahamas Ministry of Tourism office is at the port, but depending on where your ship is berthed, it may be a short walk across the parking lot or a long hike. You'll also find a Ministry of Tourism Information Center at the International Bazaar on West Sunrise Highway. Pick up maps, brochures, and information from either office.

Getting Around Everything in Freeport/Lucaya is far apart, so you need to sign up for a shore excursion, take a cab, or rent a car or moped.

By Bus Buses serve downtown Freeport and Lucaya; the fare is about 75¢. Service between Freeport and Lucaya costs $1.

By Car Car rentals average $60–$85 daily, and a significant deposit is required. In Lucaya, contact **Avis** (tel. 242/373–1102).

By Bicycle, Moped, or Scooter Rental mopeds and bicycles are available dockside in Freeport. Rates for bicycles start at about $10 per day, with a $50 deposit; scooters cost $40 per day with a $50–$100 deposit. Helmets are mandatory.

By Taxi Metered taxis meet all the incoming cruise ships. Rates are $2 for the first ¼ mile and 30¢ for each additional ¼ mile. A taxi tour costs $12–$18 an hour, but rates for longer trips are negotiable. Always settle the fare in advance. Taxis are also available in most major tourist areas. Try **Freeport Taxi** (tel. 242/352–6666).

Exploring Freeport/ Lucaya

Numbers in the margin correspond to points of interest on the Freeport/Lucaya map.

You will enjoy driving or riding around Freeport/Lucaya as long as you remember to drive on the left. Broad, landscaped "dual carriageways"—British for highways—and tree-lined streets wind through parks, past lovely homes, and along lush, green fairways.

❶ **Churchill Square** and the Freeport town center is where residents shop and tend to business. If you're hungry, **Mum's Coffee Shop and Bakery,** at 7 Yellow Pine Street, has delicious homemade breads, soups, and sandwiches. Head north on the Mall to Settler's Way ❷ East, then turn right and follow the tree-lined highway to the **Rand Memorial Nature Center.** The 100-acre park, composed of natural woodland, preserves more than 400 indigenous varieties of subtropical plants, trees, and flowers. It is also a sanctuary for thousands of native and migratory birds. A mile of well-marked nature trails leads to a 30-foot waterfall. Guided walks are conducted by the resident naturalists.

Leaving the nature center, continue east on Settler's Way, then turn ❸ south (right) onto West Beach Road to the **Garden of the Groves** (admission free; closed Wed.). The 11-acre park features some 5,000 varieties of rare and familiar subtropical and tropical trees, shrubs, plants, and flowers. Well-marked paths lead past clearly identified plants, a fern gully and grotto, and a tiny, stone interdenominational chapel.

From here, head for the sea, then turn right onto Royal Palm Way ❹ and drive until you come to the **Underwater Explorers Society** (UNEXSO), the famous scuba-diving school of the Bahamas, which trains more than 2,500 divers annually. *Tel. 242/373–1244. Dive lesson and 1 dive $89; snorkeling trip including all equipment $15. Open daily 8–6.*

❺ Within walking distance is **Lucayan Harbour,** with a 50-slip marina at which *El Galleon* is moored. This replica of a 16th-century Spanish galleon offers day and dinner cruises.

❻ The **Dolphin Experience** at Sanctuary Bay is the world's largest dolphin sanctuary. A $25 ferry ride from the UNEXSO dive shop takes you there to see the dolphins and take pictures. For $59, you can wade into the waist-deep water and cavort with the dolphins for about 20 minutes.

Shopping

The **International Bazaar and Straw Market** is on West Sunrise Highway, next to the Princess Casino. You enter through the 35-foot, red-lacquer Torii Gate, traditional symbol of welcome in Japan. Within the bazaar are a straw market and exotic shops with merchandise from around the world. Most items are priced at 20%–40% below U.S. *retail* prices, which means that you may or may not be getting a bargain when compared with prices in discount stores at home. Two dozen countries are represented in the 10-acre bazaar, with nearly a hundred shops. The vendors in the straw market expect you to haggle over the price, but don't bargain in the stores. For a less touristy experience, go to **Churchill Square** and the Freeport town center. An open-air produce market offers mangoes, papayas, and other fruit for snacking as you walk. To the east of Freeport is **Port Lucaya,** an attractive waterfront marketplace with 85 shops, boutiques, restaurants, and lounges. You'll need to drive or take a taxi to get here from downtown Freeport.

Sports

Diving

One of the most famous scuba schools and NAUI centers in the world is the **Underwater Explorers Society** (UNEXSO), adjacent to Port Lucaya (*see* Exploring Freeport/Lucaya, *above*). Beginners can learn to dive for $89, which includes three hours of professional instruction in the club's training pools, and a shallow reef dive. For ex-

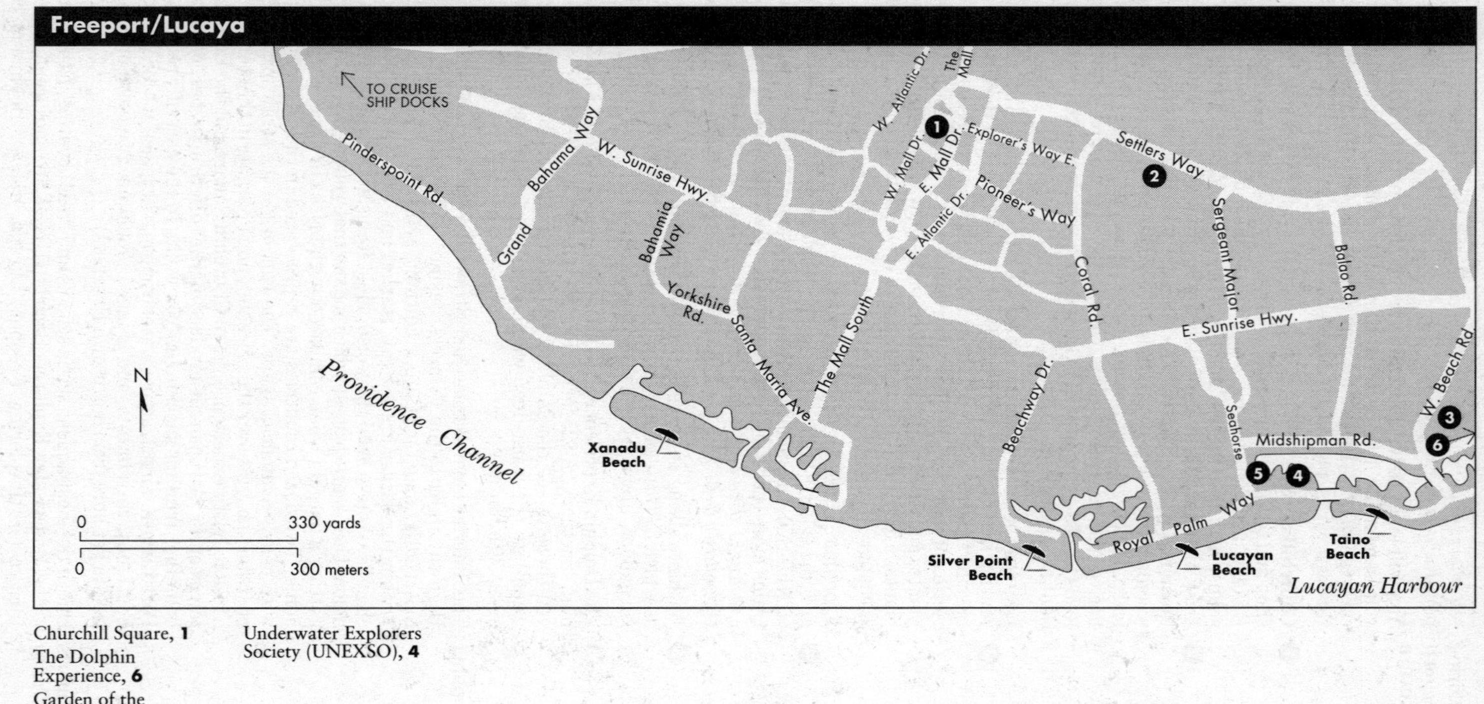

Churchill Square, **1**
The Dolphin Experience, **6**
Garden of the Groves, **3**
Lucayan Harbor, **5**
Rand Memorial Nature Center, **2**
Underwater Explorers Society (UNEXSO), **4**

perienced divers, there are three trips daily (tel. 242/373–1244 or 800/992–3483, or write to UNEXSO, Box F-2433, Freeport, Grand Bahama).

Fishing Contact **Reef Tours** (tel. 242/373–5880). Boat charters cost $300 for a half day, $600 for a full day.

Golf Grand Bahama's four championship 18-hole courses are among the best in the Caribbean: **Bahamas Princess Hotel & Golf Club** (2 courses, tel. 242/352–6721), **Fortune Hills Golf & Country Club** (tel. 242/373–4500), and **Lucayan Golf & Country Club** (tel. 242/373–1066). Fees are about $35 for nine holes.

Parasailing and Windsurfing Contact the **Clarion Atlantik Beach** (Royal Palm Way, tel. 242/373–1444) or **Bahamas Sea Adventures** (at the Radisson Hotel, tel. 242/373–3923). Parasail rides cost $20–$25 for seven minutes. Windsurfing boards cost $10–$15 an hour; private lessons cost $25–$30.

Tennis Cruise passengers are welcome at several hotels. Try **Xanadu Beach Resort** (3 clay courts, tel. 242/352–6782) and the **Lucayan Beach Resort & Casino** (4 courts, tel. 242/373–7777). Court time costs $5 an hour.

Beaches The closest beach to the cruise-ship dock is **Xanadu Beach,** which has a mile of white-sand beach. South of Port Lucaya stretch three delightful beaches: **Fortune Beach, Smith's Point,** and **Taino Beach,** where sunbathers will also find the Stone Crab (tel. 242/373–1442)—a popular seafood restaurant.

Dining

$$ **Pub on the Mall.** Opposite the International Bazaar, this splendid English pub has authentic atmosphere and decor. The Prince of Wales Lounge serves good fish-and-chips and steak-and-kidney pie. Bass Ale is on tap. Baron's Hall serves superb dinners at night—try the coquilles St. Jacques, Cornish game hen, or roast beef with Yorkshire pudding. *At Ranfurly Circus, tel. 242/352–5110. AE, MC, V.*

$ **Pusser's Co. Store and Pub.** Fashioned after an old Welsh pub, this amiable establishment overlooking Port Lucaya is part bar, part restaurant, and part maritime museum. It has a nautical decor with antique copper measuring cups and Tiffany lamps suspended from the wood-beam ceiling. Locals swap tall tales and island gossip with tourists over rum-based Pusser's Painkillers. Solid English fare is favored: shepherd's pie, fisherman's pie, steak-and-ale pie. *Port Lucaya Marketplace, tel. 242/373–8450. AE, MC, V.*

Nassau

The 17th-century town of Nassau, the capital of the Bahamas, has witnessed Spanish invasions and hosted pirates, who made it their headquarters for raids along the Spanish Main. The new American Navy seized Ft. Montagu here in 1776, when they won a victory without firing a shot.

The cultural and ethnic heritage of old Nassau includes the Southern charm of British loyalists from the Carolinas, the African tribal traditions of freed slaves, and a bawdy history of blockade-running during the Civil War and rum-running in the Roaring Twenties. Over it all is a subtle layer of civility and sophistication, derived from three centuries of British rule.

Reminders of the island's British heritage are everywhere in Nassau. Court justices sport wigs and scarlet robes. The police wear colonial garb: starched white jackets, red-striped navy trousers, tropical pith helmets. Traffic keeps to the left, and the language has a British-colonial lilt, softened by a slight drawl. New Providence Island's charm, however, is often lost in its commercialism. Downtown Nassau's colonial facade is barely visible, painted over with duty-free-shop signs. Away from town, high-rise resorts and glittering casinos line the beaches. Lovely Old Nassau sold its soul to keep the tourists coming, and come they do in ever-increasing numbers.

Shore Excursions The following are good choices in Nassau. They may not be offered by all cruise lines. Times and prices are approximate.

Undersea Creatures **Coral World.** A 100-foot observation tower soars above the landscape, but the real views are of turtles, stingrays, and starfish. Budget about three hours, but you can stay as long as you want—the ferry back to the cruise-ship docks leaves every half hour. *Cost: $21 ($24 with ferry transfers).*

Snorkeling Adventure. The Bahamas is an underwater wonderland. On this tour you can learn to snorkel, then join an escorted tour or set off on your own. *2½–3 hrs. Cost: $20–$25.*

Coming Ashore Cruise ships dock at one of three piers on Prince George's Wharf. Taxi drivers who meet the ships may offer you a $2 ride into town, but the historic government buildings and duty-free shops lie just outside the dock area. The one- or two-block walk takes 5 to 10 minutes. As you leave the pier, look for a tall pink tower: Diagonally across from here is the tourist information office. Stop in for maps of the island and downtown Nassau. On most days you can join a free one-hour walking tour conducted by well-trained guides. Outside the office, an ATM dispenses U.S. dollars.

Getting Around

By Bus Jitney service runs to most points on the island. Walk from the pier to Frederick Street between Bay Street and Woodes Rogers Walk to catch a bus. The fare is 75¢ and buses run until 8:30 PM.

By Carriage Across from the docks, along Rawson Square, are surreys drawn by straw-hatted horses that will take you through the old city and past some of the nearby historic sites. The cost is $10 for two for 25 minutes, but verify prices before getting on.

By Car Car-rental rates begin at $50 a day; a substantial deposit is required. **Hertz** (tel. 242/327–6866) has an office in downtown Nassau.

By Ferry A ferry commutes between the dock area and Paradise Island ($2 round-trip). Another goes to Coral World ($3 round-trip).

By Scooter Scooters may be rented as you exit Prince George's Wharf. Rates average $25 per half day, $40 per full day. Helmets are mandatory.

By Touring Car or Taxi As you disembark from your ship you will find a row of taxis and luxurious air-conditioned limousines. The latter are Nassau's fleet of tour cars, useful and comfortable for a guided tour of the island. Taxi fares are fixed at $2 for the first ¼ mile, 30¢ each additional ¼ mile. Sightseeing tours cost about $20–$25 per hour.

Exploring Nassau *Numbers in the margin correspond to points of interest on the Nassau map.*

❶ ❷ As you leave the cruise wharf, you enter **Rawson Square.** Directly across Bay Street is **Parliament Square.** Dating from the early 1800s and patterned after southern U.S. colonial architecture, this cluster of yellow, colonnaded buildings with green shutters is striking. In the center of the square is a statue of the young Queen Victoria, and the **Bahamas House of Parliament.**

❸ At the head of Elizabeth Avenue is the **Queen's Staircase,** a famous Nassau landmark. Its 66 steps, hewn from the coral limestone cliff by slaves in the late 18th century, were designed to provide a direct route between town and **Ft. Fincastle** at the top of the hill. The staircase was named more than a hundred years later, in honor of the 66 years of Queen Victoria's reign.

❹ Climb the staircase to reach **Ft. Fincastle.** The fort, shaped like the bow of a ship, was built in 1793. It never fired a shot in anger but

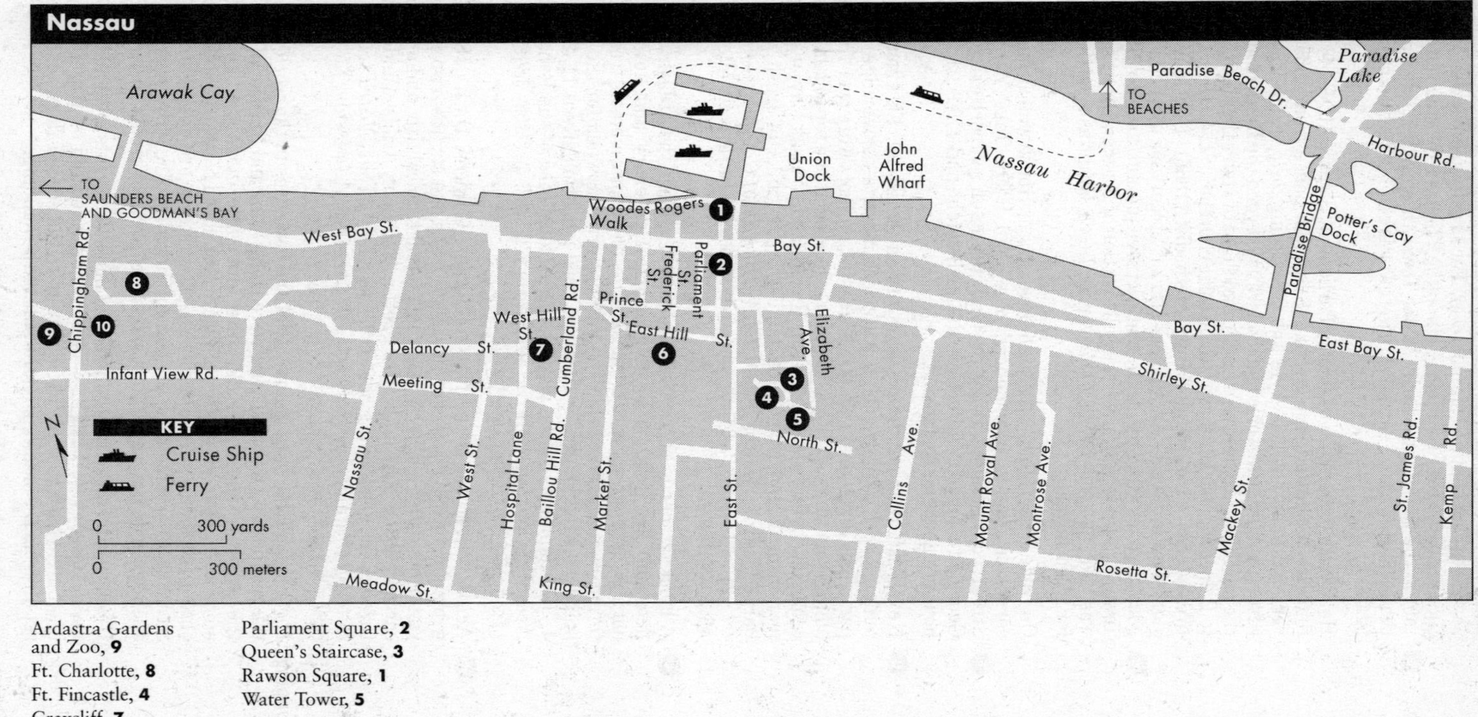

Ardastra Gardens and Zoo, **9**
Ft. Charlotte, **8**
Ft. Fincastle, **4**
Graycliff, **7**
Gregory Arch, **6**
Nassau Botanic Gardens, **10**
Parliament Square, **2**
Queen's Staircase, **3**
Rawson Square, **1**
Water Tower, **5**

served as a lookout and signal tower. For a really spectacular view of the island of New Providence, climb the 225 steps (or ride the elevator) to the top of the nearby **Water Tower.** Rising to 126 feet, more than 200 feet above sea level, the tower is the highest point on the island.

Head back toward the harbor to Parliament Street. At No. 48 you'll find **Green Shutters,** a charming Bahamian house from 1865, converted into an English-style pub (*see* Dining, *below*). On East Hill Street, you'll see historic mansions. Just beyond the **Bank House,** on the north side of the street, is a broad flight of stairs that leads down to Prince Street. Here are two historic churches, **St. Andrew's Kirk, Presbyterian** (1810) and **Trinity Methodist** (1866). Continue west along Prince Street. As you pass Market Street look up the hill for a good view of **Gregory Arch,** the picturesque entrance to **Grant's Town.** Known as the "over-the-hill" section of Nassau, Grant's Town was laid out in the 1820s by Governor Lewis Grant as a settlement for freed slaves.

On Duke Street, follow the high Government House wall around the corner to Baillou (pronounced blue) Hill Road. Take West Hill Street; across Baillou Hill is the **Graycliff** hotel, a superb example of Georgian colonial architecture, dating from the mid-1700s, that now houses a gourmet restaurant.

Next, visit the most interesting fort on the island, **Ft. Charlotte,** built in 1787 replete with a waterless moat, a drawbridge, ramparts, and dungeons. Like Ft. Fincastle, no shots were ever fired in anger from this fort. Ft. Charlotte is located at the top of a hill and commands a fine view of Nassau Harbor and Arawak Cay, a small, man-made island that holds huge storage tanks of fresh water barged in from Andros Island. *Off W. Bay St. at Chippingham Rd., tel. 242/322–7500. Admission free. Local guides conduct tours Mon.–Sat. 8:30–4.*

A block farther west, on Chippingham Road, are the **Ardastra Gardens and Zoo,** with 5 acres of tropical greenery and flowering shrubs, an aviary of rare tropical birds, and exotic animals from different parts of the world. The gardens are renowned for the pink, spindly legged, marching flamingos that perform daily at 11, 2, and 4. The flamingo, by the way, is the national bird of the Bahamas. *Near Ft. Charlotte, off Chippingham Rd., tel. 242/323–5806. Admission: $7.50. Open daily 9–5.*

Across the street is the **Nassau Botanic Gardens.** On its 18-acre grounds are 600 species of flowering trees and shrubs; two freshwater ponds with lilies, water plants, and tropical fish; and a small cactus garden that ends in a grotto. The many trails wandering through the gardens are perfect for leisurely strolls. *Near Ft. Charlotte, off Chippingham Rd., tel. 242/323–5975. Admission: $1. Open daily 8–4:30.*

Shopping

Forbes magazine once claimed that the two cities in the world with the best buys on wristwatches were Hong Kong and Nassau. Most of the stores selling these and other duty-free items are clustered along an eight-block stretch of Bay Street in Old Nassau or spill over onto a few side streets downtown. Most stores are open Monday–Saturday 9–5; some close at noon on Thursday. The straw market is open seven days a week. Most shops accept major credit cards.

If you're interested in old-fashioned maps and prints, seek out **Balmain Antiques** (tel. 242/323–7421). Though located on Bay Street, it's a little hard to find: The doorway to the second-floor gallery is set off from the sidewalk on the side of the building.

Sports

Fishing

Contact **Chubasco Charters** (tel. 242/322–8148) or **Brown's Charters** (tel. 242/324–1215). Boat charters cost $300 for a half day, $600 for a full day.

Golf Three excellent 18-hole championship courses are open to the public: **Crystal Palace Golf Course** (opposite the Wyndham Ambassador Hotel, tel. 242/327–6000, 800/222–7466 in the United States), **Paradise Island Golf Club** (eastern end of Paradise Island, tel. 242/363–3925, 800/321–3000 in the United States), and **South Ocean Beach & Golf Resort** (adjacent to Divi Bahamas Beach Resort, tel. 242/362–4391). Fees are $45–$70 for 18 holes, $22–$27 for nine holes.

Parasailing and Windsurfing Windsurfing is available at **Le Meridien Royal Bahamian Hotel** (tel. 242/327–6400). Board rental costs $12 an hour; lessons cost $30. Parasailing is available from **Sea Sports Ltd.** (in front of the Nassau Beach Hotel, tel. 242/327–6058). A six-minute ride costs $30.

Beaches **Paradise Beach,** the Bahamas' most famous beach, stretches for more than a mile on the western end of Paradise Island. The $3 admission includes a welcome drink, towels, and the use of changing rooms and locker. The **Western Esplanade** sweeps westward from the British Colonial Hotel on Bay Street (a 10-minute walk from the cruise-ship pier). It's just across the street from shops and restaurants, and it has rest rooms, a snack bar, and changing facilities. A little farther west, just past the bridge that leads to Coral World, is **Saunders Beach. Goodman's Bay,** a bit farther west of Saunders, is popular with Bahamians for picnics and cookouts on weekends and holidays.

Dining

$$$ **Graycliff.** Situated in a magnificent, 200-year-old colonial mansion, Graycliff is filled with antiques and English country-house charm. The outstanding Continental and Bahamian menu includes beluga caviar, grouper *au poivre vert,* and chateaubriand, with elegant pastries and flaming coffees for dessert. The wine cellar is excellent. *W. Hill St., across from Government House, tel. 242/322–2796 or 800/633–7411. Reservations essential. Jacket required. AE, DC, MC, V.*

$$ **Green Shutters.** Shades of Fleet Street! This very British pub is a cozy place awash with wood paneling. Steak-and-kidney pie, bangers and mash, and shepherd's pie are featured alongside such island favorites as cracked conch and Bahamian crawfish tail. *48 Parliament St., tel. 242/325–5702. AE, MC, V.*

$$ **Poop Deck.** Coiled rope wraps around beams, life preservers hang on the walls, and port and starboard lights adorn the newel posts of this favorite haunt of Nassau residents. Tables overlook the harbor and Paradise Island. Cuisine is exceptional Bahamian-style seafood, served in a festive, friendly atmosphere. The food is spicy, the wine list extensive. Save room for guava duff, a warm guava-layered local dessert, and a Calypso coffee, spiked with secret ingredients. *E. Bay St. (an 8-min cab ride from pier), tel. 242/393–8175. AE, DC, MC, V.*

$ **Shoal Restaurant and Lounge.** Saturday mornings at 9 you'll find hordes of jolly Bahamians digging into boiled fish and johnnycake, the marvelous specialty of the house. A bowl of this peppery dish, filled with chunks of boiled potatoes, onions, and grouper, keeps the locals coming back to this dimly lit, basic, and off-the-tourist-beat "Ma's kitchen," where standard Nassau dishes, including peas 'n' rice and cracked conch, are served. If it suits you, you'll find native mutton here, too, which is sometimes hard to find. *Nassau St., tel. 242/323–4400. Reservations not accepted. AE.*

Nightlife Some ships stay late into the night or until the next day so that passengers can enjoy Nassau's nightlife. You'll find nonstop entertainment nightly along Cable Beach and on Paradise Island. All the larger hotels offer lounges with island combos for listening or dancing, and restaurants with soft guitar or piano background music.

Casinos The three casinos on New Providence Island—**Crystal Palace Casino, Paradise Island Resort and Casino,** and **Ramada Inn Casino**—open early in the day, remain active into the wee hours of the morning, and offer Continental gambling and a variety of other entertainment. Visitors must be 18 or older to enter a casino, 21 or older to gamble.

Discos **Club Waterloo** (tel. 242/393–7324), on East Bay Street, is one of Nassau's most swinging nightspots. Disco and rock can be heard nightly at **Club Pastiche** (tel. 242/363–3000), at the Paradise Island Resort and Casino.

Local Entertainment The **Drum Beat Club** (tel. 242/322–4233) on West Bay Street, just up from the Best Western British Colonial Hotel, features the legendary Peanuts Taylor, still alive and well and beating away at those tom-toms; his band and gyrating dancers put on two shows nightly at 8:30 and 10:30.

Bermuda

Blessed with fabulous beaches and surrounded by a turquoise sea, Britain's oldest colony and most famous resort island lies isolated in the Atlantic Ocean, more than 500 miles from Cape Hatteras, North Carolina, the nearest point on the U.S. mainland. Although it looks like one island, Bermuda actually consists of about 150 islands—the six largest connected by bridges and causeways—all arranged in the shape of a giant fishhook. Bermuda, which is 21 square miles, is never more than a mile wide. The islands are surrounded by coral reefs that offer not only protection from Atlantic storms but wonderful scuba diving as well.

Bermuda's residents are known as "onions"—after the sweet, succulent Bermuda onion that was their livelihood a century ago. Their homes are studies in color—pink and yellow, lime and turquoise—all topped with stepped white roofs that funnel rainwater into cisterns. (The islands have no freshwater supply of their own.)

Bermuda was stumbled upon accidentally by Spaniard Juan de Bermudez in 1503. In 1609 the British ship *Sea Venture*, commanded by Sir George Somers and on its way to Jamestown, Virginia, struck one of the reefs that surround the islands. Some of the shipwrecked colonists stayed to build a settlement. Bermuda has thrived ever since and is now home to nearly 60,000 residents.

In spite of its proximity to the American mainland, Bermuda has maintained a distinctly British visage. Cricket and pubs, for instance, are very much a part of Bermudian life. Today, Bermudians are protective of their country, and change is not undertaken lightly. To avoid road congestion and air pollution, the number of cars is limited to one per residential household. There are no rental cars, so most visitors buzz around the island on mopeds or scooters. You can also take public transportation or hire a taxi.

Proper dress is stressed on Bermuda. Tourists in short shorts are frowned upon, and bathing suits are unacceptable away from the beach. Bare feet are not acceptable in public, nor is appearing without a shirt or in just a bathing-suit top.

Bermuda has long been a favorite destination of cruise passengers, and it is usually a cruise's only port of call. Most ships make seven-day loops from New York, with three days spent at sea and four days tied up in port. Three Bermuda harbors serve cruise ships: Hamilton (the capital), St. George's, and the Royal Naval Dockyard. Concerned about overcrowding, the Bermudian government limits the number of regular cruise-ship visits. Cruise lines with weekly sailings are Celebrity, Majesty, NCL, and Royal Caribbean. Lines that call occasionally include Crystal, Cunard, Holland America, and Seabourn. (For seasonal itineraries, *see* Chapter 4.)

When to Go The Bermuda cruise season runs from April through October, when temperatures are in the 70s and 80s. One or two ships sail here in November.

Currency The Bermuda dollar (BD$) is pegged on a par with the U.S. dollar, so there is no need to exchange currency. Most shops take credit cards, but a few hotels and restaurants do not. U.S. traveler's checks, however, are widely accepted. Ask for change in U.S. dollars and coins; all shopkeepers have them. All other currencies must be exchanged at banks for local tender.

Passports and Visas U.S. citizens need proof of citizenship. A passport is preferable, but a stamped birth certificate or voter registration card with photo ID are also acceptable. Canadian and British citizens need a valid passport.

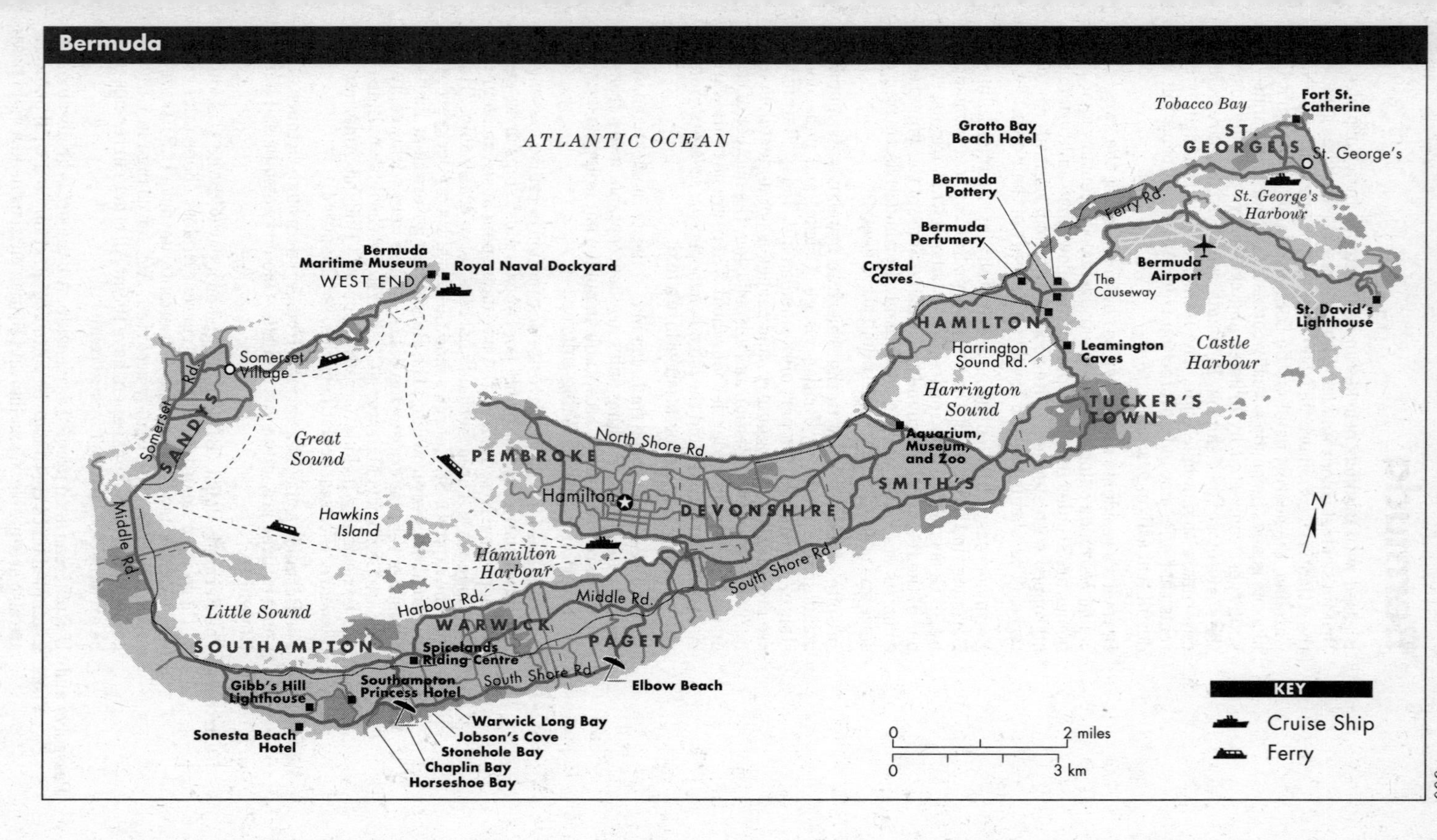

Bermuda
ATLANTIC OCEAN
Tobacco Bay
Fort St. Catherine
ST. GEORGE'S
St. George's
St. George's Harbour
Grotto Bay Beach Hotel
Bermuda Pottery
Bermuda Perfumery
Crystal Caves
Ferry Rd.
The Causeway
Bermuda Airport
St. David's Lighthouse
Castle Harbour
Bermuda Maritime Museum
WEST END
Royal Naval Dockyard
HAMILTON
Harrington Sound Rd.
Leamington Caves
Harrington Sound
TUCKER'S TOWN
Somerset Village
Somerset Rd.
SANDYS
Great Sound
PEMBROKE
North Shore Rd.
Aquarium, Museum, and Zoo
SMITH'S
Hamilton
DEVONSHIRE
N
Hawkins Island
Middle Rd.
Hamilton Harbour
South Shore Rd.
Harbour Rd.
Middle Rd.
Little Sound
WARWICK
PAGET
SOUTHAMPTON
Spicelands Riding Centre
South Shore Rd.
Gibb's Hill Lighthouse
Southampton Princess Hotel
Elbow Beach
Sonesta Beach Hotel
Warwick Long Bay
Jobson's Cove
Stonehole Bay
Chaplin Bay
Horseshoe Bay
0 2 miles
0 3 km
KEY
Cruise Ship
Ferry

Telephones and Mail Calling home from Bermuda is as easy as it is from any city in the United States, and public phones can be found everywhere, including the docks. As a rule, cruise ships sell local stamps at the front desk, and you can send postcards from an onboard mailbox as well, eliminating the need to find a post office.

Shore Excursions The following are good choices in Bermuda. They may not be offered by all cruise lines. Times and prices are approximate.

Island Sights **St. George's Highlight Tour.** A quick overview of the area around St. George's includes Ft. St. Catherine, Ft. William, Gates Fort, the Unfinished Church, Somers Garden, Tobacco Bay, and the government housing complex. The guide is informative and will point out the popular shopping areas. *2–4 hrs. Cost: $30–$36 (prices are for ships docked at St. George's or the West End).*

West End Highlight Tour. Visit Island Pottery, the Bermuda Art Centre, the Crafts Market, Maritime Museum, Heydon Trust Chapel, and Gibb's Hill Lighthouse during a drive through Somerset. This tour is a must if you are docked in Hamilton and won't go to the West End on your own. *3 hrs. Cost: $35 (price is for ships docked in Hamilton).*

Undersea Creatures **Bermuda Glass-Bottom Boat Cruise.** A tame but pleasant cruise through the harbor and over reefs. You can feed the fish from the boat. *2 hrs. Cost: $30.*

Helmet Diving. Walk on the bottom of the sea, play with fish, and learn about coral, all without getting your hair wet. Helmets cover your head and feed you air from the surface. *3½ hrs. Cost: $44.*

Snorkeling Tour. Equipment, lessons, and an underwater guided tour are included. Underwater cameras are available for an extra charge. *3¾ hrs. Cost: $44.*

Coming Ashore Ships dock in Hamilton on Front Street, at the doorstep to the capital's prestigious shops. Passengers whose ships tie up at St. George's have an easy walk from either Ordnance Island or Penno's Wharf to Bermuda's equivalent of Colonial Williamsburg. The pier at the Royal Naval Dockyard, on the West End, is within walking distance of the restored fortifications that now house the Maritime Museum, but you'll have to rent a moped or take public transportation to other sites of interest. Free ferry service is provided to and from Hamilton.

The Bermuda Department of Tourism maintains an information booth in the Hamilton cruise-ship terminal, on King's Square in St. George's, in Hamilton at 8 Front Street, and at the Royal Naval Dockyard in the West End.

Getting Around

By Bus Buses are a good way to get around, although some stop running in the evening. A fare of $4 (exact change) will get you just about anywhere on the island. A three-day pass, which is ideal for cruise passengers, costs $15 and entitles you to unlimited use in all zones and ferry passage between Hamilton and the West End. This can be purchased at the central bus terminal next to City Hall on Washington Street in Hamilton. Bus stops are marked by green-and-white or pink-and-blue striped posts, and the pink-and-blue buses are easy to spot. Most operate about every 15–25 minutes, except on weekends.

By Carriage Horse-drawn carriages line up along Front Street in Hamilton, near the cruise-ship dock. A ride costs $20 per half hour.

By Ferry Ferry service between the West End and Hamilton costs $3.50 one-way, and an extra $3.50 for a moped; the ride takes about 30 minutes. If your ship is tied up at the Royal Navy Dockyard, this crossing is free. Other ferries connect various points in Paget and Warwick for $2. Bicycles can be taken aboard for no charge, but mopeds and scooters are not allowed.

By Moped and Scooter Most visitors to Bermuda drive around on mopeds or scooters. However, be careful: The number of accidents is considerable. Mopeds can be rented all over the island at a daily rate of about $30. Riders are required to wear a strapped helmet. Most gas stations are open Monday–Saturday 7 AM–7 PM. A few remain open until 11 PM; some are also open on Sunday. Stop by a tourist information office to pick up a map for the Railway Trail, which is an especially fun ride.

By Taxi Taxis are plentiful and meet every ship. The blue flag signifies that the driver has passed a written examination to qualify as a guide. The drivers of these blue-flag taxis do not charge more than other taxi drivers. Meter rates are $2.60 for pickup plus 20¢ for each additional minute. A 25% surcharge is added between 10 PM and 6 AM. You can also hire a taxi by the hour. Rates are $30 per hour, with a three-hour minimum for up to six passengers.

Exploring Hamilton *Numbers in the margin correspond to points of interest on the Hamilton map.*

One of the most-photographed landmarks in Bermuda's capital is
1 the **Birdcage,** where a policeman sometimes directs traffic.

2 **Par-la-Ville Park** was once the private garden of William B. Perot, Bermuda's first postmaster and the creator of the famous 1848 Perot Stamp. His post office is still in operation here. The huge rubber tree was planted by Perot in 1847.

3 In what used to be William B. Perot's home you'll find the **Bermuda Public Library and Museum of the Bermuda Historical Society.** *Admission to public library free. Open weekdays 9:30–6, Sat. 9:30–5. Museum admission free, donation suggested. Open Mon.–Sat. 9:30–12:30 and 1:30–4:30.*

4 **City Hall,** a handsome modern structure with a traditional Bermudian feeling and a weather vane in the shape of the *Sea Venture,* houses the permanent displays of the Bermuda National Gallery. Works by the Old Masters as well as by painters who visited Bermuda from the 19th to 20th centuries can be seen here. The second floor of the West Wing is home to the Bermuda Society of Arts Gallery, with its changing exhibits of work by local artists in a range of media. City Hall is also home to a theater that hosts many Bermuda Festival events. *Admission to Bermuda National Gallery: $3. Open Mon.–Sat. 10–4, Sun. 12:30–4. Admission to Bermuda Society of Arts Gallery free, donation suggested. Open weekdays 10–4, Sat. 9–noon.*

5 Bermuda's **Cathedral of the Most Holy Trinity,** the seat of the Anglican Church of Bermuda, was consecrated in 1911. Commonly called the Bermuda Cathedral, it was built mainly from native limestone; decorative touches are of marble, granite, and English oak. *Open daily 8–4:45.*

6 **Sessions House** is easily recognized by its Italianate towers and colonnade decorated with red terra-cotta. In this building, the House of Assembly meets upstairs under the portraits of King George III and Queen Charlotte. The Speaker of the House, the Supreme Court chief justice, and barristers all wear the traditional English wig and black robes. Climb up to the visitor galleries on the upper floors. *Admission free. Open weekdays 9–4:30.*

7 For a spectacular panoramic view of the city and harbor, head to **Ft. Hamilton.** Visitors approach the main gate over a moat—now dry and filled with exotic plants—which can be reached from the fort's underground galleries. On the upper level, now a grassy slope filled with park benches, the Royal Arms of Queen Victoria are emblazoned on the main armaments. *Admission free. Open daily 9–5.*

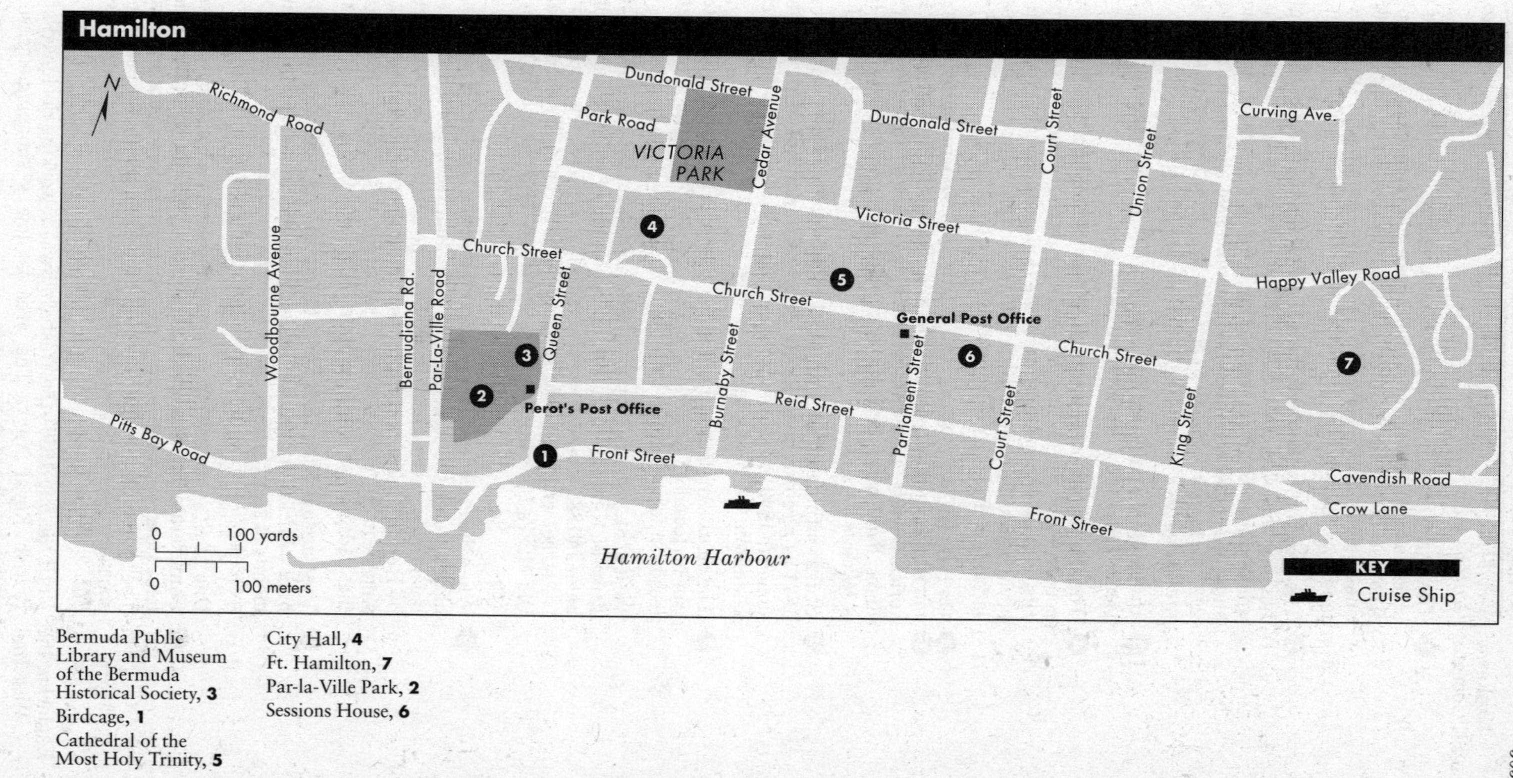

Bermuda Public Library and Museum of the Bermuda Historical Society, **3**
Birdcage, **1**
Cathedral of the Most Holy Trinity, **5**
City Hall, **4**
Ft. Hamilton, **7**
Par-la-Ville Park, **2**
Sessions House, **6**

Exploring St. George's *Numbers in the margin correspond to points of interest on the St. George's map.*

1 The heart of St. George's is **King's Square,** where replicas of the stocks and pillory that stood on the site 300 years ago are on display. Another 17th-century form of punishment was the ducking stool, one of which can be seen near the cruise-ship dock at Ordnance Island.

2 The beautifully restored **Town Hall** follows the lines of the original building that was erected in 1782 and is still in use as the town's administrative headquarters. "The Bermuda Journey" multimedia show presented here depicts Bermuda's past and present. *Tel. 441/ 297–1642. Admission to Town Hall free. Open Mon.–Sat. 9–4. "Bermuda Journey" admission: $3. Call for show times.*

3 **Bridge House** dates back to around 1700. It now belongs to the National Trust and houses an art gallery.

4 The **Old State House,** Bermuda's oldest surviving stone house, was constructed in 1620. The first building on the island constructed entirely of native limestone, the State House was built in the Italianate style because Governor Butler believed Bermuda to be on the same latitude as Italy. *Admission free. Open Wed. 10–4.*

5 6 On Duke of York Street is the entrance to **Somers Gardens,** created out of a former swampland. On Kent Street is the **St. George's Historical Society,** a museum set in a 1725 home that shows how Bermudians lived more than two centuries ago. *Admission: $1. Open weekdays 10–4.*

7 Still awaiting completion is the **Unfinished Church.** It was begun in 1874 as a replacement for St. Peter's Church, but work was abandoned in 1899 so that the funds could be used to rebuild the church in Hamilton, which had been destroyed by fire.

8 The oldest Anglican church in the Western Hemisphere, **St. Peter's,** can be found on Church Lane. The tombstones offer a fascinating lesson in social history.

West of St. Peter's Church are two interesting lanes leading down to Duke of York Street. Silk Alley, also called Petticoat Lane, got its name in 1834 when two newly emancipated slave girls walked down the street with their new, rustling silk petticoats. The other is called Old Maid's Lane because some spinsters lived along here a century ago.

9 When the **President Henry Tucker House** was built in 1711, it was not hanging over the street, as it is today, but faced a broad expanse of lawn that went down to the harbor. The house was acquired in 1775 by Henry Tucker, who was president of the town council during the American Revolution and whose family was divided over the conflict. *Admission: $4. Open Mon.–Sat. 9:30–4:30.*

10 The **Carriage Museum** is worth taking an hour to admire the custom-built vehicles that traveled along the island's roads before the automobile arrived in 1946. *Admission free, donation suggested. Open weekdays 10–5.*

11 One of St. George's more surprising historical attractions is the **Confederate Museum.** During the U.S. Civil War, this part of the island sided with the southern Confederates for economic reasons. The town of St. George became the focus of gunrunning between the southern United States and Europe. *Admission: $4. Open Mon.–Sat. 9:30–4:30.*

Exploring the West End Until the mid-1950s the West End was a working dockyard of the British Royal Navy. The area is now a shopping/sightseeing minivillage for tourists.

Bridge House, **3**
Carriage Museum, **10**
Confederate Museum, **11**
King's Square, **1**
Old State House, **4**
President Henry Tucker House, **9**
St. George's Historical Society, **6**
St. Peter's, **8**
Somers Gardens, **5**
Town Hall, **2**
Unfinished Church, **7**

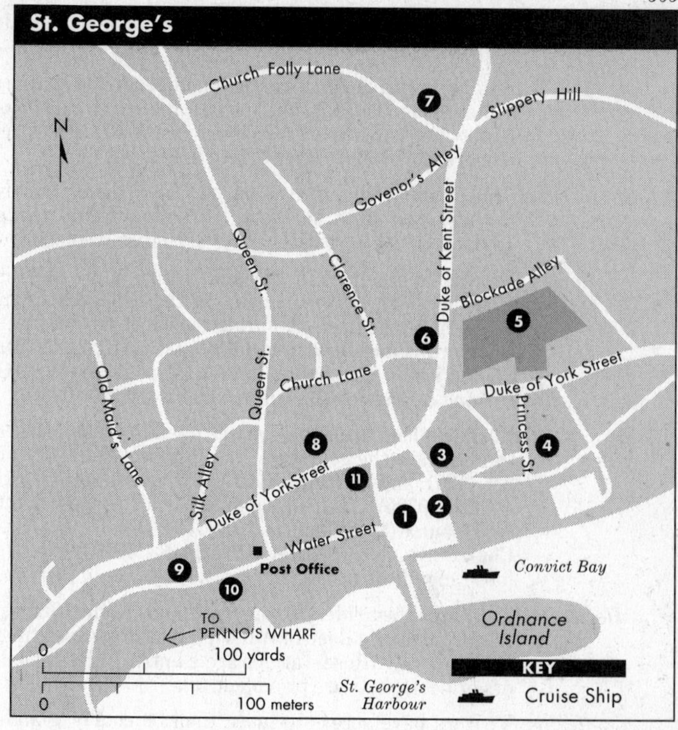

The **Maritime Museum,** in the inner fortifications of the Royal Naval Dockyard, is the most spectacular of the restored buildings. On the grounds are exhibits of Bermuda's seagoing history. A self-guided tour starts in the Queen's Exhibition Hall—originally built in 1850 to store gunpowder—and continues to the gun emplacements that surround the dockyard. Displays in the museum's several buildings include relics from Bermuda's famous shipwrecks. *Admission: $7.50. Open daily 10–5.*

Across the street from the Maritime Museum, the old Cooperage now houses the **Neptune Cinema,** which shows first-run films from the United States and Europe, and the Frog & Onion pub (*see* Dining, *below*). *Admission: $7.*

The **Craft Market,** in the adjacent Bermuda Arts Centre, displays the work of local artisans. The Dockyard also has two nightclubs, branches of Hamilton-based stores, and stalls selling ice cream and pizza. In the nearby village of Somerset are more restaurants and branch shops of the main department stores in Hamilton.

Shopping There is no sales tax in Bermuda—the price you see is what you pay. This is a place to shop for luxury items, and topping the list of good buys are cashmere sweaters, bone china, Irish linens, Scottish tweeds, perfumes, and liquor. Local handicrafts include pottery and cedar ware.

Hamilton The majority of stores are located on Front Street and in the arcades of Reid Street. Bermuda's top department stores, all located on Front Street, Hamilton, are **H.A.&E. Smith's, A.S. Cooper, St. Michael's,** and **Trimingham's.** Each is a full-service department store, with good buys in cashmere and woolens. Smith's is arguably the best men's clothier in Bermuda.

Archie Brown & Son, on Front Street, carries affordably priced lamb's-wool sweaters, while several outlets of the **English Sports**

Shop stock some of Britain's finest woolens, particularly men's sports coats.

Fine jewelry and gems can be found at several locations of **Crisson's** and of **Astwood Dickinson.** The best for fine china is **Bluck's,** found on Front and Reid streets, at Clocktower Mall at the Dockyard, and on Somers Wharf and Water Street in St. George's.

St. George's **Frangipani** is one of St. George's best shops, selling resort-style clothes. Just west on Water Street, opposite the post office, is **Taylor's,** which carries an array of British woolens.

Sports

Fishing Fishing is excellent in Bermuda, with numerous boats going out from just about every marina on the island. Do some comparison shopping at the tourist information booths. Or contact the **Bermuda Charter Fishing Boat Association** (tel. 441/292–6246), the **Bermuda Sport Fishing Association** (tel. 441/295–2370), or **St. George's Game Fishing & Cruising Association** (tel. 441/297–8093).

Golf Bermuda has seven golf courses open to cruise passengers. Among the best are the courses at the **Belmont Hotel** (Warwick, tel. 441/236–1301) and **Marriott's Castle Harbour Resort** (Tucker's Town, tel. 441/293–0795). Challenging links can also be found at the **Port Royal Golf Course** (Southampton, tel. 441/234–0972) and **St. George's Golf Course** (St. George's, tel. 441/297–8353). All are 18 holes. Greens fees range from $30 to $90.

Horseback Riding The "breakfast rides" at the **Spicelands Riding Centre** (tel. 441/238–8212), on Middle Road in Warwick, are an invigorating way to start a Bermuda day. Reservations are a must. Riders should wear sneakers or boots; hats are provided.

Tennis Visitors have access to more than 60 courts island-wide. Hourly rates for nonguests are about $10–$20 per hour; tennis balls are quite expensive. The best courts are found at the **Southampton Princess Hotel** (Southampton, tel. 441/238–1005), the **Belmont Hotel** (Warwick, tel. 441/236–1301), the **Elbow Beach Hotel** (Paget, tel. 441/236–3535), and the **Sonesta Beach Hotel** (Southampton, tel. 441/238–8122).

Water Sports Bermuda's clear waters are perfect for scuba diving, helmet diving, and snorkeling. Check at the tourist information booths to find out which operators are offering dives and snorkel tours. Excellent programs are offered by **Nautilus Diving** (at the Southampton Princess, tel. 441/238–2332), **Blue Waters Divers** (at Robinson's Marina in Sandys, tel. 441/234–1034), and **South Side Scuba** (at the Grotto Bay Beach Hotel, tel. 441/293–2915).

Waterskiing is allowed only in certain protected waters, and by law can be offered only by licensed skippers. **Island Waterskiing** (Grotto Bay Beach Hotel, tel. 441/293–2915) and **Bermuda Waterski Centre** (Robinson's Marina, Somerset, tel. 441/234–3354) both offer lessons and outings.

Windsurfers should contact **Mangrove Marina Ltd.** (Mangrove Bay, Somerset, tel. 441/234–0914), **Pompano Beach Club Watersports Centre** (tel. 441/234–0222), and **South Side Scuba Water Sports** (Grotto Bay Beach Hotel and Marriott's Castle Harbour Resort, tel. 441/293–2915). Board rental is $20 per hour; one-hour lessons are $25–$35.

Beaches Bermuda has some of the most beautiful beaches in the world. The cream of the crop are along the south shore from Southampton to Tucker's Town: **Horseshoe Bay, Chaplin Bay, Stonehole Bay, Jobson's Cove, Warwick Long Bay,** and **Elbow Beach.** Some are long sweeps of unbroken pink sand; others are divided by low coral cliffs into protected little coves. All are easily accessible by bicycle, moped, or taxi.

Dining Many restaurants require gentlemen to wear a jacket and tie and women to be appropriately dressed. When the gratuity is not included in the bill, an overall tip of 10%–15% is the accepted amount. Reservations are recommended for most restaurants.

Category	Cost*
$$$$	over $50
$$$	$35–$50
$$	$20–$35
$	under $20

**per person for a three-course meal, excluding drinks, service, and sales tax*

$$$$ **Fourways Inn.** At the very top of fine dining in Bermuda is this gourmet restaurant in an 18th-century Georgian home. The menu is impressive; specialties include fresh mussels simmered in white wine and cream, fresh veal sautéed in lemon butter, Caesar salad, and strawberry soufflé. The wine list is excellent. A gourmet brunch is offered on Sunday in cruise season. *Paget, tel. 441/236–6517. Reservations essential. AE, MC, V.*

$$$ **Once Upon a Table.** Many locals consider this the finest restaurant on Bermuda. Guests dine in an 18th-century home, surrounded by Victorian furnishings. Dishes include rack of lamb and roast duckling, served on elegant china. *Serpentine Rd., Hamilton, tel. 441/295–8585. Jacket and tie. AE, DC, MC, V. No lunch.*

$$ **Frog & Onion.** An instant hit with locals when it opened in 1992, this pub-style eatery is housed in one of the dockyard's restored 19th-century buildings. Despite its cavernous size and soaring ceilings, the restaurant manages a cozy ambience, thanks in part to subdued lighting. Seafood and pub grub are recommended over the steak offerings. *Cooperage Bldg., Dockyard, tel. 441/234–2900. MC, V.*

$$ **Pub on the Square.** Smack on King's Square in St. George's, this British-style pub is nothing fancy but offers cool draft beer, juicy hamburgers, and fish-and-chips. *King's Sq., St. George's, tel. 441/297–1522. AE, MC, V.*

Caribbean

Nowhere in the world are conditions better suited to cruising than in the ever-warm, treasure-filled Caribbean Sea. Tiny island nations, within easy sailing distance of one another, form a chain of tropical enchantment that curves from Cuba in the north all the way down to the coast of Venezuela. There is far more to life here than sand and coconuts, however. The islands are vastly different, with their own cultures, topographies, and languages. Colonialism has left its mark, and the presence of the Spanish, French, Dutch, Danish, and British is still felt. Slavery, too, has left its cultural legacy, blending African overtones into the colonial/Indian amalgam. The one constant, however, is the weather. Despite the islands' southerly position, the climate is surprisingly gentle, due in large part to the cooling influence of the trade winds.

The Caribbean is made up of the Greater Antilles and the Lesser Antilles. The former consists of those islands closest to the United States: Cuba, Jamaica, Hispaniola (Haiti and the Dominican Republic), and Puerto Rico. (The Cayman Islands lie south of Cuba.) The Lesser Antilles, including the Virgin, Windward, and Leeward islands and others, are greater in number but smaller in size, and constitute the southern half of the Caribbean chain. Cruise lines often include Caracas, Venezuela, and Mexico's Yucatán Peninsula in their Caribbean itineraries as well.

More cruise ships ply these waters than any others in the world. There are big ships and small ships, fancy ships and party ships. In peak season, it is not uncommon for several ships to disembark thousands of passengers into a small town on the same day—a phenomenon not always enjoyed by locals. Despite some overcrowding, however, the abundance of cruise ships in the area allows you to choose the itinerary that suits you best. Whether it's shopping or scuba diving, fishing or sunbathing, you're sure to find the Caribbean cruise of your dreams. (For seasonal itineraries, *see* Chapter 4.)

When to Go Average year-round temperatures throughout the Caribbean are 78°F–85°F, with a low of 65°F and a high of 95°F; downtown shopping areas always seem to be unbearably hot. High season runs from December 15 to April 14; during this most fashionable, most expensive, and most crowded time to go, reservations up to a year in advance are necessary for many ships. A low-season (summer) visit offers certain advantages: Temperatures are virtually the same as in winter (even cooler on average than in parts of the U.S. mainland), island flora is at its height, and the water is smoother and clearer. Some tourist facilities close down in summer, however, and many ships move to Europe, Alaska, or the northeastern United States.

Hurricane season runs from June through October. Although cruise ships stay well out of the way of these storms, hurricanes and tropical storms—their less-powerful relatives—can affect the weather throughout the Caribbean for days, and damage to ports can force last-minute itinerary changes.

Currency Currencies vary throughout the islands, but U.S. dollars are widely accepted. Don't bother changing more than a few dollars into local currency for phone calls, tips, and taxis.

Passports and Visas American citizens boarding ships in the United States usually need neither a passport nor visas to call at ports in the Caribbean. However, carrying a passport is always a good idea. Citizens of Canada and the United Kingdom should consult with their travel agent or cruise line regarding any documentation they may need for a Caribbean cruise.

Shore Excursions Typical excursions include a bus tour of the island or town, a visit to a local beach or liquor factory, boat trips, snorkeling or diving, and charter fishing. As far as island tours go, it's always safest to take a ship-arranged excursion, but it's almost never cheapest. You also sacrifice the freedom to explore at your own pace and the joys of venturing off the beaten path.

If you seek adventure, find a knowledgeable taxi driver or tour operator—they're usually within a stone's throw of the pier—and wander around on your own. A group of four to six people will find this option more economical and practical than will a single person or a couple.

Renting a car is also a good option on many islands—again, the more people, the better the deal. But get a good island map before you set off, and be sure to find out how long it will take you to get around. The boat will leave without you unless you're on a ship-arranged tour.

Conditions are ideal for water sports of all kinds; scuba diving, snorkeling, windsurfing, sailing, waterskiing, and fishing excursions abound. Your shore-excursion director can usually arrange these activities for you individually if the ship offers no formal excursion.

Many ships throw beach parties on a private island or an isolated beach in the Bahamas, the Grenadines, or (depending on the current political climate) Haiti. These parties are either included in your fare, with snorkeling gear and other water-sports equipment extra, or offered as an optional tour for which you pay.

Golf and tennis are popular among cruise passengers, and several lines—particularly NCL, Royal Caribbean, and Seabourn—offer special packages ashore. Most golf courses rent clubs, although many passengers bring their own.

Dining Cuisine on the Caribbean's islands is hard to classify. The region's history as a colonial battleground and ethnic melting pot creates plenty of variety. The gourmet French delicacies of Martinique, for example, are far removed from the hearty Spanish casseroles of Puerto Rico and even farther from the pungent curries of St. Lucia.

The one quality that defines most Caribbean cooking is its essential spiciness. Seafood is naturally quite popular. Some of it is even unique to the region, such as Caribbean lobster: Clawless and tougher than other types, it is more like crawfish than Maine lobster. And no island menu is complete without at least a half dozen dishes featuring conch, a mollusk similar to escargot that is served in the form of chowders, fritters, salads, and cocktails. Dress is generally casual—though in Caracas men should not wear shorts.

Category	Cost*
$$$	over $30
$$	$15–$30
$	under $15

**per person for a three-course meal, excluding drinks, service, and sales tax*

Antigua

Some say Antigua has so many beaches that you could visit a different one every day for a year. Most have snow-white sand, and many are backed by lavish resorts offering sailing, diving, windsurfing, and snorkeling.

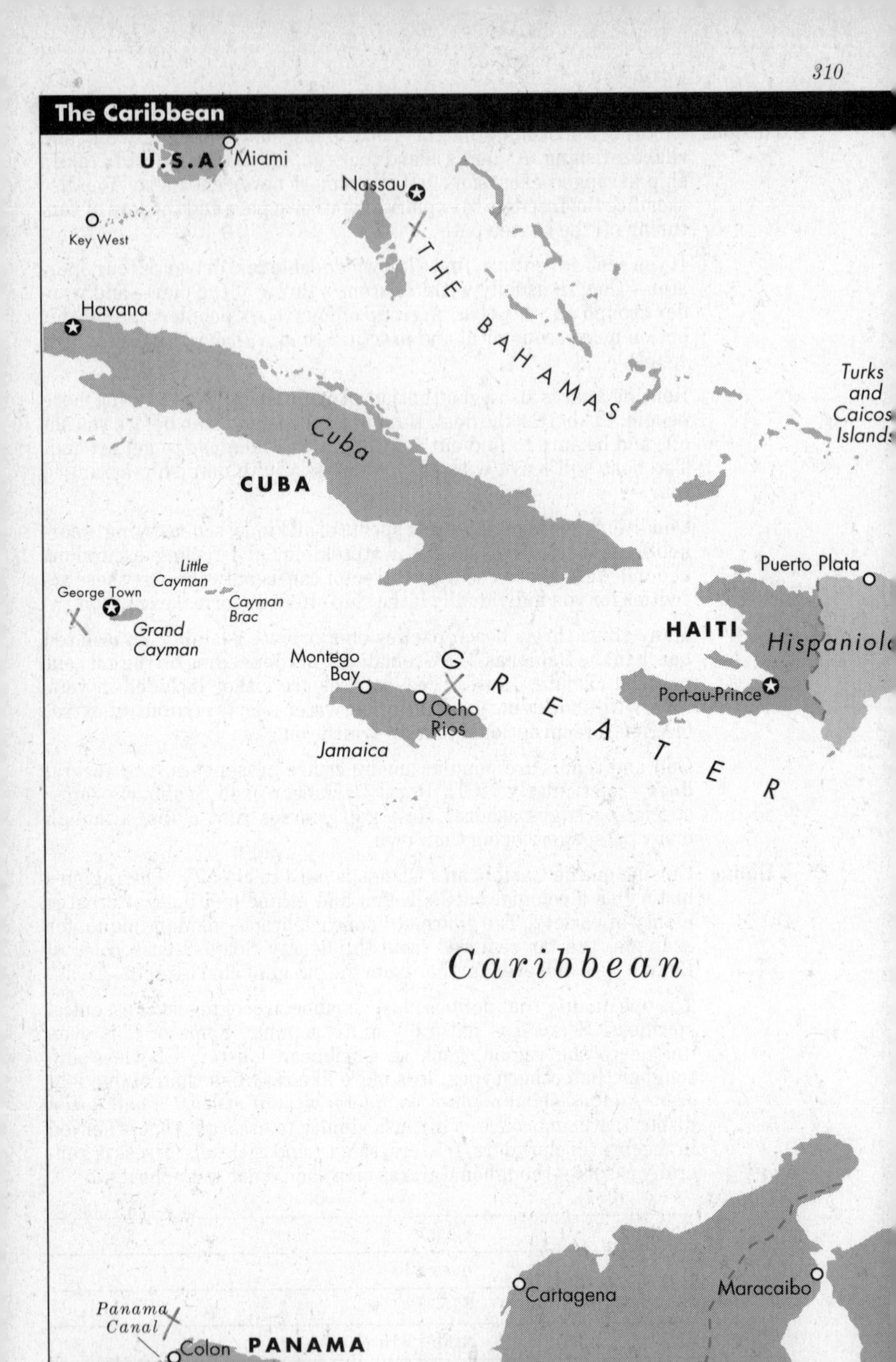
The Caribbean
U.S.A.
Miami
Key West
Nassau
THE BAHAMAS
Havana
Cuba
CUBA
Turks and Caicos Islands
Little Cayman
George Town
Cayman Brac
Grand Cayman
Puerto Plata
HAITI
Hispaniola
Montego Bay
Ocho Rios
Jamaica
GREATER
Port-au-Prince
Caribbean
Cartagena
Maracaibo
Panama Canal
Colon
PANAMA
Panama City
COLOMBIA

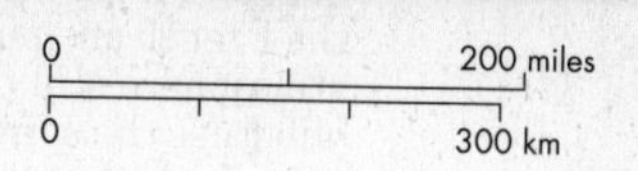
0
200 miles
0
300 km

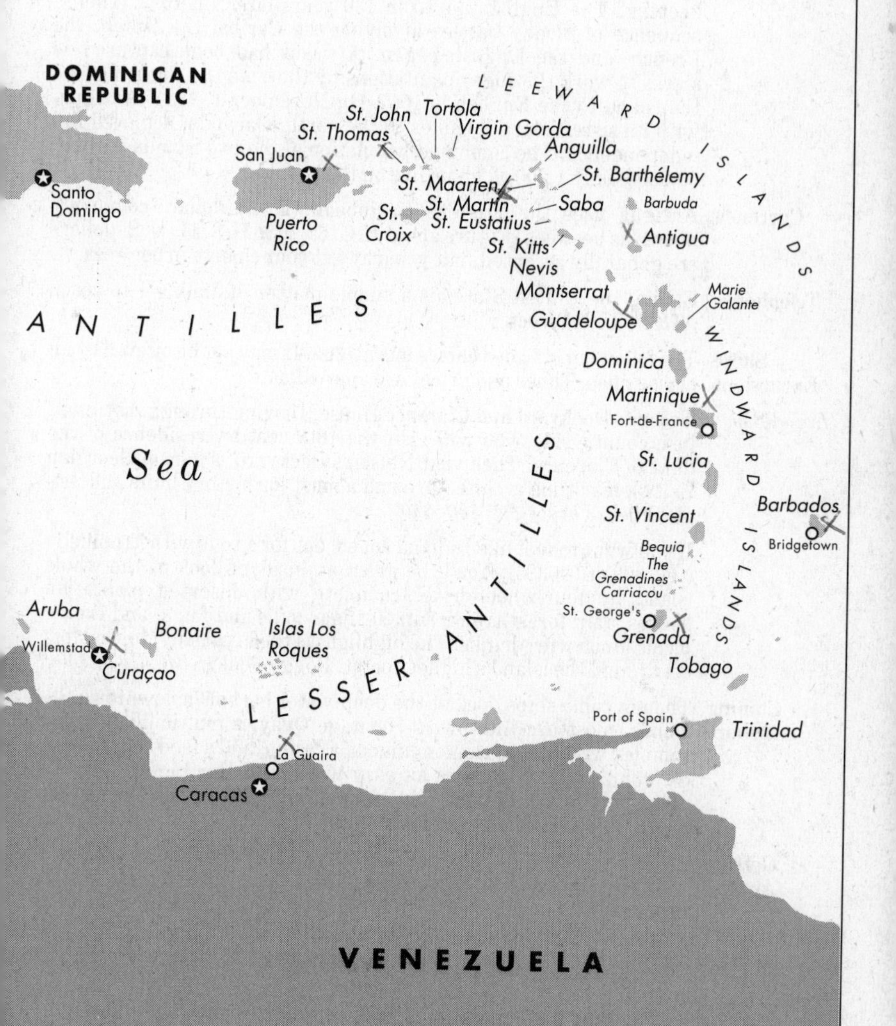
N
ATLANTIC OCEAN
DOMINICAN REPUBLIC
Santo Domingo
San Juan
Puerto Rico
St. John
St. Thomas
Tortola
Virgin Gorda
St. Croix
LEEWARD ISLANDS
Anguilla
St. Barthélemy
St. Maarten
St. Martin
Saba
St. Eustatius
St. Kitts
Nevis
Barbuda
Antigua
Montserrat
Guadeloupe
Marie Galante
Dominica
WINDWARD ISLANDS
Martinique
Fort-de-France
St. Lucia
St. Vincent
Barbados
Bridgetown
Bequia
The Grenadines
Carriacou
St. George's
Grenada
Tobago
Port of Spain
Trinidad
ANTILLES
Sea
LESSER ANTILLES
Aruba
Willemstad
Curaçao
Bonaire
Islas Los Roques
La Guaira
Caracas
VENEZUELA

The larger of the British Leeward Islands, Antigua was the headquarters from which Lord Horatio Nelson made his forays against the French and pirates in the late 18th century. A decidedly British atmosphere still prevails, underscored by a collection of pubs that will raise the spirits of every Anglophile. Cruise passengers with a taste for history will want to explore English Harbour and its carefully restored Nelson's Dockyard, as well as tour an 18th-century Royal Naval base, old forts, historic churches, and tiny villages. Hikers can wander through a tropical rain forest lush with pineapples, bananas, and mangoes. Those of an archaeological bent will head for the megaliths of Greencastle to seek out some of the 30 excavations of ancient Indian sites.

About 4,000 years ago Antigua was home to a people called the Siboney. They disappeared mysteriously, and the island remained uninhabited for about 1,000 years. When Columbus sighted the 108-square-mile island in 1493, the Arawaks had already set up housekeeping. The English moved in 130 years later, in 1623. Then a sequence of bloody battles involving the Caribs, the Dutch, the French, and the English began. Africans had been captured as slaves to work the sugar plantations by the time the French ceded the island to the English in 1667. On November 1, 1981, Antigua, with its sister island 30 miles to the north, Barbuda, achieved full independence. The combined population of the two islands is about 90,000—only 1,200 of whom live on Barbuda.

Currency Antigua uses the Eastern Caribbean (E.C.) dollar, commonly known as beewees. Figure about E.C. $2.70 to U.S. $1. U.S. dollars are generally accepted, but you may get your change in beewees.

Telephones Calling the United States is a simple matter of dialing 1 to reach **AT&T**'s USADirect.

Shore Excursions The following is a good choice in Antigua. It may not be offered by all cruise lines. Times and prices are approximate.

Island Sights **Nelson's Dockyard and Clarence House.** Driving through Antigua's lush countryside, you will visit the 18th-century residence of the duke of Clarence. Then visit Nelson's Dockyard, a gem of Georgian British maritime architecture and a must for history buffs and Anglophiles. *3 hrs. Cost: $30–$40.*

If you want to feel like Indiana Jones, opt for a tour with **Tropikelly** (tel. 809/461–0383). You'll be given an insider's look at the whole island by four-wheel-drive, complete with deserted plantation houses, rain-forest trails, ruined sugar mills and forts, and even a picnic lunch with drinks. The highlight is the luxuriant tropical forest around the island's highest point, Boggy Peak. *5 hrs. Cost: $60.*

Coming Ashore Though some ships dock at the deep-water harbor in downtown St. John's, most use the town's Heritage Quay, a multimillion-dollar complex with shops, condominiums, a casino, and a food court. Most St. John's attractions are an easy walk from Heritage Quay; the older part of the city is eight blocks away. A tourist information booth is in the main docking building.

Getting Around Avoid public buses. They're unreliable and hard to find. If you don't want to explore St. John's on foot, hire a taxi. If you intend to tour beyond this port city consider renting a car or hiring a taxi driver/guide.

By Car To rent a car, you'll need a valid driver's license and a temporary permit, which is available through the rental agent for $12. Rentals average about $50 per day, with unlimited mileage. Driving is on the left, and Antiguan roads are generally unmarked and full of potholes. Rental agencies are on High Street in St. John's, or they can be called from the terminal. Contact **Budget** (tel. 809/462–3009 or

800/648–4985), **Carib Car Rentals** (tel. 809/462–2062), or **National** (tel. 809/462–2113 or 800/468–0008), all in St. John's.

By Taxi Taxis meet every cruise ship. They are unmetered; fares are fixed, and drivers are required to carry a rate card. Tip drivers 10%. All taxi drivers double as guides, and you can arrange an island tour for about $20 per person, for up to four passengers. A tour of the Royal Dockyard takes about three hours and costs up to $60 for four. The most reliable and informed driver-guides are at **Capital Car Rental** (High St., St. John's, tel. 809/462–0863).

Exploring Antigua

Numbers in the margin correspond to points of interest on the Antigua map.

1 **St. John's** is home to about 40,000 people (nearly half the island's population). The city has seen better days, but there are some notable sights.

At the far south end of town, where Market Street forks into Valley and All Saints roads, locals jam the **marketplace** every Friday and Saturday to buy and sell fruits, vegetables, fish, and spices. Be sure to ask before you aim a camera, and expect the subject of your shot to ask for a tip.

If you have a serious interest in archaeology, see the historical displays at the **Museum of Antigua and Barbuda.** The colonial building that houses the museum is the former courthouse, which dates from 1750. *Church and Market Sts., tel. 809/462–1469. Admission free. Open weekdays 8:30–4, Sat. 10–1.*

Two blocks east of the Museum of Antigua and Barbuda on Church Street is **St. John's Cathedral.** The Anglican church sits on a hilltop, surrounded by its churchyard. At the south gate are figures said to have been taken from one of Napoléon's ships. A previous structure on this site was destroyed by an earthquake in 1843, so the interior of the current church is completely encased in pitch pine to forestall heavy damage from future quakes. *Between Long and Newcastle Sts., tel. 809/461–0082. Admission free.*

2 A favorite car excursion is to follow Fort Road northwest out of town. After 2 miles you'll come to the ruins of **Ft. James,** named for King James II. If you continue on this road, you'll arrive at **Dickenson Bay,** with its string of smart, expensive resorts on one of the many beautiful beaches you will pass.

3 In the opposite direction from St. John's, 8 miles south on All Saints Road is **Liberta,** one of the first settlements founded by freed slaves. East of the village, on Monk's Hill, are the ruins of Ft. George, built in 1669.

4 **Falmouth,** 1½ miles farther south, sits on a lovely bay, backed by former sugar plantations and sugar mills. St. Paul's Church, dating from the late 18th and early 19th centuries, held services for the military in Nelson's time; it has been restored and is now used for Sunday worship.

5 **English Harbour,** the most famous of Antigua's attractions, lies on the coast just south of Falmouth. The Royal Navy abandoned the station in 1889, but it has been restored as Nelson's Dockyard, which epitomizes the colonial Caribbean. Within the compound are crafts shops, hotels, a marina, and restaurants. The Admiral's House Museum has several rooms displaying ship models, a model of English Harbour, and various artifacts from Nelson's days. *Tel. 809/463–1053. Admission: $2. Open daily 8–6.*

The English Harbor area has a number of other attractions. On a ridge overlooking Nelson's Dockyard is Clarence House, built in 1787 and once the home of the duke of Clarence. As you leave the dockyard, turn right at the crossroads in English Harbour and drive

Dows Hill
Interpretation Center, **6**
English Harbour, **5**
Falmouth, **4**
Ft. James, **2**
Liberta, **3**
St. John's, **1**

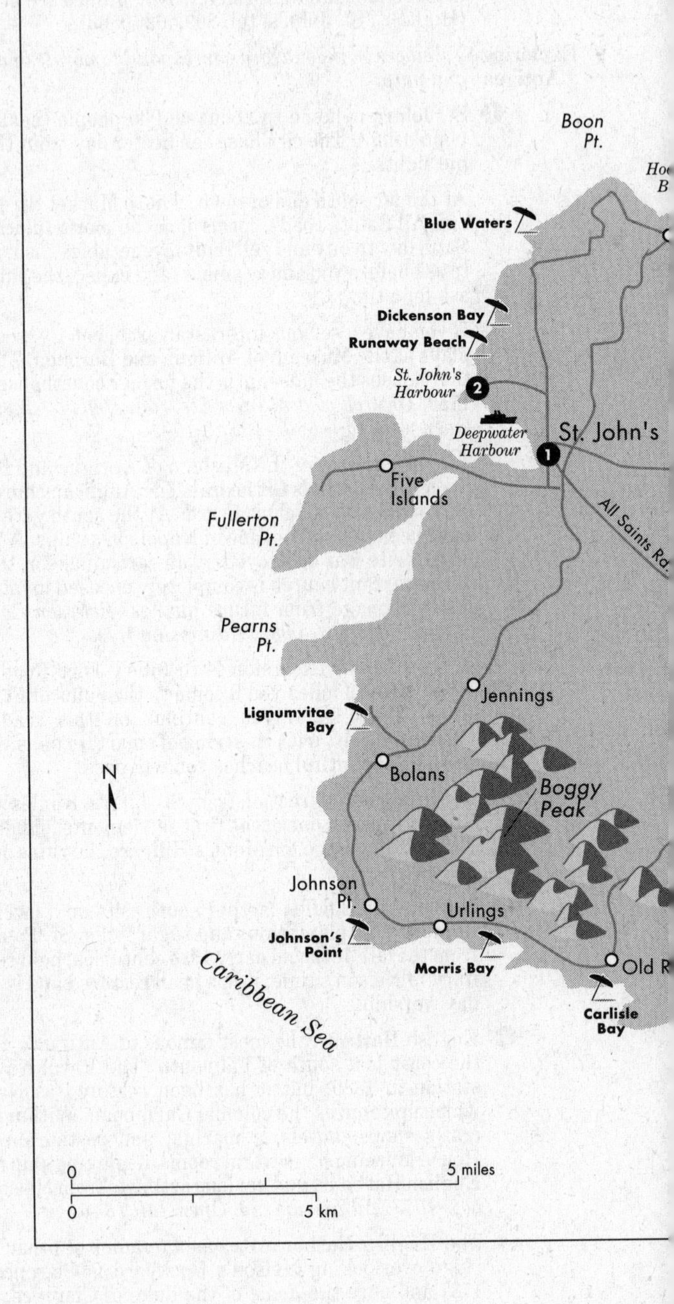

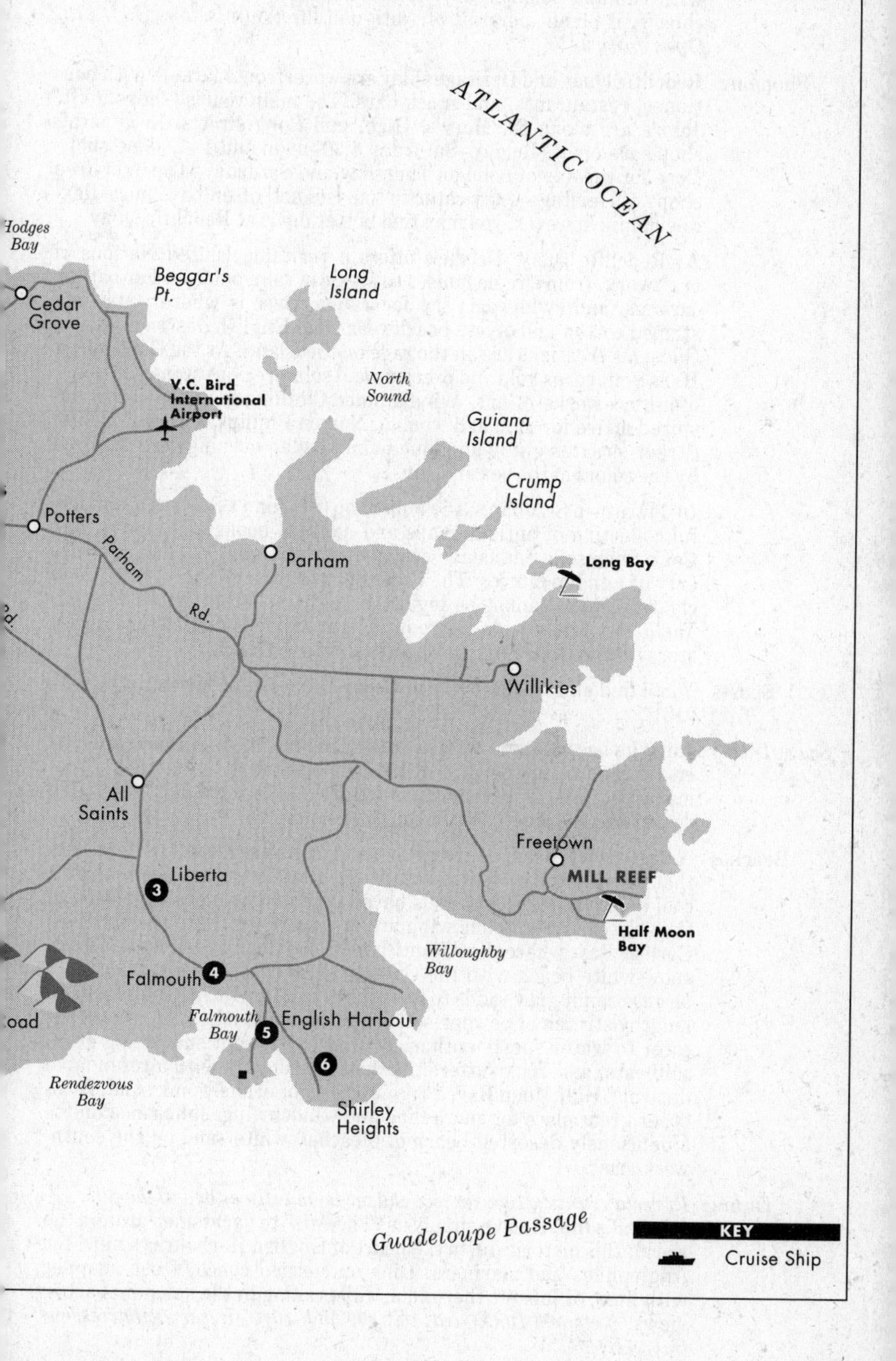
ATLANTIC OCEAN
Hodges Bay
Beggar's Pt.
Long Island
Cedar Grove
North Sound
V.C. Bird International Airport
Guiana Island
Crump Island
Potters
Parham Rd.
Parham
Long Bay
Willikies
All Saints
Freetown
MILL REEF
Liberta
Half Moon Bay
Willoughby Bay
Falmouth
Falmouth Bay
English Harbour
Rendezvous Bay
Shirley Heights
Guadeloupe Passage
KEY
Cruise Ship

up to Shirley Heights for a spectacular harbor view. Nearby, the **6** **Dows Hill Interpretation Center** chronicles the island's history and culture from Amerindian times to the present. A highlight of the center is its multimedia presentation in which illuminated displays, incorporating lifelike figures and colorful tableaux, are presented with running commentary, television, and music—resulting in a cheery, if bland, portrait of Antiguan life. *Admission: E.C. $15. Open daily 9–5.*

Shopping **Redcliffe Quay** and **Heritage Quay** are waterfront markets with boutiques, restaurants, and snack bars. The main tourist shops in St. John's are along **St. Mary's, High,** and **Long streets.** In general, shops are open Monday–Saturday 8:30–noon and 1–4; some shops close for the day at noon on Thursday and Saturday. The duty-free shops of Heritage Quay cater to tourists and often have more flexible hours; however, you may find better deals at Redcliffe Quay.

At Redcliffe Quay, **Decibels** offers a veritable United Nations of craftwork, from Creole houses to Mexican raku pottery. For batiks, sarongs, and swimwear, try **Jacaranda. Base** is where you'll find striped cotton-and-Lycra beachwear from English designer Steven Giles; his creations are all the rage on the island. At the **Goldsmitty,** Hans Smit turns gold and precious and semiprecious stones into one-of-a-kind works of art. **Windjammer Clothing** sells nautically inspired attire for men and women. **Noreen Phillips,** across Redcliffe Street, creates glitzy appliqued and beaded eveningwear inspired by the colors of the sea and sunset.

In downtown St. John's, the **Map Shop** (St. John's St.) has a wonderful collection of antique maps and nautical books and charts, and **CoCo Shop** sells Sea Island cotton designs, Daks clothing, and Liberty of London fabrics. The **Cigar Shop** (Heritage Quay) has Cuban cigars. (These cannot be legally brought into the United States.) You'll also find a wide range of duty-free shops and factory-outlet stores, from **Body Shop** to **Benetton, Polo** to **Gucci.**

Sports
Golf You'll find an 18-hole course at **Cedar Valley Golf Club** (tel. 809/462–0161).

Scuba Diving Antigua has plenty of wrecks, reefs, and marine life. **Dockyard Divers** (St. Johns, tel. 809/464–8591), run by British ex–merchant seaman Captain A. G. Finchman, is one of the oldest and most reputable diving and snorkeling outfits on the island.

Beaches Antigua's 366 beaches are public, and many are dotted with resorts that provide water-sports-equipment rentals and a place to grab a cool drink. Since most hotels have taxi stands, you can get back to the ship easily. The following are just a few excellent possibilities: **Carlisle Bay,** where the Atlantic meets the Caribbean Sea, is a long, snow-white beach with the Curtain Bluff resort as a backdrop. A large coconut grove adds to its tropical beauty. **Dickenson Bay** has a lengthy stretch of powder-soft white sand and a host of hotels that cater to water-sports enthusiasts (most will rent snorkeling gear, sailboats, and Windsurfers to cruise passengers with a refundable deposit). **Half Moon Bay,** a ¾-mile crescent of shell-pink sand, is another great place for snorkeling and windsurfing. **Johnsons Point** is a deliciously deserted beach of bleached white sand on the southwest coast.

Dining *In restaurants a 10% service charge is usually added to the bill.*

$$ **Admiral's Inn.** Known simply as "The Ads" to yachtsmen around the world, this historic inn in the heart of English Harbour is a must for Anglophiles and mariners. Dine on curried conch, fresh snapper with lime, or lobster thermidor while taking in the splendid harbor views. *Nelson's Dockyard, tel. 809/460–1027. Reservations essential. AE, MC, V.*

$$ **Redcliffe Tavern.** Set amid the courtyards of Redcliffe Quay, on the second floor of a colonial warehouse, this appealing restaurant has an inventive menu that is part northern Italian, part Continental, part Creole, and all fresh. Antique water-pumping equipment, salvaged from all over the island, adds to the unusual dining experience. *Redcliffe Quay, St. John's, tel. 809/461–4557. AE, MC, V.*

Aruba

Though the "A" in the ABC (Aruba, Bonaire, Curaçao) Islands is small—only 19.6 miles long and 6 miles at its widest—the island's national anthem proclaims "the greatness of our people is their great cordiality," and this is no exaggeration. Once a member of the Netherlands Antilles, Aruba became independent within the Netherlands in 1986, with its own royally appointed governor, a democratic government, and a 21-member elected parliament. Long secure in a solid economy, with good education, housing, and health care, the island's population of about 81,500 regards tourists as welcome guests and treats them accordingly. Waiters serve you with smiles and solid eye contact. English is spoken everywhere. In addition to the ships that call at Aruba on southern Caribbean itineraries, the island is the home port for Seawind's *Seawind Crown.*

The island's distinctive beauty lies in the stark contrast between the sea and the countryside: rocky deserts, cactus jungles, secluded coves, and aquamarine panoramas with crashing waves. It's famous mostly, however, for its casinos.

Currency Arubans accept U.S. dollars, so you've no need to exchange money, except for pocket change for bus fare or pay phones. Local currency is the Aruban florin (AFl). At press time, U.S. $1 will get you AFl 1.77 cash or AFl 1.79 in traveler's checks. Note that the Netherlands Antilles florin used in Bonaire and Curaçao is not accepted on Aruba.

Telephones International calls are placed at the phone center in the cruise terminal. To reach the United States, dial 001, the area code, and the local number.

Shore Excursions The following are good choices on Aruba. They may not be offered by all cruise lines. Times and prices are approximate.

Island Sights **Aruba Town and Countryside Drive.** A comprehensive town-and-country bus tour takes in all the island sights. After the tour, passengers may stay in town, on the beach, or at the casino. *3 hrs. Cost: $25.*

Undersea Creatures **Atlantis Submarine.** Aboard a 65-foot submarine, passengers dive 50–90 feet below the surface along Aruba's Barcadera Reef. *1½ hrs. Cost: $68.*

Glass-Bottom Boat Tour. The view of undersea creatures is less dramatic than aboard the *Atlantis* submarine, but the price is less expensive, too. *1½ hrs. Cost: $25.*

Coming Ashore Ships tie up at the Aruba Port Authority cruise terminal; inside are a tourist information booth and duty-free shops. From here, you're a five-minute walk from various shopping districts and downtown Oranjestad. Just turn right out of the cruise-terminal entrance.

Getting Around

By Bus Buses run hourly between the beach hotels and Oranjestad. They also stop across the street from the cruise terminal on L.G. Smith Boulevard. Round-trip fare is $1.50, exact change.

By Car It's easy to rent a car, Jeep, or motorbike in Aruba, and most roads are in excellent condition. Contact **Avis** (tel. 297/8–28787), **Budget** (tel. 297/8–28600), or **Hertz** (tel. 297/8–24545). Rates begin at about $45 a day.

By Taxi Taxis can be flagged down on the street. Because cabs have no meters, rates are fixed but should be confirmed before you get in. All drivers have participated in the government's Tourism Awareness Programs and have received a Tourism Guide Certificate. An hour tour of the island by taxi will cost about $35 for up to four people.

Exploring Aruba *Numbers in the margin correspond to points of interest on the Aruba map.*

❶ Aruba's charming capital, **Oranjestad,** is best explored on foot. If you're interested in Dutch architecture, begin at the corner of Oude School Straat and go three blocks toward the harbor to Wilhelminastraat, where some of the buildings date back to Oranjestad's 1790 founding. Walk west and you'll pass old homes, a government building, and the Protestant church. When you reach Shuttestraat again, turn left and go one block to Zoutmanstraat.

The small **Archaeology Museum** in Oranjestad has two rooms of Indian artifacts, farm and domestic utensils, and skeletons. *Zoutmanstraat 1, tel. 297/8–28979. Admission free. Open weekdays 8–noon and 1:30–4:30.*

Ft. Zoutman, the island's oldest building, was built in 1796 and used as a major fortress in skirmishes between British and Curaçao troops. The Willem III tower was added in 1868. The fort's Historical Museum displays island relics and artifacts in an 18th-century Aruban house. *Oranjestraat, tel. 297/8–26099. Admission: $1.25. Open weekdays 9–noon and 1:30–4:30.*

Just behind the St. Francis Roman Catholic Church is the **Numismatic Museum,** displaying coins and paper money from more than 400 countries. *Zuidstraat 27, tel. 297/8–28831. Admission free. Open weekdays 7:30–noon and 1–4:30.*

The "real" Aruba—or what's left of its wild, untamed beauty—can be experienced only by taking a car or taxi into the countryside. (Be aware that there are no public bathrooms anywhere, except in a few restaurants.)

❷ The 541-foot peak of **Hooiberg** (Haystack Hill) is located mid-island; you can climb 562 steps to the top for an impressive view. To get there from Oranjestad, turn onto Caya C.F. Croes (shown on island maps as 7A) toward Santa Cruz; the peak will be on your right.

For a shimmering panorama of blue-green sea, drive east on L.G. Smith Boulevard toward San Nicolas. Turn left where you see the drive-in theater. At the first intersection, turn right, then follow the ❸ curve to the right to **Frenchman's Pass,** a dark, luscious stretch of highway arbored by overhanging trees. Legend claims the French and native Indians warred here during the 17th century for control of the island.

❹ Near Frenchman's Pass are the cement ruins of the **Balashi Gold Mine** (follow the directions to Frenchman's Pass, above, and then take the dirt road veering to the right), a lovely place to picnic, listen to the parakeets, and contemplate the towering cacti. A gnarled divi-divi tree stands guard at the entrance.

❺ The area called **Spanish Lagoon** is where pirates once hid to repair their ships (follow L.G. Smith Boulevard, which crosses straight over the lagoon). It's a picturesque place for a picnic or to enjoy the island scenery.

❻ **San Nicolas** is Aruba's oldest village. In the 1980s, the town, with its oil refinery, was a bustling port with a rough-and-tumble quality; now it's dedicated to tourism, with the Main Street promenade full of interesting kiosks. Charlie's Bar (Zeppenfeldstraat 56) on the main street is a popular tourist lunch spot, good for both gawking at the thousands of license plates, old credit cards, baseball pennants, and hard hats covering every inch of the walls and ceiling, and for gorging on "jumbo and dumbo" shrimp.

Shopping Caya G.F. Betico Croes in Oranjestad is Aruba's chief shopping street. The stores are full of Dutch porcelains and figurines, as befits the island's Netherlands heritage. Also consider the Dutch cheeses (you are allowed to bring up to one pound of hard cheese through U.S. Customs), hand-embroidered linens, and any product made from the native plant aloe vera, such as sunburn cream, face masks, and skin fresheners. There is no sales tax, and Arubans consider it rude to haggle.

Artesania Aruba (L.G. Smith Blvd. 178, tel. 297/8–37494) has charming home-crafted pottery and folk objets d'art. **Aruba Trading Company** (Caya G.F. Betico Croes 12, tel. 297/8–22602) discounts brand-name perfumes and cosmetics (first floor), and jewelry and men's and women's clothes (second floor) up to 30%. **Gandleman's Jewelers** (Caya G.F. Betico Croes 5–A, tel. 297/8–34433) sells jewelry, including a full line of watches. **Wulfsen & Wulfsen** (Caya G.F. Betico Croes 52, tel. 297/8–23823) is one of Holland's best stores for fine-quality clothes and shoes.

Sports
Fishing Contact **De Palm Tours** in Oranjestad (tel. 297/8–24400 or 297/8–24545) for information on fishing charters.

Golf An all-new, 18-hole, par-71 golf course, Tierra del Sol (Malmokweg, tel. 297/8–67800), opened in 1995 on the northwest coast near the California Lighthouse. Designed by Robert Trent Jones, the course combines Aruba's native beauty, such as the flora, cacti, and rock formations, with the lush greens of the world's best courses. The $115 greens fee includes a golf cart. Club rentals are $25–$40. The **Aruba Golf Club** near San Nicolas (tel. 297/8–42006) has a nine-hole course with 20 sand and five water traps, roaming goats, and lots of cacti. Greens fees are $7.50 for nine holes, $10 for 18. Caddies and rental clubs are available.

Hiking **De Palm Tours** (tel. 297/8–24400 or 297/8–24545) offers a guided three-hour trip to remote sites of unusual natural beauty accessible only on foot. The fee is $25 per person, including refreshments and transportation; a minimum of four people is required.

Horseback Riding At **Rancho El Paso** (tel. 297/8–63310), one-hour jaunts ($15) take you through countryside flanked by cacti, divi-divi trees, and aloe-vera plants; two-hour trips ($30) go to the beach as well. Wear lots of sunblock.

Water Sports **De Palm Tours** (tel. 297/8–24400 or 297/8–24545) has a near monopoly on water sports, including equipment and instruction for scuba diving, snorkeling, and windsurfing. However, **Pelican Watersports** (tel. 297/8–31228 or 297/8–24739) and **Red Sail Sports** (tel. 297/8–61603), may offer cheaper rates on water-sports packages, including snorkeling, sailing, windsurfing, fishing, and scuba diving.

Beaches Beaches in Aruba are not only beautiful but clean. On the north side the water is too choppy for swimming, but the views are great. **Palm Beach**—which stretches behind the Americana, Aruba Palm Beach, Holiday Inn, Hyatt, Radisson, and Wyndham hotels—is the center of Aruban tourism, offering the best in swimming, sailing, and fishing. In high season, however, it's packed. **Manchebo Beach**, by the Bucuti Beach Resort, is an impressively wide stretch of white powder and Aruba's unofficial topless beach. On the island's eastern tip, tiny **Baby Beach** is as placid as a wading pool and only 4 or 5 feet deep—perfect for tots and bad swimmers. Thatched shaded areas provide relief from the sun. You'll see topless bathers here from time to time as well.

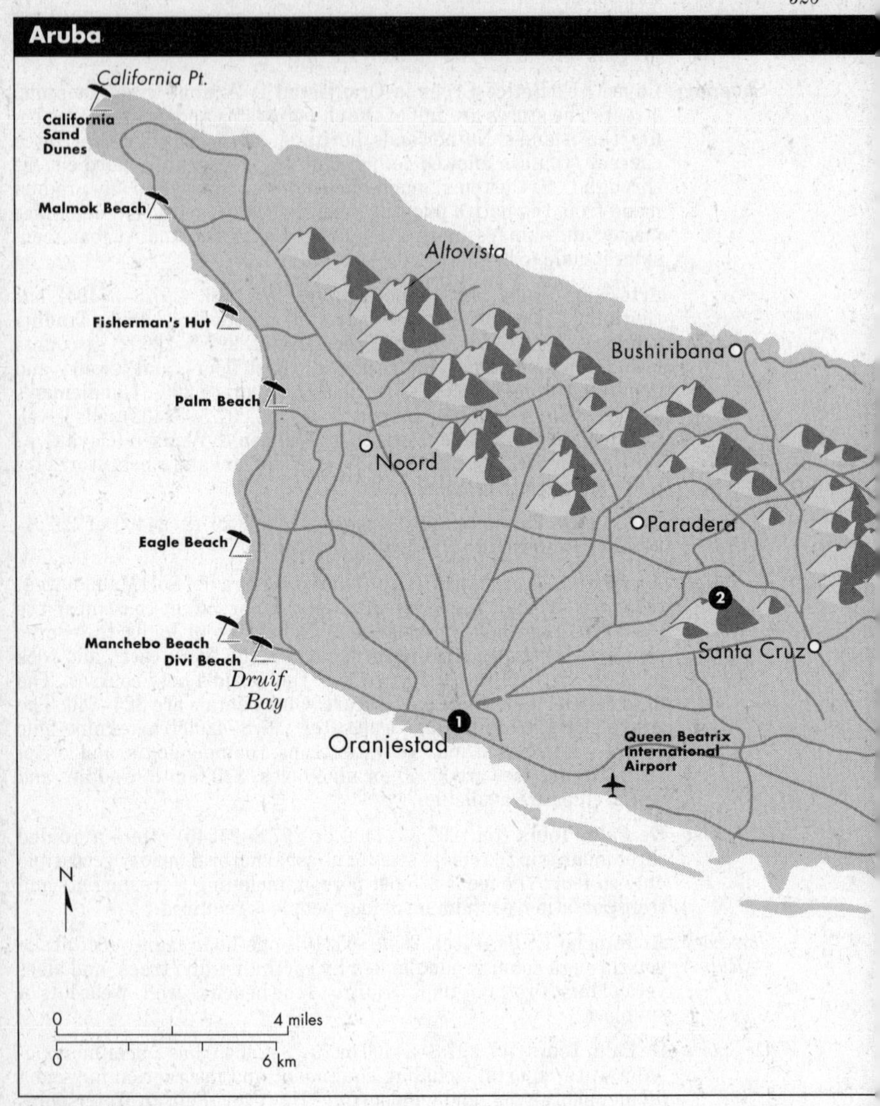

Balashi Gold Mine, **4**
Frenchman's Pass, **3**
Hooiberg (Haystack Hill), **2**
Oranjestad, **1**
San Nicolas, **6**
Spanish Lagoon, **5**

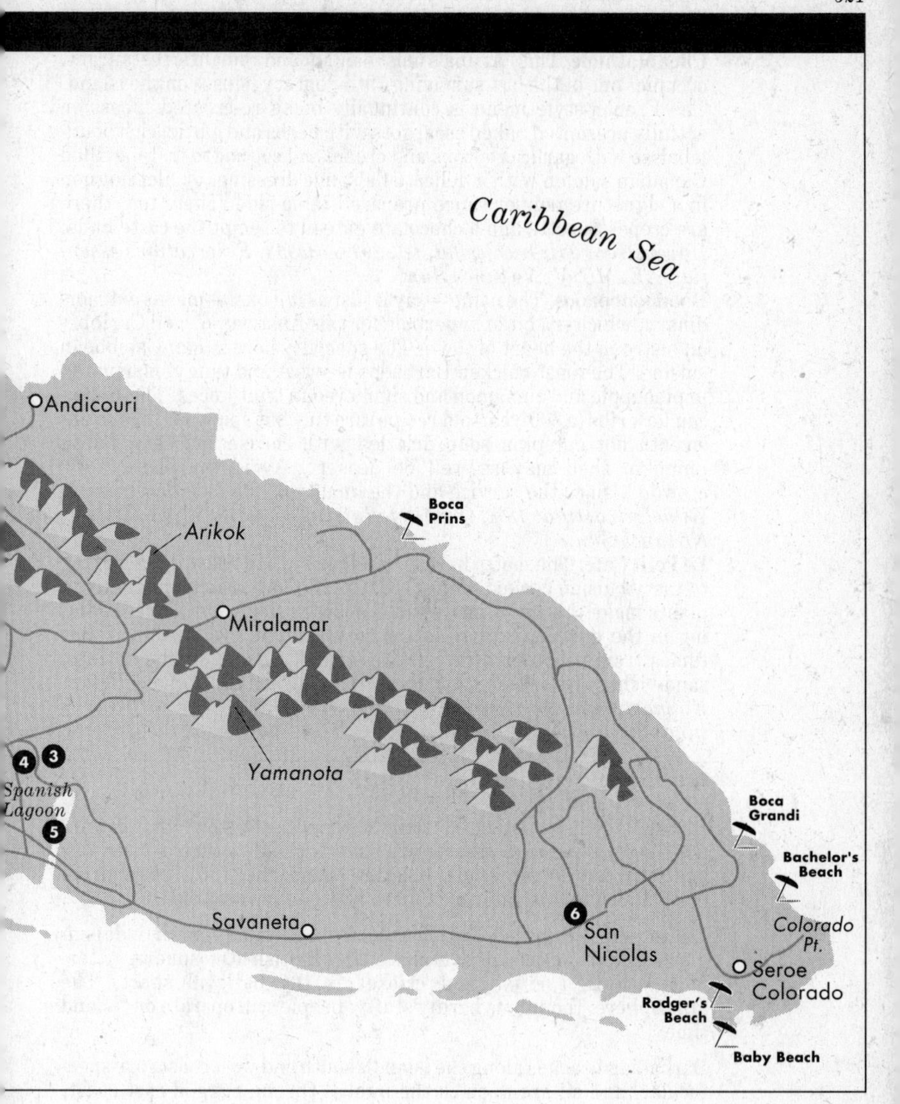
Caribbean Sea
Andicouri
Arikok
Boca Prins
Miralamar
Yamanota
Spanish Lagoon
Savaneta
San Nicolas
Boca Grandi
Bachelor's Beach
Colorado Pt.
Seroe Colorado
Rodger's Beach
Baby Beach

Dining *Restaurants usually add a 10%–15% service charge.*

$$$ **Chez Mathilde.** This, Aruba's most elegant and romantic restaurant, occupies one of the last surviving 19th-century houses on the island. The French-style menu is continually being re-created. Feast on artfully presented baked escargots with herbs and garlic, rich bouillabaisse with garlic croutons and cream and cognac to taste, grilled Canadian salmon with a delicate balsamic dressing, or filet mignon in a signature pepper sauce prepared table-side. Then, too, there are crêpes Suzette and a chocolate gâteau to tempt the taste buds. *Havenstraat 23, Oranjestad, tel. 297/8–34968. Reservations essential. AE, MC, V. No lunch Sun.*

$–$$ **Boonoonoonoos.** The name—say it just as it looks!—means extraordinary, which is a bit of hyperbole for this Austrian-owned Caribbean bistro in the heart of town. The specialty here is Pan-Caribbean cuisine: The roast chicken Barbados is sweet and tangy, marinated in pineapple and cinnamon and simmered in fruit juices. The Jamaican jerk ribs (a 300-year-old recipe) are tiny but spicy, and the satin-smooth hot pumpkin soup drizzled with cheese and served in a pumpkin shell may as well be dessert. Avoid the place if it's crowded, since the service and the quality of the food deteriorate. *Wilhelminastraat 18A, Oranjestad, tel. 297/8–31888. AE, MC, V. No lunch Sun.*

$ **Le Petit Café.** The motto here is "Romancing the Stone"—referring to tasty cuisine cooked on hot stones. The low ceiling and hanging plants make this an intimate lunch spot for shoppers. Alfresco dining in the bustling square lets diners keep an eye on things, but fumes from nearby traffic tend to spoil the meal. Jumbo shrimp, sandwiches, ice cream, and fresh fruit dishes are light delights. *Emmastraat 1, Oranjestad, tel. 297/8–26577. AE, DC, MC, V. No lunch Sun.*

Barbados

Barbados is a sophisticated island with a life of its own that continues long after cruise passengers have packed up their suntan oils and returned to their ships. A resort island since the 1700s, Barbados has slowly cultivated a civilized attitude toward tourists.

Under uninterrupted British rule for 340 years—until independence in 1966—Barbados retains a very British atmosphere. Afternoon tea is a ritual and cricket is the national sport. The atmosphere, though, is hardly stuffy; people still operate on "island time."

Barbadian beaches along the island's south and west coasts are spectacular, and all are open to the public. On the rugged east coast, where "Bajans" themselves have vacation homes, the Atlantic surf pounds against gigantic boulders. The northeast is dominated by rolling hills and valleys covered by impenetrable acres of sugarcane. Elsewhere on the island are historic plantations, stalactite-studded caves, a wildlife preserve, and tropical gardens, which are linked by almost 900 miles of good roads. Bridgetown, the capital, is a busy city with more traffic than charm.

Currency One Barbados dollar (BDS$) equals about U.S. 50¢. Both currencies are accepted everywhere on the island. Always ask which currency is being quoted.

Telephones Public phones are at the cruise-ship terminal. Use the same dialing procedure as in the United States, or dial for assistance for collect and credit-card calls.

Shore Excursions The following are good choices on Barbados. They may not be offered by all cruise lines. Times and prices are approximate.

Island Sights **Harrison's Cave.** After a bus tour of the island's central parishes, passengers board an electric tram for a one-hour tour of this series of limestone caves. A highlight is the 40-foot underground waterfall that plunges into a deep pool. *3 hrs. Cost: $33.*

Undersea Creatures **Atlantis Submarine.** A 50-foot sub dives as deep as 150 feet below the surface for an exciting view of Barbados's profuse marine life. Most passengers find this trip to the depths to be a thrilling experience. *1½ hrs. Cost: $70.*

Coming Ashore Up to eight ships at a time can dock at Bridgetown's Deep Water Harbour, on the northwest side of Carlisle Bay. The cruise-ship terminal has duty-free shops and a post office, telephone station, tourist information desk, and taxi stand. To get downtown, follow the Careenage. By foot, it will take you about 15 minutes, or you can take a cab for $1.50 each way. Taxi tours of the island are available for $16 per hour.

Getting Around

By Bus The bus system is good, connecting Bridgetown with all parts of the island, but the buses can be crowded. Service is frequent, but somewhat irregular, so leave plenty of time to make it back to the ship. The fare is BDS$1.50 wherever you go.

By Car Barbados is a pleasure to tour by car, provided you take along a map and don't mind asking directions. Driving is on the left. You'll need an international driver's license or Barbados driving permit to rent a car; get one at the rental agency for $5 with your valid home license. Contact **National** (tel. 809/426–0603) or **P&S Car Rentals** (tel. 809/424–2052). Cars with automatic transmission cost $65–$70 per day. Gas costs about $3 a gallon.

By Taxi Taxis await ships at the pier. The fare to Paradise, Brandon, or Brighton beaches runs $3–$5; to Holetown it's $7. Drivers accept U.S. dollars and expect a 10% tip. Taxis operate at a fixed hourly rate of $16, and drivers will cheerfully narrate a tour.

Exploring Barbados *Numbers in the margin correspond to points of interest on the Barbados map.*

Bridgetown

❶ The narrow strip of sea known as the Careenage made early **Bridgetown** a natural harbor. Here, working schooners were careened (turned on their sides) to be scraped of barnacles and repainted. Today, the Careenage serves mainly as a berth for pleasure yachts.

At the center of the bustling city is **Trafalgar Square.** The monument to Lord Nelson predates its London counterpart by about two decades. Also here are a war memorial and a three-dolphin fountain commemorating the advent of running water in Barbados in 1865.

The **House of Assembly** and **Parliament buildings** house the third-oldest Parliament of the British Commonwealth and are adjacent to Trafalgar Square. A series of stained-glass windows depicting British monarchs adorns these Victorian Gothic government buildings.

George Washington is said to have worshiped at **St. Michael's Cathedral** on his only trip outside the United States. The structure was nearly a century old when he visited in 1751; destroyed twice by hurricanes, it was rebuilt in 1780 and again in 1831.

Queen's Park, northeast of downtown Bridgetown, is the site of an immense baobab tree more than 10 centuries old. The historic Queen's Park House, former home of the commander of the British troops, has been converted into a theater and a restaurant. *Open daily 9–5.*

The intriguing **Barbados Museum** (about a mile south of downtown Bridgetown on Highway 7) has artifacts dating to Arawak days (around 400 B.C.), mementos of military history and everyday life in the 19th century, wildlife and natural history exhibits, a well-

Andromeda Gardens, **7**
Barbados Wildlife Reserve, **9**
Bridgetown, **1**
Codrington Theological College, **11**
Farley Hill, **8**
Flower Forest, **5**
Folkestone Marine Park, **2**
Gun Hill Signal Station, **6**
Harrison's Cave, **3**
Ragged Point Lighthouse, **12**
St. Nicholas Abbey, **10**
Welchman Hall Gully, **4**

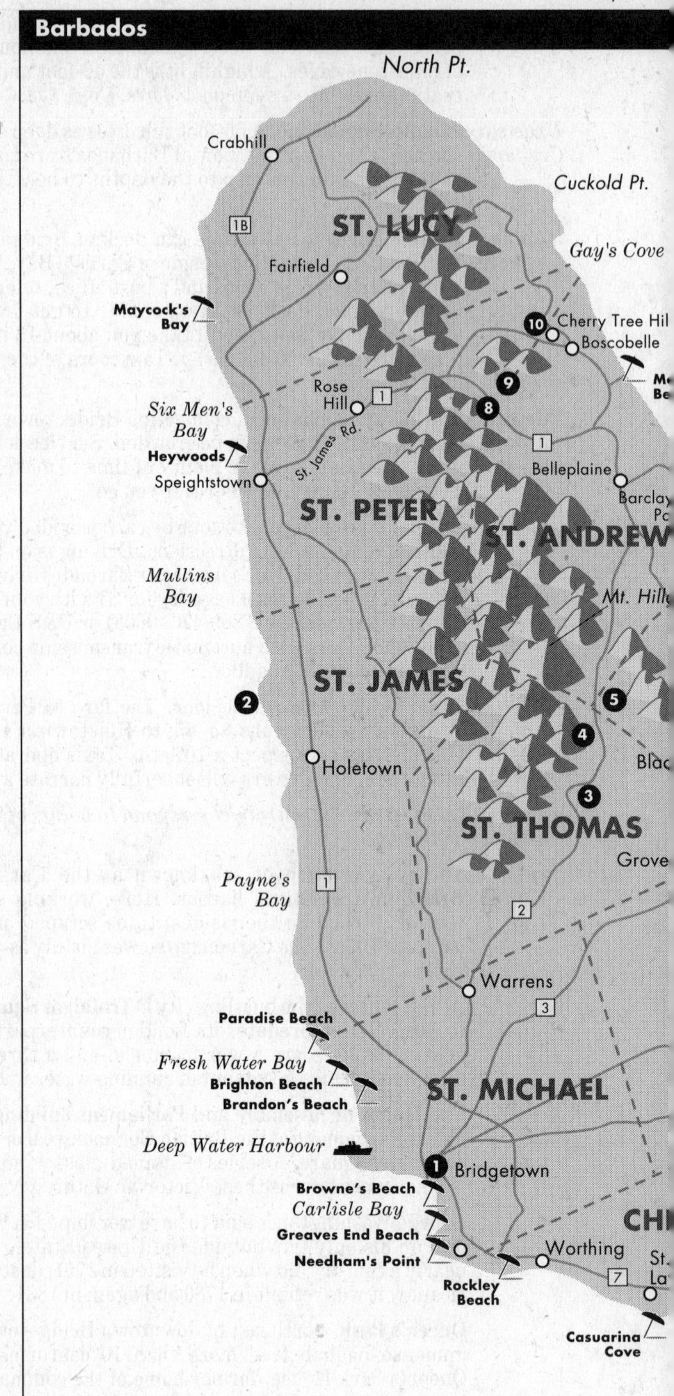

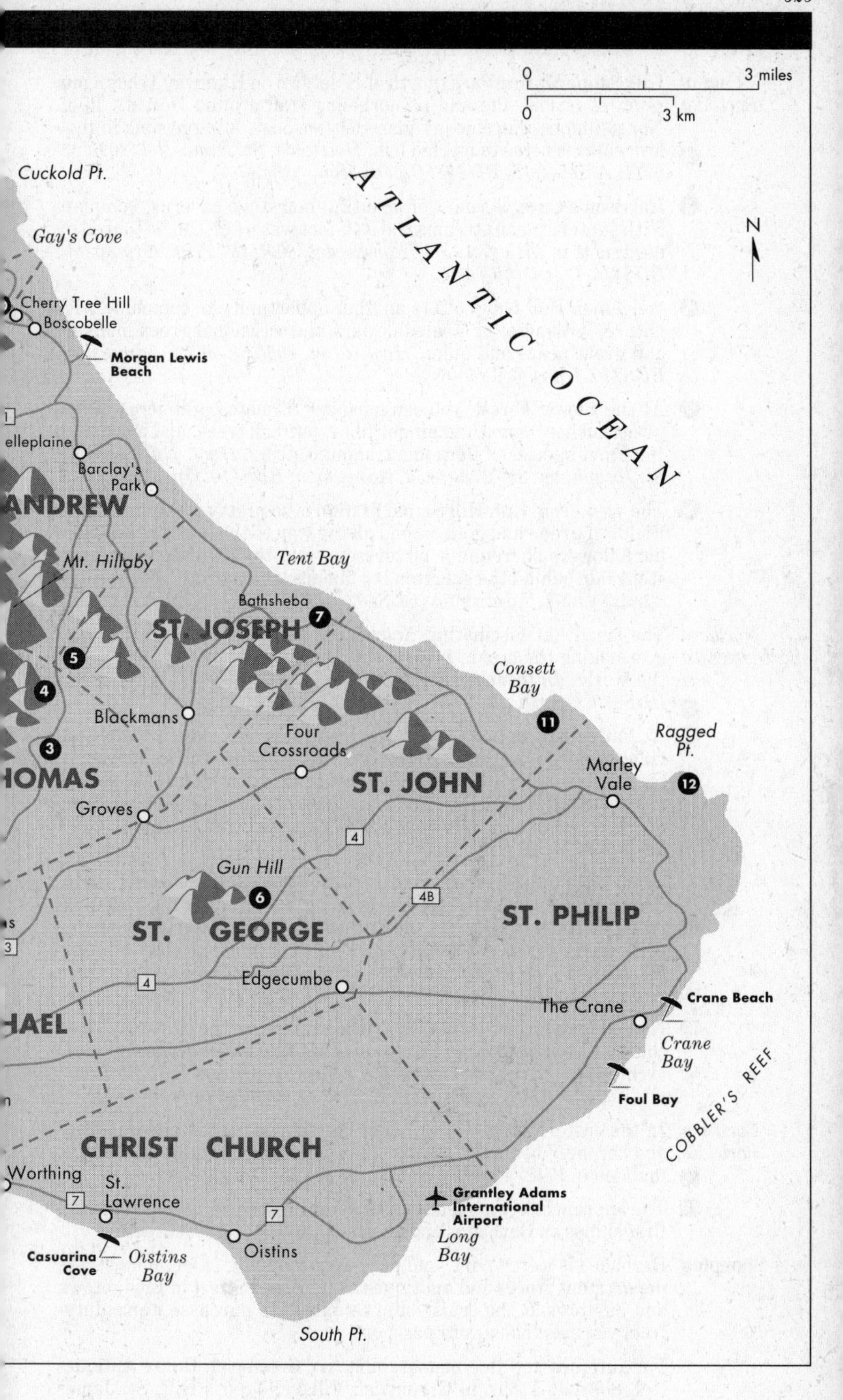

0
3 miles
0
3 km
ATLANTIC OCEAN
N
Cuckold Pt.
Gay's Cove
Cherry Tree Hill
Boscobelle
Morgan Lewis Beach
elleplaine
Barclay's Park
ANDREW
Mt. Hillaby
Tent Bay
Bathsheba
ST. JOSEPH
Consett Bay
Blackmans
Four Crossroads
Ragged Pt.
Marley Vale
HOMAS
ST. JOHN
Groves
Gun Hill
ST. PHILIP
ST. GEORGE
Edgecumbe
The Crane
Crane Beach
Crane Bay
HAEL
Foul Bay
COBBLER'S REEF
CHRIST CHURCH
Worthing
St. Lawrence
Grantley Adams International Airport
Long Bay
Casuarina Cove
Oistins Bay
Oistins
South Pt.

stocked gift shop, and a good café. *Garrison Savannah, tel. 809/427–0201. Admission: BDS$10. Open Mon.–Sat. 9–5, Sun. 2–6.*

Central Barbados

❷ **Folkestone Marine Park** (north of Holetown on Highway 1) has a museum of marine life and a snorkeling trail around Dottin's Reef. Nonswimmers can ride in a glass-bottom boat. A barge sunk in shallow water is home to myriad fish. *Holetown, St. James, tel. 809/422-2314. Admission: BDS$1. Closed Mon.*

❸ **Harrison's Cave,** a series of beautiful limestone caverns, complete with subterranean streams and a 40-foot waterfall, can be toured by electric tram. *Hwy. 2, St. Thomas, tel. 809/438–6640. Admission: BDS$15. Open daily 9–6.*

❹ **Welchman Hall Gully** offers another opportunity to commune with nature, with acres of labeled flowers, the occasional green monkey, and great peace and quiet. *Hwy. 2, tel. 809/438–6671. Admission: BDS$10. Open daily 9–5.*

❺ At the **Flower Forest,** you can meander through eight acres of fragrant bushes, canna and ginger lilies, puffball trees, and more than 100 other species of flora in a tranquil setting. *Hwy. 2, Richmond, St. Joseph, tel. 809/433–8152. Admission: BDS$10. Open daily 9–5.*

❻ The view from **Gun Hill Signal Station** is so pretty it seems unreal. Fields of green and gold extend all the way to the horizon, and brilliant flowers surround a picturesque gun tower. The white limestone lion behind the garrison is a famous landmark. *St. George, tel. 809/429–1358. Admission: BDS$8.*

Northern Barbados/East Coast

❼ The small but fascinating **Andromeda Gardens,** set into the cliffs overlooking the ocean, holds unusual plant specimens from around the world. *Bathsheba, St. Joseph, tel. 809/433–9384. Admission: BDS$10. Open daily 9–5.*

❽ At **Farley Hill** national park, you can roam through the imposing ruins of a once-magnificent plantation great house and its surrounding gardens, lawns, and towering royal palms. This part of Barbados has been dubbed the Scotland area because of its rugged landscape. *St. Peter, no phone. Admission: BDS$3 per car; walkers free. Open daily 8:30–6.*

❾ You'll encounter herons, land turtles, screeching peacocks, innumerable green monkeys, geese, brilliantly colored parrots, a kangaroo, and a friendly otter at the **Barbados Wildlife Reserve.** The fauna roam freely, so step carefully and keep your hands to yourself. *Farley Hill, St. Peter, tel. 809/422–8826. Admission: BDS$20. Open daily 10–5.*

❿ Named for a former owner, **St. Nicholas Abbey** is the oldest house on the island (circa 1650) and well worth visiting for its stone and wood architecture in the Jacobean style. *Near Cherry Tree Hill, St. Lucy, tel. 809/422–8725. Admission: BDS$5. Open weekdays 10–3:30.*

Southern Barbados

⓫ In the eastern corner of St. John Parish, the coral-stone buildings and serenely beautiful grounds of **Codrington Theological College,** founded in 1748, stand on a cliff overlooking Consett Bay.

⓬ The appropriately named **Ragged Point Lighthouse** is where the sun first shines on Barbados and its dramatic Atlantic seascape.

Shopping

Barbados is a free port, and duty-free shopping is found mostly in department stores and boutiques along **Broad Street** in Bridgetown and in stores at the cruise-ship terminal. To purchase items duty-free, you must show your passport.

For antiques and fine memorabilia, try **Greenwich House Antiques** (tel. 809/432–1169), in Greenwich Village, Trents Hill, St. James Parish. **Antiquaria** (tel. 809/426–0635), on Spring Garden Highway,

St. Michael's Row, next to the Anglican cathedral in Bridgetown, is another good place to search for antiques.

Exclusive designs in "wearable art" by Carol Cadogan are available at **Cotton Days Designs** in Ramsgate Cottage, Lower Bay Street, opposite St. Patrick's Cathedral in Bridgetown (tel. 809/427–7191), and on the Wharf in Bridgetown. **Origins—Colours of the Caribbean** (tel. 809/436–8522), on the Wharf in Bridgetown, is worth visiting for its original—and expensive—handmade clothing and accessories.

At Bridgetown's **Pelican Village Handicrafts Center** (tel. 809/426–4391), on the Princess Alice Highway near the Cheapside Market, you can watch goods and crafts being made before you purchase them; rugs and mats are good buys.

Stores are generally open weekdays 9–5 and Saturdays 8–1.

Sports

Fishing **Blue Jay Charters** (tel. 809/422–2098) has a 45-foot, fully equipped fishing boat with a knowledgeable crew. Call for information on fishing charters.

Golf Several courses are open to cruise passengers: **Almond Beach Village** (9 holes $12.50, tel. 809/422–4900), **Club Rockley Barbados** (9 holes $22.50, tel. 809/435–7873), **Royal Westmoreland Golf Club** (18 holes $90, tel. 809/422–4653), and **Sandy Lane Club** (18 holes $120, tel. 809/432–1145).

Horseback Riding The **Caribbean International Riding Center** (St. Joseph, tel. 809/433–1246) offers one- or two-hour scenic trail rides for cruise-ship passengers. Prices begin at BDS$55, and transportation is included.

Water Sports Waterskiing, snorkeling, and parasailing are available on most beaches of St. James and Christ Church parishes. Windsurfing is best learned on the south coast at **Benston Windsurfing Club Hotel** (Maxwell, Christ Church Parish, tel. 809/428–9095). For scuba divers, Barbados is a rich and varied underwater destination. Two good dive operators are the **Dive Shop Ltd.** (Aquatic Gap, St. Michael, near Grand Barbados Beach Resort, tel. 809/426–9947) and **Dive Boat Safari** (Barbados Hilton, St. Michael, tel. 809/427–4350).

Beaches All beaches in Barbados are open to cruise passengers. The west coast has the stunning coves and white-sand beaches dear to the hearts of postcard publishers, plus calm, clear water for snorkeling, scuba diving, and swimming. **Payne's Bay,** south of Holetown, is the site of several fine resorts—including the Sandy Lane Hotel, which welcomes passengers to its beach. **Greave's End Beach** is south of Bridgetown at Aquatic Gap. In Worthing, on the south coast, **Sandy Beach** has shallow, calm waters and a picturesque lagoon. It's ideal for families. If you don't mind a short drive along Highway 7, the **Crane Beach Hotel,** where the Atlantic meets the Caribbean, is a great find. Waves pound in, but a reef makes it safe for good swimmers, and the sands are golden. For refreshment, there's the hotel's dining room on the cliff above.

Dining *A 5% tax and 10% service charge are added to most restaurant bills. When no service charge is added, tip waiters 10%–15%.*

$ **Bonito Beach Bar & Restaurant.** When you tour the rugged east coast, plan to arrive in Bathsheba at lunchtime and stop here for a wholesome West Indian meal, a fresh-fruit punch, and a spectacular view of the pounding Atlantic surf. *Coast Rd., Bathsheba, tel. 809/433–9034. No credit cards.*

$ **Waterfront Cafe.** A sidewalk table overlooking the Careenage is the perfect place to enjoy a drink, snack, burger, or "Bajan" meal. It's a popular gathering place for locals and tourists alike. *Bridge House, Bridgetown, tel. 809/427–0093. MC, V.*

Caracas/La Guaira, Venezuela

The busy harbor of La Guaira is the port for nearby Caracas, the capital of Venezuela. Most passengers go directly from the dock into air-conditioned excursion buses for the 15-mile (45-minute) drive into the big city. Those who want to explore historical La Guaira will find the colonial zone most interesting.

Caracas is a bustling, multiethnic, cosmopolitan city of 6 million people. It isn't the safest spot in the world, so passengers should travel in groups if touring the capital city on their own. In La Guaira, too, it's best to explore in a group or with a local taxi driver/guide: the colonial district is filled with "bandidos." And unless you want to stick out like a sore thumb, and a rather rude one at that, men should wear long slacks, and women should wear slacks or a short-sleeve dress.

Due to its rapid growth, Caracas is a hodgepodge of styles. Many of the buildings, such as Centro Banaven, a black, glass-sided box, display innovative touches; but there is also a healthy share of neoclassical buildings, such as the 19th-century Capitol and the 20th-century Fine Arts Museum, as well as heavier, neo-Gothic structures. The colonial dwellings of La Guaira are fascinating symbols of affluence long gone: Few have been restored, and they stand in silent, weathered testimony to the passage of time.

Currency The monetary unit is the bolivar (Bs). At press time the dollar exchange stood at Bs 100 on the free market. Store owners prefer U.S. dollars, however, and may even give you a discount for paying in greenbacks.

Telephones International calls, which are quite expensive, are best made from a CANTV office. Ask at the cruise terminal for the nearest one. For operator-assisted international calls, dial 122. AT&T now offers a collect-call service to the United States: Dialing 800/11120 connects you directly with an English-speaking operator.

Shore Excursions The following are good choices in Caracas. They may not be offered by all cruise lines. Times and prices are approximate.

Angel Falls and Canaima Lagoon. A jet ride carries you into the lush jungle interior and over Angel Falls—at 3,212 feet, the world's highest waterfall. After landing, you travel by canoe to a resort jungle camp to see another waterfall and the rich vegetation up close. Lunch is followed by a swim in a lagoon, with enough time to hike and explore. Not all ships offer this unforgettable tour. If yours doesn't, ask your shore-excursion director if it can be arranged for you. *9 hrs. Cost: $200.*

Caracas. If you want to see the city, a shore excursion is a much better choice than hiring a car. This half-day tour will show you all you need to see, and still leave you time to explore the area around the ship. *4 hrs. Cost: $30.*

Coming Ashore Cruise ships dock at a modern terminal with souvenir stands and shops inside. Taxi drivers will quote negotiable prices for the round-trip ride to Caracas. Pay no more than $60, and never pay in advance or you may be left stranded. If you plan to explore La Guaira, it's best to hire an English-speaking driver/guide. Although the colonial zone is just a short distance east of the cruise-ship terminal, the walk along the highway is neither particularly scenic nor safe. Pay no more than $15–$20 to see the sights and return to the ship.

Getting Around

By Subway The modern and handsome Metro, with its elegant French cars, covers 13 miles between Propatria in the west and Palo Verde in the east. A million passengers a day ride the quiet, rubber-wheeled trains in air-conditioned comfort. It is such a pleasant experience that some city-tour shore excursions include a jaunt on the subway as a highlight. Individual fares are from Bs 13 to Bs 16.

By Taxi Taxis are the best means of independent exploration. Private tours can be arranged just inside the cruise-ship terminal.

Exploring La Guaira Begin a quick survey of the colonial district at **Plaza Vargas,** on the main shore road. Locals gather here around the statue of José Maria Vargas, a Guaireño who was Venezuela's third president. Across the plaza is Calle Bolívar, running between the shore road and the mountains. Lined by the cool and cavernous warehouses of another century's trade and by one- and two-story houses with their colonial windows and red-tile roofs, the street funnels the sea breezes like voices from a more gracious age. Have your driver/guide wait for you at the plaza while you walk down this narrow street.

With your back to the water (you'll be facing the mountains), turn right out of Plaza Vargas to find one of the best-preserved colonial buildings: **Boulton Museum,** a pink house with an ample wood balcony. It will be on your left as you walk down Calle Bolívar. Inside is a treasury of paintings, maps, documents, pistols, and other miscellany collected by the family of John Boulton, occupants of the house for more than 140 years. Unfortunately, the museum is now closed.

At the foot of Calle Bolívar, turn right and pass the post office. Next door is one of the most important old buildings in La Guaira, **Casa Guipuzcoana.** Built in 1734, it was the colony's largest civic structure, housing first the Basque company that held a trading monopoly for 50 years, then the customs office. Restored as a cultural center, it is now the Vargas District Town Hall. Follow the main shore road back to Plaza Vargas, where your driver should be waiting for you.

Exploring Caracas *Numbers in the margin correspond to points of interest on the Caracas map.*

❶ Caracas radiates from its historic center, **Plaza Bolívar.** The old Cathedral, City Hall, and Foreign Ministry (or Casa Amarilla) all face Plaza Bolívar, a pleasant, shady square with benches, pigeons, and the fine equestrian statue of Simón Bolívar, who was born only a block away. Nearby also are the Capitol, the presidential offices in Miraflores Palace, and the 30-story twin towers of the Simón Bolívar Center in El Silencio.

❷ The symbol of modern Caracas is the concrete **Parque Central,** with its two 56-story skyscrapers. Built over 16 years, the office and apartment complex was finished in 1986. Designed for 10,000 people, with seven condominiums and two towers, Parque Central encompasses not only shops, supermarkets, and restaurants, but also schools, a swimming pool, a convention center, a hotel, and the Museum of Contemporary Art. A pedestrian bridge links Parque Central to the Museum of Natural Sciences, the Museum of Fine Arts, and Los Caobos Park. Beyond this bower of mahogany trees, once a coffee plantation, lies the circular fountain of Plaza Venezuela.

Across the *autopista* (highway) from Plaza Venezuela are the ❸ **Botanical Gardens** and the City University campus. In its courtyards and buildings are a stained-glass wall by Fernand Léger; murals by Léger and Mateo Manaure; sculptures by Antoine Pevsner, Jean Arp, and Henry Laurens; and, in the Aula Magna Auditorium, acoustic "clouds" by Alexander Calder.

The great fountain with colored lights in Plaza Venezuela is part of the urban renewal undertaken by the Caracas Metro. The Metro has changed the face of Caracas. When entire avenues were torn up, architects and landscapers converted the commercial street of Sabana Grande into a pedestrian boulevard of shops, popular sidewalk cafés, potted plants, and chess tables.

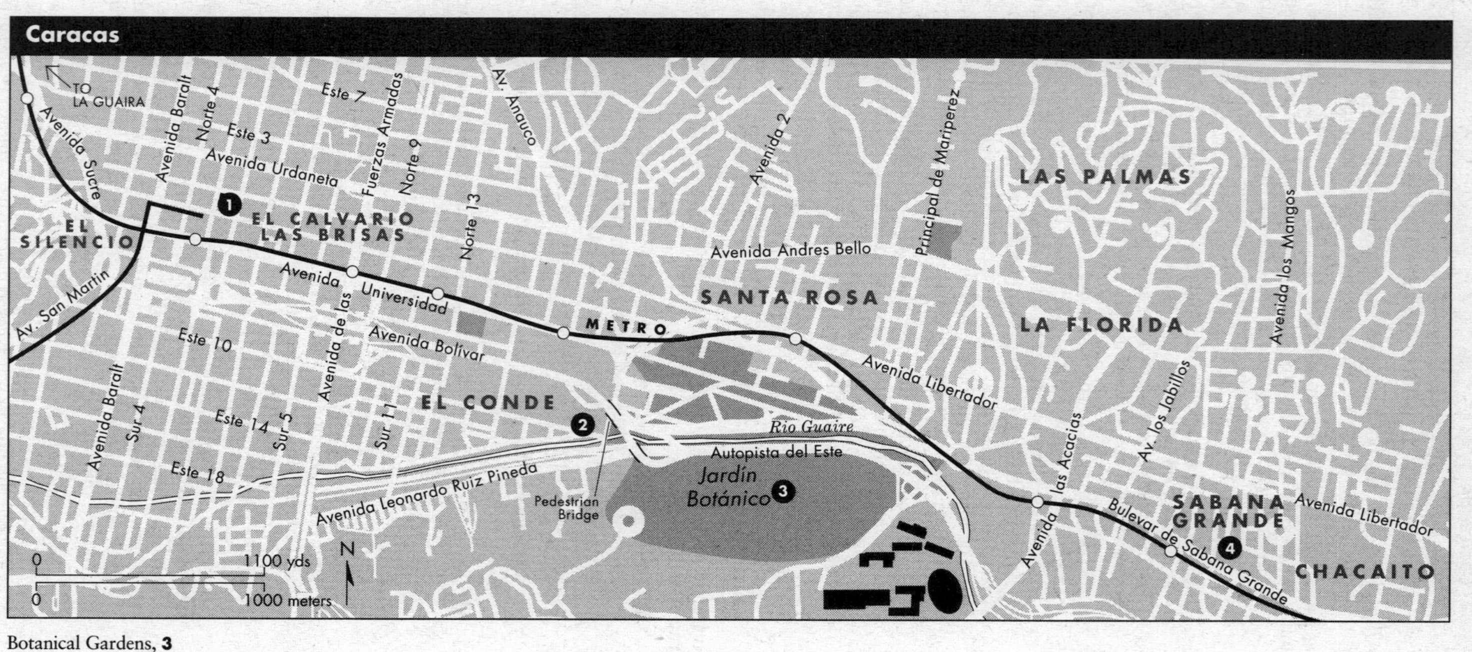

Botanical Gardens, **3**
Bulevar de Sabana Grande, **4**
Parque Central, **2**
Plaza Bolívar, **1**

Cars are banned between the Radio City theater and Chacaito, the ❹ pedestrian mall popularly known as the **Bulevar de Sabana Grande.** People of all ages and nationalities come to savor the best cappuccino and conversation in town, from midday to midnight.

Shopping Many of Caracas's sophisticated shops are in modern complexes known as *centros commerciales*, less stocked with imports than formerly, since devaluation has put foreign goods beyond most local shoppers' purses. Caracas is a buyer's market for fine clothing, tailored suits, elegant shoes, leather goods, and jewelry.

For wholesale jewelry go to **Edificio La Francia,** whose nine floors off Plaza Bolívar hold some 80 gold workshops and gem traders; profit margins are low, so buys are attractive. Since alluvial gold is found in Venezuela, nuggets of *cochanos* are made into pendants, rings, and bracelets. Expert gold designer **Panchita Labady,** who originated the popular gold orchid earrings and pins, works in a small shop at No. 98 Calle Real de Sabana Grande, opposite Avenida Los Jabillos (tel. 02/712016).

Devil's masks are much sought after for colorful souvenirs. Used in ritual dances marking the Corpus Christi Festival (usually in early June), they are made of brightly painted papier-mâché. A good place to find these and other uniquely Venezuelan gifts is El Taller de La Esquina, Nivel Galeria, in the Paseo Las Mercedes shopping center. Explore other *artesanía* (folk art) shops in Paseo Las Mercedes.

Dining *There is a 10% service charge in Venezuelan restaurants, and it is customary to tip the waiter another 10%.*

$$–$$$ **La Estancia.** Black-and-white photos of famous bullfighters seem right at home in this traditional Spanish-style restaurant. But despite the obvious Spanish influence, criollo dishes are the house specialty. Start with the lobster bisque and move on to the *parillas* (criollo-style grill) or rabbit or chicken basted in orange sauce. *Av. Principal de la Castellana, Esquina Urdaneta, tel. 02/261–2363. AE, MC, V.*

$ **Le Coq d'Or.** This is probably the best French restaurant for the money in Caracas. The menu varies, but it's always dependable. *Calle Los Mangos at Av. Las Delicias (between Bulevar de Sabana Grande and Av. Francisco Solano), tel. 02/761–0891. AE. Closed Mon.*

Cozumel, Mexico

Sun-saturated Cozumel, its ivory beaches fringed with coral reefs, fulfills the tourist's vision of a tropical Caribbean island. More Mexican than Cancún and far less developed, Cozumel surpasses its better-known, fancier neighbor to the north in several ways. It has more—and lovelier—secluded beaches, superior diving and snorkeling, more authentically Mexican cuisine, and a greater diversity of handicrafts at better prices.

Life on this flat jungle island centers on the town of San Miguel. The duty-free shops stay open as long as a ship is in town, and most of the salespeople speak English. With the world-renowned Palancar Reef nearby, San Miguel is also a favorite among divers.

Cozumel has become a mainstay for ships sailing on western Caribbean itineraries. As more and more cruise passengers arrive, the island has grown more commercial. Waterfront shops and restaurants have taken on a more glitzy appearance—gone are the hole-in-the-wall craft shops and little diners, replaced by high-dollar duty-free shops, gem traders, and slick eateries. There are also no less than half a dozen American fast-food chains and a Hard Rock Cafe.

Cruise ships visiting just for the day call at Cozumel; ships staying for two days usually call at Cozumel on one day and anchor off Playa del Carmen, across the channel on the Yucatán Peninsula, on the other. From here, excursions go to Cancún or to the Mayan ruins at Tulum, Cobá, and Chichén Itzá.

Currency In Mexico, the currency is the peso, written N$ (for nuevo peso). At press time, the exchange rate was about N$7 to $1.

U.S. dollars and credit cards are accepted at most restaurants and large shops. Most taxi drivers take dollars as well. There is no advantage to paying in dollars, but there may be an advantage to paying in cash. To avoid having to change unused pesos back to dollars, change just enough to cover what you'll need for public transportation, refreshments, phones, and tips. Use up your Mexican coins; they can't be changed back to dollars.

Telephones The best place to make long-distance calls is at the Calling Station (Av. Rafael E. Melgar 27 and Calle 3 S, tel. 987/21417), where you'll save 10%–50%. You can also exchange money here. It is open mid-December–April, daily 8 AM–11 PM; the rest of the year, it's open Monday–Saturday 9 AM–10 PM and Sunday 9–1 and 5–10.

Shore Excursions The following are good choices in Cozumel. They may not be offered by all cruise lines. Times and prices are approximate.

Archaeological Sites

Chichén Itzá. This incredible and awe-inspiring ruin of a great Mayan city is a 45-minute flight from Cozumel or a 12-hour round-trip bus ride from Playa del Carmen. A box lunch is included. *Full day. Cost: $130 (by plane), $85 (by bus).*

Tulum Ruins and Xel-ha Lagoon. An English-speaking guide leads a tour to this superbly preserved ancient Mayan city, perched on the cliffs above a beautiful beach. A box lunch is usually included. A stop is made for a swim in the glass-clear waters of Xel-ha. The tour leaves from Playa del Carmen. *7–8 hrs. Cost: $70.*

San Gervasio and Cozumel Island. If you want to see Mayan ruins but don't want to spend a full day on a tour, this excursion to a local archaeological site is a good alternative. Time is also allotted for swimming and snorkeling at the Playa Sol beach. *4 hrs. Cost: $32.*

Undersea Creatures

Glass-Bottom Boat. For those who don't dive, a tour boat with a see-through floor takes passengers to the famed Paraiso and Chankanaab sites to view schools of tropical fish. *2 hrs. Cost: $27.*

Snorkeling. This region has been acknowledged by experts from Jacques Cousteau to *Skin Diver Magazine* as one of the top diving destinations in the world. If your ship offers a snorkeling tour, take it. Equipment and lessons are included. *3 hrs. Cost: $30.*

Coming Ashore As many as six ships call at Cozumel on a busy day, tendering passengers to the downtown pier in the center of San Miguel or docking at the international pier 4 miles away. From the downtown pier you can walk into town or catch the ferry to Playa del Carmen. Taxi tours are also available. Sample prices are $6 to the Chankanaab Nature Park, $12 to the Playa Sol beach, and $35 to the Mayan ruins at San Gervasio. An island tour, including the ruins and other sights, costs about $60. The international pier is close to many beaches, but you'll need a taxi to get into town. Fortunately, cabs meet incoming ships, so there's rarely a wait. Expect to pay $4 for the ride into San Miguel from the pier.

Once in town, you can find a tourist information directory on the main square, immediately across from the downtown pier, and an information office upstairs in the Plaza del Sol mall, at the east end of the square (open weekdays 9 AM–2:30 PM).

Getting Around

By Ferry To get to Playa del Carmen from Cozumel, you can take a ferry or a jetfoil from the downtown pier. It costs about $10 round-trip and takes 40–60 minutes each way. Travelers prone to seasickness should take medications before embarking. Ferries depart every hour; the last ferry back to Cozumel leaves around 8:30 PM, but be sure to double-check because the schedule changes frequently.

By Car or Moped Mopeds are great fun, and you can circumnavigate the island on one tank of gas. The only gas station is at the corner of Avenida Juárez and Avenida 30 (open 7 AM–midnight). Wear a helmet and be careful: Accidents are frequent on Cozumel. Four-wheel drive is recommended if you're planning to explore the many dirt roads around the island. For two- or four-wheel rentals, contact **Auto Rent** (tel. 987/20844, ext. 712), **Budget** (tel. 987/21732), **National Interrent** (tel. 987/23263), or **Rentadora Cozumel** (tel. 987/21429). Rates start at about $50 per day in summer, $75 in winter. Mopeds cost about half the price of a car.

In Playa del Carmen you can rent a car from **PlayaCar Rental** (tel. 987/30241).

By Taxi Taxis are everywhere in Cozumel. Stands are on Avenida Melgar, just north of the downtown pier, and in front of all the major hotels. At Playa del Carmen, you can usually find a cab just off the ferry pier. Taxis to surrounding towns and archaeological sites are not cheap unless you're traveling in a group. Expect to pay about $45 to Cancún and $25 to Tulum or Akumal. Agree on the fare in advance.

Exploring Cozumel San Miguel is tiny—you cannot get lost—and best explored on foot. The main attractions are the small eateries and shops that line the streets. Activity centers on the ferry and the main square, where the locals congregate in the evenings. The lovely **Museo de le Isla de Cozumel,** with exhibits devoted to the island environment and to the ecosystem of the surrounding reefs and water, is on the main coastal drag, near the ferry dock. On the second floor are displays on Mayan and colonial life and on modern-day Cozumel. *Av. Melgar and Calle 4 N. Admission: $3. Open daily 10–6.*

It's not necessary to go to the mainland to explore ancient Mayan and Toltec ruins because Cozumel has several sites of archaeological interest. Start with a visit to the **Cozumel Archaeological Park,** five minutes by cab from the downtown pier/plaza area. Three thousand years of pre-Columbian Mexican culture and art are showcased here. More than 65 full-size replicas of Toltec, Mexicas, and Mayan statues and stone carvings are surrounded by jungle foliage. A guided walking tour, included in the admission price, takes about an hour. *65th Av. S, tel. 987/20914. Admission: $3. Open daily 8–6.*

To see the largest Mayan and Toltec site on Cozumel, head inland to the jungle. The ruins at **San Gervasio** once served as the island's capital and probably its ceremonial center, dedicated to the fertility goddess Ixchel. What remains today are numerous ruins scattered around a plaza and a main road leading to the sea (probably a major trade route). There's no interpretive signage, so you'll need to hire a guide in order to get much out of your visit. Guides charge $12 for groups of up to six, so try to get a group together aboard ship. *Admission: $1 to private road, $3.50 for ruins. Open daily 8–5.*

To sample Cozumel's natural beauty, head south out of town on Avenida Melgar; after 6½ miles your first stop will be the **Chankanaab Nature Park.** The natural aquarium has been designated an underwater preserve for more than 50 species of tropical fish, as well as crustaceans and coral. Snorkeling and scuba equipment can be rented, and instruction and professional guides are available, along with gift shops, snack bars, and a restaurant (open 10–5) serving fresh seafood. *Admission: $5. Open daily 6–5:30.*

Shopping San Miguel's biggest industry—even bigger than diving—is selling souvenirs and crafts to cruise-ship passengers. The primary items are ceramics, onyx, brass, wood carvings, colorful blankets and hammocks, reproductions of Mayan artifacts, shells, silver, gold, sportswear, T-shirts, perfume, and liquor. Almost all stores take U.S. dollars.

The shopping district centers on the Plaza del Sol and extends out along Avenida Melgar and Avenida 5 S and N. Good shops for Mexican crafts are **Los Cinco Soles** and **La Concha** (both on Av. Melgar) and **Unicornio** (Av. 5a S1, just off the Plaza del Sol). The most bizarre collection of shops on the island is the **Cozumel Flea Market,** on Avenida 5 N between Calles 2 and 4, which sells reproductions of erotic Mayan figurines, antique masks, rare coins, and Xtabentún, the local anise-and-honey liqueur. Down the street at Avenida 5 N #14, **Arte Na Balam** sells high-quality Mayan reproductions, jewelry, batik clothing, and a typical array of curios. For atmosphere, fresh fruit, and other foods, go to the **Municipal Market** at Avenida 25 S and Calle Salas.

Passengers whose ships dock at the International Pier can shop dockside at a complex selling T-shirts, handicrafts, trinkets, and more.

Sports

Fishing

In Cozumel contact **Yucab Reef Diving and Fishing Center** (tel. 987/24110) or **Club Naútico Cozumel** (tel. 987/20118 or 800/253–2701 in the U.S.)

Scuba Diving and Snorkeling

Cozumel is famous for its reefs. In addition to **Chankanaab Nature Park,** another great dive site is **La Ceiba Reef,** in the waters off La Ceiba and Sol Caribe hotels. Here lies the wreckage of a sunken airplane that was blown up for a Mexican disaster movie. Cozumel's dive shops include **Aqua Safari** (tel. 987/20101), **Blue Angel** (Hotel Villablanca, tel. 987/21631), **Dive Paradise** (tel. 987/21007), and **Fantasia Divers** (tel. 987/22840 or 800/336–3483 in the U.S.) and **Michelle's Dive Shop** (tel. 987/209470).

Dining

Although it is not common in Mexico, a 10%–15% service charge may be added to the bill. Otherwise, a 10%–20% tip is customary.

$$ **Pancho's Backyard.** A jungle of greenery, trickling fountains, ceiling fans, and leather chairs set the tone at this inviting restaurant, located on the cool patio of Los Cincos Soles shopping center. The menu highlights local standards such as black-bean soup, *carmone al carbon* (grilled prawns), and fajitas. Round out your meal with coconut ice cream in Kahlua. *Av. Rafael Melgar N 27 at Calle 8 N, tel. 987/22141. AE, MC, V. Closed Sun. No lunch Sat.*

$$ **Rincón Maya.** This is the top place on the island for Yucatecan cuisine, and it's a popular spot with locals and divers. Lobster and fresh fish *a la plancha* (grilled) and *poc chuc* (marinated grilled pork) are among the excellent dishes. The decor is festive; a colorful mural, hats, masks, and fans adorn the walls. *Av. 5A S between Calles 3 and 5 S, tel. 987/20467. No credit cards. No lunch.*

$ **Prima Pasta & Pizza Trattoria.** Since Texan Albert Silmai opened this northern Italian diner just south of the plaza, he's attracted a strong following of patrons, who come for the hearty, inexpensive pizzas, calzones, sandwiches, and pastas. The breezy dining area, located on a second-floor terrace above the kitchen, smells heavenly and has a charming Mediterranean mural painted on two walls. *A. Rosado Salas 109, tel. 987/24242. MC, V.*

Nightlife

After 10 PM, **Carlos 'n' Charlie's** (Av. Melgar 11 between Calles 2 and 4 N, tel. 987/20191) and **Chilly's** (Av. Melgar near Av. Benito Juarez, tel. 987/21832) are the local equivalent of college fraternity parties. The new **Hard Rock Cafe** (Av. Rafael Melgar 2A near Av. Benito Juarez) is similarly raucous. A favorite with ships' crews is **Scaramouche** (Av. Melgar at Calle Rosada Salas, tel. 987/20791), a dark, cavernous disco with a crowded dance floor surrounded by tiered seating.

Curaçao

Try to be on deck as your ship sails into Curaçao. The tiny Queen Emma Floating Bridge swings aside to open the narrow channel. Pastel gingerbread buildings on shore look like dollhouses, especially from the perspective of a large cruise ship. Although the gabled roofs and red tiles show a Dutch influence, the riotous colors of the facades are peculiar to Curaçao. It is said that an early governor of Curaçao suffered from migraines that were irritated by the color white, so all the houses were painted in colors.

Thirty-five miles north of Venezuela and 42 miles east of Aruba, Curaçao is, at 38 miles long and 2 to 7½ miles wide, the largest of the Netherlands Antilles. Although always sunny, it is never stiflingly hot here, due to the cooling influence of the constant trade winds. Water sports attract enthusiasts from all over the world, and the reef diving is excellent.

History books still don't agree as to whether Alonzo de Ojeda or Amerigo Vespucci discovered Curaçao, only that it happened around 1499. In 1634 the Dutch came and promptly shipped off the Spanish settlers and the few remaining Indians to Venezuela. To defend itself against French and British invasions, the city built massive ramparts, many of which now house unusual restaurants and hotels.

Today, Curaçao's population, which comprises more than 50 nationalities, is one of the best educated in the Caribbean. The island is known for its religious tolerance, and tourists are warmly welcomed and almost never pestered by vendors and shopkeepers.

Currency U.S. dollars are fine, so don't worry about exchanging money, except for pay phones or soda machines. The local currency is the guilder or florin, indicated by "fl" or "NAf" on price tags. The official rate of exchange at press time was NAf 1.77 to U.S.$1.

Telephones The telephone system is reliable, and there's an overseas phone center in the cruise-ship terminal. Dialing to the United States is exactly the same as dialing long distance within the United States.

Shore Excursions The following are good choices in Curaçao. They may not be offered by all cruise lines. Times and prices are approximate.

Island Sights **Country Drive.** This is a good tour if you'd like to see Westpunt and Mt. Christoffel but don't want to risk driving an hour there yourself. Other stops are the Museum of Natural History, Boca Tabla, and Knip Beach. *3½ hrs. Cost: $25.*

Undersea Creatures **Sharks, Stingrays, and Shipwrecks.** Curaçao's seaquarium, a marine park, and two sunken ships reached by a 30-minute submarine trip highlight this tour of the island's marine environment. *3 hrs. Cost: $40.*

Coming Ashore Ships dock at the cruise-ship terminal just beyond the Queen Emma Bridge, which leads to the floating market and the shopping district. The walk from the berth to downtown takes around 10 minutes. Easy-to-read tourist information maps are posted dockside and in the shopping area. The terminal has a duty-free shop, a telephone office, and a taxi stand.

Getting Around Willemstad is small and navigable on foot; you needn't spend more than two or three hours wandering around here. English, Spanish, and Dutch are widely spoken. Narrow Santa Anna Bay divides the city into the Punda, where the main shopping district is, and the Otrabanda (literally, the "other side"), where the cruise ships dock. The Punda is crammed with shops, restaurants, monuments, and markets. The Otrabanda has narrow winding streets full of colonial homes notable for their gables and Dutch-influenced designs.

You can cross from the Otrabanda to the Punda in one of three ways: Walk across the Queen Emma Pontoon Bridge; ride the free ferry, which runs when the bridge swings open (at least 30 times a day) to let seagoing vessels pass; or take a cab across the Juliana Bridge (about $10).

By Car To rent a car, call **Avis** (tel. 599/9–611255), **Budget** (tel. 599/9–683466), or **National** (tel. 599/9–683489). All you'll need is a valid U.S. or Canadian driver's license. Rates begin at $50 per day.

By Bike, Moped, or Scooter If you want to explore farther into the countryside, mopeds are an inexpensive alternative to renting a car or hiring a taxi. Scooters ($20), mopeds ($15), and bikes ($12.50) can be rented from Easy Going (tel. 599/9–695056).

By Taxi Taxis are not metered, so confirm the price before getting in. Taxis meet every cruise ship, and they can be picked up at hotels. Otherwise, call **Central Dispatch** (tel. 599/9–616711). A taxi tour for up to four people will cost about $25 an hour.

Exploring Curaçao *Numbers in the margin correspond to points of interest on the Curaçao map.*

Willemstad A quick tour of downtown **Willemstad** covers a six-block radius. The ❶ first landmark that cruise passengers come upon is the **Queen Emma Bridge,** which the locals call the Lady. The toll to cross the original bridge, built in 1888, was 2¢ per person if wearing shoes and free if barefoot. Today it's free, regardless of what is on your feet.

On the Punda side of the city, **Handelskade** is where you'll find Willemstad's most famous sight, the colorful colonial buildings that line the waterfront. The original red roof tiles came from Europe on trade ships as ballast.

At press time, the bustling **floating market** was temporarily located across Waaigat Channel while its traditional location on Sha Caprileskade was undergoing renovation. Each morning, dozens of Venezuelan schooners arrive laden with tropical fruits and vegetables. Any produce bought at the market should be thoroughly washed before eating.

The Wilhelmina Drawbridge connects the Punda with the once-flourishing district of **Scharloo.** The early Jewish merchants built stately homes in Scharloo, and many of these intriguing structures (some dating back to the 17th century) have been meticulously renovated by the government. If you cross the bridge to admire the architecture along Scharlooweg, steer clear of the waterfront end (Kleine Werf) of the district, which is now a red-light district.

The Punda's **Mikveh Israel-Emmanuel Synagogue** was founded in 1651 and is the oldest temple still in use in the Western Hemisphere. It draws 20,000 visitors a year. Enter through the gates around the corner on Hanchi Snoa. A museum in the back displays Jewish antiques and fine Judaica. *Hanchi Di Snoa 29, tel. 599/9–611067. Small donation expected. Open weekdays 9–11:45 and 2:30–5.*

At the end of Columbusstraat lies **Wilhelmina Park.** The statue keeping watch is of Queen Wilhelmina, a popular monarch of the Netherlands who gave up her throne to her daughter Juliana after her Golden Jubilee in 1948. At the far side of the square is the impressive Georgian facade of the McLaughlin Bank and, to its right, the courthouse with its stately balustrade.

Guarding the waterfront at the foot of the Pontoon Bridge are the mustard-color walls of **Ft. Amsterdam**; take a few steps through the archway and enter another century. In the 1700s the structure was actually the center of the city and the most important fort on the island. Now it houses the governor's residence, the Fort Church, the ministry, and several other government offices. Outside the entrance, a series of gnarled wayaka trees has small, fanciful carvings of a dragon, a giant squid, and a mermaid.

Western Curaçao

The road that leads to the northwest tip of the island winds through landscape that Georgia O'Keeffe might have painted—towering cacti, flamboyant dried shrubbery, aluminum-roofed houses. In these parts you may see fishermen hauling in their nets, women pounding cornmeal, and donkeys blocking traffic. Landhouses—large estate homes, most of which are closed to the public—can often be glimpsed from the road.

❷ **Christoffel Park** is a good hour from Willemstad (so watch your time) but worth a visit. This fantastic 4,450-acre garden and wildlife preserve with Mt. Christoffel at its center consists of three former plantations. As you drive through the park, watch for tiny deer, goats, and other small wildlife that might suddenly dart in front of your car. If you skip everything else on the island, it's possible to drive to the park and climb 1,239-foot Mt. Christoffel, which takes from two to three strenuous hours. The island panorama you get from the peak is amazing—on a clear day you can even see the mountain ranges of Venezuela, Bonaire, and Aruba. *Savonet, tel. 599/9–640363. Admission: $9. Open Mon.–Sat. 8–4, Sun. 6–3.*

Eastern Curaçao

❸ At the **Curaçao Seaquarium,** more than 400 varieties of exotic fish and vegetation are displayed. Outside is a 495-yard-long artificial beach of white sand, well-suited to novice swimmers and children. There's also a platform overlooking the wreck of the steamship SS *Oranje Nassau* and an underwater observatory where you can watch divers and snorkelers swimming with stingrays and feeding sharks. *Tel. 599/9–616666. Admission: $12.50. Open daily 8:30 AM–10 PM.*

❹ Near the airport is **Hato Caves,** where you can take an hour-long guided tour into various chambers containing water pools, a voodoo chamber, fruit bats' sleeping quarters, and Curaçao Falls—where a stream of silver joins a stream of gold. Hidden lights illuminate the limestone formations and gravel walkways. This is one of the better Caribbean caves open to the public. *Tel. 599/9–680378. Admission: $4. Open daily 10–5.*

❺ **Curaçao Underwater Marine Park** (*see* Sports, *below*) is the best spot for snorkeling—though the seabed is sadly litter-strewn in places. The park stretches along the southern shore, from the Princess Beach Hotel in Willemstad to the eastern tip of the island.

Along the southern shore, several private yacht clubs attract sports anglers from all over the world for international tournaments. Stop at Santa Barbara Beach, especially on Sunday, when the atmosphere approaches party time. ❻ **Caracas Bay** is a popular dive site, with a sunken ship so close to the surface that even snorkelers can view it clearly.

Shopping

Curaçao has some of the best shops in the Caribbean, but in many cases the prices are no lower than in U.S. discount stores. Hours are usually Monday–Saturday 8–noon and 2–6. Most shops are within the six-block area of Willemstad described above. The main shopping streets are Heerenstraat, Breedestraat, and Madurostraat, where you'll find **Bamali** (tel. 599/9–612258) for Indonesian batik clothing and leather. **Fundason Obra di Man** (Bargestraat 57, tel. 599/9–612413) sells native crafts and curios. If you've always longed for Dutch clogs, tulips, delftware, Dutch fashions, or chocolate, try **Clog Dance** (De Rouvilleweg 9B, tel. 599/9–623280).

Arawak Craft Factory (tel. 599/9–627249), conveniently located between the Queen Emma Bridge and the cruise-ship terminal, is open whenever ships are in port. You can buy a variety of tiles, plates, pots, and tiny landhouse replicas here.

Curaçao

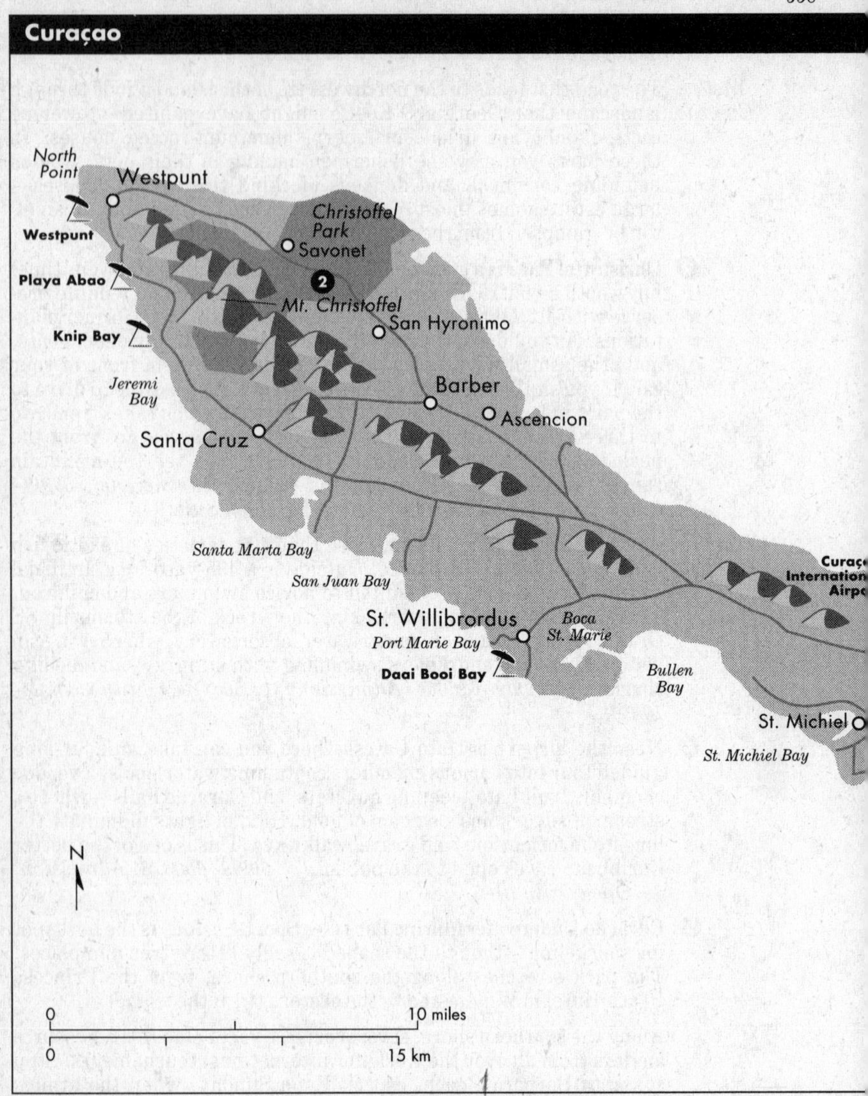

Caracas Bay, **6**
Christoffel Park, **2**
Curaçao Seaquarium, **3**
Curaçao Underwater Marine Park, **5**
Hato Caves, **4**
Willemstad, **1**

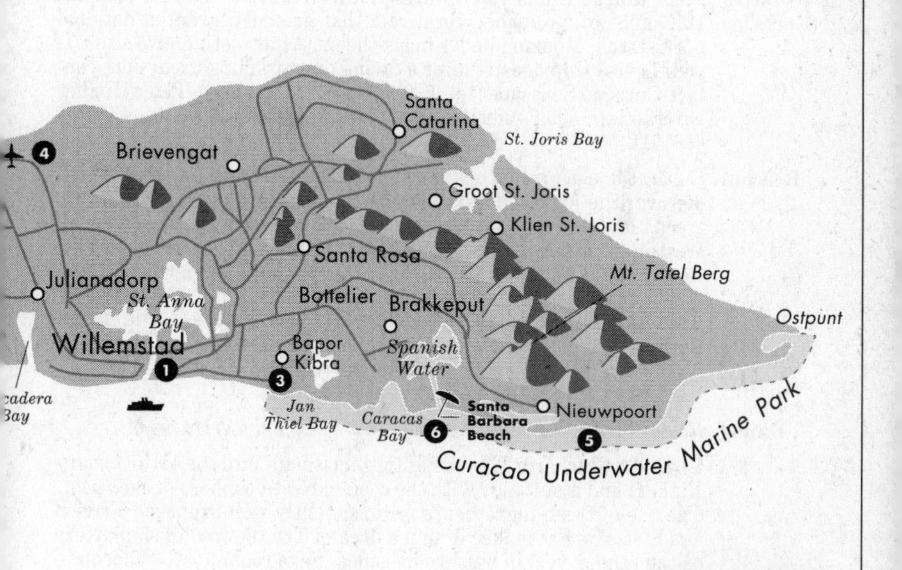

Caribbean Sea
Santa Catarina
St. Joris Bay
Brievengat
Groot St. Joris
Klien St. Joris
Santa Rosa
Mt. Tafel Berg
Julianadorp
St. Anna Bay
Bottelier
Brakkeput
Ostpunt
Willemstad
Bapor Kibra
Spanish Water
Jan Thiel Bay
Caracas Bay
Santa Barbara Beach
Nieuwpoort
Curaçao Underwater Marine Park
KEY
Cruise Ship

Julius L. Penha & Sons (Heerenstraat 1, tel. 599/9–612266), in front of the Pontoon Bridge, sells French perfumes, Hummel figurines, linen from Madeira, delftware, and handbags from Argentina, Italy, and Spain. The store also has an extensive cosmetics counter. **Boolchand's** (Heerenstraat 4B, tel. 599/9–616233) handles an interesting variety of merchandise behind a facade of red-and-white-checked tiles. Stock up here on French perfumes, British cashmere sweaters, Italian silk ties, Dutch dolls, Swiss watches, and Japanese cameras. **Little Switzerland** (Breedstraat 44, tel. 599/9–612111) is the place for duty-free shopping; here you'll find perfumes, jewelry, watches, crystal, china, and leather goods at significant savings. Try **New Amsterdam** (Gomezplein 14, tel. 599/9–612469) for hand-embroidered tablecloths, napkins, and pillowcases.

Sports

Hiking

Christoffel Park (*see* Exploring Curaçao, *above*) has a number of challenging trails.

Scuba Diving and Snorkeling

The **Curaçao Underwater Marine Park** (tel. 599/9–618131) is about 12½ miles of untouched coral reef that has been granted national park status. Mooring buoys mark the most interesting dive sites. If your cruise ship doesn't offer a diving or snorkeling excursion, contact **Curaçao Seascape** (tel. 599/9–625000, ext. 6056), **Peter Hughes Divers** (tel. 599/9–658911), or **Underwater Curaçao** (tel. 599/9–618131).

Beaches

Curaçao doesn't have long, powdery stretches of sand. Instead you'll discover the joy of inlets: tiny bays marked by craggy cliffs, exotic trees, and scads of interesting pebbles and washed up coral. Westpunt, on the northwest tip of the island, is rocky, with very little sand, but shady in the morning and with a bay view worth the one-hour trip. On Sunday watch the divers jump from the high cliff. Knip Bay has two parts: Groot (Big) Knip and Kleine (Little) Knip. Both have alluring white sand, and Kleine Knip is shaded by (highly poisonous) manchineel trees. Take the road to the Knip Landhouse, then turn right; signs will direct you.

Dining

Restaurants usually add a 10%–15% service charge to the bill.

$$$ **Bistro Le Clochard.** This romantic gem is built into the 18th-century Rif Fort and is suffused with the cool, dark atmosphere of ages past. The use of fresh ingredients in consistently well-prepared French and Swiss dishes makes dining a dream. Try the fresh fish platters or the tender veal in mushroom sauce. Save room for the chocolate mousse. *On the Otrabanda Rif Fort, tel. 599/9–625666. AE, DC, MC, V. Closed Sun. No lunch Sat.*

$ **Jaanchi's Restaurant.** Tour buses stop regularly at this open-air restaurant for lunches of mouthwatering native dishes. The main-course specialty is a hefty platter of fresh fish, conch, or shrimp with potatoes or funchi (a starch similar to cornbread) and vegetables. Bring a camera to capture the colorful sugarbirds that swarm Jaanchi's feeder on the terrace. *Westpunt 15, tel. 599/9–640126. AE, DC, MC, V.*

Grand Cayman

The largest and most populous of the Cayman Islands, Grand Cayman is one of the most popular cruise destinations in the western Caribbean, largely because it doesn't suffer from the ailments afflicting many larger ports: panhandlers, hasslers, and crime. Instead, the Cayman economy is a study in stability, and residents are renowned for their courteous behavior. Though cacti and scrub fill the dusty landscape, Grand Cayman is a diver's paradise, with translucent waters and a colorful variety of marine life protected by the government.

Compared with other Caribbean ports, there are fewer things to see on land; instead, the island's most impressive sights are underwa-

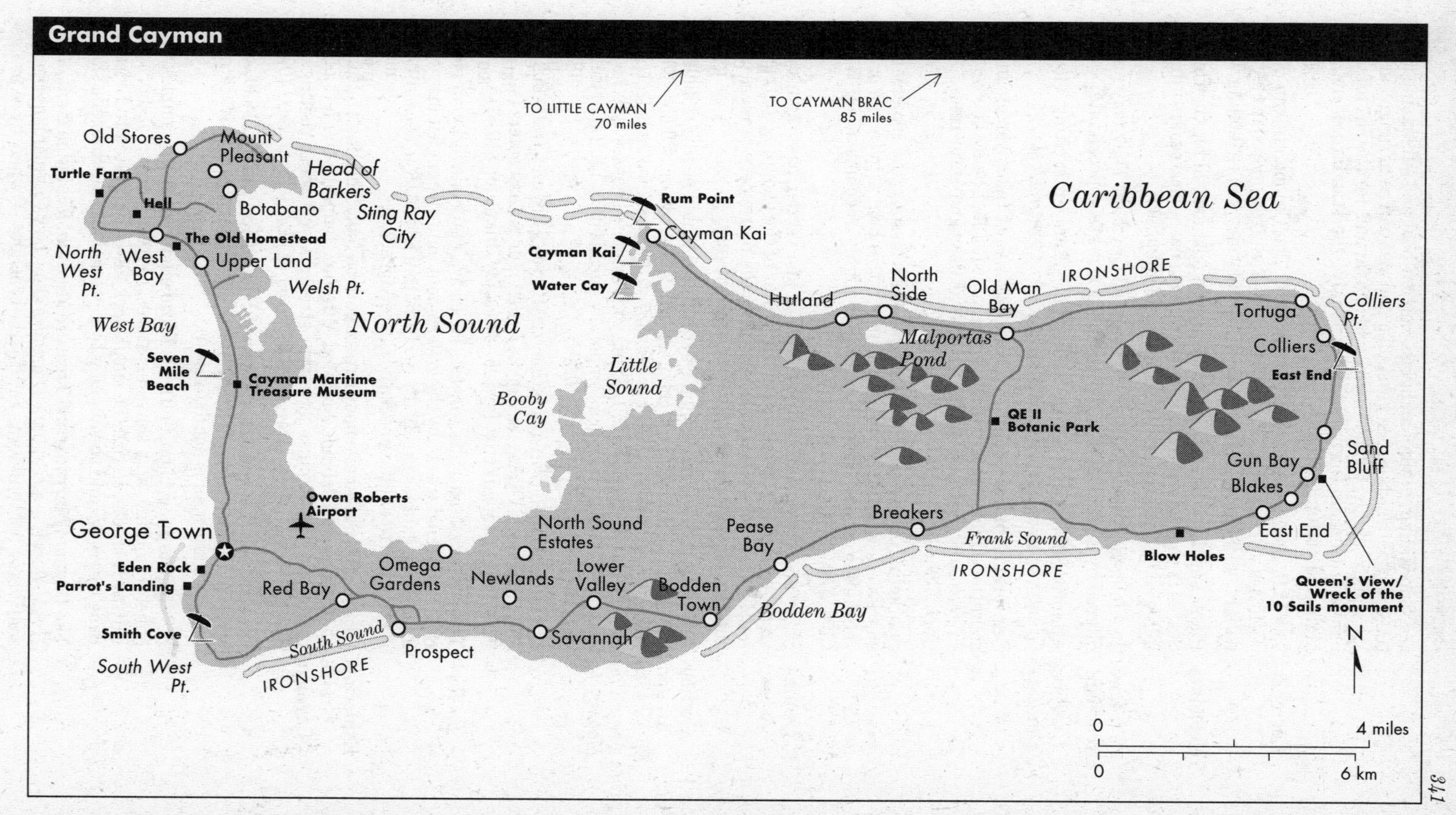
Grand Cayman
TO LITTLE CAYMAN
70 miles
TO CAYMAN BRAC
85 miles
Caribbean Sea
Old Stores
Mount Pleasant
Turtle Farm
Hell
Head of Barkers
Botabano
Sting Ray City
North West Pt.
West Bay
The Old Homestead
Upper Land
Welsh Pt.
West Bay
North Sound
Seven Mile Beach
Cayman Maritime Treasure Museum
Rum Point
Cayman Kai
Cayman Kai
Water Cay
Little Sound
Booby Cay
Hutland
North Side
Old Man Bay
IRONSHORE
Malportas Pond
QE II Botanic Park
Tortuga
Colliers Pt.
Colliers
East End
Sand Bluff
Gun Bay
Blakes
East End
Blow Holes
Queen's View/ Wreck of the 10 Sails monument
Owen Roberts Airport
George Town
Eden Rock
Parrot's Landing
Smith Cove
South West Pt.
Red Bay
South Sound
IRONSHORE
Omega Gardens
Prospect
North Sound Estates
Newlands
Lower Valley
Savannah
Bodden Town
Pease Bay
Bodden Bay
Breakers
Frank Sound
IRONSHORE
N
0
4 miles
0
6 km

ter. Snorkeling, diving, and glass-bottom-boat and submarine rides top every ship's shore-excursion list and also can be arranged at major aquatic shops. Grand Cayman is also famous for the 554 offshore banks in George Town; not surprisingly, the standard of living is high, and nothing is cheap.

Currency The U.S. dollar is accepted everywhere. The Cayman Island dollar (C.I.$) is worth about U.S.$1.20. Prices are often quoted in Cayman dollars, so make sure you know which currency you're dealing with.

Telephones Phone service is better here than on most islands. Calling the United States is the same as calling long distance in the States: Just dial 01 followed by the area code and telephone number.

Shore Excursions The following are good choices in Grand Cayman. They may not be offered by all cruise lines. Times and prices are approximate.

Undersea Creatures **Atlantis Submarine.** A real submarine offers an exciting view of Grand Cayman's profuse marine life. *1 hr 40 min. Cost: $75.*

Seaworld Explorer Cruise. A glass-bottom boat takes you on an air-conditioned, narrated voyage where you sit 5 feet below the water's surface and see sunken ships, tropical fish, and coral reefs. *1 hr. Cost: $29.*

Snorkeling Adventure. Novices can take lessons and experienced snorkelers will find good adventure on this boat trip to one or two snorkeling sites—Sting Ray City is highly recommended. *2 hrs. Cost: $30.*

Coming Ashore Ships anchor in George Town Harbor and tender passengers onto Harbour Drive, placing you in the center of the shopping district. A tourist information booth is located on the pier where tenders land, and taxis line up for disembarking passengers.

Getting Around

By Bicycle, Car, Moped, or Motorcycle If you want to see more than George Town, you'll need a vehicle. To rent a car, contact **Ace Hertz** (tel. 809/949–2280 or 800/654–3131), **Budget** (tel. 809/949–5605 or 800/527–0700), or **Cico Avis** (tel. 809/949–2468 or 800/228–0668). Bring your driver's license, and the rental agency will issue you a temporary permit ($5). Rental prices for cars range from $40 to $55 a day.

For two-wheeled transportation, try **Bicycles Cayman** (tel. 809/949–5572), **Cayman Cycle** (tel. 809/947–4021), or **Soto Scooters** (tel. 809/947–4363). Mopeds rent for $25–$30 a day, bikes for $10–$15.

By Taxi Taxis offer island-wide service. Fares are determined by an elaborate rate structure set by the government, and although it may seem expensive, cabbies rarely try to rip off tourists. Ask to see the chart if you want to double-check the quoted fare.

Exploring Grand Cayman George Town is small enough to explore on foot. The small but fascinating **Cayman Islands National Museum,** found to the left of the tender landing and just across the street, is well worth visiting. *Tel. 809/949–8368. Admission: C.I.$5. Open weekdays 9–5, Sat. 10–4.*

On Cardinal Avenue is the **General Post Office,** built in 1939, with strands of decorative colored lights and about 2,000 private mailboxes (island mail is not delivered).

Behind the general post office is **Elizabethan Square,** a complex that houses clothing and souvenir stores. At the corner of Fort and Edward streets, notice the small clock tower dedicated to Britain's King George V and the huge fig tree pruned into an umbrella shape.

The **Cayman Maritime and Treasure Museum,** located in front of the Hyatt Hotel, is a real find. Dioramas show how Caymanians became seafarers, boatbuilders, and turtle breeders. Owned by a professional treasure-salvaging firm, the museum displays a lot of artifacts from shipwrecks. A shop offers excellent buys on authentic

BISTRO

ancient coins and jewelry. *W. Bay Rd., tel. 809/947–5033. Admission: $5. Open Mon.–Sat. 9–5.*

The **Old Homestead,** formerly known as the West Bay Pink House, is probably the most photographed home in Grand Cayman. This picturesque pink-and-white cottage was built in 1912 of wattle and daub around an ironwood frame. Tours are led by Mac Bothwell, a cheery guide who grew up in the house.

Near the Old Homestead is the tiny village of **Hell,** which is little more than a patch of incredibly jagged rock formations called ironshore. The big attractions here are a small post office, which sells stamps and postmarks cards from Hell (the postcard of bikini beauties emblazoned "When Hell Freezes Over" gives you the idea), and lots of T-shirt and souvenir shops. *W. Bay Rd., tel. 809/949–7639. Admission: $5. Open Mon.–Sat. 8–5.*

The **Cayman Island Turtle Farm** is the most popular attraction on the island. Here you'll see turtles of all ages, from day-old hatchlings to huge 600-pounders that can live to be 100. In the adjoining café, sample turtle soup or turtle sandwiches. *W. Bay Rd., tel. 809/949–3893. Admission: $5. Open daily 9–5.*

Many legends are associated with **Pedro's Castle,** built in 1780 and the oldest structure on Grand Cayman. In 1877 it was struck by lightning, and it remained in ruins until the 1960s, when a restaurateur bought the building.

At **Bodden Town**—the island's original capital—you'll find an old cemetery on the shore side of the road. Graves with A-frame structures are said to contain the remains of pirates, but, in fact, they may be those of early settlers. A curio shop serves as the entrance to what's called the Pirate's Caves, partially underground natural formations that are more hokey than spooky, with fake treasure chests and mannequins in pirate garb.

Queen Elizabeth II Botanic Park is a 60-acre wilderness preserve showcasing the variety of habitats and plants native to the Caymans. Interpretive signs identify the flora along the mile-long walking trail. Halfway along the trail is a walled compound housing the rare blue iguana—it's found only in remote sections of the islands. *Frank Sound Rd., tel. 809/947–9462. Admission: $3. Open daily 7:30–5:30.*

On the way to the East End are the **Blow Holes,** a great photo opportunity as waves crash into the fossilized coral beach, forcing water into caverns and sending geysers shooting up through the ironshore.

Beyond the Blow Holes is the village of **East End,** the first recorded settlement on Grand Cayman. Farther on, as the highway curves north, you'll come to Queen's View lookout point. There's a monument commemorating the legendary Wreck of the Ten Sails, which took place just offshore.

Shopping

Grand Cayman is known for its turtle and black-coral products, but these are banned in the United States. **Fort Street** and **Cardinal Avenue** are the main shopping streets in George Town. On Cardinal Avenue is **Kirk Freeport Plaza,** with lots of jewelry shops, and the **George Town Craft Market,** with more kitschy souvenirs than crafts. On South Church Street and in the Hyatt Hotel, **Pure Art** (tel. 809/949–4433) features the work of local artists. The **Tortuga Rum Company**'s (tel. 809/949–7701) scrumptious rum cake makes a great souvenir; most shops on Grand Cayman carry it.

Sports

Fishing

For fishing enthusiasts, Cayman waters are abundant with blue and white marlin, yellowfin tuna, sailfish, dolphinfish, bonefish, and wahoo. If your ship does not offer a fishing excursion, about 25 boats are available for charter. Ask at the tourist information booth on the pier.

Scuba Diving and Snorkeling Contact **Bob Soto's Diving Ltd.** (tel. 809/947–4631 or 800/262–7686), **Don Foster's Dive Grand Cayman** (tel. 809/949–5679 or 800/833–4837), and **Parrot's Landing** (tel. 809/949–7884 or 800/448–0428). The best snorkeling is off the **Ironshore Reef** (within walking distance of George Town on the west coast) and in the reef-protected shallows of the north and south coasts, where coral and fish are much more varied and abundant.

Beaches The west coast, the island's most developed area, is where you'll find the famous **Seven Mile Beach.** The white, powdery beach is free of both litter and peddlers, but it is also Grand Cayman's busiest vacation center, and most of the island's resorts, restaurants, and shopping centers are located along this strip. The Holiday Inn rents Aqua Trikes, Paddle Cats, and Banana Rides.

Dining *Many restaurants add a 10%–15% service charge.*

$$$ **Lantana's.** Try the American-Caribbean cuisine at this fine eatery, where the decor is as imaginative and authentic as the food, and both are of top quality. Lobster quesadillas, blackened king salmon over cilantro linguine with banana fritters and cranberry relish, incredible roasted garlic soup, and apple pie are favorites from the diverse menu. *Caribbean Club, W. Bay Rd., Seven Mile Beach, tel. 809/947–5595. AE, D, MC, V. No lunch weekends.*

$$ **Crow's Nest.** With the ocean as its backyard, this secluded seafood restaurant, located about a 15-minute drive south of George Town, is a great spot for snorkeling as well as lunching. The shark du jour, herb-crusted dolphin with lobster sauce, and the shrimp and conch dishes are excellent, as is the chocolate fudge rum cake. *S. Sound Rd., tel. 809/949–9366. AE, MC, V. No lunch Sun.*

Grenada

Nutmeg, cinnamon, cloves, cocoa...the aroma fills the air and all memories of Grenada (pronounced gruh-*nay*-da). Only 21 miles long and 12 miles wide, the Spice Island is a tropical gem of lush rain forests, green hillsides, white-sand beaches, secluded coves, and exotic flowers.

Until 1983, when the U.S.–eastern Caribbean intervention catapulted this little nation into the headlines, Grenada was a relatively obscure island hideaway for lovers of fishing, snorkeling, or simply lazing in the sun. Grenada has been back to normal for more than a decade now, a safe and secure vacation spot with enough good shopping, restaurants, historical sites, and natural wonders to make it a popular port of call. Tourism is growing each year, but the expansion of tourist facilities is carefully controlled. New construction on the beaches must be at least 165 feet back from the high-water mark, and no building can stand taller than a coconut palm. As a result, Grenada continues to retain its distinctly West Indian identity.

Currency Grenada uses the Eastern Caribbean (E.C.) dollar. The exchange rate is about E.C.$2.70 to U.S.$1, although taxi drivers, stores, and vendors will frequently calculate at a rate of E.C.$2.50. U.S. dollars are readily accepted, but always ask which currency is referred to when asking prices. Unless otherwise noted, prices quoted here are in U.S. dollars.

Telephones U.S. and Canadian telephone numbers can be dialed directly. Pay phones and phone cards are available at the welcome center, on the Carenage in St. George's, where cruise-ship passengers come ashore.

Shore Excursions The following are good choices in Grenada. They may not be offered by all cruise lines. Times and prices are approximate.

Island Sights **City and Spice Tour.** Tour St. George's, then ride north along the spectacular west coast, through small villages and lush greenery, to a spice plantation and the nutmeg-processing station in Gouyave. *4 hrs. Cost: $40.*

Nature Tours **Bay Gardens Tour.** Explore St. George's forts and historical sites, then venture just outside the city to Bay Gardens, a private horticultural paradise, where 450 species of island flowers and plants are cultivated in patterns mimicking their growth in the wild. *2 hrs. Cost: $16.*

Grand Étang Tour. View the sights in the capital, then travel north through Grenada's central mountain range to the rain forest, Crater Lake, and Grand Étang Forest Centre. *3 hrs. Cost: $30.*

Coming Ashore Big cruise ships anchor outside St. George's Harbour and tender passengers to the east end of the Carenage, a horseshoe-shape thoroughfare that surrounds the harbor. Smaller ships can dock beside the welcome center, where water taxis, cabs, and walking-tour guides ($5 per hour) can be hired. From here, you can easily walk to town or take a taxi ($3 one-way). The capital can be toured easily on foot, but be prepared to climb up and down steep hills.

Getting Around If you plan to spend your day in port exploring picturesque St. George's, you'll need no more than your feet for transportation. If you want to explore outside the town, hiring a taxi or arranging a guided tour is more sensible than renting a car.

By Minivan Privately owned minivans can be hired just outside the welcome center. Pay E.C.$1, and hold onto your hat.

By Taxi Taxis are plentiful, and fixed rates to popular island destinations are posted at the welcome center on the Carenage. Hiring a cab on an hourly basis runs $15 per hour; island tours cost $16–$50.

By Water Taxi Water taxis are the quickest way to get to the beach. The fare is $4 round-trip to Grand Anse; $10 to Morne Rouge.

Exploring Grenada *Numbers in the margin correspond to points of interest on the Grenada map.*

St. George's ❶ **St. George's** is one of the most picturesque and authentic West Indian towns in the Caribbean. Pastel-painted buildings with orange-tile roofs line the Carenage, facing the harbor. Small, rainbow-colored houses rise up from the waterfront and disappear into steep green hills. On weekends, a windjammer is likely to be anchored in the harbor, giving the entire scene a 19th-century appearance.

On the bay side of St. George's, facing the sea and separated from the harbor by the Sendall Tunnel, the **Esplanade** is the location of the open-air meat and fish markets. At high tide, waves sometimes crash against the sea wall. This area is also the terminus of the minibus route.

Ft. George, built by the French in 1708, rises high above the entrance to the harbor. No shots were ever fired from the fort until October 1983, when Prime Minister Maurice Bishop and some of his followers were assassinated in the courtyard. The fort now houses Grenada's police headquarters but is open to the public. The 360-degree view from the fort is magnificent. *Admission free. Open daily during daylight hrs.*

Don't miss picturesque **Market Square,** a block from the Esplanade on Granby Street. It's open weekday mornings but really comes alive every Saturday from 8 AM to noon. The atmosphere is colorful, noisy, and exciting. Vendors sell baskets, spices, fresh produce, clothing, and other items.

A couple of blocks from the harbor, the **National Museum** has a small, interesting collection of archaeological and colonial artifacts—such as the young Josephine Bonaparte's marble bathtub and old rum-making equipment–and recent political memorabilia documenting

Concord Falls, **2**
Dougaldston Estate, **3**
Grand Étang National Park, **5**
Grenville, **6**
Nutmeg Processing Cooperative, **4**
St. George's, **1**
Westerhall, **7**

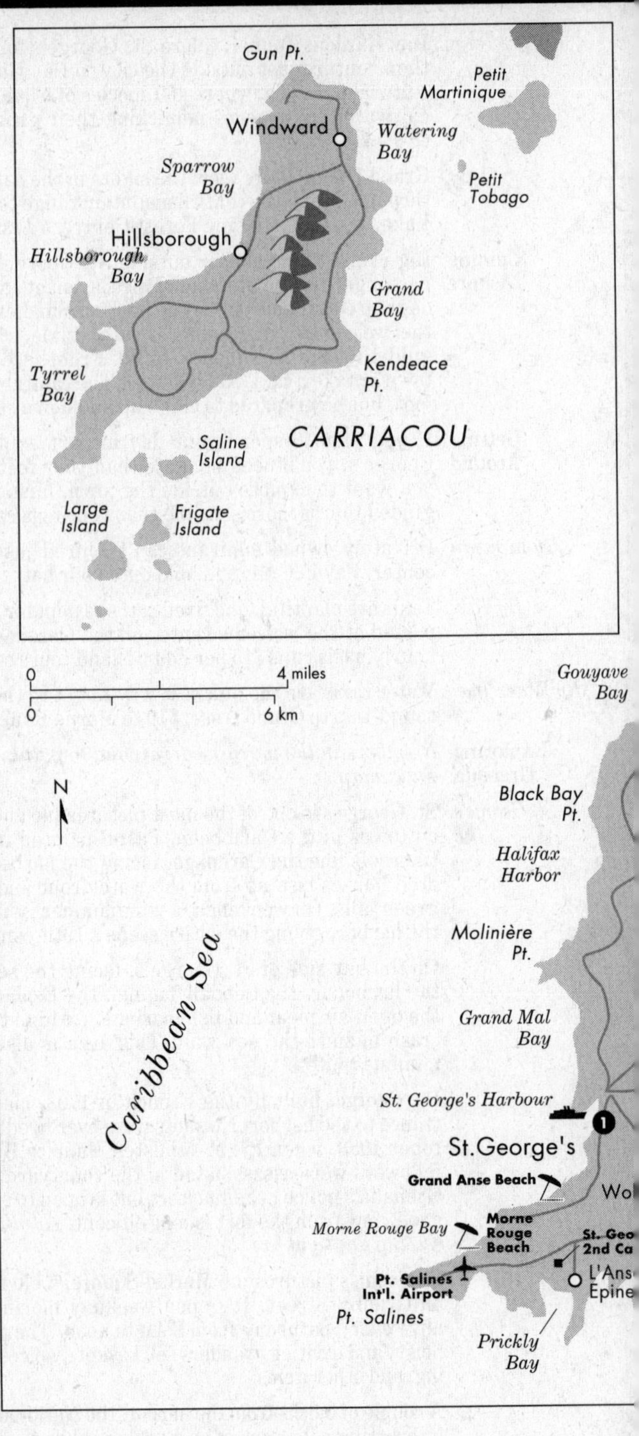

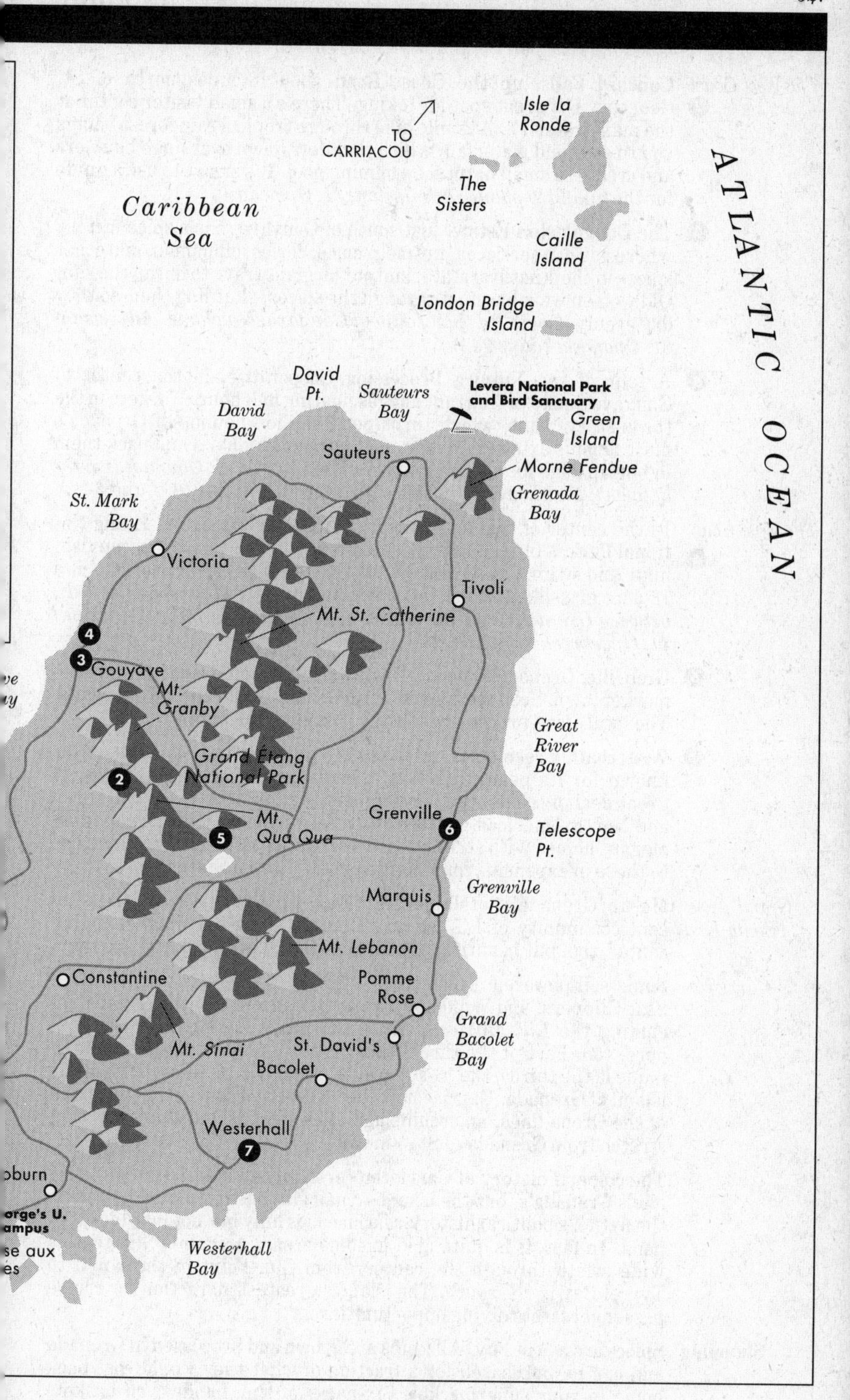

TO CARRIACOU
Isle la Ronde
The Sisters
Caille Island
London Bridge Island
ATLANTIC OCEAN
Caribbean Sea
David Pt.
Sauteurs Bay
Levera National Park and Bird Sanctuary
Green Island
David Bay
Sauteurs
Morne Fendue
Grenada Bay
St. Mark Bay
Victoria
Tivoli
Mt. St. Catherine
Gouyave
Mt. Granby
Great River Bay
Grand Étang National Park
Grenville
Mt. Qua Qua
Telescope Pt.
Marquis
Grenville Bay
Mt. Lebanon
Constantine
Pomme Rose
Grand Bacolet Bay
Mt. Sinai
St. David's
Bacolet
Westerhall
Westerhall Bay

the intervention. *Young and Monckton Sts., tel. 809/440–3725. Admission: $1. Open weekdays 9–4:30, Sat. 10–1:30.*

The West Coast

❷ **Concord Falls,** up the Coast Road about 8 miles north of St. George's, is a great spot for hiking. There's a small visitor center at the main waterfall. A 2-mile hike through tropical rain forest beings you to a second waterfall, which thunders down over huge boulders and creates a small natural swimming pool. It's smart to use a guide for the hike. *No phone. Admission: $1. Open daily 9–4.*

❸ The **Dougaldston Estate,** just south of Gouyave, has a spice factory where you can see cocoa, nutmeg, mace, cloves, cinnamon, and other spices in their natural state, laid out on giant trays to dry in the sun. Old women walk barefoot through the spices, shuffling them so they dry evenly. *Coast Rd. just south of Gouyave. No phone. Admission $1. Open weekdays 9–4.*

❹ A tour of the **Nutmeg Processing Cooperative,** in the center of Gouyave, makes a fragrant and fascinating half hour. Workers in the three-story plant, which turns out 3 million pounds of Grenada's most famous export per year, sort nutmegs by hand and pack them in burlap bags for shipping worldwide. *Coast Rd., Gouvave (center of town). No phone. Admission: $1. Open weekdays 10–1 and 2–4.*

The East Coast

❺ In the center of this lush, mountainous island is **Grand Étang National Park,** a bird sanctuary and forest reserve where you can fish, hike, and swim. Crater Lake, in the crater of an extinct volcano, is a 13-acre glasslike expanse of cobalt-blue water. *Main Interior Rd., between Grenville and St. George's, tel. 809/440–6160. Admission: $1. Open weekdays 8:30–4.*

❻ **Grenville,** Grenada's second-largest city, is reminiscent of a French market town. Schooners set sail from Grenville for the outer islands. The local spice-processing factory is open to the public.

❼ **Westerhall,** a residential area about 5 miles east of St. George's, is known for its beautiful villas, gardens, and panoramic views. A great deal of residential development is happening here. European and North American retirees and local businesspeople are building elegant homes with striking views of the sea at prices that compare to those in expensive communities in the United States.

Grand Anse/South End

Most of Grenada's hotels and nightlife are in Grand Anse or the adjacent community of L'Anse aux Epines. There's a small shopping center, too, but beautiful Grand Anse Beach is the main attraction.

Carriacou

Some sail-powered cruise ships, such as the vessels of Club Med, Star Clippers, and Windstar, call at Carriacou. A few tall ships, including the *Lili Marleen, Sea Cloud,* and *Yankee Clipper,* stop here, too. Part of the three-island nation of Grenada (Petit Martinique is the third), the 13-square-mile island is 16 miles north of the island of Grenada. Carriacou is the largest and southernmost island of the Grenadines, an archipelago of 32 small islands and cays that stretch from Grenada to St. Vincent.

The colonial history of Carriacou (pronounced kair-ee-uh-koo) parallels Grenada's, but the island's small size has restricted its role in the nation's political history. Carriacou is hilly but not lush like Grenada. In fact, it is quite arid in some areas. A chain of hills cuts a wide swath through the center, from Gun Point in the north to Tyrrel Bay in the south. The island's greatest attraction for cruise passengers is its diving opportunities.

Shopping

Spices are a best buy. All kinds are grown and processed in Grenada and can be purchased for a fraction of what they would cost back home in your supermarket. Six-packs of tiny handwoven baskets lined with bay leaves and filled with spices (about $8) make good souvenirs. Small bottles filled with fresh nutmeg, cinnamon, curry powder, cloves, peppercorns, and other spices (about $2 each) are an alternative. These are available from vendors along the Carenage and just outside the welcome center.

For Caribbean art and antique engravings, visit **Yellow Poui Art Gallery** (tel. 809/444–3001), at the corner of Cross Street and the Esplanade in St. George's. **Tikal** (Young St., tel. 809/440–2310) is a long-established boutique with exquisite handicrafts, baskets, artwork, jewelry, carvings, batik items, and fashions—both locally made and imported from Africa and Latin America. **Art Fabrik** (Young St., tel. 809/440–0568) is a batik studio where you can watch artisans create the designs by painting fabric with hot wax. You can buy batik by the yard or fashioned into batik clothing and other items.

Stores in St. George's are generally open weekdays 8–4 or 4:30, Saturday 8–1; most are closed on Sunday, though some shops open and vendors appear if ships are in port.

Sports

Golf The **Grenada Golf & Country Club** (tel. 809/444–4128) near Grand Anse has a nine-hole golf course and is open to cruise passengers. Fees are E.C.$7.

Water Sports Major hotels on Grand Anse Beach have water-sports centers where you can rent small sailboats, Windsurfers, and Sunfish. For **scuba diving**, contact Dive Grenada at Cot Bam restaurant (tel. 809/444–1092) or Grand Anse Aquatics, Ltd. at Coyaba Beach Resort (tel. 809/444–4129). Both dive operators are on Grand Anse Beach. On Carriacou, try Silver Beach Diving near Hillsborough (tel. 809/443–7882) or Tanki's Watersport Paradise, Ltd. on L'Esterre Bay (tel. 809/443–8406).

Beaches Grenada has 45 white-sand beaches along its 80 miles of coastline. Beaches are all open to cruise passengers, and some great stretches of sand are just 15 minutes from the dock in St. George's. **Grand Anse,** the most spectacular and most popular, is a gleaming 2-mile curve of clear, gentle surf. **Morne Rouge Beach,** a little southwest of Grand Anse, is less crowded and has a reef offshore that's terrific for snorkeling.

Dining *Some restaurants add a 10% service charge to your bill. If not, a 10%–15% gratuity should be added for a job well done.*

$$ **Coconut's Beach, The French Creole Restaurant.** Take local seafood, add butter, wine, and Grenadian herbs, and you have excellent French Creole cuisine. Throw in a beautiful setting at the northern end of Grand Anse Beach, and this West Indian cottage becomes a delightful spot for a meal. Lobster is prepared in a dozen different ways. Coconut's is open daily from 10 AM to 10 PM. The restaurant is set on the north end of Grand Anse beach; a water taxi is a fun way to arrive. *Grand Anse Beach, tel. 809/444–4644. AE, MC, V.*

$$ **The Nutmeg.** Fresh seafood, homemade West Indian dishes, great hamburgers, and the view of the harbor are reasons why local residents and visitors like the Nutmeg. It's on the second floor, so you can watch the harbor traffic through the large open windows as you eat. *The Carenage, St. George's, tel. 809/440–2539. AE, D, MC, V.*

$$ **Rudolf's.** This informal pub offers fine West Indian fare—such as crab back, *lambi* (conch), and delectable nutmeg ice cream—along with fish-and-chips, sandwiches, and burgers—and the best gossip on the island. *The Carenage, St. George's, tel. 809/440–2241. MC, V. Closed Sun.*

Guadeloupe

On a map, Guadeloupe looks like a giant butterfly resting on the sea between Antigua and Dominica. Its two wings—Basse-Terre and Grande-Terre—are the two largest islands in the 659-square-mile Guadeloupe archipelago. The Rivière Salée, a 4-mile seawater channel flowing between the Caribbean and the Atlantic, forms the "spine" of the butterfly. A drawbridge over the channel connects the two islands.

If you're seeking a resort atmosphere, casinos, and white sandy beaches, your target is Grande-Terre. On the other hand, Basse-Terre's Natural Park, laced with mountain trails and washed by waterfalls and rivers, is a 74,100-acre haven for hikers, nature lovers, and anyone yearning to peer into the steaming crater of an active volcano.

This port of call is one of the least touristy (and least keen on Americans). Guadeloupeans accept visitors, but their economy does not rely on tourism. Pointe-à-Pitre, the port city, is a kaleidoscope of smart boutiques, wholesalers, sidewalk cafés, a pulsating meat and vegetable market, barred and broken-down buildings, little parks, and bazaarlike stores. Though not to everyone's liking, the city has more character than many other island ports.

French is the official language, and few locals speak English—although Guadeloupeans are very similar to Parisians in that if you make an attempt at a few French words, they will usually open up. (It's sensible to carry a postcard of the ship with the name of where it is docked written in French. This will come in handy in an emergency.) Like other West Indians, many Guadeloupeans do not appreciate having their photographs taken. Always ask permission first, and don't take a refusal personally. Also, many locals take offense at short shorts or swimwear worn outside bathing areas.

Currency Legal tender is the French franc, composed of 100 centimes. At press time, the rate was 4.65F to $1.

Telephones To call the United States from Guadeloupe, dial 191, the area code, and the local number. For calls within Guadeloupe, dial the six-digit number.

Shore Excursions The following is a good choice in Guadeloupe. It may not be offered by all cruise lines. Time and price are approximate.

Pointe-à-Pitre/Island Drive. Grande-Terre's various districts and residential areas are surveyed in this half-day drive that includes a visit to Ft. Fleur d'Epée and a refreshment stop at a hotel. *3 hrs. Cost: $40.*

Coming Ashore Cruise ships dock at the Maritime Terminal of Centre St-John Perse in downtown Pointe-à-Pitre, about a block from the shopping district. To get to the tourist information office, walk along the quay for about five minutes to the Place de la Victoire. The office is across the road at the top of the section of the harbor called La Darse (*see* Exploring Guadeloupe, *below*), just a few blocks from your ship. There's also a small tourist information booth in the terminal, but its hours and the information available are limited.

Getting Around

By Car Guadeloupe has 1,225 miles of excellent roads (marked as in Europe), and driving around Grande-Terre is relatively easy. Cars can be rented at **Avis** (tel. 590/82–33–47), **Budget** (tel. 590/82–95–58), **Hertz** (tel. 590/82–00–14), or **Thrifty** (tel. 590/91–42–17). Rentals begin at about $60 a day. There is a small Hertz office at the Maritime Terminal.

By Taxi Taxi fares are regulated by the government and posted at taxi stands. Fares are more expensive here than on other islands. If your French is good, you can call for a cab (tel. 590/82–00–00, 590/83–09–55, or 590/20–74–74). Tip drivers 10%. Before you agree to use a taxi driver as a guide, make sure you speak a common language.

By Moped Vespas can be rented at **Vespa Sun** in Pointe-à-Pitre (tel. 590/91–30–36).

Exploring Guadeloupe

Numbers in the margin correspond to points of interest on the Guadeloupe map.

1 **Pointe-à-Pitre,** a city of some 100,000 people, lies almost on the "backbone" of the butterfly, near the bridge that crosses the Salée River. Bustling and noisy, with its narrow streets, honking horns, and traffic jams, it is full of pulsing life. The most interesting area, with food and clothing stalls, markets, tempting pastry shops, and modern buildings, is compact and easy to see on foot.

The **Musée St-John Perse** is dedicated to the Guadeloupean poet who won the 1960 Nobel Prize in literature. Inside the restored colonial house is a complete collection of his poetry, as well as many of his personal effects. *Corner rue Noizières and Achille René-Boisneuf, tel. 590/90–07–92. Admission: 10F. Open Thurs.–Tues. 8:30–12:30 and 2:30–5:30.*

The **Marketplace** is a cacophonous and colorful place where locals bargain for papayas, breadfruit, christophines, tomatoes, and a vivid assortment of other produce. *Between rues St-John Perse, Frébault, Schoelcher, and Peynier.*

The **Musée Schoelcher** honors the memory of Victor Schoelcher, the 19th-century Alsatian abolitionist who fought slavery in the French West Indies. Exhibits trace his life and work. *24 rue Peynier, tel. 509/82–08–04. Admission: 10F. Open weekdays 8:30–11:30 and 2–5.*

Place de la Victoire, surrounded by wood buildings with balconies and shutters and lined by sidewalk cafés, was named in honor of Victor Hugues's 1794 victory over the British. The sandbox trees in the park are said to have been planted by Hugues the day after the victory. During the French Revolution a guillotine here lopped off the heads of many an aristocrat.

The imposing **Cathedral of St. Peter and St. Paul** has survived havoc-wreaking earthquakes and hurricanes. Note the lovely stained-glass windows. *rue Alexandre Isaac.*

Basse-Terre

If you have a car, high adventure is yours by driving across Basse-Terre, which swirls with mountain trails and lakes, waterfalls, and hot springs. Basse-Terre is the home of the Old Lady, as the Soufrière volcano is called, and of the capital, also called Basse-Terre.

2 On the west coast of the island lie the two mountains known as **Les Mamelles** (The Breasts). The pass that runs between Les Mamelles to the south and a lesser mountain to the north offers a spectacular view. Trails ranging from easy to arduous lace the surrounding mountains.

You don't have to be much of a hiker to climb the stone steps leading
3 from La Traversée to the **Zoological Park and Botanical Gardens.** Titi the raccoon is the mascot of the park, which also features cockatoos, iguanas, and turtles. *Tel. 590/98–83–52. Admission: 25F. Open daily 9–4:30.*

Shopping

For serious shopping in Pointe-à-Pitre, browse the boutiques and stores along **rue Schoelcher, rue Frébault,** and **rue Noizières.** The market square and stalls of **La Darse** are filled mostly with vegetables, fruits, and housewares, but you will find some straw hats and dolls.

There are dozens of shops in and around the cruise terminal, **Centre St-John Perse.** Many stores here offer a 20% discount on luxury items purchased with traveler's checks or major credit cards. You can find good buys on anything French—perfume, crystal, wine, cosmetics, and scarves. As for local handcrafted items, you'll see a lot of junk, but you can also find island dolls dressed in madras, finely woven straw baskets and hats, salako hats made of split bamboo, madras table linens, and wood carvings.

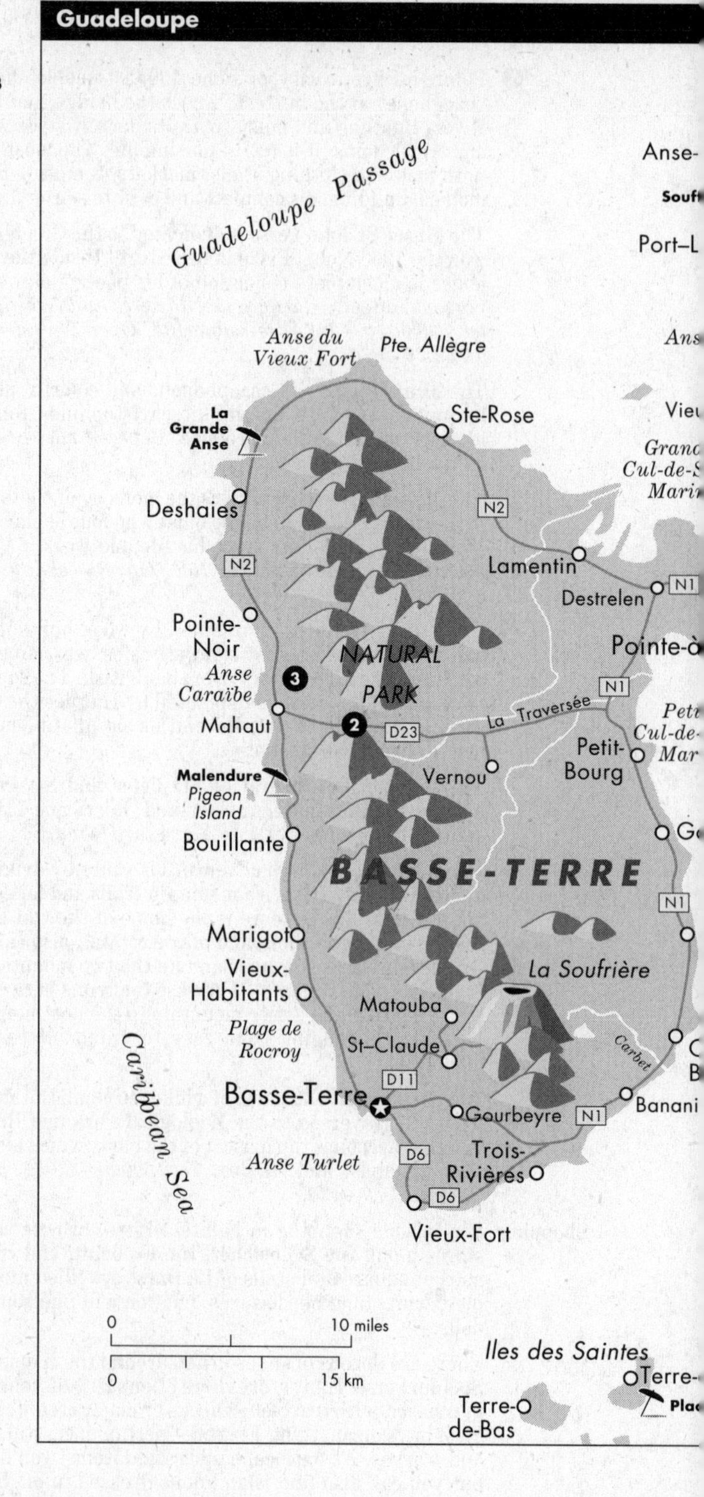
Guadeloupe
Guadeloupe Passage
Anse du Vieux Fort
Pte. Allègre
La Grande Anse
Ste-Rose
Deshaies
N2
Lamentin
Destrelen
N1
Pointe-Noir
Anse Caraïbe
NATURAL PARK
Mahaut
D23
La Traversée
Vernou
Petit-Bourg
Malendure
Pigeon Island
Bouillante
BASSE-TERRE
Marigot
Vieux-Habitants
La Soufrière
Matouba
Plage de Rocroy
St-Claude
Carbet
D11
Basse-Terre
Gourbeyre
Caribbean Sea
Anse Turlet
D6
Trois-Rivières
Vieux-Fort
Bananier
0
10 miles
15 km
Iles des Saintes
Terre-de-Bas

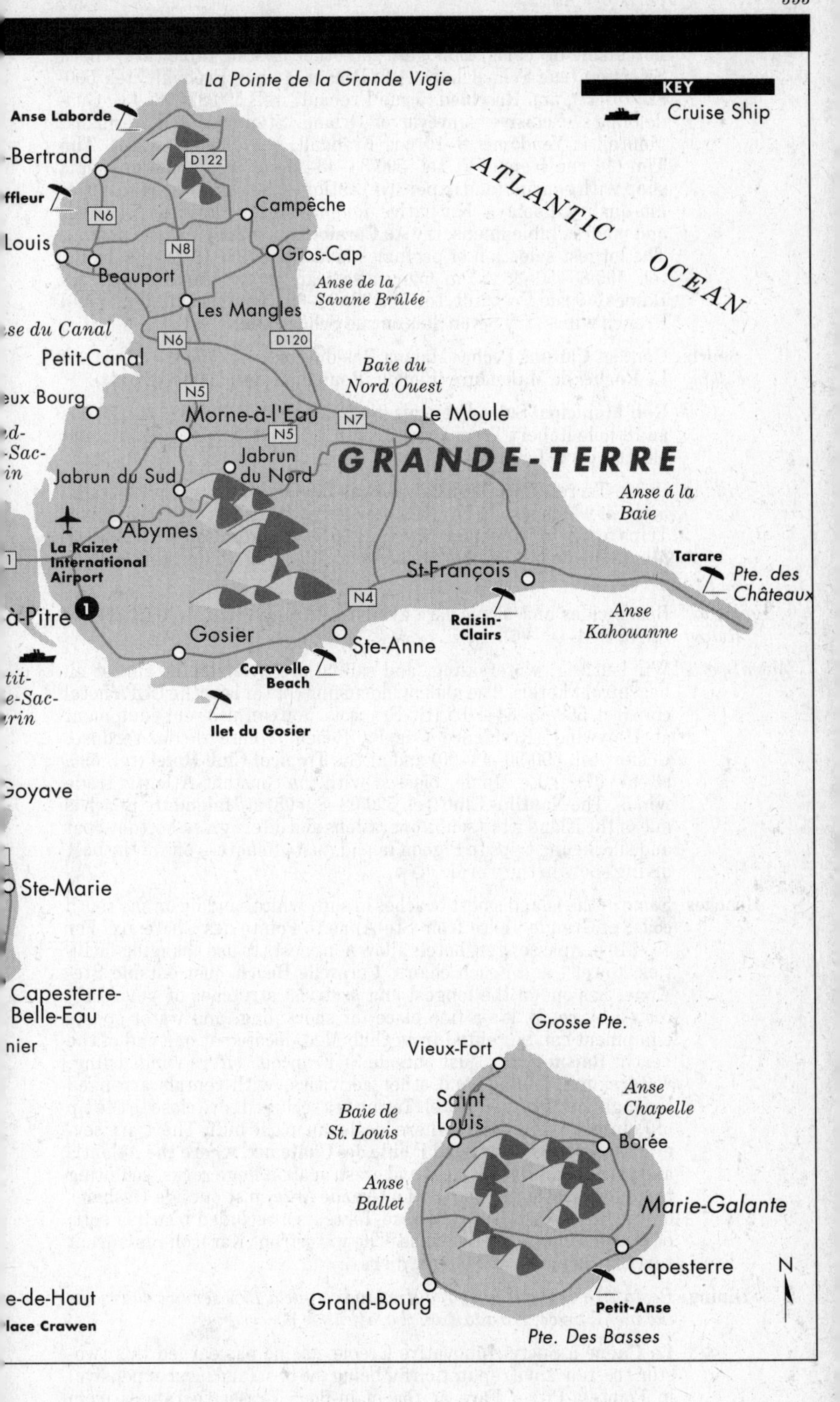
La Pointe de la Grande Vigie
KEY
Cruise Ship
ATLANTIC OCEAN
Anse Laborde
-Bertrand
D122
ffleur
N6
Campêche
Louis
N8
Gros-Cap
Beauport
Anse de la Savane Brûlée
Les Mangles
se du Canal
N6
D120
Petit-Canal
Baie du Nord Ouest
N5
eux Bourg
Morne-à-l'Eau
N7
Le Moule
N5
Jabrun du Nord
GRANDE-TERRE
Jabrun du Sud
Anse á la Baie
Abymes
La Raizet International Airport
Tarare
St-François
Pte. des Châteaux
N4
à-Pitre
Raisin-Clairs
Anse Kahouanne
Gosier
Ste-Anne
Caravelle Beach
Ilet du Gosier
Goyave
Ste-Marie
Capesterre-Belle-Eau
Grosse Pte.
Vieux-Fort
Saint Louis
Anse Chapelle
Baie de St. Louis
Borée
Anse Ballet
Marie-Galante
Capesterre
N
Grand-Bourg
Petit-Anse
e-de-Haut
Pte. Des Basses

The following shops are all in Pointe-à-Pitre: For Baccarat, Lalique, Porcelaine de Paris, Limoges, and other upscale tableware, check **Selection** (rue Schoelcher), **A la Pensée** (44 rue Frébault, tel. 590/82–10–47), and **Rosebleu** (5 rue Frébault, tel. 590/82–93–43). Guadeloupe's exclusive purveyor of Orlane, Stendhal, and Germaine Monteil is **Vendôme** (8–10 rue Frébault, tel. 590/83–42–44). **Tim Tim** (16 rue Henri IV, tel. 590/83–48–71) is an upscale nostalgia shop with elegant (and expensive) antiques; be sure to see the museum-quality displays. For native *doudou* dolls, straw hats, baskets, and madras table linens, try **Au Caraibe** (4 rue Frébault, no phone). The largest selection of perfumes is at **Phoenicia** (8 rue Frébault, tel. 590/83–50–36). You many also want to try **Au Bonheur des Dames** (49 rue Frébault, tel. 590/82–00–30). For discount liquor and French wines, try **Seven Sins** on rue Schoelcher.

Sports

Fishing Contact **Caraibe Peche** (Marina Bas-du-Fort, tel. 590/90–97–51) or **Le Rocher de Malendure** (Pigeon, Bouillante, tel. 590/98–28–84).

Golf **Golf Municipal Saint-François** (St-François, tel. 590/88–41–87) has an 18-hole Robert Trent Jones course, an English-speaking pro, and electric carts for rent.

Hiking Basse-Terre's **Parc Tropical de Bras-David** is abundant with trails, many of which should be attempted only with an experienced guide. Trips for up to 12 people are arranged by **Organisation des Guides de Montagne de la Caraibe** (Maison Forestière, Matouba, tel. 590/81–05–79).

Horseback Riding Beach rides and picnics are available through **Le Criolo** (St-Felix, tel. 590/84–04–06).

Water Sports Windsurfing, waterskiing, and sailing are available at almost all beachfront hotels. The main windsurfing center is at the **UCPA** hotel club (tel. 590/88–64–80) in St-François. You can also rent equipment at **Holywind** (Résidence Canella Beach, Pointe de la Verdure, Gosier, tel. 590/90–44–00) and at the **Tropical Club Hotel** (tel. 590/93–97–97) at Le Moule, blessed with the constant Atlantic trade winds. The **Nautilus Club** (tel. 590/98–89–08) at Malendure Beach is one of the island's top scuba operations and offers glass-bottom-boat and snorkeling trips to Pigeon Island, just offshore—one of the best diving spots in the world.

Beaches Some of the island's best beaches of soft, white sand lie on the south coast of Grande-Terre from Ste-Anne to Pointe des Châteaux. For $5–$10 per passenger, hotels allow nonguests to use changing facilities, towels, and beach chairs. **Caravelle Beach,** just outside Ste-Anne, has one of the longest and prettiest stretches of sand. Protected by reefs, it's a fine place for snorkeling, and water-sports equipment can be rented from Club Med, located at one end of the beach. **Raisin-Clairs,** just outside St-François, offers windsurfing, waterskiing, sailing, and other activities, with rentals arranged through the Méridien Hotel. **Tarare** is a secluded cove close to the tip of Pointe des Châteaux, where locals tan in the buff. There are several secluded coves around **Pointe des Cháteaux,** where the Atlantic and Caribbean waters meet and crash against huge rocks, sculpting them into castlelike shapes. **La Grande Anse,** just outside Deshaies on the northwest coast of Basse-Terre, is a secluded beach of soft, beige sand sheltered by palms. The waterfront Karacoli restaurant serves rum punch and Creole dishes.

Dining *Restaurants are legally required to include a 15% service charge in the menu price. No additional gratuity is necessary.*

$$$ **La Canne à Sucre.** Innovative Creole cuisine has earned this two-story restaurant a reputation for being the best (and most expensive) in Pointe-à-Pitre. Fare at the main-floor Brasserie ranges from crayfish salad with smoked ham to skate in puff pastry with saffron sauce. Dining upstairs is more elaborate and twice as expensive.

Quai No. 1, Port Autonome, tel. 590/82-10-19. AE, V. No lunch Sat.

$$ **Le Rocher de Malendure.** The setting on a bluff above Malendure Bay overlooking Pigeon Island makes this restaurant worth a special trip for lunch. The tiered terrace is decked with flowers, and the best choices on the menu are fresh fish, but there are also meat selections, such as veal in raspberry vinaigrette and tournedos in three sauces. *Malendure Beach, Bouillante, tel. 590/98-70-84. DC, MC, V. No dinner Sun.*

Jamaica

The third-largest island in the Caribbean, the English-speaking nation of Jamaica enjoys a considerable self-sufficiency based on tourism, agriculture, and mining. Its physical attractions include jungle mountains, clear waterfalls, and unforgettable beaches, yet the country's greatest resource may be its people. Although 95% of Jamaicans trace their bloodlines to Africa, their national origins also lie in Great Britain, the Middle East, India, China, Germany, Portugal, and South America, as well as in many other islands in the Caribbean. Their cultural life is a wealthy one; the music, art, and cuisine of Jamaica are vibrant with a spirit easy to sense but as hard to describe as the rhythms of reggae or the streetwise patois.

Don't let Jamaica's beauty cause you to relax the good sense you would use in your own hometown. Resist the promise of adventure should any odd character offer to show you the "real" Jamaica. Jamaica on the beaten track is wonderful enough, so don't take chances by wandering too far off it.

Currency Currency-exchange booths are set up on the docks at Montego Bay and Ocho Rios whenever a ship is in port. The U.S. dollar is accepted virtually everywhere, but change will be made in local currency. Check the value of the J$ on arrival—it fluctuates greatly. At press time the exchange rate was J$40 to U.S.$1.

Telephones Direct telephone, telegraph, telefax, and telex services are available in communication stations at the ports. Phones take phone cards, which are available from kiosks or variety shops.

Shore Excursions The following are good choices in Jamaica. They may not be offered by all cruise lines. Times and prices are approximate.

Natural Beauty **Prospect Plantation.** The beautiful gardens of Prospect Plantation are the highlight of this tour, with a brief stop at Dunn's River Falls. *3½ hrs. Cost: $39.*

Rafting on the Martha Brae River. Glide down this pristine river in a 30-foot, two-seat bamboo raft, admiring the verdant plant life along the river's banks. *4 hrs. Cost: $45.*

Coming Ashore

In Montego Bay A growing number of cruise ships are using the city of Montego Bay (nicknamed "Mo Bay"), 67 miles to the west of Ocho Rios, as their Jamaican port of call. The cruise port in Mo Bay is a $10 taxi ride from town. There is one shopping center within walking distance of the Montego Bay docks. The Jamaica Tourist Board office is about 3½ miles away on Gloucester Avenue.

In Ocho Rios Most cruise ships dock at this port on Jamaica's north coast, near the famous Dunn's River Falls. Less than a mile from the Ocho Rios cruise-ship pier are the Taj Mahal Duty Free Shopping Center and the Ocean Village Shopping Center, where the Jamaica Tourist Board maintains an office. Getting anywhere else in Ocho Rios will require a taxi.

Getting Around Neither Montego Bay nor Ocho Rios is a walking port, and driving is not recommended for cruise passengers. Jamaicans are not admired for their driving skills, and driving is on the left. Furthermore, you

Jamaica

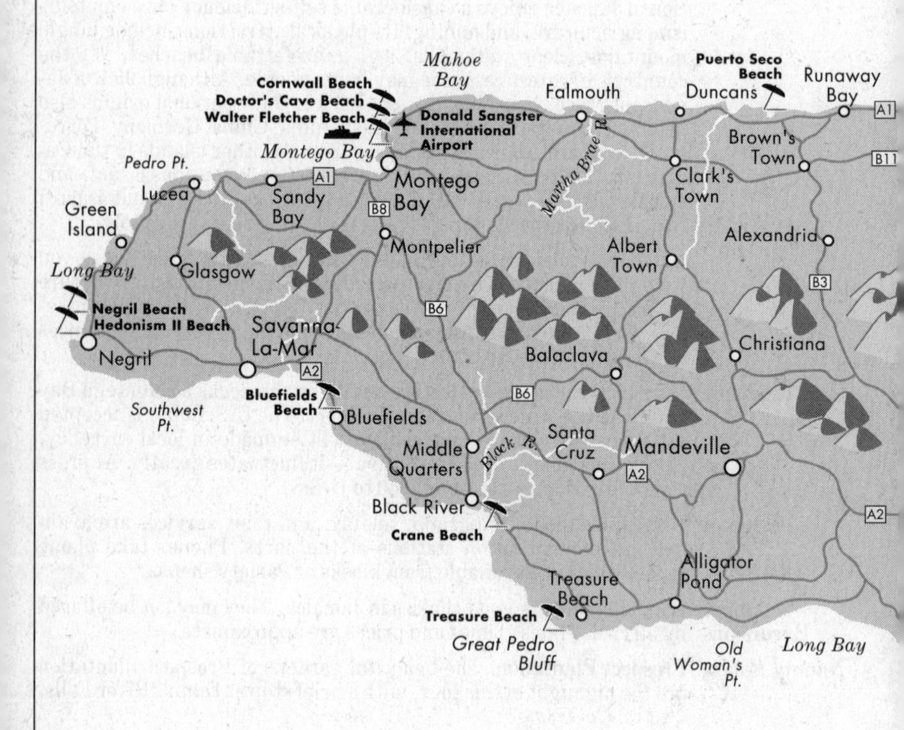

Mahoe Bay
Puerto Seco Beach
Runaway Bay
Cornwall Beach
Doctor's Cave Beach
Walter Fletcher Beach
Donald Sangster International Airport
Falmouth
Duncans
A1
Brown's Town
B11
Montego Bay
Pedro Pt.
Lucea
Sandy Bay
Montego Bay
Clark's Town
Martha Brae R.
Green Island
B8
Alexandria
Montpelier
Albert Town
Long Bay
Glasgow
B3
Negril Beach
Hedonism II Beach
B6
Savanna-La-Mar
Christiana
Negril
Balaclava
A2
Bluefields Beach
Bluefields
Southwest Pt.
Santa Cruz
Mandeville
Middle Quarters
Black R.
Black River
Crane Beach
Alligator Pond
Treasure Beach
Treasure Beach
Great Pedro Bluff
Old Woman's Pt.
Long Bay

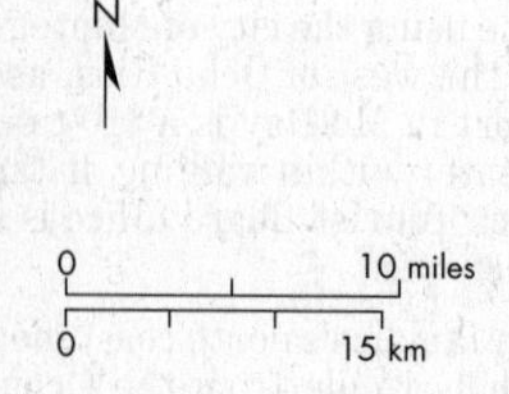

N
0
10 miles
0
15 km

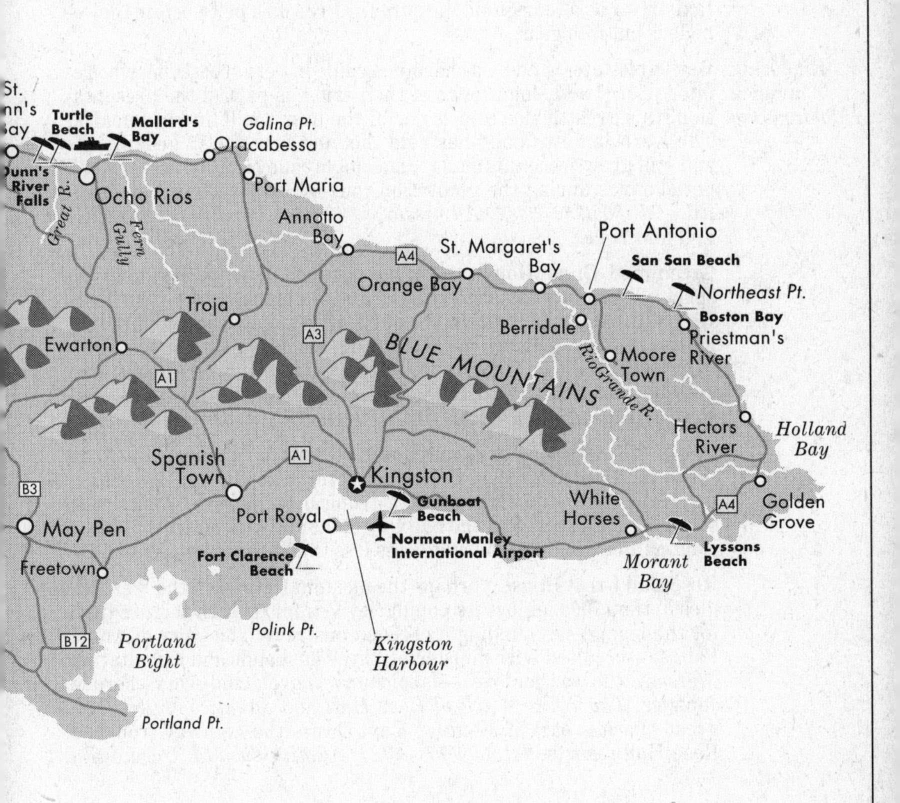

St.
nn's
ay
Turtle Beach
Mallard's Bay
Galina Pt.
Oracabessa
unn's River Falls
Ocho Rios
Great R.
Fern Gully
Port Maria
Annotto Bay
Port Antonio
San San Beach
Northeast Pt.
St. Margaret's Bay
Orange Bay
A4
Boston Bay
Priestman's River
Berridale
Troja
Ewarton
A3
BLUE MOUNTAINS
Moore Town
Rio Grande R.
A1
Hectors River
Holland Bay
Spanish Town
A1
Kingston
Gunboat Beach
White Horses
Golden Grove
A4
B3
May Pen
Port Royal
Norman Manley International Airport
Lyssons Beach
Morant Bay
Fort Clarence Beach
Freetown
Polink Pt.
B12
Portland Bight
Kingston Harbour
Portland Pt.
Caribbean Sea
KEY
Cruise Ship

must reserve a car and send a deposit *before* you reach Jamaica. Rates are about $75–$100 per day.

By Moped Mopeds are available for rent, but as with renting a car, this is not the best Caribbean port for cruise passengers to drive in. Daily rates run from about $45. Deposits of $200 or more or a signed credit card slip are usually required. Ask at the tourist office for rental shops near your port.

By Taxi Some of Jamaica's taxis are metered; rates are per car, not per passenger. Cabs can be flagged down on the street. All licensed and properly insured taxis display red Public Passenger Vehicle (PPV) plates. Licensed minivans also bear the red PPV plates. If you hire a taxi driver as a tour guide, be sure to agree on a price *before* the vehicle is put into gear.

Exploring Jamaica

Montego Bay

Barnett Estates. Led by a charming guide in period costume who relates poetry and sings songs of the period as part of the presentation, this great-house tour is one of the best you'll find in Jamaica. The Kerr-Jarrett family has held the land here for 11 generations and still grows coconut, mango, and sugarcane on 3,000 acres; you'll get samples during the plantation tour by jitney. *Granville Main Rd., tel. 809/952–2382. Admission: $30. Call for hrs of operation and tour times.*

Greenwood Great House, 15 miles east of Montego Bay, has no spooky legend to titillate visitors, but it's much better than Rose Hall at evoking the atmosphere of life on a sugar plantation. Highlights of Greenwood include oil paintings of the family, china specially made for them by Wedgwood, a library filled with rare books, fine antique furniture, and a collection of exotic musical instruments. *Tel. 809/953–1077. Admission: $10. Open daily 9–6.*

One of the most popular excursions in Jamaica is rafting on the **Martha Brae River** (tel. 809/952–0889 for reservations), a gentle waterway filled with the romance of a tropical wilderness. Wear your swimsuit for a plunge at the halfway point and pick a raft that has a comfortable cushion. The ride costs less than $40 for two people.

Rose Hall Great House, perhaps the most impressive in the West Indies in the 1700s, enjoys its popularity less for its architecture than for the legend surrounding its second mistress. The story of Annie Palmer—credited with murdering three husbands and a plantation overseer who was her lover—is told in two novels sold everywhere in Jamaica: *The White Witch of Rose Hall* and *Jamaica Witch.* The great house is east of Montego Bay, across the highway from the Rose Hall resorts. *Tel. 809/953–2323. Admission: $15. Open daily 9–6.*

Ocho Rios

Dunn's River Falls is 600 feet of cold, clear mountain water splashing over a series of stone steps to the warm Caribbean. Don a swimsuit, climb the slippery steps, take the hand of the person ahead of you, and trust that the chain of hands and bodies leads to an experienced guide. The climb leaders are personable, reeling off bits of local lore while telling you where to step. Take a towel and wear tennis shoes. *Tel. 809/974–2857. Admission: $5. Open daily 9–5.*

The tour of **Prospect Plantation** is the best of several offerings that delve into the island's former agricultural lifestyle. It's not just for specialists; virtually everyone enjoys the beautiful views over the White River Gorge and the tour by jitney through a plantation with exotic fruits and tropical trees. Horseback riding through 1,000 acres is available, with one hour's notice, for about $20 per hour. *Tel. 809/974–2058. Admission: $12. Open daily 10:30–3:30; tours at 11, 1:30, and 3:30.*

Shopping

Jamaican artisans express themselves in resort wear, hand-loomed fabrics, silk-screening, wood carvings, and paintings. Jamaican rum makes a great gift, as do Tia Maria (Jamaica's famous coffee liqueur) and Blue Mountain coffee. Cheap sandals are good buys (about $20 a pair).

While you should not rule out a visit to the "crafts markets" in Mo Bay and Ocho Rios, you should consider first how much you like pandemonium and haggling over prices and quality. If you're looking to spend money, head for **City Centre Plaza, Half Moon Village, Miranda Ridge Plaza, Montego Bay Shopping Center, St. James's Place,** and **Westgate Plaza** in Montego Bay; in Ocho Rios, the shopping plazas are **Pineapple Place, Ocean Village,** the **Taj Mahal, Coconut Grove,** and **Island Plaza.** Some cruise lines run shore excursions devoted exclusively to shopping.

For Jamaican and Haitian paintings, go to the **Gallery of West Indian Art** (1 Orange La., Montego Bay, tel. 809/952–4547). A corner of the gallery is devoted to hand-turned pottery and beautifully carved birds and jungle animals. Six miles east of the docks in Ocho Rios is **Harmony Hall** (tel. 809/975–4222), a huge house that has been converted into an art gallery, restaurant, and bar. Wares here include arts and crafts, carved items, ceramics, antiques, books, jewelry, fudge, spices, and Blue Mountain coffee.

Sports

Golf

The best courses are at the **Half Moon Club** (tel. 809/953–2560) and **Tryall** (tel. 809/956–5681) in Montego Bay or **Runaway Bay** (tel. 809/973–2561) and **Sandal's Golf and Country Club** (tel. 809/974–2528) in Ocho Rios. Rates range from $25 to $50 for 18 holes at the Ocho Rios courses to $110 and higher at the Half Moon Club and Tryall.

Horseback Riding

Chukka Cove (St. Ann, tel. 809/972–2506), near Ocho Rios, is the best equestrian facility in the English-speaking Caribbean. Riding is also available at **Prospect Plantation** (Ocho Rios, tel. 809/974–2058) and **Rocky Point Stables** (Half Moon Club, Montego Bay, tel. 809/953–2286).

Beaches

Doctor's Cave Beach at Montego Bay is getting crowded, attracting Jamaicans and tourists alike. The 5-mile stretch of sugary sand has been spotlighted in so many travel articles and brochures that it's no secret to anyone anymore. Two other popular beaches near Montego Bay are **Cornwall Beach,** farther up the coast, which has food and drink options, and **Walter Fletcher Beach,** on the bay near the center of town. Fletcher offers protection from the surf on a windy day and has unusually calm waters for swimming. The recently opened **Rose Hall Beach Club,** east of central Mo Bay near Rose Hall Great House, is a secluded area (far less crowded than beaches in town) with changing rooms and showers, a water-sports center, volleyball and other beach games, and a beach bar and grill. Ocho Rios appears to be just about as busy as Mo Bay these days, and the busiest beach is **Ocho Rios public beach** stretching behind Jamaica Grande and Club Jamaica. Next door is **Turtle Beach,** the islanders' favorite place to swim in Ocho Rios.

Dining

Many restaurants add a 10% service charge to the bill. Otherwise, a tip of 10%–15% is customary.

In Montego Bay

$$$

Sugar Mill. One of the finest restaurants in Jamaica, the Sugar Mill (formerly the Club House) serves seafood with flair on a terrace. Steak and lobster are usually garnished in a pungent sauce that blends Dijon mustard with Jamaica's own Pickapeppa. *At Half Moon Golf Course, Montego Bay, tel. 809/953–2228. AE, DC, MC, V.*

$

Pork Pit. Enjoy Jamaica's fiery jerk pork at this open-air hangout. Plan to arrive around noon, when the first jerk is lifted from its bed of coals and pimiento wood. *Gloucester Av. across from Walter Fletcher Beach, Montego Bay, tel. 809/952–1046. Reservations not accepted. No credit cards.*

In Ocho Rios
$$–$$$

Almond Tree. This very popular restaurant prepares Jamaican dishes enlivened by a European culinary tradition. The swinging rope chairs of the terrace bar and the tables perched above a lovely Caribbean cove are great fun. *83 Main St., Ocho Rios, tel. 809/974–2813. Reservations essential. AE, DC, MC, V.*

$–$$

Evita's. The setting here is a sensational, nearly 100-year-old gingerbread house high on a hill overlooking Ocho Rios Bay (but also convenient from Mo Bay). More than 30 kinds of pasta are served here, ranging from lasagna Rastafari (vegetarian) and fiery "jerk" spaghetti to rotelle *Colombo* (crabmeat with white sauce and noodles). There are also excellent fish dishes from which to choose *Mantalent Inn, tel. 809/974–2333. AE, MC, V.*

Key West

The southernmost city in the continental United States was originally a Spanish possession. Along with the rest of Florida, Key West became part of American territory in 1821. During the late 19th century, Key West was Florida's wealthiest city per capita. The locals made their fortunes from "wrecking"—rescuing people and salvaging cargo from ships that foundered on nearby reefs. Cigar making, fishing, shrimping, and sponge gathering also became important industries.

Capital of the self-proclaimed "Conch Republic," Key West today makes for a unique port of call for the 10 or so ships that visit each week. A genuinely American town, it nevertheless exudes the relaxed atmosphere and pace of a typical Caribbean island. Major attractions for cruise passengers are the home of the Conch Republic's most famous citizen, Ernest Hemingway; the birthplace of now-departed Pan American World Airways; and, if your cruise ship stays in port late enough, the island's renowned sunset celebrations.

Shore Excursions

The following are good choices in Key West. They may not be offered by all cruise lines. Times and prices are approximate.

Island Sights

Historic Homes Walking Tour. You'll see three notable Key West residences—the Harry S. Truman Little White House, the Donkey Milk House, and the Audubon House and Gardens—on a short guided stroll through the historic district. *2 hrs. Cost: $16.*

Undersea Creatures

Reef Snorkeling. The last living coral reefs in continental America are your boat's destination. Changing facilities, snorkeling gear, and unlimited beverages are included. *3 hrs. Cost: $38.*

Coming Ashore

Cruise ships dock at Mallory Square or near Truman Annex. Both are within walking distance of Duval and Whitehead streets, the two main tourist thoroughfares. For maps and other tourism information, the Chamber of Commerce (402 Wall St.) is found just off Mallory Square.

Getting Around

Key West is easily explored on foot. There is little reason to rent a car or hire a cab; public transportation is virtually nonexistent. If you plan to venture beyond the main tourist district, a fun way to get around is by bicycle or scooter.

By Taxi

The **Maxi-Taxi Sun Cab System** (tel. 305/294–2222) and **Five 66666** (tel. 305/296–6666) provide service in and around Key West. Taxis meet ships at the pier, but they are not recommended for sightseeing.

By Bicycle or Moped

Key West is a cycling town. In fact, there are so many bikes around that cyclists must watch out for one another as well as for cars. Try renting from **Keys Moped & Scooter** (tel. 305/294–0399) or **Moped Hospital** (tel. 305/296–3344); both can be found on Truman Avenue. Bikes rent for about $3–$5 per day, mopeds cost $10 for three hours.

By Tour Train or Trolley

The **Conch Tour Train** (tel. 305/294–5161) provides a 90-minute, narrated tour of Key West that covers 14 miles of island sights. Board at the Front Street Depot every half hour. The first train leaves at 9 AM and the last at 4:30 PM.

Old Town Trolley (tel. 305/296–6688) operates 12 trackless, trolley-style buses for 90-minute, narrated tours of Key West. You may get off at any of 14 stops and reboard later.

Exploring Key West

Numbers in the margin correspond to points of interest on the Key West map.

1 **Mallory Square** is named for Stephen Mallory, secretary of the Confederate Navy, who later owned the Mallory Steamship Line. On nearby Mallory Dock, a nightly sunset celebration draws street performers, food vendors, and thousands of onlookers.

2 Facing Mallory Square is **Key West Aquarium,** which houses hundreds of brightly colored tropical fish and other fascinating sea creatures from local waters. *1 Whitehead St., tel. 305/296–2051. Admission: $6.50. Open daily 9–6; guided tours and shark feeding at 11, 1, 3, and 4:30.*

3 The **Mel Fisher Maritime Heritage Society Museum** symbolizes Key West's "wrecking" past. On display are gold and silver bars, coins, jewelry, and other artifacts recovered in 1985 from two Spanish treasure ships that foundered in 1622. *200 Greene St., tel. 305/294–2633. Admission: $6. Open daily 9:30–5.*

4 At the end of Front Street, the **Truman Annex** is a 103-acre former military parade ground and barracks. Also here is the Harry S. Truman Little White House Museum, in the former president's vacation home. *111 Front St., tel. 305/294–9911. Admission: $7. Open daily 9–5.*

5 The **Audubon House and Gardens** commemorates ornithologist John James Audubon's 1832 visit to Key West. On display are a large collection of the artist's engravings. *205 Whitehead St., tel. 305/294–2116. Admission: $7.50. Open daily 9:30–5.*

6 At **301 Whitehead Street,** a sign proclaims the birthplace of Pan American World Airways, the first U.S. airline to operate scheduled international air service. The inaugural flight took off from Key West International Airport on October 28, 1927.

7 Built in 1851, **Hemingway House** was the first dwelling in Key West to have running water and a fireplace. Ernest Hemingway bought the place in 1931 and wrote eight books here. Descendants of Hemingway's cats still inhabit the grounds. Half-hour tours begin every 10 minutes. *907 Whitehead St., tel. 305/294–1575. Admission: $6.50. Open daily 9–5.*

8 Up the block from Hemingway House and across the street, behind a white picket fence, is the **Lighthouse Museum,** a 66-foot lighthouse built in 1847 and an adjacent 1887 clapboard house where the keeper lived. You can climb the 98 steps to the top for a spectacular view of the island. *938 Whitehead St., tel. 305/294–0012. Admission: $5. Open daily 9:30–5.*

9 At the foot of Whitehead Street, a huge concrete marker proclaims this spot to be the **Southernmost Point** in the United States. Turn left on South Street. To your right are two dwellings that both claim to be the Southernmost House. Take a right onto Duval Street, which ends at the Atlantic Ocean, and you will be at the Southernmost Beach.

10 The **Wrecker's Museum** is said to be the oldest house in Key West. It was built in 1829 as the home of Francis Watlington, a sea captain and wrecker. It now contains 18th- and 19th-century period furnish-

Key West

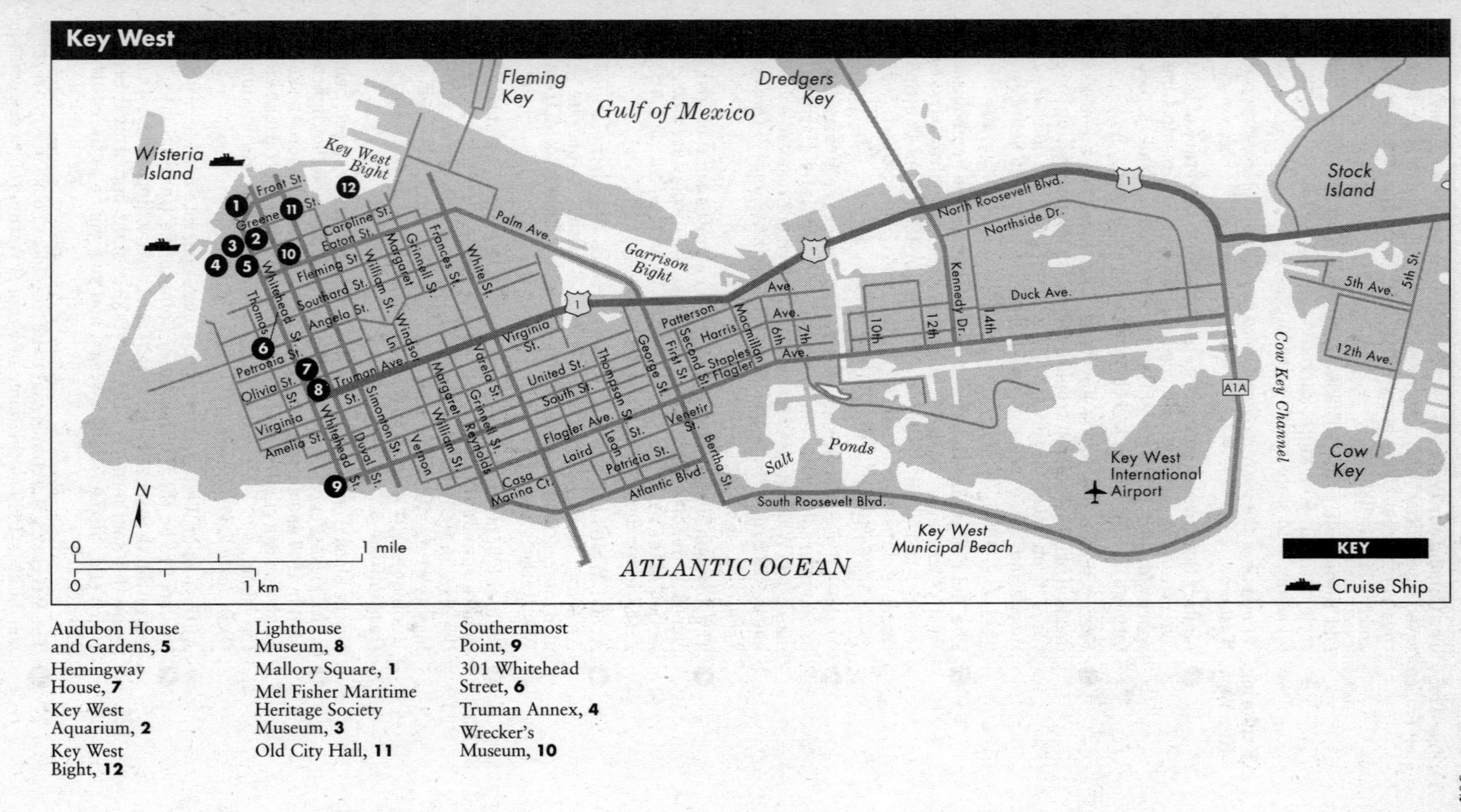

Audubon House and Gardens, **5**
Hemingway House, **7**
Key West Aquarium, **2**
Key West Bight, **12**
Lighthouse Museum, **8**
Mallory Square, **1**
Mel Fisher Maritime Heritage Society Museum, **3**
Old City Hall, **11**
Southernmost Point, **9**
301 Whitehead Street, **6**
Truman Annex, **4**
Wrecker's Museum, **10**

ings. *322 Duval St., tel. 305/294–9502. Admission: $3. Open daily 10–4.*

11 For a look at Key West as it was, visit the restored **Old City Hall** (510 Greene St.). Inside is a permanent exhibit of old Key West photographs, dating back to 1845.

12 **Key West Bight,** also known as Harbor Walk, remains the last funky area of Old Key West. Numerous charter boats and classic yachts call its slips home, and there's a popular waterfront bar called the Schooner Wharf (*see* Pub Crawling, *below*). The Reef Relief Environmental Center (tel. 305/294–3100) has videos, displays, and free information about the coral reef.

Shopping Passengers looking for T-shirts, trinkets, and other souvenirs will find them all along Duval Street and around the cruise-ship piers. **Fast Buck Freddie's** (500 Duval St., tel. 305/294–2007) sells such novelties as battery-operated alligators that eat Muenster cheese, banana leaf–shape furniture, fish-shape flatware, and every flamingo item anyone has ever dreamed up. **H.T. Chittum & Co.** (725 Duval St., tel. 305/292–9002) sells Key West–style apparel and accessories, from aviator hats to fish-cleaning knives. **Key West Island Bookstore** (513 Fleming St., tel. 305/294–2904) is the literary bookstore of the large Key West writers' community, while **Lucky Street Gallery** (919 Duval St., tel. 305/294–3973) carries the work of Key West artists and others.

Sports

Diving **Captain's Corner** (tel. 305/296–8865) leads excursions to reefs and wrecks for spear fishing or lobstering and archaeological and treasure hunting.

Fishing and Boating A variety of fishing vessels, glass-bottom boats, and sailing charters sail from Key West. The ***Discovery*** (tel. 305/293–0099) and ***Fireball*** (tel. 305/296–6293) are two glass-bottom boats, and the ***Wolf*** (tel. 305/296–9653) is a schooner that sails on day and sunset cruises with live music. The ***Linda D III*** and ***Linda D IV*** (tel. 305/296–9798 or 800/299–9798), captained by third-generation Key West seaman Bill Wickers, run full- and half-day sportfishing outings. The Chamber of Commerce on Front Street, by the pier, has a full list of other operators.

Golf **Key West Resort Golf Course** (tel. 305/294–5232) is an 18-hole course on the bay side of Stock Island. Fees are $62 for 18 holes, including a cart.

Snorkeling The northernmost living coral reef in the Americas and clear, warm Gulf of Mexico waters make Key West a good choice for getting your flippers wet (*see* Shore Excursions, *above*, and Beaches, *below*).

Beaches Facing the Gulf of Mexico, **Simonton Street Beach,** at the north end of Simonton Street and near the cruise-ship piers, is a great place to watch the boats come and go in the harbor. On the Atlantic Ocean, **Fort Zachary Taylor State Historic Site** has several hundred yards of beach near the western end of Key West. The beach is relatively uncrowded; snorkeling is good here. **Smathers Beach** features almost 2 miles of coarse sand alongside South Roosevelt Boulevard. Vendors along the road will rent you rafts, Windsurfers, and other beach toys. **Southernmost Beach** is found at the foot of Duval Street (*see* Exploring, *above*).

Dining

$$$ **Pier House Restaurant.** Steamships from Havana once docked at this pier jutting into the Gulf of Mexico. Now, it's an elegant place to dine, indoors or out, and to watch the boats glide by. The menu highlights American and Caribbean cuisine. Specialties include such dishes as grilled tuna with cracked peppercorns and lobster ravioli in a creamy pesto sauce. *1 Duval St., tel. 305/296–4600. AE, DC, MC, V.*

$–$$ **Half Shell Raw Bar.** "Eat It Raw" is the motto, and even during the off-season this oyster bar keeps shucking. You eat at shellacked picnic tables in a shed, with model ships, life buoys, and old license plates hung overhead. If shellfish isn't to your taste, try the broiled dolphin sandwich or linguine seafood marinara. *Land's End Marina, tel. 305/294–7496. Reservations not accepted. MC, V.*

Pub Crawling Three spots stand out for first-timers among the many local saloons frequented by Key West denizens. **Capt. Tony's Saloon** (428 Greene St.) is where Ernest Hemingway used to hang out when it was called **Sloppy Joe's.** The current **Sloppy Joe's** is found nearby at 201 Duval Street and has become a landmark in its own right. **Schooner Wharf** (Key West Bight; *see* Exploring Key West, *above*) is the most authentically local saloon and doesn't sell T-shirts. All are within easy walking distance of the cruise-ship piers.

Martinique

One of the most beautiful islands in the Caribbean, Martinique is lush with wild orchids, frangipani, anthurium, jade vines, flamingo flowers, and hundreds of hibiscus varieties. Trees bend under the weight of tropical treats such as mangoes, papayas, bright red West Indian cherries, lemons, and limes. Acres of banana plantations, pineapple fields, and waving sugarcane fill the horizon.

The towering mountains and verdant rain forest in the north lure hikers, while underwater sights and sunken treasures attract snorkelers and scuba divers. Martinique is also wonderful if your idea of exercise is turning over every 10 or 15 minutes to get an even tan, or if your adventuresome spirit is satisfied by a duty-free shop.

The largest of the Windward Islands, Martinique is 4,261 miles from Paris, but its spirit and language are decidedly French, with more than a soupçon of West Indian spice. Tangible, edible evidence of that fact is the island's cuisine, a superb blend of classic French and Creole dishes.

Fort-de-France is the capital, but at the turn of the 20th century, St-Pierre, farther up the coast, was Martinique's premier city. Then, in 1902, volcanic Mont Pelée blanketed the city in ash, killing all its residents—save for a condemned man in prison. Today, the ruins are a popular excursion for cruise passengers.

Currency Legal tender is the French franc, which consists of 100 centimes. At press time, the rate was 4.65F to U.S.$1. Dollars are accepted, but if you're going to shop, dine, or visit museums on your own, it's better to convert a small amount of money into francs.

Telephones It is not possible to make collect calls from Martinique to the United States on the local phone system, but you can usually use an AT&T card. There are no coin telephone booths on the island. If you must call home and can't wait until the ship reaches the next port, go to the post office and purchase a Telecarte, which looks like a credit card and is used in special booths marked TELECOM. Long-distance calls made with Telecartes are less costly than operator-assisted calls.

Shore Excursions The following is a good choice on Martinique. It may not be offered by all cruise lines. Time and price are approximate.

Island Sights **Martinique's Pompeii.** By bus or taxi, drive through the lush green mountains, past picturesque villages, to St-Pierre, stopping at the museum there. This is one of the best island tours in the Caribbean. *2½–4 hrs. Cost: $50–$60.*

Coming Ashore Cruise ships that dock call at the Maritime Terminal east of the city. The only practical way to get into town is by cab ($16 round-trip). To get to the Maritime Terminal tourist information office, turn right and walk along the waterfront. Ships that anchor in the Baie des

Flamands (*see* Exploring Martinique, *below*) tender passengers directly to the downtown waterfront. A tourist office is just across the street from the landing pier in the Air France building. Guided walking tours ($15 for 1½ hrs.) can be arranged at the nearby open-air marketplace.

Getting Around

By Car

Martinique has about 175 miles of well-paved roads marked with international road signs. Streets in Fort-de-France are narrow and clogged with traffic, country roads are mountainous with hairpin turns, and the Martiniquais drive with controlled abandon. If you drive in the country, be sure to pick up a map from one of the tourist offices; an even better one is the *Carte Routière et Touristique*, available at any local bookstore.

For rental cars, contact **Avis** (tel. 596/70–11–60), **Budget** (tel. 596/63–69–00), or **Hertz** (tel. 596/60–64–64). Count on paying $60 a day.

By Ferry

Weather permitting, *vedettes* (ferries) operate daily between Fort-de-France and the marina Méridien, in Pointe du Bout, and between Fort-de-France and the beaches of Anse-Mitan and Anse-à-l'Ane. The Quai d'Esnambuc is the arrival and departure point for ferries in Fort-de-France. The one-way fare is 16F; round-trip, 27F.

By Taxi

Taxis are relatively expensive. At press time, metered taxi fares were about to be introduced. Under the old system, rates were regulated by the government. The minimum charge was 10F (about $2.90), but a journey of any distance could easily cost upwards of 50F. Before you agree to use a taxi driver as a guide, make sure his English is good.

Exploring Martinique

Numbers in the margin correspond to points of interest on the Martinique map.

Fort-de-France

❶ On the island's west coast, on the beautiful Baie des Flamands, lies the capital city of **Fort-de-France.** Its narrow streets and pastel buildings with ornate wrought-iron balconies are reminiscent of the French Quarter in New Orleans—but whereas New Orleans is flat, Fort-de-France is hilly.

Bordering the waterfront is **La Savane,** a 12½-acre landscaped park filled with gardens, tropical trees, fountains, and benches. It's a popular gathering place and the scene of promenades, parades, and impromptu soccer matches. Near the harbor is a marketplace where beads, baskets, pottery, and straw hats are sold. The crafts here are among the nicest in the Caribbean.

On rue de la Liberté, which runs along the west side of La Savane, look for the **Musée Départmentale de la Martinique.** Artifacts from the pre-Columbian Arawak and Carib periods include pottery, beads, and part of a skeleton that turned up during excavations in 1972. One exhibit examines the history of slavery; costumes, documents, furniture, and handicrafts from the island's colonial period are on display. *9 rue de la Liberté, tel. 596/71–57–05. Admission: 15F. Open weekdays 8:30–1 and 2:30–5, Sat. 9–noon.*

Rue Schoelcher runs through the center of the capital's primary shopping district—a six-block area bounded by rue de la République, rue de la Liberté, rue Victor Sévère, and rue Victor Hugo (*see* Shopping, *below*).

The Romanesque **St-Louis Cathedral** (west of rue Victor Schoelcher), whose steeple rises high above the surrounding buildings, has lovely stained-glass windows. A number of Martinique's former governors are interred beneath the choir loft.

The **Bibliothèque Schoelcher** (pronounced shell-cher), a wildly elaborate Byzantine-Egyptian-Romanesque public library, is named after Victor Schoelcher, who led the fight to free the slaves in the French West Indies in the 19th century. The eye-popping structure

Ajoupa-Bouillon, **4**
Balata, **2**
Bellefontaine, **8**
Fort-de-France, **1**
Le Carbet, **7**
Le Morne Rouge, **3**
Musée Gauguin, **6**
St-Pierre, **5**
Schoelcher, **9**

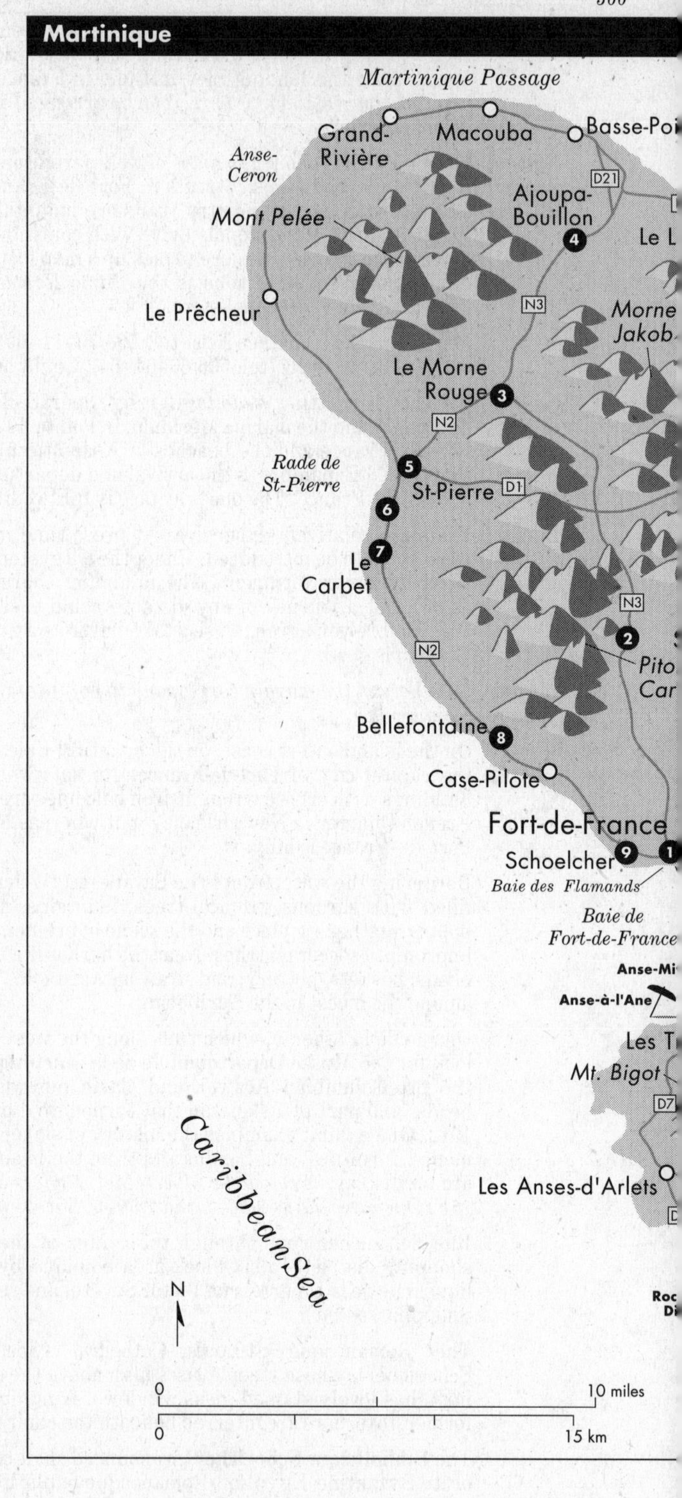

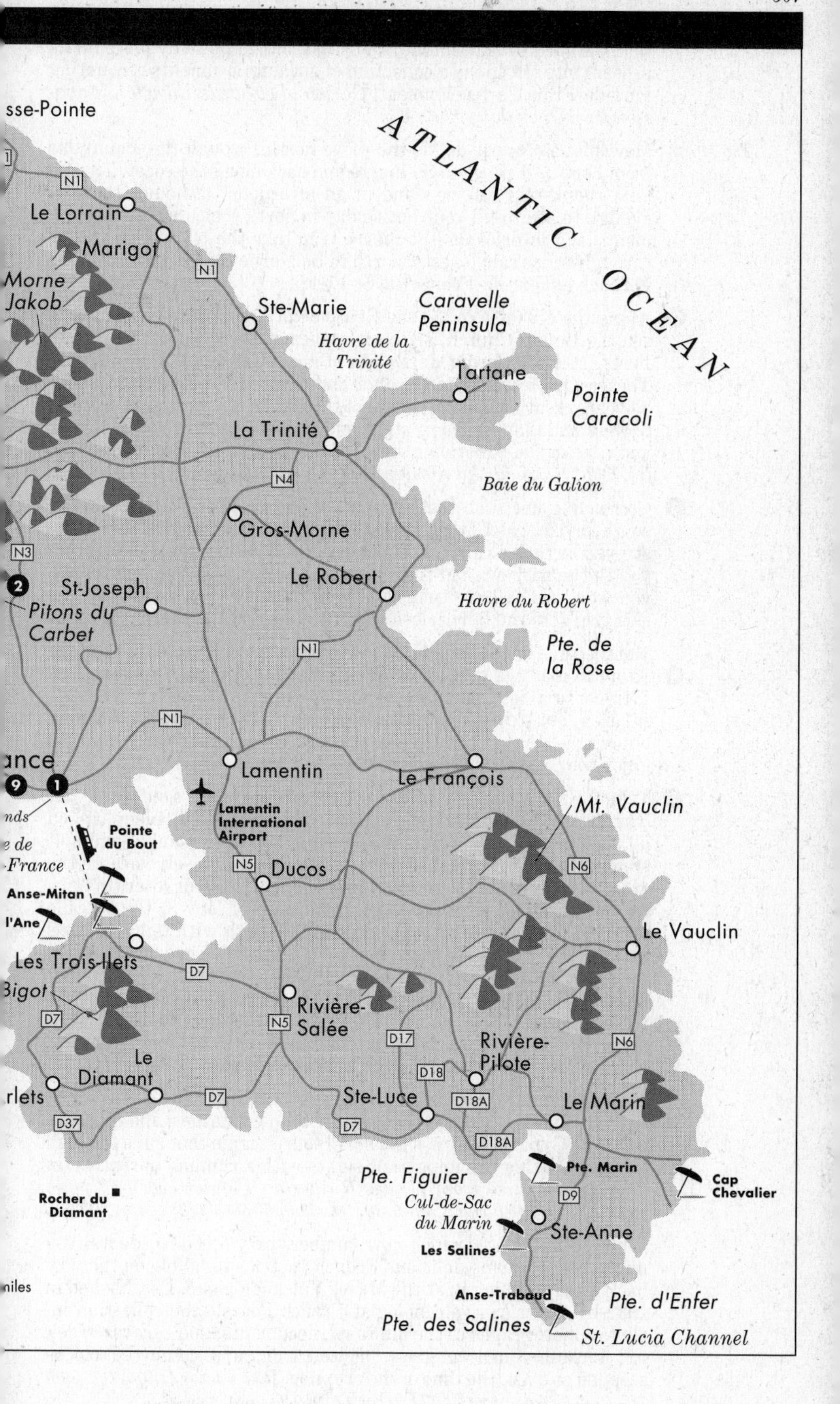
sse-Pointe
ATLANTIC OCEAN
N1
Le Lorrain
Marigot
Morne Jakob
N1
Ste-Marie
Caravelle Peninsula
Havre de la Trinité
Tartane
Pointe Caracoli
La Trinité
N4
Baie du Galion
Gros-Morne
N3
Le Robert
St-Joseph
Pitons du Carbet
Havre du Robert
N1
Pte. de la Rose
N1
ance
Lamentin
Le François
nds
Lamentin International Airport
Mt. Vauclin
Pointe du Bout
e de
France
N5
Ducos
N6
Anse-Mitan
l'Ane
Le Vauclin
Les Trois-Ilets
D7
Bigot
Rivière-Salée
D7
N5
D17
Rivière-Pilote
N6
Le Diamant
D18
rlets
D7
Ste-Luce
D18A
Le Marin
D37
D7
D18A
Pte. Marin
Pte. Figuier
Cap Chevalier
Rocher du Diamant
D9
Cul-de-Sac du Marin
Ste-Anne
Les Salines
niles
Anse-Trabaud
Pte. d'Enfer
Pte. des Salines
St. Lucia Channel

was built for the 1889 Paris Exposition, after which it was dismantled, shipped to Martinique, and reassembled piece by piece on its present site. Inside is a collection of ancient documents recounting Fort-de-France's development. *Corner of rue de la Liberté. Admission free. Open daily 8:30–6.*

The North Martinique's "must do" is the drive north through the mountains from Fort-de-France to St-Pierre and back along the coast. The 40-mile round-trip can be done in an afternoon, although there is enough to see to fill your entire day in port. A nice way to see the lush island interior and St-Pierre is to take the N3, which snakes through dense rain forests, north to Le Morne Rouge; then take the N2 back to Fort-de-France via St-Pierre.

❷ Along the N3 (also called the Route de la Trace), stop at **Balata** to see the **Balata Church,** an exact replica of Sacré-Coeur Basilica in Paris, and the **Jardin de Balata** (Balata Gardens). Jean-Phillipe Thoze, a professional landscaper and devoted horticulturist, spent 20 years creating this collection of thousands of varieties of tropical flowers and plants. There are shaded benches where you can relax and take in the panoramic views of the mountains. *Rte. de Balata, tel. 596/72–58–82. Admission: 30F. Open daily 9–5.*

❸ Continuing north on the N3, you'll reach **Le Morne Rouge,** on the southern slopes of Mont Pelée. This town was, like St-Pierre, destroyed by the volcano and is now a popular resort. Signs will direct you to the narrow road that takes you halfway up the mountain—you won't really have time to hike to the 4,600-foot peak, but this side trip gets you fairly close and offers spectacular views.

❹ Northeast of here on the N3, a few miles south of **Basse-Pointe** on the Atlantic coast, is the flower-filled village of **Ajoupa-Bouillon.** This 17th-century settlement in the midst of pineapple fields is a beautiful area, but skip it if you've never seen St-Pierre and are running out of time. From Le Morne Rouge, you'll need a good three hours to enjoy the coastal drive back to Fort-de-France.

❺ Take the N2 west a few miles to **St-Pierre,** the island's oldest city. It was once called the Paris of the West Indies, but Mont Pelée changed all that in the spring of 1902, when it began to rumble and spit steam. By the first week in May, all wildlife had wisely vacated the area, but city officials ignored the warnings, needing voters in town for an upcoming election. On the morning of May 8, the volcano erupted, belching forth a cloud of burning ash with temperatures above 3,600°F. Within three minutes, Mont Pelée had transformed St-Pierre into Martinique's Pompeii. The entire town was annihilated, its 30,000 inhabitants calcified. There was only one survivor: a prisoner named Siparis, who was saved by the thick walls of his underground cell. He was later pardoned and for some time afterward was a sideshow attraction at the Barnum & Bailey Circus.

You can wander through the site to see the ruins of the island's first church, built in 1640; the theater; the toppled statues; and Siparis's cell. The Cyparis Express is a small tourist train that runs through the city, hitting the important sights with a running narrative (in French). *Departs from pl. des Ruines du Figuier every 45 mins weekdays 9:30–1 and 2:30–5:30, tel. 596/55–50–92. Tickets: 30F.*

While in St-Pierre, which now numbers only 6,000 residents, you might pick up some delicious French pastries to nibble on the way back after stopping in at the **Musée Vulcanologique.** Established in 1932 by American volcanologist Franck Perret, the collection includes photographs of the old town, documents, and excavated relics, including molten glass, melted iron, and contorted clocks stopped at 8 AM, the time of the eruption. *Rue Victor Hugo, tel. 596/78–15–16. Admission: 15F. Open daily 9–noon and 3–5.*

A short way south is **Anse-Turin,** where Paul Gauguin lived briefly in 1887 with his friend and fellow artist Charles Laval. The **Musée Gauguin** traces the history of the artist's Martinique connection through documents, letters, and reproductions of paintings he completed while on the island. *Tel. 596/77-22-66. Admission: 15F. Open daily 9-5:30.*

Continuing down the coast, **Le Carbet** is where Columbus is believed to have landed on June 15, 1502. In 1635, Pierre Belain d'Esnambuc arrived here with the first French settlers.

On your way back to port, you'll pass two of the island's more interesting towns. **Bellefontaine** is a small fishing village with pastel houses spilling down the hillsides and colorful boats bobbing in the water. Just north of Fort-de-France, **Schoelcher** is home of the University of the French West Indies and Guyana.

Shopping French products, such as perfume, wines, liquors, designer scarves, leather goods, and crystal, are all good buys in Fort-de-France. In addition, luxury goods are discounted 20% when paid for with traveler's checks or major credit cards. Look for Creole gold jewelry, white and dark rums, and handcrafted straw goods, pottery, and tapestries.

Small shops carrying luxury items proliferate around the cathedral in Fort-de-France, particularly on rue Victor Hugo, rue Moreau de Jones, rue Antoine Siger, and rue Lamartine. Look for Lalique, Limoges, and Baccarat at **Cadet Daniel** (72 rue Antoine Siger, tel. 596/71-41-48) and at **Roger Albert** (7 rue Victor Hugo, tel. 596/71-71-71), which also sells perfume. A wide variety of dolls, straw goods, tapestries, and pottery is available at the **Caribbean Art Center** (Centre de Métiers Art, opposite the tourist office, Blvd. Alfassa, tel. 596/70-32-16). The **Galerie Arti-Bijoux** (89 rue Victor Hugo, tel. 596/63-10-62) has some unusual and excellent Haitian art at reasonable prices.

Sports
Fishing For charter excursions, contact **Bathy's Club** (Hótel Méridien, Anse-Mitan, tel. 596/66-00-00).

Golf **Golf de l'Impératrice Joséphine** (tel. 96/68-32-81) has an 18-hole Robert Trent Jones course with an English-speaking pro, a pro shop, a bar, and a restaurant. Located at Trois-Ilets, a mile from the Pointe du Bout resort area and 18 miles from Fort-de-France, the club offers special greens fees for cruise-ship passengers.

Hiking **Parc Naturel Régional de la Martinique** (Caserne Bouille, Fort-de-France, tel. 596/73-19-30) organizes inexpensive guided hiking tours. Information is available at the island tourist offices.

Horseback Riding Excursions and lessons are available at the **Black Horse Ranch** (near La Pagerie in Trois-Ilets, tel. 596/68-37-69), **La Cavale** (near Diamant on the road to the Novotel hotel, tel. 596/76-22-94), and **Ranch Jack** (near Anse-d'Arlets, tel. 596/68-37-67).

Water Sports Hobie Cats, Sunfish, and Sailfish can be rented by the hour from hotel beach shacks. If you're a member of a yacht club, show your club membership card and enjoy the facilities of **Club de la Voile de Fort-de-France** (Pointe Simon, tel. 596/70-26-63) and **Yacht Club de la Martinique** (blvd. Chevalier, Ste-Marthe, tel. 596/63-26-76). To explore the old shipwrecks, coral gardens, and other undersea sites, you must have a medical certificate and insurance papers. Among the island's dive operators are **Bathy's Club** (Hotel Méridien, Anse-Mitan, tel. 596/66-00-00) and the **Sub Diamant Rock** (Diamant-Novotel, tel. 596/76-42-42).

Beaches Topless bathing is prevalent at the large resort hotels. Unless you're an expert swimmer, steer clear of the Atlantic waters, except in the area of Cap Chevalier and the Caravelle Peninsula. **Pointe du Bout** has small, white-sand beaches, most of which are commandeered by resort hotels. **Anse-Mitan,** south of Pointe du Bout, is a white-sand beach with superb snorkeling. **Anse-à-l'Ane** offers picnic tables and a nearby shell museum; bathers cool off in the bar of the Calalou Hotel. **Grande-Anse** is less crowded—the preferred beach among people who know the island well. **Les Salines** is the best of Martinique's beaches, whether you choose to be with other sun worshipers or to find your own quiet stretch of sand. However, it's an hour's drive from Fort-de-France and 5 miles beyond Ste-Anne.

Dining *All restaurants include a 15% service charge in their menu prices.*

$$$ **Relais Caraibes.** For a leisurely lunch, a magnificent view of Diamond Rock, and possibly a swim in the pool, head out to this tasteful restaurant and hotel. (A taxi will take you there for about 180F from Fort-de-France, less from Pointe du Bout.) Dishes include a half lobster in two sauces, fresh-caught fish in a basil sauce, and fricassee of country shrimp. *La Cherry (on the small road leading to the Diamant-Novotel), Le Diamant, tel. 596/76-44-65. AE, MC, V. Closed Mon.*

$ **Le Second Soufflé.** The chef uses fresh vegetables and fruits—nutrition is a top priority here—to make soufflés ranging from aubergine (eggplant) to *filet de ti-nain* (small green bananas) with chocolate sauce and other tempting creations, such as eggplant ragout and okra quiche. *27 rue Blénac, Fort-de-France, tel. 596/63-44-11. No credit cards. No lunch Sat.*

St. Croix

St. Croix is the largest of the three U.S. Virgin Islands that form the northern hook of the Lesser Antilles. Its position, 40 miles south of its sisters, is far removed from the hustle and bustle of St. Thomas.

Christopher Columbus landed here in 1493, skirmishing briefly with the native Carib Indians. Since then, the three U.S. Virgin Islands have played a colorful, if painful, role as pawns in the game of European colonialism. Theirs is a history of pirates and privateers, sugar plantations, slave trading, and slave revolt and liberation. Through it all, Denmark had staying power; from the 17th to the 19th century, Danes oversaw a plantation slave economy that produced molasses, rum, cotton, and tobacco. Many of the stones you see in buildings or tread on in the streets were once used as ballast on sailing ships, and the yellow fort of Christiansted is a reminder of the value once placed on this island treasure.

Currency The U.S. dollar is the official currency of St. Croix.

Telephones Calling the United States from St. Croix works the same as within the states. Local calls from a public phone cost 25¢ for every five minutes.

Shore Excursions The following are good choices on St. Croix. They may not be offered by all cruise lines. Times and prices are approximate.

Island Sights **Plantation Hike.** At the ruins of this plantation, discovered outside Frederiksted in 1984, you can glimpse into St. Croix's past as you hike through the verdant rain forest. *3 hrs. Cost: $25–$30.*

Tee Time **Golf at Carambola.** Robert Trent Jones designed this 18-hole, par-72 course, considered one of the Caribbean's finest. Includes shared golf cart and greens fees. *Half day. Cost: $58.*

Coming Ashore Smaller ships (fewer than 200 passengers) dock in Christiansted, larger ones in Frederiksted. Information centers are found near both piers. In Christiansted, pick up a copy of the "Walking Tour Guide" at the visitor center. Both towns are easily explored on foot; beaches are nearby.

Getting Around

By Car Driving is on the left-hand side of the road, although steering wheels are on the left-hand side of the car. Rentals are available from **Avis** (tel. 809/778–9355) and **Budget** (tel. 809/778–9636), which are both near the airport; **Caribbean Jeep & Car** (tel. 809/773–4399) in Frederiksted; and **Olympic** (tel. 809/773–2208) in Christiansted. Rates begin at about $50 daily.

By Taxi Taxis of all shapes and sizes are available at the cruise piers and at various shopping and resort areas; they also respond quickly when telephoned. Taxis do not have meters, so you should check the list of standard rates available from the visitor centers and settle the fare with your driver before you start. Taxi drivers are required to carry a copy of the official rates and must show it to you when asked. Remember, too, that you can hail a taxi that is already occupied. Drivers take multiple fares and sometimes even trade passengers at midpoints. Try **St. Croix Taxi Association** (tel. 809/778–1088) or **Antilles Taxi Service** (tel. 809/773–5020).

Exploring St. Croix

Numbers in the margin correspond to points of interest on the St. Croix map.

❶ Next to the cruise-ship pier in **Frederiksted** is the restored Ft. Frederik, completed in the late 18th century. Here, in 1848, the slaves of the Danish West Indies were freed by Governor Peter van Scholten. Down Market Street is the Market Place, where you can buy fresh fruit and vegetables early in the morning.

Around the corner on Prince Street is the Old Danish School, designed in the 1830s and now part of the Ingeborg Nesbett Clinic. St. Paul's Episcopal Church, a mixture of classic and Gothic Revival architecture, is two blocks south on Prince Street; it has survived several hurricanes since its construction in 1812 and became Episcopal when the United States purchased the island in 1917. A few steps away, on King Cross Street, is Apothecary Hall, which survived the great fire of 1878. Walk south and turn right on Queen Cross Street to the Old Public Library, or Bell House, which now houses an arts-and-crafts center and the Dorsch Cultural Center for the performing arts. Back at the waterfront, walk up Strand Street to the fish market. By the cruise-ship pier is Victoria House, on your right. Once a private home and the town's best example of Victorian gingerbread architecture, it was recently renovated.

❷ South of Frederiksted is the **West End Salt Pond,** rife with mangroves and little blue herons. In the spring, large leatherback sea turtles clamber up the white sand to lay their eggs. You will also see brown pelicans.

❸ If you follow Centerline Road out of town, you'll soon come to the **Estate Whim Plantation Museum.** The lovingly restored estate, with windmill, cookhouse, and other buildings, gives a real sense of what life was like for the owners of St. Croix's sugar plantations in the 1800s. The great house, with a singular oval shape and high ceilings, features antique furniture and utensils, as well as a major apothecary exhibit. Note the house's fresh and airy atmosphere—the waterless moat was used not for defense but for gathering cooling air.

❹ About a mile east of Estate Whim Plantation, on Centerline Road, are the **St. George Village Botanical Gardens,** 17 lush and fragrant acres amid the ruins of a 19th-century sugarcane plantation village.

❺ At the **Cruzan Distillery** rum is made with pure rainwater, making it (so it is said) superior to any other. Visitors are welcome for a tour and a free rum-laced drink (the concoction changes daily).

❻ For a good view of Salt River Bay, where Columbus landed, make your way along Northside Road to **Judith's Fancy.** Once home to the governor of the Knights of Malta, this old great house and tower are

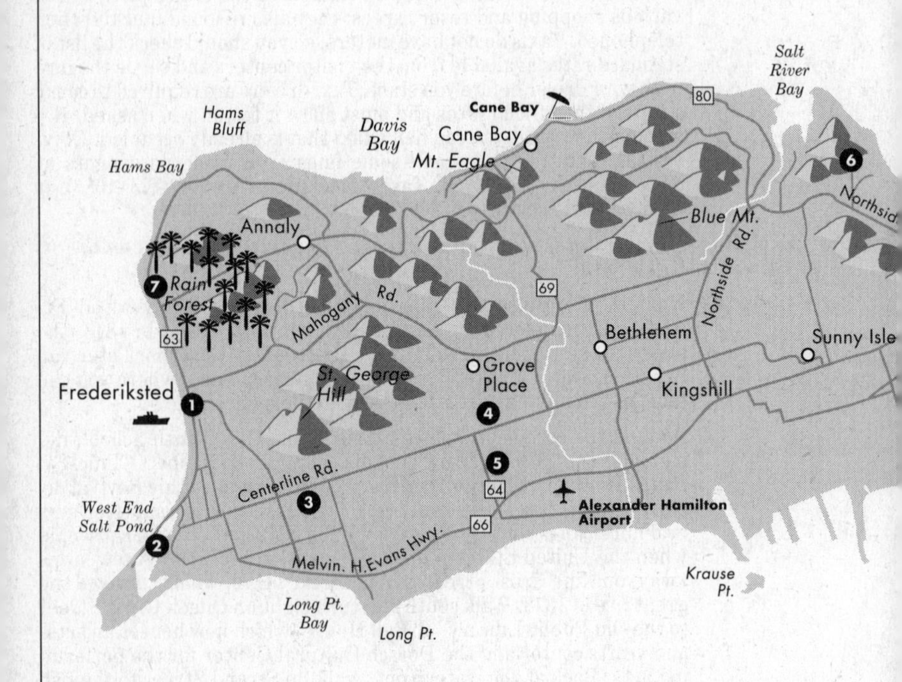

Christiansted, **8**
Cruzan Distillery, **5**
Estate Whim Plantation Museum, **3**
Frederiksted, **1**
Judith's Fancy, **6**
St. George Village Botanical Gardens, **4**
Sprat Hall Plantation, **7**
West End Salt Pond, **2**

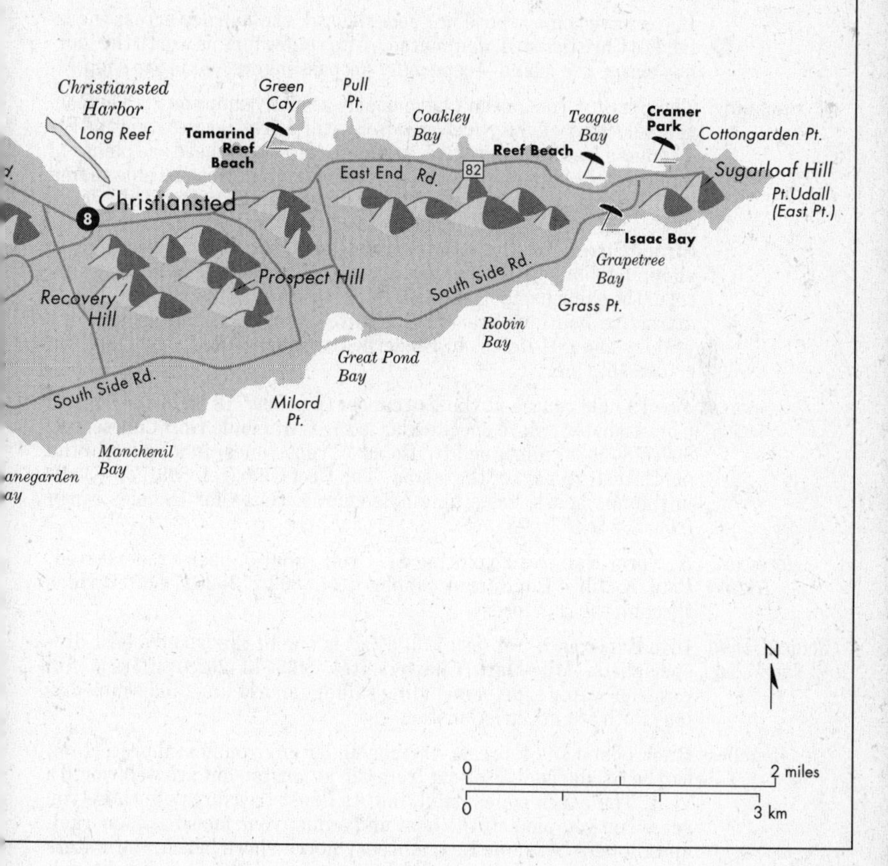
Buck Island
Buck Island Beach
Christiansted Harbor
Long Reef
Green Cay
Pull Pt.
Tamarind Reef Beach
Coakley Bay
Teague Bay
Cramer Park
Cottongarden Pt.
Reef Beach
East End Rd.
82
Sugarloaf Hill
Pt.Udall (East Pt.)
Christiansted
8
Isaac Bay
Grapetree Bay
Prospect Hill
South Side Rd.
Recovery Hill
Grass Pt.
Robin Bay
Great Pond Bay
South Side Rd.
Milord Pt.
Manchenil Bay
anegarden
ay
N
0
2 miles
0
3 km

now in ruins. The "Judith" comes from the name of a woman buried on the property.

7 **Sprat Hall Plantation** (Route 63) has been owned and run for generations by the Hurd Family, who has established quite a reputation for home-cooked food. The beautiful great house is the oldest in the Virgin Islands. Pull up a chair at the breezy Sprat Hall Beach Restaurant to sip on a cooling soda or rum drink and munch on the famous pumpkin fritters while you gaze through beach seagrapes at the glistening Caribbean.

8 If you have come ashore in Frederikstad, the journey across the island to **Christiansted,** dominated by its yellow fort, is worth the journey across the island—especially for passengers looking to shop.

Shopping Though St. Croix doesn't have nearly as many shops as St. Thomas, the selection of duty-free goods is still fairly large. Many of St. Thomas's leading shops have branches here, and there are plenty of independent merchants who carry items you may not be able to find in Charlotte Amalie. The best shopping is in **Christiansted,** where most shops are in the historic district near the harbor. **King Street, Strand Street,** and the arcades that lead off them comprise the main shopping district. The longest arcade is **Caravelle Arcade,** in the hotel of the same name. **Gallows Bay,** just east of Christiansted, has an attractive boutique area that features unusual island-made silver jewelry and gift items. In **Frederiksted,** a handful of shops face the cruise-ship pier.

Sports

Golf The 18-hole course at the **Buccaneer** (tel. 809/773–2100) is close to Christiansted. More spectacular is the **Carambola Golf Course** (tel. 809/778–5638), designed by Robert Trent Jones, in a valley in the northwestern part of the island. The **Reef Club** (tel. 809/773–8844), in the northeast, has a nine-hole course. Rates for 18 holes range from $35 to $77.

Horseback Riding At Sprat Hall (*see* Exploring St. Croix, *above*), near Frederiksted, **Paul & Jill's Equestrian Stables** (tel. 809/772–2627) offer rides through the rain forest.

Scuba Diving and Snorkeling **Dive Experience** (tel. 809/773–3307) is one of the island's best dive specialists. **Mile-Mark Charters** (tel. 809/773–2628) offers a full range of water sports, including sailing, snorkeling, and scuba diving. Both are in Christiansted.

Beaches **Buck Island** and its reef, which is under environmental protection, can be reached only by boat from Christiansted but are well worth a visit. The beach is beautiful, but its finest treasures are those you see when you plop off the boat and adjust your face mask, snorkel, and flippers. At **Cane Bay,** a breezy north-shore beach, the waters are not always gentle but the diving and snorkeling are wondrous, and there are never many people around. Less than 200 yards out is the drop-off, called Cane Bay Wall. Three miles north of Frederiksted you'll find **Rainbow Beach** where you can enjoy the sand, snorkel at a small nearby reef, and get a bite to eat at the bar. **Tamarind Reef Beach** is a small but attractive beach with good snorkeling east of Christiansted. Green Cay and Buck Island seem smack in front of you and make the view arresting.

Dining

$$ **Le St. Tropez.** A dark-wood bar and soft lighting add to the Mediterranean feel at this pleasant bistro, tucked into a courtyard off Frederiksted's main thoroughfare. Daily specials highlight local seafood, while light French cuisine, such as quiches, brochettes, and crepes, are the menu's mainstays. *67 King St., Frederiksted, tel. 809/772–3000. AE, D, MC, V. Closed Sun.*

$ **Camille's.** This tiny, lively spot is perfect for lunch or a light supper. Sandwiches and burgers are the big draw, but each day there's a seafood special—often wahoo or mahimahi. *Queen Cross St., Christiansted, tel. 809/773–2985. No credit cards. No lunch Sun.*

St. Lucia

Lush St. Lucia—a ruggedly beautiful island, with towering mountains, a dense tropical rain forest, fertile green valleys, and hundreds of acres of banana plantations—sits in the middle of the Windward Islands. Nicknamed "the Helen of the West Indies" because of its natural beauty, St. Lucia is distinguished from its eastern Caribbean neighbors by its unique geological sites. The Pitons, twin peaks on the island's southwest coast that have become a symbol of this island, soar to more than 2,400 feet above the ocean floor. Nearby, just outside the French colonial town of Soufrière, is a "drive-in" volcano with bubbling sulphur springs that attract visitors for their curative waters. Visitors come to St. Lucia for the ecotouring opportunities and to enjoy resort life at some of the Caribbean's most spectacular properties. The island's offshore reefs attract world-class scuba divers.

Battles between the French and English resulted in St. Lucia changing hands 14 times before 1814, when England finally won possession. In 1979, the island became an independent state within the British Commonwealth of Nations. The official language is English, although most people also speak a French Creole patois.

Currency St. Lucia uses the Eastern Caribbean (E.C.) dollar. The exchange rate is about E.C.$2.65 to U.S.$1. U.S. dollars are readily accepted, but you'll usually get change in E.C. dollars. Major credit cards and traveler's checks are also widely accepted.

Telephones Long-distance connections from St. Lucia are excellent, and numbers can be dialed directly. International telephone and telex services are available at Pointe Seraphine, where most ships dock.

Shore Excursions The following is a good choice in St. Lucia. It may not be offered by all cruise lines. Time and price are approximate.

Natural Beauty **La Soufrière and the Pitons.** Travel by air-conditioned bus along the winding West Coast Road for a spectacular view of the Pitons; visit La Soufrière volcano and its sulfur springs and nearby Diamond Botanical Gardens and Mineral Baths. A buffet lunch accompanies this scenic overview of the island. *8 hrs. Cost: $45.*

Coming Ashore Most cruise ships call at the capital city of Castries, on the island's northwest coast. Two docking areas are used: Pointe Seraphine, a duty-free shopping complex and cruise-ship terminal, or the downtown industrial dock across the harbor. Ferry service connects the two dock areas.

On some cruise itineraries, vessels call instead at Soufrière, farther south on the island's west coast. Ships calling at Soufrière drop anchor and tender passengers ashore.

Tourist information offices are located at Pointe Seraphine and along the waterfront, on Bay Street, in Soufrière. Neither Castries nor Soufrière offers much of interest for visitors, although downtown Castries is within walking distance of the pier. Instead, most of St. Lucia's worthwhile attractions are found beyond these two port cities. You can hire a taxi at the docks to see the outlying sights, but the most cost-efficient way to see the island is on a ship-organized shore excursion.

Getting Around Passengers who choose to explore on their own have the option of renting a car or hiring a taxi.

By Car To rent a car, you must have a valid driver's license and credit card and also buy a temporary St. Lucian license, which costs U.S.$12. Rates begin at about U.S.$50 a day for a Jeep and U.S.$75 for a car with standard transmission. Remember that driving is on the *left* side of the road. Rental agencies at or convenient to Pointe Seraphine include **Avis** (tel. 809/452–2700), **Budget** (tel. 809/452–

0233), **Hertz** (tel. 809/452–0679), and **National** (tel. 809/450–8721). In Soufrière, contact **Cool Breeze Jeep/Car Rental,** (tel. 809/459–7729).

By Taxi Taxis are unmetered, but the government has issued a list of suggested fares. From Pointe Seraphine, a 10–20 minute ride north to Rodney Bay should cost about $10–$15. For trips to Soufrière, at least an hour's drive to the south, expect to pay $20 per hour for up to four people. A tour of the entire island takes about six hours and costs about $120. Whatever your destination, negotiate the price with the driver before you depart, and be sure that you both understand whether the rate you've agreed upon is in E.C. or U.S. dollars. Drivers expect a 10% tip.

Exploring St. Lucia *Numbers in the margin correspond to points of interest on the St. Lucia map.*

Castries Area

1 **Government House,** the official residence of the governor-general of St. Lucia, is one of the island's few remaining examples of Victorian architecture. *On Government House Rd., Castries.*

2 Driving up **Morne Fortune,** the "hill of good fortune," you'll see beautiful tropical plants—frangipani, lilies, bougainvillea, hibiscus, and oleander. *South of Castries.*

Ft. Charlotte, on the Morne, was begun in 1764 by the French as the *Citadelle du Morne Fortune* and completed after 20 years of battling and changing hands. Its old barracks and batteries have been converted to government buildings and local educational facilities, but you can view the remains—redoubts, a guardroom, stables, and cells.

3 **Gros Islet.** This quiet little fishing village north of Rodney Bay jumps on Friday nights, when a street festival with live music attracts locals and tourists alike.

The Castries **Market** is open every day but most crowded on Friday and Saturday mornings, when farmers bring their produce to town. Across the street, also in a new building, is the Vendor's Arcade, where you can buy souvenirs and handicrafts. *Corner of Jeremie and Peyier Sts., Castries.*

4 According to island tales, pirate Jambe de Bois (Wooden Leg) used **Pigeon Island** as his hideout. Now a national park, Pigeon Island has a beach, calm waters for swimming, restaurants, and picnic areas. On the grounds you'll see ruins of barracks, batteries, and garrisons dating from the French and British battles for control of St. Lucia. The island is easily reached by a causeway. *Pigeon Island, St. Lucia Trust, tel. 809/450–8167. Admission: E.C.$10. Open daily 9–5.*

Soufrière Area

5 It's an hour's drive on the new, but winding, West Coast Road from Castries to **Soufrière,** a French colonial town that was named for the nearby volcano. The mountainous region of St. Lucia is breathtakingly lush, and the road that snakes along the coast offers spectacular views of the Pitons, the rain forest, and the sea.

6 In 1713 Louis IV provided funds for the construction of curative baths on this site. Today, you can walk through the **Diamond Mineral Baths and Botanical Garden**'s beautifully kept grounds to Diamond Falls, then slip into your swimsuit for a dip in the steaming sulfur baths. *Soufrière Estate, tel. 809/452–4759, Admission: E.C.$5. Open daily 10–5.*

7 **La Soufrière,** the drive-in volcano, is southeast of the town of Soufrière. More than 20 pools of black, belching, smelly sulfurous waters bubble, bake, and steam on the surface. *Bay St., tel. 809/459–5500. Admission: E.C.$3, includes guided tour. Open daily 9–5.*

8 The incredible **Pitons** have become the symbol of St. Lucia. These perfectly shaped pyramidal cones, covered with thick tropical vege-

tation, rise precipitously out of the azure sea. Petit Piton, at 2,619 feet, is taller than Gros Piton (2,461 feet), although Gros is broader.

Shopping As tourism is increasing in St. Lucia, so are the options for shopping. Local products include silk-screened fabric and clothing, pottery, wood carvings, cocoa and coffee, and baskets and other straw items. The only duty-free shopping is at Pointe Seraphine.

Artsibit (corner of Brazil and Mongiraud Sts., Castries, tel. 809/452–7865) features works by top St. Lucian artists.

Bagshaw Studios (at Pointe Seraphine and on La Toc Rd., La Toc Bay, tel. 809/452–7570) sells clothing and household items created from unique silk-screened and hand-printed fabrics that are designed, printed, and sold only on St. Lucia.

Caribelle Batik (Old Victoria Rd., The Morne, tel. 809/452–3785) welcomes visitors to watch artisans creating batik clothing and wall hangings.

Eudovic Art Studio (Morne Fortune, 15 mins south of Castries, tel. 809/452–2747) sells trays, masks, and figures that are carved in the studio from mahogany, red cedar, and eucalyptus wood.

Made in St. Lucia (Gablewoods Mall, north of Castries, tel. 809/453–2788) sells only items made on the island—sandals, shirts, hot sauces, costume jewelry, carved wooden items, clay cooking pots, original art, and more—all at reasonable prices.

Noah's Arkade (Jeremie St. Castries and Pointe Seraphine, tel. 809/452–2523) has hammocks, straw mats, baskets and hats, and carvings, as well as books about and maps of St. Lucia.

Pointe Seraphine, the cruise-ship terminal, is a modern, Spanish-style complex where 33 shops sell designer perfume, china and crystal, jewelry, watches, leather goods, liquor, and cigarettes; to get the duty-free price, you must show your boarding pass or cabin key. Native crafts are also sold here.

Soufrière is not much of a shopping port, although there's a small arts center where handicrafts are sold and a batik studio at the Humming Bird Resort. Both are along the waterfront at the north end of town.

Sports
Fishing Among the sea creatures in these waters are dolphin, Spanish mackerel, barracuda, and white marlin. For half- or full-day fishing excursions, contact **Captain Mike's** (Vigie Bay Marina, Castries, tel. 809/452–7044) or **Mako Watersports** (Rodney Bay Marina, tel. 809/452–0412).

Golf The golf courses on St. Lucia are scenic and good fun, but they're not of a professional caliber. Nine-hole courses are at both **Sandals St. Lucia** (La Toc Rd., Castries, tel. 809/452–3081) and **St. Lucia Golf Club** (Cap Estate, tel. 809/452–8523). A caddy is required at Sandals. Greens fees are about U. S. $20 at either for 18 holes; club rentals are $10.

Hiking St. Lucia is laced with trails, but you should not attempt the challenging peaks on your own. The **Forest and Land Department** (tel. 809/450–2231) can provide you with a guide. The **St. Lucia National Trust** (tel. 809/452–5005) offers tours of several sites, including Pigeon Island (*see* Exploring St. Lucia, *above*).

Horseback Riding For trail rides, contact **International Riding Stables** (Gros Islet, tel. 809/452–8138), **Trim's Riding School** (Cas-en-Bas, tel. 809/452–8273), **North Point Riding Stables** (Gros Islet, tel. 809/450–8853), or **Jalousie Plantation** (Soufrière, tel. 809/459–7666). A half-hour ride runs about U.S.$30.

Scuba Diving **Scuba St. Lucia** (tel. 809/459–7355) is a PADI five-star training facility that offers daily beach and boat dives, resort courses, underwater

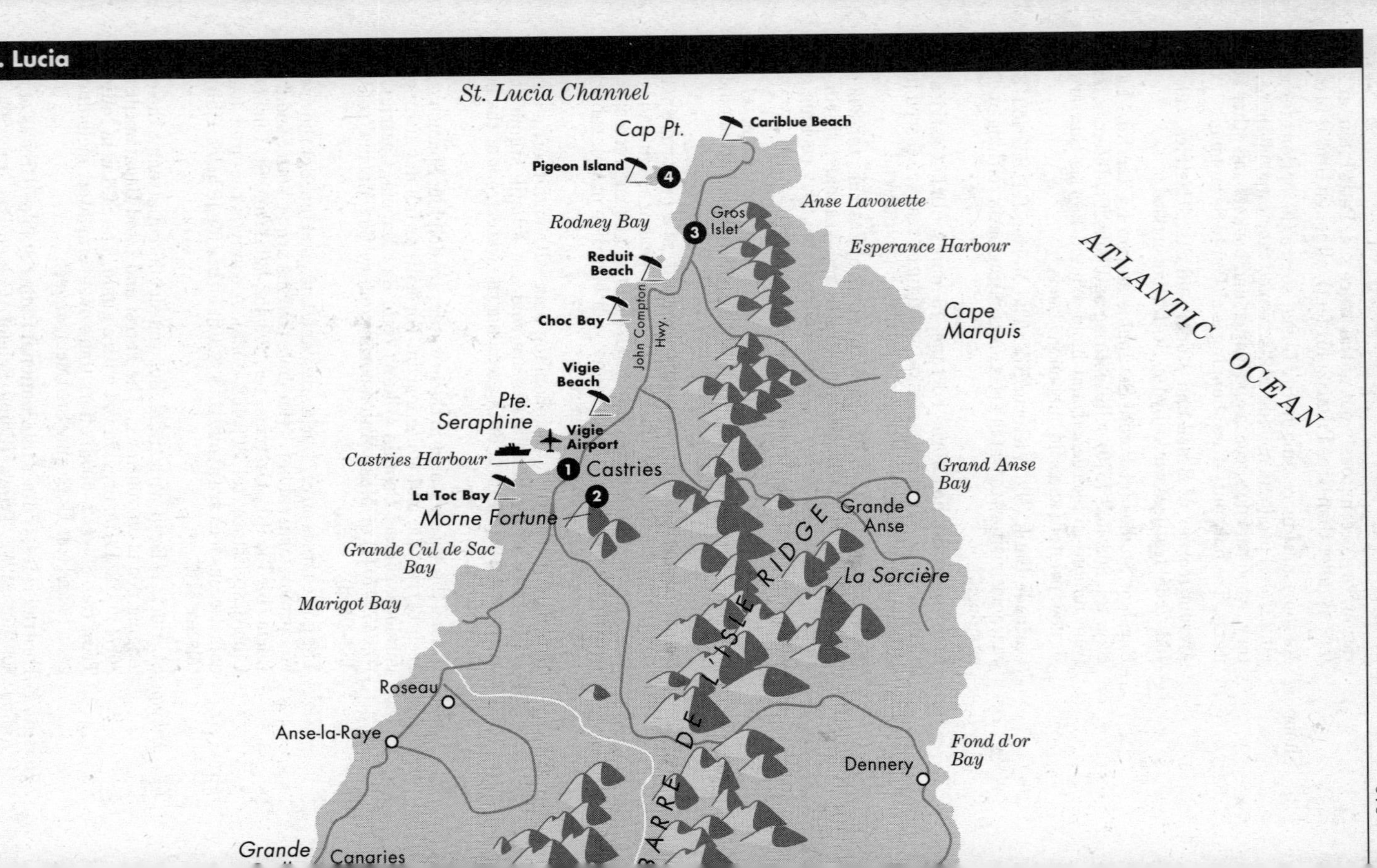

St. Lucia
St. Lucia Channel
Cap Pt.
Cariblue Beach
Pigeon Island
4
Anse Lavouette
Rodney Bay
3
Gros Islet
Esperance Harbour
ATLANTIC OCEAN
Reduit Beach
Choc Bay
John Compton Hwy.
Cape Marquis
Vigie Beach
Pte. Seraphine
Vigie Airport
Castries Harbour
1
Castries
Grand Anse Bay
La Toc Bay
2
Grande Anse
Morne Fortune
Grande Cul de Sac Bay
BARRE DE L'ISLE RIDGE
La Sorcière
Marigot Bay
Roseau
Anse-la-Raye
Fond d'or Bay
Dennery
Grande
Canaries

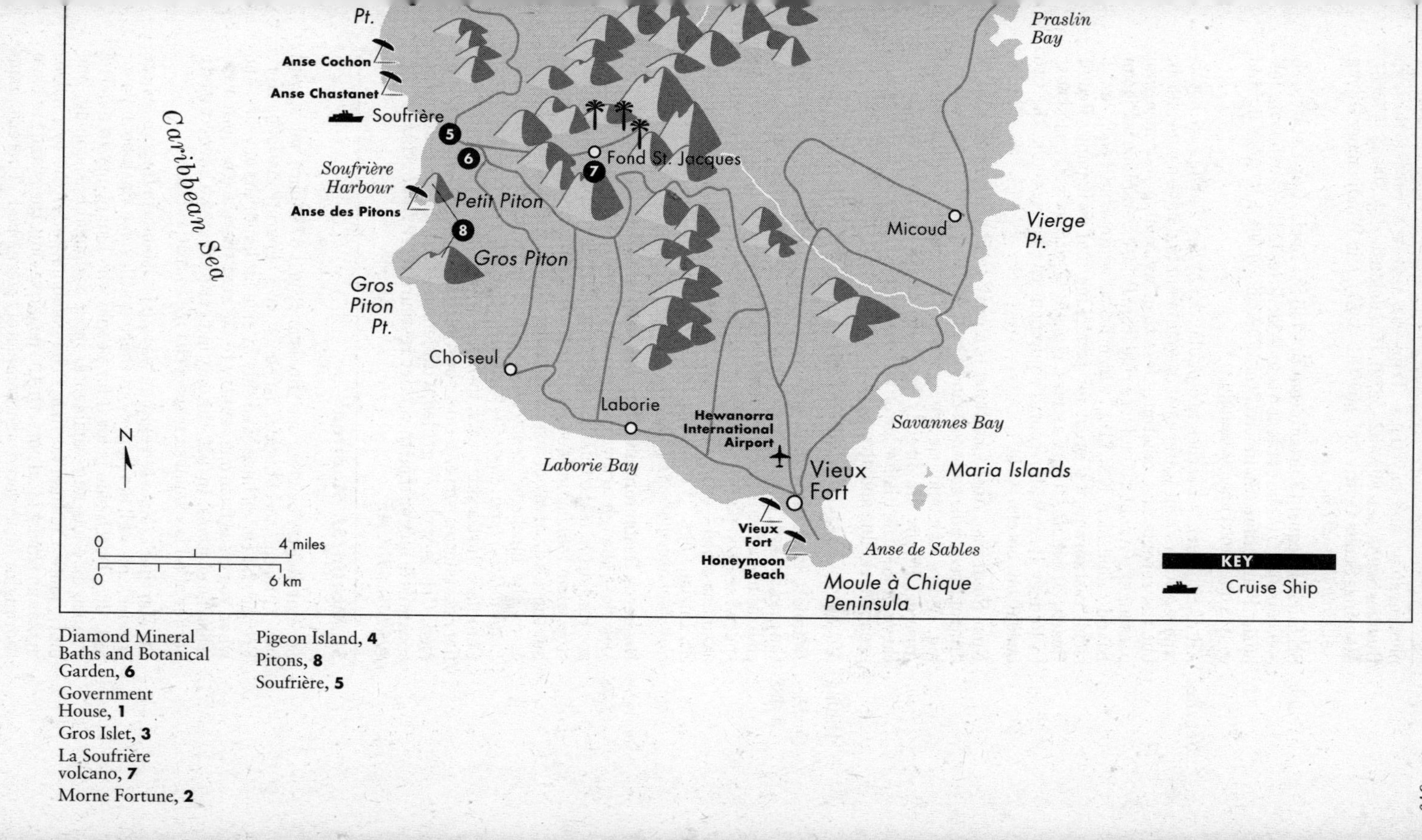

Diamond Mineral Baths and Botanical Garden, **6**
Government House, **1**
Gros Islet, **3**
La Soufrière volcano, **7**
Morne Fortune, **2**
Pigeon Island, **4**
Pitons, **8**
Soufrière, **5**

photography, and day trips. Trips can also be arranged through **Buddies Scuba** (tel. 809/452–5288), **Dive Jalousie** (tel. 809/459–7666), **Moorings Scuba Centre** (tel. 809/451–4357), and **Windjammer Diving** (tel. 809/452–0913).

Tennis **St. Lucia Racquet Club** (adjacent to Club St. Lucia, Cap Estate, tel. 809/450–0551) is one of the top tennis facilities in the Caribbean. **Jalousie Plantation** (Soufrière, tel. 809/459–7666) has four lighted courts open to cruise passengers.

Beaches All of St. Lucia's beaches are public. Many are flanked by hotels where you can rent water-sports equipment and have a rum punch, but the resorts are sometimes less than welcoming to cruise-ship passengers. About a 30-minute ride from Pointe Seraphine is **Pigeon Island** (admission E.C.$10), which has a white-sand beach and a small restaurant; it's great for picnicking and swimming. **Reduit Beach,** 20 minutes from Castries, is a long stretch of beige sand next to Rodney Bay. Water-sports equipment can be rented at the two beachfront hotels.

Near Soufrière, **Anse Chastanet** is a gray-sand beach with a backdrop of green hills and the island's best reefs for snorkeling and diving. A dive shop and bar are located on the beach. The black-sand **Anse des Pitons** sits directly between the Pitons and is accessible through Jalousie Plantation or by boat from Soufrière. It, too, offers great snorkeling and diving.

Dining *Most restaurants add a 10% service charge to the bill.*

Castries
$$–$$$ **Jimmie's.** It's a 10- to 15-minute ride from the ship, but worth it for the great views. Popular with locals as well as visitors, Jimmie's specializes in seafood—from Creole stuffed crab for an appetizer to the special seafood platter for an entrée. Dessert lovers had better be in a banana mood—everything from fritters to ice cream is made with St. Lucian "figs." *Vigie Cove, Castries, tel. 809/452–5142. Reservations not accepted. AE, MC, V.*

Soufrière
$$$$ **Dasheene Restaurant and Bar.** The breathtaking view—the Pitons look close enough to touch—plus some of the best food on St. Lucia are reasons to make this open-air perch high in the mountains your stop when touring in the area. Fresh-caught fish is always special, but there's an array of inspired salads, sandwiches and even a burger on the luncheon menu. Dinner, of course, is more elaborate. *Ladera Resort, tel. 809/459–7323. AE, DC, MC, V.*

$ **Camilla's.** Just a short walk from the wharf, this friendly, second-floor restaurant serves local dishes, such as the catch of the day curried, Creole-style, or grilled with lemon sauce. The list of tropical cocktails is bigger than the entire restaurant! *12 Boulevard St., tel. 809/459–5379. AE.*

St. Martin/St. Maarten

St. Martin/St. Maarten: one tiny island, just 37 square miles, with two different accents, and ruled by two separate nations. Here French and Dutch have lived side by side for hundreds of years, and when you cross from one country to the next there are no border patrols, no customs. In fact, the only indication that you have crossed a border at all is a small sign and a change in road surface.

St. Martin/St. Maarten epitomizes tourist islands in the sun, where services are well developed but there is still some Caribbean flavor left. The Dutch side is ideal for people who like plenty to do. The French side has more ambience, more fashionable shopping, and much more Continental flair. The combination of the two halves makes an almost ideal port. On the negative side, the island has been thoroughly discovered and completely developed. There is gambling, but table limits are so low that high rollers will have a better time gamboling on the beach. It can be fun to shop, and you'll find an occasional bargain, but many goods (particularly electronics) are cheaper in the United States. At press time, this island was still feeling some aftereffects of the devastating hurricane in fall 1995. Some resorts were closed, and much of the land was left barren—only now is it beginning to fully recover.

Though Dutch is the official language of St. Maarten, and French of St. Martin, almost everyone speaks English. If you hear a language you can't quite place, it's Papiamento, a Spanish-based Creole.

Currency Legal tender on the Dutch side is the Netherlands Antilles florin (guilder), written NAf; on the French side, it's the French franc (F). In general, the exchange rate is about NAf 1.80 to U.S.$1, and 5F to U.S.$1. There's little need to exchange money, though, as dollars are accepted everywhere.

Telephones
Intra-Island Calls To phone from the Dutch side to the French side, dial 06 plus the local number. From the French side to the Dutch side, dial 011–5995 plus the local number. Remember that a call from one side to the other is an international call and not a local one.

Overseas Calls At the Landsradio in Philipsburg, St. Maarten, there are facilities for overseas calls and an AT&T USADirect telephone. On the French side, it's not possible to make collect calls to the United States, but you can make credit-card calls from a phone on the side of the tourist office in Marigot. The operator will assign you a PIN number, valid for as long as you specify. Calls to the United States are about $4 per minute. To call from other public phones, you'll need to go to the special desk at Marigot's post office and buy a Telecarte, which looks like a credit card.

Shore Excursions The following is a good choice in St. Martin/St. Maarten. It may not be offered by all cruise lines. Time and price are approximate.

Undersea Creatures **Snorkel Tour.** Take a boat to a beach, where you will be taught how to snorkel, then given the choice of joining a group or setting off on your own. Refreshments may be served. *3 hrs. Cost: $27.*

Coming Ashore Except for a few vessels that stop on the French side, cruise ships drop anchor off the Dutch capital of Philipsburg or dock in the marina at the southern tip of the Philipsburg harbor. If your ship anchors, tenders will ferry you to the town pier in the middle of town, where taxis await passengers. Next to the pier, on Wathey Square, is the Tourist Bureau, where you can pick up information and maps. If your ship docks at the marina, downtown is a 15-minute taxi ride away. The walk is not recommended.

Getting Around
By Bus One of the island's best bargains, public buses cost from 80¢ to $2 and run frequently between 7 AM and 7 PM, from Philipsburg through Cole Bay to Marigot.

By Car The island's roads are good, and it would be quite difficult to get lost. Because everything is within an easy drive of Philipsburg and taxis are very expensive, this is a good port for renting a car. The cost is about $35 a day. It's best to reserve a car before you leave home, especially at the height of the winter season. Contact **Avis** (tel. 800/331–1212), **Budget** (tel. 800/527–0700), **Hertz** (tel. 800/654–3131), or **National** (tel. 800/328–4567).

By Taxi Taxis are government-regulated and costly. Authorized taxis display stickers of the St. Maarten Taxi Association. Taxis are also available at Marigot.

Exploring St. Martin/ St. Maarten *Numbers in the margin correspond to points of interest on the St. Martin/St. Maarten map.*

The Dutch Side The Dutch capital of **Philipsburg,** which stretches about a mile along an isthmus between Great Bay and Salt Pond, is easily explored on foot. It has three parallel streets: Front Street, Back Street, and Pond Fill. Little lanes called *steegjes* connect Front Street (which ❶ has been recobbled and its pedestrian area widened) with Back Street, which is considerably less congested because it has fewer shops. Altogether, a walk from one end of downtown to the other takes a half hour, even if you stop at a couple of stores.

The first stop for cruise passengers should be **Wathey Square,** in the middle of the isthmus, which bustles with vendors, souvenir shops, and tourists. The streets to the right and left are lined with hotels, duty-free shops, restaurants, and cafés, most in West Indian cottages decorated in pastels with gingerbread trim. Narrow alleyways lead to arcades and flower-filled courtyards with yet more boutiques and eateries.

To explore beyond Philipsburg, start at the west end of Front Street. The road (which becomes Sucker Garden Road) leads north along Salt Pond and begins to climb and curve just outside town.

❷ The first right off Sucker Garden Road leads to **Guana Bay Point,** from which you get a splendid view of the island's east coast, tiny deserted islands, and little St. Barts in the distance.

❸ **Dawn Beach,** an excellent snorkeling beach, lies on the east coast of the island, just below Oyster Pond, and has an active sailing community.

The French Side

Cruise passengers following the main road north out of Philipsburg will come first to **Orléans.** This settlement, also known as the French ❹ Quarter, is the island's oldest.

❺ North of Orléans is the **French Cul de Sac,** where you'll see the French colonial mansion of St. Martin's mayor nestled in the hills. From here the road swirls south through green hills and pastures, past flower-entwined stone fences.

❻ Past L'Espérance Airport is the town of **Grand Case,** known as the "Restaurant Capital of the Caribbean." Scattered along its mile-long main street are more than 20 restaurants serving French, Italian, Indonesian, and Vietnamese fare, as well as fresh seafood. Along the shore, vendors known as *lolos* sell delicious barbecued chicken, beef on skewers, and other delicacies.

❼ The capital of the French side is **Marigot.** (If you're coming from Grand Case, follow the signs south to rue de la République.) Marina Port La Royale is the shopping complex at the port; rue de la République and rue de la Liberté, which border the bay, are also filled with duty-free shops, boutiques, and bistros. The road south from Marigot leads to the official border, where a simple marker, placed here in 1948, commemorates 300 years of peaceful coexistence. This road will bring you back to Philipsburg.

Shopping

Prices can be 25%–50% below those in the United States and Canada for French perfume, liquor, cognac and fine liqueurs, crystal, linens, leather, Swiss watches, and other luxury items. However, it pays to know the prices back home; not all goods are a bargain. Caveat emptor: Although most merchants are reputable, there are occasional reports of inferior or fake merchandise passed off as the real thing. When vendors bargain excessively, their wares are often suspect.

In Philipsburg, Front Street is one long strip of boutiques and shops; **Old Street,** near the end of Front Street, is packed with stores, boutiques, and open-air cafés. At Philipsburg's **Shipwreck Shop,** look for Caribelle batiks, hammocks, handmade jewelry, the local guava-berry liqueur, and herbs and spices. You'll find almost 100 boutiques in the **Mullet Bay** and **Maho** shopping plazas. In general, you will find smarter fashions in Marigot than in Philipsburg. In Marigot, wrought-iron balconies, colorful awnings, and gingerbread trim decorate the shops and tiny boutiques in the **Marina Port La Royale** and on the main streets, **rue de la Liberté** and **rue de la République.**

Sports

Fishing

Contact **Sea Brat, Black Fin,** or **Pita** at Bobby's Marina, Philipsburg (tel. 599/5–22366) for information on fishing charters.

Golf

Mullet Bay Resort (tel. 599/5–52801) has an 18-hole championship course. Green fees are $90 for 18 holes and $50 for nine holes.

Water Sports

Myriad boats can be rented at **Lagoon Watersports** (tel. 599/5–52801) and **Caribbean Watersports** (tel. 590/87–58–66). NAUI-, SSI-, and PADI-certified dive centers offer scuba instruction, rentals, and trips. On the Dutch side, try **Trade Winds Dive Center** (tel. 599/5–75176) and **St. Maarten Divers** (tel. 599/5–22446). On the French side, there's **Lou Scuba** (tel. 590/87–22–58) and **Blue Ocean** (tel. 590/87–89–73), both PADI-certified.

Beaches

The island's 10 miles of beaches are all open to the public. Those occupied by resort properties charge a small fee (about $3) for changing facilities, and water-sports equipment can be rented at most hotels. Some of the 37 beaches are secluded; some are in the thick of things. Topless bathing is common on the French side. Nude bathing can be found at Orient Beach, Cupecoy Beach, and Baie Longue. If you take a cab to a remote beach, be sure to arrange a specific time for the driver to return for you. Don't leave valuables unattended on the beach.

Baie Longue, the island's best beach, is a mile-long curve of white sand at the western tip, offering excellent snorkeling and swimming but no facilities. **Cupecoy Beach** is a narrower, more secluded curve of white sand just south of Baie Longue near the border. There are no facilities, but a truck often pulls up with cold beer and sodas. Clothing becomes optional at the western end of the beach. This is also the island's gay beach.

Dining

By law, restaurants on the French side figure a service charge into the menu prices, so no tips are expected. On the Dutch side, most restaurants add 10%–15% to the bill.

Dutch Side

$–$$

Chesterfield's. Burgers and salads are served at lunch, but menus are more elaborate for dinner on this indoor/outdoor terrace overlooking the marina. Specialties include French onion soup, roast duckling with fresh pineapple and banana sauce, and chicken Cordon Bleu. The Mermaid Bar is popular with yachtsmen. *Great Bay Marina, Philipsburg, tel. 599/5–23484. AE, MC, V.*

$

Shiv Sagar. Authentic East Indian cuisine, emphasizing Kashmiri and Mogul specialties, is served in this small, mirrored room fragrant with cumin and coriander. Marvelous tandooris and curries are offered, but try one of the less-familiar preparations such as *madrasi machi* (red snapper cooked in a blend of hot spices). A large selection of vegetarian dishes is also offered. There's a friendly open-air bar out front. *3 Front St., Philipsburg, tel. 599/5–22299. AE, D, DC, MC, V. Closed Sun.*

French Side

$$$

Le Poisson d'Or. At this posh and popular restaurant set in a stone house, the waters of the bay beckon from the 20-table terrace as you feast on hot foie gras salad in raspberry vinaigrette; smoked lobster boiled in tea with parsley cream sauce; or veal with Roquefort, hazelnut, and tarragon sauce. The young chef, François Julien, cooks with enthusiasm, but his cuisine must compete for attention with the striking setting. *Off rue d'Anguille, Marigot, tel. 590/87–72–45. AE, MC, V. No lunch Tues. in low season.*

$$

La Crêperie du Soleil. This charming little eatery on the beach in quaint Grand Case offers all kinds of delicious crepes, from sweet to salty. Owners David and Véronique are most gracious and helpful in making the decision of which delectable treat to have. They also offer grilled lobster, fresh fish, chicken kebabs, salads, and pastas.

Dawn Beach, **3**
French Cul de Sac, **5**
Grand Case, **6**
Guana Bay Point, **2**
Marigot, **7**
Orléans, **4**
Philipsburg, **1**

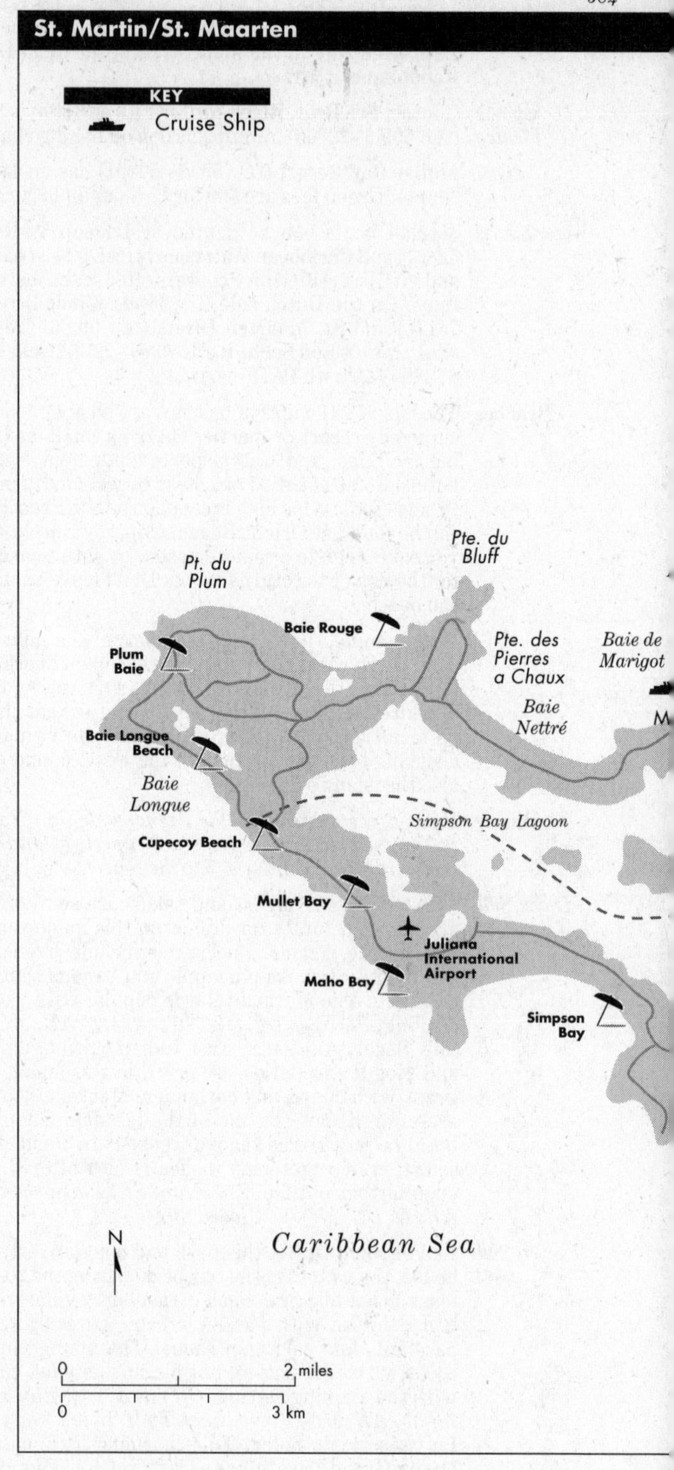

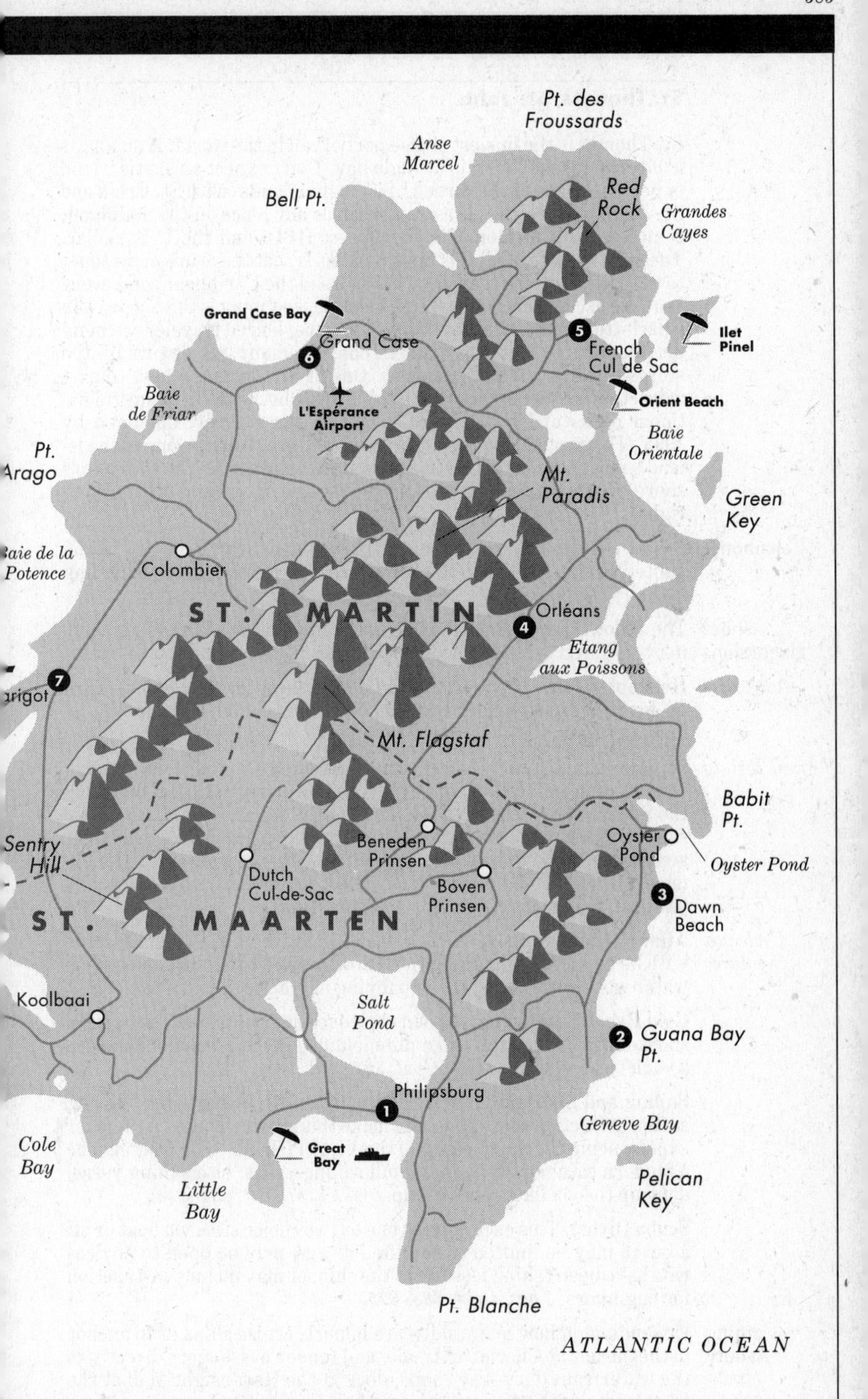

Pt. des Froussards
Anse Marcel
Bell Pt.
Red Rock
Grandes Cayes
Grand Case Bay
Grand Case
Ilet Pinel
French Cul de Sac
Orient Beach
Baie de Friar
L'Espérance Airport
Baie Orientale
Pt. Arago
Mt. Paradis
Green Key
Colombier
ST. MARTIN
Orléans
Etang aux Poissons
Mt. Flagstaf
Babit Pt.
Oyster Pond
Oyster Pond
Beneden Prinsen
Dutch Cul-de-Sac
Boven Prinsen
Dawn Beach
ST. MAARTEN
Koolbaai
Salt Pond
Guana Bay Pt.
Philipsburg
Geneve Bay
Cole Bay
Great Bay
Pelican Key
Little Bay
Pt. Blanche
ATLANTIC OCEAN

Don't forget the chocolate fondue for dessert. *Blvd. de Grand Case, Grand Case, tel. 590/87-92-32. MC, V.*

St. Thomas/St. John

St. Thomas is the busiest cruise port of call in the world. As many as a dozen ships may visit in a single day. Don't expect an exotic island experience: One of the three U.S. Virgin Islands (with St. Croix and St. John), St. Thomas is as American as any place on the mainland, complete with McDonald's franchises, HBO, and the U.S. dollar. The positive side of all this development is that there are more tours to choose from here than anywhere else in the Caribbean, and every year the excursions get better. Of course, shopping is the big draw in Charlotte Amalie, the main town, but experienced travelers remember the days of "real" bargains. Today, so many passengers fill the stores that it's a seller's market. One of St. Thomas's best tourist attractions is its neighboring island, St. John, with its beautiful national parks and beaches. St. Thomas was severely damaged by 1995's Hurricane Marilyn; at press time Coral World—one of the island's most popular attractions—was still closed. Ask at your ship's shore-excursion desk for the current status of this and other island sights.

Telephones It's as easy to call home from St. Thomas as from any city in the United States. And public phones are all over the place, including right on the dock.

Shore Excursions The following are good choices in St. Thomas/St. John. They may not be offered by all cruise lines. Times and prices are approximate.

Adventure

Helicopter Tour. If you haven't taken a helicopter tour before, sign up for this exciting aerial tour of St. Thomas and surrounding islands. *1–2 hrs, includes 1-hr flight time. Cost: $50–$100.*

Natural Beauty

St. John Island Tour. Either your ship tenders you in to St. John in the morning before docking at St. Thomas, or you take a bus from the St. Thomas docks to the St. John ferry. On St. John, an open-air safari bus winds through the national park to a beach for snorkeling, swimming, and sunbathing. (If you have the option, go to Honeymoon Beach instead of Trunk Bay.) All tours end with a ferry ride back to St. Thomas. *4–4½ hrs. Cost: $22–$50.*

Undersea Creatures

Atlantis Submarine. A surface boat ferries you out to a submarine with large picture windows; the *Atlantis* dives to explore the underwater world, with good accompanying narrative. *2 hrs. Cost: $72.*

Coki Beach Snorkeling. A good choice for novices who want to learn snorkeling (instruction and equipment usually are included) and see a variety of wildlife. *3 hrs. Cost: $21–$22.*

Sailing and Snorkeling Tour. A romantic sail, a snorkeling lesson, and an attractive snorkeling site make this an excellent excursion for experiencing the true beauty of the Virgin Islands. The boat may be a modern catamaran, a single-hull sailing yacht, or a sailing vessel done up to look like a pirate ship. *3½–4 hrs. Cost: $32–$45.*

Scuba Diving. This excursion to one or two choice sites via boat or off a beach may be limited to certified divers, may be open to novices who have been taking lessons on the ship, or may include instruction for beginners. *3 hrs. Cost: $38–$75.*

Coming Ashore Depending on how many ships are in port, cruise ships drop anchor in the harbor at Charlotte Amalie and tender passengers directly to the waterfront duty-free shops, dock at the Havensight Mall at the eastern end of the crescent-shaped bay, or dock at Crown Bay Marina a few miles west of town. The distance from Havensight to the duty-free shops is 1½ miles, which can be walked in less than half an hour, or a taxi can be hired for $5 per person, one-way ($2.50 if there is more than one passenger). Tourist information offices are located at the Havensight Mall (Bldg. No 1) for docking passengers and downtown at the eastern end of the waterfront shopping strip for those coming ashore by tender. Both distribute free island and downtown shopping maps. From Crown Bay, it's also a half-hour walk or a $3 cab ride ($2.50 for more than one passenger).

Getting Around

By Car

St. Thomas is an excellent port for cruise passengers to rent a car. Driving is on the left side of the road, though steering wheels are on the left side of the car. Car rentals are available from numerous agencies, including **ABC Rentals** (by Havensight Mall, tel. 809/776–1222), **Budget** (Marriott's Frenchman Reef Hotel, tel. 809/776–5774), and **Hertz** (near the airport, tel. 809/774–1879). Rates for one day range from $55 to $70.

By Ferry

You can get to St. John on your own via ferry from Charlotte Amalie. The cost is $7 round-trip. Get ferry schedules and information from the tourist information offices at Havensight or in Charlotte Amalie.

By Taxi

Taxis meet every ship. They don't have meters, but rates are set. Check with the shore-excursion director for correct fares and agree on the price before getting in the cab. Most taxis are minivans, which take multiple fares and charge per person. Many of them will give you a guided tour of the island for far less than you'd pay for a ship-sponsored excursion. The most popular destination, Magens Bay, costs $6.50 from town and $7.50 from the Havensight pier, per person, one way.

Exploring St. Thomas

Numbers in the margin correspond to points of interest on the St. Thomas map.

Charlotte Amalie

❶

Charlotte Amalie is a hilly, overdeveloped shopping town. There are plenty of interesting historical sights here, and much of the town is quite pretty. So while you're shopping, take the time to see at least a few of the sights. For a great view of the town and the harbor, begin at the beautiful Spanish-style Hotel 1829, whose restaurant (*see* Dining, *below*) is one of the best on St. Thomas. A few yards farther up the road is the base of the 99 Steps, a staircase "street" built by the Danes in the 1700s. Go up the steps (there are more than 99) and continue to the right to Blackbeard's Castle, originally Ft. Skysborg. The massive five-story watchtower was built in 1679. It's now a dramatic perch from which to sip a drink and admire the harbor from the small hotel and restaurant.

Government House (on Kongen's Gade) dates back to 1867 and is the official residence of the governor of the U.S. Virgin Islands. Inside are murals and paintings by Pissarro.

Frederick Lutheran Church is the second-oldest Lutheran church in the Western Hemisphere. Its walls date to 1793.

Emancipation Garden honors the 1848 freeing of the slaves and features a smaller version of the Liberty Bell. As you stand in the park facing the water, you'll see a large red building to your left, close to the harbor; this is Ft. Christian, St. Thomas's oldest standing structure (1627–87) and a U.S. national landmark. The building was used at various times as a jail, governor's residence, town hall, courthouse, and church. The clock tower was added in the 19th century. It now houses a museum filled with historical artifacts.

The lime-green edifice on Kings Wharf is the **Legislature Building** (1874), seat of the 15-member U.S.V.I. Senate since 1957.

The South Shore and East End

❷

Route 32 brings you into **Red Hook,** which has grown from a sleepy little town, connected to the rest of the island only by dirt roads, into an increasingly self-sustaining village. There's luxury shopping at American Yacht Harbor, or you can stroll along the docks and visit

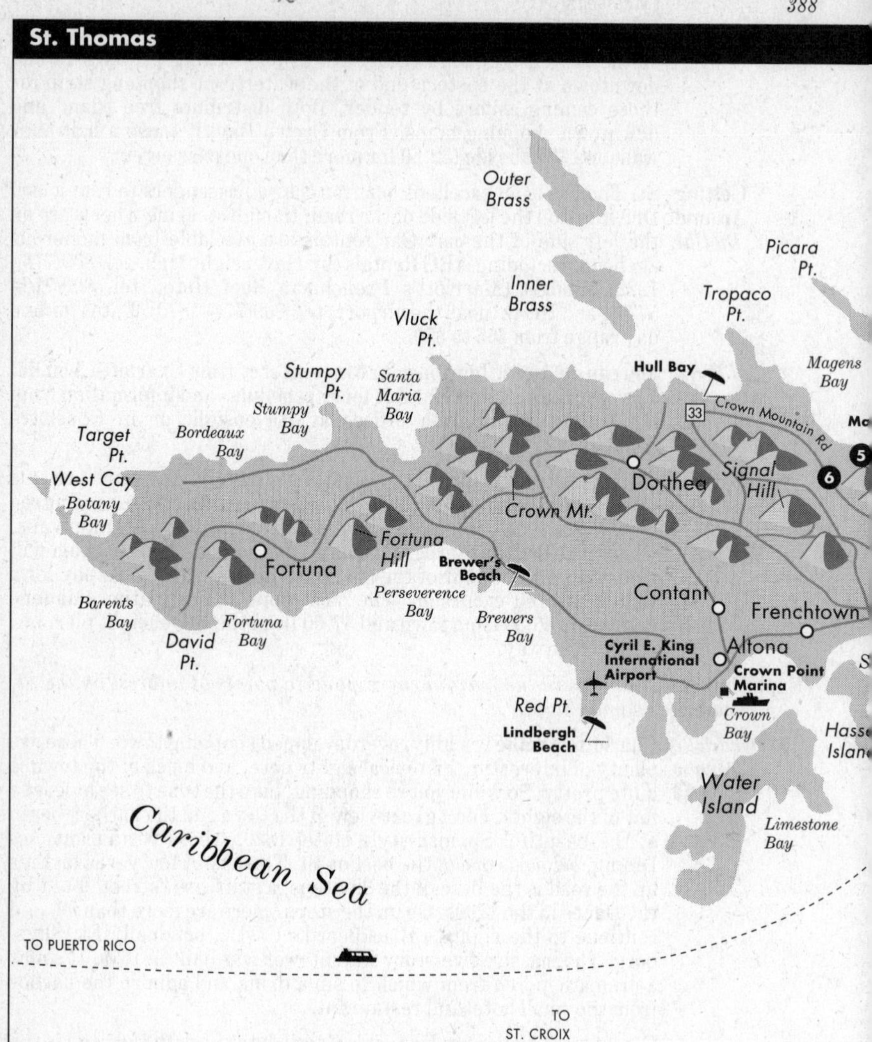

Charlotte Amalie, **1**
Coral World, **3**
Drake's Seat, **5**
Mountain Top, **6**
Red Hook, **2**
Tillett's Gardens, **4**

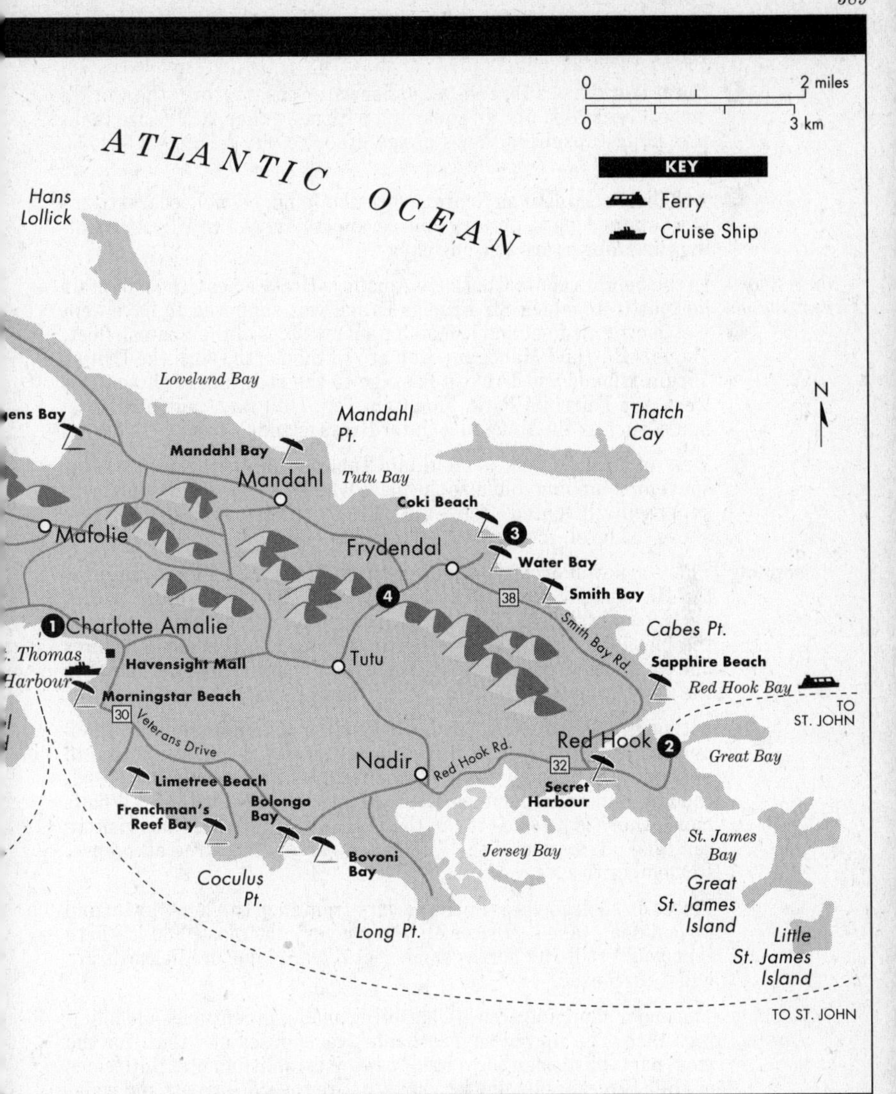

0
2 miles
0
3 km
KEY
Ferry
Cruise Ship
ATLANTIC OCEAN
Hans Lollick
Lovelund Bay
Mandahl Pt.
Thatch Cay
N
Mandahl Bay
Mandahl
Tutu Bay
Coki Beach
3
Mafolie
Frydendal
Water Bay
4
Smith Bay
38
Smith Bay Rd.
Cabes Pt.
1 Charlotte Amalie
Tutu
Havensight Mall
Sapphire Beach
Red Hook Bay
Morningstar Beach
TO ST. JOHN
30
Veterans Drive
Red Hook
2
Great Bay
Nadir
Red Hook Rd.
32
Limetree Beach
Secret Harbour
Frenchman's Reef Bay
Bolongo Bay
St. James Bay
Jersey Bay
Bovoni Bay
Coculus Pt.
Great St. James Island
Long Pt.
Little St. James Island
TO ST. JOHN

with sailors and fishermen, stopping for a beer at The Blue Marlin or Larry's Warehouse.

❸ **Coral World** has a three-level underwater observatory, the world's largest reef tank, and an aquarium with more than 20 TV-size tanks providing capsulized views of sea life. *Rte. 38, tel. 809/775–1555. Admission: $14. Open daily 9–6.*

❹ At **Tillett's Gardens** on Route 38 (*see* Shopping, *below*), local artisans craft stained glass, pottery, and ceramics. Artist Jim Tillett's paintings and fabrics are also on display.

North Shore/ Center Islands

❺ In the heights above Charlotte Amalie is **Drake's Seat,** the mountain lookout from which Sir Francis Drake was supposed to have kept watch over his fleet and looked for enemy ships of the Spanish fleet. Magens Bay and Mahogany Run are to the north, with the British Virgin Islands and Drake's Passage to the east. Off to the left, or west, are Fairchild Park, Mountain Top, Hull Bay, and smaller islands, such as the Inner and Outer Brass islands.

❻ West of Drake's Seat is **Mountain Top,** not only a tacky mecca for souvenir shopping, but also the place where the banana daiquiri was supposedly invented. There's a restaurant here and, at 1,500 feet above sea level, some spectacular views.

Shopping

There are well over 400 shops in Charlotte Amalie alone, and near the Havensight docks there are at least 50 more, clustered in converted warehouses. Even die-hard shoppers won't want to cover all the boutiques, since a large percentage peddle the same T-shirts and togs. Many visitors devote their shopping time on St. Thomas to the stores that sell handicrafts and luxury items.

Although those famous "giveaway" prices no longer abound, shoppers on St. Thomas can still save money. Today, a realistic appraisal puts prices on many items at about 20% off stateside prices, although liquor and perfume often are priced 50%–70% less. What's more, there is no sales tax in the U.S. Virgin Islands, and visitors can take advantage of the $1,200-per-person duty-free allowance. Remember to save receipts.

Prices on such goods as linens do vary from shop to shop—if you find a good deal, take it. Prices on jewelry vary the most, and it's here that you'll still run across some real finds. Major credit cards are widely accepted.

Shopping Districts

The major shopping area is Charlotte Amalie, in centuries-old buildings that once served as merchants' warehouses and that, for the most part, have been converted to retail establishments. Both sides of **Main Street** are lined with shops, as are the side streets and walkways between Main Street and the waterfront. These narrow lanes and arcades have names like Drake's Passage, Royal Dane Mall, Palm Passage, Trompeter Gade, Hibiscus Alley, and Raadet's Gade. The **Bakery Square Shopping Mall** (1 block north of Main St. off Nye Gade) has about 15 boutiques. The streets adjacent to Bakery Square, notably Back Street, Nye Gade, Garden Street, Kongen's Gade, and Norre Gade, are also very good areas for browsing. At **Havensight Mall,** near the deep-water port where many cruise ships dock, you'll find branches of downtown stores, as well as specialty shops and boutiques.

Charlotte Amalie

Unless otherwise noted, the following stores have branches both downtown and in Havensight Mall and are easy to find. If you have any trouble, shopping maps are available at the tourist offices and often from your ship's shore-excursion desk. U.S. citizens can carry back a gallon, or six "fifths," of liquor duty-free.

A.H. Riise Gift Shops: Waterford, Wedgwood, Royal Crown, Royal Doulton, jewelry, pearls, ceramics, perfumes, watches; liquors, cordials, and wines, including rare vintage cognacs, Armagnacs, ports, and Madeiras; tobacco and imported cigars; fruits in brandy; barware from England. **Al Cohen's Discount Liquor** (Havensight only): discount liquors. **Amsterdam Sauer** (downtown only): one-of-a-kind fine jewelry. **Blue Diamond** (downtown only): 14-karat and 18-karat jewelry crafted by European goldsmiths. **Boolchand's:** cameras, audio-video equipment.

The **Caribbean Marketplace** (Havensight Mall only): Caribbean handicrafts, including Caribelle batiks from St. Lucia; bikinis from the Cayman Islands; Sunny Caribee spices, soaps, teas, and coffees from Trinidad. **Down Island Traders** (downtown only): hand-painted calabash bowls; jams, jellies, spices, and herbs; herbal teas made of rum, passion fruit, and mango; high-mountain coffee from Jamaica; Caribbean handicrafts. The **English Shop:** china and crystal from Spode, Limoges, Royal Doulton, Portmeirion, Noritaki, and Villeroy & Boch.

The Gallery (downtown only): Haitian and local oil paintings, metal sculpture, wood carvings, painted screens and boxes, figures carved from stone, oversize papier-mâché figures. **G'Day** (downtown only): umbrellas, artwork, sportswear. **Gucci:** wallets, bags, briefcases, totes, shoes. **H. Stern:** gems and jewelry. **Janine's Boutique** (downtown only): women's and men's apparel and accessories from European designers and manufacturers, including Louis Feraud, Valentino, Christian Dior, Pierre Cardin. **Java Wraps** (downtown only): Indonesian batik, swimwear, leisure wear, sarongs, ceremonial Javanese puppets. **The Leather Shop:** Fendi, Bottega Veneta, other fine leather goods. **Little Switzerland:** Lalique, Baccarat, Waterford, Swarovski, Riedel, Orrefors, and other crystal; Villeroy & Boch, Aynsley, Wedgwood, Royal Doulton, and other china; Rolex watches. **MAPes MONDe Ltd.** (in A.H. Riise, downtown): old-fashioned maps and engravings of Caribbean scenes. **Opals of Australia** (downtown only): the name says it all.

Pampered Pirate (downtown only): Caribbean handicrafts, spices, sauces, jams, and Jamaican coffee; gold chain by the inch. **Royal Caribbean** (no affiliation with the cruise line): cameras, cassette players, audio-video equipment. **Sea Wench** (Havensight Mall only): swimwear, lingerie. **Traveler's Haven** (Havensight Mall only): leather bags, backpacks, vests, money belts. **Tropicana Perfume Shoppes** (downtown only): fragrances for men and women.

Tillett's Gardens

Tillett's Gardens and Craft Complex (Estate Tutu, tel. 809/775–1405; *see* Exploring St. Thomas, *above*) is more than worth the cab fare to reach it. Jim Tillet's artwork is on display, and you can watch craftsmen and artisans produce watercolors, silk-screened fabrics, pottery, enamel work, candles, and other handicrafts.

St. John

Opportunities for duty-free shopping are more limited and the prices a bit higher on St. John. One popular spot is **Wharfside Village,** an attractive, compact mall of some 30 shops overlooking Cruz Bay Harbor. **Mongoose Junction,** just north of Cruz Bay across from the Park Service visitor center, is one of the most pleasant places to shop in the Caribbean. Built from native stone, the graceful staircases and balconies wind among the shops, a number of which sell handicrafts designed and fashioned by resident artisans.

Sports

Fishing

Call **American Yacht Harbor** at Red Hook (tel. 809/775–6454) if you're interested in some serious angling.

Golf

Scenic **Mahogany Run** (tel. 809/775–5000), north of Charlotte Amalie, has a par-70, 18-hole course and a view of the British Virgin Islands. The rate for 18 holes is $85, cart included.

Water Sports

Underwater Safaris (tel. 809/774–1350) is at the Ramada Yacht Haven Motel and Marina, near Havensight. Other reliable scuba and snorkeling operators are **Chris Sawyer Diving Center** (tel. 809/775–7320) and **Aqua Action** (tel. 809/775–6285).

Beaches

St. Thomas

All beaches in the U.S. Virgin Islands are public, but occasionally you'll need to stroll through a resort to reach the sand. Government-run **Magens Bay** is lively and popular because of its spectacular loop of white-sand beach, more than a half mile long, and its calm waters. Food, changing facilities, and rest rooms are available. **Secret Harbour** is a pretty cove for superb snorkeling; go out to the left, near the rocks. **Morningstar Beach**, close to Charlotte Amalie, has a mostly sandy sea bottom with some rocks; snorkeling is good here when the current doesn't affect visibility. **Sapphire Beach** has a fine view of St. John and other islands. Snorkeling is excellent at the reef to the east, near Pettyklip Point, and all kinds of water-sports gear can be rented. Be careful when you enter the water; there are many rocks and shells in the sand.

St. John

Trunk Bay is the main beach on St. John, mostly because of its underwater snorkeling trail. However, experienced snorkelers may find it tame and picked over, with too little coral or fish. Lifeguards are on duty.

Dining

Some restaurants add a 10%–15% service charge to the bill.

$$$ **Hotel 1829.** Candlelight flickers over old stone walls and across the pink table linens at this restaurant on the gallery of a lovely old hotel. The award-winning menu and wine list are extensive, from Caribbean rock lobster to rack of lamb; many items, including a warm spinach salad, are prepared table-side. The restaurant is justly famous for its dessert soufflés: chocolate, Grand Marnier, raspberry, and coconut. *Government Hill, a few steps up from Main St., Charlotte Amalie, tel. 809/776–1829. Reservations essential. AE, D, MC, V. No lunch.*

$ **Gladys' Cafe.** Even if the food was less tasty and the prices higher, it would be worth visiting just to see Gladys smile. Antiguan by birth, she won a local following as a waitress at Palm Passage before opening her own restaurant for breakfast and lunch in a courtyard off Main Street in Charlotte Amalie. Try the Caribbean lobster roll, the barbecue ribs, Gladys's hot chicken salad, or one of the filling salad platters. *17 Main St., tel. 809/774–6604. AE. No dinner.*

San Juan, Puerto Rico

Although Puerto Rico is part of the United States, few cities in the Caribbean are as steeped in Spanish tradition as San Juan. Old San Juan has restored 16th-century buildings, museums, art galleries, bookstores, 200-year-old houses with balustrade balconies overlooking narrow, cobblestone streets—all within a seven-block neighborhood. In contrast, San Juan's sophisticated Condado and Isla Verde areas have glittering hotels, flashy Las Vegas–style shows, casinos, and discos.

Out in the countryside is the 28,000-acre El Yunque rain forest, with more than 240 species of trees growing at least 100 feet high. You can also visit dramatic mountain ranges, numerous trails, vast caves, coffee plantations, old sugar mills, and hundreds of beaches. No wonder San Juan is one of the busiest ports of call in the Caribbean. Like any other big city, San Juan has its share of crime, so guard your wallet or purse, and avoid walking in the area between Old San Juan and the Condado.

Telephones

You can use the long-distance telephone service office in the cruise-ship terminal, or call from any pay phone. A phone center by the Paseo de la Princesa charges 40¢ a minute for calls to the United States.

Shore Excursions

The following are good choices in San Juan. They may not be offered by all cruise lines. Times and prices are approximate.

Local Flavors **Bacardi Rum Distillery.** After seeing how it is made, you can sample and buy some Bacardi rum. *2 hrs. Cost: $15.*

San Juan Nightlife Tour. Several major hotels (like the Condado Plaza) have very exciting revues, especially those that feature flamenco or Latin dancers. Admission includes a drink or two. *3 hrs. Cost: $26–$34.*

Natural Beauty **El Yunque Rain Forest.** A 45-minute drive heads east to the Caribbean National Forest, where you may walk along various trails, see waterfalls, and climb the observation tower. The trip may include a stop at Luquillo Beach. *4 hrs. Cost: $20.*

Coming Ashore Cruise ships dock within a couple of blocks of Old San Juan. The Paseo de la Princesa, a tree-lined promenade beneath the city wall, is a nice place for a stroll, where you can admire the local crafts and stop at the refreshment kiosks. A tourist information booth and long-distance telephone office are found in the cruise-terminal area. From here a 10- or 15-minute taxi ride to New San Juan costs $8–$10. A five-minute ride to the Condado costs $3–$4.

Getting Around

By Bus The **Metropolitan Bus Authority** operates buses that thread through San Juan. The fare is 25¢, and the buses run in exclusive lanes, against traffic, on all major thoroughfares, stopping at yellow posts marked *Parada* or *Parada de Guaguas.* The main terminal is Intermodal Terminal, at Marina and Harding streets in Old San Juan.

By Car U.S. driver's licenses are valid in Puerto Rico. All major U.S. car-rental agencies are represented on the island. Contact **Avis** (tel. 787/721–4499 or 800/331–1212), **Budget** (tel. 787/791–3685 or 800/527–0700), **Hertz** (tel. 787/791–0840 or 800/654–3131), or **L & M Car Rental** (tel. 787/725–8416). Prices start at $30 a day. If you plan to drive across the island, arm yourself with a good map and be aware that many roads up in the mountains are unmarked, and many service stations require cash. To keep you on your toes, speed limits are posted in miles, distances in kilometers, and gas prices are per liter.

By Taxi Taxis line up to meet ships. Metered cabs authorized by the Public Service Commission charge an initial $1; each additional ⅒ mile is 10¢. Waiting time is 10¢ for each 45 seconds. Demand that the meter be turned on, and pay only what is shown, plus a tip of 10%–15%.

By Trolley If your feet fail you in Old San Juan, climb aboard the free open-air trolleys that rumble through the narrow streets. Take one from the docks or board anywhere along the route.

Exploring Old San Juan *Numbers in the margin correspond to points of interest on the Old San Juan map.*

Old San Juan Old San Juan, the original city founded in 1521, contains authentic and carefully preserved examples of 16th- and 17th-century Spanish colonial architecture. Graceful wrought-iron balconies decorated with lush green hanging plants extend over narrow, cobblestoned streets. Seventeenth-century walls still partially enclose the old city. Designated a U.S. National Historic Zone in 1950, Old San Juan is packed with shops, open-air cafés, private homes, tree-shaded squares, monuments, plaques, pigeons, people, and traffic jams. It's faster to walk than to take a cab. Nightlife is quiet, even spooky during the low season; you'll find more to do in New San Juan, especially the Condado area.

❶ **San Cristóbal,** the 18th-century fortress that guarded the city from land attacks, is known as the Gibraltar of the West Indies. San Cristóbal is larger than El Morro (*see below*), and offers spectacular views of both Old San Juan and the new city. *Tel. 787/729–6960. Admission free. Open daily 9–5.*

❷ **Plaza de Armas** is the original main square of Old San Juan. The plaza has a lovely fountain with statues representing the four seasons.

Casa de los Contrafuertes, **6**
City Hall, **4**
Dominican Convent, **9**
El Morro (Fuerte San Felipe del Morro), **11**
La Fortaleza, **10**
La Intendencia, **3**
Pablo Casals Museum, **7**
Plaza de Armas, **2**
San Cristóbal, **1**
San José Church, **8**
San Juan Cathedral, **5**

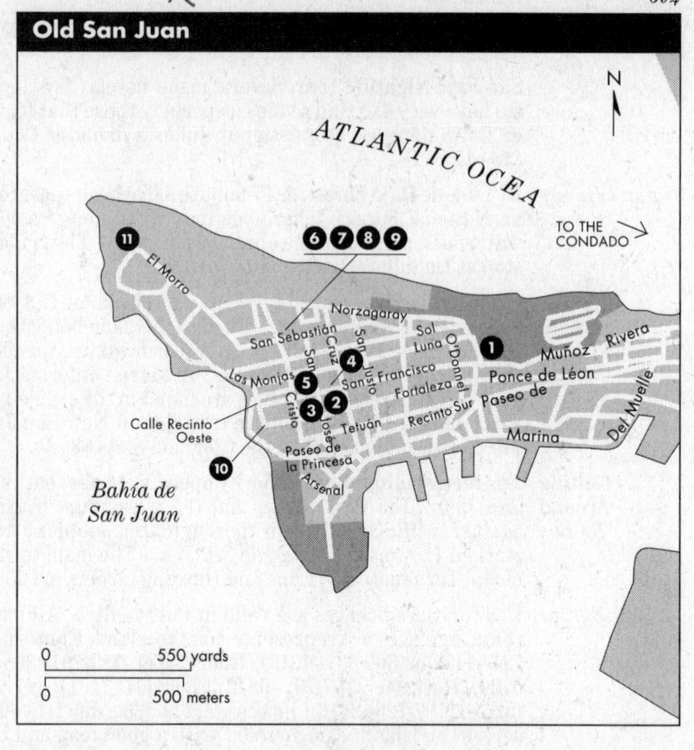

❸ West of the main square stands **La Intendencia,** a handsome, three-story neoclassical building that was home to the Spanish Treasury from 1851 to 1898. *Calle San José at Calle San Francisco. Admission free. Open weekdays 8–noon and 1–4:30.*

❹ On the north side of the Plaza de Armas is **City Hall,** called the *alcaldía.* Built between 1604 and 1789, it was fashioned after Madrid's city hall, with arcades, towers, balconies, and a lovely inner courtyard. An art gallery is on the first floor. *Tel. 787/724–7171, ext. 2391. Open weekdays 8–4.*

❺ The remains of Ponce de León are in a marble tomb near the transept in the **San Juan Cathedral** on Calle Cristo. This great Catholic shrine of Puerto Rico had humble beginnings in the early 1520s as a thatch-top wood structure that was destroyed by a hurricane. It was reconstructed in 1540, when the graceful circular staircase and vaulted ceilings were added, but most of the work on the church was done in the 19th century. *153 Calle Cristo. Open daily 8–4.*

❻ **Casa de los Contrafuertes**—also known as the Buttress House because buttresses support the wall next to the plaza—is one of the oldest remaining private residences in Old San Juan. Inside is the Pharmacy Museum, a re-creation of an 18th-century apothecary shop, and the Latin American Graphic Arts Museum and Gallery. *101 Calle San Sebastián, Plaza de San José, tel. 787/724–5477. Admission free. Open Wed.–Sun. 9–4:30.*

❼ The **Pablo Casals Museum** contains memorabilia of the famed Spanish cellist, who made his home in Puerto Rico for the last 20 years of his life. *101 Calle San Sebastián, Plaza de San José, tel. 787/723–9185. Admission: $1. Open Tues.–Sat. 9:30–5.*

❽ In the center of Plaza San José is the **San José Church.** With its series of vaulted ceilings, it is a fine example of 16th-century Spanish Gothic architecture. *Calle San Sebastián, tel. 787/725–7501. Admission free. Open Mon.–Sat. 8:30–4; Sun. mass at 12:15.*

9 Next door to the San José Church is the **Dominican Convent.** Also built in the 16th century, the building now houses an ornate 18th-century altar, religious manuscripts, artifacts, and art. *98 Calle Norzagaray, tel. 787/721–6866. Admission free. Chapel museum open Mon.–Sat. 9–5.*

10 **La Fortaleza,** on a hill overlooking the harbor, is the Western Hemisphere's oldest executive mansion in continuous use. Built as a fortress, the original 16th-century structure has seen numerous changes, including the addition of marble and mahogany, medieval towers, and stained-glass galleries. Guided tours are conducted every hour on the hour in English, on the half hour in Spanish. *Tel. 787/721–7000, ext. 2211. Admission free. Open weekdays 9–4.*

11 San Juan's most famous sight is undoubtedly **El Morro** (Fuerte San Felipe del Morro), set on a rocky promontory on the northwestern tip of the old city. Rising 140 feet above the sea, the massive, six-level Spanish fortress is a labyrinth of dungeons, ramps, turrets, and tunnels. Built to protect the port, El Morro has a commanding view of the harbor and Old San Juan. Its small museum traces the history of the fortress. *Tel. 787/729–6960. Admission free. Open daily 9–5.*

New San Juan

In **Puerta de Tierra,** a half mile east of the pier, is Puerto Rico's white marble Capitol, dating from the 1920s. Another mile east, at the tip of Puerta de Tierra, tiny Ft. San Jeronimo perches over the Atlantic like an afterthought. Added to San Juan's fortifications in the late 18th century, the structure barely survived the British attack of 1797.

Santurce, the district between Miramar on the west and the Laguna San José on the east, is a busy mixture of shops, markets, and offices. The classically designed Sacred Heart University is home of the Museum of Contemporary Puerto Rican Art (tel. 787/268–0049).

San Juan Environs

From San Juan, Route 2 leads west to the **Caparra Ruins,** where, in 1508, Ponce de León established the island's first settlement. The ruins are those of an ancient fort. Its small Museum of the Conquest and Colonization of Puerto Rico contains historic documents, exhibits, and excavated artifacts. *Km 6.6 on Rte. 2, tel. 787/781–4795. Admission free. Open Wed.–Sun. 9–4.*

Past the Caparra Ruins, Route 2 brings you to **Bayamón.** In the Central Park, across from the city hall, are some historic buildings and a 1934 sugarcane train that runs through the park.

Along Route 5 from Bayamón to Catano, you'll find the **Barrilito Rum Plant.** On the grounds is a 200-year-old plantation home and a 150-year-old windmill, which is listed in the National Register of Historic Places.

The **Bacardi Rum Plant,** along the bay, conducts 45-minute tours of the bottling plant, museum, and distillery, which has the capacity to produce 100,000 gallons of rum a day. (Yes, you'll be offered a sample.) *Km 2.6 on Rte. 888, tel. 787/788–1500. Admission free. Tours Mon.–Sat. 9:30–3:30; closed holidays.*

Shopping

San Juan is not a free port, and you won't find bargains on electronics and perfumes. However, shopping for native crafts can be fun. Popular souvenirs and gifts include *santos* (small, hand-carved figures of saints or religious scenes), hand-rolled cigars, handmade lace, carnival masks, Puerto Rican rum, and fancy men's shirts called *guayaberas*.

Old San Juan is filled with shops, especially on **Calles Cristo, La Fortaleza,** and **San Francisco.** You can get discounts on Hathaway shirts and clothing by Christian Dior and Ralph Lauren at **Hathaway Factory Outlet** (203 Calle Cristo, tel. 787/723–8946) and on raincoats at the **London Fog Factory Outlet** (156 Calle Cristo, tel. 787/722–4334). For one-of-a-kind local crafts, head for **Puerto Rican Arts & Crafts** (204 Calle La Fortaleza, Old San Juan, tel. 787/725–5596) or the **Haitian Gallery** (367 Calle Fortaleza, tel. 787/725–0986).

Sports

Golf There are four 18-hole courses shared by the **Hyatt Dorado Beach Hotel** and the **Hyatt Regency Cerromar Beach Hotel** (Dorado, tel. 787/796–1234). You'll also find 18-hole courses at **Palmas del Mar Resort** (Humacao, tel. 787/852–6000), **Club Ríomar** (Rio Grande, tel. 787/887–3964), **Punta Borinquén** (Aquadilla, tel. 787/890–2987), and **Bahia Beach Plantation** (Rio Grande, tel. 787/256–5600).

Hiking Dozens of trails lace **El Yunque.** Information is available at the Sierra Palm Visitor Center (Km 11.6, Rte. 191).

Water Sports Virtually all the resort hotels on San Juan's Condado and Isla Verde (*see* Beaches, *below*) strips rent paddleboats, Sunfish, and Windsurfers.

Beaches By law, all of Puerto Rico's beaches are open to the public (except for the Caribe Hilton's artificial beach in San Juan). The government runs 13 public beaches (*balnearios*), which have lockers, showers, and picnic tables; some have playgrounds and overnight facilities. *Admission free; parking $1. Open Tues.–Sun. 8–5 in summer, 9–6 in winter.*

Isla Verde is a white sandy beach close to metropolitan San Juan. Backed by several resort hotels, the beach offers picnic tables and good snorkeling, with equipment rentals nearby.

Dining *A 10%–15% tip is expected in restaurants.*

$$$ **La Chaumière.** Reminiscent of a French inn, this intimate yet bright white restaurant serves a respectable onion soup, oysters Rockefeller, rack of lamb, and veal Oscar, in addition to daily specials. *327 Calle Tetuán, tel. 787/722–3330. AE, DC, MC, V. Closed Sun. No lunch.*

$–$$ **Amadeus.** The atmosphere of this restaurant is gentrified Old San Juan, with an ever-changing menu of 20 appetizers, including *tostones* with sour cream and caviar, plantain mousse with shrimp, and Buffalo wings. Entrées on the nouvelle Caribbean menu range from Cajun-grilled mahimahi, to creamy pasta dishes, to chicken and steak sandwiches. *106 Calle San Sebastián, tel. 787/722–8635. AE, MC, V. Closed Mon.*

Nightlife Almost every ship stays in San Juan late or even overnight to give passengers an opportunity to enjoy the nightlife—the most sophisticated in the Caribbean.

Casinos By law, all casinos are in hotels. Alcoholic drinks are not permitted at the gaming tables, although free soft drinks, coffee, and sandwiches are available. The atmosphere is quite refined, and many patrons dress to the nines, but informal attire is usually fine. Casinos set their own hours, which change seasonally, but generally operate from noon to 4 AM. Casinos are located in the following hotels: **Condado Plaza Hotel, Caribe Hilton, Carib Inn, Clarion Hotel, Dutch Inn, El San Juan, Ramada, San Juan Marriott,** and **Sands.**

Discos In Old San Juan, young people flock to **Lazers** (251 Cruz St., tel. 787/721–4479). In Puerta de Tierra, Condado, and Isla Verde, the thirty-something crowd heads for **Amadeus** (El San Juan Hotel, tel. 787/791–1000), **Isadora's** (Condado Plaza Hotel, tel. 787/721–1000), and **Club Ibiza** (La Concha Hotel, tel. 787/721–6090).

Nightclubs The Sands Hotel's **Calypso Room** has a flamenco show nightly except Monday. El San Juan's **Tropicoro** presents international revues and, occasionally, top-name entertainers. The Condado Plaza Hotel has the **Copa Room,** and its **La Fiesta** sizzles with steamy Latin shows. Young professionals gather at **Egypt** (tel. 787/725-4664 or 787/725-4675), where the design is 1950s and the music mixes oldies and current dance hits.

Europe and the Mediterranean

For sheer diversity, there is no cruise destination quite like Europe. From the majesty of Norway's fjords to the ruins of ancient Greece, the Old World has more than one could possibly hope to see in a single cruise vacation.

The hardest part of cruising in Europe is deciding what to see. Do you want to sail the Mediterranean, with ports of call in Greece, Turkey, Israel, Egypt, and Spain? Or would you prefer Northern Europe, perhaps including a few cities in the former Soviet Union? Or maybe Western Europe, with the glamorous beaches and resort cities of the French Riviera? You will have to choose.

Select your ship as carefully as you choose your itinerary. Look especially at the mix of passengers: Are they all North Americans or a mix of Americans and Europeans? If the latter sounds interesting to you, *see* Chapter 2.

When to Go Cruise lines sail in Europe from April to November. Peak season runs from May through August; the weather is usually at its best during this time, which means you will be joining the crowds. Early spring and late fall are a good time to visit if you want to avoid the fray—and get lower prices. Temperatures can be very comfortable, and it is possible to swim in the Mediterranean through early October. Some lines operate European itineraries year-round featuring the Canary Islands, a popular spot among Europeans for winter getaways.

Currency Currencies vary by country, and U.S. dollars are accepted at some ports. It is advisable to change only a small amount on your ship or ashore for purchasing trinkets or snacks. When making major purchases and eating at better restaurants, use credit cards, which offer the best exchange rate.

Passports and Visas All U.S. citizens will need a passport to travel to Europe. Several countries, including Israel, Egypt, and Russia, require visas. Your cruise documents will specify whether visas are needed, and, generally, the line or your travel agent can obtain the visa for you for a fee.

What to Pack A priority item for cruising Europe is a comfortable pair of shoes—walking is the best and sometimes only way to really explore in port. Wardrobes will be determined by your cruise itinerary. In the Mediterranean, casual summer wear will do. In countries such as Egypt, Turkey, and Morocco, women will want to dress conservatively, covering their arms and legs. Pack clothing that can be layered and that is suitable for hot days and cooler evenings.

Telephones and Mail Unless money is no object, don't use the satellite phones aboard ship. At major ports where ships dock, there typically will be telephones near or at the pier. If you ship is tendering into port, ask at the shore-excursion office for the nearest calling center.

As a rule, cruise ships sell local stamps at the front desk, and you can send postcards from an onboard mailbox as well, eliminating the need to find a post office.

Shore Excursions Due to its diversity and wealth of attractions, Europe is well suited to shore excursions, which are usually bus tours. However, depending on the port, you may want to explore on your own. Often, this is possible on foot. In larger ports, you can hire a local guide at the pier. A group of four to six will find this more economical and practical than will a couple or a single person. Renting a car is often more of a pain than a pleasure, given the limited time you have ashore. On some islands, motor scooters are an option—but they are notoriously dangerous. It's better to hire a car and driver. Ask your shore-excursions office for recommended companies in each port.

Amsterdam, The Netherlands

If you've come to Holland expecting to find its residents shod in wooden shoes, you're years too late; if you're looking for windmills at every turn, you're looking in the wrong place. The bucolic images that brought tourism here in the decades after World War II have little to do with the Netherlands of the '90s. Modern Holland is a marriage of economic power and cultural wealth, a mix not new to the Dutch: In the 17th century, for example, money raised through colonial outposts was used to buy or commission portraits and paintings by young artists such as Rembrandt, Hals, Vermeer, and van Ruisdael.

Amsterdam is the focal point of the nation. Small and densely packed with fine buildings, many dating from the 17th century or earlier, it is easily explored on foot. The heart of the city consists of canals, with narrow streets radiating out like spokes of a wheel.

Currency The unit of currency in Holland is the guilder, written as NLG (for Netherlands guilder), Fl., or simply F. Each guilder is divided into 100 cents. At press time, the exchange rate for the guilder was 1.7 Fl. to the U.S. dollar.

Telephones Direct-dial international calls can be made from any phone booth. To reach an **AT&T** long-distance operator, dial 06/022–9111; for **MCI,** dial 06/022–9122; for **Sprint,** dial 06/022–9119.

Shore Excursions The following is a good choice in Amsterdam. It may not be offered by all cruise lines. Time and price are approximate.

City Tour Cruise. By motor coach and canal boat, you'll see Amsterdam's major sights, including the Royal Palace, New Church, and Rijksmuseum. The route also passes some of Amsterdam's architectural highlights, such as Mint Tower and Weeping Tower. *3 hrs. Cost: $50.*

Coming Ashore Ships dock at the cruise terminal; it's about a 10-minute drive to the main square. Central Station, the hub of the city, is the most convenient point to begin sightseeing. Across the street, in the same building as the Old Dutch Coffee House, is a tourist information center that offers helpful advice.

Getting Around Amsterdam is a small, congested city of narrow streets, which makes it ideal for exploring on foot. The most enjoyable way to get to know Amsterdam is by taking a boat trip along the canals. There are frequent departures from points opposite Central Station. Taxis are expensive: A 3-mile ride costs around Fl. 20. Rental bikes are readily available for around Fl. 10 per day. Several rental companies are close to Central Station.

Exploring Amsterdam *Numbers in the margin correspond to points of interest on the Amsterdam map.*

1 **The Centraal Station** (Central Station), designed by P. J. H. Cuijpers, was built in 1884–89 and is a good example of Dutch architecture at its most flamboyant. The street directly in front of the station square is Prins Hendrikkade.

2 The most important of Amsterdam's museums is the **Rijksmuseum** (State Museum), easily recognized by its towers. It was founded in 1808, but the current, rather lavish, building dates from 1885. The museum's fame rests on its unrivaled collection of 16th- and 17th-century Dutch masters. Of Rembrandt's masterpieces, make a point of seeing *The Nightwatch*, concealed during World War II in caves in Maastricht. The painting was misnamed because of its dull layers of varnish; in reality it depicts the Civil Guard in daylight. Also worth

Europe
Reykjavik
ICELAND
NORWAY
Bergen
SCOTLAND
NORTHERN IRELAND
Edinburgh
North Sea
Belfast
IRELAND
Irish Sea
Dublin
GREAT BRITAIN
DENMARK
WALES
Hamburg
Cardiff
ENGLAND
HOLLAND
Amsterdam
London
The Hague
Rotterdam
ATLANTIC OCEAN
English Channel
Brussels
BELGIUM
Bonn
Frankfurt
Paris
LUXEMBOURG
FRANCE
Zürich
Bern
SWITZERLAND
Lyon
Milan
Nice
Marseille
Monaco
Florence
PORTUGAL
ANDORRA
Madrid
Lisbon
Barcelona
Corsica
SPAIN
Seville
Granada
Sardinia
Balearic Islands
Gibraltar
Mediterranean Sea
MOROCCO
ALGERIA
TUNISIA
0
400 miles
0
600 km

FINLAND
Gulf of Bothnia
Oslo
SWEDEN
Helsinki
Gulf of Finland
St. Petersburg
Stockholm
ESTONIA
Tartu
Gothenburg
Kattegat
Riga
Moscow
LATVIA
Copenhagen
LITHUANIA
Baltic Sea
Kaunas
RUSSIA
RUSSIA
Vilnius
Kaliningrad
Minsk
Berlin
POLAND
BELARUS
Warsaw
NY
Cracow
Kiev
Prague
CZECHOSLOVAKIA
UKRAINE
Vienna
MOLDOVA
Budapest
Kishinev
AUSTRIA
HUNGARY
SLOVENIA
Zagreb
ROMANIA
CROATIA
Novi Sad
Bucharest
BOSNIA AND HERZEGOVINA
Belgrade
Black Sea
Sarajevo
SERBIA
Adriatic Sea
BULGARIA
Priština
MONTENEGRO
Sofia
Rome
Skopje
Titograd
MACEDONIA
Istanbul
Tirane
Naples
ALBANIA
Ankara
GREECE
TURKEY
Aegean Sea
Ionian Sea
Sicily
Athens
CYPRUS
MALTA
Crete
Mediterranean Sea

searching out are Frans Hals's family portraits, Jan Steen's drunken scenes, Van Ruysdael's romantic but menacing landscapes, and Vermeer's glimpses of everyday life bathed in his usual pale light. *Stadhouderskade 42, tel. 020/6732121. Admission: Fl. 12.50. Open Tues.–Sun. 10–5.*

❸ The not-to-be-missed **Rijksmuseum Vincent van Gogh** (Vincent van Gogh Museum) contains the world's largest collection of the artist's works—200 paintings and nearly 500 drawings—as well as works by some 50 of his contemporaries. *Paulus Potterstraat 7, tel. 020/5705200. Admission: Fl. 10. Open daily 10–5.*

❹ The **Stedelijk Museum** (Municipal Museum) has a stimulating collection of modern art and ever-changing displays of contemporary art. Before viewing the works of Cézanne, Chagall, Kandinsky, and Mondrian, check the list of temporary exhibitions in Room 1. *Paulus Potterstraat 13, tel. 020/5732911. Admission: Fl. 7.50. Open daily 11–5.*

❺ Arguably the most famous house in Amsterdam is **Anne Frankhuis** (Anne Frank House), which was immortalized by the poignant diary kept by the young Jewish girl from 1942 to 1944, when she and her family hid here from the German occupying forces. A small exhibition on the Holocaust can also be seen in the house. *Prinsengracht 263, tel. 020/5567100. Admission: Fl. 8. Open June–Aug., Mon.–Sat. 9–7, Sun. 10–7; Sept.–May, Mon.–Sat. 9–5, Sun. 10–5.*

The infamous *rosse buurt* or red-light district is bordered by Amsterdam's two oldest canals (Oudezijds Voorburgwal and Oudezijds Achterburgwal). In the windows at canal level, women in sheer lingerie slouch, stare, or do their nails. Although the area can be shocking, with its sex shops and porn shows, it is generally safe. If you do decide to explore the area, take care; purse-snatchers and pickpockets are a problem.

❻ Dominating Dam Square is the **Het Koninklijk Paleis te Amsterdam** (Royal Palace at Amsterdam), a vast, well-proportioned structure that was completed in 1655. It is built on 13,659 pilings sunk into the marshy soil. The great pedimental sculptures are an allegorical representation of Amsterdam surrounded by Neptune and mythological sea creatures. *Dam, tel. 020/6248698. Admission: Fl. 5. Open Tues.–Thurs. 1–4; daily noon–4 during Easter, summer, and fall holidays. Sometimes closed for state events.*

From 1639 to 1658, Rembrandt lived at Jodenbreestraat 4, now the ❼ **Museum Het Rembrandthuis** (Rembrandt's House). For more than 20 years, the ground floor was used by the artist as living quarters; the sunny upper floor was his studio. It contains a superb collection of his etchings. From St. Antonies Sluis Bridge, just by the house, there is a canal view that has barely changed since Rembrandt's time. *Jodenbreestraat 4–6, tel. 020/6249486. Admission: Fl. 7.50. Open Mon.–Sat. 10–5, Sun. 1–5.*

Beer lovers will want to visit the **Heinekenontvangstgebouw,** formerly the Heineken Brewery. The guided weekday tours (year-round 9:30 and 11, additional summer tours at 1 and 2:30) take in a slide presentation, the old brewery stables, and, of course, include free beer at the end of the tour. *Van der Helstraat, tel. 020/5239436. Admission: Fl. 2. Children under 18 not admitted.*

Shopping

Amsterdam is a cornucopia of interesting markets and quirky specialty shops selling antiques, art, and diamonds. The chief shopping districts, which have largely been turned into pedestrian-only areas, are the **Leidsestraat, Kalverstraat,** and **Nieuwendijk.** The **Rokin,** hectic with traffic, houses a cluster of boutiques and renowned antiques shops selling 18th- and 19th-century furniture, antique jewelry, Art Deco lamps, and statuettes. By contrast, some of the **Nieuwe**

Spiegelstraat's old curiosity shops sell a less expensive range of goods. Haute couture and other fine goods are at home on **P. C. Hooftstraat, Van Baerlestraat,** and **Beethovenstraat.** For trendy small boutiques and unusual crafts shops, locals browse through the **Jordaan.** For A-to-Z shopping in a huge variety of stores, visit the new **Magna Plaza** shopping center, built inside the glorious old post office behind the Royal Palace.

Athens/Piraeus, Greece

Athens is essentially a village that outgrew itself, spreading out from the original settlement at the foot of the Acropolis. Back in 1834, when it became the capital of modern Greece, the city had a population of fewer than 10,000. Now it houses more than a third of the Greek population—around 4 million. A modern concrete city has engulfed the old village and now sprawls for 388 square kilometers (244 square miles), covering almost all the surrounding plain from the sea to the encircling mountains.

The city is crowded, dusty, and overwhelmingly hot during the summer. It also has an appalling air-pollution problem. Still, Athens is an experience not to be missed. Its tangible vibrancy makes it one of the most exciting cities in Europe, and the sprawling cement has failed to overwhelm the few astonishing reminders of ancient Athens.

Currency The Greek monetary unit is the drachma (dr.). At press time, there were approximately 241 dr. to the U.S. dollar.

Telephones Although you can buy phone cards with up to 5,000 dr. credit, if you plan to make and pay for several international phone calls, go to an OTE office; there are several branches in Athens. For an **AT&T** long-distance operator, dial 00/800–1311; **MCI,** 00/800–1211; **Sprint,** 00/800–1411.

Shore Excursions The following are good choices in Athens. They may not be offered by all cruise lines. Times and prices are approximate.

Athens and the Acropolis. A must for the first-time visitor. Drive by motor coach to Athens, passing the Olympic Stadium, the former Royal Palace, and the Tomb of the Unknown Warrior on the way to the Acropolis, where a guide will lead an extensive walking tour. *4 hrs. Cost: $40.*

Agora and Plaka. The Acropolis, where Sophocles once taught, and Athens's old shopping district are the centerpieces of this half-day tour into historic Greece. *4 hrs. Cost: $38.*

Coming Ashore Cruise ships dock at Piraeus, 10 kilometers (6 miles) from Athens's center. From Piraeus, you can take the nearby metro right into Omonia Square. The trip takes 20 minutes and costs 100 dr. Alternatively, you can take a taxi, which may well take longer due to traffic and will cost around 1,100 dr. Cruise lines nearly always offer bus transfers for a fee.

The central area of modern Athens is small, stretching from the Acropolis to Mt. Lycabettus, with its little white church on top. The layout is simple: Three parallel streets—Stadiou, Venizelou (a.k.a. Panepistimiou), and Akademias—link two main squares—Syntagma and Omonia.

Getting Around Many of the sights you'll want to see, and most of the hotels, cafés, and restaurants, are within the central area of Athens, and it's easy to walk everywhere. Taxis are plentiful except during rush hours, public-transportation strikes, and rainstorms. Most drivers speak basic English and are familiar with the city center. There is an additional 140 dr. charge for trips from the port.

Anne Frankhuis, **5**
Centraal Station, **1**
Het Koninklijk Paleis te Amsterdam, **6**
Museum Het Rembrandthuis, **7**
Rijksmuseum, **2**
Rijksmuseum Vincent van Gogh, **3**
Stedelijk Museum, **4**

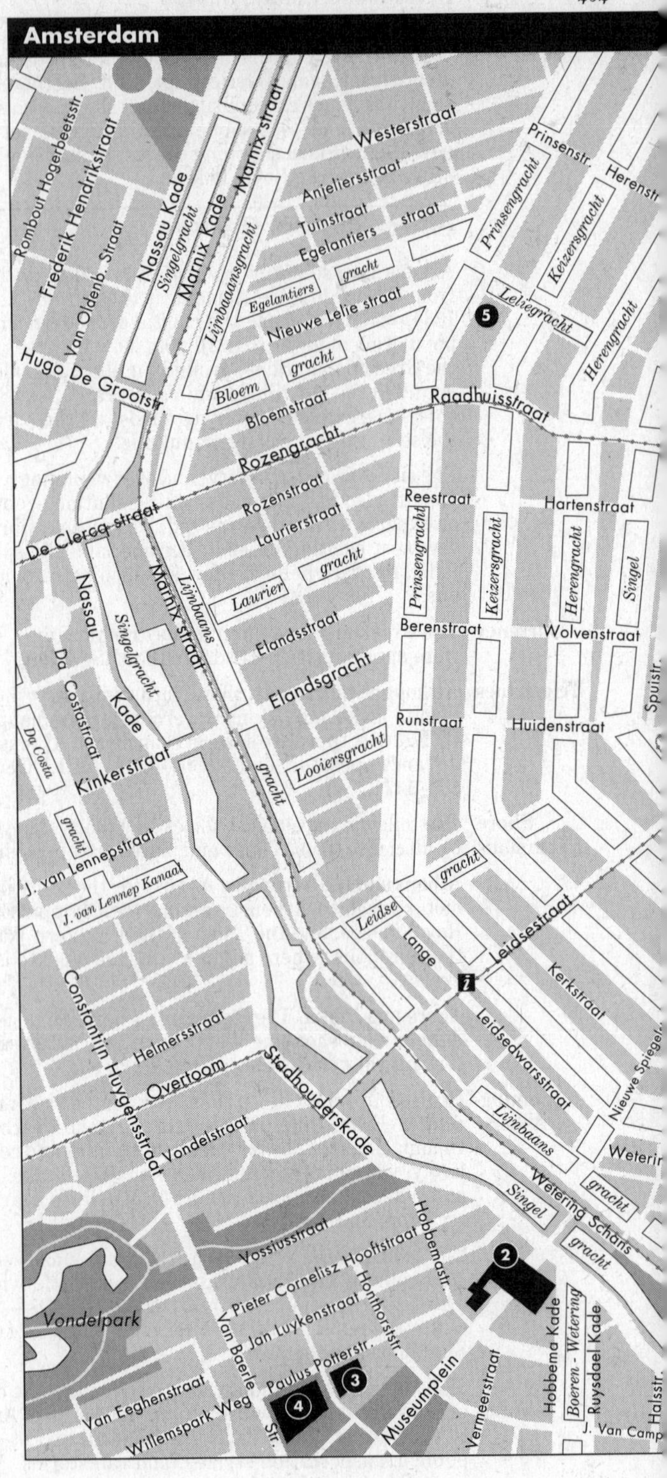

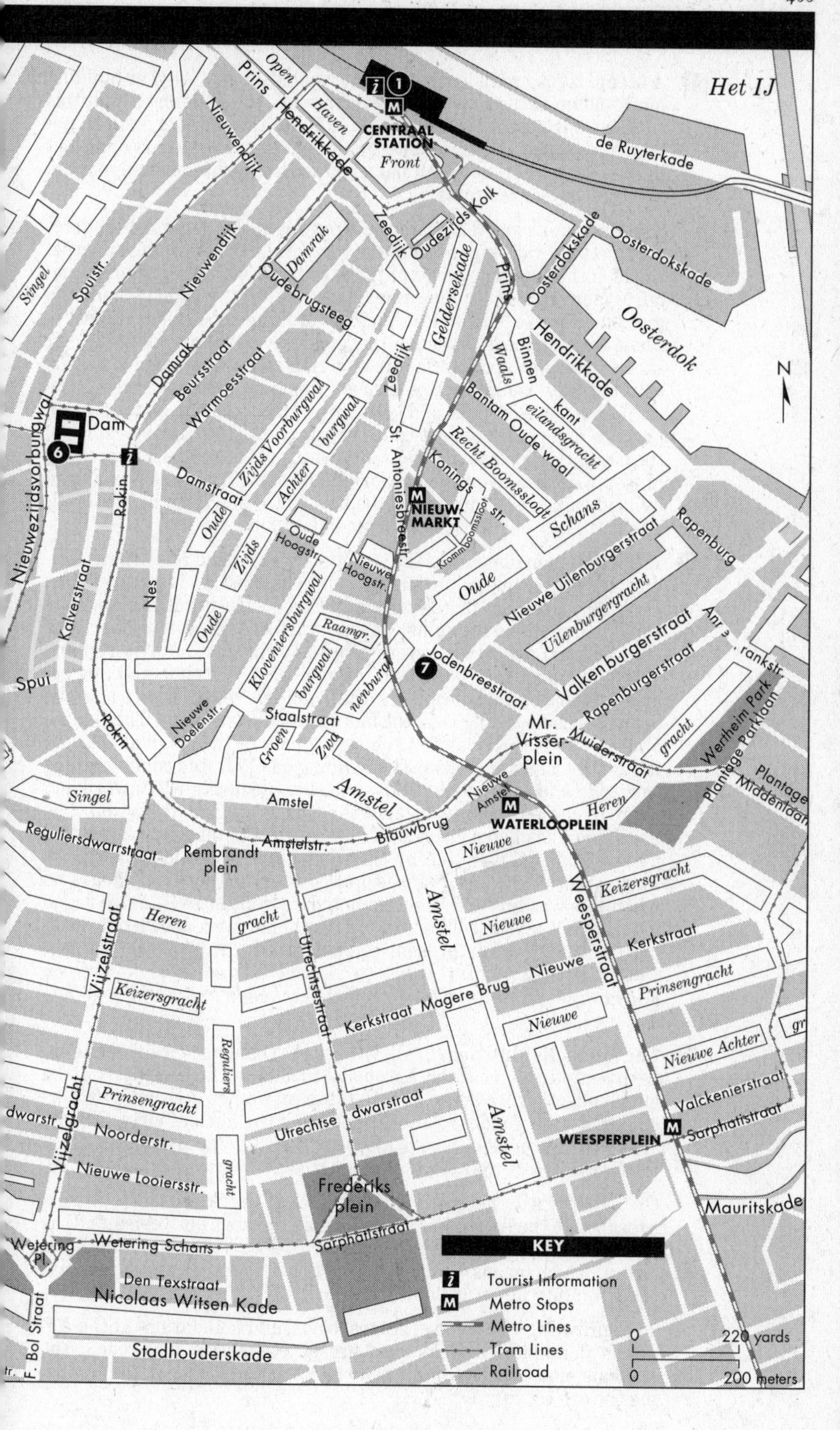
Het IJ
Centraal Station
Front
Open Haven
Prins Hendrikkade
de Ruyterkade
Oosterdokskade
Oosterdok
Nieuwendijk
Singel
Spuistr.
Damrak
Oudebrugsteeg
Zeedijk
Oudezijds Kolk
Gelderskade
Beursstraat
Warmoesstraat
Dam
Nieuwezijdsvorburgwal
Damstraat
Rokin
Nieuwmarkt
St. Antoniesbreestr.
Binnen Bantam
Oude waal
Recht Boomssloot
Konings str.
Schans
Rapenburg
Nieuwe Uilenburgerstraat
Uilenburgergracht
Kloveniersburgwal
Raamgr.
Kalverstraat
Nes
Spui
Jodenbreestraat
Valkenburgerstraat
Rapenburgerstraat
Staalstraat
Mr. Visser-plein
Muiderstraat
Wertheim Park
Plantage Parklaan
Plantage Middenlaan
Amstel
Waterlooplein
Blauwbrug
Reguliersdwarrstraat
Rembrandt plein
Amstelstr.
Herengracht
Keizersgracht
Vijzelstraat
Utrechtsestraat
Kerkstraat
Magere Brug
Weesperstraat
Prinsengracht
Nieuwe Achter
Valckenierstraat
Weesperplein
Sarphatistraat
Utrechtse dwarstraat
Noorderstr.
Nieuwe Looiersstr.
Frederiks plein
Mauritskade
Wetering Pl.
Wetering Schans
Den Texstraat
Nicolaas Witsen Kade
Stadhouderskade
F. Bol Straat
KEY
Tourist Information
Metro Stops
Metro Lines
Tram Lines
Railroad
0 220 yards
0 200 meters

Exploring Athens *Numbers in the margin correspond to points of interest on the Athens map.*

❶ A steep, zigzag path leads to the **Acropolis.** After a 30-year building moratorium at the time of the Persian wars, the Athenians built this complex during the 5th century BC to honor the goddess Athena, patron of the city. It is now undergoing conservation as part of an ambitious 20-year rescue plan launched with international support in 1983 by Greek architects.

The first ruins you'll see are the Propylaea, the monumental gateway that led worshipers from the temporal world into the spiritual world of the sanctuary; now only the columns of Pentelic marble and a fragment of stone ceiling remain. Above, to the right, stands the graceful Temple of Wingless Victory (or Athena Nike), so called because the sculptor depicted the goddess of victory without her wings in order to prevent her from flying away. The elegant and architecturally complex Erechtheion temple, most sacred of the shrines of the Acropolis and later turned into a harem by the Turks, has now emerged from extensive repair work. Dull, heavy copies of the Caryatids (draped maidens) now support the roof. The Acropolis Museum houses five of the six originals, their faces much damaged by acid rain; only four are on display, since one is being restored. The sixth is in the British Museum in London.

❷ The **Parthenon** dominates the Acropolis and indeed the Athens skyline. It was completed in 438 BC and is the most architecturally sophisticated temple of that period. Even with hordes of tourists wandering around the ruins, you can still feel a sense of wonder. The architectural decorations were originally finished in vivid red and blue paint, and the roof was of marble tiles, but time and neglect have given the marble pillars their golden-white shine, and the beauty of the building is all the more stark and striking. The British Museum houses the largest remaining part of the original 532-foot frieze (the Elgin Marbles). The building has 17 fluted columns along each side and eight at the ends, and these lean slightly inward and bulge to cleverly counterbalance the natural optical distortion. The Parthenon has had a checkered history: It was made into a brothel by the Romans, a church by the Christians, and a mosque by the Turks. The Turks also stored gunpowder in the Propylaea, and when this was hit by a Venetian bombardment in 1687, a fire raged for two days and 28 columns of the Parthenon were blown out, leaving the temple in its present condition. *Tel. 01/321–0219. Admission: 2,000 dr., joint ticket to Acropolis and museum. Open weekdays 8–6:30 (8–4:30 in winter), weekends and holidays 8:30–2:30.*

❸ The **Acropolis Museum,** just below the Parthenon, contains some superb sculptures from the Acropolis, including the Caryatids and a large collection of colored *korai* (statues of women dedicated by worshipers to the goddess Athena, patron of the ancient city). *Tel. 01/323–6665. Admission: 2,000 dr., joint ticket to the Acropolis. Open weekdays 8–6:30 (8–4:30 in winter), weekends and holidays 8–2:30.*

On Areopagus, the rocky outcrop facing the Acropolis, St. Paul preached to the Athenians; the road leading down between it and the hill of Pnyx is called Agiou Pavlou (St. Paul). To the right stands the ❹ **Agora,** which means "marketplace," the civic center and focal point of community life in ancient Athens.

The sprawling confusion of stones, slabs, and foundations at the Agora is dominated by the best-preserved temple in Greece, the ❺ **Hephaisteion** (often wrongly referred to as the Theseion), built during the 5th century BC.

The impressive **Stoa of Attalos II,** reconstructed by the American School of Classical Studies in Athens with the help of the Rockefel-

❻ ler Foundation, houses the **Museum of the Agora Excavations.** *Tel. 01/321–0185. Admission: 1,200 dr. Open Tues.–Sun. 8:30–2:45.*

❼ The **Plaka** is almost all that's left of 19th-century Athens. During the 1950s and '60s, the area became garish with neon as nightclubs moved in and residents moved out. Renovation in recent years has restored the Plaka, with its winding lanes, neoclassical houses, and sights such as the Greek Folk Art Museum (Kidathineon 17), the Tower of the Winds (a 1st-century BC water clock near the Roman Agora), and the Monument of Lysikrates (in a park off Lysikratous). Above the Plaka, at the base of the Acropolis, is Anafiotika, the closest thing you'll find to a village in Athens. To escape the city bustle, take some time to wander among its whitewashed, bougainvillea-framed houses and its tiny churches. *Stretching east from the Agora.*

❽ Make time to see the **National Archaeological Museum.** Despite being somewhat off the tourist route, a good 10-minute walk north of Omonia Square, it is well worth the detour. It houses one of the most exciting collections of antiquities in the world, including sensational archaeological finds made by Heinrich Schliemann at Mycenae; 16th-century BC frescoes from the Akrotiri ruins on Santorini; and the 6½-foot-tall bronze sculpture *Poseidon*, an original work of circa 470 BC, possibly by the sculptor Kalamis, which was found in the sea off Cape Artemision in 1928. *28 Oktovriou (Patission) 44, tel. 01/821–7717. Admission: 2,000 dr. Open Mon. 11–5, Tues.–Fri. 8–7 (8–5 in winter), weekends and holidays 8:30–3.*

❾ The **Museum of Cycladic Art's** collection spans 5,000 years, with nearly 100 exhibits of the Cycladic civilization (3000–2000 BC), including many of the slim marble figurines that so fascinated artists such as Picasso and Modigliani. *Neofytou Douka 4, tel. 01/722–8321. Admission: 400 dr. Open Mon. and Wed.–Fri. 10–4, Sat. 10–3.*

❿ Housed in an 1848 mansion built by an eccentric French aristocrat is the **Byzantine Museum.** Since the museum is undergoing renovation, not all its pieces are on display, but it has a unique collection of icons and the very beautiful 14th-century Byzantine embroidery of the body of Christ, in gold, silver, yellow, and green. Sculptural fragments provide an excellent introduction to Byzantine architecture. *Vasilissis Sofias 22, tel. 01/721–1027. Admission: 500 dr. Open Tues.–Sun. 8:30–3.*

Shopping Better tourist shops sell copies of traditional Greek jewelry, silver filigree, enamel, Skyrian pottery, onyx ashtrays and dishes, woven bags, attractive rugs (including flokatis—shaggy wool rugs, often brightly colored), worry beads called *koboloi* in amber or silver, good leather items, and furs. Furs made from scraps are inexpensive. Some museums sell replicas of small items that are in their collections. The best handicrafts are sold in the **National Welfare Organization shop** (Ypatias 6), near the Cathedral of Athens, and the **Center of Hellenic Tradition** (Pandrossou 36, in Monastiraki). Other shops sell dried fruit, packaged pistachios, and canned olives. Natural sponges also make good gifts.

Barcelona, Spain

Barcelona thrives on its business acumen and industrial muscle. Its hardworking citizens are proud to have and use their own language (Catalan)—with street names, museum exhibits, newspapers, radio programs, and movies all in this native tongue. A recent milestone was the realization of a long-cherished goal—to host the Olympic Games, held in Barcelona in summer 1992. This thriving metropolis has a rich history and an abundance of sights. For medieval atmosphere, few places can rival the narrow alleys of its Gothic Quarter. Barcelona has a sophistication built on its obsession with design, from Antoni Gaudí at the turn of the century right up to the present

Acropolis, **1**
Acropolis Museum, **3**
Agora, **4**
Byzantine Museum, **10**
Hephaisteion, **5**
Museum of Agora Excavations, **6**
Museum of Cycladic Art, **9**
National Archaeological Museum, **8**
Parthenon, **2**
Plaka, **7**

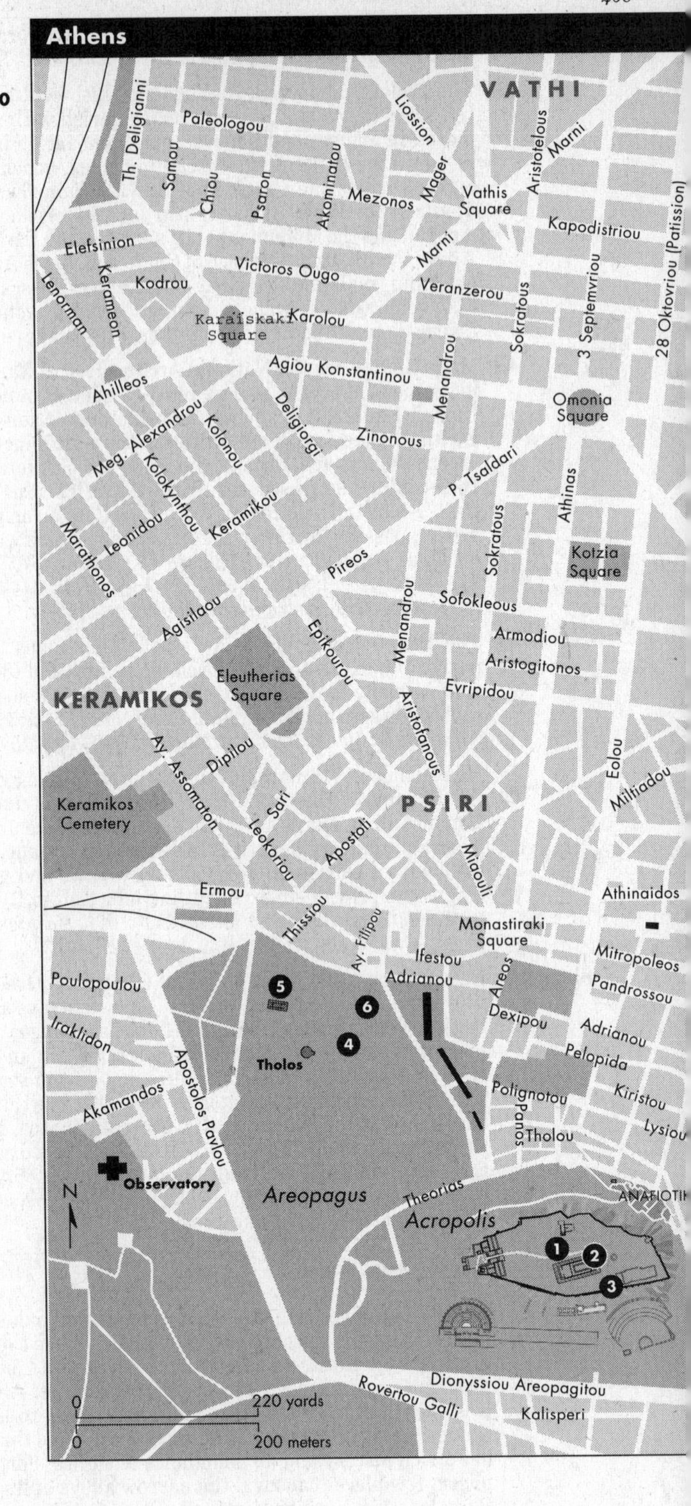

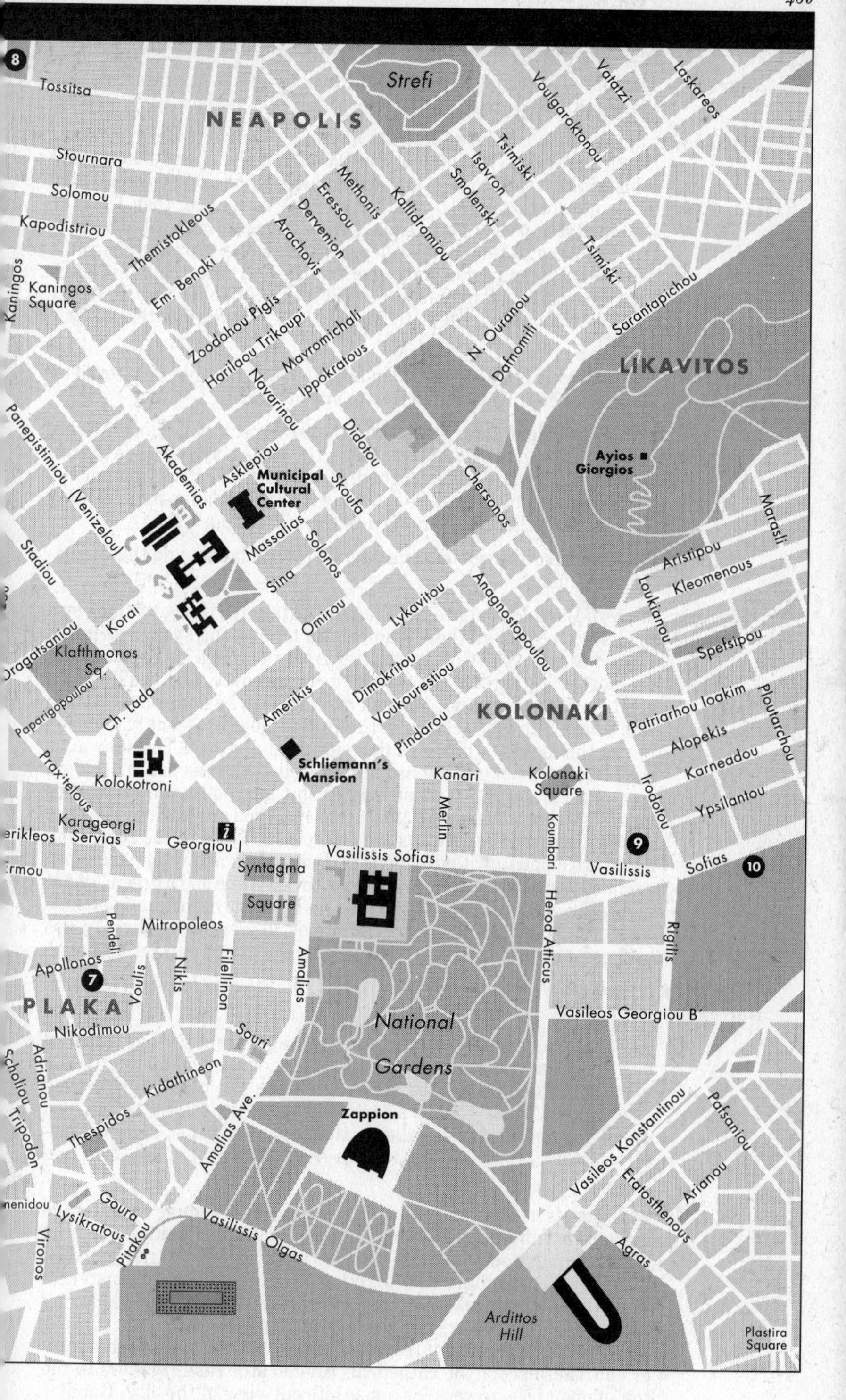
8
Tossitsa
Strefi
NEAPOLIS
Stournara
Solomou
Kapodistriou
Laskareos
Vatatzi
Voulgaroktonou
Tsimiski
Isavron
Smolenski
Methonis
Kallidromiou
Eressou
Dervenion
Arachovis
Themistokleous
Em. Benaki
Kaningos
Kaningos Square
Zoodohou Pigis
Harilaou Trikoupi
Mavromichali
Ippokratous
Navarinou
N. Ouranou
Dafnomili
Sarantapichou
LIKAVITOS
Ayios Giorgios
Panepistimiou (Venizelou)
Akademias
Asklepiou
Municipal Cultural Center
Didotou
Skoufa
Chersonos
Stadiou
Massalias
Solonos
Sina
Marasli
Aristipou
Kleomenous
Loukianou
Korai
Omirou
Lykavitou
Anagnostopoulou
Spefsipou
Dragatsaniou
Klafthmonos Sq.
Paparigopoulou
Ch. Lada
Amerikis
Dimokritou
Voukourestiou
Pindarou
KOLONAKI
Patriarhou Ioakim
Ploutarchou
Alopekis
Karneadou
Ypsilantou
Praxitelous
Kolokotroni
Schliemann's Mansion
Kanari
Merlin
Kolonaki Square
Irodotou
Karageorgi Servias
Georgiou I
Vasilissis Sofias
Koumbari
9
Vasilissis
Sofias
10
Syntagma Square
Mitropoleos
Pendeli
Herod Atticus
Rigilis
Apollonos
7
Voulis
Nikis
Filellinon
Amalias
PLAKA
Vasileos Georgiou B'
Nikodimou
Souri
National Gardens
Adrianou
Scholiou
Kidathineon
Tripodon
Thespidos
Zappion
Amalias Ave.
Pafsaniou
Vasileos Konstantinou
Eratosthenous
Arianou
Goura
Lysikratous
Vasilissis Olgas
Pitakou
Vironos
Agras
Ardittos Hill
Plastira Square

day. Make time to see the elegance and distinction of its **Moderniste Eixample** area and the fantasies of Gaudí's whimsical imagination.

Currency The unit of currency in Spain is the peseta (pta.). At press time, the exchange rate was about 129 ptas. to the U.S. dollar.

Telephones Calling home can be done from any pay phone marked TELÉFONO INTERNACIONAL. Use 50-pta. (or 100-pta. if the phone takes them) coins initially, then coins of any denomination to prolong your call. Dial 07 for international calls, wait for the tone to change, then 1 for the United States or 0101 for Canada. For lengthy international calls, go to the *telefónica,* a telephone office, where an operator assigns you a private booth and collects payment at the end of the call; this is the least expensive and by far the easiest way of phoning abroad. **AT&T** (tel. 900/99–00–11), **MCI** (tel. 900/99–00–14), **Sprint** (tel. 900/99–00–13).

Shore Excursions The following is a good choice in Barcelona. It may not be offered by all cruise lines. Time and price are approximate.

Barcelona Highlights. This comprehensive excursion winds its way from the pier to the Gothic Quarter. Along the way you'll see the unfinished Sagrada Familia cathedral and visit Montjuïc, one of the city's highest points, before reaching Plaza Catalunya for a walking tour of the Gothic Quarter. *3½ hrs. Cost: $30–$50.*

Coming Ashore Ships visiting Barcelona dock near Portal de la Pau and the Columbus Monument.

Getting Around Modern Barcelona above the Plaça de Catalunya is mostly built on a grid system, though there's no helpful numbering system as in the United States. The Gothic Quarter from the Plaça de Catalunya to the port is a warren of narrow streets, however, and you'll need a good map to get around. Most sightseeing can be done on foot—you won't have any other choice in the Gothic Quarter—but you'll need to use the metro or buses to link sightseeing areas. The subway is the fastest way of getting around, as well as the easiest to use. You pay a flat fare of 135 ptas. no matter how far you travel. City buses run from about 5:30 or 6 AM to 10:30 PM, though some stop earlier. Again, there's a flat-fare system (135 ptas.). Plans of the routes followed are displayed at bus stops. Taxis are black and yellow and when available for hire show a LIBRE sign in the daytime and a green light at night. The meter starts at 350 ptas., and there are small supplements for rides to the port. There are cab stands all over town; cabs may also be flagged down on the street. Make sure the driver puts on his meter.

Exploring Barcelona *Numbers in the margin correspond to points of interest on the Barcelona map.*

❶ At the Plaça de la Seu, step inside the magnificent Gothic **cathedral** built between 1298 and 1450, though the spire and Gothic facade were not added until 1892. Highlights are the beautifully carved choir stalls, Santa Eulàlia's tomb in the crypt, the battle-scarred crucifix from Don Juan's galley in the Lepanto Chapel, and the cloisters. *Tel. 93/315–1554. Admission free. Open daily 7:45–1:30 and 4–7:45.*

❷ Barcelona's most eccentric landmark is Gaudí's **Temple Expiatori de la Sagrada Família** (Expiatory Church of the Holy Family). Far from finished at his death in 1926—Gaudí was run over by a tram and died in a pauper's hospital—this striking creation will cause consternation or wonder, shrieks of protest or cries of rapture. In 1936, during the Spanish Civil War, the citizens of Barcelona loved their crazy temple enough to spare it from the flames that engulfed all their other churches except the cathedral. An elevator takes visitors to the top of one of the towers for a magnificent view of the city. Gaudí is buried in the crypt. *Tel. 93/455–0247. Admission: 700 ptas. Open Sept.–May, daily 9–7; June–Aug., daily 9–9.*

3 One of Barcelona's most popular attractions, the **Museu Picasso** is actually two 15th-century palaces that provide a striking setting for the collections donated in 1963 and 1970, first by Picasso's secretary, then by the artist himself. The collection ranges from early childhood sketches to exhibition posters done in Paris shortly before his death. Of particular interest are his Blue Period pictures and his variations on Velázquez's *Las Meninas. Carrer Montcada 15–19, tel. 93/319–6310. Admission: 650 ptas; Wed. ½ price, free 1st Sun. of month. Open Tues.–Sat. 10–8, Sun. 10–3.*

4 **Santa Maria del Mar** is Barcelona's best example of a Mediterranean Gothic church and is widely considered the city's loveliest. It was built between 1329 and 1383 in fulfillment of a vow made a century earlier by Jaume I to build a church for the Virgin of the Sailors. Its simple beauty is enhanced by a stunning rose window and magnificent soaring columns. *Open weekends 9–12:30 and 5–8.*

An impressive square built in the 1840s in the heart of the Gothic 5 Quarter, the **Plaça Sant Jaume** features two imposing buildings facing each other. The 15th-century Ajuntament, or City Hall, has an impressive black and gold mural (1928) by Josep María Sert (who also painted the murals for New York's Waldorf Astoria) and the famous Saló de Cent, from which the Council of One Hundred ruled the city from 1372 to 1714. You can wander into the courtyard, but to visit the interior, you will have to ask permission in the office beforehand. The Palau de la Generalitat, seat of the Catalan Regional Government, is a 15th-century palace open to the public on Sunday mornings only. *Carrer Ferran.*

Head to the bottom of Rambla and take an elevator to the top of the 6 **Monument a Colon** (Columbus Monument) for a breathtaking view over the city. Columbus faces out to sea, pointing, ironically, east. (Nearby you can board the cable car that crosses the harbor to Barceloneta or goes up to Montjuïc.) *Admission: 300 ptas. Open Tues.–Sat. 10–2 and 3:30–6:30, Sun. 10–7.*

7 The **Museu Marítim** (Maritime Museum) is housed in the 13th-century Drassanes Reiales, the old Royal Shipyards. The museum is packed with ships, figureheads, nautical paraphernalia, and several early navigation charts, including a map by Amerigo Vespucci and the oldest chart in Europe, the 1439 chart of Gabriel de Valseca from Mallorca. *Plaça Portal de la Pau 1, tel. 93/318–3245. Admission: 350 ptas., Wed. 175 ptas., free 1st Sun. of month. Open Tues.–Sat. 10–2 and 4–7, Sun. 10–2.*

8 Gaudí's **Palau Güell** mansion was built between 1885 and 1890 for his patron, Count Eusebi de Güell, and is the only one of Gaudí's houses that is open to the public. *No. 3, Nou de la Rambla. Admission: 350 ptas. Open Tues.–Sat. 10–1:30 and 4–7:30.*

Above the Placa de Catalunya you come into modern Barcelona and an elegant area known as the **Eixample,** which was laid out in the late 19th century as part of the city's expansion scheme. Much of the building here was done at the height of the Moderniste movement, a Spanish and mainly Catalan offshoot of art nouveau, whose leading exponents were the architects Gaudí, Domènech i Montaner, and Puig i Cadafalch. The principal thoroughfares of the Eixample are the Rambla de Catalunya and the Passeig de Gràcia, where some of the city's most elegant shops and cafés are found.

Moderniste houses are one of Barcelona's special drawing cards, so 9 walk up Passeig de Gràcia until you come to the **Mançana de la Discòrdia,** or Block of Discord, between Consell de Cent and Aragó. Its name is a pun on the word *mançana,* which means both "block" and "apple." The houses here are quite fantastic. At No. 43 is Gaudí's Casa Batlló. Farther along the street on the right, on the 10 corner of Provença, is Gaudí's **Casa Milà** (Passeig de Gràcia 92), more

Casa Milà, **10**
Cathedral, **1**
Mançana de la Discòrdia, **9**
Monument a Colon, **6**
Museu Nacional d'Art de Catalunya, **11**
Museu Marítim, **7**
Museu Picasso, **3**
Palau Güell, **8**
Plaça Sant Jaume, **5**
Santa Maria del Mar, **4**
Temple Expiatori de la Sagrada Família, **2**

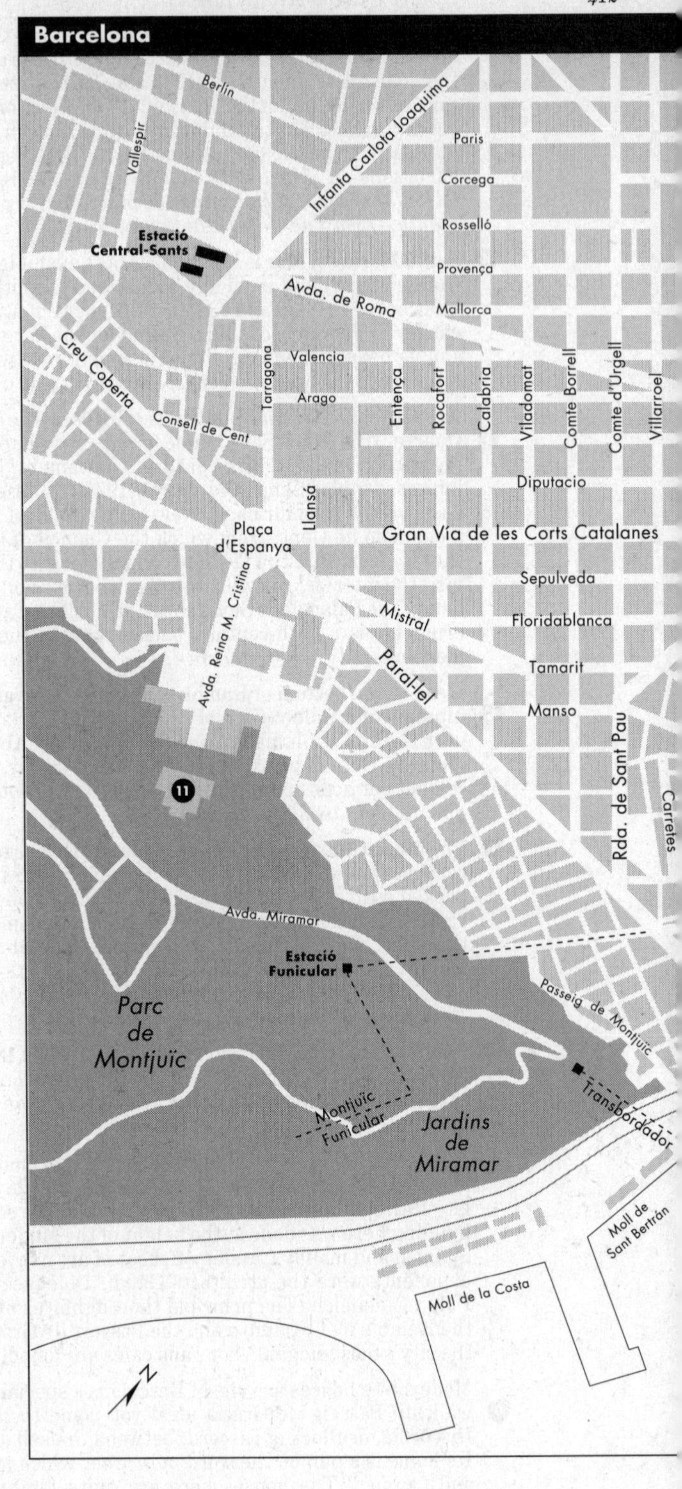

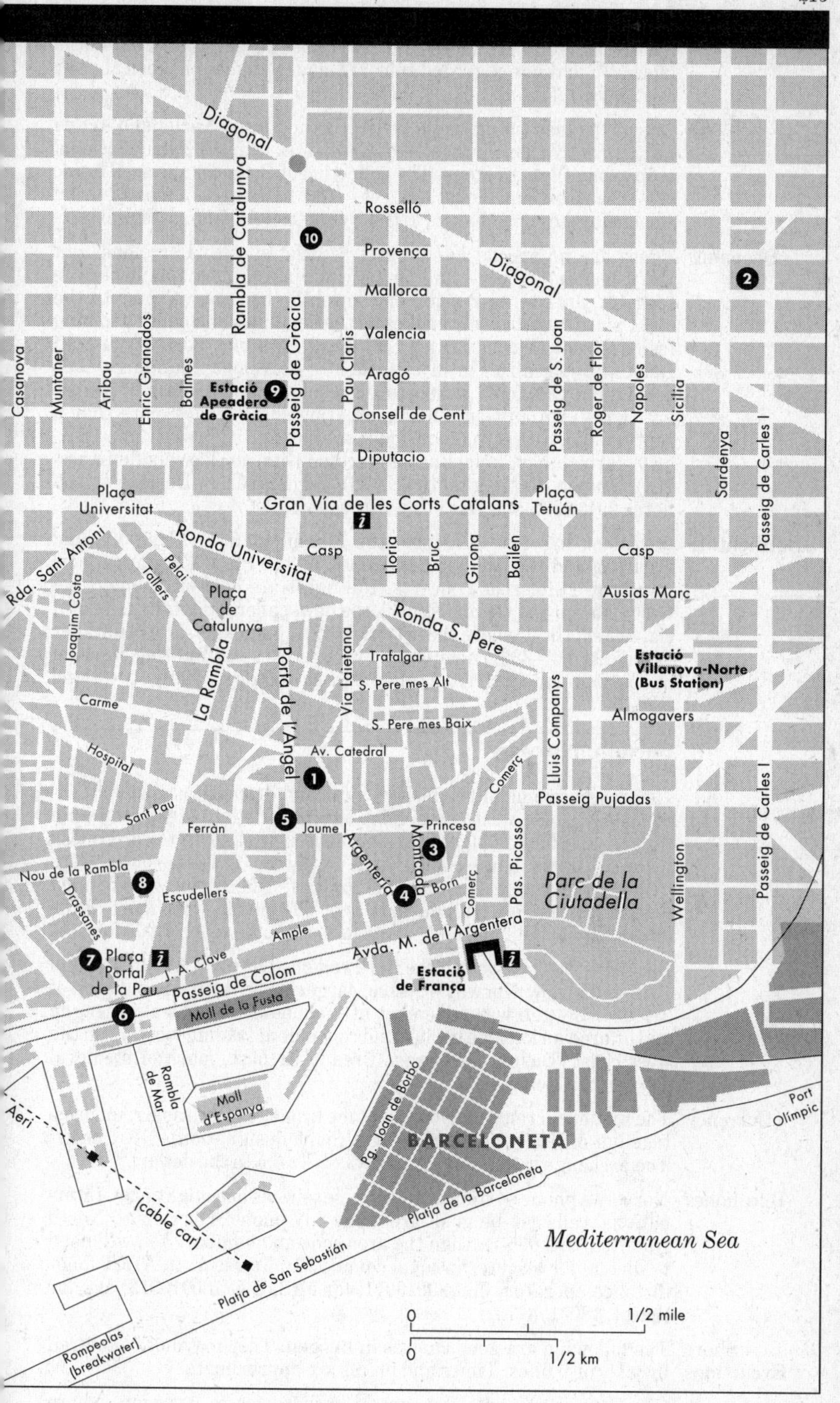

Diagonal
Rambla de Catalunya
Rosselló
Provença
Diagonal
Mallorca
Valencia
Aragó
Consell de Cent
Diputacio
Casanova
Muntaner
Aribau
Enric Granados
Balmes
Estació Apeadero de Gràcia
Passeig de Gràcia
Pau Claris
Passeig de S. Joan
Roger de Flor
Napoles
Sicilia
Sardenya
Passeig de Carles I
Plaça Universitat
Gran Vía de les Corts Catalans
Plaça Tetuán
Rda. Sant Antoni
Ronda Universitat
Casp
Lloria
Bruc
Girona
Bailén
Casp
Ausias Marc
Joaquim Costa
Pelai
Tallers
Plaça de Catalunya
Ronda S. Pere
Estació Villanova-Norte (Bus Station)
La Rambla
Porta de l'Angel
Via Laietana
Trafalgar
S. Pere mes Alt
S. Pere mes Baix
Carme
Almogavers
Lluis Companys
Hospital
Av. Catedral
Comerç
Passeig Pujadas
Sant Pau
Ferràn
Jaume I
Princesa
Moncada
Argenteria
Born
Comerç
Pas. Picasso
Parc de la Ciutadella
Wellington
Passeig de Carles I
Nou de la Rambla
Drassanes
Escudellers
Ample
Avda. M. de l'Argentera
Plaça Portal de la Pau
J. A. Clave
Passeig de Colom
Estació de França
Moll de la Fusta
Rambla de Mar
Moll d'Espanya
Pg. Joan de Borbó
BARCELONETA
Port Olímpic
Aeri
(cable car)
Platja de la Barceloneta
Mediterranean Sea
Platja de San Sebastián
Rompeolas (breakwater)
0
1/2 mile
0
1/2 km

often known as La Pedrera. Its remarkable curving stone facade with ornamental balconies actually ripples around the corner of the block. To arrange a guided tour of Gaudí's phantasmagorical roof, call 93/488–3592.

⓫ One of the leading attractions here is the **Museu Nacional d'Art de Catalunya** (National Museum of Catalan Art) in the Palau Nacional atop a long flight of steps. The collection of Romanesque and Gothic art treasures—medieval frescoes and altarpieces, mostly from small churches and chapels in the Pyrenees—is simply staggering.

Shopping There are no special handicrafts associated with Barcelona, but you'll have no trouble finding typical Spanish goods anywhere in town. If you're into fashion and jewelry, then you've come to the right place, as Barcelona makes all the headlines on Spain's booming fashion front. **Xavier Roca i Coll** (Sant Pere mes Baix 24, just off Laietana) specializes in silver models of Barcelona's buildings. Barcelona and Catalonia have passed along a playful sense of design ever since Antoni Gaudí began creating shock waves more than a century ago. Stores and boutiques specializing in design items (jewelry, furnishings, knickknacks) include **Gimeno** (Passeig de Gracia 102), **Vinçon** (Passeig de Gràcia 96), **Bd** (Barcelona Design, at Mallorca 291–293), and **Dos i Una** (Rosselló 275).

Bullfighting Barcelona has two bullrings, the **Monumental,** on Gran Vía and Carles I, and the smaller **Les Arenes,** on the Plaça d'Espanya, now mainly used for rock concerts. Bullfights are held on Sundays between March and October; check the newspaper for details. The official ticket office, where there is no markup on tickets, is at Muntaner 24 (tel. 93/453–3821) near Gran Vía. There's a **Bullfighting Museum** at the Monumental ring, open March–October, daily 10–1 and 5:30–7.

Bergen, Norway

Norway has some of the most remote and dramatic scenery in Europe. Along the west coast, deep fjords knife into steep mountain ranges. In older villages, wooden houses spill down toward docks where Viking ships—and later, whaling vessels—once were moored. Norway is most famous for its fjords, which were formed during an ice age a million years ago. The entrances to most fjords are shallow, about 500 feet, while inland depths reach 4,000 feet.

Bergen is the gateway to the fjord region. The town was founded in 1070 and is now Norway's second-largest city, with a population of 219,000. Bergen was a member of the medieval Hanseatic League and offered an ice-free harbor and convenient trading location on the west coast. Despite numerous fires in its past, much of medieval Bergen has remained.

Currency The unit of currency in Norway is the krone, written as Kr. on price tags but officially written as NOK (bank designation), NKr, or kr. The exchange rate at press time was NKr 6.5 to the dollar.

Telephones Norway's phone system is not as expensive as one might fear. International calls can be made from any pay phone. For calls to North America, dial 095–1, then the area code and number. You will need to dial 00 for an international connection. To reach an **AT&T** long-distance operator, dial 80019011; for **MCI,** dial 180019912; and for **Sprint,** 180019877.

Shore Excursions The following are good choices in Bergen. They may not be offered by all cruise lines. Times and prices are approximate.

City Tour. Head past the central harbor area to Bryggen, where rows of gabled merchants' houses line the streets. Stop at Troldhaugen, once the estate of composer Edvard Grieg, for a tour and concert. The estate is near Nordaas Lake and is surrounded by a park. *3 hrs. Cost: $35.*

Museum and Haakon's Hall. Visit King Haakon's Hall, a royal ceremonial hall inaugurated in 1261. This tour also visits the Old Bergen Museum, an open-air collection of early 19th century houses relocated here. *3 hrs. Cost: $35.*

Coming Ashore Ships calling at Bergen dock at the harbor area at Bryggen. Seven surrounding mountains set off the weathered wooden houses, cobbled streets, and Hanseatic-era warehouses along the waterfront. Bergen is small and easily toured by foot.

Exploring Bergen The best way to get a feel for Bergen's medieval trading heyday is to visit the **Hanseatisk Museum** on the Bryggen. One of the oldest and best-preserved of Bergen's wooden buildings, it is furnished in 16th-century style. The guided tour is excellent. *Admission: NKr 30. Open June–Aug., daily 9–5; May and Sept., daily 11–2; Oct.–Apr., Mon., Wed., Fri., Sun. 11–2.*

On the western end of the Vågen is the **Rosenkrantz tårnet** (tower), part of the Bergenhus, the 13th-century fortress guarding the harbor entrance. The tower and fortress were destroyed during World War II, but were meticulously restored during the '60s and are now rich with furnishings and household items from the 16th century. *Admission: NKr 15. Open mid-May–mid-Sept., daily 10–4; mid-Sept.–mid-May, Sun. noon–3, or upon request.*

From Ævregaten, the back boundary of Bryggen, you can walk through the meandering back streets to the popular **Fløybanen,** the funicular (a cable railway in which ascending cars counterbalance descending cars). It climbs a steep 1,070 feet to the top of Fløyen, one of the seven mountains guarding the city.

Canary Islands, Spain

Traditionally a popular spot for winter holidays, Spain's Canary Islands are becoming a year-round destination favored by sunseekers and nature lovers alike. The Canaries lie 70 miles off the coast of southern Morocco in the Atlantic Ocean and enjoy mild, sunny weather throughout the year, except for the north coast of Tenerife, which has above-average rainfall for the Canaries and below-average temperatures year-round. Each of the seven volcanic islands in the archipelago is distinct. Some have lush tropical vegetation, poinsettias as tall as trees, and banana plantations, while others are arid and resemble an exotic moonscape of lava rock and sand dunes. Mt. Teide (12,198 feet), Spain's highest peak, snowcapped for much of the year, is here. The islands are also home to national parks and dozens of other protected ecological zones in which visitors can hike through mist-shrouded forests of virgin laurel trees, climb mountains, eat food cooked by nature over volcanic craters, or scuba dive off long stretches of unspoiled coastline.

Currency The unit of currency in the Canary Islands is the peseta (pta.). At press time, the exchange rate was about 129 ptas. to the U.S. dollar.

Telephones Calling abroad can be done from any pay phone marked TELÉFONO INTERNACIONAL. Use 50-pta. (or 100-pta. if the phone takes them) coins initially, then coins of any denomination to prolong your call. Dial 07 for international calls, wait for the tone to change, then dial 1 for the United States or 0101 for Canada. **AT&T** (tel. 900/99–00–11), **MCI** (tel. 900/99–00–14), **Sprint** (tel. 900/99–00–13).

Shore Excursions The following are good choices in the Canary Islands. They may not be offered by all cruise lines. Times and prices are approximate.

In Tenerife **Mount Teide and Countryside.** A motor coach takes you through the Esperanza mountain range to Mount Teide National Park with picturesque scenery along the way. *4½ hrs. Cost: $40.*

Botanical Gardens. This motor-coach excursion takes you to the Orotava Valley, with its banana plantations and views of Mount Teide, before reaching the Botanical Gardens. Next head to the La Paz resort and its seawater pools. *4 hrs. Cost: $40.*

In Lanzarote **Timanfaya National Park and Winery Tour.** By motor coach, this tour visits the park of Timanfaya (fire mountains), before heading off to El Golfo, Los Hervideros, and Janubio, which feature a variety of different forms of volcanic activity. A visit to the La Geria vineyards includes a tasting. *4 hrs. Cost: $40.*

Coming Ashore

Ships dock in Tenerife at the Santa Cruz pier in the island's provincial capital.

Getting Around

Most visitors rent a car or Jeep—it is by far the best way to explore the countryside. **Hertz** and **Avis** have locations in both Tenerife and Lanzarote, though better rates can be obtained from the Spanish company **Cicar** (tel. 928/27–73–08), located at airports.

Exploring the Canary Islands

Tenerife

The **Museo Arqueológico Provincial** (Provincial Archeology Museum), contains ceramics and mummies from the stone-age culture of the Guanches, the native people who inhabited the islands before they were conquered and colonized by the Spanish in the 15th century. *Bravo Murillo 5, tel. 922/24–20–90.*

The best thing to visit in Santa Cruz is the colorful weekday-morning market, **Mercado de Nuestra Señora de Africa,** which sells everything from tropical fruits and flowers to canaries and parrots. *Av. de San Sebastín. Open Mon.–Sat. 5 AM–noon.*

Inland, past banana plantations, almond groves, and pine forests, is the entrance to **Mt. Teide National Park** (visitor center open daily 9–4). Before arriving at the foot of the mountain, you pass through a stark landscape called Las Cañadas del Teide, a violent jumble of rocks and minerals created by millions of years of volcanic activity. A cable car (admission 1,000 ptas.; open daily 9–5, last trip up at 4) will take you within 534 feet of the top of Mt. Teide, where there are good views of the southern part of the island and neighboring Gran Canaria.

Also worth a visit are the north-coast towns of **Icod de los Vinos,** which boasts a 3,000-year-old, 57-foot-tall dragon tree once worshiped by the ancient Guanches and a plaza surrounded by typical wood-balconied Canarian houses; and, farther west, **Garachico,** the most peaceful and best-preserved village on this touristy isle.

Lanzarote

The **Parque National Timanfaya,** popularly known as the fire mountains, takes up much of the southern part of the island. Here you can have a camel ride, take a guided coach tour of the volcanic zone, and eat lunch at one of the world's most unusual restaurants, El Diablo, where meat is cooked over the crater of a volcano using the earth's natural heat. *4 km/2½ mi north of Yaiza, tel. 928/84–00–57. Admission: 850 pts. Open daily 9–5.*

The **Jameos del Agua** (Water Cavern) is a natural wonder, created when molten lava streamed through an underground tunnel and hissed into the sea. Ponds in the caverns are home to a unique species of albino crab. The site also features an auditorium with fantastic acoustics for concerts and a restaurant-bar. *Rte. GC710, 21 km/13 mi north of Arrecife.*

Shopping

In Tenerife Tenerife is a free port, meaning no value-added tax is charged on luxury items such as jewelry and electronics. The streets are packed with shops selling these items, but the prices do not represent a significant savings for Americans. The Canary Islands are famous for lacy, hand-embroidered tablecloths and place mats. The largest selection is available in Puerto de la Cruz at **Casa Iriarte** (San Juan 17). Contemporary crafts and traditional musical instruments can be found at the government-sponsored shop **Casa Torrehermosa** (Tomas Zerolo 27) in Orotava.

Beaches
In Tenerife
Las Teresitas beach, 7 kilometers (4 miles) east of Santa Cruz, was constructed using white sand imported from the Sahara Desert and is popular with local families. **Playa del Medano,** on the southern coast, a large bay surrounded by yellow sand, is considered the best beach on Tenerife.

In Lanzarote
Playa de la Garita is a wide bay with crystal-clear water that's great for snorkeling. The **Playa Blanca** resort area, reached by traveling down hard-packed dirt roads on Punta de Papagayo, features white-sand beaches.

Copenhagen, Denmark

When Denmark ruled Norway and Sweden in the 15th century, Copenhagen was the capital of all three countries. Today it is still a lively northern capital, with about 1 million inhabitants. It's a city meant for walking, the first in Europe to recognize the value of pedestrian streets in fostering community spirit. As you stroll through the cobbled streets and squares, you'll find that Copenhagen combines the excitement and variety of big-city life with a small-town atmosphere. If there's such a thing as a cozy metropolis, you'll find it here.

You're never far from water, be it sea or canal. The city itself is built upon two main islands, Slotsholmen and Christianshavn, connected by drawbridges. Walk down Nyhavn Canal, an area formerly haunted by a fairly salty crew of sailors. Now it's gentrified, and the 18th-century houses lining it are filled with chic restaurants. You should linger, too, in the five main pedestrian streets known collectively as Strøget, with shops, restaurants, cafés, and street musicians and vendors. In summer Copenhagen moves outside, and the best views of city life are from the sidewalk cafés in the sunny squares. The Danes are famous for their friendliness and have a word—*hyggelig*—for the feeling of well-being that comes from their own brand of cozy hospitality.

Currency The monetary unit in Denmark is the krone (kr., DKr, or DKK), which is divided into 100 øre. At press time, the krone stood at about 5.9 kr. to the dollar.

Telephones For international calls dial 00, then the country code, the area code, and the number. To reach an **AT&T** long-distance operator, dial 8001–0010; for **MCI,** dial 8001–0022; and for **Sprint,** 8001–0877.

Shore Excursions The following are good choices in Copenhagen. They may not be offered by all cruise lines. Times and prices are approximate.

City Tour. This quick overview of the sights takes you to a Renaissance castle, City Hall Square, Tivoli Gardens, Christiansborg Palace, the Borsen Stock Exchange, the Canal District, and the courtyard of Amalienborg Palaces. *3 hrs. Cost: $35.*

Royal Castle Tour. Castle aficionados can see two on this tour: Christiansborg Palace and Rosenborg Castle, as well as other sites. *3 hrs. Cost: $50.*

Coming Ashore Ships visiting Copenhagen dock at Langelinie Pier, a short distance from the central part of the city.

Getting Around Copenhagen is a city for walkers, not drivers. Attractions are relatively close together, and public transportation is excellent. Buses and suburban trains operate on a ticket system and divide Copenhagen and its environs into three zones. Tickets are validated on the time system: On the basic ticket, which costs 10 kr. for an hour, you can travel anywhere in the zone in which you started. Taxis are not cheap, but all are metered. The base charge is 12 kr., plus 8–10 kr. per kilometer.

Exploring Copenhagen

Numbers in the margin correspond to points of interest on the Copenhagen map.

1 Copenhagen's best-known attraction is **Tivoli.** In the 1840s, the Danish architect Georg Carstensen persuaded King Christian VIII that an amusement park was the perfect opiate of the masses, preaching that "when people amuse themselves, they forget politics." In the season from May to September, about 4 million people come through the gates. Tivoli is more sophisticated than a mere amusement park: It offers a pantomime theater and an open-air stage; elegant restaurants; and numerous classical, jazz, and rock concerts. On weekends there are elaborate fireworks displays. Try to see Tivoli at least once by night, when the trees are illuminated along with the Chinese Pagoda and the main fountain. *On Vesterbrogade, tel. 33/15–10–01. Admission: 40 kr. Open mid-Apr.–mid-Sept., daily 10 AM–midnight.*

2 The hub of Copenhagen's commercial district is Rådhus Pladsen, which is dominated by the mock-Renaissance building **Københavns Rådhus** (city hall), completed in 1905. A statue of Copenhagen's 12th-century founder, Bishop Absalon, sits atop the main entrance. Inside, you can see the first World Clock, an astrological timepiece invented and built by Jens Olsen and put in motion in 1955. If you're feeling energetic, take a guided tour partway up the 350-foot tower for a panoramic view. *Rådhus Pladsen, tel. 33/66–25–82. Admission: tour 20 kr., tower 10 kr. Open Mon.–Wed. and Fri. 9:30–3, Thurs. 9:30–4, Sat. 9:30–1. Tours in English weekdays at 3, Sat. at 10. Tower tours Mon.–Sat. at noon; additional tours June–Sept. at 10 and 2.*

3 The city's **Nationalmuseet** (National Museum) houses extensive collections that chronicle Danish cultural history to modern times and displays Egyptian, Greek, and Roman antiquities. Viking enthusiasts may want to see the Runic stones in the Danish cultural-history section. *Ny Vestergade 10, tel. 33/13–44–11. Admission: 30 kr. Open Tues.–Sun. 10–5.*

4 Castle Island is dominated by the massive gray **Christiansborg Slot** (Christiansborg Castle). The complex, which contains the Folketinget (Parliament House) and the Royal Reception Chambers, is on the site of the city's first fortress, built by Bishop Absalon in 1167. While the castle was being built at the turn of the century, the National Museum excavated the ruins beneath the site. *Christiansborg ruins, tel. 33/92–64–92. Admission: 12 kr. Open May–Sept., daily 9:30–3:30; Oct.–Apr., Sun. and Tues.–Fri. 9:30–3:30. Folketinget, tel. 33/37–55–00. Admission free. Tour times vary; call ahead. Reception Chambers: 27 kr. Opening and tour times vary; call ahead. Closed Jan.*

5 The 19th-century Danish sculptor Bertel Thorvaldsen is buried at the center of the **Thorvaldsens Museum.** He was greatly influenced by the statues and reliefs of classical antiquity. In addition to his own works, there is a collection of paintings and drawings by other artists illustrating the influence of Italy on Denmark's Golden Age artists. *Porthusgade 2, tel. 33/32–15–32. Admission free. Open Tues.–Sun. 10–5.*

6 With its steep roofs, tiny windows, and gables, the **Børsen,** the old stock exchange, is one of Copenhagen's treasures. It is believed to be the oldest building still in use—although it functions only on special occasions. It was built by the 16th-century monarch King Christian

IV, a scholar, warrior, and architect of much of the city. The king is said to have had a hand in twisting the tails of the four dragons that form the structure's distinctive green copper spire.

7 **Amalienborg** has been the principal royal residence since 1784. Among the museum's highlights are the study of King Christian IX (1818–1906) and the drawing room of his wife, Queen Louise. The collection also includes rococo banquet silver, highlighted by a bombastic Viking-ship centerpiece, and a small costume collection. *Amalienborg Museum, tel. 33/12–21–86. Admission: 35 kr. Open Mar.–late Oct., daily 11–4; late Oct.–Feb., Tues.–Sun. 11–4.*

8 The **Frihedsmuseet** (Liberty Museum) in Churchillparken gives an evocative picture of the heroic Danish Resistance movement during World War II, which managed to save 7,000 Jews from the Nazis by hiding them in homes and hospitals, then smuggling them across to Sweden. *Churchillparken, tel. 33/13–77–14. Admission free. Open Sept. 16–Apr., Tues.–Sat. 11–3, Sun. 11–4; May–Sept. 15, Tues.–Sat. 10–4, Sun. 10–5.*

9 Near the Langelinie, which on Sunday is thronged with promenading Danes, is **Den Lille Havfrue** (Little Mermaid), the 1913 statue commemorating Hans Christian Andersen's lovelorn creation and the subject of hundreds of travel posters.

10 **Rosenborg Slot,** a Renaissance castle—built by Renaissance man Christian IV—houses the Crown Jewels, as well as a collection of costumes and royal memorabilia. Don't miss Christian IV's pearl-studded saddle. *Øster Voldgade 4A, tel. 33/15–32–86. Admission: 40 kr. Castle open late Oct.–Apr., Tues., Fri., and Sun. 11–2; treasury open daily 11–3. Both open May and Sept.–late Oct., daily 11–3; June–Aug., daily 10–4.*

The **Statens Museum for Kunst** (National Art Gallery) features a collection that ranges from modern Danish art to works by Rubens, Dürer, and the Impressionists. Particularly fine are the museum's 20 Matisses. *Sølvgade 48–50, tel. 33/91–21–26. Admission: 20 kr. (30 kr. for special exhibitions). Open Tues.–Sun. 10–4:30, Wed. until 9 PM.*

Shopping Strøget's pedestrian streets are synonymous with shopping. For glass, try **Holmegaard** (Æstergade 15, tel. 33/12–44–77), where handcrafted bowls, glasses, and vases are available. Just off the street is Pistolstræde, a typical old courtyard that has been lovingly restored and is filled with intriguing boutiques. **Magasin** (Kongens Nytorv 13, tel. 33/11–44–33), one of the largest department stores in Scandinavia, offers everything in terms of clothing and gifts, as well as an excellent grocery. **Illum** (Æstergade 52, tel. 33/14–40–02) is similar to Magasin, with another fine basement grocery and eating arcade. Don't confuse Illum with **Illums Bolighus** (Amagertorv 10, tel. 33/14–19–41), where designer furnishings, porcelain, quality clothing, and gifts are displayed in near-gallery surroundings. **Royal Copenhagen Porcelain** (Amagertorv 6, tel. 33/13–71–81) carries both old and new china and porcelain patterns and figurines. **Georg Jensen** (Amagertorv 4 and Æstergade 40, tel 33/11–40–80) is one of the world's finest silversmiths and gleams with a wide array of silver patterns and jewelry. Don't miss the **Georg Jensen Museum** (Amagertorv 6, tel. 33/14–02–29), which showcases glass and silver beauties, ranging from tiny, twisted-glass shot glasses to an $85,000 silver fish dish.

Corfu, Greece

The northernmost of the seven major Ionian islands, Corfu has a lively history of conquest and counterconquest. All told, beginning with Classical times, Corfu has been ruled by the Corinthians, the

Amalienborg, **7**
Børsen, **6**
Christiansborg Slot, **4**
Den Lille Havfrue, **9**
Frihedsmuseet, **8**
Københavns Rådhus, **2**
Nationalmuseet, **3**
Rosenborg Slot, **10**
Thorvaldsens Museum, **5**
Tivoli, **1**

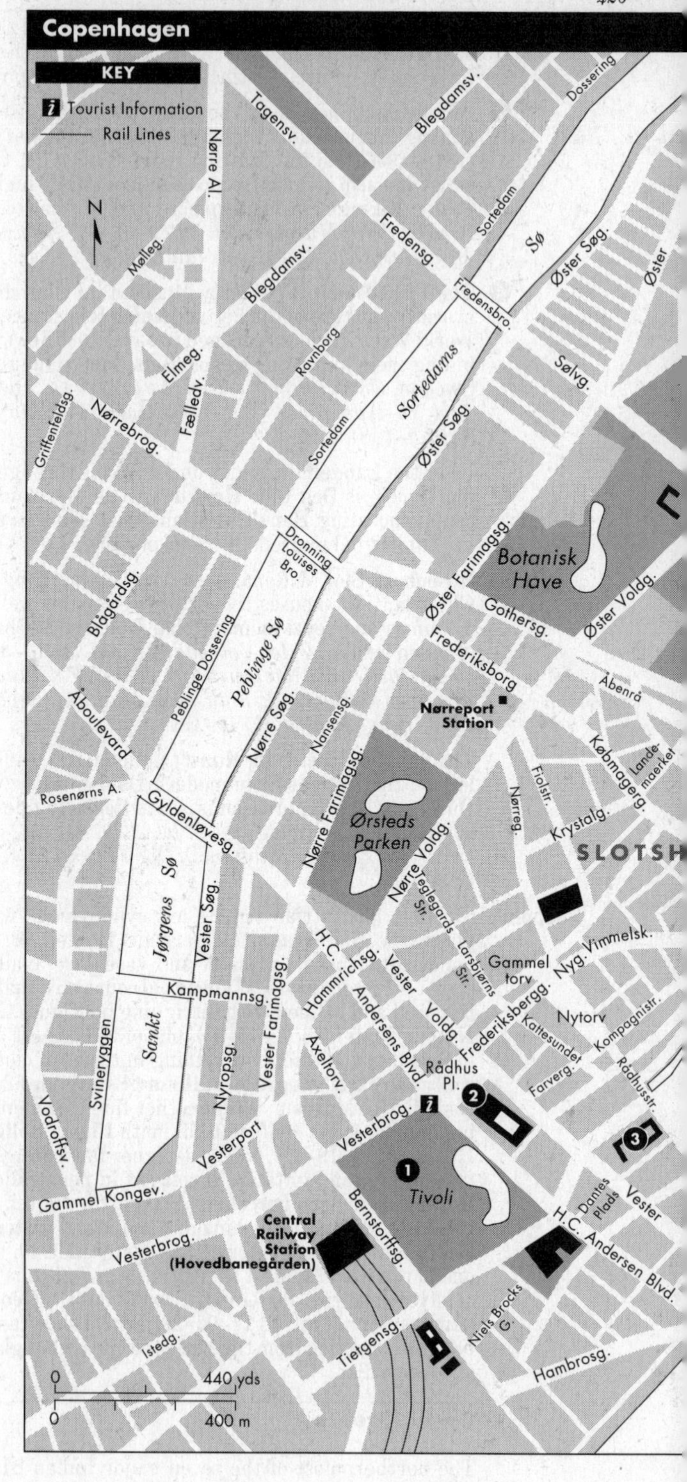

Langeliniebrd.
Dag Hammarskjölds Al.
Kristianiag.
Farimagsg.
Østbaneg.
Folke Bernadottes Al.
Østerport Station
Oslo Plads
Stockholmsg.
Øster Anlæg
Churchill-parken
Forbindelsesv.
Langelinie
Yderhavn
Grøningen
St. Kongensg.
Rigensg.
Esplanaden
Sølvg.
Fredericiag.
Bredg.
Amalieg.
Kongens Have
Kronprincesseg.
Store Kongensg.
Toldbodg.
Dronningens Tværg.
Adelg.
Borgerg.
Sankt Annæ Plads
Vognmagerg.
Gammelmønt
Pilestræde
Gothersg.
Ny Østerg.
Kongens Nytorv
Nyhavn
Nyhavn Canal
Inderhavn
HOLMEN
Kr. Bernikg.
Østerg.
Amagertorv
Højbro
Bremerholm
Holmenskanal
Heibergsg.
Læderstr.
Holbergsg.
Gammel Strand
Havnegade
Vindelbrog
Christiansborg Slotsplads
Chr. IV's Bro
Børsg.
Knippelsbro
Tøjhusgade
Frederiksholms Kanal
Christians Brygge
Voldg.
CHRISTIANSHAVN
Sankt Annæg.
Torveg.
Dronningensg.
Princessg.
Christianshavns Voldg.
Langerbrog.
Langebro
Amager Blvd.
Stadsgraven
Amagerbrog.
Vermlandsg.

tyrants of Syracuse, the kings of Epirus and of Macedonia, the Romans, the Norman and Angevin kings, the Venetians, and the British, and it was finally ceded to Greece in 1864. The climate of the island is rainy, which makes it green. Moderated by westerly winds, scored with fertile valleys, and punctuated by enormous, gnarled olive trees, the island is perhaps the most beautiful in Greece.

Currency The Greek monetary unit is the drachma (dr.). At press time, there were approximately 241 dr. to the U.S. dollar.

Telephones Although you can buy phone cards with up to 5,000 dr. credit, if you plan to make and pay for several international phone calls, go to an OTE office. For an **AT&T** long-distance operator, dial 00/800–1311; **MCI,** 00/800–1211; **Sprint,** 00/800–1411.

Shore Excursions The following are good choices in Corfu. They may not be offered by all cruise lines. Times and prices are approximate.

Paleocastritsa, Achilleion and Corfu Town. Visit the pretty resort of Paleocastritsa and the 100-year-old Achilleion Palace, and drive past the major sights of the town. *4 hrs. Cost: $40.*

City tour with Achilleion and Kanoni. Visit the famed and funky Achilleion Palace, the village of Kanoni, and enjoy a walking tour of Corfu. *4 hrs. Cost: $40.*

Coming Ashore Most cruise ships dock at Corfu Town.

Getting Around Radio-dispatched taxis are available, and rates, set by the government, are reasonable. The bus network on the island is extensive, and buses tend to run fairly close to their schedules. Motorbike rentals are available, but caution is advised.

Exploring Corfu The **New Fortress** was built by the Venetians and added to by the French and the British. It was a Greek naval base until 1992, when it was opened to the public. Tourists can now wander through the fascinating maze of tunnels, moats, and fortifications. A classic British citadel stands at its heart, and there are stunning views of Corfu Town, the sea, and the countryside in all directions. The best times to come here are early morning and late afternoon. *Above the Old Port on north side of Corfu Town.*

The huge parade ground on the land side of the canal is the **Esplanade,** central to life in Corfu Town. It is bordered on the west by a street lined with a row of tall houses and arcades, called Liston, which was once the exclusive preserve of Corfiot nobility. Now the arcades are lively with cafés that spill out onto the square in the evening. Cricket matches are played on the northern side of the Esplanade.

The narrow streets that run west from the Esplanade lead to the medieval parts of the city, where Venetian buildings stand cheek-by-jowl with the 19th-century ones built by the British. This is a great shopping area—you can buy nearly anything on earth.

The **Archaeological Museum** displays artifacts from the excavation of Paleopolis. Note the Gorgon from the pediment of the 6th-century BC Temple of Artemis. *Tel. 0661/30680. Admission: 400 dr. Open Tues.–Sun. 8:30–3.*

The village of **Analipis** crowns the site of the ancient town's Acropolis, and a path leads to a spring where Venetians watered their ships. Continue through the gardens and parks to the ruins of the Archaic Temple of Artemis and past the lagoon of Halikiopoulou to the tip of the peninsula, called Kanoni, one of the world's most beautiful spots.

Achilleion Palace is a monument to bad taste redeemed by beautiful gardens stretching to the sea. The palace was built in the late 19th century by an Italian architect for Empress Elizabeth of Austria.

The palace is a hodgepodge of a pseudo-Byzantine chapel, a pseudo-Pompeian room, and a pseudo-Renaissance dining hall, culminating in a hilariously vulgar fresco of *Achilles in His Chariot*. *19 km/12 mi from Corfu town, tel. 0661/56210. Admission: 400 dr. Open 8:30–7 in season.*

Shopping The downside of Corfu's popularity with tourists is that merchants have become greedy, at times charging outrageous prices in order to squeeze as much money as possible out of visitors. Ask your ship's cruise or shore-excursion director for the names of reputable shops.

Beaches The resort areas of Ermones and Glyfada, which are south of the popular resort area Paleokastritsa, offer good sunning. On the north coast, Roda and Sidari have good beaches.

Crete, Greece

The mountains, blue-gray and barren, split with deep gorges and honeycombed with caves, define both landscape and lifestyle in Crete. No other Greek island is so large and rugged. To Greeks, Crete is the Great Island, where rebellion was endemic for centuries—against Arab invaders, Venetian colonialists, Ottoman pashas, and German occupiers in World War II. Situated in the south Aegean, Crete was the center of Europe's earliest civilization, the Minoan, which flourished from about 2000 BC to 1200 BC. It was struck a mortal blow in about 1450 BC by some unknown cataclysm, now thought to be political.

Currency The Greek monetary unit is the drachma (dr.). At press time, there were approximately 241 dr. to the U.S. dollar.

Telephones Although you can buy phone cards with up to 5,000 dr. credit, if you plan to make and pay for several international phone calls, go to an OTE office. For an **AT&T** long-distance operator, dial 00/800–1311; **MCI,** 00/800–1211; **Sprint,** 00/800–1411.

Shore Excursions The following are good choices in Crete. They may not be offered by all cruise lines. Times and prices are approximate.

Knossos and the Museum. After a tour of the Archaeological Museum, you'll visit Knossos, the largest Minoan palace. *4 hrs. Cost: $50.*

Chania and Akrotiri. This excursion explores the old town of Chania before heading to Akrotiri peninsula to see the tomb of Eleftherios Venizelos and the Ayia Triada Monastery. *Half day. Cost: $45.*

Coming Ashore Most ships dock at Heraklion. A few tie up at Souda Bay, which is about 15 minutes from Chania. Smaller vessels may dock at Ayios Nikolaos.

Getting Around You can rent cars, Jeeps, and motorbikes in all the island's towns. Bus companies offer regular service between main towns.

Exploring Crete The most important Minoan remains are housed in the **Archaeological Museum in Heraklion,** Crete's largest. A visit here compares with a visit to any of the great museums of western Europe. *Plateia Eleftherias, tel. 081/226–092. Admission: 1,500 dr. Open Mon. noon–3, Tues.–Fri. 8–7 (8–5 in winter), weekends and holidays 8:30–3.*

The partly reconstructed **Palace of Knossos** will give you a feeling for the Minoan world. Note the simple throne room, which contains the oldest throne in Europe, and the bathrooms with their efficient plumbing. The palace was the setting for the legend of the Minotaur, a monstrous offspring of Queen Pasiphae and a bull, which King Minos confined to the labyrinth under the palace. *Tel. 081/231–940. Admission: 1,500 dr. Open Tues.–Sun. 8:30–3.*

Ayios Nikolaos on the Gulf of Mirabellow was built just a century ago by Cretans and is good for an afternoon of strolling and shopping. *24 km/15 mi from Heraklion.*

Beaches In addition to archaeological treasures, Crete can boast of beautiful mountain scenery and a large number of beach resorts along the north coast. One is **Mallia,** which contains the remains of another Minoan palace and has good sandy beaches. Two other beach resorts, **Ayios Nikolaos** and the nearby **Elounda,** are farther east. The south coast offers good beaches that are quieter.

Dublin, Ireland

Dublin is a small city with a population of just over 1 million. Even so, it has a distinctly cosmopolitan air, one that complements happily the individuality of the city and the courtesy and friendliness of its inhabitants. Originally a Viking settlement, Dublin is situated on the banks of the River Liffey. The Liffey divides the city north and south, with the more lively and fashionable spots, such as the Grafton Street shopping area, to be found on the south side. Most of the city's historically interesting buildings date from the 18th century, and, although many of its finer Georgian buildings disappeared in the over- enthusiastic redevelopment of the '70s, enough remain, mainly south of the river, to recall the elegant Dublin of the past. The slums romanticized by writers Sean O'Casey and Brendan Behan have virtually been eradicated, but literary Dublin can still be recaptured by those who want to follow the footsteps of Leopold Bloom's progress, as described in James Joyce's *Ulysses.* And Trinity College—alma mater of Oliver Goldsmith, Jonathan Swift, and Samuel Beckett, among others—still provides a haven of tranquillity.

Currency The unit of currency in Ireland is the pound, or punt (pronounced poont), written as IR£ to avoid confusion with the pound sterling. The currency is divided into 100 pence (written *p*). Although the Irish pound is the only legal tender in the republic, U.S. dollars and British currency are often accepted in large hotels and shops licensed as *bureaux de change.* The rate of exchange at press time was 65 pence to the U.S. dollar and 95 pence to the British pound sterling.

Telephones For calls to the United States and Canada, dial 001 followed by the area code. To reach an **AT&T** long distance operator, dial 1–800/550–000; for **MCI,** dial 1–800/551–001; and for **Sprint,** dial 1–800/552–001.

Shore Excursions The following is a good choice in Dublin. It may not be offered by all cruise lines. Time and price are approximate.

City Tour. Two of Dublin's main attractions, St. Patrick's Cathedral and Trinity College, are the highlight of this excursion, which passes other city sights, such as St. Stephen's Square, Georgian Dublin, the River Liffey, and the Customs House. *3½ hrs. Cost: $38.*

Coming Ashore Ships dock at the Ocean Pier in the city's industrial port area, about a 20-minute drive to downtown.

Getting Around Dublin is small as capital cities go—the downtown area is positively compact—and the best way to see the city and soak in the full flavor is on foot. Taxis are located beside the central bus station, at train stations, at O'Connell Bridge, at St. Stephen's Green, at College Green, and near major hotels. They are not of a uniform type or color. Make sure the meter is on. The initial charge is IR£2; the fare is displayed in the cab. A one-mile trip in city traffic costs about IR£3.50.

Exploring Dublin *Numbers in the margin correspond to points of interest on the Dublin map.*

❶ **O'Connell Bridge** is the city's most central landmark. Look closely and you will notice a strange feature: The bridge is wider than it is long. The north side of O'Connell Bridge is dominated by an elaborate memorial to Daniel O'Connell, "the Liberator," erected as a tribute to the great 19th-century orator's achievement in securing Catholic emancipation in 1829. Today O'Connell Street is the city's main shopping area.

Henry Street, a pedestrian-only shopping area, leads to the colorful **Moore Street Market,** where street vendors recall their most famous ancestor, Molly Malone, by singing their wares—mainly flowers and fruit—in the traditional Dublin style.

❷ The **General Post Office,** known as the GPO, occupies a special place in Irish history. It was from the portico of its handsome classical facade that Padraig Pearse read the Proclamation of the Republic on Easter Monday 1916. You can still see the scars of bullets on its pillars from the fighting that ensued. The GPO remains the focal point for political rallies and demonstrations and is used as a viewing stand for VIPs during the annual St. Patrick's Day parade. *Henry St.*

❸ Charlemont House, whose impressive Palladian facade dominates the top of Parnell Square, now houses the **Hugh Lane Municipal Gallery of Modern Art.** Sir Hugh Lane, a nephew of Lady Gregory, who was Yeats's curious, high-minded aristocratic patron, was a keen collector of Impressionist paintings. The gallery also contains some interesting works by Irish artists, including Yeats's brother Jack. *Parnell Sq., tel. 01/674–1903. Admission free. Open Tues.–Fri. 9:30–6, Sat. 9:30–5, Sun. 11–5.*

❹ The Parnell Square area is rich in literary associations. They are explained and illustrated in the **Dublin Writers Museum,** which opened in 1991 in two carefully restored 18th-century buildings. Paintings, letters, manuscripts, and photographs relating to Joyce, O'Casey, Shaw, Yeats, Behan, Synge, and others are on permanent display. There are also temporary exhibitions, lectures, and readings, as well as a bookshop. *18–19 Parnell Sq. N, tel. 01/872–2077. Admission: IR£2.25. Open Mon.–Sat. 10–5, Sun. 1–5.*

❺ A must for every visitor is a stop at **Trinity College.** The college, familiarly known as TCD, was founded by Elizabeth I in 1592 and offered a free education to Catholics—provided that they accepted the Protestant faith. As a legacy of this condition, right up until 1966, Catholics who wished to study at Trinity had to obtain a dispensation from their bishop or face excommunication. Today more than 70% of Trinity's students are Catholics, a clear indication of how far away those days seem to today's generation. The college's facade, built between 1755 and 1759, consists of a magnificent portico with Corinthian columns. The design is repeated on the interior, so the views from outside the gates and from the quadrangle inside are the same. On the sweeping lawn in front of the facade are statues of two of the university's illustrious alumni—statesman Edmund Burke and poet Oliver Goldsmith. Other famous students include the philosopher George Berkeley, (who gave his name to the San Francisco–area campus of the University of California), Jonathan Swift, Thomas Moore, Oscar Wilde, John Millington Synge, Henry Grattan, Wolfe Tone, Robert Emmet, Bram Stoker, Edward Carson, Douglas Hyde, and Samuel Beckett.

The 18th-century building on the left, just inside the entrance, is the chapel. There's an identical building opposite, which is the Examination Hall. The oldest buildings are the library in the far right-hand corner and a row of red brick buildings known as the Rubrics, which contain student apartments; both date from 1712.

Custom House, **15**
Dublin Castle, **11**
Dublin Writers Museum, **4**
Four Courts, **14**
Genealogical Office, **9**
General Post Office, **2**
Guinness Brewery, **12**
Hugh Lane Municipal Gallery of Modern Art, **3**
Irish Whiskey Corner, **13**
Leinster House, **7**
National Gallery, **6**
National Museum, **8**
O'Connell Bridge, **1**
St. Patrick's Cathedral, **10**
Trinity College, **5**

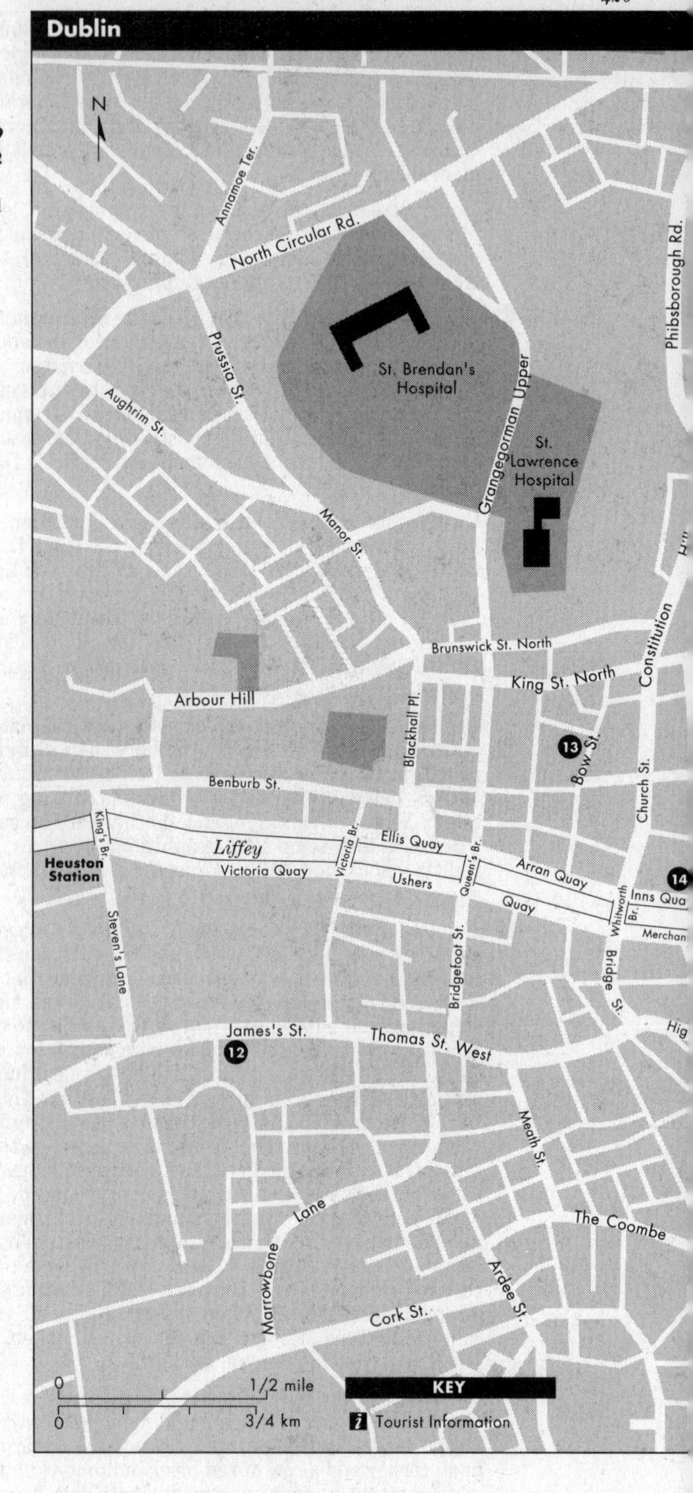

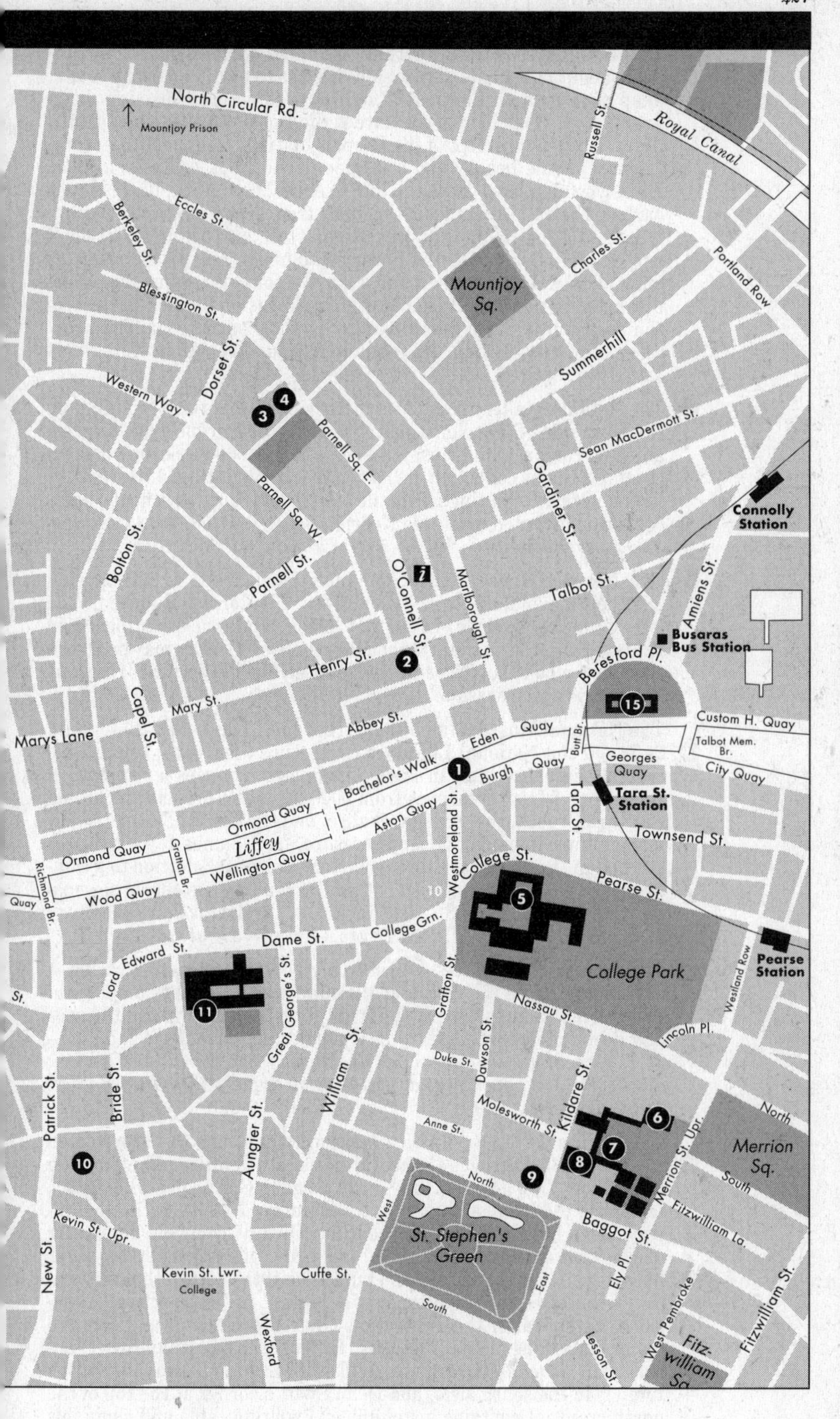
North Circular Rd.
Mountjoy Prison
Royal Canal
Russell St.
Eccles St.
Berkeley St.
Blessington St.
Charles St.
Portland Row
Mountjoy Sq.
Dorset St.
Summerhill
Western Way
Parnell Sq. E.
Parnell Sq. W.
Sean MacDermott St.
Gardiner St.
Connolly Station
Bolton St.
Parnell St.
O'Connell St.
Marlborough St.
Talbot St.
Amiens St.
Busaras Bus Station
Henry St.
Beresford Pl.
Capel St.
Mary St.
Abbey St.
Custom H. Quay
Marys Lane
Eden Quay
Butt Br.
Talbot Mem. Br.
Bachelor's Walk
Burgh Quay
Georges Quay
City Quay
Tara St.
Tara St. Station
Ormond Quay
Aston Quay
Westmoreland St.
Townsend St.
Liffey
Grattan Br.
Wellington Quay
College St.
Pearse St.
Richmond Br.
Quay
Wood Quay
College Grn.
Dame St.
Lord Edward St.
College Park
Pearse Station
Westland Row
Great George's St.
Grafton St.
Nassau St.
Lincoln Pl.
William St.
Dawson St.
Duke St.
Kildare St.
Molesworth St.
Anne St.
North
Merrion Sq.
Merrion St. Upr.
South
Patrick St.
Bride St.
Aungier St.
West
St. Stephen's Green
Fitzwilliam La.
Baggot St.
Kevin St. Upr.
New St.
Kevin St. Lwr.
College
Cuffe St.
East
Ely Pl.
Fitzwilliam St.
West Pembroke
Lesson St.
Wexford
Fitz-william Sq.

Ireland's largest collection of books and manuscripts is housed in the **Trinity College Library.** There are 3 million volumes gathering dust here; about half a mile of new shelving has to be added every year to keep pace with acquisitions. The library is entered through the library shop. Its principal treasure is the Book of Kells, a beautifully illuminated manuscript of the Gospels, dating from the 8th century. Because of the beauty and the fame of the Book of Kells, at peak hours you may have to wait in line to enter the library; it's less busy early in the day. Apart from the many treasures it contains, the aptly named Long Room is impressive in itself, stretching for 213 feet and housing 200,000 of the library's volumes, mostly manuscripts and old books. Originally it had a flat plaster ceiling, but the perennial need for more shelving resulted in a decision to raise the level of the roof and add the barrel-vaulted ceiling and the gallery bookcases. *Tel. 01/677–2941. Admission: I£2.50. Open Mon.–Sat. 9:30–4:45, Sun. noon–5.*

❻ The **National Gallery** is the first in a series of important buildings on the west side of Merrion Square. It is one of Europe's most agreeable and compact galleries, with more than 2,000 works on view, including a major collection of Irish landscape painting, 17th-century French works, paintings from the Italian and Spanish schools, and a collection of Dutch masters. *Merrion Sq., tel. 01/661–5133. Admission free. Open Mon.–Sat 10–5:30, Thurs. until 8:30, Sun. 2–5.*

❼ The **Leinster House,** seat of the Irish Parliament, is an imposing 18th-century building with two facades: Its Merrion Square facade is designed in the style of a country house, while the other facade, in Kildare Street, is in the style of a town house. Visitors may be shown the house when Dáil Eireann (pronounced dawl Erin), the Irish Parliament, is not in session.

❽ The **National Museum** (admission free; open Tues.–Sat. 10–5, Sun. 2–5) and the **National Library** each feature a massive, colonnaded rotunda entrance built in 1890. The museum houses a remarkable collection of Irish treasures from 6000 BC to the present, including the Tara Brooch, the Ardagh Chalice, and the Cross of Cong. Every major figure in modern Irish literature, from James Joyce onward, studied in the National Library at some point. In addition to a comprehensive collection of Irish authors, it contains extensive newspaper archives. *Kildare St., tel. 01/661–8811. Admission free. Open Mon. 10–9, Tues.–Wed. 2–9, Thurs.–Fri. 10–5, Sat. 10–1.*

❾ The **Genealogical Office**—the starting point for ancestor tracing—also incorporates the **Heraldic Museum,** which features displays of flags, coins, stamps, silver, and family crests that highlight the uses and development of heraldry in Ireland. *2 Kildare St., tel. 01/661–8811. Genealogical Office: open weekdays 10–5. Heraldic Museum: admission free; open weekdays 10–12:30 and 2:30–4. Guided tours Mar.–Oct., IR£1.*

❿ Legend has it that St. Patrick baptized many converts at a well on the site of **St. Patrick's Cathedral** in the 5th century. The building dates from 1190 and is mainly early English Gothic in style. At 305 feet, it is the longest church in the country. Its history has not always been happy. In the 17th century, Oliver Cromwell, dour ruler of England and no friend of the Irish, had his troops stable their horses in the cathedral. It wasn't until the 19th century that restoration work to repair the damage was begun. St. Patrick's is the national cathedral of the Protestant Church of Ireland and has had many illustrious deans. The most famous was Jonathan Swift, author of *Gulliver's Travels,* who held office from 1713 to 1745. Swift's tomb is in the south aisle, and Dean Swift's corner at the top of the north transept contains his pulpit, his writing table and chair, his portrait, and his death mask. Memorials to many other celebrated figures from Ireland's past line the walls of St. Patrick's. *Patrick St., tel. 01/475–4817. Admission: IR£1.*

⓫ Guided tours of the lavishly furnished state apartments in **Dublin Castle** are offered every half hour and provide one of the most enjoyable sightseeing experiences in town. Only fragments of the original 13th-century building survive; the elegant castle you see today is essentially an 18th-century building. The state apartments were formerly the residence of the English viceroys and are now used by the president of Ireland to entertain visiting heads of state. The state apartments are closed when in official use, so phone first to check. *Off Dame St., tel. 01/677–7129. Admission: IR£2.50. Open weekdays 10–12:15 and 2–5, weekends 2–5.*

⓬ The **Guinness Brewery,** founded by Arthur Guinness in 1759 and covering 60 acres, dominates the area to the west of Christ Church. Guinness is proud of its brewery and invites visitors to attend a 30-minute film, shown in a converted hops store next door to the brewery itself. After the film, you can sample the famous black beverage. *Guinness Hop Store, Crane St., tel. 01/453–6700. Admission: IR£2.50. Open weekdays 10–3.*

⓭ **Irish Whiskey Corner** is just behind St. Michan's. A 90-year-old warehouse has been converted into a museum to introduce visitors to the pleasures of Irish whiskey. There's an audiovisual show and free tasting. *Bow St., tel. 01/872–5566. Admission: IR£3. Tours weekdays at 3:30 or by appointment.*

Off the River Liffey are two of Dublin's most famous landmarks, both of them the work of 18th-century architect James Gandon and ⓮ both among the city's finest buildings. The first is the **Four Courts,** surmounted by a massive copper-covered dome, giving it a distinctive profile. It is the seat of the High Court of Justice of Ireland. The building was completed between 1786 and 1802, then gutted in the Civil War of the '20s; it has since been painstakingly restored. You ⓯ will recognize the same architect's hand in the **Custom House,** farther down the Liffey. Its graceful dome rises above a central portico, itself linked by arcades to the pavilions at either end.

Shopping

Although the rest of the country is well supplied with crafts shops, Dublin is the place to seek out more specialized items—antiques, traditional sportswear, haute couture, designer ceramics, books and prints, silverware and jewelry, and designer hand-knit items.

The city's most sophisticated shopping area is around **Grafton Street. St. Stephen's Green Center** contains 70 stores, large and small, in a vast Moorish-style glass-roof building on the Grafton Street corner. **Molesworth** and **Dawson streets** are the places to browse for antiques; **Nassau** and **Dawson streets,** for books; the smaller cross streets for jewelry, art galleries, and old prints. The pedestrian **Temple Bar** area, with its young, offbeat ambience, has a number of small art galleries, specialty shops (including music and books), and inexpensive and adventurous clothes shops. The area is further enlivened by buskers (street musicians) and street artists.

Tweeds and Woolens

Ready-made tweeds for men can be found at **Kevin and Howlin,** on Nassau Street, and at **Cleo Ltd.,** on Kildare Street. The **Blarney Woollen Mills,** on Nassau Street, has a good selection of tweed, linen, and woolen sweaters in all price ranges. The **Woolen Mills,** at Ha'penny Bridge, has a good selection of hand-knits and other woolen sweaters at competitive prices.

Edinburgh/Leith, Scotland

Scotland and England *are* different—and let no Englishman tell you otherwise. Although the two nations have been united in a single state since 1707, Scotland retains its own marked political and social character, with, for instance, legal and educational systems quite distinct from those of England. And by virtue of its commanding geographic position, on top of a long-dead volcano, and the survival of a large number of outstanding buildings carrying echoes of the nation's history, Edinburgh ranks among the world's greatest capital cities. The key to understanding Edinburgh is to make the distinction between the Old and New Towns. Until the 18th century, the city was confined to the rocky crag on which its castle stands, straggling between the fortress at one end and the royal residence, the Palace of Holyroodhouse, at the other. In the 18th century, during a civilizing time of expansion known as the "Scottish Enlightenment," the city fathers fostered the construction of another Edinburgh, one a little to the north. This is the New Town, whose elegant squares, classical facades, wide streets, and harmonious proportions remain largely intact and are still lived in today.

Currency The British unit of currency is the pound sterling, divided into 100 pence (p). Scottish banks issue Scottish currency, of which all coins and notes—with the exception of the £1 notes—are accepted in England. At press time, exchange rates were approximately US$1.54 to the pound.

Telephones The cheapest way to make an overseas call is to dial it yourself. But be sure to have plenty of coins or Phonecards close at hand. After you have inserted the coins or card, dial 010 (the international code), then the country code—for the United States it is 1—followed by the area code and local number. To reach an **AT&T** long-distance operator, dial 0500890011; for **MCI,** dial 0800890202, and for **Sprint,** dial 0800890877 (from a British Telecom phone) or 0500890877 (from a Mercury Communications phone). To make a collect or other operator-assisted call, dial 155.

Shore Excursions The following is a good choice in Edinburgh. It may not be offered by all cruise lines. Time and price are approximate.

City Tour. Survey Old Town and New Town, visiting Edinburgh Castle. Pass by sights such as Princes Street, St. Giles Cathedral, the Royal Mile, and Holyrood Palace. *4½ hrs. Cost: $40.*

Coming Ashore Ships dock at Leith, the port for Edinburgh. It is about a 15-minute drive to Edinburgh from the pier.

Getting Around Walking is the best way to tour the old part of the city. It can be tiring, so wear comfortable shoes. Taxi and bus services also are available.

Exploring Edinburgh *Numbers in the margin correspond to points of interest on the Edinburgh map.*

❶ **Edinburgh Castle,** the brooding symbol of Scotland's capital and the nation's martial past, dominates the city center. The castle's attractions include the city's oldest building—the 11th-century St. Margaret's Chapel; the Crown Room, where the Regalia of Scotland are displayed; Old Parliament Hall; and Queen Mary's Apartments, where Mary, Queen of Scots, gave birth to the future King James VI of Scotland (who later became James I of England). In addition, military features of interest include the Scottish National War Memorial and the Scottish United Services Museum. *Tel. 0131/244–3101. Admission: £5. Open Apr.–Sept., daily 9:30–5; Oct.–Mar., daily 9:30–4:15.*

❷ **The Royal Mile,** the backbone of the Old Town, starts immediately below the Castle Esplanade, the wide parade ground that hosts the annual Edinburgh Military Tattoo—a grand military display staged during a citywide festival every summer. The Royal Mile consists of a number of streets, running into each other—Castlehill, Lawnmarket, High Street, and Canongate—leading downhill to the Palace of Holyroodhouse, home to the Royal Family when they visit

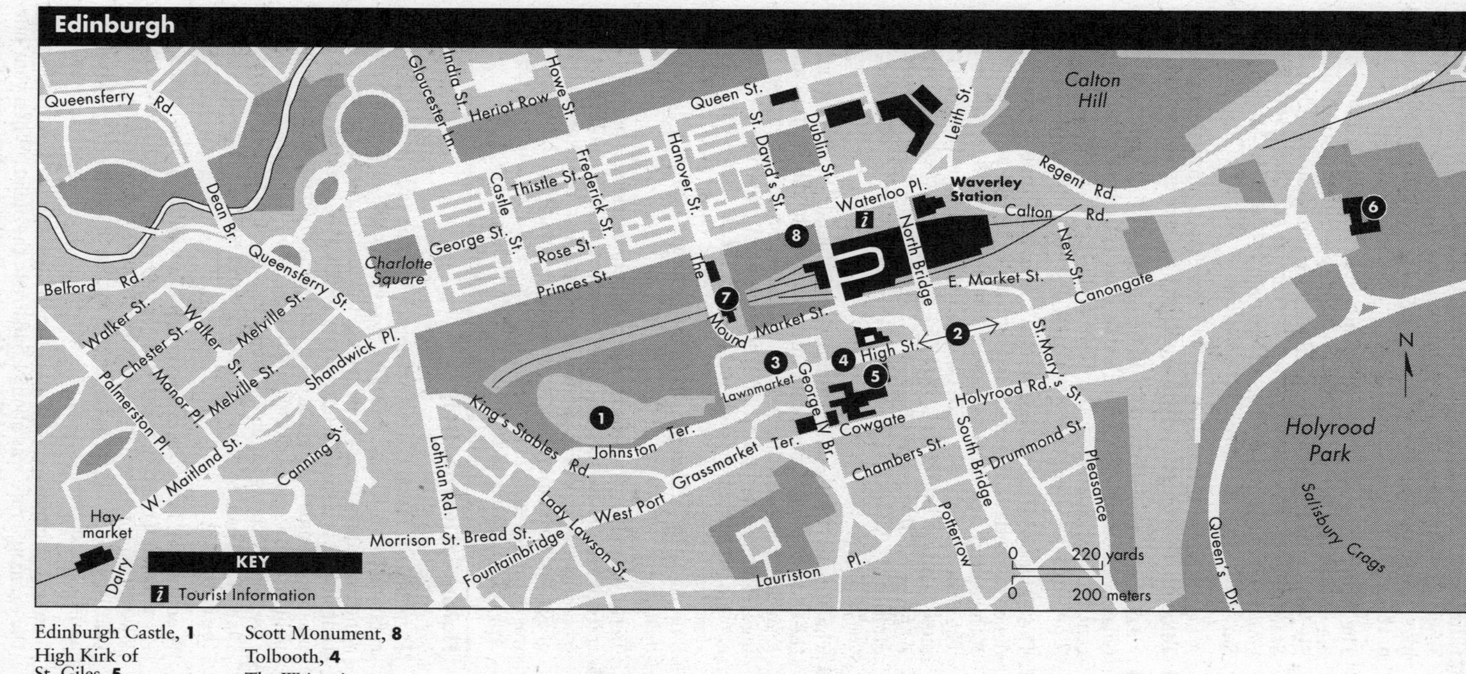

Edinburgh Castle, **1**
High Kirk of St. Giles, **5**
National Gallery of Scotland, **7**
Palace of Holyroodhouse, **6**
The Royal Mile, **2**
Scott Monument, **8**
Tolbooth, **4**
The Writers' Museum, **3**

Edinburgh. Tackle this walk in leisurely style; the many original Old Town "closes," narrow alleyways enclosed by high tenement buildings, are rewarding to explore and give a real sense of the former life of the city.

❸ **The Writers' Museum,** housed in Lady Stair's House, is a town dwelling of 1622 that recalls Scotland's literary heritage with exhibits on Sir Walter Scott, Robert Louis Stevenson, and Robert Burns. *Lady Stair's Close, Lawnmarket, tel. 0131/225–2424, ext. 4901. Admission free. Open June–Sept., Mon.–Sat. 10–6; Oct.–May, Mon.–Sat. 10–5, Sun. 2–5 during the festival.*

A heart shape set in the cobbles of High Street marks the site of the ❹ **Tolbooth,** the center of city life until it was demolished in 1817.

❺ Near the former site of the Tolbooth stands the **High Kirk of St. Giles,** Edinburgh's cathedral; parts of the church date from the 12th century, the choir from the 15th. *High St. Admission free. Open Mon.–Sat. 9–5 (7 in summer), Sun. 2–5 and for services.*

❻ The **Palace of Holyroodhouse,** still the Royal Family's official residence in Scotland, was founded by King James IV at the end of the 15th century and was extensively remodeled by Charles II in 1671. The state apartments, with their collections of tapestries and paintings, can be visited. *Tel. 0131/556–7371. Admission: £3.50. Open Apr.–Oct., Mon.–Sat. 9:30–5:15, Sun. 10:30–4:30; Nov.–Mar., Mon.–Sat. 9:30–3:45, Sun. 10–3:45; closed during royal and state visits.*

❼ The **National Gallery of Scotland,** on the Mound, the street that joins the Old and New Towns, contains works by the old masters and the French Impressionists and has a good selection of Scottish paintings. This is one of Britain's best national galleries and is small enough to be taken in easily on one visit. *Tel. 0131/556–8921. Admission free; charge for special exhibitions. Open Mon.–Sat. 10–5, Sun. 2–5. Print Room, weekdays 10–noon and 2–4 by arrangement.*

To the east along Princes Street is the unmistakable soaring Gothic ❽ spire of the 200-foot-high **Scott Monument,** built in the 1840s to commemorate the celebrated novelist of Scots history. There is a statue of Sir Walter and his dog within. The views from the top are well worth the 287-step climb. *Tel. 0131/225–2424. Admission: £1. Open Apr.–Sept., Mon.–Sat. 9–6; Oct.–Mar., Mon.–Sat. 9–3.*

Florence/Livorno, Italy

Founded by Julius Caesar, Florence has the familiar grid pattern common to all Roman colonies. Except for the major monuments, which are appropriately imposing, the buildings are low and unpretentious. It is a small, compact city of ocher and gray stone and pale plaster; its narrow streets open unexpectedly into spacious squares populated by strollers and pigeons. At its best, it has a gracious and elegant air, though it can at times be a nightmare of mass tourism. Plan, if you can, to visit Florence in early spring or late fall to avoid the crowds.

A port call in Florence is a visit to the birthplace of the Italian Renaissance, and the city bears witness to the proud spirit and unparalleled genius of its artists and artisans. In fact, there is so much to see that it is best to savor a small part rather than attempt to absorb it all in a muddled vision.

Currency The unit of currency in Italy is the lira (plural, lire). At press time, the exchange rate was about 1,546 lire to the dollar. When your purchases run into hundreds of thousands of lire, beware of being shortchanged, a dodge that is practiced at ticket windows and cashiers' desks, as well as in shops and even banks. Always count your change before you leave the counter.

Telephones To place international calls, many travelers go to the Telefoni telephone exchange (usually marked TELECOM), where the operator assigns you a booth, can help place your call, and will collect payment when you have finished. To dial an international call, insert a phone card, dial 00, then the country code, area code, and phone number. For **AT&T,** dial access number 172–1011; for **MCI,** dial access number 172–1022; for **Sprint,** dial access number 172–1877. You will be connected directly with an operator in the United States.

Shore Excursions The following is a good choice in Florence. It may not be offered by all cruise lines. Time and price are approximate.

City and Coastal Tour. Stop at Pisa on the way to Florence from the port of Livorno to see the Leaning Tower. In Florence visit the Piazza del Duomo, the Accademia Museum or Pitti Palace, the Piazza del Signoria, the Loggia dei Lanzi and the Church of Santa Croce. *10 hrs. Cost: $145, including lunch.*

Coming Ashore Ships dock at Livorno, which is a little more than an hour from Florence. Most cruise lines sell bus transfers to Florence for independent sightseeing for about $70.

Getting Around Once in the city, you can see most of Florence's major sights on foot, as they are packed into a relatively small central area. Wear comfortable shoes and wander to your heart's content: It is easy to find your way around in Florence. The system of street addresses is unusual, with commercial addresses (those with an *r* in them, meaning *rosso*, or red) and residential addresses numbered separately (32/r might be next to or a block away from plain 32).

Taxis wait at stands. Use only authorized cabs, which are white with a yellow stripe or rectangle on the door. The meter starts at 3,200 lire. To call a taxi, phone 055/4798 or 055/4390.

Exploring Florence The best place to begin a tour of Florence is **Piazza del Duomo,** where the cathedral, bell tower, and baptistery stand in the rather cramped square.

The lofty **cathedral of Santa Maria del Fiore** is one of the longest in the world. Begun by master sculptor and architect Arnolfo di Cambio in 1296, its construction took 140 years to complete. Inside, the church is cool and austere, a fine example of the architecture of the period. Among the sparse decorations, take a good look at the frescoes on the left wall and on the dome. The dome itself is a great architectural and technical achievement and was the inspiration of such later domes as the one for St. Peter's in Rome and even the Capitol in Washington. You can climb to the cupola gallery, 463 fatiguing steps up between the two skins of the double dome, for a fine view of Florence and the surrounding hills. *Dome entrance is in left aisle of cathedral. Admission: 5,000 lire. Open Mon.–Sat. 10–5. Cathedral (small admission fee may be charged) open Mon.–Sat. 10–5:30, Sun. 1–5.*

Next to the cathedral of Santa Maria del Fiore is Giotto's 14th-century **bell tower,** richly decorated with colored marble and sculpture reproductions (the originals are in the Museo dell'Opera del Duomo). The 414-step climb to the top is less strenuous than that to the cupola. *Piazza del Duomo. Admission: 5,000 lire. Open Mar.–Oct., daily 8:30–7; Nov.–Feb., daily 9–4:30.*

In front of the cathedral is the **baptistery** (open Mon.–Sat. 1:30–6:30, Sun. 9–1), one of the city's oldest and most beloved edifices, where, since the 11th century, Florentines have baptized their children. The most famous of the baptistery's three portals is Ghiberti's east doors (facing the Duomo), dubbed the "gates of Paradise" by Michelangelo; gleaming copies now replace the originals, which have been removed to the Museo dell'Opera del Duomo (Cathedral Museum).

Along Via Calzaiuoli you'll come upon **Piazza della Signoria,** the heart of Florence and the city's largest square. During the long and controversial process of replacing the paving stones over the past few years, well-preserved remnants of Roman and medieval Florence came to light and were thoroughly examined and photographed before being buried again and covered with the new paving. In the center of the square a slab marks the spot where in 1497 Savonarola—the Ayatollah Khomeini of the Middle Ages—induced the Florentines to burn their pictures, books, musical instruments, and other worldly objects—and where a year later he was hanged and then burned at the stake as a heretic.

The **Uffizi Gallery** houses Italy's most important collection of paintings. The palace was built to house the administrative offices of the Medicis, onetime rulers of the city. Later their fabulous art collection was arranged in the Uffizi Gallery on the top floor, which was opened to the public in the 17th century—making this the world's first public gallery of modern times. The emphasis is on Italian art of the Gothic and Renaissance periods. Make sure you see the works by Giotto, and look for the Botticellis in Rooms X–XIV, Michelangelo's *Holy Family* in Room XXV, and the works by Raphael next door. In addition to its art treasures, the gallery offers a magnificent close-up view of Palazzo Vecchio's tower from the little coffee bar at the end of the corridor. Authorities have done wonders in repairing the damage caused by a bomb in 1993. *Loggiato Uffizi 6, tel. 055/23885. Admission: 12,000 lire. Open Tues.–Sat. 9–7, Sun. 9–2.*

The **Accademia Gallery** houses Michelangelo's famous *David.* Skip the works in the exhibition halls leading to the main attraction; they are of minor importance, and you'll gain a length on the tour groups. Michelangelo's statue is a tour de force of artistic conception and technical ability, for he was using a piece of stone that had already been worked on by a lesser sculptor. Take time to see the forceful *Slaves,* also by Michelangelo; the rough-hewn, unfinished surfaces contrast dramatically with the highly polished, meticulously carved *David.* Michelangelo left the *Slaves* "unfinished" as a symbolic gesture: to accentuate the figures' struggle to escape the bondage of stone. *Via Ricasoli 60, tel. 055/214375. Admission: 12,000 lire. Open Tues.–Sat. 9–7, Sun. 9–2.*

The remarkable **Medici Chapels** contain the tombs of practically every member of the Medici family, and there were a lot of them, for they guided Florence's destiny from the 15th century to 1737. Cosimo I, a Medici whose acumen made him the richest man in Europe, is buried in the crypt of the Chapel of the Princes, and Donatello's tomb is next to that of his patron. The chapel upstairs is decorated in a dazzling array of colored marble. In Michelangelo's New Sacristy, his tombs of Giuliano and Lorenzo de' Medici bear the justly famed statues of *Dawn* and *Dusk,* and *Night* and *Day. Piazza Madonna degli Aldobrandini, tel. 055/213206. Admission: 9,000 lire. Open Tues.–Sat. 9–2, Sun. 9–1.*

Don't be put off by the grim look of Bargello, a fortresslike palace that served as residence of Florence's chief magistrate in medieval times, and later as a prison. It now houses Florence's **Museo Nazionale** (National Museum), a treasure house of Italian Renaissance sculpture. In a historically and visually interesting setting, it displays masterpieces by Donatello, Verrocchio, Michelangelo, and many other major sculptors. This museum is on a par with the Uffizi, so don't shortchange yourself on time. *Via del Proconsolo 4, tel. 055/238-8606. Admission: 8,000 lire. Open Tues.–Sat. 9–2, Sun. 9–1.*

The **Ponte Vecchio** is Florence's oldest bridge. It seems to be just another street lined with goldsmiths' shops until you get to the middle and catch a glimpse of the Arno flowing below. Spared during World War II by the retreating Germans (who blew up every other bridge in the city), it also survived the 1966 flood. It leads into the Oltrarno District, which has its own charm and still preserves much of the atmosphere of old-time Florence, full of fascinating craft workshops.

The church of **Santo Spirito** is important as one of Brunelleschi's finest architectural creations, and it contains some superb paintings, including a Filippino Lippi *Madonna*. Santo Spirito is the hub of a colorful neighborhood of artisans and intellectuals. An **outdoor market** enlivens the square every morning except Sunday; in the afternoon, pigeons, pet owners, and pensioners take over. An arts-and-crafts fair is held in the square on the second Sunday of the month. The area is definitely on an upward trend, with new cafés, restaurants, and upscale shops opening every day.

Shopping Florence offers top quality for your money in leather goods, linens and upholstery fabrics, gold and silver jewelry, and cameos. Straw goods, gilded wooden trays and frames, hand-printed paper desk accessories, and ceramic objects make good inexpensive gifts. Many shops offer fine old prints.

The most fashionable streets in Florence are **Via Tornabuoni** and **Via della Vigna Nuova.** Goldsmiths and jewelry shops can be found on and around the **Ponte Vecchio** and in the **Santa Croce area,** where there is also a high concentration of leather shops.

The **Loggia del Mercato Nuovo** on Via Calimala is crammed with souvenirs and straw and leather goods at reasonable prices; bargaining is acceptable here. *Open Mon.–Sat. 8–7 (closed Mon. AM).*

Outside the Church of San Lorenzo, you'll find yourself in the midst of the sprawling **San Lorenzo Market,** dealing in everything and anything, including some interesting leather items. *Piazza San Lorenzo, Via dell'Ariento. Open Tues.–Sat. 8–7.*

French Riviera

Few places in the world have the same pull on the imagination as France's fabled Riviera, the Mediterranean coastline stretching from St-Tropez in the west to Menton on the Italian border. Cooled by the Mediterranean in the summer and warmed by it in winter, the climate is almost always pleasant—and the cities crowded—in July and August.

Although the Riviera's coastal resorts seem to live exclusively for the tourist trade and have often been ruined by high-rise blocks, the hinterlands remain relatively untarnished. The little villages perched high on the hills behind medieval ramparts seem to belong to another century. One of them, St-Paul-de-Vence, is the home of the Maeght Foundation, one of the world's leading museums of modern art. Artists, attracted by the light, have played a considerable role in popular conceptions of the Riviera, and their presence is reflected in the number of modern art museums: the Musée Picasso at Antibes, the Musée Renoir and the Musée d'Art Moderne Mediterranée at Cagnes-sur-Mer, and the Musée Jean Cocteau near the harbor at Menton. Wining and dining are special treats on the Riviera, especially if you are fond of garlic and olive oil. Bouillabaisse, a spicy fish stew, is the most popular regional specialty.

The tiny principality of Monaco, which lies between Nice and Menton, is included in this section, despite the fact that it is a sovereign state. Although Monaco has its own army and police force, its language, food, and way of life are French.

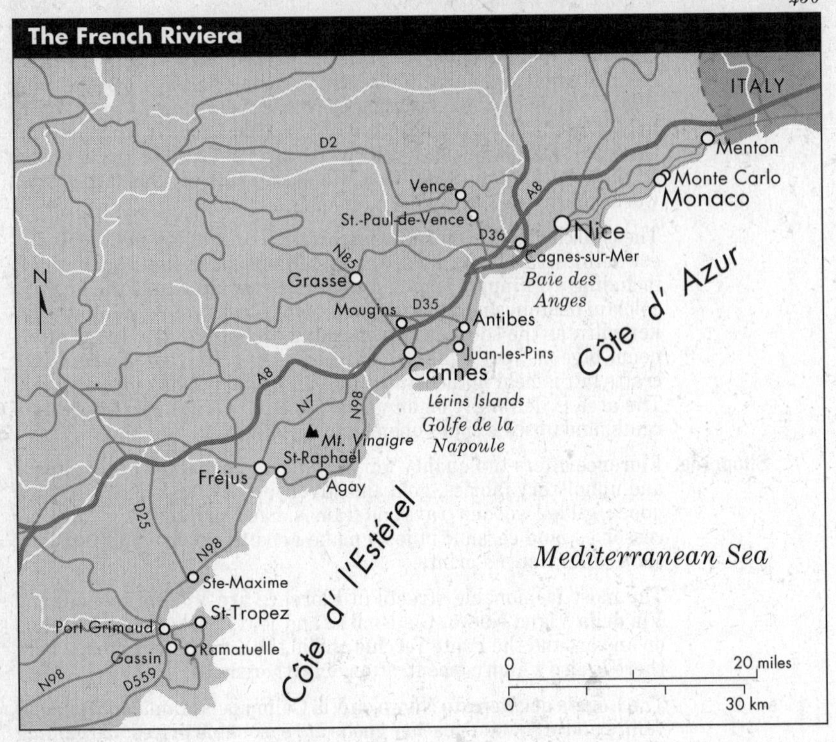

Currency The unit of French currency is the franc, subdivided into 100 centimes. At press time, the dollar bought 5.18 francs.

Telephones To call abroad, dial 19 and wait for the tone, then dial the country code, area code, and number. To reach an **AT&T** long-distance operator, dial 19–0011; for **MCI,** dial 19–0019; and for **Sprint,** 19–0087. Dial 12 for local operators.

Shore Excursions The best way to spend time in the French Riviera is to wander the city streets, lunch at a café, or head to the beach. Depending on where you're docked, your cruise line may offer excursions to other nearby towns.

Coming Ashore Only small ships dock at St-Tropez or Monaco. Most larger ones will dock or drop anchor at Nice or Cannes, where you can hire a car, catch a train, or take a shore excursion to St-Tropez or Monaco.

Exploring the Riviera The towns of the French Riviera are easily and best seen on foot. Only if you wish to travel between towns will you need additional transportation.

St-Tropez Between the old and new ports is the **Musée de l'Annonciade,** set in a cleverly converted chapel, which houses paintings by artists drawn to St-Tropez between 1890 and 1940—including Paul Signac, Matisse, Derain, and Van Dongen. *Quai de l'Épi, tel. 94–97–04–01. Admission: 22 frs. Open June–Sept., Wed.–Mon. 10–noon and 3–7; Oct.–May, Wed.–Mon. 10–noon and 2–6.*

A long climb up to the **citadel** is rewarded by a splendid view over the old town and across the gulf to Ste-Maxime, a quieter, more working-class family resort with a decent beach and reasonably priced hotels.

St-Tropez is also a good base for visiting **Port Grimaud,** a pastiche of an Italian fishing village, and the nearby hilltop villages: the old Provençal town of **Ramatuelle** and the fortified village of **Gassin.**

In Cannes Cannes is for relaxing—strolling along the seafront on the **Croisette** and getting tanned on the beaches. Near the eastern end of La Croisette is the Parc de la Roserie, where some 14,000 roses nod their heads in the wind.

The **Palais des Festivals** is where the famous film festival is held each May, and it is near the Cannes harbor.

Only a few steps inland is the old town, known as the **Suquet,** with its steep, cobbled streets and its 12th-century watchtower.

In Nice The **place Masséna** is the logical starting point for an exploration of Nice. This fine square was built in 1815 to celebrate a local hero: one of Napoléon's most successful generals.

The **Promenade des Anglais,** built by the English community here in 1824, is only a short stroll past the fountains and the **Jardin Albert Ier.** It now carries heavy traffic but still forms a splendid strand between town and sea.

Just up rue de Rivoli is the **Palais Masséna,** a museum concerned with the Napoleonic era. *65 rue de France, tel. 93–88–11–34. Admission free. Open Dec.–Oct., Tues.–Sun. 10–noon and 2–5 (3–6 May–Sept.).*

Farther west, along rue de France and right up avenue des Baumettes, is the **Musée des Beaux-Arts Jules-Chéret,** Nice's fine-arts museum, built in 1878 as a palatial mansion for a Russian princess. The rich collection of paintings includes works by Renoir, Degas, and Monet; Oriental prints; sculptures by Rodin; and ceramics by Picasso. *33 av. des Baumettes, tel. 93–62–18–12. Admission free. Open May–Sept., Tues.–Sun. 10–noon and 3–6; Oct. and Dec.–Apr., Tues.–Sun. 10–noon and 2–5.*

The narrow streets in the old town are the prettiest part of Nice: Take the rue de l'Opéra to see **St-François-de-Paule** church (1750) and the **opera house.** At the northern extremity of the old town lies the vast **place Garibaldi**—all yellow-ocher buildings and formal fountains.

The **Musée Chagall** is just off the boulevard de Cimiez, near the Roman ruins. The museum was built in 1972 to house the Chagall collection, including the 17 huge canvases of *The Message of the Bible,* which took 13 years to complete. *Av. du Dr-Ménard, tel. 93–81–75–75. Admission: 27 frs. Open July–Sept., Wed.–Mon. 10–7; Oct.–June, Wed.–Mon. 10–12:30 and 2–5:30.*

A 17th-century Italian villa amid the Roman remains contains two museums: the **Musée Archéologique,** with a plethora of ancient objects, and the renovated **Musée Matisse,** with paintings and bronzes by Henri Matisse (1869–1954). *164 av. des Arènes-de-Cimiez, tel. 93–81–08–08. Musée Matisse admission: 25 frs. Open Apr.–Sept., Wed.–Mon. 11–7; Oct.–Mar., Wed.–Mon. 10–5. Musée Archéologique, admission free. Open Dec.–Oct., Tues.–Sat. 10–noon and 2–5, Sun. 2–5.*

In Monaco For more than a century Monaco's livelihood was centered in its splendid copper-roof **casino.** The oldest section dates from 1878 and was conceived by Charles Garnier, architect of the Paris opera house. It's as elaborately ornate as anyone could wish, bristling with turrets and gold filigree, and masses of interior frescoes and bas-reliefs. There are lovely sea views from the terrace, and the gardens out front are meticulously tended. The main activity is in the American Room, where beneath the gilt-edged ceiling, busloads of tourists feed the one-armed bandits. *Pl. du Casino, tel. 92–16–21–*

21. Persons under 21 not admitted. Admission: 50 frs (American Room free). Open daily noon–4 AM; closed May 1.

The **Musée National des Automates et Poupées d' Autrefois** (Museum of Antique Dolls and Automatons) has a compelling collection of 18th- and 19th-century dolls and mechanical figures, the latter shamelessly showing off their complex inner workings. It's magically set in a 19th-century seaside villa (designed by Garnier). *17 av. Princesse-Grace, tel. 93–30–91–26. Admission: 26 frs. Open daily 10–12:15 and 2:30–6:30.*

Monaco Town, the principality's old quarter, has many vaulted passageways and exudes an almost tangible medieval feel. The magnificent **Palais du Prince** (Prince's Palace), a grandiose Italianate structure with a Moorish tower, was largely rebuilt in the last century. Here, since 1297, the Grimaldi dynasty has lived and ruled. The spectacle of the Changing of the Guard occurs each morning at 11:55; inside, guided tours take visitors through the state apartments and a wing containing the **Palace Archives** and **Musée Napoléon** (Napoleonic Museum). *Pl. du Palais, tel. 93–25–18–31. Palace admission: 40 frs. Open June–Oct., daily 9:30–12:30 and 2–6:30. Musée Napoléon and Palace Archives admission: 20 frs. Open Tues.–Sun. 9:30–6:30.*

Monaco's **cathedral** is a late-19th-century neo-Romanesque confection in which Philadelphia-born Princess Grace lies entombed in splendor along with past members of the Grimaldi dynasty. *4 rue Colonel Bellando de Castro.*

The **Musée Historial des Princes de Monaco** (Waxworks Museum) is a Monégasque Madame Tussaud's, with none-too-realistic wax figures stiffly portraying various episodes in the Grimaldi history. The waxworks may not convince, but the rue Basse is wonderfully atmospheric. *27 rue Basse, tel. 93–30–39–05. Admission: 24 frs. Open May–Sept., daily 9–8; Oct.–Dec., daily 10:30–6; Jan.–Apr., daily 9–6:30.*

Next to the St-Martin Gardens—which contain an evocative bronze monument in memory of Prince Albert I (Prince Rainier's great-grandfather, the one in the sou'wester and flying oilskins, benignly guiding a ship's wheel)—is the **Musée Océanographique** (Oceanography Museum and Aquarium). This museum is also an internationally renowned research institute, founded by the very Prince Albert who is remembered outside as an eminent marine biologist; the well-known underwater explorer Jacques Cousteau is the present director. The aquarium is the undisputed highlight, however, where a collection of the world's fish and crustacea—some colorful, some drab, some the stuff of nightmares—live out their lives in public. *Av. St-Martin, tel. 93–15–36–00. Admission: 60 frs. Open Sept.–Oct. and May–June, daily 9:30–7; Nov.–Apr., daily 9:30–6; July and Aug., daily 9–8.*

Before heading back inland, take a stroll to the eastern tip of the rock, to the **Fort Antoine Theater** (av. de la Quarantaine, tel. 93–30–19–21), a converted 18th-century fortress that certainly looks a lot prettier now than it would have in more warlike times, covered as it is in ivy and flowering myrtle and thyme. In the summer, this is an open-air theater that seats 350.

The Moneghetti area is the setting for the **Jardin Exotique** (Garden of Exotic Plants), where 600 varieties of cacti and succulents cling to the rock face, their improbable shapes and sometimes violent coloring further testimony that Mother Nature will try anything once. Your ticket also allows you to explore the caves next to the gardens and to visit the adjacent **Museum of Prehistoric Anthropology.** *Blvd. du Jardin Exotique, tel. 93–15–80–06. Admission: 39 frs. Open Oct.–May, daily 9–5:30; June–Sept., daily 9–7.*

Beaches

In Cannes Many of Cannes's beaches are private, but that doesn't mean you can't use them, only that you must pay for the privilege. The Croisette offers splendid views of the Napoule Bay.

In St-Tropez Close to town are **Plage des Greniers** and the **Bouillabaisse,** but most people prefer a 10-kilometer (6-mile) sandy crescent at **Les Salins** and **Pampellone.** These beaches are about 3 kilometers (2 miles) from town.

Gibraltar

The Rock of Gibraltar acquired its name in AD 711 when it was captured by the Moorish chieftain Tarik at the start of the Arab invasion of Spain. It became known as Jebel Tariq (Rock of Tariq), later corrupted to Gibraltar. After successive periods of Moorish and Spanish domination, Gibraltar was captured by an Anglo-Dutch fleet in 1704 and ceded to the British by the Treaty of Utrecht in 1713. This tiny British colony, whose impressive silhouette dominates the straits between Spain and Morocco, is a rock just 5⅘ kilometers (3⅗ miles) long, ¾ kilometer (½ mile) wide, and 1,394 feet high.

Currency Gibraltar's official language is English and the currency is the British pound sterling. At press time, $1 = 1.54.

Shore Excursions The following is a good choice in Gibraltar. It may not be offered by all cruise lines. Time and price are approximate.

The Rock. By taxi, you'll climb the 1,400-foot-high Rock of Gibraltar for a panoramic view of the town and harbor. Includes a visit to Ape's Den, home of Barbary apes. *1½ hrs. Cost: $32.*

Coming Ashore Cruise ships dock at Gibraltar's pier. From here, you can walk or take a taxi or shuttle to the center of town.

Getting Around Since Gibraltar is just over 3 miles long and only half a mile wide, getting around is not a major problem.

Exploring Gibraltar **Punta Grande de Europa** (Europa Point) is the Rock's most southerly tip. Stop here to admire the view across the Straits to the coast of Morocco, 22½ kilometers (14 miles) away. You are standing on what in ancient times was called one of the two Pillars of Hercules. Across the water in Morocco, a mountain between the cities of Ceuta and Tangier formed the second pillar. Plaques explain the history of the gun installations here, and, nearby on Europa Flats, you can see the Nun's Well, an ancient Moorish cistern, and the Shrine of Our Lady of Europe, venerated by sailors since 1462.

Jews Gate is an unbeatable lookout point over the docks and Bay of Gibraltar to Algeciras in Spain. From here you can gain access to the Upper Nature Preserve, which includes St. Michael's Cave (*see below*), the Apes' Den, the Great Siege Tunnel, and the Moorish Castle. *Engineer Rd. Admission to preserve, including all sites: £4.50, plus £1.50 per vehicle. Open daily 10–6.*

St. Michael's Cave, a series of underground chambers adorned with stalactites and stalagmites, provides an admirable setting for concerts, ballet, and drama. *Queen's Rd.*

Apes' Den, near the Wall of Charles V, is where you'll find the famous Barbary apes, a breed of cinnamon-colored, tailless monkeys, natives of the Atlas Mountains in Morocco. Legend holds that as long as the apes remain, the British will continue to hold the Rock. Winston Churchill himself issued orders for the maintenance of the ape colony when its numbers began to dwindle during World War II. *Old Queen's Rd.*

The **Great Siege Tunnel** (Old Queen's Rd.) is found at the northern end of the Rock. These huge galleries were carved out during the

Great Siege of 1779–83. Here, in 1878, the governor, Lord Napier of Magdala, entertained former president Ulysses S. Grant at a banquet in St. George's Hall. From here, the Holyland Tunnel leads out to the east side of the Rock above Catalan Bay.

The recently refurbished **Gibraltar Museum**'s exhibits recall the history of the Rock throughout the ages. *Gibraltar Museum, Bomb House La., tel. 9567–74289. Admission: £1.50. Open weekdays 10–6, Sat. 10–2.*

Greek Islands

The islands of the Aegean have colorful legends—the Minotaur in Crete; the lost continent of Atlantis, which some believe was Santorini; and the Colossus of Rhodes, to name a few. Each island has its own personality. Mykonos has windmills, dazzling whitewashed buildings, hundreds of tiny churches and chapels on golden hillsides, and small fishing harbors. Visitors to volcanic Santorini sail into what was once a vast volcanic crater and anchor near the island's forbidding cliffs. In Rhodes, a bustling modern town surrounds a walled town with a medieval castle.

Currency The Greek monetary unit is the drachma (dr.). At press time, there were approximately 241 dr. to the U.S. dollar.

Telephones Although you can buy phone cards with up to 5,000 dr. credit, if you plan to make and pay for several international phone calls, go to an OTE office. For an **AT&T** long-distance operator, dial 00/800–1311; **MCI,** 00/800–1211; **Sprint,** 00/800–1411.

Shore Excursions The following excursions are good choices in the Greek Islands. They may not be offered by all cruise lines. Times and prices are approximate.

In Mykonos The best way to explore Mykonos is on your own, wandering through the narrow whitewashed streets. Some lines may offer excursions to the neighboring island of Delos.

In Santorini **Akrotiri & Wine Tasting.** Visit the excavated town of Akrotiri, and then continue on your bus to a winery for a tasting. *4 hrs. Cost: $45.*

Oia. By motor coach, ride to the cliff-top village of Oia, where there will be time to wander through the town. *4 hrs. Cost: $30.*

In Rhodes **Mount Philerimos and Rhodes Town.** Visit the Church of Our Lady on the plateau of Philerimos and walk through the old walled portion of Rhodes Town to the Palace of Grand Masters. *4½ hrs. Cost: $40.*

Lindos. Drive 30 miles to Lindos Village and up the summit of the Acropolis to see ruins and to shop in the village. *4½ hrs. Cost: $40.*

In Lesbos **Island Tour.** Breeze through the island's highlights, including the Church of Taxiarches, Theofilos Museum, Theriade Museum, and Agiasso Village. *4½ hrs. Cost: $38.*

Coming Ashore Depending on which Greek Islands your ship visits—and how many port calls it makes—you may dock, tender, or both.

In Mykonos Ships tender passengers to the main harbor area along the Esplanade in Mykonos Town.

In Santorini If your ship doesn't dock below Thira and tender passengers ashore, it will dock at or tender you to the new port, Athinios, where visitors are met by buses and taxis. The bus ride into Thira takes about a half hour, and from there you can make connections to Oia.

In Rhodes Ships dock at Mandraki Harbor, once the ancient port of Rhodes. Rhodes Town stretches in front of the port.

In Lesbos Cruise ships visiting Lesbos tender passengers to the main town of Mytilini, where most of the town's sights are clustered.

Getting Around Most port cities in the Greek Islands are compact enough to explore on foot. There are, however, several outlying towns worth visiting; for these you'll need to hire a driver or rent a car.

In Mykonos Mykonos Town is well suited to walking. Taxis and buses will take you to other points of interest. Motorbikes also can be rented.

In Santorini If you dock below Thira, you can take the cable car to and from the harbor to the town, or, if you like a little adventure, try the donkey service. Buses and taxis will take you around town. Many people rent mopeds, but they're not recommended as a safe means of traveling about the island.

In Rhodes It is possible to tour the island in one day only if you rent a car. Walking is advisable in Rhodes Town. Taxis can take you to other nearby sights and beaches.

In Lesbos A car is handy on Lesbos if you want to explore the island, and rentals cost around $60 a day. Bus service is relatively expensive and infrequent.

Exploring the Greek Islands

Mykonos Besides their sun-kissed beaches, the Greek Islands offer a diverse mix of historical, architectural, and cultural attractions. The **Archaeological Museum** houses funerary sculptures discovered on the neighboring islet of Rhenea. *Ayios Stefanos Rd., north end of port, tel. 0289/22325. Admission: 400 dr. Open Tues.–Sun. 8:30–3.*

The most famous of the island's churches is the **Church of Paraportiani.** The sloping, white-washed conglomeration of four chapels, mixing Byzantine and vernacular idioms, has been described as a "confectioner's dream gone mad," and its position on a promontory facing the sea sets off the unique architecture. *Ayion St.*

Little Venice is a neighborhood where a few old houses have been turned into bars. In the distance across the water are the famous windmills. *Walk on Mitropoleos Georgouli toward the water.*

The **Old Folk Museum** is housed in an 18th-century house and features one bedroom furnished and decorated in the fashion of the period. On display are looms and lace-making devices, Cycladic costumes, old photographs, and Mykoniot musical instruments. *Near Little Venice, tel. 0289/22591 or 0289/22748. Admission free. Open Mon.–Sat. 5:30–8:30, Sun. 6:30–8:30.*

About 40 minutes by boat from Mykonos and its 20th-century holiday pleasures is the ancient isle of **Delos**—the legendary sanctuary of Apollo. Its Terrace of the Lions, a remarkable group of nine Naxian marble sculptures from the 7th century BC, is a must. Worth seeing, too, are some of the houses of the Roman period, with their fine floor mosaics.

The best of the mosaics from Delos's ruins are in the island's **Archaeological Museum.** *Tel. 0289/22–259. Admission to archaeological site (including entrance to museum): 1,200 dr. Open Tues.–Sun. 8:30–3.*

Santorini Santorini's volcano erupted during the 15th century BC, destroying its Minoan civilization. At **Akrotiri,** on the south end of the island, the remains of a Minoan city buried by volcanic ash are being excavated. The site, believed by some to be part of the legendary Atlantis, should be a must on your sightseeing list. *13 km/8 mi from Fira, tel. 0286/81–366. Admission: 1,200 dr. Open Tues.–Sun. 8:30–3.*

Oia, the serene town at the northern tip, is charming and has spectacular views despite being packed with visitors in the summer. This is the place, if your time ashore allows, to watch the sunset. Oia, 14 kilometers (8½ miles) from Thira, has the usual souvenir and handicrafts shops and several reasonably priced jewelry shops. Be sure to try the local wines. The volcanic soil produces a unique range of flavors, from light and dry to rich and aromatic.

The capital, **Fira,** midway along the west coast of the east rim, is no longer just a picturesque town but a major tourist center, overflowing with discos, shops, and restaurants.

At **Ancient Thira,** a cliff-top site on the east coast of the island, a well-preserved ancient town includes a theater and agora, houses, fortifications, and ancient tombs. *Take taxi partway up Mesa Vouna then hike to summit, no phone. Admission free. Open Tues.–Sun. 8:30–3.*

For an enjoyable but slightly unnerving excursion, take the short boat trip to the island's still-active small offshore volcanoes, called the **Kamenes** (Burnt Islands). You can descend into a small crater, hot and smelling of sulfur, and swim in the nearby water, which has been warmed by the volcano.

Rhodes The fascinating **old walled city,** near the harbor, was built by crusaders—the Knights of St. John—on the site of an ancient city. The knights ruled the island from 1309 until they were defeated by the Turks in 1522.

Within the fine medieval walls, on the Street of the Knights, stands the **Knights' Hospital,** now the Archaeological Museum, housing ancient pottery and sculpture, including two famous statues of Aphrodite. *Tel. 0241/27–657. Admission: 800 dr. Open Tues.–Fri. 8:30–7 (8:30–3 in winter), weekends and holidays 8:30–3.*

Another museum that deserves your attention is the restored and moated medieval **Palace of the Grand Masters.** Destroyed in 1856 by a gunpowder explosion, the palace was renovated by the Italians as a summer retreat for Mussolini. Note its splendid Hellenistic and Roman floor mosaics. *Tel. 0241/23–359. Admission: 1,200 dr. Open Tues.–Fri. 8:30–7 (8:30–3 in winter), weekends and holidays 8:30–3.*

The walls of Rhodes's Old Town are among the greatest medieval monuments in the Mediterranean. For 200 years the knights strengthened them, making them up to 40 feet thick in places and curving the walls to deflect cannonballs. You can take a guided walk on part of the 4-kilometer (2½-mile) road along the top of the walls every Tuesday and Saturday (call 0241/21–954 for information).

The enchanting village of **Lindos** is about 60 kilometers (37 miles) down the east coast from Rhodes Town. Take a donkey from the village center and ride or put on your comfortable shoes and walk up the steep hill to the ruins of the ancient **Acropolis of Lindos,** which is slowly being restored. The sight of its beautiful colonnade with the sea far below is unforgettable. Look for little St. Paul's Harbor, beneath the cliffs of the Acropolis; seen from above, it appears to be a lake, as the tiny entrance from the sea is obscured by the rocks. *Tel. 0244/31–258. Admission: 1,200 dr. Open Tues.–Sun. 8:30–2:40.*

Lesbos Above **Mytilini** looms the stone castle built by the Byzantines on a 600 BC temple of Apollo. It was repaired by Francesco Gateluzzi of the famous Genoese family. Inside there's only a crumbling prison and a Roman cistern, but a visit is worth it for the fine views. *Tel. 0251/27297. Admission: 400 dr. Open daily sunrise–sunset.*

One of Greece's best art museums is at **Varia,** home of the early 20th-century painter Theophilos. Eighty of his paintings can be seen. *4 km/2½ mi south of Mytilini, tel. 0251/28179. Admission: 250 dr. Open Tues.–Sun. 9–1 and 4:30–8.*

The **Theriade Library and Museum of Modern Art** includes Theriade's publications "Minotaure" and "Verved" and his collection of works, mostly lithographs, by Picasso, Matisse, Chagall, and Miro. *Next to Varia, tel. 0251/28179. Admission: 500 dr. Open Tues.–Sun. 9–2 and 5–8.*

The 18th-century monastery **Taxiarchis Michail** is famous for its black icon of Archangel Michael. Visitors used to make a wish and press a coin to the archangel's forehead; if it stuck, the wish would be granted. Owing to wear and tear on the icon, the practice is now forbidden. *In town of Mandamados, 37 km/23 mi northwest of Mytilini.*

At the foot of Mt. Olympos, the island's highest peak, sits **Agiassos** village. It remains a lovely settlement, with gray stone houses, cobblestone lanes, a medieval castle, and the church of Panayia Vrefokratousa. The latter was founded in the 12th century to house an icon believed to be the work of St. Luke.

In the main town of **Mytilini** there is a traditional Lesbos house, restored and furnished in 19th-century style, that people are permitted to visit. Call to arrange a time with owner Marika Vlachou. *Mitropleos 6, tel. 0251/28550. Admission free by appointment only.*

Shopping

In Mykonos Mykonos is the best of the Greek islands for shopping. The main shopping street in Mykonos runs perpendicular to the harbor and is lined with jewelry stores, clothing, boutiques, cafés, and candy stores.

In Santorini For locally made items head to Oia, where you will find the best art galleries, antiques shops, craft shops, and stores that sell Byzantine reproductions. Boutiques abound in Thira as well.

In Rhodes Many attractive souvenir and handicrafts shops are located in the Old Town, particularly on Sokratous Street, and just outside the walls vendors sell decorative Rhodian pottery, local embroidery, sea sponges, and relatively inexpensive jewelry.

In Lesbos Lesbos is famous for its chestnuts, olive oil, and ouzo. Agiassos is known for its wood crafts.

Beaches

In Mykonos Within walking distance of Mykonos Town are **Tourlos, Ayios Stefanos,** and **Ayios Ioannis. Psarou,** on the south coast, protected from wind by hills and surrounded by restaurants, offers a wide selection of water sports and is considered the finest beach.

In Santorini There is a red-sand beach below Akrotiri on the southwest shore. Long black-sand/volcanic beaches are found in Kamari and Perissa.

In Rhodes Rhodes town and the more sheltered east coast have exquisite stretches of beach, while the west side can be choppy. **Elli** beach in town has fine sand. Much of the coast is developed, so you can reach the best beaches only through the hotels that occupy them. There also is a long nice stretch of beach between Haraki and Vlicha Bay.

In Lesbos Some of the most spectacular beaches are sandy coves in the southwest, including the stretch from Skala Eressou to Sigri. **Vatera,** one of the island's best beaches, lies southwest of Agiassos on the southeast side of the island.

Helsinki, Finland

Helsinki is a city of the sea, built on peninsulas and islands along the Baltic shoreline. Streets curve around bays, bridges arch over the nearby islands, and ferries carry traffic to destinations farther offshore. The smell of the sea hovers over the city, while the huge ships that ply the Baltic constantly come and go from the city's harbors. Helsinki has grown dramatically since World War II, and now accounts for about one-sixth of the Finnish population. The city covers a total of 433 square miles and includes 315 islands. Most of the city's sights, hotels, and restaurants, however, are located on one peninsula—forming a compact hub of special interest to cruise passengers.

Currency The unit of currency in Finland is the Finnmark, divided into 100 penniä. At press time, the exchange rate was about FIM 4.69 to the dollar. Credit cards are widely accepted, even in many taxicabs. Traveler's checks can be changed only in banks.

Telephones You can dial directly to the United States from anywhere in Finland. To make a direct international phone call from Finland, dial 990, then the appropriate country code and phone number. For an **AT&T** long-distance operator, dial 9800–10010; for **MCI,** 9800–10280; for **Sprint,** 9800–10284.

Shore Excursions The following is a good choice in Helsinki. It may not be offered by all cruise lines. Time and price are approximate.

City Tour. The National Museum, Senate Square, the Esplanade, and other Helsinki landmarks are the highlights of this half day on the town. *3 hrs. Cost: $35.*

Coming Ashore Ships calling at Helsinki dock harborside near Market Square. From here, you can easily spend the day exploring the city center on foot.

Getting Around If you want to use public transportation, your best buy is the Helsinki Card, which gives unlimited travel on city public transportation, as well as free entry to many museums, a free sightseeing tour, and a variety of other discounts. Streetcars can be very handy and route maps and schedules are posted at most downtown stops. Single tickets are sold on board. Taxis are all marked TAKSI. The meters start at FIM 18, with the fare rising on a kilometer basis. A listing of all taxi companies appears in the white pages under *Taksi*—try to choose one that is located nearby, because they charge from point of dispatch. Many accept credit cards.

Exploring Helsinki *Numbers in the margin correspond to points of interest on the Helsinki map.*

❶ The **Kauppatori** (Market Square) is frequented by locals and tourists alike. All around are stalls selling everything from colorful, freshly cut flowers to ripe fruit, from vegetables trucked in from the hinterland to handicrafts made in small villages. Look at the fruit stalls—mountains of strawberries, raspberries, blueberries, and, if you're lucky, cloudberries. Closer to the dock are fresh fish, caught that morning in the Baltic Sea and still flopping. *At South Harbor, harborside.*

❷ On the Pohjoisesplanadi (North Esplanade) is the **Presidentinlinna** (President's Palace), built as a private home in 1818 and converted for use by the czars in 1843. It was the official residence of Finnish presidents from 1919–1993. It still houses the presidential offices and is the scene of official receptions. Just up the street is the city hall.

At the district of **Katajanokka,** 19th-century brick warehouses are slowly being renovated to form a complex of boutiques, arts-and-crafts studios, and restaurants. You'll find innovative designs at these shops, and the restaurants tend to offer lighter fare, which can make this a tempting area in which to stop for lunch.

❸ **Senaatintori** (Senate Square), the heart of neoclassical Helsinki, is ❹ dominated by the domed **Tuomiokirkko** (Lutheran cathedral). The square is the work of Carl Ludvig Engel. The harmony created with the Tuomiokirkko, the university, and the state council building places you amid one of the purest styles of European architecture. Senaatintori has a dignified, stately air, enlivened in summer by sun worshipers who gather on the wide steps leading up to Tuomiokirkko and throughout the year by the bustle around the Kiseleff Bazaar on the square's south side. *North of City Hall.*

❺ Worth taking a look at is the old brick **Market Hall**—with its voluminous displays of meat, fish, and other gastronomic goodies. *Along western shore of South Harbor on Eteläranta St. Open weekdays 8–5, Sat. 8–2.*

❻ The **Railway Station** and its square form the bustling commuting hub of the city. The station's huge red-granite figures are by Emil Wikström, but the solid building they adorn was designed by Eliel Saarinen, one of the founders of the early 20th-century National Romantic style.

❼ The **Valtion Taidemuseo Ateneum** (Finnish National Gallery) is on the south side of the square, facing the National Theater. *Admission: FIM 10. Open Tues. and Fri. 9–6, Wed. and Thurs. 9–8, weekends 11–5.*

In front of the main post office, west of the railway station, is the ❽ **statue of Marshal Mannerheim,** gazing down Mannerheimintie, the major thoroughfare named in his honor. Perhaps no man in Finnish history is so revered as Marshal Baron Carl Gustaf Mannerheim, the military and political leader who guided Finland through much of the turbulent 20th century. When he died in Switzerland on January 28, 1951, his body was flown back to lie in state in the cathedral. For three days, young war widows, children, and soldiers filed past his bier.

❾ About half a mile along, past the colonnaded red-granite **Parliament** ❿ **House,** stands **Finlandiatalo** (Finlandia Hall), one of the last creations of Alvar Aalto, and, a bit farther up Mannerheimintie, the new ⓫ **Suomen Kansallisoppera** (Finnish National Opera), a striking example of Scandinavian architecture. If you can't make it to a concert there, take a guided tour. Behind the hall and the opera house lies the inland bay of Töölönlahti, and almost opposite the hall stands the ⓬ **Suomen Kansallismuseo** (National Museum), another example of National Romantic exotica in which Eliel Saarinen played a part. *Admission: FIM 15. Open June–Aug., Wed.–Sun. 11–5, Tues. 11–8; Sept.–May, Wed.–Sun. 11–4, Tues. 11–8.*

Finlandiatalo, **10**
Kauppatori, **1**
Market Hall, **5**
Parliament House, **9**
Presidentinlinna, **2**
Railway Station, **6**
Senaatintori, **3**
Statue of Marshal Mannerheim, **8**
Suomen Kansallismuseo, **12**
Suomen Kansallisoppera, **11**
Temppeliaukion Kirkko, **13**
Tuomiokirkko, **4**
Valtion Taidemuseo Ateneum, **7**

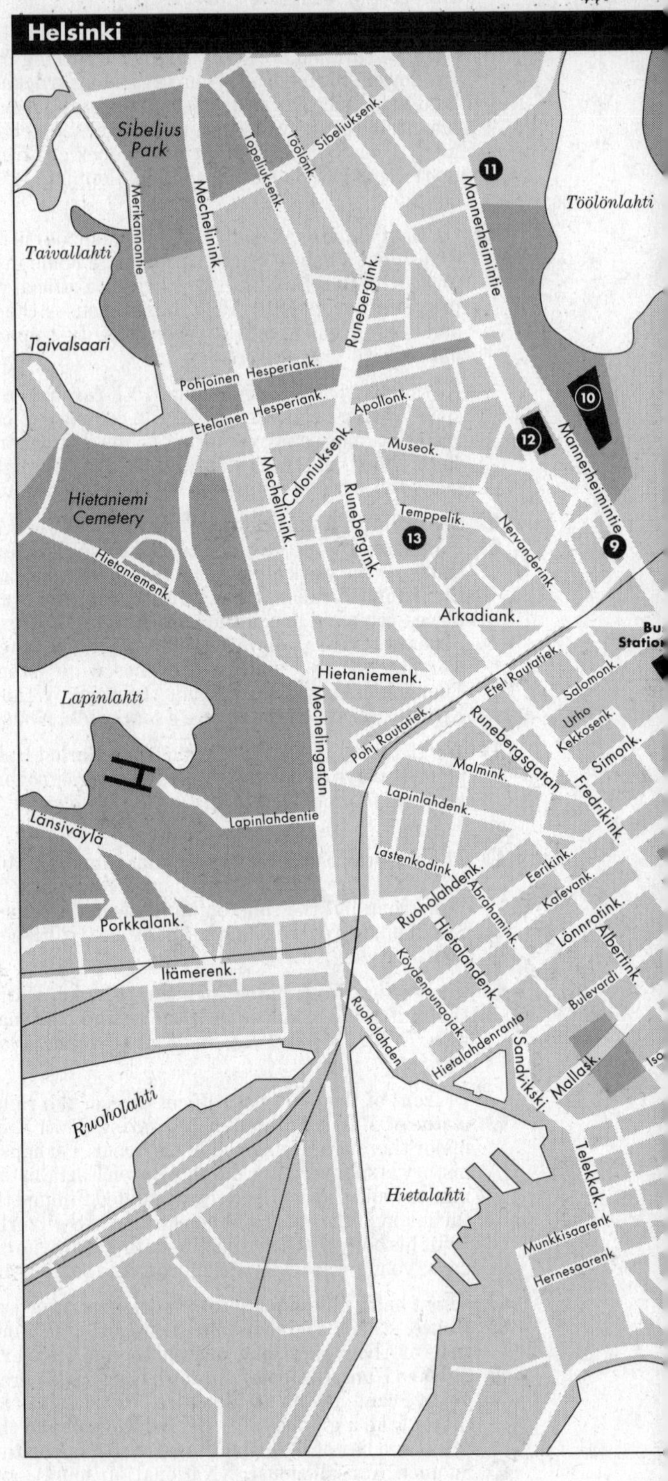

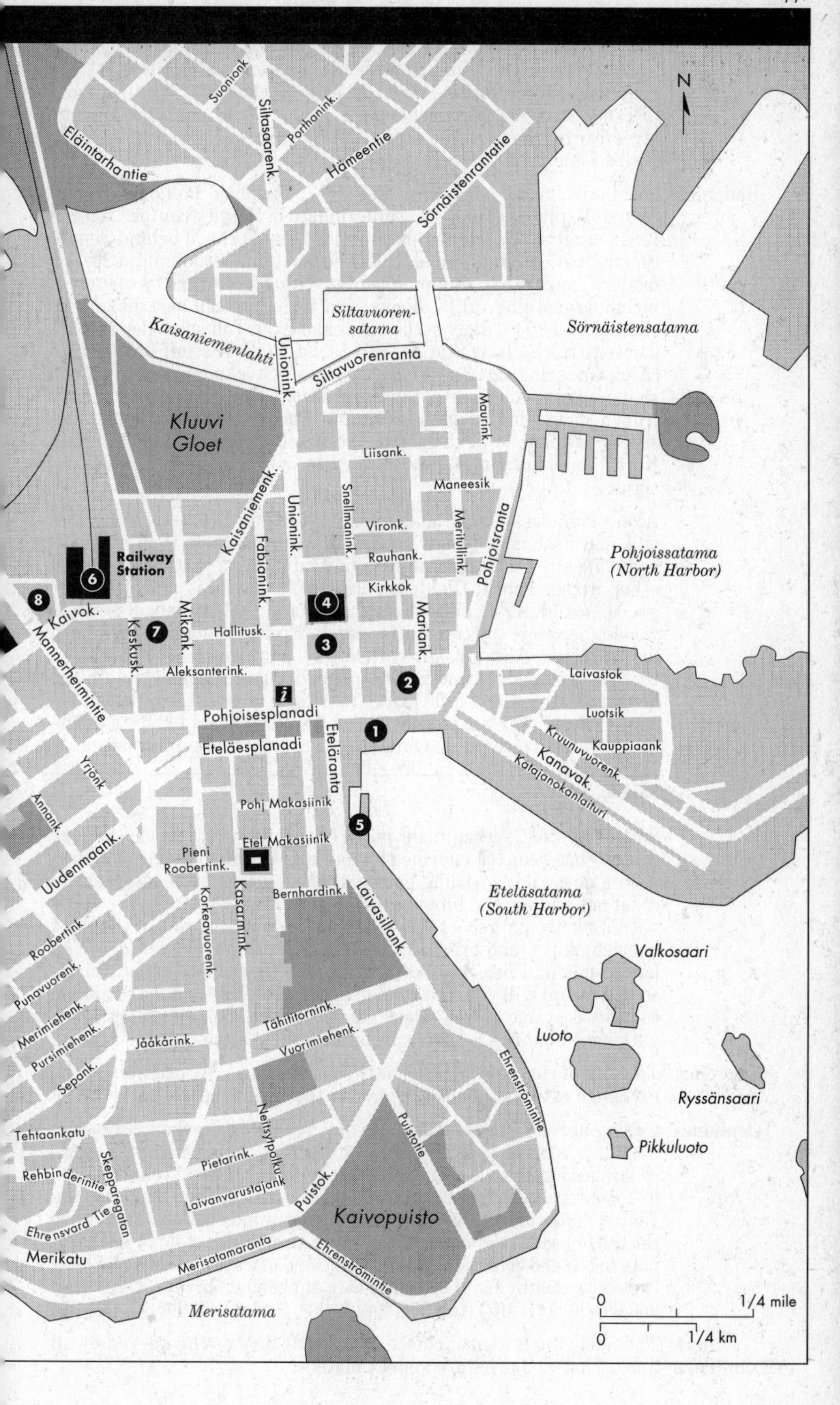
N
Suonionk.
Siltasaarenk.
Porthanink.
Eläintarhantie
Hämeentie
Sörnäistenrantatie
Siltavuoren-
satama
Sörnäistensatama
Kaisaniemenlahti
Unionink.
Siltavuorenranta
Kluuvi
Gloet
Maurink.
Liisank.
Maneesik.
Snellmanink.
Kaisaniemenk.
Unionink.
Fabianink.
Vironk.
Meritullink.
Pohjoisranta
Pohjoissatama
(North Harbor)
Rauhank.
Railway
Station
Kirkkok.
Mariank.
Kaivok.
Mikonk.
Keskusk.
Hallitusk.
Mannerheimintie
Aleksanterink.
Laivastok.
Pohjoisesplanadi
Eteläranta
Luotsik.
Eteläesplanadi
Kruunuvuorenk.
Kauppiaank.
Kanavak.
Katajanokanlaituri
Yrjönk.
Annank.
Pohj Makasiinik.
Etel Makasiinik.
Uudenmaank.
Pieni
Roobertink.
Korkeavuorenk.
Kasarmink.
Bernhardink.
Laivasillank.
Eteläsatama
(South Harbor)
Roobertink.
Valkosaari
Punavuorenk.
Merimiehenk.
Tähtitorniink.
Pursimiehenk.
Jääkärink.
Vuorimiehenk.
Luoto
Sepänk.
Ehrenströmintie
Ryssänsaari
Neitsytpolku
Puistotie
Tehtaankatu
Pikkuluoto
Skepparegatan
Pietarink.
Rehbinderintie
Laivanvarustajank.
Puistok.
Kaivopuisto
Ehrensvard Tie
Merikatu
Merisatamaranta
Ehrenströmintie
Merisatama
0
1/4 mile
0
1/4 km

Tucked away in a labyrinth of streets to the west is the strikingly
⑬ modern **Temppeliaukion Kirkko** (Temple Square Church). Carved out of solid rock and topped with a copper dome, this landmark is a center for church services and concerts. (From here it's only a short distance back to Mannerheimintie, where you can pick up any streetcar for the downtown area.) *Lutherinkatu 3. Open daily 11–8; closed Tues. 1–2 PM and during concerts and services.*

Shopping Helsinki's prime shopping districts run along **Pohjoisesplanadi** (North Esplanade) and **Aleksanterinkatu** in the city center. You can find a number of antiques shops in the neighborhood behind Senate Square, called **Kruununhaka. The Forum** (Mannerheimintie 20) is a modern, multistory shopping center with a wide variety of stores, including clothing, gifts, books, and toys. You can also make purchases until 10 PM daily in the shops along the Tunneli underpass underneath the Railway Station. Some shops in the **Kiseleff Bazaar Hall** (Aleksanderinkatu 28), which once housed Stockmann's and now has shops selling handicrafts, toys, and knitwear, are open on Sundays from noon to 4 in the summer. **Kaunis Koru,** which sells Finnish-designed jewelry, is next door to the Kiseleff Bazaar Hall. **Kalevala Koru** (Unioninkatu 25) has jewelry based on ancient Finnish designs.

Along Pohjoisesplanadi and on the other side Eteläesplanadi, you will find Finland's design houses. **Hackman Arabia** (Pohjoisesplanadi 25) sells Finland's well-known Arabia china, Iittala glass, and other items. **Pentik** (Pohjoisesplanadi 27) features artful leather goods. **Aarikka** (Pohjoisesplanadi 25–27 and Eteläesplanadi 8) offers wooden jewelry, toys and gifts. **Artek** (Eteläesplanadi 18) is known for its Alvar Alto–designed furniture and ceramics. **Marimekko** (Pohjoisesplanadi 31 and Eteläesplanadi 18) sells women's clothing, household items, and gifts made from its famous textiles. **Design Forum Finland** (Eteläesplanadi 8), which often hosts exhibits of the latest Finnish design innovations, can provide more information.

Ibiza, Spain

Settled by the Carthaginians in the 5th century BC, Ibiza in the 20th century has been transformed by tourism. From a peasant economy, it became a wild, anything-goes gathering place for the international jet set and for the hippies of the 1960s—only to enter the 1990s with its principal resort, Sant Antoni, regarded as one of the most boorish, noisy, and brash on the Mediterranean. And yet, of the islands, only on Ibiza (and Formentera, the tiny island just off Ibiza's southern tip) will you find women in the fields dressed in the simple country costume of long black skirt and wide-brimmed straw hat, gathering almonds in their aprons or herding errant goats.

Currency The unit of currency in Spain is the peseta (pta.). At press time, the exchange rate was about 129 ptas. to the U.S. dollar.

Telephones Calling abroad can be done from any pay phone marked TELÉFONO INTERNACIONAL. Use 50-pta. (or 100-pta. if the phone takes them) coins initially, then coins of any denomination to prolong your call. Dial 07 for international, wait for the tone to change, then dial 1 for the United States or 0101 for Canada. For lengthy international calls, go to the telefónica, a telephone office, where an operator assigns you a private booth and collects payment at the end of the call; this is the least expensive and by far the easiest way of phoning abroad. **AT&T** (tel. 900/99–00–11), **MCI** (tel. 900/99–00–14), **Sprint** (tel. 900/99–00–13).

Shore Excursions The following is a good choice in Ibiza. It may not be offered by all lines. Time and price are approximate.

Island Tour. Explore Eivissa, wander the old town, and visit the cathedral and castle. Stop at the beaches of Las Salinas and San Antoni. *Half day. Price: $38.*

Coming Ashore Ships calling at Ibiza dock in the harbor at Eivissa. You can explore the town on foot, but to see the outlying areas of the island you will need to take a taxi or bus.

Exploring Ibiza Once a quiet fisherman's quarter, **Sa Penya** is the part of Eivissa that turned into a tourist mecca in the 1960s and it is full of restaurants and shops.

Dalt Vila, the walled upper town, is entered through Las Tablas, its main gate. On each side of the gate stands a statue, Roman in origin; both are now headless.

Inside the upper town, a ramp continues to the right and opens onto a long, narrow plaza lined with cafés. At the top of the hill lies the **cathedral,** which sits on the site of religious constructions from each of the cultures that have ruled Eivissa since the Phoenicians. Built in the 13th and 14th centuries and renovated in the 18th century, the cathedral has a Gothic tower and a Baroque nave. The painted panels above a small vault adjoining the sacristy depict souls in purgatory being consumed by flames and tortured by devils while angels ascend to heaven. *At top of Carrer Major. Admission: 250 pts. Open Sun.–Fri. 10–1 and 4–6:30, Sat. 10–1.*

The **Museu Dalt Vila** (Museum of Archaeology) in the upper town has a collection of Phoenician, Punic, and Roman artifacts. *Plaça Catedral 3, tel. 971/30–12–31. Admission: 450 pts. Open Mon.–Sat. 10–1.*

A passageway leads between the cathedral and castle to the **Bastion of Sant Bernardo.** (There's a great view here of the wide bay.)

A Punic necropolis, with more than 3,000 tombs, has been excavated at **Puig des Molins.** Many of the artifacts can be seen at the Museu Puig d'Es Molins (Punic Archaeological Museum), adjacent to the site. *Via Romana 31, tel. 971/30–17–71. Admission: 450 pts. Open Mon.–Sat. 10–1.*

The **Museu d'Art Comtemporani** (Museum of Contemporary Art) is housed in the gateway's arch. *Ronda Pintor Narcis Putget s/n/, tel. 971/130–27–23. Admission: 350 pts. Open daily 10:30–1 and 6–8:30.*

Irish Coast and Cork

Hilly Cork is Ireland's second-largest city. The road to Cork City passes through the beautiful wooded glen of Glanmire and along the banks of the River Lee. In the center of Cork, the Lee divides in two, giving the city a profusion of picturesque quays and bridges. The name Cork derives from the Irish *corcaigh* (pronounced corky), meaning a marshy place. The city received its first charter in 1185 and grew rapidly in the 17th and 18th centuries with the expansion of its butter trade. It is now the major metropolis of the south, with a population of about 138,000.

Currency The unit of currency in Ireland is the pound, or punt (pronounced poont), written as IR£ to avoid confusion with the pound sterling. The currency is divided into 100 pence (written *p*). Although the Irish pound is the only legal tender in the republic, U.S. dollars and British currency are often accepted in large hotels and shops licensed as bureaux de change. The rate of exchange at press time was 65 pence to the U.S. dollar and 95 pence to the British pound sterling.

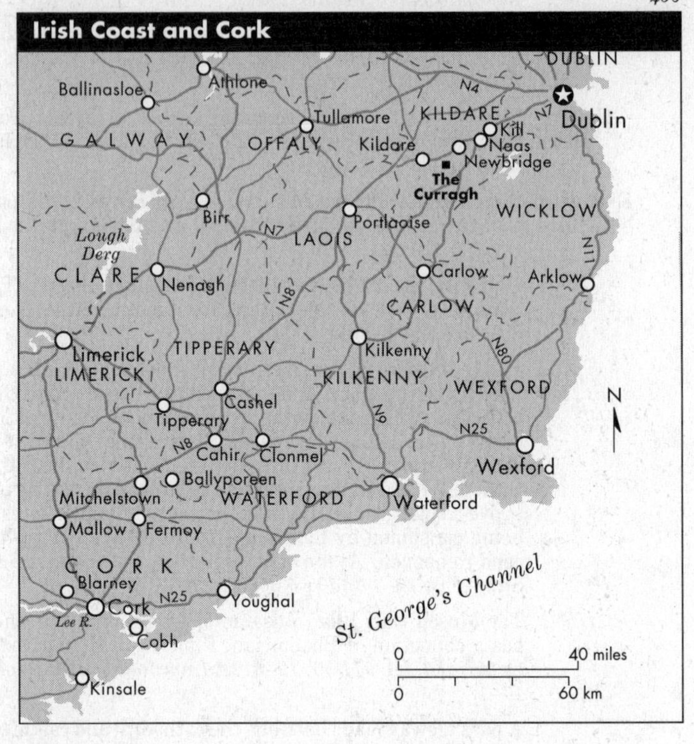

Telephones For calls to the United States and Canada, dial 001 followed by the area code. To reach an **AT&T** long distance operator, dial 1–800/550–000; for **MCI,** dial 1–800/551–001; and for **Sprint,** dial 1–800/552–001.

Shore Excursions The following are good choices in Cork. They may not be offered by all cruise lines. Times and prices are approximate.

Cork City and Blarney Tour. This is a good choice for passengers who want to visit Blarney. Upon reaching the village, you'll walk up the castle's steps to reach the famous Blarney stone. The tour also includes highlights of Cork city. *4 hrs. Cost: $42.*

Cobh Island and Whiskey Distillery. Drive through the seaside resort town of Cobh, the countryside, and Cork to reach Midleton for a visit to the Jameson Irish Whiskey Heritage Center. *4 hrs. Cost: $42.*

Coming Ashore Ships dock at the harbor of Cobh, which is around 15 miles from the main district of Cork.

Getting Around Once in the compact main district of Cork, the best way to see the city and soak in its full flavor is on foot.

Exploring Cork Patrick Street is the focal point of Cork. Here, you will find the city's most famous statue, that of **Father Theobald Mathew** (1790–1856), who led a nationwide temperance crusade, no small feat in a country as fond of a drink as this one.

In the hilly area to the north of Patrick Street is the famous 120-foot **Shandon Steeple,** the bell tower of St. Anne's Church. It is shaped like a pepper pot and houses the bells immortalized in the song *The Bells of Shandon.* Visitors can climb the tower; read the inscriptions on the bells; and, on request, have them rung over Cork. *Admission: IR£1, with bell tower IR£1.50. Open May–Oct., Mon.–Sat. 9:30–5; Nov.–Apr., Mon.–Sat. 10–3:30.*

Cobh is an attractive hilly town dominated by its 19th-century **cathedral.** It was the first and last European port of call for transatlantic liners, one of which was the ill-fated *Titanic*. Cobh has other associations with shipwrecks: It was from here that destroyers were sent out in May 1915 to search for survivors of the *Lusitania*, torpedoed by a German submarine with the loss of 1,198 lives.

Cobh's maritime past and its links with emigration are documented in a new IR£2 million heritage center known as the **Queenstown Project,** which opened in the town's old railway station in 1993. *Tel. 021/813–591. Admission: IR£3.50. Open Feb.–Nov., daily 10–6.*

Most visitors to Cork want to kiss the famous **Blarney Stone** in the hope of acquiring the "gift of the gab." Blarney itself, 8 kilometers (5 miles) from Cork City, should not, however, be taken too seriously as an excursion. All that is left of Blarney Castle is its ruined central keep containing the celebrated stone. This is set in the battlements, and to kiss it, you must lie on the walk within the walls, lean your head back, and touch the stone with your lips. Nobody knows how the tradition originated, but Elizabeth I is credited with giving the word *blarney* to the language when, commenting on the unfulfilled promises of Cormac MacCarthy, Lord Blarney of the time, she remarked, "This is all blarney; what he says, he never means." In Blarney village there are several good crafts shops, and the outing provides a good opportunity to shop around for traditional Irish goods at competitive prices. *Tel. 021/385–252. Admission: IR£3. Open Mon.–Sat. 9 to sundown, Sun. 9–5:30.*

Shopping Patrick Street is the main shopping area of Cork, and there you will find the city's two major department stores, **Roches** and **Cash's.** Cash's has a good selection of Waterford crystal. The liveliest place in town to shop is just off Patrick Street, to the west, near the city-center parking lot, in the pedestrian-only **Paul Street** area. **Mendows & Byrne** of Academy Street stocks the best in modern Irish design, including tableware, ceramics, knitwear, handwoven tweeds, and high fashion. The **Donegal Shop,** in Paul Street Piazza, specializes in made-to-order tweed suits and rainwear. At the top of Paul Street is the **Crawford Art Gallery,** which has an excellent collection of 18th- and 19th-century views of Cork and mounts adventurous exhibitions by modern artists. *Emmet Pl., tel. 021/273–377. Admission free. Open weekdays 10–5, Sat. 9–1.*

Istanbul, Turkey

Turkey is one place to which the phrase "East meets West" really applies, both literally and figuratively. It is in Turkey's largest city, Istanbul, that the continents of Europe and Asia meet, separated only by the Bosporus, which flows 29 kilometers (18 miles) from the Black Sea to the Sea of Marmara. On the vibrant streets of this city of 12 million people, miniskirts and trendy boots mingle with head scarves and prayer beads. People from as far away as Ghana, Sri Lanka, and the Philippines and as nearby as the central Asian republics and the former Soviet Union make their way to Istanbul in search of better lives.

Although most of Turkey's landmass is in Asia, Turkey has faced West politically since 1923, when Mustapha Kemal, better known as Atatürk, founded the modern republic. He transformed the remnants of the shattered Ottoman Empire into a secular state with a Western outlook. So thorough was this changeover—culturally, politically, and economically—that in 1987, 49 years after Atatürk's death, Turkey applied to the European Community (EC) for full membership. It has been a member of the North Atlantic Treaty Organization (NATO) since 1952.

Istanbul is noisy, chaotic, and exciting. Spires and domes of mosques and medieval palaces dominate the skyline. At dawn, when the muezzin's call to prayer rebounds from ancient minarets, many people are making their way home from the nightclubs and bars, while others are kneeling on their prayer rugs, facing Mecca. Day and night, Istanbul has a schizophrenic air to it. Women in jeans, business suits, or elegant designer outfits pass women wearing the long skirts and head coverings that villagers have worn for generations. Donkey-drawn carts vie with old Chevrolets and Pontiacs or shiny Toyotas and BMWs for dominance of the loud, narrow streets, and the world's most fascinating Oriental bazaar competes with Western boutiques for the time and attention of both tourists and locals.

Currency The monetary unit is the Turkish lira (TL). At press time, the exchange rate was 79,205 TL to the dollar. These rates are subject to wide fluctuation, so check close to your departure. Be certain to retain your original exchange slips when you convert money into Turkish lira—you will need them to reconvert the money. Because the Turkish lira is worth a lot less than most currencies, it's best to convert only what you plan to spend.

Telephones For all international calls dial 00, then dial the country code, area or city code, and the number. You can use the higher-price cards for this or reach an international operator by dialing 132. To reach an **AT&T** long distance operator, dial 00800-12277, for **MCI,** dial 00800-11177, and for **Sprint,** 00800-14477.

Shore Excursions The following are good choices in Istanbul. They may not be offered by all lines. Times and prices are approximate.

City Tour. Visit the major city sights, including the Hippodrome, Blue Mosque, Hagia Sophia, and Topkapí Palace Museum. *4 hrs. Cost: $35.*

Tour plus Bazaar. This tour hits all the major sights but also includes lunch and shopping at the Grand Bazaar, which should be a must on anyone's list of things to do. *8 hrs. Cost: $85.*

Coming Ashore Ships dock on the Bosporus in Istanbul on the newer Asian side of the city. Across the Galata Bridge lie the city's main attractions.

Getting Around The best way to get around all the magnificent monuments in Sultanahmet in Old Istanbul is to walk. They're all within easy distance of one another, along streets filled with peddlers, shoe-shine boys, children playing, and craftsmen working. To get to other areas, you can take metered taxis, which are plentiful, inexpensive, and more comfortable than city buses. A new tram system runs from Topkapí, via Sultanahmet, to Sirkeci.

Exploring Istanbul *Numbers in the margin correspond to points of interest on the Istanbul map.*

Old Istanbul (Sultanahmet)

❶ The number-one attraction in Istanbul is **Topkapí Palace** (Topkapí Saray), on Seraglio Point in Old Istanbul, known as Sultanahmet. The palace, which dates from the 15th century, was the residence of a number of sultans and their harems until the mid-19th century. To avoid the crowds, try to get there by 9 AM, when the gates open. If you're arriving by taxi, tell the driver you want the Topkapí Saray in Sultanahmet, or you could end up at the remains of the former Topkapí bus terminal on the outskirts of town.

Sultan Mehmet II built the first palace during the 1450s, shortly after the Ottoman conquest of Constantinople. Over the centuries, sultan after sultan added ever more elaborate architectural fantasies, until the palace eventually ended up with more than four courtyards and some 5,000 residents, many of them concubines and eunuchs. Topkapí was the residence and center of bloodshed and drama for the Ottoman rulers until the 1850s, when Sultan Abdül Mecit moved with his harem to the European-style Dolmabahçe Palace, farther up the Bosporus coast.

❷ ❸ In Topkapí's outer courtyard are the **Church of St. Irene** (Aya Irini), open only during festival days for concerts, and the **Court of the Janissaries** (Merasim Avlusu), originally for members of the sultan's elite guard.

Adjacent to the ticket office is the **Bab-i-Selam** (Gate of Salutation), built in 1524 by Suleyman the Magnificent, who was the only person allowed to pass through it. In the towers on either side, prisoners were kept until they were executed beside the fountain outside the gate in the first courtyard.

In the second courtyard, amid the rose gardens, is the **Divan-i-Humayun,** the assembly room of the council of state, once presided over by the grand vizier (prime minister). The sultan would sit behind a latticed window, hidden by a curtain so no one would know when he was listening, although occasionally he would pull the curtain aside to comment.

One of the most popular tours in Topkapí is the **Harem,** a maze of nearly 400 halls, terraces, rooms, wings, and apartments grouped around the sultan's private quarters on the west side of the second courtyard. Forty rooms are restored and open to the public. Next to the entrance are the quarters of the eunuchs and about 200 of the lesser concubines, who were lodged in tiny cubicles, as cramped and uncomfortable as the main rooms of the Harem are large and opulent. Tours begin every half hour.

In the third courtyard is the **Treasury** (Hazine Dairesi), four rooms filled with jewels, including two uncut emeralds, each weighing 3½ kilograms (7.7 pounds), that once hung from the ceiling. Here, too, you will be dazzled by the emerald dagger used in the movie *Topkapí* and the 84-carat "Spoonmaker" diamond, which according to legend, was found by a pauper and traded for three wooden spoons.

In the fourth and last courtyard of the Topkapí Palace are small, elegant summerhouses, mosques, fountains, and reflecting pools scattered amid the gardens on different levels. Here you will find the **Erivan Kiosk,** also known as the Revan Kiosk, built by Murat IV in 1636 to commemorate the successful Erivan campaign. In another kiosk in the gardens, called the **Golden Cage** (Iftariye), the closest relatives of the reigning sultan lived in strict confinement under what amounted to house arrest. The custom began during the 1800s after the old custom of murdering all possible rivals to the throne had been abandoned. The confinement of the heirs apparently helped keep the peace, but it deprived them of any chance to prepare themselves for the formidable task of ruling a great empire. *Topkapı Palace, tel. 212/512–0480. Admission: $4.25, harem $1. Open Wed.–Mon. 9:30–5:30.*

❹ To the left as you enter the outer courtyard of Topkapí Palace, a lane slopes downhill to three museums grouped together: the **Archaeological Museum** (Arkeoloji Müzesi), which houses a fine collection of Greek and Roman antiquities, including finds from Ephesus and Troy; the **Museum of the Ancient Orient** (Eski Şark Eserleri Müzesi), with Sumerian, Babylonian, and Hittite treasures; and the **Tiled Pavilion** (Çinili Köşkü), which houses ceramics from the early Seljuk and Osmanli empires. The admission price covers all three museums. *Tel. 212/520–7740. Admission: $2. Open Tues.–Sun. 9:30–5.*

❺ Just outside the walls of Topkapí Palace is **Hagia Sophia** (Church of the Divine Wisdom), one of the world's greatest examples of Byzantine architecture. Built in AD 532 under the supervision of Emperor Justinian, it took 10,000 men six years to complete. Hagia Sophia is

Archaeological Museum, **4**
Blue Mosque, **6**
Church of St. Irene, **2**
Court of the Janissaries, **3**
Dolmabahçe Palace, **11**
Flower Arcade, **10**
Galata Tower, **9**
Hagia Sophia, **5**
Hippodrome, **7**
Museum of Turkish and Islamic Arts, **8**
Topkapi Palace, **1**

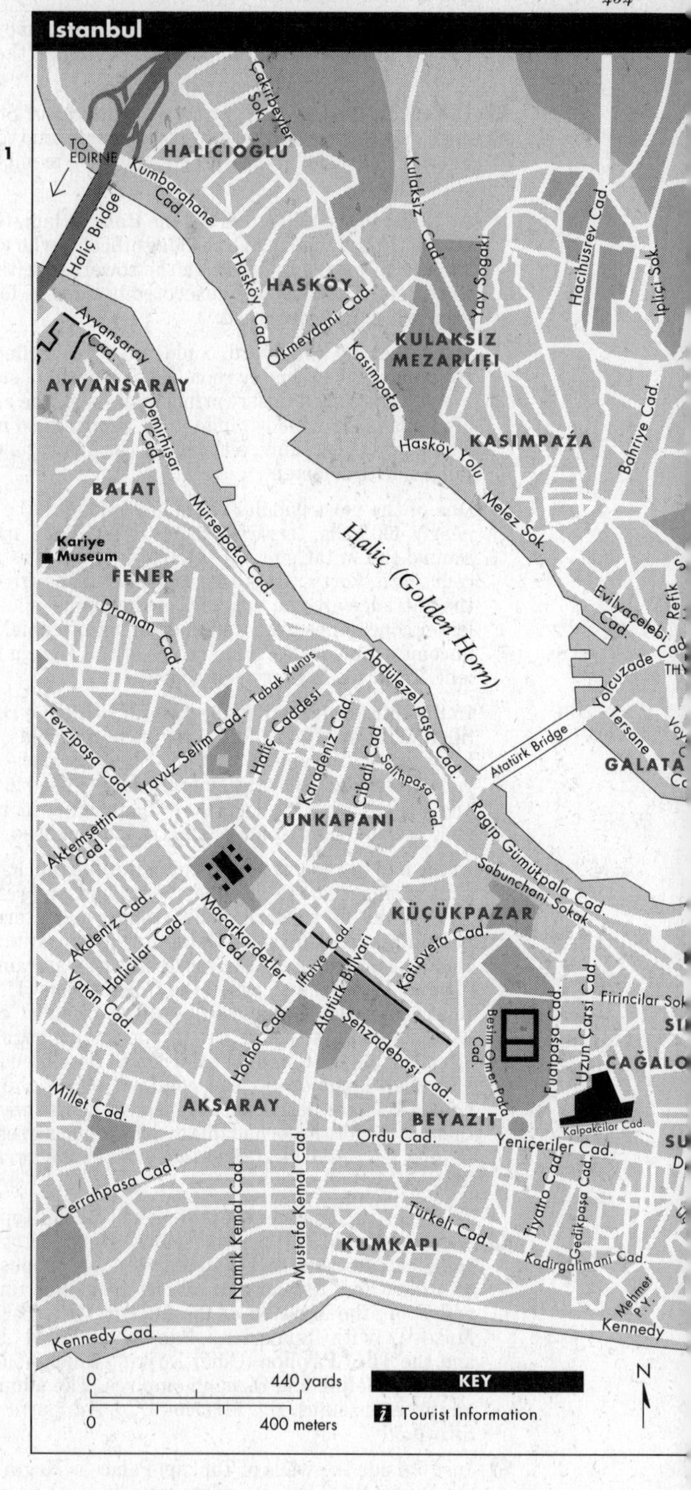

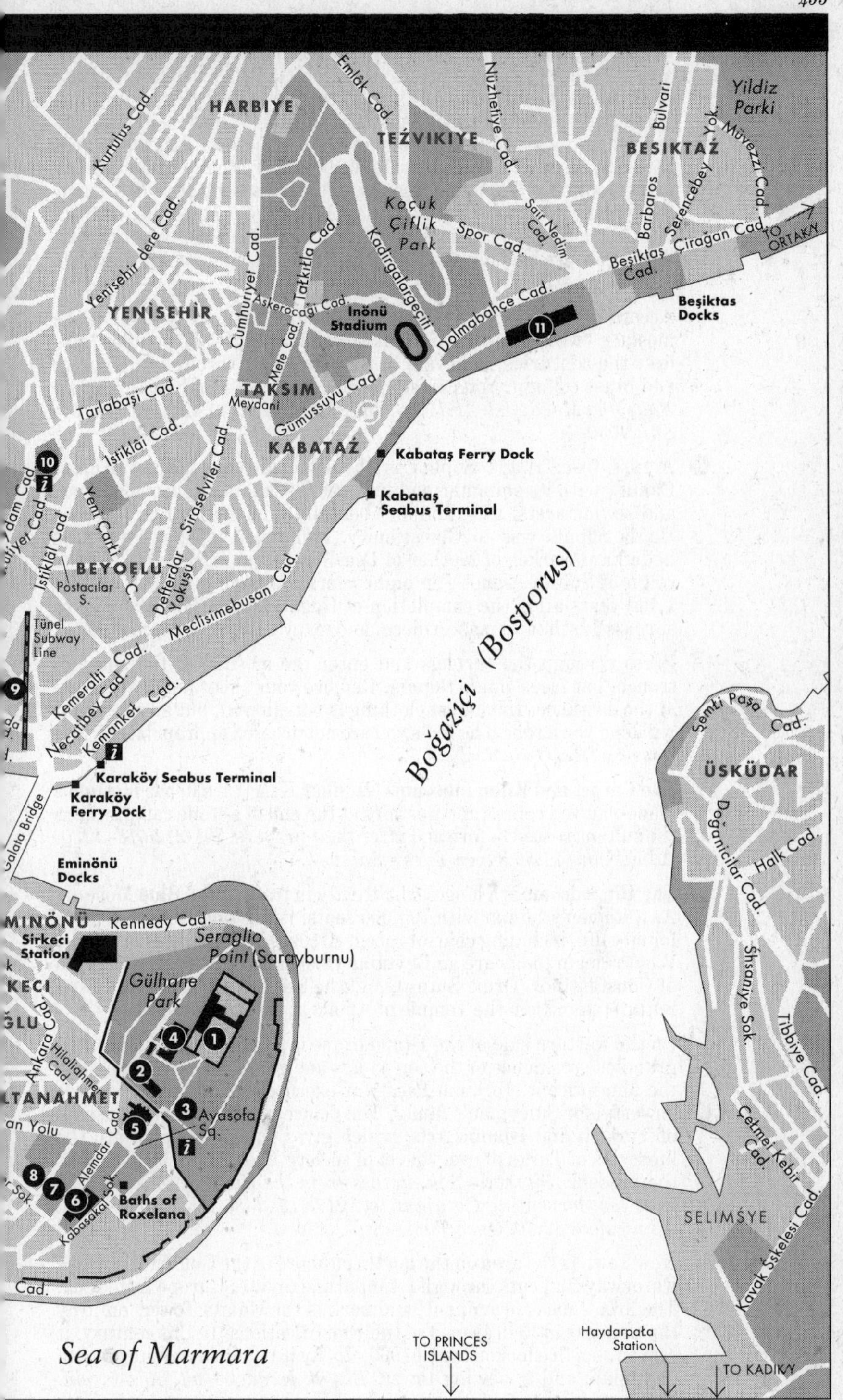
HARBIYE
TEŹVIKIYE
BESIKTAŹ
Yildiz Parki
Emlâk Cad.
Nüzhetiye Cad.
Bulvari
Müvezzi Cad.
Yıl.
Kurtulus Cad.
Koçuk Çiflik Park
Spor Cad.
Sair Nedim Cad.
Barbaros
Serencebey
Çirağan Cad.
TO ORTAKY
Beşiktaş Cad.
Beşiktas Docks
Yenisehir dere Cad.
Cumhuriyet Cad.
Tatkitla Cad.
Kadirgalargeçiti
YENİSEHİR
Askerocaği Cad.
Inönü Stadium
Dolmabahçe Cad.
Mete Cad.
TAKSIM
Meydani
Gümüssuyu Cad.
Tarlabaşi Cad.
Istiklâi Cad.
Siraselviler Cad.
KABATAŹ
Kabataş Ferry Dock
Kabataş Seabus Terminal
Yeni Çarti C.
Istiklâl Cad.
BEYOĖLU
Postacılar S.
Defferdar Yokușu
Meclisimebusan Cad.
Tünel Subway Line
Kemeraltı Cad.
Necatibey Cad.
Kemankeł Cad.
Karaköy Seabus Terminal
Karaköy Ferry Dock
Galata Bridge
Boğaziçi (Bosporus)
Şemti Paşa Cad.
ÜSKÜDAR
Doğanicilar Cad.
Halk Cad.
Eminönü Docks
MINÖNÜ
Kennedy Cad.
Sirkeci Station
Seraglio Point (Sarayburnu)
KECI
GLU
Gülhane Park
Ankara Cad.
Hilaliahmer Cad.
LTANAHMET
an Yolu
Ayasofa Sq.
Alemdar Cad.
Kabasakal Sok.
Baths of Roxelana
Cad.
Shsaniye Sok.
Tibbiye Cad.
Çetmei Kebir Cad.
SELIMŚYE
Kavak Śskelesi Cad.
Sea of Marmara
TO PRINCES ISLANDS
Haydarpała Station
TO KADIKY
1
2
3
4
5
6
7
8
9
10
11

made of ivory from Asia, marble from Egypt, and columns from the ruins of Ephesus. The dome was the world's largest until the dome at St. Peter's Basilica was built in Rome 1,000 years later. Hagia Sophia was the cathedral of Constantinople for 900 years, surviving earthquakes and looting Crusaders until 1453, when it was converted into a mosque by Mehmet the Conqueror. Minarets were added by succeeding sultans. Hagia Sophia originally had many mosaics depicting Christian scenes, which were plastered over by Suleyman I, who felt they were inappropriate for a mosque. In 1935, Atatürk converted Hagia Sophia into a museum. Shortly after that, American archaeologists discovered the mosaics, which were restored and are now on display.

According to legend, the **Sacred Column,** in the north aisle of the mosque, "weeps water" that can work miracles. It's so popular that, over the centuries, believers have worn a hole through the marble and brass column. You can stick your finger in it and make a wish. *Ayasofya Meyd., tel. 212/522–1750. Admission: $4.25. Open Tues.–Sun. 9:30–5.*

❻ Across from Hagia Sophia is the **Blue Mosque** (Sultan Ahmet Camii), with its shimmering blue tiles, 260 stained-glass windows, and six minarets, as grand and beautiful a monument to Islam as Hagia Sophia was to Christianity. Mehmet Aga, also known as Sedefkar (Worker of Mother of Pearl) built the mosque during the reign of Sultan Ahmet I in eight years, beginning in 1609, nearly 1,100 years after the completion of Hagia Sophia. His goal was to surpass Justinian's masterpiece, and many believe he succeeded.

Press through the throngs and enter the mosque at the side entrance that faces Hagia Sophia. Remove your shoes and leave them at the entrance. Immodest clothing is not allowed, but an attendant will lend you a robe if he feels you are not dressed appropriately. *Admission free. Open daily 9–5.*

The **Carpet and Kilim museums** (Hünkar Kasri) are in the mosque's stone-vaulted cellars and upstairs at the end of a stone ramp, where the sultans rested before and after their prayers. *Tel. 212/518–1330. Admission: $1.50. Open Tues.–Sat. 9–4.*

❼ The **Hippodrome** is a long park directly in front of the Blue Mosque. As a Roman stadium with 100,000 seats, it was once the focal point for city life, including chariot races, circuses, and public executions. What remain today are an **Egyptian Obelisk** (Dikilitas), the **Column of Constantinos** (Örme Sütun), and the **Serpentine Column** (Yilanli Sütun) taken from the Temple of Apollo at Delphi in Greece.

On the western side of the Hippodrome is **Ibrahim Paşa Palace,** the grandiose residence of the son-in-law and grand vizier of Suleyman the Magnificent. Ibrahim Paşa was executed when he became too ❽ powerful for Suleyman's liking. The palace now houses the **Museum of Turkish and Islamic Arts,** which gives superb insight into the lifestyles of Turks of every level of society, from the 8th century to the present. *Şifahane Sok, across from the Blue Mosque, in line with the Serpentine Column, tel. 212/518–1385 or 212/518–1805. Admission: $2.50. Open Tues.–Sun. 9:30–5.*

New Town New Town is the area on the northern shore of the Golden Horn, the waterway that cuts through Istanbul and divides Europe from Asia. ❾ The area's most prominent landmark is the **Galata Tower,** built by the Genoese in 1349 as part of their fortifications. In this century, it served as a fire lookout until 1960. Today it houses a restaurant and nightclub, and a viewing tower. *Büyük Hendek Cad. Admission: $1. Open daily 9–8.*

❿ North of the tower is the **Flower Arcade** (Çiçek Pasaji), off Istiklâl Caddesi, a lively blend of tiny restaurants, bars, and street musicians. Strolling farther on Istiklâl Caddesi is an experience in itself. The busy pedestrian road is lined with shops, restaurants, banks, and cafés in turn-of-the-century buildings. The restored original 19th-century tram still carries people from Tunel to Taksim Square. On the side streets you'll find Greek and Armenian churches, bars, and other establishments; in the narrow, poorer residential alleys, you'll see laundry hanging between the old buildings, as you dodge through the children at play.

⓫ The **Dolmabahçe Palace** was built in 1853 and, until the declaration of the modern republic in 1923, was the residence of the last sultans of the Ottoman Empire. It was also the residence of Atatürk, who died here in 1938. The palace, floodlit at night, is an extraordinary mixture of Hindu, Turkish, and European styles of architecture and interior design. Queen Victoria's contribution to the lavishness was a chandelier weighing 4½ tons. Guided tours of the palace take about 80 minutes. *Gümüssuyu Cad., tel. 212/258–5544. Admission: $4.80. Open Apr.–Oct., Tues.–Sun. 9–4; Nov.–Mar., Tues.–Sun. 9–3.*

Shopping The **Grand Bazaar** is what it sounds like: a smattering of all things Turkish—carpets, brass, copper, jewelry, textiles, and leather goods. A shopper's paradise, it lies about ¼ mile northwest of the Hippodrome (*see* Exploring, *above*), a 15-minute walk or 5-minute taxi ride. Also called the Covered Bazaar, this maze of 65 winding, covered streets hides 4,000 shops, tiny cafés, and restaurants. Originally built by Mehmet the Conqueror in the 1450s, it was ravaged by two modern-day fires, one in 1954 that virtually destroyed it, and a smaller one in 1974. In both cases, the bazaar was quickly rebuilt. It's filled with thousands of curios, including carpets, fabrics, clothing, brass ware, furniture, icons, and gold jewelry. *Yeniçeriler Cad. and Fuatpaşa Cad. Admission free. Open Apr.–Oct., Mon.–Sat. 8:30–7; Nov.–Mar., Mon.–Sat. 8:30–6:30.*

Tünel Square, a quick, short metro ride up from Karaköy, is a quaint group of stores with old prints, books, and artifacts.

Bargaining The best part of shopping in Turkey is visiting the *bedestans* (bazaars), all brimming with copper and brass items, hand-painted ceramics, alabaster and onyx goods, fabrics, richly colored carpets, and relics and icons trickling in from the former Soviet Union. The key word for shopping in the bazaars is "bargain." You must be willing to bargain, and bargain hard. It's great fun once you get the hang of it. As a rule of thumb, offer 50% less after you're given the initial price and be prepared to go up by about 25% to 30% of the first asking price. It's both bad manners and bad business to underbid grossly or to start bargaining if you're not serious about buying. Outside the bazaars prices are usually fixed. Beware of antiques: Chances are you will end up with an expensive fake, but even if you do find the genuine article, it's illegal to export antiques of any type.

Limassol, Cyprus

The Mediterranean island of Cyprus was once a center for the cult of Aphrodite, the Greek goddess who is said to have risen naked and perfect from the sea near what is now the beach resort of Paphos. Wooded and mountainous, with a 751-kilometer-long (466-mile-long) coastline, Cyprus lies just off the southern coast of Turkey. Oranges, olives, lemons, grapes, and cherries grow here, and fish are plentiful. The summers are hot and dry; the springs, gentle.

Cyprus's strategic position in the eastern Mediterranean has made it subject to regular invasions by powerful armies. Greeks, Phoenicians, Assyrians, Egyptians, Persians, Romans, and Byzantines—have all ruled here. The influence of diverse cultures adds to the island's appeal to cruise passengers. Many fortifications built by the Crusaders and the Venetians still stand. The tomb of the Prophet

Mohammed's aunt (Hala Sultan Tekke), on the shores of the great salt lake near Larnaca, is one of Islam's most important shrines. A piece of the true cross is said to exist in the Monastery of Stavrovouni, and Paphos has the remains of a pillar to which St. Paul was allegedly tied and beaten for preaching Christianity.

The upheavals are not over. Following independence in 1960, the island became the focus of Greek–Turkish contention. Currently nearly 80% of the population are Greek Cypriots and 18% are Turkish Cypriots. Since 1974 Cyprus has been divided by a thin buffer zone—occupied by United Nations (UN) forces—between the Turkish Cypriot north and the Greek Cypriot south. The zone cuts right through the capital city of Nicosia. Talks aimed at uniting the communities into one bizonal federal state have been going on for years, lately under the auspices of the UN's secretary general.

Currency The monetary unit in the Republic of Cyprus is the Cyprus pound (C£), which is divided into 100 cents. At press time, there was C£0.45 to the U.S. dollar.

Telephones To reach an **AT&T** long-distance operator, dial 080–90010; for **MCI,** 080–90000; for **Sprint,** 080–90001. Public phones may require a deposit of a coin or phone card when you call these services.

Shore Excursions The following are good choices in Limassol. They may not be offered by all cruise lines. Times and prices are approximate.

Paphos Castle. A drive along the southwest of Cyprus leads to vineyards, coastal scenery, and the Paphos castle for a tour. *4½ hrs. Cost: $35.*

Kolossi Castle and Curium Ruins. Visit a Crusader castle and Cyprus's Greek and Roman ruins after a drive through the countryside. *3½ hrs. Cost: $32.*

Omodos Village. The chief attraction of this tour is the Church of the Holy Cross, where there is a silver cross reputed to be a piece of the original cross of Jesus's crucifixion. *3½ hrs. Cost: $34.*

Coming Ashore Ships dock at Limassol, a commercial port and wine-making center on the south coast. The city is a bustling, cosmopolitan town popular with tourists. Luxury hotels, apartments, and guest houses stretch along 12 kilometers (7 miles) of seafront. The nightlife is lively. In central Limassol, the elegant modern shops of Makarios Avenue contrast with those of the old part of town, where you'll discover local handicrafts.

Getting Around Shared taxis accommodate four to seven passengers and are a cheap, fast, and comfortable way of traveling. Drivers are bound by law to use and display a meter. Ask the driver what it will cost before you depart, and don't be afraid to barter. In-town journeys range from C£1.50 to about C£3.

Exploring Limassol Near the old port is **Limassol Fort,** a 14th-century castle built on the site of an earlier Byzantine fortification. According to tradition, Richard the Lionhearted married his future queen of England here in 1191.

The **Cyprus Medieval Museum** at Limassol Fort displays a variety of medieval armor and relics. *Tel. 05/330132. Admission: 50¢. Open weekdays 7:30–5, Sat. 9–5, Sun. 10–1.*

For a glimpse of Cypriot folklore, visit the **Folk Art Museum** on St. Andrew's Street. The collection includes national costumes and fine examples of the island's crafts and woven materials. *Tel. 05/362303. Admission: 30¢. Open Mon. and Wed.–Fri. 8:30–1:30 and 4–7 (winter 3–5:30), Tues. 8:30–1:30.*

The **Troodos Mountains,** north of Limassol, are popular in summer for the shade of their cedar and pine forests and the coolness of their springs. Small, painted churches in the Troodos and Pitsilia foothills are rich examples of a rare indigenous art form. Asinou Church and St. Nicholas of the Roof, south of Kakopetria, are especially noteworthy. Nearby is the Tall Trees Trout Farm, a shady oasis serving delicious fresh fish meals. Be sure to visit the Kykko Monastery, whose prized icon of the Virgin is reputed to have been painted by St. Luke.

Curium (Kourion), west of Limassol, has numerous Greek and Roman ruins. There is an amphitheater, where actors occasionally present classical and Shakespearean drama. Next to the theater is the Villa of Eustolios, a summerhouse that belonged to a wealthy Christian. A nearby Roman stadium has been partially rebuilt. Three kilometers (2 miles) farther along the main Paphos road is the Sanctuary of Apollo Hylates (Apollo of the woodlands), an impressive archaeological site. *Admission: C£1. Open daily 7:30–sunset (winter 7:30–5:30).*

Other places to visit include **Kolossi Castle,** a Crusader castle of the Knights of St. John, a 15-minute drive outside Limassol; and the fishing harbor of **Latchi** on the west coast, 32 kilometers (20 miles) north of Paphos. Near Latchi are the **Baths of Aphrodite,** where the goddess of love is said to have seduced swains. The wild and undeveloped Akamas Peninsula is perfect for a hike.

Lisbon, Portugal

Portugal's capital presents unending treats for the eye. Its wide boulevards are bordered by black-and-white mosaic sidewalks made of tiny cobblestones called *calçada*. Modern, pastel-colored apartment blocks vie for attention with Art Nouveau houses faced with decorative tiles. Winding, hilly streets provide scores of *miradouros,* natural vantage points that offer spectacular views of the river and the city. Lisbon is not easy to explore on foot. The steep inclines of many streets present a tough challenge to cruise passengers, and places that appear to be close to one another on a map are sometimes on different levels. Yet the effort is worthwhile—judicious use of trams, the funicular railway, and the majestic city-center vertical lift (also called the *elevador*) make walking tours enjoyable even on the hottest summer day.

Currency The unit of currency in Portugal is the escudo, which can be divided into 100 centavos. At press time, the exchange rate was about 157$00 to the U.S. dollar.

Telephones Long-distance calls cost less from 8 PM to 7 AM. Collect calls can also be made from post offices. Access numbers to reach American long-distance operators are: for **AT&T,** 050–171288; for **MCI,** 0010–480–0112; for **Sprint,** 050–171877.

Shore Excursions The following are good choices in Lisbon. They may not be offered by all cruise lines. Times and prices are approximate.

Lisbon Highlights. See the Jeronimos Monastery, the Royal Coach Museum, Alfama, Alto Do Parque, and Belem Tower. *4 hrs. Cost: $40.*

Walking the City. Tour the Alfama district on foot, visiting St. George's Castle, Santa Justa Elevator, Rossio Square, and Black Horse Square. *4 hrs. Cost: $32.*

Coming Ashore Ships dock at the Fluvial terminal, adjacent to Praça do Comércio. Lisbon is a hilly city, and the sidewalks are paved with cobblestones, so walking can be tiring, even when you're wearing comfortable shoes.

Getting Around Lisbon's tram service is one of the best in Europe and buses go all over the city. A Tourist Pass for unlimited rides on the tram or bus costs 400$00 for one day's travel. Cabs can be easily recognized by a lighted sign on green roofs. There are taxi stands in the main squares, and you can usually catch one cruising by, though this can be difficult late at night. Taxis are metered and take up to four passengers at no extra charge. Rates start at 300$00.

Numbers in the margin correspond to points of interest on the Lisbon map.

Exploring Lisbon

The Moors, who imposed their rule on most of the southern Iberian Peninsula during the 8th century, left their mark on Lisbon in many ways. The most visible examples are undoubtedly the imposing **Castelo de São Jorge** (St. George's Castle), set on one of the city's highest hills, and the Alfama, a district of narrow, twisting streets that wind their way up toward the castle. The best way to tour this area of Lisbon is to take a taxi to the castle and walk down.

❶

Although the **Castelo de São Jorge** is Moorish in construction, it stands on the site of a fortification used by the Visigoths in the 5th century. The castle walls enclose the ruins of a Muslim palace that was the residence of the kings of Portugal until the 16th century; there is also a small village with a surviving church, a few simple houses, and souvenir shops. Panoramic views of Lisbon can be seen from the walls, but visitors should take care, because the footing is uneven and slippery. *Admission free. Open Apr.–Sept., daily 9–9; Oct.–Mar., daily 9–7.*

❷ **Alfama,** a warren of streets below St. George's Castle, is a jumble of whitewashed houses, with their flower-laden balconies and red-tile roofs resting on a foundation of dense bedrock. It's a notorious place for getting lost, but it's relatively compact, and you'll keep coming upon the same main squares and streets.

❸ The **Museu de Artes Decorativas** (Museum of Decorative Arts) is housed in a 17th-century mansion. More than 20 workshops teach rare handicrafts—bookbinding, ormolu, carving, and cabinetmaking. *Largo das Portas do Sol 2. Admission: 500$00. Open Tues.–Sun. 10–5:30.*

❹ The **Sé** (cathedral), founded in 1150 to commemorate the defeat of the Moors three years earlier, has an austere Romanesque interior enlivened by a splendid 13th-century cloister. *Largo da Sé. Admission to cathedral free, cloister 300$00. Open daily 9–noon and 2–6.*

❺ **Rossío** (officially, Praça Dom Pedro IV), Lisbon's principal square, which in turn opens on its northwestern end into the Praça dos Restauradores, can be considered the beginning of modern Lisbon. Here the broad, tree-lined Avenida da Liberdade begins its northwesterly ascent, and ends just over 1.6 kilometers (1 mile) away at the green expanses of the Parque Eduardo VII.

❻ In the **Parque Eduardo VII,** rare flowers, trees, and shrubs thrive in the *estufa fria* (cold greenhouse) and the *estufa quente* (hot greenhouse). *Parque Eduardo VII. Admission to greenhouses: 75$00. Open winter, daily 9–5; summer, daily 9–6.*

❼ The renowned **Fundação Calouste Gulbenkian** is a cultural trust whose museum houses treasures collected by Armenian oil magnate Calouste Gulbenkian (1869–1955) and donated to the people of Portugal. There are superb examples of Greek and Roman coins, Persian carpets, Chinese porcelain, and paintings by such old masters as Rembrandt and Rubens, as well as Impressionist and pre-Raphaelite works. *Av. de Berna 45, tel. 01/795–0236. Admission: 200$00, free Sun. Open June–Sept., Tues., Thurs., Fri., and Sun. 10–5, Wed. and Sat. 2–7:30; Oct.–May, Tues.–Sun. 10–5.*

❽ In the cozy, clublike lounge at the **Instituto do Vinho do Porto** (Port Wine Institute), visitors can sample from more than 300 types and

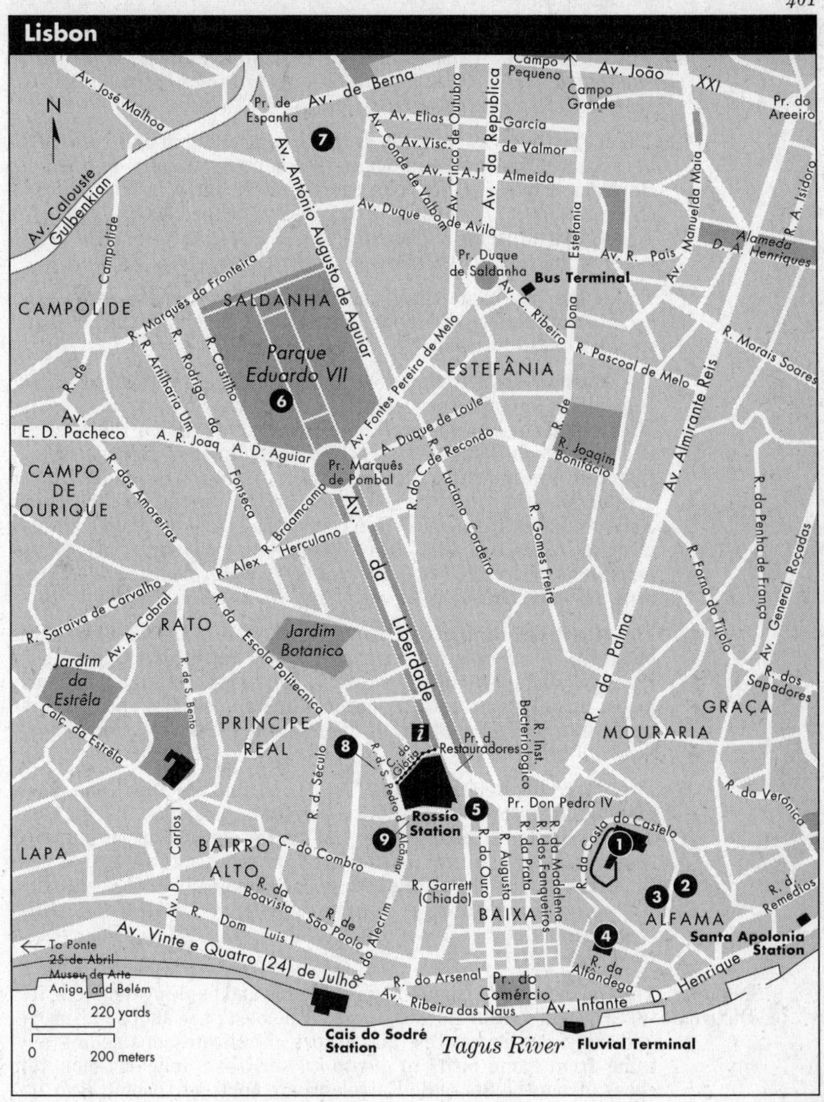

Alfama, **2**

Castelo de São Jorge, **1**

Fundação Calouste Gulbenkian , **7**

Igreja de São Roque, **9**

Instituto do Vinho do Porto, **8**

Museu de Artes Decorativas, **3**

Parque Eduardo VII, **6**

Rossío, **5**

Sé, **4**

vintages of Portugal's most famous beverage—from the extra-dry white varieties to the older ruby-red vintages. *Rua S. Pedro de Alcântara 45, tel. 01/342–3307. Admission free. Prices of tastings vary, starting at 160$00. Open Mon.–Sat. 10–10.*

9 The highly decorative **Igreja de São Roque** (Church of St. Roque) is best known for the flamboyant 18th-century Capela de São João Baptista (Chapel of St. John the Baptist), but it is nonetheless a showpiece in its own right. Adjoining the church is the Museu de Arte Sacra (Museum of Sacred Art). *Church open daily 8:30–6. Museum admission: 250$00. Museum open Tues.–Sun. 10–5.*

To see the best examples of that uniquely Portuguese, late-Gothic architecture known as Manueline, head for **Belém,** at the far southwestern edge of Lisbon.

The **Mosteiro dos Jerónimos** (Jerónimos Monastery), in the Praça do Império, is an impressive structure conceived and planned by King Manuel I at the beginning of the 16th century to honor the discoveries of Vasco da Gama. Construction began in 1502 and was largely financed by treasures brought back from the so-called *descobrimentos*—the "discoveries" made by the Portuguese in Africa, Asia, and South America. Don't miss the stunning double cloister with its arches and pillars heavily sculpted with marine motifs. *Admission to church free, cloisters: 400$00. Open June–Sept., Tues.–Sun. 10–6:30; Oct.–May, Tues.–Sun. 10–1 and 2:30–5.*

The **Museu de Marinha** (Maritime Museum) is at the west end of the Mosteiro dos Jerónimos monastery. Its huge collection reflects Portugal's long seafaring tradition, and exhibits range from early maps, model ships, and navigational instruments to entire fishing boats and royal barges. *Admission: 300$00, free Sun. Open Tues.–Sun. 10–5.*

The **Torre de Belém** (Belém Tower) is another fine example of Manueline architecture, with openwork balconies, loggia, and domed turrets. Although it was built in the early 16th century on an island in the middle of the River Tagus, today the tower stands near the north bank—the river's course has changed over the centuries. *Av. de India. Admission: 400$00 June–Sept., 250$00 Oct.–May. Open June–Sept., Tues.–Sun. 10–6:30; Oct.–May, Tues.–Sun. 10–1 and 2:30–5.*

Shopping Districts

The **Baixa,** one of Lisbon's main shopping and banking districts, features a small crafts market, some of the best shoe shops in Europe, glittering jewelry stores, and a host of delicatessens selling anything from game birds to *queijo da serra*—a delicious mountain cheese from the Serra da Estrela range north of Lisbon. *Rua Augusta between the Rossío and the River Tagus.*

On Avenida Engeneiro Duarte Pacheco, west of Parque Eduardo VII, the blue-and-pink towers of the **Amoreiras,** a huge modern shopping center (open daily 9 AM–11 PM), dominate the Lisbon skyline.

The ***feira da ladra*** (flea market) is held on Tuesday morning and all day Saturday in the Largo de Santa Clara behind the Church of São Vicente, near the Alfama district.

London/Southampton, England

Southampton—a traditional terminal port for transatlantic crossings and the starting point for many historic voyages, including that of the Mayflower—is the port for ships calling at London, a city with a vibrant artistic, cultural, and commercial life. Modern London began to evolve in the Middle Ages, more than 600 years ago, and still standing is much of the work of Christopher Wren, the master architect chiefly responsible for reconstruction after the disastrous Great Fire of 1666. Traditionally London has been divided between the City, to the east, where its banking and commercial interests lie, and Westminster to the west, the seat of the royal court and of government. Today the distinction between the two holds good, and even the briefest exploration will reveal each area's distinct atmosphere. It is also in these two areas that you will find most of the grand buildings that have played a central role in British history: the Tower of London and St. Paul's Cathedral, Westminster Abbey and the Houses of Parliament, Buckingham Palace, and the older royal palace of St. James's.

Currency The British unit of currency is the pound sterling, divided into 100 pence (p). At press time, exchange rates were approximately U.S.$1.54 to the pound.

Telephones The cheapest way to make an overseas call is to dial it yourself. But be sure to have plenty of coins or Phonecards close at hand. After you have inserted the coins or card, dial 010 (the international code), then the country code—for the United States, it is 1—followed by the area code and local number. To reach an **AT&T** long-distance operator, dial 0500890011; for **MCI,** dial 0800890202, and for **Sprint,** dial 0800890877 (from a British Telecom phone) or 0500890877 (from a Mercury Communications phone). To make a collect or other operator-assisted call, dial 155.

Shore Excursions Most cruise lines use Southampton as an embarkation or disembarkation point. Your best bet is to add a few days to your cruise to visit London. You can either arrange your own package or book a line's pre- or post-cruise package.

The following is a good choice should you want to tour sights near Southampton. It may not be offered by all cruise lines. Time and price are approximate.

Salisbury and Stonehenge. An hour from Southampton lies Salisbury Cathedral, which was built in 1220 AD. After a walk through town and lunch, continue to Stonehenge. *Full day. Cost: $90.*

Coming Ashore Ships dock at the Southampton terminal. Southampton's attractions are a short drive from the pier; London is about an hour and a half from Southampton by bus. Places such as Winchester, Stonehenge, Salisbury, and Bath are not far from Southampton.

Getting Around London, although not simple of layout, is a rewarding walking city, and this remains the best way to get to know its nooks and crannies. If you want, you can take "the tube," London's extensive Underground system, which is by far the most widely used form of city transportation. Trains run both beneath and above the ground out into the suburbs, and all stations are clearly marked with the London Underground circular symbol. (A SUBWAY sign refers to an under-the-street crossing.)

There are 10 basic lines, which are all named. The Central, District, Northern, Metropolitan, and Piccadilly lines all have branches, so be sure to note which branch is needed for your particular destination. Electronic platform signs tell you the final stop and route of the next train, and most signs also indicate how many minutes you'll have to wait for the train to arrive. One-day Travelcards are a good buy. These allow unrestricted travel on the tube, most buses, and British Rail trains in the Greater London zones and are valid weekdays after 9:30 AM, weekends, and all public holidays. They cannot be used on airbuses, night buses, or for certain special services. The price is £2.80–£3.80.

London's black taxis are famous for their comfort and for the ability of their drivers to remember the mazelike pattern of the capital's streets. Hotels and main tourist areas have stands where you wait your turn to take one of the taxis that drive up. You can also hail a taxi if the flag is up or the yellow FOR HIRE sign is lighted.

Exploring London

Numbers in the margin correspond to points of interest on the London map.

Westminster is the royal backyard—the traditional center of the royal court and of government. Here, within a kilometer or so of one another, are virtually all of London's most celebrated buildings (St. Paul's Cathedral and the Tower of London excepted), and there is a strong feeling of history all around you. Generations of kings and queens and their offspring have lived here since the end of the 11th century, in no less than four palaces, three of which (Buckingham, St. James's, and Westminster) still stand.

❶ **Trafalgar Square** dates from about 1830. A statue of Lord Nelson, victor over the French in 1805 at the Battle of Trafalgar, at which he lost his life, stands atop a column. Huge stone lions guard the base of the column, which is decorated with four bronze panels depicting naval battles against France and cast from French cannons captured by Nelson. The bronze equestrian statue on the south side of the square is of the unhappy Charles I; he is looking down Whitehall toward the spot where he was executed in 1649.

❷ In the **National Gallery,** which occupies the long neoclassical building on the north side of Trafalgar Square, is a comprehensive collection of paintings, with works from virtually every famous artist and school from the 14th to the 19th century. The gallery is especially strong on Flemish and Dutch masters, Rubens and Rembrandt among them, and on Italian Renaissance works. The Sainsbury Wing houses the early Renaissance collection. *Trafalgar Sq., tel. 0171/839–3321; 0171/839–3526 (recorded information). Admission free; charge for Sainsbury Wing exhibitions. Open Mon.–Sat. 10–6, Sun. 2–6; June–Aug., Wed. until 8.*

At the foot of Charing Cross Road is a second major art collection, ❸ the **National Portrait Gallery,** which contains portraits of well-known (and not so well-known) Britons, including monarchs, statesmen, and writers. *2 St. Martin's Pl., tel. 0171/930–1552. Admission free. Open weekdays 10–5, Sat. 10–6, Sun. 2–6.*

❹ **Buckingham Palace** is the London home of the queen and the administrative hub of the entire royal family. When the queen is in residence (normally on weekdays except in January, August, September, and part of June), the royal standard flies over the east front. Inside there are dozens of splendid state rooms used on such formal occasions as banquets for visiting heads of state. The private apartments of Queen Elizabeth and Prince Philip are in the north wing. Behind the palace lie some 40 acres of private gardens, a wildlife haven. The ceremony of the Changing of the Guard takes place in front of the palace at 11:30 daily, May through July, and on alternate days during the rest of the year. It's advisable to arrive early, since people are invariably stacked several deep along the railings, whatever the weather. Parts of Buckingham Palace are open to the public during August and September; the former chapel, bombed during World War II, rebuilt in 1961, and now the Queen's Gallery, shows paintings from the vast royal art collections from March through December. *Buckingham Palace Rd., tel. 0171/493–3175. Admission: £8. Queen's Gallery, tel. 0171/799–2331. Admission: £3. Open Tues.–Sat. and bank holidays 10–5, Sun. 2–5; closed between exhibitions.*

❺ **Parliament Square** is flanked, on the river side, by the Palace of Westminster. Among the statues of statesmen long since dead are those of Churchill, Abraham Lincoln, and Oliver Cromwell, the Lord Protector of England during the country's brief attempt at being a republic (1648–60).

❻ **Westminster Abbey** is the most ancient of London's great churches and the most important, for it is here that Britain's monarchs are crowned. It is unusual for a church of this size and national importance not to be a cathedral. The abbey dates largely from the 13th and 14th centuries, although Henry VII's Chapel, an exquisite example of the heavily decorated late-Gothic style, was not built until the early 1600s, and the twin towers over the west entrance are an 18th-century addition. There is much to see inside, including the touching tomb of the Unknown Warrior, a nameless World War I soldier buried, in memory of the war's victims, in earth brought with his corpse from France; and the famous Poets' Corner, where England's great writers—Milton, Chaucer, Shakespeare, et al—are memorialized, and some are actually buried. Behind the high altar are the royal tombs, including those of Queen Elizabeth I; Mary, Queen of Scots; and Henry V. In the Chapel of Edward the Confessor stands the Coronation Chair. Among the royal weddings that have taken place here are those of the present queen and most recently, in 1986, the duke and duchess of York. *Broad Sanctuary, tel. 0171/222–5152. Admission to the nave is free; to Poets' Corner and Royal Chapels: £4 (Royal Chapels, free Wed. 6–7:45 PM). Open weekdays 9–4, Sat. 9–2 and 3:45–5; Sun. all day for services only; museum and cloisters open Sun.; closed weekdays to visitors during services; Royal Chapels closed Sun. No photography except Mon. eve.*

❼ **Hyde Park,** which covers about 340 acres, was originally a royal hunting ground, while Kensington Gardens, which adjoins it to the west, started life as part of the royal Kensington Palace. These two parks contain many fine trees and are a haven for wildlife. The sandy track that runs along the south edge of the parks has been a fashionable riding trail for centuries. Though it's called Rotten Row, there's nothing rotten about it. The name derives from *route du roi* (the King's Way)—the route William III and Queen Mary took from their home at Kensington Palace to the court at St. James's. There is boating and swimming in the Serpentine, the S-shaped lake formed by damming a stream that used to flow here. Refreshments are served at the lakeside tearooms, and the Serpentine Gallery (tel. 0171/402–6075) holds noteworthy exhibitions of modern art.

❽ London's **Science Museum** is the leading national collection of science and technology, with extensive hands-on exhibits on outer space, astronomy, computers, transportation, and medicine. *Tel. 0171/938–8000; 0171/938–8123 (recorded information). Admission: £4.50. Open Mon.–Sat. 10–6, Sun. 11–6.*

❾ The **Natural History Museum** is housed in an ornate late-Victorian building with striking modern additions. As in the Science Museum, its displays on topics such as human biology and evolution are designed to challenge visitors to think for themselves. *Cromwell Rd., tel. 0171/938–9123; 0142/692–7654 (recorded information). Admission: £5; free weekdays 4:30–5:50. Open Mon.–Sat. 10–6, Sun. 2:30–6.*

❿ The **Victoria and Albert Museum** (or V&A) originated in the 19th century as a museum of decorative art and has extensive collections of costumes, paintings, jewelry, and crafts from every part of the globe. The collections from India, China, and the Islamic world are especially strong. *Cromwell Rd., tel. 0171/938–8500; 0171/938–8441 (recorded information). Suggested voluntary contribution: £4.50. Open Mon.–Sat. 10–5:50, Sun. 2:30–5:50.*

⓫ The **British Museum** houses a vast and priceless collection of treasures, including Egyptian, Greek, and Roman antiquities; Renaissance jewelry; pottery; coins; glass; and drawings from virtually every European school since the 15th century. It's best to pick out one section that particularly interests you—to try to see everything would be an overwhelming and exhausting task. Some of the high-

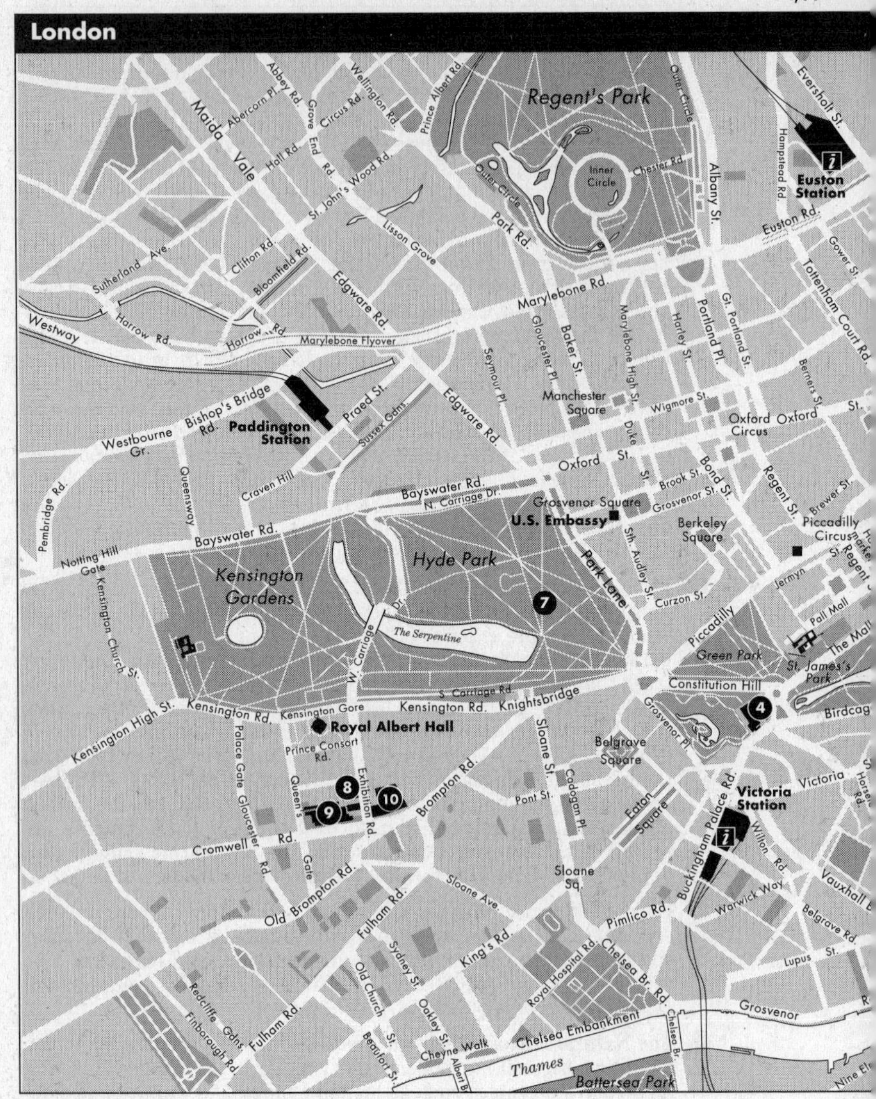

British Museum, **11**
Buckingham Palace, **4**
Hyde Park, **7**
Lloyd's of London, **13**
National Gallery, **2**
National Portrait Gallery, **3**
Natural History Museum, **9**
Parliament Square, **5**
St. Paul's Cathedral, **12**
Science Museum, **8**
Tower of London, **14**
Trafalgar Square, **1**
Victoria and Albert Museum, **10**
Westminster Abbey, **6**

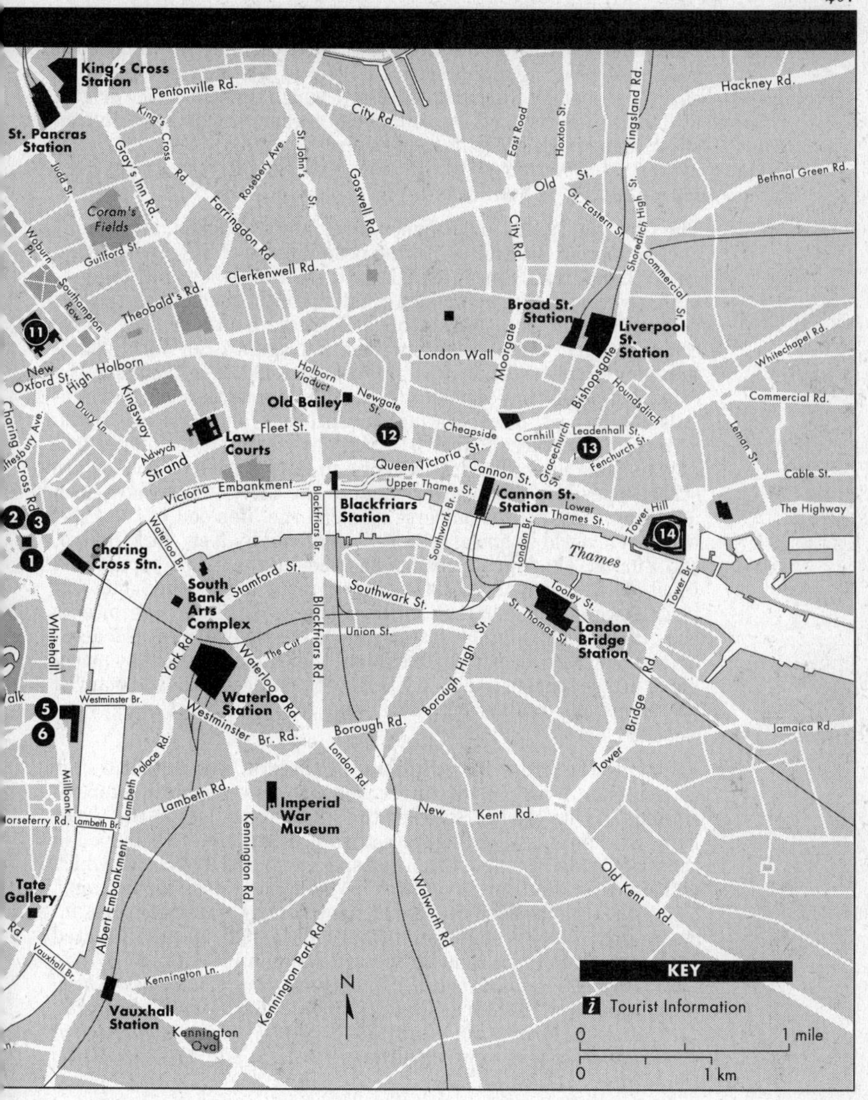
King's Cross Station
St. Pancras Station
Pentonville Rd.
City Rd.
Hackney Rd.
Kingsland Rd.
East Road
Hoxton St.
Old St.
Bethnal Green Rd.
Gt. Eastern St.
Shoreditch High St.
Commercial St.
Gray's Inn Rd.
King's Cross Rd.
Rosebery Ave.
St. John's St.
Goswell Rd.
City Rd.
Farringdon Rd.
Judd St.
Coram's Fields
Guilford St.
Woburn Pl.
Southampton Row
Clerkenwell Rd.
Theobald's Rd.
Broad St. Station
Liverpool St. Station
London Wall
Moorgate
Bishopsgate
Whitechapel Rd.
Houndsditch
Commercial Rd.
New Oxford St.
High Holborn
Holborn Viaduct
Newgate St.
Old Bailey
Kingsway
Drury Ln.
Fleet St.
Law Courts
Cheapside
Cornhill
Leadenhall St.
Fenchurch St.
Gracechurch St.
Leman St.
Charing Cross Rd.
Aldwych
Strand
Queen Victoria St.
Cannon St.
Cable St.
Victoria Embankment
Upper Thames St.
Blackfriars Br.
Blackfriars Station
Southwark Br.
Cannon St. Station
London Br.
Lower Thames St.
Tower Hill
The Highway
Waterloo Br.
Charing Cross Stn.
Stamford St.
Thames
South Bank Arts Complex
Southwark St.
Tooley St.
St. Thomas St.
Tower Br.
Blackfriars Rd.
Union St.
London Bridge Station
Whitehall
York Rd.
The Cut
Waterloo Rd.
Borough High St.
Waterloo Station
Westminster Br.
Westminster Br. Rd.
Borough Rd.
London Rd.
Tower Bridge Rd.
Jamaica Rd.
Millbank
Lambeth Palace Rd.
Lambeth Rd.
Imperial War Museum
New Kent Rd.
Horseferry Rd.
Lambeth Br.
Kennington Rd.
Old Kent Rd.
Tate Gallery
Albert Embankment
Walworth Rd.
Vauxhall Br.
Kennington Park Rd.
Kennington Ln.
Vauxhall Station
Kennington Oval
N
KEY
Tourist Information
0
1 mile
0
1 km

lights are the Elgin Marbles, sculptures that formerly decorated the Parthenon in Athens; the Rosetta Stone, which helped archaeologists interpret Egyptian script; a copy of the Magna Carta, the charter signed by King John in 1215 to which is ascribed the origins of English liberty; and the Mildenhall treasure, a cache of Roman silver found in East Anglia in 1842. *Great Russell St., tel. 0171/636–1555; 0171/580–1788 (recorded information). Admission free. Open Mon.–Sat. 10–5, Sun. 2:30–6.*

The City, the traditional commercial center of London, is the most ancient part of the capital, having been the site of the great Roman city of Londinium. Since those days, the City has been built and rebuilt several times. The wooden buildings of the medieval City were destroyed in the Great Fire of 1666. There were further waves of reconstruction in the 19th century, and then again after World War II to repair the devastation wrought by air attacks. The 1980s saw the construction of many mammoth office developments, some undistinguished, others incorporating adventurous and exciting ideas. Throughout all these changes, the City has retained its unique identity and character. The lord mayor and Corporation of London are still responsible for the government of the City, as they have been for many centuries. Commerce remains the lifeblood of the City, which is a world financial center rivaled only by New York, Tokyo, and Zurich. The biggest change has been in the City's population. Until the first half of the 19th century, many of the merchants and traders who worked in the City lived there, too. Today, despite its huge daytime population, scarcely 8,000 people live in the 677 acres of the City. Try, therefore, to explore the City on a weekday morning or afternoon. On weekends its streets are deserted, and many of the shops and restaurants, and even some of the churches, are closed.

⓬ Following the Great Fire, **St. Paul's Cathedral** was rebuilt by Sir Christopher Wren, the architect who was also responsible for designing 50 City parish churches to replace those lost in the Great Fire. St. Paul's is Wren's greatest work. Fittingly, he is buried in the crypt under a simple Latin epitaph, composed by his son, which translates as: "Reader, if you seek his monument, look around you." The cathedral has been the site of many famous state occasions, including the funeral of Winston Churchill in 1965 and the ill-fated marriage of the Prince and Princess of Wales in 1981. *Tel. 0171/248–2705. Admission to cathedral free; Ambulatory (American Chapel), Crypt, and Treasury: £3; to galleries: £2.50; combined ticket: £5. Cathedral open Mon.–Sat. 7:30–6, Sun. 8–6; the Ambulatory, Crypt, and Galleries open weekdays 10–4:15, Sat. 11–4:15. Tours weekdays 11, 11:30, 2, 2:30.*

⓭ One of the most striking pieces of contemporary City architecture is the headquarters of **Lloyd's of London,** designed by the modernist architect Richard Rogers, whose other famous work is Paris's Pompidou Center. The underwriters of Lloyd's provide insurance for everything imaginable, from oil rigs to a pianist's fingers, though they suffered a crash in 1993, with most of the so-called Names, whose millions formed Lloyd's backbone, losing major money. *1 Lime St., tel. 0171/623–7100. Admission free.*

⓮ The **Tower of London** is one of London's most famous sights and one of its most crowded, too. Come as early in the day as possible and head for the Crown Jewels, so you can see them before the crowds arrive. The tower served the monarchs of medieval England as both fortress and palace. Every British sovereign from William the Conqueror in the 11th century to Henry VIII in the 16th lived here, and it remains a royal palace, in name at least. *Tower Hill, tel. 0171/709–0765. Admission: £7.95. Open Mar.–Oct., Mon.–Sat. 9:30–6, Sun. 10–6; Nov.–Feb., Mon.–Sat. 9:30–4. Subject to weather and availa-*

bility of guides, tours are conducted about every 30 mins until 3:30 in summer, 2:30 in winter.

Shopping Shopping is one of London's great pleasures. Different areas retain their traditional specialties. **Chelsea** centers on the King's Road; once synonymous with ultrafashion, it still harbors some designer boutiques, plus antiques and home-furnishings stores. **Covent Garden** is a something-for-everyone neighborhood, with clothing chain stores and top designers, stalls selling crafts, and shops selling gifts of every type—bikes, kites, herbs, beads, hats, you name it. Crowded **Oxford Street** is past its prime and lined with tawdry discount shops. Selfridges, John Lewis, and Marks and Spencer are good department stores, though, and there are interesting boutiques secreted off Oxford Street, just north of the Bond Street tube stop, in little St. Christopher's Place and Gees Court.

Perpendicular to Oxford Street lies **Regent Street,** with possibly London's most pleasant department store, Liberty's, as well as Hamley's, the capital's toy mecca. Shops around once-famous **Carnaby Street** stock designer youth paraphernalia and 57 varieties of T-shirts. **South Molton Street** offers high-price high-style fashion—especially at Browns—and the tailors of Savile Row are of worldwide repute. In **St. James's** the English gentleman buys the rest of his gear: handmade hats, shirts, and shoes, silver shaving kits, and hip flasks. Here is also the world's best cheese shop, Paxton & Whitfield. Nothing in this neighborhood is cheap, in any sense.

Kensington's main drag, **Kensington High Street,** is a smaller, classier version of Oxford Street, with some larger stores at the eastern end. Try Kensington Church Street for expensive antiques, plus a little fashion. Neighboring **Knightsbridge** has Harrods, of course, but also Harvey Nichols, the top clothes stop, and many expensive designers' boutiques along Sloane Street, Walton Street, and Beauchamp Place.

Piccadilly is a busy street lined with some grand and very English shops (including Hatchards, the booksellers; Swaine, Adeney Brigg, the equestrian outfitters; and Fortnum and Mason, the department store that supplies the queen's groceries). **Jermyn Street,** south of Piccadilly, is famous for upscale shops that sell accessories for the gentleman's wardrobe, from handmade shoes to bespoke hats (his suits come from nearby Savile Row). Shops along **Duke Street** and **Bury Street** specialize in paintings, the former in old masters, the latter in early English watercolors. Don't be put off by the exclusive appearance of these establishments—anyone is free to enter, and there is no obligation to buy. **King Street** is home to Christie's, the fine-art auctioneer, and to Spink and Son, renowned for Asian art.

There are three special shopping streets in Mayfair, each with its own specialties. **Savile Row** is the home of gentlemen's tailors. Nearby **Cork Street** has many dealers in modern and classical art. **Bond Street** (divided into two parts, Old and New, though both are some 300 years old) is the classiest shopping street in London, the home of haute couture, with such famous names as Gucci, Hermès, and Chanel, and costly jewelry from such shops as Asprey, Tiffany, and Cartier.

North of Kensington Gardens is the lively **Notting Hill** district, full of restaurants and cafés where young people gather. The best-known attraction in this area is Portobello Road, where the lively antiques and bric-a-brac market is held each Saturday (arrive early in the morning for the best bargains). The street is also full of regular antiques shops that are open most weekdays.

The Piazza, the **Victorian Market Building,** is now a vibrant shopping center, with numerous boutiques, crafts shops, and cafés. On the south side of the market building is the lively and much less formal Jubilee market, with crafts and clothing stalls.

Napoli Coast, Italy

Campania (the region of Naples, the Amalfi coast, and other sights) is where most people's preconceived ideas of Italy become a reality. You'll find lots of sun, good food that relies heavily on tomatoes and mozzarella, acres of classical ruins, and gorgeous scenery.

Currency The unit of currency in Italy is the lira (plural, lire). At press time, the exchange rate was about 1,546 lire to the dollar. When your purchases run into hundreds of thousands of lire, beware of being shortchanged, a dodge that is practiced at ticket windows and cashiers' desks, as well as in shops and even banks. Always count your change before you leave the counter.

Telephones To place international calls, many travelers go to the Telefoni telephone exchange, where the operator assigns you a booth, can help place your call, and will collect payment when you have finished. Telefoni exchanges (usually marked TELECOM) are found in all cities. To dial an international call, insert a phone card, dial 00, then the country code, area code, and phone number. The cheaper and easier option, however, will be to use your AT&T, MCI, or Sprint calling card. For **AT&T,** dial access number 172–1011; for **MCI,** dial access number 172–1022; for **Sprint,** dial access number 172–1877. You will be connected directly with an operator in the United States.

Shore Excursions The following are good choices on the Napoli Coast. They may not be offered by all cruise lines. Times and prices are approximate.

In Naples **Naples and Pompeii.** See the main attractions of Naples before traveling by motor coach to the ruins at Pompeii. *3½ hrs. Cost: $55.*

Heraculaneum and Naples. The well-preserved ruins at Heraklion and downtown Naples are the focus of this two-town tour. *3½ hrs. Cost: $52.*

In Sorrento **Excavations at Pompeii.** Here's another chance to see the ruins at Pompeii. *4 hrs. Cost: $55.*

Amalfi Drive. Journey for two hours along the seaboard between Sorrento and Amalfi, where you will have some free time to stroll. *5½ hrs. Cost: $70.*

In Capri Capri is a place to wander, not tour. Cruise lines will arrange round-trip tickets on the public jetfoil for passengers wishing to visit Capri.

In Amalfi Cruise lines often offer excursions featuring the Amalfi coast, from Naples or Sorrento. You can also arrange to hire a car, often through the ship's tour desk.

Coming Ashore Ships calling on the Napoli Coast generally drop anchor offshore. Nearby towns are easily reached from the major ports of call.

In Naples Ships calling at Naples tender passengers ashore from Naples Bay. You'll probably do a lot of walking in Naples, since the buses are crowded and taxis get stalled in traffic. Keep a firm grip on your pocketbook and camera.

In Sorrento Ships calling at Sorrento tender passengers to shore from the town's harbor. Sorrento is best explored on foot, since motor coaches must remain in designated areas.

In Capri The trip on the public jetfoil to Capri is about a 20-minute ride from Sorrento or about a 40-minute ride from Naples. A cog railway or bus service takes you up to the town of Capri from the marina.

In Amalfi Amalfi is a within driving distance of Naples or Sorrento. Once in town, you will want to wander around on foot.

Exploring the Napoli Coast

Naples

The 17th-century **Palazzo Reale** (Royal Palace), built during the rule of the Bourbons, is still furnished in the lavish Baroque style that suited the Bourbons so well. *Piazza del Plebiscito, tel. 081/413888. Admission: 8,000 lire. Open Apr.–Oct., Tues.–Sun. 9–7:30; Nov.–Mar., Tues.–Sun. 9–1:30.*

The massive stone **Castel Nuovo,** which was built by the city's Aragon rulers in the 13th century, has some rooms recently opened to the public that contain sculptures and frescoes that date from the 14th and 15th centuries. *Admission: 5,000 lire. Open weekdays 9–2, Sat. 9–1.*

A favorite Neapolitan song celebrates the quiet beauty of the church of **Santa Chiara,** which was built in the early 1300s in Provençal Gothic style. Directly across is the oddly faceted stone facade and elaborate Baroque interior of the church of the **Gesù** (Via Benedetto Croce). *Off Via Toledo, also known as Via Rome.*

The museum in the **Certosa di San Martino,** a Carthusian monastery restored in the 17th century, contains an eclectic collection of Neapolitan landscape paintings, royal carriages, and *presepi* (Christmas crèches). Check out the view from the balcony off Room 25. *Certosa di San Martino, tel. 081/578–1769. Admission: 8,000 lire. Open Tues.–Sun. 9–2.*

The **Museo Archeologico Nazionale** is dusty, unkempt, and undergoes perpetual renovations, but it holds one of the world's great collections of antiquities. Greek and Roman sculptures, vividly colored mosaics, countless objects from Pompeii and Herculaneum, and an equestrian statue of the Roman emperor Nerva are all worth seeing. *Piazza Museo, tel. 081/440166. Admission: 12,000 lire. Open May–Sept., Mon.–Sat. 9–7, Sun. 9–1; Oct.–Apr., Mon.–Sat. 9–2, Sun. 9–1.*

The **Museo di Capodimonte,** housed in an 18th-century palace built by Bourbon king Charles III, is surrounded by a vast park that must have been lovely when it was better cared for. In the picture gallery are some fine Renaissance paintings; climb the stairs to the terrace for a magnificent view of Naples and the bay. Downstairs you can visit the State Apartments and see the extensive collection of porcelain, much of it produced in the Bourbons' own factory right here on the grounds. *Parco di Capodimonte, tel. 081/744–1307. Admission: 12,000 lire. Open Apr.–Oct., Tues.–Sun. 9–7:30; Nov.–Mar., Tues.–Sun. 9–2.*

Near Naples is **Pompeii,** where an estimated 2,000 residents were entombed on that fateful August day when Mt. Vesuvius erupted in AD 79. The ancient city of Pompeii was much larger than nearby Herculaneum, and excavations have progressed to a much greater extent (though the remains are not as well preserved, owing to some 18th-century scavenging for museum-quality artwork, most of which you are able to see at Naples's Museo Archeologico Nazionale; *see above*). This prosperous Roman city had an extensive forum, lavish baths and temples, and patrician villas richly decorated with frescoes. It's worth buying a detailed guide of the site to give meaning and understanding to the ruins and their importance. Be sure to see the Villa dei Misteri, whose frescoes are in mint condition. Perhaps that is a slight exaggeration, but the paintings are so rich with detail and depth of color that one finds it difficult to believe that they are more than 1,900 years old. Have lots of small change handy to tip the guards at the more important houses so they will unlock the gates for you. *Pompeii Scavi, tel. 081/861–0744. Admission: 10,000 lire. Open daily 9–1 hr before sunset (ticket office closes 2 hrs before sunset).*

Sorrento The **Museo Correale,** an attractive 18th-century villa, houses an interesting collection of decorative arts (furniture, china, and so on) and paintings of the Neapolitan school. *Via Correale. Admission: 5,000 lire; gardens only, 3,000 lire. Open Apr.–Sept., Mon. and Wed.–Sat. 9–12:30 and 4–6, Sun. 9–12:30; Oct.–Mar., Mon. and Wed.–Sat. 9–12 and 3–5, Sun. 9–8.*

Capri Stroll the **Piazzetta,** a choice place from which to watch the action, and window-shop expensive boutiques or browse in souvenir shops along Via Vittorio Emanuele on your way to the **Gardens of Augustus,** which have gorgeous views. The town of Capri is deliberately commercial and self-consciously picturesque.

To get away from the crowds, hike to **Villa Jovis,** one of the many villas that Roman emperor Tiberius built on the island, at the end of a lane that climbs steeply uphill. The walk takes about 45 minutes, with pretty views all the way and a final spectacular vista of the entire Bay of Naples and part of the Gulf of Salerno. *Villa Jovis, Via Tiberio. Admission: 4,000 lire. Open daily 9–1 hr before sunset.*

In Anacapri there is the little church of **San Michele,** off Via Orlandi, where a magnificent hand-painted majolica-tile floor shows you an 18th-century vision of the Garden of Eden. You'll need to take a bus or a jaunty open taxi. *Open Easter–Oct., daily 7–7; Nov.–Easter, daily 10–3.*

Villa San Michele is the charming former home of Swedish scientist-author Axel Munthe. *Via Axel Munthe. Admission: 5,000 lire. Open May–Sept., daily 9–6; Nov.–Feb., daily 10:30–3:30; Mar., daily 9:30–4:30; Apr. and Oct., daily 9:30–5.*

Amalfi The main historical attraction is the **Duomo** or Cathedral of St. Andrew, which shows a mix of Moorish and early Gothic influences. The interior is a 10th-century Romanesque skeleton in an 18th-century Baroque dress. *Admission free. Open daily 7–noon and 4–6:30.*

The village of **Ravello,** 8 kilometers (5 miles) north of Amalfi, is not actually on the coast, but on a high mountain bluff overlooking the sea. The road up to it is a series of switchbacks, and the village itself clings precariously on the mountain spur. The village flourished during the 13th century and then fell into a tranquillity that has remained unchanged for the past six centuries.

The center of Ravello is **Piazza Duomo,** with its cathedral, founded in 1087 and recently restored. Note the fine bronze 12th-century doors and, inside, two pulpits richly decorated with mosaics: one depicting the story of Jonah and the whale; the other—more splendid—carved with fantastic beasts and resting on a pride of lions.

The 11th-century **Villa Rufolo** in Ravello is where the composer Richard Wagner once stayed, and there is a Wagner festival every summer on the villa's garden terrace. There is a Moorish cloister with interlacing pointed arches, beautiful gardens, an 11th-century tower, and a belvedere with a fine view of the coast. *Admission: 3,000 lire. Open summer, daily 9:30–1 and 3–7:30; winter, daily 9:30–1 and 2–4:30.*

At the entrance to the **Villa Cimbrone** is a small cloister that looks medieval but was actually built in 1917, with two bas-reliefs: one representing nine Norman warriors, the other illustrating the seven deadly sins. Then, the long avenue leads through peaceful gardens scattered with grottoes, small temples, and statues to a belvedere and terrace, where, on a clear day, the view stretches out over the Mediterranean Sea. *Admission: 5,000 lire. Open daily 8:30–1 hr before sunset.*

Norwegian Coast and Fjords

Norway's Far North, land of the summertime midnight sun, offers picturesque scenery and quaint towns. The fjords continue northward from Bergen all the way to Kirkenes, at Norway's border with Finland and Russia. Norway's Far North is for anyone eager to hike, climb, fish, bird-watch for seabirds, see Samiland (land of the Sami, or "Lapps"), or experience the unending days of nighttime sun in June and July.

The major towns north of Bergen are Ålesund, Trondheim, Bodø, Narvik, Tromsø, Hammerfest, and Kirkenes. The best way to reach these places is by ship, whether cruise ship or coastal ferry (*see* Chapter 2).

Currency The unit of currency in Norway is the krone, written as Kr. on price tags but officially written as NOK (bank designation), NKr, or kr. The exchange rate at press time was NKr 6.5 to the dollar.

Telephones Norway's phone system is not as expensive as one might fear. International calls can be made from any pay phone. For calls to North America, dial 095–1, then the area code and number. You will need to dial 00 for an international connection. To reach an **AT&T** long-distance operator, dial 80019011; for **MCI,** dial 180019912; and for **Sprint,** 180019877.

Coming Ashore Ships calling at Tromsø, Bodø, and Trondheim dock in the harbor, which is the lifeline of all the towns along the Norwegian coast.

Getting Around Attractions are close by the pier, and the best way to explore these ports is on foot.

Shore Excursions The following are good choices in the towns along Norway's coast. They may not be offered by all cruise lines. Times and prices are approximate.

In Trondheim **City Tour.** A visit to an open-air folk museum is the highlight of this tour, which also visits Nidaros Cathedral, which is built on the grave of St. Olav, who founded the city in AD 997. *3 hrs. Cost: $35.*

City View with Ringve Museum. You'll drive through the city on your way to the Ringve Museum of Musical Instruments, which is housed in a manor overlooking the fjord. *3 hrs. Cost: $38.*

In Bodø **Tour of Kjerringoy.** From Bodø, head off for Kjerringoy, which gained independence from Norway in 1800. Once there, you'll have time to wander the city's Central Square and streets. *Half day. Cost: $15.*

In Tromsø **Museum, Cathedral, and Cable Car.** Visit the Tromsø Museum before driving around the island of Troms. Pass Lake Prestvtn, where the Northern Lights Observatory is located, to reach Tromsø Bridge for a visit to Tromsdalen Church, known as the Arctic Cathedral. The tour includes a ride on the cable car to Storsteinen. *3½ hrs. Cost: $40.*

Museum, Cathedral, and Planetarium. Visit the museum and cathedral as well as the Northern Lights Planetarium, which opened in 1989. At the planetarium you will see a film on a 360-degree screen about, of course, the Aurora Borealis. *3 hrs. Cost: $40.*

Exploring Trondheim Construction of Scandinavia's largest medieval building, **Nidaros Domkirke** (cathedral), started in 1320 but was not completed until the early 1920s. For centuries, Niadaros Domkirke drew religious pilgrims. Norwegian kings were crowned here, and the crown jewels are still on display.

Scandinavia's two largest wooden buildings are in Trondheim. One is the rococo **Stiftsgården,** a royal palace built in 1774. The other is a student dormitory.

Exploring Bodø Bodø was bombed by the Germans in 1940. The stunning, contemporary **Bodø Cathedral,** its spire separated from the main building, was built after the war. Inside are rich, modern tapestries; outside is a war memorial.

The **Nordland County Museum** depicts the life of the Sami, as well as regional history. *Prinsengt. 116, tel. 75526128. Admission free. Open weekdays 9–3, weekends noon–3.*

Exploring Tromsø Be sure to see the spectacular **Ishavskatedral** (cathedral), with its eastern wall made entirely of stained glass, across the long stretch of **Tromsø bridge.** Coated in aluminum, the bridge's triangular peaks make a bizarre mirror for the midnight sun.

Be sure to walk around old Tromsø (along the waterfront) and to visit the **Tromsø Museum,** which concentrates on science, the Sami, and northern churches. *Lars Thøringsvei 10, Folkeparken; take Bus 27 or 22. Admission: NKr 10. Open June–Aug., daily 9–9; Sept.–May, weekdays 8:30–3:30, Sat. noon–3, Sun. 11–4.*

Oslo, Norway

Although it's one of the world's largest capital cities in area, Oslo has only about 475,000 inhabitants. The foundations for modern Norwegian culture were laid here in the 19th century, during the period of union with Sweden, which lasted until 1905. Oslo blossomed at this time, and Norway produced its three greatest men of arts and letters: composer Edvard Grieg (1843–1907), dramatist Henrik Ibsen (1828–1906), and painter Edvard Munch (1863–1944). The polar explorers Roald Amundsen and Fridtjof Nansen also lived during this period.

In recent years, the city has taken off: Shops are open late, and pubs, cafés, and restaurants are crowded at all hours. The downtown area is compact, but the geographic limits of Oslo spread out to include forests, fjords, and mountains, which give the city a pristine airiness that complements its urban dignity. Explore downtown on foot, then venture beyond via bus, streetcar, or train.

Currency The unit of currency in Norway is the krone, written as Kr. on price tags but officially written as NOK (bank designation), NKr, or kr. The exchange rate at press time was NKr 6.5 to the dollar.

Telephones Norway's phone system is not as expensive as one might fear. International calls can be made from any pay phone. For calls to North America, dial 095–1, then the area code and number. You will need to dial 00 for an international connection. To reach an **AT&T** long-distance operator, dial 80019011; for **MCI,** dial 180019912; and for **Sprint,** 180019877.

Shore Excursions The following are good choices in Oslo. They may not be offered by all cruise lines. Times and prices are approximate.

City Spotlight. From Vigeland Sculpture Park, where master sculptor Gutav Vigeland created a world of human figures and animals in stone, iron, and bronze, to Holmenkollen, the cradle of ski jumping, this half-day of sightseeing takes in all the major attractions. *3 hrs. Cost: $35.*

Munch Museum and Scandinavian Design. Art lovers won't want to miss this tour, which takes in the Munch Museum and the Museum of Scandinavian Design, with its diverse collection of arts and crafts from AD 600 to the present. *3 hrs. Cost: $34.*

Coming Ashore Ships dock in Oslo's harbor. You can walk right into the main part of the city from the pier. The waterfront toward the central harbor is the heart of Oslo and head of the fjord. Aker Brygge, a new quayside shopping and cultural center, with a theater, cinemas, and galleries among the shops, restaurants, and cafés, is a great place to hang out. You don't have to buy anything—just sit amid the fountains and statues and watch the activities.

Getting Around

A taxi is available if the roof light is on. There are taxi stands at Oslo Central Station and usually alongside Narvesen newsstands, or call 22388090; during peak hours, though, you may have to wait. The city boasts good public transportation.

Exploring Oslo

Numbers in the margin correspond to points of interest on the Oslo map.

Oslo's main street, **Karl Johans gate,** runs right through the center of town, from Oslo Central Station uphill to the Royal Palace. Half its length is closed to traffic, and it is in this section that you will find many of the city's shops and outdoor cafés.

❶ The **Slottet** (Royal Palace) is the king's residence. The neoclassical palace, completed in 1848, is as sober, sturdy, and unpretentious as the Norwegian character. The surrounding park is open to the public, though the palace is not. The changing of the guard happens daily at 1:30. When the king is in residence—signaled by a red flag—the Royal Guard strikes up the band.

❷ The **Universitet** (University) is made up of three big buildings. The main hall of the university is decorated with murals by Edvard Munch (1863–1944), Norway's most famous artist. The *aula* (hall) is open only during July. The Nobel Peace Prize is presented there each year on December 10. *Walk down Karl Johans gate. Admission to hall free. Open July, weekdays noon–2.*

❸ **Nasjonalgalleriet** (the National Gallery) is Norway's largest public gallery. It has a small but high-quality selection of paintings by European artists, but of particular interest is the collection of works by Scandinavian Impressionists. Edvard Munch is represented here, although most of his work is in the Munch Museum (*see below*). *Universitetsgt. 13. Admission free. Open Mon., Wed., Fri., and Sat. 10–4, Thurs. 10–8, Sun. 11–3.*

❹ The **Historisk Museum** (Historical Museum) is in back of the National Gallery. In addition to displays of daily life and art from the Viking period, the museum has an ethnographic section with a collection related to the great polar explorer Roald Amundsen, the first man to reach the South Pole. *Frederiksgt. 2. Admission free. Open summer, Tues.–Sun. 11–3; winter, Tues.–Sun. noon–3.*

❺ The **Nationaltheatret** (National Theater) is watched over by the statues of Bjørnstjerne Bjørnson and Henrik Ibsen. Bjørnson was the nationalist poet who wrote Norway's anthem. Internationally lauded playwright Ibsen wrote *Peer Gynt* (he personally requested Edvard Grieg's musical accompaniment), *A Doll's House*, and *Hedda Gabler*, among others. He worried that his plays, packed with allegory, myth, and sociological and emotional angst, might not have appeal outside Norway. Instead, they were universally recognized and changed the face of modern theater.

❻ The **Stortinget** (Parliament) is a bow-fronted, yellow-brick building that stretches across the block. It is open to visitors by request when Parliament is not in session: A guide will take you around the frescoed interior and into the debating chamber. *Karl Johans gt. 22, tel. 22313050. Admission free. Guided tours July–Aug. Public gallery open weekdays 11–1.*

❼ **Oslo Domkirke** (cathedral), consecrated in 1697, is modest by the standards of those in some other European capital cities, but the interior is rich with treasures, such as the Baroque carved wooden altarpiece and pulpit. The ceiling frescoes by Hugo Lous Mohr were done after World War II. Behind the cathedral is an area of arcades,

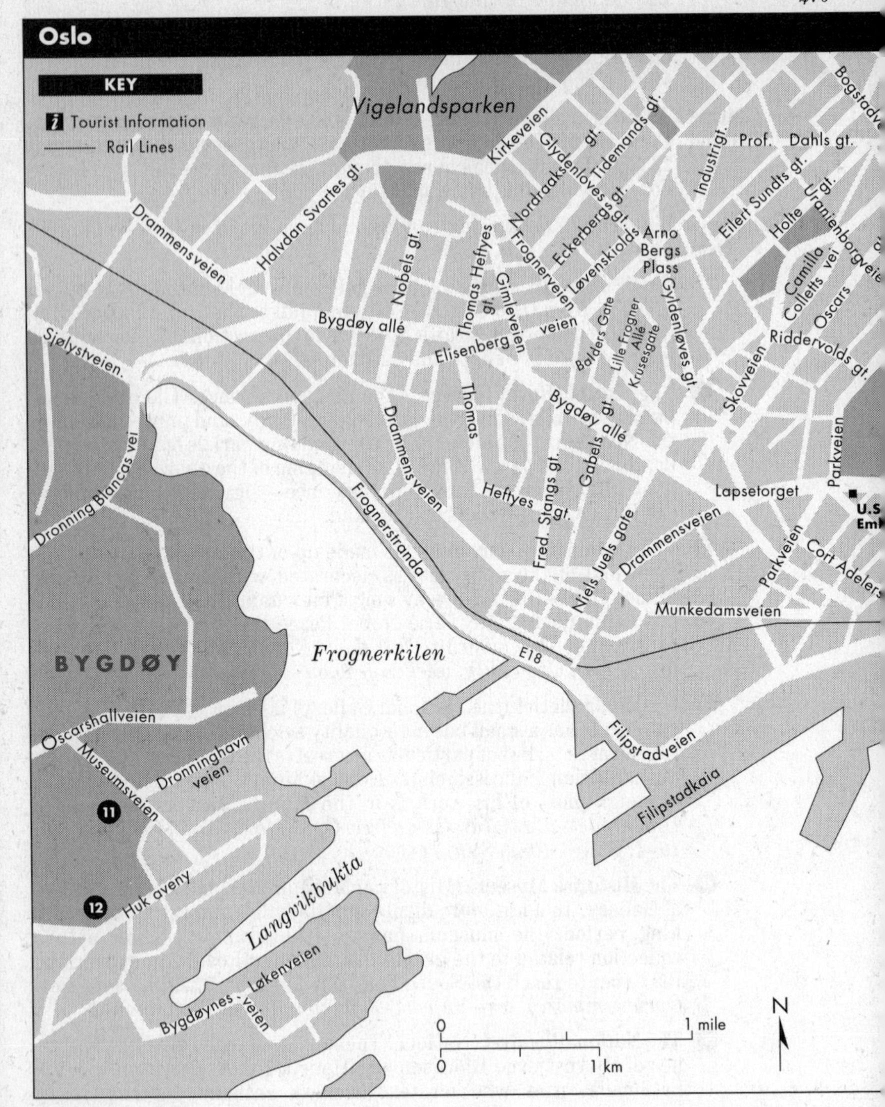

Akershus Slott, **8**
Forsvarsmuseet and Hjemmefrontmuseum, **9**
Historisk Museum, **4**
Munch-museet, **13**
Nasjonalgalleriet, **3**
Nationaltheatret, **5**
Norsk Folkemuseum, **11**
Oslo Domkirke, **7**
Rådhuset, **10**
Slottet, **1**
Stortinget, **6**
Universitet, **2**
Vikingskipshuset, **12**

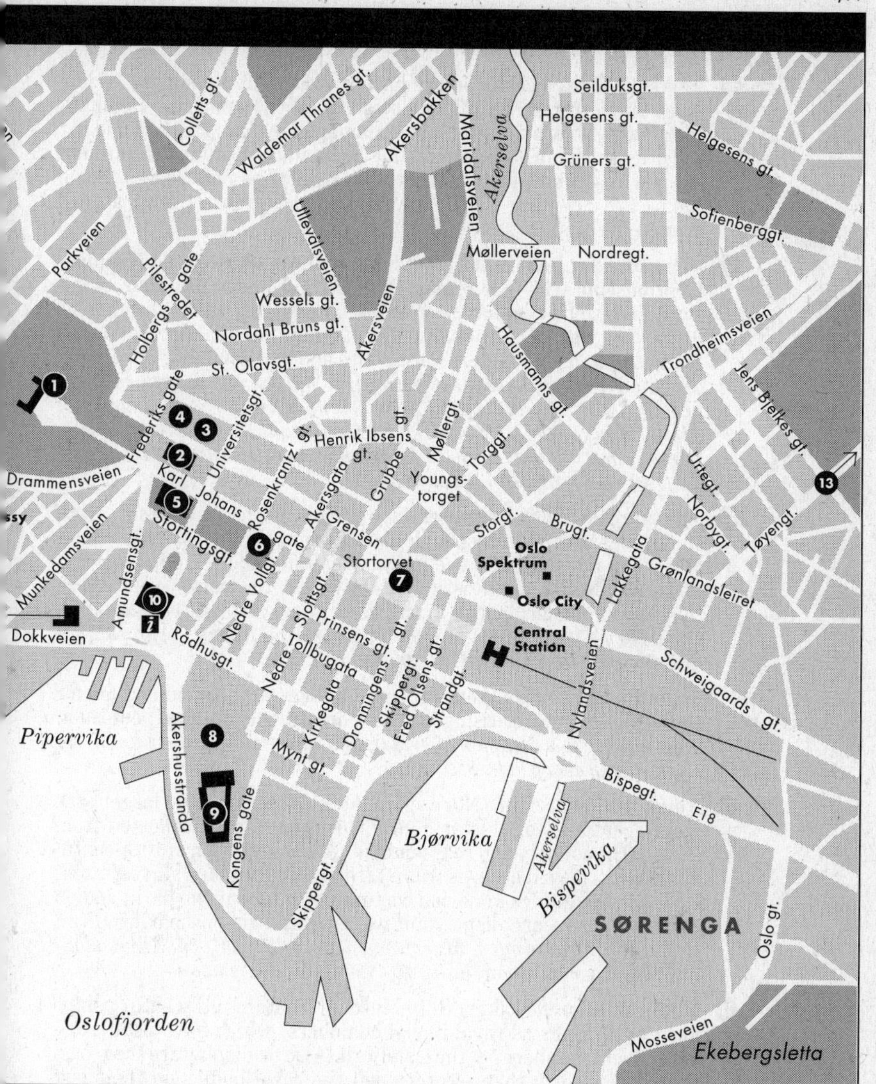
Seilduksgt.
Helgesens gt.
Grüners gt.
Helgesens gt.
Sofienberggt.
Colletts gt.
Waldemar Thranes gt.
Akersbakken
Maridalsveien
Akerselva
Ullevålsveien
Parkveien
Pilestredet
Holbergs gate
Møllerveien
Nordregt.
Wessels gt.
Nordahl Bruns gt.
Akersveien
Hausmanns gt.
Trondheimsveien
Jens Bjelkes gt.
St. Olavsgt.
Frederiks gate
Universitetsgt.
Rosenkrantz' gt.
Henrik Ibsens gt.
Grubbe gt.
Møllergt.
Torggt.
Youngs-torget
Drammensveien
Karl Johans gate
Akersgata
Grensen
Storgt.
Brugt.
Urtegt.
Norbygt.
Tøyengt.
Munkedamsveien
Amundsensgt.
Stortingsgt.
Nedre Vollgt.
Stortorvet
Oslo Spektrum
Oslo City
Lakkegata
Grønlandsleiret
Dokkveien
Rådhusgt.
Slottsgt.
Prinsens gt.
Central Station
Nylandsveien
Schweigaards gt.
Nedre Tollbugata
Kirkegata
Dronningens gt.
Skippergt.
Fred Olsens gt.
Strandgt.
Pipervika
Akershusstranda
Mynt gt.
Bispegt.
E18
Kongens gate
Bjørvika
Akerselva
Bispevika
SØRENGA
Skippergt.
Oslo gt.
Oslofjorden
Mosseveien
Ekebergsletta

small restaurants, and street musicians. *Stortorvet 1. Admission free. Open weekdays 10–3.*

8 **Akershus Slott,** a castle on the harbor, was built during the Middle Ages but restored in 1527 by Christian IV of Denmark—Denmark then ruled Norway—after it was damaged by fire. He then laid out the present city of Oslo (naming it Christiania, after himself) around his new residence; Oslo's street plan still follows his design. Some rooms are open for guided tours, and the grounds form a park around the castle.

9 The grounds of Akershus Slott house **Forsvarsmuseet** and **Hjemmefrontmuseum** (the Norwegian Defense and Resistance museums). Both give you a feel for the Norwegian fighting spirit throughout history and especially during the German occupation, when the Nazis set up headquarters on this site and had a number of patriots executed here. *Akershus Castle and museums: Entrance from Festningspl., tel. 22412521. Admission: NKr 15. Guided tours of castle, May–Sept., Mon.–Sat. 11, 1, and 3, Sun. 1 and 3. Forsvarsmuseet and Hjemmefrontmuseum open June–Aug., weekdays 10–6; Sept.–May, weekdays 10–4.*

10 The large redbrick **Rådhuset** (city hall) is on the waterfront. Note the friezes in the courtyard, depicting scenes from Norwegian folklore, then go inside and see murals depicting daily life in Norway, historical events, and Resistance activities. You can set your watch by the astronomical clock in the inner courtyard. *Admission free. Open May–Aug., Mon.–Sat. 9–5, Sun. noon–4; Sept.–Apr., Mon.–Sat. 9–3:30. Tours weekdays 10, noon, 2.*

From Pipervika Bay, you can board a ferry in the summertime for the seven-minute crossing of the fjord to the **Bygdøy** peninsula, where there is a complex of seafaring museums. *Ferries run May–Sept., daily every ½ hr 8:15–5:45.*

11 **Norsk Folkemuseum** (Norwegian Folk Museum) is a large park where centuries-old historic farmhouses have been collected from all over the country and reassembled. A whole section of 19th-century Oslo was moved here, as was a 12th-century wooden stave church. Look for the guides in period costume throughout the park, and on Sundays, there are displays of weaving and sheepshearing. *First ferry stop, Dronningen. Museumsvn. 10, tel. 22437020. Admission: NKr 50. Open summer, daily 10–6; winter, daily noon–4.*

12 **Vikingskipshuset** (Viking Ship Museum) contains 9th-century ships used by Vikings as royal burial chambers, which have been excavated from the shores of the Oslofjord. Also on display are the treasures and jewelry that accompanied the royal bodies on their last voyage. The ornate craftsmanship evident in the ships and jewelry dispels any notion that the Vikings were skilled only in looting and pillaging. *Huk aveny 35. Admission: NKr 20. Open Nov.–Mar., daily 11–3; Apr. and Oct., daily 11–4; May–Aug., daily 9–6; Sept., daily 11–5.*

13 **Munch-museet** (Munch Museum). In 1940, four years before his death, Munch bequeathed much of his work to the city of Oslo; the museum opened in 1963, the centennial of his birth. Although only a fraction of its 22,000 items—books, paintings, drawings, prints, sculptures, and letters—are on display, you can still get a sense of the tortured expressionism that was to have such an effect on European painting. *Tøyengt. 53. Admission: NKr 40. Open June–Sept.*

15, Tues.–Sat. 10–6, Sun. noon–6; Sept. 16–May, Tues., Wed., Fri, Sat. 10–4, Thurs. 10–6, Sun. noon–6.

Shopping Oslo has a wide selection of pewter, silver, glass, sheepskin, leather, and knitwear. Prices on handmade articles are government-controlled.

Many of the larger stores are between Stortinget and the cathedral; much of this area is for pedestrians only. The **Basarhallene,** at the back of the cathedral, is an art and handicrafts boutique center. Oslo's newest shopping area, **Aker Brygge,** was once a shipbuilding wharf. Located right on the waterfront, it is a complex of booths, offices, and sidewalk cafés. Also check out **Bogstadveien/Hegdehaugsveien,** which runs from Majorstua to Parkveien. This street offers a good selection of stores and has plenty of places to rest your tired feet and quench your thirst. Shops stay open until 5 (Thursday until 7).

Paris/Le Havre, France

Le Havre is the port city for Paris, one of Europe's most treasured and beautiful cities. Most cruise passengers will find a day far too short to truly explore the city. However, Paris is a compact city, and with the possible exception of the Bois de Boulogne and Montmartre, you can easily walk from one sight to the next. The city is divided in two by the River Seine, with two islands (Ile de la Cité and Ile St-Louis) in the middle. The south, or Left, Bank has a more intimate, bohemian flavor than the haughtier Right Bank. The east–west axis from Châtelet to the Arc de Triomphe, via the rue de Rivoli and the Champs-Elysées, is the principal thoroughfare for sightseeing and shopping on the Right Bank.

Currency The unit of French currency is the franc, subdivided into 100 centimes. At press time, the dollar bought 5.18 francs.

Telephones To call abroad, dial 19 and wait for the tone, then dial the country code, area code, and number. To reach an **AT&T** long-distance operator, dial 19–0011; for **MCI,** dial 19–0019; and for **Sprint,** 19–0087. Dial 12 for local operators.

Shore Excursions The following is a good choice from Le Havre. It may not be offered by all cruise lines. Time and price are approximate.

Paris. Journey by coach to Paris, where you will tour the Cathedral of Notre Dame, the Eiffel Tower, Place de la Concorde, and have time to shop. Glimpse the tree-lined Champs-Elysé and Arc de Triomphe, Place de l'Opera, and Pont Neuf. Includes lunch. *10 hrs. Cost: $150.*

Coming Ashore Ships dock at Le Havre. The trip to Paris is approximately three hours each way. Cruise lines will typically sell transfers for around $100 to Paris for those who want to explore on their own.

Getting Around Once you're in the city, you'll find that Paris's monuments and museums are within walking distance of one another. A river cruise is a pleasant way to get an overview. The most convenient form of public transportation is the *métro*; buses are a slower alternative, though they do allow you to see more of the city. Taxis are not expensive but are not always easy to hail, either.

There are 13 métro lines crisscrossing Paris and the nearby suburbs, and you are seldom more than a five-minute walk from the nearest station. It is essential to know the name of the last station on the line you take, since this name appears on all signs within the system. A connection (you can make as many as you please on one ticket) is called a *correspondance.* At junction stations, illuminated orange signs bearing the names of each line terminus appear over the corridors that lead to the various correspondances.

There is no standard vehicle or color for Paris taxis, but all offer good value. Daytime rates (7 to 7) within Paris are about 2.80 francs per kilometer, and nighttime rates are around 4.50 francs, plus a basic charge of 12 francs. Cruising cabs can be hard to find. There are numerous taxi stands, but you have to know where to look. Cruise passengers should be aware that taxis seldom take more than three people at a time.

Exploring Paris *Numbers in the margin correspond to points of interest on the Paris map.*

1 The most enduring symbol of Paris, and its historic and geographic heart, is **Notre Dame Cathedral,** around the corner from Cité métro station. Notre Dame has been a place of worship for more than 2,000 years; the present building is the fourth on this site. It was begun in 1163, making it one of the earliest Gothic cathedrals, although it was not finished until 1345. The 387-step climb up the towers is worth the effort for a perfect view of the famous gargoyles and the heart of Paris. *Cathedral admission free. Towers admission: 31 frs. Open daily 10–5. Treasury (religious and vestmental relics) admission: 15 frs. Open Mon.–Sat. 10–6, Sun. 2–6.*

2 The Hôtel de Cluny houses the **Musée National du Moyen-Age,** a museum devoted to the late Middle Ages and Renaissance. Look for the *Lady with the Unicorn* tapestries and the beautifully displayed medieval statues. *6 pl. Paul-Painlevé. Admission: 27 frs, 18 frs on Sun. Open Wed.–Mon. 9:30–5:15.*

3 **The Sorbonne,** Paris's ancient university, is where students used to listen to lectures in Latin, which explains why the surrounding area is known as the Quartier Latin (Latin Quarter). The Sorbonne is the oldest university in Paris—indeed, one of the oldest in Europe—and has for centuries been one of France's principal institutions of higher learning.

4 The **Panthéon,** with its huge dome and elegant colonnade, is reminiscent of St. Paul's in London but dates from a century later (1758–89). The Panthéon was intended to be a church, but during the French Revolution it was earmarked as a secular hall of fame. Its crypt contains the remains of such national heroes as Voltaire, Rousseau, and Zola. The interior is empty and austere, with principal interest centering on Puvis de Chavannes's late-19th-century frescoes, relating the life of Geneviève, patron saint of Paris. *On rue Cujas. Admission: 26 frs. Open daily 10–5:30.*

5 Rue de Navarre and rue Lacépède lead to the **Jardin des Plantes** (Botanical Gardens), which have been on this site since the 17th century. The gardens have what is reputedly the oldest tree in Paris, an acacia Robinia (allée Becquerel) planted in 1636. Natural science enthusiasts will be in their element at the various museums, devoted to insects (Musée Entomologique), fossils and prehistoric animals (Musée Paléontologique), and minerals (Musée Minéralogique). The Grande Galerie de l'Evolution, with its mind-blowing collection of stuffed and mounted animals (some now extinct), reopened in 1994 to popular acclaim. *Admission: 12–40 frs. Museums open Wed.–Mon. 9–11:45 and 1–4:45.*

6 You can hardly miss the sturdy pointed tower of **St-Germain-des-Prés,** the oldest church in Paris (begun around 1160, though the towers date from the 11th century). Note the colorful nave frescoes by the 19th-century artist Hippolyte Flandrin, a pupil of Ingres. *On blvd. St-Germain.*

7 The **Musée d'Orsay** is one of Paris's newest tourist attractions. Its imaginatively housed collections of the arts (mainly French) span the period 1848–1914 and take up three floors, but the visitor's immediate impression is one of a single, vast hall. This is not surpris-

ing: The museum was originally built in 1900 as a train station. *1 rue Bellechasse, tel. 40–49–48–14. Admission: 35 frs. Open Tues., Wed., Fri., Sat. 10–5:30; Thurs. 10–9:30; Sun. 9–5:30.*

8 The **Musée Rodin** is among the most charming of Paris's individual museums. An old house (built in 1728) and a pretty garden are filled with the vigorous sculptures of Auguste Rodin (1840–1917). The garden also has hundreds of rosebushes, with dozens of different varieties. *77 rue de Varenne. Admission: 27 frs, 18 frs Sun. Open Tues.–Sun. 10–5.*

9 No one will want to miss Paris's most famous landmark, the **Eiffel Tower.** It was built by Gustave Eiffel for the World Exhibition of 1889. Recent restorations haven't made the elevators any faster—long lines are inevitable—but decent shops and two good restaurants have been added. Such was Eiffel's engineering precision that even in the fiercest winds the tower never sways more than a few centimeters. Standing beneath it, you may have trouble believing that it nearly became 7,000 tons of scrap iron when its concession expired in 1909. Only its potential use as a radio antenna saved the day; it now bristles with a forest of radio and television transmitters. The view from 1,000 feet up will enable you to appreciate the city's layout and proportions. *Admission: on foot, 12 frs; by elevator, 20–53 frs, depending on the level. Open July–Aug., daily 9 AM–midnight; Sept.–June, Sun.–Thurs. 9 AM–11 PM, Fri., Sat. 9 AM–midnight.*

10 Along avenue Foch, the widest and grandest boulevard in Paris, you will come to the **Arc de Triomphe.** This 164-foot arch was planned by Napoléon to celebrate his military successes; yet Napoléon had been dead for 15 years when the Arc de Triomphe was finally finished in 1836. From the top of the Arc you can see the "star" effect of Etoile's 12 radiating avenues and admire two special vistas: one down the Champs-Elysées toward place de la Concorde and the Louvre, and the other down avenue de la Grande Armée toward La Tête Défense, a severe modern arch surrounded by imposing glass and concrete towers. Halfway up the Arc is a small museum devoted to its history. *Admission: 31 frs. Open daily 10–5:30.*

The **Champs-Elysées** is the site of colorful national ceremonies on July 14 and November 11; its trees are often decked with French tricolors and foreign flags to mark visits from heads of state. It is also where the cosmopolitan pulse of Paris beats strongest. The gracefully sloping 2-kilometer (1¼-mile) boulevard was originally laid out in the 1660s by André Le Nôtre as a garden sweeping away from the Tuileries. There is not much sign of that as you stroll past the cafés, restaurants, airline offices, car showrooms, movie theaters, and chic arcades that occupy its upper half, although the avenue was spruced up in the early 1990s with wider sidewalks and an extra row of trees.

11 **The Louvre** was begun as a fortress in 1200 (the earliest parts still standing date from the 1540s) and completed under Napoléon III in the 1860s. The museum's sheer variety can seem intimidating. The main tourist attraction is Leonardo da Vinci's *Mona Lisa* (known in French as *La Joconde*), painted in 1503. The latest research, based on Leonardo's supposed homosexuality, would have us believe that the subject was actually a man! The *Mona Lisa* may disappoint you: It's smaller than most imagine, it's kept behind glass, and it's invariably encircled by a mob of tourists. Turn your attention instead to some of the less-crowded rooms and galleries nearby, where Leonardo's fellow Italians are strongly represented: Fra Angelico, Giotto, Mantegna, Raphael, Titian, and Veronese. El Greco, Murillo, and Velázquez lead the Spanish; Van Eyck, Rembrandt, Frans Hals, Brueghel, Holbein, and Rubens underline the achievements of northern European art. English paintings are highlighted by works

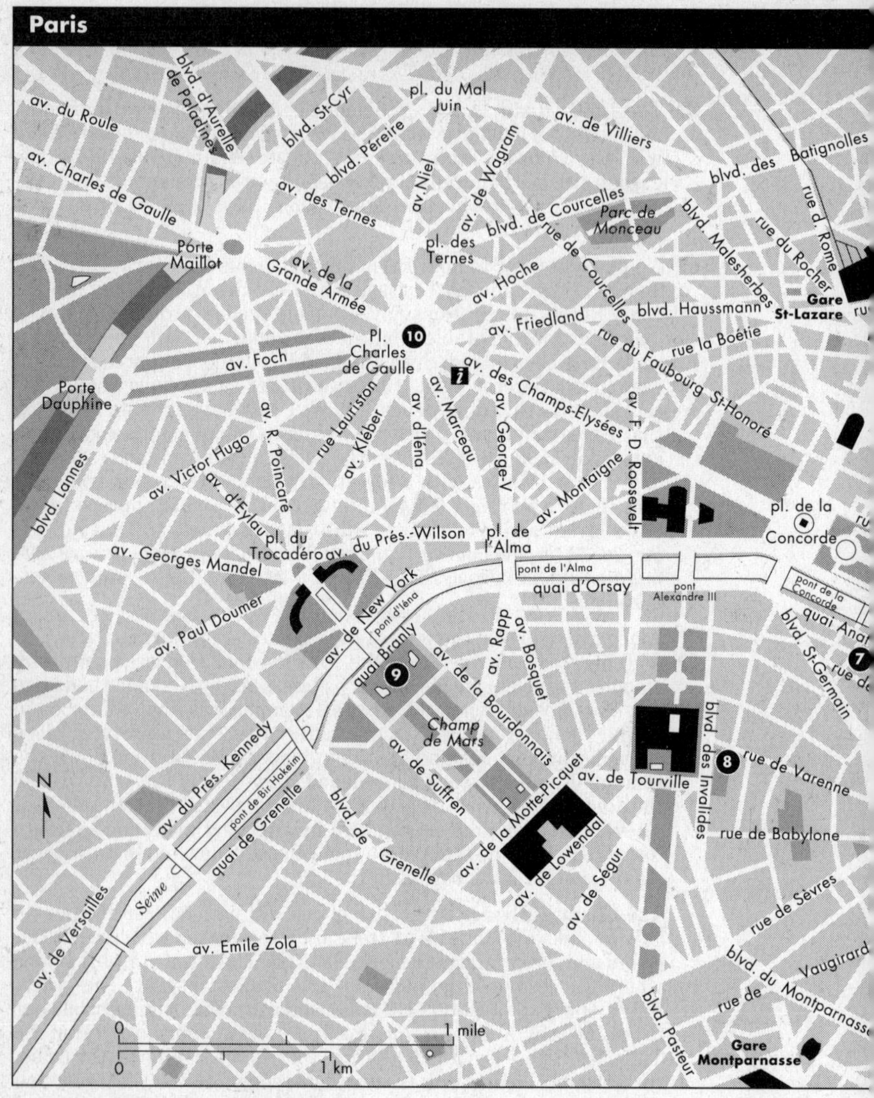

Arc de Triomphe, **10**
Eiffel Tower, **9**
Jardin des Plantes, **5**
The Louvre, **11**
Musée d'Orsay, **7**
Musée National du Moyen-Age, **2**
Musée Rodin, **8**
Notre Dame Cathedral, **1**
Panthéon, **4**
St-Germain-des-Prés, **6**
The Sorbonne, **3**

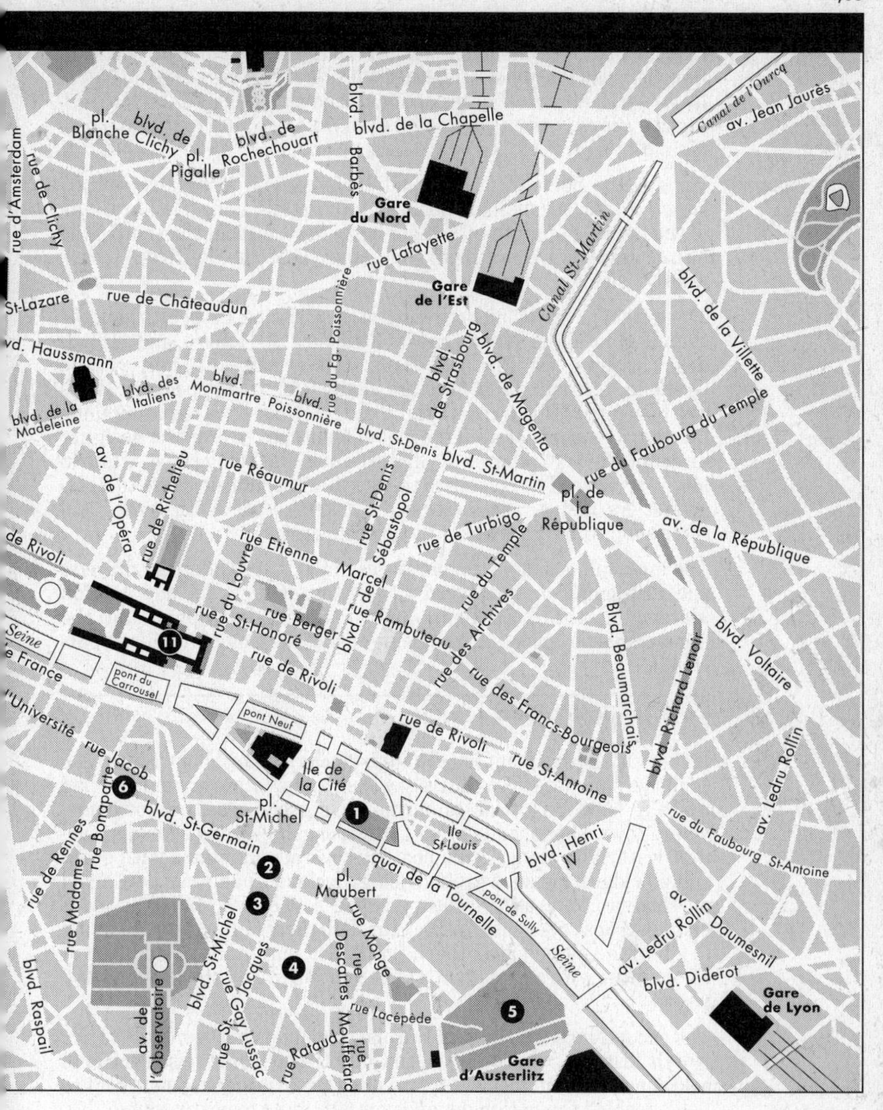

pl. Blanche
blvd. de Clichy
pl. Pigalle
blvd. de Rochechouart
blvd. de la Chapelle
blvd. Barbès
Canal de l'Ourcq
av. Jean Jaurès
rue d'Amsterdam
rue de Clichy
Gare du Nord
rue Lafayette
Gare de l'Est
Canal St-Martin
St-Lazare
rue de Châteaudun
rue du Fg.-Poissonnière
blvd. de la Villette
blvd. Haussmann
blvd. de Strasbourg
blvd. de Magenta
blvd. des Italiens
blvd. Montmartre
blvd. Poissonnière
blvd. de la Madeleine
blvd. St-Denis
blvd. St-Martin
rue du Faubourg du Temple
av. de l'Opéra
rue de Richelieu
rue Réaumur
rue St-Denis
Sébastopol
pl. de la République
de Rivoli
rue Etienne Marcel
rue de Turbigo
av. de la République
rue du Louvre
rue du Temple
rue St-Honoré
rue Berger
blvd. de
rue Rambuteau
rue des Archives
Blvd. Beaumarchais
blvd. Richard Lenoir
blvd. Voltaire
Seine
e France
pont du Carrousel
rue de Rivoli
rue des Francs-Bourgeois
pont Neuf
l'Université
rue Jacob
Ile de la Cité
rue St-Antoine
av. Ledru Rollin
pl. St-Michel
Ile St-Louis
rue du Faubourg St-Antoine
blvd. St-Germain
blvd. Henri IV
rue de Rennes
rue Bonaparte
quai de la Tournelle
pl. Maubert
rue Madame
pont de Sully
av. Ledru Rollin
av. Daumesnil
blvd. St-Michel
rue St-Jacques
rue Monge
rue Descartes
Seine
blvd. Diderot
Gare de Lyon
blvd. Raspail
av. de l'Observatoire
rue Gay Lussac
rue Lacépède
rue Rataud
rue Mouffetard
Gare d'Austerlitz
1
2
3
4
5
6
11

of Lawrence, Reynolds, Gainsborough, and Turner. Highlights of French painting include works by Poussin, Fragonard, Chardin, Boucher, and Watteau—together with David's *Coronation of Napoléon*, Géricault's *Raft of the Medusa*, and Delacroix's *Liberty Guiding the People. Admission: 40 frs, 20 frs after 3 PM and Sun. Open Mon. and Wed. 9 AM–9:45 PM, Thurs.–Sun. 9–6.*

Shopping Paris is the home of fashion and perfume. Old prints are sold by *bouquinistes* (secondhand booksellers) in stalls along the Left Bank of the Seine. For state-of-the-art home decorations, the shop in the **Musée des Arts Décoratifs** in the Louvre (107 rue de Rivoli) is well worth visiting.

The top shops are along both sides of the Champs-Elysées, along the avenue Montaigne and the rue du Faubourg St-Honoré, and at place des Victoires. On the Left Bank, St-Germain-des-Prés, rue de Grenelle, and rue de Rennes are centers for small specialty shops and boutiques. If you're on a tight budget, search for bargains along the shoddy streets around the foot of Montmartre or in the designer discount shops (Cacharel, Rykiel, Dorotennis) along rue d'Alésia in Montparnasse. The streets to the north of the Marais, close to Arts-et-Métiers métro, are historically linked to the cloth trade, and some shops offer garments at wholesale prices.

The most famous department stores in Paris are **Galeries Lafayette** and **Printemps,** on boulevard Haussmann. Others include **Au Bon Marché** on the Left Bank (métro: Sèvres-Babylone) and the **Samaritaine,** overlooking the Seine east of the Louvre (métro: Pont-Neuf).

Reykjavík, Iceland

Iceland is anything but icy. Though glaciers cover about 10% of the country, summers are relatively warm, and winters are milder than those in New York. Coastal farms lie in green, pastoral lowlands, where cows, sheep, and horses graze alongside raging streams. Distant waterfalls plunge from heather-covered mountains with great spiked ridges and snowcapped peaks. Iceland's name can be blamed on Hrafna-Flóki, a 9th-century Norse settler who failed to plant enough crops to see his livestock through their first winter. Leaving in a huff, he passed a northern fjord filled with pack ice and cursed the country with a name that's kept tourism in cold storage for 1,100 years.

The second-largest island in Europe, Iceland is in the middle of the North Atlantic, where the warm Gulf Stream from the south meets cold currents from the north, providing a choice environment for the fish on which the nation depends for 80% of its export revenue. Beneath some of the country's glaciers are burning fires that become visible during volcanic eruptions—fires that heat the country's hot springs and geysers. The springs, in turn, provide warmth for the country's homes, hospitals, and public swimming pools, keeping the nation's air smokeless and smogless.

Currency The Icelandic monetary unit is the króna (plural krónur), which is equal to 100 aurar and is abbreviated ISK. At press time, the rate of exchange was ISK 67 to the dollar.

Telephones For collect calls and assistance with overseas calls, dial 09; for local calls dial 02; for information dial 03; for direct international calls dial 00.

Shore Excursions The following are good choices in Iceland. They may not be offered by all cruise lines. Times and prices are approximate.

Golden Circle. Iceland's natural wonders are the focus of this tour, which visits Thingvellir National Park, Gulifoss (the Golden Waterfall), and Strokkur Geyser. You'll also see the second-largest glacier in Iceland and post-glacial lava fields. *5 hrs. Cost: $69.*

City Sights. Reykjavík's naturally heated outdoor swimming pool is a highlights of a half-day of sightseeing, which also visits the Arabaer Folk Museum and the National Museum and drives by the University, Old Town, the Parliament, the Cathedral and residential areas. *3 hrs. Cost: $40.*

Coming Ashore

Ships calling in Iceland berth at the dock in Reykjavík. The most interesting sights are in the city center, within easy walking distance of one another.

Getting Around

Buses run from 7 AM to midnight. The flat fare for Reykjavík and suburbs is ISK 100. Taxi rates start at about ISK 300; few taxi rides exceed ISK 700. The best taxis to call are: Hreyfill (tel. 568–5522), BSR (tel. 561–1720), and Bæjarleiðir (tel. 553–3500).

Exploring Reykjavík

The heart of Reykjavík is **Austurvöllur,** a small square in the center of the city. The 19th-century Alþingi (Parliament building), one of the oldest stone buildings in Iceland, faces the square. In the center of the square is a statue of Jón Sigurðsson (1811–79), the national hero who led Iceland's fight for independence, which it achieved fully in 1944.

Next to Alþingi is the **Dómkirkjan** (Lutheran cathedral), a small, charming stone church. Behind it is Tjörnin, a natural pond next to Reykjavík City Hall. One corner of the pond does not freeze; here thermal springs feed warm water, making it an attraction for birds year-round.

Overlooking Tjörnin stands the **National Gallery,** which houses a collection of Icelandic art.

At Lækjartorg square, on the right, is the **Bernhöftstorfa** district, a small hill with colorful two-story wooden houses from the mid-19th century, where no modernizing efforts have been made. For a century and a half, the largest building has housed the oldest educational institution in the country, Menntaskólinn í Reykjavík, a college whose graduates have from the early days dominated political and social life in Iceland.

Leading west out of Lækjartorg square is Austurstræti, a semi-pedestrian shopping street with the main post office on the right. From here you can take Buses 10 or 110 from the bus station for a 20-minute ride to the **Arbæjarsafn** (Open-Air Museum), a "village" of 18th- and 19th-century houses. *Tel. 558–4094. Admission: ISK 300. Open June–Aug., Tues.–Sat. 10–6; Sept., weekends 10–6; Oct.–May, by appointment.*

At the **Ásmundur Sveinsson Gallery,** a few originals of this social realist sculptor are in the surrounding garden, which is accessible at all times free of charge. *v/Sigtún, tel. 553–2155. Admission: ISK 200. Open June–Sept., daily 10–4; Oct.–May, Tues., Thurs., and weekends 1–4.*

The **Náttúrufræðistofnun** (Museum of Natural History), on Hlemmtorg square along with the city's main bus station, exhibits various items from stuffed peacocks to giant sea turtles. *Tel. 552–9822. Admission free. Open Tues. and Thurs.–Sun. 1:30–4:30.*

The **Hallgrímskirkja** features a 210-foot gray stone tower that dominates the city's skyline. The church, which took more than 40 years to build and was completed in the '80s, is open to the public. The church tower offers a panoramic view of the city and its spacious suburbs. *Tel. 551–0745. Admission to tower: ISK 200. Open daily 10–6.*

The **Einar Jónsson Museum** is devoted to the works of Iceland's leading early-20th-century sculptor. His monumental sculptures have a strong symbolic and mystical content. *v/Skólavörðuholt. Admission: ISK 100. Open weekends, 1:30–4. Sculpture garden open daily, 11–4.*

At the campus of the **University of Iceland** (founded 1911) is the outstanding [P]jóðminjasafn (National Museum). On display are Viking artifacts, national costumes, weaving, wood carving, and silver works. *Suðurgata 41, tel. 552–8888. Small admission fee. Open June–Sept., daily 1:30–4; Oct.–May, Tues., Thurs., and weekends 1:30–4.*

Shopping Many of the shops that sell the most attractive Icelandic woolen goods and arts and crafts are on Aðalstræti, Hafnarstræti, and Vesturgata streets. The **Icelandic Handcrafts Center** (Falcon House, Hafnarstræti 3, tel. 551–1784) stocks Icelandic woolens, knitting and tapestry materials, and handmade pottery, glassware, and jewelry. At the **Handknitting Association of Iceland,** (Skólavörðustígur 9, tel. 552–1890 or 552–1912) you can buy high-quality hand-knitted items through a knitters' cooperative. **Rammagerðin** (Hafnarstræti 19, tel. 551–7910) stocks a wide range of Icelandic-made clothes, souvenirs, and books. For original Icelandic arts and crafts direct from the artists, try **Hjá Þeim** (Skólavörðustigur 6b, tel. 551–2350). On weekends, try the harborside **Kolaport** flea market (tel. 562–5030).

Rome/Civitavecchia, Italy

Civitavecchia is the port city for Rome, where antiquity is taken for granted. Successive ages have piled the present on top of the past—building, layering, and overlapping their own particular segments of Rome's 2,500 years of history to form a remarkably varied urban complex. Most of the city's major sights are located in a fairly small area known as the *centro*. At its heart lies ancient Rome, where the Forum and Colosseum stand. It was around this core that the other sections of the city grew up through the ages: medieval Rome, which covered the horn of land that pushes the Tiber toward the Vatican and extended across the river into Trastevere; and Renaissance Rome, which was erected upon medieval foundations and extended as far as the Vatican, creating beautiful villas on what was then the outskirts of the city.

Currency The unit of currency in Italy is the lira (plural, lire). At press time, the exchange rate was about 1,546 lire to the dollar. When your purchases run into hundreds of thousands of lire, beware of being shortchanged, a dodge that is practiced at ticket windows and cashiers' desks, as well as in shops and even banks. Always count your change before you leave the counter.

Telephones To place international calls, many travelers go to the Telefoni telephone exchange, where the operator assigns you a booth, can help place your call, and will collect payment when you have finished. Telefoni exchanges (usually marked TELECOM) are found in both cities. To dial an international call, insert a phone card, dial 00, then the country code, area code, and phone number. For **AT&T,** dial access number 172–1011; for **MCI,** dial access number 172–1022; for **Sprint,** dial access number 172–1877. You will be connected directly with an operator in the United States.

Shore Excursions Due to the limited amount of time you will have in the city and its wealth of sights, it is a good idea to select a tour in Rome. The following is a good choice in Rome. It may not be offered by all cruise lines. Time and price are approximate.

Highlights and History. Drive by motor coach to the city to tour the Colosseum, the Vatican Museum and St. Peter's Basilica. Along the way pass Aventine and the Palatine Hills, the Circus Maximus, the Pyramid of Caius Cestius, and the Forum. *10½ hrs. Cost: $155.*

Coming Ashore Ships dock at Civitavecchia, about one hour and 45 minutes to Rome by bus. Cruise lines usually will sell bus transfers to Rome for those who want to explore independently.

Getting Around The layout of the centro is highly irregular, but several landmarks serve as orientation points to identify the areas that most visitors come to see: the Colosseum, the Pantheon and Piazza Navona, St. Peter's, the Spanish Steps, and Villa Borghese. You'll need a good map to find your way around; newsstands offer a wide choice. The important thing is to relax and enjoy Rome. Don't try to see everything, but do take time to savor its pleasures. If you are in Rome during a hot spell, do as the Romans do: Sightsee a little, take a break during the hottest hours, then resume sightseeing.

The best way to see Rome once you arrive is to choose an area or a sight that you particularly want to see, reach it by bus or metro, then explore the area on foot. Wear comfortable, sturdy shoes, preferably with thick rubber soles to cushion you against the cobblestones. You can buy transportation-route maps at newsstands and at ATAC (bus company) information and ticket booths. The metro provides the easiest and fastest way to get around. Taxis wait at stands and, for a small extra charge, can also be called by telephone. The meter starts at 6,400 lire. Use the yellow or the newer white cabs only, and be very sure to check the meter. To call a cab, phone 06/3570, 06/3875, 06/4994, or 06/88177.

Exploring Rome *Numbers in the margin correspond to points of interest on the Rome map.*

❶ In the valley below the Campidoglio is the **Foro Romano** (Roman Forum). Once only a marshy hollow, the forum became the political, commercial, and social center of Rome, studded with public meeting halls, shops, and temples. As Rome declined, these monuments lost their importance and eventually were destroyed by fire or the invasions of barbarians. Rubble accumulated (though much of it was carted off later by medieval home builders as construction material), and the site reverted to marshy pastureland; sporadic excavations began at the end of the 19th century. You don't really have to try to make sense of the mass of marble fragments scattered over the area of the Roman Forum. Just consider that 2,000 years ago this was the center of the Mediterranean world. Wander down the Via Sacra and climb the Palatine Hill, where the emperors had their palaces and where 16th-century cardinals strolled in elaborate Italian gardens. From the belvedere you have a good view of the Circus Maximus. *Entrances on Via dei Fori Imperiali, Piazza Santa Maria Nova, and Via di San Gregorio, tel. 06/699–0110. Admission: 12,000 lire. Open Apr.–Sept., Mon.–Sat. 9–6, Sun. 9–1; Oct.–Mar., Mon.–Sat. 9–3, Sun. 9–1.*

❷ Rome's most famous ancient ruin, the **Colosseum,** was inaugurated in AD 80 with a program of games and shows that lasted 100 days. On opening day alone 5,000 wild animals perished in the arena. The Colosseum could hold more than 50,000 spectators; it was faced with marble, decorated with stuccos, and had an ingenious system of awnings to provide shade. Try to see it both in daytime and at night, when yellow floodlights make it a magical sight. The Colosseum, by the way, takes its name from a colossal, 118-foot statue of Nero that stood nearby. You must pay a fee to explore the upper levels. *Piazza del Colosseo, tel. 06/700–4261. Admission: 8,000 lire to upper levels. Open Apr.–Sept., Mon.–Tues. and Thurs.–Sat. 9–7, Sun. and Wed. 9–1; Oct.–Mar., Mon.–Tues. and Thurs.–Sat. 9–3.*

❸ The **Baths of Caracalla** numbered among ancient Rome's most beautiful and luxurious, were inaugurated by Caracalla in 217 and used until the 6th century. An ancient version of a swanky athletic club, the baths were open to the public; citizens could bathe, socialize, and exercise in huge pools and richly decorated halls and libraries, now towering ruins. *Via delle Terme di Caracalla. Admission: 8,000 lire. Open Apr.–Sept., Tues.–Sat. 9–6, Sun.–Mon. 9–1; Oct.–Mar., Tues.–Sat. 9–3, Sun.–Mon. 9–1.*

4 The **Spanish Steps,** named for the Spanish Embassy to the Holy See, opposite the American Express office, are a popular rendezvous, especially for the young people who throng this area.

5 **Fontana di Trevi** (Trevi Fountain) is a spectacular fantasy of mythical sea creatures and cascades of splashing water. Legend has it that visitors must toss a coin into the fountain to ensure their return to Rome, but you'll have to force your way past crowds of tourists and aggressive souvenir vendors to do so. The fountain as you see it was completed in the mid-1700s, but there had been a drinking fountain on the site for centuries. Pope Urban VIII almost sparked a revolt when he slapped a tax on wine to cover the expenses of having the fountain repaired.

6 One of Rome's oddest sights is the crypt of the **Church of Santa Maria della Concezione** on Via Veneto, just above the Fountain of the Bees. In four chapels under the main church, the skeletons and scattered bones of some 4,000 dead Capuchin monks are arranged in decorative motifs, a macabre practice peculiar to the Baroque age. *Via Veneto 27, tel. 06/462850. Admission free, but donations encouraged. Open daily 9–noon and 3–6.*

Via della Conciliazione, the broad avenue leading to St. Peter's Basilica, was created by Mussolini's architects by razing blocks of old houses. This opened up a vista of the basilica, giving the eye time to adjust to its mammoth dimensions and thereby spoiling the effect Bernini sought when he enclosed his vast square (which is really 7 oval) in the embrace of huge quadruple colonnades. In **Piazza San Pietro** (St. Peter's Square), which has held up to 400,000 people at one time, look for the stone disks in the pavement halfway between the fountains and the obelisk. From these points the colonnades seem to be formed of a single row of columns all the way around.

When you enter St. Peter's Square (completed in 1667), you are entering Vatican territory. Since the Lateran Treaty of 1929, **Vatican City** has been an independent and sovereign state, which covers about 108 acres and is surrounded by thick, high walls. Its gates are watched over by the Swiss Guards, who still wear the colorful dress uniforms designed by Michelangelo. Sovereign of this little state is John Paul II, 264th pope of the Roman Catholic Church.

At noon on Sunday, the pope appears at his third-floor study win- 8 dow in the **Vatican Palace,** to the right of the basilica, to bless the crowd in the square. (Note: Entry to St. Peter's, the Vatican Museums, and all other sites within Vatican City, e.g., the Gardens, is barred to those wearing shorts, miniskirts, sleeveless T-shirts, and otherwise revealing clothing. Women should carry scarves to cover bare shoulders and upper arms or wear blouses that come to the elbow. Men should dress modestly, in slacks and shirts.) Free 90-minute tours of St. Peter's Basilica are offered in English daily (usually starting about 10 AM and 3 PM) by volunteer guides. They start at the information desk under the basilica portico.

9 **St. Peter's Basilica** is one of Rome's most impressive sights. It takes a while to absorb the sheer magnificence of it, however, and its rich decoration may not be to everyone's taste. Its size alone is overwhelming, and the basilica is best appreciated when providing the lustrous background for ecclesiastical ceremonies thronged with the faithful. The original basilica was built in the early 4th century AD by the emperor Constantine, over an earlier shrine that supposedly marked the burial place of St. Peter. After more than a thousand years, the old basilica was so decrepit it had to be torn down. The task of building a new, much larger one took almost 200 years

and employed the architectural genius of Alberti, Bramante, Raphael, Peruzzi, Antonio Sangallo the Younger, and Michelangelo, who died before the dome he had planned could be completed. Finally, in 1626, St. Peter's Basilica was finished. The basilica is full of extraordinary works of art. Among the most famous is Michelangelo's *Pietà* (1498), seen in the first chapel on the right just as you enter the basilica. Michelangelo has four *Pietàs* to his credit. The earliest and best known can be seen here. Two others are in Florence, and the fourth, the *Rondanini Pietà,* is in Milan.

At the end of the central aisle is the bronze statue of **St. Peter,** its foot worn by centuries of reverent kisses. The bronze throne above the altar in the apse was created by Bernini to contain a simple wood and ivory chair once believed to have belonged to St. Peter. Bernini's bronze *baldacchino* (canopy) over the papal altar was made with metal stripped from the portico of the Pantheon at the order of Pope Urban VIII, one of the powerful Roman Barberini family. His practice of plundering ancient monuments for material to implement his grandiose schemes inspired the famous quip, *"Quod non fecerunt barbari, fecerunt Barberini"* ("What the barbarians didn't do, the Barberini did").

As you stroll up and down the aisles and transepts, observe the fine mosaic copies of famous paintings above the altars, the monumental tombs and statues, and the fine stuccowork. Stop at the **Treasury** (Historical Museum), which contains some priceless liturgical objects.

The entrance to the so-called **Vatican Grottoes,** or crypt, is in one of the huge piers at the crossing. It's best to leave this visit for last, as the crypt's only exit takes you outside the church. The crypt contains chapels and the tombs of many popes. It occupies the area of the original basilica, over the necropolis, the ancient burial ground where evidence of what may be St. Peter's burial place has been found. To see the roof and dome of the basilica, take the elevator or climb the stairs in the courtyard near the exit of the Vatican Grottoes. From the roof you can climb a short interior staircase to the base of the dome for an overhead view of the interior of the basilica. Only if you are in good shape should you attempt the very long, strenuous, and claustrophobic climb up the narrow stairs to the balcony of the lantern atop the dome, where the view embraces the Vatican Gardens as well as all of Rome. *St. Peter's Basilica, tel. 06/6988–4466. Open Apr.–Sept., daily 7–7; Oct.–Mar., daily 7–6. Treasury (Museo Storico-Artistico): entrance in Sacristy. Admission: 3,000 lire. Open Apr.–Sept., daily 9–6:30; Oct.–Mar., daily 9–5:30. Roof and dome: entrance in courtyard to the left as you leave basilica. Admission: 6,000 lire, including use of elevator to roof, 5,000 lire if you climb spiral ramp on foot. Open Apr.–Sept., daily 8–6; Oct.–Mar., daily 8–5. Vatican Grottoes (Tombs of the Popes): entrance alternates among piers at crossing. Admission free. Open Apr.–Sept., daily 7–6; Oct.–Mar., daily 7–5.*

❿ The collections in the **Vatican Museums** cover nearly 8 kilometers (5 miles) of displays. If you have time, allow at least half a day for Castel Sant'Angelo and St. Peter's and another half day for the museums. Posters at the museum entrance plot out a choice of four color-coded itineraries; the shortest takes about 90 minutes, the longest more than four hours, depending on your rate of progress.

No matter which tour you take, it will include the famed **Sistine Chapel.** In 1508, Pope Julius II commissioned Michelangelo to fresco the more than 10,000 square feet of the chapel's ceiling. For four years Michelangelo dedicated himself to painting over fresh plaster, and the result was his masterpiece. Recently completed cleaning operations have removed centuries of soot and revealed its original and surprisingly brilliant colors.

Baths of Caracalla, **3**
Church of Santa Maria della Concezione, **6**
Colosseum, **2**
Fontana di Trevi, **5**
Foro Romano (Roman Forum), **1**
Pantheon, **11**
Piazza San Pietro, **7**
Spanish Steps, **4**
St. Peter's Basilica, **9**
Vatican Museums, **10**
Vatican Palace, **8**

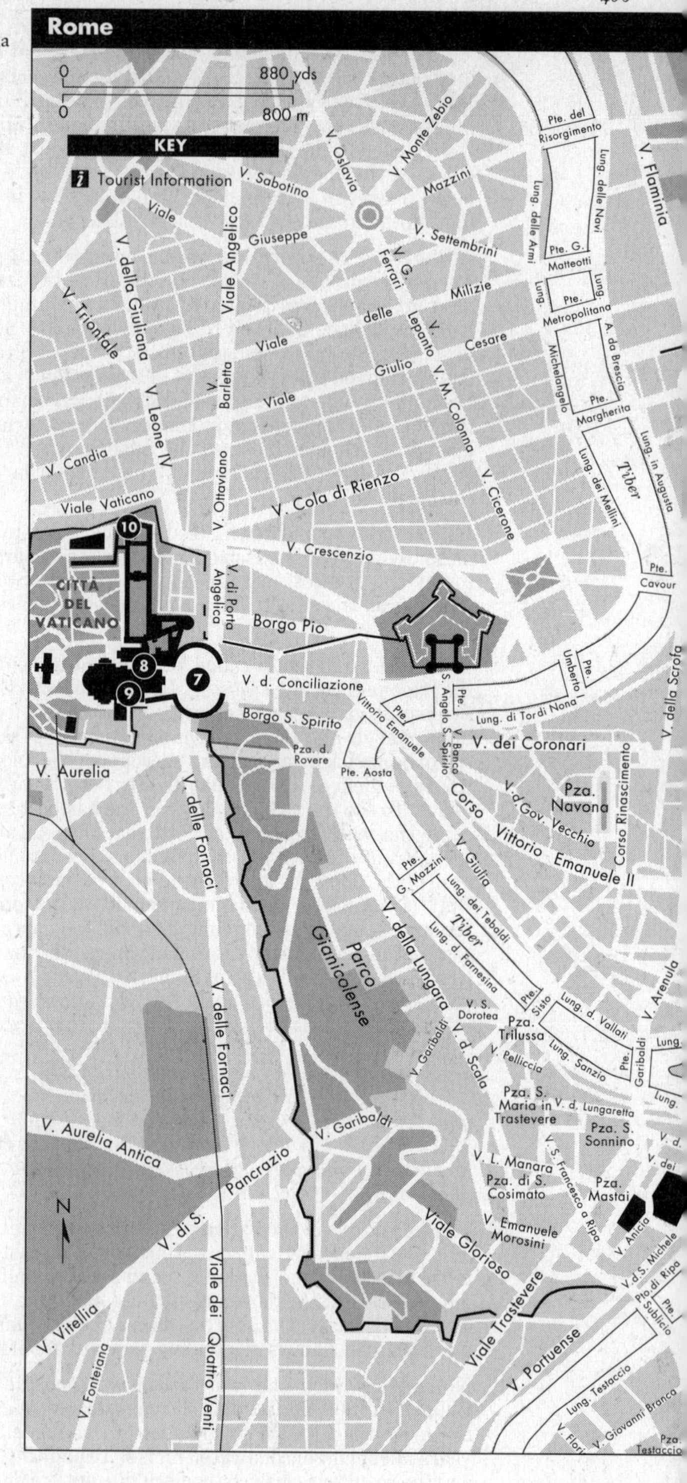

Villa Borghese
Zoological Gardens
Botanical Gardens
Pincio
Galoppatoio
Villa Medici
V. Ulisse Aldrovandi
Viale delle Belle Arti
Vle. G. Washington
V. Pietro Raimondi
Viale dell' Uccelliera
Viale P. Canonica
V. d. Magnolie
Viale d. Museo Borghese
V. Pinciana
V. Po
V. Salaria
V. Tagliamento
Viale Regina Margherita
V. Nomentana
Pza. Fiume
Pza. Alessandria
Ple. di Porta Pia
Porta Pinciana
Corso d'Italia
V. Campania
V. Piemonte
V. Romagna
V. Piave
Viale d. Policlinico
Viale Castro Pretorio
Vle. G. Annunzio
Viale del Muro Torto
V. Trinità d. Monti
V. del Babuino
V. del Corso
V. di Ripetta
V. Vittoria
Pza. di Spagna
Pza. Augusto Imperatore
V. Tomacelli
V. Condotti
V. d. Pta. Pinciana
V. Vitt. Veneto
V. Boncompagni
V. Quintino Sella
V. Sallustiana
V. Ludovisi
V. L. Bissolati
V. XX Settembre
V. Goito
V. Palestro
V. Gaeta
V. Cernaia
V. F. Crispi
V. Sistina
V. d. Due Macelli
V. Barberini
Pza. d. Repubblica
V. Volturno
V. Vicenza
MONTE QUIRINALE
V. Tritone
V. d. Scuderie
Giardini del Quirinale
V. d. Quattro Fontane
V. Torino
Stazione Termini
V. Castro Pretorio
Viale Pretoriano
Pza. Colonna
Palazzo del Quirinale
V. Napoli
V. A. Depretis
V. G. Amendola
V. Marsala
V. Nazionale
V. Milano
V. d. S. Maria Maggiore
Sta. Maria Maggiore
V. Giovanni Giolitti
V. F. Turati
V. C. Battisti
V. IV Novembre
V. d. Plebiscito
Pza. Venezia
V. d. Serpenti
V. Panisperna
V. Cavour
V. Quattro Cantoni
V. Carlo Alberto
V. Napoleone III
Vittoriano
MONTE CAPITOLINO
MONTE VIMINALE
V. Giovanni Lanza
V. d. Statuto
Pza. Vittorio Emanuele II
V. Pr. Umberto
V. Pr. Eugenio
V. Conte Verde
V. dei Fori Imperiali
MONTE ESQUILINO
Viale del Monte Oppio
V. Mecenate
V. Merulana
Foro Romano
V. d. Cenci
V. d. Teatro di Marcello
V. di S. Teodoro
V. d. Domus Aurea
V. Rugg. Bonghi
V. Labicana
Viale Manzoni
V. Emanuele Filiberto
Lung. d. Pierleoni
Pte. Cestio
Anguillara
Pte. Palatino
Salumi
Genovesi
MONTE PALATINO
V. S. Giovanni in Laterano
V. di S. Gregorio
V. Claudia
S. Giovanni in Laterano
Pza. Giovanni XXIII
Lung. Ripa
Tiber
Circo Massimo
V. dei Cerchi
V. del Circo Massimo
COLLE AVENTINO
Lung. Aventino
Pza. SS. Giovanni e Paolo
MONTE CELIO
V. di S. Stefano Rotondo
Ple. Romolo e Remo
Pza. di Pta. Capena
V. di S. Erasmo
V. dell' Amba Aradam
V. Magna Grecia
V. S. A. Magno
V. d. S. Sabina
V. S. Prisca
V. d. Navicella
V. delle Terme Caracalla
Pza. d. Emporio
MONTE AVENTINO
Viale Aventino
V. Aventina
Parco di Porta Capena
V. Guido Baccelli
Pza. di Porta Metronia
V. Gallia
V. Pannonia
V. Anselmo
Pza. Albania
V. M. Gelsomini
V. Marmorata
V. d. Porta Latina
1
2
3
4
5
6
11

You can try to avoid the tour groups by going early or late, allowing yourself enough time before the closing hour. In peak season, the crowds definitely detract from your appreciation of this outstanding artistic achievement. To make sense of the figures on the ceiling, buy an illustrated guide or rent a taped commentary. A pair of binoculars also helps.

The Vatican collections are so rich that unless you are an expert in art history, you will probably want only to skim the surface, concentrating on pieces that strike your fancy. Some of the highlights that might be of interest include the newly reorganized Egyptian collection and the *Laocoön*, the *Belvedere Torso*, and the *Apollo Belvedere*, which inspired Michelangelo. The Raphael Rooms are decorated with masterful frescoes, and there are more Raphaels in the *Pinacoteca* (Picture Gallery). At the Quattro Cancelli, near the entrance to the Picture Gallery, a rather spartan cafeteria provides basic nonalcoholic refreshments. *Viale Vaticano, tel. 06/6988–3332. Admission: 13,000 lire, free last Sun. of month. Open Easter period and July–Sept., weekdays 8:45–5, Sat. 8:45–2; Oct.–June, Mon.–Sat. 8:45–2. Ticket office closes 1 hr before museums close. Closed Sun., except last Sun. of month, and religious holidays: Jan. 1, Jan. 6, Feb. 11, Mar. 19, Easter Sun. and Mon., May 1, Ascension Thurs., Corpus Christi, June 29, Aug. 15–16, Nov. 1, Dec. 8, Dec. P25–26.*

⓫ Originally built in 27 BC by Augustus's general Agrippa and rebuilt by Hadrian in the 2nd century AD, the **Pantheon** is one of Rome's finest, best-preserved, and perhaps least appreciated ancient monuments. Romans and tourists alike pay little attention to it, and on summer evenings it serves mainly as a backdrop for all the action in the square in front. It represents a fantastic feat of construction, however. The huge columns of the portico and the original bronze doors form the entrance to a majestic hall covered by the largest dome of its kind ever built, wider even than that of St. Peter's. In ancient times the entire interior was encrusted with rich decorations of gilt bronze and marble. *Piazza della Rotonda. Open Mon.–Sat. 9–2, Sun. 9–1.*

Shopping Shopping is part of the fun of being in Rome. The best buys are leather goods of all kinds, from gloves to handbags and wallets to jackets; silk goods; and high-quality knitwear. Shops are closed on Sunday and on Monday morning; in July and August, they close on Saturday afternoon as well. Romans themselves do much of their shopping along **Via Cola di Rienzo** and **Via Nazionale.**

Seville, Spain

Seville—Spain's fourth-largest city and capital of Andalucía—is one of the most beautiful and romantic cities in Europe. Here in this city of the sensuous Carmen and the amorous Don Juan, famed for the spectacle of its Holy Week processions and April Fair, you'll come close to the spiritual heart of Moorish Andalucía. The downside to a visit to Seville is that petty crime, much of it directed against tourists, is rife. Take only the minimum amount of cash with you when going ashore. If you're unlucky, it's an equally depressing fact that the police have adopted a distinctly casual attitude to such thefts and often combine indifference to beleaguered tourists with rudeness in about equal measure.

Currency The unit of currency in Spain is the peseta (pta.). At press time, the exchange rate was about 129 ptas. to the U.S. dollar.

Telephones Calling abroad can be done from any pay phone marked *teléfono internacional.* Use 50-pta. (or 100-pta. if the phone takes them) coins initially, then coins of any denomination to prolong your call. Dial 07 for international calls, wait for the tone to change, then 1 for the United States or 0101 for Canada. For lengthy international calls, go to the telefónica, a telephone office, where an operator assigns you a private booth and collects payment at the end of the call; this is the least expensive and by far the easiest way of phoning abroad. **AT&T** (tel. 900/99–00–11), **MCI** (tel. 900/99–00–14), **Sprint** (tel. 900/99–00–13).

Shore Excursions The following is a good choice in Seville. It may not be offered by all cruise lines. Time and price are approximate.

Seville Tour. Travel through Seville's past and present on this comprehensive excursion that explores the city's religious, ethnic, and historical diversity. *8½ hrs. Cost: $135.*

Coming Ashore Ships dock at Cádiz for Seville. The drive to and from Seville is around two hours each way.

Getting Around Once in the city, you can walk from some sights to others; hop a cab or even take a horse-drawn carriage to reach other areas.

Exploring Seville *Numbers in the margin correspond to points of interest on the Seville map.*

❶ A must is a visit to the **cathedral,** begun in 1402, a century and a half after St. Ferdinand delivered Seville from the Moors. This great Gothic edifice, which took just over a century to build, is traditionally described in superlatives. It's the biggest and highest cathedral in Spain, the largest Gothic building in the world, and the world's third-largest church after St. Peter's in Rome and St. Paul's in London. And it boasts the world's largest carved wooden altarpiece. Despite such impressive statistics, the inside can be dark and gloomy, with too many overly ornate Baroque trappings. You'll want to pay your respects to Christopher Columbus, whose mortal vestiges are enshrined in a flamboyant mausoleum in the south aisle. Borne aloft by statues representing the four medieval kingdoms of Spain, it's to be hoped the great voyager has found peace at last, after the transatlantic quarrels that carried his body from Valladolid to Santo Domingo and from Havana to Seville. *Admission to cathedral and Giralda (*see below*): 550 ptas. Open Mon.–Sat. 10–5, Sun. 10–4. Cathedral also open for Mass.*

Every day the bell that summons the faithful to prayer rings out from a Moorish minaret, a relic of the Arab mosque whose admirable tower of Abu Yakoub the Sevillians could not bring themselves to destroy. Topped in 1565–68 by a bell tower and weather vane and ❷ called the **Giralda,** this splendid example of Moorish art is one of the marvels of Seville. In place of steps, a gently sloping ramp climbs to the viewing platform 230 feet high. St. Ferdinand is said to have ridden his horse to the top to admire the view of the city he had conquered. Seven centuries later your view of the Golden Tower and shimmering Guadalquivir will be equally breathtaking. *Open same hrs as cathedral and visited on same ticket.*

❸ The high, fortified walls of the **Alcázar** belie the exquisite delicacy of the palace's interior. It was built by Pedro the Cruel—so known because he murdered his stepmother and four of his half-brothers—who lived here with his mistress María de Padilla from 1350 to 1369. Don't mistake this for a genuine Moorish palace, as it was built more than 100 years after the reconquest of Seville; rather, its style is Mudéjar—built by Moorish craftsmen working under orders of a Christian king. *Plaza del Triunfo, tel. 95/422–7163. Palace and gardens admission: 600 ptas. Open Tues.–Sat. 10:30–5, Sun. 10–1.*

❹ The **Barrio de Santa Cruz,** with its twisting alleyways, cobbled squares, and whitewashed houses, is a perfect setting for an operetta. Once the home of Seville's Jews, it was much favored by 17th-century noblemen, and today boasts some of the most expensive properties in Seville. All the romantic images you've ever had of

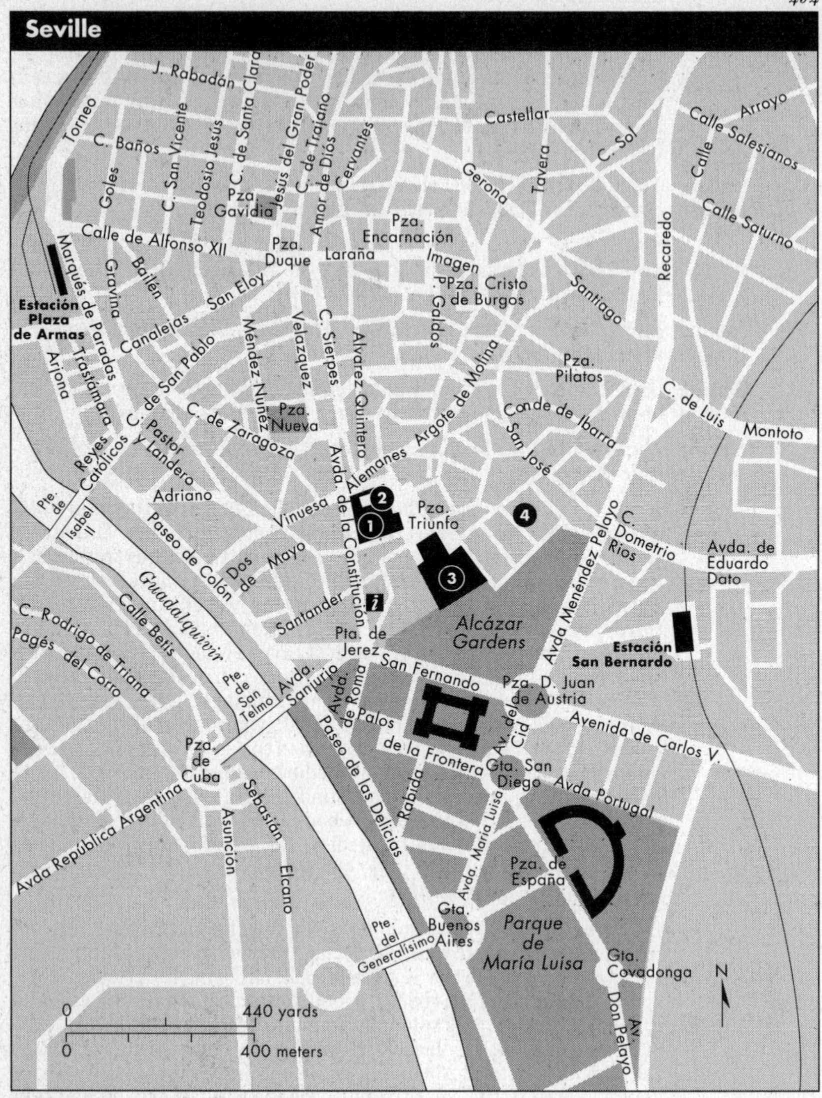

Alcázar, **3**
Barrio de Santa Cruz, **4**
Cathedral, **1**
Giralda, **2**

Spain will come to life here: Every house gleams white or deep ocher yellow, wrought-iron grilles adorn the windows, and every balcony and patio is bedecked with geraniums and petunias. Ancient bars nestle side by side with antiques shops.

Stockholm, Sweden

The city of Stockholm, built on 14 small islands among open bays and narrow channels, is a handsome, civilized place, full of parks, squares, and airy boulevards; yet it is also a bustling, modern metropolis. Glass-and-steel skyscrapers abound, but in the center you are never more than five minutes' walk from twisting, medieval streets and waterside walks.

Currency The unit of currency in Sweden is the krona (plural kronor), which is divided into 100 öre and is written as SKr, SEK, or kr. At press time, the exchange rate was 6.7 kronor to the dollar.

Telephones Calls can be made from any pay phone. For calls to the United States and Canada, dial 009, then 1 (the country code), then wait for a second dial tone before dialing the area code and number. You can make calls from Telebutik offices. To reach an **AT&T** long-distance operator, dial 020/795611; for **MCI,** dial 020/795922; and for **Sprint,** 020/799011.

Shore Excursions The following are good choices in Stockholm. They may not be offered by all lines. Times and prices are approximate.

City and Vasa Museum. Visit City Hall and Golden Hall, the site of the Nobel Prize banquet. Pass the Senate Building and Royal Opera House on the way to the Vasa Ship Museum. *3 hrs. Price: $40.*

Royal Palace and Millesgarden. A complete tour of the royal residence precedes a visit to Millesgarden, the home, studio, and gardens of Sweden's famous modern sculptor, Carl Milles. In-between, you'll stroll the streets of Old Town and drive through Stockholm Center past the Royal Opera House. *3 hrs. Cost: $42.*

Coming Ashore Ships berth at Stockholm's pier within view of the Royal Palace in Old Town.

Getting Around The most cost-effective way of getting around Stockholm is to buy a Stockholmskortet (the Key to Stockholm card). Besides unlimited transportation on city subway, bus, and rail services, it offers free admission to 60 museums and several sightseeing trips. The card costs SKr 175 for 24 hours. It is available from the tourist information centers at Sweden House and the Kaknäs TV tower, and at the Hotellcentralen accommodations bureau at the central train station.

Maps and timetables for all city transportation networks are available from the Stockholm Transit Authority (SL) information desks at Sergels Torg, the central train station, and at Slussen in Gamla Stan. You can also obtain information by phone (tel. 08/600–1000).

The subway system, known as T-banan (the *T* stands for tunnel), is the easiest and fastest way of getting around the city. Station entrances are marked with a blue T on a white background. The T-banan has about 100 stations and covers more than 60 route-miles. Trains run frequently between 5 AM and 2 AM.

A 10-kilometer (6-mile) taxi ride will cost SKr 93 between 6 AM and 7 PM on weekdays; weekend prices are SKr 110, including Moms (value-added tax). Major taxi companies are Taxi Stockholm (tel. 08/150000), Taxikurir (tel. 08/300000), and Taxi 020 (tel. 020/850400).

Exploring Stockholm *Numbers in the margin correspond to points of interest on the Stockholm map.*

Anyone in Stockholm with limited time should give priority to a tour of **Gamla Stan** (the Old Town), a labyrinth of narrow, medieval streets, alleys, and quiet squares on the island just south of the city center. Ideally, you should devote an entire day to this district.

❶ **Stadshuset** (city hall) was constructed in 1923 and is now one of the symbols of Stockholm. Lavish mosaics adorn the walls of the Golden Hall, and the Prince's Gallery features a collection of large murals by Prince Eugen, brother of King Gustav V. Take the elevator halfway up, then climb the rest of the way to the top of the 348-foot tower for a magnificent view of the city. *Tel. 08/785–9074. Admission: SKr 30. Tours daily at 10 and noon; also at 11 and 2 in summer. Tower admission: SKr 15. Tower open May–Sept., daily 10–4:30.*

❷ You should get to **Kungliga Slott** (Royal Palace), preferably by noon, when you can see the colorful changing-of-the-guard ceremony. The smartly dressed guards seem superfluous, as tourists wander at will into the palace courtyard and around the grounds. Several separate attractions are open to the public. Be sure to visit the Royal Armory, with its outstanding collection of weaponry and royal regalia. The Treasury houses the Swedish crown jewels, including the regalia used for the coronation of King Erik XIV in 1561. You can also visit the State Apartments, where the king swears in each successive government. *Tel. 08/789–8500. Admission: SKr 50 for Armory; SKr 30 for Treasury; SKr 30 for State Apartments. Call ahead for opening hrs, as they are subject to change.*

A short walk from the city center is the large island of **Djurgården,** where attractions include Waldemarsudde (tel. 08/662–2800), an art museum in the former summer residence of Swedish prince Eugen, on a peninsula in Djurgården.

The *Vasa*, a restored 17th-century warship, is one of the oldest preserved war vessels in the world and has become Sweden's most popular tourist sight. It sank ignominiously in Stockholm Harbor on its maiden voyage in 1628, reportedly because it was not carrying sufficient ballast. Recovered in 1961, the ship has been restored to its original appearance and is housed in a spectacular museum, ❸ **Vasamuseet,** which opened in 1990. It has guided tours, films, and displays. *Gälarvarvet, tel. 08/666–4800. Admission: SKr 45. Open Thurs.–Tues. 10–5, Wed. 10–8.*

❹ **Gröna Lund Tivoli,** Stockholm's version of the famous Copenhagen amusement park, is a family favorite, with roller coasters as well as tamer delights. *Tel. 08/670–7600. Open late Apr.–early Sept. Call ahead for prices and hrs, as they are subject to change.*

❺ **Nordiska Museet** (the Nordic Museum) provides insight into the way Swedish people have lived over the past 500 years. The collection includes displays of peasant costumes, folk art, and Sami culture. Families with children should visit the delightful "village life" play area on the ground floor. *Tel. 08/666–4600. Admission: SKr 40. Open Tues.–Sun. 11–5.*

Shopping **Västerlånggatan,** one of the main streets in the Old Town, is a popular shopping area brimming with boutiques and antiques shops. Walk down to the Skeppsbron waterfront, then head back toward the center over the Ström bridge, where anglers cast for salmon.

Turkish Coast

Some of the finest reconstructed Greek and Roman cities, including the fabled Pergamum, Ephesus, Aphrodisias, and Troy, are found along the Aegean. Bright yellow road signs pointing to historical sites or to those currently undergoing excavation are everywhere here. There are so many Greek and Roman ruins, in fact, that some haven't yet been excavated and others are going to seed. Grand or small, all the sites are steeped in atmosphere and are best explored early in the morning or late in the afternoon, when there are fewer crowds. You can escape the heat of the day on one of the sandy beaches that line the coast.

Currency The monetary unit is the Turkish lira (TL). At press time, the exchange rate was 79,205 TL to the dollar. These rates are subject to wide fluctuation, so check close to your departure. Be certain to retain your original exchange slips when you convert money into Turkish lira—you will need them to reconvert the money. Because the Turkish lira is worth a lot less than most currencies, it's best to convert only what you plan to spend.

Telephones For all international calls dial 00, then dial the country code, area or city code, and the number. You can use the higher-price cards for this, or reach an international operator by dialing 132. To reach an **AT&T** long distance operator, dial 00800-12277; for **MCI,** dial 00800-11177; and for **Sprint,** 00800-14477. The country code for Turkey is 90.

Shore Excursions The following are good choices along the Turkish coast. They may not be offered by all cruise lines. Times and prices are approximate.

In İzmir **City Tour.** Visit the fairly well-preserved Velvet Fortress and Archeological Museum followed by a belly-dancing performance and a folkloric show. *3¾ hrs. Cost: $30.*

Ephesus. Drive 1 hour and 15 minutes to reach Ephesus, once the Roman Capital of Asia Minor, where you'll tour the spellbinding ruins of Ephesus. Major sights include the Great Theater, the Library of Celsus, the Temple of Hadrian, and Curetes Street. *4½ hrs. Cost: $45.*

In Kuşadası **Ancient Ephesus.** This is the tour to take—it explores one of the best-preserved ancient cities of the world. Be prepared to do a lot of walking. *4 hrs. Cost: $35.*

In Bodrum The Castle of Bodrum is easily explored on your own, and is within walking distance of the tender drop-off point.

Wooden Boat Ride. Sail one of the wooden boats that line Bodrum's harbor to small coves and bays for swimming and snorkeling. *3½ hrs. Cost: $59.*

Coming Ashore Whether your ship docks or drops anchor along the Turkish Coast, landing sites are conveniently located for independent exploration.

In İzmir Ships calling at İzmir's harbor dock along the waterfront boulevard called Kordon. Depending on what you want to see, you can walk, take a bus, or hire a taxi to explore the sights.

In Kuşadası Ships either dock or tender passengers ashore at Kuşadası. Shops and restaurants are within walking distance of the port.

In Bodrum Ships calling at Bodrum tender passengers ashore in the main harbor. Walking Bodrum's streets is truly the best and most pleasurable way to explore local sights.

Exploring the Turkish Coast

İzmir The center of the city is **Kültürpark,** which is a large green park that is the site of İzmir's industrial fair from late August until late September.

On top of İzmir's highest hill is the **Kadifekale** (Velvet Fortress), built in the 3rd century BC by Lysimachos. It is easily reached by dolmuş and is one of the few ancient ruins that was not destroyed in the fire after the war for Turkish independence.

At the foot of the hill is the restored **Agora,** the market of ancient Smyrna. The modern-day marketplace is in Konak Square, a maze of tiny streets filled with shops and covered stalls. *Open Mon.–Sat. 8–8.*

Kuşadası The major attraction near Kuşadası is **Ephesus,** a city created by the Ionians in the 11th century BC and now one of the grandest recon-

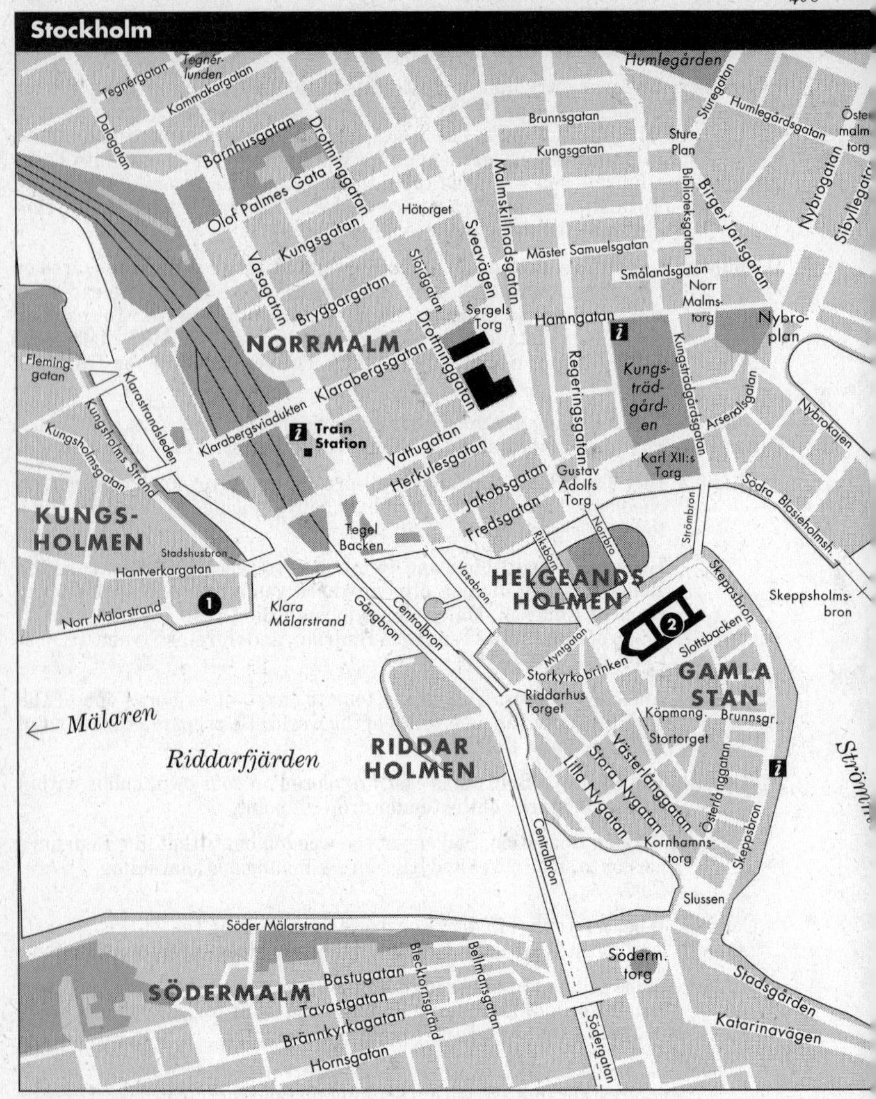

Gröna Lund Tivoli, **4**
Kungliga Slott, **2**
Nordiska Museet, **5**
Stadshuset, **1**
Vasamuseet, **3**

Karlaplan
Kommendörsgatan
Sibyllegatan
ÖSTERMALM
Narvavägen
Banérgatan
Karlavägen
LADUGÅRDSGÄRDET
Linnégatan
Oxenstiernsgatan
Artillerigatan
Skeppargatan
Grevgatan
Styrmangatan
Storgatan
Linnégatan
Gärdesgatan
Skarpögatan
Riddargatan
Strandvägen
Strandvägen
Djurgårdsbron
Djurgårdsbrunnsviken
5
Rosendalsvägen
3
SKEPPSHOLMEN
Svensksundsvägen
DJURGÅRDEN
Alkärret
Djurgårdsvägen
Falkenbergsg.
Sirishovsvägen
Allmänna Gränd
Djurgårds Slätten
Sollidsbacken
Singelbacken
KASTELL-HOLMEN
4
Baltic
Saltsjön
BECKHOLMEN
N
KEY
Tourist Information
Rail Lines
0
500 yards
0
500 meters

structed ancient sites in the world. It is the showpiece of Aegean archaeology. Ephesus was a powerful trading port and the sacred center for the cult of Artemis, Greek goddess of chastity, the moon, and hunting. The Ionians built a temple in her honor, one of the Seven Wonders of the Ancient World. During the Roman period, it became a shrine for the Roman goddess Diana. Today, waterlogged foundations are all that remain of the temple. Allow yourself the full day for Ephesus.

Bodrum One of the outstanding sights in Bodrum is **Bodrum Castle,** known as the Castle of St. Peter. Located between the two bays, the castle was built by crusaders in the 11th century. It has beautiful gardens and the Museum of Underwater Archaeology. *Castle and museum admission: $2.50. Open Tues.–Sun. 8:30–noon and 1–5.*

The peninsula is downright littered with ancient Greek and Roman ruins, although getting to some of them involves driving over rough dirt roads. Five kilometers (3 miles) from Bodrum is **Halikarnas,** a well-preserved 10,000-seat Greek amphitheater built in the 1st century BC and still used for town festivals. *Admission free. Open daily 8:30–sunset.*

Varna, Bulgaria

Bulgaria, a land of mountains and seascapes, of austerity and rustic beauty, lies in the eastern half of the Balkan peninsula. From the end of World War II until recently, it was the closest ally of the former Soviet Union and presented a rather mysterious image to the Western world. This era ended in 1989 with the overthrow of Communist party head Todor Zhivkov. Since then, Bulgaria has gradually opened itself to the West as it struggles along the path toward democracy and a free-market economy.

Founded in 681, Bulgaria was a crossroads of civilization even before that date. Archaeological finds in Varna, on the Black Sea coast, give proof of civilization from as early as 4600 BC. Bulgaria was part of the Byzantine Empire from AD 1018 to 1185 and was occupied by the Turks from 1396 until 1878. The combined influences are reflected in Bulgarian architecture, which has a truly Eastern feel. Five hundred years of Muslim occupation and nearly half a century of Communist rule did not wipe out Christianity, and there are many lovely, icon-filled churches to see.

Currency The unit of currency in Bulgaria is the lev (plural leva), divided into 100 stotinki. At press time, the exchange rate was 133 leva to the U.S. dollar. All unspent leva must be exchanged before you depart the country, and you will need to present your official exchange slips to prove that the currency was legally purchased—so exchange only as much as you plan to spend.

Telephones In Bulgaria, calls can be made from public telephones in the post offices. To place a call to the United States via an **AT&T USADirect** international operator, dial 00–1800–0010; for **Sprint Express,** dial 00–800–0877. There is a new system of international telephones—modern, direct-dial phones with no coin slots—that operate only with special cards paid for in leva. Directions for buying the cards are given, often in English, on the phones.

Shore Excursions The following is a good choice in Varna. It may not be offered by all cruise lines. Time and price are approximate.

Varna Tour. You'll see the city's major sites before visiting one of the area's renowned Black Sea spas. *Half day. Cost: $42.*

Coming Ashore Ships calling at Varna dock at the city harbor. Varna's main sights can be reached on foot. Buses are inexpensive; make sure to buy your ticket in advance from the kiosks near the bus stops.

Exploring Varna

Begin with the **Archeologicheski Musei,** one of the great—if lesser-known—museums of Europe. The splendid collection includes the world's oldest gold treasures from the Varna necropolis of the 4th millennium BC, as well as Thracian, Greek, and Roman treasures, and richly painted icons. *41 Osmi Primorski Polk Blvd., tel. 052/23-70-57. Open Tues.–Sat. 10–5.*

The monumental **cathedral** (1880–86) is worth a look for its lavish murals. Opposite the cathedral, in the city gardens, is the Old **Clock Tower,** built in 1880 by the Varna Guild Association.

On the corner of Knyaz Boris I Boulevard and Shipka Street are the remains of the **Roman fortress wall.**

The **Holy Virgin Church** of 1602 also features the substantial remains of the **Roman baths,** dating from the 2nd to the 3rd century AD. Buy the excellent English guidebook here to get the most out of your visit. *On Han Krum St.*

The **Naval Museum** displays the early days of navigation on the Black Sea and the Danube. *No. 2 Primorski Blvd., tel. 052/22-26-55. Open weekdays 8–4.*

The extensive and luxuriant **Marine Gardens** command a wide view over the bay. In the gardens there are restaurants, an open-air theater, and the fascinating Copernicus Astronomy Complex. *Tel. 052/22-28-90. Open weekdays 8–noon and 2–5.*

Eight kilometers (5 miles) north along the coast from Varna is **Sveti Konstantin,** Bulgaria's oldest Black Sea resort. Small and intimate, it spreads through a wooded park near a series of sandy coves. Warm mineral springs were discovered here in 1947, and the five-star Grand Hotel Varna, the most luxurious on the coast, offers all kinds of hydrotherapy under medical supervision.

The lively **Zlatni Pjasâci,** better known as **Golden Sands,** lies 16 kilometers (10 miles) nort of Varna. It's known for its extensive leisure amenities, mineral-spring medical centers, and sports and entertainment facilities.

Just over 4 kilometers (2 miles) inland from Golden Sands is **Aladja Rock Monastery,** one of Bulgaria's oldest, cut out of the cliff face and made accessible to visitors by sturdy iron stairways.

Venice, Italy

For hundreds of years Venice was the unrivaled mistress of trade between Europe and the Orient, and the staunch bulwark of Christendom against the tide of Turkish expansion. Though the power and glory of its days as a wealthy city-republic are gone, the art and exotic aura remain. The majority of its magnificent palazzi are slowly crumbling, but somehow in Venice the shabby, derelict effect is magically transformed into one of supreme beauty and charm. Hot and sultry in the summer, Venice is much more welcoming in early spring and late fall.

Currency

The unit of currency in Italy is the lira (plural, lire). At press time, the exchange rate was about 1,546 lire to the dollar. When your purchases run into hundreds of thousands of lire, beware of being shortchanged, a dodge that is practiced at ticket windows and cashiers' desks, as well as in shops and even banks. Always count your change before you leave the counter.

Telephones

To place international calls, many travelers go to the Telefoni telephone exchange (usually marked TELECOM), where the operator assigns you a booth, can help place your call, and will collect payment when you have finished. To dial an international call, insert a phone card, dial 00, then the country code, area code, and phone number. For **AT&T,** dial access number 172–1011; for **MCI,** dial access number

172–1022; for **Sprint,** dial access number 172–1877. You will be connected directly with an operator in the United States.

Shore Excursions The following are good choices in Venice. They may not be offered by all cruise lines. Times and prices are approximate.

Island Tour. See Venice from the water on this boat tour that visits a 10th-century monastery on San Giorgio Maggiore and the famous glass factory on Murano Island. *3½ hrs. Cost: $40.*

Venice Tour. Visit St. Mark's Square and Cathedral, Doge's Palace, and the Bridge of Sighs. *2½ hrs. Cost: $42.*

Coming Ashore Ships typically dock in Venice at the main port terminal, an unappealing building whose saving grace is its relative nearness to St. Mark's Square.

Getting Around Cruise passengers may find that getting around Venice presents some unusual problems: the complexity of its layout (the city is made up of more than 100 islands, all linked by bridges); the bewildering unfamiliarity of waterborne transportation; the apparently illogical house numbering system and duplication of street names in its six districts; and the necessity of walking whether you enjoy it or not. It's essential to have a good map showing all street names and water-bus routes; buy one at any newsstand, and count on getting lost more than once.

Walking is the only way to reach many parts of Venice, so wear comfortable shoes. ACTV water buses run the length of the Grand Canal and circle the city. There are several lines, some of which connect Venice with the major and minor islands in the lagoon. Line 1 is the Grand Canal local, calling at every stop, and continuing via San Marco to the Lido. (It takes about 45 minutes from the station to San Marco.) The fare is 3,500 lire on most lines. A 24-hour tourist ticket costs 14,000 lire. Timetables are posted at every landing stage, but there is not always a ticket booth operating. You may get on a boat without a ticket, but you will have to pay a higher fare on the boat. Landing stages are clearly marked with name and line number, but check before boarding, particularly with the 52 and 82, to make sure the boat is going in your direction.

Motoscafis, or water "taxis," are excessively expensive, and the fare system is as complex as Venice's layout. A minimum fare of about 50,000 lire gets you nowhere, and you'll pay three times as much to get from one end of the Grand Canal to the other. Always agree on the fare before starting out.

Few tourists know about the two-man gondolas that ferry people across the Grand Canal at various fixed points. It's the cheapest and shortest gondola ride in Venice, and it can save a lot of walking. The fare is 600 lire, which you hand to one of the gondoliers when you get on. Look for TRAGHETTO signs.

Exploring Venice *Numbers in the margin correspond to points of interest on the Venice map.*

❶ Even the pigeons have to fight for space on **Piazza San Marco,** the most famous piazza in Venice, and pedestrian traffic jams clog the surrounding byways. Despite the crowds, San Marco is the logical starting place for exploring Venice.

❷ The **Basilica di San Marco** (St. Mark's Basilica) was begun in the 11th century to hold the relics of St. Mark the Evangelist, the city's patron saint, and its richly decorated facade is surmounted by copies of the four famous gilded bronze horses (the originals are in the basilica's upstairs museum). Inside, golden mosaics sheathe walls and domes, lending an extraordinarily exotic aura: half Christian church, half Middle Eastern mosque. Be sure to see the Pala d'Oro, an eye-filling 10th-century altarpiece in gold and silver, studded with precious gems and enamels. From the atrium, climb the steep stairway to the museum: The bronze horses alone are worth the effort. *Basilica is open from early morning, but tourist visits are only allowed Mon.–Sat. 9:30–5, Sun. 2–5. No admission to those wearing shorts or other revealing clothing. Pala d'Oro and Treasury tel. 041/522–5205. Admission: 3,000 lire. Open Apr.–Sept., Mon.–Sat. 9:30–5, Sun. 2–5; Oct.–Mar., Mon.–Sat. 10–4, Sun. 2–4, although these times may vary slightly. Gallery and Museum admission: 3,000 lire. Open Apr.–Sept., daily 9:30–5; Oct.–Mar., daily 10–4.*

❸ During Venice's heyday, the **Palazzo Ducale** (Doge's Palace) was the epicenter of the Serene Republic's great empire. More than just a palace, it was a combination White House, Senate, Supreme Court, torture chamber, and prison. The building's exterior is striking; the lower stories consist of two rows of fragile-seeming arches, while above rests a massive pink-and-white marble wall, whose solidity is barely interrupted by its six great Gothic windows. The interior is a maze of vast halls, monumental staircases, secret corridors, and the sinister prison cells and torture chamber. The palace is filled with frescoes, paintings, and a few examples of statuary by some of the Renaissance's greatest artists. Don't miss the famous view from the balcony, overlooking the piazza and St. Mark's Basin and the church of San Giorgio Maggiore across the lagoon. *Piazzetta San Marco, tel. 041/522–4951. Admission: 10,000 lire. Open Apr.–Oct., daily 9–7; Nov.–Mar., daily 9–4. Last entry 1 hr before closing time.*

❹ For a pigeon's-eye view of Venice take the elevator up to the top of the **Campanile di San Marco** (St. Mark's bell tower) in Piazza San Marco, a reconstruction of the 1,000-year-old tower that collapsed one morning in 1912, practically without warning. Fifteenth-century clerics found guilty of immoral acts were suspended in wooden cages from the tower, sometimes to live on bread and water for as long as a year, sometimes to die of starvation and exposure. Look for them in Carpaccio's paintings of the square, which hang in the Accademia (*see below*). *Piazza San Marco, tel. 041/522–4064. Admission: 5,000 lire. Open Easter–Sept., daily 9:30–7; Oct., daily 10–6; Nov.–Easter, daily 10–4:30; closed most of Jan.*

❺ The **Galleria dell'Accademia** (Accademia Gallery) is Venice's most important picture gallery and a must for art lovers. Try to spend at least an hour viewing this remarkable collection of Venetian art, which is attractively displayed and well lighted. Works range from 14th-century Gothic to the Golden Age of the 15th and 16th centuries, including oils by Giovanni Bellini, Giorgione, Titian, and Tintoretto, and superb later works by Veronese and Tiepolo. *Campo della Carità, tel. 041/522–2247. Admission: 12,000 lire. Open Fri.–Mon. 9–2, Tues.–Thurs. 9–7.*

❻ The church of Santa Maria Gloriosa dei Frari—known simply as the **Frari**—is one of Venice's most important churches, a vast, soaring Gothic building of brick. Since it is the principal church of the Franciscans, its design is suitably austere to reflect that order's vows of poverty, though paradoxically it contains a number of the most sumptuous pictures in any Venetian church. Chief among them are the magnificent Titian altarpiece, the immense *Assumption of the Virgin*, over the main altar. Titian was buried here at the ripe old age of 88, the only one of 70,000 plague victims to be given a personal church burial. *Campo dei Frari. Admission: 1,000 lire. Special visiting hrs: Mon.–Sat. 2:30–6. Open Apr.–Oct., Mon.–Sat. 9–noon, Sun. 3–6; Nov.–Mar., Mon.–Sat. 9:30–noon, Sun. 3–5:30.*

Just off Piazzetta di San Marco (the square in front of the Doge's Palace) you can catch Vaporetto 1 at either the San Marco or San Zaccaria landing stages (on Riva degli Schiavoni), to set off on a boat tour along the **Grand Canal.** Serving as Venice's main thoroughfare, the canal winds in the shape of an S for more than 3½ kilometers

Venice

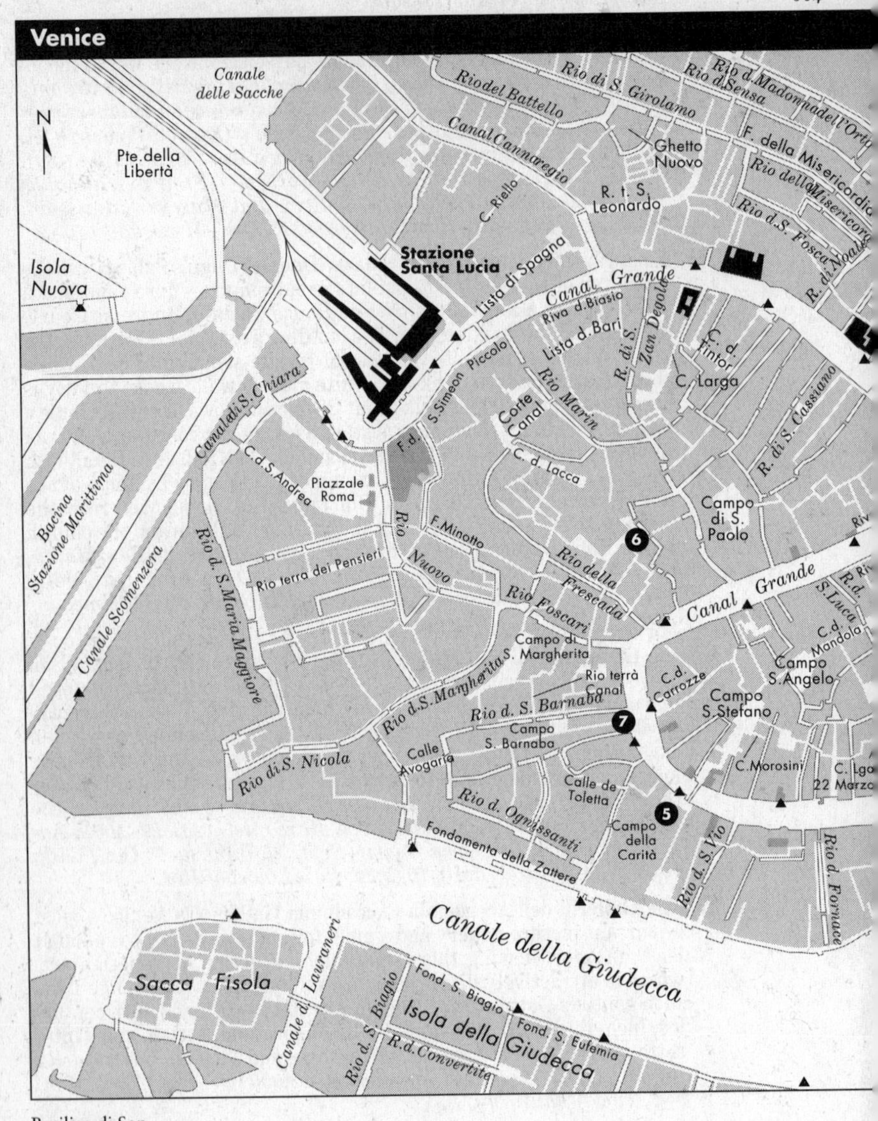

Basilica di San Marco, **2**

Ca' Rezzonico, **7**

Campanile di San Marco, **4**

Frari, **6**

Galleria dell'Accademia, **5**

Palazzo Ducale, **3**

Piazza San Marco, **1**

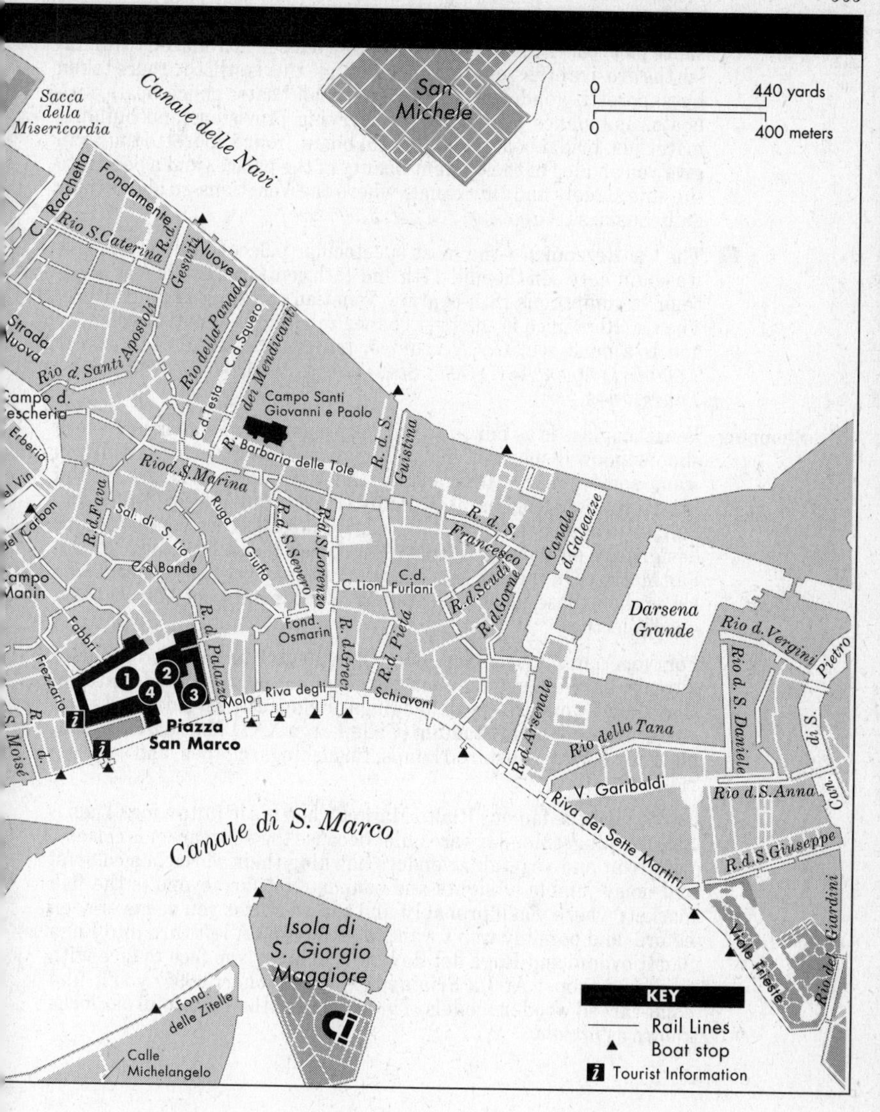

San Michele
0 440 yards
0 400 meters
Sacca della Misericordia
Canale delle Navi
Fondamente Nuove
C. Racchetta
Rio S.Caterina
R.d. Gesuiti
Strada Nuova
Rio d. Santi Apostoli
Rio della Panada
C.d.Squero
R. dei Mendicanti
C.d.Testa
Campo Santi Giovanni e Paolo
R. Barbaria delle Tole
R. d. S. Guistina
Campo d. Pescheria
Erberia
Riod.S.Marina
R.d.Fava
Sal. di S. Lio
Ruga Giuffa
R.d. S.Severo
Rd.S.Lorenzo
C.d.Bande
Campo Manin
C.Lion
C.d. Furlani
R. d. S. Francesco
R.d.Scudi
R.d.Gorne
Canale d.Galeazze
Darsena Grande
Rio d. Vergini
Pietro
Rio d. S. Daniele
di S.
Can.
Fabbri
Frezzaria
Fond. Osmarin
R. d.Greci
R.d. Pietà
R. d. Palazzo
Molo
Riva degli Schiavoni
Piazza San Marco
S. Moisè
R. d.
R.d.Arsenale
Rio della Tana
V. Garibaldi
Rio d.S.Anna
Riva dei Sette Martiri
R.d.S.Giuseppe
Canale di S. Marco
Isola di S. Giorgio Maggiore
Viale Trieste
Rio dei Giardini
Fond. delle Zitelle
Calle Michelangelo
KEY
Rail Lines
Boat stop
Tourist Information

(2 miles) through the heart of the city, past some 200 Gothic-Renaissance palaces. Although restrictions have been introduced to diminish the erosive effect of wash on buildings, this is still the route taken by vaporetti, gondolas, water taxis, mail boats, police boats, fire boats, ambulance boats, barges carrying provisions and building materials, bridal boats, and funeral boats. Your vaporetto tour will give you an idea of the opulent beauty of the palaces and a peek into the side streets and tiny canals where the Venetians go about their daily business. *Vaporetto 1. Cost: 3,500 lire.*

7 The **Ca' Rezzonico**—the most spectacular palace in all of Venice—was built between the mid-17th and 18th centuries and is now a museum of sumptuous 18th-century Venetian paintings and furniture. The Ca' Rezzonico is the best chance to glimpse Venetian splendor and is a must-see. *Ca' Rezzonico, tel. 041/522–4543. Admission: 8,000 lire. Open Apr.–Oct., Sat.–Thurs. 10–5; Nov.–Mar., Sat.–Thurs. 10–4.*

Shopping Venetian glass is as famous as the city's gondolas, and almost every shop window displays it. There's a lot of cheap glass for sale; if you want something better, among the top showrooms are **Venini** (Piazzetta dei Leoncini 314), **Pauly** (Piazza San Marco 73–77), and **Salviati** (Piazza San Marco 79B). Carlo Moretti's chic, contemporary designs are on show at **L'Isola** (Campo San Moisè 1468, near Piazza San Marco). On the island of Murano, where prices are generally no lower than those in Venice, **Domus** (Fondamenta dei Vetrai) has a good selection.

For Venetian fabrics, **Norelene** (Calle della Chiesa 727, in Dorsoduro, near the Guggenheim) has stunning hand-painted material that makes wonderful wall hangings or elegantly styled jackets and chic scarves. **Venetia Studuim** (Calle Larga XXII Marzo 2430), is famous for Fortuny-inspired lamps, furnishings, clothes, and accessories.

Try to visit the famous **Rialto Market** when it's in full swing (Tues.–Sat. mornings; Mondays are quiet because the fish market is closed), with fruit and vegetable vendors hawking their wares in a colorful and noisy jumble of sights and sounds. Not far beyond is the fish market, where you'll probably find sea creatures you've never seen before (and possibly won't want to see again). A left turn into Ruga San Giovanni and Ruga del Ravano will bring you face to face with scores of shops: At **La Scialuppa** (Calle Saoneri 2695) you'll find hand-carved wooden models of gondolas and their graceful oar locks known as *forcole*.

The Hawaiian Islands

It's hard to believe such a gentle paradise sprang from such a violent beginning—mighty volcanic explosions. Over the centuries, crashing surf, strong sea winds, and powerful rivers carved and chiseled the great mountains and lush valleys that are Hawaii's pride.

Polynesian explorers stumbled upon these islands in the 4th century AD while navigating the South Pacific in their huge voyaging canoes. A succession of native rulers began in 1795 with King Kamehameha I and ended with the deposition of Queen Liliuokalani in 1893, when a provisional government was installed. In 1900 Hawaii was established as a U.S. territory, and in 1959 it became the 50th state. Today the islands retain a mystique that makes Hawaii America's most exotic state, with 132 islands and atolls stretching across 1,600 miles of ocean.

At one time many a ship brought travelers to the Hawaiian Islands, but when Pan Am's amphibious *Hawaii Clipper* touched down on Pearl Harbor's waters in 1936, it marked the beginning of the end of regular passenger-ship travel here. Since then, visitors have been flown in, and only a few cruise lines now pass through the islands. Among them are Carnival, Crystal, Holland America, Princess, Royal Caribbean, and Seabourn. One line, American Hawaii, sails exclusively in Hawaii. Its 800-passenger ship, the SS *Independence*, leaves Honolulu on seven-day cruises that visit the Big Island, Maui, and Kauai. (For seasonal itineraries, *see* Chapter 4.)

When to Go Hawaii is always temperate, sunny, and a pleasure. Although rainfall is slightly greater from December through February, the sun is rarely hidden behind the clouds for a solid 24-hour period. Summer is big with families, as are holidays. February and March are also busy cruising months because whales are most abundant during this period.

Passports and Visas Canadians need only prove their place of birth, with a passport, birth certificate, or similar document. Other foreign citizens require a passport and visa.

Shopping Distinctively Hawaiian gifts include Aloha shirts and muumuu dresses, rich roasted Kona coffee, macadamia nuts, pineapples, and hand-carved wood. In general, major stores and shopping centers are open from 9 or 10 AM to 5 PM; some have evening hours.

Retail outlets abound in the Aloha State, from major tourist centers to small villages. Shopping malls are prevalent; many run free shuttles from the pier for cruise passengers. The largest on Oahu is the **Ala Moana Center,** which is just west of Waikīkī—home of the **Royal Hawaiian Shopping Center.** Outside Waikīkī are **Ward Warehouse,** the **Kahala Mall,** and **Pearlridge Center.**

On the Neighbor Islands smaller strips of shops are the rule, but larger stores exist in Kauai's **Kukui Grove Center** in Līhue, Maui's **Kaahumanu Center,** and the Big Island's **Prince Kūhiō Plaza** in Hilo. Kauai is known for its mom-and-pop shops and family-run boutiques. Exclusive shops are abundant in the luxury hotels.

Dining Hawaii's melting-pot population accounts for its great variety of epicurean delights. You can dine on Japanese sashimi, Thai curry, Hawaiian *laulau* (fish, meat, and other ingredients wrapped and steamed in ti leaves), Chinese roast duck, and a mouthwatering array of French, German, Korean, American, Mexican, Indian, Italian, and Greek dishes.

There are, of course, a few uniquely tropical tastes, especially when it comes to fruit. Bananas, papayas, and pineapples grow throughout the year, while the prized mangos, watermelons, and litchis appear in summer. Seafood is equally exotic, with such delicacies as mahimahi (dolphinfish), *ōpakapaka* (pink snapper), *ulua* (crevelle), and *ahi* (yellowfin tuna).

Many tourists rate a trip to a luau among the highlights of their stay. At these feasts, you're likely to find the traditional *kālua* pig, often roasted underground in an *imu* (oven); *poi*, the starchy, bland paste made from the taro root; and laulau.

Category	Cost*
$$$$	over $50
$$$	$30–$50
$$	$15–$30
$	under $15

**per person for a three-course meal, excluding drinks, service, and 4.17% sales tax*

The Big Island of Hawaii

Nearly twice the size of the other Hawaiian Islands combined, the Big Island is also the most diverse. With 266 miles of coastline of black-lava, white-coral, and green-olivine beaches, and with cliffs of lava and emerald gorges slashing into jutting mountains, the Big Island is so large and so varied that ships call at two ports, Hilo and Kona.

Shore Excursions The following are good choices on the Big Island. They may not be offered by all cruise lines. Times and prices are approximate.

In Hilo **Volcanoes and Nuts.** Discover the sights, sounds, and tastes of the Big Island on this attraction-filled half-day tour. Travel from sea level to 4,000 feet, from desert to rain forest, and see steam vents and lava flows and explore an ancient lava tunnel. Includes a stop at a macadamia-nut farm, where you can buy freshly roasted nuts, chocolate-covered nuts, and nut-flavored coffee. *Half day. Cost: $35.*

Volcanoes by Helicopter. Hover over the still-active craters of Kīlauea, which have been erupting steadily for more than a decade. If you're lucky, they'll be oozing lava. *45-min flight. Cost: $125.*

In Kona **Deep-Sea Fishing.** Fish the waters around Kona, renowned for their abundance of billfish. Blue marlin and yellowfin tuna are other prizes here. Bait, tackle, and ice are provided. *3 hrs. Cost: $95.*

Spectacular Snorkeling. At least once during your cruise, put on your flippers and mask to explore below Hawaii's crystal-clear waters. A variety of snorkeling excursions are offered. *3–4½ hrs. Cost: $40–$60.*

Coming Ashore *In Hilo* Ships dock in an industrial area of tank farms and freight depots; the only thing within walking distance for cruise passengers is the Big Island Candies factory gift shop. It's about half a mile away from the pier. Make a right as you exit the dock area—it's a little ways down on the left. Across Hilo Bay, you can see the Big Island's small collection of resorts on Banyan Drive. There's also a Japanese garden, landscaped with bonsai trees and reflecting pools, and a small beach. It's about 2 miles away. The island's major attraction, **Volcanoes National Park,** is 30 miles from the ship. There's a State of Hawaii visitor information booth inside the cruise terminal.

In Kona Ships drop anchor off Kailua-Kona and tender passengers to shore. Walk off the tender and you're across the street from the tony shopping complex of the King Kamehameha Hotel. Just a short stroll away is historic Hulihee Palace; from here, the village of Kailua extends about a mile down the coast.

Getting Around

By Car

If you choose to tour the Big Island on your own, you'll need a car. **Avis** (tel. 800/331–1212), **Hertz** (tel. 800/654–3131), and **Budget** (tel. 800/527–0700) are among the national agencies with locations in both Hilo and Kona. In Hilo, also try **Harper's** (tel. 808/969–1478). American Hawaii ships can arrange car rentals through their shore-excursions offices. Prices start at around $40 a day for a compact.

By Historic Auto

An antique Sampan—an open-air, station wagon–like vehicle—runs on a continuous circuit in Hilo between the pier and Banyan Drive, the Nani Mau Gardens and shopping centers. A single trip is $2; for $10 you can ride all day (Hilo Sampan Co., tel. 808/935–6955).

By Taxi

Several companies advertise guided tours by taxi, but it is an expensive way to travel: The trip around the island costs more than $300. Meter rates are $2 for pickup and $1.60 per mile. In Hilo, call **Ace Taxi** (tel. 808/935–8303) or **Hilo Harry's** (tel. 808/935–7091). In Kona, try **Paradise Taxi** (tel. 808/329–1234) or **Marina Taxi** (tel. 808/329–2481).

Beaches

Don't believe anyone who tells you the Big Island lacks beaches; it actually has 80 or more. Small but beautiful, swimmable white-sand beaches dot the Kohala coastline. The surf is rough in summer, and few public beaches have lifeguards. In Hawaii beaches change constantly; a new black-sand beach, **Kamoamoa,** was formed in 1989 by molten lava encountering cold ocean waters. It was just as suddenly closed in 1992 by lava flow from Kīlauea, which has been erupting since 1983. Lava also covered the Harry K. Brown and Kaimū beaches in 1990.

Near Kona

The closest beach to ships that call at Kona is White Sands, a 10-minute drive from the tender landing. Another five minutes down the coast is Kahalu'u, a coarse-sand beach good for swimming, sunning, and snorkeling.

Near Hilo

Three small beaches can be found 10–15 minutes from the pier. **James Keahola** is a white-sand beach with rest rooms and picnic tables. **Onekahakaha** also has facilities and picnic tables. **Leleiwi Beach Park** is a lava-rock beach with small, protected coves for swimming. **Punaluu Beach Park** is 27 miles from Volcanoes National Park, on the south side of the island. Turtles swim in the bay and lay their eggs in the black sand. Fishponds are just inland. There are rest rooms across the road.

Dining

$$

Merriman's. It's worth the 30-minute drive from Kailua-Kona to cowboy country in Kamuela to sample Peter Merriman's imaginative cuisine. The menu features beef and veal dishes named for local ranchers along with vegetarian selections. An exhibition kitchen allows diners to watch the chef prepare his creations. *'Opelo Plaza II, corner of Rte. 19 and 'Opelo Rd., Kamuela, tel. 808/885–6822. AE, MC, V.*

$–$$

Harrington's. At this popular and reliable steak-and-seafood restaurant located right near the docks, two outstanding dishes are fresh ono or mahimahi meunière, served with brown butter, lemon, and parsley; and Slavic steak, thinly sliced and slathered with garlic butter. *135 Kalanianaole St., Hilo, tel. 808/961–4966. MC, V.*

Kauai

Nicknamed "the Garden Isle," Kauai is Eden epitomized. In the mountains of Kōkee, lush swamps ring with the songs of rare birds, while the heady aroma of ginger blossoms sweetens the cool rain forests of Hāena. Time and nature have carved elegant spires along the remote northern shore, called the Nā Pali Coast, while seven powerful rivers give life to the valleys where ancient Hawaiians once dwelled.

The Hawaiian Islands

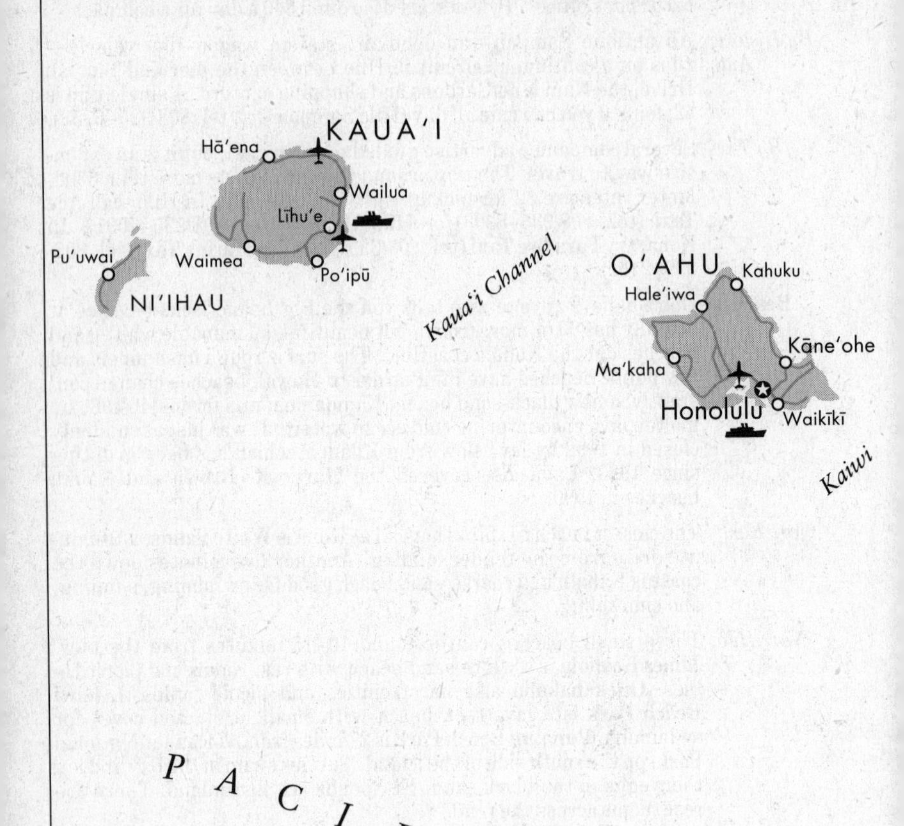

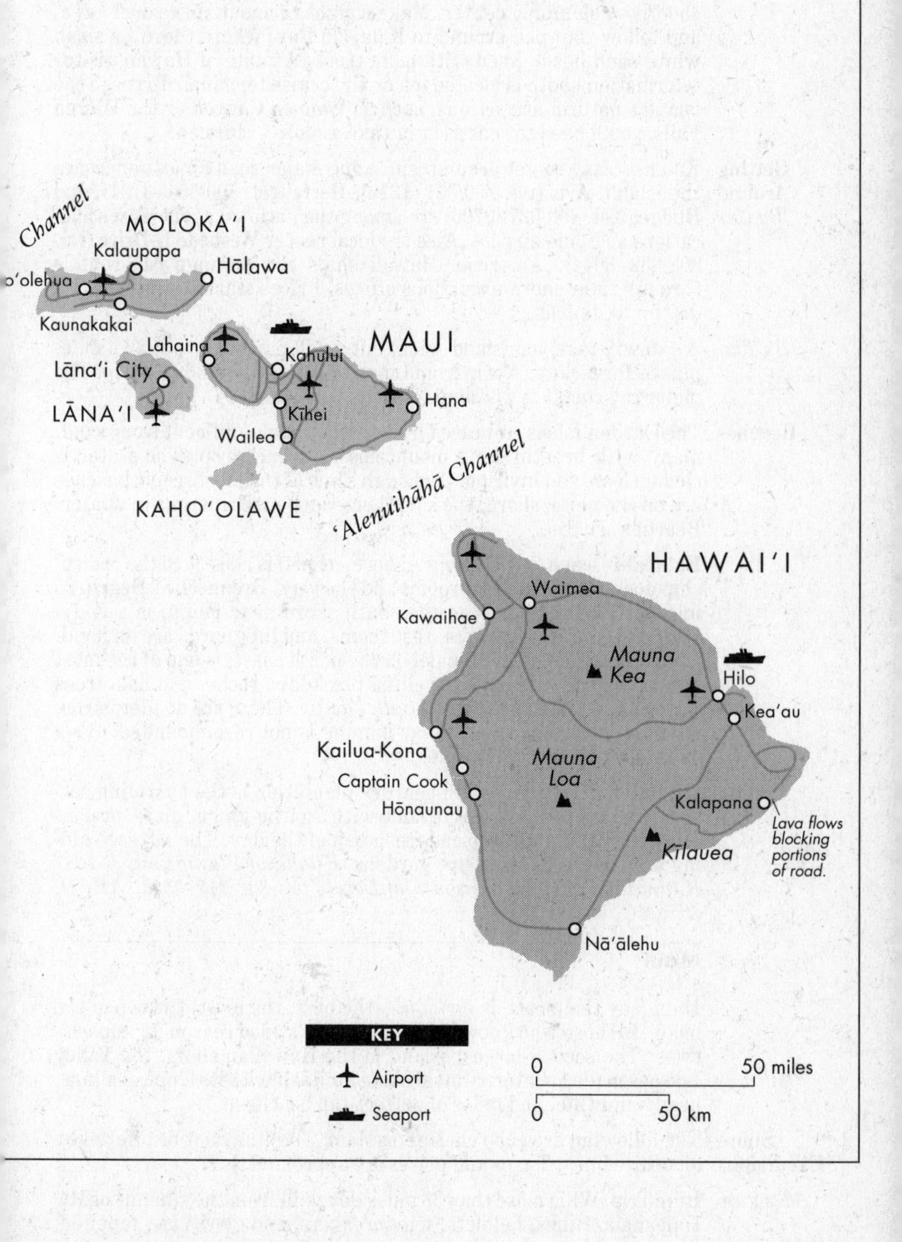
N
Channel
MOLOKA'I
Kalaupapa
Hālawa
o'olehua
Kaunakakai
Lahaina
MAUI
Kahului
Lāna'i City
LĀNA'I
Kīhei
Hana
Wailea
KAHO'OLAWE
'Alenuihāhā Channel
HAWAI'I
Waimea
Kawaihae
Mauna Kea
Hilo
Kea'au
Kailua-Kona
Mauna Loa
Captain Cook
Hōnaunau
Kalapana
Lava flows blocking portions of road.
Kīlauea
Nā'ālehu
KEY
Airport
Seaport
0
50 miles
0
50 km

Shore Excursions The following are good choices on Kauai. They may not be offered by all cruise lines. Times and prices are approximate.

Natural Beauty **Helicopter Tour.** Get a bird's-eye view of Kauai's canyons, waterfalls, and rain forests. *25–50 mins. Cost: $75–$125.*

Waimea Canyon. A quick and convenient way to see Waimea Canyon, known as the "Grand Canyon of the Pacific," without renting a car. *Half day. Cost: $35.*

Coming Ashore Ships calling along the "Coconut Coast" dock at Nāwiliwili, a picturesque if somewhat industrial harbor in the shadows of the Hoary Head mountain range. A five-minute walk from the dock is the Anchor Cove shopping center. Make a right turn out of the dock area, and follow the road around to Kalapakī Bay, where there's a small white-sand beach lined with palm trees. A State of Hawaii visitor information booth is located inside the cruise terminal. To reach the island's natural attractions, such as **Waimea Canyon** or the **Wailua Falls,** you'll need to rent a car or take a shore excursion.

Getting Around

By Car Kauai is easy to get around, since one major road almost encircles the island. **Avis** (tel. 800/331–1212), **Hertz** (tel. 800/654–3131), and **Budget** (tel. 800/527–0700) are among the national agencies with locations at Līhue airport. Also try local renter **Westside U-Drive** (tel. 808/332–8644). American Hawaii ships can arrange car rentals through their shore-excursions offices. Prices start at around $40 a day for a compact.

By Taxi A cab will take you island-wide, but you'll pay dearly, at $2 a mile, plus $2 for pickup. A trip from Līhue to Poipū costs $36, plus tip. The major cab company is **Kauai Cab** (tel. 808/246–9554).

Beaches The Garden Isle is embraced by stretches of magnificent ivory sand, many with breathtaking mountains as a backdrop. The water is clean, clear, and inviting. Although some of the most scenic beaches are on the north shore, the surf there can be treacherous in winter. Beaches are free.

Kalapakī Beach (*see* Coming Ashore, *above*) is closest to the cruise-ship dock. There are rest rooms and showers. **Brennecke's Beach,** 25 minutes from the ship on the south shore near Poipū, is a body-surfer's paradise. Showers, rest rooms, and lifeguards are on hand. **Lumahai Beach,** near Hanalei on the north coast, is one of the most scenic beaches. Its majestic cliffs, black lava rocks, and hala trees were the setting for the film *South Pacific*. There are no lifeguards, showers, or rest rooms, and swimming is not recommended. It's a 45-minute drive from the pier.

Dining

$$ **Gaylord's.** A gracious 19th-century plantation is the charming setting in which to enjoy rack of lamb with a garlic-ginger glaze, or pan-blackened and highly spiced fresh fish of the day. The alfresco dining area opens to extensive gardens. *Kilohana Plantation, 3–2087 Kaumualii Hwy., 1 mi south of Līhue, tel. 808/245–9593. AE, D, DC, MC, V.*

Maui

Maui, say the locals, is *no ka oi*—the best, the most, the top of the heap. To those who know Maui well, there's good reason for superlatives. The second-largest island in the Hawaiian chain, the Valley Isle has made an international name for itself with its tropical allure, heady nightlife, and miles of perfect-tan beaches.

Shore Excursions The following are good choices on Maui. They may not be offered by all cruise lines. Times and prices are approximate.

Adventure **Bike Trip.** Whiz more than 38 miles downhill from the summit of Mt. Haleakalā. Bikes, helmets, windbreakers, and gloves are supplied;

riders must bring their own eye protection and wear closed shoes. For a truly unforgettable experience, choose the sunrise departure. This trip can be dangerous; participants must be 12 or older. *7½ hrs. Cost: $50 and up.*

Natural Beauty **Haleakalā Crater.** A motor coach takes you through Maui's beautiful interior to the Haleakalā crater, the world's largest dormant volcano. The summit lies at 10,000 feet. *Half day. Cost: $30.*

Hāna Drive. This drive along Maui's rugged north and east coasts is beautiful but long and winding. It's more exciting to drive it yourself, but take this excursion if you don't rent a car. *Full day. Cost: $72.*

Coming Ashore

In Kahului Most ships calling in Maui tie up at Kahului. Some may instead call at Lahaina, sea conditions permitting. Ships calling at Kahului dock in an industrial harbor. To reach the island's natural attractions, such as **Īao Valley State Park, Haleakalā Crater,** or the **Hāna Highway,** you'll need to rent a car or take a shore excursion.

In Lahaina Ships that call at Lahaina drop anchor just offshore and tender passengers directly into the heart of this historic old whaling town. Along Front Street, the main drag, there are restaurants, shops, and a few small museums. A free shuttle bus runs from the Cinema Center (just across from the harbor) to the Kāanapoli beach resort area. To reach the island's major natural attractions, you'll need to rent a car or take a shore excursion.

Getting Around

By Car **Avis** (tel. 800/331–1212), **Hertz** (tel. 800/654–3131), and **Budget** (tel. 800/527–0700) are among the many national agencies with locations at Kahului Airport. American Hawaii ships can arrange car rentals through their shore-excursions offices. Prices start at around $40 a day for a compact.

By Taxi For short hops this can be a convenient way to go, but you'll have to call for pickup—even busy West Maui lacks curbside taxi service. Rates are $2 for pickup and $1.75 per mile. In Kahului and Central Maui, call **Kīhei Taxi** (tel. 808/879–3000). In Lahaina, contact **West Maui Taxi** (tel. 808/667–2605).

Beaches Maui has more than 100 miles of coastline. Not all of this is beach, but striking white crescents do seem to be around every bend. Closest to ships that anchor off Lahaina are the beaches of **Kihei,** which stretch along the south coast of Maui. Another 10 minutes away are the white-sand beaches of **Wailea.** For passengers docking in Kahului, the beaches of Kanaha are close by. **Kaihalulu Beach** is a gorgeous cove with good swimming and snorkeling on the Hāna Coast. Though a bit hard to reach, this red-sand beach is worth the hike. No facilities are available.

Dining

$$$ **David Paul's Lahaina Grill.** Cap off a day of sightseeing and shopping with dinner at this amiable grill. Chef David Paul revises the menu regularly, marrying imaginative sauces and side dishes to poultry, meat, and seafood. Vanilla-bean rice, for example, is an innovative complement for grilled ōpakapaka. *127 Lahainaluna Rd., Lahaina, tel. 808/667–5117. AE, D, DC, MC, V.*

$$$ **Haliimaile General Store.** Owner-chef Beverly Gannon did wonders with this onetime camp store in a pineapple field, turning it into a charming outpost that serves some of the best food in the state. Duck, prepared a number of ways, is the specialty of the house. *Haliimaile Rd., 2 mi north of Pukalani, tel. 808/572–2666. MC, V.*

$$$ **Mama's Fish House.** Looking for the best seafood on Maui? Head to this Old Hawaii restaurant a mile from Pāia in a lovely oceanfront setting. Try the stuffed fish Lani, a fresh fillet baked with shrimp stuffing. *Hāna Hwy. (Hwy. 36), Pāia, tel. 808/579–8488. AE, D, MC, V.*

$$–$$$ **Avalon Restaurant and Bar.** The decor at this most trendy spot is 1940s Hawaii. The "Hawaiian regional" cuisine features dishes

made from local Hawaiian ingredients. *Mariner's Alley, 844 Front St., Lahaina, tel. 808/667–5559. AE, D, DC, MC, V.*

Oahu

The person who dreamed up Oahu's nickname, "the Gathering Place," was prophetic. Hawaii's most populated island boasts an eclectic blend of people, places, customs, and cuisines. Its geography ranges from peaks and plains to rain forests and beaches. The sands of Waikīkī brim with honeymooners, couples celebrating anniversaries, Marines on holiday, and every other type of tourist imaginable. Beaches to the west and north are surprisingly unspoiled and uncrowded.

On cruises that begin and end in Honolulu, you can visit Oahu as part of your pre- or post-cruise vacation. American Hawaii Cruises offers hotel packages and shore excursions for those with late flights home.

Shore Excursions The following is a good choice in Oahu. It may not be offered by all cruise lines. Time and price are approximate.

Pearl Harbor and the *Arizona* Memorial. A Navy launch takes you to the submerged hull of the U.S.S. *Arizona*, where 1,178 men lost their lives when the ship was sunk during the attack on Pearl Harbor. *Half day. Cost: $20.*

Coming Ashore Ships dock downtown at Aloha Tower, where there's a new waterfront complex of shops and restaurants. At the far side of the marketplace is the Hawaii Maritime Museum. Look for the tall ship, the *Falls of Clyde*, moored out front. There's a State of Hawaii visitor information desk inside the cruise terminal. A $1 trolley runs to the beaches and resorts of Waikīkī, a 20-minute drive from Aloha Tower.

American Hawaii passengers on fly/cruise packages will be shuttled from the airport to the pier. For those arriving independently, taxis wait outside the airport exit; the fare to the pier is about $15.

Getting Around

By Car Don't bother renting a car unless you're planning to travel outside Waikīkī, in which case a number of highly competitive car-rental companies offer deals and discounts. When making hotel or plane reservations, ask if there's a car tie-in. At peak times—summer, Christmas vacation, and February—reservations are a must. **Avis** (tel. 800/331–1212), **Hertz** (tel. 800/654–3131), and **Budget** (tel. 800/527–0700) are among the many national agencies with locations in Honolulu.

By Bus The fare to anywhere on the island is $1 (exact change or a one-dollar bill), including one free transfer; ask for one when boarding.

By Taxi Meter rates are $1.50–$2.00 at the drop of the flag, plus $1.95 for each additional mile. The two biggest cab companies are **Charley's** (tel. 808/531–1333) and **SIDA of Hawaii** (tel. 808/836–0011).

Beaches **Waikīkī** (*see* Coming Ashore, *above*) is a 2½-mile chain of beaches extending from the Hilton Hawaiian Village to the base of Diamond Head. The sand is harder and coarser, and the beaches more crowded, than at some of the less-frequented spots out of town, but food stands and equipment rentals are more abundant here. Other than Waikīkī, **Ala Moana Beach Park,** a 10-minute drive from the cruise-ship pier, is the most popular beach in Honolulu. A protective reef keeps its waters calm. Amenities include playing fields, changing houses, indoor and outdoor showers, lifeguards, grills, concession stands, and tennis courts.

Dining

$$$$ **Orchids.** You can't beat this eatery's seaside setting: Diamond Head looms in the distance, and fresh orchids are everywhere. The popovers are huge, the salads light and unusual. The Sunday brunch

buffet is a big hit. *Halekulani Hotel, 2199 Kālia Rd., Waikīkī, tel. 808/923–2311. AE, DC, MC, V.*

$$$ **Golden Dragon.** Local Chinese consider this the best Chinese food in town. Set right by the water, it has stunning red-and-black decor. Best bets are stir-fried lobster with *haupia* (coconut) and Szechuan beef. *Hilton Hawaiian Village, 2005 Kālia Rd., Waikīkī, tel. 808/949–4321. AE, DC, MC, V.*

$$ **Gordon Biersch Brewery Restaurant.** Snuggling up to Honolulu Harbor, this indoor-outdoor eatery is the busiest in Aloha Tower Marketplace. Oahu-born chef Kelly Degala's spicy food goes well with the beer, which is brewed on the premises. *Aloha Tower, Honolulu, tel. 808/599–4877. AE, D, DC, MC, V.*

Mexican Riviera

Along the Mexican Riviera's 2,000-mile coast, cruise passengers find the exotic and the familiar. Among the McDonald's and Pizza Huts and the Fords and Chevys are adobe cantinas, breathtaking parasailing, and high-cliff divers. Although Spanish and various Indian dialects predominate, most Mexicans involved in tourism speak some English.

The transformation of once sleepy fishing villages—most notably, Acapulco, Puerto Vallarta, and Mazatlán—into booming cities has been a direct result of the swarms of tourists who come by land, by air, and by sea. And the growth has not been gentle. Although the area's recorded history stretches back more than 400 years, cruise passengers will find few significant landmarks or archaeological sites. (These are more common along Mexico's Caribbean coast; *see* Cozumel, *above.*) If it's authentic history and genuine culture you want, go elsewhere. But for sun, sea, and sports, the colorful Mexican west coast is a fine choice. Indeed, Mexico's beaches compare favorably with the best in the world. Their talcum-powder sands are white, wide, and beckoning; the water is warm and clear.

Loop cruises of 3, 4, 7, and sometimes 10 days usually depart from Los Angeles for the Mexican Riviera. Among the lines sailing here are Carnival, Crystal, and Royal Caribbean. (For seasonal itineraries, *see* Chapter 4.)

When to Go November through March is the Mexican Riviera's cruising season—most ships reposition to Alaska for the summer. Still, it is possible to cruise here year-round, and prices are lowest from April through October. June has the best weather, though it is remarkably good almost all year, with daytime temperatures averaging from 82°F to 90°F. During the June–October rainy season, very brief showers can be expected.

Currency In Mexico, the currency is the peso, written N (for neuvo peso). At press time, the exchange rate was about N7 to 1.

U.S. dollars and credit cards are accepted at most restaurants and large shops. Most taxi drivers take dollars as well. There is no advantage to paying in dollars, but there may be an advantage to paying in cash. To avoid having to change unused pesos back to dollars, change just enough to cover what you'll need for public transportation, refreshments, phones, and tips. Use up your Mexican coins; they can't be changed back to dollars.

Passports and Visas Although U.S. and Canadian citizens do not need a passport or visa to enter or leave Mexico, they must fill out a tourist card, issued by the cruise line, a Mexican embassy or consulate, or any airline flying to Mexico. This is free, but you must show proof of citizenship (passport or birth certificate) to have it validated. British travelers need a passport and a tourist card.

Telephones and Mail Until recently, phoning home from the Mexican Riviera could be frustrating because phone lines were few and the sound quality was poor. Since the introduction of AT&T USADirect service, calling has become much easier with better connections. You must use "Ladatel" phones, located on the dock in Acapulco, Mazatlán, Puerto Vallarta, and Zihuatanejo. Dial 95–800–462–4240 to be connected with an English-speaking operator, who will take your **AT&T** credit-card number or place a collect call for you. **MCI** users should dial 95–800–674–7000; **Sprint** users should dial 95–800–877–8000.

As a rule, cruise ships sell local stamps at the front desk, and you can send postcards from an onboard mailbox as well, eliminating the need to find a post office.

The Mexican Riviera

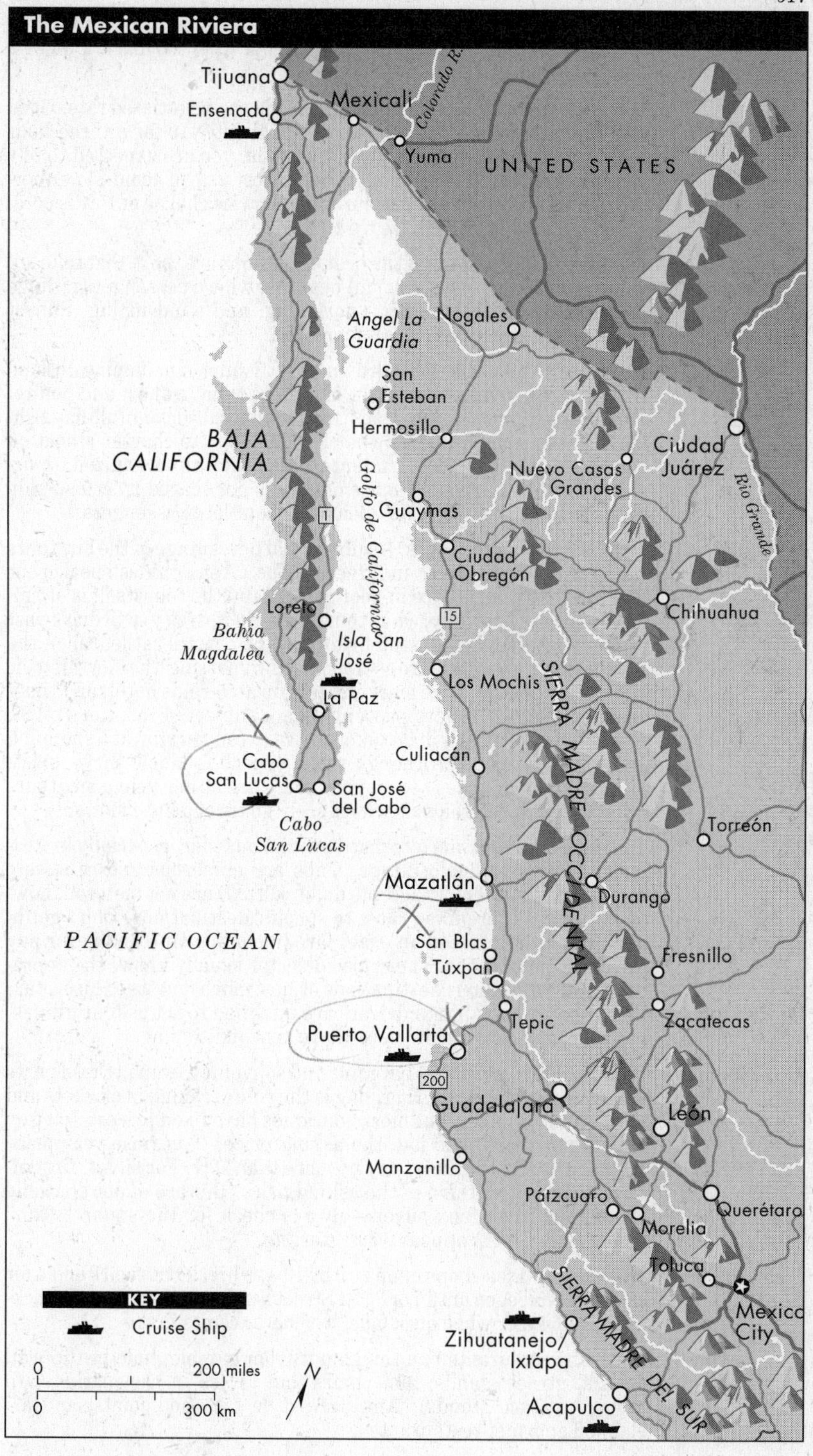

Tipping Everyone wants a dollar; not everyone expects one. It's wise to carry some pesos for those times when a dollar tip is too much. Don't tip less than N$4 or N$5.

For taxi rides, tips are usually included in the negotiated rate. Good taxi tours, however, merit a small tip; about N10 for a three-hour tour is average. If you stop for a cold soda, you are expected to buy your driver a bottle. Bus-tour guides expect a tip of about $1 per person per half-day tour. In restaurants a service charge of 15% is occasionally included; otherwise tip 10%–15%.

Shore Excursions Not surprisingly, some of the best excursions are those that take advantage of the area's wonderful beaches, where passengers indulge in parasailing, waterskiing, snorkeling, and windsurfing. Sunset sails and booze cruises are also popular.

Deep-sea fishing has long drawn sportfishing fans hoping to land trophy-size marlin and sailfish, as well as tuna, wahoo, and bonito. Most ships sailing the Mexican Riviera offer half-day or full-day fishing at rates comparable to what it would cost to charter a boat on your own. It's therefore prudent to take the ship-organized excursions: The locals' relaxed sense of time is not shared by cruise-ship captains, who will—and do—leave without late passengers.

And be wary of land tours. A substantial percentage of the bus tours range from mediocre to indifferent. Too often, guides speak poor English, the vehicles are in poor repair, and the tour itself is of limited interest. Typically, a bus tour of the *ciudad* (city) will drive past the *malecón* (sea wall), stop briefly at the central cathedral on the *zócalo* (main town square)—and then, bypassing the few historic sites or authentic native markets, pull up at various hotels and time-share properties, where passengers are subjected to a sales pitch. Finally, passengers will be taken for an extended stop at a shopping area or crafts shop. Although a few superb folkloric shows exist, most dance companies seen on bus tours are either young amateurs or jaded semiprofessionals who merely go through the motions.

Taxis are a worthwhile alternative to the bus tour, especially in Acapulco and Zihuatanejo/Ixtapa. Cabs are numerous and relatively cheap, and every driver accepts dollars. Taxis are not metered, however, nor are there fixed rates to specific destinations. Don't get in until you've negotiated an exact fare (including tip), and never pay the driver in advance. The cruise director usually knows the appropriate fare to various destinations or how much it costs to hire a taxi by the hour. Not all taxi drivers are qualified to act as tour guides, however, and cabs almost never have air-conditioning.

Shopping It's possible to get great bargains and souvenirs, even in those ports where cruise ships call. Haggling is the rule of thumb in markets and with street vendors, but most boutiques have fixed prices. Start by offering no more than half the asking price, then raise your price very slowly. At the most, pay no more than 70%. For silver, first offer a quarter to a third of the asking price. Beware of disreputable shops that hawk faux silver—always check for the stamp ".925," which must by law appear on all sterling.

Most resort-area shops open at 9 or 10 AM, break between 2 and 4 for siesta, then reopen until 7 or 8 PM. Street vendors generally start packing up at 6 PM or when dusk falls, whichever comes first.

Dining Mexican restaurants run the gamut from humble, hole-in-the-wall shacks, street stands, and chairs and tables in the markets, to *taquerías* (taco stands), American-style fast-food joints, and acclaimed gourmet restaurants.

Seviche—raw fish and shellfish (*mariscos*) marinated in lime juice and topped with cilantro, onion, tomato, and chili—is almost a national dish, though it originated in Acapulco. Shrimp, lobster, and oysters can be huge and succulent; the safest time to eat oysters is October–March. Avoid all foods sold by street vendors—especially meat and fruit—no matter how tempting. Tacos *al pastor*—thin pork slices grilled on a revolving spit and garnished with cilantro, onions, and chili—are delicious but dangerous for most non-Mexican stomachs.

Thursday is **the** day for eating *pozole,* a hearty stew made with hominy, chicken, and pork (with pickled pig's knuckles usually served separately). It comes in three colors (red, green, or white, depending on the spices used). If you're not keen on spiciness, ask that your food be prepared *no muy picante.* Stick to bottled beverages, and ask for your drinks *sin hielo* (without ice), unless you're in one of the bigger hotels or restaurants frequented by tourists. Then, ask if the ice is made with *agua purificado,* in which case it's okay to drink; the cubes have passed the test if they're uniform in size and have holes in the middle. If you're a beer drinker, try a *michelada,* a glass of icy cold brew with a splash of fresh squeezed lime in a salt-rimmed glass.

Category	Cost*
$$$$	over $35
$$$	$25–$35
$$	$15–$25
$	under $15

**per person for a three-course meal, excluding drinks, service, and 10% sales tax*

Acapulco

As the ship enters the harbor, passengers should be on deck for a panoramic view of Acapulco's gently curving, high-rise-studded waterfront backed by a series of dramatic hills. Distant mountains are shrouded in haze. As the ship passes Roqueta Island, a rock jutting almost straight up in the air, you see hundreds of boats and a sprawling fort. Acapulco, the largest city on the Mexican Riviera, bustles with crowded markets, trendy discos, fashionable restaurants, and spectacular gardens and scenery.

Shore Excursions The following is a good choice in Acapulco. It may not be offered by all cruise lines. Time and price are approximate.

Adventure **Helicopter Flightseeing:** A spectacular view of Acapulco's bay is the reward for those brave enough to step aboard one of these choppers. The copter then flies over the cliff divers at La Quebrada and the Acapulco Princess hotel and beach. *Flight time 15–30 mins. Cost: $45–$90.*

Coming Ashore The municipal pier, where cruise ships dock, is alive with food hawkers, souvenir vendors, taxi drivers, and small boys ready to dive for coins. From the pier, it's a short stroll to Costera Miguel Alemán, the main boulevard that wraps around the harbor and includes the city's famous hotel zone. A taxi stand is located at the cruise terminal; a ride to the hotel zone shouldn't cost more than $5, to the main flea market about $3.

Getting Around For those who choose not to walk, a variety of wheeled vehicles may be employed to explore the city:

By Bus Public buses are cheap and can be a fun way to see the town. The bus marked HORNOS follows the Costera from the pier to the hotel zone; the fare is N$1.50 (N$2 for air-conditioned models).

By Carriage Buggy rides are available up and down the hotel zone on weekends. Bargain before you get in—fares are about $20 for a half hour.

By Taxi Taxis are cheap and plentiful. Fares are negotiable; Volkswagen Beetles are cheapest. Flagging a cab in the street costs less than getting one at a hotel or at the cruise terminal, where hourly rates for tours run about $20 for a vehicle that seats four to eight.

Exploring Acapulco *Numbers in the margin correspond to points of interest on the Acapulco map.*

Though it is within walking distance of the docks, in Old Acapulco you'll find more Mexicans than tourists. Colors are earthier, odors more pungent, and air-conditioning almost nonexistent. Near the municipal pier is the **zócalo,** a pleasant plaza crisscrossed with shaded promenades and alive with shoe-shine stands, vendors, children, and old men ogling a new generation of lovers. Sunday means music in the grandstand. The church of **Nuestra Señora de la Soledad** is a modern oddity, with a stark white facade and blue and yellow spires.

Opposite the pier and towering over it is **El Fuerte de San Diego,** built in the 18th century as protection from pirates. An earlier fort, finished in 1616, was destroyed by an earthquake. Today the fort's air-conditioned rooms offer archaeological, historical, and anthropological exhibits, covering early Mexican exploration and Spanish trade. *Calle Hornitos and Av. Costera Miguel Alemán. Admission: about $4. Open Tues.–Sun. 10:30–5.*

La Quebrada, where world-famous cliff divers perform daily, is a 15–20 minute walk west, up a rather steep hill, so consider a taxi (the fare is about $7). A $2-per-person entrance fee gives you access to a platform beside the **Plaza las Glorias El Mirador Hotel,** an excellent vantage point, or you can see the cliff-diving show while having drinks and dinner at the hotel's **La Perla** nightclub. Cliff-diving exhibitions are scheduled daily at 1 PM and every hour from 7:30 to 10:30 PM.

Shopping The best bargains are found in the public markets. In places like **El Mercado de Artesanías** in the hotel zone, **Noa Noa** near Papagayo Park, and any of the several open-air markets set up around town, you can haggle for woven blankets, puppets, colorful wood toys, leather, baskets, hammocks, jewelry, and handmade wood furniture, but beware of pickpockets.

Along the Costera east of the cruise pier, between Continental Plaza and Papagayo Park, is where you'll find many upscale boutiques. The **Galería Rudic** (across from the Continental Plaza, tel. 74/84–48–44) has great prices on authentic Mexican fine art. For silver jewelry and flatware, go to **Taxco Exporta** (La Quebrada 315, tel. 74/83–25–51). The expensive and formal **Esteban's,** the most glamorous shop in Acapulco, is on the Costera, across the street from the Club de Golf (tel. 74/84–04–84).

Sports
Fishing Try the **Pesca Deportiva,** the dock across from the zócalo. Boats accommodating four to eight people cost $200 to $500 a day. Excursions leave at about 7 AM and return at 2 PM. Most fishing operations get a license for you; otherwise, go to the **Secretaría de Pesca,** above the central post office at Costera Miguel Alemán 215.

Golf Two great 18-hole golf courses are shared by the **Princess and Pierre Marqués** hotels (tel. 74/69-10-00 for both properties). Greens fees are $85 for cruise passengers. At the **Club de Golf Acapulco** (tel. 74/84–07–82), a public nine-hole course on the Costera Miguel Alemán, next to the Centro Internacional Acapulco, the fee is about $19 for nine holes, about $26 for 18 holes.

Water Sports Water sports of all kinds can be arranged at any of the big beachfront hotels. Rates for the most popular activities are: Broncos (one-person motorboats; $30 per half hour), parasailing (about $15–$25 for 10 minutes), sailing ($20–$30 an hour), snorkeling (equipment rental $10 per day), waterskiing (about $25–$30 per half hour), windsurfing ($15 per hour).

Beaches Acapulco's beaches are legendary. Smack in the middle of Acapulco Bay, **Playa Condesa** is a tourist-riddled stretch of sand that's especially popular with singles. The atmosphere is fun and festive, but the undertow is especially strong here. Stretching west of Papagayo Park, **Playa Hornos** is crammed with Mexican tourists who know a good thing: Graceful palms shade the sand, and scads of casual eateries are within walking distance. On the far eastern side of the bay, **Playa Icacos** is less populated than other beaches on the Costera. The morning waves are especially calm.

Dining
$$$$ **Blackbeard's.** The pirate-ship motif here sports walls decked with fishing nets and wood figureheads, and booths with maps on the tables. Photos of movie stars who've eaten here, from Bing Crosby to Liz Taylor, hang in the much-used lounge. A luscious salad bar and jumbo shrimp, lobster, and steak portions keep 'em coming back. Part of the restaurant is a disco. *Costera Miguel Alemán 101, tel. 74/84–25–49. AE, MC, V.*

$$ **Beto's.** By day you can eat and enjoy live tropical music beachside; by night, this *palapa*-style restaurant is transformed into a dim and romantic dining area lighted by candles and paper lanterns. Whole red snapper, lobster, and seviche are recommended. *Costera Miguel Alemán 99, tel. 74/84–04–73. AE, MC, V.*

$$ **Carlos 'n Charlie's.** This is *the* happening eatery in Acapulco; the line forms well before the doors open at 6 PM. An atmosphere of controlled craziness is cultivated through prankster waiters, a jokey menu, and the eclectic decor. Ribs, stuffed shrimp, and oysters are among the more serious choices; but more in keeping with the party atmosphere are the addictive nachos (taco chips topped with melted cheeses and fiery jalapeño peppers). *Costera Miguel Alemán 112, tel. 74/84–12–85 or 74/84–00–39. AE, DC, MC, V. No lunch.*

$$ **Pipo's.** The owners are a mother-and-son team who have been preparing some of the best seafood in Acapulco for years. Seating is in the air-conditioned interior or on a terrace overlooking life on the Costera. This no-frills restaurant is a favorite spot for *Acapulqueños,* many of whom can be seen enjoying the house special seviche *de marisco* (cold seafood salad in a spicy lime and tomato marinade). *Almirante Bretón 3 off the Costera and near Centro Internacional Acapulco, tel. 74/84–01–65. AE, MC, V.*

Nightlife Cruise ships often dock in Acapulco late into the night or for two days so that passengers can take advantage of the city's discos and nightclubs.

Discos The discos open late, around 10:30 PM, and stay open until sunrise. Most clubs have a cover charge of $10–$20 (except for **News,** which is $28). Sometimes you get a drink or two with that, perhaps even access to an open bar; sometimes you don't. Lines are common but usually move quickly. Since many discos are bunched together in the hotel zone, you can easily hop from one to another.

As if the spectacle of a crowded, pulsating dance floor weren't enough, a huge glass wall at **Extravaganzza** provides a breathtaking wraparound view of the harbor. *Carretera Escénica to Las Brisas, next to Los Rancheros restaurant, tel. 74/84–71–54.*

For stargazing, Hollywood-style, go to **Fantasy**; it's expensive, exclusive, and one of the few places in Acapulco where you're supposed to dress to the nines. *On Carretera Escénica, just below Las Brisas and near Extravaganzza, tel. 74/84–67–27.*

News is billed as a "disco and concert hall." It's enormous, with seating for 1,200 in booths and love seats. Theme parties and competi-

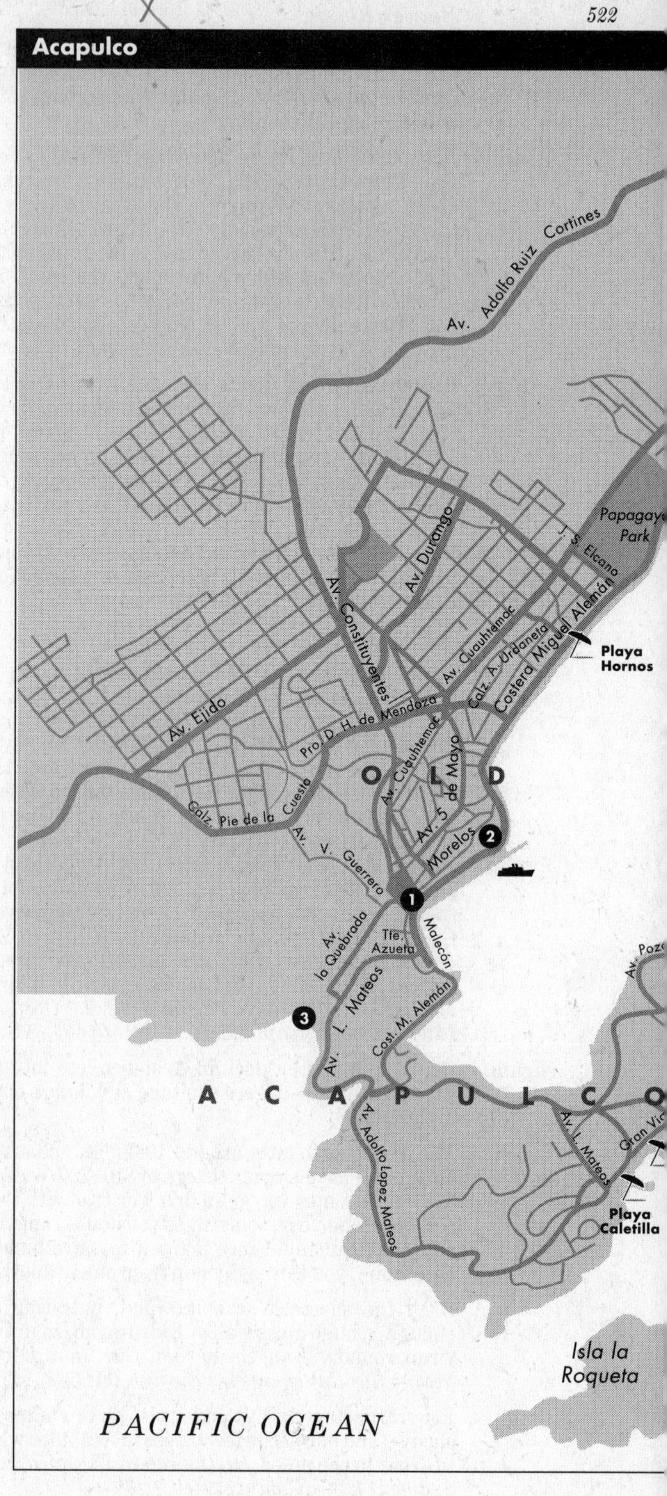
Acapulco
Av. Adolfo Ruiz Cortines
J. S. Elcano
Av. Durango
Av. Constituyentes
Costera Miguel Alemán
Playa Hornos
Av. Cuauhtemoc
Calz. A. Urdaneta
Av. Ejido
Pro. D. H. de Mendoza
OLD
Av. Cuauhtemoc
Av. 5 de Mayo
Morelos
2
Calz. Pie de la Cuesta
Av. V. Guerrero
1
Av. la Quebrada
Tte. Azueta
Malecón
3
Av. L. Mateos
Cost. M. Alemán
A C A P U L C O
Av. Adolfo Lopez Mateos
Av. L. Mateos
Playa Caletilla
Isla la Roqueta
PACIFIC OCEAN

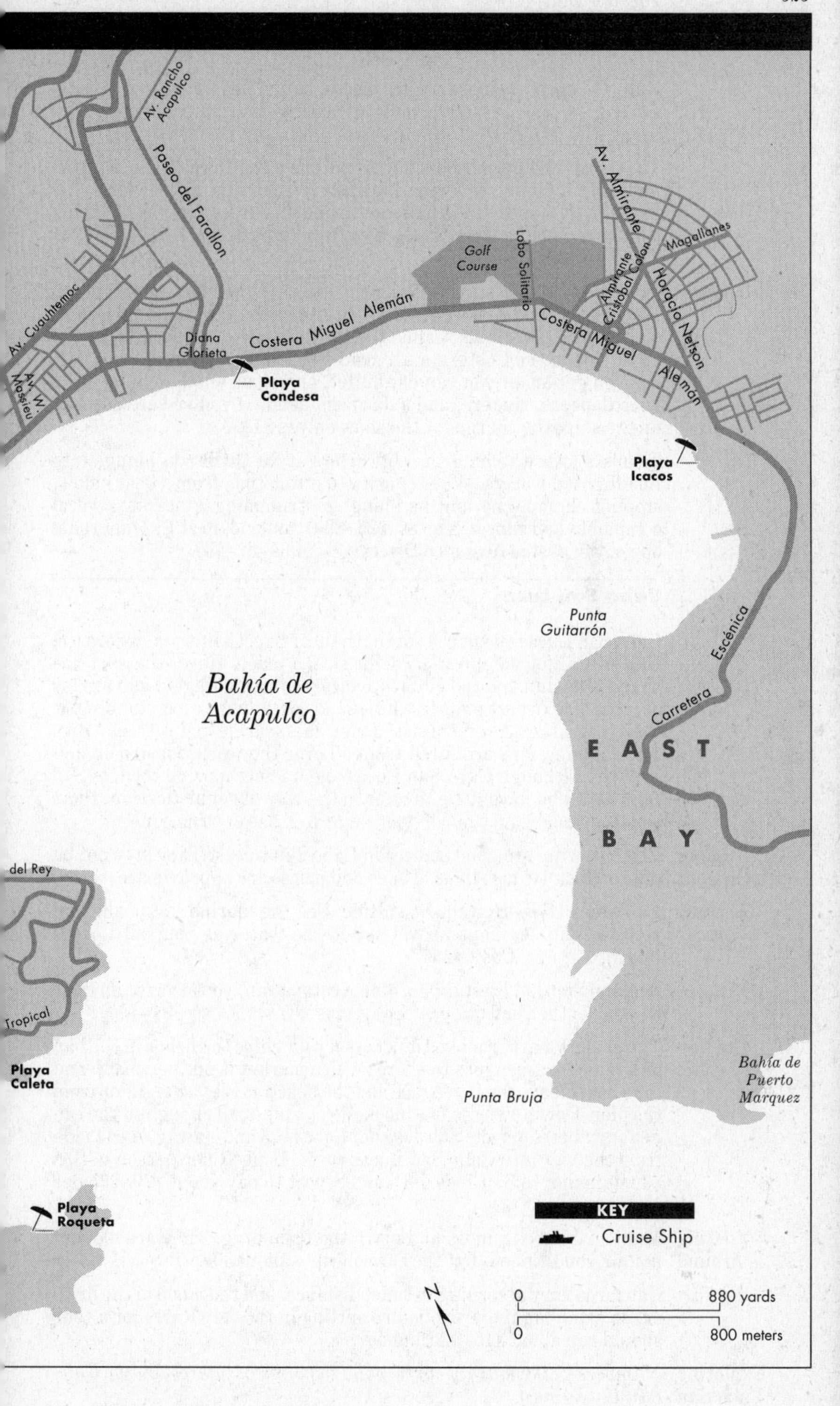

Av. Rancho Acapulco
Paseo del Farallon
Av. Cuauhtemoc
Av. W. Massieu
Diana Glorieta
Costera Miguel Alemán
Playa Condesa
Golf Course
Lobo Solitario
Av. Almirante
Almirante Cristobal Colon
Magallanes
Horacio Nelson
Costera Miguel Alemán
Playa Icacos
Punta Guitarrón
Carretera Escénica
Bahía de Acapulco
EAST BAY
del Rey
Tropical
Playa Caleta
Punta Bruja
Bahía de Puerto Marquez
Playa Roqueta
KEY
Cruise Ship
N
0
880 yards
0
800 meters

tions are offered nightly. *Costera Miguel Alemán, across from Hyatt Regency, tel. 74/84–59–02.*

Baby O, one of the best singles discos, resembles a cave in a tropical setting. A big 18-to-30 crowd of mostly tourists dominates the scene. *Costera Miguel Alemán near News, tel. 74/84–74–74.*

The decor of **D'Paradisse** is black, and the place has a fabulous after-midnight light show. As many as 500 vivacious night crawlers compete for the tables and chairs arranged on three levels overlooking the dance floor. *Across the Costera from Baby O, tel. 74/84–88–15 or 74/84–88–16.*

Entertainment

One of Acapulco's best folkloric shows is performed Monday, Wednesday, and Friday at 7:30 at the **Acapulco International Center** (tel. 74/84–62–28), also called the convention center, located on the right side of the Costera, near Icacos beach. For about $24 per person you get an all-you-can-eat buffet, open bar, and a rousing show with dancers, singers, and a mariachi band. If you've eaten dinner on the ship, the charge for the show only is $14.

Tourists love watching the cliff divers at **La Quebrada** plunge into floodlighted waters. Where better to watch than from a boat below, sipping champagne and listening to strumming guitars? Several companies sell sunset cruises ($25–$30) that end up at La Quebrada; one of the best is **Acapulco Divers** (tel. 74/84–82–74).

Cabo San Lucas

Cabo San Lucas sits at the southern tip of Baja California, where the Gulf of California and the Pacific Ocean meet. Here, the surf has shaped the dun-colored cliffs into bizarre jutting fingers and arches of rock. The desert ends in white-sand coves, with cacti standing at their entrances like sentries under the soaring palm trees. Big-game-fishing fans are lured from all over the world for marlin and sailfish. Although Cabo San Lucas and its neighboring town of San José del Cabo have little to offer in the way of sophistication, their isolation and beauty make them superb cruise destinations.

Shore Excursions

The following are good choices in Cabo San Lucas. They may not be offered by all cruise lines. Times and prices are approximate.

Undersea Creatures

Los Arcos Glass-Bottom-Boat Ride: See the marine life below and pelicans and sea lions above and on the water as you sail Lovers Beach. *1–2 hrs. Cost: $15.*

Sail and Snorkel Fiesta: Boarding a catamaran, you stop for an hour to snorkel then sail out past Los Arcos. *2½ hrs. Cost: $25–$30.*

Coming Ashore

The shallow harbor makes it necessary for ships to anchor in the bay and tender passengers to shore. A flea market is on the wharf, and tour boats leave for Los Arcos and the beach at Playa del Amor from the pier. Downtown is a few blocks away and small enough so you can get anywhere on foot. San José del Cabo is 23 miles away. A cab ride from the pier into Cabo San Lucas costs about $1 per person with a $3 minimum; to San José del Cabo expect to pay about $20–$25 per carload.

Getting Around

Municipal buses run up and down the main drag. They are old and not air-conditioned, but they are cheap—about 30¢.

By Taxi

Cab fares vary according to time, distance, and the mood of the driver, so establish the price before getting in the car. Rates for a tour should run about $15–$20 an hour.

Exploring Cabo San Lucas

Numbers in the margin correspond to points of interest on the Cabo San Lucas map.

1 The main downtown street of Cabo San Lucas, Avenida Lázaro Cárdenas, passes a small **zócalo.** Most shops, services, and restaurants

X Great

Los Arcos, **2**
Zócalo, **1**

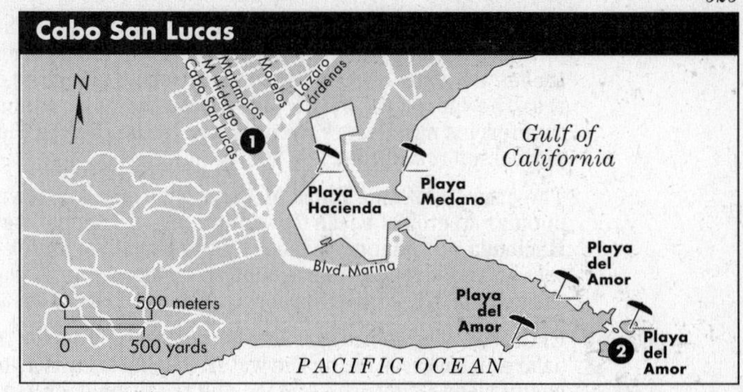

are between the avenida and the waterfront, two blocks east. From the inner harbor you can see the spectacular natural rock arches called **Los Arcos,** but they are more impressive from the water. **2**

About 15 minutes from town is a dramatic desert, populated by wild horses and incredible cacti.

Shopping Along the waterfront and on its side streets, Cabo San Lucas is a shopper's mecca; the selection of handicrafts and sportswear is especially good. As you step off the tender at the pier is the **Mercado de Artesanías,** a maze of thatched booths selling mediocre silver jewelry, mass-produced wood sculptures, T-shirts, and other souvenirs. Sportswear shops—**Ferrioni, Bye-Bye, Fila,** and **Benetton**—are clustered around the **Plaza Cabo San Lucas,** on Avenida Madero near the waterfront, and at **Plaza Bonita,** at the marina in the inner harbor. **Temptations** (Lázaro Cárdenas and Matamoros, on the same block as the Giggling Marlin restaurant; *see* Dining, *below*) has some chic and original designs for women, including the María de Guadalajara line. **La Paloma** in town is another good spot for souvenirs, and the boutiques in the **Mexican Village** at the Hacienda Hotel are popular with tourists. **El Dorado Gallery,** across from the marina, is a must. Its two rooms are filled with sculptures in ceramic, papier-mâché, brass, and copper; the creations of Mario González; and contemporary Mexican paintings and handicrafts.

Sports
Fishing Long known as a deep-sea fisherman's paradise, the best fishing on the Baja is found here. You can charter a 28-foot cruiser for about $300 a day from the Cabo San Lucas marina. Contact **The Palmilla Fleet** (tel. 114/2-0582), **La Gaviota** (tel. 114/3-0430), **Picis Fleet** (tel. 114/3–0588), or **Pesca Deportiva Solmar** (Hotel Solmar, tel. 114/3-0022).

Golf Over the past few years, Los Cabos' desert-by-the-sea setting has become known as one of the world's newest and most unusual golf destinations. Advance reservations are recommended, but not required to tee off at **Palmilla Golf Club** (tel. 114/8-8525; greens fee $121 for 18 holes) and **Cabo del Sol Golf Club** (tel. 114/3-3149; greens fee $120 for 18 holes). Good courses can also be found at the **Westin Hotel** (tel. 114/2-9000; greens fees $110 for 18 holes and $65 for 9 holes), and at the **Melia Hotel** (tel. 114/4-0000; greens fees $101 for 18 holes). Other popular links are at the **Cabo San Lucas Country Club** (tel. 114/3-4654; greens fees $65 for 9 holes) and at the public **Fonatur Campo Golf** course (tel. 114/2-0905; greens fees $15 for 9 holes).

Scuba Diving Los Arcos is the prime diving and snorkeling area, but several good rocky points are off the coast. Contact **Amigos del Mar** (near the sportfishing docks, tel. 114/3-0022), **Cabo Acuadeportes** (at the Cabo San Lucas, Hacienda, Plaza Las Glorias, and Pueblo Bonito hotels, tel. 114/3-0117), **Cabo Divers** (Blvd. Marina and Av. Madero, tel. 114/3-0747), **Palmilla Divers** (at the resort of the same name, tel. 114/2-0582), and **Tío Water Sports** (tel. 114/3-1000).

Beaches **Playa del Amor** sits at the end of the peninsula, with the Gulf of California on one side and the Pacific on the other. The beach and nearby arches are some of the most romantic spots along the Mexican Riviera. The surf on the Pacific side is too rough for swimming. A water taxi ferries passengers from the tender landing to the beach for $5 per person round-trip.

The crowded 2-mile **Playa Medano,** just north of town, is the most popular stretch of beach for sunbathing and people-watching. **Playa Hacienda,** in the inner harbor by the Hacienda Hotel, has calm waters and good snorkeling around the rocky point. A water taxi from the marina in the inner harbor to the hotel costs about $2 per person.

Dining

$$$ **El Galeón.** The choice seats at this posh eatery across from the marina are on terraces facing the water. The interior is an assemblage of heavy wood furniture. Seafood and traditional Italian fare are prepared expertly. Drop in for the piano music, which starts at 6 PM. *By the road to Hotel Finesterra, tel. 114/3–0443. AE, MC, V.*

$$ **Giggling Marlin.** Five large color TVs broadcast major sporting events and other U.S. programs at this bar-restaurant, raking in a huge crowd during the Super Bowl, World Series, and other important spectacles. Though the menu is extensive—burgers, sandwiches, tostadas, burritos, steaks—regulars advise sticking with tacos or the nachos smothered in cheese and topped with guacamole. *Av. Matamoros and Blvd. Marina, tel. 114/3–0606. MC, V.*

$$ **Las Palmas.** Playa Medano's most popular hangout is headquarters to beach-volleyball competitors, dune-buggy enthusiasts, and beach bums of all types. The barbecued ribs are great; even better is the quail, lobster, and steak combo. *Tel. 114/3–0447. MC, V.*

$$ **Salsita.** Right on the Plaza Bonita with a view of the marina, this restaurant and bar is for those who love standard Mexican favorites; try the *antojitos* (mixed appetizers). *Tel. 114/3–7440. MC, V.*

$$ **Whale Watcher's Bar.** No guesses are necessary about what to do once you've ordered at this restaurant. Located at the Hotel Finisterra, it has an outdoor fireplace, mariachi music, and "tipico" Mexican dishes (try the antojitos, mixed appetizers), and the view is spectacular. *Tel. 114/3–3000. AE, MC, V.*

Mazatlán

Mazatlán (an Aztec word meaning "place of the deer") is the only major city on the Mexican Riviera with a raison d'être other than welcoming droves of tourists. With 400,000 inhabitants, it's a thriving seaport, home to Latin America's largest shrimp fleet and other commercial-fishing boats (totaling over 800 vessels). Nearly 40 million tons of shrimp are processed here each year, effectively making Mazatlán the shrimp capital of the world. Long before the first cruise ships called and the tourist hotels were built, Mazatlán was a year-round mecca for sportfishermen and hunters in search of sailfish and marlin, duck and quail. Hunting is on the wane now as time-share condos and high-rises pop up, but the Mazatlán waterfront still has the feel of a working fishing town rather than a tourist resort.

Shore Excursions The following is a good choice in Mazatlán. It may not be offered by all cruise lines. Time and price are approximate.

Sierra Madre Tour: Go inland and up into the mountains, to visit the ancient towns of Copala and Concordia, with their baroque houses, wonderfully unspoiled plazas, a deserted silver mine, and shopping stopovers. Lunch is served in a local cantina that frequently features amateur musicians. *4–6½ hrs. Cost: about $40.*

Coming Ashore Cruise ships tie up along a narrow channel leading from the Pacific Ocean, but passengers must take a short shuttle ride to the nearby cruise terminal. The downtown zócalo, where you'll find the cathedral and the *mercado municipal* (flea market), is about 12 blocks away.

Getting Around Mazatlán is spread far and wide, and walking from one section of town to another can take hours.

By Bus Air-conditioned minibuses, marked SABALO-CENTRO, run along the coastal road to the town plaza. The fare is N$1, but the driver will accept a U.S. dollar if you don't have any pesos.

By Taxi Taxis are cheap and readily available. Fares are set, with the city divided into four zones. One-way fares for a private car range from $5 to $10 per carload, depending on your destination. If you don't mind sharing, so-called "ecotaxis" cost only $1.50 to $2.25, also depending upon your destination. You can flag one down anywhere, but you may have to make stops for other passengers. Or, for a real adventure, try hopping on one of the open-air *pulmonía* (pneumonia) taxis, which look like a combination carriage and golf cart. The cost is slightly less than that for the ecotaxis.

Exploring Mazatlán *Numbers in the margin correspond to points of interest on the Mazatlán map.*

Mazatlán has two faces: the glitzy resort area known as the Zona Dorado and the authentically Mexican part of town. Downtown is filled with buses and locals rushing to and from work and the market.

❶ Head for the gold spires of the **Mazatlán Catedral.** Built in 1890 and made a basilica in 1935, it has an ornate triple altar, with murals of angels overhead and many small altars along the sides. Dress appropriately (no shorts or tank tops) to enter. Steps away, at the Plazuela Machado, peek in at the restored **Angela Peralta Theater,** Mazatlán's former opera house.

❷ Across the street is the **zócalo, Plaza Revolución,** with a fascinating gazebo: It looks like a '50s diner inside the lower level, with a wrought-iron bandstand on top. The green and orange tile on the walls, the ancient jukebox, and the soda fountain serving shakes, burgers, and hot dogs couldn't make a more surprising sight. Facing the zócalo are the City Hall, banks, the post office, and a telegraph office.

For a great view, take a taxi to the end of the peninsula, where you ❸ climb **Cerro del Crestón** (Summit Hill). At the top is **El Faro** (505 ft ❹ high), the second-tallest lighthouse in the world.

❺ The tallest building in Mazatlán houses the **Cervezaría del Pacífico** brewery, home of one of the country's best-loved beers. It is open for free daily tours (corner of Germán Evers and Melchior Ocampo Sts., tel. 69/81-3021).

❻ North of downtown in the Zona Dorada is the **Acuario Mazatlán,** an aquarium with tanks of sharks, sea horses, eels, lobsters, and multicolor saltwater and freshwater fish. *Av. de los Deportes 111, tel. 69/81–7815. Admission: $5.50. Open daily 9:30–6:30.*

Shopping Most tourists head for the **Mazatlán Arts and Crafts Center** (tel. 69/13–5022) in the Zona Dorada, a market where you can watch artists at work. You'll find some of the best prices on the Mexican Riviera here, although the handicrafts are only average. On the next block is **Sea Shell City** (tel. 69/13–1301), and there are dozens of other shops on the surrounding streets. **La Carreta,** at the El Cid and Playa Mazatlán hotels, is another worthwhile handicrafts center. The enormous **Mercado Central,** between calles Juárez and Serdan, sells produce, meat, fish, and handicrafts at competitive prices as well.

Sports
Fishing Mazatlán has the largest charter fishing fleet on the Mexican Riviera. Charters cost $200–$400 for two to five people; a chair on a shared boat runs about $65. Contact **Bill Heimpel's Star Fleet** (tel. 69/

Acuario Mazatlán, **6**
Cerro del Crestón, **3**
Cervezaría del Pacífico, **5**
El Faro, **4**
Mazatlán Catedral, **1**
Zócalo (Plaza Revolución), **2**

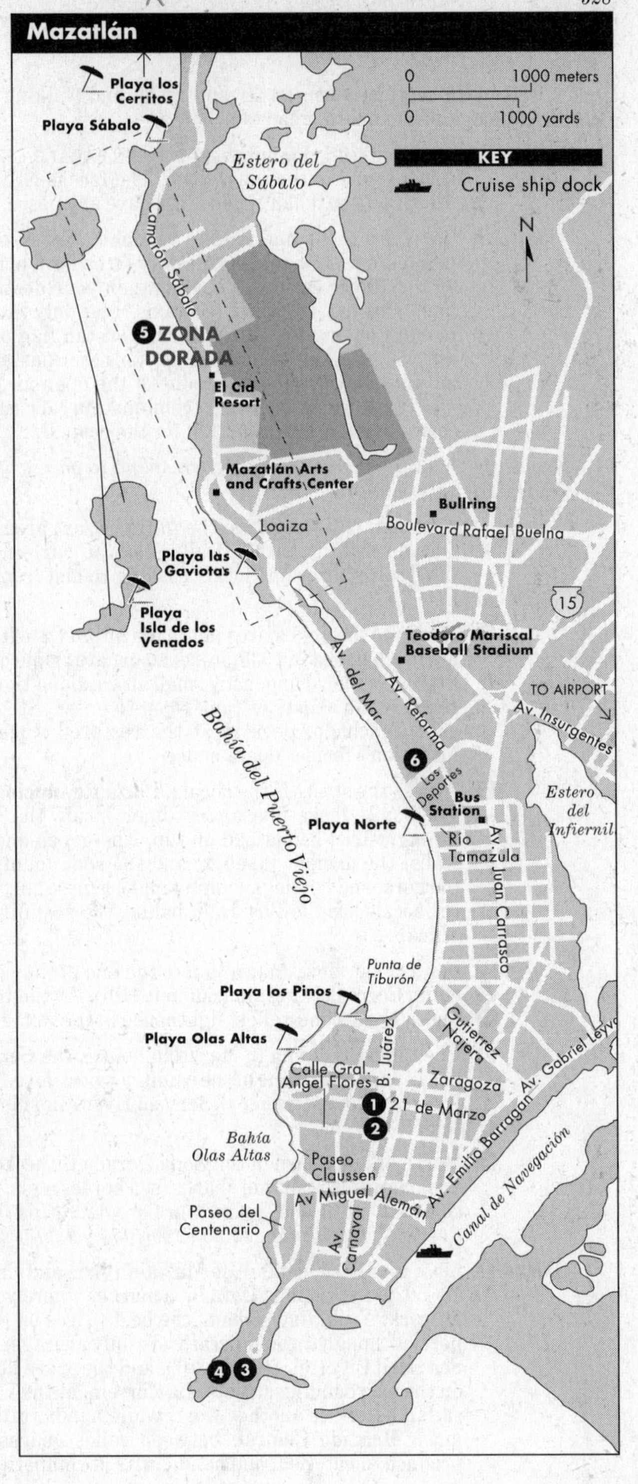

82–2665), **De Oro** (tel. 69/82–3130), **Estrella** (tel. 69/82–3878), **Flota Bibi** (tel. 69/81–3640), or **Flota American Fleet** (tel. 69/81–5992).

Water Sports Rent Jet Skis, Hobie Cats, and Windsurfers from most hotels, and look for parasailing along the Zona Dorado. Mazatlán doesn't have good diving spots.

Beaches **Playa los Cerritos,** the northernmost beach on the outskirts of town, runs from Camino Real Resort to Punta Cerritos, and is the cleanest and least populated. It's too rough for swimming but great for surfing. The two most popular beaches are along the Zona Dorado—**Playa Sábalo** and **Playa las Gaviotas.** Here you'll find as many vendors selling blankets, pottery, lace tablecloths, and silver jewelry as you will find sunbathers. Boats, Windsurfers, and parasailers line the shores. Boats make frequent departures from the Zona Dorado hotels for **Playa Isla de los Venados** on Deer Island. You can buy tickets at the El Cid Hotel (about $8 round-trip). The amphibious vehicle leaves 10 AM, noon, and 2 PM, returning every two hours until 4 PM. It's only a 20-minute ride, but the difference is striking: The beach is pretty, uncluttered, and clean, and you can hike around the southern point of the island to small, secluded coves covered with shells.

Dining

$$$ **Sr. Peppers.** This is an elegant yet unpretentious place, with ceiling fans, lush foliage, candlelit tables, and choice steaks and lobsters cooked over a mesquite grill. You can bop around the dance floor to live music. *Av. Camarón Sábalo, across from Camino Real Hotel, tel. 69/84–0120. AE, DC, MC, V.*

$$ **Costa Marinera.** At one of the best seafood houses on the Mexican Riviera, try the fresh fish and the generous seafood platter, grilled on a hibachi at your table and piled high with frogs' legs, shrimp, oysters, octopuses, and more, covered with melted cheese. Also good is the shrimp *machaca*, sautéed in olive oil with tomatoes, chives, and chilis. *Privada del Camarón and Privada de la Florida, tel. 69/14–1928. AE, MC, V.*

$$ **Señor Frog.** Almost every gringo eventually ends up here. Bandido waiters carry tequila bottles and shot glasses in their bandoliers, and patrons stand on tables to sign their names on the ceiling. Barbecued ribs and chicken, served with corn on the cob, and heaping portions of standard Mexican dishes are the specialties. The tortilla soup is excellent. *Av. del Mar 225, tel. 69/82–8270. DC, MC, V.*

$$ **Mamucas.** Another one of the superb seafood places in town, Mamucas is popular with locals and gringos alike. Try the "are my eyes bigger than my stomach" test with the mixed seafood grill. The owner claims that an order of sugar-sweet grilled shrimp brochettes and an ice-cold beer will cure anything from a broken heart to a sunburn to a toothache. *Av. Simón Bolívar 404, tel. 69/81–3490. MC, V.*

$$ **El Shrimp Bucket.** This cheerful and casual eatery, located in the Hotel La Siesta, is where the popular Carlos Anderson chain began. Of course, there is shrimp—boiled, grilled, fried, whatever. Try the *camarón empanizado* (breaded fried shrimp in spicy ketchup and beer sauce). If you're more in the mood for red meat, try the *carne tampiqueña*, a grilled beef fillet served with a chili and guacamole sauce. *Paseo Olas Altas 11-126, tel. 69/81–6350. AE, MC, V.*

Puerto Vallarta

Puerto Vallarta was an unknown fishing village until John Huston filmed *Night of the Iguana* here in 1964 with Richard Burton, who brought along his girlfriend Liz Taylor. The torrid romance (which locals claim blossomed under the tropical magic of the sun and moon) made international headlines and launched Puerto Vallarta as one of the most popular resorts on the Riviera. The sweeping Bahía de Banderas bay, stretching up to where your ship will dock, is the second-largest natural bay in the world.

The area between the airport and Old Town, including the new Marina Vallarta complex, is overdeveloped; luxury high-rise hotels block sea views and mar the landscape. Downtown and the area south of the Río Cuale, however, have avoided the raw boomtown look that afflicts so many Mexican towns. Here, efforts are made to retain the image of the charming fishing village that once was: You'll still find the traditional whitewashed houses with red-tile roofs and lush bougainvillea, cobblestone streets, and fleets of colorful fishing boats hauling in their afternoon catches.

Shore Excursions

The following are good choices in Puerto Vallarta. They may not be offered by all cruise lines. Times and prices are approximate.

City History

Puerto Vallarta City Tour: An overview of the city includes a visit to Gringo Gulch (the prestigious part of town that many expatriates call home), where Taylor and Burton built a bridge over the street to join their houses. (Called "Casa Kimberly," it is today a bed-and-breakfast inn.) Other stops include Mismaloya Beach, where *Night of the Iguana* was filmed, and time for shopping downtown. *3 hrs. Cost: $25.*

Natural Beauty

Vallarta Horseback Riding: Ride through the lush hillside or along the shore to a beach for a swim. *2½–4 hrs. Cost: $30–$55.*

Coming Ashore

Cruise ships dock nearly 3 miles from downtown. Taking a bus tour or hiring a taxi is recommended if you want to see all of the large, sprawling town, but you can easily cover the downtown area on foot once you get there; a cab ride into town costs $2 per person; it will cost $5 per carload to return (*see* By Taxi, *below*). A cab ride to a beach costs $5 per person, and about twice that back to the pier.

Getting Around

By Bus

Buses are cheap and crisscross the city, but figuring out which goes where is too much effort for most passengers with only a few hours ashore.

By Car

Rental cars and motorbikes are expensive, but they may be the only practical way to visit the beaches at Boca de Tomatlán if you can't catch a convenient van or taxi. Contact **Avis** (Carretera Aeropuerto Km 2.5, tel. 322/1–1158), **Budget** (Carretera Aeropuerto Km 5, tel. 322/1–1888), **Dollar** (Paseo de las Palmas 1728, tel. 322/3–1354), **Hertz** (Paseo de las Palmas 1602, tel. 322/2–0024), **National** (Carretera Aeropuerto Km 1.5, tel. 322/2–0515), and **Quick** (Carretera Aeropuerto Km 1.5, tel. 322/2–4010).

By Taxi

Cabs are the best way to travel between the pier and town or to the beaches. There are two types: Volkswagen *combis* or vans pick up passengers only at the pier. Yellow union cabs cruise the downtown and beach areas and return passengers to the pier. Combis/vans and union cabs charge different rates; either way, negotiate the fare before getting in. Combi tours should cost $20–$30 per hour, depending on the size of the car and if it's air-conditioned. There is a three-hour minimum, and a good guide should be able to show you the town and the outskirts in that time.

Exploring Puerto Vallarta

Numbers in the margin correspond to points of interest on the Puerto Vallarta map.

There are three major regions: the northern hotels and resorts, the downtown, and the Río Cuale and Playa de los Muertos. Exploring downtown is best done on foot. Holes in the old cobblestone streets have recently been filled with cement, but you'll still want to wear comfortable walking shoes.

❶ Along the ***malecón,*** or sea wall, is the bronze sea horse that has become the town's trademark. A lovely promenade of palm trees and benches, the malecón and the beachfront are peppered with touristy sing-along bars, open-air restaurants, and boutiques.

City Hall, **6**
La Iglesia de Nuestra Señora de Guadalupe, **4**
Malecón, **1**
Museo Arqueológico, **3**
Playa Mismaloya, **7**
Plaza de Armas, **5**
Río Cuale Island, **2**

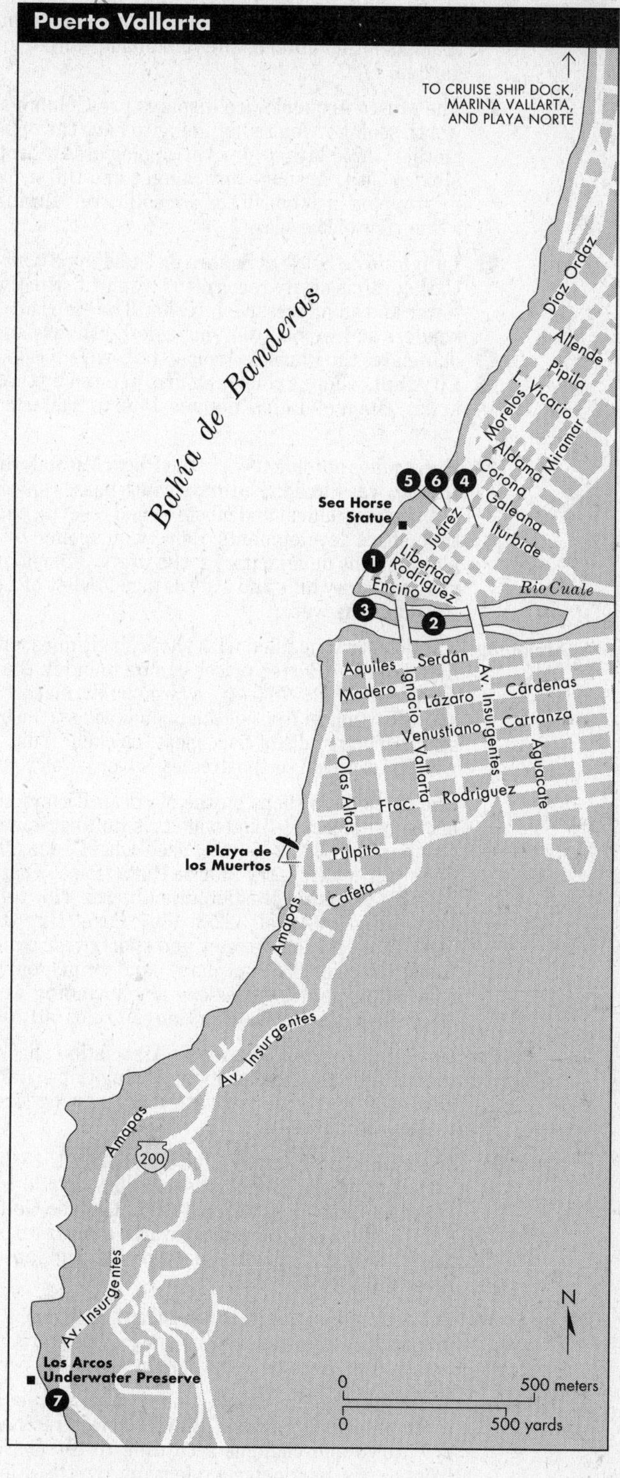

❷ **Río Cuale Island** is home to purveyors of paintings, folk art, stuffed iguanas, other interesting handmade wares, and a small botanical garden.

❸ The **Museo Arqueológico** displays pre-Columbian artifacts that are worth seeing if you're not going to have the opportunity to visit the mother ship, Museo de Antropología (Anthropology Museum) in Mexico City. Assuage any hunger and thirst from all this strolling by stopping in at one of the appealing restaurants on the island with a fine view of the sea.

❹ **La Iglesia de Nuestra Señora de Guadalupe** (Our Lady of Guadalupe Cathedral) is easily recognized by the distinctive crown on its clock tower and an impressive interior. The steps are often crowded with vendors and women weaving colored shawls and bags. A cathedral ❺ dominates the **Plaza de Armas,** the town's zócalo. On the north side is ❻ **City Hall,** where a colorful mural painted by the town's most famous artist, Manuel Lepe, depicts Puerto Vallarta before the tourist boom.

❼ Eight miles outside town is the **Playa Mismaloya,** where *Night of the Iguana* was filmed. The drive south passes spectacular homes, some of the town's oldest and most refined resorts, and a slew of condo and time-share developments. Somewhat spoiled by the huge hotel complex La Jolla de Mismaloya, the pretty Mismaloya cove is backed by rugged, rocky hills and affords a good view of Los Arcos, a rock formation in the water.

Shopping The downtown is filled with shops, boutiques, and stalls charging inflated prices. Better prices can be found in the **Mercado Municipal** (open daily 9 AM–7:30 PM), a large public market at Avenida Miramar and Libertad, in front of the inland bridge (the one farthest from the sea). Among stalls of fish, meat, chicken, fruit, and vegetables, you will find serapes, cotton dresses, silver jewelry, and leather goods.

One of the best shops on the Mexican Riviera for handmade leather boots, belts, jackets, and wallets is **Rolling Stones** (on the Malecón at Galeana, tel. 322/2–5798; Paseo Díaz Ordaz 802, tel. 322/3–1769). For silver jewelry, try **Mar de Plata** (Paseo Díaz Ordaz 824, tel. 322/2–6727) or **Sergio Bustamante** (Juárez 275, tel. 322/2–1129; Paseo Díaz Ordaz 700A, tel. 322/3–1407; Paseo Díaz Ordaz 542, tel. 322/2–5480). For costume jewelry and sportswear by local designers, visit **Keico** (Morelos 335, no phone) and **Primadonna Boutique** (Ignacio 335, no phone). For Mexican art, including works by Tamayo and Lepe, look into the **Galería Uno** (Morelos 561, tel. 322/2–0908).

Sports

Fishing Head over to the **Fishermen's Association** shack at the north end of the malecón to find out about fishing trips. Large group boats cost about $60 per person; private charters range from $150–$400 for up to six passengers.

Golf **Los Flamingos Country Club** (tel. 322/7–1515) has an 18-hole course carved from the jungle; reservations should be made a day in advance and include transportation. **Club de Golf Marina** (tel. 322/1–0171) is another good course; water comes into play on 11 holes, with the fairway dotted with lakes, ponds, and lagoons. Greens fees are around $75 for 18 holes.

Water Sports Snorkeling and diving are best at **Los Arcos,** a natural underwater preserve on the way to Mismaloya, but you'll have to take a motor launch from Boca de Tomatlán for about $15 per person, round-trip.

Beaches Beaches at Puerta Vallarta, many with coarse sand, are not the best on the Mexican Riviera. **Playa Norte** stretches from the wharf to downtown and changes according to the character of the hotel it fronts. It's particularly pleasant by the Fiesta Americana and Krystal hotels. Within walking distance of town, **Playa de los Muertos** (Beach of the Dead) is said to have been the site of a battle between pirates and Indians. Budget travelers hang out here, along with myriad vendors selling kites, blankets, and jewelry. No matter which beach you pick, soaking up the sun can work up an appetite, so try one of the local specialties offered by seaside vendors: *sarandeado*, barbecued fish on a stick.

Dining

$$ **El Dorado.** This is a popular beachfront hangout for American expatriates. The eclectic menu includes spaghetti, burgers, and crepes, but stick with Dorado-style fish, broiled with a thick layer of melted cheese. *Amapas and Pulpito, tel. 322/2-1511. AE, MC, V.*

$–$$ **Mr. Tequilla's Grill.** Set on a second-floor perch above the malecón, this place is worth a visit for the view alone. The menu includes tasty Mexican sandwiches, fresh seafood, and build-your-own tacos with oysters, peppers, and mushrooms among the fillings. Live music adds to the fun. *Galena 101–104, tel. 322/2-5725. AE, MC, V.*

$–$$ **Carlos O'Brian's.** Sooner or later *everyone* has at least a beer or margarita at this oceanside institution. It's an informal place, decorated with old historical photographs and a winged cow hanging from the ceiling. House specialties include juicy barbecued spareribs and *molcajete azteca* (strips of beef in a red-chili and onion sauce, served with refried beans and tortillas). *Paseo Diaz Ordaz 786, tel. 322/2-1444. AE, MC, V.*

Zihuatanejo/Ixtapa

Few Mexican resorts can claim the graceful balance between old and new reflected in the twin resort towns of Zihuatanejo (pronounced zee-wha-tah-*nay*-ho and meaning the land of women) and Ixtapa (eek-TAH-pah, "the white place," in the ancient Nahuatl dialect of the native indigenous settlers). Until the early 1970s Zihuatanejo was just another sleepy fishing village and neighboring Ixtapa was a swampy coconut plantation. But with some of the most beautiful beaches anywhere, the area could not go undiscovered by tourism. Certain developers would like to turn Ixtapa into another Cancún, but the Mexican government's master plan is to avoid that kind of growth. So Ixtapa today is an isolated oasis of about a dozen hotels, and Zihuatanejo is a charming village of small hotels and restaurants less glitzy than Ixtapa's. Hoping to boost tourism, investors have built a $500 million marina complex at the end of Ixtapa's hotel row, and two new 18-hole golf courses, including one designed by Robert Trent Jones. For now, at least, the area has something Cancún lacks: a quiet, easy pace and a way of life more closely resembling a fishing village than a resort.

In this wild, rugged part of Mexico, Spanish colonization was never very successful. As a result, many natives, including the craftspeople who come here from surrounding mountain villages to sell their wares, still speak one of five Indian dialects. But everyone is friendly, and despite the language barrier, it's somehow easier to make yourself understood here (even if communication is in sign language) than it is in other Mexican Riviera ports.

Shore Excursions The following is a good choice in Ixtapa. It may not be offered by all cruise lines. Time and price are approximate.

Undersea Creatures **Sail and Snorkel Tour:** A catamaran takes you to a less-populated beach, such as one in Manzanillo, for an hour of snorkeling. Drinks and snacks are served. *2½–3 hrs. Cost: $39.*

Coming Ashore Ships anchor in Zihuatanejo's harbor and tender passengers ashore to the town pier, in the center of the crescent-shape bay. To the right of the tender landing, the town covers about 2 square miles of brick-lined, closely fitted, sunbaked brick streets, and the main shopping area is concentrated in a few blocks near the town pier.

Getting Around While small Zihuatanejo is easily managed on foot, Ixtapa is 10 minutes away via the main highway.

By Bus Buses run between Zihuatanejo and the Ixtapa Hotel Zone approximately every 10 minutes for about N$1.

By Taxi The fare from Zihuatanejo to Ixtapa is about $3 per carload. Taxis are small, fitting three passengers comfortably. Minibuses also run between Zihuatanejo and Ixtapa; the fare is about $2 round-trip. Getting anywhere within the Ixtapa Hotel Zone is about $2–$3.

Exploring Zihuatanejo/ Ixtapa Zihuatanejo's charm lies in its narrow, sun-baked streets and its little shops and boutiques. The local **Museo Arqueológico** (Archeology Museum) and a folk-art store are beside the main church.

Ixtapa is strictly a resort town, with hotels strung for miles along the beach. Aside from the main boulevard, there is little to explore. However, with several malls clustered together, it's a shopping nirvana, and you'll find plenty of restaurants at the malls and in the resort hotels.

Shopping
Zihuatanejo Budget at least an hour here. Unlike elsewhere on the Mexican Riviera, merchants leave you alone and let you browse. (But locals will often approach you on the street, wanting to sell you packs of gum for $1.) Locally produced goods include wood carvings, ceramics, weavings, and leather goods. Indians display handicrafts in a **street market** on Cinco de Mayo. **Casa Marina** (tel. 755/4–2373), on the waterfront, has four distinctive shops: **El Embarcadero** has a large selection of indigenous embroidered clothing made of hand-loomed cotton, as well as wool rugs and wall hangings; **El Jumil** has native masks and hand-carved figurines; **La Zapoteca** has handwoven wool Zapotec rugs and Yucatán hammocks; and **Manos** has toys, baskets, hats, and copper. **Coco Cabaña** (tel. 755/4–2518), the folk-art store on Vicente Guerrero, behind Coconuts restaurant, is fabulous.

Ixtapa In Ixtapa browse at the **La Puerta** shopping mall along the Hotel Zone. It has more boutiques than Zihuatanejo does, with pricey merchandise by such designers as Ralph Lauren and Christian Dior, as well as a number of shops selling handicrafts and casual clothing and beachwear by local designers. There is also an open-air market for local crafts.

Sports
Fishing Big-game fishing here ranks among the world's best, with trophy-size sailfish, blue and black marlin, yellowfin tuna, and dorado. You can charter a boat at the **Municipal Beach**'s Zihuatanejo Pier and at **Playa Quieta** in Ixtapa. Rates range from $150 to $350 per day.

Golf The 18-hole **Ixtapa Golf Club** (tel. 755/3–1062) also is a wildlife preserve extending from a coconut plantation down to the sea. The new **Marina Golf Course** (tel. 755/3–1410) in the Marina Ixtapa area just north of the hotel zone, has 18 championship-caliber holes set amidst meandering canals. The greens fee at both courses is about $45–$50 per person.

Water Sports Waterskiing, windsurfing, snorkeling, diving, and sailing can be arranged at the Hotel Zone beaches in Ixtapa and on La Ropa Beach in Zihuatanejo. Waterskiing costs about $25 a half hour.

Beaches Zihuatanejo has some very fine swimming spots, and there's really no reason to travel to Ixtapa to spend the day at a beach. A taxi ride from the pier to the popular stretch of sand at Playa la Ropa costs about $2.

A few steps from downtown, the **Playa Principal** (Municipal Beach) curves around Zihuatanejo Bay. It's lined with restaurants and hotels. **Playa la Ropa,** a calm, safe swimming beach, is across the bay—about a $2 taxi ride one-way. **Las Gatas** is reached by water taxis, which are usually *panga* boats (outboard skiffs). Buy a ticket at the kiosk on the town pier (also $2) and hail one of the boats for the short ride across the harbor. There are several small restaurants and facilities here. Snorkeling equipment can be rented to explore the man-made breakwater that shelters the beach. One of the best swimming options is at the **Puerto Mío Hotel.** For the price of a drink and a snack you can spend the day at the stunning tile pool, cut into a cliff overlooking a small cove.

Dining
Zihuatanejo
$$

La Sirena Gorda. Right next to the pier and across from the municipal beach is the home of the very creative "Chubby Mermaid." Seafood tacos, octopus kebabs, conch and cactus salad, and a sizzling surf-n-turf platter are enough to lure any sailor out of the water. Open for breakfast, lunch, and dinner. *Paseo del Pescador y Playa Municipal, tel. 755/4-2687. MC, V.*

$–$$ **Casa Elvira.** An institution here since the 1950s, where the lobster and *huachinango* (white fish grilled with tomato, chilis, and onion) are perfumed with the sea. In high season, this joint is jammed. The food and the service are impeccable. *Paseo del Pescador 8 (a block away from La Sirena Gorda), tel. 755/4-2061. MC, V.*

$ **La Bocana.** This favorite with locals and visitors has been here for ages. Service is good, and so's the food. Musicians sometimes stroll through. *Juan Alvarez 13, tel. 755/4-3545. MC, V.*

$ **Puntarenas.** Home-cooked, authentic Mexican food in a no-nonsense setting makes this a favorite with locals and visitors in the know. *Across the bridge at the end of Juan Alvarez, no phone. No credit cards. Closed Easter–mid-Dec. No dinner.*

Ixtapa
$$$

Las Esferas. This is a complex of two restaurants and a bar in the Westin Brisas (formerly known as the Camino Real) hotel. **Portofino** specializes in Italian cuisine and is decorated with multicolor pasta and scenes of Italy. In **El Mexicano** you get Mexican food along with Mexican ambience—bright pink tablecloths, Puebla jugs, and a huge, colorful "tree of life" folk-art sculpture. *Playa Vista Hermosa, tel. 755/3-2121, ext. 3444. AE, DC, MC, V.*

$$ **Carlos 'n Charlie's.** Hidden away at the end of the beach is an outpost of the famous Anderson's chain. Pork, seafood, and chicken are served in a Polynesian setting. *Next to Posada Real Hotel, tel. 755/3-0035. AE, DC, MC, V.*

$$ **Da Baffone.** Italian dishes are the specialties of this restaurant, one of three eateries in La Puerta mall. *Tel. 755/3-11-22. AE, MC, V.*

New England and Canada

Less crowded and less expensive than Alaska, New England and Canada's Maritimes offer beautiful scenery, historical sights, and wildlife (including whales). Prime attractions of a cruise in this area are Nova Scotia's tiny fishing villages, the historic St. Lawrence River valley, and hillsides ablaze with autumn colors. Major ports are New York, Newport, Boston, Halifax, and Québec City. Among the lines that sail here seasonally are American Canadian, Cunard, Dolphin, Holland America, Princess, Seabourn, and Silversea. Small ships, such as those in the fleets of American Canadian Caribbean Line and Clipper Cruise Line, also sail inland: ACCL navigates upstate New York's canal and lock system—a stunning trip in the summer and autumn; while Clipper explores New York's Hudson River valley every fall. (For seasonal itineraries, *see* Chapter 4.)

When to Go Cruises leave during the summer and through early autumn. The best cruising time is early fall, when the leaves are turning color, or summer if you enjoy jazz and arts festivals. Some ships offer only a couple of cruises between their summer season in Europe and their Caribbean season, so the number of berths is limited. For that reason, few bargains are offered.

Boston

Boston is a popular terminus and port of call. Once staid and settled, the city has over the past decade become revitalized, with new developments breeding a flurry of economic activity. The historic shrines and glittering new skyscrapers along the Freedom Trail make for an excellent walking tour that contrasts Colonial America with corporate America. The influence of the hugely successful Faneuil Hall and Quincy Market has spread to restored and brand-new buildings along the waterfront with many new restaurants and shops. The Back Bay, too, has many eating and shopping attractions for visitors. In addition, the city offers world-class art museums and three major collegiate centers—Harvard, Boston University, and Boston College—which contribute a youthful influence that percolates throughout "Bean Town."

Coming Ashore Cruise ships dock at the Black Falcon Cruise Terminal, about a mile from downtown. Taxis generally meet incoming ships. The ride into town costs about $4. Buses run from the dock to downtown every 20 minutes, Monday–Friday 7 AM–6 PM. The fare is $1. Maps and brochures are available inside the terminal; the nearest manned information booth is at South Station.

Exploring Boston For traditionalists, a walk through Boston should start on **Beacon Hill,** taking in all the little side streets; then wind past **Government Center,** heading for the back corners of the North End, where landmarks such as **Paul Revere's House** and the **Old North Church** reveal themselves at every turn. Continue through the downtown streets, through the Common and the Public Garden and along a Beacon Street that still belongs to the ghost of Oliver Wendell Holmes. As afternoon shadows lengthen, walk along the Charles River toward **Harvard Square,** as Archibald MacLeish did on the night he decided to become a poet rather than a lawyer. Cross the river into **Cambridge** and consider what possessed men to build a college in what in 1636 was the wilderness.

Newport

Now trendy but once genteel, the seaside community of Newport, Rhode Island, offers a very manageable day of exploring. Newport is best known for its Colonial beginnings and turn-of-the-century high-society splendor: Along Bellevue Avenue and Ocean Drive you

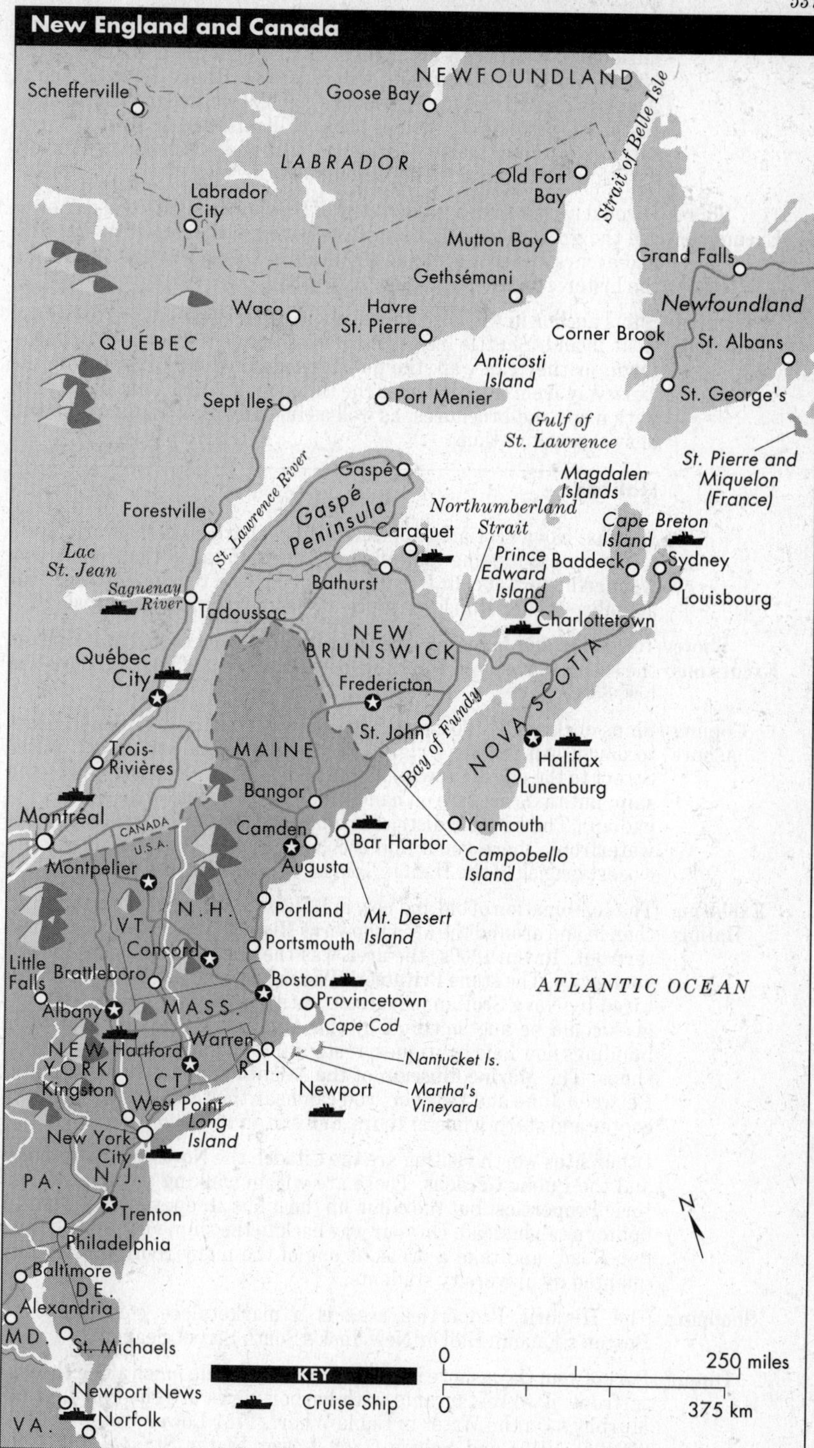
New England and Canada
NEWFOUNDLAND
Schefferville
Goose Bay
LABRADOR
Strait of Belle Isle
Old Fort Bay
Labrador City
Mutton Bay
Grand Falls
Gethsémani
Newfoundland
Waco
Havre St. Pierre
Corner Brook
St. Albans
QUÉBEC
Anticosti Island
St. George's
Sept Iles
Port Menier
Gulf of St. Lawrence
St. Pierre and Miquelon (France)
Gaspé
Magdalen Islands
St. Lawrence River
Gaspé Peninsula
Northumberland Strait
Forestville
Caraquet
Cape Breton Island
Lac St. Jean
Prince Edward Island
Baddeck
Sydney
Bathurst
Louisbourg
Saguenay River
Tadoussac
Charlottetown
NEW BRUNSWICK
Québec City
NOVA SCOTIA
Fredericton
St. John
Bay of Fundy
Trois-Rivières
MAINE
Halifax
Lunenburg
Bangor
Montreal
CANADA
U.S.A.
Camden
Yarmouth
Bar Harbor
Augusta
Campobello Island
Montpelier
N.H.
Portland
Mt. Desert Island
VT.
Portsmouth
Concord
Little Falls
Brattleboro
Boston
ATLANTIC OCEAN
Provincetown
Albany
MASS.
Cape Cod
NEW YORK
Hartford
Warren
Nantucket Is.
R.I.
CT.
Newport
Martha's Vineyard
Kingston
West Point
Long Island
New York City
PA.
N.J.
Trenton
Philadelphia
Baltimore
DE.
Alexandria
MD.
St. Michaels
KEY
Cruise Ship
Newport News
Norfolk
VA.
0
250 miles
0
375 km
N

can see the summer mansions (several sumptuous ones are open as museums). Newport is also famous as a Navy town, and a visit to the Naval War College Museum will illustrate Rhode Island's role in America's naval history. Newport's colonial waterfront boasts more restored 18th-century homes than Williamsburg or Boston, first-rate restaurants, fashionable shops, jazz and folk festivals, a lively nightlife, and special events throughout the year.

Shore Excursions If you'd rather take a guided tour of Newport's sights, good choices are the guided walking tour of the waterfront district (2 hrs, $18) and excursions that combine a ride along Ocean Drive with tours of the historic mansions (2–4 hrs, $20–$35).

Coming Ashore Ships anchor in the East Passage and tender passengers to nearby Goat Island. Shuttle buses transfer passengers from here to downtown, or they can walk the quarter-mile distance. Just across the causeway from Goat Island is the Gateway Visitors Center, stocked with maps and brochures, as well as friendly local staffers who will answer any questions.

Halifax

Halifax, Nova Scotia, has one of the finest harbors in the world, with a history of shipping and understated hospitality that makes it a wonderful port of call. If you are on one of the very few cruises that actually start or stop here, a pre- or post-cruise stay is a must.

Shore Excursions To see the sights beyond the town itself, a good choice in Halifax is the scenic drive along the rugged south shore and Peggy's Cove (3½ hrs, $50.)

Coming Ashore Ships dock at Pier 20/21 near the railway station, a 15-minute walk to downtown. (Make a right out of the terminal and follow Water Street to the edge of town.) A shuttle bus is usually arranged by the ship, but taxis also are on hand. The ride to downtown costs $5 (Canadian). The historic district is a pleasant half-mile walk along the waterfront; there you'll find the Nova Scotia Visitor Center. The closest branch of the Halifax Tourist Office is at Old City Hall.

Exploring Halifax The combination of old and new in Halifax is nowhere more apparent than in and around the area known as **Historic Properties,** on the waterfront. In the 1800s, the area was the center of business for the young city. The stone **Privateer's Warehouse** housed the cargoes captured by Nova Scotian privateers until the captured ships and cargoes could be auctioned off by the Admiralty. The area's historic buildings now hold boutiques, restaurants, nightclubs, and souvenir shops. The **Marine Museum of the Atlantic** has excellent exhibits. Between June and October, you can hear the town crier, take helicopter and stern-wheeler tours, and sail on the *Bluenose II*.

Other sites worth visiting are the **Citadel,** the **Nova Scotia Museum,** and the **Public Gardens.** These are within walking distance of Historic Properties, but the climb up the hill is steep; you may want to opt for a cab instead. On your way back to the ship, visit Spring Garden Road, and take a break at one of the many rooftop cafés frequented by university students.

Shopping The Historic Properties area is a marketplace comparable to Boston's Faneuil Hall or New York's South Street Seaport.

Dining Part of your day ashore in Halifax should include lunch along the waterfront. Two restaurants with harbor views are the **Sail Loft** (at Murphy's On the Water in Cable Wharf, 1751 Lower Water St., tel. 902/420–1015) and **Salty's** (1869 Lower Water St., tel. 902/423–6818). Both are in the Historic Properties area.

Montréal

In contrast to Québec City (*see below*), Montréal is a thoroughly modern city, although it also has a French accent and its own charming historic district. Montréal is so clean and organized that most visitors feel safe and comfortable as they wander its many vibrant neighborhoods, or *quartiers*.

Coming Ashore Ships dock within a few blocks of Place Jacques-Cartier, the main square in Old Montréal. Taxis are plentiful in the port area, and there are three Métro stations in Old Montréal to carry you to the Underground City and elsewhere. (Montréal's Métro is clean, quiet, and efficient.) The closest information booth is at 174 Notré Dame East, near Place Jacques-Cartier.

Exploring Montréal Downtown are boutiques, department stores, and 21 museums. Among these are such gems as the **Canadian History Museum,** the **Art Deco Museum,** the **International Humor Museum,** and the **Montreal Museum of Fine Arts.** Buildings linked by the **Underground City** include several posh hotels and 11 shopping malls. Close to the docks, the **Latin Quarter** has a Métro station at Berride Montigny on St-Denis. Lower St-Denis has a typical student-quarter atmosphere, with bookstores, art galleries, and bistros. In summer, musicians in town for the Jazz Festival gather here for jam sessions. Off St-Denis, 19th-century homes on **St-Louis Square** surround a fountain and flower market. The square's west side leads to the **Prince Arthur pedestrian mall,** lined with restaurants (many of them inexpensive) and outdoor cafés. A healthy walk will lead you to **Place Jacques-Cartier** in Old Montréal, where you will see many historic sites.

Québec City

The birthplace of French-colonial North America, Québec City is a jewel. Perched high on a cliff overlooking the St. Lawrence River, it is rich in charm and history. Extremely proud of their heritage, Québecois have preserved dozens of buildings (many dating to the 17th century), battle sites, and monuments. The result is a charming blend of winding cobblestone streets and old houses reminiscent of Europe. In fact, Québec is so full of architectural treasures that in 1985 UNESCO declared it a World Heritage Treasure site, ranking it with Egypt's pyramids and India's Taj Mahal.

Shore Excursions Good choices in Québec City are a tour that combines sights in the old and new cities (2½ hrs, $20), an escorted walking tour of the old city (2½ hrs, $18), and, in season, a fall foliage drive through the countryside (3½ hrs, $40).

Coming Ashore Ships dock downtown, below the cliffs and a few steps from the old walled city. Taxis are always near the dock, which is next to the ferry terminal. Typically, a tourist guide meets the ship to answer questions and provide maps, but in summer you can look for friendly youths on scooters handing out maps on street corners in the old town.

To reach the old city on foot, make your way from the ship across rue Dalhousie to rue du Marché. At the statue of Louis XIV, make a right to walk to the upper city. Immediately after the arch, you'll see a staircase on your left. Follow this to the heart of the upper city.

Exploring Québec City Most of the Old World charm is found in **Vieux Québec,** the historic walled city. The **Lower City** is the place to browse through art galleries and superb boutiques. Then take the funicular, or elevator tram, into the upper city (for about $1 [Canadian]) to stand on **Dufferin Terrace,** with its boardwalk and panoramic view of the waterway below. To your right is the **Château Frontenac,** probably the most photographed building in Canada. Street musicians and jugglers turn the **Place d'Armes** into an open-air theater in summer. Nearby is **Trésor Street,** the colorful artists' alley (*see* Shopping, *below*).

Shopping **Rue du Trésor,** in the upper city, is the place to find local artists displaying their work. The most popular subject is scenes of Old Quebec; most prints are priced from $5 to $50. For Canadian fashions, visit **Boutique Zazou** (31 Petit Champlain, tel. 418/694–9990) in the lower city.

Dining The upper city's rue St. Louis is lined with restaurant after restaurant. **Cafe de Paris** (66 rue St. Louis, tel. 418/694–9626) stands out for its interesting specials, such as salmon in vinegar-raspberry sauce, rabbit in mustard sauce, or chicken in asparagus sauce.

Other Ports

As a cruise destination, New England and Canada remain relatively unspoiled, and full of charm, history, and a fresh perspective on very beautiful lands. Besides the major ports outlined above, places of interest include the historic French fortress city of Louisbourg, Nova Scotia; the quaint but upscale island of Nantucket, Massachusetts; resort towns on the coastline of Maine; the scenic St. Lawrence River and Saguenay Fjord; and Campobello Island on the Bay of Fundy, site of President Franklin D. Roosevelt's summer home.

Panama Canal and Central America

Transit of the Panama Canal takes only one day. The rest of your cruise will be spent on islands in the Caribbean or at ports along the Mexican Riviera. Increasingly, Panama Canal itineraries include stops in Central America; some may also call along the northern coast of South America. Most Panama Canal cruises are one-way trips, part of a 10- to 14-day cruise between the Atlantic and Pacific oceans. Shorter loop cruises enter the canal from the Caribbean, sail around Gatún Lake for a few hours, and return to the Caribbean.

The Panama Canal is best described as a water bridge that "raises" ships up and over Central America, then down again, using a series of locks or water steps. Artificially created Gatún Lake, 85 feet above sea level, is the canal's highest point. The route is approximately 50 miles long, and the crossing takes from 8 to 10 hours. Cruise ships pay more than $100,000 for each transit, which is less than half of what it would cost them to sail around Cape Horn, at the southern tip of South America.

Just before dawn, your ship will line up with dozens of other vessels to await its turn to enter the canal. Before it can proceed, two pilots and a narrator will come on board. The sight of a massive cruise ship being raised dozens of feet into the air by water is so fascinating that passengers will crowd all the forward decks at the first lock. If you can't see, go to the rear decks, where there is usually more room and the view is just as intriguing. Later in the day you won't find as many passengers up front.

On and off throughout the day, commentary is broadcast over ship's loudspeakers, imparting facts and figures as well as anecdotes about the history of the canal. The canal stands where it does today not because it's the best route but because the railroad was built there first, making access to the area relatively easy. The railway had followed an old Spanish mule trail that had been there for more than 300 years.

When to Go In spring and autumn a number of cruise ships use the Panama Canal to reposition between the Caribbean and Alaska. However, several ships offer regular transcanal and loop cruises throughout the winter season. (For seasonal itineraries, *see* Chapter 4.)

Currency Passengers won't need to change money to transit the canal, but some ships stop in Costa Rica; in the San Blas Islands, off Panama; and at Cartagena, Colombia. In Costa Rica, the currency is the colón. At press time, one U.S. dollar was worth about 163 colónes. In Panama, the balboa and the U.S. dollar are regular currency and both have the same value. In Colombia, the monetary unit is the peso, with one U.S. dollar worth about 580 pesos.

Passports and Visas No passport or visa is necessary to transit the Panama Canal because passengers do not disembark. A passport is needed for passengers on cruises that call in Costa Rica, the San Blas Islands, or Cartagena.

Cartagena, Colombia

Cartagena, Colombia, is one of the Western Hemisphere's most fascinating cities. Seventeenth-century walls divide Cartagena into the "old" and "new" cities. In the old city, houses are in the Iberian style: thick walls, high ceilings, central patios, gardens, and balconies. The streets are narrow and crooked, designed for protection during assault. The cityscape is filled with historical sites, forts,

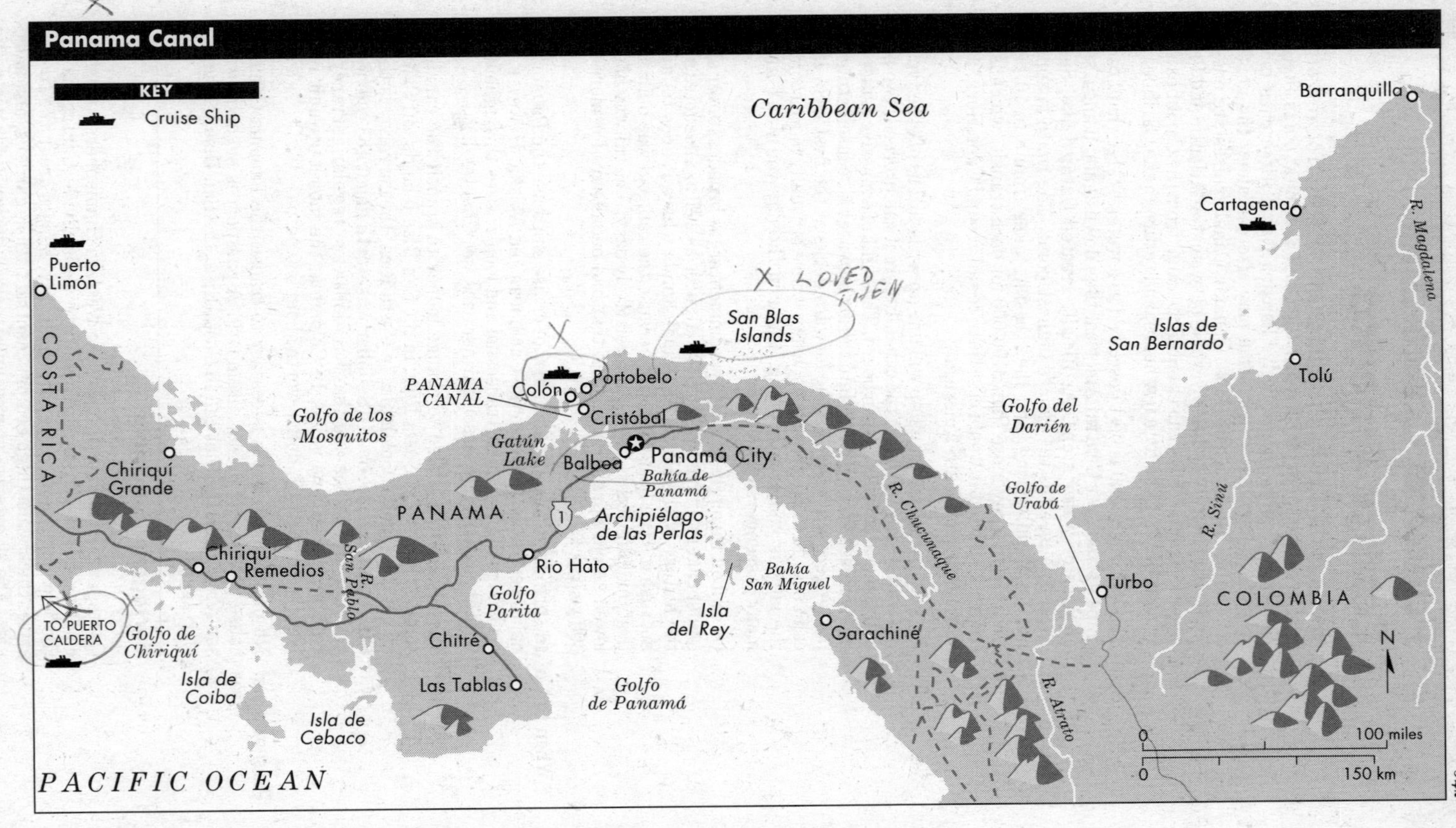
Panama Canal
KEY
Cruise Ship
Caribbean Sea
Barranquilla
Cartagena
R. Magdalena
Puerto Limón
COSTA RICA
San Blas Islands
Islas de San Bernardo
Tolú
Portobelo
PANAMA CANAL
Colón
Cristóbal
Golfo de los Mosquitos
Golfo del Darién
Gatún Lake
Balboa
Panamá City
Bahía de Panamá
Chiriquí Grande
PANAMA
Archipiélago de las Perlas
Golfo de Urabá
R. Sinú
R. Chucunaque
Chiriqui
Remedios
R. San Pablo
Rio Hato
Bahía San Miguel
Turbo
COLOMBIA
TO PUERTO CALDERA
Golfo de Chiriquí
Golfo Parita
Isla del Rey
Garachiné
Chitré
Las Tablas
Isla de Coiba
Golfo de Panamá
R. Atrato
Isla de Cebaco
N
0
100 miles
0
150 km
PACIFIC OCEAN

and museums. Among Cartagena's major exports are coffee and emeralds—Colombia supplies 70% of the world's supply of these gems.

Shore Excursions The best choice in Cartagena for the first-time visitor is the city tour (3½ hrs, $26), which takes you through the city, stopping at a hilltop monastery for a sweeping view, and into the old town for a survey of the historic attractions and shopping.

Costa Rica

Costa Rica is emerging as a popular port of call on Panama Canal itineraries, due to its growing reputation as a land of unspoiled rain forests, abundant wildlife, and friendly locals. Twenty-seven percent of the land is protected wilderness—home to 850 species of birds, 200 species of mammals, and 35,000 species of insects. Some itineraries include a scenic sail into the Golfo Dulce, whose shores are lined with remote beaches and untouched rain forest teeming with wildlife.

Coming Ashore Most ships call at Puerto Caldera, located 5 miles from Puntarenas on the Pacific Coast, or Puerto Limon, on the Caribbean coast. Both double as cargo ports, and since most attractions are located some distance away or involve guided nature walks, it's a good idea to book a shore excursion. From Puerto Caldera, a local taxi to Puntarenas costs approximately U.S. $12 each way, but its beaches are polluted and there is little of interest for cruise passengers. A small selection of stands at the port sells coffee, souvenir oxcarts, wood, leather and T-shirts.

Shore Excursions From Puerto Caldera, the best choice for nature lovers is a walk through the Carara Biological Reserve, a half hour from the ship, where you can see crocodiles, toucans, and sloths (4 hrs, $55). (Skip the nine-hour excursion to the more famous Los Angeles Cloud Forest, where you'll spend only about an hour actually in the forest.) Shoppers won't want to miss a trip to the artisan city of Sarchi (5 hrs, $45). A 10-hour tour to the capital city of San Jose, two hours from the ship, costs $95.

Good choices from Puerto Limon include river rafting on the Rio Reventazon (8 hrs, $78) and riding the historic Green Train through banana plantations (2½ hrs, $68).

Puerto Quetzal, Guatemala

Guatemala is home to a vibrant Indian culture, colonial cities, and stunning mountain scenery. Most ships call at Puerto Quetzal, a lively cargo and cruise port located on Guatemala's flat Pacific coast. Families and school groups pose for photos in front of the cruise ship, friendly hawkers approach with handcrafted silver belts, and locals slurp ices purchased from a two-wheel cart. You can easily spend a morning bargaining for leather, jewelry, rugs and embroidered belts at the open-air market set up amid sacks of grain at the port. Otherwise, it's a good idea to book a shore excursion. Local taxes aren't necessarily reliable, and it's about U.S. $50 per person each way to the colonial town of Antigua or Guatemala City, a two-hour drive away. The closest town, San Jose, is dirty and offers little of interest to cruise passengers.

Shore Excursions The Mayan ruins of Tikal are perhaps Guatemala's most famous attraction, and with good reason: They're known as the greatest Mayan site yet discovered, with 3,000 unique buildings nestled in thick jungle. But it's neither cheap nor easy to get there from the ship: The trip involves buses, walking, and a one-hour flight by chartered aircraft (10 hrs, $354). Less costly and complicated options include a tour of historic Antigua, with its cobblestone streets and brightly colored buildings (8 hrs, $104) or an excursion to the Guatemala Highlands and Lake Atitlan, whose crystal-clear waters are ringed by mountains on all sides (9 hrs, $140).

The San Blas Islands

The beautiful islands of the **San Blas** archipelago are home to the Cuna Indians, whose women are famous for handworked stitching. These women are a charming sight, with their embroidered *molas*, strings of necklaces, gold jewelry in their noses, and arm and ankle bracelets. Some cruise lines organize shore excursions to Cuna villages on outlying islands. Travel is by motorized dugout canoe. A native dance performance may be scheduled, and native crafts are usually for sale. If you are wavering between two Panama Canal cruises, take the one that stops at the San Blas Islands.

South America

Sailing to South America to escape the cold northern winter is one of cruising's more exotic adventures. The most common itineraries, sometimes known as Caribazon cruises, combine Caribbean ports of call with a navigation of the Amazon River. Other itineraries sail down to Rio de Janeiro to coincide with Carnival; a few head even farther south, rounding the tip of the continent at Tierra del Fuego. The grandest of all is a circumnavigation of South America, which takes in all the major ports in about 50 days.

The Amazon region has figured so prominently in novels and films that most people arrive with several preconceived notions. Often they expect an impenetrable jungle, herds of animals, flocks of swooping birds, and unfriendly Indians. In reality, ground cover is sparse, trees range from 50 to 150 feet in height, little animal life can be spotted, and the birds nest in the tops of the high trees. However, the natural romance of the Amazon River, the free-flowing water, and the hint of mystery remain.

Most of the Amazon basin has been explored and charted. The river itself is 3,900 miles long—the second-longest in the world—and has 17 tributaries, each over 1,000 miles long. About one-third of the world's oxygen is produced by the vegetation, and one-fifth of all the fresh water in the world is carried by the Amazon. Although more than 18,000 plant species thrive here, the extremely heavy rainfall leaches the soil of its nutrients and makes organized cultivation impractical. Poor in agricultural possibilities, the Amazon is rich in other products, including gold, diamonds, lumber, rubber, oil, and jute.

Listed below are brief overviews of South America's major cruise ports; your shore-excursion director will have detailed information on getting around these ports, choosing excursions, and exchanging currency. At press time, the major cruise lines sailing to South America were Costa, Crystal, Cunard, Holland America, Princess, Radisson Seven Seas, Royal Olympic, Seabourn, Silversea, and Special Expeditions. (For seasonal itineraries, *see* Chapter 4.) Alternative sailings to South America can be found aboard some European cruise lines, such as Costa, and passenger-freighter lines, such as Ivaran (*see* Chapter 2).

When to Go South America's cruising season is short—from the end of October to early March. The few ships going there tend to be booked quickly, so make your reservations early.

Health Travelers to the Amazon, and other South American rural areas and small cities, are advised to get vaccinated against yellow fever and to take medication to prevent malaria. There are no formal vaccination requirements for entry, but the **Centers for Disease Control** (tel. 404/639–2572) in Atlanta offers up-to-the-minute advice on health precautions. Call their **International Travellers Hotline** for information on your destination. In addition to malaria and yellow fever, you'll be warned about hepatitis A (for which immune serum globulin is recommended), hepatitis B, typhoid fever, and cholera. Contact your health department for immunization information. Local offices of the **U.S. Public Health Service** (a division of CDC) handle inquiries. There are branches in Chicago, Hawaii, Los Angeles, Miami, New York, San Francisco, and Seattle.

Passports and Visas Brazil requires valid passports and tourist visas of visitors whose countries demand visas of Brazilians. This includes the United States and Canada, but not the United Kingdom. A tourist visa, valid for 90 days, is easily obtainable from a Brazilian consulate and free if you apply in person and bring your passport, a 2″-by-3″ passport photo, and a round-trip ticket. Check requirements with your cruise line if your itinerary includes other countries.

South America

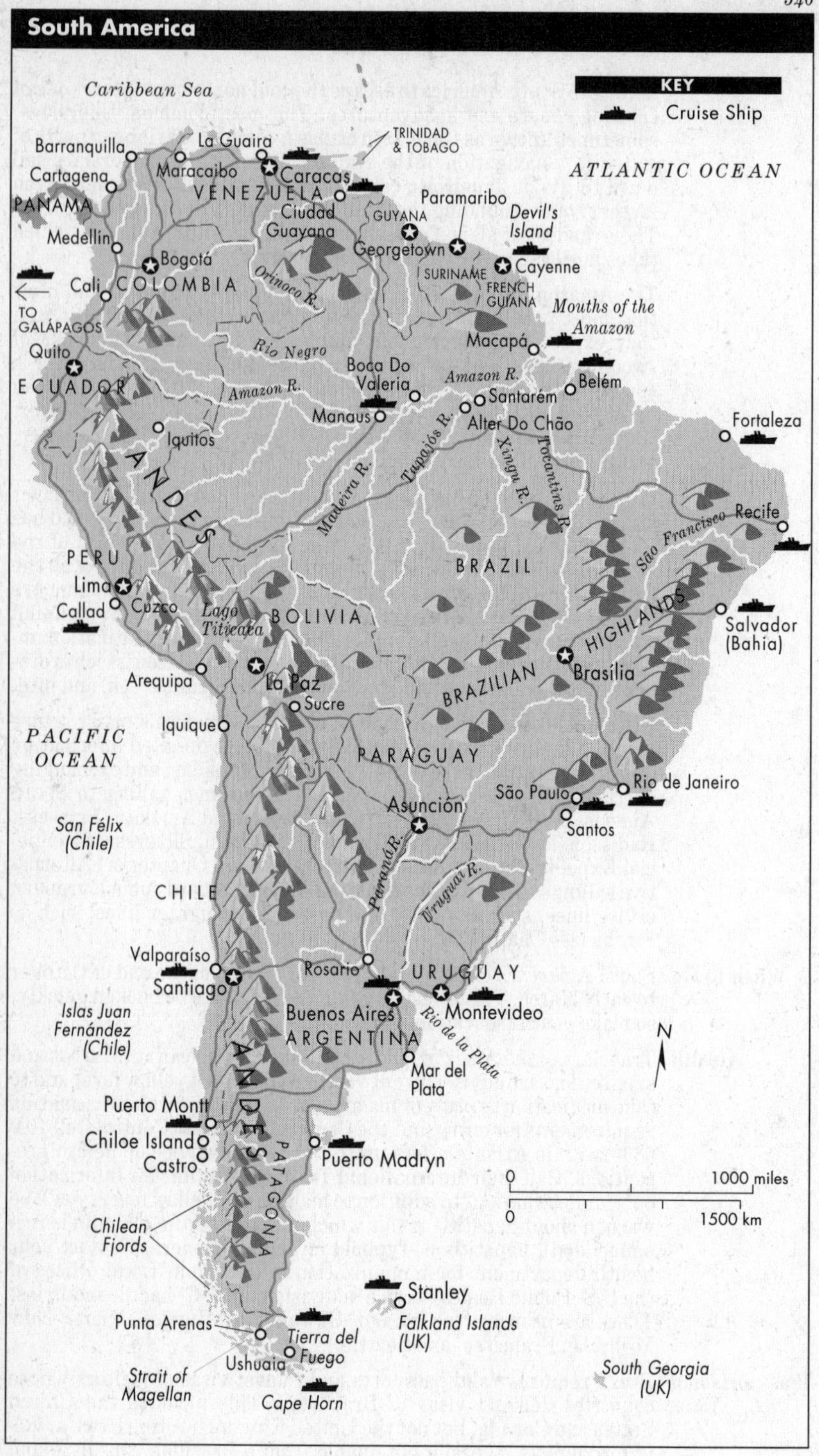

Alter do Chão/Santarém, Brazil

Cruise ships that call at Alter do Chão generally spend half the day here and half at nearby Santarém—they're both on the Amazon about midway between Belém and Manaus. Shopping for such local handicrafts as masks, blowguns, earrings, necklaces, and straw baskets is a major pastime. You'll find the same wares sold by literally the same merchants in both towns.

Coming Ashore Ships drop anchor off Alter do Chão and tender passengers directly to the main square downtown. Most worthwhile sights are within walking distance. At Santarém, ships dock just a few minutes' walk from the downtown shopping district. Ships run shuttle buses to the **Mercado Modelo** (handicrafts market) for about $10 per person, but taxis are readily available and cheaper at $3–$5 per carload.

Exploring Alter do Chão/ Santarém There are no formal shore excursions in Alter do Chão, a small village on the Tapajós River with lush vegetation and fine river swimming. After tendering ashore, passengers can shop; visit the **Museum of Indigenous Art,** with exhibits and artifacts representing 58 Amazonian Indian tribes; or watch folk dances performed by local children. For a small fee ($2–$4), local fishermen will row you across the little harbor to a small but very clean beach.

Santarém, founded in 1661, is a city of 250,000 people. It's notable for its riches of timber, bauxite, and gold, and the colorful **waterfront** makes for an engaging stroll. There are no formal excursions here, either. Browsing and shopping are the major pursuits for cruise passengers.

Belém, Brazil

The Brazilian city of Belém is the gateway to the Amazon, 90 miles from the open sea. It has ridden the ups and downs of Amazon booms and busts since 1616, alternately bursting with energy and money and slumping into relative obscurity. This is evident in the city's architecture: Ultramodern high-rises mingle with older red-tile-roof buildings, and colonial structures survive alongside rubber-era mansions and ostentatious monuments.

Shore Excursions The following are good choices in Belém. They may not be offered by all cruise lines. Times and prices are approximate.

Belém City and the Goeldi Museum. Includes visits to the Ver-o-Peso market; the Goeldi Museum; the marble, turn-of-the-century Basilica of Our Lady of Nazareth; and a stop at the enormous, neoclassical Teatro de la Paz. *Half day. Cost: $35.*

Brazilian Jungle River Cruise. Cruise in riverboats into creeks and channels of the Guama River. Stop at Santa Maria Island for a walk into the Amazon rain forest, which can be muddy and is always hot and humid. *Half day. Cost: 50.*

Coming Ashore Ships must anchor quite far offshore. With the strong local current, the tender ride can take 15–20 minutes one-way. Passengers land at a floating dock about a half-hour ride outside town. Taxis are available, but few drivers speak English.

Exploring Belém In the "old city" you will find the **Our Lady of Nazare** church, with its ornate interior; the former **city palace**; and the **Bolonha Palace.** Walk to the **Praça da Republica,** facing the Municipal Theatre, to see the Victorian marble statues. Nearby is the **handicrafts center**, run by the state tourism office; at this daily fair you will find wood, leather, and straw objects, plus handmade Indian goods and examples of the region's colorful and distinctive pottery, called *marajoara.* In addition to the **Goeldi Museum**'s extensive collection of Indian artifacts and excellent photographs, there is a **zoo** with many local animals in their natural surroundings. The **Ver-o-Peso**

market is short on cleanliness but long on local color, with vendors offering medicinal herbs, regional fruits, miracle roots from the jungle, alligator teeth, river fish, and good-luck charms for body and soul.

Boca de Valeria, Brazil

Calling tiny, undeveloped Boca de Valeria a port is a bit generous. Passengers are often met by a group of 50 or so Native Americans, who canoe into port when a ship arrives. The big draw here is a chance to capture on film little boys holding their pet monkeys, sloths, and alligators; and little girls selling beaded necklaces. If you're one of the first ashore, you'll get a fascinating, though somewhat contrived, picture of an Amazon village.

Coming Ashore Boca de Valeria is so small that cruise ships set up inflatable docks for disembarkation by tender at this village east of Manaus. There are no facilities, restaurants, or tourist offices. Crew members sometimes bring ashore coolers of refreshments. Exploring is done solely on foot along dirt paths.

Buenos Aires, Argentina

Buenos Aires has been called the most sophisticated city in South America. Most cruise lines recognize its late-night appeal by calling here overnight. Spending the evening in this city that never sleeps gives you the chance to see an Argentine folk dance or even venture out to a tango parlor on your own. Pre- or post-cruise packages in Buenos Aires or to Iguazú Falls are extremely popular.

Shore Excursions The following are good choices in Buenos Aires. They may not be offered by all cruise lines. Times and prices are approximate.

A Day in the Pampas. Drive out of the city into the nearby pampas to visit an *estancia* (ranch). Watch a performance of traditional gaucho guitar music and a show of horsemanship. A barbecue lunch is served. *7 hrs. Cost: $60–$80.*

Buenos Aires City Tour. This drive through Buenos Aires gives you a feel for this sprawling, architecturally rich city, with its broad boulevards, narrow colonial streets, and famous landmarks, such as the Casa Rosada (the pink "White House"), the tomb of Evita Perón, the Obelisk, and the Teatro Colón. *Half day. Cost: $25.*

Steak Dinner and Tango Show. This tour combines an Argentine steak dinner at one of the city's barbecue and *parilla* (grill) restaurants with a stage show of tango Argentino and gaucho (cowboy) folk dancing. *5 hrs. Cost: $70–$89.*

Coming Ashore Ships dock in the deep-water harbor. The most interesting shopping areas are a long walk or short taxi ride away. Taxis are available at the passenger terminal, and most drivers speak at least a smattering of English. The 10–15 minute ride into town costs $3–$5.

Caracas/La Guaira, Venezuela

Cruises that call along the Venezuelan coast are most often sailing on a southern Caribbean itinerary (*see* Caribbean, *above*).

Cartagena, Colombia

Cruises that call at Colombia's capital city are most often sailing on a Panama Canal itinerary (*see* Panama Canal, *above*).

Devil's Island, French Guiana

Many cruises that advertise a stop at Devil's Island may actually put ashore at another of French Guiana's three Iles du Salut, of which Devil's Island (Ile Royale) is one. All three were prisons, and today tourism is unwilling—and unable—to push back the rampant jungle. The area is picturesque, lush, and haunting, so don't forget your camera.

Coming Ashore Passengers tender ashore to explore the remains of the penal colony and follow the footpath that encircles the island.

Fortaleza, Brazil

Several hundred miles southeast of Belém, Fortaleza is Brazil's fifth-largest city. A long drought devastated this agrarian region during the 1980s, and only in recent years has Fortaleza begun to recover. On the Atlantic, you'll find wonderful (usually crowded) beaches and some of the best lobster and fresh fish in South America. Its famed lace industry is fast turning Fortaleza into one of Brazil's top fashion centers.

Shore Excursions The following is a good choice in Fortaleza. It may not be offered by all cruise lines. Time and price are approximate.

City Tour. Includes the gothic-style cathedral; the monument to former president of Brazil Castello Branco; the fortress; and a visit to an artisan's center—in the old city jail—to shop for such local handicrafts as lacework, leather, wooden figures, and sand paintings in bottles. *Half day. Cost: $35.*

Coming Ashore Ships dock within walking distance of the beaches. You can stroll along the waterfront and watch vendors parade by, dangling live crabs from sticks. An artisan's center, a marketplace, seafood restaurants, and other attractions are minutes away by bus or taxi.

Galápagos Islands, Ecuador

Ecuador's "Enchanted Isles," the Galápagos archipelago includes 13 major islands and dozens of islets. This 3-million-year-old cluster of volcanic islands is home to giant tortoises (after which the Galápagos Islands are named); marine iguanas; sea lions; and such rare birds as the blue-footed boobies, cormorants, and albatross.

At press time, foreign cruise ships were prohibited by the Ecuadorian government from calling at the Galápagos. For local cruise operators that visit the Galápagos, *see* Chapter 2.

Manaus, Brazil

A sprawling city of nearly 1.5 million people, Manaus is built in the densest part of the jungle, some 1,000 miles up the Amazon. After years of dormancy, it has reestablished its role as the key city of the Amazon. A number of cruise lines use it as the embarkation or disembarkation port for Caribazon sailings, making Manaus an ideal jumping-off point for a pre- or post-cruise overnight jungle experience.

Of the excursions listed below, the two river tours are most worthwhile. Because it's possible to tour the opera house by day, you may wish to skip the fabricated evening performance. You can hire a taxi to show you the sights described in the city shore excursion. Some jewelry companies, such as **H. Stern** and **Amsterdam Sauer,** give free taxi tours (stopping only upon request), provided you agree to end with a showroom visit.

Shore Excursions The following are good choices in Manaus. They may not be offered by all cruise lines. Times and prices are approximate.

Alligator Spotting. On this nighttime version of the Amazon River tour (*see below*), motorized canoes venture into alligator-populated creeks. Guides search for gators with a strong flashlight, spotting the creatures' gleaming red eyes in the darkness. Once hypnotized by the bright light, the alligator can be lifted by the guide for photographs and then released unharmed. *3 hrs. Cost: $55.*

Amazon River Tour. A local riverboat plies the black-tinted Rio Negro, until it meets the caramel-colored Solimoes River; they eventually blend to form the Amazon. At Lake Janauaca, motorized canoes whisk you along small *igarapés* (creeks) into the jungle. Water levels permitting, you'll cross a wooden bridge to view Victoria Regia water lilies. *4½ or 7 hrs. Cost: $48–$55.*

An Evening Performance at Teatro Amazonas (Manaus Opera House). Attend a 50-minute folklore performance, designed especially for cruise passengers, which provides an historic overview of Manaus's native population, rubber-boom times, and the city today. *1½ hrs. Cost: $45.*

Manaus City Tour. Visit the Victorian–style Municipal Market, housing meat, fruit, hat, and herb vendors; the turn-of-the-century Teatro Amazonas Opera House; the Indian Museum; and the Natural Science Museum, which showcases piranhas, electric eels, butterflies, beetles, and tarantulas. *3 hrs. Cost: $38.*

Coming Ashore Ships tie up at the floating dock, which comes alive with a festive atmosphere as peddlers, vendors, and other locals gather to greet the ships. Within walking distance is the **Mercado Municipal** (Municipal Market).

Exploring Manaus The **custom house** and **lighthouse** were imported piece by piece from England and reassembled alongside the floating dock, which was built to accommodate the annual 40-foot rise and fall of the river. Vestiges of Manaus's opulent rubber-boom days remain, including the famous **Teatro Amazonas Opera House,** where Jenny Lind once sang and the Ballets Russes once danced. Completed in 1910 and restored to its former splendor in 1990, the building is adorned with French ironwork and works of art and chinaware. Take a taxi to the suburbs to the **Salesian Mission Museum** to see a documentary on the now vanished "Floating City"; also visit the **Indian Museum** operated by the same religious order. For insight into the rubber-boom period, visit a **rubber plantation.** For shopping, try the **Credilar Teatro,** an imposing edifice of native red stone and glass.

Montevideo, Uruguay

An increasing number of cruise ships have begun calling at this sprawling capital city of nearly 2 million. Although Montevideo has no regal colonial past, this well-laid-out metropolis is a pleasant place to relax.

The best way to see the sights is on a ship-arranged city tour. From the harbor, a tour can take you past the downtown area's art deco– and nouveau-style buildings, the Prado district, and monuments, and then down the Rambla (the riverfront drive).

You can combine the city tour with a visit to an estancia (ranch) for a traditional barbecue of beef, chicken, and sausages, then watch a gaucho (cowboy) show of folkloric music and horsemanship. Another popular option is spending the day at the South American resort of Punta Del Este, on the Atlantic Ocean.

Coming Ashore Ships dock a long walk or short taxi ride from the city. Taxis are fairly inexpensive, and it's fairly easy to find drivers who speak English.

Many cabs are vintage 1920s–1950s autos. The restaurants immediately around the port area are a good choice for lunch.

Port Stanley, Falkland Islands (United Kingdom)

Although there are no formal shore excursions, some cruise ships—mostly expedition vessels—call here for a day. The islands (of which there are several hundred) are located 350 miles east of Cape Horn. The war in 1982 between Great Britain and Argentina put the Falkland Islands on the map.

The pretty town of Port Stanley is a bit of old England transplanted to the South Atlantic. Among its attractions for cruise passengers are an excellent museum and shopping for hand-knit woolen goods.

Puerto Madryn/Ushuaia, Argentina

These two ports, several hundred miles apart on Argentina's east coast, are becoming increasingly popular with cruise ships.

A day in Puerto Madryn might be spent driving around **Peninsula Valdes** to observe some of the 13,000 sea elephants reclining on the pebbled beaches. Another option is a drive to Punta Tombo through the Patagonian countryside to watch the thousands of migrating birds, including tuxedo-clad Magellan penguins, which gather here annually.

From Ushuaia, the southernmost town in the world (population 20,000), visit **Tierra del Fuego National Park,** take a catamaran ride to see the wildlife of the **Beagle Channel,** or spend a full day on **Fagnano Lake,** where you'll see a beaver dam and peat bogs and have lunch in a country inn.

Rio de Janeiro, Brazil

The approach to Rio de Janeiro by ship is one of cruising's most breathtaking sights, as the famous peak of Sugar Loaf grows ever bigger on the horizon. Rio is blessed with deep green, mountainous jungles; a profusion of birds, butterflies, and flowers; and long stretches of soft, sandy beaches lined with tall palm trees. To these natural blessings people have added colorful parades, colonial buildings vying for space with dramatic skyscrapers, and music everywhere—from honking automobile horns to soft singing voices to the thump of recorded drums accompanying street dancers. Several ships offer cruises that coincide with Carnival (the four days before Ash Wednesday) and reserve grandstand seats for their passengers; if you enjoy crowds and pageantry, nowhere is more exciting.

At any time of year, though, the city offers many museums and historical sites, distinctive coffeehouses, and remarkable districts where shopping is good and affordable: You can buy a fine leather coat for less than a cloth one would cost back home. At the beaches you can watch barely clothed youths sunbathing and playing volleyball. Or head up to **Pão de Açúcar** (Sugar Loaf) for a rousing samba show. Be aware, however, that Rio is home to a great many poor settlers living in a country rife with economic problems. Watch your valuables, and don't walk down empty streets.

Shore Excursions

The following is a good choice in Rio de Janeiro. It may not be offered by all cruise lines. Time and price are approximate.

Rio's Beaches and Sugar Loaf. Drive through the Reboucas Tunnel (the longest in Brazil) and along the famous beaches of Leblon, Ipanema, and Copacabana. Ride the cable car to the peak of Pão de Açúcar (Sugar Loaf). A stop is made for shopping. *Half day. Cost: $35.*

Coming Ashore Ships dock in the oldest part of the city. Restaurants and shops are found just outside the pier area, where an impromptu flea market springs up whenever a ship pulls in. The beaches and hotel district are a half-hour taxi ride away; cabs are readily available at the dock. Free car tours (stopping only upon request) are supplied by jewelers such as H. Stern, but only if you agree to end your sightseeing at their showroom.

Salvador, Brazil

With a rich colonial past evident in its churches, forts, and other historical buildings, Salvador is known to Brazilians as the most Brazilian of their cities. For this it draws not only upon its history (Salvador was the country's first capital), but also upon its colors, tastes, sounds, and aromas—a blend of African, Native American, and European cultures. Salvador moves to its own rhythm, slow and sensual, more at ease than Rio and blessed with miles of practically untouched beaches. Plunge into the **Upper City,** home to Brazil's best-preserved colonial architecture. Walking around, you may happen upon a street exhibition of *capoeira*, a fight dance that originated in Bahia. Don't miss the chance to sample the special Bahian cuisine.

Shore Excursions The following is a good choice in Salvador. It may not be offered by all cruise lines. Time and price are approximate.

City tour. Includes visits to the **Mercado Modelo** (public market), the Upper City and colonial section, the Church of São Francisco and Carmo church (Salvador has nearly 200 churches), and Largo do Pelourinho—a plaza of Latin America's finest colonial buildings. Shops near the plaza sell Bahian costumes and jewelry. *Half day. Cost: $35.*

Coming Ashore Ships dock within sight of the Upper City. There is a funicular to the colonial district, but it is more prudent to take a taxi. Cabs are readily available outside the pier; drivers speak at least a smattering of English.

Santos/São Paulo

Santos is São Paulo's port. São Paulo, overflowing with more than 14 million residents, is one of the largest cities in the world. It's the richest area in South America, the fastest growing, and the pride of all Brazilians. Sprawling over 589 square miles, São Paulo is covered by a semipermanent blanket of smog. Skyscrapers dominate the horizon in jagged concrete clusters. Coffee plantations made São Paulo what it is today; now a variety of industries thrive.

Santos is a lovely tropical retreat of sun worshiping and swimming. Apart from the historic Basilica of Santo Andre, the city offers little in the way of culture.

Shore Excursions The following are good choices in Santos/São Paulo. They may not be offered by all cruise lines. Times and prices are approximate.

Santos Beach Party. Swimmers can choose among two swimming pools or the beach at the resort island of Ilha Porchat. *Half day. Cost: $45.*

São Paulo city tour. From Santos a two-hour bus ride passes banana plantations and oil refineries before glimpsing the skyscrapers of downtown São Paulo. A stop is made at Butanta Institute, where snakes are raised for antivenom. Lunch is included. *6–7 hrs. Cost: $100.*

Coming Ashore Santos has the largest dock area in South America. Ships tie up next to a small outdoor mall, where there is shopping for coffee and handicrafts. São Paulo is about 40 miles away.

Less Visited Ports

Brazil A few cruise ships call at **Recife** on the east coast of Brazil or, as part of an Amazon River itinerary, Macapá, Parintins, or the Anavilhanas archipelago.

Chile Ships visiting **Santiago,** the capital, call at **Valparaíso,** two to three hours away. Farther south, from **Puerto Montt,** passengers can explore the lake country of southern Chile. Down around Chile's tip, **Punta Arenas** provides an opportunity for adventurous travelers to board a flightseeing plane to view the White Continent, **Antarctica**; to take a drive up to Observation Point for a panoramic view of the city or of the **Strait of Magellan**; or to drive alongside Otway Bay to the **Penguin Caves.**

Peru Calls may include **Callao,** the port city for **Lima,** the capital, which is half an hour away. From Lima, passengers can visit **Machu Picchu,** the ancient fortress of the Incas, high in the Andes Mountains. Calls are contingent upon Peru's unstable political conditions. Check with your travel agent or cruise line.

Southeast Asia

Like an awakening giant stretching its arms and looking around, the far-off lands in Asia are emerging as the world's newest cruise destinations. Their diverse ports of call are, arguably, the most exotic to be found on any itinerary.

The romantic allure of Asia has yet to be overrun with tourists, although rapid change makes these ports a study in contrasts. Today, Asian cities span every degree of development, from booming, bustling Hong Kong and Singapore—with their sophisticated restaurants and world-class shopping—to small island villages on Ko Samui and Bali, where older ways of life and traditions are followed.

Typical cruise itineraries sail from Hong Kong; Bangkok, Thailand; or Singapore. Exotic locales between the major ports make up the balance of itineraries. Each country differs greatly from the others, with its own language, cuisine, and culture. For many people, a cruise to Asia is a once-in-a-lifetime trip. Especially for those taking their first trip to the region, a cruise offers a comprehensive tour of the most well-known destinations as well as remote ports. A cruise also is the easiest way to visit less-developed locales in style, comfort, and safety.

Listed below are brief overviews of some of the region's most popular ports of call. Your shore-excursion director will have detailed information on getting around these ports, choosing excursions, and exchanging currency. At press time, the major lines sailing in the region were Crystal, Cunard, Holland America, Orient Lines, Princess, Radisson Seven Seas, Renaissance, Royal Caribbean, Seabourn, Silversea, and Star Clippers. (For seasonal itineraries, *see* Chapter 4.)

When to Go Generally, most lines schedule sailings during the dry season, which typically runs from December through early April.

Currency Currencies vary by country, and U.S. dollars are accepted in many—but not all—ports. Don't change a significant amount of money into local currency, which will be needed only for snacks or trinkets. In your final port of call, you may also need local currency for transfers and departure taxes at the airport. Credit-card purchases offer the best exchange rate.

Health There are no formal vaccinations requirements for entry to an Asian country frequented by cruise ships, but the **Centers for Disease Control** (tel. 404/639-2572) in Atlanta offers up-to-the-minute advice on health precautions. Call their International Travellers Hotline for information on your destination. It is unlikely you will need to get vaccinations, but booster shots should be up to date. (*See* Cruise Primer for more information on health.)

Passports and Visas All passengers will need a valid passport. Those visiting China or Vietnam will be required to get a visa, which can be obtained either through your cruise line or a travel agent.

Telephones and Mail Unless money is no object, don't use the satellite phones aboard ship. At major ports where ships dock, there typically will be telephones near or at the pier (*see* individual ports of call, *below*). If your ship is tendering into port, ask at the shore-excursion office for the nearest calling center.

As a rule, cruise ships sell local stamps at the front desk, and you can send postcards from an onboard mailbox as well, eliminating the need to find a post office.

Shore Excursions Typically, shore excursions in Asia include a motor coach or minibus tour of an island or town, with visits to major attractions and shops. It is always safest to take the ship excursions, but not always necessary depending on the port and how adventurous you are. In cities with traffic-clogged roads, it may be best to book the ship excursion. Otherwise, you run the risk of missing the ship. In some Asian destinations, the city may be an hour or more away from where the ship docks. If you prefer to explore independently in such cases, hiring a car and driver is a good alternative, but always ask your shore-excursion office for local recommendations.

Bali, Indonesia

Some still refer to Bali as the "Last Paradise." Others say its beaches have been overwhelmed by mass tourism, which has diminished the charm of the most famous of Indonesia's 13,677 islands. Regardless, Bali retains its magic. Here, distinctive architecture and holy mountains compete for attention with surf-swept beaches.

A large part of the island's appeal is its people, the Balinese, whose religion is a unique form of Hinduism blended with Buddhism and animism. To the Balinese, every living thing contains a spirit; when they pick a flower as an offering to the gods, they first say a prayer to the flower. Maintaining harmony is the life work of every Balinese.

The island is only 140 kilometers (84 miles) long by 80 kilometers (48 miles) wide. Bali has three main beach areas on the southern coast: Kuta, Sanur, and Nusa Dua. Many of Bali's cultural attractions are inland, to the north and east of Denpasar, the island's capital.

Currency Indonesia's unit of currency is the rupiah. At press time $1 = 2,334 Rp.

Telephones In most cases you are best off using hotel phones despite the surcharges; an operator can help with translation and information. If you want to avoid using hotel phones, the most economical way to call is from the nearest Kantor Telephone & Telegraph office. When calling the States, you can also use **AT&T**'s USADirect Service. Dialing 008–0110 will put you in touch with an AT&T operator.

Shore Excursions The following are good choices in Bali. They may not be offered by all cruise lines. Times and prices are approximate.

Island Sights **Besakih and Klungkung.** A scenic 43-mile drive to Besakih, Bali's oldest temple, reveals a countryside of rice-terraced slopes and views of sacred Mt. Agung. At Klungkung, former capital of the Bali kingdom, the floating pavilion and the old Royal Court of Justice are visited. Stops are also made for shopping at arts-and-crafts centers, time permitting. *4 hrs. Cost: $27. Longer tours with lunch, $60.*

Bali Arts and Crafts. This tour of notable arts attractions includes a visit by minibus to Werdi Budaya, an arts complex in Denpasar; Celuk, a center for intricate gold and silver work; Mas, home of wood-carvers; and Ubud, a rural community famous for its painters, studios, art schools, and a museum housing traditional and modern paintings. *4 hrs. Cost: 35.*

Mengwi, Alas Kedaton and Tanah Lot. *The* tour for photographers and temple buffs. Travel by minibus through Denpasar to the Pura Taman Ayun of Mengwi, the second-largest temple complex in Bali. Continue to the famous Monkey Forest of Pura Alas Kedaton, where hundreds of monkeys roam the 17th century temple's grounds. (Hold on to your belongings.) The last stop is at the dramatic sea temple of Tanah Lot. *4 hrs. Cost: 27.*

Coming Ashore Cruise ships visiting Bali dock at Benoa Harbor. Taxis are available in the main tourist areas. They are unmetered, but fares within the Kuta–Sanur–Nusa Dua area are fixed. Renting guided cars or Jeeps is convenient and popular. The ship's shore-excursion office should be able to assist with these reservations.

Southeast Asia
CHINA
Guangzhou
Macau
HONG KON
Mandalay
UNION OF MYANMAR (BURMA)
LAOS
Luang Prabang
Hanoi
Haiphong
HAINAN
Vientiane
Pegu
Yangon (Rangoon)
Chiang Mai
Hue
Danang
THAILAND
Korat
Bangkok
Angkor Wat
VIETNAM
CAMBODIA (KAMPUCHEA)
Andaman Sea
Phnom Penh
Ho Chi Minh City (Saigon)
Isthmus of Kra
Gulf of Thailand
Phuket
Songkhla
South China Sea
Kota Kinabalu
George Town
WEST MALAYSIA
MALAYSIA
BRUNEI
SABAH
Medan
Strait of Malacca
Kuala Lumpur
SARAWAK
Kuching
SINGAPORE
BORNEO
SUMATRA
Karimata Strait
KALIMANTAN
KEPULAUAN
Jambi
INDONESIA
INDIAN OCEAN
Palembang
Banjarmasin
GREATER SUNDA ISL
Jakarta
Java Sea
Bandung
Surabaya
Yogyakarta
JAVA
LES
BALI
LOMBOK
0
500 miles
0
750 km
N

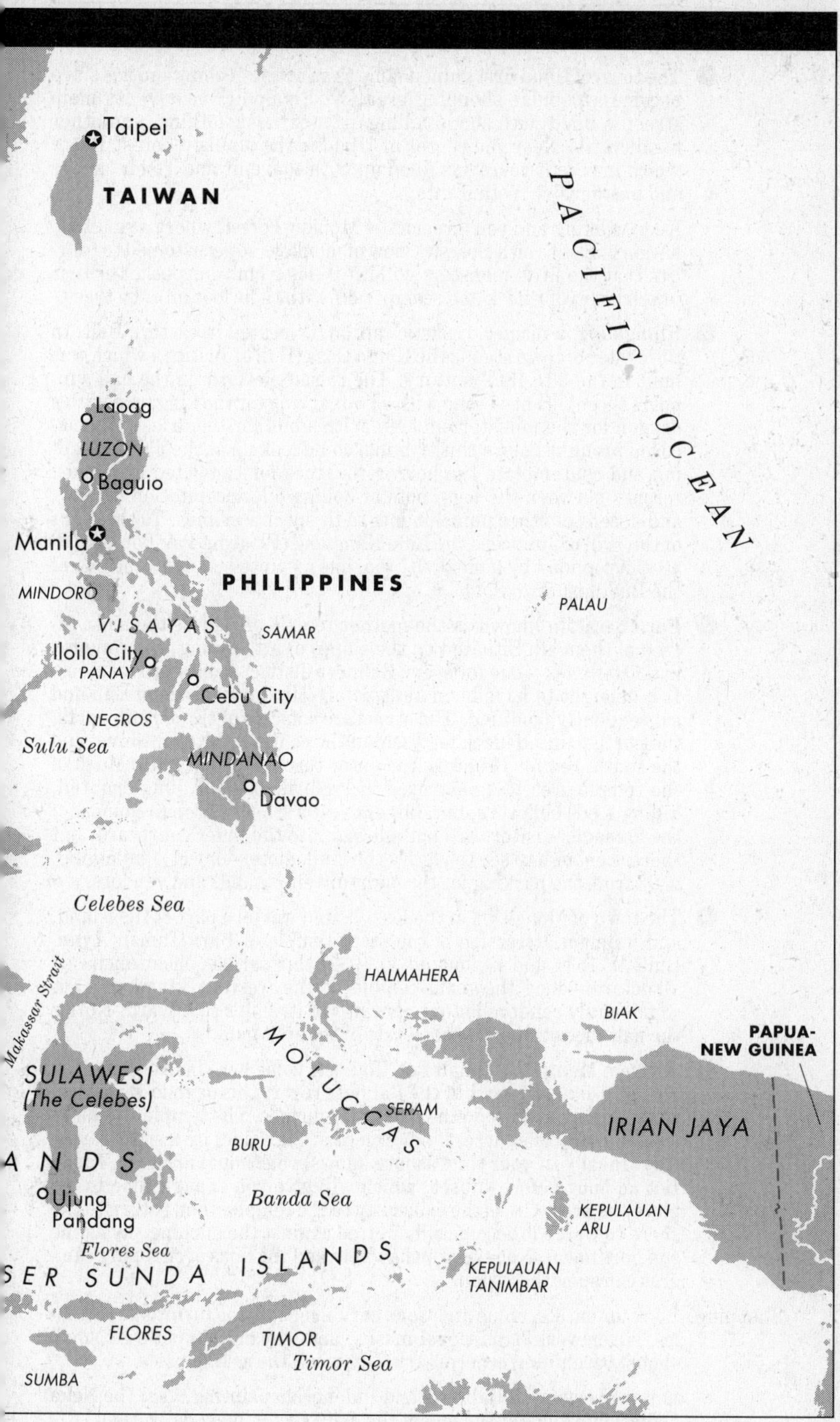

Taipei
TAIWAN
PACIFIC OCEAN
Laoag
LUZON
Baguio
Manila
PHILIPPINES
MINDORO
PALAU
VISAYAS
SAMAR
Iloilo City
PANAY
Cebu City
NEGROS
Sulu Sea
MINDANAO
Davao
Celebes Sea
Makassar Strait
HALMAHERA
BIAK
PAPUA-
NEW GUINEA
MOLUCCAS
SULAWESI
(The Celebes)
SERAM
IRIAN JAYA
BURU
ANDS
Ujung
Pandang
Banda Sea
KEPULAUAN
ARU
Flores Sea
SER SUNDA ISLANDS
KEPULAUAN
TANIMBAR
FLORES
TIMOR
Timor Sea
SUMBA

Exploring Bali *Numbers in the margin correspond to points of interest on the Bali map.*

1 The town of **Ubud** first gained fame as an artists' colony and has since become a popular shopping area (*see* Shopping, *below*). Its main street is lined with shops selling art, textiles, clothing, and other handicrafts. Near the center of Ubud is the Monkey Forest Road, which in recent years has filled up with souvenir and T-shirt shops and inexpensive restaurants.

Keep walking and you'll reach the **Monkey Forest,** where a small donation will get you a close-up view of monkeys so accustomed to tourists that the little monsters will lift items from your pocket or tear jewelry off your neck and scamper off with their loot into the trees.

2 **Klungkung,** a former dynastic capital, is located in eastern Bali. In the center of town stands the Kerta Gosa (Hall of Justice), which was built in the late 18th century. The raised platform in the hall supports three thrones—one with a lion carving for the king, one with a dragon for the minister, and one with a bull for the priest. The accused brought before this tribunal could look up at the painted ceiling and contemplate the horrors in store for convicted criminals: torches between the legs, pots of boiling oil, decapitation by saw, and dozens of other punishments to fit specific crimes. To the right of the Hall of Justice is the Bale Kambang (Floating Pavilion), a palace surrounded by a moat. It, too, has a painted ceiling, this one of the Buddhist *Suta Sota*.

3 **Pura Besakih,** known as the mother temple of Bali, is the most sacred of them all. Situated on the slopes of Mt. Agung, the complex has 30 temples—one for every Balinese district—on seven terraces. It is thought to have been built before Hinduism reached Bali and subsequently modified. The structure consists of three main parts, the north painted black for Vishnu; the center, white for Shiva; and the south, red for Brahma. You enter through a split gate. Much of the temple area was destroyed in 1963 when Mt. Agung erupted, killing 1,800 believers, but diligent restoration has repaired most of the damage. Visitors are not allowed into the inner courtyard, but there is enough to see to justify the 2-kilometer-long (1¼-mile-long) walk from the parking lot through souvenir stands and vendors.

4 The town of **Mengwi** is in the less-visited western part of the island, and its main attraction is the state temple of Pura Taman Ayun. Built in 1634 and renovated in 1937, this serene, moat-encircled structure—once the main temple of the western kingdom—has wonderfully rendered stone carvings in its inner courtyard. Notice the half-face of Boma on each side of the split gate.

5 South of Mengwi is **Tanah Lot.** Tourists come here in droves for the postcard-like setting, but the Balinese revere this pagoda-style temple as deeply as they do the mountain shrines. The temple stands on a small rocky islet accessible (except at high tide) by a small causeway. Ideally (if your time ashore allows) you should arrive at Tanah Lot an hour before sunset, which will give you enough time to explore the area. Cross the causeway to the temple, then return to the shore to watch it become silhouetted against the burning sky as the sun goes down. Not even the hawkers and the lines of snapping cameras can spoil the vision.

Shopping Look for batiks, stone and wood carvings, bamboo furniture, ceramics, silver work, traditional masks, and wayang puppets. At small shops, bargaining is necessary. Offer half the asking price.

For an overview of Balinese and Indonesian painting, visit the **Neka Gallery** in Ubud (at the end of the main street; open daily 9–4).

The **Rudana Gallery** in Ubud exhibits collectors' pieces of hand-painted batik, as well as more affordable prints (tel. 0361/26564; open daily 9–7).

Batubulan is known for its resident stone carvers, whose workshops and displays line the road.

Celuk is a village of silver- and goldsmiths, with lots of workshops and salesrooms to roam about.

Beaches Kuta has one of the world's most splendid golden-sand beaches, but it's extremely commercial and somewhat tawdry. **Sanur Beach**'s hotels, restaurants, and shops are more spread out, so the pace here is less hectic than in Kuta. The beach is less dramatic, too. Nusa Dua, a former burial ground, consists of two tiny islands linked to the mainland with a reinforced sand spit. Its beaches are wide and peaceful.

Bangkok/Laem Chabang, Thailand

Laem Chabang serves as the port city for Bangkok, Thailand's capital. Bangkok is an amazing sensory kaleidoscope in which temples and palaces of spectacular beauty stand alongside ramshackle homes on the banks of evil-smelling *klongs* (canals). Appetizing odors of exotic street food mix with the earthy pungency of open drains; graceful classical dancers perform on stages next door to bars where go-go girls gyrate in clinical nakedness, and BMWs stall in traffic jams while *tuk-tuks* (three-wheel cabs) scoot between them.

A foreigner's reaction to Bangkok is often as confused as the city's geography. Bangkok has no downtown, and the streets, like the traffic, seem to veer off in every direction. The oldest quarter clusters around the eastern bank of the Chao Phraya River, which winds between Bangkok and Thonburi, where the Thais first established their capital in 1782.

In the last 20 years, the face of Bangkok has changed. Before the Vietnam War, and before Bangkok became an R&R destination for American servicemen, the city had a population of 1.5 million. Then, the flaunting of U.S. dollars attracted the rural poor to the city. Within two decades, it grew to 6 million, 40 times the size of any other city in Thailand. Space in which to live and breathe is inadequate. Air pollution is the worst in the world (policemen directing traffic are now required to wear masks), and traffic jams the streets from morning to evening. Yet, while hurtling headlong into the world of modern commercialism and technology, Bangkok strangely gives a sense of history and timelessness, even though it is only some 200 years old.

Currency In Thailand, the basic unit of currency is the baht. There are 100 satang to one baht. At press time, $1 equals 24 baht.

Telephones Calls to home can easily be made from any hotel. You can also use the overseas telephone facilities next to the general post office. The center is open 24 hours and has **AT&T** USADirect phones. These phones place you in direct contact with an AT&T operator, who will accept your AT&T credit card or place the call collect. For **MCI**'s Call USA, dial 001–999–1–2001; ask the operator at that number for customer service. If you wish to receive assistance for an overseas call, dial 100/233–2771. For local telephone inquiries, dial 13 for an English-speaking operator.

Shore Excursions On many Asian cruise itineraries, Bangkok is a point of embarkation or disembarkation rather than a port of call. To fully enjoy the city's sights, you should book a pre- or post-cruise stay if it is not included in your package.

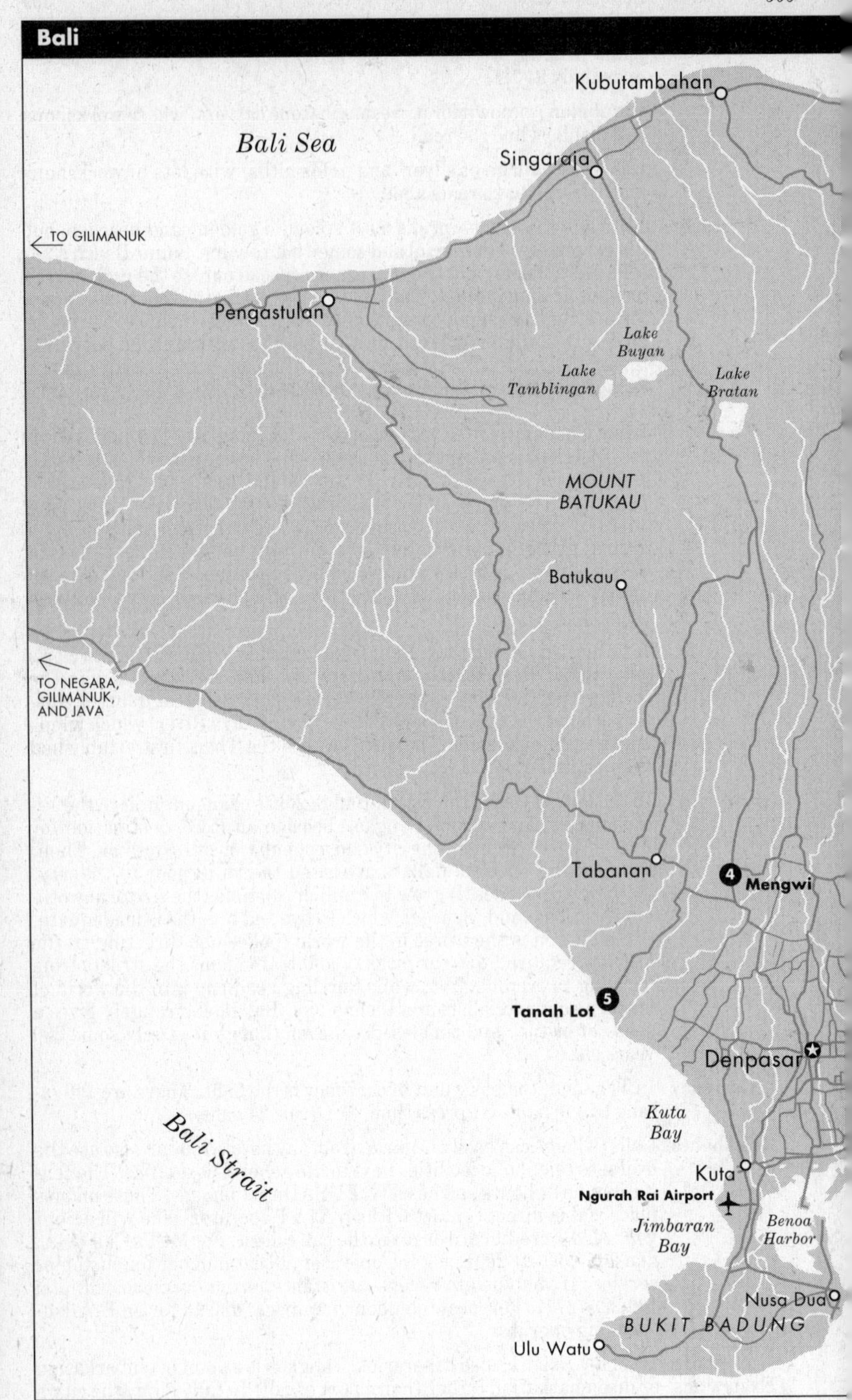
Bali
Bali Sea
Kubutambahan
Singaraja
TO GILIMANUK
Pengastulan
Lake Buyan
Lake Tamblingan
Lake Bratan
MOUNT BATUKAU
Batukau
TO NEGARA, GILIMANUK, AND JAVA
Tabanan
4 Mengwi
5 Tanah Lot
Denpasar
Kuta Bay
Kuta
Ngurah Rai Airport
Jimbaran Bay
Benoa Harbor
Nusa Dua
BUKIT BADUNG
Ulu Watu
Bali Strait

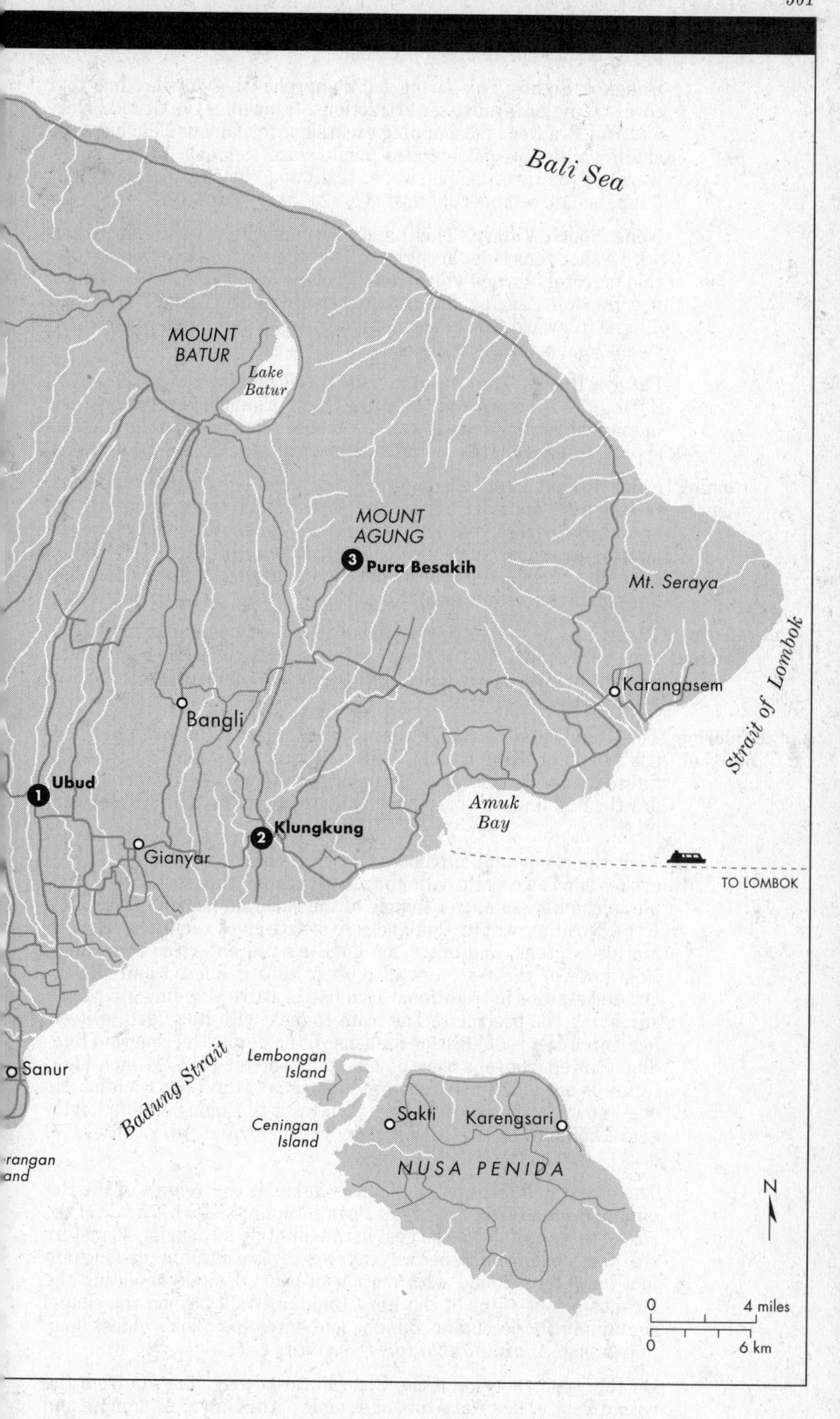
Bali Sea
MOUNT BATUR
Lake Batur
MOUNT AGUNG
3 Pura Besakih
Mt. Seraya
Karangasem
Strait of Lombok
Bangli
1 Ubud
Amuk Bay
2 Klungkung
Gianyar
TO LOMBOK
Sanur
Badung Strait
Lembongan Island
Ceningan Island
Sakti
Karengsari
NUSA PENIDA
N
0
4 miles
0
6 km

The following are good choices in Bangkok for those staying only a day. Time and price are approximate.

Bangkok Sights. This tiring but comprehensive one-day bus tour covers Bangkok's must-see attractions. It includes the Grand Palace and Wat Pra Keo and shopping excursions for famous Thai buys, including silks, precious stones, niello ware, celadon, bronze tableware, silverware, lacquerware, teakwood carvings, shadow play puppets, and temple rubbings. *8 hrs or more. Cost: $80.*

Nong Nooch Village. This highly recommended excursion begins with a short bus ride through the Thai countryside and takes you to this privately owned village on 250 acres of lush parkland. A show features folk dancing, Thai boxing, sword fighting, and a Thai wedding. Afterward, you're free to stroll the grounds inhabited by deer, swans, and monkeys. *4 hrs. Cost: $35.*

Pattaya Beach. This was a popular R&R destination for U.S. GIs during the Vietnam War. Few lines have organized excursions, but individual arrangements can be made. The beach offers water sports, funky and fine shopping, and great seafood in outdoor cafés.

Coming Ashore

Ships dock at Laem Chabang, an industrial port which is approximately a 2½-hour drive from Bangkok. Guided taxis can usually be arranged through your ship's shore-excursion office, but there are no cabs available at pier-side. The port city of Laem Chabang is edged by pineapple, tapioca, and sugarcane plantations. The coastline is fringed with beautiful beaches.

Getting Around

Traffic in Bangkok is horrendous and the city center is more than two hours away from the ship. Passengers who wish to explore independently rather than join a ship-organized tour are advised to hire a guided car.

Exploring Bangkok

The **Grand Palace** is Bangkok's major landmark. This is where Bangkok's founder, King Rama I, built his palace and walled city in 1782. Subsequent Chakri monarchs enlarged the walled city, though today the buildings are used only for state occasions and royal ceremonies.

Visit the compound of palaces first, because none of the buildings evokes such awe as the adjoining royal chapel, the most sacred temple in the kingdom, the **Temple of the Emerald Buddha** (Wat Phra Keo). No other wat in Thailand is so ornate and so embellished with murals, statues, and glittering gold. As you enter the compound, take note of the 6-meter-tall (20-foot-tall) helmeted and tile-encrusted statues in traditional Thai battle attire standing guard and surveying the precincts. The main chapel, with its gilded, glittering, three-tier roof, dazzles the senses. Inside sits the Emerald Buddha. Carved from one piece of jade, the ¾-meter-high (31-inch-high) figure is one of the most venerated images of the Lord Buddha. No one knows its origin, but history places it in Chiang Rai, in northeast Thailand, in 1464. *Admission charge. Open daily 8:30–11:30 and 1–3:30.*

The oldest and largest temple in Bangkok is the **Temple of the Reclining Buddha** (Wat Po, or Wat Phya Jetuphon). Much is made of the size of this statue—the largest in the country, measuring 46 meters (151 feet) in length. Especially noteworthy are his 3-meter-long (10-foot-long) feet, inlaid with mother-of-pearl designs depicting the 108 auspicious signs of the Lord Buddha. Walk beyond the chapel containing the Reclining Buddha and enter Bangkok's oldest open university. *Admission charge. Open daily 7–5.*

On the western bank of the Chao Phraya River, not far from the Grand Palace, lies **Wat Arun,** or Temple of the Dawn. At sunrise and dusk, it is inspiring. Within the square courtyard, the temple's architecture is symmetrical, containing five Khmer-style *prangs* (stupas). The central prang, towering 86 meters (282 feet), is surrounded by its four attendant prangs in the corners. All of the prangs are covered in mosaics of broken Chinese porcelain. The surrounding grounds are a peaceful haven in which to relax and watch the sun go down. More-energetic passengers may want to climb the steep steps of the central prang for the view over the Chao Phraya River. *Admission charge. Open daily 8–5:30.*

Unless you can get an early start to visit some temples and beat the heat, the **National Museum** should be your first stop. This extensive museum has one of the world's best collections of Southeast Asian art in general, and Buddhist and Thai art in particular. As a result, it offers the best opportunity to trace Thailand's long history, beginning with ceramic utensils and bronze ware from the Ban Chiang civilization, thought to have existed 5,000 to 6,000 years ago. *Admission charge. Open Wed.–Fri. and weekends 9–noon and 1–4.*

One of Bangkok's must-see attractions is **Jim Thompson's House,** a compound of traditional Thai architecture and Southeast Asian furnishings. After World War II, American Jim Thompson stayed in Thailand and took it upon himself to revitalize the silk industry, which had virtually become extinct. His project and product met with tremendous success. That in itself would have made Thompson into a legend, but in 1967 he went to the Malaysian Cameron Highlands for a quiet holiday and was never heard from again. *Tel. 02/215–0122. Admission charge. Open Mon.–Sat. 9–4:30.*

Shopping Bangkok offers some of the best shopping in the world—provided you have enough stamina to deal with the crowds. Specialties include bronze ware, carved wood, dolls, jewelry, lacquerware, precious stones, rattan, Thai celadon, and silk. Prices are fixed in department stores. In stores selling artifacts, price is open to negotiation, and in bazaars and street-side stalls, bargaining is essential. Expect to pay about 30% less than the vendor's asking price.

Dining Laem Chabang has some restaurants, but due to concerns about hygiene, none are recommended. Check with your ship's shore-excursions office for advice on dining in Bangkok.

Canton (Guangzhou), China

Strategically located near Hong Kong on the South China Sea, Canton has become one of China's major seaports and a convenient port of call for ships with Southeast Asian itineraries. Five million people live in this sprawling metropolis, which boasts more than 3,000 state-owned factories turning out virtually everything from buses to sewing machines.

Currency If you are taking the tour (as most people do), you don't need to worry about changing money while in China. U.S. dollars are widely accepted in local shops; some also will take traveler's checks. Many street vendors accept U.S. dollars, too.

Telephones Canton is not a good place to make telephone calls. Fortunately, a port call here usually falls immediately before or after Hong Kong (*see below*), which is a good stop for calling home.

Shore Excursions The following is a good choice in Canton. It may not be offered by all cruise lines. Time and price is approximate.

Window on China. This long, full-day excursion is worth it for a diverse look at local Chinese life. Stops along the way include a visit to a kindergarten. There's time for shopping and a break for lunch at a local hotel. *7–8 hrs. Cost: $99.*

Coming Ashore Most ships dock at Shekou, a container port about an hour and a half from the city of Canton. China is strict about requiring a visa. Be sure to arrange for one before you leave home, or you will not be allowed off the ship when you arrive in port. You must also carry your visa with you at all times while ashore.

Getting Around Although it is a bit complicated, you can get to and from Canton on your own. There are no taxis pier-side, but one can be arranged for you ahead of time through your ship's shore-excursion office. A taxi ride for up to four people to the city will cost about $60 one-way. Some taxis accept U.S. dollars; more widely accepted are Hong Kong dollars. Try to have your shore-excursion office establish the currency at the time they arrange for your taxi. Your best bet, however, is to change enough money for your round-trip taxi ride, plus a little more.

Exploring Canton To see the major sights of this far-flung city, your best bet is to sign up for the comprehensive shore excursion described above. However, if you'd prefer to explore on your own, the riverfront offers a fascinating glimpse of the hustle-and-bustle of modern-day China. The **Pearl River** flows right though the center of town, and from its banks you can see the daily comings and goings of the ferryboats, junks, sampans, and freighters that have fueled China's booming economy.

Shopping Ceramics and embroideries are among the merchandise sold in stores and by enterprising street vendors. The tour also stops at the Friendship Store, which offers a wide variety of crafts.

Dining Canton is home to some of the Chinese dishes most popular among North Americans, such as sweet-and-sour pork, cashew chicken, and fried rice. The shore excursion stops at a major hotel for a hearty meal, with an excellent and tasty variety on the menu. If you're dining on your own, stay away from the street food, as tempting as it may be, and opt instead for one of the large hotels. You'll still get wonderful Chinese cuisine and be assured of better standards of hygiene.

Ho Chi Minh City, Vietnam

Vietnam was shut off from the outside world for more than 25 years and has the unspoiled beauty of Thailand before developers arrived. Since it opened its doors, though, there has been an explosion in construction. Now is a good time to visit Vietnam, before it becomes the next Bangkok or Hong Kong.

Ho Chi Minh City was once an elegant city, but it's a bit shabby now. The city still retains its Asian–colonial French hybrid charm. Mostly, though, it's the city's dynamism—reawakened after years of isolation—that captivates the visitor.

Currency The unit of currency is the dong. At press time, U.S.$1 equals approximately 11,000 dong. The Vietnamese are dollar-hungry, and it's advisable to bring dollars rather than other currencies. Dollars are used to pay for major purchases, so U.S.$25 per day in dong should more than cover your needs. Carry lots of $1 and $5 bills—but watch out for pickpockets.

Telephones Telephone calls are best made from hotels.

Shore Excursions The following are good choices in Ho Chi Minh City. They may not be offered by all cruise lines. Times and prices are approximate.

City Tours **Ho Chi Minh Highlights.** A minibus takes you to Cholon, the city's Chinatown; Giac Lam Pagoda and Binh Tay Market; the National History Museum; Reunification Hall; and the former Presidential Palace. Along the way you'll see the neo-Romanesque Notre Dame Cathedral, the colonial-style Central Post Office, and the People's Committee City Hall; your tour will also pass by the Continental, Rex, and Caravelle hotels en route to a lacquer workshop. *4–5 hrs. Cost: $45.*

Evening in Saigon. If your ship stays in port overnight, don't miss this fascinating experience. A mix of familiar and exotic foods are served at dinner, usually in an ornate room in the historic Rex Royal Court Hotel. Singers and dancers perform during the meal, which is followed by a tour of Chinatown. *3 hrs. Cost: $65.*

Outside the City

Countryside and Cu Chi Tunnels. This is an arduous trip, but it's well worth the effort. Travel for two hours by bus to the Cu Chi underground tunnels used by the Viet Cong to fight the French and, later, American forces. Sensitive travelers may find the photo displays upsetting, and the cramped tunnels can bring on feelings of claustrophobia. *5 hrs. Cost: $44.*

Mekong Delta. This tour of the countryside is a wonderful look at where 80% of the Vietnamese people live. The highlight of the tour is a brief stop at a typical Vietnamese farm, where passengers can meet the family and tour their home. *4 hrs. Cost: $60.*

Coming Ashore

Most ships dock downtown on the Saigon River, a 15-minute walk from the main shopping district. Larger ships may dock a few miles farther down the river. Passengers on ships that stay overnight usually have a 10 PM curfew (11 PM for those on organized tours).

Getting Around

For a quick jaunt to local sights, late-model, metered, air-conditioned cabs are readily available at the pier. Their drivers have a working command of English and readily accept U.S. dollars. The typical cost of a ride from the ship to the shopping district is $2–$5; an hour-long drive through the city should cost about $9. Tipping is generally not expected, unless you hire your driver as a guide. If you want to tour independently, hire a car and driver through a tour agency (ask your ship's shore-excursion office to recommend a company).

For a traditional view of the sights, hire a *cyclo* (a bicycle on which the passenger sits in front while the driver pedals from behind). A tour of the side streets and historic monuments should only cost a couple of dollars, but agree on the fee before you climb aboard.

Exploring Ho Chi Minh City

For a Vietnamese perspective of recent and historical events, there are two museums celebrating Vietnam's fight for independence.

The **Revolutionary Museum** (65 Ly Tu Trong St., tel. 08/99741) pays tribute to the heroes who fought against the French and the Americans.

The **Exhibit of War Crimes** (28 Vo Van Tan St., tel. 08/90325), in the building that once housed the U.S. Information Service, is devoted to capitalist atrocities against the Vietnamese.

For a look at Vietnam's vibrant culture, the **National History Museum** houses a small but interesting collection of artifacts. Most delightful is the water-puppet theater. *Nguyen Binh Khiem St., tel. 08/298146. Open Tues.–Sun.*

Of the city's several pagodas, the **Giac Lam Pagoda** (118 Lac Long Quan) is the city's oldest and the best to visit. It dates from 1744 and is built in the Vietnamese style.

The 200-kilometer (125-mile) network of **Cu Chi Tunnels,** where the Viet Cong hid under the feet of Allied troops, is not for the weak at heart because of explicit photography displays, but it is something important to see. Cu Chi Tunnels are 35 kilometers (22 miles) from Ho Chi Minh City as the crow flies, but 75 kilometers (47 miles) by road.

Shopping

You'll find some interesting browsing along the streets of downtown—there are small shops, an enclosed market, and sidewalk vendors. T-shirts with Vietnamese logos typically sell for as little as $1–$2.50; stone and wood carvings can be purchased for $2–$10;

lacquerware ranges in price from a few dollars to $100 for more elaborate pieces.

Embroidery is a tremendous buy. Try the **Mai-a-Anh boutique** (81 Mac Thi.) or the **C. Minh Huong** (85 Mac Thi). You can buy traditional Vietnamese water puppets for about $12 at the National History Museum (*see* Exploring Ho Chi Minh City, *above*).

Be careful when shopping in Ho Chi Minh City. Beggars are aggressive and pickpockets pervasive. Keep a tight grip on your purse and carry your wallet in a front pocket.

Dining No matter how tempted you are by the wonderful smells, do not eat food from street vendors. Never drink the water and stick to restaurants with reputations for safe dining (ask your shore-excursions manager). Three good choices for typical Vietnamese fare on Dong Khoi Street are **Lemon Grass, Vietnam House,** and **Maxim's,** which is still famous for its lavish dinners and dancing.

Hong Kong

Hong Kong is the New York City of Asia. Few visitors can avoid being swept up in the energy, excitement, and apparent confusion of Hong Kong. This vibrancy is just as much an attraction as the tens of thousands of shops selling the world's luxuries duty-free.

The colony consists of 51.5-square-kilometer (32-square-mile) Hong Kong Island, the 5.6 square kilometers (3.5 square miles) of mainland Kowloon, and the assorted islands and hinterland of the New Territories, which cover about 588 square kilometers (365 square miles). As small as it is, Hong Kong wields enormous economic clout.

The territory's deep, sheltered harbor was the reason Hong Kong became part of the British Empire in 1841. This year, on June 30, the British government leaves, and the territory reverts to Chinese sovereignty. Beijing has pledged that Hong Kong will become a Special Administrative Region, with its own economic, educational, and judicial system, for a guaranteed 50 years.

Currency The unit of currency in Hong Kong is the Hong Kong dollar. At press time, $1 equals 8 Hong Kong dollars.

Telephones Hong Kong is a good Asian port for phoning home. Long-distance calls can easily be made from any hotel. Calls can also be placed from Hong Kong Telecom International (Exchange Square, Central, tel. 2845-1281, and TST Hermes House, Kowloon, tel. 2732–4243). You can dial direct from specially marked silver-colored phone booths, which take phonecards, available from the Hong Kong Telephone Companies retail shops and 7-11 convenience stores throughout the island. **AT&T**'s USADirect service allows direct calls to the United States from coin-operated phones by using their access code from Hong Kong (tel. 800–1111). To reach an **MCI** operator, dial 800–1121; **Sprint**'s access number is 800–1877.

For local calls, try the multilingual telephone information service (tel. 2801–7177; open weekdays 8 AM–6 PM, weekends and holidays 9 AM–5 PM).

Shore Excursions Hong Kong is usually a port of embarkation or disembarkation rather than a port of call. If your cruise line does not include a pre- or post-cruise package, you should stay at least a night to explore the territory.

The following is a good choice for a day in Hong Kong. The tour may not be offered by all cruise lines. Time and price are approximate.

Island Drive. Travel to Victoria Peak, with its views of towering office buildings and the harbor from a 1,800-foot-high vantage point.

Continue to Aberdeen Fishing village, home to several floating restaurants. Includes a sampan ride. *4 hrs. Cost: $37.*

Coming Ashore Ships dock at the Ocean Terminal, near the Star Ferry Pier, a convenient starting place for any tour of Kowloon. Here you will also find the bus terminal, with traffic going to all parts of Kowloon and the New Territories. Inside the terminal, and in the adjacent Harbour City, are miles of air-conditioned shopping arcades. There is also a visitor information booth run by the Hong Kong Tourist Association. A ferry will take you to Hong Kong Island.

Getting Around The driving conditions are difficult, traffic is constantly jammed, and parking is usually impossible. But public transportation is excellent, and the taxis are inexpensive.

By Subway The Mass Transit Railway (MTR, tel. 2750–0170) is a splendid, air-conditioned subway that links Hong Kong Island to the shopping area of Tsim Sha Tsui and to parts of the New Territories. Trains are frequent, safe, and easy to use.

By Taxi Taxis in Hong Kong are usually red and have a roof sign that lights up when the taxi is available.

Exploring Hong Kong *Numbers in the margin correspond to points of interest on the Hong Kong and Kowloon map.*

❶ The **Star Ferry,** in the Central District, is one of the main attractions for first-time visitors. Since 1898, the ferry has been the gateway to Hong Kong Island from Kowloon. The charge is minimal: HK$1.50 first class, HK$1.20 second class; the tram from Central to Causeway Bay and beyond is HK$1.

❷ Take your camera and head for the upper deck of the **Peak Tram,** the steepest funicular railway in the world. The tram dates back to 1880 and rises from ground level to **Victoria Peak** (1,305 feet), offering a panoramic view of Hong Kong. From Victoria Peak on a clear day, you can see across the islands to mainland China. Both residents and tourists use the tram, which has five stations. The tram runs every 10–15 minutes daily from 7 AM to midnight. There is a free shuttle bus to and from the Star Ferry and from next to City Hall, at Edinburgh Place, to the tram. *Between Garden Rd. and Cotton Tree Dr. Fare: HK$12 one-way, HK$19 round-trip.*

❸ In the midst of antiques and curio shops is the **Man Mo Temple** (Hollywood Rd.). Built in 1847, it is Hong Kong Island's oldest temple and is dedicated to Man, the god of literature, and Mo, the god of war. The statue of Man is dressed in green and holds a writing brush. Mo is dressed in red and holds a sword. To their left is a shrine to Pao Kung, god of justice, whose face is painted black. To the right is Shing Wong, god of the city. Coils of incense hang from the roof beams, filling the air with a heavy fragrance. The temple bell, cast in Canton in 1847, and the drum next to it are sounded to attract the attention of the gods when a prayer is being offered.

❹ **Hong Kong Park** (between Garden Rd. and Cotton Tree Dr.) is a 25-acre marvel in the heart of the Central District. It contains lakes, gardens, sports areas, a rain-forest aviary with 500 species of birds, and a greenhouse filled with 200 species of tropical and arid-region plants.

The **Flagstaff House,** the city's oldest colonial building (built in 1846) and former official residence of the commander of the British forces, is located in the Hong Kong park. The building now houses the **Museum of Tea Ware** and holds displays on everything connected with the art of serving tea from the 7th century onward. *Cotton Tree Dr., tel. 2869–0690. Admission free. Open Thurs.–Tues. 10–5.*

❺ **Causeway Bay,** one of Hong Kong's best shopping areas, also has a wide range of restaurants and a few sightseeing attractions. Much of

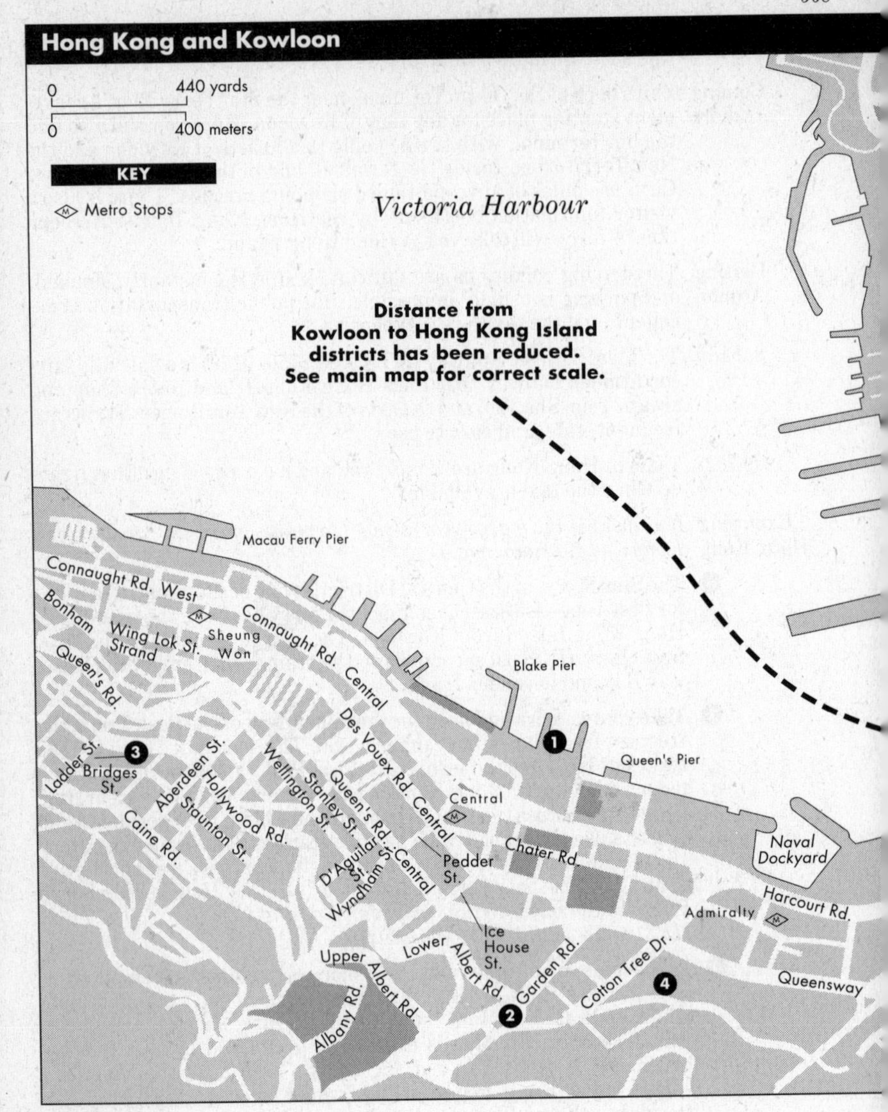
Hong Kong and Kowloon
0
440 yards
0
400 meters
KEY
Metro Stops
Victoria Harbour
Distance from Kowloon to Hong Kong Island districts has been reduced. See main map for correct scale.
Macau Ferry Pier
Connaught Rd. West
Bonham
Wing Lok St.
Strand
Sheung Won
Connaught Rd. Central
Queen's Rd.
Blake Pier
Des Voeux Rd. Central
Ladder St.
Bridges St.
Aberdeen St.
Hollywood Rd.
Staunton St.
Caine Rd.
Wellington St.
Stanley St.
Queen's Rd. Central
D'Aguilar St.
Wyndham St.
Central
Pedder St.
Queen's Pier
Chater Rd.
Naval Dockyard
Harcourt Rd.
Admiralty
Ice House St.
Lower Albert Rd.
Upper Albert Rd.
Albany Rd.
Garden Rd.
Cotton Tree Dr.
Queensway

Causeway Bay, **5**
Hong Kong Park, **4**
Man Mo Temple, **3**
Peak Tram, **2**
Star Ferry, **1**

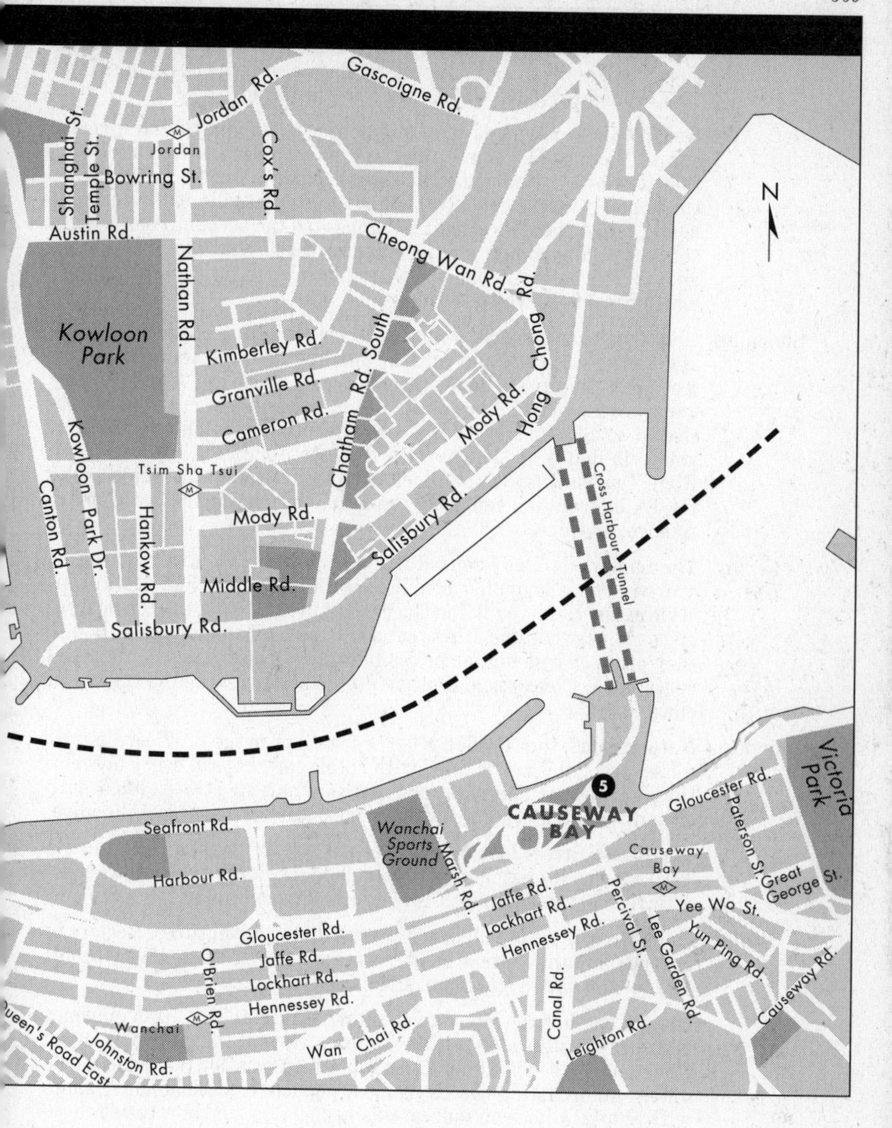
Gascoigne Rd.
Jordan Rd.
Jordan
Shanghai St.
Temple St.
Bowring St.
Cox's Rd.
Austin Rd.
Cheong Wan Rd.
Kowloon Park
Nathan Rd.
Kimberley Rd.
Granville Rd.
Cameron Rd.
Chatham Rd. South
Mody Rd.
Hong Chong Rd.
Tsim Sha Tsui
Mody Rd.
Salisbury Rd.
Cross Harbour Tunnel
Canton Rd.
Kowloon Park Dr.
Hankow Rd.
Middle Rd.
Salisbury Rd.
Seafront Rd.
Harbour Rd.
Wanchai Sports Ground
Marsh Rd.
CAUSEWAY BAY
Gloucester Rd.
Paterson St.
Victoria Park
Causeway Bay
Great George St.
Jaffe Rd.
Lockhart Rd.
Hennessey Rd.
Percival St.
Yee Wo St.
Lee Garden Rd.
Yun Ping Rd.
Gloucester Rd.
Jaffe Rd.
Lockhart Rd.
Hennessey Rd.
O'Brien Rd.
Wanchai
Queen's Road East
Johnston Rd.
Wan Chai Rd.
Canal Rd.
Leighton Rd.
Causeway Rd.

the district can be easily reached from Central by the tram, which runs along Hennessy Road, or by the MTR to Causeway Bay Station. If you come by taxi, a good starting point is the Excelsior Hotel (281 Gloucester Rd.), which overlooks the harbor.

Kowloon is a peninsula jutting out from mainland China, directly across Victoria Harbour from the Central District. Legend has it that Kowloon was named by a Chinese emperor who fled here during the Sung Dynasty (960–1279). He counted eight hills on the peninsula and called them the Eight Dragons—so the account goes—but a servant reminded him that an emperor is also considered a dragon, and so the emperor called the region *Gau-lung* (nine dragons), which became Kowloon in English.

Shopping Goods such as cameras, sound systems, computers, precious gems and metals, fabrics, and furs are brought into the territory duty-free. But shop rents have soared, forcing prices up. The best bargains are found in factory outlets. A little bargaining can be productive in small shops; a lot is expected in the lanes and markets. If you're in doubt about where to shop for items, stick to the Hong Kong Tourist Association's member shops. Pick up the guide at the HKTA information center in the Star Ferry terminal (*see* Coming Ashore, *above*).

In the Central District **The Landmark** (Des Voeux Rd. and Pedder St., Central) is a rather overwhelming shopping complex, with an atrium and European-style cafés. Here you'll find Gucci, Tiffany, and all of the top designer boutiques that line 5th Avenue and the Champs-Elysées, though they often charge higher prices because of the stratospheric retail rents here. Concerts and other events are presented here free of charge.

In Kowloon **Nathan Road,** the "Golden Mile," runs north in the Kowloon district for several miles and is filled with hotels and shops of every description. To the left and right are mazes of narrow streets lined with even more shops crammed with every possible type of merchandise.

The **Kansu Street Jade Market** (Kansu St., off Nathan Rd., Yau Ma Tei.) carries everything from fake jade pendants to precious carvings. The best time to visit is from 10 AM to noon daily.

Dining Hong Kong is resplendent with great dining adventures. Be sure to try the dim sum—bite-size morsels of meat, seafood, and vegetables wrapped in dough and fried, steamed, braised, or boiled.

Hong Kong has too many good dining choices to list, from gourmet European restaurants with a stunning view of the city to open-air street markets. The Hong Kong Tourist Association publishes a free dining guide listing the city's most popular establishments, along with helpful advice on sauces, cuisines, prices, and how to use chopsticks. Pick one up at the information center at the Star Ferry terminal (*see* Coming Ashore, *above*.)

Ko Samui, Thailand

Once an island destination for backpackers, Ko Samui still is regarded as more idyllic than Phuket (*see below*), with fewer hotels, restaurants, and café-bars. The island, about 500 kilometers (310 miles) from Bangkok and 30 kilometers (18½ miles) off Surat Thani, in the Gulf of Siam, can be easily toured in a day. But cruise ships call here for the sun and sand, not for sightseeing. The best beaches, those with glistening white sand and clear waters, are on the island's east coast. Beaches on the other coasts either have muddy sand or rocky coves.

Currency In Thailand, the basic unit of currency is the baht. There are 100 satang to one baht. At press time, $1 equals 24 baht.

Shore Excursions The following are good choices in Ko Samui. The tours may not be offered by all cruise lines. Times and prices are approximate.

Island Tour. Visit all the major sites, including the Big Buddha Monastery and the monkey theater. Some tours include a stop at the Butterfly Garden. *3 hrs. Cost: $46.*

Beach Time. Take a drive to the Butterfly Garden, where a buffet lunch will be served, and then relax on the beach. *4 hrs. Cost: $64.*

Coming Ashore Passengers come ashore aboard local tenders in Na Thon, a bustling town with shops and restaurants. Most of the restaurants and souvenir shops are along the waterfront. Commercial shops and banks line the parallel street one block inland.

Getting Around If you want to explore Ko Samui on your own, it's best to rent your own transportation. Jeeps are expensive (around B1,200 plus B175 for a collision damage waiver), but they're the safest, although most people choose motor scooters, which can be obtained for about B175 per day. Gravel, potholes, and erratic driving make riding dangerous, and each year some travelers return home with broken limbs. Some never return at all.

Exploring Ko Samui On the north coast, east of Na Thon, the first major tourist area is **Maenam.** Its long, curving, sandy beach is lapped by gentle waters that are great for swimming.

Bophut (Big Buddha) is a bay separated by a small headland from Maenam. The dramatic sunsets attract photographers and romantics.

Along the north shore lies **Ko Fan,** a little island with a huge sitting Buddha covered in moss. Try to visit at sunset, when the light off the water shows the Buddha at its best.

For the finest beach, go to **Chaweng Beach,** with glistening white sand. But this is also Ko Samui's most congested beach, crammed with guest houses and tourists.

Many visitors make a pilgrimage to Lamai Beach to visit the point marking the end of Lamai. Here stand two rocks, named **Hin Yaa** (Grand Mother Rock) and **Hin Ta** (Grand Father Rock). Erosion has shaped the rocks to resemble weathered and wrinkled intimate private parts.

Kota Kinabalu, Sabah (Malaysia)

Kota Kinabalu, called Jesselton when Sabah was the British crown colony of North Borneo, was razed during World War II, thus its local name Api-Api (fires). It was renamed in 1963, when Sabah and Sarawak joined independent Malaysia. Little of historic interest remains—the oldest part of the city is vintage 1950s. The multistory shop houses sell hardware and other practical goods; the upper floors are residences. The central market on the waterfront sells produce and handicrafts. Next to the central market is a smaller collection of stalls selling produce from the Philippines. The main attraction of the city is its proximity to the revered Mt. Kinabalu—the tallest peak in Southeast Asia.

Currency Malaysia ringgit are also called Malaysia dollars. The units are called sen (100 sen equals M$1). At press time, exchange rates were M$2.5 equals U.S.$1.

Telephone Local phone books give pages of information in English on international calling, rates, and locations of telephone offices. Public phones that take telephone cards are found at strategic locations around the city. The cards, Kadfon and Unicard, can be purchased at 7-11 or Hop-In stores. Pay phones take 10-sen coins for local calls.

Shore Excursions The following are good choices in Kota Kinabalu. The tours may not be offered by all cruise lines. Times and prices are approximate.

About the City **Kota Kinabalu Sightseeing.** By motor coach, visit the Saba State Museum, Likas Bay, and Kampung Likas, a typical Malaysian fishing village. *2½ hrs. Cost: $33.*

Mountain Peaks **Kinabalu National Park.** This tour goes by motor coach to the Kinabalu National Park, which is nestled below Mount Kinabalu. Take a 45-minute walk or just enjoy lunch at a nearby hotel. Continue to Pekan Nabalu, a village with handicrafts for sale, as well as to Tamparuli, with its swinging suspension bridge. *4–8 hrs. Cost: $45–$65.*

Coming Ashore Ships dock near downtown. Walk down the gangway and another 10 minutes to the pier gate, and you'll find taxis waiting. From here, the main section of town is a half-hour walk or a $5 cab ride away.

Getting Around Cabs are expensive and are unmetered. Agree on the price with your driver before setting out.

Exploring Kota Kinabalu Kota Kinabalu's main draw is the **Sabah Museum,** on a hilltop off Jalan Penampang, about 3 kilometers (2 miles) from the city center. The building resembles a traditional longhouse, and its contents are a good introduction to local history, archaeology, botany, and ethnography. *Bukit Istana Lama, tel. 088/53199. Admission free. Open Sat.–Thurs. 9–6.*

If you don't take the shore excursion described above, hire a car to take you to **Mt. Kinabalu National Park.** (Remember, though, it will be a long and expensive ride). Nature lovers can walk miles of well-marked trails through jungle dense with wild orchids, carnivorous pitcher plants, bamboo, mosses and vines, and unusual geologic formations. The wildlife is shy, but you are likely to see exotic birds and possibly a few orangutans. Towering above the park is the 4,100-meter (13,500-foot) Mt. Kinabalu.

Shopping This is one Asian port where you may need to change money, as many merchants do not accept U.S. dollars.

Two Kota Kinabalu shops specializing in local products are **Borneo Handicrafts** (ground floor, Lot 51, Jln. Gaya, tel. 088/714081) and **Sabah Handicraft Centre** (ground floor, Lot 49, Bandaran Berjaya, tel. 088/221230).

Beaches The best beaches are on the islands of **Tuanku Abdul Rahman National Park,** a 15-minute speedboat ride from the pier in downtown Kota Kinabalu. Here serenity and privacy prevail. Pretty coral formations and exotic marine life attract snorkelers and divers.

Kuala Lumpur, Malaysia

Kuala Lumpur (KL) is a city of contrasts. Gleaming new skyscrapers sit next to century-old, two-story shop houses. On six-lane superhighways, rush-hour traffic often appears to be an elongated parking lot, but nearly a quarter of the population still lives in traditional *kampongs* within the city, giving KL as much a rural feel as urban.

KL was founded by miners who discovered tin where the Kelang and Gombak rivers form a broad delta. Those pioneers were a rough, hardy lot, and the city retains some of that early boomtown character. Despite its bustling, cosmopolitan style, KL is at heart an earthy place, where people sit around the *kedai kopi* (coffeehouse) and talk about food, religion, and business. It also is the center of the federal government, and since government is dominated by Malays and business by Chinese, the tone of the city is as much influenced by the easygoing Malays as by the energetic Chinese.

Currency Malaysia ringgit are also called Malaysia dollars. The units are called sen (100 sen equals M$1). At press time, exchange rates were M$2.5 equals U.S.$1.

Telephone Local phone books give pages of information in English on international calling, rates, and locations of telephone offices. Public phones that take telephone cards are found at strategic locations around the city. The cards, Kadfon and Unicard, can be purchased at 7-11 or Hop-In stores. Pay phones take 10-sen coins for local calls.

Shore Excursions The following are good choices in Kuala Lumpur. The tours may not be offered by all cruise lines. Times and prices are approximate.

Capital Sights. Travel by motor coach to the Buddhist Temple of Thean on the city's outskirts. Also visit the National Monument, National Museum, Royal Selangor Pewter Factory, Malayan Railway building, and Independence Square, with lunch at a deluxe hotel. *7¾ hrs. Cost: $89.*

Colonial KL. Features the National Museum, Orchid Garden, Hibiscus Garden, Bird Park, Butterfly Park, Malayan Railway building, and Royal Palace, with lunch at one of the city's stately colonial mansions. *7¾ hrs. Cost: $104.*

Coming Ashore Ships dock at Port Klang, an industrial city about a 1½-hour drive from the city.

Getting Around Most cruise lines offer round-trip motor-coach transportation ($35) to Kuala Lumpur from Port Klang for passengers wanting to explore on their own. (Tickets may be sold in the line's shore-excursion office.) Once in KL, walking is the best way to get around the city center's three main areas, called the Golden Triangle. For short distances, you can always hop on a minibus or hail a taxi, which are metered.

Exploring Kuala Lumpur The **National Museum** (Muzium Negara) is modeled after an old-style Malay village house, enlarged to institutional size. In addition to displays on Malay folk traditions and Chinese culture, the museum's exhibits trace the stages of British colonization, from the old East India Company in the late 18th century to Britain's withdrawal in the mid-20th. Photos and text outline the Japanese occupation during World War II and Malaysia's moves toward federation status in 1948 and independence in 1957. A natural-history exhibit upstairs is devoted to indigenous wildlife, with stuffed flying lemurs, birds, insects, and poisonous snakes. In all, it's worth a visit. *Jln. Damansara, tel. 03/238–0255. Admission free. Open daily 9–6; closed for Fri. prayers, 12:15–2:45 PM.*

The **Lake Gardens** (behind the National Museum) are where you can enjoy a leisurely stroll and join city dwellers relaxing, picnicking, and boating on the lake. Also in the park is the National Monument, a bronze sculpture dedicated to the nation's war dead, and an orchid garden with more than 800 species.

The four-story **National Art Gallery** was the old Majestic Hotel until its conversion into a museum in 1984. The permanent collection serves as an aesthetic introduction to Malaysia and its people, and it emphasizes contemporary modes—conceptual pieces, pop images, bold sculptures, humorous graphics, and realistic landscapes. The gallery is a bit funky, with its ceiling fans, linoleum-covered floors, and some dimly lighted rooms, but it's still a treat. The museum shop sells witty posters, prints and cards, and arty T-shirts at reasonable prices. *1 Jln. Sultan Hishamuddin, tel. 03/230–0157. Admission free. Open daily 10–6, except for the Fri. prayer break.*

Shopping Malaysia offered few bargains until duty-free shopping reduced prices a few years ago. Now most quality radios, watches, cameras, and calculators are slightly cheaper in Kuala Lumpur than in Singapore; look for a duty-free sticker in shop windows. Fashion, too, has come to KL, and at prices far better than in Singapore. You can also pick up inexpensive clothing, from jeans to shirts, for much less than in the United States and Europe. If you can't find a particular product or service, call **Infoline** (tel. 03/230–0300), a telemarketing company that will try to steer you in the right direction. It also gives advice on restaurants and nightspots.

Don't miss a lively bazaar in the heart of Kuala Lumpur, the **Central Market.** Housed in a renovated Art Deco building that used to be the city's produce market, it was converted into a series of stalls and shops in 1986. Now the 50-year-old market, painted apricot and baby blue, is the commercial, cultural, and recreational hub of downtown from 10 to 10 daily. Some 250 tenants do business within the two-story, block-long market. Demonstrations of such disappearing arts as batik block printing, Kelantan silversmithing, and the weaving of *kain songket*—a lush (and expensive) fabric made with gold threads—draw crowds to an area called the *kampong*. Cultural programs are presented daily, highlighting such Malaysian fare as *wayang kulit*, gamelan orchestras, Chinese opera, lion dances, and traditional Malay dances. Some 40 food vendors serve Malaysian dishes at reasonable prices. This is a great place to sample new dishes.

Dining At press time, Port Klang had no recommended restaurants. For choices in KL, ask your shore-excursions manager.

Phuket, Thailand

In the 1970s, the word got out about Phuket's long, white-sand beaches, cliff-sheltered coves, waterfalls, mountains, fishing and seafood, clear waters, scuba diving, and fiery sunsets. Entrepreneurs built massive developments, at first clustered around Patong, and then spread out. Most formerly idyllic deserted bays and secluded havens now have at least one hotel impinging on their beauty. But for all the development, Phuket still retains its charm.

Currency In Thailand, the basic unit of currency is the baht. There are 100 satang to one baht. At press time, $1 = 24 baht.

Shore Excursions The following are good choices in Phuket. The tours may not be offered by all cruise lines. Times and prices are approximate.

Phuket City and Cultural Show. By motor coach, visit Phuket's largest collection of Buddhist temples en route to the Thai Village, where a 45-minute show is performed. *4½ hrs. Cost: $39.*

Phang Nga Bay. Phang Nga Bay is famous for its dramatic limestone isles. Other sights on this boat tour include Koh Panyi, a sea-gypsy village with houses built on stilts, and Koh Khao Ping Gun, where the James Bond film, *The Man with the Golden Gun*, was filmed in 1974. *8½ hrs. Cost: $65.*

Coming Ashore Ships calling at Phuket anchor off Karon Beach, which is divided into two areas, Karon Noi and Karon Yai (*see* Beaches, *below*).

Getting Around Taxi fares are mostly fixed. *Songthaews*, the minibuses that seat six people, have no regular schedule, but all use Phuket Town as their terminal. As Phuket has so many different beaches, your own transportation offers the most convenience for exploring. Ask your ship's shore-excursion office about arrangements. Driving poses few hazards, except for those on motor scooters—potholes and gravel can cause spills, and some roads are not paved.

Exploring Phuket About one-third of the island's population lives in **Phuket Town,** the provincial capital. The town is busy, and drab, modern, concrete buildings have replaced the old Malay-colonial-influenced architecture. A few hours of browsing through the tourist shops are not wasted, however. Most of the shops and cafés are along Phang-Nga Road and Rasda Road.

Wat Chalong is the largest and most famous part of a grouping of 20 Buddhist temples—all built since the 19th century.

The **Thai Cultural Village,** in a 500-seat amphitheater, presents various aspects of southern Thai culture, including classical Thai dance, shadow puppets, exhibition Thai boxing, sword fighting, and an "elephants at work" show. *Thepkasati Rd., tel. 076/214–860. Admission charge. Show times: 10:15, 11, 4:45, 5:30.*

Beaches Avoid Patong, an enclave of massage parlors and hustlers selling trinkets. Head instead for **Kata Beach,** 17 kilometers (10½ miles) southwest of Phuket Town. The sunsets are as marvelous as ever, but the peace and quiet are fading fast. Club Med has moved in, but there are still stretches of sand with privacy.

Near Kata is **Kata Noi Beach** (*noi* means small) in the shelter of a forest-clad hill. The bay is surrounded by verdant hills and is truly beautiful, but huge crowds spill out of the Le Meridien Hotel resort. For a little more privacy, try **Karon Yai,** which is good for swimming and surfing.

Nai Harn is a gloriously beautiful bay, protected by Man Island. On the north side, a huge, white-stucco, stepped building, the Phuket Island Yacht Club, rises from the beach in stark contrast to the verdant hillside. From the Yacht Club's terrace, the view of the sun, dropping into the Andaman Sea behind Man Island, is superb. The beach is good for sunning and swimming in the dry season, but beware of the steep drop-off.

Singapore

To arrive in Singapore is to step into a world where the muezzin call to prayer competes with the bustle of capitalism; where old men play mah-jongg in the streets and white-clad bowlers send the ball flying down well-tended cricket pitches; where Chinese fortune-tellers and high-priced management consultants advise the same entrepreneur. This great diversity of lifestyles, cultures, and religions thrives within the framework of a well-ordered society. Singapore is a spotlessly clean—some say sterile—modern metropolis, surrounded by green, groomed parks and populated by 2.7 million extremely polite, well-mannered people.

The diverse population of Malays, Chinese, Indians, and a small mix of Eurasians, Filipinos, Armenians, and Thais, contributes significantly to the nation's cultural mix. The British and the heritage of their colonial stay are profoundly felt, even though Singapore has been an independent nation since 1965.

Currency The local currency is the Singapore dollar (S$), which is divided into 100 cents. At press time, the exchange rate was approximately U.S.$1 equals S$1.50.

Telephones Singapore is another good Asian port for phoning home. Long-distance calls can easily be placed from any hotel. **AT&TDirect** phones can also be found at the General Post Office and at many of the post offices around the city center, such as the one in the Raffles City shopping complex.

Shore Excursions Singapore is usually a port of embarkation or disembarkation rather than a port of call. If your cruise line does not include a pre- or post-cruise package, you should stay at least a day to explore the city's vast offerings.

The following are good choices in Singapore. The tours may not be offered by all cruise lines. Times and prices are approximate.

Singapore City Drive. By bus, drive through Little India and past colonial buildings, including Victoria Theater, the Supreme Court, and City Hall. Next comes China Town, the National Museum, and the Botanical Gardens. *3½ hrs. Cost: $24.*

Raffles's Traditions. Arrive by boat at Clifford Pier in Marina Bay, where Stamford Raffles first landed, and walk around Clarke Quay where warehouses have been converted to restaurants and shops. Then a trishaw, a three-wheeled pedicab, will take you to the Raffles Hotel and Museum for a tour and Singapore sling at the famous Long Bar. *4 hrs. Cost: $72.*

Coming Ashore Ships dock at the new Singapore Cruise Center, which is located in the city, across from Sentosa Island.

Getting Around Singapore is easy to find your way about, whether you take the super-clean and efficient subway (the MRT) or buses.

By Bus Buses are much cheaper than taxis and—with a little practice—easy to use. (Stops have signs pointing out sightseeing attractions.) During rush hours, they can be quicker than cabs, since there are special bus lanes along the main roads. Some buses are air-conditioned, and service is frequent—usually every 5 to 10 minutes on most routes. If you plan to explore by bus, pick up the excellent ***Bus Guide,*** available for S$1 at any bookstore. The minimum fare is S$.50, the maximum S$1.10 for non-air-conditioned buses, S$.80 to S$1.70 for air-conditioned buses. Exact change is necessary.

By Subway The MRT consists of two lines that run north–south and east–west and cross at the City Hall and Raffles Place interchanges. The system includes a total of 42 stations along 67 kilometers (42 miles). All cars and underground stations are air-conditioned, and the trains operate between 5:45 AM and midnight daily. Fares start at S$.60 for about two stations; the maximum fare is S$1.50.

By Taxi There are more than 10,000 taxis in Singapore, strictly regulated and metered. Many are air-conditioned. Taxis may be found at stands or hailed from any curb not marked with a double yellow line.

Exploring Singapore *Numbers in the margin correspond to points of interest on the Singapore City map.*

Singapore City

1 The neoclassical **Empress Place** building was constructed in the 1860s as the new courthouse and has housed nearly every government body. Now, after a S$22 million renovation, Empress Place is a cultural exhibition center. Its vast halls, high ceilings, and many columns give a majestic drama to exhibitions from around the world, though most of the major exhibits are art collections from China. *1 Empress Pl., tel. 336–7633. Admission charge. Open daily 9:30–9:30.*

2 The **National Museum and Art Gallery,** housed in a grand colonial building topped by a giant silver dome, originally opened as the Raffles Museum in 1887. Included in its collection are 20 dioramas depicting the republic's past; the Revere Bell, donated to the original St. Andrew's Church in 1843 by the daughter of American patriot Paul Revere; the 380-piece Haw Par Jade Collection, one of the largest of its kind; ethnographic collections from Southeast Asia; and many historical documents. The Art Gallery displays contemporary works by local artists. *Stamford Rd., tel. 330–9562. Admission charge. Open Tues.–Sun. 9–4:30.*

3 The **Raffles Hotel** has seen many ups and downs, especially during World War II, when it was first a center for British refugees, then quarters for Japanese officers, then a center for released Allied prisoners of war. After the war the hotel deteriorated. It survived mostly as a tourist attraction, trading on its heritage rather than its facilities. However, in late 1991, after two years of gutting, rebuilding, and expansion, Raffles reopened as the republic's most expen-

sive hotel. The casual tourist is no longer welcome to roam, but instead is channeled through new (albeit colonial-style) buildings to a museum of memorabilia, a multimedia show (with free performances at 10, 11, 12:30, and 1), or a reproduction of the famous Long Bar, where the Singapore sling was created. (A Raffles sling now costs S$14.65, which includes service and tax but not the glass—that's another S$7.05.) If you're hungry, there's the new Empress Café; if you want to shop, there are 60 boutiques. (By walking to the end of the new attractions and turning left, you can reach the original Tiffin Room and the Bar and Billiard Room.)

❹ In **Merlion Park** stands a statue of Singapore's tourism symbol, the Merlion—half lion, half fish. In the evening, the statue—on a point of land looking out over the harbor—is floodlit, its eyes are lighted, and its mouth spews water.

Singapore Island

Sri Mariamman Temple is the oldest Hindu temple in Singapore. Its pagodalike entrance is topped by one of the most ornate *gopurams* (pyramidal gateway towers) you are ever likely to see. Hundreds of brightly colored statues of deities and mythical animals line the tiers of this towering porch; glazed cement cows sit, seemingly in great contentment, atop the surrounding walls. Inside are some spectacular paintings that have been recently restored.

At the Sakya Muni Buddha Gaya Temple, also known as the **Temple of 1,000 Lights,** you can—for a small donation—pull the switch that lights countless bulbs around a 15-meter (50-foot) Buddha. The entire temple, as well as the Buddha statue, was built by the Thai monk Vutthisasala, who, until he died at the age of 94, was always in the temple, ready to explain Buddhist philosophy to anyone who wanted to listen. The monk also managed to procure relics for the temple: a mother-of-pearl-inlaid cast of the Buddha's footstep and a piece of bark from the bodhi tree under which he received enlightenment. Around the pedestal supporting the great Buddha statue is a series of scenes depicting the story of his search for enlightenment; inside a hollow chamber at the back is a re-creation of the scene of the Buddha's last sermon.

Cliché though it may be, at the **Singapore Zoological Gardens,** humans visit animals as guests in their habitat. The zoo is designed according to the open-moat concept, wherein a wet or dry moat separates the animals from the people. Try to arrive in time for the buffet breakfast. The food itself is not special, but the company is. At 9:30 AM, Ah Meng, a 24-year-old orangutan, comes by for her repast. At various times throughout the day, there are performances by snakes, monkeys, fur seals, elephants, free-flying storks, and other of the zoo's 1,700 animals from 160 species. Elephant rides are available for S$2. For S$1.50, visitors can travel from one section of the zoo to another by train. *80 Mandai Lake Rd., tel. 269–3411. Admission charge. Open daily 8:30–6.*

The **Night Safari** claims to be the world's first nighttime wildlife park. Here 80 acres of jungle provide a home to 100 species of wildlife that are more active at night than during the day. Some 90% of tropical animals are, in fact, nocturnal, and to see them active—instead of snoozing, which is what you are likely to catch them doing if you visit during the day—gives their behavior a new dimension. Night Safari uses the same moat concept as the zoo to create an open natural habitat; the area is floodlit with enough light to see the animals' colors, but not enough to limit their nocturnal activity. Visitors are transported on a 45-minute tram ride along 3.2 kilometers (2 miles) of loop roads, stopping frequently to admire the beasts and their antics. Another 1.3 kilometers (.8 mile) of trails allows you to walk among the animals. *80 Mandai Lake Rd. (about 250 yards from entrance to zoo), tel. 269–3411. Admission: S$15. Open daily 6:30–midnight.*

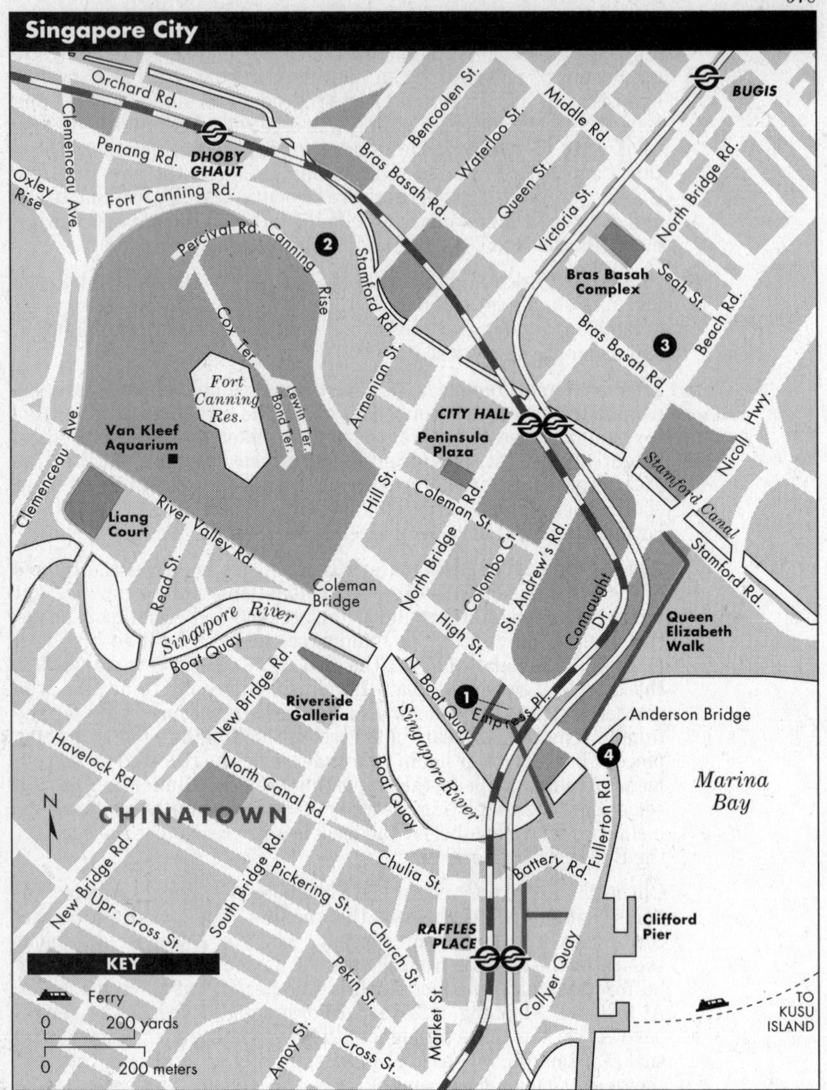

Empress Place, **1**
Merlion Park, **4**
National Museum and Art Gallery, **2**
Raffles Hotel, **3**

Near city center are the **Botanic Gardens,** an ideal place to escape the bustle of downtown Singapore (and only a short bus ride away). They began in Victorian times as a collection of tropical trees and plants. The beautifully maintained gardens now spread over some 74 acres, with a large lake, masses of shrubs and flowers, and magnificent examples of many tree species, including 30-meter-high (98-foot-high) fan palms. An orchid bed boasts specimens representing 250 varieties, some of them very rare. *Corner of Napier and Cluny Rds., tel. 474–1163. Admission free. Open weekdays 5 AM–11 PM, weekends 5 AM–midnight. Via Bus 7, 14, 105, 106, or 107, it's a 10-min ride to the Botanic Gardens from Orchard Rd.*

Shopping Bargaining is widely practiced in Singapore; the type of store determines the potential "discount." Only department store prices are fixed—it's a good idea to visit one first to establish the base price of an item, then shop around. The heart of Singapore's preeminent shopping district is **Orchard Road,** which is lined with modern shopping complexes and hotels.

Dining The **Telok Ayer Market,** the largest Victorian cast-iron structure left in Southeast Asia, was a thriving fish market in 1822. It was redesigned as an octagonal structure by George Coleman in 1894. Now it has reopened as a planned food court, with hawker stalls offering the gamut of Asian fare. By day it's busy with office workers. After 7 PM Boon Tat Street closes to traffic, and the mood turns festive: The hawkers wheel out their carts, and musicians give street performances until midnight. Only time will tell whether the high prices will drive away the locals.

4 Itineraries

Sailing Schedules

Itineraries begin with fall 1996 and run through summer 1997. Ports of call are described in Chapter 3. Ship deployments and itineraries are subject to change; ports of call may also vary with departure date. Check with your cruise line or travel agent.

Abercrombie & Kent

Explorer **Early Fall:** A 34-night westbound **transatlantic** crossing from Tenerife (Canary Islands) to Port Stanley (Falkland Islands). **Mid-Fall–Winter:** Thirteen-, 14-, and 18-night **Antarctica** cruises sail round-trip from Ushuaia (Argentina) or between Ushuaia and Port Stanley. **Spring:** Ten- and 17-night **Amazon** cruises between Belem (Brazil) and Iquitos (Peru) or Iquitos and Manaus (Brazil) include calls at Alter do Chao and other ports in Brazil and Peru.

Alaska Sightseeing/Cruise West

Spirit of Alaska **Fall:** Seven-night **Canada's Inside Passage** loops depart Seattle. **Winter:** No cruises scheduled. **Early Spring:** Same as fall. **Mid-Spring–Summer:** Seven-night **Alaska** cruises between Juneau and Ketchikan call at Glacier Bay National Park, Skagway, Haines, Sitka, and Wrangell.

Spirit of Columbia **Fall:** Seven-night **Columbia and Snake river** loops depart Portland (Oregon). **Winter:** No cruises scheduled. **Spring–Summer:** Same as fall.

Spirit of Discovery **Fall:** Three- and four-night **California Wine Country** loops depart San Francisco. **Winter:** No cruises scheduled. **Early Spring:** Seven-night **Puget Sound and San Juan Islands** loops depart Seattle. **Mid-Spring–Summer:** Two- and three-night **Prince William Sound** loops depart Whittier (Alaska).

Spirit of Endeavour **Mid-Spring–Summer:** Seven-night **Inside Passage** cruises between Seattle and Juneau call at Ketchikan, Sitka, Skagway, and Haines.

Spirit of Glacier Bay **Fall:** Seven-night **Puget Sound** loops from Seattle. **Winter:** No cruises scheduled. **Mid-Spring–Summer:** Ten-night **Inside Passage** cruises sail between Seattle and Juneau. Three- and four-night **Glacier Bay** loops depart Juneau, calling at Sitka and Admiralty Island.

Spirit of '98 **Fall–mid-Spring:** No cruises scheduled. **Mid-Spring–Summer:** Ten- and seven-night **Inside Passage** cruises between Seattle and Juneau call at Skagway, Haines, Sitka, and Ketchikan.

American Canadian Caribbean Line

Caribbean Prince **Fall:** Eleven-night **New England and Canada** cruises sail between Warren (Rhode Island) and Québec City. A 14-night **eastern seaboard** cruise sails from Warren to Palm Beach Gardens (Florida). **Winter:** Eleven-night **Central America** loops depart Belize City. Eleven-night **Central America** cruises sail between Roatan (off Honduras) and Belize City. **Spring–Summer:** Same as fall. A 14-night **New England and Canada** cruise sails between Québec City and Warren.

Mayan Prince **Fall:** Same as *Caribbean Prince*. **Winter:** An 11-night **Panama Canal** transit calls at the San Blas Islands and other ports of call. **Spring–Summer:** Same as fall. Five-night **New England** cruises sail round-trip from Warren (Rhode Island).

Niagara Prince **Fall:** Fourteen-night **mid-America** cruises sail between Chicago and New Orleans. A 15-night **Great Lakes** cruise sails between Chicago and Warren (Rhode Island). **Winter:** Eleven-night **Virgin Islands** loops depart St. Thomas. Eleven-night **Venezuela** cruises sail between Trinidad and Tobago. Eleven-night **southern Caribbean** cruises call at Aruba, Bonaire, and Curaçao. **Spring–Summer:** Eleven-night **Bahamas** loops depart Nassau. Fourteen-night **mid-America** cruises and a 15-night **inland waterways** cruise (same as fall). An 11-night **Great Lakes** cruise sails between Warren and Buffalo (New York).

American Hawaii Cruises

Independence **Year-round:** Seven-night **Hawaii** loops depart Honolulu, calling at Kona, Hilo, Kahului, and Nawiliwili.

Carnival Cruise Lines

Carnival Destiny **Year-round:** Seven-night **eastern Caribbean** loops depart Miami, calling at San Juan, St. Croix, and St. Thomas. Seven-night **western Caribbean** loops depart Miami, calling at Cozumel/Playa del Carmen, Grand Cayman, and Ocho Rios.

Celebration **Fall–mid-Spring:** Seven-night **eastern Caribbean** loops depart Miami, calling at San Juan, St. Thomas/St. John, and St. Maarten/St. Martin. **Mid-Spring–Summer:** Seven-night **western Caribbean** loops depart Tampa or New Orleans, calling at Grand Cayman and Cozumel/Playa del Carmen.

Ecstasy **Year-round:** Three-night **Bahamas** loops depart Miami, calling at Nassau. Four-night **western Caribbean** loops depart Miami, calling at Key West and Cozumel/Playa del Carmen.

Fantasy **Year-round:** Three-night **Bahamas** loops depart Port Canaveral, calling at Nassau. Four-night **Bahamas** loops depart Port Canaveral, calling at Nassau and Freeport/Lucaya.

Fascination **Year-round:** Seven-night **southern Caribbean** loops depart San Juan, calling at St. Thomas, Guadeloupe, Grenada, La Guaira/Caracas, and Aruba.

Holiday **Year-round:** Three-night **Baja Mexico** loops depart Los Angeles, calling at Ensenada. Four-night **Baja Mexico** loops depart Los Angeles, calling at Ensenada and Catalina Island.

Imagination **Year-round:** Seven-night **western Caribbean** loops depart Miami, calling at Cozumel/Playa del Carmen, Grand Cayman, and Ocho Rios.

Inspiration **Year-round:** Seven-night **southern Caribbean** loops depart San Juan, calling at St. Thomas, St. Maarten/St. Martin, Dominica, Barbados, and Martinique.

Jubilee **Year-round:** Seven-night **Mexican Riviera** loops depart Los Angeles, calling at Puerto Vallarta, Cabo San Lucas, and Mazatlán.

Sensation **Year-round:** Seven-night **eastern Caribbean** loops depart Miami, calling at San Juan, St. Thomas, and St. Maarten/St. Martin.

Tropicale **Early Fall:** Eleven-night **Hawaii** cruises between Honolulu and Vancouver or Ensenada (Mexico) call at Kaului, Hilo, Kona, and Nawiliwili. A 14-night **Panama Canal** transit from Los Angeles to San Juan calls at Puerto Vallarta, Zihuatenejo/Ixtapa, Acapulco, Puerto Caldera, Curaçao, and St. Thomas. **Late Fall–early Spring:** Ten-night **southern Caribbean** loops depart San Juan, calling at St. Thomas, Martinique, Barbados, Grenada, St. Lucia, St. Barts, Antigua, and St. Maarten/St. Martin. Eleven-night **Panama Canal** loops depart San Juan, calling at St. Thomas, St. Barts, St. Lucia, Aruba, and Ocho Rios. A 16-night Panama Canal transit from Tampa to Vancouver calls at Cartagena, Acapulco, Zihuatenejo/Ixtapa, Puerto Vallarta, Cabo San Lucas, and Los Angeles. **Mid-Spring–Summer:** Seven-night **Inside Passage/Gulf of Alaska** cruises between Vancouver and Seward (Alaska) call at Juneau, Ketchikan, Skagway, and Sitka or Valdez.

Celebrity Cruises

Century **Year-round:** Seven-night **eastern Caribbean** loops depart Fort Lauderdale, calling at San Juan, St. Thomas, St. Maarten/St. Martin, and Nassau. Seven-night **western Caribbean** loops depart Fort Lauderdale, calling at Ocho Rios, Grand Cayman, Cozumel/Playa del Carmen, and Key West.

Galaxy **Fall–Spring:** Seven-night **western Caribbean** loops depart Fort Lauderdale, calling at Key West, Cozumel/Playa del Carmen, Montego Bay, and Grand Cayman. **Summer:** A 10-night **Inside Passage** cruise from Los Angeles to Vancouver calls at San Francisco, Victoria, Sitka, Juneau, Ketchikan, and Glacier Bay National Park. Seven-day **Inside Passage** loops depart Vancouver, calling at Juneau, Skagway, Haines, Ketchikan, and Yakutat Bay (Hubbard Glacier). A 12-night **Inside Passage** cruise from Vancouver to Los Angeles calls at Ketchikan, Skagway, Juneau, Victoria, San Francisco, Misty Fjords National Monument, and Glacier Bay National Park.

Horizon **Fall–Spring:** A 17-night **Panama Canal** transit from Los Angeles to San Juan calls at San Diego, Cabo San Lucas, Acapulco, Puerto Caldera, the San Blas Islands, Cartagena, and Aruba. Seven-night **Caribbean** loops depart San Juan, calling at Catalina Island, Martinique, Barbados, Antigua, and St. Thomas. **Summer:** Seven-night **Inside Passage** loops depart Vancouver, calling at Ketchikan, Juneau, Skagway, and Haines. Seven-night **Inside Passage/Gulf of Alaska** cruises between Vancouver and Seward (Alaska) call at Sitka, Juneau, Skagway, Ketchikan, and Valdez.

Meridian **Fall–Spring:** Ten- and 11-night **Caribbean** and **Caribbean/Panama Canal** loops depart San Juan and include calls at Aruba, Caracas/La Guaira, Grenada, Barbados, St. Lucia, Martinique, St. Maarten/St. Maarten, St. Thomas, St. John, Cartagena, and the San Blas Islands. An 11-night **Caribbean** cruise from Fort Lauderdale to San Juan calls at Nassau, Tortola, St. Maarten/St. Maarten, Antigua, Martinique, Barbados, Grenada, and St. Thomas. **Spring–Summer:** Seven-night **Bermuda** loops depart New York or Fort Lauderdale, calling at King's Wharf. Ten- and 11-night **Caribbean** and **Caribbean/Panama Canal** loops (same as fall).

Zenith **Fall–Winter:** Seven-night **Caribbean** loops depart San Juan, calling at St. Thomas, Guadeloupe, Grenada, Caracas/La Guaira, and Aruba. A seven-night **Caribbean** cruise between San Juan and New York calls at St. Thomas, St. Maarten, and Bermuda. **Spring–Summer:** Seven-night **Bermuda** loops depart New York, calling at Hamilton and St. George's.

Clipper Cruise Line

Nantucket Clipper **Fall:** Seven- to 14-night **New England and Canada** or **eastern seaboard** loops depart New York or sail between Quincy (Massachusetts) and Alexandria (Virginia), Alexandria and New York, Charleston (South Carolina) and Jacksonville (Florida), or Jacksonville and Alexandria. **Winter:** Seven-night **Virgin Islands** loops depart St. Thomas. **Spring:** Seven- to 14-night **New England and Canada** cruises (same as fall). **Summer:** Ten- and 11-night **Great Lakes** cruises sail between Québec City and Toledo (Ohio). Seven- to 14-night **New England and Canada** cruises (same as fall).

Yorktown Clipper **Early Fall:** A 10-night **Pacific Northwest** cruise sails between Seattle and Portland. Five-night **northern California** cruises depart San Francisco. Seven-night **Sea of Cortez** cruises sail between La Paz and Cabo San Lucas (Mexico). **Late Fall–Winter:** Eight-night **Costa Rica/Panama Canal** cruises sail between Colon (Costa Rica) and Puerto Caldera (Costa Rica). Ten-night **Lesser Antilles and Orinoco River (Venezuela)** cruises sail between Curaçao and Trinidad.

Seven-night **Caribbean** cruises sail between St. Lucia and St. Kitts. **Spring: Costa Rica/Panama Canal, Sea of Cortez** and **northern California** cruises (same as fall). **Summer:** A 14-night **Inside Passage** cruise between Seattle and Juneau calls at Haines, Skagway, Glacier Bay National Park, Wrangell, Ketchikan, the San Juan Islands, and Victoria. Seven-night **Inside Passage** cruises between Juneau and Ketchikan call at Glacier Bay National Park, Inian Islands, Sitka, Baranof Island, and Wrangell.

Club Med

Club Med 1 **Mid-Fall–late Spring:** Seven-night **Caribbean** loops depart Martinique and include calls at Barbados, St. Lucia, Carriacou, St. Thomas, St. Maarten/St. Martin, San Juan, and other islands. **Late Spring–Summer:** An 18-night eastbound **transatlantic crossing** sails from Martinique to Lisbon (Portugal). Three- to seven-night **Mediterranean** and **Canary Islands** cruises depart Lisbon, Malaga (Spain), Toulon and Cannes (France), Rome/Civitavecchia and Naples (Italy), Athens/Piraeus (Greece), and Istanbul (Turkey), and include calls at the Greek Islands, the Napoli Coast, Barcelona, the French Riviera, and the Turkish Coast.

Club Med 2 **Year-round:** Seven-night **French Polynesia** loops depart Papeete, Tahiti.

Commodore Cruise Line

Enchanted Isle **Year-round:** Seven-night **western Caribbean** loops depart New Orleans, calling at Cozumel/Playa del Carmen, Grand Cayman, and Montego Bay.

Costa Cruise Lines

CostaAllegra **Fall–mid-Spring:** South America cruises with port calls to be announced. **Mid-Spring–Summer:** Northern Europe and Mediterranean cruises with port calls to be announced.

CostaClassica **Fall–mid-Spring: Caribbean** cruises with port calls to be announced. **Mid-Spring–Summer:** Seven-night **Mediterranean** loops depart Venice and include calls on the Greek Islands, Athens/Piraeus, and other ports.

CostaMarina **Fall–mid-Spring:** South America cruises with port calls to announced. **Mid-Spring–Summer:** Seven-night **northern Europe** and **Norwegian Fjords** loops from Copenhagen include calls at Stockholm, Helsinki, Bergen, and Oslo.

CostaRiviera **Fall–mid-Spring:** To be announced.

CostaRomantica **Fall–mid-Spring:** Seven-night **eastern Caribbean** loops depart Port Everglades, calling at San Juan, St. Thomas, Serena Cay/Casa de Campo, and Nassau. **Western Caribbean** loops call at Key West, Cozumel/Playa del Carmen, Ocho Rios, and Grand Cayman. **Mid-Spring–Summer:** Seven-night **western Mediterranean** loops depart Genoa (Italy) and include calls on the Napoli Coast, the French Riviera, the Canary Islands, and Barcelona.

CostaVictoria **Fall–mid-Spring:** Seven-night **eastern Caribbean** loops depart Port Everglades, calling at San Juan, St. Thomas, Serena Cay/Casa de Campo, and Nassau. **Western Caribbean** loops call at Key West, Cozumel/Playa del Carmen, Ocho Rios, and Grand Cayman. **Mid-Spring–Summer:** Seven-night **Mediterranean** loops depart Venice and include calls on the Turkish Coast, Athens/Piraeus, and other ports.

Daphne **Fall–mid-Spring:** To be announced.

EugenioCosta **Fall–mid-Spring:** Ten- and 11-night **Canary Islands** loops departing Genoa (Italy) include a call at Barcelona and other ports.

Crystal Cruises

Crystal Harmony **Early Fall:** Eleven- and 12-night **Southeast Asia** cruises between Beijing and Hong Kong or Bangkok/Laem Chabang (Thailand), or between Hong Kong and Singapore, include calls at Ho Chi Minh City, Kota Kinabalu, Sabah, and Canton. **Late Fall:** Eleven- and 14-night **South Pacific** cruises sail between Singapore and Sydney (Australia) or Sydney and Auckland (New Zealand). A 27-night eastbound **trans-Pacific** cruise from Auckland to Los Angeles calls at Honolulu and Lahaina. A seven-night **Mexican Riviera** cruise from Los Angeles to Acapulco calls at San Diego, Cabo San Lucas, Mazatlan, Puerto Vallarta, and Zihuatenejo/Ixtapa. **Winter:** Ten-, 11-, and 12-night **Panama Canal** transits between Acapulco and New Orleans, San Juan, or Fort Lauderdale include calls at Puerto Limon, Puerto Caldera, the San Blas Islands, Huatulco, Cozumel/Playa del Carmen, Galveston, Grand Cayman, Aruba, St. Maarten/St. Martin, St. Thomas, St. Barts, and Puerto Quetzal. **Spring–Summer:** A 12-night eastbound **transatlantic** crossing from Fort Lauderdale to Lisbon (Portugal) calls at Bermuda. Twelve-night **Mediterranean** cruises between Athens/Piraeus and Lisbon or Rome/Civitavecchia include calls on the French Riviera, Venice, the Napoli Coast, and the Greek Islands. Twelve-night **Baltic Sea/northern Europe** cruises between Greenwich (England) and Copenhagen or Hamburg include calls at Oslo, Helsinki, Edinburgh/Leith, Stockholm, and Bergen. Twelve-night **Mediterranean/Europe** cruises between Rome/Civitavecchia and Greenwich include calls on the French Riviera, Lisbon, and other ports.

Crystal Symphony **Fall:** A 12-night westbound **transatlantic** crossing from Lisbon (Portugal) to Barbados includes a call on the Canary Islands. Ten-, 11-, and 12-night **Panama Canal** cruises sail between Acapulco and Barbados, New Orleans, or Fort Lauderdale, and include calls at St. Lucia, St. Vincent, Aruba, Huatulco, Cozumel/Playa del Carmen, Puerto Quetzal, Puerto Caldera, Puerto Limon, and the San Blas Islands. **Winter:** A 12-night **eastern Caribbean** loop from Fort Lauderdale calls at Nassau, Antigua, St. Lucia, Barbados, St. Maarten/St. Martin, and St. John/St. Thomas. A 14-night **Panama Canal** transit from Fort Lauderdale to Los Angeles calls at Grand Cayman, Aruba, and Acapulco. A 21-night westbound **Pacific crossing** from Los Angeles to Sydney (Australia) includes a call at Honolulu. A 19-night **Southeast Asia** cruise from Sydney to Hong Kong includes a call at Bali and other ports. A 16-night **Asia** cruise from Hong Kong to Bombay (India) includes a call at Singapore and other ports. **Spring:** A 22-night **Indian Ocean** cruise sails from Bombay to Cape Town. A 25-night westbound **transatlantic/South America/Caribbean** cruise from Cape Town (South Africa) to Fort Lauderdale includes calls at Rio de Janeiro, Salvador, Recife, Barbados, and St. Thomas. An 11-night **Panama Canal** cruise from Fort Lauderdale to Acapulco calls at Cozumel/Playa del Carmen, Grand Cayman, and Puerto Caldera. A seven-night **Mexican Riviera** cruise from Acapulco to San Francisco calls at Puerto Vallarta, Mazatlan, Cabo San Lucas, and Los Angeles. **Summer:** Twelve-night **Inside Passage** loops from San Francisco call at Victoria, Vancouver, Ketchikan, Juneau, Skagway, Glacier Bay National Park, and Sitka.

Cunard Line Limited

Cunard Countess **Year-round:** Seven-night **southern Caribbean** loops depart San Juan, calling at St. Maarten/St. Martin, Dominica, Grenada, St. Lucia, St. Kitts, and St. Thomas or Tortola, Antigua, Martinique, Barbados, and St. Thomas.

Cunard Dynasty **Fall–Spring:** A 14-night **Panama Canal** transit from Los Angeles to Fort Lauderdale calls at Acapulco, Puerto Caldera, Cartagena, Colombia, and Ocho Rios. Ten- and 11-night **Panama Canal** transits between Fort Lauderdale and Acapulco include calls at Cozumel/Playa del Carmen, Grand Cayman, Puerto Caldera, Ocho Rios, and Key West. **Summer: Alaska** cruises with ports of call to be announced.

Queen Elizabeth 2 **Fall–early Winter:** A five-night **New England and Canada** loop departs New York. Five-night **transatlantic crossings** depart New York or London/Southampton. An eight-night **Iberia** loop departs London/Southampton and includes a call at Lisbon. An eight-night **Canary Islands** loop departs London/Southampton. A 15-night **Caribbean** loop departs New York, calling at Fort Lauderdale, St. Thomas, Aruba, Caracas/La Guaira, Grenada, Barbados, St. Maarten/St. Martin, and Martinique. **Mid-Winter–Spring:** A 103-night **world cruise** sails round-trip from New York or Fort Lauderdale. Five-night **transatlantic crossings** depart New York or London/Southampton. **Summer: Mediterranean, North Cape/Iceland,** and **Bermuda** cruises with ports of call to be announced.

Royal Viking Sun **Late Fall–mid-Winter:** Fourteen-night **Mediterranean** cruises sail between Barcelona (Spain) and Istanbul, Istanbul and Genoa (Italy), or Genoa and Venice, and include calls at Florence/Livorno, Rome/Civitavecchia, the Napoli Coast, Athens/Piraeus, the Greek Islands, and the Turkish Coast. An 18-night **Mediterranean/Red Sea** cruise from Venice to Mombasa (Kenya) calls on the Greek Islands and the Turkish Coast. A 22-night westbound **transatlantic crossing** sails from Mombasa to Rio de Janeiro (Brazil). A 14-night **Amazon/Caribbean** cruise from Rio de Janeiro to Fort Lauderdale calls at Salvador de Bahia, Devil's Island, Barbados, and St. Thomas. An 18-night **Panama Canal** transit from Fort Lauderdale to San Francisco calls at Cozumel/Playa del Carmen, Acapulco, Mazatlan, Aruba, and Puerto Caldera. **Mid-Winter–Spring:** A 99-night **world cruise** sails between San Francisco and Fort Lauderdale. **Summer: Mediterranean, northern Europe,** and **North Cape** cruises with ports of call to be announced.

Sea Goddess I **Fall–Winter:** Seven-, 10- and 11-night **Mediterranean** and **Red Sea** cruises sail between Athens/Piraeus and Venice, Istanbul and Alexandria (Egypt), or Haifa (Israel) and Istanbul, and call on the Greek Islands and the Turkish Coast. **East Africa/Seychelles** cruises with ports of call to be announced.

Sea Goddess II **Fall:** Ten- and 11-night **Panama Canal** transits between Acapulco and Aruba include calls at Puerto Caldera, the San Blas Islands, Cartagena, and other ports. A 14-night **Panama Canal** transit from Acapulco to St. Thomas also calls at Curaçao and St. Barts. Seven-night **Caribbean** loops depart St. Thomas, calling at St. John, St. Maarten/St. Martin, St. Barts, Antigua, Virgin Gorda, and Jost Van Dyke. **Winter: Indian Ocean** and **Southeast Asia** cruises with ports of call to be announced. **Spring–Summer: Mediterranean** cruises with ports of call to be announced.

Vistafjord **Fall:** Fourteen-night **Mediterranean and Mediterranean/Canary Island** cruises sail between Venice and Athens/Piraeus, Genoa (Italy) and Barcelona (Spain), or Barcelona and Malaga (Spain), and include calls at Istanbul, the Turkish Coast, the Napoli Coast, the Greek Islands, Ibiza, Lisbon, and Gibraltar. A 21-night westbound **transatlantic crossing** from Malaga to Fort Lauderdale calls at the Canary Islands, Barbados, Grenada, St. Lucia, Guadeloupe, St. John, Antigua, and St. Thomas. A 16-night **Caribbean** loop departs Fort Lauderdale, calling at San Juan, St. Croix, Barbados, St. Lucia, Grenada, Caracas/La Guaira, Aruba, and St. Thomas. An 11-night **Caribbean** loop departs Fort Lauderdale, calling at San Juan, St. Thomas, St. Kitts, Aruba, and Grand Cayman. **Winter:** A 49-night **South America** loop departs Fort Lauderdale and includes calls at

Barbados, Devil's Island, Montevideo, Rio de Janeiro, Buenos Aires, Valparaiso, Puerto Montt, the Chilean Fjords, Port Stanley, Aruba, and Grand Cayman. **Spring:** Fifteen-night **Panama Canal** transits between Los Angeles and Fort Lauderdale may call at Acapulco, Puerto Vallarta/Zihuatanejo/Ixtapa, Puerto Caldera, Aruba, Cartagena, and Grand Cayman. A 15-night eastbound **transatlantic crossing** from Fort Lauderdale to Genoa calls at St. Thomas, the Canary Islands, and Gibraltar. **Mid-Spring**–Summer: **Mediterranean** and **Europe** cruises with ports of call to be announced.

Delta Queen Steamboat Company

American Queen **Year-round:** Three- to 14-night river cruises on the **Mississippi River System** depart New Orleans, Memphis, St. Louis, St. Paul, Cincinnati, Pittsburgh, and Louisville.

Delta Queen **Year-round:** Three- to 12-night river cruises on the **Mississippi River System** depart New Orleans, Memphis, St. Louis, St. Paul, Louisville, Cincinnati, Nashville, Pittsburgh, Chattanooga, Little Rock, Tulsa, and Galveston.

Mississippi Queen **Year-round:** Three- to 11-night river cruises on the **Mississippi River System** depart New Orleans, Memphis, St. Louis, St. Paul, Louisville, Cincinnati, Nashville, Pittsburgh, and Chattanooga.

Dolphin Cruise Line

IslandBreeze **Early Fall:** Two-night cruises to nowhere depart New York. Five-night **New England and Canada** loops depart New York, calling at Newport, Portland, and Halifax. **Mid-Fall–early Spring:** Seven-night **Caribbean/Panama Canal** cruises depart Montego Bay (Jamaica), calling at Cartagena, the San Blas Islands, and Puerto Limon. **Mid-Spring–Summer:** Same as early fall.

OceanBreeze **Year-round:** Three-night **Bahamas** loops depart Miami, calling at Nassau and Blue Lagoon Island. Four-night **Mexican Yucatan** loops depart Miami, calling at Cozumel/Playa del Carmen and Key West.

SeaBreeze **Year-round:** Seven-night **eastern Caribbean** loops depart Miami, calling at Nassau, San Juan, and St. Thomas/St. John. Seven-night **western Caribbean** loops call at Grand Cayman, Montego Bay, and Cozumel/Playa del Carmen.

Holland America Line

Maasdam **Early Fall:** Nine-, 11-, and 12-night **Mediterranean** cruises depart Athens/Piraeus or Rome/Civitavecchia and include calls on the Turkish Coast, the Greek Islands, Venice, the Napoli Coast, the French Riviera, Barcelona, and Lisbon. A 10-night westbound **transatlantic crossing** from Lisbon (Portugal) to Fort Lauderdale calls at Hamilton. **Late Fall–early Winter:** Ten-night **Panama Canal** transits between Fort Lauderdale and Acapulco include calls at Grand Cayman, Puerto Caldera, and Puerto Quetzal. Ten-night **Panama Canal** transits between New Orleans and Acapulco call at Puerto Quetzal, Grand Cayman and Cozumel/Playa del Carmen. **Spring–Summer:** A 10-night eastbound **transatlantic crossing** from Fort Lauderdale to Lisbon includes a call at Nassau. **Mediterranean** cruises (same as early fall). Twelve-night **western Europe** cruises sail between Rome/Civitavecchia and Copenhagen and include calls at Amsterdam, Lisbon, and Oslo. Twelve-night **northern Europe** cruises sail between London/Dover and Copenhagen and include calls at Bergen, the Norwegian Coast, Oslo, Helsinki, and Stockholm.

Nieuw Amsterdam **Fall–mid-Spring:** A 20-night **Panama Canal** transit from Vancouver to New Orleans includes calls at Cabo San Lucas, Acapulco, Puerto

Caldera, Aruba, and Ocho Rios. Seven-night **western Caribbean** loops depart New Orleans, calling at Montego Bay, Grand Cayman, and Cozumel/Playa del Carmen. **Mid-Spring–Summer:** A 21-night **Panama Canal** transit from New Orleans to Vancouver includes calls at Grand Cayman, Montego Bay, Cartagena, Puerto Caldera, Acapulco, Zihuatenejo/Ixtapa, Puerto Vallarta, Los Angeles, and Victoria. Seven-night **Inside Passage** loops depart Vancouver, calling at Juneau, Skagway, Glacier Bay National Park, and Ketchikan.

Noordam **Fall–mid-Spring:** A 19-night **Panama Canal** transit from Vancouver to Tampa calls at Victoria, San Francisco, San Diego, Cabo San Lucas, Acapulco, Puerto Caldera, Cartagena, and Grand Cayman. Seven-night **western Caribbean** loops depart Tampa, calling at Key West, Cozumel/Playa del Carmen, Ocho Rios, and Grand Cayman. **Late Spring–Summer:** A 12-night **Panama Canal** cruise with ports of call to be announced. Seven-night **Inside Passage/Gulf of Alaska** cruises between Vancouver and Seward (Alaska) call at Ketchikan, Juneau, Sitka, and Valdez.

Rotterdam **Fall:** A 50-night **Central/South America** cruise from Los Angeles to Fort Lauderdale calls at 18 ports, including Acapulco, Puerto Quetzal, Puerto Caldera, Puerto Arenas, Valparaiso, Puerto Montt, Montevideo, Port Stanley, Salvador, Recife, Rio de Janeiro, Devil's Island, and Curaçao. **Winter:** A 14-night **Panama Canal** transit from Fort Lauderdale to Los Angeles includes calls at Curaçao, Puerto Caldera, Acapulco, Cabo San Lucas. A 102-day **world cruise** includes a 20-night **Hawaii/South Pacific** segment from Los Angeles to Auckland (New Zealand), a 25-night **South Pacific/Asia** segment from Auckland to Hong Kong, and a 19-night **Southeast Asia** segment from Hong Kong to Bombay (India). **Spring:** A 24-night **Mediterranean** cruise from Bombay to Rome/Civitavecchia calls at Istanbul, Crete, and other ports. A 14-night westbound **transatlantic crossing** from Rome/Civitavecchia to Fort Lauderdale calls at Lisbon and New York. A 17-night **Panama Canal** transit from Fort Lauderdale to Los Angeles calls at Nassau, San Juan, Aruba, Puerto Quetzal, Zihuatanejo/Ixtapa, Acapulco, and other ports. **Summer:** Seven-night **Inside Passage/Gulf of Alaska** cruises between Vancouver and Seward (Alaska) call at Ketchikan, Juneau, Sitka, and Valdez.

Ryndam **Early Fall:** A 20-night **Panama Canal** transit from Vancouver to Fort Lauderdale calls at Los Angeles, Puerto Vallarta, Zihuatenejo/Ixtapa, Acapulco, Puerto Caldera, Curaçao, St. Thomas, and Nassau. **Late Fall–mid-Spring:** Ten-night **Caribbean** loops depart Fort Lauderdale, calling at St. Maarten/St. Martin, St. Lucia, Barbados, and Antigua or Guadeloupe, St. John/St. Thomas, and Nassau. **Mid-Spring–Summer:** A 16-night **Panama Canal** transit with ports of call to be announced. Seven-night **Inside Passage/Gulf of Alaska** cruises between Vancouver and Seward (Alaska) call at Ketchikan, Juneau, Sitka, and Valdez.

Statendam **Early Fall:** A 21-night **Panama Canal** transit from Vancouver to Fort Lauderdale calls at Victoria, San Francisco, San Diego, Cabo San Lucas, Puerto Vallarta, Acapulco, Puerto Quetzal, the San Blas Islands, Cartagena, and Grand Cayman. **Late Fall–mid-Spring:** Ten-night **southern Caribbean** loops depart Fort Lauderdale, calling at Curaçao, Caracas/La Guaira, Grenada, Dominica, St. Thomas/St. John, and Nassau. A 13-night **Panama Canal** transit with ports of call to be announced. Sixteen- and 19-night **Hawaii** cruises with ports of call to be announced. **Mid-Spring–Summer:** Seven-night **Inside Passage** loops depart Vancouver, calling at Juneau, Skagway, Glacier Bay National Park, and Ketchikan.

Veendam **Early Fall:** Ten-night **New England and Canada** cruises depart New York or Montréal, and include calls at Newport, Boston, Portland, Sydney/Ingonish, Charlottetown, and Québec City. A 12-night **Bermuda/New England and Canada** loop departs New York, calling at

Hamilton, Boston, Portland, Bar Harbor, St. John, Halifax, and Newport. **Mid-Fall–Winter:** Seven-night **eastern Caribbean** loops depart Fort Lauderdale, calling at Nassau, San Juan, and St. Thomas/St. John. Seven-night **western Caribbean** loops call at Key West, Cozumel/Playa del Carmen, Ocho Rios, and Grand Cayman. **Winter–mid-Spring:** Seven-night **Caribbean** loops depart Fort Lauderdale, calling at St. Kitts, St. John/St. Thomas, and Nassau. **Mid-Spring–Summer:** A 20-night **Panama Canal** transit from Fort Lauderdale to Vancouver calls at Curaçao, Puerto Quetzal, Acapulco, Zihuatenejo/Ixtapa, Puerto Vallarta, San Francisco, Seattle, and other ports. Seven-night **Inside Passage** loops depart Vancouver, calling at Juneau, Skagway, Glacier Bay National Park, and Ketchikan.

Westerdam **Fall–Winter:** A 20-night **Panama Canal** transit from Vancouver to New Orleans calls at Los Angeles, Puerto Vallarta, Zihuatenejo/Ixtapa, Acapulco, Puerto Quetzal, Cartagena, Grand Cayman, and Ocho Rios. Seven-night **eastern Caribbean** loops depart Fort Lauderdale, calling at St. Maarten/St. Martin, St. Thomas/St. John, and Nassau. **Spring–Summer:** Seven-night **eastern Caribbean** loops (same as winter). **Western Caribbean** loops depart Fort Lauderdale, calling at Key West, Cozumel/Playa del Carmen, Ocho Rios, and Grand Cayman.

Majesty Cruise Line

Royal Majesty **Late Fall–mid-Spring:** Three-night **Bahamas** loops depart Miami, calling at Nassau and Key West. Four-night **Mexican Yucatan** loops depart Miami, calling at Key West and Cozumel/Playa del Carmen. **Late Spring–Summer:** Seven-night **Bermuda** loops depart Boston, calling at St. George's.

Norwegian Cruise Line

Dreamward **Fall–Spring:** Seven-night **western Caribbean** loops depart Fort Lauderdale, calling at Grand Cayman, Cozumel/Playa del Carmen, Cancun, and Great Stirrup Cay. **Summer:** Seven-night **Bermuda** loops depart New York, calling at St. George's and Hamilton.

Leeward **Year-round:** Three-night **Bahamas** loops depart Miami, calling at Great Stirrup Cay, and Nassau or Key West. Four-night **Mexican Yucatan** loops depart Miami, calling at Key West and Cozumel/Playa del Carmen or Cozumel and Cancun.

Norwegian Crown **Fall–Winter:** Seven-night **western Caribbean** loops depart Fort Lauderdale, calling at Grand Cayman, Cozumel/Playa del Carmen, Great Stirrup Cay, and Key West. **Spring–Summer:** Twelve-night **western Europe** cruises depart London/Dover or Lisbon (Portugal) and include calls at Amsterdam, Barcelona, Cork, Dublin, Paris/Le Havre, and Edinburgh/Leith. Twelve-night **northern Europe** loops depart London/Dover, and include calls at Helsinki, Stockholm, Copenhagen, and Oslo. A 12-night **Norwegian Fjords/North Cape** loop departs London/Dover and includes a call at Bergen and other Norwegian ports.

Norway **Year-round:** Seven-night **eastern Caribbean** loops depart Miami, calling at St. Maarten/St. Martin, St. Thomas/St. John, and Great Stirrup Cay. Seven-night **western Caribbean** loops depart Miami, calling at Ocho Rios, Grand Cayman, Cozumel/Playa del Carmen, and Great Stirrup Cay.

Seaward **Year-round:** Seven-night **southern Caribbean** loops depart San Juan, calling at Barbados, Martinique, St. Maarten/St. Martin, Antigua, and St. Thomas or Aruba, Curaçao, Tortola, and St. Thomas.

Windward **Fall–Winter:** Seven-night **southern Caribbean** loops depart San Juan, calling at Barbados, St. Lucia, St. Barts, St. Thomas, and

Tortola. **Late Spring–Summer:** Seven-night **Inside Passage** loops depart Vancouver, calling at Skagway, Haines, Juneau, and Ketchikan. Some departures call at Glacier Bay National Park.

Orient Lines

Marco Polo **Fall–early Winter:** A 23-night **Middle East/Africa** cruise-tour from Athens/Piraeus to Mombasa (Kenya) calls at five ports and includes a three-night safari. A 16-night **Africa/Seychelles** cruise-safari departs Nairobi for Mombasa. A 22-night **Africa to Asia** cruise-tour departs Nairobi for Singapore. **Winter:** A 23-night **Southeast Asia** cruise-tour from Singapore to Sydney calls in Australia and along the Java Sea. Segments are available. Eleven- to 20-night **Australia, New Zealand, and South Pacific** cruise-tours depart Auckland (New Zealand), Sydney (Australia), and Christchurch (New Zealand). **Spring:** Fifteen- to 24-night **Southeast Asia** cruise-tours depart Singapore, Hong Kong, or Bangkok/Laem Chabang (Thailand) and include calls in Vietnam, Bali, Kuala Lumpur, and other ports. An 18-night **Asia/India** cruise-tour from Singapore to Bombay (India) includes calls in Malaysia, Thailand, Sri Lanka, and India. A 20-night **Middle East** cruise-tour from Bombay to Athens/Piraeus includes calls in Egypt, Jordan, and Israel. **Summer:** Eleven- to 17-night **Mediterranean** cruise-tours between Athens/Piraeus and Istanbul or Barcelona (Spain) call on the Greek Islands and along the Italian and French Rivieras.

Premier Cruise Lines

Star/Ship Atlantic **Year-round:** Three- and four-night **Bahamas** loops depart Port Canaveral, calling at Nassau and Freeport/Lucaya.

Star/Ship Oceanic Same as *Star/Ship Atlantic*, above.

Princess Cruises

Crown Princess **Early Fall:** An 18-night **Panama Canal** transit from Vancouver to Fort Lauderdale calls at San Diego, Cabo San Lucas, Acapulco, Puerto Quetzal, Grand Cayman, and Princess Cays. **Mid-Fall–Spring:** Ten-night **southern Caribbean** loops depart Fort Lauderdale, calling at Nassau, Princess Cays, St. Maarten/St. Martin, Dominica, Barbados, Guadeloupe, and St. Thomas. **Mid-Spring–Summer:** Seven-night **Inside Passage/Gulf of Alaska** cruises between Vancouver and Seward (Alaska) call at Ketchikan, Juneau, Skagway, and Glacier Bay National Park.

Dawn Princess **Spring:** Seven-night **southern Caribbean** loops depart San Juan, calling at Grenada, Barbados, Guadeloupe, St. Maarten/St. Martin, and St. Thomas. **Mid-Spring–Summer:** Seven-night **Inside Passage/Gulf of Alaska** cruises between Vancouver and Seward (Alaska) call at Ketchikan, Juneau, Skagway, and Glacier Bay National Park.

Island Princess **Fall:** A 12-night **western Europe** cruise from London/Southampton to Rome/Civitavecchia includes calls at Paris/Le Havre, Lisbon, Gibraltar, Seville, Barcelona, and Florence/Livorno. A 14-night **Black Sea** cruise from Athens/Piraeus to Rome/Civitavecchia includes calls at Istanbul, Varna, and the Greek Islands. Twelve- and 14-night **Mediterranean** and **Mediterranean/Red Sea** cruises sail between Rome/Civitavecchia and Athens/Piraeus and include calls on the Greek Islands, Limassol, and Istanbul. A 17-night **India/Red Sea** cruise from Rome/Civitavecchia to Bombay includes a call on the Greek Islands and other ports. **Winter:** An 11-night **India/Asia** cruise from Bombay to Singapore includes calls at Phuket and Kuala Lumpur. Fourteen-night **Southeast Asia** cruises between Singapore and Hong Kong include calls at Bangkok/Laem Chabang, Ko Samui, Ho Chi Minh City, Kota Kinabalu, Sabah, and Canton. A 14-night

Spice Islands loop from Singapore includes calls at Kuala Lumpur, Phuket, and Bali. A 23-night **Africa/Asia** cruise from Singapore to Cape Town (South Africa) includes calls at Kuala Lumpur and Phuket. **Spring–Summer:** A 14-night **Mediterranean** cruise from Athens/Piraeus to Rome/Civitavecchia includes calls at Istanbul, Limassol, and the Greek Islands. Twelve-night **Mediterranean** cruises between Rome/Civitavecchia and London/Southampton include calls at Florence/Livorno, the French Riviera, Barcelona, Gibraltar, Seville, Lisbon, and Paris/Le Havre. Twelve-night **British Isles** and **western Europe** loops depart London/Southampton and include calls at Dublin, Edinburgh/Leith, Paris/Le Havre, and Amsterdam. Fourteen-night **Scandinavia/Russia** loops depart London/Southampton and include calls at Amsterdam, Copenhagen, Stockholm, and Helsinki. Twelve-night **Mediterranean** cruises between Rome/Civitavecchia and Athens/Piraeus include calls on the French Riviera, the Greek Islands, Istanbul, and the Napoli Coast.

Pacific Princess **Fall:** Twelve-night **Mediterranean** cruises between Barcelona (Spain) and Venice include calls at Florence/Livorno, the Napoli Coast, Rome/Civitavecchia, the Turkish Coast, Athens/Piraeus, and the Greek Islands. **Winter–Spring:** A 19-night westbound **transatlantic crossing** from Barcelona to San Juan includes calls at Gibraltar, Devil's Island, Barbados, Dominica, and St. Thomas. Fourteen-night **Panama Canal** transits between San Juan and New Orleans call at St. Thomas, Guadeloupe, Grenada, Caracas/La Guaira, Aruba, Puerto Limon, and Cozumel/Playa del Carmen. Fourteen- and 17-night **South America** and **South America/Amazon** cruises sail between San Juan and Santiago (Chile) or Buenos Aires (Argentina) and Manaus (Brazil), and include calls at Montevideo, Puerto Madryn, Ushuaia, Port Stanley, Punta Arenas, Puerto Montt, Recife, and other ports. A 19-night **South America/Africa/Europe** cruise from Manaus to Lisbon (Portugal) includes calls at Alter do Chao, Santarem, the Canary Islands, and Gibraltar. **Summer:** Same as fall.

Regal Princess **Fall–Mid-Spring:** Ten-night **Panama Canal** loops depart Fort Lauderdale, calling at Princess Cays, Puerto Limon, Cartagena, and Cozumel/Playa del Carmen. Fifteen-night **Panama Canal** transits between Fort Lauderdale and Los Angeles include calls at Princess Cays, St. Thomas, Cartagena, Puerto Limon, Acapulco, and Cabo San Lucas. **Mid-Spring–Summer:** Seven-night **Inside Passage** loops depart Vancouver, calling at Juneau, Skagway, Sitka, and Glacier Bay National Park.

Royal Princess **Early Fall:** Ten-night **New England and Canada** cruises between New York and Montréal call at Newport, Boston, Bar Harbor, St. John, Halifax, and Québec. **Mid-Fall–mid-Spring:** Ten-night **Panama Canal** transits between Acapulco and San Juan call at Puerto Caldera, Cartagena, Aruba, and St. Thomas. Eleven-night **Panama Canal** transits between San Juan and Acapulco call at St. Thomas, Martinique, Grenada, Caracas/La Guaira, and Curaçao. **Mid-Spring–Summer:** A 15-night eastbound **transatlantic crossing** from New York to Rome/Civitavecchia includes calls at Lisbon, Gibraltar, Barcelona, the French Riviera, and Florence/Livorno. A 13-night **Mediterranean** cruise from Rome/Civitavecchia to Athens/Piraeus includes calls on the Napoli Coast, Venice, the Greek Islands, and Istanbul. A 13-night **western Europe** cruise from Athens/Piraeus to London/Southampton includes calls on the Greek Islands, Rome/Civitavecchia, Florence/Livorno, the French Riviera, Barcelona, Lisbon, and Gibraltar. Thirteen-night **Scandinavia/Russia** loops depart London/Southampton and include calls at Oslo, Copenhagen, Stockholm, and Helsinki. A 13-night **Norwegian Fjord/North Cape** loop departs London/Southampton and includes calls along the Norwegian Coast, Oslo, and Bergen. A 13-night **Iceland/British Isles** loop departs London/Southampton and includes calls at Edinburgh/ Leith, Reykjavik, and Dublin.

Sky Princess **Fall–mid-Spring:** Nineteen-night **Alaska/Far East** cruises between Vancouver and Osaka/Kyoto (Japan) include calls at Juneau and Glacier Bay National Park. Fourteen-night **Southeast Asia** cruises between Bangkok/Laem Chabang (Thailand) and Hong Kong include calls at Canton, Kota Kinabalu, Sabah, and Singapore. A 14-night **Spice Islands** loop from Singapore includes calls at Kuala Lumpur, Phuket, and Bali. Nineteen-night **Asia/South Pacific** cruises between Bangkok/Laem Chabang and Sydney (Australia) include calls at Ho Chi Minh City, Singapore, and Bali. Fourteen-night **Far East** cruises sail between Hong Kong and Osaka/Kyoto. Fourteen-night **Australia/New Zealand** cruises sail between Sydney and Auckland. Sixteen-night **South Pacific** cruises sail between Sydney and Papeete (Tahiti). Eleven-night **Hawaii/French Polynesia** cruises between Papeete and Honolulu include calls at the Big Island and Maui. **Mid-Spring–Summer:** Eleven-night **Inside Passage** loops depart San Francisco, calling at Victoria, Vancouver, Juneau, Skagway, and Ketchikan.

Star Princess **Fall–mid-Spring:** An 11-night **Panama Canal** transit from Acapulco to Fort Lauderdale calls at Puerto Limon, Cartagena, St. Thomas, and Princess Cays. Seven-night **eastern Caribbean** loops depart Fort Lauderdale, calling at Nassau, Princess Cays, St. Croix, and St. John/St. Thomas. A 10-night **southern Caribbean** loop departs Fort Lauderdale, calling at Nassau, Princess Cays, St. Thomas, Guadeloupe, Barbados, Dominica, and St. Maarten/St. Martin. **Mid-Spring –Summer:** Seven-night **Inside Passage/Gulf of Alaska** cruises between Vancouver and Seward (Alaska) call at Ketchikan, Juneau, Skagway, and Glacier Bay National Park or Hubbard Glacier.

Sun Princess **Fall–early Spring:** A 16-night **Panama Canal** transit from Los Angeles to Fort Lauderdale includes calls at Cabo San Lucas, Acapulco, Cozumel/Playa del Carmen, Puerto Limon, Cartagena, Montego Bay, and Grand Cayman. Seven-night **western Caribbean** loops depart Fort Lauderdale, calling at Princess Cays, Montego Bay, Grand Cayman, and Cozumel/Playa del Carmen. **Mid-Spring–Summer:** Seven-night **Inside Passage/Gulf of Alaska** cruises between Vancouver and Seward (Alaska) call at Ketchikan, Juneau, Skagway, and Glacier Bay National Park.

Radisson Seven Seas Cruises

Hanseatic **Late Fall–Winter:** A 17-night **South America** cruise sails from the Galapagos Islands to Puerto Montt (Chile). A 20-night **South America/Antarctica** cruise from Puerto Montt to Buenos Aires (Argentina) includes calls at Punta Arenas and Port Stanley. Ten-night **Antarctica** loops sail from Ushuaia (Argentina). Seven-, nine-, 11- and 14-night **South America/Amazon** cruises sail between Rio de Janeiro (Brazil) and Belem (Brazil), Belem and Manaus, and Manaus and Cayenne (French Guiana). **Spring:** To be announced. **Summer:** Ten- and 11-night **North Cape** loops depart Honningsvag (Norway) or sail between Honningsvag and Lubeck (Germany). A 14-night **Greenland and Iceland** cruise sails between Hamburg (Germany) and Sondre Stromfjord (Greenland). A 24-night **Northwest Passage** cruise sails between Sondre Stromfjord and Nome (Alaska).

Radisson Diamond **Early Fall:** Seven-night **Mediterranean** cruises depart Rome/ Civitavecchia, Piraeus/Athens, or Istanbul and call on the Napoli Coast, the Greek Islands, and the Turkish Coast. A 10-night **Mediterranean/Canary Islands** cruise from Rome/Civitavecchia to Las Palmas (Spain) calls at Barcelona, Gibraltar, and the Canary Islands. A 19-night westbound **transatlantic crossing** sails from Las Palmas to San Juan. **Late Fall–early Spring:** An eight-night **Panama Canal** transit from San Juan to Puerto Caldera (Costa Rica) calls at Curaçao, Cartagena, and the San Blas Islands. Eleven- or 15-night **Panama Canal** transits between Puerto Caldera and Charleston (South Carolina) include calls at Grand Cayman, Cozumel/Playa del Carmen, and Fort Lauderdale. Seven-, eight, and nine-night **Panama Canal** transits between Puerto Caldera and San Juan or Aruba include calls at Curaçao, Cartagena, and the San Blas Islands. Four- and five-night **Caribbean** loops depart San Juan, calling at Tortola, St. Barts, St. Maarten/St. Martin, and St. Thomas. **Late Spring:** A nine-night eastbound **transatlantic crossing** sails from San Juan to Las Palmas (the Canary Islands). **Summer:** To be announced.

Song of Flower **Fall:** Seven-night **Mediterranean** cruises depart Athens/Piraeus or Istanbul, and include calls on the Turkish Coast, Greek Islands, and Venice. A nine-night **Mediterranean/Red Sea** cruise from Istanbul to Aqaba (Jordan) includes calls on the Turkish Coast, the Greek Islands, and Limassol. **Winter:** A 14-night **Southeast Asia** cruise from Bombay (India) to Singapore includes calls at Phuket and Kuala Lumpur. Seven-night **Southeast Asia** cruises between Singapore and Rangoon (Myanmar) include calls at Kuala Lumpur and Phuket. Eight- and 11-night **Southeast Asia** cruises sail between Singapore and Bali (Indonesia). Eleven-night **Southeast Asia/Far East** cruises between Singapore and Hong Kong may include a call at Ho Chi Minh City and other ports. A seven-night **Far East** loop departs Hong Kong, calling at Canton and other ports. **Spring:** A 10-night **Indian Ocean** cruise sails from Rangoon to Bombay. Twelve- and 13-night **Middle East** cruises sail between Dubai (United Arab Emirates) and Aqaba. Nine-night **Mediterranean/Red Sea** cruises between Aqaba and Athens/Piraeus call on the Greek Islands and the Turkish Coast. **Summer: Mediterranean** and **northern Europe** cruises with ports of call to be announced.

Renaissance Cruises

Renaissance III At press time, no cruises were scheduled. Contact Renaissance Cruises for more information.

Renaissance IV At press time, no cruises were scheduled. Contact Renaissance Cruises for more information.

Renaissance V **Early Fall:** Eleven-night **Mediterranean** cruise-tours sail between Rome/Civitavecchia and Barcelona (Spain) or Athens/Piraeus, and include calls on the French Riviera, Florence/Livorno, and the Napoli Coast. **Late Fall–Spring:** Thirty-five-night **Mediterranean/Asia** cruise-tours between Athens/Piraeus and Singapore include calls at Phuket, Kuala Lumpur, and other ports. Seventeen-night **Southeast Asia** cruise-tours sail from Bali (Indonesia) to Singapore. **Summer:** Thirteen-night **northern Europe** cruise-tours between Copenhagen and Stockholm include a call at Helsinki and other ports.

Renaissance VI **Fall–Spring:** Same as *Renaissance V*. **Summer:** Eleven-night **Mediterranean** cruise-tours between Barcelona (Spain) and Rome/Civitavecchia include calls on the French Riviera and Florence/Livorno.

Renaissance VII **Fall:** Eleven-night **Mediterranean** cruise-tours between Athens/Piraeus and Istanbul include calls on the Greek Islands and Turkish Coast. **Winter–Spring:** Fifteen-night **Seychelles and Africa** cruise-tours travel between Nairobi (Kenya) and Luxor (Egypt). **Summer: Mediterranean** cruises (same as fall). Eleven-night **Mediterranean** cruise-tours from Rome/Civitavecchia to Athens/Piraeus include calls on the Napoli Coast.

Renaissance VIII **Fall–Spring:** Mediterranean (same as *Renaissance VII*). **Summer:** Northern Europe (same as *Renaissance V*).

Royal Caribbean Cruise Line

Grandeur of the Seas **Year-round:** Seven-night **eastern Caribbean** loops depart Miami, calling at Labadee, San Juan, St. Thomas, and CocoCay.

Legend of the Seas **Fall:** Ten-night **Hawaii** sailings between Vancouver and Honolulu, or Honolulu and Ensenada (Mexico), call at Hilo, Kona, Kaunakakai, Kahului, and Port Allen. **Winter–mid-Spring:** Ten- and 11-night **Panama Canal** transits between Acapulco and San Juan call at St. Thomas, Santo Domingo, Curaçao, and Puerto Caldera. **Mid-Spring–Summer:** Seven-night **Inside Passage** loops depart Vancouver, calling at Skagway, Haines, Juneau, and Ketchikan.

Majesty of the Seas **Year-round:** Seven-night **western Caribbean** loops depart Miami, calling at Grand Cayman, Cozumel/Playa del Carmen, Ocho Rios, and Labadee.

Monarch of the Seas **Year-round:** Seven-night **southern Caribbean** loops depart San Juan, calling at Martinique, Barbados, Antigua, St. Maarten/St. Martin, and St. Thomas.

Nordic Empress **Fall:** Three- and four-night **Bahamas** loops depart Miami, calling at Nassau and CocoCay. Four-night cruises also call at Freeport/Lucaya. **Winter–Spring:** Three- and four-night **southern Caribbean** loops depart San Juan, calling at St. Thomas/St. John and St. Maarten/St. Martin. Four-night cruises also call at St. Croix. **Summer:** Three- and four-night **Bahamas** loops depart Port Canaveral, calling at Nassau and CocoCay.

Song of America **Fall:** Seven-night **Bermuda** loops depart New York, calling at St. George's and Hamilton. **Winter–mid-Spring:** Seven-night **Mexican Riviera** loops depart Los Angeles, calling at Cabo San Lucas, Mazatlan, and Puerto Vallarta. A 14-night **Panama Canal** transit from Los Angeles to San Juan calls at Acapulco, Puerto Caldera, Aruba, and St. Thomas/St. John. **Mid-Spring–Summer:** Same as fall.

Song of Norway **Fall–Spring:** A 10-night **Panama Canal** transit from Acapulco to San Juan calls at Puerto Caldera, Curaçao, and St. Thomas/St. John. Ten- and 11-night **southern Caribbean** cruises between Miami and San Juan include calls at CocoCay, St. Barts, St. Lucia, Grenada, Dominica, St. Maarten/St. Martin, and St. Thomas/St. John. **Summer:** Ten- and 11-night **Inside Passage** loops depart Vancouver, calling at Victoria, Sitka, Skagway, Haines, Juneau, Ketchikan, and Wrangell.

Sovereign of the Seas **Fall:** Seven-night **eastern Caribbean** loops depart Miami, calling at Labadee, San Juan, St. Thomas, and CocoCay. **Winter:** Three- and four-night **Bahamas** loops depart Miami, calling at Nassau and CocoCay. Four-night cruises also call at Freeport/Lucaya.

Splendour of the Seas **Early Fall:** Twelve-night **Mediterranean** loops depart Barcelona (Spain) and include calls on the French Riviera, Florence/Livorno, the Napoli Coast, Venice, and Rome/Civitavecchia. A 15-night westbound **transatlantic crossing** from Barcelona to Miami calls at Gibraltar, Lisbon, the Canary Islands, and St. Maarten/St. Martin. **Late Fall–Spring:** Seven-night **southern Caribbean** loops depart San Juan, calling at Aruba, Curaçao, St. Maarten/St. Martin, and St. Thomas/St. John. A 13-night eastbound **transatlantic crossing** from San Juan to Barcelona includes calls at Barbados and the Canary Islands. **Summer:** Twelve-night **Mediterranean** loops depart Barcelona and include calls on the French Riviera, Florence/Livorno, the Napoli Coast, Rome/Civitavecchia, and Venice. A 12-night **western Europe** cruise from Barcelona to Harwick (England) includes calls at Lisbon, Paris/Le Havre, Oslo, and Copenhagen. Twelve-night **Scandinavia/Russia** loops depart Harwick and include calls at Oslo, Stockholm, Helsinki, and Copenhagen. Twelve-night **North Cape/Norwegian Fjords** loops depart Harwick and call along the Norwegian fjords and Bergen. Twelve-night **British Isles** loops depart

Harwick and include calls at Paris/Le Havre, Dublin, and Amsterdam.

Sun Viking **Year-round:** Thirteen- and 14-night **China** cruises sail between Beijing (China) and Hong Kong. Fourteen-night **Southeast Asia** loops depart Singapore, and 15-night cruises sail between Singapore and Bangkok/Laem Chabang (Thailand) and include calls at Bali, Kuala Lumpur, Phuket, and Ko Samui. Fourteen- and 15-night **Far East** cruises between Hong Kong and Singapore or Bangkok/Laem Chabang call at Canton, Ho Chi Minh City, and Ko Samui.

Viking Serenade **Year-round:** Three- and four-night **West Coast** loops depart Los Angeles, calling at Catalina Island and Ensenada.

Royal Olympic Cruises

Odysseus **Fall:** Three- and four-night **Mediterranean** loops depart Athens/Piraeus, calling at the Greek Islands and Turkish Coast. A 20-night westbound **transatlantic crossing** cruise from Athens/Piraeus to Rio de Janeiro (Brazil) calls at Gibraltar, Recife, and Salvador de Bahia. **Winter:** Eleven- and 12-night **South America** cruises between Rio de Janeiro and Buenos Aires (Argentina) call at Montevideo, Puerto Madryn, and other ports. Fourteen-night **Straits of Magellan** cruises between Puerto Montt (Chile) and Buenos Aires call at Puerto Madryn, Ushuaia, Punta Arenas, and Puerto Natales. **Spring:** A 15-night eastbound **transatlantic crossing** from Rio de Janeiro to Lisbon (Portugal) includes calls at Salvador de Bahia and the Canary Islands. Twelve-night **Mediterranean** cruises between Lisbon and Athens/Piraeus include calls at Gibraltar, Florence/Livorno, Rome/Civitavecchia, and the French Riviera. **Summer: Mediterranean** cruises (same as fall).

Olympic **Fall:** Three- and four-night **Mediterranean** loops depart Athens/Piraeus, calling on the Greek Islands and the Turkish Coast. **Winter:** No cruises scheduled. **Spring–Summer:** Same as fall.

Orpheus **Fall:** Seven-night **Mediterranean** loops depart Athens/Piraeus, calling on the Greek Islands and Crete. **Winter:** No cruises scheduled. **Spring–Summer:** Same as fall.

Stella Oceanis **Fall:** Seven-night **Mediterranean** loops depart Athens/Piraeus, calling on the Greek Islands and the Turkish Coast. **Winter:** Seven- and 12-night **Red Sea** loops depart Suez (Egypt) or sail between Suez and Athens/Piraeus. **Spring–Summer:** Same as fall.

Stella Solaris **Fall–early Spring:** A 23-night westbound **transatlantic crossing** from Athens/Piraeus to Miami includes calls at Florence/Livorno, the French Riviera, Barcelona, the Canary Islands, and Trinidad. A 10-night **Caribbean** cruise from Miami to Fort Lauderdale calls at Nassau, San Juan, Curaçao, St. Lucia, and St. Thomas. A 27-night **Caribbean/Amazon** loop departs Fort Lauderdale and includes calls at St. Thomas, St. Lucia, Barbados, Grenada, Tobago, Manaus, Alter de Chao, Antigua, San Juan, and other ports. Twelve-night **Panama Canal** loops depart Galveston (Texas) and include calls at Grand Cayman, the San Blas Islands, Puerto Limon, Cozumel/Playa del Carmen, and Gatun Lake. A 12-night **western Caribbean** loop departs Galveston, calling at Grand Cayman, Cozumel/Playa del Carmen, and other ports. A seven-night **western Caribbean** loop departs Galveston, calling at Cozumel/Playa del Carmen, Mexico, Grand Cayman, and Key West. A 23-night eastbound **transatlantic crossing** from Galveston to Athens/Piraeus calls at Key West, Fort Lauderdale, Nassau, Lisbon, the French Riviera, Florence/Livorno, and Civitavecchia/Rome. **Mid-Spring–Summer:** Seven-night **Mediterranean** loops depart Athens/Piraeus, calling on the Greek Islands, Istanbul, and the Turkish Coast.

Triton **Fall:** Seven-night **Mediterranean** loops depart Athens/Piraeus, calling on the Greek Islands, Istanbul, and the Turkish Coast. **Winter:** No cruises scheduled. **Spring–Summer:** Same as fall.

Seabourn Cruise Line

Seabourn Legend **Early Fall:** A 14-night **New England and Canada** loop departs New York, calling at Halifax, Montréal, and other ports. A seven-night **Bermuda** loop departs New York, calling at Hamilton. A 12-night **eastern seaboard/Bahamas** cruise sails from New York to Fort Lauderdale. **Late Fall–Winter:** Fourteen-night **Caribbean/Panama Canal** cruises sail between Fort Lauderdale and Curaçao. A seven-night **Caribbean** loop departs Curaçao. An eight-night **Mexico** loop departs Tampa. A 15-night **Central America** loop departs Tampa and includes calls at Cozumel/Playa del Carmen, Grand Cayman, and other ports. An 18-night **Caribbean/Panama Canal** cruise from Tampa to Antigua calls at Cancun, the San Blas Islands, Cartagena, Curaçao, Barbados, Grenada, St. Lucia, and other ports. A seven-night **Caribbean** cruise from San Juan to Fort Lauderdale calls at St. Barts, St. Maarten/St. Martin, St. Thomas, and Virgin Gorda. A 12-night **Caribbean/Orinoco River** cruise from Curaçao to St. Thomas calls at Barbados, St. Lucia, St. Barts, St. Maarten/St. Martin, and other ports. A seven-night **Caribbean** cruise from St. Thomas to Barbados includes calls at St. Maarten/St. Martin, St. Barts, Antigua, St. Lucia, and Grenada. A nine-night **Caribbean** cruise sails from Barbados to West Palm Beach. **Spring:** A 23-night **Panama Canal** transit from Fort Lauderdale to San Diego calls at Cozumel/Playa del Carmen, the San Blas Islands, Puerto Caldera, Acapulco, Puerto Vallarta, Mazatlan, Cabo San Lucas, and other ports. Eleven-night **Hawaii** cruises between Ensenada (Mexico) and Honolulu call at Lahaina and other ports. Three- and five-night **California** loops depart San Diego and San Francisco or sail between San Diego and San Francisco. **Summer:** Ten-night **Inside Passage** cruises between Vancouver and Seattle call at Victoria, Petersburg, Juneau, Skagway, Haines, Sitka, and Ketchikan. A 14-night cruise also calls at Eureka and San Francisco. A 10-night **Inside Passage** cruise from San Francisco calls at Victoria and Ketchikan.

Seabourn Pride **Fall:** An 11-night **Hawaii** cruise from Ensenada (Mexico) to Honolulu calls at Kona, Lanai, and Lahaina. Fourteen-night **Pacific crossings** between Honolulu and Papeete (Tahiti) include calls on Kauai and the Big Island. Ten-, 12-, 13-, and 14-night **South Pacific** cruises sail between Papeete and Lautoka (Fiji), Lautoka and Sydney (Australia), Sydney and Auckland (New Zealand), Auckland and Papeete, or Papeete and Honolulu. **Winter:** A 16-night **Mexico** loop departs San Diego, calling at Cabo San Lucas, Zihuatenejo/Ixtapa, Acapulco, Manzanillo, Puerto Vallarta, and Santa Catalina Island. A 22-night **South America** cruise from Cabo San Lucas (Mexico) to Valparaiso (Chile) calls at Zihuatenejo/Ixtapa, Acapulco, Puerto Caldera, and other ports. A 22-night **South America** cruise from Valparaiso to Rio de Janeiro (Brazil) calls at Puerto Montt, Punta Arenas, Puerto Madryn, Buenos Aires, Montevideo, and other ports. A 15-night **Amazon** cruise from Rio de Janeiro to Manaus (Brazil) includes calls at Salvador de Bahia, Recife, Belem, and Alter do Chao. A 15-night **Amazon/Caribbean** cruise from Manaus to Fort Lauderdale includes calls at ports along the Amazon, Devil's Island, St. John, Antigua, and San Juan. **Spring–Summer:** A 13-night eastbound **transatlantic crossing** from Fort Lauderdale to Lisbon (Portugal) includes a call at Hamilton. A 12-night **Mediterranean/Canary Islands** loop departs Lisbon and includes calls at the Canary Islands and Seville. A 14-night **western Europe** cruise sails from Lisbon to London/Southampton. Fourteen-night **northern Europe** cruises depart London/Southampton and Copenhagen and include calls at Edinburgh/Leith, Dublin, Stockholm, Helsinki, and Bergen.

Seabourn Spirit **Fall:** Ten-, 12-, and 14-night **Mediterranean** cruises depart Lisbon (Portugal), Barcelona (Spain), Rome/Civitavecchia, or Athens/Piraeus, and include calls in Seville, the French Riviera, Florence/Livorno, the Napoli Coast, the Greek Islands, Istanbul, and the Turkish Coast. **Winter:** Nine-, 12-, and 13-night **Africa/Seychelles** cruises sail between Haifa (Israel) and Mombasa (Kenya), Mombasa and Victoria (Seychelles), and Victoria and Singapore. Ten-, 13-, and 14-night **Southeast Asia** cruises depart Singapore or Hong Kong and include calls at Ko Samui, Phuket, Bangkok/Laem Chabang, Ho Chi Minh City, and Bali. **Spring–Summer:** Fourteen-night **Mediterranean** cruises sail between Haifa and Rome/Civitavecchia, Rome/Civitavecchia and Nice (France), Rome/Civitavecchia and Istanbul, or Istanbul and Haifa, and include calls on the Turkish Coast and Istanbul, the Greek Islands, Athens/Piraeus, the Napoli Coast, Rome/Civitavecchia, Florence/Livorno, the French Riviera, and Barcelona.

Seawind Cruise Line

Seawind Crown **Year-round:** Seven-night **southern Caribbean** loops depart Aruba, calling at Curaçao, Grenada, Barbados, and St. Lucia, or Trinidad, Tobago, Barbados, and Martinique.

Silversea Cruises

Silver Cloud **Early Fall:** Ten-night **New England and Canada** cruises between New York and Montréal call at Halifax, Québec City, Boston, Newport, and other ports. An eight-night **eastern seaboard** cruise sails from New York to Nassau. **Late Fall–mid-Winter:** A 10-night **Caribbean** cruise from Nassau to Fort Lauderdale calls at Grand Cayman, Aruba, and other ports. Six-night cruises between Fort Lauderdale and Barbados call at St. Maarten/St. Martin, Dominica, St. Lucia, Antigua, and Virgin Gorda. Ten-night **Caribbean/Amazon** cruises between Barbados and Manaus (Brazil) call at Devil's Island and along the Amazon River. A 14-night **Caribbean** loop departs Fort Lauderdale, calling at St. Maarten/St. Martin, Antigua, Martinique, Barbados, St. Lucia, Guadeloupe, and other ports. **Mid-Winter–mid-Spring:** Sixteen- to 21-day **South America** cruises between Buenos Aires (Argentina) and Valparaiso (Chile) include calls at Montevideo, Puerto Madryn, Ushuaia, Port Stanley, Punta Arenas, and Puerto Montt. **Mid-Spring–Summer:** A 14-night eastbound **transatlantic crossing** from Rio de Janeiro (Brazil) to Lisbon (Portugal) includes calls at Salvador, Recife, and the Canary Islands. Ten-, 12-, and 14-night **northern Europe** and **Baltic** cruises depart London/Southampton, St. Petersburg (Russia), or Copenhagen, and include calls at Bergen, the Norwegian Coast, Helsinki, and Stockholm.

Silver Wind **Fall:** A 14-night **Mediterranean** cruise from Athens/Piraeus to Barcelona (Spain) includes calls on the Napoli Coast, Ibiza, and the Canary Islands. An 11-night **Mediterranean** cruise from Barcelona to Venice includes calls on the Napoli Coast and Corfu. A 10-night **Mediterranean/Red Sea** cruise from Istanbul to Haifa (Israel) calls at Athens/Piraeus, the Greek Islands, the Turkish Coast, and Limassol. Seven and nine-night **Africa** loops depart Mombasa (Kenya) or sail between Mombasa and Mahe. A 14-night **Indian Ocean/Southeast Asia** cruise sails from Mombasa to Singapore. **Winter:** A 14-night **Southeast Asia** loop departs Singapore and includes a call at Phuket and other ports. Thirteen- and 14-night **Southeast Asia** cruises sail between Singapore and Bangkok/Laem Chabang (Thailand) or Cairns (Australia), or Bangkok/Laem Chabang and Hong Kong, and include calls at Bali, Ho Chi Minh City, and Ko Samui. Fourteen-night **Australia/New Zealand** cruises sail between Cairns and Auckland (New Zealand) or between Auckland and Sydney

(Australia). **Spring:** Thirteen- and 14-night **Southeast Asia** cruises sail between Hong Kong and Bangkok/Laem Chabang or Singapore and may include calls at Ho Chi Minh City, Ko Samui, and other ports. A 14-night **Southeast Asia/India** cruise from Singapore to Bombay (India) includes a call at Phuket and other ports. A 16-night **Middle East** cruise sails from Bombay to Haifa. **Summer:** Seven-, 10-, 11-, 12-, and 14-night **Mediterranean** cruises depart Istanbul, Athens/Piraeus, Venice, Rome/Civitavecchia, Monte Carlo, or Barcelona (Spain), and include calls on the Greek Islands, the Napoli Coast, Ibiza, the Canary Islands, the French Riviera, Florence/Livorno, and the Turkish Coast.

Society Expeditions

World Discoverer **Early Fall: South Pacific** cruises to be announced. **Mid-Fall–Winter: Antarctica** and **Chilean Fjords** cruises call at Santiago, Puerto Montt, Ushuaia, Port Stanley, and a variety of small islands and research stations. Some itineraries visit the Chilean fjords. **Early Spring:** same as early fall. **Mid-Spring–Summer: Bering Strait** cruises depart Homer (Alaska) or Seward (Alaska), calling at the Aleutian Islands, the Pribolof Islands, and the Russian Far East. **Inside Passage/Gulf of Alaska** cruises depart Homer or Seward, calling at Prince William Sound, Glacier Bay National Park, Tracy Arm, and Sitka. **Aleutian Islands** loops depart Seward, calling along the Alaskan Peninsula and the Russian Far East.

Special Expeditions

Polaris **Fall:** Sixteen-night **Amazon** cruises between Belém (Brazil) and Iquitos (Peru) call at Manaus and explore the upper Amazon, lower Amazon, and Rio Negro. Twenty-six- and 34-night **South America** cruises to be announced. **Winter:** Eight-night **Costa Rica and Panama** cruises sail between Colón (Panama) and Puerto Caldera (Costa Rica). Thirteen-night **Panama Canal** transits between Balboa (Panama) and Belize call at the San Blas Islands and ports in Nicaragua and Honduras. **Spring–Summer:** A 16-night eastbound **transatlantic crossing** to be announced. **Western and northern Europe** cruises include calls at Dublin, Edinburgh/Leith, Amsterdam, Helsinki, Oslo, Stockholm, and Copenhagen.

Sea Bird, Sea Lion **Fall:** Seven-night **Pacific Northwest** cruises sail between Vancouver and Seattle. Seven-night **Columbia and Snake Rivers** loops depart Portland (Oregon). **Winter:** Eight- and nine-night **Baja California** whale-watching cruises to be announced. **Spring–Summer: Columbia and Snake Rivers** cruises (same as fall). Eleven-night **Alaska/British Columbia** cruises between Juneau and Seattle call at Glacier Bay National Park, Sitka, Ketchikan, and the San Juan Islands. Eight- and nine-night **Alaska** cruises between Juneau and Sitka call at Skagway, Glacier Bay National Park, and Haines.

Star Clippers

Star Clipper **Fall–Winter:** Seven-night **Caribbean** loops depart Barbados, calling at Martinique, Dominica, St. Lucia, Tobago, and Bequia or Carriacou, Grenada, Union Island, St. Vincent, and St. Lucia. **Mid-Spring:** A 31-day eastbound **transatlantic crossing** sails from Barbados to Cannes (France). **Late Spring–Summer:** Seven-day **Mediterranean** loops depart from Cannes.

Star Flyer **Fall–Winter:** A 35-day **Indian Ocean** crossing sails from Rhodes to Phuket (Thailand). Seven-day **Southeast Asia** cruises sail between Singapore and Phuket. **Early Spring:** A 35-night **Indian Ocean crossing** sails between Phuket and Athens/Piraeus. **Mid-Spring–Summer:** Seven-night **Mediterranean** cruises sail between Athens/Piraeus and Kuşadası (Turkey), round-trip from Kuşadası, or between Kuşadası and Rhodes (Greece) and include calls on the Greek Islands and Turkish Coast.

Windstar Cruises

Wind Song **Year-round:** Seven-night **French Polynesia** loops depart Papeete (Tahiti).

Wind Spirit **Early Fall:** Six-, seven-, 10-, 12-, and 13-night **Mediterranean** cruises depart Athens/Piraeus, Istanbul, or Rome/Civitavecchia, and include calls on the Greek Islands, the Turkish Coast, the Napoli Coast, the French Riviera, Ibiza, and Lisbon. **Late Fall–early Spring:** Seven-, 10-, and 11-night **Caribbean** loops depart St. Thomas and include calls at St. Croix, St. John, St. Lucia, Barbados, Martinique, St. Maarten/St. Martin, Guadeloupe, and other islands. **Early Spring–Summer:** A 14-night eastbound **transatlantic crossing** sails from St. Thomas to Lisbon (Portugal). Ten- and 12-night **Mediterranean** cruises depart Rome/Civitavecchia and Lisbon and include a call at Barcelona and other ports. Seven-night **Mediterranean** cruises depart Athens/Piraeus and Istanbul and include calls on the Greek Islands and the Turkish Coast.

Wind Star **Early Fall:** Seven-, 10-, and 12-night **Mediterranean** and **Canary Islands** cruises depart Athens/Piraeus, Istanbul, Barcelona (Spain), or Madeira (Portugal), and include calls on the Greek Islands, Turkish Coast, French Riviera, Gibraltar, Ibiza, and the Canary Islands. **Late Fall–mid-Spring:** Seven-, nine-, and 12-night **Caribbean** loops depart Barbados and include calls at St. Maarten/St. Martin, Martinique, Carriacou, Grenada, St. Lucia, Guadeloupe, and other islands. **Mid-Spring–Summer:** A 14-night eastbound **transatlantic crossing** sails from Barbados to Lisbon (Portugal). Fourteen-night **Mediterranean** cruises depart Lisbon and include calls at Gibraltar and the French Riviera. Seven- and 14-night **Mediterranean** cruises depart Nice (France) and include calls on the Napoli Coast and the Greek Islands. Seven-night **Mediterranean** cruises depart Athens/Piraeus and Istanbul and call on the Greek Islands and the Turkish Coast.

World Explorer Cruises

SS Universe Explorer **Winter:** Fourteen-night **Western Caribbean/Central America/South America** loops depart Nassau, calling at Calica, Puerto Cortes, Puerto Limon, Cristobal, Cartagena, and Ocho Rios. **Summer:** Fourteen-night **Inside Passage/Gulf of Alaska** loops depart Vancouver, calling at Ketchikan, Sitka, Seward, Valdez, Skagway, Juneau, Wrangell, Victoria, and Glacier Bay National Park.

Index